Purchasing and Supply Chain Management

SIXTH EDITION

Robert M. Monczka
Arizona State University and CAPS Research

Robert B. Handfield
North Carolina State University

Larry C. Giunipero
Florida State University

James L. Patterson
Western Illinois University

CENGAGE
Learning®

Australia • Brazil • Mexico • Singapore • United Kingdom • United States

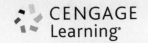

Purchasing and Supply Chain Management, Sixth Edition
Robert M. Monczka, Robert B. Handfield, Larry C. Giunipero, James L. Patterson

Vice President, General Manager, Social Science & Qualitative Business:
Erin Joyner

Product Director: Joe Sabatino

Associate Content Developer: Conor Allen

Senior Product Assistant: Brad Sullender

Marketing Manager: Heather Mooney

Marketing Coordinator: Eileen Corcoran

Art and Cover Direction, Production Management, and Composition:
Lumina Datamatics, Inc.

Media Developer: Chris Valentine

Intellectual Property
   Analyst: Christina Ciaramella
   Project Manager: Betsy Hathaway

Manufacturing Planner: Ron Montgomery

Cover Image: © Carlos Castilla/Shutterstock

For product information and technology assistance, contact us at
Cengage Learning Customer & Sales Support, 1-800-354-9706

For permission to use material from this text or product, submit all requests online at **www.cengage.com/permissions**
Further permissions questions can be emailed to
permissionrequest@cengage.com

Unless otherwise noted, all items © Cengage Learning

Library of Congress Control Number: 2014950274

Student Edition ISBN: 978-1-285-86968-1

Cengage Learning
20 Channel Center Street
Boston, MA 02210
USA

Cengage Learning is a leading provider of customized learning solutions with office locations around the globe, including Singapore, the United Kingdom, Australia, Mexico, Brazil, and Japan. Locate your local office at:
www.cengage.com/global

Cengage Learning products are represented in Canada by Nelson Education, Ltd.

To learn more about Cengage Learning Solutions, visit
www.cengage.com

Purchase any of our products at your local college store or at our preferred online store **www.cengagebrain.com**

Printed in the United States of America
Print Number: 02   Print Year: 2015

Brief Contents

Cases 813

Contents

Part 2   Purchasing Operations and Structure   37

Preface

The Sixth Edition of *Purchasing and Supply Chain Management* reflects the ever-changing face of supply management and the increased recognition in boardrooms of organizations across every industry. The challenges experienced by organizations are calling for a new type of supply manager with many different capabilities. Students seeking to pursue a career in supply management may choose to focus on one or more of these areas as they consider where in supply management they wish to focus.

- Internal Consultant—Ability to connect, listen, and deliver business value to internal stakeholders. Building a strong P2P system to drive improved procurement transaction excellence and driving results that matter to the business.

- Market Intelligence & Cost Modeling Analytics—Deployment of total cost analytic modeling and cost to serve capabilities, application of analytical cost modeling approaches for decision support, and building supply market intelligence data gathering and knowledge dissemination capabilities. Deep knowledge and understanding of macro economic forces and ability to relate them to future market movements and forecasts.

- Financial Acumen—Knowledge of currency, capital markets, and contribution of procurement to P&L and balance sheet. Ability to contribute to CFO and other financial leadership discussions and debates. Ability to build logistics cost models, understand contribution of supply management to capitalization, facility productivity, and other key metrics.

- Risk Mitigation—Knowledge of different sources of risk, ability to build risk profiles, link recognition of risks to risk mitigation and scenario planning, and understanding how to manage disasters when they occur. Building a business case for risk mitigation planning.

- Supplier Coach—Ability to deploy supplier development to drive improvement in high-need categories or regions, especially in emerging countries where local content is required. Becoming a customer of choice and driving improvement in supplier capabilities. Harnessing supplier innovation and developing solutions to stakeholder requirements.

- Relationship Broker—Managing teams in multicultural environments, managing virtual teams, and understanding pros and cons of different organizational models (centralization vs. decentralization). Working with global engineering teams and understanding of technical knowledge. Managing outsourced relationships and services. Driving supplier innovation and linking to internal teams.

- Legal Expertise—Building relational contracts, understanding legal contractual language, terms and conditions, legal clauses, and vernacular. Building good price and cost modeling indices for contracting, and managing risks and rewards through improved contract structure. Best practices in on-going contract management. Managing conflicts that emerge post-contract signing. Dealing with IP issues when working with suppliers.

- Talent Management—Building a pipeline of leadership and supply management expertise, mentoring, and leadership development.

The Sixth Edition emphasizes these competencies through new material and emphasis on traditional competencies that have become more important recently. This new edition includes a number of new topics, including cases in health care, oil and gas, and financial services, industries that have downplayed the role of strategic supply management in the past.

In addition, some of the subjects that are newly introduced or expanded upon in this edition include:

- Cross-functional teaming
- Procurement analytics
- Application of mobile technologies in the supply chain
- Supplier integration into new product development
- Software as a service applications for procurement
- Social networking and cloud applications
- The role of "big data" in procurement
- Supplier development
- Cost modeling and market intelligence
- The role of procurement logistics in globalization
- "Should cost" modeling
- Supplier collaboration for cost savings ideas
- Negotiation simulations
- Contracting and Internet law
- Supply chain risk management
- Sustainability in the supply chain
- The importance of labor and human rights in procurement contracts and codes of conduct
- The role of transportation infrastructure and government regulation in global logistics
- Public procurement and acquisition
- Crowd-sourcing and open innovation
- Impact of sourcing strategies on revenue, capital asset management, and share price of the enterprise
- Deployment of category management
- Expanded and comprehensive cases, sourcing snapshots, and good practice examples pulled from direct interviews with senior procurement executives

We are proud of this new edition and believe that it reflects many themes that are only beginning to emerge in industries worldwide.

Course Description

Purchasing and Supply Chain Management is intended for college and university courses that are variously titled purchasing, materials management, supply chain management, sourcing management, supply management, and other similar titles. The text is also well suited for training seminars for buyers, and portions of it have been used in executive education forums. Chapters have been used in both undergraduate and M.B.A. classes in supply management, business strategy, operations management, and logistics. Some instructors may also elect to apply sections of the book to undergraduate or graduate classes in operations management.

The text is appropriate for either an elective or a required course that fulfills AACSB International: The Association to Advance Collegiate Schools of Business requirements for coverage of supply chain management issues. Most of the cases included in the book are based on actual companies and all were adapted and modified through classroom use by the authors.

Course Objectives

Depending on the placement of a course in the curriculum or the individual instructor's philosophy, this book can be utilized to satisfy a variety of objectives:

1. Students should be made aware of the demands placed on purchasing and supply chain managers by business stakeholders, both internally and externally to the firm.

2. As prospective managers, students need to understand the impact of purchasing and supply chain management on the competitive success and profitability of modern organizations.

3. Students should appreciate the ethical, contractual, risk management, sustainability, and legal issues faced by purchasing and supply chain professionals.

4. Students must understand the increasingly strategic nature of purchasing, especially the fact that it involves much more than simply buying goods and services.

5. Students entering or currently in the workforce must understand the influence of purchasing on other major functional activities, including product design, information system design, e-commerce, manufacturing planning and control, inventory management, human resource development, financial planning, forecasting, sales, quality management, and many other areas.

Unique to This Edition

Many of the insights and topics presented throughout this book are based on examples developed through discussions with top purchasing executives and from various research initiatives, including research published by CAPS Research, work at the North Carolina State University Supply Chain Resource Consortium, and a project on supplier integration funded by the National Science Foundation. The text also has a chapter format that includes an opening vignette, a set of sourcing snapshots, and a concluding good practice example that illustrates and integrates each chapter's topics. New and updated vignettes and examples, discussion questions, and additional readings provide up-to-date illustrations of the concepts presented in each chapter. In addition, as mentioned earlier, a number of new or enhanced topics are included.

The concept of cross-functional teaming and collaboration is emphasized throughout this book. Therefore, many of the case exercises require a team effort on the part of students. We recommend that the instructor have students work in teams for such projects to prepare them for the team environment found in most organizations.

Structure of the Book

This book is subdivided into six parts and twenty chapters that provide thorough coverage of purchasing and supply chain management.

Part 1: Introduction

Chapter 1 introduces the reader to purchasing and supply chain management. This chapter defines procurement and sourcing, introduces the notion of the supply chain, and summarizes the evolution of purchasing and supply chain management as an organizational activity.

Part 2: Purchasing Operations and Structure

The chapters in Part 2 provide an in-depth understanding of the fundamentals surrounding the operational activity called supply management. These chapters focus primarily on the fundamentals of purchasing as a functional activity. Without a solid understanding of purchasing basics, appreciating the important role that purchasing can play is difficult.

Chapter 2 provides an overview of the purchasing process by presenting the objectives of world-class purchasing organizations, the responsibilities of professional purchasers, the purchasing cycle, and various types of purchasing documents and types of purchases. In addition, this chapter now includes health care and services supply management case examples and snapshots. The Procure-to-Pay (P2P) cycle has been updated with new research in the process.

Chapter 3 examines various categories and types of purchasing policy and procedure. Ethical issues in procurement are emphasized here. This chapter includes updates on corporate social responsibility and sustainability as a component of purchasing policy and procedures as well as an updated list on the best companies for social responsibility and diversity in procurement.

Chapter 4 examines purchasing as a boundary-spanning function. Much of what purchasing involves requires interacting and working with other functional areas and suppliers. This chapter examines the intra-firm linkages between purchasing and other groups, including suppliers.

Chapter 5 focuses on purchasing and supply chain organization. This includes a discussion of purchasing in the organizational hierarchy, how the purchasing function is organized, and the placement of purchasing authority, including the center-led approach. The chapter also describes the team approach as part of the organizational structure.

Part 3: Strategic Sourcing

A major premise underlying this book is that purchasing is a critical process and makes as important a contribution as manufacturing, marketing, or engineering to the pursuit of a firm's strategic objectives. Progressive firms have little doubt about purchasing's impact on total quality, cost, delivery, technology, and responsiveness to the needs of external customers. Part 3 addresses what firms must do to achieve a competitive advantage from their procurement and sourcing processes. Realizing these advantages requires shifting our view of purchasing from a tactical or clerically oriented activity to one focusing on strategic supply management. This type of management involves developing the strategies, approaches, and methods for realizing a competitive advantage and improvement from the procurement and sourcing process, particularly through direct involvement and interaction with suppliers.

Chapter 6 develops an understanding of how firms set purchasing strategies and category management. This process should include a vision and plan of what a firm must do in its purchasing/sourcing efforts to support the achievement of corporate goals and objectives. Clearly, the category strategy development process should be the starting point for any discussion of strategic supply management. This chapter contains an updated section on strategic category management, reflecting the latest developments in the field. There are also discussions of insourcing versus outsourcing as a component of strategy, with examples featuring Boeing Corporation, illustrating how the economic recession is impacting category management strategies. There is also a new section on how to perform market intelligence and risk assessments for category management, as well as fresh information on stakeholder engagement.

Chapter 7 focuses on one of the most important processes performed by firms today—supplier evaluation, selection, and measurement. Selecting the right suppliers helps ensure that buyers receive the right inputs to satisfy their quality, cost, delivery, and technology requirements. Choosing the right suppliers also requires doing due diligence via supplier visits. Performing the selection process correctly creates the foundation for working closely with suppliers while continually enhancing performance.

Chapter 8 describes how a progressive and proactive buying firm incorporates supplier quality into its supplier selection and supplier performance evaluation processes. Improving supplier quality can also create substantial tactical and strategic competitive advantages that may not be available to competing firms. Six Sigma, ISO 9000, and ISO 14000 applications have been updated, and there are new sections on The Seven Wastes (Honda's BP process) and Basic Contents of a Supplier Quality Manual.

Chapter 9 describes what firms must do to manage and develop world-class supply-base performance. A focus on supplier development, managing supply base risk, and sustainability in the supply chain is provided. New sections to this chapter include Managing Supply Base Risk and Managing Sustainability in the Supply Base.

Finally, Chapter 10 focuses on worldwide sourcing, which is an important part of strategic supply management as firms search globally for the best resources.

Part 4: Strategic Sourcing Process

Chapter 11 focuses on strategic cost management, cost/price analysis, and target costing. Progressive firms focus on cost control and reduction with suppliers as a way to improve (i.e., reduce) purchase price over time. This chapter details various types of costs, presents cost analysis techniques, and discusses the factors that affect a supplier's price. The chapter also discusses total cost analysis, cost-based pricing, use of pricing indicators for category management and other innovative techniques designed to provide accurate and timely cost data. New sections on both strategic cost management and target costing at Honda of America and pricing indicators for different categories are included, as well as best practice research on strategic cost management based on a 2009 study.

Purchasing professionals rely on an assortment of tools, techniques, and approaches for managing the procurement and supply chain process.

Chapter 12 presents various quantitative tools that purchasers use when problem solving and pursuing performance improvements. Process mapping, value analysis, price break analysis, and the learning curve can help purchasers achieve specific outcomes such as reducing cost/price, improving quality, reducing time, or improving delivery performance from suppliers.

Chapter 13 deals with supply management negotiation. Effective supply managers must know how to plan for and negotiate value-adding contracts within a buyer-seller relationship. Increasingly, procurement contracts emphasize far more issues than simply purchase price. Buyers and sellers may negotiate cost reductions, delivery requirements, higher quality levels, payment terms, access to technology, or anything else important to the parties. The Negotiation Framework in Supply Management section has been revised, and The Impact of Electronic Media on Negotiations has been updated and expanded.

Chapter 14 addresses the fundamentals of contracting. The formal contracting process creates the framework for conducting business between two or more firms. As such, an understanding of contracting is essential when attempting to manage costs within a buyer-seller relationship. Contract management best practices are viewed in light of recent events and supply chain risk.

Chapter 15 addresses the major legal considerations in purchasing, including the legal authority of the purchasing manager. The chapter also discusses sources of U.S. law, warranties, purchase order contracts, breaches of contract, and patent and intellectual property rights. Because contracting is a part of the legal process, this chapter naturally follows the contracting chapter.

Part 5: Critical Supply Chain Elements

Part 5 describes the major activities that relate to or directly support supply chain management. Some of these activities involve specific disciplines, such as inventory management or transportation; other activities relate to the development of supply chain support systems. These systems include performance measurement systems and computerized information technology systems. The activities presented in this part may or may not be a formal part of the purchasing organization. These activities and systems, however, are key elements of purchasing and supply chain management.

Without them, purchasing most likely cannot pursue its goals and objectives effectively. Therefore, purchasing students must be familiar with a range of supply chain activities.

Chapter 16 focuses on overall lean thinking in supply management, including the management of a firm's inventory investment. The money that a firm commits to inventory usually involves a significant commitment of financial resources. This chapter discusses the function of inventory within a firm, factors leading to inventory waste, creating a lean supply chain, approaches for managing a firm's inventory investment, and future trends related to managing inventory.

The purchase of transportation and other services is another important supply consideration. We have witnessed major changes in transportation over the last two decades or so, many of which have affected supply management. Since Congress deregulated the U.S. transportation industry in the early 1980s, the role of the buyer has changed dramatically. More than ever, supply management is involving itself in the evaluation, selection, and management of transportation modes and carriers. Even if a buyer does not get involved directly with transportation, having a working knowledge of this dynamic area is critical.

Chapter 17 highlights supply management's role in procuring transportation, as well as services buying, presents a decision-making framework for developing a transportation procurement strategy, discusses ways to control and influence inbound transportation, and evaluates trends affecting the purchase of transportation services, such as performance based logistics. Four sections in this chapter have been revised or updated.

Information technology systems are changing business. Purchasing, too, can benefit from the development of current information technology systems.

Chapter 18 examines the role of technology in supply chain information systems and electronic commerce. The chapter addresses the newer Internet-based electronic linkages between firms as well as traditional electronic data interchange (EDI). The chapter also discusses the impact of social networking, blogs, and cloud computing in addition to advanced and future e-purchasing and supply systems' applications. The use of information technology systems greatly enhances supply management's ability to operate at the highest levels of efficiency and effectiveness.

Chapter 19 focuses on performance measurement and evaluation with a new emphasis on innovation sourcing and an update on trends. Increasingly, firms must develop valid measurement systems that reveal how well a firm is performing, including the performance of its purchasing and supply chain management efforts. These systems need to be clearly linked to overall company objectives. Measurement systems support procurement and sourcing decision making by providing accurate and timely performance data. This chapter examines why firms measure performance, defines various purchasing performance measurement categories, and discusses how to develop a purchasing performance measurement system, including a balanced scorecard. In this chapter, data on supply strategy performance results has been updated.

Part 6: Future Directions

Chapter 20 focuses on what purchasing and supply chain management will look like by 2018. These trends, which are adapted directly from recent surveys and studies of key executive managers from a variety of global organizations, can help students identify how the field of purchasing and sourcing management is changing and what skills they will need to develop in view of these changes. The latest predictions are included from CAPS Research Executive Assessments of Supply, a joint CAPS Research, A.T. Kearney, and ISM study focused on supply strategies for the decade ahead, and other research studies and discussions with supply executives.

Case Studies and Instructor's Resources

Purchasing and Supply Chain Management features new and revised cases throughout the book. These cases were thoroughly tested in the classroom and used within the industry. A test bank, PowerPoint® presentations, and other ancillary instructional materials are available on the book's companion website to help instructors identify how best to use and interpret the text and cases. Of particular interest are the negotiation and supplier selection cases, which allow students to experience personally the purchasing decision-making process in real time. Access the companion website by going to www.cengagebrain.com and searching for this book by its title.

Acknowledgments

We very much appreciate the work of Conor Allen, Associate Content Developer at Cengage Learning, and Joseph Malcolm, Associate Program Manager at Lumina Datamatics, in making this Sixth Edition possible.

Robert M. Monczka

Robert B. Handfield

Larry C. Giunipero

James L. Patterson

About the Authors

Robert M. Monczka, Ph.D., is former Distinguished Research Professor of Supply Chain Management in the W. P. Carey School of Business at Arizona State University and is Professor Emeritus at the Eli Broad Graduate School of Management, Michigan State University. He also served as Director of Strategic Sourcing and Supply Chain Strategy Research at CAPS Research, where he led initiatives focused on sourcing and supply strategy innovation, development, and implementation. Dr. Monczka has published more than 200 books and articles and is a frequent speaker at professional meetings. He has consulted worldwide with leading companies in the Fortune 100 and has received two National Science Foundation grants to study supply strategy. He is also a recipient of the J. Shipman Gold Medal Award, supply management's highest honor.

Robert B. Handfield, Ph.D., is Bank of America University Distinguished Professor of Supply Chain Management in the College of Management at North Carolina State University. He is also Co-Director of the Supply Chain Resource Cooperative (http://scrc.ncsu .edu). He is Consulting Editor of the *Journal of Operations Management* and on the editorial board of several leading academic journals. His research focuses on strategic sourcing, supply market intelligence, supplier relationship management, and sourcing overseas. He has served in consulting and executive education roles for more than 20 Fortune 500 companies.

Larry C. Giunipero, Ph.D., CPSM, C.P.M., is Professor of Purchasing and Supply Chain Management at Florida State University. He has published more than 60 articles in various academic journals. His research interests focus on supply management, including supply chain sourcing strategies and relationships, supply management skills and competencies, risk management, global sourcing and e-purchasing. He has served as a consultant and/ or executive trainer in more than 25 Fortune 1000 organizations both domestically and globally.

James L. Patterson, Ph.D., C.P.M., A.P.P., is Assistant Dean and Associate Professor of Supply Chain Management in the College of Business and Technology at Western Illinois University–Quad Cities. A Michigan State University Ph.D. alumnus in SCM, he holds lifetime C.P.M. and A.P.P. credentials from the Institute for Supply Management. He has been honored twice as *Outstanding Teacher of the Year* for WIU's College of Business and Technology and four times in *Who's Who Among America's Teachers*. He is currently President of the Quad-City Foreign Trade Zone #133 and a longtime reviewer for the *Journal of Supply Chain Management.* His research interests include supply chain risk management, supply chain fraud, negotiation and conflict resolution, and strategic sourcing strategy.

Introduction

Chapter 1   Introduction to Purchasing and Supply Chain Management

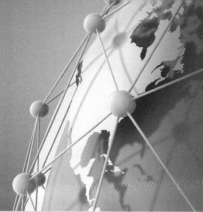

Introduction to Purchasing and Supply Chain Management

CHAPTER 16

Learning Objectives

After completing this chapter, you should be able to

- Understand the differences between purchasing and supply management
- Understand the differences between supply chains and value chains
- Identify the activities that are part of supply chain management
- Appreciate the importance of supply chain enablers
- Identify the historical stages of purchasing's evolution

Chapter Outline

CSX Purchasing and Supply: Managing into the Winds of Change

Michael O'Malley, a University of Illinois graduate, knows all about the winds of change from his days in his hometown of Chicago (aka the Windy City). When O'Malley was named vice president of Procurement & Supply Chain Management at CSX Transportation several months ago, he felt that changes were needed to get his sourcing team on a faster track. Since his appointment to the job, he has put the company's procurement and supply chain function on the "strategic and global" track to twenty-first century excellence.

CSX is one of four Class 1 Railroads in the United States. In 2013 the company had sales of over $12 billion and net earnings of $1.86 billion ($1.83/share). With a barrel of crude oil fluctuating in the $70 to $125 range the past three years and fuel prices in the $2.50 to $3.00 a gallon range, railroads have become a favorite of many shippers interested in taking advantage of their superior fuel efficiency. The U.S. railroads' low cost-per-ton-mile allows them to compete very favorably with other transportation modes. Railroads own both the land and the rails that support the movement of freight via locomotives and railcars. Keeping a modern railroad running, however, requires that significant amounts of money be reinvested into infrastructure. The firm plans to spend approximately $ 5 billion during 2014, which requires a skilled procurement and supply chain group to manage that spend effectively.

Supporting this favorable business growth trend and sustaining high levels of customer service, while controlling materials costs, posed major challenges for the CSX procurement and supply chain department. Meeting the challenge was compounded by a changing supply base. O'Malley states, "A reduction in the number of railroads and the subsequent consolidation of purchases resulted in a downsizing of our domestic supply base." With the growth in shipments experienced by the U.S. Class 1 Railroads, the limited number of domestic suppliers is a concern.

O'Malley and his buying team's $5 billion annual purchase expenditures are spread over a broad group of products and services. The CSX procurement and supply chain management group purchase over 100,000 unique items necessary to keep 21,000 route miles of track, about 100,000 freight cars, and over 4,300 locomotives moving freight to customers. The geographic range is large, consisting of 23 eastern states and the District of Columbia, as well as two Canadian provinces. CSX serves thousands of localities and customers and connects to more than 70 ocean, river and lake ports. CSX's intermodal business links customers to railroads via trucks and terminals. CSXT also serves thousands of production and distribution facilities through track connections to approximately 240 short-line and regional railroads. This extensive network reaches nearly two-thirds of the population in the United States.

"Based on the demands of our operating environment, the shrinking supply base, and the need to continuously add value to the company from a supply perspective, it was a no-brainer that we had to develop a more global perspective," says O'Malley.

His goal was to raise the skill levels of his organization to meet the global as well as other challenges required of a twenty-first century supply function. Toward that end, O'Malley requires all current employees and new hires to further develop their skill sets and attain the status of Certified Professional in Supply Management (CPSM). Currently over 70 percent of his supply management professionals are CPSM certified. "As we move to an even more strategic focus, CSX must continue to raise the bar and focus its resources on development of its highly talented professionals. The CPSM provides a basic foundation for this growth, and we are leveraging that base to develop our strategic approach to sourcing." says O'Malley.

"The journey from a domestic to a global supply base, coupled with a more strategic focus in our supply group, allows our team to make a significant and lasting impact," O'Malley states. Michael reorganized his resources and formed a team focused on developing current suppliers and growing the supply base. The mission of the new team is to identify commodities with sourcing sensitivities, and then develop new or existing suppliers to meet the needs of the company from a global perspective.

An early success was the development of a new steel rail supplier from Eastern Europe. With this addition, CSX now sources its steel rail from two domestic rail mills, a Japanese mill, and a recently approved mill in the Czech Republic. Assistant Vice President-Engineering Thomas Holmes led the team that identified this new opportunity, noting that "CSX has worked hard to ensure we have a strong base of suppliers, both global and domestic, who are prepared to meet all our rail infrastructure needs."

On the locomotive side of the business, O'Malley has his Assistant Vice President-Mechanical Frank Carbone scouring the globe for wheels, brake shoes, and freight car parts. "Many of the commodities in the marketplace where we play are becoming global," states Carbone. So, in another effort to enhance the skill set of his purchasing team, CSX had its key managers and staff attend a series of global sourcing workshops. "The customized workshops provided our team with a much deeper understanding of global sourcing issues and required relationships," he states. To date, the department has several global sourcing initiatives in the pipeline. Some are pending approval from standards agencies like the American Association of Railroads (AAR), while others require physical, metallurgical or service testing to ensure their integrity.

"We won't cut corners," says O'Malley. To support that statement, the company combined resources from around CSX to centralize and expand supplier quality and product performance efforts into his group. With the cooperation and support of the Mechanical (freight cars and locomotives) and Engineering (track and structures) departments, the group was centralized in Procurement and Supply Chain Management and its scope was expanded to include all critical materials for these key internal customers.

Complementing the global push is CSX's extensive involvement in e-commerce. The railroads have a long history of doing business electronically, beginning with their pioneering efforts in using EDI with their customers. CSX continues the use of electronic tools to facilitate sourcing. According to Neil Versteeg, Director of Process Improvement, "98.6 percent of our purchasing expenditures are now transmitted electronically. Versteeg further states, "On an average month we run about 2,000 items a day over our Oracle system."

Putting the right structure in place to achieve results in all these different, yet related areas is no easy task. "I felt my core team was somewhat disjointed and hindered the ability to make rapid decisions," states O'Malley. "I needed to streamline our organization and become able to identify and seize market opportunities quickly." O'Malley's vision is to have a lean, responsive supply management organization that anticipates and meets the needs of CSX. "I want to be like a Home Depot... by having a quality product available, at a convenient place and at the right cost, while working with both our suppliers and internal customers to provide a very high level of cooperation and customer service after the sale."

O'Malley is pushing his procurement team to work at a more strategic level, providing services to their business partners that add value and support the company's growth objectives. "In today's rapidly changing environment we need skilled, open-minded supply professionals who can deliver results to our organization regardless of economic conditions and in any area of spend." I view our purchasing and supply area as a major contributor to the bottom line and critical to the service capabilities of our railroad company." Accomplishing their mission requires a staff of dedicated professionals who can ensure availability of the locomotives, cars, track, and maintenance parts needed to keep CSX trains running at a very demanding operating capacity. O'Malley is optimistic that their sourcing group will continue to build on their string of recent successes. The winds of business change are strong, but at CSX Purchasing and Materials O'Malley feels his staff has the skills and talent to successfully navigate those changing winds.

Source: L. Giunipero, Interview with E. Michael O'Malley and CSX supply management personnel, June & September 2013.

Introduction

As the CSX story illustrates, the development of strategic purchasing practices can help a company maintain or improve its competitive position in a rapidly changing business environment. In reality, it is only recently that managers would even place the words "strategic" and "purchasing" in the same sentence. Prior to the twenty-first century, the life of many purchasing professionals was comfortable and predictable. When someone required something, a buyer sent a request to suppliers for competitive bids, awarded short-term contracts based on price, enjoyed a free lunch or ball game with salespeople, and figured out how to meet not-too-demanding performance measures. Although the buying position did not carry much prestige, it was a stable job.

This model worked relatively well until new competitors from around the world showed there was a better way to manage purchasing and the supply base. New and better methods helped these competitors achieve dramatic reductions in cost, exponential improvements in quality, and unheard-of reductions in the time it takes to develop new products. This new model featured closer relationships with important suppliers, performing due diligence on suppliers before awarding long-term contracts, conducting worldwide Internet searches for the best sources of supply, and inviting key suppliers to participate in product and process development. Furthermore, executive managers began to require purchasing professionals to achieve demanding performance improvements. What really changed the purchasers' comfortable world, and ended the era of free lunches, was global competition. Borrowing a phrase from Thomas Friedman, the world is flat, and competition is now 24/7, anywhere and anytime.[1]

As is illustrated in the CSX story, global sourcing is a requirement and no longer a luxury for most firms. This chapter introduces the reader to the changing world of purchasing and supply chain management. The world has dramatically changed during the first 14 years of the twenty-first century, and the rate of change will continue to accelerate going forward. The first section of this chapter describes the new competitive environment where we now operate—an environment that affects every major industry. We next present the reasons why purchasing has taken on increased importance. Third, we clarify the confusing terminology that surrounds purchasing and supply chain management. The next sections present the activities that are part of supply chain management, discuss the four enablers of purchasing and supply chain excellence, and review the historic evolution of purchasing and supply chain management. The last section outlines the contents of this book.

A New Competitive Environment

Today's business climate features increasing numbers of world-class competitors, domestically and internationally, that are forcing organizations to improve their internal processes to stay competitive. Sophisticated customers, both industrial and consumer, no longer talk about price increases—they demand price reductions! Information that is available over the Internet will continue to alter the balance of power between buyers and sellers. An abundance of competitors and choices have conditioned customers to want higher quality, faster delivery, and products and services tailored to their individual needs at a lower total cost. The widespread use of "social media" through Twitter and blogs spread information about products and services at an accelerated rate. If a company is not meeting its requirements, consumers will quickly "spread the word" and they will find someone who is more accommodating.

In the work environment, mobile devices permit constant contact with job activities enabling purchasers to be connected on a 24/7 basis. One of the major facilitators of increased mobility is the dramatic drop in cost of storing and retrieving data. Part of this efficiency is driven by "cloud-based" storage systems that provide all sized firms and individuals access to massive amounts of data at very low costs. The lines between work, play, buying, and promotion are both blurred and shifting to the individual. These trends in mobility have significant impact on where and when work is performed in purchasing.

While historically, the speed at which information moved was slower than current times, firms still valued customer loyalty. In the 1960s and 1970s, companies began to develop detailed market strategies that focused on creating and capturing this loyalty. Before long, organizations also realized that this required a strong engineering, design, and manufacturing function to support these market requirements. Design engineers had to translate customer requirements into product and service specifications, which then had to be produced at a high level of quality at a reasonable cost. As the demand for new products increased throughout the 1980s, organizations had to become flexible and responsive to modify existing products, services, and processes, or to develop new ones to meet ever-changing customer needs.

As organizational capabilities improved further in the 1990s, managers began to realize that material and service inputs from suppliers had a major impact on their ability to meet customer needs. This led to an increased focus on the supply base and the responsibilities of purchasing. Managers also realized that producing a quality product was not enough. Getting the right products and services to customers at the right time, cost, and place, and in the right condition, and quantity constituted an entirely new type of challenge. The twenty-first century has spawned a whole set of time-reducing information technologies and logistics networks aimed at meeting these new challenges.

The availability of low-cost alternatives has led to unprecedented shifts toward outsourcing and offshoring. The impact of China as a major world competitor poses tremendous challenges for U.S. firms in both the manufacturing and services sectors. Because the services sector now accounts for over 70 percent of the Gross Domestic Product, new strategies are required for effective supply management in this sector. Recent economic trends in Chinese wages, complexity of supply chains, and well publicized quality problems have caused firms to reassess the economics of Chinese sourcing strategies. Chinese labor rates increased 14 percent in 2012 and are up 71 percent since 2008.[2] Supply strategies must now evaluate the economics of *re-shoring* and *near-shoring*. **Re-shoring** involves bringing some sourcing back to the United States, while **near-shoring** involves evaluating suppliers located closer to United States. Such suppliers may be located in Mexico and Central and South America.

All these changes have made twenty-first century organizations realize how important it is to actively manage their *supply base*. The supply base consists of all the suppliers that provide and organization with its materials and services. In some organization's this supply base extends to the network of downstream firms responsible for delivery and aftermarket service of the product to the end customer. The realization that competitive advantage could be achieved by managing both upstream (suppliers) and downstream (customers) flows led to a focus on *supply chains* and *supply chain management*.

Several factors are driving an emphasis on supply chain management. First, the *low cost and increased availability of information resources* among entities in the supply chain allow easy linkages that eliminate time delays in the network. Second, the *level of competition* in both domestic and international markets requires organizations to be fast, agile, and flexible. Third, *customer expectations and requirements* are becoming much more demanding. Fourth, the *ability of an organization's supply chain to identify and mitigate risk* minimizes disruptions in both supply and downstream product or services to mitigate the impact on lost sales. As customer demands increase, organizations and their suppliers must be responsive or face the prospect of losing market share. Competition today is no longer between firms; it is between the supply chains of those firms. The companies that configure the best supply chains will be the market winners and gain competitive advantage.

Why Purchasing Is Important

Increasing Value and Savings

As companies struggle to increase customer value by improving performance, many companies are turning their attention to purchasing and supply management. Consider, for example, CSX, the company featured at the beginning of this chapter. Almost 45 percent of the total sales of CSX is expended with suppliers for the purchase of materials and services. It does not take a financial genius to realize the impact that suppliers can have on a firm's total cost. Furthermore, many features that make their way into final products originate with suppliers. The supply base is an important part of the supply chain. Supplier capabilities can help differentiate a producer's final good or service, increasing their value to the final customer.

In the manufacturing sector, the percentage of purchases to sales averages 55 percent. This means that for every dollar of revenue collected on goods and services sales, more than half goes back to suppliers. It is not difficult to see why purchasing is clearly a major area for cost savings. Cost savings also encompasses avoiding costs through early involvement with design and proactively responding to supplier requests for price increases.

Building Relationships and Driving Innovation

As mentioned above, savings come in different forms; the traditional approach is to bargain hard for price reductions. A newer approach is to build relations with suppliers to jointly pull costs out of the product or service and expect suppliers to contribute innovative ideas that continually add value to a firm's products and services.

Examples of supply managers building these relationships are occurring in many industries. For example, that's what happened a few years ago when two senior executives, one from Shell and one from Hewlett-Packard (HP), were having a conversation. HP is a strategic supplier of end-user services, service desk, and hardware to Shell and, as part of Shell's focus on supplier relationship management, the executives meet to discuss business value. Because both companies focus on innovation, the conversation eventually turned to what's new in R&D. The HP executive talked about research into a new wireless printer head the size of a postage stamp that works by picking up vibrations (using sensing technology). The information piqued Shell's interest because its deep-water oil explorations use sensing technology to discover rock formations that could hold oil several miles under the ocean. That simple conversation sparked a collaboration between the two companies to produce a system to sense, collect, and store geophysical data.[3]

David H. Cummins, senior supplier manager, strategic sourcing for Shell Global Projects U.S. in Houston, says the example proves that dedication to uncovering supplier value and capabilities is a never-ending process. "The value that was uncovered was part of a conversation that had nothing to do with the current services provided," he says. "Finding hidden capabilities is about putting each other's brains to work on challenges and to come up with something that is new and tangible. Very often capabilities are revealed when you are having deep conversations about mutual interests."[4]

For these relationships to work, both the buyer and supplier must agree to acceptable paybacks from their investments so that each realizes a positive gain. If the suppliers' strategic intent is to be the customer of choice, then they need to provide necessary technical infrastructure to assist the buyer. As the above example illustrates, when both parties cooperate, a climate of trust emerges between the parties setting the stage for innovative ideas.

Improving Quality and Reputation

Purchasing and supply management also has a major impact on product and service quality. In many cases, companies are seeking to increase the proportion of parts, components, and services they outsource in order to concentrate on their own areas of specialization and competence. This further increases the importance of the relationships among purchasing, external suppliers, and quality. The following example illustrates this important link between supplier quality and product quality. Lululemon Athletica is a provider of high-end yoga pants and other athletic gear for women. The company experienced vibrant growth in its athletic apparel until supplier quality problems created a "brand nightmare." In March of 2013, the apparel maker had to recall its yoga pants as they were too "shear." This sheerness created a "see through" look that did not sit well with high-end consumers who had paid a premium for the product. Lululemon's supplier claimed it was making the pants in accordance with the specifications. The results showed otherwise and eliminating the sheer pants from the market proved more difficult than expected. While steps have been taken to correct the problem, the toll on the company has been significant. In June of 2013 came the announcement that CEO Christine Day would leave her position. Lululemon's stock price was also affected by both these events, and it slid from $79 a share earlier in the year to $61 in late June of 2013.[5] This example illustrates the importance of the supplier quality in the selection process and how a poor quality input affects the entire supply chain, including finished product and brand name reputation. This example further illustrates how lapses in managing supplier quality can potentially tarnish a firm's reputation.

Reducing Time to Market

Purchasing, acting as the liaison between suppliers and engineers, can also help improve product and process designs. For example, companies that involve suppliers early, compared to companies that do not involve suppliers, achieve an average 20 percent improvement on materials costs, material quality, and product development times. Development teams that include suppliers as members also report they receive more improvement suggestions from suppliers than teams that do not involve suppliers. Thus, involving suppliers early in the design process is a way purchasing can begin to add new value and contribute to increasing competitiveness.

Managing Supplier Risk

Every time purchasing places an order with a supplier a potential risk arises; this risk could be as minor as a late delivery or as major as loss of an entire supplier due to bankruptcy or natural disaster (fire, etc.). The example in the paragraph above illustrates the major impact poor quality can have on an organization. Unfortunately, poor quality is only one supply threat; others include natural disasters, financial instability, operational problems, transportation delays, and so on. These risks are magnified by sourcing strategies that emphasized global sourcing, single sourcing, and JIT inventory. Certainly there were benefits realized from these strategies, however, often the increased vigilance necessary to mitigate and manage these additional risks was not established. For example, the 2011 tsunami that hit Japan left Honda and Toyota with supply shortages for months and cost millions of dollars in sales. Progressive supply managers must continually monitor their supply base for risk and develop business continuity plans to mitigate these risks.

Generating Economic Impact

The power of organizational purchasers as a group is significant. The *ISM Report on Business* is one of the most closely followed indicators of economic activity. This monthly survey of purchasing managers in both the manufacturing and non-manufacturing sectors is closely monitored by the financial sector, and the results of both reports have the power to move financial markets. The *ISM Report on Business* is a change index, and generally a rating over 50 indicates the economy is expanding. A full discussion of the *ISM Report on Business* can be found at http://www.ism.ws/ISMReport/

Contributing to Competitive Advantage

Many executives will agree that a focus on effective purchasing has become a critical way to gain competitive advantage. An indication of this enhanced status, reputation, and recognition is the higher salaries being paid to purchasing professionals. The most recent *Inside Supply Management* magazine salary survey showed an average annual income of $103,793.

Entry level professionals averaged $51,600 annually, supply managers $102,300, and those classified as vice presidents $217,100. Having a bachelor's degree counts, as they earned 20 percent more than colleagues with a high school degree and 13 percent more than those purchasers with an associate's degree. Continuing education through certification also fattens the wallet. Those purchasers who attained their Certified Professional in Supply Management (CPSM) earned 9 percent more than those without a CPSM designation.[6] This study also reported that bonuses averaged over 13 percent of base salaries. The bonus was based on a combination of company, department, and individual performance.

Managing talent requires a constant focus on finding, developing, and promoting individuals who will contribute to making the supply management department recognized as a strategic contributor to the organization. One major integrated oil company developed a core training program for its purchasing/supply chain management group (PSCM) to develop talent. The program consisted of a four-phased approach and recognized experience differences. The four phases were: (1) PSCM common buying processes; (2) PSCM curriculum consisting of classes in areas such as contracting, negotiations, strategic cost management, and so on; (3) Professional accreditation and education such as the CPSM and MBA programs; and (4) Professional leadership development program. This program recognized the differences between those with one to three years of experience and those with four years and above. Finding, developing, and retaining top-tier talent is vital to furthering supply management's impact on company strategies and competitiveness.

Understanding the Language of Purchasing and Supply Chain Management

Anyone who has written about purchasing and supply chain management has defined the various terms associated with these concepts one way or another, making confusion about the subjects a real possibility. How, for example, is purchasing different from supply management? Are supply chains and value chains the same? What is supply chain management? What is an extended enterprise? It is essential to define various terms before proceeding with this book.

Purchasing and Supply Management

We need to recognize the differences between purchasing and supply management. Purchasing is a functional group (i.e., a formal entity on the organizational chart) as well as a functional activity (i.e., buying goods and services). The purchasing group performs many activities to ensure it delivers maximum value to the organization. Examples include supplier identification and selection; buying, negotiation, and contracting; supply market research; supplier measurement and improvement; and purchasing systems development. Purchasing has been referred to as doing "the five rights": getting the right quality, in the right quantity, at the right time, for the right price, from the right source. In this text we will interchange the terms "purchasing" and "procurement."

Supply management is not just a new name for purchasing but a more inclusive concept. We feel supply management is a *strategic approach to planning for and acquiring the organization's current and future needs through effectively managing the supply base, utilizing a process orientation in conjunction with cross-functional teams (CFTs) to achieve the organizational mission.* Similar to our definition, the Institute for Supply Management defines supply management as *the identification, acquisition, access, positioning, and management of resources and related capabilities an organization needs or potentially needs in the attainment of its strategic objectives.*[7] Exhibit 1.1 depicts the key elements in our definition of supply management.

Supply management requires pursuing strategic responsibilities, which are those activities that have a major impact on the long-term performance of the organization. These long-term responsibilities are not pursued in isolation, but should be aligned with the overall mission and strategies of the organization. These strategies exclude routine, simple, or day-to-day decisions that may be part of traditional purchasing responsibilities. The routine ordering and follow-up of basic operational supplies is not a strategic responsibility. The development of the systems that enable internal users to order routine supplies, however, is considerably more important.

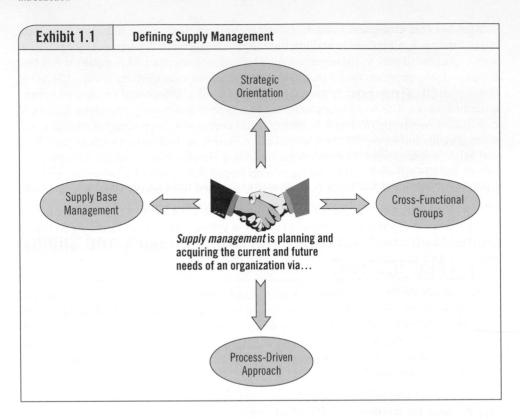

Exhibit 1.1 | Defining Supply Management

Strategic Orientation

Supply Base Management

Cross-Functional Groups

Supply management is planning and acquiring the current and future needs of an organization via…

Process-Driven Approach

Supply management is a broader concept than purchasing. Supply management is a progressive approach to **managing the supply base** that differs from a traditional arm's-length or adversarial approach with sellers. It requires purchasing professionals to work directly with those suppliers that are capable of providing world-class performance and advantages to the buyer. Think of supply management as a strategic and supercharged version of basic purchasing.

Supply management often takes a **process approach** to obtaining required goods and services. We can describe supply management as the process of identifying, evaluating, selecting, managing, and developing suppliers to realize supply chain performance that is better than that of competitors. We will interchange the terms "purchasing," "supply management," and "strategic sourcing" throughout this book.

Supply management is **cross-functional**, meaning it involves purchasing, engineering, supplier quality assurance, the supplier, and other related functions working together as one team, early on, to further mutual goals. Instead of adversarial relationships, which characterize traditional purchasing, supply management features a long-term, win-win relationship between a buying company and specially selected suppliers. Except for ownership, the supplier almost becomes an extension of the buying company. Supply management also recognizes the mutual benefits to both parties, through shared information, provisions for on-site resources, and frequent help to suppliers in exchange for dramatic and continuous performance improvements, including steady price reductions. In short, supply management is a new way of operating, involving internal operations and external suppliers to achieve advances in cost management, product development, cycle times, and total quality control.

Organizationally, leading and coordinating strategic supply management activities have largely become the responsibility of the functional group called purchasing. Practicing professionals often use the terms "supply management" and "purchasing" interchangeably. Through the above discussion we have sought to clarify some of the differences while recognizing that good purchasing and supply management practices can have significant impact on the organization's overall performance.

Supply Chains and Value Chains

Over time, researchers and practitioners have developed dozens of definitions to describe supply chains and supply chain management. One group of researchers has indicated that defining supply chain management both as a philosophy and as a set of operational activities creates confusion.[8] These researchers break down the concept into three areas and separate supply chains from supply chain orientation and from supply chain management.

A **supply chain** is a set of three or more organizations linked directly by one or more of the upstream or downstream flows of products, services, finances, and information from a source to a customer. It is important to acknowledge that anytime business is conducted a supply chain will exist. A **supply chain orientation** is a higher-level recognition of the strategic value of managing operational activities and flows within and across a supply chain. **Supply chain management** then, endorses a supply chain orientation and involves proactively managing the two-way movement and coordination of goods, services, information, and funds (i.e., the various flows) from raw material through end user. According to this definition, supply chain management requires the coordination of activities and flows that extend across boundaries. Organizations that endorse a supply chain orientation are likely to emphasize supply chain management.[9]

Regardless of the definition or supply chain perspective used, we should recognize that supply chains are composed of interrelated activities that are *internal* and *external* to a firm. These activities are diverse in their scope; the participants who support them are often located across geographic boundaries and often come from diverse cultures.

Although many activities are part of supply chain management (which a later section discusses), an improved perspective visualizes supply chains as composed of processes rather than discrete, often poorly aligned activities and tasks. A *process* consists of a set of interrelated tasks or activities designed to achieve a specific objective or outcome. New-product development (NPD), customer-order fulfillment, supplier evaluation and selection, and demand and supply planning are examples of critical organizational processes that are part of supply chain management. Recent product recalls of consumer products such as automobiles, toys, peanut butter, and dog food have placed increasing emphasis on a new supply chain concept: the **reverse supply chain**; its goal is to rapidly identify and return these tainted products back through the supply chain. Toyota's much publicized quality breakdowns that created acceleration and braking problems led to massive recalls and forced Toyota to temporarily suspend the sales of certain models.

In this case the creation of a reverse supply chain was necessary to fix defective brakes and gas pedals was necessary to fix these problems and restore confidence in the Toyota brand.

Value chains vs. Supply chains

A question that often arises, and one that has no definite answer, involves the difference between a value chain and a supply chain. Michael Porter, who first articulated the value chain concept in the 1980s, argues that a firm's **value chain** is composed of primary and support activities that can lead to competitive advantage when configured properly. The accumulation of these activities results in the total value added by the firm. Exhibit 1.2 presents a modified version of Porter's value chain model. This exhibit also defines some important supply chain-related terms and places them in their proper context.

One way to think about the difference between a value chain and a supply chain is to conceptualize the supply chain as a subset of the value chain. All personnel within an organization are part of a value chain. The same is not true about supply chains. The primary activities, or the horizontal flow across Exhibit 1.2, represent the operational part of the value chain, or what some refer to as the supply chain. At an organizational level, the value chain is broader than the supply chain, because it includes all activities in the form of primary and support activities. Furthermore, the original value chain concept focused primarily on internal participants, whereas a supply chain, by definition, is both internally and externally focused.

To reflect current thinking, we must expand the original value chain model, which focused primarily on internal participants, to include suppliers and customers who reside well upstream and downstream from the focal organization. Multiple levels of suppliers and customers form the foundation for the **extended value chain** or the **extended enterprise** concept, which states that success is a function of effectively managing a linked group of firms past first-level suppliers or customers. In fact, progressive firms understand that managing cost, quality, and delivery requires attention to suppliers that reside several tiers from the producer. The extended enterprise concept recognizes explicitly that competition is no longer between firms but rather between coordinated supply chains or networks of firms.

Notice that Exhibit 1.2 identifies purchasing as a support activity. This means that purchasing provides a service to internal customers. Although purchasing is the central link with suppliers that provide direct materials, which is the upstream or left-hand side of Exhibit 1.2, purchasing can support the materials and service requirements of any internal group. *Direct materials* are those items provided by suppliers and used directly during production or service delivery. Purchasing is becoming increasingly responsible for sourcing *indirect goods* and services required by internal groups. Examples of indirect items include personal computers, office and janitorial supplies, health care contracts, transportation services, advertising and media, and travel. Although indirect items are not required for production, they are still vital to the effective running of an organization. The right-hand side of the model illustrates the customer, or downstream, portion of the supply chain. Because meeting or exceeding customer expectations is the lifeblood of any organization, it should become the focal point of supply chain activities.

Exhibit 1.2 presents a relatively straightforward and linear view of the value and supply chain, which is often not the case. First, the flows of materials, information, funds, and knowledge across a supply chain are often fragmented and uncoordinated. The "hand-off" points from one group to the next or from one organization to the next usually provide opportunity for improvements. Second, the value chain model shows suppliers linking with inbound logistics and then operations. Although this is usually the case with direct materials, indirect items and finished goods sourced externally can result in suppliers delivering to any part of the supply chain.

Supply Chains Illustrated

The increasing importance of supply chain management is forcing organizations to rethink how their purchasing and sourcing strategies fit with and support broader business and supply chain objectives. Supply chains involve multiple organizations as we move toward the raw material suppliers or downstream toward the ultimate customer. Simple supply chains pull materials directly from their origin, process them, package them, and ship them to consumers.

A good example of a simple supply chain involves cereal producers (see Exhibit 1.3). A cereal company purchases the grain from a farmer and processes it into cereal.

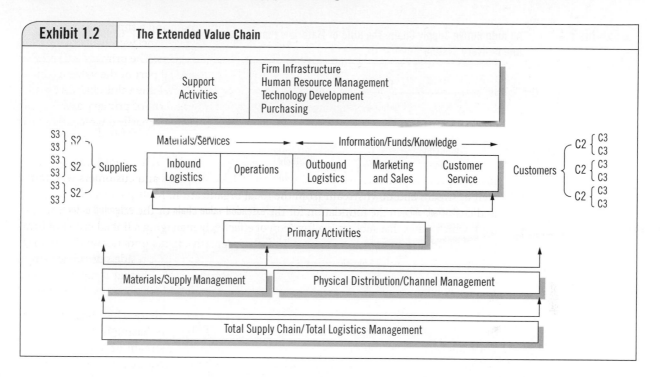

Exhibit 1.2   The Extended Value Chain

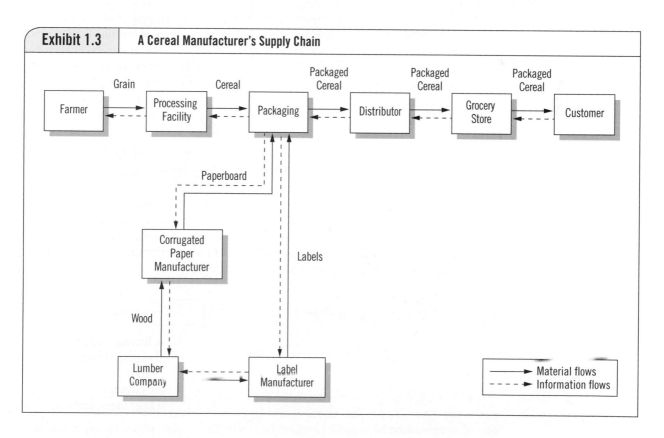

Exhibit 1.3   A Cereal Manufacturer's Supply Chain

Exhibit 1.4	An Automotive Supply Chain: The Role of Materials Planning and Logistics in the Production and Delivery System

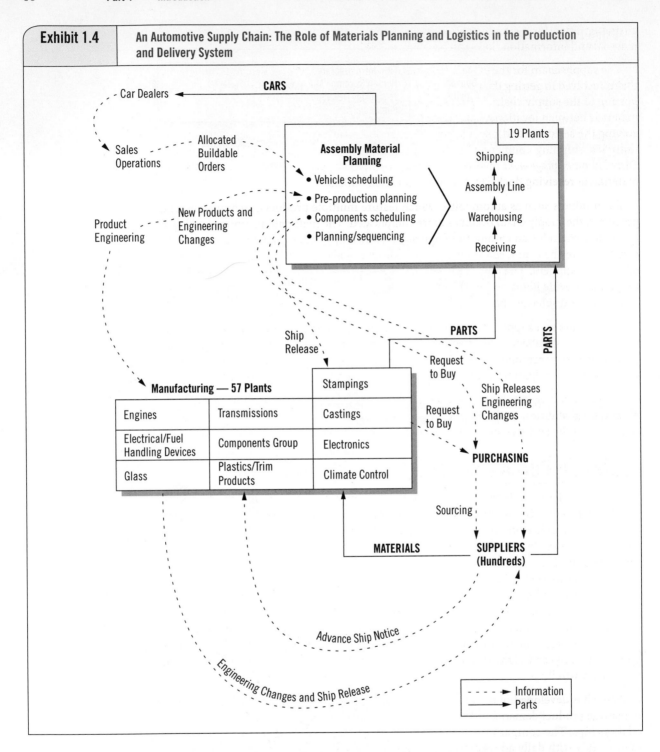

The cereal company also purchases the paperboard from a paper manufacturer, which purchased the trees to make the paper, and labels from a label manufacturer, which purchased semifinished label stock to make the labels. The cereal is then packaged and sent to a distributor, which in turn ships the material to a grocer, who then sells it to an end customer. Even for a simple product such as cereal, the number of transactions and of material and information flows can be considerable.

The supply chain for the cereal manufacturer features an extensive distribution network that is involved in getting the packaged cereal to the final customer. Within the *downstream* portion of the supply chain, logistics managers are responsible for the actual movement of materials between locations. One major part of logistics is *transportation management,* in volving the selection and management of external carriers (trucking companies, airlines, railroads, shipping companies) or the management of internal private fleets of carriers. *Distribution management* involves the management of packaging, storing, and handling of materials at receiving docks, warehouses, and retail outlets.

For products such as automobiles, which feature multiple products, technologies, and processes, the supply chain becomes more complicated. The materials, planning, and logistics supply chain for an automotive company is shown in Exhibit 1.4, which illustrates the complexity of the chain, spanning from automotive dealers back through multiple levels or tiers of suppliers. The automotive company's supplier base includes the thousands of firms that provide items ranging from raw materials, such as steel and plastics, to complex assemblies and subassemblies, such as transmissions, brakes, and engines.

Participants in a supply chain are willing to share such information only when there is trust between members. Thus, the management of relationships with other parties in the chain becomes paramount. Effective supply chain organizations are built on *relationships* (sometimes called "partnerships" or "alliances") that require shared resources.

For instance, organizations may provide dedicated capacity, specific information, technological capabilities, or even direct financial support to other members of their supply chain so that the entire chain can benefit.

Achieving Purchasing and Supply Chain Benefits

When the pieces come together, can the assumption of a supply chain orientation with the right kinds of activities really produce the results envisioned by proponents? Consider the rebirth of Apple Computer, which had *BusinessWeek* asking in 1997, "Is Apple mincemeat?"[10] Apple made a great comeback through an impressive, steady stream of new and innovative products such as the iPod, iPod Nano, iPhone, iPad and the new iPhone 5s and less expensive iPad. Apple has reengineered itself from being considered "mincemeat" to now once again being a great company. While recent increased competition from android phones and other mobile devices have slowed Apple's growth, the company is still a powerhouse. It was ranked by Gartner as the number 1 supply chain company for the sixth straight year. The ratings are based on five criteria: Gartner analysts' opinion, peer opinion, three-year weighted return on assets, inventory turns, and three-year weighted revenue growth.[11]

Apple has developed of an impressive array of purchasing and supply chain activities to manage product demand, inventory investment, channel distribution, and supply chain relationships. The company consistently maintains a manageable product line, forecasts sales weekly with daily adjustments to production, and expects suppliers to manage inventory for standard parts and components. Apple also formalized a partnership with a supplier to build components close to Apple facilities with just-in-time (JIT) delivery, created a direct ship distribution network through the Web, and simplified its finished goods distribution channel. Apple is even re-shoring by returning some of its production to the United States.

The Supply Chain Umbrella-Management Activities

A large set of activities besides purchasing are part of supply chains. As previously discussed, management's ability to align, coordinate, integrate, and synchronize these activities and the physical, information, and monetary flows is supply chain management. What are the activities that are part of this concept called supply chain management? The management activities that are covered by the supply chain umbrellas are illustrated in Exhibit 1.5 and briefly described in the following paragraphs.

Purchasing

Most organizations include purchasing as a major supply chain activity. Because purchasing is the central focus of this book, there is no need to provide more detail here.

Inbound Transportation

Larger organizations usually have a specialized traffic and transportation function to manage the physical and informational links between the supplier and the buyer. Transportation is a major cost for many organizations; as a result there are usually opportunities to coordinate the purchase of transportation services.

Quality Control

As previous examples have shown, quality control is vital to all organizations. Today's focus on supplier quality has shifted from detecting defects at the time of receipt or use to

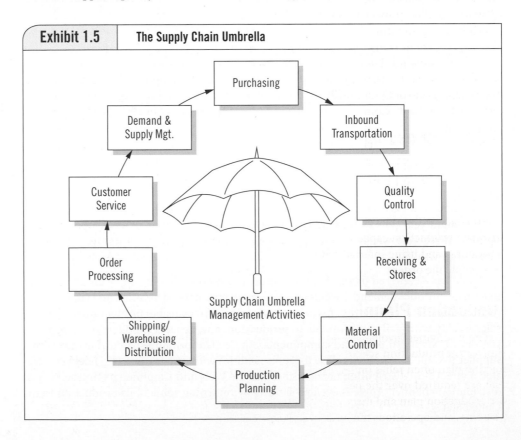

Exhibit 1.5   The Supply Chain Umbrella

prevention early in the materials-sourcing process. Progressive organizations work directly with suppliers to develop proper quality control procedures and processes.

Demand and Supply Planning

Demand planning schedules the firm's output. This includes forecasts of anticipated demand, inventory adjustments, orders taken but not filled, and spare-part and aftermarket requirements. Supply planning is the process of taking demand data and developing a supply, production, and logistics network capable of satisfying demand requirements.

Receiving, Materials Handling, and Storage

All inbound material must be physically received as it moves from a supplier to a purchaser. In a non-just-in-time environment, material must also be stored or staged. Receiving, materials handling, and storage are responsible for the physical control over inventory. Receipts from users indicating that services have been performed are also run through receiving to trigger invoice payment.

Materials or Inventory Control

The terms "materials control" and "inventory control" are sometimes used interchangeably. Within some organizations, however, these terms have different meanings. The *materials control* group is often responsible for determining the appropriate quantity to order based on projected demand and then managing materials releases to suppliers. This includes generating the materials release, contacting a supplier directly concerning changes, and monitoring the status of inbound shipments. The *inventory control* group is often responsible for determining the inventory level of finished goods required to support customer requirements, which emphasizes the physical distribution (i.e., outbound or downstream) side of the supply chain.

Order Processing

Order processing helps ensure that customers receive material when and where they require it and represents the key link between the producer and the external customer.

Problems with order processing have involved accepting orders before determining if adequate production capacity is available, not coordinating order processing with order scheduling, and using internal production dates rather than the customer's preferred date to schedule the order.

Production Planning, Scheduling, and Control

These activities involve determining a time-phased schedule of production, developing short-term production schedules, and controlling work-in-process production. The production plan often relies on forecasts from marketing to estimate the volume of materials that are required over the near term. Because operations is responsible for carrying out the production plan and meeting customer-order due dates, order processing, production planning, and operations must work together closely.

Shipping/Warehousing/Distribution

The *shipping* activity involves physically getting a product ready for transportation to the customer. Shipping activities include: (1) proper packaging to prevent damage, (2) attaching any special labeling requirements, (3) completing all required shipping documents, and (4) arranging transportation with an approved carrier. For obvious reasons, shipping and outbound transportation must work together closely.

Before a product is shipped to the customer, it may be stored for a period in a warehouse or distribution center. This is particularly true for companies that produce according to a forecast in anticipation of future sales. Increasingly, as companies attempt to make a product only after receiving a customer order and information systems become more sophisticated, this part of the supply chain may become less important.

Outbound Transportation

Many organizations have outsourced the transportation link to their customers. Full-service transportation providers called **third party logistics providers (3PLs)** are designing and managing entire distribution networks for their clients. Firms operating in this space include familiar names such as UPS, DHL, CH Robinson, and Ryder.

Customer Service

Customer service includes a wide set of activities that attempt to keep a customer satisfied with a product or service. The three primary elements of customer service are pre-transaction, transaction, and post-transaction activities.

Four Enablers of Purchasing and Supply Chain Management

Now that we have a better understanding of the terminology surrounding purchasing and supply chain management, we must recognize that excellence in these areas does not just happen. A commitment to the four enablers of purchasing and supply chain excellence permits firms to reap real benefits (see Exhibit 1.6). These enablers provide the support that makes the development of progressive strategies and approaches possible. Later chapters present these four areas in detail.

The four enablers model shows that firms have certain guiding philosophies and business requirements that are the foundation of all supply chain activities. These guiding philosophies and requirements may relate to areas such as globalization, customer responsiveness, or supply chain integration. The four enablers, in turn, support the development of strategies and approaches that not only align with an organization's philosophies and requirements but also support the attainment of purchasing, supply chain, and organizational objectives and strategies.

Capable Human Resources

The key to the success of any company is the quality of its employees. This is certainly true for purchasing. Exhibit 1.6 identifies, from previous research, the various kinds of knowledge and skills demanded of today's supply chain professional. Previous research indicated that the top five knowledge areas for purchasers should include: (1) supplier relationship

Exhibit 1.6 | **Four Pillars of Purchasing and Supply Chain Excellence**

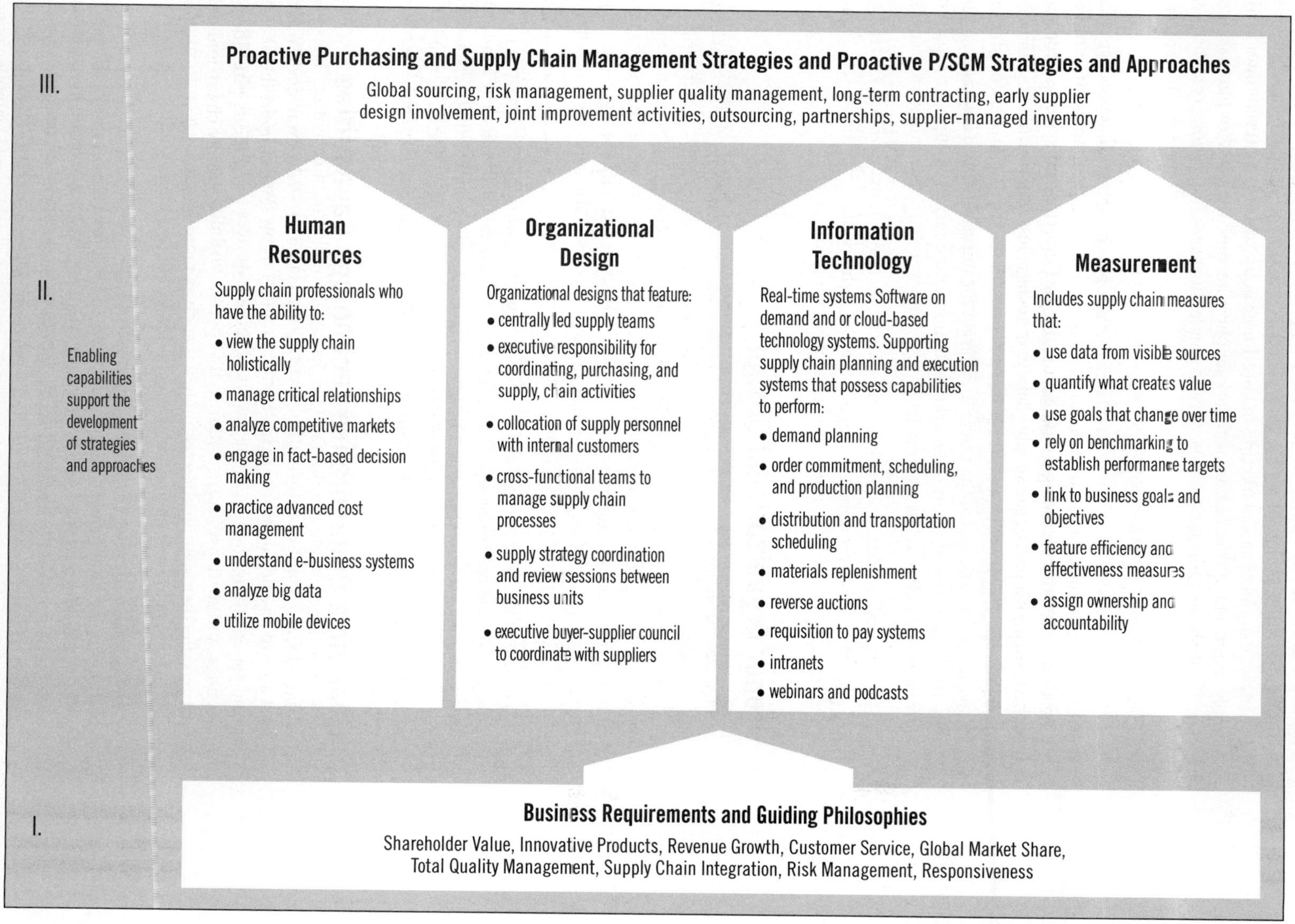

III.

II.

Enabling
capabilities
support the
development
of strategies
and approaches

I.

Proactive Purchasing and Supply Chain Management Strategies and Proactive P/SCM Strategies and Approaches

Global sourcing, risk management, supplier quality management, long-term contracting, early supplier
design involvement, joint improvement activities, outsourcing, partnerships, supplier-managed inventory

Human Resources

Supply chain professionals who
have the ability to:

- view the supply chain
  holistically
- manage critical relationships
- analyze competitive markets
- engage in fact-based decision
  making
- practice advanced cost
  management
- understand e-business systems
- analyze big data
- utilize mobile devices

Organizational Design

Organizational designs that feature:

- centrally led supply teams
- executive responsibility for
  coordinating, purchasing, and
  supply, chain activities
- collocation of supply personnel
  with internal customers
- cross-functional teams to
  manage supply chain
  processes
- supply strategy coordination
  and review sessions between
  business units
- executive buyer-supplier council
  to coordinate with suppliers

Information Technology

Real-time systems Software on
demand and or cloud-based
technology systems. Supporting
supply chain planning and execution
systems that possess capabilities
to perform:

- demand planning
- order commitment, scheduling,
  and production planning
- distribution and transportation
  scheduling
- materials replenishment
- reverse auctions
- requisition to pay systems
- intranets
- webinars and podcasts

Measurement

Includes supply chain measures
that:

- use data from visible sources
- quantify what creates value
- use goals that change over time
- rely on benchmarking to
  establish performance targets
- link to business goals and
  objectives
- feature efficiency and
  effectiveness measures
- assign ownership and
  accountability

Business Requirements and Guiding Philosophies

Shareholder Value, Innovative Products, Revenue Growth, Customer Service, Global Market Share,
Total Quality Management, Supply Chain Integration, Risk Management, Responsiveness

management, (2) total cost analysis, (3) purchasing strategies, (4) supplier analysis, and (5) competitive market analysis.[12] Effective supply chain management requires close collaboration with suppliers as well as internal coordination with engineering, procurement, logistics, customers, and marketing to coordinate activities and material flows across the supply chain. These *relationships* with key suppliers become the basis for purchasing strategies. The Babson College Good Practice Example illustrates how suppliers and the college benefit from developing these strong ties with key outsourced suppliers. At Babson, these strong ties require bi-weekly meetings to search for ways to provide increased value.

Cost management has become an integral part of purchasing and supply chain management. With an inability to raise prices to customers, cost management becomes essential to long-term success. Purchasing specialists at a major U.S. chemical company, for example, evaluate major supply decisions using *total cost models* with data provided by suppliers and other sources. Another company requires its teams to identify upstream cost drivers past immediate suppliers, which the teams then target for improvement. These analyses of total cost are then imposed upon the market situation and analysis of supplier capabilities to arrive at an overall purchasing strategy.

Gaining access to the right skills will require a sound human resources strategy that includes internal development of high-potential individuals, recruiting talent from other functional groups or companies, and hiring promising college graduates.

Proper Organizational Design

Organizational design refers to the process of assessing and selecting the structure and formal system of communication, division of labor, coordination, control, authority, and responsibility required to achieve organizational goals and objectives, including supply chain objectives.[13] Formal charts portray only a portion of the workings of an organization. For example, many organizations are now utilizing center-led supply management structures. These hybrid forms of organization utilize various coordinating mechanisms that are not part of a formal organizational chart.

The use of teams as part of supply chain design will continue to be important. However, managers should use teams selectively. Few studies have established a clear connection between teaming and higher performance, and even fewer have quantitatively assessed the impact of teaming on corporate performance. The use of organizational work teams to support purchasing and supply chain objectives does not guarantee greater effectiveness.[14]

Real-Time Collaborative Technology Capabilities

The development of information technology (IT) software and platforms that support an end-to-end supply chain have grown rapidly in the twenty-first century. There are cloud-based storage systems, a new wave of mobile devices that permit skyping for visual meetings, and shared software platforms that permit visibility between all size supply chain partners. Further identification technologies such as radio frequency identification (RFID) and voice recognition systems are getting better and better.

For example, the e-supply chain company ULTRIVA which states on its website "Ultriva solutions are helping manage the supply chains and improve the inventory velocity of leading organizations at 150 plants in 20 countries. This cloud-based e-solutions provider's product is being used to transact over $2 billion of material spend on an annual basis and have contributed to over $400 million in inventory savings for its customers."[15] Cloud-based solutions continue to gain acceptance in supply management. **Cloud computing** refers to the shared software and information that users access via the web. Rather than storing information on their own physical servers or computer hard drives, users rely on servers that are maintained by the cloud computing software providers (e.g., IBM Smart Cloud). According to Gartner, Inc., the adoption rates are highest in the areas of collaborative (1) sourcing and procurement, (2)demand planning, (3) global trade management (GTM), and (4) transportation management systems (TMS).[16]

These categories follow the two general software categories of planning and execution. Planning software seeks to improve forecast accuracy, optimize production scheduling, reduce working capital costs, shorten cycle times, cut transportation costs, and improve customer service. Execution software helps obtain materials and manage physical flows from suppliers through downstream distribution to ensure that customers receive the right products at the right location, time, and cost. It can be summed up as "lean logistics," "lean operations," and "lean supply."

Regardless of the type of information technology platform or software used, supply chain systems should capture and share information across functional groups and organizational boundaries on a real-time or near-real-time basis. This may involve transmitting the location of transportation vehicles using global positioning systems (GPSs), using Internet-based systems to transmit material requirements to suppliers, or using bar code technology to monitor the timeliness of receipts from suppliers. RFID tags are being used in more applications to capture real-time data about material and product movement across the supply chain.

Examples regarding the relationship between information technology and supply chain excellence are not hard to find. SanDisk Corporation is a global leader in flash memory storage solutions. By using JDA's software, SanDisk was able to improve its on-time deliveries to over 90 percent and was able to facilitate improved collaboration with its channel partners. This increased delivery performance was achieved with less inventory as turnover increased from three to eight in terms of petabytes of storage.[17]

Right Measures and Measurement Systems

The right measures and measurement systems represent the fourth pillar supporting purchasing and supply chain excellence. Unfortunately, there are many roadblocks between measurement and improved performance. Some of these include (1) too many metrics, (2) debate over the correct metrics, (3) constantly changing metrics, and (4) old data. Overcoming these roadblocks requires that the organization know what it wants to measure, has a process in place to measure it, and has accessibility to the right data. The next step involves taking action on the measurement data.[18] Finally, as with any planning system, the targets are revised to reflect the realities of the marketplace, competition, and changing goals of the organization.

Why is measurement so important? First, objective measurement supports fact-based rather than subjective decision making. Second, measurement is also an ideal way to communicate requirements to other supply chain members and to promote continuous improvement and change. When suppliers know their performance is being monitored, they are likely to perform better. Many firms use the measurement system not only to improve future supplier performance but also to recognize outstanding performance. For example, Lockheed-Martin Corporation awarded Southwest Research Institute (SwRI) its STAR supplier award.[19] Of Lockheed's Electronic Systems' 4700 suppliers, only 38 have received the STAR award. Measurement also conveys what is important by linking critical measures to desired business outcomes. The measurement process also helps determine if new initiatives are producing the desired results. Finally, measurement may be the single best tool to control purchasing and supply chain activities and processes.

Although there is no definitive or prescriptive set of supply chain measures, and there certainly is no one best way to measure supply chain performance, we do know that effective measures and measurement systems satisfy certain criteria. These criteria, which Exhibit 1.6 summarizes, provide a set of principles with which to assess supply chain measures and measurement systems.

These four enablers support the pursuit of progressive approaches and strategies that begin to define purchasing and supply chain excellence. If organizations ignore these areas, they will see their ability to develop progressive practices and approaches fall short of competitors that have stressed these enabling areas.

The Evolution of Purchasing and Supply Chain Management

As has been highlighted in this chapter, dramatic changes have affected purchasing over the past decade. An appreciation of how we arrived at where we are today requires a brief understanding of the evolution of purchasing and supply chain management; although some might argue the last decade resembled a revolution. This evolution covers seven periods, spanning the last 160 years.

Period 1: The Early Years (1850–1900)

Some observers define the early years of purchasing history as beginning after 1850. There is evidence, however, that the purchasing function received attention before this date. Charles Babbage's book on the economy of machinery and manufacturers, published in 1832, referred to the importance of the purchasing function. Babbage also alluded to a "materials man" responsible for several different functions. Babbage wrote that a central officer responsible for operating mines was "a materials man who selects, purchases, receives, and delivers all articles required."[20]

In the textile industry, the selling agent often handled purchasing and was also responsible for the output, quality, and style of the cloth. The selling agent was responsible for all purchasing decisions, because the grade of cotton purchased was a factor in determining the quality of the cloth produced. Customer orders were transformed into purchase orders (POs) for cotton and subsequently into planned production.[21]

The greatest interest in and development of purchasing during the early years occurred after the 1850s. During this period, the growth of American railroads made them one of the major forces in the economy. Railroads were vital to the country's ability to move goods from the more developed Eastern and Midwestern markets to less developed Southern and Western markets. By 1866, the Pennsylvania Railroad had given the purchasing function departmental status, under the title of Supplying Department. A few years later, the head purchasing agent at the Pennsylvania Railroad reported directly to the president of the railroad. The purchasing function was such a major contributor to the performance of the organization that the chief purchasing manager had top managerial status.[22]

The comptroller of the Chicago and Northwestern Railroad wrote the first book exclusively about the purchasing function, *The Handling of Railway Supplies—Their Purchase and Disposition* in 1887. He discussed purchasing issues that are still critical today, including the need for technical expertise in purchasing agents along with the need to centralize the purchasing department under one individual. The author also commented on the lack of attention given to the selection of personnel to fill the position of purchasing agent.

The growth of the railroad industry dominated the early years of purchasing development. Major contributions to purchasing history during this period consisted of early recognition of the purchasing process and its contribution to overall company profitability. The late 1800s signaled the beginning of organizing purchasing as a separate corporate function requiring specialized expertise. Before this period, this separation did not exist.

Period 2: Growth of Purchasing Fundamentals (1900–1939)

The second period of purchasing evolution began around the turn of the twentieth century and lasted until the beginning of World War II. Articles specifically addressing the industrial purchasing function began appearing with increasing regularity outside the railroad trade journals. Engineering magazines in particular focused attention on the need for qualified purchasing personnel and the development of materials specifications.

This era also witnessed the development of basic purchasing procedures and ideas. In 1905, the second book devoted to purchasing—and the first nonrailroad purchasing book— was published. *The Book on Buying* contained 18 chapters; each written by a different author.[23] The editors devoted the first section of the book to the "principles" of buying. The second section described the forms and procedures used in various company purchasing systems.

Purchasing gained importance during World War I because of its role in obtaining vital war materials. The central focus of purchasing during this period was on the procurement of raw material versus buying finished or semifinished goods. Ironically, the years during World War I did not feature publication of any major purchasing books. Harold T. Lewis, a respected purchasing professional during the 1930s through the 1950s, noted that there was considerable doubt about the existence of any general recognition of purchasing as being important to a company. Lewis noted that from World War I to 1945, at least a gradual, if uneven, recognition of the importance of sound procurement to company operation developed.

Period 3: The War Years (1940–1946)

World War II introduced a new period in purchasing history. The emphasis on obtaining (scarce) materials during the war influenced a growth in purchasing interest. In 1933, only nine colleges offered courses related to purchasing. By 1945, this number had increased to 49 colleges. The membership of the National Association of Purchasing Agents increased from 3,400 in 1934, to 5,500 in 1940, to 9,400 in the autumn of 1945. A study conducted during this period revealed that 76 percent of all purchase requisitions contained no specifications or stipulation of brand. This suggested that other departments within the firm recognized the role of the purchasing agent in determining sources of supply.[24]

Period 4: The Quiet Years (1947–Mid-1960s)

The heightened awareness of purchasing that existed during World War II did not carry over to the postwar years. John A. Hill, a noted purchasing professional, commented about the state of purchasing during this period: "For many firms, purchases were simply an inescapable cost of doing business which no one could do much about. So far as the length and breadth of American industry is concerned, the purchasing function has not yet received in full measure the attention and emphasis it deserves."[25]

Another respected purchasing professional, Bruce D. Henderson, also commented about the state of affairs facing purchasing. In his words, "Procurement is regarded as a negative function—it can handicap the company if not done well but can make little positive contribution."[26] He noted that purchasing was a neglected function in most organizations because it was not important to mainstream problems. He went on to say that some executives found it hard to visualize a company becoming more successful than its competitors because of its superior procurement.

Articles began appearing during this period describing the practices of various companies using staff members to collect, analyze, and present data for purchasing decisions. Ford Motor Company was one of the first private organizations to establish a commodity research department providing short- and long-term commodity information.[27] Ford also created a purchase analysis department to give buyers assistance on product and price analysis.

The postwar period saw the development of the value analysis (VA) technique, pioneered by General Electric in 1947. GE's approach concentrated on the evaluation of which materials or changes in specifications and design would reduce overall product costs. Although important internal purchasing developments occurred during this era, there is no denying that other disciplines such as marketing and finance overshadowed purchasing. The emphasis during the postwar years and throughout the 1960s was on satisfying consumer demand and the needs of a growing industrial market. Furthermore, firms faced stable competition and had access to abundant material—conditions that historically have diminished the overall importance of purchasing. The elements that would normally cause an increase in the importance of purchasing were not present during these quiet years of purchasing history.

Period 5: Materials Management Comes of Age (Mid-1960s–Late 1970s)

The mid-1960s witnessed a dramatic growth of the materials management concept. Although interest in materials management grew during this period, the concept's historical origins date to the 1800s, when U.S. railroads organized under the materials management concept during the latter half of the nineteenth century. They combined related functions such as purchasing, inventory control, receiving, and stores under the authority of one individual.

External events directly affected the operation of the typical firm. The Vietnam War, for example, resulted in upward price and materials availability pressures. During the 1970s, firms experienced materials problems related to oil "shortages" and embargoes. The logical response of industry was to become more efficient, particularly in the purchase and control of materials leading to the concept of "materials management."

The overall objective of materials management was to solve materials problems from a total system viewpoint rather than the viewpoint of individual functions or activities. The various functions that might fall under the materials umbrella included materials planning and control, inventory planning and control, materials and procurement research, purchasing, incoming traffic, receiving, incoming quality control, stores, materials movement, and scrap and surplus disposal.

The behavior of purchasing during this period was notable. Purchasing managers emphasized multiple sourcing through competitive bid pricing and rarely viewed the supplier as a value-added partner. Buyers maintained arm's-length relationships with suppliers. Price competition was the major factor determining supply contracts.

Overall, the function was relegated to secondary status in many companies. Dean Ammer's classic 1974 article in the *Harvard Business Review* categorized top management's view of purchasing as passive, risk averse, and a dead-end job. Ammer felt overcoming this perception could be accomplished by active purchasing, which is measured in terms of meeting overall company objectives and contributing to bottom-line profitability.[28] He argued that the purchasing executive should be part of non-purchasing decisions, for the entire organization loses when purchasing is not part of the organization's consensus on major decisions.[29] Finally, Ammer suggested that the function should have sufficient stature to report to top management or a division manager. However, this happened in only 37 percent of his responding firms.[30]

Period 6: The Global Era (Late 1970s–1999)

The purchasing strategies and behaviors that evolved over the last half century were inadequate when the severe economic recession of the early 1980s and the emergence of foreign global competitors occurred. America had lost its quality edge and researchers and experts proposed methods such as "statistical process control" and "total quality management" as remedies.

The global era, and its effect on the importance, structure, and behavior of purchasing, has already proved different from other historical periods. These differences include the following:

- Never in our industrial history has competition become so intense so quickly.
- Global firms increasingly captured world market share and emphasized different strategies, organizational structures, and management techniques compared with their American counterparts.
- The spread and rate of technology change during this period was unprecedented, with product life cycles becoming shorter.
- The ability to coordinate worldwide purchasing activity by using international data networks and the World Wide Web (via intranets) emerged.

This intensely competitive period witnessed the growth of supply chain management. Now, more than ever, firms began to take a more coordinated view of managing the flow of goods, services, funds, and information from suppliers through end customers. Managers began to view supply chain management as a way to satisfy intense cost and other improvement pressures.

Period 7: Integrated Supply Chain Management (The Twenty-First Century)

Purchasing and supply chain management today reflects a growing emphasis concerning the importance of suppliers. Supplier relationships are shifting from an adversarial approach to a more cooperative approach with selected suppliers. The activities that the twenty-first century purchasing organization must put in place are quite different from those of the recent past. Supplier development, supplier design involvement, the use of full-service suppliers, total cost supplier selection, supplier relationship management, strategic cost management, enterprise-wide systems (enterprise resource planning, or ERP) hosted on the "cloud" and integrated Internet linkages and shared databases available 24/7 are now seen as ways to create new value within the supply chain. However, newer concepts continue to emerge, including enabling innovation in the supply base, contributing to top-line revenue growth, using mobile devices to monitor supply and managing risks of a global supply chain. Purchasing behavior is shifting dramatically to support the performance requirements of the new era.

It is possible to reach three conclusions about twenty-first century purchasing. First, the reshaping of purchasing's role in the emerging global economy is under way, in response to the challenges presented by worldwide competition and rapidly changing technology and customer expectations. Second, the overall importance of the purchasing function is increasing, particularly for firms that compete in industries characterized by worldwide competition and rapid change. Third, purchasing must continue to become more integrated with customer requirements, as well as with operations, logistics, human resources, finance, accounting, marketing, and information systems. This evolution will take time to occur fully, but the integration is inevitable.

The history and evolution of purchasing and supply chain management provides an appreciation for the growth, development, and increased stature of the profession over the last 150 years. Each historical period has contributed something unique to the development of purchasing, including the events that have shaped today's emphasis on integrated supply chain management.

Looking Ahead

This book comprises 20 chapters, divided into six parts including this introduction. The remainder of this book addresses the major tasks and challenges facing the modern purchasing professional operating within the context of a dynamic supply chain.

Part 2, *Purchasing Operations and Structure* Chapters 2 through 5, provides a basic understanding of the functional activity called purchasing. Without a solid understanding of basic purchasing processes, policies, and organization, appreciating the important role that purchasing has within a supply chain is difficult. Today's supply management professional has a strategic focus, and Chapter 4 addresses supply management integration.

With this understanding, Part 3, *Strategic Sourcing* considers how purchasing evaluates, selects, manages, and improves supplier performance. Chapters 6 through 10 present strategic sourcing activities, which are activities that can affect the competitiveness of a firm. The ability to realize advantages from our purchasing and supply efforts requires shifting our view of purchasing from a tactical or clerically oriented activity to one that focuses on strategic supply management.

Part 4, *Strategic Sourcing Process* recognizes that purchasing professionals must play a major role in improving supply chain performance. Chapters 11 through 15 present an assortment of tools, techniques, and approaches for managing the procurement and sourcing process, including an understanding of contracting and legal issues.

Part 5, *Critical Supply Chain Elements* deals extensively with the critical elements of integrated supply chains from supplier through customer. The activities and topics presented in Chapters 16 through 19 may or may not be a formal part of the purchasing organization. They are, however, integral stepping stones to effective supply chain management.

Part 6, *Future Directions* contains a single chapter that presents future directions identified during research and experience with many organizations. The trends identified in Chapter 20 help us identify how the field of purchasing and supply chain management is changing, what is behind these changes, and how best to respond. As we move further into the twenty-first century, this section must change on a continuous basis to reflect the dynamic changes occurring in purchasing and supply chain management.

Good Practice Example	*Taking an Entrepreneurial Approach to Purchasing at Babson College*

Teresa Pitaro, the Director of Business Services for Babson College, and her team of Purchasing managers are acting like entrepreneurs and as a result changing the culture of Babson. Prior to joining Babson in 2006, Teresa has held positions of increasing responsibility at Raytheon, TJX, and Staples. She is a Babson alumna, holding both undergraduate and MBA degrees from the school.

Pitaro's Purchasing team of Anne Krueger, C.P.M., Kerrie Dunn C.P.M., and Lori Sullivan collectively have engineered copy center, bookstore, and transportation deals. They have extended their influence to become an integral part of construction sourcing. This job was previously performed by facilities managers with minimal or no Purchasing input. Finally, they have found new ways to leverage their office supply buy through a university consortium. All this has been accomplished while automating the buying process and giving their internal customers (i.e., faculty and staff) more responsive service.

Considering that Babson has the premier entrepreneurship program in the country, according to *U.S. News and World Report,* the supply team's approach fits well with the culture. The academic world has traditionally been characterized as somewhat rigid and bureaucratic, following traditional rules and regulations engrained by decades of use. Purchasing is no exception. It, too, operated in a clerical, paper-intense atmosphere. But true to the very definition of an entrepreneur, Pitaro believes there is always the ability to innovate, especially given the Babson culture.

"The challenges at Babson require us to continually challenge old ways of doing business," says Pitaro. "Buying can usually be segmented into buying processes and internal customer groups," adds Purchasing Manager Anne Krueger. Pitaro has had her team of Krueger, Dunn, and Sullivan focus their activities on three buying processes and their associated customers:

1. *Process driven buying* empowers the customer to purchase from contracts that the Purchasing group negotiates. Office supplies are the best example of this type of purchase. Working with the Boston Consortium, a group of 15 Boston area universities, a very attractive contract was negotiated with a major supplier of office products. In some cases savings between 5–8% were realized from the previous contract. Additionally, a procurement card (P-Card) contract was negotiated by the Purchasing group that provides additional price discounts over a certain volume level. These rebates are then put in a general budget at Babson to fund additional operating needs. *Marketplace* is an e-procurement tool provided by the Consortium that has potential to further streamline and automate the Purchasing process for the College in the future.

2. *Nontraditional spend* buying process involves expanding Purchasing's influence into spend categories that have been traditionally purchased by other functions. Examples in this category include construction and renovation projects. Previously, construction-related purchases were performed by Facilities with little involvement by Purchasing. An independent consultant report confirmed this. Recently, Kerrie Dunn, with support from Babson's Facilities Management team, was able to get Purchasing involved early in the planning stages of new construction projects. This included successfully bidding Construction Management services for the renovations of two buildings on campus.

3. *Centralized Contracted services* buying process involves using the expertise of suppliers that team with the college to provide products used on a daily, ongoing basis. Pitaro has focused her efforts on meeting with user groups to identify opportunities in these areas to lower costs and improve service while reducing risk. Examples of this category of spend include, copy/print services, bus transportation and dining and bookstore services. Most of these contracts involve ongoing collaborative efforts with both suppliers and internal customers.

"Our Purchasing department is no different from most companies in the private sector," says Teresa. As she sees it, today's challenge is twofold:

1. Centralize buying efforts to capture complete usage across various users, and then collaborate with suppliers to continually reduce total costs.

2. Leverage technology to simplify and automate repetitive activities while capturing and disseminating information/knowledge.

"We can't forget that faculty and staff want maximum freedom in sourcing, so our challenge is to preserve their independence-and still improve the way we manage the $161 million in college operational spending every year," Pitaro goes on to explain how Babson's Purchasing group plans to address these challenges.

Process Change-The P Card System

Procurement card systems (P-Card) are now a standard at many organizations. They enable users to acquire low dollar purchases from contracts established by Purchasing. Babson had a P-Card system in place for several years, but it was stagnant and not growing. Purchasing undertook a total review of the program and negotiated a new P-Card program through a new vendor. They focused on three critical areas: (1) service, (2) reporting capability, and (3) rebate structure. The results were impressive; they doubled card offered rebate from (.75% to 1.5%). Secondly, they further streamlined program process to provide improved service. As a result, the number of P-Card adopters increased from 310 to 403 (out of a total of 650+ faculty and staff). Purchases through the P-Card program have increased to $7 million, with the increased rebate percentages providing additional revenue for Babson. Sullivan, Krueger, and Pitaro are now exploring ways to automate the reconciliation process. "We want to further automate so we can reduce the paperwork now involved with the 300–400 monthly reconciliation reports received," says Teresa.

Under the office supplies contract, negotiated through the consortium, a total savings of 5–8% were realized. Further, the winning supplier provided a portal customized to Babson's "look and feel." Pitaro feels the next step in this evolution is integrating the P-Card system into office supplies. "The procurement card program has greatly streamlined the process of acquiring small dollar items and allows our internal customers to order at their convenience," adds Lori.

Another process automation tool being evaluated is an e-procurement tool called *Marketplace*. *Marketplace* is used by members of the Boston Consortium Group and is operated by an outside vendor partner who services and maintains the system. Currently, it is focused on buy side, with some customized pay side for certain members, and contains the offerings of suppliers of scientific laboratory equipment, computers, and office supplies. Plans are now underway to improve the development of the automated pay side, with the goal of having an entire procure to pay system. Pitaro's group is continually monitoring the system developments and its potential uses and applications at Babson. Pitaro's group is also continuing to investigate other systems that are available in the market and that may be used by other institutions.

Nontraditional Spend Influence

Previously, Purchasing only placed the orders for construction projects after Facilities managers had selected the supplier(s). "In the past, the typical Purchasing process was initiated with the Facilities manager coming to the Purchasing department with the contractor already selected," stated Teresa. Once Pitaro's group emphasized the importance of a bid process and worked with Facilities to implement it, they were able to "bring more discipline to the process," she states. This insures that the money spent on these high dollar projects is better managed. In the contracts negotiated to date, Kerrie has successfully been able to complete a range of projects from remodeling, to construction manager selection and new construction projects. Now bids are appropriately structured, comparisons made between contractors on key dimensions, and negotiations and final supplier selection have been seamless. This increased process discipline is evidenced in programs such as inviting the finalists (3–4 contractors) to a scope/bid review meeting. The result is a formal construction bidding, award, and contract management process that have been streamlined. An additional benefit is reduced risk as Purchasing and Risk Management collectively do their "due diligence" on contractors to insure financial stability and insurability. Considering Babson is embarking on a new six-year master plan, this involvement could not have come at a better time. Kerrie knows Babson will be quite busy managing construction purchases for the foreseeable future.

Centralizing The Spend

Among Pitaro's first endeavors was to reinforce the idea and benefit of centralized purchasing, operating on a foundation of service. "Creating an effective, efficient process requires consistent campus-wide use," says Teresa. "To achieve this goal, our Purchasing department would have to be recognized by our customers as capable of reducing complexity and adding value, knowledge, and skill to the process." Two examples of these efforts are the bus transportation and print/copy management services contracts.

"Before we looked at the transportation area we had every department calling their favorite bus company for their transportation needs," states Pitaro. On a campus like ours we have *bus transportation* needs for athletics, student groups, field trips for various classes, and so on. First, bus transportation needs were identified through a committee of stakeholders across campus. Not surprisingly, the largest user was Athletics ($150,000/year).

Anne also identified other internal customers (other than Athletics) who were using whatever bus service they wanted for travel to and from various events. Utilizing her own entrepreneurial spirit, she collected usage numbers on the trips taken via bus/charter at Babson during a school year. Athletics had previously negotiated their own contract independent of Purchasing. "Getting them on board was key as they utilize a large number of busses for our athletic events," stated Anne.

Next, Krueger built a request for proposal (RFP) that was sent out to 14 charter bus firms. All 14 were invited to attend a Question & Answer session about the proposal. The initial proposals were evaluated and reduced to three suppliers. Evaluations on the financials, operations, and risk perspective were analyzed along with price and capabilities in a weighted-scoring matrix. Babson wanted detailed information on the emergency safety procedures, driver selection policy, and the actual safety record. For example, what background checks were performed prior to hiring drivers? Was it clear that drivers would not be permitted to text or use cell phones while driving? Liability insurance and indemnification was also important. Next, the fleet inventory was analyzed. Student activities may require a small, 15-passenger minivan up to a full size bus. Finally the age of the vehicle fleet and maintenance procedures were analyzed, along with the replacement cycle.

If the potential suppliers passed these initial screens then pricing was analyzed. Fuel surcharges and various trip charges, depending on the travel required, were priced (1) by mileage, (2) by day, and (3) by overnight costs. After months of negotiation and refinements, a contract was finalized for a three-year period, resulting in a nice cost savings for Babson.

In addition to cost savings, users have the ability to book their bus(es) via phone, email, or online. However, the selected bus contractor and Babson Purchasing would like to see more use of the online system. As a result, Purchasing scheduled an on-campus event open house with the new bus vendor for users to insure that they can understand the online process, meet the new vendor representatives, and can come out and view the new busses.

Print/copy management involves multifunctional devices used for printing, copying, scanning, and faxing. There were over 90 of these devices at Babson. The incumbent supplier provided this equipment and ran the central on-site copy center for a minimum of 15 years. "We felt the incumbent had begun to take the business for granted and as a result service levels deteriorated," said Pitaro. "We wanted better customer service and improved maintenance of machines." "Service was a sore spot on campus," she said. According to Teresa, "The incumbent supplier lost track of value and we needed to see what the market had to offer." Purchasing moved swiftly to request proposals from three new suppliers and the incumbent. This effort led to selecting a new supplier for all of the centralized print/copy business. The final negotiated price was several hundred thousand dollars lower than the current supplier with improved service levels. The new supplier also focused on driving sustainability into the print business. "They measure ways to reduce carbon footprint of what we are printing," states Pitaro. "Babson has a focus on sustainability and now we have a way to track this." "It was not a priority of the previous supplier," she states.

"Our ability to negotiate these centrally managed contracts provides users much better service at lower rates," states Pitaro.

Consortium participation. Krueger believes her efforts with the Boston Consortium Group consisting of mostly the Chief Financial Officer's from 15 Boston area universities will allow for further opportunities to leverage centralized spend. A major office supplies deal is already in place and more deals are in the works. Phil DeChiara, the executive director of the Consortium is physically located close to Babson's Purchasing on the Franklin W. Olin College of Engineering campus. While Mr. DeChiara does not see the main mission of the group as a buying consortium, he does realize there are many buying opportunities available to member universities.

Collaboration

On a university campus, Purchasing's various customers can be finicky users. Satisfying these many interests has its challenges. On Babson's campus, there are many *snack vending machines.* Purchasing had consolidated these machines with one supplier, but needed to look at customer satisfaction. Anne Krueger and Steve Heaslip (who manages the snack vending machines) worked together on the new snack vending RFP and conducted a focus group on student desires in their snack machines. One of the suppliers proposed a totally healthy food selection in the vending machines. However, students wanted a blend of healthy and traditional snacks. As a result, the mix of products were altered to include both types and the "healthy only" snack food alternative was abandoned.

Anne and Steve also evaluated headcounts of residents and office staff, studied traffic flow, and benchmarked their findings against other schools. "Collaborating with internal customers is a key element of a vending machine contract," states Krueger.

"At Babson, we aren't experts in every field, for example bookstore and campus dining," says Teresa. "In these areas, contracted service companies require a more collaborative approach," she adds.

Bookstore operations Leveraging a supplier's expertise, whether it is in raw materials testing or third-party fulfillment and distribution, was a major tool in realizing success. The common perception is that outsourcing reduces supply options and service management flexibility. Pitaro feels differently. "It actually increases capabilities," she says, "as I can leverage the talent, skills, and assets of both Babson and the supplier." To make this "outsourced/in-house operation" effective, a cultural shift had to take place. Suppliers need freedoms and restrictions, as well as incentives and guidelines that are similar to those of an internal department.

"I try never to fall into the trap of thinking that our internal customer is always right, or that the supplier is holding out and can always do better," says Pitaro. "Once you replace 'us' and 'them' with 'we,' the returns come quickly!"

The incumbent bookstore supplier had been on campus for several years. This on-site status made it essentially a sole source of branded merchandise items, books, and miscellaneous convenience items. In conjunction with a consultant who was familiar with bookstore operations, Pitaro's group crafted an RFP to three suppliers. The result was maintaining the incumbent supplier, but with renegotiated terms and a focus on improved service and terms. "We felt that the market had changed and the incumbent had lost focus on how the market had changed," stated Pitaro. Working hand in hand with the supplier to improve value, the bookstore was renovated; a one-time donation was made to Babson as part of the new six-year contract. Babson was also able to renegotiate the percentage of sales commission it receives. With current annualized sales of almost $3 million per year, this amount is substantial. Now both parties have an interest in keeping the store fresh and current.

Every other week, Pitaro meets with the bookstore manager and a Babson Student Affairs Director. They review questions such as how to make the space more attractive, how to market the Babson brand to students, alumni, and others, and how to continually analyze and provide the goods and services that students want in the store. They also identify other student needs based on their observations and student comments on use. They then challenge the supplier to propose a creative solution. "Once we agree on the changes necessary, we totally empower the supplier," states Pitaro. "We respect and support the supplier's rights, encourage them in company-driven experiments, and collaborate on improving their offerings," she states.

Food Services Perhaps no service on campus gets more scrutiny than *food services*. Babson's relationship with Sodexo has continued for over 25 years. This partnership is periodically reviewed and renegotiated. Renegotiations focus on efficiencies gained and thus reductions in annual operating fees. The current contract has an overhead component as well as a profit-sharing arrangement. Any operating surpluses are shared between Babson and Sodexo. Sales are meal plans, retail operations, and catering. Operating statements consist of revenue from meal plans, catering and retail operations (pay as you go), and less controllable and non-controllable expenses. Periodically, our internal audit team will review the rates of the food service contract against the invoiced amounts.

Collaborative meetings are held bi-weekly between the General Manager of Sodexo, Teresa, and the Director of Residence Life. "This campus department knows its particular customer—the students in this case—and this interface with suppliers improves the process for both parties," states Pitaro.

For example, Sodexo dining tracks how many students are served during 15-minute intervals of each day and how much of each entrée is consumed per day. The goal is to add this type of data to information along with additional consumer surveys and research to assure that we are providing the best food product, when, where, and how the student desires. This data enables working with suppliers to determine the benefits, risks, and effects of various staffing options, service and materials changes, merchandising, advertising, and promotion plans that they may be considering. Sodexo's General Manager at Babson also meets with meets with the Student Government Association (SGA) representatives twice a semester to discuss food services on campus, including quality, variety, and possible enhancements. The General Manager of Sodexo teaches Babson students twice a year (spring and fall semester) in an Organizational Effective Management (OEM) class.

Water filtration embodies a unique way to gain acceptance for a sustainable solution to reduce use of plastic bottles. Water stations are located across campus. There were five suppliers identified by Anne in Purchasing and the Sustainability Office that provided water filtration devices for these water stations. Students were challenged to test the various filtration devices and select the best "taste." The supplier who won was awarded the contract. The result was an increase in the use of recyclable containers.

Overall, working together with suppliers created goals, measurements for success, and a communication system that assures clear and constant understanding of action steps and timing. "Cooperation and communication at that level insures that there's no mystery about performance requirements," Pitaro adds.

Professionalism

Krueger, Dunn, and Sullivan form an experienced team, with combined, extensive college Purchasing experience. "I'm very fortunate," Pitaro states, "to have a staff that's not just talented and experienced, but service-minded." Pitaro wanted to communicate the staff's knowledge and professionalism as well. Both Dunn and Krueger are Certified Purchasing Managers (C.P.M.s) Teresa's goal is to enhance her group's common knowledge, experience, and camaraderie while illustrating their desire to continually enhance the level of professionalism. To that end, they have established a long-term goal of obtaining their Certified Professional in Supply Management (CPSM).

"We are obviously in an environment that values expertise," she continues, "but it takes more than education. It takes motivation to enhance credibility. We need to continually increase our level of knowledge, professionalism and service."

"We want to be viewed as fast and flexible, with creative solutions to sourcing."

Pitaro summarizes her philosophy by stating "In this day and age it is crucial to maximize the buying power of every tuition dollar we have to do more with less!"

To that end, Pitaro is well on her way to achieving her goal: "To maximize our department's ability to leverage campus-wide buying power, benchmark resources, negotiate better terms, eliminate duplicate spending, and manage contract services."

Source: L. Giunipero, Personal interviews with Teresa Pitaro, Anne Krueger, and Phil DeChiara 2013. (Author Note: The foundation for Babson's supply management progress started with Peter Russo previous Director who left in 2010. Teresa, Anne, Kerrie, and Lori are continuing to build on this foundation while developing their own philosophies through implementing new programs.)

KEY TERMS

cloud computing, 22

cross-functional, 12

extended enterprise, 14

extended value chain, 14

ISM Report on Business, 10

managing the supply base, 12

near-shoring, 8

organizational design, 22

process approach, 12

purchasing, 11

re-shoring, 8

reverse supply chain, 13

strategic responsibilities, 11

supply chain, 13

supply chain management, 13

supply chain orientation, 13

supply management, 11

third party logistics providers (3PLs), 20

value chain, 13

DISCUSSION QUESTIONS

1. Why are more top managers recognizing the importance of purchasing/supply management?

2. What is the difference between purchasing and supply management? What is the difference between a supply chain orientation and supply chain management?

3. What is the difference between a supply chain and a value chain?

4. Do you think organizational purchasers should behave like entrepreneurs? Why or why not?

5. What are some of the factors that might influence how important purchasing is to the success of an organization?

6. What knowledge and skills do you feel are required for a purchasing professional?

7. Why does the collective behavior of supply managers have such an impact on economic trends?

8. Why are supply base innovation and risk management two future areas that will consume more of the supply manager's day?

9. Discuss the four enablers of purchasing and supply chain excellence.

10. Would you agree that the importance of the individual supply chain management activities vary with the type of business (e.g., purchasing vs. inbound transportation) and provide examples?

11. Briefly discuss each of the seven periods in the evolution of purchasing and supply management. What do you forecast for the future?

ADDITIONAL READINGS

Bhote, K. R. (1989), *Strategic Supply Management: A Blueprint for Revitalizing the Manufacturing-Supplier Partnership*, New York: American Management Association, p. 13.

Fearon, H. (1965), "The Purchasing Function within 19th Century Railroad Organization," *Journal of Purchasing*, pp. 1–7.

Giunipero, L., Hooker, R., Joseph, S., Yoon, T., and Brudvig, S. (2008, October), "A Decade of SCM Literature: Past, Present, and Future Implications," *Journal of Supply Chain Management*, 44(4), 66–86.

Giunipero, L., Handfield, R., and El Tantawy, R. (2006), "Supply Management's Evolution: Key Skill Sets for the Purchaser of the Future," *International Journal of Production and Operations Management*, 26(7), 822–844.

Gonzalez-Benito, J. (2007), "A Theory of Purchasing's Contribution to Business Performance," *Journal of Operations Management*, 25(4), 901–917.

Handfield, R., and Onitsuka, M. (1995), "Process and Supply Chain Management Evolution in the American Cotton Textile Industry," *St. Andrew's University Economic and Business Review*, December, pp. 1–35.

Henderson, B. D. (1975, Summer), "The Coming Revolution in Purchasing," *Journal of Purchasing and Materials Management*, 11(2), 44–50.

Hill, J. A. (1975, Summer), "The Purchasing Revolution," *Journal of Purchasing and Materials Management*, 11(3), 18–19.

Lee, H. (2004), "The Triple-A Supply Chain," *Harvard Business Review*, October, pp. 102–112.

Lusch, R. (2011) "Reframing Supply Chain Management: A Service Dominant Logic Perspective," *Journal of Supply Chain Management*, 47(1), 14–18.

Sprague, L. G. (2007), "Evolution of the Field of Operations Management," *Journal of Operations Management*, 25(2), 219–238.

ENDNOTES

1. Friedman, T. L. (2005), *The World Is Flat*, New York: Farrar, Straus, and Giroux, p. 6.

2. Orlik, T. (2013), "Rising Wages Pose Dilemma for China," *Wall Street Journal*, May 17, pp. A1, A14.

3. Siegfried, M. (2012, October), "Dig Deep to Uncover Supplier Capabilities," *Inside Supply Management*, 23(8), 18–19.

4. Siegfried, p. 18.

5. Kowalski, M. (2013), "Will Lululemon Athletica Unravel at the Seams?" *USA TODAY*, June 24, p. 1.

6. Tracey, T. (2013, May), "ISM's 2013 Salary Survey," *Inside Supply Management*, 24(4), 18–21.

7. Flynn, A., Harding, M. L., Lallatin, C. S., Pohlig, H. M., and Sturzl, S. R. (Eds.), (2009), *ISM Glossary of Key Supply Management Terms* (5th ed.), Tempe, AZ: Institute for Supply Management.

8. Mentzer, J., DeWitt, W., Keebler, J., Min, S., Nix, N., Smith, C., and Zacharia, Z. (2001), "Defining Supply Chain Management," *Journal of Business Logistics*, 22(2), 1–25.

9. Mentzer et al., pp. 3, 11, 17.

10. "1997-2007: The Ten-Year Apple Comeback," October 15, 2007, 9rules.com/apple/notes/8244/

11. Blanchard, D. (2013), "Top Industry Supply Chains of 2013," *Industry Week* May 30, http://www.industryweek.com/top-25#slide-0-field_images-71802

12. Giunipero, L., and Handfield, R. (2004), *Purchasing Education and Training II*, Tempe, AZ: CAPS Research, 74 pages.

13. Hamel, G., and Pralahad, C. K. (1994), *Competing for the Future*, Cambridge, MA: Harvard Business School Press, as reported in Hellriegel, D., Slocum, J. W., and Woodman, R. W. (2001), *Organizational Behavior*, Cincinnati, OH: South-Western, p. 474.

14. Trent, R. J. (2003), *Supply Management Organizational Design Effectiveness Study*, Working paper, Lehigh University, Bethlehem, PA.

15. ULTRIVA website http://www.ultriva.com, accessed June 20, 2013.

16. McCrea, B. (2013), "Analysts Report That Cloud-Based Adoption Increased 40 Percent This Year for Supply Chain Software," *Supply Chain*, 247, http://www.supplychain247.com/article/analysts_report_that_cloud_based_adoption_increased_40_percent_this_year/gt_nexus, accessed July 2, 2013.

17. McCrea, B. (2013), "Scan Disk and the Adaptive Supply Chain," http://www.jda.com/company/display-collateral/pID/2464, accessed June 21, 2013.

18. Hofman, D. (2007), "Getting to World-Class Supply Chain Measurement," *Purchasing*, October 1, pp. 15–17. www.purchasing.com/article/CA6389475.html?ref=nbra&q=+World+Class+supply+chain+Measurement+systems+2007+

19. Hofman, D. (2012), "SwRI Earns Its Second Lockheed Martin STAR Supplier Award," SwRI press release, February 20, http://www.swri.org/9what/releases/2012/lockheed-star.htm

20. Babbage, C. (1968), *On the Economy of Machinery and Manufacturers* (2nd ed.), London: Charles Knight Publishing, p. 202, as reported in Fearon, H. (1968), "History of Purchasing," *Journal of Purchasing, February*, p. 44.

21. Handfield, R., and Onitsuka, M. (1995), "Process and Supply Chain Management Evolution in the American Cotton Textile Industry," *St. Andrew's University Economic and Business Review, December*, pp. 1–35.

22. Fearon, H. (1968), "History of Purchasing," *Journal of Purchasing*, February, pp. 44–50, reprinted in *Journal of Purchasing and Materials Management*, 1989, 71–81.

23. Fearon, p. 47.

24. Fearon, p. 48.

25. Hill, J. A. (1975), "The Purchasing Revolution," *Journal of Purchasing Management, Summer*, pp. 18–19. (Note: This is a reprint of a speech given by John Hill in 1953.)

26. Henderson, B. D. (1975), "The Coming Revolution in Purchasing," *Journal of Purchasing and Materials Management*, Summer, p. 44. (Note: This is a reprint of an article first published in 1964.)

27. Browning, A. J. (1947), "Purchasing—A Challenge and an Opportunity," *Purchasing*, December, pp. 99–101.

28. Ammer, D. S. (1974), "Is Your Purchasing Department a Good Buy?" *Harvard Business Review*, March–April, pp. 136–158.

29. Ammer, p. 158.

30. Ammer, p. 158.

Purchasing Operations and Structure

Part 2

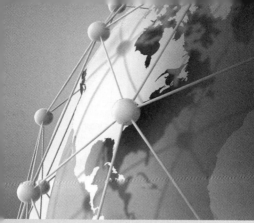

The Purchasing Process

CHAPTER 2

Learning Objectives

After completing this chapter, you should be able to

- Understand the key objectives of any supply management function
- Understand the responsibilities of the supply management function
- Understand the purchasing process and the role of e-procurement tools in the process
- Understand the different types of purchases made by organizations
- Understand how organizations are seeking to improve the procurement process

Chapter Outline

Thyssen-Krupp: The New "Amazon" of Industrial Material Services

ThyssenKrupp is one of the big steel producers in Europe and is getting ready to move to a completely different supply chain model. The company competes in a number of areas, including steel, in Europe, steel in Americas, Materials Services, Inoxum, Elevator Technology, Plant Technology, Components Technology, and Marine Systems. The Chairman of the Board, Dr. Ing. Heinrich Hiesinger, spoke about the massive period of change the company is going through. He noted in his speech that "we want to align our businesses to those of the future. One quarter of the company will be sold, and we have made major headway—and merged our company, we are selling off steel companies in Brazil and in the United States. Our main capability is that we see ourselves as an engineering company—and the importance of the company is our know-how. In the years to come, steel will only be 30% of revenue and we will be a totally different company. The other segments are becoming more important—elevators, escalators, fertilizers, and 90% of diamonds go through our services, and also services for manufacturing industries."

The latter category represented a true source of supply chain innovation. Hiesinger spoke of becoming the "Amazon of Material Services." Material services and logistics management will become TK's core activity. The company has 500 branches in 40 countries and does global distribution of materials including plastic, copper, and iron ore. The distribution business does more and more warehousing and general inventory management. They have 1,500,000 items available ex stock in Germany alone, and a warehousing, logistics and information logistics system with hub and spoke warehouses. "It is like being an Amazon for small to medium sized businesses. They place orders, and we try to deliver in 24 hours. Steel distribution now accounts for only 15% of sales for this unit. Most of the demand is driven by final end customer requirements—and a new business model was generated for logistics as we move out of steel production."

In doing so, Hiesinger spoke about how far reaching the subject of logistics is in a traditional company and how decisive it will be for the success of the company. Changing a business model from being a large clunky steel producer, to a nimble Internet provider of material to industrial businesses is no easy feat. He noted that "The importance of connecting IT and people is key. Global connectedness means that our customers expect us to be connecting them to service locations and we have 130 plants worldwide, about 2000 service stations and 2/3 of our staff is located abroad. To keep this network running smoothly there is no longer a distinction between manufacturing and industry. Logistics is a relevant and compelling part of any company and this will make us more successful and efficient in the interest and benefit of the company. It is critical for us to be networked and connected. We need to use IT and automated purposes and it is not a simple task. Many of our people are traditional steel manufacturing engineers, and the concept of an IT-enabled supply chain is very difficult for them to comprehend. Very deliberately we know once we are connected, we can react flexibly to changing environments. Services may be developed in Germany, but we need to connect with others in other parts of the world for success."

One of the biggest messages was that "there is no longer a distinction between production and logistics. Thinking this way is far from the reality of a global economy. The share of value creation in your own company is going down more and more. In today's global environment, customer satisfaction is determined more by logistics and influenced in the first days or weeks, more so than the technical elements of the product itself. Keep a focus on the customer to the delivery point will lose opportunities for growth. Production is not the issue any more."

Compelling words indeed....and a harbinger of more change to come in the world of industrial manufacturing.

Introduction

Many people new to procurement/purchasing/supply management often have the wrong impression about how complex this function really is. A typical response is "Why can't you just go out and buy the stuff I need! I do all of my shopping online at Amazon—why can't I do that at work?" In fact, the purchasing process is a good deal more complicated than doing your Christmas shopping online at Amazon or Best Buy or Target. The purchasing process has a major impact on organizational competitiveness, and supply managers are continuously working to improve its efficiency and effectiveness. As shown in the opening vignette, procurement and automation of the procurement function are playing a big role in business strategy and can create new market models for organizations in the global economy.

In this chapter, we cover the major types of activities and responsibilities that supply managers follow in conducting their duties, and explore the importance of information technology in achieving these objectives. As shown in Exhibit 2.1, the **purchasing process** is used to identify user requirements, evaluate the user needs effectively and efficiently, identify suppliers who can meet that need, develop agreements with those suppliers, develop the ordering mechanism, ensure payment occurs promptly, ascertain that the need was effectively met, and drive continuous improvement. In every step of this process, managers are challenged to ensure that internal users are satisfied with both the process and the outcome. This chapter introduces the following topics and ideas associated with purchasing in multiple industries:

- Purchasing objectives
- Purchasing responsibilities
- E-procurement and the procure-to-pay process
- Types of purchases
- Purchasing process improvements
- Good practice example at Coke Consolidated

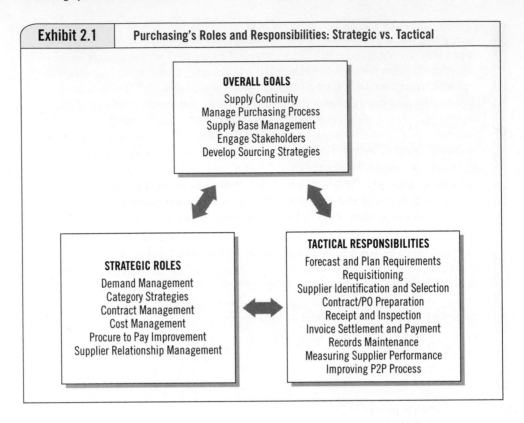

Exhibit 2.1	Purchasing's Roles and Responsibilities: Strategic vs. Tactical

OVERALL GOALS

Supply Continuity
Manage Purchasing Process
Supply Base Management
Engage Stakeholders
Develop Sourcing Strategies

STRATEGIC ROLES

Demand Management
Category Strategies
Contract Management
Cost Management
Procure to Pay Improvement
Supplier Relationship Management

TACTICAL RESPONSIBILITIES

Forecast and Plan Requirements
Requisitioning
Supplier Identification and Selection
Contract/PO Preparation
Receipt and Inspection
Invoice Settlement and Payment
Records Maintenance
Measuring Supplier Performance
Improving P2P Process

Purchasing Objectives

The objectives of a world-class purchasing organization have evolved far beyond the traditional mantra of ensuring we "get a good price!" To understand how this role has changed, let's review the major objectives of a world-class purchasing organization.

Objective 1: Supply Assurance

Purchasing must perform a number of activities to satisfy the operational requirements of **internal customers**, which is the traditional role of the purchasing function. More often than not, purchasing supports the needs of operations through the purchase of services, raw materials, components, subassemblies, and repair and maintenance items. Purchasing may also support the requirements of physical distribution centers responsible for storing and delivering replacement parts or finished products to end customers. Purchasing also supports engineering and technical groups (such as IT), particularly during new-product/service development and outsourcing of key processes. As noted by one executive, "purchasing exists because a decision was made to outsource something that could have been done internally." In effect, purchasing occurs because that outsourced product or service still needs to be managed, or performance will atrophy.

With the dramatic increase in outsourcing, enterprises are relying increasingly on external suppliers to provide not just materials and products, but information technology, services, and design activities as well. As a greater proportion of the responsibility for managing key business processes shifts to suppliers, purchasing must support this strategy by providing an uninterrupted flow of high-quality goods and services that internal customers require. Supporting this flow requires purchasing to do the following:

1. Source products and services at the right price.
2. Source them from the right source.
3. Source them at the right specification that meets users' needs.
4. Source them in the right quantity.
5. Arrange for delivery/service performance at the right time to the right internal customer.

Supply managers must be responsive to the materials and support needs of their internal users (sometimes also called internal customers). Failing to respond to the needs of internal customers will diminish the confidence these users have in purchasing, and they may try to negotiate contracts themselves (a practice known as **maverick buying**).

Objective 2: Manage the Sourcing Process Efficiently and Effectively

Purchasing must manage its internal operations efficiently and effectively, by performing the following:

- Determining staffing levels
- Developing and adhering to administrative budgets
- Providing professional training and growth opportunities for employees
- Introducing improved buying channels within the procure-to-pay systems that lead to improved spending visibility, efficient invoicing and payment, and user satisfaction

Purchasing management has limited resources available to manage the purchasing process and must continuously work toward improved utilization of these resources. Limited resources include employees working within the department, external consulting, training, travel, and IT budget limitations, other budgeted funds, time, information, and knowledge. Organizations are therefore constantly looking for people who have developed the skills necessary to deal with the wide variety of tasks faced by purchasing. Procurement people must be focused on continuously improving transactional-level work through efficient purchasing systems that keep suppliers satisfied, which makes life easier for internal users.

Talent management is proving to be an important task for procurement, as the need for qualified purchasing personnel is growing globally. As organizations expand their production boundaries to emerging countries such as Brazil, Russia, India, China, and other parts of Asia, the challenge of finding people in these regions is increasing.

Objective 3: Supplier Performance Management

One of the most important objectives of the purchasing function is the selection, development, and maintenance of suppliers, a process that is sometimes described as **supplier performance management (SPM)**. Purchasing must keep abreast of current conditions in supply markets to ensure that purchasing (1) selects suppliers that are competitive, (2) identifies new suppliers that have the potential for excellent performance and develops closer relationships with these suppliers, (3) improves existing suppliers, and (4) develops new suppliers that are not competitive with current suppliers. In so doing, purchasing can select and manage a supply base capable of providing performance advantages in product cost, quality, technology, delivery, and new-product development.

Supplier performance management requires that purchasing pursue better relationships with external suppliers and develop reliable, high-quality supply sources. This objective also requires that purchasing work directly with suppliers to improve existing capabilities and develop new capabilities. In some cases, supply managers may need to challenge internal customers who want to add new but unqualified suppliers to the supply base. A good part of this text focuses on how purchasing can effectively meet these objectives.

Objective 4: Develop Aligned Goals with Internal Stakeholders

Global organizations have traditionally maintained organizational structures that have resulted in limited cross-functional interaction and cross-boundary communication. Purchasing must communicate closely with functional groups that represent their internal customers. Internal customers are sometimes called **stakeholders**, in that they have a significant stake in the outcome of purchasing's decision. As such, purchasing's activities are largely driven by stakeholder requirements. If a supplier's components are defective and causing problems for manufacturing, then purchasing must find ways to improve supplier quality. Similarly, if marketing is planning to launch a major advertising and promotion campaign, then purchasing must work to understand supplier capabilities and help build effective service-level agreements and pricing. In order to achieve this objective, purchasing must work closely alongside these internal stakeholder groups, which may mean having procurement professionals who are embedded in these groups, which may include marketing, manufacturing, engineering, technology, IT, human resources, and finance.

Objective 5: Develop Integrated Supply Strategies That Support Business Goals and Objectives

Perhaps the single most important objective for supply management is to support business goals and objectives. Although this sounds easy, it is not always the case that purchasing goals match organizational goals. This objective implies that purchasing can directly affect (positively or negatively) the long-term growth, revenue, and operating outcomes and plans of stakeholders and business units. For example, let's assume an organization has an objective of reducing the amount of working capital across its supply chain. Purchasing can work with suppliers to deliver smaller quantities more frequently, leading to inventory reductions and lower working capital levels. Such policies will show up as improved performance on the firm's balance sheet and income statements. In so doing, purchasing can be recognized as a strategic asset that provides a powerful competitive advantage in the marketplace.

Unfortunately, it is often the case that supply management fails to develop strategies and plans that align with or support organizational strategies or the plans of other business functions. There are a number of reasons why purchasing may fail to integrate their plans with company plans. First, purchasing personnel have not historically participated in senior forums discussing strategic business plans, because they have often been regarded as a tactical support function. Second, executive management has frequently been slow to recognize the value that a world-class procurement organization can provide to the business. As these two conditions are rapidly changing, supply management executives have been promoted to a higher role and are being invited to engage and participate in the strategic planning process. Some of the industries that have already recognized the value of strategic supply include automotive, consumer goods, electronics, and manufacturing. A supply management executive actively involved in business strategy discussions can provide critical supply market intelligence, budget forecasts, and other insights that contribute to more effective strategic business planning. Examples of such inputs include:

- Updates on supply market conditions and trends (e.g., material price increases, shortages, changes in suppliers) and translation of these impacts on key business outcomes

- Identification of emerging materials and service technologies to support company strategies in key performance areas, particularly during new-product development

- Development of supply options and contingency plans to reduce risk

- Support the requirements for a diverse and globally competitive supply base

Strategic Supply Management Roles and Responsibilities

Functional groups carry out certain duties on behalf of the organization. We refer to this as a function's responsibility or **span of control**. Purchasing must have the legitimate authority to make decisions that fall within their span of control. Span of control is established through senior management policies and support. Although internal customers influence many important decisions, final authority for certain matters must ultimately be assigned to the purchasing department. This section details those decision areas that are rightfully part of purchasing's operating authority in most organizations. (Further details on the factors that influence how senior management determines purchasing's span of control are discussed in Chapter 5.)

Sourcing Snapshot

Healthcare Purchasing Mission Statement

A major hospital in the Midwest hired a new Chief Procurement Officer, whose prior experience was working in the oil and gas sector. Upon his arrival, his first meeting was held with the CEO of the hospital chain. The CEO shared with him the high level statistics of the system. The health system had approximately $2 billion annual revenue, and with 12,000 employees in two states, making it one of largest Integrated Delivery Networks (IDN) in the Midwest, as it owned and operated 15 hospitals and 30+ clinics in this region. When the new CPO asked the CEO how much the spend under management was, the response was that there was approximately $200M in spend. "That doesn't sound right," he noted to himself. Sure enough, after further investigation, the CPO discovered that the total spend of the hospital was $600M! After further discussion and many meetings with stakeholders, the CPO developed a mission statement for the supply management group, that set targets for scope of responsibility and for savings.

Healthco is projected to spend an estimated $600M annually with third party suppliers. Our comprehensive Spend Analysis shows our major categories of spend (80/20) that we have across Healthco, and hence we will focus and target our strategic management on those 4 to 6 major categories with **the aim of managing risk of supply and improving financial performance** process for managing this spend today is heavily disbursed, with each business area mostly managing its materials and services expenditures independently. A significant opportunity for improved spend coordination and more sophisticated supply category strategies exists. First, we must ensure that all business areas are aware of contracts in place and are maximizing their take-up/compliance and second, since a significant amount of our spend is not covered by agreements, a clear opportunity for establishing new and smart contracts is here.

We estimate that a deliberate and focused effort to better manage our major supply categories should mitigate Supply Chain risk and yield sustainable cost savings of approximately 4–10% *price improvement* **on the spend under review. However, the real prize will be capturing the additional–130% total cost improvement** per above by creating deeper supplier relationships and fundamentally changing the way Healthco buys and utilizes materials and services.

The ultimate prize will not be an easy one to achieve. **It requires a coordinated effort across the enterprise that relentlessly focuses on seamless execution of robust category strategies and incorporating new ways of getting work done that is driven by a structured review of existing practices and integration of leading-edge thinking.** We can only achieve this level of return if we are committed to investing the time and resources required to fundamentally change our Supply Chain model. As leading change management experts are apt to quote … *"The definition of insanity is doing what you have always done and expecting a different result."*

Source: Michael DeLuca, Interview by Robert Handfield World Health Congress, January 25, 2010, Dallas, TX.

Figure 2.2 shows some of the more common strategic roles and responsibilities. We will cover each of these briefly, then provide more detail in later chapters.

Spend Analysis

Spend analysis is the process of collecting historical data by commodity, relative to demand from the lines of business, with the exception of personnel expenses, occupancy, and corporate spend. The data should go into the appropriate level of unit-level detail required for analysis and commodity management, and should also be rolled up at an aggregate level on every element of what we spend. The result is a common understanding of historical spend relative to demand from each end user within an organization, based on accurate information collected through defined and automated procure-to-pay systems. Spend analysis requires that you drive all spend to a UNIT of consumption and a RATE of consumption. The output of spend analysis is used to drive demand management, commodity management, and risk management strategies. It is fundamental to communicate to the business partners to ensure understanding of where they spent their money and why it was spent.

Demand Management and Specifications/SOW's

Demand management is the process of using UNIT and RATE consumption levels to forecast and estimate future consumption in an internal functional customer, and providing guidance and input on how to optimize usage and educating the user on the tradeoffs. Demand management activities may involve (but are not limited to):

- Optimization of sourcing strategies based on how much the team projects they will be buying
- Proactively setting policies, procedures, and measurement systems that throttle the consumption and total expenditures of a unit of category of spend

- Ensuring appropriate levels of capacity in the supply base required to minimize risk
- Establishing a fixed set of standards to limit options, and restricting the supply base to include only preferred suppliers who comply with risk and compliance requirements
- Challenging product and service specifications to drive out costs while ensuring the same level of performance.

The authority to review and challenge specifications (for products or for services) is also within purchasing's span of control in managing demand, although internal stakeholders sometimes dispute this right. Purchasing personnel work hard to develop knowledge and expertise about a wide variety of materials and services but must also make this knowledge work to an organization's benefit. The right to question allows purchasing to review specifications where required. In the case of services, it also allows purchasing to ensure that the work being performed is correctly documented and performed. For example, purchasing may question whether a lower-cost material can still meet an engineer's stress tolerances. They may also question the rate at which a consultant or maintenance provider is charging for a specific project or activity, and revise the work statement accordingly. A review of different requisitions may also reveal that different users actually require the same material or services. By combining purchase requirements, purchasing can often achieve a lower total cost.

Category Management and Supplier Evaluation/Selection

Category management is the process of developing insights into stakeholder requirements, comparing these to external industry intelligence, supply base capabilities and operational risks, and developing a strategy to align internal requirements with external supply market conditions. Sourcing events are a specific activity contained within the strategy used to explore the market to identify competitive value. A critical element in the strategy is a business case that identifies the rationale for the plan, a risk mitigation plan, and the business value derived from the strategy. The output of a category strategy is a plan for negotiating a contract, a supplier scorecard used to monitor the relationship, as well as a sourcing workplan developed for communication of the strategy to the internal user.

In many cases, category management requires having senior executive's acknowledge that, ultimately, purchasing has the strategic responsibility to evaluate and select suppliers. It is important to retain this right to avoid maverick buying and selling—a situation that occurs when sellers seek to "go around" purchasing, and instead directly contact and attempt to sell to end users (stakeholders). Instead, purchasing should work with stakeholders and include them on the category team, to ensure that they have input into category strategies to evaluate and select suppliers. Engineering, for example, can support the category team by evaluating supplier product and process performance capabilities. The right to evaluate and select suppliers also does not mean that sales representatives are not allowed to talk with non-purchasing personnel. However, non-purchasing personnel cannot make commitments to the seller or enter into contractual agreements without some formal interaction with purchasing, either through a category team or through contract negotiation. The selection decision in category teams requires that the members reach a consensus in selecting suppliers.

Contract Management

An important area of control is that purchasing has the right to determine how to award purchase contracts. Will purchasing award a contract based on competitive bidding, negotiation, or a combination of the two approaches? If purchasing takes a competitive bidding approach, how many suppliers will it request to bid? Purchasing should also lead or coordinate negotiations with suppliers. Again, this does not mean that purchasing should not use personnel from other functions to support the negotiation process. It means that purchasing retains the right to control the overall process, act as an agent to commit an organization to a legal agreement, and negotiate a purchase price. Because the source process involves multiple communications among internal customers, purchasing, sales, and the suppliers' internal functions, the right to be the primary contact with suppliers during the contracting process is retained by supply management. However, involving stakeholders as part of the contracting process can improve the transfer of information and knowledge between buying and selling organizations, resulting in a mutually beneficial contract.

Purchasing departments historically have maintained a policy that suppliers have contact only with purchasing personnel. Although this makes sense from a control standpoint, some firms today are beginning to relax this policy. Today, we recognize that purchasing must act as the primary contact with suppliers, but that other functions should be able to interact directly with suppliers as needed. However, purchasing is ultimately responsible for developing and validating a contract with suppliers. Hence, "contract management is a process associated with defining the contract, defining roles and responsibilities of both parties, and advising when to modify and ensure appropriate escalation." In doing so, purchasing ensures accuracy of contracting terms and conditions ("T's and C's"), and alignment with the category strategy, required service-level agreements, and periodic audits to ensure that post-delivery invoices are aligned with contracted requirements. In addition, contract management should be used to trigger proactive sourcing events before contracts expire. Often, this occurs through maintenance of a contract database, which allows internal users to reference documented relationships, while keeping the contracts current, protected, and referenced. When there are disparities between what a supplier is delivering and the terms of the contract, then contract compliance actions may be required to establish resolution of disparate standard terms and conditions.

Cost Management

Once the contract is signed, purchasing's job is not over. In fact, it is just the beginning. One of the most important roles from here on is cost management, involving continuous cost improvement. Cost management involves unbundling the price paid and understanding the total cost of ownership over the life cycle of a product or service to deliver a target cost and a unit rate to determine if it is priced competitively in the marketplace. Cost management may involve different decision-support tools and databases to create insights into:

- The cost of supporting a process or commodity
- The gap between cost drivers and the assumed business case
- Identifying the business case (e.g., is it a reasonable expense after we deliver it to the customer?)
- The total cost of offering a service, including all of the elements of receiving, use, and disposal over the life cycle of the offering
- Development of cost models in the initial stages of category management prior to supplier negotiations

Managing the Procure-to-Pay Process

Improving the Procure-to-Pay ("P2P") system involves automation of all transactional activities associated with the thread of events that occur from the time of buying a good or service, through the release mechanism, to the point of issuing payment, including:

- Requisitioning
- RFX
- Contract award
- Orders
- Approval
- Receipt
- Payment

Covered in more detail in this chapter, P2P process improvement is associated with establishing controls on the front end of this process to minimize the need to monitor the back end and drive efficiencies, which free resources to work on strategic initiatives. An effective P2P system ensures automated capture of clean, usable spend, invoice, performance, and Accounts Payable / General Ledger data as input into future spend analysis, demand management, commodity strategy development, and cost management activities.

Supplier Relationship Management

Supplier relationship management (SRM) is the end-to-end process of managing a supplier through the entire sourcing life cycle, which includes first identifying the abilities of a particular company with regard to performing a service for the internal customer, completing a sourcing event, negotiating a contract, executing an order, and determining payment. This involves all aspects of the relationship including:

- Day-to-day transactions
- Identification and mitigation of operational risk and deliverables
- Business continuity planning
- Understanding the suppliers' business challenges
- Identification of opportunities to improve value and reduce cost
- Establishing scorecard metrics for improvement and reviewing progress toward these objectives
- Contract T's and C's
- Leveraging the flow of information between key internal process owners and the supplier to create value

When problems are identified, this may drive a supplier development initiative, which is a hands-on six sigma approach to support suppliers to achieve quality delivery and cost targets. Supplier development occurs when there is an existing supplier who is performing at a certain level that has deficiencies—and working to fill the gaps in performance—or when the supplier relationship is not generating the savings projected. This is a critical component for minority suppliers (covered in a later chapter).

Establish a Supply Management Strategy

A supply management strategy is, very simply, an overarching plan for designing the organization, assigning resources, and aligning these resources against the demands placed on the supply chain by the business. Supply management strategies are reviewed at the highest level of the organization, and they drive a workplan that establishes how different businesses must work together to meet the organizational needs through stable and robust processes.

Characteristics of a mature, well-developed supply strategy include:

- A <u>repeatable</u> and <u>well-defined</u> process for building strategy and governance around defining, planning, managing, and receiving products and services for a business
- Clear alignment with executive vision and internal user-specific business goals
- A process based on well-developed supplier market intelligence and input from executives and internal customers
- Established goals and metrics for short-term project plans, as well as a definite five-year plan that provides year over year performance improvements
- Establishes procurement transformation initiatives that involve improving the maturity of the procurement function to elevate strategic value and impact
- Established communication plan to inform senior management and all lines of business updated and reviewed quarterly against defined goals and objectives

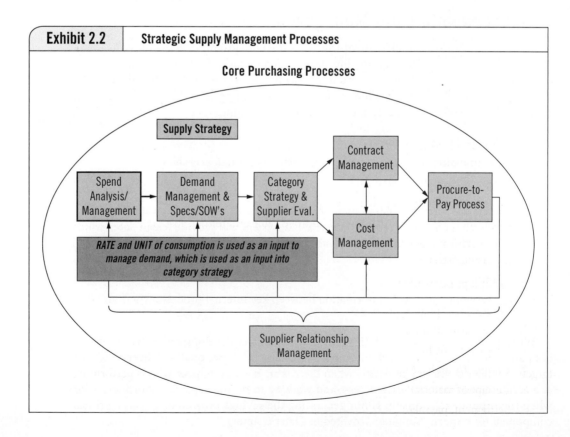

Exhibit 2.2   **Strategic Supply Management Processes**

In the next section, we cover one of these components—the procure-to-pay cycle—in more detail. Components of these purchasing responsibilities are often called the "tactical" components of procurement activity, as they involve management of the many daily transactions that occur as part of an organization's external spending activity. However, just because they are deemed "tactical," that does not mean they are not important (as we shall see).

Improving the Procure-to-Pay Process

In this section, we examine in detail the purchasing process, which includes all the steps that must be completed when someone within the organization requires a product, material, or service. As stated in the chapter introduction, purchasing is a process made up of all activities associated with identifying needs, locating and selecting suppliers, negotiating terms, and following up to ensure supplier performance. Though there are strategic activities associated with managing high level processes associated with developing suppliers, measuring their performance, establishing new performance initiatives, and the like, the fact remains that procurement must still manage the "day to day" activities of buying products and services, and handling these transactions efficiently. These buying activities are highlighted in Exhibit 2.3; these are often referred to as the procure-to-pay cycle, purchase to pay process, (or sometimes the "P2P" process for short). This term includes all of the steps required, from the initial identification of requirements, to the procurement/purchasing of the item, through the receipt of the goods, and finally, to the payment of the supplier once the goods are received.

There are two things to keep in mind as we describe the P2P process. First, the relative effort a company spends on P2P activities will differ greatly from one situation to another. The purchasing process leading to a $30 billion contract for military jets is very different from that for a routine purchase of office supplies. As such, there is a need to dedicate the appropriate amount of resources and time to a purchase situation that makes sense. Purchasing organizations are often strapped for staff and rarely have a lot of excess resources. An efficient P2P process is therefore critical to ensure the best utilization of people to the right set of activities.

Second, as you look at the steps in the procure-to-pay cycle shown in Exhibit 2.3, recognize that companies can often gain a competitive advantage by performing these activities better than their competitors. Many organizations, for example, use electronic procurement ("e-procurement") solutions to automate routine purchase order preparation, whereas others use sourcing management teams to improve the outcome of supplier evaluation and selection efforts. Finally, an effective P2P system will provide "clean data," which is critical to perform a good spend analysis (as we discussed earlier), which in turn will make purchasing's strategic activities more effective.

This section presents the P2P process as a cycle consisting of six major stages:

1. Forecast and plan requirement
2. Need clarification (requisition)
3. Supplier identification/selection
4. Contract/purchase order generation
5. Receipt of material or service and documents
6. Settlement, payment, and measurement of performance

Exhibit 2.3	The Purchasing Process

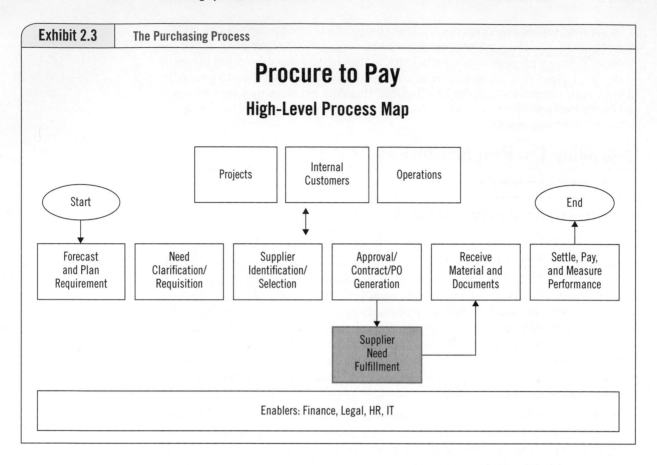

Procure to Pay
High-Level Process Map

These stages may vary in different organizations, depending on whether purchasing is sourcing a new or a repetitively purchased item, and also whether there is a detailed approval process for purchases that exceed a specific dollar amount. New items require that purchasing spend much more time up front evaluating potential sources. Repeat items usually have approved sources already available. Exhibit 2.3 illustrates a typical purchasing process used in many enterprises, with some typical contingency elements shown.

A document flow accompanies the movement of orders and material throughout the procure-to-pay process. Historically, preparing and managing the proper purchasing documents has been a time-consuming process. Most firms have streamlined the document flow process to reduce the paperwork and handling required for each purchase. The suite of tools used to achieve efficiency in purchasing transactions is broadly defined as e-procurement. Companies are using e-procurement tools to manage the flow of documents by (1) automating the document generation process and (2) electronically transmitting purchase documents to suppliers. The benefits of electronically generating and transmitting purchasing-related documents include the following:

1. A virtual elimination of paperwork and paperwork handling
2. A reduction in the time between need recognition and the release and receipt of an order
3. Improved communication both within the company and with suppliers
4. A reduction in errors

5. A reduction in overhead costs in the purchasing area
6. A reduction in the time spent by purchasing personnel on processing purchase orders and invoices, and more time spent on strategic value-added purchasing activities

The electronic documents often used in the process are represented in Exhibit 2.3 by boxes, which we will now discuss.

Sourcing Snapshot

Rockwell Collins P2P and Supplier Portal

Rockwell Collins is a growing company selling communications and avionics systems to both government and commercial customers with sales of over $4B. The company provides pilot controls to the flight deck of the new Boeing 787 Dreamliner.

In 2005, the material and supply operation at Rockwell Collins was already good enough to win *Purchasing*s Medal of Professional Excellence. Not one to rest on his laurels, Roger Weiss, Vice President, Material and Supply, has taken steps to make the operation even more strategic, positioning it to play an even more important role in the company's future growth. The role relies heavily on the success of its supply chain.

"We are truly dependent on our supply chain to make that happen, to continue to grow at the rate we've been growing," says Weiss. "Programs driven by the government and commercial industry are forcing us to become more supply chain focused. We simply can't do everything in-house.

Phil Krotz, Director of Lean Supply, says that all the key strategies the material and supply operation had in place when Rockwell Collins received *Purchasing* medal have served them well. The team's efforts to lower inventory levels continue to be successful, he says. They've also reduced shortages by 30%, helping to ensure an ample supply of material to the company's facilities across the U.S.

Automating procurement activities have helped offset business growth: Material and supply has not had to add resources in the past year. "We let our processes and systems do the tactical work," he says.

In fact, the team now is concentrating its efforts on more strategic activities. For example, Kevin Meyers, Senior Director of Enterprise Sourcing, is working on the organization's planning processes.

"We believe that if we focus on our material planning processes up front that we will be able to reap further benefits in asset management and inventory, as well as have a more stable supply chain," says Krotz. That involves more discipline and integration with the company's marketing and sales organization.

Use of the material and supply team's supplier portal, www.supplycollins.com, has increased from 25,000 visits per month a year ago to more than 40,000 today. More than 1,700 suppliers have signed on to use the portal, which encompasses more than 95% of the company's direct spend.

The team has automated more than 75% of the company's procure-to-pay process, resulting in another recognition: Rockwell Collins received the R. Gene Richter award for leadership and innovation in supply management in the technology category at the annual Institute for Supply Management conference in 2006.

The team also is more focused on containing costs and strategic sourcing. In an inflationary market with rising raw material and energy prices, they've been able to maintain and slightly decrease the company's cost structure, Krotz says. They've taken a new approach to sourcing, now looking at, for example, an entire display system rather than a single component. "We establish teams to identify cost drivers within the system and work with our supply base to look at value engineering or other avenues that we could perform to lower our overall costs," he says.

As Director of Lean Supply, one of Krotz's responsibilities is supplier development. He's taking the company's lean initiatives a step further, by deploying Six Sigma techniques with suppliers. "With our lean tools, we're creating flow and looking to reduce variability in those processes so there's very little variation in, say, performance or size or parts as they are being produced." This will help to further reduce costs.

The material and supply team has created a supplier dossier, or what Krotz calls a one-stop shop for supplier information. Developed for Rockwell Collins employees who work with suppliers, the dossier contains data gathered from www.supplycollins.com, the company's SAP system and supplier information available through Dun & Bradstreet. Says Krotz, "The better informed you are when dealing with someone the better the result."

They're also developing a dashboard that displays performance metrics so that first thing on Monday morning Weiss can get a reading on the health of the business and determine what he and the team need to do to meet their commitments to the corporation. Now, quality and delivery metrics appear on the dashboard with inventory and purchase price variance measures to be up and running shortly. The dashboard consists of three levels, with the first providing a summary of the four measures. Levels two and three provide a deeper dive into the data.

"The benefit is that now we are all looking at the same metrics, calculated in the same way, from the same data sources," says Krotz. "In the past, we had to reconcile data and make sure that we pulled it in the same manner from each location. The dashboard is going to help us manage business-critical metrics on a more proactive basis."

Source: Avery, S. (2006) "Rockwell Collins Builds on Success," *Purchasing*, October 19.

Forecast and Plan Requirement

The purchasing cycle begins with the identification of a need (a requirement). In most cases, procurement personnel have an annual or biannual planning process, whereby they will review the spending pattern for the organization (through a spend analysis, discussed later in the chapter) and prepare a forecast of what will be purchased. In some cases, there may be a whole set of new requirements that have not been planned for (such as for new product requirements). In such cases, purchasing personnel meet with internal customers to discuss their needs for the coming year. In world-class organizations, supply management is the only allowable channel for sourcing of external inputs (products or services) from suppliers. This is often captured in the metric of "percent of spend captured/managed." To accomplish this objective of managing all third party spend, supply management will need to work with a large number of stakeholders, including marketing, operations, engineering, R&D, finance, information technology, human resources, and other internal customers. Through a structured dialogue, purchasing will understand and plan for what these customers will be buying and translate this into a forecast that is shared with suppliers. (In Chapter 3, we will discuss the sourcing process that takes place to identify which suppliers are to receive the business associated with fulfilling this need.)

A projected need may take the form of a component (e.g., a set of fasteners), raw material (e.g., resins), subassembly (e.g., a motor), or even a completely finished item (e.g., a computer). In other cases, the need may be a service, such as the need to contract with an ad agency for a new marketing campaign, airline and hotel travel for client meetings, or a food service to provide lunches at the company cafeteria. Because purchasing is responsible for acquiring products and services for the entire organization, the information flows between the purchasing function and other areas of the organization can be extensive.

Of course, not all needs can be forecasted ahead of time. Situations arise when an internal customer has a need that comes up suddenly, which is not planned for and for which there is no preexisting supplier identified to provide the product or service required. Such needs are often handled through a **spot buy** approach, which is also discussed within the context of the P2P process. For example, marketing may need to purchase a set of pens and cups for a special promotion and may alert purchasing on sudden notice of this need. If it was not planned for, then purchasing must work with marketing to quickly identify a supplier to provide these products on short notice at the lowest possible cost with an acceptable level of quality and delivery time.

When creating a forecast for a needed product or service, internal customers may not always be able to express exactly what it is they will need at a future point in time. For example, a chemical plant maintenance group may say that they will need replacement parts for their equipment, but they may not be able to provide details on the exact nature of the specific parts they will need, nor the exact time they will need them. In such cases, purchasing may negotiate agreements with distributors for parts supply agreements. In other cases, a stakeholder may request to work with a specific service provider for temporary services, consulting services, or software programming, but they cannot express exactly the type of labor requirement needed. Purchasing will then seek to create a contract with predefined costs for different classes of workers who can provide these services on short notice.

Needs Clarification: Requisitioning

At some point, however, internal customers identify their need for a product or service and communicate to purchasing exactly what they need and when it is required.

Internal users communicate their needs to purchasing in a variety of ways including purchase requisitions from internal users, forecasts and customer orders, routine reordering systems, stock checks, and material requirements identified during new-product development. Let's take a closer look at these electronic (or paper) documents that communicate internal customer requirements to purchasing.

Purchase Requisitions/Statement of Work

The most common method of informing purchasing of material needs is through a **purchase requisition** (An example is shown in Exhibit 2.4.) Users may also transmit their needs by phone, by word of mouth, or by a computer-generated method. Although there are a variety of purchase requisition formats, every requisition should contain the following:

- Description of required material or service
- Quantity and date required
- Estimated unit cost
- Operating account to be charged
- Date of requisition (this starts the tracking cycle)
- Date required
- Authorized signature

Exhibit 2.4	The Purchasing Requisition

AnyCompany

TO: PURCHASING DEPARTMENT, PLEASE FURNISH THE FOLLOWING

	OUR P.O. NUMBER	**REQUISITION** **No. 36010**
ACCOUNT CODE NO./A.F.E. NO./A.F.M. NO./W.O. NO./EQUIP. NO.	REQUESTED BY	VENDOR NO.
DATE DATE DELIVERY REQ'D. F.O.B.	DEPARTMENT OR LOCATION	TERMS
TO BE USED FOR	COST ESTIMATE	APPROVAL
	APPROVAL REQUIRED BY	

SUGGESTED SUPPLIER	SHIPPING INSTRUCTIONS
	☐ TAXABLE ☐ TAX EXEMPT

ITEM NO.	QUANTITY	PART NO.	DESCRIPTION	PRICE

DELIVER TO	INSPECTION REQUIRED	
☐ CONFIRMING ORDER TO DATE	BY	METHOD

COPIES OF PURCHASE ORDER TO	☐ ACKNOWLEDGMENT COPY	☐ PURCHASING APPROVAL OF INVOICE REQUIRED

REASON FOR AWARD
  ☐ Low Bid   ☐ Blanket Order   ☐ Priority Source
  ☐ Only Bid   ☐ Only Approved Source   ☐ Commitment made outside of Purchasing Department
  ☐ Only Available Source   ☐ Emergency   ☐ Low Bidder not acceptable (explanation attached)
  ☐ National Account/Contract Supplier ☐ Small Purchase   ☐ Other – or additional comments

CORPORATE FORMS MANAGEMENT

Although varieties of formats exist, a minimum a purchase requisition should include a detailed description of the material or service, the quantity, date required, estimated cost, and authorization. This form of communication for a specific need is called a requisition. A requisition is an electronic or paper form that provides some critical information about the need. A typical requisition will provide a description of the product (e.g., a valve), the material and color (brass, red valve), the quantity required (20 red brass valves), the intended purpose (20 red brass valves to be used in a maintenance project for equipment XYZ), and the required date for delivery (three weeks).

Sometimes a service is required. For instance, marketing may want to purchase an advertising campaign, R&D may need a clinical trial, or human resources may need to print a brochure. In this case, the user will complete a **statement of work (SOW)** that specifies the work that is to be completed, when it is needed, and what type of service provider is required. Note that an SOW may need to include multiple details regarding expectations for a variety of criteria, including required training, site safety, liability and insurance, uniforms, background checks, and other related issues.

A standard purchase requisition or SOW is used most often for routine, noncomplex items that are increasingly being transmitted through online requisition systems linking users with purchasing. An online requisition system is an internal system designed primarily to save time through efficient communication and tracking of material requests. Users should utilize these systems only if they require purchasing involvement. It is possible that users have access to other systems that will allow them to purchase an item directly from a supplier, such as a corporate procurement card. In that case, requisitions forwarded to purchasing are unnecessary.

There are wide differences across organizations in the quality and use of electronic purchase requisition systems. A system that simply requires users to submit to purchasing what they require for electronic transmission is similar to electronic mail. This type of system provides little added value except to speed the request to purchasing. Conversely, one system studied was so complex that users were afraid to use it. They bypassed online requisitioning and relied instead on the phone or intra-company mail.

Although the user may suggest a supplier, purchasing has final selection authority. For routine, off-the-shelf items, the requisition may contain all the information that purchasing requires. However, for technically complex or nonstandard items, purchasing may require additional information or specifications with the requisition. Examples of such specifications include the grade of material, method of manufacture, and detailed measurements and tolerances. Purchasing may send an acknowledgment of the receipt of the purchase requisition to the requestor. This acknowledgment often takes the form of a confirming order requisition. The acknowledgment may be a separate form notifying the user that purchasing has received and is processing the requisition, or it may be a copy of the original requisition. The confirmation verifies the accuracy of the user's purchase request.

Traveling Purchase Requisitions/Bar Codes

Material needs are also communicated through a traveling purchase requisition—a form consisting of a label or bar code with information about whom the item is purchased from. Information on the card or the database entry associated with the bar code can include the following:

- Description of item
- List of approved suppliers

- Prices paid to suppliers
- Reorder point
- Record of usage

A traveling requisition can be helpful because it can conserve time when reordering routine materials and supplies. When stock levels reach a specified reorder point, an employee notifies purchasing by forwarding the traveling requisition maintained with the inventory, or by electronically scanning the bar code into the ordering system. The employee notes the current stock level and desired delivery date. To eliminate the need to research information, the traveling requisition includes information required by a buyer to process an order. This system saves time because it provides information for the item on the card (or in the database) that otherwise would require research by a buyer. For example, the traveling requisition can include a list of approved suppliers, prices, a history of usage and ordering, and leadtime information. Historical ordering information is noted directly on the record over a period of time. As inventory systems continue to become computerized (even at smaller companies), traveling requisitions are used less frequently. With an automated system, buyers simply enter the order requirement, and the system generates a purchase requisition or automatically places an order.

Forecasts and Customer Orders

Customer orders can trigger a need for material requirements, particularly when changes to existing products require new components. Customer orders can also signal the need to obtain existing materials. As companies increasingly customize products to meet the needs of individual customers, purchasing must be ready to support new material requirements. Market forecasts can also signal the need for material. An increasing product forecast, for example, may signal the need for additional or new material. If a supplier is already selected to provide that material, then an automated ordering system such as a material requirements planning (MRP) system may forward the material request to suppliers automatically.

Reorder Point System

A reorder point system is a widely used way to identify purchase needs. Such a system uses information regarding order quantity and demand forecasts unique to each item or part number maintained in inventory. Each item in a reorder point system, which is usually computerized, has a predetermined order point and order quantity. When inventory is depleted to a given level, the system notifies the materials control department (or the buyer, in some organizations) to issue a request to a supplier for inventory replenishment. This signal might be a blinking light on a screen, a message sent to the materials control department's e-mail address, or a computer report. Most reorder point systems are automated, using predetermined ordering parameters (such as an economic order quantity, which considers inventory holding and ordering costs). Electronic systems (such as material requirements planning systems) can instantly calculate reorder point parameters. Most systems can also calculate the cost tradeoffs between inventory holding costs, ordering costs, and forecast demand requirements. Reorder point systems are used for production and nonproduction items.

An automated reorder point system efficiently identifies purchase requirements. This type of system can routinely provide visibility to current inventory levels and requirements of thousands of part numbers. The reorder point system is the most common method for transmitting routine material order requests today, particularly for companies that maintain spare part distribution centers.

Stock Checks

Stock checks (or cycle counts) involve the physical checking of inventory to verify that system records (also called the **record on hand**, or **ROH**) match actual on-hand inventory levels—also called the **physical on hand (POH)** levels. If the physical inventory for an item is below the system quantity, an adjustment to that part's record can trigger a reorder request for additional inventory. Why might physical inventory be less than what the computerized system indicates should be on hand? Placing material in an incorrect location, damage that is not properly recorded, theft, and short shipments from the supplier that receiving did not notice all can contribute to the POH being less than the ROH. For example, at one major hardware retailer, missing inventory on the shelf may be located in another area of the store, or may simply be missing because of a problem with the incorrect item being entered into the system.

Smaller firms that rely on standard, easy-to-obtain items often use stock checks to determine material ordering requirements. In this environment, the stock check consists of physically visiting a part location to determine if there is enough inventory to satisfy user requirements. No purchase reorder is necessary if there is enough inventory to cover expected requirements.

Sourcing Snapshot

Subject Matter Expert Insights into P2P Processes

As part of a research study, a number of senior procurement executives from a variety of different industries were interviewed to get their responses to the same problems associated with the P2P cycle. Each of these individuals provided a different perspective on how to improve the P2P process, but some common themes validated many of the vendors' suggested recommendations as well.

Robust Processes and Training

A critical element identified by all of the subject-matter experts was the need to develop standardized processes and training around the P2P process. Specifically, roles and duties of the different people involved in the process must be clearly defined, training should emphasize how invoices and requests should be processed, and the reasons why deviation from the process is unacceptable as well as what the consequences for deviating are should be explained. This ensures that everyone not only is compliant, but understands the need and rationale behind the compliance. Part of the process redesign effort should also focus on simplifying processes to reduce complexity. If there is no need for a specific channel for purchasing, then eliminate it.

On-Site Relationship Managers

An important point that many respondents noted was the need to establish dedicated roles around on-site relationship managers from procurement who were on site to manage invoices, service entries, and the like. The simple fact is that many maintenance and project managers do not think in terms of procurement, but rather are focused on people, equipment, and schedules; they do not have the time or patience required to ensure that the correct entries are put into a P2P system. The relationship manager can also act as the liaison between the supplier and the maintenance organization, to ensure prompt payment, resolution of issues, and improvement of processes.

Simplified Online Portals to Minimize Human Intervention

A number of SMEs described the need to eliminate the manual intervention of multiple untrained individuals in entering information into systems such as SAP. Many ERP systems have modules for purchasing and plant maintenance, but they all require significant configuration. On the other hand, a number of bolt-on packages are also available, but our SMEs advise against these because of the high probability of interface issues associated with deployment.

Improve Forecasting for Maintenance and Planning for Emergencies That can Flex with Different Situations That Arise

The need to improve forecasting processes is a critical element in ensuring that maintenance needs are met. Although maintenance is often an emergency, there are many scheduled maintenance activities that can be planned and communicated to suppliers. Even in emergency situations, having a plan in place with a designated supplier can avoid many of the problems that occur downstream in the P2P cycle. Too often, data, invoices, service entries, and other key elements are entered incorrectly as a result of a fundamental lack of planning and forecasting. These elements need to be incorporated into the design of new P2P systems.

Reduce Complexity in Catalogs and Buying Channels to Streamline Procurement

Many of the experts also emphasized that the need to reduce complexity in the interface systems through pre-defined procurement buying channels is critical to improving the entire P2P cycle. There is no need for users to have multiple channels for procurement. However, establishing the credibility for users to be able to use only these channels also requires significant management support.

Source: R. Handfield, "Best Practices in the Procure-to-Pay Cycle," *Practix*, March 2006, Center for Advanced Purchasing Management, http://www.caps.org

Cross-Functional Sourcing Teams

When users contact purchasing with a specific need, we say that purchasing is operating in a manner. When purchasing works directly with internal stakeholders to anticipate future requirements, such as during new-product development, or with physician councils in a health care provider, purchasing is acting *proactively*. What does it mean to anticipate a requirement? If purchasing is part of new-sourcing requirements team, then the opportunity exists to work with stakeholders and helping them to define the need early in the process. When involved earlier in the process, category team leader can begin to identify potential suppliers for expected requirements rather than having to react to a supply requirement demand on short notice, resulting in a suboptimal outcome. Anticipating requirements can contribute to faster cycle times and better supplier evaluation and selection. As firms continue to be forced to reduce the time required to develop new products, stakeholder engagement will increasingly be the means through which organizations identify, and hopefully anticipate, material requirements in the purchasing process cycle.

No matter how the need is clarified, the outcome is that a requisition document is completed by a requisitioner. A requisitioner is someone who is authorized by purchasing to complete the needs clarification process. In some cases, the person who expresses the need can also be the requisitioner. This occurs in cases where the supplier has already been qualified, and the individual who has the need can go to a supplier's online catalog, order the product or service directly (e.g., through Amazon), and pay for the item using a company purchasing credit card. In such cases, the item is typically low cost, and it is not worth the expense and trouble of completing an entire requisition and going through the entire P2P cycle.

Description

Within the requisitioning process, it is important to include a description of what is to be sourced. Why? If the time is not spent to describe the product or service, purchasing will have no idea of what to go out and purchase! How purchasing accomplishes this will differ dramatically from one situation to another. There are a variety of methods for communicating the user's requirements. **Description by market grade** or **description by industry standard** might be the best choice for standard items, where the requirements are well understood and there is common agreement between supply chain partners about what certain terms mean. **Description by brand** is used when a product or service is proprietary, or when there is a perceived advantage to using a particular supplier's products or services. A builder of residential communities, for example, might tell the purchasing staff to purchase R21 insulation, an industry standard, for walls and to buy finish-grade lumber, a market grade, for the trim and fireplace mantels. In addition, it might also specify brands such as Georgia-Pacific's Catawba hardboard siding, Kohler faucets, and TruGreen-Chemlawn lawn treatment for all the homes. As you can see, brand names, market grades, and industry standards provide purchasing with an effective and accurate shortcut for relaying the user's needs to potential suppliers.

More detailed and expensive methods of description will be needed when the items or services to be purchased are more complex, when standards do not exist, or when the user's needs are harder to communicate. Three common methods include description by specification, description by performance characteristics, and prototypes or samples.

In some cases, an organization may need to provide very detailed descriptions of the characteristics of an item or service. We refer to such efforts as **description by specification**. Specifications can cover such characteristics as the materials used, the manufacturing or service steps required, and even the physical dimensions of the product. In contrast, **description by performance characteristic** focuses attention on the outcomes the customer wants, not on the precise configuration of the product or service. The assumption is that the supplier will know the best way to meet the customer's needs. A company purchasing hundreds of PCs from Dell Computer might demand: (1) 24-hour support available by computer or phone and (2) 48-hour turn-around time on defective units. How Dell chooses to meet these performance characteristics may be described in their detailed proposal.

Firms often develop prototypes or samples to share with their suppliers. Prototypes can provide critical information on the look or feel of a product or service. Such information is often difficult to convey in drawings or written descriptions. Note that prototypes or samples are not limited to physical products. An excellent example is a prototype information system that a company might share with potential software vendors. The prototype may include sample output screens and reports. Through the prototype, the company can give its software vendors a clearer idea of how the company expects its users to interact with the system. However, prototypes may be in lower volumes than higher production quantities, and process validation must also be accompanied by prototype validation.

Supplier Identification and Selection

Once the need and the description of the need are identified, one of two things can happen: (1) The need is fulfilled by a supplier that has an existing contractual relationship with the buying company. (2) The need is fulfilled by a new supplier that is not currently qualified to provide products and services to the firm.

In the first case, the P2P process moves quite smoothly. Through the need forecasting process, purchasing personnel have already identified which suppliers will be used to source the need, and they have already taken steps to evaluate and prequalify the supplier. Qualification is important, as the purchasing firm must ascertain that the supplier meets several criteria and evaluate whether it is qualified to do business and meet the needs of their internal customers in a satisfactory manner. This evaluation process is described in some detail in Chapter 3.

In the second case, where a supplier is not identified or when the internal customer requests that the need be fulfilled by a specific supplier of their choosing, purchasing faces a more difficult challenge. Because there is no existing contract with the supplier, they may balk at approving the need fulfillment from this supplier. When internal customers purchase directly from nonqualified suppliers and try to bypass purchasing in the process, this is known as maverick spending. That is, customers are acting as a maverick, that is they do not wish to use suppliers already deemed by purchasing as qualified to fulfill the need. Although some level of maverick spending is always going to occur in an organization, there are significant risks that can occur when it reaches high proportions.

Maverick spending is acceptable when there is little risk associated with the purchase. For example, if someone needs to purchase a box of copy paper, there is little risk when an internal customer goes to the local Staples store and purchases a box using the company procurement card. In fact, purchasing will often encourage them to do so, because going through the entire requisitioning process for a small item does not represent a productive use of their time in managing these types of expenses. However, when high levels of maverick spending occur repeatedly throughout the company, it can result in major lost opportunities to control cost and also expose the firm to undue risk and loss of control over the purchasing process.

Let's assume for the moment that a qualified supplier is able to provide the product or service, and that the supplier has been through the evaluation process. For some items, firms may maintain a list of **preferred suppliers** that receive the first opportunity for new business. A preferred supplier has demonstrated its performance capabilities through previous purchase contracts and therefore receives preference during the supplier selection process. By maintaining a preferred supplier list, purchasing personnel can quickly identify suppliers with proven performance capabilities.

In cases when there is not a preferred supplier available, purchasing must get involved in selecting a supplier to fulfill that need. Final supplier selection occurs once purchasing completes the activities required during the supplier evaluation process. Selecting suppliers is perhaps one of the most important activities performed by companies. Errors made during this part of the purchasing cycle can be damaging and long lasting. Competitive bidding and negotiation are two methods commonly used for final supplier selection when there is not a preferred supplier.

Bidding or Negotiating?

Identifying potential suppliers is different from reaching a contract or agreement with suppliers. Competitive bidding and negotiation are two methods commonly used when selecting a supplier. Competitive bidding in private industry involves a request for bids from suppliers with whom the buyer is willing to do business. This process is typically initiated when the purchasing manager sends a **request for quotation (RFQ)** form to the supplier. The objective is to award business to the most qualified bidder. Purchasers often evaluate the bids based on price. If the lowest bidder does not receive the purchase contract, the buyer has an obligation to inform that supplier of the reason it was not chosen for the contract. Competitive bidding is effective under certain conditions:

- Volume is high enough to justify this method of business.
- The specifications or requirements are clear to the seller. The seller must know or have the ability to estimate accurately the cost of producing the item.
- The marketplace is competitive, which means it has an adequate number of qualified sellers that want the business.
- Buyers ask for bids only from technically qualified suppliers who want the contract, which in turn means they will price competitively.
- Adequate time is available for suppliers to evaluate the requests for quotation.
- The buyer does not have a preferred supplier for that item. If a preferred supplier exists, the buyer may simply choose to negotiate the final details of the purchase contract with that supplier.

Buyers use competitive bidding when price is a dominant criterion and the required item (or service) has straightforward material specifications. In addition, competitive bidding is often used in the defense industry and for large projects (e.g., construction projects and information system development). If major nonprice variables exist, then the buyer and seller usually enter into direct negotiation. Competitive bidding can also be used to narrow the list of suppliers before entering contract negotiation.

Negotiation is logical when competitive bidding is not an appropriate method for supplier selection. Face-to-face negotiation is the best approach in the following cases:

- When any of the previously mentioned criteria for competitive bidding are missing. For example, the item may be a new or technically complex item with only vague specifications
- When the purchase requires agreement about a wide range of performance factors, such as price, quality, delivery, risk sharing, and product support
- When the buyer requires early supplier involvement
- When the supplier cannot determine risks and costs
- When the supplier requires a long period of time to develop and produce the items purchased. This often makes estimating purchase costs on the part of the supplier difficult

As firms continue to develop closer relationships with selected suppliers, the negotiation process becomes one of reaching agreement on items in a cooperative mode. One thing is certain: the process that buyers use to select suppliers can vary widely depending on the required item and the relationship that a buyer has with its suppliers. For some items, a buyer may know which supplier to use before the development of final material specifications. For standard items, the competitive bid process will remain an efficient method to purchase relatively straightforward requirements. The bid process can also reduce the list of potential suppliers before a buyer begins time-consuming and costly negotiation. Chapter 14 discusses negotiation in detail.

After bids have been received or the negotiation has taken place, the sourcing team will select a supplier and then move on to authorize the purchase through the purchase approval process.

Request for Quotation

If the requisition requests an item for a higher dollar amount with no existing supplier, then purchasing may obtain quotes or bids from potential suppliers. Purchasing forwards a request for quotation to suppliers, inviting them to submit a bid for a purchase contract. The form provides space for the information that suppliers require to develop an accurate quotation, including the description of the item, quantity required, date needed, delivery location, and whether the buyer will consider substitute offers. Purchasing can also indicate the date by which it must receive the supplier's quotation. The supplier completes the form by providing name, contact person, unit cost, net amount, and any appropriate payment terms. The supplier then forwards the request for quotation to the buyer for comparison with other quotations. The normal practice for a buyer is to request at least three quotations. Purchasing evaluates the quotations and selects the supplier most qualified to provide the item.

Specifications or Blueprints

If the requested item is complex or requires an untested or new production process, purchasing can include additional information or attachments to assist the supplier. This might include detailed blueprints, samples, or technical drawings. Electronic cloud-based systems also permit electronic sharing of these documents using Computer Aided Design (CAD) systems. In addition, buyers can use requests for quotation as a preliminary approach to determine if a potential supplier even has the capability to produce a new or technically complex item. A buyer must identify suppliers with the required production capability before requesting detailed competitive bids. Further quotation and evaluation can then occur to identify the best supplier.

If the purchase contract requires negotiation between the buyer and seller (rather than competitive bidding), purchasing sends a **request for proposal (RFP)** to a supplier. In many firms, RFQs and RFPs are synonymous. However, in the latter case, the item's complexity requires that a number of issues besides price need to be included in the supplier's response.

Evaluate Suppliers

As shown in Exhibit 2.2, when the size of the purchase dictates that a detailed evaluation is required for a new purchase, supplier evaluation may be required. The potential evaluation of suppliers begins after determining that a purchase need exists (or is likely to exist) and the development of material specifications occurs. For routine or standard product requirements with established or selected suppliers, further supplier evaluation and selection is not necessary, and the approval process may be generated. However, potential sources for new items, especially those of a complex nature, require thorough investigation to be sure that purchasing evaluates only qualified suppliers.

The source evaluation process requires the development of a list of potential suppliers. This list may be generated from a variety of sources, including market representatives, known suppliers, information databases, and trade journals.

Buyers use different performance criteria when evaluating potential suppliers. These criteria are likely to include a supplier's capabilities and past performance in product design, commitment to quality, management capability and commitment, technical ability, cost performance, delivery performance, and the ability to develop process and product technology. These factors are weighted in the supplier evaluation process. Specific examples of such weighting schemes appear in Chapter 8 on supplier evaluation. Final evaluation often requires visits to supplier plants and facilities. Because the resources to conduct such visits are limited, the purchaser must take great care in deciding which suppliers to visit.

In recent years, firms have also begun to utilize an electronic competitive bidding tool called a **reverse auction** or an **e-auction**. These mechanisms work exactly like an auction, but in reverse. That is, the buyer identifies potential qualified suppliers to go online to a specific website at a designated time and bid to get the business. In such cases, the lowest bid will often occur as suppliers see what other suppliers are bidding for the business, and in an effort to win the contract, bid it lower. Although they are somewhat ruthless, reverse auctions have been found to drive costs much lower when there is adequate competition in a market.

Approval, Contract, and Purchase Order Preparation

After the supplier is selected or a requisition for a standard item is received, purchasing grants an approval to purchase the product or service. This is accomplished through several different approaches, depending on the type of system in place.

Purchase Order

The drafting of a **purchase order**, sometimes called a **purchase agreement** takes place after supplier selection is complete. Purchase orders often contain a large number of details regarding policies, because it is effectively a **legally binding document**. For that reason, most purchase orders include details on standard legal conditions that the order (i.e., the contract) is subject to. Information may include details on the quantity of material (or service quantity), material specification, quality requirements, price, delivery date, method of delivery, ship-to address, purchase order number, and order due date. This information, plus the name and address of the purchasing company, appears on the front side of the order. Exhibit 2.5 presents an example of a purchase order, and Exhibit 2.6 illustrates a typical set of conditions and instructions.

Companies with an older paper system have a cumbersome process (see Exhibit 2.3). Approximately seven to nine copies typically accompany the purchase order. In cloud-based electronic environments, a file containing a copy of the PO is sent to each department's computer mailbox. The supplier receives the original copy of the purchase order along with a file copy. The supplier signs the original and sends it back to the buyer. This acknowledges that the supplier has received the purchase order and agrees with its contents. In legal terms, the transmittal of the purchase order constitutes a contractual offer, whereas the acknowledgment by the supplier constitutes a contractual acceptance. Offer and acceptance are two critical elements of a legally binding agreement.

Purchasing forwards a copy of the purchase order (either electronically or manually) to accounting (accounts payable), the requesting department, receiving, and traffic.

Exhibit 2.5	Purchase Order

CORPORATE FORMS MANAGEMENT

ACCOUNT CODE NUMBER/A.F.E. NO./A/F/M/ NO.	REQUESTED BY	REQUISITION NO.	VENDOR NO.

AnyCompany

PURCHASE ORDER

No.

PURCHASE ORDER NUMBER MUST BE SHOWN ON ALL DOCUMENTS, ACKNOWLEDGEMENTS, SHIPPING PAPERS, PACKING SLIPS, PACKAGES, INVOICES AND CORRESPONDENCE.

INVOICE IN TRIPLICATE ATTN: ACCOUNTS PAYABLE

DATE WRITTEN	DATE DELIVERY REQUIRED	F.O.B.	DEPARTMENT OR LOCATION	TERMS

TO

SHIPPING INSTRUCTIONS

THIS ORDER SUBJECT TO CONDITIONS ON REVERSE SIDE

☐ TAXABLE   ☐ TAX EXEMPT

ITEM NO	QUANTITY	DESCRIPTION	PRICE

– IMPORTANT –
IF YOU CANNOT DELIVER THIS MATERIAL OR SERVICE BEFORE DATE REQUIRED PLEASE NOTIFY US **IMMEDIATELY**

NOTICE:
EQUIPMENT, MATERIALS AND/OR SERVICE UNDER THIS CONTRACT MUST COMPLY WITH ALL APPLICABLE STATE AND FEDERAL SAFETY CODES FOR PLACES OF EMPLOYMENT, INCLUDING OSHA.

AnyCompany

_____
PURCHASING AGENT   ASST   BUYER

☐   ☐

AN EQUAL EMPLOYMENT OPPORTUNITY EMPLOYER

Exhibit 2.6	A Typical Set of Conditions and Instructions for a Purchase Order

1. Any different or additional terms or conditions in Seller's (Contractor's) acknowledgment of this order are not binding unless accepted in writing by Buyer.

2. Seller shall comply with all applicable state, federal, and local laws, rules, and regulations.

3. Seller expressly covenants that all goods and services supplied will conform to Buyer's order; will be merchantable, fit, and sufficient for the particular purpose intended; and will be free from defects, liens, and patent infringements. Seller agrees to protect and hold harmless Buyer from any loss or claim arising out of the failure of Seller to comply with the above, and Buyer may inspect and reject nonconforming goods and may, at Buyer's option, either return such rejected goods at Seller's expense, or hold them pending Seller's reasonable instructions.

4. The obligation of Seller to meet the delivery dates, specifications, and quantities, as set forth herein, is of the essence of this order, and Buyer may cancel this order and Seller shall be responsible for any loss to or claim against Buyer arising out of Seller's failure to meet the same.

5. Buyer reserves the right to cancel all or any part of this order that has not actually been shipped by Seller, in the event Buyer's business is interrupted because of strikes, labor disturbances, lockout, riot, fire, act of God or the public enemy, or any other cause, whether like or unlike the foregoing, if beyond the reasonable efforts of the Buyer to control.

6. The remedies herein reserved shall be cumulative, and additional to any other or further remedies provided in law or equity. No waiver of a breach of any provision of this contract shall constitute a waiver of any other breach, or of such provisions.

7. The provisions of this purchase order shall be construed in accordance with the Uniform Commercial Code as enacted in the State of Georgia.

8. Government Regulations:

   (1) Seller's and Buyer's obligations hereunder shall be subject to all applicable governmental laws, rules, regulations, executive orders, priorities, ordinances, and restrictions now or hereafter in force, including but not limited to (a) the Fair Labor Standards Act of 1938, as amended; (b) Title VII of the Civil Rights Act of 1964, as amended; (c) the Age Discrimination in Employment Act of 1967; (d) Section 503 of the Rehabilitation Act of 1973; (e) Executive Order 11246; (f) the Vietnam Era Veteran's Readjustment Assistance Act of 1974; and the rules, regulations, and orders pertaining to the above.

   (2) (2)Seller agrees that (a) the Equal Opportunity Clause; (b) the Certification of Nonsegregated Facilities required by Paragraph (7) of Executive Order 11246; (c) the Utilization of Minority Business Enterprises and the Minority Business Enterprises Subcontracting Program Clauses; (d) the Affirmative Action for Handicapped Worker's Clause; and (e) the Affirmative Action for Disabled Veterans and Veterans of the Vietnam Era Clause are, by this reference, incorporated herein and made a part hereof.

   (3) Seller agrees (a) to file annually a complete, timely, and accurate report on Standard Form 100 (EEO–1) and (b) to develop and maintain for each of its establishments a written affirmative action compliance program which fulfills the requirements of 41 C.F.R. 60–1.40 and Revised Order No. 4 (41 C.F.R. 60–2.1 et seq.).

Purchasing usually keeps several copies for its records. There are good reasons for allowing other departments to view purchase orders and incoming receipts:

- The accounting department gains visibility to future accounts payable obligations. It also has an order against which to match a receipt for payment when the material arrives.

- The purchase order provides the requesting department with an order number to include in its records.

- The requestor can refer to the purchase order number when inquiring into the status of an order.

- Receiving has a record of the order to match against the receipt of the material. Receiving also can use outstanding purchase orders to help forecast its inbound workload.

- Traffic becomes aware of inbound delivery requirements and can make arrangements with carriers or use the company's own vehicles to schedule material delivery.

- Purchasing uses their copies of the purchase order for follow-up and monitoring open orders.
- Orders remain active in all departments until the buying company acknowledges receipt of the order and agrees that it meets quantity and quality requirements.

Note that firms are increasingly using e-procurement systems to perform these processes and are moving toward a paperless office. Most of the major ERP systems such as Oracle, SAP, Red Prairie, and others have e-procurement system modules.

Blanket Purchase Order

For an item or group of items ordered repetitively from a supplier, purchasing may issue a **blanket purchase order**—an open order, usually effective for one year, covering repeated purchases of an item or family of items. Exhibit 2.7 on p. 69 provides an example of such a form. Blanket orders eliminate the need to issue a purchase order whenever there is a need for material. After a buyer establishes a blanket order with a supplier, the ordering of an item simply requires a routine order release. The buyer and seller have already negotiated or agreed upon the terms of the purchase contract. With a blanket purchase order, the release of material becomes a routine matter between the buyer and seller.

Almost all firms establish blanket purchase orders with their suppliers. In fact, blanket orders have historically been the preferred method for making the purchasing process more efficient and user friendly. Buyers usually prefer a purchase order for initial purchases or a one-time purchase, which purchasing professionals may also call a "spot buy." Blanket purchase orders are common for production items ordered on a regular basis or for the routine supplies required to operate. A maintenance supplies distributor, for example, may have a purchase order covering hundreds of items. It is not unusual for the buyer or seller to modify a purchase order to reflect new prices, new quantity discount schedules, or the adding or deleting of items.

The blanket purchase order is similar to the purchase order in general content and is distributed to the same departments that receive a copy of a purchase order. The major difference between a purchase order and a blanket purchase order is the delivery date and the receiving department. This information on the blanket order remains open because it often differs from order to order.

When negotiating a blanket purchase order, the buyer and supplier evaluate the anticipated demand over time for an item or family of items. The two parties agree on the terms of an agreement, including quantity discounts, required quality levels, delivery lead times, and any other important terms or conditions. The blanket purchase order remains in effect during the time specified on the agreement. This time period is often, but not always, six months to a year. Longer-term agreements covering several years are becoming increasingly common with U.S. firms. Most buyers reserve the right to cancel the blanket order at any time, particularly in the event of poor supplier performance. This requires an **escape clause** that allows the buyer to terminate the contract in the event of persistently poor quality, delivery problems, and so on.

Material Purchase Release

Buyers use material purchase releases to order items covered by blanket purchase orders. Purchasing specifies the required part number(s), quantity, unit price, required receipt date, using department, ship-to address, and method of shipment and forwards this to the supplier. Purchasing forwards copies of this form to the supplier, accounting, receiving, and traffic. Purchasing retains several copies for its records. The copy to the supplier serves as a notification of a required item or items. Accounting receives a copy so it can

Exhibit 2.7	Blanket Purchase Order

CORPORATE FORMS MANAGEMENT

ACCOUNT CODE NUMBER/A.F.E. NO./A.F.M. NO. Refer to Blanket Order Release	REQUESTED BY J. M. Smith	REQUISITION NO. 20659	VENDOR NO. 02867

AnyCompany
Corporate Purchasing
Street Address
Any City, State 00000
Telephone

PURCHASE ORDER

No.   34833

PURCHASE ORDER NUMBER MUST BE SHOWN ON ALL DOCUMENTS, ACKNOWLEDGEMENTS, SHIPPING PAPERS, PACKING SLIPS, PACKAGES, INVOICES AND CORRESPONDENCE.

SEND INVOICE TO:
ATTN: ACCOUNTS PAYABLE

DATE WRITTEN	DATE DELIVERY REQUIRED	F.O.B.	DEPARTMENT OR LOCATION	TERMS
1/ 3/ 11	As Requested	Our Plant	Various	2% 10, Net 30

TO

Miller Plumbing Supply Company
1616 S. E. 3rd Avenue
Anytown, Any State 90641

SHIPPING INSTRUCTIONS

☑ ATTN: SUPPLY ROOM

☐

☑ TAXABLE   ☐ TAX EXEMPT

ITEM NO.	QUANTITY	DESCRIPTION	PRICE
		<u>BLANKET PURCHASE ORDER</u> This Blanket Purchase Order is issued to cover our purchases of <u>valves, pipe and fittings</u> from you for the period 1/3/11 through 6/30/11. Prices are not to exceed your proposal dated 12/15/10 for the period of this order. This order is not a commitment for any material until actual releases are made on our standard Blanket Order Release form #GP-3809 by an authorized AnyCompany employee whose name appears below. All shipments, deliveries, and pick-ups will be accompanied by a delivery ticket or packing slip. All packing slips, delivery tickets, invoices and any other documents relating to this order must reference this Blanket Purchase Order number and the applicable Blanket Order Release number. AnyCompany reserves the right to cancel this order at any time without cost or obligation for any items not released against this order. Personnel authorized to make releases against this Blanket Purchase Order: THIS PURCHASE ORDER SUPERSEDES PURCHASE ORDER #40019, DATED JULY 1, 2009.	

– IMPORTANT –
IF YOU CANNOT DELIVER THIS MATERIAL OR SERVICE
BEFORE DATE REQUIRED PLEASE NOTIFY US **IMMEDIATELY.**

AnyCompany

John M. Doe

PURCHASING AGENT   ☐ ASST   ☐ BUYER

THIS ORDER SUBJECT TO CONDITIONS ON REVERSE SIDE

NOTICE: EQUIPMENT, MATERIALS AND/OR SERVICE UNDER THIS CONTRACT MUST COMPLY WITH ALL APPLICABLE STATE AND FEDERAL SAFETY CODES FOR PLACES OF EMPLOYMENT, INCLUDING OSHA.

AN EQUAL EMPLOYMENT OPPORTUNITY EMPLOYER

match the quantity received against the quantity ordered for payment purposes. Receiving must have visibility of incoming orders so it can compare ordered quantities with received quantities. As with other forms, this part of the process is increasingly becoming electronic.

Different types of material releases exist. Organizations often use the material release as a means to provide visibility to the supplier about forecasted material requirements as well as actual material requirements. One U.S. automobile producer provides suppliers with an 18-month forecast for replacement parts. The first three months of the release are actual orders. The remaining nine months represent forecasted requirements that help the supplier plan.

In other cases, a more detailed contract is required above and beyond a simple purchase order. A contract is typically required if the size of the purchase exceeds a predetermined monetary value (e.g., $1,000), or if there are risks associated with doing business with a supplier where the potential for conflict and problems is not negotiated prior to the purchase. Because purchasing professionals buy products and services as a career, it is not surprising that they deal regularly with contracts. It is therefore critical that purchasing managers understand the underlying legal aspects of business transactions and develop the skills to manage those contracts and agreements on a day-to-day basis. Once a contract has been negotiated and signed, the real work begins. From the moment of signing, it is the purchasing manager's responsibility to ensure that all of the terms and conditions of the agreement are fulfilled. If the terms and conditions of a contract are breached, purchasing personnel are also responsible for resolving the conflict. In a perfect world, there would be no need for a contract, and all deals would be sealed with a handshake. However, contracts are an important part of managing buyer-supplier relationships as they explicitly define the roles and responsibilities of both parties, as well as how conflicts will be resolved if they occur (which they almost always do).

Purchasing contracts can be classified into different categories based on their characteristics and purpose. Almost all purchasing contracts are based on some form of pricing mechanism and can be categorized as a variation on two basic types: fixed-price and cost-based contracts. In a fixed-price contract, the price stated in the agreement does not change, regardless of fluctuations in general overall economic conditions, industry competition, levels of supply, market prices, or other environmental changes. Cost-based contracts are generally applicable when the goods or services procured are expensive, complex, and important to the purchasing party or when there is a high degree of uncertainty regarding labor and material costs. In this case, the suppliers are reimbursed all of their actual costs plus some agreed on operational margin and overhead amount. The differences in contracts will be discussed later in Chapter 14.

Receipt and Inspection

This phase of the purchasing cycle involves the physical transmittal of purchase requirements (see Exhibit 2.1 with further details in Exhibit 2.8). This should be a fairly routine, although not necessarily the most efficient, part of the purchasing cycle. Some organizations transmit orders electronically, whereas others send material releases through the mail or by fax. Purchasing or materials planning must minimize the time required to release and receive material. **Electronic acknowledgment and receipt** involves the electronic transfer of purchase documents between the buyer and seller, and can help shorten order cycle time. Purchasing or a materials control group must monitor the status of open purchase orders. There may be times when a purchaser has to expedite an order or work with a supplier to avoid a delayed shipment. A buyer can minimize order follow-up by selecting only the best suppliers and developing stable forecasting and efficient ordering systems. The receiving process should also be made as efficient as possible by using bar code technology to receive and place supplier deliveries in inventory.

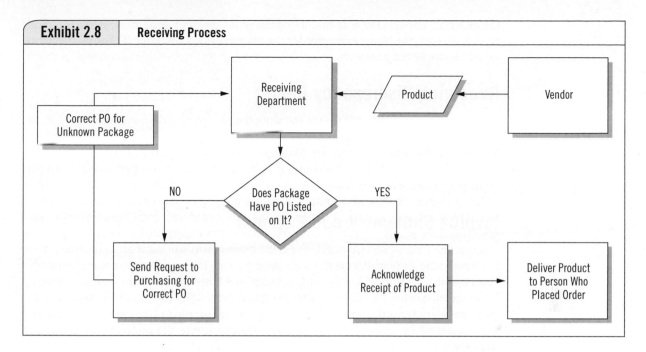

Exhibit 2.8 | **Receiving Process**

The shipping and receiving processes require several other important documents that also can be electronic, including the material packing slip, the bill of lading, and the receiving discrepancy report.

Material Packing Slip

The **material packing slip**, which the supplier provides, details the contents of a shipment. It contains the description and quantity of the items in a shipment. It also references a specific purchase order and material release number for tracking and auditing purposes. A packing slip is a critical document when receiving material at a buyer's facility. The receiving agent uses the packing slip to compare the supplier packing slip quantity against the actual physical receipt quantity. Furthermore, the packing slip quantity should match the material release quantity. The comparison between material release quantity and packing slip quantity is critical. It determines if suppliers have over- or undershipped.

Bill of Lading

Transportation carriers use a **bill of lading** to record the quantity of goods delivered to a facility. For example, the bill of lading may state that ABC carrier delivered three boxes to a buyer on a certain date. This prevents the purchaser from stating a week later that it received only two boxes. The bill of lading details only the number of boxes or containers delivered. Detailing the actual contents of each container is the supplier's responsibility; that information appears on the packing slip.

The bill of lading helps protect the carrier against wrongful allegations that the carrier somehow damaged, lost, or otherwise tampered with a shipment. This document does not necessarily protect the carrier against charges of concealed damage, however. A user may discover concealed damages after opening a shipping container. Responsibility for concealed damage is often difficult to establish. The receiving company may blame the carrier. The carrier may blame the supplier or maintain that the damage occurred after delivery of the material. The supplier may maintain total innocence and implicate the carrier. While all this goes on, the buyer must reorder the material as a rush order. This can affect customer service or commitments.

Receiving Discrepancy Report

A **receiving discrepancy report** details any shipping or receiving discrepancies noted by the receiving department. It is often the job of purchasing or material control to investigate and resolve material discrepancies. Material discrepancies usually result from incorrect quantity shipments. They can also result from receiving an incorrect part number or a part number that has been incorrectly labeled.

Invoice Settlement and Payment

Once the item or service is delivered, the buying firm will issue an authorization for payment to the supplier. Payment is then made through the organization's accounts payable department. This is increasingly being accomplished through electronic means. Suppliers are more often being paid through **electronic funds transfer (EFT)**, which is the automatic transfer of payment from the buyer's bank account to the supplier's bank account. More and more organizations are moving to integrated systems where all purchase orders, receipts, and payments are made electronically.

Records Maintenance

After the product or service has been delivered and the supplier paid, a record of critical events associated with the purchase is entered into a supplier performance database. The supplier performance database accumulates critical performance data over an extended period, helping purchasing identify trends or patterns in supplier performance.

Why is it important to capture the transaction-level data associated with all purchasing processes? This answer is discussed in the next section. Specifically, from time to time the firm must identify opportunities for savings through a process known as a spend analysis. Spend analysis becomes a critical input into building sourcing strategies—the topic of the next section.

Continuously Measure and Manage Supplier Performance

One way to identify the best suppliers is to track performance after awarding a contract. Supplier measurement and management is a key part of the purchasing cycle. As shown in Exhibit 2.2, buyers should not assume that the purchasing cycle ends with the receipt of an ordered item or the selection of a supplier. Continuous measurement is necessary to identify improvement opportunities or supplier nonperformance. A later chapter discusses purchasing measurement and evaluation tools. This section simply summarizes the key points about this phase of the purchasing cycle.

A desired outcome from performance measurement is improved supplier performance. If no formal evaluation takes place, a buyer has little insight into supplier performance over time, and tracking any performance improvement that results from supplier development efforts is not possible. Without a measurement and evaluation system, a buyer lacks the quantitative data necessary to support future purchase decisions.

A major issue when evaluating supplier performance is the frequency of evaluation and feedback. For example, should a buyer receive a supplier quality performance report on a daily, weekly, monthly, or quarterly basis? Although most firms recognize the need to notify suppliers immediately when a problem arises, there is little consensus about the frequency for conducting routine or scheduled supplier evaluations. For many firms, this overall evaluation may occur only one or two times a year. Regardless of the reporting frequency, supplier performance measurement is an important part of the purchasing process cycle.

Reengineering the Procure-to-Pay Process

Many companies have P2P processes that are in disrepair and are focused on improving the P2P cycle. In reengineering the procure-to-pay process, suppliers and experts recommend that executives apply the following approach:

1. Secure top management support for the initiative and budgeting for the project. Develop a list of key benefits and deliverables that will occur as a result of the improvements. Document the cost of leaving the system "broken" in its current state.

2. Map existing processes and problems with the P2P cycle. Identify where the breakdowns are occurring and why they are occurring.

3. Understand the needs and requirements of the user groups. Many of the people involved—maintenance, planning, project management, suppliers' accounts payable, buyers, and so on—have specific issues that prevent them from using the existing system. Also, many of the specific sites may have issues that need to be considered in designing the new system.

4. Team redesign workshops should be used to bring together key subject matter experts (SMEs) from each of the business units. Suppliers should also be invited to attend and participate, as they may have solutions they have adopted with other customers that may prove to be efficient and simple to use ("Why reinvent the wheel?").

5. Explore existing technology solutions with ERP systems, as well as bolt-on applications. Map out the business requirements and ensure they are aligned with the technology solutions that are available. Begin to estimate cost of deployment, and ensure that adequate planning and due diligence are taken at this step.

6. Following the workshops, define the new process, and begin to pilot using a planned technology. Ensure that it takes place in a real environment, with actual nontrained users involved in the pilot before cutting over to the next process.

7. Train and deploy other users based on the new processes and systems. Be sure to make the training appropriate to the specific functional unit and user groups.

8. Monitor, update, and improve the system, ensuring that catalogs are kept up to date. Hold periodic meetings with suppliers and user groups to solicit input and identify problems with the systems.

As technology and business requirements evolve, the P2P cycle will probably need to be revisited from time to time to ensure it is meeting the needs of internal customers and that suppliers are satisfied with the system.

Types of Purchases

Organizations buy many different goods and services. All purchases represent a tradeoff between what an organization can either produce or service internally versus what it must purchase externally. For many items, the make-or-buy decision is actually quite simple. Few firms could manufacture their own production equipment, computers, or pencils. However, all firms require these items to support continued operations. The challenge is deciding which suppliers offer the best opportunity for items an organization must purchase externally. The following sections outline the variety of goods and services a typical purchasing department is responsible for buying. Please note that for each category, organizations should establish measures that track the amount of goods in physical inventory.

Raw Materials

The raw materials purchase category includes items such as petroleum, coal, and lumber, and metals such as copper and zinc. It can also include agricultural raw materials such as soybeans and cotton. A key characteristic of a raw material is a lack of processing by the supplier into a newly formed product. Any processing that occurs makes the raw material saleable. For example, copper requires refining to remove impurities from the metal. Another key characteristic is that raw materials are not of equal quality. Different types of coal, for example, can differ by sulfur content. Raw materials often receive a grade indicating the quality level. This allows raw materials purchases based on the required grade.

Semifinished Products and Components

Semifinished products and components include all the items purchased from suppliers required to support an organization's final production. This includes single-part number components, subassemblies, assemblies, subsystems, and systems. Semifinished products and components purchased by an automobile producer include tires, seat assemblies, wheel bearings, and car frames.

Managing the purchase of semifinished components is a critical purchasing responsibility because components affect product quality and cost. Hewlett-Packard buys its laser jet printer engines, which are a critical part of the finished product, from Canon. HP must manage the purchase of these engines carefully and work closely with the supplier. Outsourcing product requirements increases the burden on purchasing to select qualified suppliers, not only for basic components, but also for complex assemblies and systems.

Finished Products

All organizations purchase finished items from external suppliers for internal use. This category also includes purchased items that require no major processing before resale to the end customers. An organization may market under its own brand name an item produced by another manufacturer. Why would a company purchase finished items for resale? Some companies have excellent design capability but have outsourced all production capability or capacity. Examples include IBM, Hewlett-Packard, Sun, Cisco, General Motors (Geo), and others. The purchase of finished products also allows a company to offer a full range of products. Purchasing (or engineering) must work closely with the producer of a finished product to develop material specifications. Even though the buying company does not produce the final product, it must make sure the product meets the technical and quality specifications demanded by engineering and the end customer.

Maintenance, Repair, and Operating Items

Maintenance, repair, and operating (MRO) items include anything that does not go directly into an organization's product. However, these items are essential for running a business. This includes spare machine parts, office and computer supplies, and cleaning supplies. The way these items are typically dispersed throughout an organization makes monitoring MRO inventory difficult. The only way that most purchasing departments know when to order MRO inventory is when a user forwards a purchase requisition. Because all departments and locations use MRO items, a typical purchasing department can receive thousands of small-volume purchase requisitions. Some purchasers refer to MRO items as nuisance items.

Historically, most organizations have paid minimal attention to MRO items. Consequently, (1) they have not tracked their MRO inventory investment with the same concern with which they track production buying, (2) they have too many MRO suppliers, and (3) they commit a disproportionate amount of time to small orders. With the development of computerized inventory systems and the realization that MRO purchase dollar volume is often quite high, firms have begun to take an active interest in controlling MRO inventory. At FedEx, an agreement with Staples allows purchasing to be free of the burden of tracking office supply requests. Instead, Staples provides a website listing all supplies with prices; users can point and click on the items they need, and the supplier will deliver them to the users' location the next business day.

Production Support Items

Production support items include the materials required to pack and ship final products, such as pallets, boxes, master shipping containers, tape, bags, wrapping, inserts, and other packaging material. Production support items directly support an organization's production operation; this is a key distinction separating production support from MRO items. The DaimlerChrysler sourcing snapshot in Chapter 19 provides a good example of how this activity can be managed.

Services

All firms rely on external contractors for certain activities or services. An organization may hire a lawn care service to maintain the grounds around a facility or a heating and cooling specialist to handle repairs that the maintenance staff cannot perform. Other common services include machine repair, snow removal, data entry, consultants, and the management of cafeteria services. Like MRO items, the purchase of services occurs throughout an organization. Therefore, there has been a tendency to pay limited attention to them and to manage the service purchases at the facility or department level. A study by AT&T several years ago revealed that the company was spending over a billion dollars a year on consultants. As with any purchase category, careful and specialized attention can result in achieving the best service at the lowest total cost. More and more, companies are negotiating longer-term contracts with service providers just as they would with other high-dollar purchase categories.

Capital Equipment

Capital equipment purchasing involves buying assets intended for use exceeding one year. There are several categories of capital equipment purchases. The first includes standard general equipment that involves no special design requirements. Examples include general-purpose material-handling equipment, computer systems, and furniture. A second category includes capital equipment designed specifically to meet the requirements of the purchaser. Examples include specialized production machinery, new manufacturing plants, specialized machine tools, and power-generating equipment. The purchase of these latter items requires close technical involvement between the buyer and seller.

Several features separate capital equipment purchases from other purchases. First, capital equipment purchases do not occur with regular frequency. A production machine, for example, may remain in use for 10 to 20 years. A new plant or power substation may remain in operation over 30 years. Even office furniture may last over 10 years. A second feature is that capital equipment investment requires large sums of money. This can range from several thousand dollars to hundreds of millions of dollars. High-dollar contracts will require finance and executive approvals. For accounting purposes, most capital equipment is depreciable over the life of the item. Finally, capital equipment purchasing is highly sensitive to general economic conditions.

Buyers can rarely switch suppliers in the middle of a large-scale project or dispose of capital equipment after delivery because of dissatisfaction. Furthermore, the relationship between the buyer and supplier may last many years, so the buyer should also consider the supplier's ability to service the equipment. The consequences of selecting a poorly qualified supplier of capital equipment can last for many years. The reverse is also true. The benefit of selecting a highly qualified capital equipment provider can last many years.

Transportation and Third-Party Purchasing

Transportation is a specialized and important type of service buying. Few purchasing departments involved themselves with transportation issues before the early 1980s. However, legislation passed during the late 1970s and early 1980s deregulated the air, trucking, and railroad industries. This legislation allowed buyers to negotiate service agreements and rate discounts directly with individual transportation carriers. Previously, the U.S. government, through the Interstate Commerce Commission, established the rate (referred to as a **tariff**) that a transportation carrier charged. It was common for suppliers to arrange shipment to a purchaser and simply include the transportation cost as part of the purchase cost.

Purchasing personnel have become involved with transportation buying and the management of inbound and outbound material flows. It is now common for purchasing personnel to evaluate and select logistics providers the same way they evaluate and select suppliers of production items. Buyers are also selecting suppliers that are capable of providing coordinated transportation and logistics services for an entire company, including warehousing, packaging, and even assembly. Because many carriers now provide service throughout the United States, a buyer can rely on fewer transportation carriers. The cost savings available from controlling and managing logistics are significant.

Improving the Purchasing Process

Most companies spend too much time and too many resources managing the ordering of goods and service, particularly lower-value items. Some purchasing departments spend 80 percent of their time managing 20 percent of their total purchase dollars. Recent research on maintenance, repair, and operating purchases reported that while the average MRO invoice was $50, the total cost of processing an MRO transaction was $150.[1] In another example, a U.S. government agency reported that in a single year it processed 1.1 million transactions at an estimated cost of $300 per transaction! How can organizations create value through their purchasing process when they spend more time processing orders than what the orders are worth?

A recent study by Trent and Kolchin[2] addressed how organizations are improving the purchasing process by reducing the time and effort associated with obtaining lower-value goods and services. The following sections summarize the approaches and methods presented in Exhibit 2.9.

Exhibit 2.9	Methods or Approaches Organizations Expect to Emphasize to Reduce the Effort or Transactions Required to Process Low-Value Purchases		
METHOD OR APPROACH	**TOTAL SAMPLE**	**INDUSTRIAL**	**NONINDUSTRIAL**
Online requisitioning systems from users to purchasing	66.3%	64.9%	67.4%
Procurement cards issued to users	65.1	59.7	69.6
Electronic purchasing commerce through the Internet	60.9	68.8	54.3
Blanket purchase order agreements	57.4	63.7	52.2
Longer-term purchase agreements	54.4	58.4	51.1
Purchasing online ordering systems to suppliers	61.0	46.7	53.3
Purchasing process redesign	53.3	50.7	55.4
Electronic data interchange	52.7	58.4	47.8
Online ordering through electronic catalogs	51.5	49.4	53.3
Allowing users to contact suppliers directly	49.7	54.5	45.7
User online ordering systems to suppliers	49.1	51.9	46.7
	N = 169	N = 77	N = 92

*Represents the percentage of total respondents expecting to emphasize a method or approach.
Source: Trent and Kolchin, 1999.

Online Requisitioning Systems from Users to Purchasing

Online requisitioning systems are internal systems designed primarily to save time through efficient and rapid communication. Users should utilize these systems only if they require purchasing involvement to support a material or service need. If users do not require assistance, they should have access to other low-dollar systems that do not require purchasing involvement.

Advanced organizations are much more likely to allow users to request low-value purchases through internal electronic systems when the need requires purchasing involvement. Organizations that have made less progress managing low-value purchasing use company mail or the phone to receive user requests. Users should rely on efficient requisitioning systems for items that require purchasing involvement. A longer-term focus should be to create systems and processes that empower users to obtain low-value items directly from suppliers rather than involving purchasing.

Procurement Cards Issued to Users

One tool or system that most organizations agree is central to improving the purchasing process is the use of the procurement card, which is essentially a credit card provided to internal users. When users have a lower-value requirement, they simply contact a supplier and use the card to make the purchase. Cards work well for items that do not have established suppliers or are not covered by some other purchasing system. The users make the buying decisions (the money for which comes out of their department's budget) and bypass purchasing completely. The dollar value of the items covered by procurement cards is relatively low. The cost to involve purchasing or engage in a comprehensive supplier search would likely outweigh the cost of the item.

The study by Trent and Kolchin found that the average cost per transaction due to procurement card use decreased from over $80 to under $30. The primary benefits from using cards include faster response to user needs, reduced transaction costs, and reduced total transaction time. In most organizations, purchasing is responsible for introducing and maintaining the card program.

Electronic Purchasing Commerce through the Internet

Electronic purchasing commerce through the Internet refers to a broad and diverse set of activities. Using the Internet to conduct purchasing business is not extensive today, although commercial Internet usage by purchasers should increase dramatically over the next several years. The highest expected growth areas in e-commerce purchasing include the following:

- Transmitting purchase orders to suppliers
- Following up on the status of orders
- Submitting requests for quotes to suppliers
- Placing orders with suppliers
- Making electronic funds transfer payments
- Establishing electronic data interchange capability

Longer-Term Purchase Agreements

Longer-term purchase agreements usually cover a period of one to five years, with renewal based on a supplier's ability to satisfy performance expectations. These agreements can reduce the transactions costs associated with lower-value purchases by eliminating the need for time-consuming annual renewal. Furthermore, once a purchaser and a supplier reach agreement, material releasing responsibility should shift to user groups. Ideally, material releasing becomes electronic rather than manual, even for lower-value items.

Although the two approaches are conceptually similar, differences exist between a blanket purchase order, which purchasers routinely use, and longer-term purchase agreements. Both approaches rely on a contractual agreement to cover specific items or services; they may be for extended periods; they are legal agreements; and they are highly emphasized ways to manage lower-value purchases. However, blanket purchase orders are typically used more often for lower-value items than for longer-term agreements. Longer-term agreements are usually more detailed in the contractual areas they address compared with blanket purchase orders.

Cloud-Based Ordering Systems

Cloud-based procurement ordering systems involve direct electronic links from a purchaser's system to a supplier's system, often through a modem or other web-enabled technologies. A major feature of cloud-based systems is that suppliers often bear the responsibility for developing the software required to link with a customer's system. Further, the software, e-catalogs, and ordering systems reside "in the cloud" (that is, they are on a server maintained and operated by a third party system provider). In such cases, multiple suppliers may access the system through an online portal, and the buying company transacts business with these suppliers through the system. Online ordering is a logical approach once an organization has established a blanket purchase agreement or longer-term contract with a supplier. The system may be maintained through a third party, or in some cases, the supplier may provide the buyer access to their system. For example, office supply companies such as OfficeMax, Staples, and others maintain their own cloud-based catalog systems, or can configure customized systems for the buying company. Advantages of online ordering systems include the following:

- Immediate visibility to back-ordered items
- Faster order input time, which contributes to reduced order cycle times
- Reduced ordering errors

- Order tracking capabilities
- Order acknowledgment from the supplier, often with shipping commitment dates
- Ability to batch multiple items from multiple users on a single order
- Faster order cycle time from input to delivery

Suppliers establish cloud-based systems so purchasers can have dedicated access to the supplier's order-entry system. The system creates a seamless tie-in or linkage between organizations. Third-party software providers such as Coupa and Ariba provide turnkey solutions that are continuing to provide new capabilities in this space.

Purchasing Process Redesign

Most organizations recognize that purchasing process redesign efforts often precede the development of low-dollar purchase systems. Properly executed redesign efforts should lead to faster cycle times and simplified processes that result in reduced transactions costs.

The purchasing process is composed of many subprocesses, which means it can benefit from process mapping and redesign. The low-value purchase process affects hundreds or even thousands of individuals throughout a typical organization—users in every

Sourcing Snapshot

*University of Pittsburgh Health System Reengineers
Their Process*

University of Pittsburgh Medical Center System Redesign

The University of Pittsburgh Medical Center (UPMC) is a large hospital system with $8B in revenue, and over $1B in spending on medical supplies. The system has 50,000 employees, 20 hospitals, 5,000 physicians, and 4,200 beds. Two years ago, the hospital recognized the importance of supply chain management in driving operating revenue. Executives recognized that by improving profit, money could be reinvested into the hospital, drive investments in technology, and increase the number of patients who chose UPMC as their hospital of choice for surgery and care.

UPMC's supply management team faced a number of challenges in 2009. They had uncontrolled sourcing processes, with thousands of suppliers, hundreds of thousands of transactions, and a huge manual Accounts Payable process. The procurement process produced poor data quality, and there was a need to drive more compliance at the point of purchase for physicians and doctors. Several major pain points were recognized by Michael DeLuca, Director of Supply Chain. First, data quality was poor. There were bloated line item masters data files (indicating that the number of products purchased was massive, with more added daily). All purchase requisitions were paper-based and were handled manually through Accounts Payable agent. Second, there was poor supplier connectivity. Most transactions were manual, even though many suppliers had websites and online catalogs (including Grainger, Staples, HP, Sysco, and GFS). Third, the user experience for procurement was not effective. One physician complained "I can go online to Amazon and review what I want to buy before Christmas—why can't I have the same experience for medical supplies? I can't memorize all of the product identification codes and vendor codes, especially using this 'outdated' technology." There was a need to get better data out of the system, and make the buying process more efficient and easier (e.g., a "shopping cart" model similar to the Amazon experience). Fourth, there were major resource constraints. Not only were there significant layoffs as a result of the economic recession, but a series of waves of layoffs often began with purchasing staff. The rationale was that if procurement could streamline procurement processes, then not as many transactional accounts payable people were required, and that profit generated through the savings could also be generated and reinvested into the system.

DeLuca was also intent on building a capability called "strategic sourcing." This was a seven-step process that could allow category teams to focus on clinical and nonclinical purchase families, and focus more effort on these processes, and less on transactional work. His rationale was, "If I could replace three of my AP people with one good strategic sourcing manager, I could generate significant savings." He also recognized that many of the internal services, including catering, print shops, and telecoms, were not being fully utilized. For the most part, UPMC had relied on a Group Purchasing Organization to manage all of their purchased items-in order to leverage. He recognized that the GPO was NOT a one-size-fits all strategy for all their purchases, although it could be useful in some situations.

The procurement team began to put in an e-procurement system that would work through the company's PeopleSoft ERP system. The guiding principle was to improve data management. This began by tracking inventory in the system, and establishing daily replenishment levels at constrained designated locations throughout the hospital system. There were individuals assigned to strategically support the Operating Room and who challenged the OR's to show the usage on products, and to reduce procurement of those items which are not used regularly and keeping them out of inventory. The number of items in the item master database was reduced from 100,000 to 53,000, and further reductions are planned. The IT organization also developed a capability known as "punch out," which allowed a user working in a PeopleSoft ERP environment to go out to a supplier's website, and created a search capability that allowed them to find products. The website showed pictures of the items, pricing, and descriptions. Users could now create a shopping cart by pulling requested items from contracted suppliers, such as McKesson, Grainger, Airgas, or others. The website was called the UPMD Marketplace, which also allowed users to search item master data, using a tool as a point of consolidation for services (catering, print, telecom, and others). Deluca noted, "We have created a UPMC Marketplace website, which is a single point for all procurement requests, that anyone can use. It is a point and click shopping cart technology, it is easy to view products, and on the back end, the team put in standard UNSPSC codes that allow procurement to process orders in a lights out' environment. In the marketplace, there is a world of content, which allows users to filter out what they need quickly, and find those items that are required in their particular hospital. Supplier on-boarding into the system is controlled by a single procurement person, meaning that suppliers who are NOT on the system (and not approved) cannot be used, which improves compliance. The supply base ecosystem continues to grow, and suppliers are recognizing that they need to improve the content on the site to win over hospital users. The goal in 2010 is to have 30% of ALL purchase orders (POs) in a lights out' no-touch environment, which means no AP person or procurement person touches the order, and that it proceeds through the system electronically and effortlessly." Results have been impressive. UPMC has enjoyed $3M in annual savings, 40% increase in contract compliance, 100% e-enabled requisitions, 40% reduction in special buyer-assisted purchase orders, and 40% less time cleaning up the item master database. Thirty-five suppliers were on boarded in 24 months, representing close to 60% of total spend. Deluca noted, "The single biggest factor for our success was our senior leadership. Every hospital needs a 'Peyton Manning' leader who can take the team forward; who studies the business case, calls out what he sees, and drives action!"

Source: Handfield, Robert, Interview with Michael DeLuca, presenter at World Health Care Congress, January 25, 2010, Dallas, TX.

department, office, plant, and facility; accounts payable; receiving and handling; purchasing; systems; and of course, suppliers. Anyone with a need for low-value goods or services is part of the low-value purchase process.

Electronic Data Interchange

Electronic data interchange involves a communications standard that supports interorganizational electronic exchange of common business documents and information. It is a cooperative effort between a buyer and seller to become more efficient by streamlining communication processes. When used by buyers and suppliers, EDI can help eliminate some steps involved in traditional communication flows, which reduces time and cost.

Although actual volumes through EDI have increased through the 1990s, actual EDI volume does not match the expected volume that was projected by companies. In 1993, for example, purchasing professionals estimated that 60 percent of the supply base, 70 percent of total purchase dollars, and 65 percent of total purchasing transactions would flow through EDI systems. Actual 1997 volume was 28 percent of suppliers, 38 percent of total purchase dollars, and 32 percent of total purchasing transactions flowing through.

EDI systems.[3] Part of this shortfall is due to the introduction of auto fax technology. For many organizations, especially smaller organizations, auto fax is a quicker and less expensive method of communicating with suppliers. Auto fax systems automatically fax requirements to suppliers once those requirements are known by the buyer. The Internet also captures electronic volume that formerly would have passed through third-party EDI providers. The IT chapter discusses this important topic in greater detail.

Online Ordering through Electronic Catalogs

Purchasers are increasingly using this approach in conjunction with other low-dollar purchase systems. For example, one organization allows its user to identify supply sources through the Internet and then use a procurement card to process the order. The key benefit of using electronic catalogs is their powerful low-cost search capability and if users order directly instead of relying on purchasing, reduced total cycle time and ordering costs. Perhaps the greatest drawback to online ordering is the limited number of suppliers that offer electronic catalogs, along with questions about security of electronic ordering and control issues.

Allowing Users to Contact Suppliers Directly

This general method or approach involves different kinds of low-dollar systems. Procurement cards technically qualify as a system that allows users to contact suppliers directly. Online ordering systems also allow users to contact suppliers directly, or the system may involve nothing more than a multiple part form, such as a limited purchase order that users complete as they initiate an order. FedEx refers to its "pick up the phone" system, which allows users to contact suppliers directly, as its **convenience ordering system**.

Approaches that allow users to contact suppliers directly shift responsibility for the transaction from purchasing to the user. Even for items with no established supplier, purchasing still may have limited or no involvement unless the requirement reaches a predetermined dollar or activity level. If an item becomes a repetitive purchase, then purchasing may determine if the item warrants a blanket purchase order. Blanket purchase orders usually allow users to contact suppliers directly when a need arises for material.

Why is it important to capture the transaction-level data associated with all elements of the P2P process? This answer is discussed in Chapter 6 on sourcing strategy. Specifically, from time to time the firm must identify opportunities for savings through a process known as a spend analysis. A spend analysis becomes a critical input into building sourcing strategies, the topic of Chapter 6.

Good Practice Example

Redesigning the Procure-to-Pay System at Coca Cola Consolidated: The CPO Perspective

At the Coupa INSPIRE procurement conference in San Francisco held in April, 2013, the Chief Procurement Officer of Coca Cola Consolidated (located in Charlotte, NC), Patrick Hopkins, shared his views on the "4 Truths of Procurement", and how he has operationalized his views through the deployment of procure-to-pay software.

Coca Cola Consolidated, located in Greensboro North Carolina, which later moved its headquarters to Charlotte, NC, is one of the last remaining private bottlers of Coke. Coke Consolidated has come up with many innovations since then, including the introduction of Cherry Coke. Today, Coke Consolidated is one of 64 bottlers nationwide, has 6000 employees who sell a case of coke every four seconds!

When it comes to "procurement truths," Hopkinds shared what he believes are critical issues that procurement needs to think about when deploying any type procure-to-pay system. He offered these insights based on the extensive process that Coke Consolidated went through in implementing their version of the Coupa software platform.

1. The product must be in the catalog.
2. Users must be able to find what they need.
3. Data must be right.
4. Users must WANT to use the system.

When Coke first started looking at e-procurement systems, they questioned why they should go out of the current ERP system that was already deployed. They developed a list of 48 criteria that needed to be met in considering different P2P systems. The software provider, Coupa met all of them, and Coke signed a letter of intent with the provider to deploy the system. The decision was to keep the front end of the system in SAP, and use Coupa for the procure to order elements of the P2P process. The Coupa system would issue the PO to the provider, and a companion non-functional PO would reside in SAP, out of which payment would occur from the invoice. Deployment occurred December 1, 2012. Here's how the roll-out fared compared to Coke's four truths.

1. **The product must be in the catalog**. All of the items initially piloted ended up being in the catalog. The catalogs could be internally hosted using COUPA or in a "punch out" mode using the SAP system. Both forms were used to access the items. The only glitch identified was for the Grainger-based material systems, where the discounted pricing Grainger provided did not show up in the catalog pricing, so users thought they might be able to get a "better deal" as the discounted pricing was not shown. One of the other issues was to reduce the number of items Office Max had in their catalog from 10,000 to 3,000—the net savings? 10%!

2. **Users find what they need.** The team ensured that employees were well trained prior to implementation, and as a result, there was very fast response time. The metric used to determine if this criteria was met was the "binary rule" that went as follows: users were able to find their exact match or 100% of all alternatives the first time using ONE SEARCH. This refers to the

ability of the search engine to find the part using keyword searches in a description field. The system worked, and users found what they needed with zero chance of error, ensuring the right part was delivered to the right person at the right location.

3. **The data must be right.** The system was able to drive good visibility and inventory availability of material, and the accuracy of the master data file was established.

4. **Users must want to use it.** This was a critical element, the major element of success is whether users are satisfied with a P2P system. The system allows mobility across different applications, including iPhones and Android devices, and is easy to use. Patrick notes that "after we deployed, the phones were quiet, which was a great sign that things were working."

Overall the system captured spend visibility, had become device agnostic (as it was hosted in the cloud as a service), it was easy to use and streamlined the travel and expenses reimbursement process, and was easy to add new suppliers. This latter feature was important, as with everyone using the system, when people wished to add a new supplier, they were first pointed to existing suppliers who already sold the product, thereby limiting the number of suppliers expanding into the system. While deployment is still under way, Hopkins notes that "this was the most successful deployment of e-procurement since we introduced p-cards". The cloud solution makes it easy to implement and easy to intergrate into existing SAP systems.

Questions

1. What steps in the purchasing process are done electronically versus on paper?

2. Who are the users in this case that you believe Patrick Hopkins is referring to when it comes to the "four truths"?

3. Why do you think a different system was adapted instead of the SAP ERP system in this case? What do you think was the rationale?

4. Do you agree with the Four Truths? Can you cite examples of situations where you have run into the problems noted when P2P systems don't work as they should in your own purchase history?

Source: Handfield, Robert, blogpost, Supply Chain View From the Field, http://scm.ncsu.edu/blog/2013/04/10/patrick-hopkins-at-coupa-coca-colas-four-truths-of-procure-to-pay-in-action/. April 10, 2013.

CONCLUSION

This chapter provides an overview of the purchasing process, including the objectives of a world-class purchasing function, purchasing's span of control, the purchasing cycle, and the documents used to manage the purchasing process. These topics provide the foundation from which to introduce the tools, techniques, and strategies used by purchasing organizations in a competitive market. A detailed discussion of the procure-to-pay process was provided. Although the P2P process is sometimes seen as a tactical function, we emphasize here that without a solid transactional process, it is difficult for supply management to drive strategic activities.

This chapter also points out the many different categories of purchases. In addition to buying production material and items, purchasing can be responsible for buying transportation, services, packing supplies, MRO items, capital equipment, and even the corporate jet! There is no one system or approach that applies to all purchase situations. Purchases can vary according to type, importance, impact on quality, time frame for delivery, and dollar volume. We rarely find purchasing personnel who are experts in all the different types of purchases, which is why so many purchasing departments have specialized personnel. All these personnel have one thing in common, however, that is the opportunity to manage large amounts of resources through the purchasing process. By utilizing e-procurement tools, purchasing can achieve the goals of satisfying user requirements, minimizing non-value-added time, and focusing on deployment of sourcing strategies that can provide tangible value to their enterprise.

KEY TERMS

bill of lading, 71

blanket purchase order, 68

convenience ordering
    system, 81

description by brand, 61

description by industry
    standard, 61

description by market
    grade, 61

description by performance
    characteristic, 61

description by
    specification, 61

e-auction, 65

e-procurement, 52

electronic funds transfer
    (EFT), 72

electronic acknowledgment
    and receipt, 70

escape clause, 68

internal customers, 42

legally binding
    document, 65

material packing
    slip, 71

maverick buying, 43

physical on hand (POH), 59

preferred suppliers, 62

purchase agreement, 65

purchase order, 65

purchase requisition, 55

purchasing process, 41

receiving discrepancy
    report, 72

record on hand
    (ROH), 59

request for proposal
    (RFP), 64

request for quotation
    (RFQ), 63

reverse auction, 65

span of control, 45

spot buy, 55

stakeholders, 44

statement of work
    (SOW), 57

supplier performance
    management
    (SPM), 43

tariff, 76

DISCUSSION QUESTIONS

1. How can an effective purchasing department affect organizational performance?

2. Discuss the concept of the internal customer. Who are purchasing's internal customers?

3. Discuss the contributions a purchasing department can make to the corporate strategic planning process.

4. List the areas typically considered within purchasing's span of control. Explain why it is important that purchasing have authority over each of these areas.

5. Describe how purchasing becomes aware of purchase requirements.

6. How is anticipating a material requirement or need through purchasing's involvement on a new-product development team different from reacting to a purchase need?

7. Why do some firms no longer rely only on competitive bidding when awarding purchase contracts?

8. Provide a list of the major documents that are covered in a suite of e-procurement software tools.

9. Discuss the advantages of electronically transmitting and receiving purchasing documents between a buyer and seller. What are the challenges involved in implementing e-procurement tools?

10. Why is it important to measure and monitor supplier performance improvement over time?

11. How does a just-in-time purchasing and production system reduce the need for certain purchasing documents?

12. Why is purchasing becoming increasingly involved in the purchase of transportation services and other nontraditional purchasing areas?

13. Discuss how the purchase of capital equipment differs from the purchase of routine supplies.

14. Develop a list of topics that nonpurchasing personnel should be allowed to talk about with their counterparts at suppliers. Develop a list of topics that only purchasing should be allowed to talk about with suppliers.

15. What is the difference between a purchase order and a blanket purchase order? What are the advantages of using blanket purchase orders?

ADDITIONAL READINGS

Antonette, G., Sawchuk, C., and Giunipero, L. (2002), *E-Purchasing Plus* (2nd ed.), New York: JGC Enterprises.

Busch, Jason. *Spend Matters*, Compass Research White Paper series, http://www.spendmatterspro.com/pro/research-library/compass-research/

Caniato, F., Longoni, A., and Moretto, A. (2012), "Effective eProcurement Implementation Process," *Production Planning & Control: The Management of Operations*, 23(12), 935–949.

Handfield, R. (2006, March), "Best Practices in the Procure-to-Pay Cycle," *Practix*.

Neef, D. (2001), *E-Procurement: From Strategy to Implementation*, Saddle River, NJ: Prentice Hall.

Sabri, E., Gupta, A., and Beitler, M. (2006), *Purchase Order Management Best Practices: Process, Technology, and Change Management*, Fort Lauderdale, FL: J. Ross Publishing.

Timme, S. and Warberg, E., (2011, January–February), "How Supply Chain Finance Can Reduce Cash Flow," *Supply Chain Management Review*, pp. 18–23.

Trent, R. J. and Kolchin, M. G. (1999), *Reducing the Transaction Costs of Purchasing Low-Value Goods and Services*, Tempe, AZ: Center for Advanced Purchasing Studies.

ENDNOTES

1. Antonette, G., Sawchuk, C., and Giunipero, L. (2002), *E-Purchasing Plus* (2nd ed.), New York: JGC Enterprises.

2. Trent, R. J., and Kolchin, M. G. (1999), *Reducing the Transaction Costs of Purchasing Low-Value Goods and Services*, Tempe, AZ: Center for Advanced Purchasing Studies.

3. ibid.

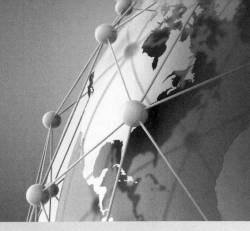

Purchasing Policy and Procedures

CHAPTER 3

Learning Objectives

After completing this chapter, you should be able to

- Understand why purchasing policies are important
- Understand the different types of purchasing policies
- Understand the different types of purchasing procedures

Chapter Outline

Ensuring Contract Compliance in a Chemical Company

Problem Statement

A major global crop science has many procurement contracts for all of its materials (both Direct and Indirect). The contracts are stored in both paper and electronic formats. Electronic forms are being stored in different locations in their systems. There was lot of data discrepancy between the contracts in paper and electronic forms. Handling of the contracts in the system is also very inefficient due to storing in different locations.

Approach

A student team reviewed all available documentation of contracts with five selected suppliers of formulation materials for the company. Contract information was reviewed from both contract systems; transactional data from the ERP system was analyzed from all orders placed between January and August of 2012 for compliance with contract terms as compared with the PO data. Analysis included a comparison of the number of POs processed in PMD with reference to an Outline Agreement (OLA), as well as an assessment of the total invoice amounts to date.

The company's contract policy and process documentation was also examined to assess whether the contracts and contract handling processes reflect stated requirements. Subject Matter Expert interviews were conducted with key individuals representing various areas of the three Procurement groups (Strategic Procurement, Procurement Solutions, and Transactional Procurement). The student team researched available articles, class texts, and other information available through The International Association for Contract & Commercial Management.

Analysis

After review of the available documentation, the team determined current contract handling practices did not accurately reflect the company's established contract management policy with respect to periodic review of contract terms and assessment at contract termination. Current contract repositories do not have the necessary settings or information to prompt this review as it is described in the policy documentation. No contract documentation could be located for two of the five formulation suppliers, although regular purchases were being made from them according to the transactional data that was provided.

The team came up with recommendations based on the gaps identified. The team also determined that there is no documentation available that specifically describes roles and responsibilities with respect to contract management. Documentation detailing the steps taken from contract signing and uploading into the various systems to monitoring performance and termination of the contract was also lacking. This increases the possibility of communication gaps and data errors.

Recommendations were to take the following actions to improve contract management processes:

- Document the contract number (generated at the time a contract is loaded into that system) into a reference field in the applicable OLA within SAP/PMD
- Develop detailed process documentation and ensure semi-annual certification by contract management officer
- Create a checklist/process to ensure responsibilities are properly transferred from one person to the next
- Modify notification systems on SAP to prompt timely contract monitoring

- Design and implement formal training for new hires as well as re-train existing staff on standardized processes
- Ensure presence of OLAs for all PO's, ensuring consistent pricing and payment terms are used for any PO to a supplier

In the long term, the team recommends a detailed review of possible software solutions to fully integrate contract management at the company. This solution would be one that supports contract generation, storage, monitoring, and analysis across the organization.

Introduction

The opening vignette illustrates an important point about purchasing policies: From time to time, it is important to review them and update them as required. Because the company's environment is constantly changing, there is a need to keep up with these changes and provide guidelines and directions to employees regarding how these changes will impact their ways of working. Policies provide the basis for action on the part of sourcing professionals, as well as a set of guidelines for the appropriate way to deal with new situations. As the purchasing and technology environment changes, policies and procedures must be kept up to date with these changes.

Most organizations have a set of policies outlining or detailing the directives of executive management across a range of topics. These directives provide guidance while at the same time placing operating constraints on personal behavior. This chapter, divided into three major sections, discusses the role of purchasing policy and procedures in today's business environment. The first section provides a general overview and discussion of the policy. This includes defining policy, the characteristics of an effective policy, the advantages and disadvantages of policy, and the policy hierarchy. The second section focuses on specific categories of purchasing policies, with a special emphasis on one area known as maverick spending. The third section presents purchasing procedures, which are operating instructions detailing functional duties and tasks.

Policy Overview

The term **policy** includes all the directives, both explicit and implied, that designate the aims and ends of an organization and the appropriate means used in their accomplishment.

Policy refers to the set of purposes, principles, and rules of action that guide an organization.[1] Rules of action refer to standard operating procedures along with any rules and regulations. Although policies are usually documented in writing, unwritten or informal policies can also exist. Informal policies are understood over time and eventually become part of an organization's culture.

What Are the Advantages and Disadvantages of Policies?

Having written and implied policies is an opportunity to define and clarify top management objectives. Policy statements are a means for executive management to communicate its leadership and views. Executive management should develop a series of high-level policy statements that provide guidance to employees at all levels.

Another advantage is that policies provide a framework for consistent decision making and action. In fact, one of the primary objectives of a policy is to ensure that personnel act in a manner consistent with executive or functional management's expectations. Finally, an effective policy provides an additional advantage by defining the rules and procedures that apply to all employees.

There are also potential disadvantages to policy development. First, a policy is often difficult to communicate throughout large organizations. Second, employees might view policies as a substitute for effective management. Policy statements are guidelines that outline management's belief or position on a topic. They are not a set of how-to instructions designed to provide specific answers for every business decision. Third, policy development can also restrict innovation and flexibility. Too many policies accompanied by cumbersome procedures can become an organization's worst enemy.

What Makes for an Effective Policy?

Several characteristics of a policy render it effective. Effective policies are action-oriented guidelines that provide guidance. They provide enough detail to direct behavior toward a specific goal or objective but are not so detailed that they discourage personnel from following the policy.

An effective policy is relevant (avoiding trivial or unimportant issues) and concise (stating a position with a minimum number of words). An effective policy is unambiguous, allowing personnel little doubt as to how to interpret the policy's intent and direction. Policies that are subject to different interpretations will, over a period of time, result in several possible outcomes. This can lead to inconsistent behavior, as people will simply ignore the policy because it is so difficult to interpret.

Sourcing Snapshot

HP is Investigated for Unethical Sales Bribes in Germany and Russia

German and Russian authorities recently launched an investigation into whether Hewlett-Packard Co. executives paid millions of dollars in bribes to win a contract in Russia. German prosecutors are exploring whether HP officials paid about $10.9 million in bribes to win a roughly $45M contract for computer products, through a German subsidiary, to the office of the prosecutor general of the Russian Federation. HP's Moscow headquarters were raided by Russian investigators. German prosecutors are looking into whether HP executives funneled the suspected bribes through a network of shell companies and accounts in multiple countries around the globe. Ironically, the computer system was intended to be a state-of-the-art system designed to provide secure communications for prosecutors through Russia! This could lead to further action by the U.S. Securities and Exchange Commission. Why? Because the Foreign Corrupt Practice Act prohibits U.S. companies from paying bribes to foreign officials, and the SEC also requires public companies to disclose any probes (such as this one) in their filings. HP's most recent filing at the time of the case only referred to the fact that "in many foreign countries illegal business practices are 'common," and that such actions "in violation of our policies . . . could have a material adverse effect on our business and our reputation." German courts can order the seizure of illicit profits if a corporation is found to be the beneficiary of a crime. Investigators are sifting through thousands of e-mails and documents to identify any sign that the 10 HP suspects were acting in an unethical and criminal manner.

Source: Crawford, David, "Germany and Russia Investigate H-P," *Wall Street Journal*, April 15, 2010, B1.

Another characteristic of effective policies is that they are timely and current, which assumes that they are periodically reviewed for clarity and conformance. A policy is ineffective or counterproductive if it is confusing, ignored, or outdated. For example, in the opening vignette, each cement plant was operating under a different set of rules, and everyone was essentially ignoring the fact that a common set of policies or procedures existed. Policy formation and review should be a dynamic activity undertaken at least once every year or so. A policy may be timely and correct but not properly enforced by management. In this case, it is management's responsibility to reeducate the workforce about the policy's intent. There is no other substitute for detailed training on policies to ensure that everyone understands how to do their jobs.

The following characteristics apply to effective policies:

- Action oriented
- Relevant
- Concise
- Unambiguous/well understood
- Timely and current
- Helpful in solving problems

Purchasing Policies—Providing Guidance and Direction

Purchasing management develops policies to provide guidance and support to the professional purchasing and support staff. These policies are general outlines clarifying purchasing management's position on a subject. Although many purchasing policies exist, most fall into one of five categories:

- Policies defining the role of purchasing
- Policies defining the conduct of purchasing personnel
- Policies defining social and minority business objectives
- Policies defining buyer-seller relationships
- Policies defining operational issues

The following discussion does not include all possible purchasing policies. Organizations will also develop policies to meet unique operational requirements.

Policies Defining the Role of Purchasing

This set of policies defines purchasing's authority. It usually addresses the objectives of the purchasing function and defines the responsibilities of the various buying levels. These policies often serve as a general or broad policy statement from which more detailed or specific policies evolve.

Origin and Scope of Purchasing Authority

Personnel at all levels must be aware of purchasing's authority to conduct business and to represent organizational interests. An executive committee usually grants this authority and develops this policy. This policy may also detail the authority of purchasing to delegate certain tasks or assignments to other departments or functions.

An important section of this policy describes the areas where purchasing authority does or does not exist. The policy may exclude the purchasing function from any responsibility for purchasing real estate, medical insurance policies, or other areas where purchasing may not have direct expertise. (However, purchasing is increasingly becoming involved in all types of purchases, including these nontraditional areas.) This policy outlines the overall authority of purchasing as granted by the executive committee while describing the limits to that authority.

Objectives of the Purchasing Function

As noted in Chapter 2, purchasing generally has the final authority over a certain spending area. This is typically set forth in a policy describing the general objectives or principles guiding the purchasing process. The following describes one company's purchasing objectives or principles:

- To select suppliers that meet purchase and performance requirements
- To purchase materials and services that comply with engineering and quality standards
- To promote buyer-seller relations and to encourage supplier contribution
- To treat all suppliers fairly and ethically
- To work closely with other departments
- To conduct purchasing operations, so they enhance community and employee relations
- To support all corporate objectives and policies
- To maintain a qualified purchasing staff and to develop the professional capabilities of that staff

Although these objectives or principles appear broad, they are important because they set forth, in writing, management's commitment to achieving a professional level of purchasing behavior. These principles are also important because they give rise to other policies that directly support purchasing activities.

Corporate Purchasing Office Responsibilities

It is also useful to understand the duties and responsibilities of the central or corporate purchasing office (if a central office exists). This policy may also detail the relationship of the corporate office to purchasing centers located at the divisional, business unit, or plant level. The corporate purchasing office is usually a staff position directing, supporting, and coordinating the purchasing effort. This policy can provide guidance concerning the role of the corporate purchasing staff in the following areas:

- Carry out executive policies
- Develop and publish functional purchasing and material policies and procedures to support efficient and effective purchasing operations at all levels
- Coordinate strategy development between purchasing departments or centers to maximize purchasing leverage of critical commodities
- Evaluate the effectiveness of purchasing operations
- Provide expert support to purchasing departments (e.g., international sourcing assistance, contract negotiations, systems development)
- Perform other tasks typically associated with a corporate support staff

Exhibit 3.1 illustrates a policy detailing corporate purchasing office responsibilities.

Exhibit 3.1	**Example of a Functional Purchasing Policy**

ABC Technologies Purchasing Policy

Policy Number: 2   Applies to Corporate Staff

Divisional Purchasing

Plant Buyers

Date: 1-1-04

Subject: Corporate Purchasing Office Responsibilities

This policy outlines the responsibilities and authority of the Corporate Purchasing office and staff and its relationship to Division Purchasing and Buying Units.

Executive policy E-7 sets forth the principles supporting the organization and management of ABC Technologies and its operating Divisions:

ABC Technologies, by executive policy, is organized on a line and staff basis, with divisional operations largely decentralized. It is corporate policy to assign responsibility and delegate authority concerning operational matters to executive divisional management. All responsibilities not delegated to divisional management remain as official responsibilities of the corporate staff.

The Corporate Purchasing staff is one of the corporate staffs referred to in executive policy E-7. As such, it retains responsibility for the following functions, activities, and duties:

- Responsibility for carrying out and ensuring that each division and buying unit adheres to each corporate policy as stated by executive management.
- Responsibility for developing and publishing functional purchasing and material policies and procedures. The purpose of this is to support efficient and effective purchasing operations throughout the company.
- Coordinate strategy development between divisional purchasing and other buying units to support company-wide efficiencies and reduced duplication of effort.
- Develop systems to evaluate companywide purchasing performance and operations.
- Provide expert support to purchasing departments and buying units throughout the company.
- Assume responsibility for (1) tasks typically associated with a corporate support staff and (2) tasks not directly assigned to divisional or plant purchasing.

This policy reaffirms the autonomy of the divisions and other buying centers to conduct operational purchasing duties and functions. It also reaffirms the company's commitment to efficient companywide purchasing operations through a strong corporate support staff.

Policies Defining the Conduct of Purchasing Personnel

These policies outline management's commitment to ethical and honest behavior while guiding personnel who are confronted with difficult situations. Some business practices are technically not illegal but are potentially unethical or questionable.

Because of this, purchasing management must develop policies that provide guidance in these gray areas. Because purchasing personnel act as legal agents and representatives, they must uphold the highest standards as defined by executive policy and the law.

Ethics Policy

Most organizations, particularly medium- and larger-sized ones, have a written policy describing management's commitment to ethical purchasing behavior. Chapter 15 discusses purchasing ethics in considerable detail.

Reciprocity Policy

A formal policy often exists, which details management's opposition to reciprocal purchase agreements. **Reciprocity** discussed in the purchasing ethics section of Chapter 15, occurs when suppliers are pressured to purchase the buyer's products or services as a condition of securing a purchase contract. A reciprocity policy usually describes management's opposition to the practice and lists the type of behavior to avoid. Personnel must not engage in behavior that suggests any of the following:

- A buyer gives preference to suppliers that purchase from the buyer's organization.
- A buyer expects suppliers to purchase the buying company's products as a condition for securing a purchase contract.
- A buyer looks favorably on competitive bids from suppliers that purchase the buyer's products.

This area requires an executive management policy because disagreement occurs regarding this topic. Reciprocity is relatively easy to control once management issues a policy on the subject.

Good Practice Example | *Sustainable Supply Base Management in the Energy Industry*

The mining and petroleum refinement industry is a very diverse group of companies that have operations around the world. Many of the companies deal with the same issues surrounding supply chain management, labor and human rights, and sustainability efforts with varying degrees of success in handling these complex issues. The industry as a whole sponsor a wide range of programs and activities related to labor and human rights as well as sustainability. Some of the companies have more defined standards for these efforts—including them in contracts—though others lack transparency in the steps they take to ensure the environment and the people in the countries they work are protected.

Labor and human rights as well as sustainability efforts are heavily influenced by the overall control the company has on its supply chain. Research showed that those companies which place a strong emphasis on supply chain relationship management perform better in their efforts to protect the environment and the employees of companies they do business with are respected. The mining and petroleum refinement industry faces challenges that many other industries do not—in that they have operations spanning the globe—a fact that can make it by nature difficult to control. However, companies within the industry have stepped up in large part to ensure that they track where money is being spent, how it is being spent, and finally ensuring that their operations do not have a negative impact on the world and the people in it.

Key Sustainability Issues Facing Energy Companies

- Reliance on coal
- Reliance on foreign sources of fossil fuel energy from politically unsettled areas makes supplier sustainability harder to measure and monitor than in other industries
- Emergence of natural gas as a domestic energy resource and the political, environmental, and economic benefits and consequences associated with it
- Limited number of suppliers

- Increasing demand for fuel and mined resources
- Efficiency in all stages of refining fossil fuels (e.g., transportation of crude oil to appropriate refineries, Keystone Pipeline controversy)
- Expense of constructing new nuclear plants or hydroelectric dams
- Emergence of new alternative energy technologies (e.g., wind and solar), associated legislative requirements for implementation, and economic impacts
- Other geopolitical hurdles in areas where resources are located

A student research team at the Supply Chain Resource Cooperative (http://scm.ncsu.edu) at North Carolina State University evaluated 16 large Fortune 500 mining and energy refinement companies to determine the supply chain maturity of each, utilizing the Supply Chain Sustainability Index (developed by the Supply Chain Resource Cooperative). This framework incorporates assessments regarding supplier relationship management (SRM), labor and human rights management (LHR), and environmental sustainability. Each indicator is ranked from 1 to 5 (ad hoc-worst, optimized-best) according to the result of group discussion. Company research was conducted through reviewing corporate websites, public media outlets, and third party research.

Best Practice Examples:

Chevron

- Chevron has a cutting edge supplier management system that allows them to have oversight and control over their suppliers no matter where they are in the world.
- Chevron has a supplier recognition program that highlights the success and best practices of its suppliers.
- Chevron has a long history of focusing on the needs of the communities in which it is involved. This includes funding for schools and medical centers in Africa and environmental improvement efforts in South America.
- Its use of small businesses and diverse suppliers has been award winning and it focuses on using local suppliers to meet many of its supply requirements.

Freeport McMoran

- Freeport McMoran Global Supply Chain has developed a unique initiative called the "Hour- glass," which requires them and their suppliers to jointly examine the supply chain process to reduce waste and increase profit.
- Since 2005, Freeport McMoran has sought independent verification of its annual sustainability reports, including selected performance data statements on processes and achievements and conformance to the Global Reporting Initiative (GRI) guidelines. They are implementing the International Council on Mining & Metals (ICMM) Sustainable Development Framework, including implementation of 10 Sustainable Development Principles across the Company.
- Freeport McMoran has been a member of the Voluntary Principles on Security and Human Rights since it was established in 2000, which provides guidance to their operations as well as a mechanism to promote engagement, awareness, and respect for human rights within their employee base and with governments and community partners.

Pitfalls, Opportunities, and Industry Recommendations

The mining and petroleum refining industry face huge challenges just due to the hazardous nature of their business. Additionally, the fact that they operate in geographically diverse locations having varying human rights, labor, and environmental restrictions makes their job of being sustainable throughout their supply chain even more difficult. These companies can also attract a lot of attention in case of a major failure in their operations or a disruption in their supply chain as consequences of such failures can be catastrophic to the company in terms of impact on the environment as well as loss of human lives (for example the BP oil spill in the Gulf of Mexico, 2010). For such reasons these companies have stringent health and safety norms and practices. Owing to the large size of these companies, they have the resources to invest extensively in developing their partners and suppliers. They often invest heavily in societal development programs when working in underdeveloped areas. Most of them are also heavily invested in large scale development of green initiatives (such as the Green Corridor Initiative of planting 2,50,000 trees over 5 years by Chevron), which a few companies from other industries can afford to do. On a positive note, this industry has shown its willingness to invest its developing technology which not only is currently beneficial to their line of business but also benefit the society in the long run (such as the BP biofuels Global technology Center).

These companies have shown their commitment towards developing the communities that they work with, which most of the times happen to be in less developed parts of the world. If these companies can continue with their balanced approach of exploring opportunities for maximizing their profits, seeking to contribute towards the environment and society at large, it would definitely lead to a progressive sustainable planet.

Source: R. Handfield, MBA Student Project, Supply Chain Resource Cooperative, http://scm.ncsu.edu/articles, Spring 2013.

Contacts and Visits to Suppliers

An understanding must exist regarding direct visits or other communication contacts with suppliers or potential suppliers. This policy should address not only purchasing personnel but also other departments or functions that visit or contact suppliers. Purchasing wants to control unauthorized or excessive contacts or visits because these can impose an unnecessary burden on suppliers.

Also, unauthorized supplier visits or contacts by nonpurchasing personnel undermine purchasing's legitimate authority as the principal commercial contact with suppliers. Purchasing wants to avoid situations where suppliers might interpret statements and opinions offered by nonpurchasing personnel as commitments.

Former Employees Representing Suppliers

Occasionally, an employee may leave to work for a supplier. This is a concern because the former employee probably has knowledge about business plans or other confidential information that might provide an unfair advantage over other suppliers. One way to address this issue is to establish a policy prohibiting business transactions with suppliers that employ former employees known to have inside or confidential information. This exclusion can range from a period of a few months to several years, depending on the employee and the situation. Another possibility involves including a clause in the employee's original employment contract prohibiting employment with a competitor or a supplier for a specified time. This can offset the advantage a former employee may have from his or her previous employment.[2]

Reporting of Irregular Business Dealings with Suppliers

This policy may establish a reporting mechanism for buyers or other employees to report irregular business dealings. Examples of irregular dealings include accepting bribes from suppliers, cronyism, accepting late bids, owning a stake in a supplier's company, and other types of behavior that are not considered part of the normal course of business. The policy can specify the proper office to which to report the irregularity, the safeguards in place to protect the reporting party, and the need to report suspected irregularities as soon as possible. This policy sends the message that management will not tolerate irregular business transactions involving employees.

The sourcing snapshot below suggests that even well-known Fortune 500 companies are guilty of using bribes as a mechanism to win bids. This is especially prevalent in countries where unethical actions are often dismissed and put "under the table." In any case, the repercussions for unethical behavior are severe, with the penalties far outweighing the potential benefits.

Sourcing Snapshot

IBM Makes Suppliers Accountable for the Environment

IBM announced on April 13, 2010 that it will require its 28,000 suppliers in more than 90 countries to install management systems to gather data on their energy use, greenhouse gas emissions, waste and recycling.

Those companies in turn must ask their subcontractors to do the same if their products or services end up as a significant part of IBM.'s $40 billion global supply chain. The suppliers must also set environmental goals and make public their progress in meeting those objectives.

"We will be among the first, if not the first, with these broad-based markers on our supply base and we're going to have to spend an appropriate amount of time and money to help our suppliers do what we're asking them to do," John Paterson, vice president for IBM's global supply and chief procurement officer, said in a telephone interview from Hong Kong.

"It's clear that there are real financial benefits to be had for procurers across the world to get innovative with their suppliers," Mr. Paterson added. "In the long term, as the earth's resources get consumed, prices are going to go up. We've already seen large price increases and problems with water."

"Our overall interest is to systemize environmental management and sustainability across our global supply chain, so it helps our suppliers build their own capacity in a way that's not only good for the environment but their business," supply manager Mr. Balta said. "It's about creating a system that works regardless of who is in leadership and what's in green vogue."

Mr. Paterson acknowledged the biggest challenge will be working with suppliers in regions of the world where sustainability is not as big an issue as it is in the United States and Europe. But he pointed to a recent success in China, where he said IBM helped one of its suppliers, a shipping company, redesign its own supply chain to reduce its carbon footprint by 15 percent.

Although a deadline had not been set, Mr. Paterson said he would like suppliers to be in compliance by early 2011.

"Ultimately, if a supplier cannot be compliant with requirements on the environment and sustainability, we'll stop doing business with them," he said.

Source: Woody, Todd, "I.B.M. Suppliers Must Track Environmental Data," *NY Times*, B1, April 14, 2004.

Policies Defining Social and Minority Business Objectives

In the long run it is likely in a purchaser's best interest to use its power to support social and minority business objectives. This may include supporting and developing local sources of supply or awarding business to qualified minority suppliers.

Purchasing's actions help shape a perception of good corporate citizenship. Pursuing social objectives may require the development of policies specifically defining management's position. A list of the top companies engaged in minority supplier development is shown in Sourcing Snapshot: The Best Companies for Minority Supplier Contracting.

Sourcing Snapshot

The Best Companies for Supplier Diversity

Though other awards and "Top" lists crown companies for metrics such as overall economic growth and returns to shareholders, The Div50 is an indicator of which organizations provide the best and the most business for diversity-owned companies. "In a marketplace that is increasingly becoming as sensitive to diversity as it is to revenues, awarding the top buyers of multicultural products and services is becoming a natural part of the new socioeconomic food chain. Organizations that consistently buy most products and services from diversity businesses and those which sustain the most mutually beneficial business relationships with their multicultural suppliers should be recognized not only by the business community but also by the general public. That is what we have accomplished in creating The Div50," said Kenton Clarke.

As multicultural and female owned businesses gain more buying power and their lifestyles become more affluent, multicultural markets are growing in economic muscle. This in turn attracts more corporations, as they compete for market share. The Div50 list has therefore become the consumer guide for women and minority consumers. "As a diversity business owner, I appreciate the business we receive from corporate buyers; and in turn, when I buy products and services, either personally or for my company, I am more likely to buy from the same companies that support my business or are supporting businesses like mine," said Helen Levinson, principle of Desert Rose Design headquartered in Elmhurst, Illinois.

The Div50

The Div50 is a listing of the top 50 corporate and organizational buyers of diversity products and services throughout the U.S. It represents the voice of over 1,300,000 diversity-owned (women, African Americans, Hispanics, Asians, Native American, and other multicultural groups) businesses in the U.S., in sectors such as technology, manufacturing, food service, and professional services. It has become the Gold Standard to its members and their associates and reaches millions of consumers every year. In thirteen short years, it has become a highly valued metric of corporate excellence in the diversity space.

The winning companies were honored during a special awards ceremony at DiversityBusiness.com's 13th Annual Multicultural Business Conference, which took place April 24–April 26, 2013 at the Wynn Resort in Las Vegas, Nevada.

The best companies for 2013 are shown in the following table.

TOP 50 MULTICULTURAL BUYING ORGANIZATIONS

1	Wal-Mart Stores, Inc.	26	Walgreens
2	AT & T Inc.	27	Pacific Gas & Electric
3	IBM	28	Target Corporation
4	Northrop Grumman Corporation	29	Colgate-Palmolive Company
5	Office Depot Inc.	30	Wells Fargo
6	Cisco Systems, Inc	31	General Motors
7	Verizon	32	The Home Depot, Inc
8	Raytheon Company	33	Johnson & Johnson
9	Dell	34	Nordstrom
10	Apple Inc.	35	Comcast Corporation
11	Lockheed Martin	36	General Electric
11	Time Warner Inc.	37	Pfizer
12	Toyota	38	Kraft Foods
13	Boeing Company	39	Hospira
14	The Coca-Cola Company	40	Microsoft
15	Kroger	40	MillerCoors
16	Ford	41	Turner Construction Company
17	J.C. Penney Company, Inc.	42	Ahold USA
18	Altria	43	Accenture
19	Hewlett-Packard	44	Capital One Financial Corporation
20	Blue Cross and Blue Shield Association	45	Hilton Worldwide
21	United Parcel Service	46	New York Life
22	United Technologies Corporation	47	Avis Budget Group
23	Super Valu Inc.	48	OfficeMax
24	PepsiCo Inc.	49	Metlife
25	Chrysler	50	Novation

Source: http://www.diversitybusiness.com/news/supplierdiversity/45201336.asp

Supporting Minority Business Suppliers

Supporting minority suppliers is not only the right thing to do, it is also the smart thing to do. As the nature of America's demographics and workforce continually changes, organizations will need to hire and train people with multicultural backgrounds and promote relationships with suppliers and customers from diverse backgrounds. At the same time, it is important to recognize that minority suppliers are a special class of supplier. As such, they face many problems that are unique to their special status, while also facing many of the same problems that confront nonminority suppliers. Several factors lie at the core of these problems: lack of access to capital; large firms' efforts to optimize their supply bases; inability to attract qualified managers and other professionals; and minority suppliers' relatively small size, which may lead to overreliance on large customer firms.

Management's position concerning transactions with minority business suppliers provides guidance to buyers. A minority business supplier is a business that is run or partially owned by an individual classified as a minority by the U.S. government. Such policies typically state that these suppliers should receive a fair and equal opportunity to participate in the purchasing process. The policy may outline a number of steps to achieve the policy's objectives, including the following:

- Set forth management's commitment on this subject.

- Evaluate the performance potential of small and disadvantaged suppliers to identify those qualifying for supplier assistance.

- Invite small and disadvantaged suppliers to bid on purchase contracts.
- Establish a minimum percentage of business to award to qualified small and disadvantaged suppliers.
- Outline a training program to educate buyers regarding the needs of the small and disadvantaged suppliers.

Policies supporting disadvantaged suppliers are common in contracts with the U.S. government, which encourages awarding subcontracts to small and disadvantaged suppliers. Other companies have formal procedures for including minority business suppliers.

Sourcing Snapshot

Does Your Organization Really Enforce Its Labor and Human Rights Standards?

Saying that you have no human rights abuses in your supply chain, and actually being able to verify that you do not are two different issues. Auditing and tracking of human rights compliance and violations is trickier than it sounds; auditors can be paid off in LCC countries. Even honest auditors typically announce their audits prior to arrival, allowing facilities to "sterilize" their operational environments for the day, and revert back to old habits. A more useful approach involves assessing the end-to-end sourcing process, which consists of supplier evaluation, contracting, and performance measurement, and is much more preventive in nature. Not only can organizations avoid establishing contracts with suppliers who do not manage their LHR processes, but a framework that provides ongoing monitoring and punitive measures for those who do manage to sneak through the security net is more likely to ensure compliance.

But what are the criteria for assessing LHR violations? One of the most important frameworks that has emerged is the one provided by the International Labor Organization, which provides several key guidelines for assessing compliance to fair labor standards. These are listed below. The International Labor Organization (ILO) framework is useful, but applying it to the sourcing process is more problematic. There is a need for establishing guidelines that can be applied to the sourcing process (selection, contracting, and performance measurement) that ensure that ILO human rights guidelines are explicitly considered.

There are a number of clear guidelines that spell out whether or not an organization is really serious about improving their supply chain human rights performance. These must be clearly identified in an organization's policies and procedures, and integrated into daily routines for supply managers. These include elements that align with best practices in strategic sourcing and global supply management and are described below:

- Code of Conduct: Does the organization have a code of conduct for suppliers that clearly represents acceptable and unacceptable labor practices that align with the ILO standards? Are there penalties in place to enforce compliance?
- Contracts: Do all sourcing contracts with global suppliers include clauses that mandate penalties for noncompliance to code of conduct violations?
- Reporting: Are there internal performance tracking systems, complemented by independent auditors, to track compliance to code of conduct requirements? Are these measures reviewed on an appropriate basis by senior executives?
- Supplier Enforcement: Are there on-site programs to train suppliers and to demonstrate exactly what is meant by code of conduct requirements? Are suppliers also required to adopt an aligned code of conduct policies into their own organizational governance systems?

- Second Tier Suppliers: Many suppliers simply pass on their human rights violations to smaller, second tier subcontractors. Do these Tier 1 suppliers have their own auditing systems to ensure that these Tier 2 suppliers are also compliant with code of conduct requirements?
- Evaluation: Are there internal auditing systems that audit a majority of suppliers on a regular basis (annually)? Are these completed by independent, respected auditors? Are auditor reports maintained in a database that is shared with key suppliers, as well as external parties?
- Human Resources: Are there training programs in place to ensure suppliers understand how to improve compliance to ILO requirements? Are there other mechanisms to engage the local community to support these measures?
- Lawsuits: Does the organization have a clean track record of addressing any outstanding labor and human rights lawsuits?

These building blocks provide clear and unequivocal standards that senior leaders can apply to gauge whether they are truly committed to human rights improvement in the supply chain. The standards also provide clear benchmarking guidelines that can be used to measure the level of LHR compliance of not only a single enterprise, but an industry or a region of the world.

Source: Handfield, Robert, and George, Seena, "Labor and Human Rights in the Supply Chain," Working paper, Supply Chain Resource Cooperative, http://scm.ncsu.edu, 2010.

For instance, one large pharmaceutical company has developed a process for identifying minority suppliers, which includes the following questions:

- Is the supplier fully qualified?
- Does the supplier satisfy U.S. government criteria defining a minority business?
- Does the supplier meet our standard performance requirements?
- Is the supplier price competitive?
- How much business can we give the supplier given its capacity?

Links and information having to do with minority business development can be found at http://www.mbda.gov.

A recent study on best practices conducted by the Supply Chain Resource Cooperative at North Carolina State University emphasized that companies in many industries are making great improvements in minority supplier development programs. However, until organizations can devote more resources to actively improving minority suppliers through focused supplier development programs, growth of minority suppliers in the supply base will remain problematic.

The research also suggested that almost all industries have limited resources for supplier diversity programs. One interesting observation regarding resource allocation is that industries that are rife with financial difficulties do not have the luxury to dedicate additional resources for these programs. However, in industries that are not experiencing financial difficulties, the research found that there was often a lack of executive sponsorship, which led to the same outcome: diversity does not get enough attention or budget allocation for its progress. Two important features of any supplier development initiative were identified: process improvement and leadership/corporate commitment. These elements were viewed by many executives as critical foundational elements for any minority supplier development initiative. The industry-specific best practices in how organizations developed their policies and procedures include the following:

- Mandate Tier 1 suppliers to have a Tier 2 diversity spend goal and incorporate the terms in the contracts. Tier 1 suppliers should be able to record their diversity spend / minority supplier spend online through the customer's website. Increasing Tier 2 diversity spend offsets to some extent the effect of diminishing opportunities for minority suppliers due to increased global sourcing and offshore contracting. Online tracking of minority spend in Tier 2 suppliers also increases visibility and compliance.

- Include minority suppliers in all RFQs, without exception. Policies may be defined on the basis of mutually agreed-upon terms between business units and the organization's Supplier Diversity Council. Awarding of RFQs should in all circumstances be tied to performance.

- Tie the goals and objectives of the supplier diversity program (SDP) to supply chain management strategies and supply chain job functions. Business units should also have diversity goals tied to performance to increase participation and commitment to the program.

- Incorporate supplier diversity programs within the corporate procurement organization, and assign supplier diversity advocates to specific business units. These advocates can provide training and support to buyers and drive compliance. This approach also enables consolidation of spend with the minority suppliers that are being developed by the corporate supplier diversity programs.

- Incorporate all corporate functions in which suppliers are selected and procurement commitments are made. Corporate supplier diversity committees should include management representatives from all such cross-functional areas: Advertising, Public Relations, Finance, Legal, R&D, Human Resources, Engineering, Real Estate, Traffic and Distribution, Sales, and Corporate Office Administration. This is in recognition of the fact that SDP should be a supply chain accountability and not just a corporate accountability.

Corporate Social Responsibility

Low-cost country (LCC) sourcing is now a commonplace strategy for shrinking bottom line labor and material costs in most consumer products industries, including apparel, footwear, toys, and other manufactured products. Organizations continue to scour global markets for even lower labor rates, moving from Western China to the Pearl River, and now to Vietnam, Indonesia, Malaysia, Cambodia, and North Africa. With overseas factories moving to new locations with lower labor costs, monitoring and controlling working conditions, environmental compliance, and quality control becomes an ongoing challenge. Within the rubric of "Corporate Social Responsibility," environmental infractions have generally received the bulk of attention from the international press. Recently, however, CSR and sustainability has also come to include the "human factor" implicit in this definition. Humans are also part of the environment. Although many organizations have sought to play down the importance of labor and human rights (LHR) violations in their CSR initiatives, this is beginning to change.

A set of policies outlining a position related to environmental issues is becoming increasingly important. Moreover, governments are now requiring such policies by law. These policies include the use of recycled material, strict compliance with local, state, and federal regulations, and proper disposal of waste material. The Clean Air Act of 1990 imposes large fines on producers of ozone-depleting substances and foul-smelling gases. As a result, buyers must consider a supplier's ability to comply with environmental regulations as a condition for selection. This includes, but is not limited to, the proper disposal of hazardous waste.

A good example of environmental policy involves the chemical industry, which traditionally has been a major source of industrial pollution. This industry knows that if it does not adopt a set of environmental policies, then government regulators will initiate strict regulations. Dow Chemical, for example, considers environmental concerns a critical feature of its policies and procedures.[3] As a member of the Chemical Manufacturers Association, Dow is a participant in Responsible Care, a program initiative that addresses a community's concerns regarding chemicals, including their manufacture, transportation, use, and safe disposal; health and safety issues; prompt reporting of environmental accidents; and counseling of customers. Supplier evaluation involves assessing the environmental policies of suppliers (primarily other major chemical companies). A key element of evaluation involves understanding and assessing the environmental risk associated with the particular chemical being purchased. Dow searches for suppliers that are green, according to industry standards.

Labor and human rights is much trickier to monitor via policies. The conventional view is that most companies have policies governing ethical treatment of people at suppliers' facilities, but this is not always the case. For example, companies such as Nike, Abercrombie, and Adidas extol the virtues of their ethical, child-free, factories. However, recent research suggests that organizations actually do very little to truly monitor human rights violations in their low-cost country supply chain manufacturing locations. To placate human rights activists, organizations have issued flashy corporate codes of conduct that appear on web pages or color brochures, along with pictures of smiling children and green pastures. But are these organizations truly monitoring these conditions? These organizations will be facing much more scrutiny in the next decade, and those that do not pay attention will feel the effects on their share price.

Moreover, there is increasing pressure from the value-norm driven community (the UN, Doctors Without Borders, human rights activists, customers, and the media) to consider human rights as a component of socially responsible management. This is also a growing demand from institutional investors (CALPERS, AFL-CIO, and pension fund managers), who are concerned about where their investment dollars are going, and if it violates the ethical and institutional mission of their stakeholders. In this economic climate where stocks have been hit hard by economic recessionary forces, fund managers can no longer only be concerned about the financial bottom line, but are increasingly concerned about sustainable strategies that span labor and human rights issues. As such, organizations can no longer ignore abuses and problems with a shrug, but must be able to provide demonstrable evidence through performance metrics, action-based community initiatives, and supply chain audits that they are doing the "right thing." The snapshot below provides details on guidelines that senior management can adopt in their strategic supply chain configurations, and a vision for future collaboration with global business communities and industry associations.

Policies Defining Buyer-Seller Relationships

The policies that are part of buyer-seller relationships cover a wide range of topics. Each topic, however, relates to some issue involving the supply base.

Sourcing Snapshot

Caterpillars Code of Conduct

Caterpillar is almost a century old. The company, based in Peoria, IL, has grown from a Midwest manufacturer of farm equipment into a global construction equipment powerhouse. With this growth into different countries, cultures, and markets, the company has also struggled at times to maintain the Midwest homegrown culture of integrity associated with its early roots. To that end, Jim Owens, CEO, has put forth a code of conduct that applies to all associates, based on the principle that "integrity is the foundation of all we do." An additional set of implied statements were developed that have direct implications for purchasing policy and actions of purchasing associates. In particular, the following elements stand out:

- We align our actions with our words and deliver what we promise. We build and strengthen our reputation through trust. We do not improperly influence others or let them improperly influence us. In short, the reputation of the enterprise reflects the ethical performance of the people who work here.

- We are honest and we act with integrity. We hold ourselves to the highest standard of integrity. We strive to keep our commitments. Our company's shareholders, customers, dealers, those with whom we do business (suppliers), and our fellow employees must be able to trust what we say and to believe that we will always keep our word.

- We compete fairly. Caterpillar believes that fair competition is fundamental to free enterprise. In relationships with competitors, dealers, suppliers, and customers, we avoid arrangements or understandings with competitors affecting prices, terms upon which products are sold, or the number and type of products manufactured or sold.

- We ensure accuracy and completeness of our financial reports and accounting reports. The same standards of integrity that apply to external financial reporting apply to the financial statements that we use as internal management tools.

- We are fair, honest, and open in our communications. We keep investors, creditors, securities trading markets, employees, dealers, suppliers, and the general public informed on a timely basis through public release of relevant and understandable financial and other information about our company. In releasing information about Caterpillar, we make every effort to ensure that full disclosure is made to everyone without preference or favoritism to any individual or group.

- We handle "inside information" appropriately and lawfully. A Caterpillar employee who has undisclosed information about a supplier, customer, or competitor should not trade in that company's stock, nor should an employee advise others to do so.

- We refuse to make improper payments. In dealing with public officials, other corporations, suppliers, and private citizens, we firmly adhere to ethical business practices.

- We will not seek to influence others, either directly or indirectly, by paying bribes or kickbacks, or by any other measure that is unethical or that will tarnish our reputation for honesty and integrity. Even the appearance of such conduct must be avoided.

Source: Caterpillar Code of Conduct, http://www.cat.com

Supplier Relations

The principles that guide relations with suppliers are often contained in a policy stating that buyer-seller relationships are essential for economic success. Furthermore, relationships based on mutual trust and respect must underlie the purchasing effort. This policy often describes a number of principles that support positive relationships, including the following:

- Treating suppliers fairly and with integrity
- Supporting and developing those suppliers that work to improve quality, delivery, cost, or other performance criteria
- Providing prompt payment to suppliers
- Encouraging suppliers to submit innovative ideas with joint sharing of benefits
- Developing open communication channels
- Informing suppliers as to why they did not receive a purchase contract
- Establishing a fair process to award purchase contracts

Qualification and Supplier Selection

Buyers may require guidance regarding the performance criteria used to evaluate potential sources of supply or to evaluate an existing supplier for an item not traditionally provided by suppliers. Management wants to make sure that supplier selection occurs only after purchasing has thoroughly reviewed all criteria. Supplier selection criteria include the following:

- Price/cost competitiveness
- Product quality
- Delivery performance
- Financial condition
- Engineering and manufacturing technical competence
- Management of its own suppliers
- Management capability
- Ability to work with the customer
- Potential for innovation

This policy may also outline management's position on single and multiple sourcing or the use of longer-term purchase agreements. It may also acknowledge purchasing's need to rely on nonpurchasing personnel to evaluate technical or financial criteria during the supplier selection process.

Principles and Guidelines for Awarding Purchase Contracts

The process for selecting and awarding purchase contracts is central to effective purchasing. This policy covers a number of critical topics:

- Buyer's authority to award a contract within a certain dollar limit
- Conditions where the competitive bid process is acceptable and where it is not
- Conditions outlining the use of competitive bids
- Process of analyzing sealed competitive bids

- Conditions prompting the sourcing of an item to other than the lowest bid supplier
- Conditions prompting a rebid
- Operating guidelines that pertain to the negotiation of contracts with suppliers

Although there is a trend toward less reliance on competitive bids and more on negotiated longer-term agreements, many contracts are still awarded through the competitive bid process. Routine items available from many different sources are generally purchased through competitive bidding. It is important for purchasing to have a standard set of guidelines for awarding purchase contracts to suppliers. These guidelines provide assurances that purchasing bases the awarding of contracts on a fair set of principles.

Labor or Other Difficulties at Suppliers

Management's position concerning supply or labor disruptions as well as possible courses of action provides guidelines during supplier strikes or other labor problems. One issue this policy can address is the legal removal of company-owned tooling from suppliers during a strike, so that the buyer can establish an additional source during the interruption. The policy can provide details about this issue, which can be part of the contract with the supplier, to suspend temporarily any purchase contracts or outstanding orders with a striking supplier. Since 9/11, emergency policies must be established to deal with sudden disruptions in the supply chain. In one case, a single-source supplier to Toyota had a supplying plant burn down; there was no official policy to deal with this issue. Other major automotive companies including Honda and Nissan ended up working with Toyota to help it obtain parts during this crisis.

Other Policies Dealing with Buyer-Seller Relations

Organizations must be cautious about liabilities associated with accepting and using ideas provided by suppliers interested in doing business with a purchaser. A policy may state that the buyer accepts unsolicited proposals from interested suppliers only on a non-confidential basis with no obligation or liability to the provider. Suppliers may even have to sign a waiver releasing the purchaser from liabilities in this area.

Another policy can clarify management's position on financial obligations to suppliers that provide early product design involvement. A buyer may request that suppliers submit cost reduction ideas during the early phases of new-product design. This policy can provide guidance about the extent of financial obligation to suppliers, particularly to suppliers whose ideas were not accepted.

In cases where purchasing is attempting to integrate suppliers into the new-product development process, many companies have established a policy manual written by engineering, marketing, manufacturing, and purchasing. This manual specifies the steps in developing a new product and the triggers in the process that identify when and how suppliers should be part of the process. The policy may also specify the types of nondisclosure agreements used, the criteria for sharing patents, and other joint product development policies.

Policies Defining Operational Issues

The broadest of the five purchasing policy categories involves policies that provide guidance for operational issues that confront buyers during the normal performance of duties.

Sourcing Snapshot

Walmart Commits to Sustainable Purchasing

Walmart announced a goal to eliminate 20 million metric tons of greenhouse gas (GHG) emissions from its global supply chain by the end of 2015. This represents one and a half times the company's estimated global carbon footprint growth over the next five years and is the equivalent of taking more than 3.8 million cars off the road for a year.

"Energy efficiency and carbon reduction are central issues in the world today," said Mike Duke, Walmart president and CEO. "We've been working to make a difference in these areas, both in our own footprint and our supply chain. We know that we have an opportunity to do more and the capacity to do more."

Walmart's global supply chain is many times larger than its operational footprint, and the company sources from suppliers located all over the world. This initiative has the opportunity to make a much greater impact on global emissions than a single provider.

"Like everything we do at Walmart, this commitment ends up coming down to our customers," Duke added. "Reducing carbon in the life cycle of our products will often mean reducing energy use. That will mean greater efficiency and, with the rising cost of energy, lower costs, making our business stronger and more competitive. And, as we help our suppliers reduce their energy use, costs and carbon footprint, we'll be helping our customers do the same thing."

Walmart collaborated with Environmental Defense Fund (EDF) to develop this approach that looks at the supply chain on a global scale. Other external advisers include PricewaterhouseCoopers, ClearCarbon Inc., the Carbon Disclosure Project and the Applied Sustainability Center (ASC) at the University of Arkansas. This team will identify projects, quantify reductions, engage suppliers and ensure proper procedures are followed for each GHG reduction claim.

"Today the world's largest company begins a global race for carbon pollution cuts," said Fred Krupp, president of Environmental Defense Fund. "Walmart's bold move will help companies identify steps to slash pollution and costs. As this story unfolds, it will transform a vast supply chain here at home, and around the world."

The innovative program to reduce GHGs has three main components:

- Selection—Walmart will focus on the product categories with the highest embedded carbon. This is defined as the amount of life cycle GHG emissions per unit multiplied by the amount the company sells. To find the embedded carbon, the ASC reviewed the GHG emissions associated with all Walmart product categories. This approach ensures the project team focuses on the categories that have the greatest opportunity for reductions. Reductions can come from any part of a product's life cycle.
- Action—For a project to be included as part of this goal, it must reduce GHGs from a product in the sourcing of raw materials, manufacturing, transportation, customer use or end-of-life disposal. Walmart must demonstrate it had direct influence on the reduction and show how that reduction would not have occurred without Walmart's participation.
- Assessment—Suppliers and Walmart will jointly account for the reductions. ClearCarbon will perform a quality assurance review of those claims to ensure that methodology, completeness and calculations are correct. When the claims meet the quality assurance check, PricewaterhouseCoopers will assess under consulting standards whether the defined procedures were followed consistently to quantify the reduction claim.

Source: walmartstores.com/greenhousegas, accessed April 19, 2010.

Hazardous Materials

Purchasers must take an active role in controlling hazardous waste. During the last 10 years, new regulations and policies have outlined the proper handling of toxic and hazardous material. In the period from 1899 to 1950, the U.S. government passed seven laws that involved environmental protection. From 1976 to 1978, Congress passed nine environmental laws. More recent legislation has further emphasized the need for business to have a carefully considered response to environmental initiatives. Another important trend is the requirement for an organization to be ISO 14000 certified to engage in global business transactions. ISO 14000 certification requires companies to establish an environmental management system (EMS) to deal with environmental issues.[4] An EMS requires a company to do the following:

- Create an environmental policy.
- Set appropriate objectives and targets.
- Help design and implement a program aimed at achieving these objectives.
- Monitor and measure the effectiveness of these programs.
- Monitor and measure the effectiveness of general environmental management activities within the firm.

Involvement in developing an EMS is a critical responsibility for purchasing, because the procurement of waste disposal services is often a purchasing task. For companies that routinely use or produce hazardous materials, the law requires a policy that outlines in detail the legal requirements and conditions for the handling of toxic waste. Failure to have such a policy is considered a federal offense. This policy details the responsibility of purchasing to select only those contractors that conform to local, state, and federal laws. Before awarding a contract for the hauling and disposing of dangerous materials, some policies require that the contractor provide the following detailed information:

- Evidence of valid permits and licenses
- Specification of the types of disposal services the contractor is licensed to provide
- Evidence of safeguards to prevent accidents along with contingency plans and preparations if a hazardous spill occurs
- Details of the specific process used to control hazardous material once it exits a buyer's facilities
- Evidence of adequate liability insurance on the part of the contractor
- Evidence that the waste transporter uses properly certified disposal sites

Selecting a qualified hazardous waste contractor is critical. On a larger scale, this requires a clearly expressed environmental policy. Increased government and public awareness of environmental concerns is driving this issue.

Supplier Responsibility for Defective Material

This policy outlines supplier responsibility for defective material shipments or other types of nonperformance. It usually details the various charge-back costs for which suppliers are liable in the event of nonperformance. These costs can include the cost of material rework, repackaging for return shipment, additional material handling costs, return shipping costs, or costs associated with lost or delayed production. Purchasers operating in a just-in-time environment are usually quite strict about the charges associated with supplier-caused material problems. A single defective shipment in a just-in-time production environment can shut down an entire production process, resulting, in some cases, in fines of up to $10,000 per minute (in automotive Original Equipment Manufacturers (OEMs)).

Defective material policies may also outline purchasing's authority to negotiate and settle claims against suppliers. This requires purchasing to review each nonperformance carefully to determine a fair settlement. This policy provides protection for the purchaser in the case of supplier-caused problems.

Purchased Item Comparisons

Another policy may outline management's position concerning the continued evaluation of purchased items. This evaluation may require buyers to review purchased items or services periodically to determine if existing suppliers still maintain market leadership. This evaluation can include cost, quality, delivery, and technological comparisons.

For items purchased through the competitive bid process, purchased item comparisons often mean requesting new bids for an item from qualified suppliers. This policy usually states how often management expects competitive comparisons and the general procedure for conducting a comparison. For items on longer-term purchase contracts, purchased item comparisons may involve benchmarking or comparing cost performance against leading competitors.

Other Operating Policies

Many other operating policies guide purchasing. Additional examples include policies that outline the following:

- Compliance with U.S. laws and regulations
- Restrictions on source selection outside of the purchasing function
- Proper disposal of material assets
- Purchasing's legal right to terminate a purchase contract or order
- Supplier responsibility for premium transportation costs
- Supplier-requested changes in contractual terms and conditions
- Supplier use of trademarks or logos

All of the policies just listed have something in common: they clarify management's position on a topic while providing guidance to the personnel responsible for carrying out the policy. The outcome of these policies should be consistent actions on the part of personnel at different locations or organizational levels. A basic set of policy statements outlining management's position on different topic areas should be readily available and distributed. All policies should be regularly reviewed and updated. Increasingly, progressive companies are posting their policies on their intranet.

Purchasing Procedures

Procedures are the operating instructions detailing functional duties or tasks, and a procedure manual is really a how-to manual. A large purchasing department may have hundreds of procedures detailing the accepted practice for carrying out an activity.

It is beyond the scope of this discussion to present more than a brief overview of purchasing procedures, particularly because there is no uniform set of principles to guide the development of purchasing procedures. Every organization develops a unique set of operating instructions to meet its own specific requirements.

A procedure manual serves a number of important purposes. First, the manual is a reference guide for purchasing personnel and is especially valuable to new employees who require training in how to accomplish different activities or assignments. For experienced personnel, the manual provides clarification or simply reinforces knowledge about different topics. Second, the manual provides consistency and order by documenting the steps and activities required to perform a task. A well-documented procedure manual supports efficient operations and is usually more extensive and detailed than the policy manual. The procedure manual may also specify industry best practices to follow that are identified through benchmarking comparisons with leading firms.

Simplifying procedures should be a goal whenever possible. A primary emphasis should be on the development of a concise, accurate, and complete set of operating instructions. A word of caution is in order here. A procedure is ineffective if it specifies too many steps to carry out or presents unnecessary detail. Many companies have found that the traditional procedure for developing new products does not support cooperation between departments. Existing procedures are being replaced by streamlined procedures that encourage timeliness and responsiveness. As with a policy, management must review and evaluate its procedures to make sure that they are timely and accurate and that they contribute to—rather than hinder—performance.

Exhibit 3.2 shows a purchasing procedure for a large high-technology company. This procedure, which establishes purchasing's authority to select sources of supply, includes the different sections just discussed. As with all procedures, this procedure will require future review to verify its timeliness and effectiveness. Increasingly, engineering and purchasing are located closer together to reduce product development cycle times. When this occurs, the determination of source selection often is made by a team rather than an individual. Existing procedures may no longer apply when well-established processes are changed.

Purchasing Procedural Areas

There are procedures to cover just about any subject involving purchasing. Most purchasing procedures correspond to one of the following areas.

The Purchasing Cycle

Existing procedures usually document the proper steps to follow during each stage of the purchasing cycle or process. The purchasing process is described in Chapter 2.

The Proper Use of Purchasing Forms

A typical purchasing function relies on many forms to conduct its business. Recall that Chapter 2 provided examples of commonly used purchasing documents and forms. Most of these are electronically generated or e-mailed and contained within a database. However, it is important to recognize that many companies still rely on manual and faxed forms and have not automated all of these elements. The procedure manual is a valuable source that includes a description of the proper use of each form (regardless of whether it is manual or electronically generated), the detailed meaning of each information field on the form, and a description of the proper handling and storage of each form. For the latter point, this usually includes information about where and for how long to store each

Exhibit 3.2	Examples of a Functional Purchasing Procedure

ABC Technologies Purchasing Procedure

Procedure Number: 4.3   Date: 10/1/00

Subject: Sourcing Requests from Engineering

I. INTRODUCTION

This procedure outlines the steps to follow when purchasing receives a material request from engineering with a Specified Source form attached (form SS-1). Processing a specified source request differs from processing a suggested supplier source listing. The purpose of this procedure is to evaluate engineering source requests in a fair, timely, and thorough manner.

II. RELATED POLICY

Executive policy grants purchasing the authority to obtain materials, components, and other items that meet the delivery, quality, lowest total cost, and other competitive requirements of the company. Restriction of this authority can have a serious impact on purchasing's ability to perform its required duties and assignments. Certain conditions, however, may warrant the specification of sources by departments other than purchasing.

III. RESPONSIBILITY

It is the responsibility of the direct supervisor or manager of the buyer that receives the Specified Source form to evaluate and determine the final disposition of the specified source request in accordance with the following procedure.

IV. PROCEDURE

A. Upon receipt of an SS-1 form submitted by engineering, purchasing departmental management verifies that each section of the form is properly completed.

B. Purchasing management must verify that the requested item is not currently an actively purchased item. If the item is currently purchased, purchasing must inform engineering of this.

C. For items not currently purchased, purchasing management must evaluate engineering's reasons for specifying a source for the required item. It is also within purchasing's authority to identify and evaluate equally qualified sources if the reasons for the specified source are found not to reflect acceptable purchasing or market principles.

D. If engineering's source request is accepted, purchasing management signs the Specified Source form and promptly processes the purchase order.

E. Rejected requests are sent back to engineering with reasons. To promote close working relations between purchasing and engineering, purchasing will respond to specified source requests within a reasonable amount of time. Furthermore, purchasing agrees to work with engineering to identify sources that satisfy engineering's technical requirements while meeting the commercial requirements of the company.

copy of the form along with required signatures or approvals. Storage can be manual or electronic.

The Development of Legal Contracts

The development of legal purchase contracts can require dozens of pages and address many topics. Most organizations have specific procedures for contracting with outside suppliers and individuals for goods and services. It is the purchasing employee's responsibility to become familiar with and follow the procedures covering legal contracts. Some of the topics discussed in legal contract procedures include the following:

- Basic features of the standard purchase contract
- Basic contract principles

- Execution and administration of agreements
- Essential elements of the contract
- Compliance with contract terms and performance assessment
- Formal competitive contracting procedures
- Contract development process
- Examples of sample agreements
- Legal definitions
- Use of formal contract clauses

The procedures covering the development, execution, and enforcement of legal purchase agreements and contracts are usually quite detailed (much like the contracts themselves). A purchaser may rely on a specialized staff to provide assistance in this complex procedural area.

Operational Procedures

Operational procedures provide instruction and detail across a broad range of topics. A procedure can be developed for any operational topic that benefits from following a specific set of steps, requires consistent action to promote efficiency and consistency, or carries out the directives of functional or executive policies. The following procedure topics appear in the material manual of a Fortune 500 company:

- Control of material furnished to suppliers
- Storage of purchasing documents
- Process of supplier qualification
- Use of purchasing systems (such as Ariba or others)
- Analysis of competitive quotations
- Use of single source selection
- Requirements for order pricing and analysis
- Procedures for cost analysis
- Acceptable cost reduction techniques and documentation
- Intracompany transactions
- Processing and handling of overshipments
- Supplier acknowledgment of purchase orders
- Disposition of nonconforming purchased material
- Removal of company-owned tooling from supplier

This is a small sample of the different operational topics that often require documented procedures. The topic of purchasing procedures is broad and sometimes mundane. However, an effective set of procedures can result in the efficient use of a purchasing professional's time. Procedures serve as a ready reference covering a host of questions. They also ensure that employees follow the same basic steps when performing similar tasks.

CONCLUSION

Understanding policies and procedures is essential for understanding how organizations operate and work. Policy is based on the idea that guidelines are documented and applicable to all the internal and external relations of an organization. A policy prescribes methods of accomplishment in terms broad enough for decision makers to exercise discretion while allowing employees to render judgment on an issue. Well-formulated policies and procedures support efficient, effective, and consistent purchasing operations. On the other hand, policies and procedures that are out of date, require unnecessary actions, or do not address current issues or topics will not support effective purchasing operations. As organizations expand their global sourcing activity, they are increasingly revisiting their purchasing policies and procedures, to ensure that they are keeping up with the rapid set of changes their professional associates are facing in their work lives.

KEY TERMS

policy, 88   procedures, 108   reciprocity, 93

DISCUSSION QUESTIONS

1. Write a brief policy statement that presents a position on the need for utilizing more diverse suppliers. What are the features or characteristics that your policy statement should have?

2. Why is it important to include a policy that outlines the origin and scope of purchasing authority? What might happen if such a policy did not exist?

3. Why should management periodically review its purchasing policies and procedures? What are the potential consequences if management does not review policies and procedures? How often do you think it should go through a minor or major set of rewrites?

4. What are the benefits associated with a comprehensive policy and procedure manual? Is there a downside to the manual being too comprehensive?

5. Discuss the concept of ethics. Why is the purchasing profession particularly sensitive to this topic?

6. Companies such as Walmart and IBM are enforcing environmental performance in their supply base. What do you suppose is the motivation for doing so? How does this decision impact the brand of these and other companies?

7. How important is labor and human rights in today's supply chain environment? Why is it important? What are the implications for fair trade, sourcing overseas, and policy adoption in a global sourcing environment? Why is it so difficult to monitor supplier that are guilty of violating labor and human rights guidelines?

8. What are the risks associated with backdoor (maverick) buying and selling? Why is purchasing interested in controlling this business practice?

9. Consider the elements of the code of conduct developed by Caterpillar in Sourcing Snapshot: Caterpillar's Code of Conduct. What are some specific examples of purchasing behavior that would violate elements of this code of conduct?

10. This chapter listed a number of different operational procedures. Describe and discuss three additional topic areas that might benefit from written procedures.

ADDITIONAL READINGS

Baumer, D. L., and Poindexter, J. C. (2002), *Cyberlaw and E-Commerce*, New York: McGraw-Hill.

Baumer, D. L., and Poindexter, J. C. (2004), *Legal Environment of Business in the Information Age*, New York: McGraw-Hill.

Center for Advanced Purchasing Studies. (1999), *ISO 14000: Assessing Its Impact on Corporate Effectiveness and Efficiencies*, Tempe, AZ: National Association of Purchasing Management

Duerden, J. (1995), "'Walking the Walk' on Global Ethics," *Directors and Boards*, 19(3), 42–45.

Forker, L. B., and Janson, R. L. (1990), "Ethical Practices in Purchasing," *Journal of Purchasing and Materials Management*, 26(1), 19–26.

Handfield, R., and Baumer, D. (2006), "Conflict of Interest in Purchasing Management," *Journal of Supply Chain Management*, 42(3), 41–50.

Handfield, R., and Edwards, S. (2006), "Minority Supplier Development: We're Not There Yet," *Inside Supply Management*, 17(5), 20–21.

Handfield, R., "Is There a Soul to the Enterprise?" http://scm.ncsu.edu/blog/2013/05/06/600-dead-in-bangladesh-is-there-a-soul-to-the-enterprise/, accessed July 5, 2013.

ENDNOTES

1. Klein, W. H., and Murphy, D. C. (1973), *Policy: Concepts in Organizational Guidance*, Boston: Little Brown, p. 2.

2. Ernshwiller, J. (2003), "Many Companies Report Transactions with Top Officers," *Wall Street Journal*, December 29.

3. Additional information on the responsible care program and Dow Chemical's commitment to the environment can be found at http://www.dow.com

4. Center for Advanced Purchasing Studies. (1999), *ISO 14000: Assessing Its Impact on Corporate Effectiveness and Efficiencies*, Tempe, AZ: National Association of Purchasing Management.

Supply Management Integration for Competitive Advantage

CHAPTER 4

Learning Objectives

After completing this chapter, you should be able to

- Understand why integration is important to company performance and the role that supply management plays in internal and external integration

- Understand the role of cross-functional teams in promoting integration

- Understand how supply management can work with engineering and suppliers to develop new products and services

Chapter Outline

The Critical Role of Purchasing and Integration

Background

A new product line at large global firm Electro required a winning design for the control console—essentially the electronic "control center" of its product. Though the design of new control consoles has traditionally been the most critical factor affecting product launch, Electro consistently failed to meet cost, availability and quality launch goals for the consoles during previous product launches. Electro's own internal processes that deal with console design were overly complex, and more than 10 different groups traditionally had input into the design process. Because the customer sees and touches the console, it is an important part of the product from an aesthetics perspective.

Electro had historically performed its own design work and then requested that suppliers bid on those designs. Desirous of a radically different approach and using consoles as the initial project to test a new way of doing business, the company opted to implement a cross-functional process to define design requirements, including functions, features, and costs. The cross-functional team's broad goals were to collaborate with suppliers and to solicit supplier input and feedback during the design phase of the console. Specifically, the team wanted to ensure the best design to improve manufacturability, to achieve quality and cost targets, and to establish the best supply chain for the consoles.

Approach

The design of the new product line provided a perfect opportunity for Electro to pilot a supplier collaboration project, with the problem-plagued consoles providing the ideal test bed. Furthermore, a shift toward a cross-functional project management approach for developing new products was the final factor that caused all the "stars to align." Electro asked suppliers to propose a design concept that involved a challenging curvature of the console cover, resulting in both design and manufacturing challenges for both electronic and decorative suppliers. Electro also used this opportunity to apply project management techniques when developing the new line of products and establish a company-wide set of rigorous criteria for evaluating supplier concept proposals.

In previous product launches, Electro's supply management group typically worked with a 14-to-18-month lead time before launch. Marketing and engineering would work independently for the first three months, and by the time supply management was involved it would be too late to make design changes; design and costs were locked in by then to meet a launch deadline.

Internal collaboration at Electro involved marketing/product management, design, engineering, procurement (commodity and category managers) and quality working jointly and concurrently to develop a new product. External collaboration involved a network of suppliers working together to achieve common design objectives. The primary network of suppliers included a system integrator responsible for developing the touch panel, screen controls and decorative molded covers for the product. The system integrator was also responsible for selecting and managing a network of sub-tier component suppliers, including an electronics supplier that would serve as an electronics integrator while working with the systems integrator.

With this approach, Electro asked suppliers to propose concepts, materials, and manufacturing processes that could be incorporated into the product's design during the concept phase of product development. Typically, Electro would be fairly specific about the design requirements and technology to which a supplier would then bid. On this project, Electro informed suppliers about the concept, functionality, and cost targets, then requested that suppliers create detailed designs. With this approach, designs are no longer "thrown over the wall" from one internal group to another or from Electro to suppliers.

A tier-one supplier would play the role of system integrator as it selected and managed Electro's sub-tier suppliers. For Electro, the timing was right for pursuing this new way of doing business. The procurement group was in the process of dividing responsibilities for product launch into two roles, project management and commercial, increasing the emphasis placed on project management. The company believed it had "the right people in the right places at the right time" to try new approaches to product design.

Electro adopted several terms that are specific to this new way of working with suppliers. First, the company utilized a "value management team" approach via an ongoing standing team charged with developing technology and sourcing roadmaps to meet the company's projections of consumer needs five-to-seven years out. Though suppliers do not play a formal part on this team, Electro can involve them on individual projects. The second term specific to collaboration is early supplier engagement (ESE), which refers to a specific process or project where suppliers become involved early in the product design process.

Electro utilized a two-phase strategy for collaboration:

1. A rigorous supplier selection process to identify collaboration suppliers
2. Product design, development and manufacturing process changes

Supplier Selection Process

By having an agreed-to set of internal evaluation criteria developed by a representative group of employees, Electro was able to address supplier selection much earlier than it had in previous console design projects. This allowed time to thoroughly qualify potential suppliers.

An Electro team of about 20 people from various functional groups was formed to evaluate supplier proposals. This widespread visibility to the selection process helped to gain buy-in to the final selection decisions.

Supplier design proposals were evaluated using a comprehensive set of 18 objective criteria grouped into three broad categories—desirability, viability, and feasibility. Examples of these assessment criteria included:

- Desirability—solves a problem/fits to a solution stream, believability/sellability
- Viability—speed to market, quality impact, service impact
- Feasibility—development risk, sourcing fit, development cost, logistics, cost

As a result of the proposals and their evaluations, Electro identified several clear winners. The company selected SI Industries (SII) as its system integrator and specified a supplier to provide electronics at the tier-two level. The electronics supplier serves as an integrator for the electronic component suppliers. The console project was the first time Electro had collaborated with this supplier, which was relied upon on to select the tier-two component suppliers. This aligned with Electro's strategy of making tier-one suppliers responsible for upstream supplier decisions and performance.

Product Design Process Changes

Undertaking a collaborative approach with a systems integrator required Electro to change how it did business. First, Electro had to pursue collaboration earlier in the design and development process than it traditionally had. In addition, design was now done collaboratively by internal styling and suppliers. A different set of internal groups beyond marketing and engineering at Electro needed to be involved early on compared with a more sequential or "traditional" approach to product development. For example, procurement, cost management activities (modeling and budgeting) and manufacturing were engaged earlier.

While a great deal of interpersonal communication occurred during product development, Electro and suppliers also relied on computer-aided design (CAD) systems to share data and drawings. Electro would like to explore the use of various kinds of collaborative software to support future projects. For this project Electro did not require suppliers to use a specific software package.

Results

A "perception of success" permeated this project. Numerous individuals participated in a supplier selection process that was transparent. They had ownership of the selection process and had access to a great deal of data, making buy-in to the selection decision that much easier. Supply management and engineering had ownership for supplier selection, and marketing gained access to valuable information from the suppliers on styling cost structures (e.g., at what point would increasing the number of colors cause a step change in costs?). The needs of a variety of organizational groups were met or exceeded.

Supply managers believe that the internal cross-functional teams involved with the product development and launch would rate this supplier collaboration experience as successful. The targets for product availability at launch, quality levels and costs, were met or exceeded.

Source: Value Chain Strategies for the Changing Decade: Collaboration Across the Extended Value Chain, CAPS Research, 2013.

Introduction

The opening vignette illustrates how important supply management, working with other functions and suppliers, is in determining firm performance. The area of supply delivery and availability perfect product launches and effective risk management, are all becoming increasingly important elements in the global supply chain. A single glitch in the supply chain, such as late and over budget product launches and the earthquake described in Sourcing Snapshot: Apple's I-Pod Supply Chain at Risk, can shut down multiple assembly plants and impact customer delivery, sales and company growth and profits worldwide. In this new environment of global sourcing, the need for supply management to work closely with businesses to drive cost savings, reduce disruptions and risk, and deliver innovation and value to customers becomes more important than ever.

Purchasing offices were once corporate backwaters, filled with people who did not dream of advancing to the top rungs of their organizations. Many buyers saw themselves as industrial bureaucrats, filing purchase orders with the same short list of familiar, mostly nearby suppliers. When possible, they avoided the complex process of assessing potential new suppliers, especially those in other countries and regions of the world.

Top supply managers today need different skills and often have higher aspirations. Sometimes they are financially trained, engineers, or others with operating experience that gives them more intimate knowledge of how their company's products and services are developed and produced.

Today's transformation in buying was made possible by a technological breakthrough more than a decade ago, when companies began installing computer systems that record their every transaction, and led to the advanced e-systems and analytics of today. This often revealed startling weaknesses. For instance, many companies found that different divisions—or even different offices down the hall from one another—were sometimes paying different prices for the same goods and services bought from outside suppliers.

Sourcing Snapshot

Apple's iPod Supply Chain at Risk

Could a typhoon in Manila affect what teenagers in Minneapolis find in their Christmas stockings?

A lot of high-tech gadgets are made in the Philippine Islands, including parts of Apple Computer's iPod music player. Apple depends on that Philippine link in its supply chain: in the third quarter of 2007 (July through September), Apple sold almost 9 million iPods,.

In September, researcher Nathaniel Forbes reviewed the contingency planning at a Philippines factory that assembles 1.8-inch disk drives that go into iPods. I'll call the factory "Pod Parts."

In the review, it was discovered that Pod Parts has only one factory making iPod disk drives—this one in the Philippines. If it were destroyed, it would take months, and several hundred million dollars, to build a new assembly line from scratch for 1.8-inch drives.

Apple needs at least 50,000 drives a day to make iPods, and probably more, assuming that flash memory iPods do not need disk drives. What would be the business impact (on Apple, and on Pod Parts' relationship with Apple) if Pod Parts could not deliver those drives? Sure they could—the other supplier is just down the street in Laguna Technopark—about 1 kilometer away. In fact, there are four other manufacturers in Laguna Technopark that supply Pod Parts with components for disk drives. For manufacturing efficiency, the proximity of these factories to one another is an obvious advantage. Their proximity is, however, a potential risk to the continuity of the supply chain. It is hard to imagine a natural catastrophe that would affect just one manufacturer in LTI; it is likely that they would all be affected at the same time.

Is a calamity likely? Pod Parts has a documented and tested emergency-response system, an active emergency team, and a visible and active security force. There is a municipal fire department in LTI. There are fire extinguishers all over the plant. Pod Parts is reasonably prepared for a fire or a plant-specific event. But what if a widespread national catastrophe occurred? Consider the following data:

1. The Taal volcano, 30 kilometers (18 miles) from Pod Parts, is one of 16 "Decade Volcanoes" identified as a serious potential hazard to population centers by the International Association of Volcanology and Chemistry of the Earth's Interior. The Taal volcano recorded 29 volcanic earthquakes in one day in September 2006. There were four earthquakes in the Philippines in one weekend in October 2006, including one felt in Laguna that measured 4.7 on the Richter scale.

2. Tropical storms and typhoons are a regular occurrence in the Philippines.

The area around Laguna Technopark is subject to regular flooding from storm water, requiring people to leave work early.

Pod Parts has about two days of finished product stored on-site, waiting for shipment.

The drives are just too valuable to keep in inventory. Construction of an alternative production line would be excruciatingly expensive, putting Pod Parts at a competitive disadvantage.

A disruption at Pod Parts could have a direct and serious impact on Apple's ability to produce iPods within about 48 hours.

If that interruption happened in October, it could drastically reduce the supply of iPods available at retail for Christmas. A most destructive typhoon occurred two years ago.

Source: Forbes, N., (2006, October 28) "Tuning Out Supply Chain Risk," Retrieved from http://www.zdnetasia.com/blog/bcp/0,39056819,61963177,00.htm

Purchasing managers and executives play a role as highly effective cost cutters, though that part of their job has some surprising nuances. To be sure, buyers save companies huge amounts by trolling the world for new, lower-cost sources, and this is certainly a big reason for their growing stature at many multinationals. But in an era of scarce (or abundant) commodities and the risks of disruptions to supply lines posed by terrorist attacks, striking dockworkers, or supplier bottlenecks, they also have to make sure they pick dependable sources—which might mean choosing the more expensive source just to ensure no disruptions.

Different functions or groups within any organization must work together to achieve a wide range of common goals—from the reduction of product cost and improved product quality and delivery to the development of innovative new products. Supply management plays an active role in supporting such performance objectives, interacting with and supporting the needs of groups within the organization and outside of it. How does supply management achieve this? **Supply integration** involves professionally managing suppliers and developing close working relationships with different internal groups. The central theme of this chapter is that supply management must become closely integrated with other internal and external functions to develop the capabilities that will lead to improved competitive performance. Integration spans a number of areas, including operating strategy development, finance, engineering, logistics, service operations, production, new-product development, and customer service.

The first section of the chapter defines what we mean by integration. Next we address supply management's critical internal and external linkages with various groups. The third section discusses the need to develop closer and more collaborative buyer-seller relationships to achieve improved external integration. The fourth section discusses the cross-functional sourcing team—an increasingly important approach taken to achieve supply management integration. The final section focuses on supply management's involvement in developing new products and customer order fulfillment.

Integration: What Is It?

Integration, a term often heard in the popular press, is in many cases not well defined. In this text, we define **integration** as "the process of incorporating or bringing together different groups, functions, or organizations, either formally or informally, physically or by information technology, to work jointly and often concurrently on a common business-related assignment or purpose." Although this is a very broad definition, it implies certain elements. First, that people are coming together to work together on a strategy or problem. It is no surprise that "two heads are better than one" when it comes to developing creative strategies or solving problems, but many enterprises do not apply the idea of bringing together people with a different point of view to develop supply strategies or solve a common problem. This is especially true in a global environment, with team members located all over the world. Thus, another caveat to this definition involves doing so either formally or informally, through physical methods or by information technology. Finally, integration requires that people create a common understanding of the end goal or purpose; as we will see, this is an important aspect of the success of integration strategies.

A recent study of senior executives in the United States and Europe indicated that integration is at the top of these executives' minds, in terms of what will be required in the future.[1] Moreover, when asked about the most critical skills required for supply management managers in the year 2010, executives did not list some of the more common elements such as process focus, financial analysis, or efficiency. The single most important element that senior executives look for is **relationship management (RM) skills**, defined as the ability to act ethically, listen effectively, communicate, and use creative problem solving. The ability to drive relationships is critical for firms seeking to build strong integration with internal business functions, as well as with external suppliers.

Integration can occur in many forms. It can occur through functions, such as in sourcing or new-product development teams. It can also occur through cross-location teams, where people from different business units are brought together. Finally, the most difficult and challenging form is cross-organizational teams, which involves working with suppliers, customers, or even both concurrently. Bringing different people to the table to work on a problem or supply strategy can provide significant benefits. People will generally provide input in the form of the following:

- Information
  - About their markets
  - About their own plans and requirements
- Knowledge and expertise
  - Product and service knowledge and technology
  - Process knowledge and understanding of how to make it work
- Business advantages
  - Favorable cost structures that can benefit customers
  - Economies of scale, which can also help reduce costs
  - Different perspective on an issue, which may drive a team to look at the problem from a new perspective that they had not thought of before

Some of the different methods that supply management will apply to achieve integration include the following:

- Cross-functional or cross-organizational committees and teams
- Information systems such as video-conferencing and webmail
- Integrated performance objectives and measures that drive a common goal
- Process-focused organizations that are dedicated to certain processes
- Co-location of suppliers and customers
- Buyer or supplier councils that provide input and guidance to a steering committee

Paradoxically, the very elements of sound supply chain business practice that are the cornerstones of mature spend management cultures—and a crucial foundation for supplier relationship management (SRM)—can also serve as an anchor holding back progression to the higher levels of success.

One part of breaking through is tied to the personal effectiveness of the supply chain professionals charged with doing the work. Supply management professionals must begin to work with their internal functions, not against them. This means that the key building blocks for integration (team-building, communication, and relationship management) will become more important than ever. Let us discuss the first of these integration elements: internal integration with the functional entities in their own enterprise.

Internal Integration

Supply management must maintain a number of communication flows and linkages. Exhibit 4.1 on p. 122 illustrates the two-way linkages between supply management and other key groups along with a sample of the information exchanged between these groups.

The linkages between supply management and other groups will become even stronger and more important as the role of supply management continues to develop and evolve.

Supply Management Internal Linkages

To facilitate integration with other internal functions, a number of critical communication linkages or interfaces have evolved between supply management and other departments. This need for internal integration has increased exponentially in the last five years. Many organizations have actively moved toward an outsourced environment (but now, selectively insourcing outsourced products), and in some cases are sourcing all products through low-cost-country sourcing environments or contract manufacturers. These environments are very different from North American buyer-seller situations, and supply management must play a critical role in establishing these agreements and identifying global requirements for success. Supply management must often work to become part of the global negotiations teams and become involved in supplier qualification, contract management, and logistics, working with multiple internal parties in the firm including finance, legal, logistics, marketing, and operations.

Operations

Supply management has always closely engaged with the operations group. Because the links between operations and supply management have been so close, it has not been unusual for supply management to report directly to operations. A major link between operations and supply management is through the development of global operations strategy. Because supply management directly supports operations, it must develop insights into production or service strategic plans. One area in which supply management has critical input to operations (and marketing) is through the sales and operations plan, which identifies the level of production and sales for six months to one year, as well as the required input to execute the plan. Clearly, supply management's strategies and plans must be aligned with the sales and operations plan. For example, supply management must be aware of the components and services needed by operations as they plan to fulfill customer requirements for products or services. This could include materials, software, services, travel, hotel, information technology, and outsourced labor. Because supply management is responsible for sourcing the inputs to support operation's plans, supply management managers must work with operations to coordinate the execution to plan.

Supply management and operations also maintain communication linkages through direct personnel contact. Many firms are now colocating supply management personnel directly at operating locations so supply management can respond quickly to operation's needs. For example, in many financial institutions, supply managers are co-located within the strategic business units and provide supplier relationship managers to act as a primary single point of contact between suppliers and the organization. These managers can work to identify problems, create problem resolution strategies, and act as a liaison for discussions of service management expectations.

Quality Assurance

The supply management—quality linkage has increased in importance during the last 10 years. As firms externally source a larger percentage of finished product requirements, supply management and quality assurance must work together closely to ensure that suppliers perform as expected. Joint projects involving these two groups include supplier quality training, process capability studies, and corrective action planning. This linkage has become so important that some firms have placed the responsibility for supplier quality

Exhibit 4.1   Purchasing's Communications Flows and Linkages—Redo Graphic

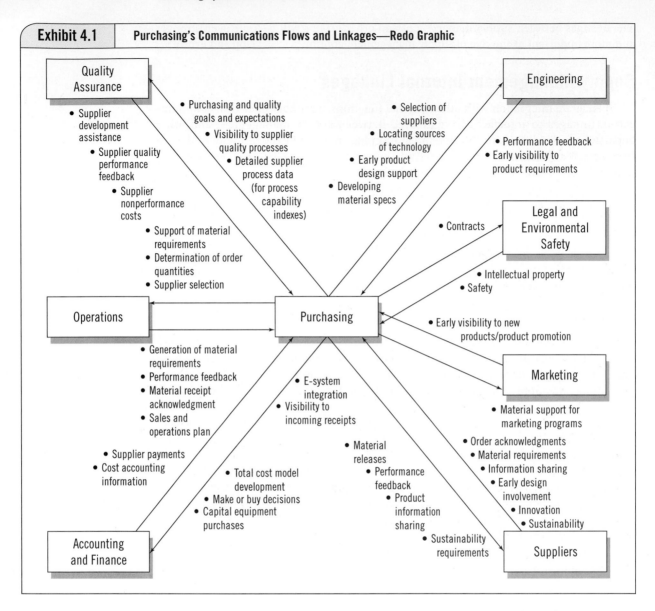

management directly with supply management. Many firms now have a dedicated supplier quality management function with a dual reporting element to both quality and supply management.

Engineering

Perhaps the most important and challenging linkages exist between supply management and engineering. The need to develop quality products in less time has drawn supply management and engineering closer over time. There are still opportunities, however, to improve the level of interaction between these two groups.

Firms can create stronger communication linkages and flows between supply management and engineering in several ways. Engineers and buyers can develop open communication by working together on product development or supplier selection teams. Supply management can also colocate a buyer within the engineering group. The buyer can maintain direct contact with product and process engineers to respond quickly to their needs. A firm can also appoint a liaison that coordinates interdepartmental communications and makes sure that each group is aware of the other group's activities. The two departments can hold regular meetings to report on items of mutual concern. Finally, many supply management groups are recruiting commodity managers with very strong technical backgrounds, who are able to talk the talk and walk the walk alongside their engineering counterparts. The key to a successful relationship between supply management and engineering is open and direct communication, which in turn should lead to increased teamwork and trust.

Engineering looks to supply management to perform certain tasks to support engineering's efforts. For example, engineering expects supply management to identify the most technically and financially capable supplier for an item and to make sure each supplier meets engineering's quality and delivery targets. In addition, engineering expects supply management to assess a supplier's production capabilities, actively involve suppliers early in the design process, and develop relationships that encourage a supplier to offer innovative ideas. Engineering also expects supply management to identify sources of new cost effective technologies that can be integrated into new products and services that are sold to global markets with different needs. It is also important to note that supply and engineering must work closely together to deal with quality risks that may arise in new products, such as the example shown in Sourcing Snapshot: Ensuring Quality Requirements: Batteries from Sony.

Finally, manufacturing and process engineering will want to ensure ongoing technical support and service during product launch and ongoing customer order fulfillment, as problems inevitably arise during this phase of the product life cycle as well.

Accounting and Finance

Supply management also maintains tactical and strategic linkages with the accounting and finance department. The strategic linkages are focused on annual cost reduction goals

Sourcing Snapshot

Ensuring Quality Requirements: Batteries from Sony

Outsourcing has its risks. Suppliers may misstate their capabilities, their process technology may be obsolete, or their performance may not meet the buyer's expectations. In other cases, the supplier may not have the capability to produce the product at the level of quality required. The most obvious example of this is the Sony battery catastrophe. Major manufacturers such as Dell, Apple, and IBM outsourced the power supply for their laptops to Sony. However, it quickly became apparent that the batteries were defective. When the batteries were made, the metal case of the cell was crimped, and microscopic shards of metal could be released into the battery, causing a short circuit that triggered overheating and in some cases, fire. After several of these incidents, Dell recalled 4.1 million batteries, and Apple recalled 1.9 million batteries. The supplier, in this case Sony, had to recall over 9.6 million laptop batteries, a problem that has rattled confidence in the company's image. Sony announced that the recalls of lithium-ion batteries will boost its costs.

and measurement and validation of achieved cost reductions. Capital equipment decisions are also closely coordinated with finance. In addition, much of the communication linkage between supply management and accounting is tactical and today is electronic. For example, as supply management transmits material releases to suppliers, it also provides information concerning inbound material requirements to the accounting department. On receipt of the ordered material, the material control system updates the supply management files from on-order or in-transit to a received status. The accounts payable system then receives the receipt information and compares the amount received to the amount ordered for payment.

Supply management may require data from the cost accounting system. For example, supply management must know handling and material rework costs for an item resulting from poor supplier performance. Supply management usually does not maintain data about individual activity costs that can increase total cost. The supply management performance measurement system also relies on input from cost accountants to help calculate the total cost of an item, which is also important in make-or-buy decisions.

Marketing/Sales

Supply management maintains indirect linkages with marketing. Many new-product ideas that supply management must support start with marketing personnel, who are the voice of a firm's end customers. Marketing also develops sales forecasts that convert into production plans. Supply management must select suppliers and request material to support both marketing and production plans.

Legal

Supply management often confers with the legal department to seek counsel on specific elements of contracts. Issues that may arise include patent ownership terms in new-product development, intellectual property, product liability claims, antitrust, long-term contracts containing escape clauses, and other legal issues. Electronic commerce also raises many legal issues that require supply management to consult with the legal department. Later chapters discuss legal issues in greater detail. Sourcing Snapshot: The New Role for Supply Management in Contracts illustrates some of the major challenges that lie ahead,

Sourcing Snapshot

The New Role for Supply Management in Contracts

More than 300 delegates joined together at a recent International Association of Commercial and Contract Managers (IACCM) Americas Conference (www.iaccm.com/americas) to debate issues related to contract management and to work together in creating a framework for the future. Representatives from top universities and business schools around the world explored cooperation in learning and research.

The emerging business environment demands increased global awareness and capabilities, better integration across business functions and external suppliers, and a more collaborative approach to relationship management. What is the role of the procurement or negotiations professional? What is the organizational model that will best equip companies for success? How do we integrate technology, skills, and organizational design to create a winning mix?

These issues were debated at this conference. Tim Cummins, CEO of IACCM, emphasized the dynamics of the new global contract management environment:

> The leaders in the community must raise their sights above logistics and purchasing savings, risk, and compliance, to understand the full value chain implications of the global networked economy. They must avoid being obsessed with tinkering with the mechanics and instead engage in the overall design of the vehicle. And to do this, they should engage with IACCM and the wider community it represents. One problem in developing professional status is that today we are an apparently random mix of job roles and titles-no one really thinks of us as a "professional community." Yet research shows we possess very similar skills and knowledge and there is more in common about the roles we perform than there is that divides us. Indeed, lawyers or doctors probably have greater differences within their ranks than we do-yet they have a composite status. One of the steps we have taken to address this is to adopt the term "commitment management" as an overarching title for the work we perform. Our community identifies, negotiates, documents, and manages the commitments required for successful realization of corporate goals from its external relationships (supplier, customer, distribution channel, strategic alliance, etc.).
>
> Another key problem is to escape from the constraining transactional focus of our work (which creates limited executive interest and results in low visibility) and instead to be visible in driving strategic performance. That means we must start collecting more data and accepting greater accountability for business outcomes. What process do we own, what results will we commit to monitoring, who will we challenge to change their process, rules, capabilities to ensure greater competitiveness, quality, or efficiency?
>
> In the end, the market will decide who survives. Our focus must be to drive the competitiveness of our business through greater speed, innovation, creativity. We must manage risks, but that means finding new and better ways to do things so they become less risky, not avoiding doing things because history or experience tells us they might be risky.

specifically with respect to the role of procurement on contract management and legal overlapping responsibilities.

Environmental Management, Health, and Safety

Supply management may also confer with personnel from the environmental, health, and safety departments to ensure that suppliers are employing safe methods of transportation and are complying with Occupational Safety and Health Administration and safety regulations. Supply management is also concerned with environmental sustainability. It works with company sustainability offices to develop strategies and practices to enhance supplier sustainability.

External Integration

Supply management represents the external face of the organization and also serves as the primary vehicle by which to integrate external suppliers and other entities into the organization. This is done by creating and maintaining linkages with groups external to the firm—these linkages are in some respects more important than supply management's internal linkages.

Supply Management's External Linkages

Supply management acts as a liaison with external parties on multiple fronts, including materials, new technology, information, and services. These parties include suppliers, government, and local communities.

Suppliers

Supply management's primary external linkages are with its suppliers. Supply management's primary responsibility is to maintain open communications with suppliers and select the suppliers with which to do business. Supply management should be the primary communication linkage with suppliers, although nonsupply management personnel may contact a supplier about a particular item or question.

Supply management has the responsibility to select suppliers and to remain the primary commercial linkage with the buying firm, including any matter involving the conditions of the purchase agreement or other issues of importance. Nonsupply management departments should not select, independently work with, or directly negotiate with potential suppliers for items for which the supply management department is responsible.

Government

Supply management sometimes maintains communication linkages with governments at different levels and locations. For example, supply management has an active role in international countertrade and often negotiates directly with foreign governments when establishing countertrade agreements. Supply management may also need to consult with federal government agencies on various matters, including the Environmental Protection Agency, the Department of Defense, the Department of External Affairs, and other agencies that have authority over issues governed by public policy.

Local Communities

Supply management may have contact with local communities and leaders. Because supply management controls a large budget, it has the potential to affect certain social goals. These goals include sourcing from local suppliers, awarding a certain percentage of business to qualified minority suppliers, environmental sustainability and establishing ethical business practices in all dealings.

Collaborative Buyer-Seller Relationships

Most purchasers and sellers now recognize a need for joint cooperation to achieve cost, quality, delivery, and time improvements. Beginning in the 1980s, progressive purchasers eliminated poor or marginal suppliers from their supply base. They then developed collaborative relationships or alliances with a selective number of the remaining suppliers.

Collaboration is defined as the process by which two or more parties adopt a high level of purposeful cooperation to maintain a trading relationship over time to achieve specified goals. The relationship is bilateral; both parties have the power to shape its nature and future direction over time. Mutual commitment to the future and a balanced power relationship are essential to the process. Although collaborative relationships are not devoid of conflict, they build mechanisms into the relationship for managing conflict.[2]

Exhibit 4.2	Characteristics of the Buyer-Seller Relationship		
	TRADITIONAL APPROACH		**COLLABORATIVE APPROACH**
Suppliers	Multiple sources played off against each other	→	One of few preferred suppliers for each major item
Cost sharing	Buyer takes all cost savings; supplier hides cost savings	→	Win-win shared rewards
Joint improvement efforts	Little or none	→	Joint improvement driven by mutual interdependence
Dispute resolution	Buyer unilaterally resolves disputes	→	Existence of conflict-resolution mechanisms
Communication	Minimal or no two-way exchange of information	→	Open and complete exchange of information
Marketplace adjustments	Buyer determines response to changing conditions	→	Buyer and seller work together to adapt to changing marketplace
Quality	Buyer inspects at receipt	→	Designed into the product

The following characteristics define a collaborative buyer-seller relationship:

- One or a limited number of suppliers for each purchased item or family of items. Remaining suppliers often provide material under long-term contracts with agreed-upon performance improvement targets.
- A win-win approach to reward sharing.
- Joint efforts to improve supplier performance across all critical performance areas.
- Joint efforts to resolve disputes.
- Open exchange of information. This includes information about new products, supplier cost data, and production schedules and forecasts for purchased items.
- A credible commitment to work together during difficult times. In other words, a purchaser does not return to old practices at the first sign of trouble.
- A commitment to quality, defect-free products having design specifications that are manufacturable and that the supplier's process is capable of producing.

Exhibit 4.2 compares the characteristics of traditional and collaborative buyer-seller relationships. Although not all relationships between purchasers and suppliers should be collaborative, the trend is toward greater use of the collaborative approach.

Advantages of Closer Buyer-Seller Relationships

A firm can gain many advantages by pursuing closer relationships with suppliers. The first is the development of mutual trust, which is the foundation of all strong relationships.

Trust

Although trust seems intangible, it refers to the belief in the character, ability, strength, and truthfulness of another party. Trust makes it possible, for example, for the seller to share cost data with a buyer, which can result in a joint effort to reduce a supplier's cost through a mutual sharing of ideas. Trust can also result in a supplier working with a purchaser early in the design of a new product.

Long-Term Contracts

Another advantage of closer buyer-seller relationships is the opportunity to evaluate which suppliers should receive longer-term contracts. Purchaser and seller both realize benefits from longer-term contracts. A long-term contract provides an incentive for a supplier to invest in new plants and equipment. This investment can make a supplier more efficient and result in lower costs to the purchaser. Longer-term contracts can also lead to the joint development of technology, risk sharing, and supplier capabilities (see Sourcing Snapshot: Suncor Energy Partners with Drilling Suppliers).

Obstacles to Closer Buyer-Seller Relationships

A number of obstacles can prevent the development of closer relationships between a purchaser and a seller. A firm must evaluate whether these obstacles are present and identify ways to overcome them if the goal is to pursue closer interfirm cooperation.

Confidentiality

The need for confidentiality regarding financial, product, and process information is the most frequently cited reason for not developing closer supplier relationships. Supply management managers are sometimes reluctant to share critical information with suppliers that may also sell to competitors. There is also the possibility that a supplier is a direct competitor or may become one in the future.

Limited Interest by Suppliers

Closer relationships may not interest all suppliers. A supplier may have the leverage or power in some relationships, particularly when it is in a monopolistic or oligopolistic industry position. In such cases, the purchaser may be unable to pursue a closer relationship simply because of the relative sizes or power positions of the two firms.

Legal Barriers

In some industries, legal antitrust concerns may act as barriers or obstacles to closer buyer-seller relationships (covered in greater detail in Chapter 14, which discusses the legal aspects of supply management).

Resistance to Change

Entire generations of supply management professionals grew up using an arm's-length approach. A shift toward a more trusting approach is not easy. Resistance to change is a powerful force that takes time, patience, and training to overcome. Also, firms that practice traditional supply chain management may not have the skills or knowledge in their workforce to evolve toward closer supplier relationships.

An example of how buyer-supplier teams can work together, despite the odds, to create mutually beneficial outcomes is described in Sourcing Snapshot: Suncor Energy Partners with Drilling Suppliers.

Critical Elements for Supplier Relationship Management

Recent research conducted by Ward, Handfield, and Cousins based on interviews with executives revealed the following critical elements for building effective supply relationships.[3]

Sourcing Snapshot

Suncor Energy Partners with Drilling Suppliers

In the oil and gas exploration business, a successful exploration and development drilling program requires strong performance from a multidisciplinary team, as well as active participation and support from many suppliers and contractors. Suncor Energy is a diversified oil and gas company based in Calgary, Alberta. As part of its strategic supplier relationship program, the Suncor Foothills Drilling—Asset Team was formed; it includes people from the drilling department and the Foothills Asset Team, as well as contractors and suppliers. This team drills mainly in the foothills of the Canadian Rocky Mountains.

The drilling business is traditionally very cyclical and somewhat secretive, with most of the actual drilling being outsourced to groups of specialized service suppliers. The on-again, off-again nature of the work can significantly damage service quality and expertise. Often the staffing of a drilling effort is determined by who is available, not by who is the best fit. The secretive nature of the business amplifies the difficulties of the service suppliers by the lack of information available for planning, forecasting, and workload leveling. To drill a well, materials and services are required from approximately 20 different suppliers. Often the information used by the service supplier is subject to change and can oftentimes be incorrect. Changes in timing or design can impact each of these suppliers significantly.

In addition to the coordination issues listed above, the technical issues related to drilling deep sour gas wells are also highly significant. Suncor has drilled wells as deep as 6400 m, with horizontal sections close to 2000 m in length. In the last five years the Foothills Drilling-Asset Team has drilled approximately 50 wells throughout the Alberta Foothills. In mountainous regions, expertise and extensive area experience go hand-in-hand with successfully drilling wells. Drilling techniques downhole have to be adapted to very challenging mountainous-type conditions. Poor drilling execution can result in safety concerns, increased costs, and lower capital returns. Even when drilling techniques are well executed, the Foothills challenges can result in significant timing fluctuations that can affect the entire supply chain network.

To overcome these challenges, a total integration of objectives was initiated to create greater influence on the factors affecting drilling performance. In essence, a greater team concept was created with one common center and full alignment. Team integration between the drilling group and the Foothills Drilling-Asset Team has extended further than previously documented for the industry. This integration has also been extended to a number of contractor services. The greater team concept has created a high trust environment that allows for accelerated learning and has enhanced integrated expertise. As a result, the key service suppliers and the different groups from Suncor work together as though they were one company with one set of objectives.

The implementation of this unified philosophy in all phases of the life cycle, as well as the creation of an environment of openness, trust, and mutual success, has resulted in substantial improvements. Based on a 2003 cost study, the team has achieved the following: (1) drilling costs reduced by 18 percent ($1.4 million/well), (2) planning times reduced by 42 percent (five months), (3) drilling times reduced by 20 percent on average, and (4) 80 percent—plus success rate on wells drilled. In addition, Foothills production volumes have tripled over the past five years. These results have been accomplished against a backdrop of 5 percent inflation. Suncor's Foothills Drilling-Asset Team has become one of the preferred employers from the service supplier perspective within its operating region. This position continues to strengthen.

Source: McCormack, K., Cavanagh, P.H., and Handfield, R. (2003) Foothills Drilling Team White Paper, Suncor Energy.

Focus on deliverables at the level of the product or service, not the centralized relationship that occurs at an abstract level and fails to get into the details of the business performance metrics. Too often, thoughts about SRM start with discussions about global contracts or broad-based partnering marketing initiatives. Although these can be seductive, they rarely produce sufficient short-term payoff to sustain the level of effort required to maintain focus on the initiative. Instead, as one group-level category manager said, "You need to provide short-term payoff on the basics before leaping into the other neat stuff. Our job is to make it a pull, not a push."[4]

- Start with the business outcome at the business unit level. This means defining a specific measurable performance indicator that means something to the business stakeholder (e.g., operational cost savings, supply continuity, process improvement suggestions, access to new technology, or process innovation).

- Let the business outcome drive the relationship process, course of action, and level of investment through initiation of projects focused on achieving the outcome.

- The overall relationship (Big R) then becomes an outcome of various relationships with different products and services that meet different business outcomes (little r's).

- Program management (Big R) drives incongruity resolution, aggregation of benefits, and opportunity analysis across lines of business.

Business cases must be clearly understood and compelling at all levels. Although well-intentioned efforts sometimes get off the ground because the business case is intuitively obvious, these efforts often are the first to founder in tougher times. Explicit documentation of time, efforts, and investments against projected payoffs is an essential component of success. A site-level procurement person who managed the little r at his location put it this way: "You've got to understand their strategic priorities and day-to-day pressures, make sure there is a direct line of sight between what we are asking them to do and how it will support their performance objectives."[5]

- Specific benefits to supplier and buyer need to be outlined with clear criteria for success and a realistic timeline for assessing leading and lagging indicator metrics.

- Benefits need to be weighed against a realistic assessment of costs of adopting a different way of working and the time and resource investment required to realize the benefits.

- Soft benefits should be rolled up to believable metrics that are meaningful to business units. Metrics need not always be financial, but need to be compelling and strategically important.

- Metrics should conform to existing available data; gathering the data should not be an additional hardship.

External RM starts with internal RM; internal alignment is key. SRM will expose and even magnify the fault lines in an organization's structure and alignment. Although governance models for SRM have been much discussed, they are often used to mask fundamental conflicts or gaps in accountabilities and responsibilities. In today's heavily matrixed environments, perfect alignment is neither possible nor desirable. Instead, procurement executives need to be conscious of the hot spots and tensions and have plans in place to manage through them.

An exasperated category manager discussing his company's SRM failings noted, "Do you have an appetite for the culture change this requires? Planning, sharing, having real dialogue, and investing the time and resources to engage at each level with real teams and open communication? In our case the answer was no."[6] To avoid this type of negative outcome, SRM initiatives should consider the following approach:

- Start with how a firm interacts with itself; where are the functional silos and who are the key decision makers at each level who determine the course of action?

- Once identified, internal conflicts between stakeholder needs within different functional silos need to be resolved before trying to change or refocus externally.

- Once established, procurement should become the initial point of contact to make and deliver on supplier commitments, but then it needs to drive the relationship into each business and transition into a facilitator role.

- Relationship management governance needs engaged relationship managers. Ideally, the business line sponsors focus on the achievement of little r business outcomes, with dedicated procurement resource leaders and senior business executive sponsors focused on Big R enterprisewide coordination.

Engineer change into the process; keep structure and key performance indicators (KPIs) dynamic. SRM is, by definition, a multiyear, long-horizon effort, at least at the Big R level. But businesses rarely have the discipline to manage beyond pressures for short-term results. Rather than try to swim against the tide, SRM advocates would do well to remember that for most business executives, "If it doesn't work in the short term, there may be no long term." The need to meet short-term goals is an important component of successful program management; each relationship must be tuned to emerging and shifting business priorities.

Otherwise, as one procurement executive said, "The big guys stop showing up at the meetings, you keep measuring things nobody cares about anymore, and it becomes just another piece of work."[7]

In managing both internal and external relationships, some of the key points to keep in mind include the following:

- Different stages of SRM require different people and skills and levels of investment and attention; the people needed to jump start the effort may not be the best ones to nurture, manage, and sustain it.

- Recruit from the business. The best supplier relationship managers are those who have worked in the business, understand the day-to-day pressures, and speak the same technical vernacular. These individuals can align the business realities for stakeholders and suppliers with the opportunities.

- Monitor internal and external shifts, and establish mechanisms that facilitate readjustment in roles, metrics, and project deliverables.

- Schedule regular site-level meetings with suppliers and stakeholders to reevaluate and revise KPIs to reflect current business priorities.

- Drive people to insight and to commitment; as one executive noted, "It's a business relationship, not a marriage." Be willing to cut bait on people or directions that are not in alignment with strategy.

The Critical Role of Cross-Functional Sourcing Teams

The pressure to improve, already intense, is expected to increase even more in the years ahead. Firms are responding to this pressure by creating organizational structures that promote cross-functional and cross-organizational communication, coordination, and collaboration. In support of this effort, cross-functional sourcing teams have become increasingly important as firms pursue leading-edge supply management strategies and practices.

Cross-functional sourcing teams consist of personnel from different functions and, increasingly, suppliers, brought together to achieve supply management or supply chain—related tasks. This includes specific tasks such as product design or supplier selection, or broader tasks such as responsibility for reducing purchased item cost or improving quality.

When executed properly, the cross-functional sourcing team approach can bring together the knowledge and resources required for responding to new sourcing demands, something that rigid organizational structures are often incapable of doing. Prior researchers on team building, such as Likert, have noted that groups and teams can accomplish much that is good, or they can do great harm. There is nothing implicitly good or bad, weak or strong, about teams, regardless of where an organization uses them.

Exhibit 4.3 segments cross-functional sourcing teams by the team's assignment (finite or continuous) and the members' personal commitment to the team (full or part time). Although some progressive firms are creating full-time sourcing team assignments, in most cases sourcing team assignments are still part time. The lower half of this matrix (finite or continuous team assignments supported by part-time members) presents a special challenge. It is often a struggle to obtain the commitment of members who have other professional responsibilities. Experience reveals that cross-functional sourcing teams are usually part-time/continuous assignments, making the use of sourcing teams a challenging way to work.

Exhibit 4.3	Purchasing at Different Organizational Levels

		Time Frame	
		Finite	Continuous
Personal Commitment	Full-Time	Move from project to project	Assigned permanently to specific team with evolving or changing responsibilities
	Part-Time	Support a specific team assignment in addition to regular responsibilities Disband after completion	Ongoing support of team assignments in addition to regular responsibilities

The following discussion of sourcing teams examines the benefits and potential draw-backs to team interaction, identifies when to form a cross-functional team (CFT), and concludes with a set of questions and answers that will explain how to make sourcing teams effective.

Benefits Sought from the Cross-Functional Team Approach

Firms commit the energy needed to form teams to realize specific performance ben-efits. When cross-functional teams meet their performance objectives, the benefits can far outweigh the cost of using teams. The following highlights some of the benefits that orga-nizations hope to realize from cross-functional sourcing teams.

Reduced Time to Complete a Task

Individuals working as a team can often reduce the time required to solve a problem or complete an assigned task. The traditional approach to completing organizational tasks often requires duplication of effort among groups, and the individual sign-off of differ-ent functional groups may take an extended period of time. The team approach supports members reaching agreement together, which can result in reduced rework and the time required to execute a decision.

Increased Innovation

Firms look to teams to develop innovative products and processes to maintain an advantage over competitors. Innovation is critical to long-term success. Research has revealed that lower levels of formal rules and procedures along with informal organizational structures support increased levels of innovation.[8]

The team approach should require fewer formal rules and qualifies as a less formal organizational structure. Teams can be a means to encourage increased innovation among members.

Joint Ownership of Decisions

The team approach requires joint agreement and ownership of decisions among different members. Through team interaction, members begin to understand each other's requirements or limitations and develop solutions that different departments can support. Perhaps the greatest benefit of team interaction is that once a team makes a decision, implementing the decision often becomes easier because of group buy-in. The stakeholders involved in carrying out the decision are more likely to do so efficiently and effectively, because the team has established cross-functional agreement and ownership regarding the change or decision.

Enhanced Communication among Functions or Organizations

Those who have worked in an organization with rigidly separated departments know the inefficiencies associated with interdepartmental communication. The problems are even worse as parties attempt to communicate across organizations. The cross-functional team approach can help reduce communication barriers because members are in direct contact with each other (either face to face or by electronic communication). For example, the team approach can help reduce design or material changes during product development because the team works together when developing product specifications.

This cross-functional team approach, by design, encourages open and timely exchange of information between members.

Realizing Synergies by Combining Individuals and Functions

A primary objective of using teams is to bring together individuals with different perspectives and expertise to perform better on a task compared to individuals or departments acting alone. The synergistic effect of team interaction can help generate new and creative ways to look at a problem or approach a task. Ideally, a team works together to solve problems that individuals could not solve as well acting alone, to create new ways to perform routine (though time-consuming) tasks, and to develop ideas that only a diverse group could develop.

Better Identification and Resolution of Problems

Teams with diverse knowledge and skills have an opportunity to quickly identify causes of problems that may affect the team or the organization. Early problem identification and correction minimizes or even prevents a problem's total impact. Furthermore, a team should assume joint ownership of problems and accept the responsibility for problem correction, which helps prevent finger-pointing for blame between departments.

The Need to Build Internal Relationships through Teams

Research[9] suggests that supply management professionals may, indeed, be placed in some of the most interpersonally demanding situations of any occupational group studied. Success depends upon the ability to navigate organizational fault lines with facility and interpersonal sophistication akin to that of the best general managers—without the organizational clout to back it up. Some of the comments below from supply management senior executives reflect the recognition of this need to create a tighter bridge between procurement professionals and business stakeholders.[10]

- "A number of our people have the perception that once the contract is done, you put it in the drawer.… We have no culture of continuous management and measurement, so this level of engagement is new for us."
- "They've got to believe that we know we are only in service to the business. There's a credibility gap and we've got to change the quality of the conversation, change the way we present information."
- "Don't give us procurement SRM tools without investing the time and money to help us adapt them to our business and make sure we know how to use them. And you can't even use the tools until you can earn a seat at the table! How're we supposed to do that?"

Critically, SRM means learning to exercise a new kind of power, one not grounded in the ability to force compliance with procurement procedures and contracting processes. Instead, procurement executives need to learn to build relationship capital that inspires trust and commitment from stakeholders and suppliers. Relationship capital is a function of the professional's ability to translate supply market data into compelling insights that solve business problems and to enable organizational connections and networking that accelerate business success.

Potential Drawbacks to the Cross-Functional Team Approach

The use of cross-functional sourcing teams does not guarantee a successful outcome to a project or assignment. The team approach requires careful management, open exchange of information between members, motivated team members, clearly understood team goals, effective team leaders, and adequate resources. There are potential drawbacks to the team approach when conditions do not support an effective team effort. Supply management managers must be willing to address these drawbacks if they begin to affect team performance.

Team Process Loss

Process loss occurs when a team does not complete its task in the best or most efficient manner, or members are not motivated to employ their resources to create a successful outcome.[11] When process loss is present, the total group effort is less than the expected sum of the individual parts. There is a potential drawback if the benefits resulting from team interaction do not outweigh team process loss. For example, a supplier selection team with twelve members, five of whom are active on the team, would experience a loss and waste from a lack of team interaction and participation.

Negative Effects on Individual Members

Membership on a team can have negative effects on individuals. Teams can exert pressure to conform to a decision or position that the member does not support. An example might involve a materials engineer who is pressured by other team members to select the lowest-price supplier, even though he or she knows that a higher-priced supplier will provide better quality.

A team may also pressure an individual to support or conform to a lower productivity norm than the individual's personal norm. Also, some individuals may feel stifled in a team setting or may not interact well with other team members. When this occurs, individual performance suffers.

Poor Team Decisions

Although it seems counter to what we popularly believe, cross-functional teams can arrive at poor decisions. **Groupthink**—the tendency of a rational group or team to arrive at a bad decision when other information is available—may become a problem for individuals in a cohesive group. By striving for group uniformity and consensus, they may suppress their motivation to appraise alternative courses of action.[12] The team may arrive at a decision that careful evaluation of all available information or critical discussion normally would not support.

When to Form a Cross-Functional Team

All organizations face resource constraints that affect the number of cross-functional teams, including sourcing teams, they can establish. Clearly, a firm cannot use the team approach for every business decision. Certain business decisions simply do not require a team approach. A team approach is useful when the task at hand satisfies certain characteristics.

A firm faced with a complex or large-scale business decision should consider the cross-functional team approach. Examples include new-product development, locating a new production facility, developing a commodity or purchase family strategy, or establishing a new business unit. These tasks are so large or complex that one person or function cannot effectively accomplish the assignment. A firm can also use the team approach when a team is likely to arrive at a better solution than a person or department acting individually. For example, supply management may be able to handle the evaluation and selection of suppliers but may benefit from a team with diverse experience whose members are better equipped to evaluate suppliers from a number of perspectives. Engineering can provide technical specifications, marketing can provide details on the features required, accounting can provide material and labor cost data estimates, and so on. In these situations, selecting a better supplier(s) for the situation at hand is more likely as better information becomes available and is analyzed by team members.

An assignment that directly affects a firm's competitive position, such as negotiation with a joint venture partner, might also benefit from the team approach. The cross-functional team approach is also useful when no single function has the resources to solve a problem that affects more than one department or function.

Improving Sourcing Team Effectiveness

The remainder of our team discussion presents a set of questions that require students and managers to think about various issues that affect the quality of sourcing team interaction and performance. Each question includes a brief discussion of major points and insights related to that question.

Question 1: Does Our Organization Consider Cross-Functional Team Planning Issues When Establishing Sourcing Teams?

Successfully using teams requires extensive planning before a team should be allowed to pursue an assignment. Ignoring these issues or the needs of team members during team formation increases the risk of team failure. The following summarizes several sourcing team planning issues:

Selecting a Task

Organizations should use teams selectively because of limited resource availability. Sourcing teams should work only on tasks that are important to an organization's success. One expert recommends selecting tasks that are meaningful. A meaningful task is one that requires members to use a variety of higher-level skills, supports giving members regular feedback about performance, results in an outcome with a significant effect on the organization and others outside the team, and provides members autonomy for deciding how they will do the work. For example, reducing purchase cost is an example of a broad performance objective.

Selecting Team Members and Leaders

Perhaps one of the most critical planning issues involves selecting the right members and leader. An effective team member is one who meets the following requirements:

- Understands the team's task—the member has task-relevant knowledge
- Has the time to commit to the team

- Has the ability to work with others in a group
- Can assume an organizational rather than strict functional perspective

Training Requirements

Interacting as a team requires a set of skills different from the skills required for traditional work. Organizations must consider carefully the training requirements of sourcing team members. Members may require training in project management, conflict resolution, consensus decision making, group problem solving, goal setting, and effective communication and listening skills.

Resource Support

An earlier study of cross-functional sourcing teams by Monczka and Trent revealed that the types of resources that cross-functional sourcing teams had access to made a major difference in team performance.[13] Adapted from work by Peters and O'Connor, we can identify 10 categories of team resources, as presented in Exhibit 4.4.[14] The resources that correlate the highest, on average, with effective sourcing teams (in order of importance) are supplier participation, required services and help from others, time availability, and budgetary support. Budgetary support is especially critical for teams whose members must travel from different geographical areas or for teams that must visit suppliers during the course of their assignment.

Other planning issues not addressed here include determining the level of sourcing team authority, the types and frequency of team evaluations and rewards, and the physical location of team members. This list of planning issues reveals that organizations must give serious attention to some important considerations before allowing sourcing teams to begin work.

Question 2: Does Executive Management Practice Subtle Control over Sourcing Teams?

A major issue involves management's willingness to exert subtle control over cross-functional sourcing teams, a process that does not mean that management dictates or supervises team activities. Instead, subtle control involves activities undertaken by management to increase the probability of team success. There are several ways that management can practice subtle control over sourcing teams:

- Authorizing the creation of the sourcing team
- Selecting the team's task
- Establishing broad objectives (with the team later establishing specific performance targets or goals)
- Selecting the team leader and members
- Requiring performance updates at regular intervals or at key milestones (What team wants to report to executive management that they have made no progress?)
- Conducting performance reviews and holding teams accountable for performance outcomes

Although management does not involve itself in a team's day-to-day activities, management must concern itself with moving the sourcing team process forward.

Exhibit 4.4	Organizational Resource Requirements

1. **Supplier Participation**

   The degree to which suppliers directly support completion of the team's task assignments when supplier involvement is required

2. **Required Services and Help from Others**

   The services and help required from others external to the team to perform the team's assignment

3. **Time Availability**

   The amount of time that can be devoted by all team members to the team's assignment

4. **Budgetary Support**

   The financial resources needed to perform the team's assigned tasks

5. **Materials and Supplies**

   The routine items that are required to perform the team's assignment

6. **Team Member Task Preparation**

   The personal preparation and experience of team members, through previous education, formal company training, and relevant job experience, required to perform the team's assignment

7. **Work Environment**

   The physical aspects of the immediate work environment needed to perform the team's assignment—characteristics that facilitate rather than interfere with team performance

8. **Executive Management Commitment**

   The overall level of support that executive management exhibits toward the cross-functional team process

9. **Job-Related Information**

   The information, including data and reports, from multiple sources required to support team performance. Examples include data on costs, technical issues, suppliers, supply market, performance targets, and requirements.

10. **Tools and Equipment**

    The specific tools, equipment, and technology required to perform the team's assignment

Source: Adapted from Peters, L.H., and O'Connor, J.O. (1980, March) "Situational Constraints and Work Outcomes: The Influences of a Frequently Overlooked Construct," *Academy of Management Review*, 3, 391–397.

Question 3: Does Our Organization Recognize and Reward Team Member Participation and Team Performance?

A direct link exists between rewards and team member effort, and also between rewards and team performance. Unfortunately, many organizations still fail to recognize the time and effort members must commit to sourcing teams, particularly members of part-time teams. This lack of recognition often causes team members to commit their time to non-team work activities.

How should organizations recognize and reward team member participation and team performance? Although no single answer exists, there are some guidelines that will help in this area. First, team membership should be part of an individual's performance review. This sends a message that team participation is valued and recognized by the organization, just like an individual's other work responsibilities. Second, along with an evaluation of the entire team's performance, management should consider assessing each individual's contribution to the team. This helps ensure that nonparticipating members do not benefit unfairly from the efforts of other team members.

Rewards and recognition that organizations offer teams cluster into four broad categories:

- Executive recognition, including plaques or mention in the company newsletter
- Monetary bonuses and other one-time cash awards
- Nonmonetary rewards, including dinners or sports and theater tickets
- Merit raises awarded during the team member's annual performance review

Rewards offer an opportunity to reinforce desired activity and behavior. It is well understood that what gets rewarded gets done. If team members are positively reinforced for high performance, they will likely exert even greater effort. Furthermore, if members receive immediate reinforcement, they will exert greater effort than if the reinforcement is delayed. If positive work is never recognized or reinforced through rewards, the positive effort will likely be extinguished.

Question 4: Do We Have the Right Person Selected as the Sourcing Team Leader?

The previously mentioned research by Monczka and Trent found that the effectiveness of the sourcing team leader is one of the strongest predictors of team success. An additional finding from that research was that most sourcing teams had formally designated leaders who usually were selected by management (see Question 3 on subtle control). Zenger and his colleagues, in extensive research with teams, found the following to be true:[15]

- Most organizations report they should give more attention, training, and support to their team leaders.
- Within days of taking a leadership role, team leaders usually realize they need a new set of skills.
- Even when shared team leadership among members is the goal, the team as a whole still reports to someone who might need advanced team-leadership skills.
- Overly structured team leaders who see themselves as "top sergeants with a few extra duties" greatly increase the chance of team failure.

We may conclude that selecting and training an effective team leader is critical to team success. Being an effective team leader means satisfying a demanding set of essential operating responsibilities and requirements while still promoting the creativity, leadership ability, and cohesiveness of team members. Unfortunately, relatively few individuals have the qualifications, experience, or training to immediately assume such a demanding leadership position.

Organizations should (1) evaluate team leader strengths and weaknesses, (2) rank team leaders, which is valuable when considering future leadership responsibilities, (3) provide feedback regarding improvement opportunities, which can lead to training that is targeted to the specific needs of the leader, and (4) allow individual leaders, teams, and organizations to take corrective action as required. A failure to select a qualified individual as team leader greatly reduces the probability of sourcing team effectiveness.

Question 5: Do Our Sourcing Teams Effectively Establish Performance Goals?

One of the most important activities relating to sourcing team interaction is the ability of teams to establish quantified goals that focus on end results (rather than desired activities). For example, a sourcing team that establishes a goal of 2 percent cost reduction for the first quarter of 2014 has likely established a more effective goal than one that establishes a goal of holding three team meetings in the first quarter.

Establishing sourcing team goals is important for several reasons. Teams with established goals often use those goals as a basis for evaluating how well the team is performing. The goals provide a benchmark for assessing progress, providing feedback, and allocating performance rewards for superior effort and results. Teams will also establish, on average, challenging rather than easy goals. Furthermore, external pressure on a team to set goals usually results in the setting of more challenging goals (recall our discussion of subtle control). We also know that teams with goals perform better, on average, than teams that are asked simply to perform their best without explicit end goals. Goal setting is a critical cross-functional team requirement.

Sourcing teams should develop goals for which they will be held accountable. This is a three-part process. The first part of the process requires a team to describe its task. For example, a team may be responsible for managing suppliers that provide a certain commodity. The second part of the process requires the team to assess its ability to achieve certain outcomes on a scale ranging from 1 (no potential) to 7 (high potential). Finally, the team identifies those areas offering the highest performance potential (usually the items within the 5 to 7 range) and develops quantified or specific objectives relating to that item. If the team believes it has the potential to improve material delivery, then it should develop an objective goal that relates to material delivery.

Question 6: Are Key Suppliers Part of the Sourcing Team Process?

The potential benefit of closer buyer-seller relationships is well understood by most organizations. Cross-functional sourcing teams are an ideal way to promote cross-organizational cooperation. Research reveals that relying on supplier involvement and input (when a team's assignment warrants involvement) demonstrates, on average, the following positive characteristics compared with teams that do not involve suppliers:[16]

- They are rated as more effective.
- They are rated as putting forth greater effort on team assignments.
- They report greater satisfaction concerning the quality of key information exchanged between the team and key suppliers.
- They report greater reliance on suppliers to directly support the team's goals, thus making the supplier a resource.
- They report fewer problems coordinating work activity between the team and key suppliers.
- They report receiving greater supplier contribution across many performance areas, including cost-reduction and quality improvement ideas, process improvement suggestions, and material-ordering and delivery cycle time reductions.

An integrated approach to supply chain management should also begin to identify key customers that should be part of sourcing teams (at least on an informal basis). Sourcing teams, with supplier involvement, can work to incorporate customer needs directly into sourcing strategies and practices.

Cross-functional sourcing teams offer all types of organizations, not just manufacturing firms, the opportunity to realize advantages across many performance areas. Underlying the development and use of sourcing teams must be a recognition that sourcing increasingly affects a firm's overall competitiveness along with the realization that cross-functional integration among supply management, manufacturing, marketing, and technical groups can improve a firm's sourcing effectiveness.

Integrating Supply Management, Engineering, and Suppliers to Develop New Products and Services

In forward-thinking enterprises, supply management plays a key role in the development of new products and services. As the main contact with suppliers, supply management is in a unique position to include suppliers early in the design process as well as to perform early evaluation of supplier capabilities. This is a task that engineering team members are not trained to do. Think about how much easier it is for supply management to support new-product development teams than for engineering to do it alone. As a team member, supply management has early visibility to new-product requirements, which allows managers to contribute directly during the design and specification of material requirements. With a more traditional approach, supply management plays a reactive role after other functions have completed their tasks. Because supply management knows more about supplier capabilities, it is a valuable resource for engineering staff faced with understanding the capabilities of suppliers, as well as the new and emerging technologies that lie on the horizon and are within reach of current or new suppliers.

Common Themes of Successful Supplier Integration Efforts

A study[17] funded by the National Science Foundation (NSF) identified the key factors that distinguished successful from unsuccessful attempts at involving suppliers in new-product development. The following key attributes of successful supplier integration initiatives were common among all of the companies studied, as shown in Exhibit 4.5 on p. 142.

Sourcing Snapshot

GM Purchasing Gets a Re-Engineering

Under Product Development Chief Tom Stephens, the purchasing division of General Motors Co. is being required to: Cooperate.

Engineers and purchasing decision makers will work together to weigh quality and cost, sometimes choosing a more expensive part if it gives more to the customer, Vice Chairman Stephens said.

Putting purchasing under Stephens' product development culminates a process undertaken when GM reorganized purchasing so its units mirrored the divisions within engineering.

For example, purchasing has a new interiors/safety unit that aligns with engineering's setup. Previously, interiors were included in a purchasing division with structures and closures. "Now they can act as a team so they can have the same objectives," Stephens said. "Cost isn't just purchasing's job, as quality isn't engineering's job, both are all of our jobs."

Because the divisions are aligned, corresponding representatives from purchasing and product development can meet with suppliers to discuss product and pricing, he said. Within the next six months, some U.S. purchasing staffers also colocate with engineering.

Stephens said the integration already is paying off. GM executives point to their recent selection of a more expensive power-steering supplier over a cheaper offer because the winning supplier offered a more desirable technology. That decision-for a future rear-wheel-drive Cadillac sedan that GM employees call the "BMW fighter"—was made jointly by purchasing and engineering, Stephens said.

Source: Thompson, C, (2009, December 14) "GM Purchasing Get a Re-engineering," *Automotive News*, 3.

Exhibit 4.5	Practices That Separate the "Best" from the Rest

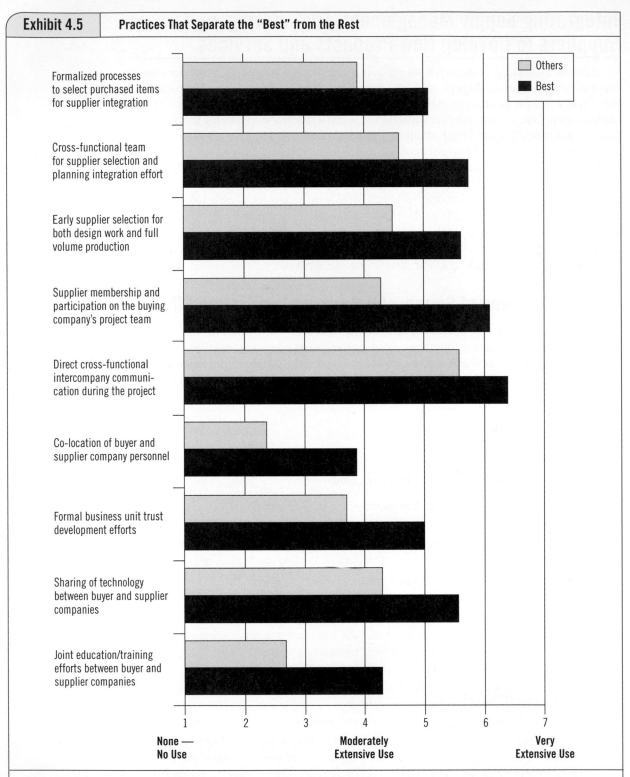

Source: Monczka, R., Frayer, D., Handfield, R., Ragatz, G., and Scannell, T. (2000) *New Product Development: Strategies for Supplier Integration*, Milwaukee, WI: ASQ Quality Press.

1. Formalized Process for Selecting Items for Supplier Integration

Supply management's involvement enables it to determine at an earlier point the materials or service requirements for a new product and provide input during the design phase based on its knowledge of materials supply markets. Supply management can recommend substitutes for high-cost or volatile materials, suggest standard items wherever possible, and evaluate longer-term materials trends. However, as we noted in Chapter 3, the right to make this decision must be formally authorized in the new-product development process, with supply management given the appropriate level of authority.

Supply management should always monitor and anticipate activity in its supply markets. For example, supply management should forecast long-term supply and prices for its basic commodities. It should monitor technological innovations that impact its primary materials or make substitute materials economically attractive. It should evaluate not only its existing suppliers but also other potential suppliers. Because team participation provides timely visibility to new-product requirements, supply management can monitor and forecast change on a continuous basis.

2. Use of Cross-Functional Teams for Supplier Evaluation and Selection

The evaluation and selection of suppliers requires a major time commitment by supply management, the group that must evaluate and select suppliers regardless of the new-product development approach used. The team approach allows supply management to anticipate product requirements earlier so it can identify the most capable suppliers.

The supplier assessment should be systematically carried out, based on hard performance data, by a cross-functional team of technical and nontechnical personnel who conduct subjective evaluations. Performance data should be weighted in such a manner that they are aligned with customer performance requirements. All of the above criteria must be tied into the evaluation/measurement system to develop a comprehensive risk assessment that answers the following questions:

- What is the likelihood that this supplier has the ability to bring the product to market?
- How does this risk assessment compare to other potential suppliers (if there are others)?
- At what point are we willing to reverse this decision if we proceed, and what are the criteria and measures for doing so?
- What is the contingency plan that takes effect in the event of reversing our decision?

3. Early Supplier Selection for Design and Volume Work

Supplier selection can occur before a new part is actually designed or reaches production. The team approach helps eliminate a source of frustration for supply management—a lack of time to evaluate, select, and develop suppliers to support new-product requirements. With the team approach, supplier selection can begin earlier in the development process, which allows supply management to perform this critical task earlier in the process and with better information.

The following elements are important in considering new or existing suppliers for integration:

- *Targets.* Is the supplier capable of hitting affordable targets regarding cost, quality, conductivity, weight, and other performance criteria?
- *Timing.* Will the supplier be able to meet product introduction deadlines?
- *Ramp-up.* Will the supplier be able to increase capacity and production fast enough to meet our market share requirements?
- *Innovation and technical.* Does the supplier have the required engineering expertise and physical facilities to develop an adequate design, manufacture it, and solve problems when they occur?
- *Training.* Do the supplier's key personnel have the required training to start up required processes and debug them?
- *Resource commitment.* If the supplier is deficient in any of the above areas, is management willing to commit resources to remedy the problem?

4. Supplier Membership and Participation on the Team

Bringing suppliers into the product development process is different from simply sharing information, and it can involve including important suppliers early in the design process of a new product, perhaps even as part of the new-product team. The benefits of early supplier involvement include gaining a supplier's insight into the design process, allowing comparisons of proposed production requirements against a supplier's existing capabilities, and allowing a supplier to begin preproduction work early. A supplier can bring a fresh perspective and new ideas to the development process.

If given the opportunity, suppliers can have a major impact on the overall timing and success of a new product. The type of involvement can also vary (see Exhibit 4.6). At one extreme, called **white box design** the supplier is given blueprints and told to make the product from them. At a more involved level, often called **gray box design** the supplier's engineers work cooperatively with the buying company's engineers to jointly design the product. At the highest level of supplier involvement, **black box design** suppliers are provided with functional specifications and are asked to complete all technical specifications, including materials to be used, blueprints, and so on. Depending on the level of involvement, the supplier may need to be a full-time member of the team, working alongside supply management, engineering, and manufacturing to bring the project to fruition.

5. Direct Cross-Functional Intercompany Communication during the Project

In the study of supplier integration, a variety of information-sharing mechanisms were employed to assess the alignment of technology roadmaps with potential suppliers. In most cases, no specific product or project was discussed at initial meetings, only the potential for a meeting of the minds. The sharing of technology roadmaps often strongly influenced the type of buyer-supplier relationship that resulted in the integration process. Very often, the buyer or supplier decided that this was not a company they were interested in doing business with because of a diverging technology road map. In cases when the supplier's current technology could be used but its long-term technology road map diverged, companies often exploited the technology for the current product or process but returned to the supply pool for future product cycles.

Team participation allows supply management to evaluate the timing of each phase of the product development project. Supply management can assess whether project timing is realistic as it applies to a new part's sourcing requirements. If the timing is not realistic,

Exhibit 4.6	Extent of Design Responsibility

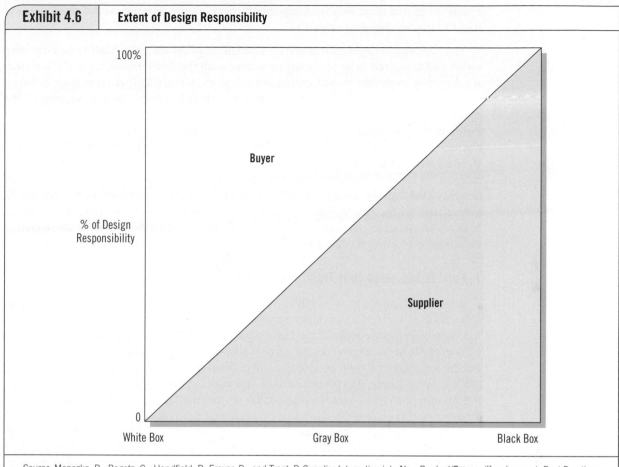

Source: Monczka, R., Ragatz, G., Handfield, R. Frayer, D., and Trent, R *Supplier Integration into New Product/Process/Development: Best Practices,* Milwaukee, WI: ASQC Quality Press, 1998.

supply management should have enough visibility to reevaluate the timing requirements or come up with plans to meet the proposed time frame. In addition, an ongoing set of milestones should be established to ensure that communication with the supplier continues and occurs at regular intervals. This can prevent the occurrence of nasty surprises if the supplier falls behind schedule in completing the project.

Sourcing Snapshot: Suncor Energy Partners with Drilling Suppliers illustrates how one company worked to closely integrate suppliers with its engineering and sourcing teams, resulting in a competitive advantage in the industry.

6. Co-Location of Buyer and Supplier Personnel

The physical co-location of a supplier engineer at a buying company is increasingly becoming a part of the normal product development process structure. One company in the study operates what it calls a "guest engineer" program through which it invites key suppliers to place an engineer in the buying company's facility for a short period of time (two to three weeks) in the very early stages of product development. During this period, the firms develop product and design specifications and assign responsibilities for development. Another buying company co-locates its personnel and the supplier's personnel at a neutral site because of union rules. The result is the same: a focused and closely integrated team who work together throughout the duration or just during critical stages of the development project.

The NSF study suggested that certain types of suppliers are more likely to be integrated earlier and may need to be physically co-located with the development team. For instance, at a Japanese computer manufacturer, the extent of interaction that takes place between product development engineers and suppliers appears to depend on the volatility of the commodity technology. Suppliers of critical nonstandard commodities are involved much earlier in the product development initiative. These suppliers are involved in face-to-face discussions with engineers on a regular basis. On the other hand, suppliers of noncritical, standard items are not integrated until the final stages of the development cycle, and communication appears to occur more in the form of computerization (e.g., computer-aided design, or CAD, is used with noncritical items such as PCBs, keyboards, and chassis). In general, face-to-face discussions are quicker, and information can be exchanged more effectively. However, in cases when suppliers are located within a day's travel of the operating divisions, co-location is often unnecessary.

7. Formal Business Unit Trust Development Efforts

A major responsibility of supply management is to provide information to suppliers involved in a new-product development project. Sharing of information can help avoid unwelcome surprises throughout the life of a project, particularly if suppliers are brought in early in the concept stage to design parts. If supply management selects capable and trustworthy suppliers, it should be able to share product information early in the development process. For example, if a component for a new part requires a specific production process, it is important to make sure the supplier has the required process capability. Early visibility to product requirements allows supply management to share critical information with suppliers that can help avoid delays. In turn, suppliers will be expected to share their information with the new-product development team. To build this level of trust may require that parties sign appropriate nondisclosure or confidentiality agreements prior to meeting. These types of agreements are covered in Chapter 16.

8. Sharing of Technology between Buyer and Supplier Companies

Supply management must work closely with engineering to determine whether there is a common convergence in technology strategies with the supplier. The most common reference to this concept is a **technology roadmap**, which refers to the set of performance criteria and products and processes an organization intends to develop or manufacture. Many companies define their technology roadmaps in terms of the next decade, whereas others employ a horizon of 50 years or even a century! Although the exact form of a technology roadmap is somewhat industry specific, it typically is defined in the following terms:

- Projected performance specifications for a class of products or processes (e.g., memory size, speed, electrical resistance, temperature, or pressure)
- An intention to integrate a new material or component (e.g., a new form of molecule or chemical)
- Development of a product to meet customer requirements that is currently unavailable in the market (e.g., new television screen technology)
- Integration of multiple complementary technologies that results in a radically new product (e.g., a combined fax/phone/modem/copier, or combining television, cable, and computer technology)
- A combination of the above as well as other possible variations

9. Joint Education and Training Efforts

Achieving this level of involvement, however, may prove difficult for personnel on both sides of the fence. Some of the typical concerns that arise in these scenarios include the following:

- Unwillingness of internal design personnel to relinquish responsibility
- Concerns over sharing proprietary information—both buyer and supplier
- Lack of business processes to support integration
- Lack of cultural alignment

To overcome these problems, personnel at both the buyer and supplier may need to be educated regarding the benefits of the integration effort, as well as be assured that the proper confidentiality agreements have been completed. In addition, engineering staff may require further education to ensure that they realize that they are not relinquishing their authority over design; another member is simply coming in to provide additional insights that will lead to a better product and a more satisfied customer.

Supplier Integration into Customer Order Fulfillment

Many companies are continuing to integrate suppliers, not just in the product development phase but also in the order fulfillment phase of the product life cycle. Suppliers can provide significant benefits in the form of lower costs, improved delivery, lower inventory, and problem-solving capabilities during the fulfillment stage of production. Supplier integration takes place in various forms, including supplier suggestion programs, buyer-seller improvement teams, and on-site supplier representatives.

Supplier Suggestion Programs

Suppliers can be an invaluable source of ideas for process improvement. They bring with them a different expertise, a different point of view, and a greater volume of ideas. Supply management groups are missing out on a great source of expertise when they do not tap into suppliers' suggestions. Suppliers may submit suggestions through an Internet site, at a formal meeting, or during supplier conferences. Typically, a supplier will submit a proposal using a standard form that identifies the nature of the improvement, impact areas, estimated savings, and business unit or functional area of application. The suggestion is assigned a tracking number, to ensure that the idea is not lost in the cracks. The suggestion then goes through a formal internal review, which may consist of multiple stages. The review team will use the following criteria in assessing the suggestion:

- Feasibility
- Resources required
- Potential savings
- Go/no-go decision
- Feedback to supplier

As a result of this review, the implementation team accepts or rejects the suggestion. Accepted suggestions may go through further refinement, and the supplier may be formally involved and given the go-ahead to proceed. Results from the suggestion will then be tracked.

Successful supplier suggestion programs tend to have several elements in common. First, the savings from the suggestion are often shared 50/50, not kept solely by the buying company. This encourages the supplier to provide further suggestions. Second, the program focuses on cost improvement, not simply cutting the supplier's margins. Third, successful buying companies provide prompt feedback to the supplier on its suggestion and also implement good suggestions promptly. This sends a clear message that the supplier's idea is being taken seriously. It is important to do more than just put the focus on suppliers' problems. Other opportunities for improvement may include those in the buying company, in intercompany communication and processes, and even within second-tier suppliers. Finally, it is critical to acknowledge the supplier's suggestion, through an awards program, newsletter, or announcement at a supplier conference.

Buyer-Seller Improvement Teams

More and more companies are involving suppliers on improvement teams in a variety of different areas. Why? Research reveals that teams that relied on supplier input and involvement (when the task warranted involvement) were more effective in their task, on average, than teams that did not involve suppliers.[18] Teams that include suppliers as participants report positive outcomes and great supplier contributions across many performance areas, including the following:

- Providing cost reduction ideas
- Providing quality improvement ideas
- Supporting actions to improve material delivery
- Offering process technology suggestions
- Supporting material-ordering cycle time reductions

Also, teams that included suppliers as participants reported other important outcomes:

- Greater satisfaction concerning the quality of information exchange between the team and key suppliers
- Higher reliance on suppliers to directly support the team's goals—the supplier is a resource
- Fewer problems coordinating work activity between the team and key suppliers
- Greater effort put forth on team assignment

A manager at Honeywell described the advantages of working on a buyer-seller improvement team when it came time to quickly identify and solve a quality problem with a major customer.[19] He noted: "Customers came to us with a product quality problem, and eventually we traced it back to the supplier. We had problems with the supplier's product, and we identified the problem as occurring because their process had shifted. Initially, we went to process quality assurance with the problem and confronted them. At first, the supplier refused to believe that it was their fault, and claimed that we were not using the material correctly. Our group leader for the product team found it difficult to coordinate with the supplier and therefore requested an in-house person from their facility to work with us. The problem was resolved through many teleconferences, meetings at their facility, checking their processes, supplier teams coming to our plant, and many exchanges on specifications via e-mail, fax, etc. They identified the problem in their process, and since then they are performing very well. There was clearly a learning phase in transitioning from a traditional relationship, but resolving this problem clearly showed how to work together to strengthen our relationship."

On-Site Supplier Representative

Many companies are encouraging suppliers to provide a permanent on-site representative who can aid the company in improving customer order fulfillment processes. The idea behind this initiative (called **vendor or supplier-managed inventory** in some circles) is to have the representative assist in managing the inventory of materials or services, provide technical support, and in some cases even aid in assembling and producing the product or service. On-site suppliers are established when the purchaser empowers a supplier representative to work on-site to perform various tasks. The supplier assumes administrative costs and assigns a full-time or part-time representative to be physically co-located on the site.

There are a number of purchase categories where an on-site supplier representative can be used, including the following:

- Waste management
- Printing services
- Spare parts inventory and other MRO items
- Computer equipment and software
- Office furniture
- Uniforms and protective equipment
- Process control equipment
- Production parts
- Transportation services
- Production maintenance

On-site representatives can be used in a number of functional areas as well.

Supply Management

An on-site supplier representative can process purchase transactions between customer and supplier using the customer's supply management system and purchase orders. In addition, the on-site rep can work cooperatively with the customer's planner to ensure timely and efficient delivery of materials. In some cases, the on-site representative can also assume a buyer-planner role and coordinate multiple facilities. It should be noted that the on-site rep places orders only at the established price and only with the supplier company involved.

Sales

An on-site supplier rep may perform the routine responsibilities of a traditional sales representative. The supplier is empowered to sell directly to internal units from an on-site location. This can often result in a reduction in the supplier's overhead cost structure for this particular customer, because a good portion of overhead goes to budgeting for a sales force.

Engineering

Preferred suppliers can reside on-site and are empowered to provide design support under the supervision of customer engineers. These full-time, on-site supplier representatives act as resident information resources. The customer can thus utilize supplier ideas and expertise at the earliest stages of product and process development.

Transportation

Overseas transportation modes (surface, air, ocean, foreign brokerage) may be combined into one location controlled at the customer's site. Suppliers of freight services provide professional on-site support to the using location and can create a command center for coordination of all inbound and outbound transportation within the supply chain.

Potential Benefits of On-Site Supplier Representatives

A number of benefits can occur for both parties in a supplier representative situation. These are also summarized in the form of a win-win proposition shown in Exhibit 4.7.

- Customer-supplier coordination and integration are increased.
- Supplier personnel work on-site to support the purchaser.
- Supply management staff is increased.
- Supplier in-plant personnel perform various buying and planning activities, allowing supply management staff to pursue other value-added activities.

Exhibit 4.7	Win-Win Elements of On-Site Supplier Representatives			
	Customer Wins with:			
Supplier Wins with:	Consignment Inventory	Direct-Floor Stocking	Releases from Rolling Forecast	Resident at Customer
More Business	X	X		X
Access to New Designs				X
Stabilized Production	X	X	X	
Fewer Transactions	X	X	X	
Quicker Payments	X			
Less Selling Expense	X	X		X
Assured Sales		X	X	X
Access to Information Earlier			X	X

The supplier also wins with the following:

- Increased supplier insight into customer needs and access to new designs
- Daily interface with customer personnel concerning current and future customer needs
- Increased supplier production efficiency
- Increased insight, leading to fewer schedule changes and surprises
- Reduced transaction costs
- Reduced inventory
- On-site material plan development using a customer's systems in a real-time mode

Although doing business in this mode is very new for most companies, more and more companies are exploring the benefits of increased supplier integration in customer order fulfillment processes, as shown in Exhibit 4.8 on p. 151.

Exhibit 4.8	Good Practice: ESI at MDR

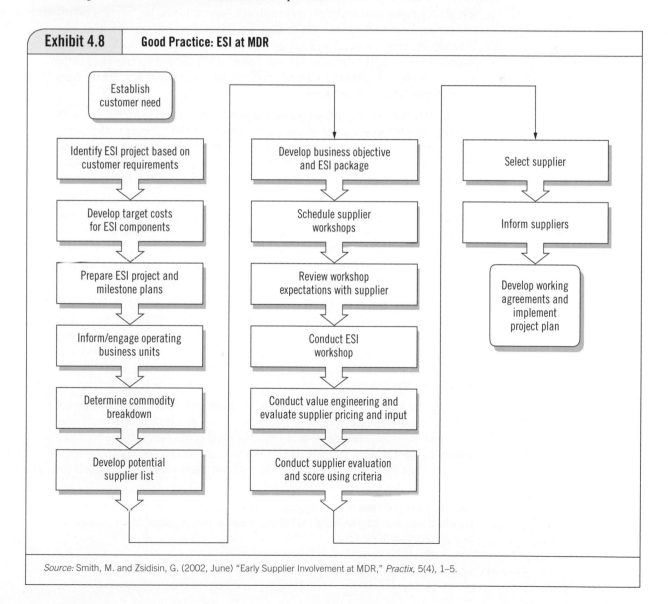

Source: Smith, M. and Zsidisin, G. (2002, June) "Early Supplier Involvement at MDR," *Practix*, 5(4), 1–5.

Good Practice Example

Globaman, Inc.—Working Across Functions and with Suppliers in Response to Crisis

Globaman, a global electronics firm, was greatly affected by the 2011 Japan tsunami, as a significant portion of its semiconductor supply was sourced from there. Supplier plants were damaged by the earthquake and flooding. For those still able to operate, power shortages made it impossible for production to resume. The suppliers' employees were also severely affected. Many mourned the loss of their relatives. Food shortages made everyday living difficult. Possible radiation exposure loomed. It was clear that recovery would take some time.

Approach

Globaman formed a task force to assess the situation and chart a recovery course. Initial estimates placed the potential profit impact in the hundreds of millions of dollars. The task force initially included only supply management, but as the magnitude of the problem became clearer it expanded to include production, logistics, quality (to qualify new suppliers) and R&D (to allow for redesign of boards if required). Sales and the CFO were also involved to help determine priority based on the specific customers being impacted and which ones Globaman should support first. In total, nearly 30 people were fully engaged with the problem.

The task force immediately started looking into broker/distributor markets as alternative sources of supply. In the first week following the disaster, the company was able to identify which suppliers were impacted. However, it did not have a comprehensive value chain map, so it took longer to know the magnitude of each supplier's impact (i.e., which specific part numbers and how much volume were impacted.) Because of this, it took longer to validate detailed information and formulate the appropriate actions.

During the second and third weeks following the tsunami, the company identified second sources outside of Japan and then developed a red/yellow/green status for each part based on the level of inventory it had on hand and worked with suppliers to ensure they were producing the critical "red" parts. In a few cases, Globaman redesigned parts or chose to substitute an older technology for a newer one that was affected by the crisis.

During the early stages of the disaster, information was sketchy and unreliable. As a result, Globaman directly sought out information rather than rely on traditional sources. It contacted electronic manufacturing services suppliers and compared their information on supply availability with what Globaman was hearing directly from the suppliers. In some cases (e.g., chemicals for manufacturing semiconductors), Globaman contacted tier three- and four-level suppliers to gain input on the status for upstream supply.

Because of the broad impact that the disaster could have on the company, supply management leadership established direct links with the managing board to gain approval for an accelerated plan to minimize impact and to elevate certain issues for executive attention. For the top five issues, Globaman's board members contacted the suppliers' top executives in Japan to gain agreement and commitment to milestones. In many cases they were even able to avoid impact because of this accelerated communication and approval process.

Over the course of the next four months, Globaman continued to work through the issues, and the majority of them were resolved by July 2011. However, the complete milestone closure could take as long as a year from that date.

A notable aspect of Globaman's event management process was the way in which it engaged with the Japanese suppliers that were affected by the tsunami. In the first week of the crisis, it chose to contact European suppliers that are also located in Japan, opting not to burden their direct contacts in Japan so as to allow those suppliers to work on their recovery. During the second week, Globaman sent condolence letters directly to Japanese suppliers.

As the Japanese suppliers began to recover, Globaman used an escalation method by contacting the supplier's top management to ensure it got high priority. Rather than just using Globaman's importance as a customer, the company offered "quid pro quo." If the suppliers prioritized Globaman's work over others, it would give Japanese customers priority for its own products in markets critical to the Japan recovery like health care and power generation, transmission and distribution.

Finally, Globaman proactively sent signals to the Japanese suppliers that it wanted to maintain sustainable relationships with them. The condolence letters let the suppliers know that this was a recovery approach and that Globaman's short-term actions (e.g., looking at second sources) was to secure near-term supply and not for the sole purpose of seeking lower prices. The company also sent "thank you" certificates to Japanese suppliers acknowledging their support of Globaman under difficult times. This reinforced the company's reputation with its suppliers by reminding them that it is interested in long-term relationships.

Results

Although Globaman incurred millions of dollars in added cost (to cover purchases from brokers, air freight, etc.), the company was able to avoid almost any operational or customer impact. (There was one minor line stoppage.) The sales organization reported that customers said that Globaman "recovered better than the competition." Additionally, some of that added expense may be covered by insurance, further reducing the financial impact.

Source: CAPS Research, Implementing Value Chain Risk Management—Case Study Findings, 2012.

CONCLUSION

This chapter discussed the need for supply management to develop closer relations with internal and external groups across the extended supply chain. To accomplish this, supply management professionals must develop a working knowledge of the principles of engineering, manufacturing, cost-based accounting, quality assurance, risk management and team dynamics. The days are over when supply management could operate in a confined area with only an occasional visit to a supplier.

Firms are using the team approach to streamline and improve the product development process. This directly affects firms that rely on innovative new products for their continued success. Supply management has a key role to play on these teams. In its role, supply management helps select suppliers for inclusion in the process, advises engineering personnel of suppliers' capabilities, and helps negotiate contracts once the product team has selected a supplier. Supply management also acts as a liaison throughout this process, in facilitating supplier participation at team meetings and helping to resolve conflicts between the supplier and the team when they occur. Supply management may also be involved in developing a target price for the supplier to aim at while planning the component or system, and helping the supplier to analyze costs and identify ways of meeting this target price. Finally, supply management may also be involved in developing nondisclosure and confidentiality agreements in cases where technology sharing occurs.

Supply management is also expected to effectively identify and manage risk across the company's extended supply chain. The increasing focus on risk management is required because of increased economic, political, and social uncertainties worldwide. In addition, physical disasters that impact a firm's profitability across global supply chains also drive an emphasis on supply chain risk management (see Good Practice Example—Globaman, Inc.). This focus requires the capability to work closely with other functions and suppliers.

Part of the increased interaction between supply management and other functions is because of the need to compete in an environment driven by reduced product cycle times. Supply management supports this effort by developing closer internal and external relationships and by participating on cross-functional teams. Those interested in the supply management profession should learn as much as they can about what it takes to compete in today's markets, including expanding their knowledge about the team approach as well as understanding how firms compete on cost, quality, time, and manage risk. The need to interact effectively with different groups plays a major role in how well supply management can accomplish its tasks.

KEY TERMS

black box design, 144

collaboration, 126

cross-functional sourcing
    teams, 132

gray box design, 144

groupthink, 135

integration, 119

meaningful task, 136

process loss, 135

relationship management
    (RM) skills, 119

supply integration, 119

technology roadmap, 146

vendor or supplier-managed
    inventory, 149

white box design, 144

DISCUSSION QUESTIONS

1. Describe the different types of integration that supply management should become actively involved in.

2. Describe the types of information and data that supply management may share with different internal and external functions.

3. What are the barriers to integration? How can they be overcome?

4. Research with cross-functional sourcing teams revealed that teams that included suppliers as active team participants put forth greater effort, on average, than teams that did not include suppliers. Discuss why the involvement of external suppliers can positively affect a team's effort.

5. Why is goal setting so important to the success of the sourcing team process? What is the role of the team leader when setting team goals?

6. Relatively few individuals have the qualifications, experience, and training to immediately assume demanding sourcing team leadership positions. Do you agree or disagree with this statement? Why?

7. Describe the traditional model of buyer-seller relationships. How is the traditional model different from the collaborative model? What are the major characteristics of the collaborative model?

8. Describe a typical technology roadmap for a manufacturer of PCs. How does this affect supply management's activities in the new-product development cycle?

9. Discuss the most important elements that characterize the most successful efforts at integrating suppliers in new-product development. How do these factors contribute to success?

10. What types of information can a supplier provide that are useful during new-product development?

11. What is the difference between a gray box and a black box approach to early supplier involvement? Under what circumstances might each approach be appropriate?

12. What criteria are most important when considering whether a supplier should be involved in a new-product development effort?

13. What are the impacts of increasing worldwide risks on supply management and the need to work closely with other functions and suppliers? Why?

ADDITIONAL READINGS

Cousins, P., Handfield, R., Lawson, B., and Peterson, K. (2006), "Creating Supply Chain Relational Capital: The Impact of Formal and Informal Socialization Processes," *Journal of Operations Management*, 24(6), 851–864.

Handfield, R., and Bechtel, C. (2001), "The Role of Trust and Relationship Structure in Improving Supply Chain Responsiveness," *Industrial Marketing Management*, 31, 1–16.

Handfield, R., Ragatz, G., Monczka, R., and Peterson, K. (1999), "Involving Suppliers in New Product Development," *California Management Review*, 42(1), 59–82.

Handfield, R., Ragatz, G., and Peterson, K. (2003), "A Model of Supplier Integration into New Product Development," *Journal of Product Innovation Management*, 20(4), 284–299.

Henke, J., and Zhang, C. (2010), "Increasing Supplier-Driven Innovation," *MITSloan Management Review*, Winter, 51(2), 41–46.

Monczka, et al., A Major Research Initiative of CAPS Research, Value Chain Strategies for the Changing Decade: Collaboration Across the Extended Value Chain, 2013.

Monczka, et al., A Major Research Initiative of CAPS Research, Value Chain Strategies for the Changing Decade: Risk Management Across the Extended Value Chain, April 2012.

Monczka, R., Frayer, D., Handfield, R., Ragatz, G., and Scannell, T. (2000), *Supplier Integration into New Product/Process Development: Best Practice*, Milwaukee, WI: ASQ Quality Press.

Monczka, R. M., and Trent, R. J. (1993), *Cross-Functional Sourcing Team Effectiveness*, Tempe, AZ: Center for Advanced Supply Management Studies.

Monczka, R. M., and Trent, R. J. (1994), "Cross-Functional Sourcing Team Effectiveness: Critical Success Factors," *International Journal of Supply Management and Materials Management*, Fall, 2–11.

Trent, R. J. (1996), "Understanding and Evaluating Cross-Functional Sourcing Team Leadership," *International Journal of Supply Management and Materials Management*, Fall, 29–36.

Trent, R. J. (1998), "Individual and Collective Team Effort: A Vital Part of Sourcing Team Success," *International Journal of Supply Management and Materials Management*, Fall, 46–54.

Ward, N., Handfield, R., and Cousins, P. (2007), "Stepping Up on SRM," *CPO Agenda*, Summer, 42–47.

ENDNOTES

1. Giunipero, L. (2004), *Purchasing Education and Training Part II*, Tempe, AZ Center for Advanced Purchasing Studies.

2. Spekman, R. E. (1988), "Strategic Supplier Selection: Understanding Long-Term Buyer Relationships," *Business Horizons*, 31(4), 76.

3. Ward, N., Handfield, R., and Cousins, P. (2007), "Stepping Up on SRM," *CPO Agenda*, Summer, 42–47.

4. Ward et al.

5. Ward et al.

6. Ward et al.

7. Ward et al.

8. Russell, R. D. (1990), "Innovation in Organizations: Toward an Integrated Model," *Review of Business*, 12(2), 19.

9. Ward et al.

10. Ward et al.

11. Steiner, I. D. (1972), *Group Process and Productivity*, New York: Academic Press, p. 88.

12. Janis, I. L. (1982), *Groupthink: Psychological Studies of Policy Decisions and Fiascoes*, Boston: Houghton Mifflin, p. 9.

13. Monczka, R. M., and Trent, R. J. (1993), *Cross-Functional Sourcing Team Effectiveness*, Tempe, AZ: Center for Advanced Supply Management Studies.

14. Peters, L. H., and O'Connor, E. J. (1980), "Situational Constraints and Work Outcomes: The Influences of a Frequently Overlooked Construct," *Academy of Management Review*, 5(3), 391–397.

15. Zenger, J., et al. (1994), *Leading Teams: Mastering the New Role*, Homewood, IL: Irwin, pp. 14–15.

16. Monczka, R. M., and Trent, R. J. (1994), "Effective Cross-Functional Sourcing Teams: Critical Success Factors," *International Journal of Supply Management and Materials Management*, 30(4), 7–8.

17. Monczka, R., Handfield, R., Ragatz, G., Frayer, D., and Scannell, T. (2000), *Supplier Integration into New Product/Process Development: Best Practices*, Milwaukee, WI: ASQ Press.

18. Monczka and Trent.

19. Monczka et al.

Purchasing and Supply Management Organization

CHAPTER 5

Learning Objectives

After completing this chapter, you should be able to

- Recognize the role of organizational design in enabling purchasing and supply management success

- Comprehend the differences between centralized, center-led and decentralized, and forms of the purchasing organization

- Understand the drivers that affect organizational design in purchasing and supply management

- Understand the cross-functional team concept and its influence and roadblocks to adoption in purchasing and supply chain

- Identify trends in the supply organization of the future

Chapter Outline

NRG, An Integrated Supply Management Organization—Post Merger

Chris Haas is the Vice President of Supply Chain at NRG Energy in Houston, Texas. This Notre Dame graduate has extensive supply management experience. Chris has held supply management positions in the automotive, railroad, contracting, and energy businesses. He came to NRG in 2010 and has fundamentally changed NRG's sourcing structure. These changes have resulted in elevating the supply chain function to a much higher strategic focus within NRG. Recently, Chris was tasked with another challenge of integrating the supply management organization of GenOn (another Independent Power Producer) into his Supply organization. "A merger is one area that I had never experienced before in my career and I needed a little of the 'luck of the Irish' to make happen," he stated.

NRG Company Background

NRG is a Fortune 300 and S&P 500 Company. It is one of the country's largest power generation and retail electricity businesses. NRG's power plants provide about 47,000 megawatts of generation capacity and its retail and thermal subsidiaries serve more than 2 million customers in 16 states. In addition to generation assets, NRG owns and operates the following subsidiary companies: NRG Energy Services; NRG Solar; NRG Residential Solar Solutions; NRG Thermal Energy Plus; eVgo; Green Mountain Energy Company; Petra Nova and Reliant Energy.

The GenOn Acquisition

GenOn was an energy company that provided electricity to wholesale customers in the United States. The company was one of the largest independent power producers in the nation with more than 14,000 megawatts of power generation capacity across the United States using natural gas, fuel oil and coal. The company, formerly known as RRI Energy, was acquired by Mirant in December of 2010. NRG completed its acquisition of GenOn Energy in December 2012 for $1.7 billion.

Independent Power Producer's Model

Wholesale generators, buy fuel and sell on wholesale market, but don't own the transmission lines. The utility business can be separated into three components: (1) power generation; (2) transmission and distribution; and (3) retail. NRG operates in the power generation and retail components of the electric business. They generate power and serve both residential and commercial customers. As a result NRG is classified as an Independent Power Producer. This is in direct contrast to a full-service utility, such as Duke Power, who serves a specific geographic area and has all three components of the utility business.

Structure starts with Internal Customers

Mr. Haas feels his supply chain organization would be classified in the "hybrid/center-led" category. However, he states that "everything is organized around serving the needs of our key customers and providing them with the support they need to accomplish their mission." NRG's spend at the macro level is categorized into the following categories: (1) Operation and Maintenance—O & M; (2) Engineering, Procurement, and Construction—EPC; (3) the Retail Business; and (4) Indirect spend.

O & M spend covers all the expenditures needed to keep power generation plants operational. There are times when the plants are scheduled for maintenance downtime prior to summer and winter peak seasons. "While a certain portion of this buy can be centralized much of it is specific to the plant," says Haas.

Engineering, Procurement and Construction (EPC) is all about purchasing all the facilities and equipment for either new power plants or retro fitting existing plants. Previously, much of this was sourced by engineers. It is now under the direction of Mr. Haas, "The dollars are significant, we bring discipline to the process and feel our strength is managing the suppliers." Another large benefit is being able to leverage the commitment of a new plant with the volume that is purchased in replacement parts and services in the O & M portion of the buy. "We are becoming more deeply involved in the contract management piece of this also and enforcing schedules and cost changes," says Haas. NRG supply managers have also discovered that contract management requires high levels of coordination with field engineers.

The retail business is a new area for NRG and this is where purchasing is buying more services. "The buys in this area are for call-center operations, advertising, marketing, etc. We are using the strategic sourcing model to bring some discipline to this area of spend," states Haas.

The classic *indirect spend* includes both goods and services at NRG. This category includes office supplies, insurance, consultants, rental cars, hotels, and IT spend. "We try to be as efficient and cost efficient as possible in this area," says Chris. The IT spend can be a major spend category in this area when both software and hardware systems are considered.

Assimilating GenOn

"While GenOn was also an IPP, and in a way they were a microcosm of NRG, their plant buyers historically operated in a very decentralized environment," said Chris. As a result they were used to making all of the buying decisions for their individual plants. "Assimilating them into our more hybrid model will be a challenge in some cases as we will be making some of their sourcing decisions centrally," says Haas. Another large challenge is making the two companies systems compatible. "We had an ERP system called Maximo and they had SAP," stated Chris. After analyzing both systems a decision was made to adopt GenOn's SAP system. "Many of our Houston area personnel were not happy with this, but we feel once they are trained on the new system we should realize major gains in inventory and sourcing efficiencies," says Haas.

The acquisition further expanded NRG's geographic footprint into the New Jersey, Pennsylvania and Ohio areas. One way to find buying commonalities across these diverse geographic regions is to have *regional purchasing summits*. At these meetings, plant buyers huddle with the headquarters strategic sourcing groups to come up with ways to uncover and then leverage common purchases. "We want them to begin to buy more volume off of our regional and central contracts," says Haas. "Our goal is to integrate GenOn buyers into the NRG fold, but we realize it will take some time and training," says Chris. Summits are held in each region also allow the corporate staff to communicate supply chain department goals, savings goals, supplier diversity initiatives, and begin to visualize how they fit into the overall strategic sourcing goals. Chris knows the new NRG Supply Chain team will "Buy like a Champion" and enable him to execute his strategy without to many bumps along the way. "GenOn is a smaller version of NRG, but one that we need to assimilate quickly and efficiently, we don't foresee any major cultural clashes and our hope is by next year all the supply chain personnel will be operating on the same systems and integrated into our hybrid purchasing structure," says Haas.

Exhibit 5.1 shows an abbreviated version of the combined NRG- GenOn supply chain organization. It illustrates how the organizational design combines the geographic, operational, business unit and strategic sourcing groups. This provides a basis for understanding the complexities associated with designing a supply organization that is both responsive and strategic. The remainder of this Chapter will focus on the issues of supply management organizational design and the scope of purchasing jobs.

Source: Larry Giunipero interview with Chris Haas, NRG June 2013.

Exhibit 5.1	NRG Supply Chain Organization—Top Level

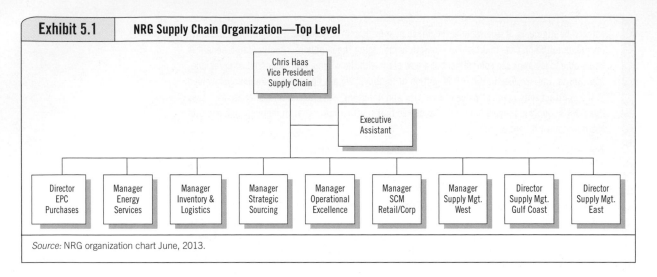

Source: NRG organization chart June, 2013.

Exhibit 5.2	P/SM Organizational Structure-Influences & Direction

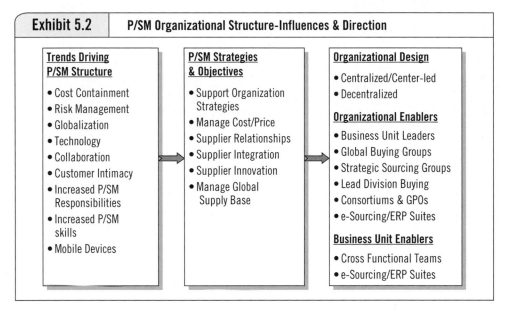

Introduction

As is evident from the NRG story, organization designs will be affected by corporate strategy such as a merger. Other factors affecting design and structure include: 1) responding to the external environmental changes, 2) the need to meet corporate goals and objectives, and 3) the firm's perception of the value of Purchasing/Supply Management (P/SM) as a value contributor to the organization's mission. Exhibit 5.2 illustrates these issues and their effect on organizational structure, and it forms the basis for our discussion of P/SM organization. Meeting corporate goals and objectives requires a flexible organizational design that is able to meet changing business conditions, yet that can take advantage of common spend categories across various business units. These are termed *center-led or hybrid forms* of buying organization. Studies have shown that a majority of P/SM organizations find this to be their organization of choice.[1]

Center-led organizations do not have the total authority that purely centralized units do; getting buy-in from various business units is implemented through many different enablers. These enablers will be discussed at both the organization and business unit level. Enablers on the organization level are mechanisms that permit coordination of common business unit spend categories at a central point. These organizational enablers have various names in different organizations. For example, Procter & Gamble uses the terms "Strategic Sourcing Groups" and "Business Unit Leaders,"[2] Meanwhile, Tyco has Global Sourcing Councils; for example, it uses four Global Travel Councils to manage its $150 million global travel spend.[3]

At both the corporate and business unit levels cross-functional teams and e-sourcing software suites combined with ERP systems provide ways to effectively gather and communicate information about the specific spend category, contract or purchase. As purchasing undertakes more of a strategic role, the organizational design should reflect this increased role and responsibility.

Organizational design refers to the process of assessing and selecting the structure and formal system of communication, division of labor, coordination, control, authority, and responsibility required to achieve organizational goals and objectives, including supply management objectives.[4] An effective (or ineffective) organizational design affects the success of purchasing and inevitably the entire organization.

P/SM Organizational Structure

The overall organizational structure of P/SM affects the: (1) location of the formal power for purchasing decisions; (2) division of purchasing tasks and activities; (3) scope of the jobs in the purchasing function; (4) patterns of communication and workflow; (5) relative job satisfaction of P/SM employees; and (6) overall effectiveness of P/SM in meeting its goals and objectives. (Exhibit 5.3)

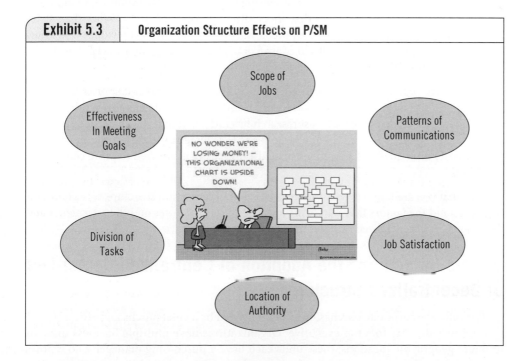

Exhibit 5.3   Organization Structure Effects on P/SM

Location of Authority Centralized or Decentralized

One of the most critical aspects of organizational design is the decision to centralize or decentralize purchasing authority. If the Chief Purchasing Officer (CPO) at corporate headquarters has the authority for the majority of the organization's purchase expenditures, then a firm maintains a **centralized** structure. If purchasing authority for the majority of purchase expenditures is at the divisional, business unit, or site level, then a firm has a more **decentralized** structure.

We can envision different purchasing organizations in terms of authority as existing on a continuum, with complete centralization at one end and complete decentralization at the other. Few organizations lie at these polar extremes; rather, most organizations lie somewhere toward one end or the other. Certain decisions or tasks, such as the evaluation and selection of suppliers that will support an entire organization, may be centrally led. The actual generation of individual purchase orders or contract releases can be located with buyers at the business unit level. Even the same item category may be subject to different authority levels. For example, a firm might centralize the authority for capital expenditure purchases over a specified dollar amount while lower-dollar capital decisions are made at a business unit level.

The one certain thing regarding organizational structure is that it will change to meet the overall strategy of the organization. In response to these changes, P/SM often evolves from a decentralized to a more centralized approach to realize savings from the more unified approach. If centralization results in bloated organizational bureaucracies and lack of both responsiveness and flexibility, there will be a push back toward more decentralized purchasing structures.

The impact of mergers, consolidations, and downsizing coupled with global competition and increased information systems visibility pushed organizations to a more centralized stance. Today's version of centralized purchasing should emphasize support, integration, and coordination of different tasks that are common across a business rather than strict control over all the activities within the purchasing process. The challenge today is to know which activities, processes, and tasks to control or coordinate centrally and which to assign to operating units.

This type of organizational structure, which combines a centralized approach for purchased items common to several business units and a decentralized approach to unique requirements, is termed **center-led.** Past research has indicated that the center-led structure was the most frequently used among large firms (54 percent using) but that it dropped in popularity after 2010 (44 percent estimated using) as firms moved to more centralized structures.[5]

Now that you are familiar with the types of P/SM organization structure, it is important to understand the factors that lead firms to adopt these structures and the advantages and disadvantages of centralized or decentralized structures.

Drivers Influencing the Adoption of Centralized/Center-Led or Decentralized Structures

Typically, the corporate purchasing group is headed by a chief purchasing officer (CPO) who reports directly to a top executive. Organizations have multiple business units in different geographic locations; these units each have a purchasing manager who reports directly to the chief executive of the facility and often has a dotted-line connection to a corporate CPO. Thus, in larger corporations with multiple locations there are local purchasing personnel plus a corporate purchasing department.

Several factors determine the degree of centralization or decentralization that an organization considers when implementing its supply structure. These interaction factors must be considered in total because decisions should not focus on just one factor. Oftentimes one of the more dominating factors will move the organization to a more hybrid form of organization. These factors include: (1) the firm's overall business strategy; (2) the similarity of purchases; (3) total purchase dollar expenditures; and (4) the overall philosophy of management.

The Firm's Overall Business Strategy

If the organization's strategy is to be responsive to individual customers in different markets, then a more decentralized approach is likely. Conversely, if the organization builds its competitive advantage by being more efficient than the competition, then a more centralized approach to supply will be favored.

Similarity of Purchases

When purchases are fairly similar across the organization, they can be combined for leverage; thus a more centralized approach is favored. Conversely, if purchases are very different across business units, an argument could be made for decentralization. This explains why Walmart's purchasing group is highly centralized, whereas in a firm like General Electric purchasing is more decentralized.

Total Purchase Dollar Expenditures

As the physical size of the purchase expenditure increases, the pressure to centralize becomes more pronounced. There is a perceived opportunity to garner savings on, and better manage, these large purchase expenditures on a centralized basis; historically, geographic dispersion resulted in more decentralized structures, whereas geographic concentration permitted centralization. However, technology has leveled the geography variable. E-sourcing software enables increased spend visibility regardless of physical location.

The Overall Philosophy of Management

If upper management is committed to operating in a decentralized mode, then oftentimes the purchasing function will be decentralized. If the management philosophy is more to control the operations from a central location, then a more centralized approach to supply will likely follow.

Advantages of Centralized/Center-led Purchasing Structures

Centralized and centrally led purchasing structures can provide some definite advantages, particularly when an organization has purchase expenditures at more than one business unit, division, or facility. The mission of the central group is to facilitate the consolidation of similar buying requirements and standardize buying processes at the various facilities. Fulfilling this mission involves many tasks, including the selection of suppliers and negotiation of purchase contracts on a corporate-wide basis. Although there are many potential benefits to centralized and centrally led purchasing, the following highlights the more important advantages.

Leverage Purchase Volumes

Historically, the primary advantage of centralized purchasing has been to achieve lower prices that are realized through combining volumes of the various business units. Leveraging the various business units spend requires undertaking spend analysis. *Spend analysis* involves using systems software to identify items purchased in common among divisions or business units. These items are then consolidated, and a purchasing strategy is developed as to how to obtain the best value for the entire organization. Depending on the items, business unit or facility purchasing personnel provide their input to the centralized sourcing team. Local supply managers also retain the authority to generate orders directly to a supplier. A firm can achieve material cost reductions by combining purchase volumes while still meeting the operating requirements of division or plant buyers.

Centrally led buying can also enhance service requirements. For example, a company-wide transportation contract results in not only cost reductions but also more uniform, consistent performance standards across all locations. General Electric established a central executive transportation committee comprised of divisional transportation managers. This committee acts as a central body to evaluate carriers for corporate transportation contracts, award corporate contracts to the best carriers, and establish uniform carrier performance standards for all divisions. By combining transportation volumes, GE realizes cost and service improvements that benefit the entire corporation.

Reduced Duplication of Purchasing Effort

Another reason for centralization is a reduction in duplication of effort. Consider an organization with 10 locations and a completely decentralized purchasing structure. This company may find itself with 10 sets of material release forms, 10 supplier quality standards, 10 supplier performance evaluation systems, 10 purchasing training manuals, and 10 different ERP systems with different communications protocols to the same suppliers. Duplication adds costs but very little in the way of unique value. It is costly and inefficient, and it creates a lack of consistency among operating units.

Coordination of Purchasing Strategies and Plans

Several strategic trends are impacting the P/SM function today. First, purchasing is becoming less of a tactical function and more of a strategic function. Second, organizations are linking corporate, operations, and purchasing plans into an overall strategic plan. These two trends require a centrally led group responsible for developing purchasing strategy at the highest levels of an organization. Without this group, an organization cannot coordinate its purchasing strategy. Chapter 6 describes the strategy development process in detail.

Coordination and Management of Company-wide Purchasing Systems

Sophisticated ERP systems, e-purchasing systems, and data warehouses are increasingly important. The design and coordination of these systems should not be the responsibility of individual units. If each division or unit is responsible for developing its own e-purchasing system or data gathering and part-numbering system, the result will be a mixture of incompatible systems.

Hewlett-Packard, historically a decentralized company, relies on a centrally led procurement group to develop and manage company-wide databases. This results in visibility to common items among HP's dozens of divisions as well as the ability to evaluate supplier performance at the corporate level. The system also supports the development of company-wide materials forecasts.

Development of Specialized Expertise

Purchasing personnel cannot become experts in all categories of spend, especially as the purchasing function becomes more complex and sophisticated. The ability to develop specialized purchasing knowledge and to support individual buying units is another advantage of a centrally led purchasing group.

Meet Corporate Goals and Manage Company-wide Change

Faced with the need to continually anticipate or adapt to changing competitive environments, firms restructure to meet these new demands. Purchasing is not spared from these structural challenges. Although no structure is perfect, there are better and worse structures at certain points in the firm's life cycle. Often top management philosophy will dictate the predominant form of organization; however, CPOs must insure that the structure of their organization best meets the overall corporate goals. To illustrate this, consider two firms with different organizational approaches to sourcing.

The first firm had a strong central focus to its major functional activities, whereas the second had over 80 highly decentralized operating companies. The decentralized company struggled to initiate change because support or compliance with corporate-wide global purchasing processes was voluntary or not a priority. The centrally focused company experienced few problems getting participants around the world to support centrally led initiatives, such as the use of company-wide suppliers selected through its global sourcing process. This example shows that managing the change process is often easier in a centrally controlled or coordinated purchasing environment.

Advantages of Decentralized Purchasing

With all the advantages that centralized purchasing appears to offer, why would any organization support a decentralized structure? Although competitive pressures encourage a more centralized approach to certain tasks, these same pressures also support the decentralized structure for other purchasing tasks. A firm can gain an advantage from placing purchasing personnel with sourcing authority directly "where the action is." So what are the potential benefits of decentralizing purchasing authority?

Speed and Responsiveness

The ability to respond quickly to user and customer requirements has always been a major justification for decentralized purchasing authority. Most purchasing professionals agree that decentralized purchasing authority often contributes to greater responsiveness and support. Organizations may resist a stronger centralized purchasing group simply because of previous negative experiences with centralized management. Some organizations fear that any centralization of authority results in slower response times.

Understanding Unique Operational Requirements

Decentralized purchasing personnel should gain a greater understanding and appreciation of local operating requirements. These personnel become familiar with the products, processes, business practices, and customers the division or plant serves. Increased familiarity allows a buyer to anticipate the needs of the departments it supports while developing solid relationships with local suppliers. This is especially important for global companies such as Colgate-Palmolive, which has facilities on every populated continent.[6]

New-Product Development Support

In organizations where new-product development occurs at the divisional or business unit level, a decentralized purchasing structure can support new-product development at earlier stages. Purchasing can support new-product development in a number of ways. First, purchasers can involve suppliers early in the product design process. They can also evaluate longer-term material product requirements, develop strategic plans, determine if substitute materials are available, and anticipate product requirements.

Ownership of Decisions Affecting Purchases

Organizations may prefer decentralized purchasing authority for an intangible reason called "ownership." In essence, ownership refers to the assumption that local personnel understand and support the objectives of the business unit or division and feel a personal commitment to a particular operation. Business unit managers are responsible for the profitability of the unit. They should have jurisdiction over purchasing because a large part of the costs and efficiency of the operation are represented in procurement.

Organizational Mechanisms to Enable Center-led Organization Design

Most organizations should benefit from a structure that retains the advantages and expertise of a centrally led purchasing group but also is responsive to the purchasing requirements of business units and individual operating locations. Implementing a center-led approach requires utilizing mechanisms that allow the central purchasing group to gain the support of the operating units. Such support is normally gained through encouraging business units to be involved through their participation in crafting an overall strategy for centralizing the particular spend category.

As previously stated, the advantage of center-led organizations is their ability to garner savings on common purchases yet allow local purchasing decisions on unique items. Given the popularity of center-led organizations, these enabling mechanisms have taken many forms and are called by many different names. Some of the more common enabling mechanisms found in center-led organizations include: (1) strategic sourcing groups; (2) lead division buying; (3) business unit leaders; (4) regional buying councils; (5) global sourcing councils; (6) corporate purchasing councils; (7) corporate steering committees; and (8) consortiums and group purchasing organizations. (Exhibit 5.4)

Strategic Sourcing Groups

In globally oriented firms these groups are often located by sourcing region. For example, P&G has strategic sourcing groups at its U.S. headquarters as well as in Switzerland, Germany, Singapore, China, and South America. The sourcing groups all use a common ERP system for spend management as well as e-purchasing providers for reverse auctions, sourcing optimization and contract management efforts.[7]

Lead Division Buying

In lead division buying, a group of operating units buys common items, typically because they produce common products. For example, one firm combined the efforts of several plants that produced transformers and distribution equipment for utility firms. The group first identified common commodities and then appointed a lead negotiator. The lead

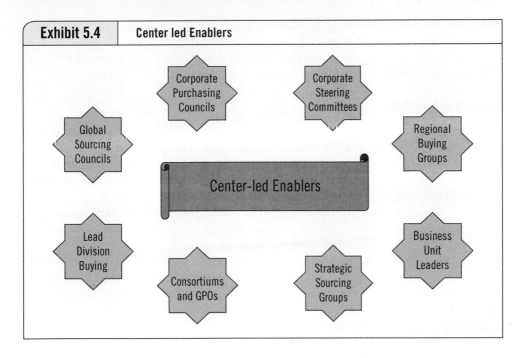

Exhibit 5.4 | Center led Enablers

negotiator was the buyer at the facility having the largest expenditure or having expertise in the commodity or item purchased.

Business Unit Leaders

Business unit leaders are P/SM employees at the corporate level who interface with the various business units cross-functional sourcing teams and provide expertise and input into the sourcing process for these units. Given their location at corporate headquarters, they have knowledge of how other business units in the company have addressed similar sourcing issues. This "business unit leader" structure also provides the Business Unit Executive with a direct contact for information and updates on critical sourcing issues. This communication with the senior executives at the business unit often facilitates "buy-in" for centralized purchasing strategies with other business units.

Global Sourcing Councils

When a key commodity is purchased by many major business units, a joint global strategy is beneficial. For example, one large diversified firm with interests in the defense and automobile parts industry has a worldwide steel-buying committee. The central corporate headquarters leads the committee, and every major steel-buying location has a representative on the committee. Demand forecasts, strategic supplier purchase plans, and negotiation strategies are established at committee meetings.

Regional Buying Groups

Regional buying groups are most advantageous where geographic concentration exists within a company. Various facilities within the particular geographic region (e.g., Pacific Northwest, the Southeast) join forces to negotiate with local and regional sources of common commodities. They generally are responsible for the purchase of large-volume items common to all facilities. They also assist individual locations that may or may not have in-house purchasing personnel to handle local purchases. Regional buying groups are useful in many service organizations (e.g., banks and insurance companies), given that they are structured on a regional basis. Regional groups also facilitate implementation of joint inventory sharing and vendor-managed inventory arrangements with suppliers.

Corporate Purchasing Councils

With smaller centrally led corporate staffs and fewer personnel at the business unit level, purchasing councils provide a way to share expertise and develop common sourcing strategies. A purchasing council is comprised of a group of buyers who purchase similar items at various facilities. A conglomerate organization had been acquiring firms at the rate of one per month for 10 years and was left with an organization of 280 factories. It was decided a center-led form of structure with purchasing councils was needed to reduce the firm's 60,000 suppliers to a manageable number. As another example, a chemical firm created an MRO council that meets as needed, and members divide up the work. The corporate representative oversees and coordinates the council members' activities. Members are given responsibility for purchases of company-wide requirements for which their division is the biggest user. National contracts are negotiated and awarded by the center-led corporate group.

Corporate Steering Committees

Steering committees are quite similar to councils except that they tend to be more advisory in nature. These committees will meet periodically and discuss strategies on the company's major purchased commodities. Steering committees will also invite large suppliers in for discussions, negotiations, performance assessments, and forecasts of purchase volumes for the coming year. They provide an opportunity for various operating-unit personnel to meet and discuss buying plans in decentralized environments.

Sourcing Snapshot

Tyco International—Using Corporate Purchasing Councils in a Decentralized Environment

Tyco International is a large conglomerate with $20 billion dollars in sales and purchases of $13 Billion annually. This spend is broken into $4 billion direct, $4 billion indirect and $5 billion intra-company. There are approximately 100,000 suppliers for direct spend and 100,000 for indirect spend.

Historically, there was no central purchasing organization at all. There were about 30 core companies that managed their purchasing separately, organizing ad hoc core teams around each purchasing area that formed as needed and then disbanded. In August 2003, Shelley Stewart, Jr., joined the company and began the process of putting some structure into its decentralized purchasing effort, finding opportunities for savings and using supply management to drive value. The first step was to pull together individual spend data from divisions throughout the company and then analyzing it for savings. Stewart's vision was to automate sourcing and other processes. This provided the information to consolidate spending and leverage the company's buying power.

An organizational design that pairs procurement professionals with leaders of the individual businesses through a *multi-council structure as* enacted. That structure has given purchasing a seat at the C-level conference table in each of the highly diversified five business units. "By partnering with the *business-unit leaders, we* focus on learning customer expectations so we can design the supply chain to meet the ultimate 'buy' expectations," says Jaime Bohnke, vice president of global supply chain. The process and systems have produced close to $2 billion dollars in savings since 2003.

Tyco takes the concept of collaboration with internal stakeholders and suppliers to new level. The key is to develop an "emotional bank account" with stakeholders, says Russ Davis, director of global sourcing, "You do it by showing results," he says.

The now structure includes *several different councils* teaming business leaders with purchasing professionals is the foundation for a more formalized council structure described below:

- At the top is the *Enterprise Supply Chain Council,* which includes vice presidents of all the businesses, and discusses common sourcing issues and sets general guide lines for purchasing at the businesses.
- Each business has its own *sourcing council*, Chaired by a sourcing professional within the business who reports to the business leader. These councils discuss sourcing issues related to the respective businesses.
- There are also separate *commodity councils,* these councils have responsibility, authority and accountability to make sourcing decisions related to the commodities on behalf of the entire company.
- *Key executives serve as champions* for certain activities.
- *Subject Experts at Corporate Purchasing* are a formal groups of domain experts called Communities of Practice (CoPs) that address process, gaps and ensure a "one-Tyco" approach to purchasing. These groups discuss business objectives, share best practices and ensure that knowledge management is institutionalized.

The future continues to bring more opportunities as Tyco is sharing its best practices pricing tools with its Marketing group and will be continuing to push for full value with suppliers.

Source: Adopted from: Congratulations to Tyco International Paul Teague. Purchasing. Boston: *Sep 17, 2009.* Vol. 138, Iss. 9; pp. 11–13.

Consortiums and Group Purchasing Organizations (GPOs)

Consortiums and Group Purchasing Organizations (GPOs) provide additional buying leverage through spend category expertise and contract management skills. A consortium is a voluntary group where buyers are in the same industry and conduct business with many of the same suppliers. These industry consortiums are legal corporations formed to facilitate the purchase of goods and services with the consortium acting as the third party. One example of a consortium is RailMarketplace.com, which is a buying consortium composed of the six largest railroads in North America. Consortiums provide additional leverage for firms and are another enabling mechanism for center-led or hybrid organizations. It is difficult to enter into a consortium without being centralized or center led since gaining maximum value is obtained by knowing the organization-wide spend for the commodities being considered for purchase. Also, government antitrust regulations prohibit the joint negotiation of items that would constitute 25 percent or more of the market.

GPOs such as Corporate United (www.corporateunited.com) combine spend from companies in different industries to leverage the best price for their clients. GPOs such as Corporate United utilize collaborative efforts of member firms to enhance spend management, reduce costs, and allow sharing of best practices through their member network. According to their website, Corporate United is comprised of more than 200 member companies, spanning every industry sector and representing over \$50 billion in aggregated spend. Corporate United helped a firm in the graphics industry solve their sourcing of temporary workers. With an annual staffing provider spend of \$4 million and multiple suppliers, the company wanted to control contingent workforce costs and achieve related process efficiencies. Current suppliers were having difficulty filling positions, and those they were able to fill had a high turnover rate. To make matters worse, the company was experiencing worksite safety and theft issues, requiring them to hire a third-party security guard to protect their employees and property. Using Corporate United's workforce solutions provider contract, the graphics firm not only received reliable employees, but also realized a 3 percent cost reduction.[8]

Sourcing Snapshot

RailMarketplace.com: Adding Value in Supply

The six largest railroads in North America (Class 1) are unique in their ability to efficiently move goods across the continent. But, they are also unique in that they have been one of the few industries in North America to have continued success with a formal buying consortium to leverage their spend.

A buying consortium is a group or association formed to jointly purchase goods and services. Consortiums are most typically made up of buyers from companies within the same industry and conduct business with many of the same suppliers. These industry consortiums are legal corporations formed to facilitate the purchase of goods and services with the consortium acting as the third party. Consortiums must strictly abide by antitrust regulations.

RailMarketplace.com (RMP) was founded in January 2001 to streamline the rail industry supply chain. The organization generates revenues from a combination of membership subscriptions and fees that are charged for sourcing services on a transaction basis. Services include conducting leveraged volume purchase projects, reverse auctions, sales of surplus materials, and managing purchase transactions. Value is also provided by non-contracting activities such as: (1) rationalizing specifications; (2) benchmarking common practices; and (3) analyzing global supply markets. The Chief Procurement Officers (CPO's) from all six Class 1 Railroads serve as board members for RMP. And, staff members from each organization, called the "core team," coordinate leadership and work to be performed on specific sourcing projects.

RMP has focused its sourcing efforts mainly on the indirect spend for the railroads. As such, contracts have been negotiated in several areas including: Office Supplies, Safety Supplies, Bottled Water, Vehicle Tires, Equipment Rentals, Computer Equipment, and Portable and Mobile Radios. Michael O'Malley, CPO for CSX Transportation states that while gaining consensus among the six firms is not always easy, the results are satisfying. "In order to achieve success on a sourcing project, compromise is necessary to gain 'social capital' for the next project," says O'Malley.

Although the heightened expectations heaped on all e-businesses at the beginning of the decade have not been fulfilled, RMP has maintained steady progress because of the ongoing commitment of the purchasing leadership at the Class 1 Railroads. It has enabled process and benchmarking reviews as well as joint contracts with suppliers. "All these value adders allow management to continue allocating manpower to RMP initiatives," states Frank Carbone Assistant Vice President of Purchasing and Materials-Mechanical and the core team representative at RMP for CSX. The other five railroads involved in the consortium are Burlington Northern Santa Fe, Canadian National, Canadian Pacific Norfolk Southern, and Union Pacific.

Source: Giunipero, L. Interview with Frank Carbone, CSX Transportation, June 2013.

Purchasing's Position within the Organizational Structure

A formal organizational structure serves several purposes that were mentioned at the beginning of the chapter. First, it details the assignment of work along with the authority that accompanies those responsibilities. Second, a formal structure helps define how a firm communicates and integrates decision making across the groups comprising the organization (a process also referred to as coordination).[9]

These job details then become a template for the various job descriptions. Job descriptions form the basis for the scope of the purchasing job, which will be discussed later. Purchasing's position or placement in an organizational structure is important since it usually indicates *organizational status* and *influence*. A function whose highest responsible executive is a manager (or even several managers) lacks the organizational importance of a function whose highest responsible executive is a senior vice president. In some organizations, the highest purchasing professional's reporting status is on a par with other major functions. In others, we have to search before finding an individual executive responsible for purchasing. Past research supported the fact that purchasing is gaining more visibility in the corporate hierarchy. The study also found that fewer chief purchasing officers (CPOs) had purchasing only backgrounds and that the CPO's term was shorter. The results of a study covering 16 years indicated that in both manufacturing and services, CPOs have greater responsibilities, report higher in the organization, and carry more significant titles than their predecessors. Additional research by these authors on first-time CPO appointments indicated that changes in corporate strategy resulted in 80 percent of first-time CPO appointments, that the CEO had a major say in who was to be selected as the CPO as well as to whom the person reported in the corporate hierarchy.[10] This section presents some of the factors influencing purchasing's position or placement in the formal organizational structure.

To Whom Does Purchasing/Supply Management Report?

A clear trend during the last 30 years is that the level of executive to whom P/SM reports has increased. Bloom and Nardone reported that "during the 1950s and early 1960s, a high percentage of the purchasing departments reported in a second-level capacity to the functional managers, most commonly production and operations."[11]

Exhibit 5.5 illustrates three possible placements of purchasing in the organizational hierarchy. In (a), purchasing is an upper-level function reporting directly to the executive vice president. In (b), purchasing is a mid-level function reporting to an executive, one level below the executive vice president, which is a common reporting level today. In (c), purchasing is a lower level function, two reporting levels from the executive vice president. In general, the higher purchasing is in the corporate structure, the greater the role it plays in supporting organizational objectives.

Factors Affecting Purchasing's Position in the Organizational Hierarchy

History

Perhaps the most important factor contributing to purchasing's position in the organizational hierarchy is history. For established organizations, early purchasing history emphasized the gradual development of the policies and procedures defining proper purchasing

Exhibit 5.5 | Purchasing at Different Organizational Levels

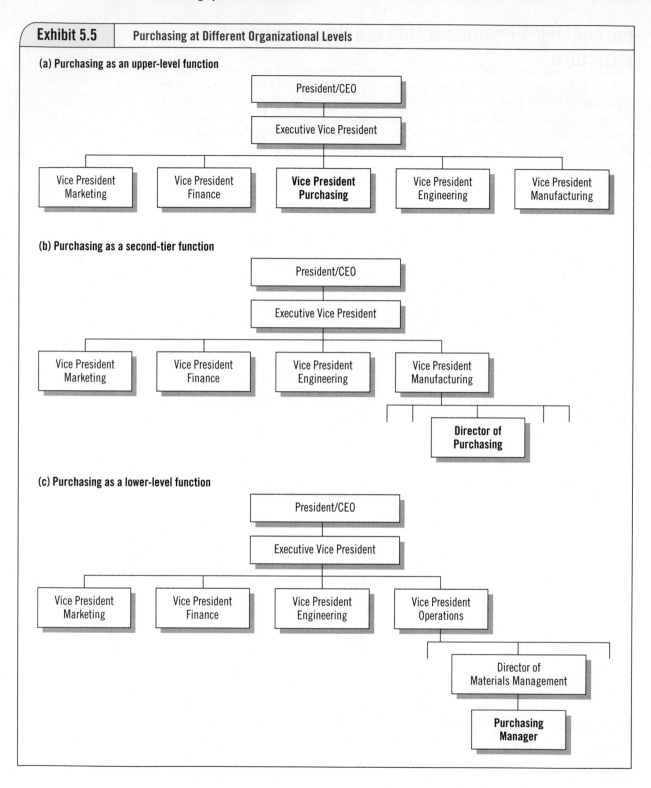

(a) Purchasing as an upper-level function

President/CEO

Executive Vice President

| Vice President Marketing | Vice President Finance | **Vice President Purchasing** | Vice President Engineering | Vice President Manufacturing |

(b) Purchasing as a second-tier function

President/CEO

Executive Vice President

| Vice President Marketing | Vice President Finance | Vice President Engineering | Vice President Manufacturing |

Director of Purchasing

(c) Purchasing as a lower-level function

President/CEO

Executive Vice President

| Vice President Marketing | Vice President Finance | Vice President Engineering | Vice President Operations |

Director of Materials Management

Purchasing Manager

from an operational perspective. Since purchasing is now receiving greater attention from executive management. The movement toward a more strategic role for P/SM is favorable for the CPO obtaining higher visibility in the corporate structure.

Impact on Organizational Performance

Moving to adopt a more strategic role means that P/SM has a more direct impact on their organization's competitiveness. P/SM's increased role as a driver of stakeholder value requires a higher position in the organizational hierarchy. If the P/SM function is to have a direct input into the corporation's strategic plans, it needs high level visibility.

The Founder's Philosophy

The philosophy of the founder (particularly when the founder still plays an active role) exerts a strong influence on an organization's formal design. This is especially true in high-technology organizations started during the last 25 years. If the founder is marketing oriented, the firm usually has a strong marketing perspective. If the founder is engineering oriented, the emphasis is usually on product and process development. The founder of Herman Miller, Inc., a producer of industrial office furniture, believed that organizations should be the "stewards" of the environment. Consequently, the purchasing department at Herman Miller emphasizes environmental responsibility in its sourcing practices.

Type of Industry

Some industries are not as driven by materials or external technological change as others. The need to constantly innovate and improve often places materials-related activities at a higher level compared with mature industries or those who traditionally treated purchasing as a lower-level function. In rapidly changing industries or those where purchased goods and services comprise a larger portion of product or service costs, management usually recognizes the need to place purchasing in a higher position within the organizational hierarchy.

Total Spend on Goods and Services

Companies such as John Deere, Honda, and Walmart spend 60 to 70 percent of their sales dollars on purchased goods and services. In the computer and telecommunications industries, companies such as Dell, Solectron, IBM, Cisco, and Hewlett-Packard, rely on suppliers for parts as well as new technology—which means that purchasing plays a critical role. A service organization spending 10 to 20 percent of its sales dollar for purchased goods and services will, on average, view purchasing differently compared with a firm spending over 60 percent.

Type of Purchased Materials and Services

The type of purchased materials affects organizational position. The purchase of routine items is quite different from the purchase of leading-edge high technology. Purchasing departments confronted with fast-paced change usually have closer contact with other functional groups and a higher organizational reporting level. When P/SM achieves a higher-level position it is better able to make an impact on managing and driving "non-traditional" spend categories such as advertising, travel, consultants, and software. Success stories that illustrate the savings realized through a disciplined sourcing process are numerous in the services area.

Scope of the Purchasing/Supply Management Job Function

The scope of P/SM jobs in larger organizations can be grouped under four major areas: (1) sourcing, negotiation, and contract management; (2) market intelligence and research; (3) operational support and follow-up; and (4) administration and data management. The specific job scope given to an individual purchaser will vary, depending on the overall structure. Within a highly centralized organization, the individual's job scope may be limited to one or two of these categories, whereas those in decentralized organizations will quite likely perform all four.

Sourcing, Negotiation, and Contract Management

This task involves identifying company spend and matching it to the best potential suppliers, negotiating with selected suppliers, and finally managing the contract. Buyers are usually responsible to purchase specific types of item(s), which may be grouped into commodities or services categories. For example, plastic injected parts are an example of a purchase commodity. Trash removal and security are examples of services. Other buyers may specialize in raw materials and are responsible for steel, copper, packaging supplies, and so on. Regardless of the commodity or service, higher-dollar items will involve extensive negotiations with suppliers. Very often, buyers will work in teams that have responsibility for negotiating contracts for the entire organization.

Market Intelligence and Research

Market intelligence involves a systematic monitoring of the supply environment to assure a continual economic supply of goods and services. An effective market intelligence program enables an organization to develop more accurate long-range materials forecasts, pinpoint commodities for value analysis, better assess supplier capabilities, and cost structures. Although some of these specialized tasks are the responsibility of individual buyers, more and more organizations recognize the benefit of having specialized research personnel. The development of product and material plans requires detailed and accurate research.

Operational Support and Follow-Up

This group includes the activities supporting the day-to-day operations of the purchasing or materials function. Expediters are part of this group. The preparation and transfer of material releases to suppliers is also part of the operational support process. Many of the tasks that qualify as operational support are being streamlined or automated, especially with the use of e-purchasing systems As a result, the number of purchasing personnel committed to these types of tasks is declining.

Administration and Data Management

There has been a surge in the amount of data available to P/SM. Reductions in the cost of data storage coupled with access to mobile technologies and databases requires an active data management system. Often in smaller and midsized businesses this data is stored on the "cloud" as opposed to company servers since it eliminates the cost of purchasing servers and IT support. Historically, this group is responsible for developing the policies and procedures that purchasing personnel follow, administering and maintaining the purchasing information system and database, determining required staffing levels, developing department plans, organizing training and seminars for buyers, and developing measurement systems to evaluate purchasing performance.

In many organizations the administration activity is the responsibility of the supply manager. He/she must make sure the purchasing department runs efficiently and meets its targeted goals within budget, and fulfills its responsibilities to both internal and external customers.

Purchasing/Supply Management Job Tasks

Today's purchasing department does much more than the traditional buying of materials, parts, and services. The job tasks assigned to purchasing are expanding to reflect the growing importance of purchasing and the performance contribution of suppliers. The following responsibilities are commonly performed tasks performed by a modern purchasing group. Not all departments perform every one of these tasks.

Buying

By definition, a primary responsibility of the purchasing function involves buying—a broad term describing the purchase of raw materials, components, finished goods, or services from suppliers, some of whom can be another operating unit within the organization. The purchase can be a one-time requirement or the release for materials against an established purchase order. The buying process requires supplier evaluation, negotiation, and selection.

Expediting

Expediting is the process of personally or electronically contacting suppliers to determine the status of past-due or near-past-due shipments. In smaller organizations, expediting is often part of the purchasing function. In larger organizations, expediters often report to a separate materials control department. The actual expediting process rarely provides new value within the purchasing process. Unfortunately, expediters are an accepted overhead cost at some organizations.

Progressive organizations recognize that a need for expediters indicates that suppliers are not performing as required, or that suppliers are not receiving realistic or stable material release schedules. It is also possible that the buying organization is making frequent and demanding schedule changes. To prevent this situation, more companies are reducing their use of expediting by developing realistic material release schedules and doing business with suppliers capable of meeting material shipment schedules.

Increasingly, purchasing is becoming less involved with expediting and inventory control. The increased sophistication and usability of enterprise systems such as ERP allow many of the traditional expediting and inventory control decisions to be put into the hands of users. Chapter 18 provides in-depth coverage of ERP systems.

Inventory Control

The inventory control function monitors the day-to-day management of purchased and in-process inventory at each using location. This activity often relies on sophisticated equations or algorithms to facilitate balancing the product or service demand requirements with the required purchase inputs for each location. In many larger companies, the individual responsible for sourcing an item is often not responsible for the maintenance or routine release of purchase requirements.

Transportation

The U.S. government deregulated transportation services in the early 1980s. Since that time, purchasing has taken an active role in the evaluation, negotiation, and final selection of transportation services and carriers. Transportation is a highly specialized activity with its own set of requirements. Chapter 17 discusses the purchase of transportation services.

Insourcing/Outsourcing

Purchasing often analyzes whether a new or existing purchase requirement should be internally or externally sourced. Certain items or services, such as standard or routine items, do not require insourcing/outsourcing evaluations. For other items, however, the analysis takes on strategic importance involving more than simple cost comparisons. Purchasing's role in make-or-buy analyses is an important one. Regarding outsourcing, purchasing must identify whether qualified suppliers exist in the marketplace. Further requirements may include supplier visits, negotiation, and monitoring supplier performance.

Value Analysis

Value analysis, a continuous improvement methodology developed by Larry Miles at General Electric during the late 1940s, is the organized study of an item's function as it relates to value and cost. Value represents the relationship between function and cost. The objective of value analysis is to enhance value by reducing the cost of a good or service without sacrificing quality, enhancing functionality without increasing cost, or providing greater functionality to the user above and beyond any increase in cost. Purchasing actively involves itself with value analysis through the study of materials, specifications, and suppliers. Chapter 12 discusses this methodology further.

Purchasing Research/Materials Forecasting

Purchasing often has responsibility for anticipating short- and long-term changes in material and supply markets. Research and forecasting are critical for any organization that sources raw materials or components. Detailed short- and long-term purchasing plans are required for items subject to technological, economic, or political change. These plans should include the historical and projected future usage of the purchased item, purchase objectives, assessment of the supply market, cost/price analysis, supplier evaluation, and the recommended procurement strategy.

Supply Management

As discussed in Chapter 1, supply management is a progressive approach to managing the supply base that differs from a traditional arm's-length or adversarial approach with sellers. It requires purchasing professionals to work directly with those suppliers that are capable of providing superior performance to the buyer.

Supply management involves purchasing, engineering, supplier quality assurance, the supplier, and other related functions working together to further mutual goals. Instead of adversarial relationships, supply management features closer relationships with specially selected suppliers. It involves frequent help to suppliers in exchange for dramatic and continuous performance improvements, including steady price reductions.

Other Responsibilities

Purchasing can also assume a variety of other responsibilities such as receiving and warehousing, managing company travel arrangements, production planning and control, commodity futures trading, global transportation and materials management, economic forecasting, and subcontracting.

Separating Strategic and Operational Purchasing

Managing day-to-day operations is quite different from managing longer-term responsibilities. Can the personnel who must manage the uninterrupted flow of materials also find time to practice strategic supply management? Do these personnel even have the right skills to shift from operational to strategic purchasing? When pressed for time, strategic responsibilities take second place to the immediate needs presented by operational issues. Strategic responsibilities lack the immediacy of tactical duties and, as a result, are often ignored.

One way to ensure that both types of assignments receive adequate attention is to separate the staff according to tactical and strategic job assignments. Separation does not mean one group or area is more important than another. Both types of assignments are important and require specialized attention. Often the group responsible for strategic activities is part of a centrally led sourcing group at a headquarters or regional location. The operational purchasing group is often located at a buying center, site, or plant.

Exhibit 5.6 highlights the characteristics of tactical and strategic buying. Both positions require buyers to work closely with internal groups while displaying the ability to think creatively. The skills required for a strategic focus, however, will be different from the skills required for an operational focus. The separation of professional duties will become increasingly common as a means to satisfy operational and strategic performance objectives.

Using Teams as Part of the Organizational Structure

We have witnessed an increased reliance on teams over the last 25 years. In purchasing and supply chain management, teams are used to evaluate and select suppliers, develop global commodity strategies, perform demand and supply planning, and carry out supplier development activities.

Teams are a group of two or more organizational members who are mutually accountable for achieving a common goal.[12] **Cross-functional teams** are composed of members from several functions in the organization. Purchasing can be a leader or member within the various cross-functional teams in the organization. Used under the right conditions, teams provide a number of benefits to organizations that include: (1) synergies gained from a wider range of knowledge through collaboration; (2) better decision making; (3) creation of a more involved workforce; and (4) facilitation of improved products and services.

Not all observers agree that the use of teams is a guarantee of greater effectiveness, however. They can waste the time and energy of members, enforce lower performance norms, create destructive conflict within and between teams, and make notoriously bad decisions. Teams can also exploit, stress, and frustrate members—sometimes all at the same time.[13]

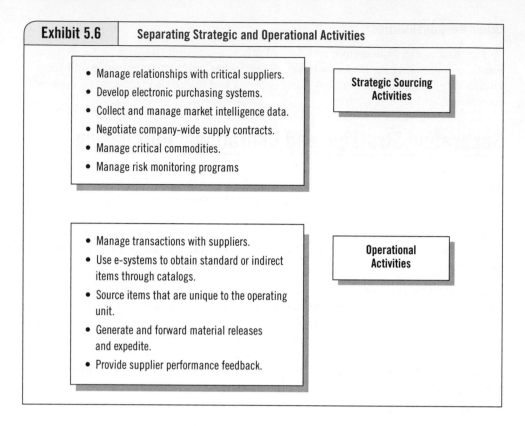

Exhibit 5.6 | **Separating Strategic and Operational Activities**

- Manage relationships with critical suppliers.
- Develop electronic purchasing systems.
- Collect and manage market intelligence data.
- Negotiate company-wide supply contracts.
- Manage critical commodities.
- Manage risk monitoring programs

Strategic Sourcing Activities

- Manage transactions with suppliers.
- Use e-systems to obtain standard or indirect items through catalogs.
- Source items that are unique to the operating unit.
- Generate and forward material releases and expedite.
- Provide supplier performance feedback.

Operational Activities

If we believe that making teams a major part of the formal organizational structure does not guarantee success, then the challenge becomes one of creating an environment where teams will be successful. Much of the success or failure of teams rests on an organization's ability to ask the right questions about using teams. Exhibit 5.7 identifies the kinds of questions that supply managers should ask when they are planning to use teams.

Although most supply managers endorse the use of teams, the reality is that there are major hurdles or challenges that can affect how well an organization uses them. First, many organizations form teams using functional group employees. In essence they are assigned to teams as *part-time members* since they are rewarded for completing their functional duties. In some organizations the rewards are through the team concept and this team assignment(s) means employees are full-time members of the team(s). Most teams within purchasing and supply chain management are staffed using the part-time member philosophy as stated above. Organizations that rely on part-time teams typically maintain their existing functional structure while adding additional team-related duties. It can be difficult to obtain commitment from members who face conflicting demands on their time.

A second hurdle that still confronts too many organizations is a *failure to recognize and reward the effort* team members put forth toward their assignments. In fact, many recognition and reward systems today encourage members not to participate on teams. Members who receive inadequate recognition for their efforts will likely direct their energy toward those areas that are recognized and rewarded. Participation may present a personal risk and create conflict once members realize that supporting a team takes time away from activities that are recognized and rewarded. Unfortunately, many companies still do not grasp the importance of this issue.

A third hurdle relates to *our individualistic national culture*. It is simply not our nature, except perhaps for sporting events, to be group or team focused, especially when compared to other countries. In his study of culture, Hofstede concluded that the United States was the most individualistic nation of all those studied.[14] Although some cultures place group needs above individual needs, this is usually not the case within the United States. Team participants may perceive that group assignments will stifle individual creativity and personal recognition. We value individualism and find that a shift away from it is often uncomfortable and threatening.

Although these barriers are important, they certainly do not represent an exhaustive list of what can affect purchasing and supply chain teams. In fact, a host of barriers may affect a specific team at a given point in time. Supply leaders must understand how to use this demanding but often difficult way to perform work.

Exhibit 5.7	Work Team Planning Guide

Identify Appropriate Team Assignments

Do assignments justify the use of teams?

Has the proper team model been identified (i.e., part-time versus full-time assignments)?

Does executive and functional management support the use of a team?

Form Work Team and Select Qualified Members and Leader

Have core versus as-needed members been identified?

Do members have the proper skills, time, and commitment to support the team?

Have team sponsors identified and selected a qualified team leader?

Are customers or suppliers part of the team if required?

Do members understand their formal team roles?

Determine Member Training Requirements

Have team member training requirements been assessed?

Is required training available on a timely basis?

Identify Resource Requirements

Are resources provided or available to support the team's task?

Determine Team Authority Levels

Have team authority levels for the team been determined?

Have team authority levels been communicated across the organization?

Establish Team Performance Goals

Has the team established objective performance goals?

Determine How to Measure and Reward Participation and Performance

Are approaches and systems in place that assess team performance and member contribution?

Are there reporting linkages to team or executive sponsors?

Is team performance effectively linked to performance reward systems?

Develop Team Charters

Has a formal charter been developed that details team mission, tasks, broad objectives, and so forth? Has the charter been communicated across the organization?

Supply Chain Management Structure

The need to coordinate and share information across organizations and functional groups has resulted in the development of higher-level positions designed to oversee various supply chain activities. Chapter 1 identifies the activities that fall under the supply chain umbrella.

A structure that coordinates the diverse activities within a supply chain contrasts greatly with one where separate supply chain groups or activities report to different executive managers. The latter model can result in each function or activity pursuing conflicting organizational goals and objectives. Organizing as an integrated supply chain structure requires traditionally separate activities to report to an executive responsible for coordinating the flow of goods, services, and information from supplier through customer. Exhibit 5.8 illustrates one possible way to structure a supply chain management organization under one executive.

Future Trends in Organizational Design

A major debate today continues to be about determining the best organizational structure, including the structure for purchasing and integrated supply chain management. The availability of mobile devices permit users to access data on an anytime anywhere basis. This has had a major impact on where work is performed and will affect how firms chose to build their formal organizational structures.

The trend today is to move away from a **vertical focus**, where work and information are managed up and down within functional groups, toward a **horizontal focus**, where work and information are managed across groups and between organizations. The horizontal organization largely eliminates hierarchy and functional or departmental boundaries. Although there will always be a need for functional groups, increasingly parts of the organization will work together horizontally in teams or groups to perform core processes. The use of cross-functional teams in managing parts of the P/SM process is an example of taking a horizontal approach.

We have also witnessed a shift over from a commodity focus to one that is end-item or *process focused*. A shift has occurred toward organizing around higher level end items or subassemblies versus purchasing parts and components.

The ideal procurement organizational model future should have certain broad features. These include *flatter hierarchies* for faster decision making and freer flow of ideas along with joint ventures and alliances with key supply chain members. Increased use of *center-led structures* that enable consolidation of common purchases coupled with decentralization of unique and transactional buying activities should provide the best that centralization and decentralization have to offer.

Rotation of managers across business units and functional groups will support the development of broad knowledge and expertise. This rotation may include **co-location** of purchasing personnel with internal customers that will provide lowered costs and improved service to internal customers. Additionally, key suppliers technical personnel will periodically co-locate in the buyer's facility to reduce the new-product development time to market cycle.

The supply chain organization of the future will rely much more on *systems capability* to enable enhanced collaboration and further improve the efficient and effective management of the flow of goods information and processes from suppliers to final customers. These technology-enabled supply chains will permit several advantages. Perhaps one of the greatest advantages will be viewing the process as circular rather than linear. This feature will allow all members, regardless of their position in the supply chain, to access inventory levels, orders, due dates, and so forth to improve their internal operations as well as customer

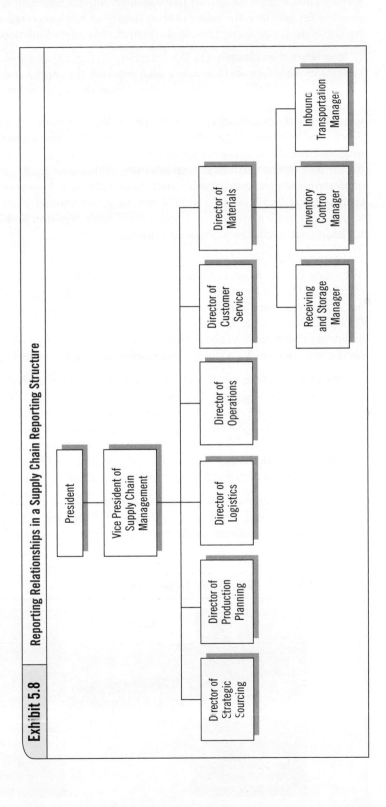

Exhibit 5.8   Reporting Relationships in a Supply Chain Reporting Structure

service. Thus, a final customer will have visibility into the shipment activity of a key supplier. Another key activity is the ability to bring together a firm's expertise in the form of a virtual team to address a problem, provide alternatives, recommend solutions, and then disband.

Open information channels via the Internet, intranets, and information technology systems make information widely available across the supply chain. This availability of information will help coordinate activities across the organizational chart. Traditionally, P/SM expanded their influence in the organizational network through personal contact with users in the organization. However, newer, Internet-based information channels allow purchasers to increase their influence by electronically sharing their knowledge across the organization. These networks are virtual and do not require physical contact. The term for the new virtual network is **social networking**. Although e-mail is still the most prevalent communication technology, organizations are increasingly relying on website providers such as LinkedIn, Facebook, and Twitter. Blogs are another form of social networking where individuals with similar interests can discuss common problems. (See Chapter 18 for additional discussion of social networking.)

The impact of social networking is very evident at the end consumer level. The influx of discussion forums, blogs, social networking sites, and review portals on the Internet is creating an increase in consumer reliance on User Generated Content (UGC) in making product and service purchase decisions. According to a recent study conducted by Research Group, 83 percent of consumers say it would be important to read user-generated content before making a decision about banking or other financial services. Another study indicated consumers rate UGC three times more influential than television advertising.[15]

One example of the use of social networking in P/SM is LinkedIn. LinkedIn is a social networking site for business professionals where members can develop a network of contacts who have similar interests. One section of LinkedIn provides access to industry experts via online groups. The Global Sourcing Council on LinkedIn provides members with a network of experts who perform global sourcing. The impact of these social networks on organizations is yet to be determined, but it is not hard to visualize with the free flow of, and immediate access to, information that it will permit flatter and more flexible organizational structures.

Thriving in an ever-changing, fast-paced environment requires new kinds of leadership and will result in newer organizational designs. A design with the right features can help a company meet the challenges of the twenty-first century (see Exhibit 5.9).

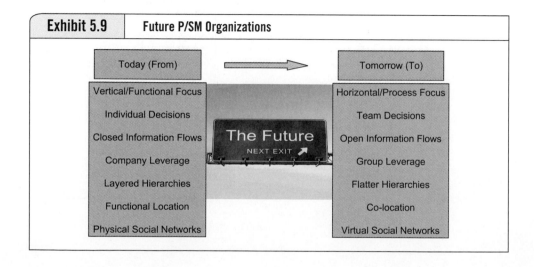

Exhibit 5.9   Future P/SM Organizations

Today (From)		Tomorrow (To)
Vertical/Functional Focus		Horizontal/Process Focus
Individual Decisions		Team Decisions
Closed Information Flows	The Future NEXT EXIT	Open Information Flows
Company Leverage		Group Leverage
Layered Hierarchies		Flatter Hierarchies
Functional Location		Co-location
Physical Social Networks		Virtual Social Networks

Sourcing Snapshot

Johnson & Johnson Uses Organizational Design to Integrate Marketing and Purchasing

Johnson & Johnson, a global company known for high-quality products and brands, is showing how the creative use of organizational design can promote integration between some important supply chain groups. Supply management professionals, who are part of the support activity called procurement, have a wide range of internal customers. One internal customer group is marketing, which is responsible for activities that could benefit from the involvement of professional supply managers.

Executive managers have assigned a sourcing manager to J&J's corporate marketing and promotion strategy team to support their efforts when developing contracts. Examples of service areas where the marketing team requires contract support include printing, convention and meeting space, media purchases, promotional displays and tradeshows, marketing research, and advertising and promotion. For example, sourcing involvement resulted in a reduction of company-wide printing suppliers from 600 to 5.

By being part of the marketing strategy team, the sourcing professional adds value to the marketing and promotion process. She verifies that every unit within the corporation is charged the same best rate from suppliers and reserves the right to audit advertising "job jackets" and costs. She controls the buying of advertising and media support while working to gain mostfavored-customer status with media suppliers. In short, she assumes a major part of the contracting process that marketing simply does not want. This allows marketing professionals to focus on those areas where they can make the greatest contribution. Although this sourcing manager currently supports only U.S. marketing, her business plan calls for providing support to worldwide marketing units over the next several years.

Source: Company interviews.

Good Practice Example   *Boston Scientific Corporation Transforms Sourcing via Center-led Structure*

When a patient learns he or she needs a procedure to diagnose or treat a condition, one of the more comforting phrases to hear from a doctor is that the procedure will be "minimally invasive." Thanks to advances in science and medicine, small catheters and stents are commonly used where open surgery was once the only medical option. Patients can recover faster, with less pain, and the costs are lower overall. Minimally invasive medicine is a platform for ongoing innovation, and companies like Boston Scientific Corporation in Natick, Massachusetts, are at the forefront of developing some of the most cutting-edge devices available to physicians around the world today.

The business of helping people live longer, healthier lives is not taken lightly in any regard. Suppliers to Boston Scientific must guarantee extremely high quality and delivery, because the smallest imperfection or delay could be life-threatening. For this reason, the entire supply chain depends on efficiency and quality. The global indirect sourcing and procurement (GISP) organization at Boston Scientific is responsible for all strategic and tactical procurement of indirect materials and services, using a center-led operating model to organize sourcing around the world. Leading this team is Karen Weinstein, vice president, global facilities and security, real estate and indirect sourcing and procurement.

Weinstein, who has been with Boston Scientific for nearly 12 years, was involved in a 2010 directive from the CEO to "optimize the company," which translated into the creation of a new indirect organization that would leverage best practices, find bottom-line savings, and improve processes. At the time, sourcing and procurement were centrally influenced. Indirect procurement was performed at all the different locations, while sourcing was performed in a "hub and spoke model," with eight different commodity managers handling a variety of commodities, from travel, to facilities, to legal and clinical services across multiple Boston Scientific locations. Each manufacturing site had a vertical operating structure, with buyers reporting to purchasing managers, who, in turn, reported to material directors.

The scattered operations meant, among other things, that procurement best practices were not communicated or leveraged on a broad basis, visibility into spend was fragmented and full value from suppliers was not being realized. For instance, Guidant Corporation, a manufacturer of cardiac medical equipment, acquired by Boston Scientific in 2006, operated with its own category managers as an independent indirect organization. Integrating Guidant into Boston Scientific's overall business model helped encourage the dramatic reorganization, says Weinstein. "We understood that standardizing our processes would, and will, help improve services to the business by maximizing our capacity and capability. This reorganization was a step toward building a culture that will serve us well into the future."

She adds that taking a fresh look at the company's procurement strategies presented opportunities to maximize working capital, as well. "After the reorganization, we extended offers to our suppliers to receive their payments more promptly than our standard payment terms in exchange for a prompt payment discount," she says. This was a win-win situation, with suppliers being paid sooner and Boston Scientific receiving a discount.

Conducting a Global Transformation

Transitioning from a decentralized to a center-led operating model is no simple endeavor, and Weinstein and the newly created GISP team approached this task from the ground up. First, the center-led operating model was broken into five regions around the globe. Each region consists of at least three Boston Scientific sites managed by one regional manager. The regional managers report to the director of procurement, who is responsible for global indirect sourcing activities. "The regional manager also has a 'strong dotted line' connecting him or her to the director of sourcing, who is responsible for cost savings goals and supplier management," explains Weinstein.

Once the regional structure was developed, the corporate indirect senior leadership team went on a worldwide tour to each site, assessing processes, management structures, policies, systems, personnel, and performance. They identified gaps, redundancies, and opportunities for procurement to play a significant role in the company. Staff was transferred or hired accordingly, and a communication plan was created to ensure all stakeholders, from the buyer to executive levels, were kept up-to-date with all the changes. Other changes, such as the restructuring of a p-card program to streamline and monitor its use, as well as new cascading metrics to measure performance globally, regionally, and by site, were all rolled out systematically and with as much transparency to stakeholders as possible.

Weinstein says three innovative solutions were the keys to developing a leaner, more flexible and effective organization, while enabling a smooth transition:

1. **A comprehensive resource activity allocation model.** The team created a comprehensive tool—the resource activity allocation model—to identify, assess, and allocate resources by region, site, and procurement/sourcing activities. One hurdle to overcome, however, was the management of attrition. As with most corporate reorganizations, attrition is

an expected issue. In this case, the attrition rate throughout the transformation was approximately 33 percent. A communication plan was put in place that included frequent updates from the executive level downward. This involved face-to-face meetings with site vice presidents, as well as monthly meetings with site material directors and weekly meetings with human resources to streamline the hiring process and facilitate the communication of organizational changes to all stakeholders.

2. **Lean principles.** Prior to the transformation, there was limited sharing of best practices across the organization, with many procurement areas focused on their own businesses and the avoidance of looking across to other sites for leveraged opportunities. Once the resource activity allocation model was in place, redundancies or gaps in the procurement activities at each site were eliminated and lean practices put into place.

3. **A global resource optimization model.** This model was developed to flex transactional resources within the Boston Scientific procurement network to optimize capacity. For example, at the start of the transition, the team found that it took 7.7 days to route a purchase request through approval and PO creation. Improvement was made to the PO process by implementing automated workflows and resource optimization, which improved efficiency by 30 percent. Gains in efficiency were used to bring more spend under control and allocate resources to other value-add areas. "This analytical tool allows us to see opportunities across staffing in procurement to maximize our effectiveness," explains Weinstein. "It gives us more strategic visibility than we would have leveraged using a more tactical execution through individual sites."

Global Indirect Summit

The GISP team also hosted a global face-to-face Indirect Summit to showcase best practices, report on prior-year achievements and develop strategic goals and objectives for the coming year. Rewards and recognition are important to keep momentum going and encourage ongoing improvement, not only among Boston Scientific procurement team members but suppliers, as well. An annual Indirect Supplier Management Awards program was launched in 2011, as an opportunity to reward top performers.

In the future, several new metrics will be added to measure integration performance. Weinstein says there are plans to measure areas such as invoice inaccuracy, spend, global cycle time and capacity utilization, among others. The point is not to simply measure numbers in a static environment, she says. "It's about using analytics intelligently to best direct activities, today and going forward."

A Hardworking Team of Professionals

None of this would have been possible without the work of a highly dedicated team of supply management and procurement professionals, says Weinstein. "We're blessed with a highly motivated team that knows the value of working in a team environment, and can play off the strengths of one another, spark open and honest dialogues throughout the organization and challenge one another," she says. "By achieving bottom-line savings and reducing risk, these efforts showcased the achievements of indirect procurement and sourcing to the C-suite."

Being competitive in the future requires objectivity as well as a way to uncover any talent gaps and mobilize to close those gaps in an efficient, timely manner. "We must assess current capabilities rigorously and dispassionately; too frequently, we try to build the future around today's players and end up short. Include a process to discover talent in the organizational hinterlands." "Talent acquisition requires serious, strategic attention to skill-set needs over the next two or three strategic time horizons," she says.

Overall, the goal for the global indirect sourcing and procurement team comes down to the mission of Boston Scientific Corporation: to improve the quality of patient care and productivity of health-care delivery. Weinstein feels honored to work with a team devoted to delivering results, now and in the future. "We need to continually challenge ourselves to seek opportunities in the unconventional areas of spend, to search the white space for value improvement," she says. "The wonderful thing is that any dollars we save can be reallocated toward further investment in R&D to create new treatment modalities to improve the quality of patient care."

Source: Adopted from Lisa Arnseth, "The Heart of a Healthy Supply Chain," *Inside Supply Management*® Vol. 23, No. 7, September 2012, pages 16–18.

CONCLUSION

Having a properly designed organizational structure along with the right people, systems, and performance measures in place is critical to purchasing success. Careful attention to assessing and selecting the structure and formal systems of communication, division of labor, coordination, control, authority, and responsibility will make the attainment of supply management objectives more likely.

Without question, the kinds of organizational design features that a firm selects often relate to the size of the firm. Larger firms differ from smaller firms in terms of scope, complexity, and available resources. They tend to have operations that are worldwide (scope), more organizational levels covering a wider array of businesses and product lines (complexity), and more resources that support the use of certain design features. As firm size increases, consolidation of common purchases can produce significant savings. Enabling this requires putting in place many of the design features to help coordinate and integrate a globally diverse, large organization. Whatever the size of the firm, progressive supply managers recognize the important relationship between organizational design and supply management effectiveness. Future organizational structures will need to be more flexible and responsive regardless of whether they are centralized, center led or decentralized. Certainly newer mobile and social networking technologies will impact the design of future organizations.

KEY TERMS

center-led, 162

centralized, 162

consortiums, 166

co-location, 180

cross-functional teams, 177

corporate purchasing councils, 166

corporate steering committees, 166

decentralized, 162

global sourcing councils, 166

group purchasing organizations, 166

horizontal focus, 180

lead division buying, 166

open information channels, 182

ownership, 166

regional buying councils, 166

social networking, 182

vertical focus, 180

DISCUSSION QUESTIONS

1. Do you feel that choosing an organizational design is simple? If so, explain why firms would change their supply management organization structure.

2. Discuss the two or three most important benefits to centralized purchasing authority. Justify your choices. Discuss the two most important benefits to decentralized purchasing authority. Justify your choices.

3. What are some of the factors that would influence whether a firm centralizes or decentralizes its supply management organization?

4. Explain how firms moving to center-led organizational design would attain "buy-in" from the business units.

5. Which of the center-led enablers could be utilized without expending a great deal of corporate P/SM's resources or requiring additional personnel?

6. Why is a function's placement in the organizational hierarchy important?

7. What factors contribute to the increasing importance of purchasing within the organizational hierarchy?

8. Discuss the logic behind physically separating strategic and operational buyers.

9. Discuss the role of consortiums and Group Purchasing Organizations.

10. You have just recently been appointed the company's Chief Purchasing Officer. You will oversee a company with worldwide operations located at 55 buying locations. Your organization has five major business groups involved with the design and manufacture of health care products (e.g., precision surgical tools, blood testing devices, and the like). Historically, the purchasing has operated in a very decentralized manner. Design an organizational structure that allows you to enact value adding strategies. Describe the reporting structure, the physical placement of personnel, the placement of purchasing authority, and the coordination of activities with other functional groups.

11. Discuss the advantages, barriers and applications of cross-functional teams in purchasing/supply management both internally and externally (e.g., evaluate and select suppliers).

12. Why would you believe that the importance of P/SM diminishes when a firm organizes under a supply chain management structure?

13. Explain how some of the popular social networking software (e.g., Facebook, LinkedIn, and so forth) could be used in purchasing and indicate the effect on future organizational structures?

14. What is the logic behind co-locating purchasing personnel with internal customers?

ADDITIONAL READINGS

Anderson, J. A. (2002), "Organizational Design: Two Lessons to Learn before Reorganizing," *International Journal of Organization Theory and Behavior*, 5(3–4), 343.

Fearon, H., and Leenders, M. (1996), *Purchasing's Organizational Roles and Responsibilities*, Tempe, AZ: Center for Advanced Purchasing Studies.

Johnson, P. F., and Leenders, M. (2007), *Supply Leadership Changes*, Tempe, AZ: Center for Advanced Purchasing Studies.

Johnson, P. F., Leenders, M., and Fearon, H. (2006), "Supply's Growing Status and Influence," *Journal of Supply Chain Management*, 42, 38–48.

Leenders, M. R., and Johnson, P. F. (2002), *Major Changes in Supply Chain Responsibilities*, Tempe, AZ: Center for Advanced Purchasing Studies.

Rogers, S. (2004), "Supply Management: 6 Elements of Superior Design," *Supply Chain Management Review*, 8(3), 48–55.

Wang, S., and He, Y. (2008, September/October), "Compensating Nondedicated Cross-Functional Teams," *Organization Science*, Linthicum, 9(5), 753–768.

ENDNOTES

1. Giunipero, L., and Handfield, R. (2004), *Purchasing Education & Training II*, Tempe, AZ: Center for Advanced Purchasing Studies (CAPS) Research, pp. 40–41.

2. Teague, P. (2008, September 11), "P&G Is King of Collaboration," *Purchasing*, 137(9), 46.

3. Avery, S. (2009, September 17), "Travel Procurement Gets a Bigger Role at Tyco," *Purchasing*, 138(9), 41.

4. Gordon, J. R. (1987), *A Diagnostic Approach to Organizational Behavior*, Boston: Allyn and Bacon, pp. 522–526.

5. Giunipero and Handfield, pp. 77–79.

6. http://www.colgate.com/app/Colgate/US/Corp/ContactUs/GMLS/HomePage.cvsp (Colgate-Palmolive website for suppliers-2013)

7. Teague, P. (2008, September 11), "2008 Medal of Professional Excellence: P&G Is King of Collaboration," *Purchasing*, p. 46.

8. www.corporateunited.com, accessed July 15, 2013.

9. Gordon, J. R. (1987), *A Diagnostic Approach to Organizational Behavior*, Boston: Allyn and Bacon, pp. 522–526.

10. Johnson, F., Leenders, M., and Fearon, H. (2006), "Supply's Growing Status and Influence: A Sixteen-Year Perspective," *Journal of Supply Chain Management*, 42(2), 33.

11. Johnson F., and Leenders, M. (2008, July), "Building a Corporate Supply Function," *Journal of Supply Chain Management*, 44(3), 39.

12. McShane, S., and Von Glinow, M. A. (2010), *Organizational Behavior*, New York: McGraw-Hill Irwin, p. 234.

13. Trent, R. J. (2004), "The Use of Organizational Design Features in Purchasing and Supply Management," *Journal of Purchasing and Supply Management*, 40(3), 4.

14. Hofstede, G. H. (1984), *Culture's Consequences: Differences in Work-Related Values*, Newbury Park, CA: Sage, p. 158.

15. Hofstede, G. H. (1984), Kellton Research Group as reported in http://www.bazaarvoice.com/research-and-insight/social-commerce-statistics/#Financialservices, accessed July 11, 2013.

Strategic Sourcing

Category Strategy Development

CHAPTER 6

Learning Objectives

After completing this chapter, you should be able to

- Understand how supply and enterprise strategies must align to drive value
- Describe what a category strategy is
- Understand the category strategy development process
- Identify the types of category strategy outcomes
- Understand e-reverse auctions
- Understand supply management transformation initiatives

Chapter Outline

Transforming Supply Management at Biogen-Idea

Although strategic sourcing capabilities are well established in industries ranging from automotive to pharmaceuticals, they are still in the formative stages in the biotechnology sector. It isn't easy to drive change in biotech companies for a number of reasons. With their external spend increasing so fast, there is great pressure on biotech companies to rethink how their sourcing structures are set up to add most value. In addition, much of the power in decision-making lies in the hands of clinical trials scientists, who often have power over procurement decisions. In a growing number of companies today, supply management is being asked to demonstrate deep insights into customer requirements and to quickly translate those insights into product offerings that often rely more on outsourced capabilities.

Biogen Idec Inc. is showing how this can happen in the biotech sector. In the last year, the company has undergone a huge shift in the way it operates its supply chain, particularly in the management of sourcing.

Headquartered in Weston, Mass. and with international headquarters in Zug, Switzerland, Biogen Idec is the world's oldest independent biotech and a *Fortune 500* company with more than $4 billion in annual revenues. The company discovers, develops, manufactures, and markets biological products for treating conditions such as multiple sclerosis and non-Hodgkin's lymphoma. It was formed from the November 2003 merger of Biogen, Inc. and IDEC Pharmaceuticals Corp.

In addition to its portfolio of drug candidates, the company has capabilities, including capacity for protein manufacturing, that are world-class in quality and scale. Biogen Idec is one of a handful of biotechs that have licensed and dedicated biological bulk-manufacturing facilities. It has a large-scale manufacturing plant in Research Triangle Park, North Carolina—one of the world's largest cell culture facilities—and a new 90,000-liter facility for producing biologics in Hillerod, Denmark.

The company's global operations (supply chain) unit reports into its pharmaceutical operations and technology (PO&T) business area. The global operations mission is to ensure the uninterrupted supply of the highest-quality products to patient sites worldwide. To meet its goals, PO&T sources an array of products and services, including active pharmaceutical ingredients, outsourced contract services, professional services, manufacturing and facilities equipment, manufacturing contract services, and raw materials and lab consumables. Like many other companies in this sector, external spend is significant in the range of several hundred million dollars annually, almost all of which can be leveraged.

Prior to 2009, support for PO&T sourcing and procurement was provided by a corporate sourcing group under a centralized business model. In September 2009, anticipating a sharp rise in the complexity of the company's supply chain, the management team launched an assessment of supply chain maturity across PO&T. Several factors had converged to spark the maturity assessment. To begin with, there were many more clinical trials in the pipeline, dealing with a range of new technologies that had not been sourced before. Concurrently, contract manufacturing spend was increasing; As a result, the executives anticipated that workload would increase in multiple PO&T areas.

Category managers were mandated to bring new sourcing efforts to the council for approval, sponsorship and commitment. For example, the council approves new supplier recommendations, non-budgeted spend with non-approved suppliers, and major strategy changes with regard to supply chain configuration. In addition, the facilitator of the council meeting—operations analytics director—is tasked with presenting the monthly KPIs on the health of PO&T suppliers as well as the spend trends to ensure adherence to overall corporate goals. By institutionalizing robust supplier approvals and/or changes, there was far less chance that suppliers would be selected based on the priorities or wishes of individual departments as opposed to organization-wide imperatives. This framework also enabled a uniform, data-driven basis for selecting which projects to pursue and to commit them to completion.

What began as a "grass-roots" transformation effort at Biogen Idec produced strong early results in the form of cost savings. The initiative was soon recognized by the executive team, but as the effort expanded, it produced results beyond cost savings, sustaining momentum and moving the organization to higher levels of process performance. This was achieved by focus on stakeholder engagement and use of an analytical sourcing framework. As a result of the partnership created between procurement and the R&D group, Biogen's sales have risen as new products have been approved by the FDA, sending their share price soaring.

Sources: Ganguly, Joydeep, Shepherd, Alasdair, Alegria, Esther, Ciamarra, Rob, and Handfield, Robert, "A Textbook Transformation: How Biogen Idec Overhauled its Supply Chain", *Supply Chain Management Review*, May/June, 2011, pp. 28–35.

Introduction

Remaining competitive means that supply management must contribute to profitability by focusing not only on cost savings, but also on contributions to top-line growth and innovation. As described in the opening vignette, supply chain strategies have often focused on outsourcing of production, but in some cases, the strategic nature of supply chain managers dictates that they recommend insourcing production and operations services. World-class supply management requires that leaders align with business unit stakeholders, understand their direct and indirect requirements for success, develop a deep insight into the global supply market's ability to meet these requirements, and negotiate contracts and manage supplier relationships that create a competitive advantage. In other cases, the sourcing process can yield a different result, (e.g., to develop the technology internally). In cases such as the Dreamliner decision, if external suppliers are not capable, then insourcing is a better alternative. Making sourcing decisions is a dynamic and difficult task, given the complexity and challenges that exist under current market conditions.

This chapter focuses on the contribution that supply management can make to a firm's competitive position and how this contribution should filter down to category management teams. A **category** refers to a specific family of products or services that are used in delivering value to the end customer. We begin by discussing how supply management executives can contribute to the strategic plan at the company-wide level. To contribute to corporate strategy, supply management must be able to translate corporate objectives into specific supply management goals. Supply management goals serve as the driver for both strategic supply management processes and detailed category strategies—specific action plans that detail how goals are achieved through relationships with suppliers. To illustrate this, we provide a step-by-step process employed by category teams that is used to define business requirements, research the supply market, and develop a plan to source the product or services. We conclude with some specific examples of category strategies that best-in-class firms are deploying to cope with an increasingly challenging set of circumstances in today's supply market.

Aligning Supply Management and Enterprise Objectives

A company's leadership team, in defining how the firm will compete and succeed in the global environment, must clearly and succinctly ask these questions to their executive team:

- What markets will the firm compete in, and on what basis?
- What are the long-term and short-term business goals the company seeks to achieve?
- What are the budgetary and economic resource constraints, and how will these be allocated to functional groups and business units?

When faced with these challenges, business unit functions must then work together to define their functional strategies, which are a set of short-term and long-term plans that will support the enterprise strategy.

The first part of this process requires that the leadership team understand its key markets and economic forecasts, and provide a clear vision of how the enterprise will differentiate itself from its competitors, achieve growth objectives, manage costs, achieve customer satisfaction, and maintain continued profitability to meet or exceed the expectations of stakeholders.

Although it is beyond the scope of this chapter to go into detail regarding corporate strategies, the economics associated with corporate strategy are fairly straightforward. An organization must take in more revenues than it spends on operating costs in the long term to grow and increase profits. As shown in Exhibit 6.1, there are two fundamental ways of balancing this equation: increase revenues or decrease costs.

Increasing revenues involves either raising prices or keeping prices stable and increasing volume. Simultaneously, costs must be held steady or must increase at a rate smaller than the rate of increasing revenues. However, this option has become increasingly more difficult to realize over the last several years. Since 2004, prices for commodities such as nickel, steel, oil and gas, coal, resin feedstocks, and copper have doubled or tripled. To combat these trends, many firms have sought new suppliers in China, India, and Asia, to counteract these higher costs with lower labor costs. (Today, labor costs in these regions continue to rise, posing a further challenge to cost containment.) As a result, inflation has been largely kept at bay, and the number of competitively priced, higher-quality products has increased. In 2013, there are only a few markets in which a seller can increase or even hold prices steady. For example, the price of automobiles has remained largely stable, even as the cost of materials going into these cars has increased dramatically.

Reducing costs has become an area of intense interest. Faced with global competition, companies are constantly searching for ways to reduce costs and pass the savings on to customers while preserving their profit margins and maintaining a return to shareholders.

Reducing the cost of materials and services has remained an important enterprise objective; another is innovation. Firms are constantly seeking to find the next new technology that will create new markets and capture a share of consumers' wallets. For instance, Apple created the iPhone, which required partnerships and joint technology development

Exhibit 6.1	How Companies Create Shareholder Value

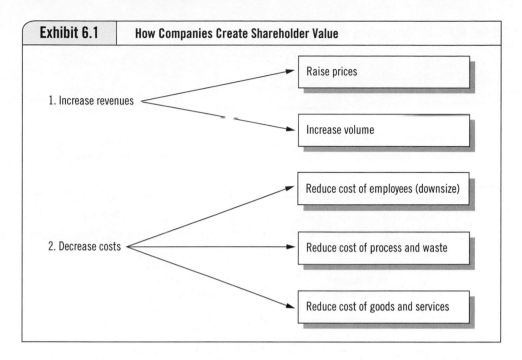

with key assembly and engineering suppliers. This collaboration launched a revolution in mobile phone technology. However, when designing a new supply chain, pursuing low cost can increase risks, such as those encountered in Low Cost Country sourcing initiatives (see Sourcing Snapshot).

Integrative Strategy Development

The process of aligning supply management goals with corporate objectives is especially important for supply management and supply chain managers. These managers often face some very broad directives from corporate management—for example, to reduce costs or to improve quality or to design a more sustainable product. The strategy development process takes place on four levels:

- Corporate Strategies: These strategies are concerned with (1) the definition of businesses in which the corporation wishes to participate and (2) the acquisition and allocation of resources to these business units.

- Business Unit Strategies: These strategies are concerned with (1) the scope or boundaries of each business and the links with corporate strategy and (2) the basis on which the business unit will achieve and maintain a competitive advantage within an industry.

- Supply Management Strategies: These strategies, which are part of a level of strategy development called functional strategies, specify how supply management will (1) support the desired competitive business-level strategy and (2) complement other functional strategies (such as marketing and operations).

- Category/Sourcing Strategies: These strategies specify how a group tasked with developing the strategy for the specific category being purchased will achieve goals that in turn will support the supply management-, business unit-, and ultimately corporate-level strategies. The term "commodity" is sometimes interchanged with the term "category" when referring to these strategies.

Exhibit 6.2	Components of Integrative Strategy Development

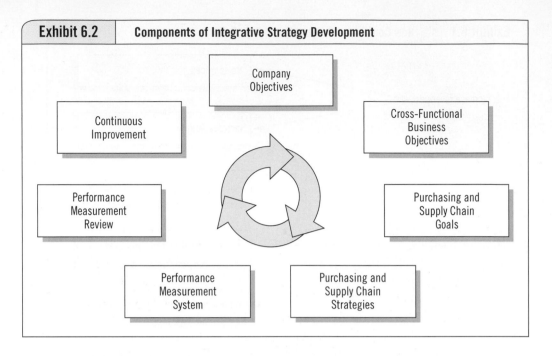

Companies that are successful in deploying supply chain strategies do so because the strategy development process is **integrative**. This means that the strategy is drafted by (or has significant input from) those people responsible for implementation.

Integrative supply chain strategies occur when corporate strategic plans are effectively "cascaded" into specific supply management and category goals, through a series of iterative planning stages (shown in Exhibit 6.2). Corporate strategy evolves from corporate objectives, which effectively evolve from a corporate mission statement drafted by the chief executive officer (CEO), functional executives, and the board of directors. Corporate strategies are crafted by the CEO, taking into consideration the organization's competitive strengths, business unit and functional capabilities, market objectives, competitive pressures and customer requirements, and macroeconomic trends. What distinguishes an integrative strategy development process is that business unit executives, as well as corporate supply management executives, provide direct input during the development of corporate strategy. This occurs through a process known as Stakeholder Engagement, described next.

Engaging Stakeholders to Build Category Strategy Objectives

Need for Engaging Stakeholders

Category strategies, by definition, need to include stakeholders as part of the team. For instance, if the team is tasked with sourcing materials for a clinical trial in a pharmaceutical company, then it makes a lot of sense to include people from clinical operations to build forecasts, establish guidelines for selecting suppliers, understand regions of the world where they will be needed, and so forth. In general, the more important the category, the more critical it is that internal stakeholders be involved. Together, the category team will develop a category strategy that provides the specific details and outlines the actions to follow in managing the category.

A general guideline to follow is that category strategies derive their direction from business unit and corporate-level objectives for success.

Before initiating any category strategy, there MUST be buy-in from the key stakeholders, especially at the senior leadership level. Without executive commitment, strategic sourcing results are unlikely to be successful. To ensure buy-in of the corporate team, supply management must clearly define the "prize" or carrot at the end of the tunnel, to obtain the go-ahead to pursue the strategy. To enable an effective category strategy, the team must:

1. Allocate resources initially, including assessment of current spend, data collection, market research, training, and people.

2. Validate the savings or contribution to other company objectives achieved by supply management.

3. Sustain the initiative through presentations to senior executives who support the move toward an integrated supply management function with other functional groups in the supply chain, including marketing, research and development, and finance.

It is imperative that strategic sourcing take their direction for building sourcing from business unit requirements. Supply management, in general, needs to build strategies that enable businesses to meet their goals, and to meet corporate objectives for cost savings, revenue, and shareholder value.

As supply management managers interact with other members within their business, as well as with corporate executives, a major set of strategic directives should begin to emerge. These strategic objectives may or may not provide details concerning how they are to be achieved. However, the process is not yet complete. Unless supply management executives can effectively translate broad-level objectives into specific supply management goals, these strategies will never be realized.

Supply management must couple each objective with a specific goal that it can measure and act upon. These specific goals become the initial step for a detailed category strategy formulation process. Remember—objectives drive goals, whether at the highest levels of an organization or at the functional or department level. The following are examples of corporate-wide supply management goals associated with various supply management objectives.

Cost-Reduction Objective

- Be the low-cost producer within our industry. (Goal: Reduce material costs by 15 percent in one year.)
- Reduce the levels of inventory required to supply internal customers. (Goal: Reduce raw material inventory to 20 days' supply or less.)

Technology/New-Product Development Objective

- Outsource non-core-competency activities. (Goal: Qualify two new suppliers for all major services by the end of the fiscal year.)
- Develop new products and services. (Goal: Develop a formal supplier integration process manual by the end of the fiscal year.)

Supply Base Reduction Objective

- Reduce the number of suppliers used. (Goal: Reduce the total supply base by 30 percent over the next six months.)

- Reduce product complexity. (Goal: Identify $300,000 in potential cost savings opportunities with two suppliers by the end of the fiscal year.)
- Increase local content in Latin America (Goal: Identify five potential suppliers in Brazil who can supply our local business in that region with $5 million of business.)

Supply Assurance Objective

- Assure uninterrupted supply from those suppliers best suited to filling specific needs. (Goal: Reduce cycle time on key parts to one week or less within six months.)

Quality Objective

- Increase quality of services and products. (Goal: Reduce average defects by 200 parts per million on all material receipts within one year.)

The next level of detail requires translating company-wide supply management goals into specific category-level goals.

Sourcing Snapshot

Apple Admits That Socially Responsible Supply Chains Need Improvement

A *New York Times* article that commented on Apple's outsourcing of its global supply chain to Asia provides insights into what has been a very secretive supply chain organization, up until the last week. The *NYT* interviewed several former Apple employees and subcontractors, and obtained insights into the decision Apple made to outsource almost its entire supply chain to Asia, with the majority of the assembly work being done by FoxxCon.

Apple's decision to outsource the Iphone to FoxCon was based on the last minute decisions by Steve Jobs to replace the screen on the iphone because it was scratched. They also describe the incredible flexibility offered by Chinese suppliers, their commitment to excellence, hard work, and resilience to changes in product requirements. No doubt, this world-class supply chain has allowed Apple to excel and provide disruptive innovations to the world, and start up thousands of businesses around its products.

But at what price? The recent release by Apple's supply chain organization clearly shows numerous ethical, environmental, and human rights violations throughout its supply chain. This is where the economics comes into play. The issue isn't so much about labor cost here. In electronics, the value driver in supply chains is upside and downside flexibility, flawless execution, and ability to deliver products with perfect quality. This is where the American workforce falls short. Several Apple executives pointed out that they considered all options before going with China—there was simply no comparison. Politicians in Washington, as well as economists calculating the numbers in the Fed, simply don't take these components into account when they develop fiscal and economic policies.

Many organizations are moving operations to new locations with lower labor costs, but this also requires that they put in systems for monitoring and controlling working conditions, environmental compliance, and quality control. Corporate Sustainability is a topic of discussion for not just political action groups, but government, investors, and most importantly—customers. All companies, not just Apple are emphasizing sustainable supply chains, which means increasing monitoring, compliance, and assessment of suppliers. New rewards and penalties are being put into place by these firms to ensure their supply chains are responsible. Not all will fail—but the importance of being clear to shareholders and customers alike about the problems they are discovering in companies is critical. Although environmental infractions have generally received the bulk of attention from the international press, sustainability has also come to include the "labor and human rights factor" implicit in this definition. Humans are also part of the environment.

These are tricky issues as there are no clear answers, just lots of questions. These issues need to be studied using a clear framework and guidelines for assessing supply chain sustainability and its relationship to business outsources, that effectively measures economic value derived from outsourcing overseas relative to the impact on the brand name, the integrity and responsibility of the leadership team, and most importantly, the "right thing to do". What that looks like remains open to debate, but it's surely time to have that discussion.

What Is a Category Strategy?

Category management is a process that carries out the following activities:

- Understand business unit requirements for the product or service.
- Conduct research on the characteristics of the supply market and the capability to fulfill these requirements.
- Evaluate specific suppliers and establish capabilities that align with business unit requirements.
- Develop a strategy that aligns supply capabilities and demand requirements.
- Determine optimal relationship characteristics and price/cost issues.
- Develop a business case for moving forward approved by senior managers.
- Develop a negotiation and contract strategy.
- Execute the negotiation and develop a contract.
- Establish a basis for ongoing management and continuous improvement of supplier management for that category, and for transitioning this responsibility to appropriate stakeholders.

The job of a category manager is threefold: (1) to engage internal stakeholders and fully understand their requirements for products and services, (2) to scan the marketplace to understand market trends, cost drivers, and risks, and (3) to build a strategy that aligns stakeholder requirements with the realities of the supply market. This chapter provides guidelines for additional tools and methodologies that may be applied, depending on the complexity of the category. These other tools will be discussed, but may not be utilized in every situation.

In developing and explaining these other tools, the application depends on the complexity and the volume of spend associated with the category. Some of the criteria for categories of spend that should have a strategy developed for them include:

- Complex projects
- Significant spend (amount may vary by company)
- High risk categories that could impact operations or customers

Category strategies are constantly in a state of change, as stakeholder requirements evolve, supply market conditions shift, or the two occur simultaneously. As such, once the category strategy is documented for the first time, it will need to be refreshed and reviewed by the sourcing council on a periodic basis to review conditions and update the strategy. Remember, category strategies are only successful when stakeholders are actively engaged. Success is a function of teamwork, research, consultation, and continuous improvement.

There are different sources of data utilized in developing a category strategy. These include business intelligence, supply market intelligence, and business requirements. By drawing on these data, category managers seek to drive several important outcomes like:

1. Minimizing risk to the enterprise
2. Reducing total cost of ownership for a category
3. Improving category performance along dimensions that are important to the stakeholder

The success of a category strategy is ultimately determined by how effectively it is deployed. To drive results, a category strategy must be effectively communicated with all parties, including stakeholders, suppliers, and internal administrators to ensure all parties are on board.

Category strategies, by definition, need to include stakeholders as part of the team. For instance, if the team is tasked with sourcing engines, then it makes a lot of sense to include people from operations as well as engineering and marketing to forecast, establish guidelines for selecting suppliers, understanding new product introduction requirements, and so on. In general, as the customer impact of the category increases, it becomes more important to involve key cross-functional team members. These individuals may be part of an "Extended Category Team," in that they come together on a periodic basis at key points in the decision process, when much of the data is collected and consolidated for them to review. Together, the category team will develop a commodity strategy that provides the specific details and outlines the actions to follow in managing the category.

Although not always the case, companies often use category teams to develop supply management strategies. Supply management strategies often apply to categories—general families of purchased products or services. Examples of major category classifications across different industries include body side moldings (automotive), microprocessors (computer), steel (metalworking), cotton (apparel), wood (pulp and paper), petroleum products (chemicals), outsourced business processes (IT programming, call centers), and office supplies (all industries). A category team is often composed of personnel from the operational group, product design, process engineering, marketing, finance, and supply management. The personnel involved should be familiar with the category being evaluated.

Difference Between Category Strategies and Strategic Sourcing

Category management is most definitely not about putting a new veneer on the strategic sourcing methodology. If procurement can be viewed as a service provider, category management becomes the primary service line, and category managers are essentially solutions assemblers who deploy the appropriate solutions/services needed by budget owners. The major difference between Strategic Sourcing and Category Management are shown in Exhibit 6.1.

The major differences in Strategic Sourcing vs. Category Management Structures are defined in Exhibit 6.1. As can be seen here, category management is an ongoing process that may be initiated by a thorough review of stakeholder engagements, but is focused on value elements that go beyond simple price savings. Strategic sourcing is often a one-time event, that is focused primarily on leveraging to drive down costs. The importance of building a full understanding of stakeholder requirements is fundamental to building category strategies.

The most common approach for building a business case in the initial stages of category management is through an annual process review of where the company is spending its money: the "spend analysis."

Conducting a Spend Analysis

As we discussed in Chapter 2, a robust procure to pay process is critical, to facilitate an accurate spend analysis. Why is it important to capture the transaction-level data associated with all purchasing processes? Because from time to time the firm must identify opportunities for savings through a process known as a spend analysis. A spend analysis becomes a critical input into building category strategies.

A **spend analysis** is an annual review of a firm's entire set of purchases. This review provides answers to the following questions:

- What did the business spend its money on over the past year? (This value is an important component in calculating the cost of goods sold in the financial statement. Purchased goods and materials are often more than 50 percent of the total cost of goods sold.)
- Did the business receive the right amount of products and services, given what it paid for them? (This is an important component involved in meeting the legal requirements of the Sarbanes Oxley Act, which requires accountability and correct reporting of financial statements to the Securities and Exchange Commission.)
- What suppliers are awarded the majority of our business volume, and did they charge an accurate price across all the divisions in comparison to the requirements in the POs, contracts, and statements of work? (This is an important component to ensure contract compliance.)
- Which divisions of the business spent their money on products and services that were correctly budgeted for? (This is an important component for planning annual budgets for spending in the coming year.)
- Are there opportunities to combine volumes of spending from different businesses, and standardize product requirements, reduce the number of suppliers providing these products, or exploit market conditions to receive better pricing? (This is an important input into strategic sourcing planning, the topic of Chapter 7 in this book.)

Moreover, a spend analysis provides insights and clarity into these questions and becomes an important planning document for senior executives in finance, operations, marketing, purchasing, and accounting. Despite the importance of this element, many firms struggle to develop a comprehensive and accurate spend analysis report. This is because purchasing was, for many years, a paper-based system, and figures were not entered correctly into accounting systems. Even with the evolution of sophisticated enterprise systems such as SAP and Oracle, purchasing transactions are often entered incorrectly, which elicits the old phrase "garbage in, garbage out." Another problem is that many enterprises have grown through mergers and acquisitions. When a new division is acquired, they may be using a different system from the acquiring company, and so the data is not easily translatable. For this reason, many firms are undergoing major initiatives to streamline procurement through electronic procurement systems that will revamp the purchase to pay process and automate different portions to capture transactions more effectively. Indeed, the research shown by Aberdeen Research in Exhibit 6.3 suggests that "best-in-class" firms are more likely to have a higher proportion of their spend under management, which has led to important improvements such as cost reductions, reduction of noncompliant purchases, supply base reduction, and electronically enabled suppliers.

Spend Analysis Spreadsheet

Assuming that a spend database is available and is reasonably accurate, how do firms produce a spend analysis? The best way to illustrate the process is to go through a specific example of a spend analysis and identify the requirements at each stage.

Exhibit 6.4 shows spend data sorted by descending dollar. Note that the dataset contains information on the general classification or "category," the primary supplier for that category, and the dollar amount spent with that supplier in that category. It is important to note that there may be multiple suppliers that supply a single category, and vice versa (multiple category classifications supplied by a single supplier). The entire spreadsheet is NOT shown in this case; in fact, the spreadsheet has over 2,500 lines in it, and this would be considered a simple spend analysis. Many datasets have literally millions of transactions in them. With this information in hand, you can proceed as follows:

1. The first step is to take this information and sort the data by category. In this case, a category is a "category" of spending.

2. From the category sort, find the total spend by category. (Hint: The subtotal or pivot table functions in Excel can help.) Calculate the total spend by category.

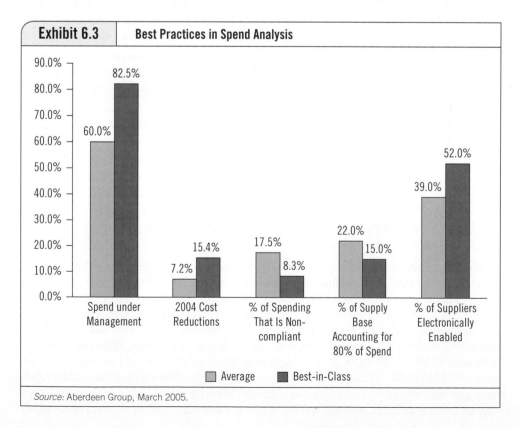

Exhibit 6.3 | **Best Practices in Spend Analysis**

■ Average   ■ Best-in-Class

Source: Aberdeen Group, March 2005.

Exhibit 6.4	Example of Spend Analysis	

SUPPLIER	CATEGORY	ANNUAL SPEND
REBATE CO	Rebate Fulfillment Call Center	$329,873,663
INVEST CO	Investments	$130,328,512
ADVERT CO	Advertising	56,134,490
REPAIR CO	Service Repairs	49,339,218
BENEFITS CO	Benefits	48,969,149
HARDWARE CO	Hardware	40,572,450
PARTCO	Service Parts	39,910,372
TELECOM	Telecommunications	31,055,599
DISPLAY CO	Store Displays	30,020,969
PENPAPER CO	Paper	29,175,843
LABOR CO	Contract Labor	27,880,363
SUPPLY CO	Paper	23,844,707
CONTRACT CO	General Contracting	22,579,113
OFFICE CO	Paper	22,257,690
GRAPHICS CO	Graphic Design	21,966,989
PAYMENT CO	Business Management Services	20,380,275
FREIGHT CO	Surface Freight	19,369,010
PAPER CO	Paper	15,603,682
SERVICE PLAN CO	Service Plan	15,478,827
SERVICE CO	Service Parts	14,868,023
CONSUMER CO	Consumer Financing	14,833,333
ENERGY CO	Energy	14,087,177

3. Make a chart of the top 10 commodities by descending dollar spend. A Pareto chart is used to show the total value of spend that occurs within each category. As shown in Exhibit 6.5, the top 10 categories of spending are rebate fulfillment and call center spending, advertising, general contracting, hardware, investments, paper, service parts, business and management services, contract labor, and telecommunications. These areas represent the highest level of spend and, therefore, the biggest opportunity for sourcing analysis and opportunities for cost savings and price reductions. But we are not done yet.

4. From the category sort, find the number of suppliers by category. (Hint: The pivot table function in Excel can help.) Perform a descending sort of number of suppliers by category.

5. Make a chart of the top ten commodities by descending number of suppliers. As shown in Exhibit 6.6, the advertising category has the highest number of suppliers within it, followed by other miscellaneous small dollar suppliers (who might be supplying office products or other noncritical items), energy, security, general contracting, and business and management services. It is amazing that this firm is using almost 2,500 different suppliers of advertising! However, this is not uncommon, as business units will often use their own local preferred supplier, because they are nearby and they know them. Although this is appropriate in

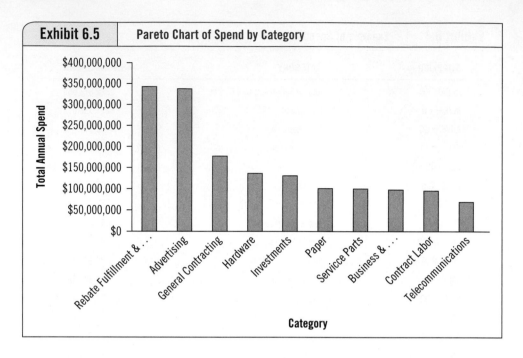

Exhibit 6.5   **Pareto Chart of Spend by Category**

Exhibit 6.6   **Pareto Chart of Spend Analysis of Suppliers by Category Group**

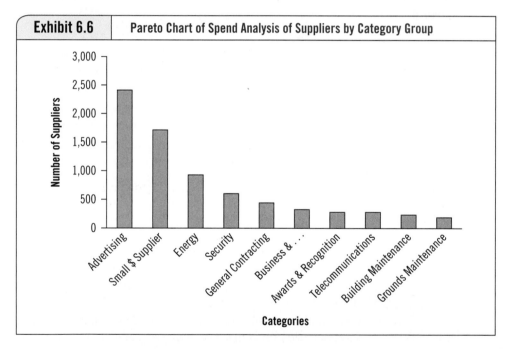

some cases, it may also be an opportunity for supply base reduction and further cost savings.

6. From the category sort, find the average spend per supplier by category. Perform an ascending sort of average spend per supplier. Exhibit 6.7 shows the categories that have the lowest volume of spending by supplier. A low spend per supplier figure is indicative that there are too many suppliers in that category, as the volume per supplier should be increased. It is interesting that none of these parameters show

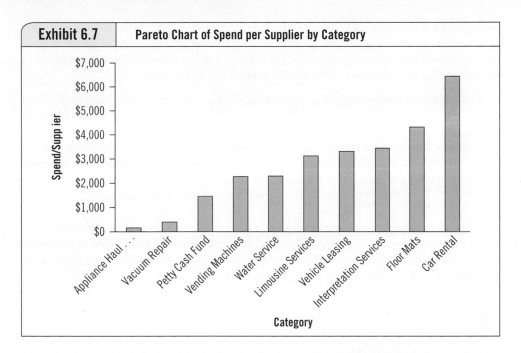

Exhibit 6.7 | **Pareto Chart of Spend per Supplier by Category**

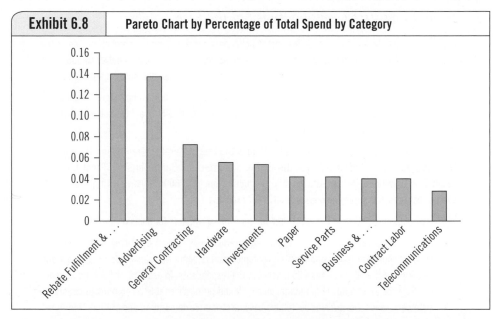

Exhibit 6.8 | **Pareto Chart by Percentage of Total Spend by Category**

up in the other two charts, suggesting that there may or may not be an opportunity worth pursuing in the categories shown in these charts.

7. Applying the concept of Pareto analysis to the chart of top 10 commodities by descending dollar spend, what are the recommendations for savings opportunities?

From Exhibit 6.5, the areas of Rebate Fulfillment and Advertising are clear areas for savings opportunities. As shown in Exhibit 6.8, total spend for this company is $2,449,428,985, of which 14 percent ($342 million) and 13.8 percent ($336 million) are in these two areas alone. Note that overall, these 10 categories constitute 65 percent of the company's total spend. Further analysis shows that rebate fulfillment only has eight suppliers, although advertising has close to 2,400! Clearly, by reducing the number of suppliers in the advertising sector, spend volumes can be leveraged and more favorable pricing can be achieved, leading to a significant cost savings (perhaps on the order of 5 to 10 percent), which could lead to a net bottom line contribution of between $17 million and $33 million

The same logic applies to general contracting, although the size of this opportunity is not as great. With close to 500 suppliers of this service, and the third highest spend ($175 million, further negotiation and supply base reduction could lead to additional savings of $8 to $17 million. Combined, these two initiatives alone could contribute up to $50 million of net savings to this enterprise, which could either be utilized in other investments, or passed on to shareholders in the form of increased profitability and shareholder value.

Not bad for a day's work!

From this analysis, the supply management team might approach the senior leadership team and ask for resources to deploy two category management teams: one in the rebate fulfillment services area, and another in the advertising sector. If approved, the deliverables might be, say, a 5 percent savings on current spend in these two areas.

Sourcing Snapshot

Global Logistics Complexity is On the Rise

Logistics complexity—in the form of fragmented channels, increased product variations, and consumer demand for customized solutions—has been increasing, according to a global study published recently by BVL International, a worldwide supply chain and logistics membership organization.

"Several trends identified in the study demonstrate that a number of major challenges lie ahead as the world becomes a more complex place in which to operate logistically," said Dr. Rob Handfield, at the NC State University Poole College of Management.

Handfield led the study for BVL in collaboration with Professor Frank Straube and Dr. Andreas Wieland from the Technische Universität Berlin, and Professor Hans-Christian Pfohl from the Technische Universität Darmstadt. The study included more than 60 interviews with global supply chain executives and survey responses from 1,757 executives.

Nine key trends emerged from the study that will have major impacts for decision-makers.

1. Customer expectations. Rising customer expectations was ranked by survey respondents as the most important trend, and meeting customer requirements was ranked as the number one logistics objective by more than 20 percent of the respondents. In essence, the results indicate that logistics and supply chain management should primarily enable a company to satisfy its customers' needs. However, as customers become ever more demanding and critical, traditional measures often fail when pursuing strategies to satisfy customers.
2. Networked economy. In the past, companies typically considered themselves to be independent players in the market, and at best, managed interfaces to direct suppliers and customers. That is no longer enough in today's networked economies. Companies are often forced to collaborate with partners both vertically and horizontally in their extended supply chain network, and these partners expect them to integrate their processes and systems. That requires network thinking rather than company thinking.
3. Cost pressure. End customers continue to expect low costs. Although other requirements such as sustainability, social issues or risk-mitigation capabilities are increasingly discussed in

the media, cost pressure seems to remain the ultimate criterion. The trend towards increased customer expectations has made it ever more difficult to reduce costs further. Logistics costs play an important role in reducing overall costs; their share of overall revenue is as low as 4 percent and 6 percent in the electronics and automotive industries, respectively. However, the survey shows that costs are on the rise, greater than 8 percent on average in manufacturing industries. A concerning result is that as many as 14 percent of the respondents cannot estimate their logistics costs.

4. Globalization. As global footprints expand, logistics performance as measured by delivery reliability has deteriorated, because of increasing customer requirements, greater volatility, and problems with infrastructure. Two out of three respondents stated that their company's logistics capability is negatively influenced by poor transportation infrastructure, which is a problem particularly in emerging markets. In sum, globalization clearly amplifies other trends and leads to an increase in complexity, particularly in regions of growth such as Russia, Eastern Europe, India, and Africa.

5. Talent shortfalls. Across all regions and sectors, talent shortages in logistics are considered one of the most important challenges in the coming years. Shortages are seen at both the operational level as well as the planning and controlling function; about 70 percent of the respondents experience a shortage of skilled labor. In the United States and Europe, talent shortages are also a function of demographics. In emerging nations strong competition from other fields like finance, strategy and IT contributes to the talent shortage in logistics. The most important strategies to cope with this talent shortage are training and qualification programs and strategic cooperation with universities and research institutions.

6. Volatility. Market turbulence on the supply and demand side has increased over the past years. This was amplified by the economic and financial crisis, which demonstrated how fluctuations in one part of the world can build up to dramatic problems in other parts of the world. Survey participants said they believe volatility will continue to increase; more than 50 percent consider it to be a very important trend in five years.

7. Sustainability pressure. This trend has emerged as a very serious topic. Already more than 55 percent of the respondents stated that green issues are part of their logistics strategy. Corporate social responsibility has also emerged as a highlight for debate. However, a great deal of uncertainty remains in the deployment of these strategies, especially relative to measurement systems, evaluation and setting goals and strategies for logistics sustainability.

8. Increased risk and disruption. The majority of companies, irrespective of size, sector, country and position in the supply chain, consider the mitigation of internal and external risks essential. Strategies for managing risk around demand and planning are also considered important. Executives concur that strategic frameworks and tools are needed for engaging the entire network in the management of risk and disruptions. Solutions focused on improving transparency of tier two suppliers, inventory and demand impede mitigation and force companies into reactive strategies. Proactive strategies should include research and development, procurement, production and sales.

9. New technology. The majority of companies are recognizing the growing need for investments in new technology, with about 60 percent of the respondents planning to invest in big data analysis tools within the next five years. These tools seek to develop capabilities around the comprehensive handling and intelligent connection of data to increase planning and control outcomes. This new wave of decentralized automated network technologies is in its infancy. Predictions from a trends study completed 8 years ago concerning the use of these technologies have not yet materialized.

Key strategies that companies plan to adopt in the coming five years include end-to-end integration, technology investments, talent management, and global process standards. The study also identifies key steps that executives need to be thinking about in shaping their logistics strategies in the next five years, including focusing on talent management and creating partnerships to drive end to end integration.

This project was completed in April 2013, supported by international partners who collaborated on interviews and survey data collection.

Sources: Robert Handfield, Blog, http://scm.ncsu.edu/blog/2013/07/18/join-bvl-international-at-the-north-american-chapter-kickoff-on-august-12-2013/

Category Strategy Development

Once the decision has been made to outsource a product or service, firms will typically use a process known as a category strategy development process to decide to whom to outsource it, as well as to decide the structure and type of relationship that should be established. A sourcing strategy is typically focused on a category of products or services, and for that reason, the strategy is sometimes called a category strategy. A category strategy is a decision process used to identify which suppliers should provide a group of products or services, the form of the contract, the performance measures used to measure supplier performance, and the appropriate level of price, quality, and delivery arrangements that should be negotiated. A typical category may include many smaller subcategories. For example, a category around information technology may include subcategories such as laptops, desktops, servers, and keyboards. If a firm outsources accounting services, the category strategy may include tax accountants and managerial accountants. The strategic sourcing decision is typically made by a cross-functional team, composed of sourcing professionals, operations managers, finance, or other stakeholders for the product or service. A stakeholder is someone who is impacted by the sourcing decision. They have a stake in the game, so to speak, so their input in the sourcing decision is critical to reaching a successful sourcing decision. The sourcing process is described below and is shown in Exhibit 6.9.

Step 1: Build the Team and the Project Charter

Companies are increasingly using a team approach to sourcing decision making by bringing together personnel, from multiple functions, who are familiar with the product to be purchased. Part of the first phase of the category management process is to identify the people who should be involved, as well as the key subject matter experts who may be part of the extended team. Once developed, the team should then define the scope of the category strategy, publish a project charter, and develop a work plan and communication plan. These steps help to define the purpose, boundaries, and goals of the process; identify the tasks involved; and provide a plan for communicating the results to the primary stakeholders.

A category team can be composed of personnel from operations, product design, process engineering, marketing, finance, and purchasing. The personnel involved should be familiar with the category being evaluated. For instance, if the team is tasked with purchasing computers, then users from information systems should be included. If the team purchases vehicles and vehicle parts, then it would be a good idea to include maintenance managers who are familiar with the characteristics of these commodities. In general, the more important the category, the more likely that cross-functional members and user

Exhibit 6.9	Strategic Sourcing Process

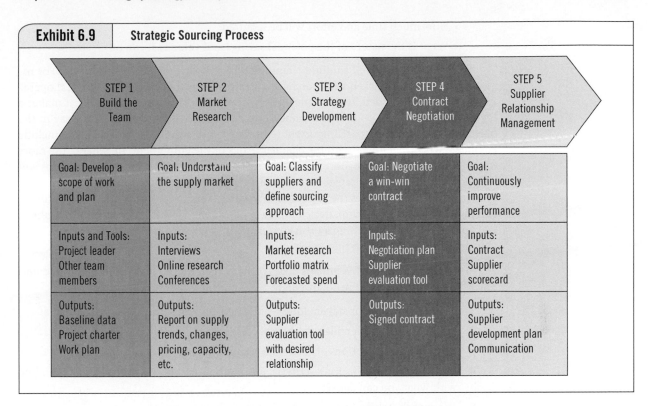

	STEP 1 Build the Team	STEP 2 Market Research	STEP 3 Strategy Development	STEP 4 Contract Negotiation	STEP 5 Supplier Relationship Management
Goal:	Goal: Develop a scope of work and plan	Goal: Understand the supply market	Goal: Classify suppliers and define sourcing approach	Goal: Negotiate a win-win contract	Goal: Continuously improve performance
Inputs and Tools:	Inputs and Tools: Project leader Other team members	Inputs: Interviews Online research Conferences	Inputs: Market research Portfolio matrix Forecasted spend	Inputs: Negotiation plan Supplier evaluation tool	Inputs: Contract Supplier scorecard
Outputs:	Outputs: Baseline data Project charter Work plan	Outputs: Report on supply trends, changes, pricing, capacity, etc.	Outputs: Supplier evaluation tool with desired relationship	Outputs: Signed contract	Outputs: Supplier development plan Communication

groups will be involved. Together, the category team will develop a category strategy that provides the specific details and outlines the actions to follow in managing the category. Strong skills in team building and leadership, decision making, influencing internal users and suppliers, and compromising in reaching a team consensus are, therefore, critical skills found in individuals who will succeed in these roles.

Every sourcing team should begin by assigning a project lead, who will coordinate meetings, project deliverables, and requirements. The project lead will assemble a group of subject matter experts from various stakeholder groups in the team to provide feedback and assist with delivering the project charter. The project charter is a clear statement of the goals and objectives of the sourcing project, which is officially announced shortly after the team's first few meetings. The project charter can be issued before or after the cross-functional sourcing team has been formed, and in fact, it can be used to garner interest from potential participants in the process. The purpose of a project charter is to demonstrate management support for the project and its manager.

It is often difficult to start out and invite people to become involved in a category strategy with no warning. As such, it is important that you think about *who* to engage in the team, as well as develop a compelling reason for *why* they need to be involved in the project. In general, it is a good idea to provide a compelling one-page project summary document that provides some key information on the following:

- What is the "burning platform" that has driven senior management to look at this category?
- What is the scope of the category?
- Who will be impacted by the decision?
- What is the process that will be followed?

- How much time and effort will be required?
- What is the nature of the potential savings and value that can be created?

The personnel involved should be familiar with the category being evaluated. For instance, if the team is tasked with purchasing comparators, then users from clinical operations should be included. If the team is renegotiating facilities contracts, then it makes a lot of sense to include plant maintenance, and ensure the plant manager has a say in the objectives and issues that are important to him or her. It would be a good idea to include engineers who are familiar with the characteristics of the equipment. In general, the more important the category, the more likely that cross-functional members and user groups will be involved. Together, the category team will develop a category strategy that provides the specific details and outlines the actions to follow in managing the category. Strong skills in team building and leadership, decision making, influencing internal users and suppliers, and compromising in reaching a team consensus are therefore critical skills found in individuals who will succeed in these roles.

An important part of this process is to consider stakeholder needs and map these out. The following steps should be followed:

1. Draw a map of your stakeholders—and check it with some of the stakeholders.
2. For each stakeholder, identify their success criteria for the project.
3. Check your perceptions of each stakeholder's success criteria.
4. Critically review all success criteria; ensure they are mutually consistent and in line with what you can deliver.
5. Work with stakeholders to reconcile any differences or gaps.
6. Check and amend success criteria on an ongoing basis.

An example is shown below:

Recognize the Need—Understanding of Stakeholder Needs

For successful interaction with stakeholders,
procurement must be able to understand the situation from a stakeholder's
perspective

Stakeholders	Example Needs
Senior Management	▶ Creation and capture of both current and future value ▶ Adherence to the corporate business strategy
Operations	▶ Assurance of supply and no discontinuity in deliveries ▶ Compliance to GMP quality standards
Supply Chain Management	▶ Reduction of temperature control deviations ▶ Inventory visibility and control of expired product
Strategic Marketing	▶ Product characteristics satisfying brand equity criteria ▶ Superb product quality ▶ Customizable product design
Transactional Services	▶ Transactional service operational efficiency ▶ Feasibility of the planned information sharing arrangements
Non-Direct Material Internal Customer (IT, Travel, Infrastructure, etc.)	▶ Freedom to customize specification ▶ Lowest achievable purchase price and ownership cost
Procurement (Other Categories, Other Geographies)	▶ Absence of possible negative effects on other categories / geographies

Stakeholder Needs Analysis Tool

Stakeholders	Example Needs	Change (H, M, L)
Conclusions (Issues to Address)		1

It is also important here to identify and name each stakeholder, and identify their readiness for change. Change is not always easy to drive, and it is important to identify first where there may be problems in driving change. Note that it is a lot easier to anticipate these issues earlier as opposed to later, as this may influence the strategy.

Steps

1. Identify and name each stakeholder.
2. Note the degree to which they are ready for change: H (high), M (medium), or L (low) readiness.
3. Note their capability for change (H, M, L).
4. Note their power (formal or informal) to make change happen (H, M, L).
5. Identify the factors which will help or inhibit the change.
6. Identify the stakeholders and factors you need to work with to make the change happen.

Stake Holder	Readiness			Capability			Power		
	H	M	L	H	M	L	H	M	L
GMP Sourcing Council			▣		▣				▣
CPO			▣	▣			▣		
Head of Quality	▣				▣			▣	

Once you have identified who may have challenges in terms of accepting change, it is also a good idea to explore the level of commitment that exists for a new strategy. Resistance to change is one end of a continuum describing people's support for change. A commitment analysis model provides a picture of where stakeholders are now in terms of commitment, and where they need to be to make change happen.

Steps

1. Name individual or groups of stakeholders.
2. Mark where they are now with X, whether they are currently opposing the change, passively letting it happen, actively supporting it, or forcefully making the change happen.
3. Mark where each stakeholder needs to be for the project to be successful (some people/groups may be in the right place, or may even need to move back).

Individual (group)	Oppose	Let Happen	Support	Make Happen
CEO			X ✓	
Sourcing Council		X	✓	
Quality			X	✓
Manufacturing				X ✓
Supply Mgmt	X	✓		
Business			✓	X

Planning for the Meeting

After you have gone through this analysis, you should have a pretty good idea of:

- Who needs to be part of the team
- Who you may have challenges with and the rationale for this lack of willingness to change
- Who you can count on to commit and support your team

Armed with this information, you need to now be very proactive and plan for the meeting. Begin by defining the challenges and objectives of the team, and identify the sponsors at a high level. Sourcing team leads do not have to "go it alone," but have a support structure in the form of a governance council who is launching the teams. This governance council, composed of senior executives, will typically identify key sourcing projects based on business impact and risk. This council can be an important driver in your arsenal to convince team members that they need to (a) engage in the team meetings and (b) participate and not hinder team progress.

If you do encounter resistance, it may be necessary to go to the associated sourcing council, and inform them of the challenges. Each council will want quarterly updates on team progress, so if a member of your cross-functional team is not showing up for meetings or avoiding it, part of the council's charter is to elicit their input.

Before pulling out these measures, however, you should spend some time meeting with each team member individually, and explaining the situation. As you should have already identified who is a naysayer and who is proactive via your stakeholder analysis, you need to leverage your promoters to advance the naysayers to the neutral category.

Step 2: Conduct Market Intelligence Research on Suppliers

The second step when developing a sourcing strategy is to fully understand the purchase requirement relative to the business unit objectives. Also involved in this step is a thorough supplier spend analysis to determine past expenditures for each category and supplier, as well as the total expenditures for the category as a percentage of the total. Note that the spend analysis identified in the prior section looked at spending for the entire company. A category spend analysis will drill down to a more granular level and identify the specific business units that are purchasing the products or services, and which suppliers they are currently using. Generally, this produces a Pareto chart as shown before; often one or a handful of suppliers are the primary sources of the majority of spending in a particular category. After understanding the spend patterns, the category team should also educate themselves as to what is happening in the marketplace, as well as what their internal customer requirements are. Just as you would perform research before buying a car (e.g., going online, reading reviews of vehicles, looking into gas mileage, and looking at repair history reports in *Consumer Reports),* teams perform the same type of market research on the supply base. This is critical in building and understanding the key suppliers, their capabilities, and their capacity to perform and meet the stakeholders' requirements.

To make an informed decision about sourcing, several pieces of information are needed. These include the following:

- Information on total annual purchase volumes. This is often an important element from the spend analysis. This analysis should show how much was spent on the category of goods or services by supplier, by business unit, and by subgroups.

- Interviews with stakeholders to determine their forecasted requirements. For example, if the annual purchase volume last year was $10 million is this figure expected to go up or down next year based on the predicted amount of work? Stakeholders should also be interviewed to determine any new sourcing elements that may not have been included in last year's figure.

- External market research identifying information on key suppliers, available capacity, technology trends, price and cost data and trends, technical requirements, environmental and regulatory issues, and any other data that is available. In effect the team must educate themselves through a detailed analysis of the marketplace and identify how best to meet the forecasted demand (generated by the spend analysis and interviews with stakeholders) given the market conditions that will occur in the next year.

The data can be collected in a number of ways. For example, the team might elect to meet with a supplier that is an expert on the marketplace, or an external consultant who specializes in studying certain markets (e.g., chemicals, resins, IT providers). These interviews are often the best source of information and are not published. Secondary data sources are published available databases, reports, websites, and so on. Examples might be a "state of the industry" report purchased from a consulting company or a publicly available database such as the Census of U.S. Manufacturers or the U.S. Department of Labor Statistics. The problem with secondary data such as these is that they are often outdated and may not provide the specific information the team is looking for.

When conducting market research, the team may use an outsourced provider such as Beroe (www.beroe-inc.com), ICE, or Global Outlook. However the data are collected, the team must also process and integrate the data to ensure that they are relevant and can be effectively communicated to stakeholders. The whole point of conducting market research is to understand the prevailing market conditions and the ability of current or potential new suppliers to deliver the product or service effectively. In that respect, supply market intelligence becomes one of the most important and critical stepping stones for an effective category strategy. As one manager noted, "Supply market intelligence may be the only competitive advantage of the future!"

Where do most firms go to find good market intelligence? There are multiple sources of market and supplier information available. The key here is to **triangulate,** which means that you need to explore, compare, and contrast data from multiple sources before you can validate it. Triangulation is part of the scientific method and requires that you establish corroborating data to validate a given hypothesis. The more data points you have supporting the hypothesis, the greater the likelihood that the hypothesis is correct. Your job is to go through these sources and identify key elements that support your hypothesis.

- Trade journals are a great place to start. These journals provide good leads and recent updates to what is happening in the industry.
- Start also with annual reports for supplier companies, as well as other customers, and make sure you read the notes to investors.
- The Internet is great and provides a ton of leads.
- Do not forget the power of books. Many people just start by using Google, which leads you to a massive set of links that may or may not be useful. A visit to a university library can lead you to some great reference books and trade journals, with multiple leads for further information.
- The power of snowball sampling is important. This means finding experts in a particular category, who can refer you to other experts whom you can also talk to.
- There are trade consultants who can provide information, but they are very often costly.
- Category managers will also visit trade association conferences and trade websites. These conferences offer a great opportunity to network and learn more from other people who know a lot about what is going on in the industry.
- You have got to be scanning the headlines.
- Suppliers are about the best sources. Do not just talk to salespeople. Talk to the line and their purchasing people.
- Investment analyst reports, as well as interviews, can provide very good information on what is happening in certain industries where they are investing.

Collecting the data is just the first part of the job. To effectively represent and communicate the market conditions, category teams may employ a number of different data representation tools to portray and explain the current situation. Three tools we will discuss here are Porter Five Forces analysis, SWOT analysis, and supplier analysis.

| Exhibit 6.10 | Porter's Five Forces Analysis |

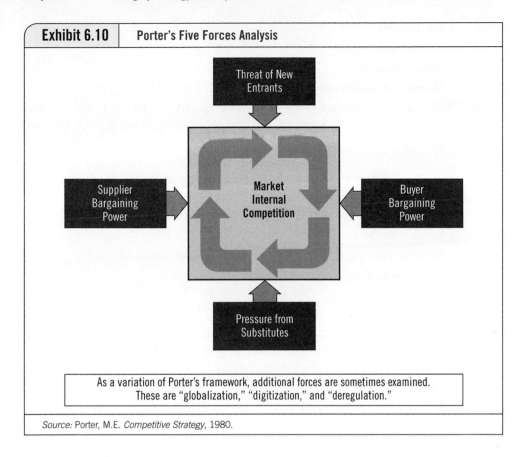

As a variation of Porter's framework, additional forces are sometimes examined. These are "globalization," "digitization," and "deregulation."

Source: Porter, M.E. *Competitive Strategy*, 1980.

Porter Five Forces

Porter Five Forces was created to describe competitive forces in a market economy. Porter Five Forces is a heavy-hitting strategy development tool that is used widely for business strategy development and sales and marketing strategies. The five forces are the forces that shape an industry (see Exhibit 6.10).

Michael Porter's industry analysis methodology was introduced in his book *Competitive Strategy*, first published in 1980 and now in its 60th printing. The powerful tool provides understanding of an industry with a simple framework.

Data for creation of a Five Forces analysis requires a review of all of the different data sources described to date in this section. It may also involve deep market intelligence through focused discussions with key stakeholders and subject matter experts. The tool helps to predict supplier and buyer behavior in the marketplace and is a critical element in shaping supply strategy. Five Forces analysis is close to a crystal ball and can be used to predict the future. It is also a helpful educational tool to lead stakeholders to understand current supply market conditions. When you understand your supplier's needs, you can figure out how you can help them help you.

The following are the five forces:

1. Higher levels of competition create more options for buyers and suppliers. Factors include the following:
   - Speed of industry growth
   - Capacity utilization

- Exit barriers
- Product differences
- Switching costs
- Diversity of competitors

2. The threat of new entrants. Examples here might be the new set of Chinese and other low-cost-country manufacturers that are entering many of the traditional U.S. manufacturing strongholds such as electronics and automobiles. Factors include the following:

- Capital markets
- Availability of skilled workers
- Access to critical technologies, inputs, or distribution
- Product life cycles
- Brand equity/customer loyalty
- Government deregulation
- Risk of switching
- Economies of scale

3. The threat of substitute products and services. For example, there are a new set of growing composites, thermosets, and carbon fibers that are replacing traditional elements such as steel. Factors influencing this include the following:

- Relative performance of substitutes
- Relative price of substitutes
- Switching costs
- Buyer propensity to substitute

4. The power of buyers. For example, as buyers begin to consolidate specifications and develop industry standards, increasing power is created over suppliers in the marketplace. Factors include the following:

- Buyer concentration
- Buyer volume
- Buyer switching costs
- Price sensitivity
- Product differences
- Brand identity
- Impact on quality or performance
- Buyer profits
- Availability of substitutes

5. The power of suppliers. As many supply markets begin to consolidate, fewer suppliers mean that a greater amount of supplier power exists in markets. Factors include the following:

- Prices of major inputs
- Ability to pass on price increases
- Availability of key technologies or other resources
- Threat of forward or backward integration

- Industry capacity utilization
- Supplier concentration
- Importance of volume to supplier

Generally speaking, summarizing these elements requires that participants take a high-level view of the marketplace and begin to brainstorm and review the implications of these changes in the marketplace.

SWOT Analysis

An analysis that examines Strengths, Weaknesses, Opportunities, and Threats (SWOT) can provide insight even with limited data. (It is often a good way to figure out what data you have and where there are gaps.) As a strategic planning tool, the goal is to minimize weakness and threats, and exploit strengths and opportunities (see Exhibit 6.11).

Supplier Analysis

Establish Benchmarks through Industry Databases   Benchmarking is an important element in building competitive strategy. Benchmarking requires identifying the critical performance criteria that are being benchmarked and identifying relative competitive performance. Industry benchmarks involve comparisons of performance with firms in the same industry, whereas external benchmarks involve best practices and performance levels achieved by firms that are not within the same industry.

The Center for Advanced Supply Management Studies has a number of supply management benchmark reports that can provide comparative insights into supply management performance. A number of reports on various components of supply strategy can also be found through consulting organizations, such as Aberdeen Group, Gartner, Procurement Strategy Council, Hackett Group, and other firms.

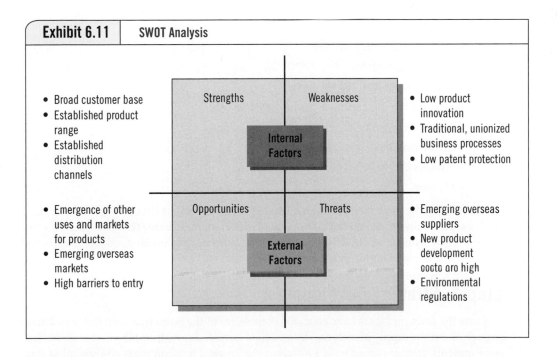

| **Exhibit 6.11** | SWOT Analysis |

Requests for Information   A request for information (RFI) is generally used before a specific requisition of an item is issued. Most organizations will issue an RFI if they have determined that there are several potential suppliers. The RFI is a solicitation document that is used by organizations to obtain general information about services, products, or suppliers. This document does not constitute a binding agreement by either the supplier or the purchaser. The information gathered from an RFI can be disseminated throughout the organization or to specific departments.

This procedure is generally used when a large or complicated purchase is being considered and the potential pool of suppliers must be prequalified. In this case, an RFI is a questionnaire or inquiry into the supplier's background. This is used to determine if the supplier meets the minimum standards needed to successfully bid on the project and, if awarded, successfully complete the project.

Value Chain Analysis   Value chain analysis is used to help identify the cost savings opportunities that exist within the supply chain. The goal is to be able to understand, identify, and exploit cost savings opportunities that may have been overlooked by business unit managers or even by suppliers in bringing the products and services to the appropriate location.

Some of the best data for value chain analysis comes from books, industry journals, and discussions with suppliers. The tool provides insights into where products originate (from dirt) and where they end up (cradle to grave). A good value chain analysis can provide insights into where in the market you need to be buying. Examples of value chain analysis are discussed in Chapter 12.

Supplier Research   Supplier research is required to identify the specific capabilities and financial health of key suppliers that are in the supply base or that may not currently be in the supply base. Some of the key elements that should be documented and included in a comprehensive supplier analysis study include the following:

- Cost structure
- Financial status
- Customer satisfaction levels
- Support capabilities
- Relative strengths and weakness
- How the buying company fits in their business
- How the company is viewed
- Core capabilities
- Strategy/future direction
- Culture

Identifying the major suppliers in a market is an important first step of any supplier analysis, especially when you are talking about global market share. This tells you who the world prefers, who the world is buying from. It is also critical to understand global capacity versus global demand and trends.

Step 3: Strategy Development

Once the team members have educated themselves to the point that they feel they know enough about the supply market conditions, the forecasted spend, and the user stakeholder requirements, they are faced with a different challenge. The team must convert all of this data into meaningful knowledge and apply some meaningful tools to structure the information so that it will render an effective decision. Two tools are most often used in this process: a portfolio analysis matrix (sometimes called the strategic sourcing matrix), and the supplier evaluation scorecard.

Portfolio Analysis

Portfolio analysis is a tool to structure and segment the supply base and is used as a means of classifying suppliers into one of four types. The objective is to categorize every purchase or family of purchases into one of four categories. The premise of portfolio analysis is that every purchase or family of purchases can be classified into one of four categories or quadrants: (1) Critical, (2) Routine, (3) Leverage, and (4) Bottleneck.[123] By effectively classifying the goods and services being purchased into one of these categories, those responsible for proposing a strategy are able to comprehend the strategic importance of the item to the business. The results of this analysis can then be compared to the current sourcing strategy for the category group, and tactics and actions defined for moving forward. Exhibit 6.12 summarizes the essential elements of strategy, tactics, and actions associated with managing categories that fall into each of the different quadrants in the matrix, and these are described in greater detail below.

Critical Category—Strategic Supplier   Generally speaking, the goals for a strategic category are to develop a competitive advantage, support and leverage the supplier's core competencies, develop best-in-class suppliers, support the company's overall strategy, and improve value-added services beyond a simple purchasing agreement. If the annual spend on the item is high, then it also makes sense for the company to establish a strategic preferred supplier. A preferred supplier designation indicates that the selected supplier should receive the business under most conditions. Formally designating a supplier as strategic builds a foundation for achieving higher levels of information sharing and improvement. In the words of Dave Nelson, a guru in supply management who has worked at Honda, John Deere, and Delphi, "If you develop the right relationship with your supply base, you can have 10,000 additional brains thinking about ways to improve your product and generate cost savings. And that is very powerful!"[4]

Routine Category   Products and services in this category are readily available and often are low in cost. Examples include janitorial services, facilities management, and office suppliers. The goal for the team is to reduce the number of items in this category through substitution, elimination of small-volume spend, elimination of duplicate SKUs, rationalization of the number of units to control costs, and simplification of the procurement process using electronic tools (e.g., electronic data interchange, auto-order systems, online vendor catalogs, and purchasing cards). For example, at GlaxoSmithKline, a pharmaceutical company, the chief procurement officer discovered that the R&D group was using 50 different types of Bunsen burners and beakers simply because scientists have particular preferences that they acquired in graduate school.

The team will also try to find suppliers that can automate the purchasing process to the greatest extent possible. For example, companies such as Staples and Office Depot will consolidate a company's purchases of paper and office supplies, and enable users to order supplies directly from their online catalog. A supplier catalog allows users to order directly through the Internet using a company procurement card (just like a credit card), with the delivery made directly to the site the next day.

Leverage Category-Preferred Supplier   As in the case of a common category, a leverage category also provides the opportunity for savings. These items or services have a high

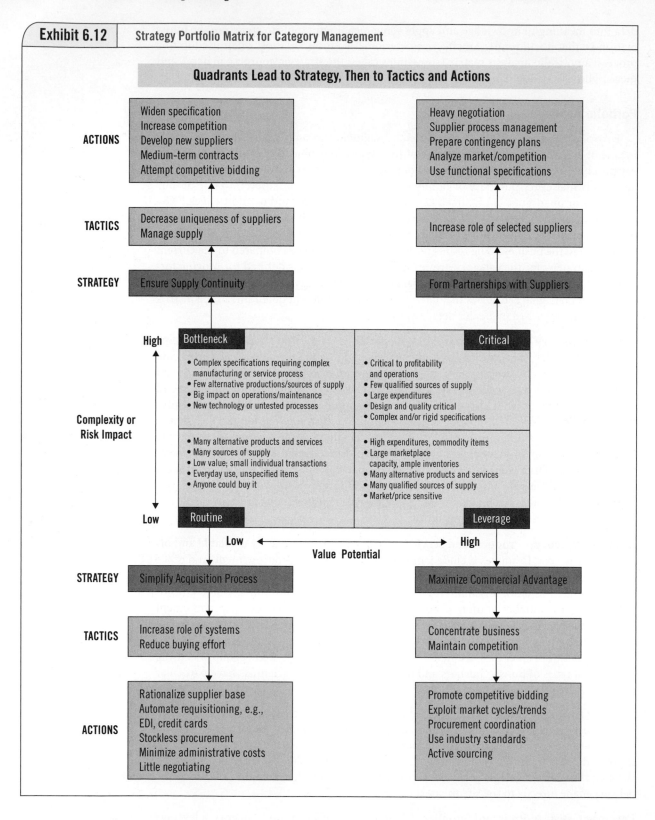

Exhibit 6.12 | Strategy Portfolio Matrix for Category Management

volume of internal consumption, are readily available, are important to the business, and represent a significant portion of spend. Because of their importance to the business, the need to maintain a high level of quality and compliance with corporate objectives is paramount. Preferred suppliers are awarded the business under these conditions with the understanding that they will be expected to significantly reduce the cost of supplying these items or services over time, in return for a significant volume of business and possible multiyear agreements. A high level of service is also expected, which may include supplier capabilities such as management of on-site inventory, e-purchasing capabilities, and ability to respond quickly to customer requirements. In so doing, the supplier will also be expected to maintain a high level of quality and to reduce the total cost to the business of managing this category.

One of the tools often used for this category of spend is an e-reverse auction (e-RA), an online auction that awards the business to the lowest bidder (as opposed to the highest bidder, as in a traditional auction; hence the terminology "reverse auction").

Bottleneck Category—Transactional Supplier   The final combination often found in developing sourcing strategy is for bottleneck commodities, which have unique requirements or niche suppliers, yet are significant to the business. Such items tend to be expensive, because of the exclusive market position maintained by the supplier. The goal of the team is to not run out and to ensure continuity of supply. In such cases, an optimal strategy might be to scan the marketplace and develop an agreement with a supplier to enable a streamlined accounts payable and receiving process. If the supplier is relatively small, this may involve sending an IT team to establish this capability at the supplier's location, with some minimal technology investment required. After a competitive bid, a detailed negotiation should take place that establishes high levels of service as critical to the business, with specific service level agreements detailed. The supplier must be validated to ensure that it can deliver in a responsive manner, is capable of handling orders from multiple locations, and is responsible for managing inventory of the item. In service agreements, the supplier must be led to understand the specific requirements around providing the service.

Supplier Evaluation

Once the portfolio analysis is completed, the team must then dive into the category and evaluate individual suppliers as to their suitability, narrowing the list down to a critical few. The ultimate result of this step is to make supplier recommendations, so the team must first identify current and potential suppliers, determine any information technology requirements, and identify opportunities to leverage the category expenditures with similar commodities.

Some of the criteria used to evaluate suppliers, as well as the tools that can be used to do so, are discussed in Chapter 7, which describes weighted point supplier evaluation systems. Here we limit ourselves to a brief description of the different criteria that a company may use to assess potential suppliers, which include the following capabilities:

- Process and design capabilities
- Management capability
- Financial condition and cost structure
- Planning and control systems
- Environmental regulation compliance
- Longer-term relationship potential
- Supplier selection scorecards

These criteria are worth talking about in more detail. Although it may not be possible to obtain all the relevant information, data that can be obtained will help the buying firm assess the potential for a successful match.

Process and Design Capabilities   Because different manufacturing and service processes have various strengths and weaknesses, the buying firm must be aware of these characteristics upfront. When the buying firm expects suppliers to perform component design and production, it should also assess the supplier's design capability. One way to reduce the time required to develop new products is to use qualified suppliers that are able to perform product design activities.

Management Capability   Assessing a potential supplier's management capability is a complicated, but important, step. Different aspects of management capability include management's commitment to continuous process and quality improvement, its overall professional ability and experience, its ability to maintain positive relationships with its workforce, and its willingness to develop a closer working relationship with the buyer.

Financial Condition and Cost Structure   An assessment of a potential partner's financial condition usually occurs during the evaluation process. Evaluation teams will typically evaluate the different financial ratios that determine whether a supplier can invest in resources, pay its suppliers and its workforce, and continue to meet its debt and financial obligations. These elements are important in determining whether the supplier will continue to be a reliable source of supply, and ensuring that supply will not be disrupted.

Planning and Control Systems   Planning and control systems include those systems that release, schedule, and control the flow of work in an organization. As we shall see in later chapters, the sophistication of such systems can have a major impact on supply chain performance.

Environmental Regulation Compliance   The 1990s brought about a renewed awareness of the impact that industry has on the environment. The Clean Air Act of 1990 imposes large fines on producers of ozone-depleting substances and foul-smelling gases, and governments have introduced laws regarding recycling content in industrial materials. As a result, a supplier's ability to comply with environmental regulations is becoming an important criterion for supply chain alliances. This includes, but is not limited to, the proper disposal of hazardous waste. (This is discussed in a later chapter.)

Since that period, corporate sustainability has emerged at the top of many corporate agendas. More and more companies are emphasizing environmental performance as a critical component of business strategy. As such, environmental objectives are often finding their way into the discussion when it comes to setting category strategy objectives. A green category strategy is one that explicitly includes environmental features and actions, including (but not limited to):

- Redesign of the product
- Substitutions of environmentally friendly materials
- Reduction of harmful materials
- Extension of the product life cycle
- Support for giving more business to environmentally conscious suppliers
- Others . . .

Examples of differences in traditional category strategy objectives, and environmental objectives are shown below:

Category Goals

- Reduce cost of purchased category by 10 percent in two years.
- Reduce defects of purchased category from 10,000 parts per million (PPM) to 1000 PPM in one year.
- Improve on-time delivery of purchased category to 99 percent with a one day window over the next three years.
- Integrate state-of-the-art components within the next six months.
- Align our company with the leading edge supplier over the next year.
- Create a motivation for Supplier X to work with our engineers in new product development.
- Have suppliers work directly with our customers on specifications.

Environmental Goals

- Reduce content of harmful substance to zero in all products within six months.
- Establish dollar savings goal of X for disposal of old parts.
- Have 10 percent of the supply base ISO 14001 compliant.
- Ensure that no new parts contain the 57 hazardous substances documented in our policies, and that volumes for existing parts be reduced to X PPM.
- Ensure that all new product packing materials comply with recycling goals.
- Ensure that all suppliers are disposing off metal molds for mass production in an environmentally appropriate manner.

Moreover, "green" category strategies go beyond "checklists" and rely on environmental management systems that identify procurement specifications, process requirements, and value stream analysis/waste stream impacts. Supplier assessment systems require audits of suppliers' processes to identify waste streams and environmental practices. Supplier development processes target potential waste areas and create incentives for moving toward a low-waste, mutually beneficial long-term relationship. Government databases are accessed to identify suppliers who have current EPA and government fines, violations, and safety incidents. Finally, environmental objectives are integrated into contractual requirements, raising the environmental performance bar for all new suppliers to meet. This area of supply management will continue to be more important in the future.

Longer-Term Relationship Potential   In some cases, a firm may be looking to develop a long-term relationship with a potential supplier. This is particularly true if the supplier is in the "Critical" quadrant, and the category of spend is high volume and critical to the company's business. This approach requires that the parties share their mutual goals, establish metrics to guide the relationship, and develop a series of ongoing discussions on how issues and conflicts can be resolved in a mutually beneficial manner. These relationships may also involve joint cost-savings projects and new-product development efforts, which are also described in a later chapter on integration.

This is not a complete list of criteria that can be applied when evaluating the possibility of a closer, longer-term relationship. This list does provide, however, a framework concerning the types of issues that are important in this area.

Supplier Segmentation

Once the portfolio analysis is completed, the team must then dive into the category, evaluate individual suppliers as to their suitability, and make recommendations for approaching them. In this step, the team must identify current and potential suppliers, and segment them into defined clusters based on (1) The relative amount of money that the buyer spends with this supplier, compared to other customers and (2) the relative attractiveness of the buyer's account relative to other customers the supplier serves.

In this step, we answer the following questions:

1. What is the current set of supplier relationships for this category?
2. How do we communications expectations for both (Buyer & Supplier) about the type of relationship we will have over long term?
3. Are there any suppliers that pose a risk to the buyer including but not limited to assurance of supply, cost, quality, and technology?
4. How should we deploy resources to develop and invest in supplier relationships?

Key inputs to segmentation are category complexity, spend with supplier, control of intellectual property (IP), number of suppliers in the market, and time develop alternate sources.

Process

1. Understand how the supplier views the buyer as a customer. Put yourself into their perspective and ask the question: does the buyer's business in this category align with the supplier's long-term business growth plan? If the answer is YES = they belong above the line. If NO = they belong below the line. This question should be considered in light of the suppliers' current and future business footprint.
2. Next, again put yourself in the supplier's shoes and answer the question: Does the supplier believe that the category under review creates value for their business? YES = put supplier on right of the vertical line, NO = put them to the left of the vertical line. The answer to this question may depend on several criteria:
   a. Does the buyer represent more than 5 to 10% of the supplier's business?
   b. Does the supplier have multiple locations? If so, perhaps only one of their facilities does a lot of business with the buyer.
   c. Does the supplier supply products or services from other categories, which combined with this category, are a large amount of revenue?
   d. Does the supplier consider the buyer's business important for its marketing and brand-affiliation? This is particularly true for smaller suppliers.

Other questions that may help determine where a supplier belongs include the following interactions with the supplier?

- Did they offer new technology to the buyer for this category in last 12 months?
- Did supplier share future growth plans to grow the business in this category?
- Have they been responsive to the category needs?
- Is it a high margin business for supplier?

Using these questions, all suppliers will be classified into one of the following segments.

CORE—In this case, the supplier views the buyer as a core customer, as the size of the account is significant to the supplier, and the account is also important from a strategic perspective. Suppliers in this category are willing to invest in the relationship and make commitments to cost improvement, performance improvement, and value adding activities, and retaining this business is a "must".

DEVELOP—In this case, the attractiveness of the buyer as a customer is significant and important to the supplier, but perhaps the historical volume of business with the buyer has been relatively low. Suppliers in this category are hungry to grow their account, and may be willing to make commitments to increase their share of the buyer's business in this category, in the hopes of moving them into the Core column.

EXPLOIT—Suppliers in this situation have a significant portion of the buyer's spend, but do not view the buyer as an important customer. The buyer offers significant value; however it is not aligned to their long-term strategy and success. As such, they are often uninterested in committing to cost reduction efforts and may in fact act to increase pricing if they do not wish to continue the relationship. This situation occurs in cases when an incumbent sole source supplier has grown his/her business over time and is confident the business cannot be lost. This may be also because of patented technologies that are unique.

NUISANCE—The final category of supplier views the buyer as an unimportant customer, and to further make the situation worse, the volume that the buyer has with this supplier is insignificant to the supplier. They are likely to provide poor service or unfavorable pricing. Suppliers in this category should be eliminated from the supply base as soon as possible (if possible!).

3. Reach consensus. Add the suppliers who may not be in top 80 percent spend now but intend to develop them. There needs to be a clear consensus as to where a supplier falls, and if possible, avoid suppliers that are "on the boundaries." As a Category Manager your ultimate goal is to have no suppliers in Exploit and Nuisance category. Suppliers in these categories will not be motivated to support your objectives because you are not a priority to them. They may charge premium and be less responsive. In addition their performance may continue to deteriorate as they will not be investing to improve the product and service. You are not their top choice and future. Category strategy must strive to achieve the goal of having no suppliers in these two quadrants.

Attractiveness of Account	High	**Development** Potential to become core	**Core** • Key Account • Will Invest
	Low	**Nuisance** • No Plans to Investigate • Ignored	**Exploit** • Not a part of future plans • Watch Price
		Low	High
		Relative Spend	

Compare Portfolio Analysis and Supplier Preference Matrix

Exhibit 6.13 | **Stages of Supply Management Strategy Evolution**

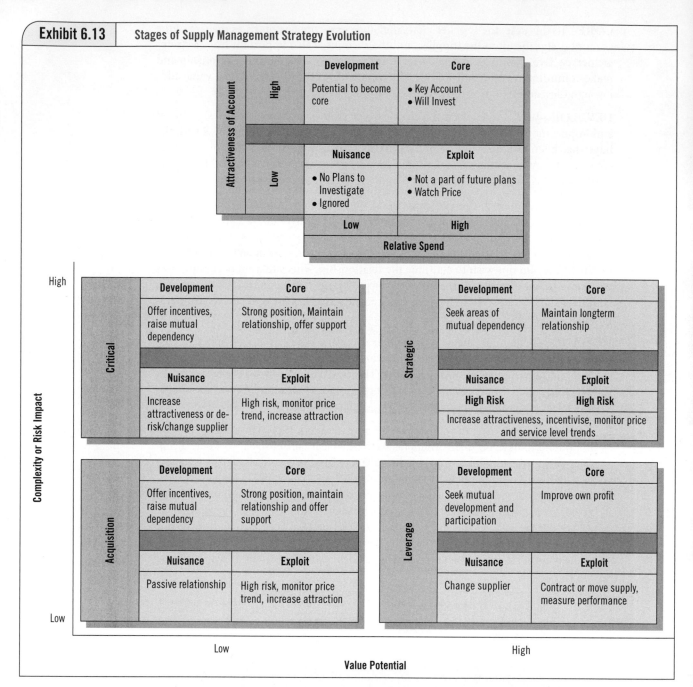

By comparing the portfolio segmentation matrix with the supplier preference matrix, a powerful combination of insights can be reached. Key to these insights is the need to identify gaps between the market reality the buyer faces in the category and the types of behaviors identified in the supply base. The team should also compare the appropriate relationship that is dictated by the Portfolio Analysis matrix, versus how suppliers are viewing you (the buyer) as a customer? The team should then logically think about options that will fit the specific situation your category team is encountering. This analysis can help the team reach a conclusion as to the appropriate strategy that will maximize opportunities for cost savings and value creation, and minimize risk. One of the outputs of this analysis is a "Long List" of suppliers that are potential candidates for sourcing this category. In addition, a list of possible risks that warrant further analysis and consideration should also be developed based on the preference analysis.

The supplier segmentation will follow this rule:

A supplier classified as "Strategic" has a significantly relative spend in the portfolio of the buyer (considering the scope of the category under study) and is currently involves any type of risk if this supplier suddenly leaves the business. Also the risk could come from spend delivered by the same supplier/holding company for another category. A strategic supplier is a core supplier.

Strategic Suppliers must be excellent in execution and innovation. Developing and being globally present, they will continuously have the ability to jointly create technical and/or commercial breakthroughs.

A **"Preferred"** supplier involves a lower level risk but still has a significant spend with the buyer. Even it is easier to resource this supplier compared to a strategic supplier, the quantity of part or level spend are significant enough that an increased risk in business continuity and performance sustainability is present. In this quadrant, the suppliers will be required to be committed to continuous join transactional/process improvements. Most of the preferred suppliers are core and some are willing to increase their long-term relationship with the buyer and become a Strategic Supplier.

"Transactional" suppliers can be easily substituted by competitors and will be challenged on a regular basis to offer the performances. On a regular basis, suppliers will be asked to compete (using eAuction/competitive bid) to demonstrate that they are the leading bidders offering the best service on price/quality and delivery.

Supplier Selection Scorecards

During the selection stage, oftentimes companies need a structured way to evaluate alternative suppliers. This can be particularly hard when the criteria include not just quantitative measures (such as costs and on-time delivery rates), but other, more qualitative factors, such as management stability or trustworthiness. A supplier selection scorecard may be used as a decision support tool. The team will assign a weight to the different categories and develop a numerical score for each supplier in each category, thereby developing a final performance score.

The need for assessment does not end with the selection decision, however. After the buyer-supplier relationship has been established, buyers also must track supplier performance over time. The ability to rank suppliers across multiple criteria can be especially helpful in identifying which suppliers are providing superior performance, and which are in need of some work.

After making the selection, using some of the different supplier evaluation tools, the team must reach a consensus on the strategy. The team may even take the suppliers' list and hold meetings with the selected suppliers to enable an effective decision. Finally, those suppliers are chosen that best fit the category strategy to be employed, based on their performance in the supplier analysis.

Step 4: Contract Negotiation

After the sourcing strategy has been determined and suppliers have been recommended, it is time to implement the strategy and negotiate the contract. Effective implementation of the strategy includes establishing tasks and time lines, assigning accountabilities and process ownership, and ensuring adequate resources are made available to the process owners. The strategy should also be communicated to all stakeholders, including suppliers and internal customers, to obtain buy-in and participation.

Before entering into contract negotiations, the category team should perform an analysis of market and pricing issues so that a fair price for both parties can be agreed upon. This analysis attempts to define the marketplace, including best price, average price, and the business unit's price, and determines expected trends in pricing. In preparation for negotiations, the buyer should develop a negotiation plan and an ideal contract. There should also be a contingency plan in case negotiations with the recommended suppliers do not go as expected. Finally, the negotiation is conducted, and a contract is signed.

For some items, firms may maintain a list of preferred suppliers that receive the first opportunity for new business. A **preferred supplier** has demonstrated its performance capabilities through previous purchase contracts and, therefore, receives preference during the supplier selection process. A **strategic supplier** is even more important, and must ideally also be preferred. By maintaining a preferred supplier list, purchasing personnel can quickly identify suppliers with proven performance capabilities. Competitive bidding and negotiation are two methods commonly used for final supplier selection when there is not a preferred supplier.

Competitive Bidding

Competitive bidding in private industry entails a request for bids from suppliers with whom the buyer is willing to do business. This process is typically initiated when the purchasing manager sends a request for quotation (RFQ) to qualified suppliers. The RFQ is a formal request for the suppliers to prepare bids, based on the terms and conditions set by the buyer. Purchasers often evaluate the resulting bids based on price. If the lowest bidder does not receive the purchase contract, the buyer has an obligation to inform that supplier why it did not receive the contract. Competitive bidding is most effective when the following conditions apply:[5]

- The buying firm can provide qualified suppliers with clear descriptions of the items or services to be purchased.
- Volume is high enough to justify the cost and effort.
- The firm does not have a preferred supplier.

Buying firms use competitive bidding when price is a dominant criterion and the required items or services have straightforward specifications. In addition, government agencies often require competitive bidding. If there are major nonprice variables, then the buyer and seller usually enter into direct negotiation. Competitive bidding can also be used to identify a short list of suppliers with whom the firm will begin detailed purchase contract negotiation.

More advanced online tools are becoming available that feature the ability to negotiate issues beyond price with multiple suppliers. With these tools, e-procurement managers no longer have to spend hours in face-to-face meetings arguing over details with suppliers. A buyer simply fills out an RFQ template and forwards the document electronically to suppliers.[6] Suppliers can respond electronically with online proposals detailing price, payment terms, shipping methods, or any other issue relevant to the buyer. These tools enable a buyer to negotiate the process simultaneously with more than one supplier, which leads to efficiencies and lower prices because of increased competition (similar to reverse auctions).

Negotiation

Negotiation is a more costly, interactive approach to final supplier selection. Face-to-face negotiation is best when the following conditions apply:

- The item is new or technically complex, with only vague specifications.
- The purchase requires agreement about a wide range of performance factors.
- The buyer requires the supplier to participate in the development effort.
- The supplier cannot determine risks and costs without additional input from the buyer.

Negotiations with a supplier should occur only when a purchaser feels confident about the level of planning and preparation put forth. However, planning is not an open-ended process; buyers must usually meet deadlines that satisfy the needs of internal customers within the purchaser's firm. Thus, the buyer faces pressure to conduct the negotiation within a reasonable amount of time.

Step 5: Supplier Relationship Management

The strategic sourcing process does not end when a contract is signed with a supplier. Although the sourcing team may disband and go their separate ways once the contract is signed, typically one member of the team will continue to work with the supplier in the role of supplier relationship manager. This individual must continuously monitor the performance of the sourcing strategy, as well as that of the supplier. The buying firm should revisit the sourcing strategy at predetermined intervals, to ensure that it is achieving its stated objectives, and may need to make modifications to the strategy if it is not working as planned or if there are changes in the market. The buying firm should also continuously monitor the performance of suppliers based on predetermined and agreed-upon criteria such as quality, delivery performance, and continuous cost improvement. And there should be a plan in place to manage any conflicts that occur with suppliers.

One of the most important tools used to monitor supplier performance is the supplier scorecard. Just like the supplier evaluation matrix, the scorecard often reflects the same set of categories used during the evaluation process, but the scores are updated typically once a quarter, and reviewed with the supplier. Over time, the nature of the classifications used in the scorecard may also change, as the stakeholders' requirements and their requests may change. Scorecards typically include the categories of price, quality, and delivery reliability used in the evaluation process, but the team may also choose to add categories such as "Responsiveness" (How quickly does the supplier return a call when there is a problem?). These scorecards are used in regularly scheduled review meetings with suppliers, so that deficiencies in performance can be noted, discussed, and acted upon.

Regular reviews must be held to determine if the strategy is successful or whether it requires modification. The review may include feedback and input from key suppliers. In any case, all suppliers should be advised of results along with future expectations. Supply management personnel play a key role in this review because they are often the primary contact for the supplier with responsibility for supplier performance measurement. Earlier decisions may have to be revisited and reevaluated if suppliers do not perform as expected.

The key goals defined in Step 2 must be revisited periodically to identify modifications to the original strategy. Key elements of the results-monitoring process include the following:

- Conduct regular review meetings (at least annually) to determine if the strategy is well aligned with an organization's objectives.
- Share results with top management to provide additional momentum to the strategy; be sure to report the performance improvements achieved through the strategy.
- Assess internal customers' and suppliers' perceptions. Are they satisfied with what has happened? If not, why not, and can the strategy be altered to improve the situation?
- Determine whether key goals are being achieved. If they are not being achieved, what is the contingency plan? If the goals are being achieved, are there any lessons to be learned?
- Provide feedback to those involved.

These strategy development steps are relatively general—they describe the steps to follow only when proposing and executing a strategy. However, the actual outcomes of the category strategy development process may vary considerably, depending on the specific category and the supply market.

Types of Supply Management Strategies

Organizations can employ a variety of different strategies that may be unique to each category. Although we cannot cover all of the possible variations of strategies that may emerge, we will briefly review some of the most common and important supply management strategies. As we will see later, certain strategies are used more often than others, depending on how advanced an organization is at the supply management strategy development process. Each of these strategies or supply management approaches is covered in greater detail in other chapters throughout the book.

Insourcing/Outsourcing

Insourcing/Outsourcing is a complex and strategic business and supply decision whether to produce a component, assembly, process or service internally (insourcing) or to purchase the same component, assembly, process or service from an outside supplier (outsourcing). The impact of such decisions is often felt for many years. The decision is now being applied to virtually every process conducted within the traditional walls of an organization and spans areas such as warehousing, distribution, transportation, production, assembly, sales, call centers, human resources, design, engineering, and even purchasing.

Insourcing/outsourcing decisions are extremely complex because they include many factors such as emerging new technologies and products, business strategies defining what is core or noncore to a business, poor performance internally or by external suppliers, significant future increases or decreases in demand, and geographical location of the demand. These decisions are also strategic as they frequently define the business model of the firm. For example, high tech firms such as Cisco, IBM, and Philips, to name a few, follow an outsourcing model where critical electronic components and subsystems are outsourced to suppliers in Asia-Pacific countries. Cost, technology leadership, and overall performance by these outsourced suppliers are viewed as providing the best opportunities for achieving and maintaining long-term competitiveness.

Insourcing/outsourcing decisions also require that purchasing play a critical team role. It is purchasing, through in-depth supply market intelligence, which can provide the necessary information about external suppliers to make a rational fact based decision whether to insource or outsource. Current and future information is required about supplier capabilities to produce and deliver goods and services, current and future technology leadership, capacity, financial condition, and overall risk/reward analysis.

In addition, purchasing is a key player in managing the business relationship with outsourced suppliers. Purchasing can strongly influence whether a good or service will be insourced or outsourced to a specific supplier(s) based on the likelihood of being able to establish a good (versus poor) working relationship with the outsourced supplier.

Well-reasoned insourcing/outsourcing decisions will be even more critical in the future as firms are forced to evaluate their business models to stay competitive and because of the growth of global sourcing.

Supply Base Optimization

Supply base optimization is the process of determining the appropriate number and mix of suppliers to maintain. Although this has also been referred to as **rightsizing**, it usually refers to reducing the number of suppliers used. Moreover, suppliers that are not capable of achieving world-class performance, either currently or in the near future, may be eliminated from the supply base. This process is continuous, because the needs of the business unit are always changing. Optimization requires an analysis of the number of suppliers required currently and in the future for each purchased item. For example, General Motors was ready to eliminate 160 suppliers worldwide that it considered poor performers in 2003 and 2004. Chapter 9 discusses supply base optimization in detail.

Supply Risk Management

Events in 2005 such as Hurricane Katrina and corresponding escalating category prices highlighted more than ever the impact of disruptions on supply chain operations and global competition. Although many events are not easily predicted, there are many other sources of supply chain disruption that have the potential to be better managed, thereby reducing the impact on firm agility and profitability.

As firms outsource a greater proportion of products and services to China, India, and other low-cost countries, the hidden perils of these approaches are often not considered, especially within the context of enterprise risk management (ERM). Global outsourcing affords many benefits in the form of lower prices and expanded market access, but only recently have senior executives begun to recognize the increased risk attributed to the higher probability of product and service flow disruptions in global sourcing networks. A major disruption in the offshore supply chain can shut down a company and have dire consequences for profitability. This was felt most drastically in the last few years, when such events as 9/11, the war in Iraq, the West Coast port workers' strike, and increased regulatory and customs delays brought supply chain operations to a standstill. In 2005, the impact of Hurricane Katrina was felt by companies relying on supplies of critical commodities produced on the Gulf Coast such as fuel, natural gas, chemicals, and resins. Other, less serious, events that can also impact customer service include fire and theft, poor communication of customer requirements, part shortages, and quality problems.

The impact of supply chain disruptions, although difficult to quantify, can be costly. A study investigated stock market reactions when firms publicly announced that they were experiencing supply chain glitches or disruptions causing production or shipping delays.[7] Results of the study of 519 supply chain problem announcements showed that stock market reactions decreased shareholder value by 10.28 percent. A follow-up study assessed the effect 827 publicly announced disruptions had on long-run stock price (one year before the disruption and two years after) and found a mean abnormal return of nearly 40 percent, along with significant increases in equity risk.[8] Their results also showed that the majority of supply chain disruptions involved parts shortages, lack of response to customer-requested changes, production problems, ramp-up problems, and quality problems.

Many recent events illustrate this phenomenon. For example, Boeing experienced supplier delivery failure of two critical parts with an estimated loss to the company of $2.6 billion. In 2002, fewer than 100 workers in the longshoremen's union strike disrupted West Coast port operations. As a result, it took six months for some containers to be delivered and schedules to return to normal. Hurricane Katrina resulted in billions of dollars of lost revenue to major retailers such as British Petroleum (BP), Shell, ConocoPhillips, and Lyondell, as well as causing gasoline shortages in many parts of the United States, resulting in lost economic activity. Most recently, a failure in supplier communication and process compliance on the Horizon caused the worst environmental disaster in the Gulf, and BP's procurement staff have spent enormous amounts of time and money to address these shortcomings (see Sourcing Snapshot). Given these and other events, it is not surprising that supply chain disruptions have caught the attention of executives.

Sourcing Snapshot

Managing Supply Chain Risk Continues to Be a Challenge

A recent survey by APQC found that 75 percent of companies in 2012 were hit by major supply disruptions (APQC, 2013). Survey findings indicate that most organizations' leaders did indeed express concern about the impact of political turmoil, natural disasters, or extreme weather. But the findings also show that the people at the front lines of the business were hamstrung by a lack of visibility into risk. Nearly half said they lacked the resources needed to adequately assess business continuity programs at supplier sites. Many relied on the suppliers filling out perfunctory, unreliable checklists.

What makes this story so compelling, is that actions taken in the last five years suggest that buying companies have still not learned from their mistakes. Despite heavy investments in "Enterprise Risk Management" systems, seventy percent of the respondents to the APQC survey say their organizations pruned their lists of suppliers over the past five years, with the intent to reduce costs. Nearly three-quarters (74%) of the companies over this same period added suppliers physically distant from their facilities, with 63 percent acknowledging that their suppliers are located in areas of the world known for high-impact natural disasters, extreme-weather events or political turmoil.

In light of these astounding facts, the results of a recent research study by Handfield and Valdares (2013) are compelling, in that they argue that a new approach for managing supplier risk is needed in a global economic environment characterized by volatility, cost pressure, increasing customer expectations, sagging logistic infrastructure, heightened government regulatory barriers, and challenging natural environments. In effect, organizations who will survive this environment need to adopt a culture of enactment, particularly with regard to supplier financial risk. The results of this research point to some important practical findings, as well as identification of area for future research on global supply network management.

The research results provide clear evidence that during the recent economic crisis of 2008–2009, proactive supply managers opened up good communication channels to better adjust their cash flow with suppliers and customers and improve financial health by finding alternative approaches for dealing with financial issues. Examples of communication involve meetings to identify the impact of the economic crisis on their cash flow, regularly scheduled information sessions to update financial conditions, discussions on contingency planning, and discussions to understand business continuity plans in the event of future economic challenges. These are simple actions, yet are powerful in terms of the level of understanding promoted. Communication in a face-to-face manner promotes trust, transparency, and openness, and is a form of enactment that reduces equivocality in that it promotes improved understanding of the risks on the part all both buyers and sellers. Communication provides feedback to simplify the problem structure, and leads to meaningful solutions that reduce supplier's financial stress as a joint solution can be sought. For example, a buying company may be able to provide increased leverage in financing options, whereas suppliers (particularly small ones) must meet their obligations through procurement cards or factoring companies, both of which are expensive options. Both alternatives amount to a 24 to 36 percent annualized cost of capital, which can further hobble a supplier's debt position for the future.

The need for clear and open communication on the financial status of organizations is an important antecedent to reduced disruptive outcomes, but is not in itself sufficient to reduce disruptions. Tangible actions must accompany communication for the impact to be felt. One of the most tangible forms of addressing financial risk is through re-negotiation of contractual. This activity involves strengthening of contractual terms, renegotiating terms that can share risks and rewards, as well as policy changes to accounts payable lead time to improve cashflow to the supplier to relieve economic duress. Proactive buyers are also administering informal Memorandums of Understanding to promote a mutual commitment to the relationship, and further enhance the level of co-destiny and aligned vision for the future. This form of "communal" trust-building behavior is often foreign to many procurement organizations, who are hesitant to make any commitment to suppliers.

Source: Handfield, R. and Valdares, Marcos, Managing Supplier Financial Risk During the 2008 Global Financial Crisis, Working Paper, 2013.

In a survey of Global 1000 companies, supply chain disruptions were perceived to be the single biggest threat to their companies' revenue streams. Although senior executives now recognize that supply chain disruptions can be devastating to an enterprise's bottom line, strategies to mitigate supply chain disruptions are typically not well developed or even initiated. A troubling statistic is that only between 5 and 25 percent of Fortune 500 companies are estimated to be prepared to handle a major supply chain crisis or disruption.

One factor that is increasing the risk exposure to supply chain disruption is the increasing propensity of companies to outsource processes to global suppliers. The complexity associated with multiple hand-offs in global supply chains increases the probability of disruptions. As the number of hand-offs required to ship products through multiple carriers, multiple ports, and multiple government checkpoints increases, so does the probability of poor communication, human error, and missed shipments. One executive we interviewed from a major electronics company noted: "We have successfully outsourced production of our products to China. Unfortunately, we now recognize that we do not have the processes in place to manage risk associated with this supply chain effectively!"[9] In this environment, questions arise such as, what steps can an organization take to design its supply chains to ensure uninterrupted material availability? Is it possible to respond in an agile manner to customer requirements in a global sourcing environment? These are issues that supply chain managers must think through in the future, to build effective contingency plans before these disruptions occur, so that there is a plan when they do occur.

Low-Cost Country Sourcing

Low-Cost Country Sourcing is an approach that requires supply management to view the entire world as a potential source for components, services, and finished goods. It can be used to access new markets or to gain access to the same suppliers that are helping global companies become more competitive. Although true global sourcing is somewhat limited in most industries; more and more companies are beginning to view the world as both a market and a source of supply. Although there has been a strong push to source from emerging BRIC (Brazil, Russia, India, and China) countries in search of lower costs, there has also been a strong push toward sourcing in these countries because of local content requirements established by governments in these areas. Specifically, many countries have regulations that require companies who sell in that country to have up to 50 percent of local content from local suppliers; meaning they will need to find domestic suppliers in the region for 50 percent of the cost of goods sold for that product to be allowed to sell in that region.

The major objective of low cost country sourcing is to provide immediate and dramatic improvements in cost and quality as determined through the category research process. The regions that are most commonly identified for these types of results are known as "Low-Cost Country" suppliers, which include Asia Pacific (China, Vietnam, India, Bangladesh, Pakistan, Thailand, Taiwan, Malaysia, and nearby regions), Latin America (Mexico, Brazil, Columbia, Argentina), and Eastern Europe (Hungary, Poland, Czechoslovakia, Romania, and so forth). In the last five years, Eastern European costs have gone up significantly. There is also an emerging set of suppliers in northern Africa that are beginning to expand their services. Global sourcing is also an opportunity to gain exposure to product and process technology, increase the number of available sources, satisfy countertrade requirements, and establish a presence in foreign markets. This strategy is not contradictory to supply base optimization because it involves locating the worldwide best-in-class suppliers for a given category. Some buyers also source globally to introduce competition to domestic suppliers. Finally, offshoring of services, such as call services, legal, and other services has increased dramatically in the last eight years, with the bulk of this work going to India.

There are several major barriers to global sourcing that must be overcome. Some serious issues are that some firms are inexperienced with global business processes and practices, and there are few personnel qualified to develop and negotiate with global suppliers or manage long material pipelines. In addition, more complex logistics and currency fluctuations require measuring all relevant costs before committing to a worldwide source.

Finally, organizations may not be prepared to deal with the different negotiating styles practiced by different cultures, and they may have to work through a foreign host national to establish contacts and an agreement. Chapter 10 addresses global sourcing in detail.

Longer-Term Supplier Relationships

Longer-term supplier relationships involve the selection of, and continuous involvement with, suppliers viewed as critical over an extended period of time (e.g., three years and beyond). In general, the use of longer-term supplier relationships is growing in importance, and there will probably be greater pursuit of these relationships through longer-term contracts. Some purchasers are familiar with the practice, whereas for others it represents a radical departure from traditional short-term approaches to supply base management.

Longer-term relationships are sought with suppliers that have exceptional performance or unique technological expertise. Within the portfolio matrix described earlier, this would involve the few suppliers that provide items and services that are critical or of higher value. A longer-term relationship may include a joint product development relationship with shared development costs and intellectual property. In other cases, it may simply be an informal process of identifying suppliers that receive preferential treatment. Chapter 14 discusses longer-term relationships and contracts.

Early Supplier Design Involvement

Early supplier design involvement and selection requires key suppliers to participate at the concept or predesign stage of new-product development. Supplier involvement may be informal, although the supplier may already have a purchase contract for the production of an existing item. Early involvement will increasingly take place through participation on cross-functional product development teams. This strategy recognizes that qualified suppliers have more to offer than simply the basic production of items that meet engineering specifications. Early supplier design involvement is a simultaneous engineering approach that occurs between buyer and seller, and seeks to maximize the benefits received by taking advantage of the supplier's design capabilities. This strategy is discussed in detail in Chapter 4; the Good Practice Example at the end of this chapter also highlights how one company has successfully employed early involvement.

Supplier Development

In some cases, purchasers may find that suppliers' capabilities are not high enough to meet current or future expectations, yet they do not want to eliminate the supplier from the supply base. (Switching costs may be high, or the supplier has performance potential.) A solution in such cases is to work directly with a supplier to facilitate improvement in a designated functional or activity area. Buyer-seller consulting teams working jointly may accelerate overall supplier improvement at a faster rate than will actions taken independently by the supplier. The basic motivation behind this strategy is that supplier improvement and success lead to longer-term benefits to both buyer and seller. This approach supports the development of world-class suppliers in new areas of product and process technology. Chapter 9 discusses supplier development in detail.

Total Cost of Ownership

Total cost of ownership (TCO) is the process of identifying cost considerations beyond unit price, transport, and tooling. It requires the business unit to define and measure the various cost components associated with a purchased item. In many cases, this includes costs associated with late delivery, poor quality, or other forms of supplier nonperformance. Total cost of ownership can lead to better decision making because it identifies all costs associated with a supply management decision and the costs associated with supplier nonperformance. Cost variances from planned results can be analyzed to determine the cause of the variance. Corrective action can then prevent further problems. TCO is discussed in detail in Chapters 10 and 11.

E-Reverse Auctions

An e-RA is an online, real-time dynamic auction between a buying organization and a group of prequalified suppliers who compete against each other to win the business to supply goods or services that have clearly defined specifications for design, quantity, quality, delivery, and related terms and conditions. These suppliers compete by bidding against each other online over the Internet using specialized software by submitting successively lower-priced bids during a scheduled time period. This time period is usually only about an hour, but multiple, brief extensions are usually allowed if bidders are still active at the end of the initial time period. See Chapter 13 for a more detailed discussion of e-Ras.

Sourcing Snapshot

Managing Sub Tier Supplier Risk

The issue of sub-tier supply risk continues to be a challenge in many of the companies we work with at the SCRC. For example, one large company has experienced big problems in the form of tier 2 supplier mechanical failures that wind up in their product. Even though they had a problem, they were totally unwilling to invest a resource to monitor and manage these suppliers. Companies need to start coming to the realization that they are part of a network. Your business may not be significant to a sub-tier, even if you are a large brand name customer. It is not enough to "put the blame on the supplier" to manage their sub-tier—it is your problem in the end! But what options are available to manage sub-tier suppliers?

If it is a quality management issue, than procurement may need to invest effort to develop sub-tiers, and drive improvement issues. However, how can you do this? One option is to write contracts that require direct reporting of sub-tier supplier performance on scorecards—but enforcing this may be difficult. Another option explored is to have third party providers to manage this.

Procurement's value to the business is increasingly driven by the knowledge of supply markets, including the sub-tier, and the ability to communicate nuggets of information based on deep intelligence and insight into the current and future state of these markets. This is not a capability that is inherently resident in many procurement organizations. Rather it is a network capability that must be developed through nurturing of external partners with their hand on the pulse of sub-tier suppliers. This requires a new form of collaboration, and regular communications to identify and work with tier 1 suppliers to help them nurture and develop the best tier 2 suppliers, and motivate them to manage them.

Source: Robert Handfield, Supply Chain View From the Field, http://scm.ncsu.edu/blog/2013/04/03/sub-tier-supplier-risk-continues-to-be-a-challenge/

The use of e-RAs has been facilitated by a number of company internal and external developments including the following:

- Buyers' and suppliers' ability to communicate in real time, worldwide, via the Internet.

- Development of robust, user-friendly Internet-based software systems to support worldwide e-RAs hosted by a third party or conducted by the buying company with little or no outside assistance.

- Significant improvements in goods and service quality and cycle-time reductions have resulted in buying companies requiring superior quality and service. Therefore, buyers have emphasized low price as a major sourcing-decision variable.

Supply Management Transformation Evolution

Many chief procurement officers are brought in to a company to help drive a major change, often referred to as "procurement transformation" or "supply chain transformation". In effect, this refers to the objective of driving the procurement function to a higher level of improvement beyond the current state. This is often viewed as a process that may take several years to achieve, because of the magnitude of change required. If we compare the level of supply management strategy evolution to the strategies available, there is clearly an implementation sequence that emerges. Exhibit 6.14 presents the sequence of supply management strategy execution based on research from multiple studies and interviews with many executives. Organizations tend to evolve through four phases as they become mature and sophisticated in their supply management strategy development.

Phase 1: Basic Beginnings

In the initial stages of supply management strategy development, supply management is often characterized as a lower-level support function. Supply management adopts essentially a short-term approach and reacts to complaints from its internal customers when deliveries are late, quality is poor, or costs are too high. The only impetus for change here is the demand for change by management. The primary role of supply managers is to ensure that enough supply capacity exists, which usually means that suppliers are viewed in an adversarial manner. However, the amount of resources for improvement is limited,

Exhibit 6.14	Stages of Supply Management Strategy Evolution		
1. BASIC BEGINNINGS	**2. MODERATE DEVELOPMENT**	**3. LIMITED INTEGRATION**	**4. FULLY INTEGRATED SUPPLY CHAINS**
• Quality/cost teams	• E-RAs	• Global sourcing	• Global supply chains with external customer focus
• Longer-term contracts	• Ad hoc supplier alliances	• Strategic supplier alliances	• Cross-enterprise decision making
• Volume leveraging	• Cross-functional sourcing teams	• Supplier TQM development	• Full-service suppliers
• Supply-base consolidation	• Supply-base optimization	• Total cost of ownership	• Early sourcing
• Supplier quality focus	• International sourcing	• Nontraditional purchase focus	• Insourcing/outsourcing to maximize core competencies of firms throughout the supply chain
	• Cross-location sourcing teams	• Parts/service standardization	• E-systems
		• Early supplier involvement	
		• Dock to stock pull systems	

usually because the highest-ranking supply management manager likely reports to manufacturing or materials management. Performance measures focus on efficiency-related measures and price reduction. Information systems are location or facility focused and primarily transaction based.

In Phase 1, supply management often focuses on supply base optimization, and more attention is paid to total quality management than to other progressive supply management strategies. In a sense, these two strategies represent the building blocks from which to pursue increasingly sophisticated strategies. A reduced supply base is necessary because of the increased two-way communication and interaction necessary for successful execution of more complicated strategies. TQM also provides the fundamental focus on process that is required to implement supply management strategies.

Phase 2: Moderate Development

The second phase of the strategy progression usually occurs as an organization begins to centrally coordinate or control some part of the supply management function across regional or even worldwide locations. Supply management councils or lead buyers may be responsible for entire classes of commodities, and company-wide databases by region may be developed to facilitate this coordination. The primary purpose of this coordination is to establish company-wide agreements to leverage volumes to obtain lower costs from volume discounts. Single sourcing with long-term agreements may eventually emerge as a policy for leveraged or consolidated purchase families. At this stage, limited cross-functional integration is occurring. In addition, e-RAs have recently been selectively used to leverage purchases and improve goods and service pricing by between 15 and 30 percent.

The approaches in Phases 1 and 2—supply base optimization, TQM, and long-term contracting—have the potential, over time, to effect a steady increase in supplier contributions and improvements, but the performance change rate may not be dramatic.

Purchasers must now begin to pursue strategic supplier relationships that focus on customer needs and the organization's competitive strategy. In Phase 2, buyers may begin to establish better relationships with critical suppliers while continuing to optimize the supply base. The supply management department may now be evaluated on the achievement of competitive objectives, and suppliers are viewed as a resource. As such, there may be some informal channels of functional integration developing between supply management, engineering, manufacturing, marketing, and accounting. Some of this may occur through infrequent cross-functional team decision making. The execution of supply management strategy still takes place primarily at the business unit or local level.

Phase 3: Limited Integration

A number of supply management initiatives discussed in this book, including concurrent engineering, supplier development, lead-time reduction, and early supplier involvement, characterize this phase. In this environment, supply management strategies are established and integrated early into the product and process design stage, and first-and second-tier suppliers are becoming actively involved in these decisions. Supply management is evaluated on the basis of strategic contribution, and resources are made available according to strategic requirements. Extensive functional integration occurs through design and sourcing teams that focus on product development, building a competitive advantage, and total cost analysis for new and existing products and services. Supply management is viewed as a key part of the organizational structure with a strong external customer focus. As such, multiple customer-oriented measurements are used to identify performance improvements. Information systems include global databases, historical price and cost information, joint strategy development efforts with other functional groups, and the beginning of total cost modeling.

Phase 4: Fully Integrated Supply Chains

In the final and most advanced phase, supply management has assumed a strategic orientation, with reporting directly to executive management and a strong external, rather than simply internal, customer focus. Non-value-added activities such as purchase order follow-up and expediting have been automated, allowing purchasers to focus their attention on strategic objectives and activities. Organizations demand a higher performance standard from suppliers. Executives take aggressive actions that will directly improve supplier capability and accelerate supplier performance contributions.

Examples of aggressive actions include developing global supplier capabilities, developing full-service suppliers, and adopting a systems thinking perspective that encompasses the entire supply chain. In such a mode, insourcing core activities add the greatest value, whereas components of the value chain are often outsourced to upstream or downstream parties that are more capable.

Such a system can directly affect the ability of the supply base to meet world-class expectations and often involves direct intervention in the supplier's operating systems and processes.

Relatively few organizations have evolved to this phase. However, for those that succeed, a number of tangible and intangible benefits accrue from the progression of supply management from a supportive role to an integrated activity. These include price reductions across all product lines ranging from 5 to 25 percent; improved quality, cost, and delivery performance in the range of 75 to 98 percent in six to eight months; and a supply base that is better than the competition's. Supply management is now in a position to influence rather than react to the supply base, and it can actually develop key suppliers in cases where a weak link exists. Moreover, all of these processes help establish the critical capabilities required of a global leader.

Observations on Supply Management Strategy Evolution

It is important that the supply management student recognize an important point about the sequence in the category management process: Few organizations have fully executed the more complex strategies found in Phases 3 and 4. This is because of a variety of factors including the relative complexity of higher-level strategies, the resources and commitment necessary to execute the strategy, the lack of a supply base optimization effort, and personnel who lack the skills and capabilities necessary for developing advanced sourcing strategies. However, those that successfully execute more sophisticated and comprehensive sourcing strategies should realize greater performance improvement over time. The following Good Practice Example illustrates how one company developed a higher-level category strategy. This strategy may be considered to be within the Phase 3–4 category of maturity.

Good Practice Example

Transforming Organizations to Be Able to Better Listen and Respond: Best Practices in Supply Market Intelligence

Organizations are facing increased uncertainty in economic markets, and are increasingly aware of the need to closely monitor market conditions and respond to these changes through improved supply chain strategies. As more organizations seek to build sourcing strategies to identify cost savings opportunities, they are recognizing that there are major shortfalls in market intelligence and cost modeling capabilities that form the basis for effective strategies and negotiation. Further, the need for integration of market intelligence into operational decisions, including budgets, profit objectives, market pricing, technology insights, global expansion, and other components of competitive strategy is generally not well executed. The result is misalignment between demand and supply planning, and major gaps in operational performance and risk mitigation.

A recent study was carried out to explore key actions that organizations are taking to remedy this situation. The research is based on interviews with subject matter experts in a number of industries who have deployed or are in the process of deploying centers of excellence for supply market intelligence, as well as surveys with 89 global supply chain executives through IACCM. Several key important insights emerged from this research.

First, organizations with successful supply market intelligence (SMI) programs excel not so much in the process of data collection and analysis, but develop a team of internal MI analysts who are proficient in defining knowledge requirements, as well as disseminating information to ensure that it is effectively applied in key business decisions. Current research suggests that successful organizations are creating Centers of Excellence for MI, with analysts co-located in multiple business units globally, but coordinating through centralized processes. MI analysts are generally responsible for $1.5 to $2 billion of organizational spend per FTE. In most firms, however, many companies are not developing dedicated teams of MI analysts, but are relying on category managers to perform this function.

Second, it is increasingly being recognized that category managers are often not well equipped to build MI analyses, because of the increasing demand for other activities. This is important, as it justifies the need for a dedicated MI function. Further, the return on investment on these individuals dictates that it does not make sense for them to be conducting routine market analyses. Over time, however, executives interviewed believe that these individuals should become full-fledged experts in their category. Best-in-class companies are all focused on having category leaders increasingly rely on an MI Center of Excellence for coordination of data collection, analysis, synthesis, and insight as a core foundational component of sourcing strategy. Internal MI analysts are best equipped if they come from an engineering, financial, supply chain, or cost accounting background. Economics and financial analyst experience will become increasingly important for MI analysis.

Third, there is an increasing trend toward outsourcing of MI data collection, synthesis, analysis and reporting. Key areas where third party providers are collecting and synthesizing data include global market analysis, benchmarking, inflation/deflationary pricing, value-chain mapping, global cost-reduction sourcing opportunities, and emerging market sales and channels. Implicit in this trend is the recognition that best-in-class companies recognize that MI is fundamentally about the application of individual and cognitive methods to weigh data and test hypotheses. As such, the primary role of an MI function is not to collect data and process it; rather, the focus of an MI team should target engagement and understanding of internal client requirements, context, and application of the information to business decisions. Proper understanding of information requirements is fundamental to a successful MI function. Analysts need to truly understand the right question before embarking on data analysis, to ensure that the appropriate hypotheses and data are collected by external Mi providers. Best-in-class organizations also rely on MI teams to process external MI reports, and explain the implications and insights through knowledge transfer mechanisms, to ensure that the intelligence is translated into meaningful insights that are useful and practical to the stakeholder.

Fourth, best-in-class companies recognize the importance of establishing expectations to clients about what can and cannot be delivered through the MI Center of Excellence. The breadth and depth of data will determine the lead time required to create the report. Clear guidelines must be communicated and acknowledged by the client, to understand the limitations regarding what can be produced within a given time horizon, as well as the appropriate types of data required for business decisions. This is an important educational process that is part of any supply chain transformation process.

Fifth, the research points to the importance of conducting performance evaluations of MI reports, and tying these back into port-mortems and lessons learned that can be filtered back into the organization. Many companies are seeking to tie MI investments to meaningful measures of cost savings. In our opinion, this is a difficult approach to apply in a systematic and standard way. Although anecdotal data can point to cost savings achieved through effective MI applied to specific projects, these are highly contextual and specific in nature. Instead, best-in-class companies are relying on a systematic evaluation of client feedback, with a long-term and strategic understanding of the importance of MI's contribution to key enterprise-wide procurement metrics and value. This requires leadership support and alignment of procurement strategy to other core organizational strategies, and an ability to link intelligence to these outcomes.

Sixth, our research suggests that most organizations are for the most part not effectively linking MI projects and insights into operational decision making. For example, in mature organizations, cost models need be aligned with savings projects and profit targets for corporate and business unit level budgeting processes. Several case studies discussed in this report provide examples of how successful organizations are at achieving this. For the most part, this requires multiple communication channels, often through simple "lunch and learn" discussions that provide opportunities for face-to-face dialogue, discussion, Q&A, and debate.

Finally, most organizations do not have a good process for a meaningful ongoing monitoring of supply risk. There are generally a good number of companies who are monitoring financial health of suppliers, but other market-level issues are often not captured. This is one of the reasons that organizations are still susceptible to intelligence failure, because of the inherent nature of surprise associated with supply market incidents. The nature of surprise is not attributable to omission or commission of information, but rather the need for contravening cognitive processes. As such, there is a need for development of talent that has the ability to develop missing hypotheses and mental models that can begin to predict the potential behavior of market participants in a specific context.

Sources: Handfield, R. (2010, January) "Transforming Your Organization to be Able to Listen and Respond," White Paper, Supply Chain Resource Cooperative Retrieved from http://scm.ncsu.edu

CONCLUSION

Category management is perhaps one of the most important ways that supply managers create value for their stakeholders. Category teams must effectively scan the market environment, conduct research on suppliers and cost drivers, analyze internal spend characteristics, and establish appropriate strategies for managing these relationships. In doing so, supply managers depict and create insights for stakeholders on key elements of their supply environment that shape their operational, financial, and market planning decisions. Effective category strategies also create the foundation for cost management, contract frameworks, and ongoing supplier performance management metrics and relationships. These elements will be discussed in greater detail in later chapters, but it is important for students to understand how to conduct research and analysis leading to these actions.

KEY TERMS

category, 193	**rightsizing**, 231	**supply base optimization**, 231
integrative, 196	**spend analysis**, 201	**strategic supplier**, 228
preferred supplier, 228	**triangulate**, 214	

DISCUSSION QUESTIONS

1. Select a category that you believe might be chosen for a strategic category analysis in the industries listed below. Describe the factors impacting each commodity, using a Porter Five Forces analysis (described earlier in this chapter). Justify why you believe the category is strategic to that industry, and the approach to be used in developing a category strategy.

   a. Oil (West Texas intermediate) versus gasoline (discuss differential)
   b. Metals
   c. Chemicals
   d. Plastic resins
   e. Shipping
   f. Wood products and other production materials
   g. Aeronautical equipment
   h. Machine tools
   i. Telecommunications
   j. Paper

2. Why has supply management traditionally not been involved in the corporate strategic planning function?

3. Explain the differences between category strategy development and strategic sourcing. How do these differences translate into different types of processes and activities required to produce an outcome in each case?

4. Describe a set of supply management goals that might be aligned with the following corporate objective made by an automotive manufacturer: "To be the number one in customer satisfaction."

5. Describe where you think the following categories—paper clips, machine tools, castings, personal computers, fuel, computer chips, printers, Styrofoam cups, paper, custom-designed networks—might fall within the portfolio matrix. Under what circumstances might one of these items fall into more than one quadrant of the matrix, or evolve from one quadrant to another?

6. Under what conditions might you consider single-sourcing an item in the leveraging category of the portfolio matrix?

7. When conducting research, what are some advantages and disadvantages of the different types of information you might obtain from the Internet? Which types of Internet sites are likely to be more reliable as compared with personal interviews?

8. Why is it important to establish a document explaining the category strategy and share it with others? What are the possible consequences of not doing so?

9. Why must organizations develop suppliers? Is supplier development a long-term trend or just a fad? Explain.

10. Supply base optimization must occur before long-term agreements can be put into place. What are the implications of this statement?

11. How long do you believe it takes a company to move from a Stage 1 phase to a Stage 4 phase of supply management strategy development? In providing your response, consider all of the changes that must take place.

12. Provide a list of companies that, based on your reading of recent articles in the popular press, fit into the category of Stage 1 companies. What companies can you think of that might fall into the category of Stage 3 or 4? Provide some justification for your lists.

13. Some companies have begun to bring production from Low Cost Countries back to North America and Europe. What are some possible explanations for this shift?

14. What do you think are the reasons that so few companies are classified as Stage 4 companies? Do you think this is likely to change?

ADDITIONAL READINGS

Craighead, C. W., Blackhurst, J., Rungtusanatham, M. J., and Handfield, R. B. (2007), "The Severity of Supply Chain Disruptions: Design Characteristics and Mitigation Capabilities," *Decision Sciences*, 38(1), 131–156.

Darnell, N., Handfield, R., and Jolley, J. (2008), "Environmental Management Systems and Green Supply Chain Management: Complements for Sustainability?" *Business Strategy and the Environment*, 18, 30–45.

D'Avanzo, R., et al. (2003), "The Link Between Supply Chain and Financial Performance," *Supply Chain Management Review*, 27(6), 40–47.

Handfield, R., Straube, F., Pfohl, H.-C., and Wieland, A. (2013), *Trends and Strategies in Logistics and Supply Chain Management*, Berlin: BVL International.

Handfield, R. (2006), *Supplier Market Intelligence*, Boca Raton, FL: Auerbach Publications.

Handfield, R., Elkins, D., Blackhurst, J., and Craighead, C. (2005), "18 Ways to Guard against Disruption," *Supply Chain Management Review*, 9(1), 46–53.

Handfield, R., and Krause, D. (1999, Winter), "Think Globally, Source Locally," *Supply Chain Management Review*, 36–49.

Handfield, R., and McCormack, K. (2005), "What You Need to Know about Sourcing in China," *Supply Chain Management Review*, 9(5), 56–62.

Handfield, R., Walton, S., and Sroufe, R. (2004, November), "Integrating Environmental Management and Supply Chain Strategies," *Business Strategy and the Environment*, 13, 1–14.

Monczka, R., and Trent, R. J. (1991), "Evolving Sourcing Strategies for the 1990s," *International Journal of Physical Distribution and Logistics Management*, 21(5), 4–12.

Monczka, R., and Trent, R. J. (1995), *Supply Management and Sourcing Strategy: Trends and Implications*, Tempe, AZ: Center for Advanced Supply Management Studies.

Porter, M. E. (1985), *Competitive Advantage: Creating and Sustaining Superior Performance*, New York: Free Press.

Wieland, A., and Handfield, R. (2013, September), "The Socially Responsible Supply Chain: An Imperative for Global Corporations," *Supply Chain Management Review*, 17(5).

ENDNOTES

1. "A Global Study of Supply Chain Leadership and Its Impact on Business Performance," Accenture and INSEAD, white paper, 2003.

2. Developed jointly with Atlanta-based UPS Consulting, the survey titled "CFOs and the Supply Chain" was carried out by CFO Research Services. Reported in "Paying Attention: Chief Financial Officers Get Involved in Managing More Supply Chains," *Traffic World*, September 2, 2003.

3. Monczka, R., Trent, R., and Handfield, R. (2002), *Purchasing and Supply Chain Management* (2nd ed.), Cincinnati, OH: South-Western.

4. Interview with Dave Nelson, North Carolina State University research study on design for order fulfillment, March 2007.

5. Dobler, D., Lee, L., and Burt, D. (1990), *Purchasing and Materials Management*, Homewood, IL: Irwin.

6. Waxer, C. (2001, June), "E-Negotiations Are In, Price-Only e-Auctions Are Out," *iSource*, 73–76.

7. Hendricks, K., and Singhal, V. (2003), "The Effect of Supply Chain Glitches on Shareholder Wealth," *Journal of Operations Management*, 21(5), 501–522.

8. Hendricks, K., and Singhal, V. (2005), "An Empirical Analysis of the Effect of Supply Chain Disruptions on Long Run Stock Price Performance and Equity Risk of the Firm," *Production and Operations Management*, 14(1), 35–52.

9. Interview with senior executive, North Carolina State research study on global supply chain risk, October 2004.

Supplier Evaluation and Selection

CHAPTER 7

Learning Objectives

After completing this chapter, you should be able to

- Recognize the seven-step supplier selection process as an enabler to world-class supplier selection
- Understand the sourcing alternatives and critical issues that supply professionals consider in determining a sourcing strategy.
- Understand the important areas to analyze when visiting suppliers.
- Identify key criteria to narrow the supplier pool
- Learn about the resources available to identify suppliers
- Understand the importance of supplier financial analysis
- Understand how to develop a quantitative supplier evaluation and selection survey

Chapter Outline

Sourcing in a Lean Responsive Organization

Fran Chinnici, the Senior Vice President, Engineering & Mechanical at the Florida East Coast Railway is faced with the job of building a procurement organization. Mr. Chinnici's job is complicated by the the rapid business changes that are driving FEC into a new era opportunities. Selecting and developing the right sources of supply are a major part of Chinnici's challenge that can help attain FEC's strategies.

Being Florida's only east coast railway, FEC is right in the center of growth. The widening of the Panama Canal is expected to be completed in 2015 and the port of Miami anticipates a large increase in freight from the Far East in addition to increased Latin American shipments. The company is also working with the State of Florida to allow joint use of its track for a high speed rail system between Miami and Orlando. Such expansion means not only sharing but building additional track. As a 29-year rail veteran experienced in operations, purchasing, and finance, Fran is well qualified to deal with these challenges. "I see my role as a conductor who carefully orchestrates the engineering and implementation of these challenges," says Chinnici.

The Penn State engineering graduate began his career as a Metallurgical Engineer in the Research and Test Department in the Chessie System in Huntington, West Virginia. He held positions of increasing responsibility in Mechanical and Transportation functions at CSX, ascending to the role of Vice President Purchasing and Materials, for 9 years.

His new executive position is unique as it requires managing both engineering and the supply chain. As Senior Vice President—Engineering and Mechanical, he is responsible for ensuring service excellence with track, design and construction projects, signaling, locomotives, and rolling equipment. By overseeing the Purchasing and Materials team, Fran ensures that these service levels are achieved at the lowest total cost of ownership.

Florida East Coast Railroad

FEC operates 351miles of mainline track and is the only railroad along Florida's east coast. FEC has interchange access with two Class I railroads in Jacksonville. This access allows FEC to provide a vital link between Florida and the nation's rail network. FEC offers the most direct and efficient North/South option for transporting freight and has a competitive advantage because of the highly congested roadways in South Florida. FEC transports an attractive freight mix of both intermodal containers and trailers. Carload traffic ranges from crushed rock, to automobiles, to food, and industrial products.

Capital investment purchases provide efficient goods movement

Fran claims, "we have a great need to purchase infrastructure and technology." "Our state is investing in its ports because we see a great opportunity to be an import and export center and the canal widening will be a huge economic boost for South Florida ports," he stated.

The Port of Miami is engaged in the FEC Rail Reconnection Project. The Project has four phases: (1) reconstruction of the Florida East Coast Railway (FEC) Port Lead, (2) rehabilitation of the bascule bridge that connects Port Miami and FEC, (3) the construction of an on-port rail facility, and (4) modifications to FEC's Rail Yard to accommodate the increase in intermodal traffic. The rail reconnection project is actually part of a larger infrastructure investment program taking place at Port Miami.

Major capital projects include the reconnection of the FEC to the Port of Miami. This connection will link to a new on-dock rail facility and the development of an Intermodal Container Transfer Facility at Port Everglades (Fort Lauderdale). Both of these projects will provide the ports with direct access to the FEC rail network and its intermodal terminals.

Chinnici envisions that the South Florida Logistics Center will save time and money of shippers by reducing drayage costs, optimizing inventory positions, and providing synergistic supply chain opportunities. The unique multi-modal logistics center will transform the way freight is moved into and out of South Florida.

Though continuing FEC's procurement spend is in the neighborhood of $75 million, the ramp up in capital expenditures and the implementation of Positive Train Control (PTC) could easily double that amount. "When we start to add track the need for rail steel increases as does the need for rail ties and ballast," says Chinnici. "Depending on our volumes we have to start thinking outside the box." "This could include looking at Chinese sources for rail steel and also working to develop a supplier of concrete ties in South Florida," says the Vice President of engineering and sourcing.

Becoming responsive and lean

Mr. Chinnici visualizes a responsive and lean purchasing organization. "We can't afford extra people, we are a class II railway and don't have the size or financial power of the class I's so we have to be more resourceful and efficient to survive." "I have a goal to upgrade the professionalism of my staff so the skills are in place to compete. In our market this will require us to quickly recognize and then seize opportunities. My buyers must know the market, suppliers and be able to craft sourcing strategies that keep our road running to provide world-class service." To that end, Chinnici is putting a people development strategy linked to a key supplier monitoring program. "At the end of the day it all starts with your people and their skill set, he says." "Selecting and developing the right suppliers becomes critical if we are to meet our corporate goals," states Chinnici. "My vision is that we will be a responsive and flexible supply group," he adds. If anyone can do it, this is one VP who has the vision and commitment to make it happen.

Source: Larry Giunipero Interview with Fran Chinnici August 2013

Introduction

One of the most important processes that organizations perform is the evaluation, selection, and continuous measurement of suppliers. Traditionally, competitive bidding was the primary method for awarding purchase contracts. In the past, it was sufficient to obtain three bids and award the contract to the supplier offering the lowest price. Enlightened purchasers now commit major resources to evaluating a supplier's performance and capability across many different areas. The supplier selection process has become so important that teams of cross-functional personnel are often responsible for visiting and evaluating suppliers. A sound selection decision can reduce or prevent a host of problems.

Supplier evaluation and selection decisions are taking on increased importance today. If a firm has reduced its supply base to a much smaller level, and if remaining suppliers usually receive longer-term agreements, the willingness or ability to switch suppliers is diminished. This makes selecting the right suppliers an important business decision.

This chapter focuses on different topics and issues pertaining to the evaluation and selection of suppliers. The first section provides an overview of the evaluation and selection process. The next sections present the various performance categories that a purchaser can include within the evaluation and selection process. The third section focuses on an approach for developing a tool or instrument for use during supplier evaluations. We next highlight the critical issues that confront a purchaser during the selection process. The chapter concludes with ways to reduce the time required for selection decisions.

The Supplier Evaluation and Selection Process

Most purchasing experts will agree that there is no one best way to evaluate and select suppliers, and organizations use a variety of different approaches. Regardless of the approach employed, the overall objective of the evaluation process should be to reduce purchase risk and maximize overall value to the purchaser.

An organization must select suppliers it can do business with over an extended period. The degree of effort associated with the selection relates to the importance of the required good or service. Depending on the supplier evaluation approach used, the process can be an intensive effort requiring a major commitment of resources (such as time and travel). This section addresses the many issues and decisions involved in effectively and efficiently evaluating and selecting suppliers to be part of the purchaser's supply base. Exhibit 7.1 highlights the critical steps involved in the supplier evaluation and selection process.

Recognize the Need for Supplier Selection

The first step of the evaluation and selection process usually involves recognizing that there is a requirement to evaluate and select a supplier for an item or service. A purchasing manager

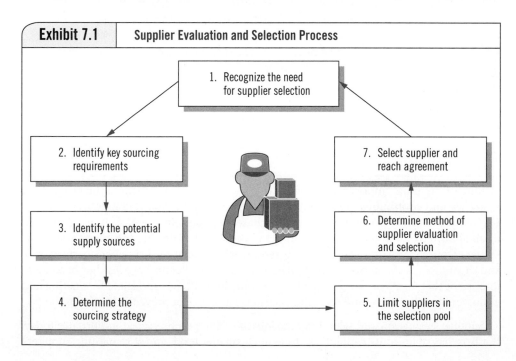

| **Exhibit 7.1** | **Supplier Evaluation and Selection Process** |

1. Recognize the need for supplier selection
2. Identify key sourcing requirements
3. Identify the potential supply sources
4. Determine the sourcing strategy
5. Limit suppliers in the selection pool
6. Determine method of supplier evaluation and selection
7. Select supplier and reach agreement

Exhibit 7.2	When Do Supplier Evaluation and Selection Decisions Arise?

- When internal users submit requisitions for goods or services
- During new-product development
- Because of poor internal or external supplier performance
- When the contract period ends
- When buying new equipment
- When expanding into new markets or product lines
- When performing market tests
- When faced with countertrade requirements
- During outsourcing analyses
- When consolidating volumes across a business
- When issuing an RFQ or conducting a reverse auction
- When current suppliers have insufficient capacity
- When reducing the size of the supply base

might begin the supplier evaluation process in anticipation of a future purchase requirement. Purchasing may have early insight into new-product development plans through participation on a product development team. In this case, engineering personnel may provide some preliminary specifications on the type of materials, service, or processes required, but will not yet have specific details. This preliminary information may be enough to justify beginning an initial evaluation of potential sources of supply. Finally, the outsourcing phenomena has created new challenges for purchasers to evaluate providers of services that often involve many less tangible and more perceptual views of quality such as consulting engineers.

The recognition that a need exists to evaluate suppliers can come about in many different ways. Exhibit 7.2 identifies the most common ways that result in a need to evaluate sources of supply. Progressive purchasing groups increasingly anticipate rather than react to supplier selection needs. The complexity and value of a required purchase will influence the extent to which a buyer evaluates potential supply sources. Regarding service buys this includes evaluating that the provider has the resources necessary to assure the reliable on-time delivery of their services. This could include a one-time report from an engineering consulting firm to a continual service such as pest control.

Identify Key Sourcing Requirements

Throughout the supplier evaluation and selection process, it is important to understand the requirements that are important to that purchase. These requirements, often determined by internal and external customers within the value chain, can differ widely from item to item. A later section discusses the various supplier performance areas where a purchaser should determine its critical sourcing requirements. Although different requirements may exist for each evaluation, certain categories—supplier quality, cost, and delivery performance—are usually included in the evaluation.

Identify Potential Supply Sources

Purchasers rely on various sources of information when identifying potential sources of supply. The degree to which a buyer must search for information or the effort put forth toward the search is a function of several variables, including how well existing suppliers can satisfy cost, quality, or other performance variables. The strategic importance or technical complexity of the purchase requirement also influences the intensity of the search.

The following offers some guidelines regarding the effort and intensity of search required during supplier evaluation:

- High capability of current suppliers + High strategic importance of requirement = **Minor to moderate information search**
- High capability of current suppliers + Low strategic importance of requirement = **Minor information search**
- Low capability of current suppliers + High strategic importance of requirement = **Major information search**
- Low capability of current suppliers + Low strategic importance of requirement = **Minor to moderate information search**

The following sections discuss various resources that may be good sources of information when seeking to identify potential suppliers.

Current Suppliers

A major source of information is current or existing suppliers. Buyers often look to existing suppliers to satisfy a new purchase requirement. The advantage of this approach is that the purchaser does not have to add and maintain an additional supplier. Also, the buyer can do business with an already familiar supplier, which may limit the time and resources required to evaluate a new supplier's capabilities.

On the negative side, using existing suppliers, although perhaps easier and quicker, may not always be the best long-term approach. A purchasing manager may never know if better suppliers are available without information on other sources. For this reason, most organizations are continuously seeking new sources of supply and are expanding this search to include global suppliers.

Selecting an existing supplier for a new purchase requirement may be an attractive option if a list of preferred suppliers is maintained. Designation as a **preferred supplier** means that a supplier consistently satisfies the performance and service standards defined by the buyer and responds to unexpected changes. A preferred supplier status conveys immediate information about the supplier's overall performance and competency. However, the buyer must still determine if a preferred supplier is capable of providing the new purchase requirement.

Sales Representatives

All purchasers receive sales and marketing information from sales representatives. These contacts can prove to be a valuable source of information about potential sources. Even if an immediate need does not exist for a supplier's services, the buyer can file the information for future reference. Detailed information on sales representatives and their product and service capabilities is available on the Internet. Information about sales representatives can be easily viewed on social media sites such as LinkedIn and Facebook.

Internet Searches and Social Media

Today, buyers routinely use the Internet to help locate potential sources that might qualify for further evaluation. Correspondingly, most sellers of all sizes have an Internet presence as part of their overall marketing efforts. Buyers are able to view pictures of the facility, find information about the management team and oftentimes a customer list. Additionally, LinkedIn, Facebook, and Twitter provide an additional resource to extract information on a potential supplier and its key employees. LinkedIn is particularly useful to locate background information about key managers at a particular supplier. There are also various interest groups by commodity or category. For example, the "Foundry and Castings User and Buyers" group consists of about 6000 members. The "Worldwide IT Buyers and Procurement" group consists of about 2500 members.

Informational Databases

Purchasers of today suffer from information overload. The use of mobile devices and increased visual capabilities of Web 2.0 provides immediate access to information about suppliers. The challenge is managing this vast array of information. Supply organizations must decide what information should be downloaded from the Internet and how it should be captured and stored in internal data warehouses or Enterprise Requirements Planning (ERP) systems.

There are several companies that can assist with providing databases where the supply organization can store information about their suppliers. These systems are also capable of providing inputs to assist in strategic sourcing or monitor if the organization's purchases are contract compliant. For example, IBM's Global Process Services Group provides software to assist buyers maintain supplier databases to locate the best suppliers as well as drive other efficiencies into the sourcing process.[1]

Databases allow the purchaser to quickly identify suppliers potentially qualified to support a requirement. The database may contain information on current products, the supplier's future technology roadmap, process capability ratios, and past performance. It is important to constantly review, update, and modify these databases to insure information accuracy. If additional suppliers are required, databases of potential supply sources are also available for purchase from external parties.

Organizational knowledge

Knowledge management is the process of capturing the sourcing knowledge and experience of an organization's purchasers in a database. This knowledge can then be shared throughout the organization.

Experienced purchasing personnel usually have strong knowledge about potential suppliers. A buyer may have worked within an industry over many years and may be familiar with the suppliers. One argument against rotating buyers too frequently between product lines or types of purchases is that a buyer may lose the expertise built up over the years. Capturing this knowledge about decision processes can improve the sourcing process for newer or less experienced purchasers.

Trade Journals

Most industries have a group or council that publishes a trade journal or magazine that routinely presents articles about different companies. These articles often focus on a company's technical or innovative development of a material, component, product, process, or service. Suppliers also use trade journals to advertise their products or services. Since most trade journals are available in electronic format, buyers can easily access and follow them.

Trade Directories

Almost all industries publish directories of companies that produce items or provide services within an industry. Such directories can be a valuable source of initial information for a buyer who is not familiar with an industry or its suppliers. Chapter 10 provides some examples of international supplier directories. A very popular directory for domestic buyers is the *ThomasNet* maintained by Thomas Publishing Company, whose mission for over 100 years has been to disseminate industrial product information. This directory can be located at www.thomasnet.com.

Trade Shows

Trade shows may be an effective way to gain exposure to a large number of suppliers at one time. Groups such as the Chemical Manufacturers Association and the American Society of Automotive Suppliers often sponsor trade shows. The International Machine Technology Show in Chicago is one of the largest trade shows held in the United States. Buyers attending trade shows can gather information about potential suppliers while also evaluating the latest technological developments. Many contacts are initiated between industrial buyers and sellers at trade shows.

Second-Party or Indirect Information

This source of information includes a wide range of contacts not directly part of the purchaser's organization. A buyer can gather information from other suppliers, such as knowledge about a non-competitor that might be valuable. Other buyers are another second-party information source. Attendees at local affiliate meetings of the Institute for Supply Management can develop informal networks of purchasers from other organizations that can provide information about potential supply sources. Most local ISM affiliates such as Purchasing Management Association of Boston (PMAB) have monthly meetings that feature presentations on current supply management practices. Additionally, PMAB's website allows members to post questions about general supply issues including difficult-to-find products or services. Other professional groups of interest to supply managers include the American Production and Inventory Control Society (APICS), the Council for Supply Chain Management Professionals (CSCMP), and the American Society for Quality Control (ASQC).

Some purchasers publicly recognize their best suppliers. Recognition may come in the form of a newspaper advertisement that highlights the achievement of superior suppliers. AT&T, for example, took out a half-page advertisement in the *Wall Street Journal* (May 14, 2013) expressing appreciation and recognition to its best suppliers. In the advertisement, AT&T recognized six outstanding suppliers out of its total supply base of 5,000. These suppliers went above and beyond in providing AT&T with better products, superior services, enhanced cost structures or best-in-class approaches that contributed to the company's success during the past year.[2] Being aware of these supplier awards allows an astute buyer to gain visibility to a group of blue-chip suppliers.

Internal Sources

Many larger companies divide the organization into different business units, each with a separate purchasing operation. Sharing information across units can occur through formal corporate purchasing councils, informal meetings, strategy development sessions,

Sourcing Snapshot

Evaluating the Risks and Challenges of Sole and Single Sourcing

Single sourcing occurs when a supply management organization purposely chooses one of many possible suppliers. The *ISM Glossary of Key Supply Management Terms* states, single sourcing is "the practice of deliberately concentrating purchases of a particular item with one source in preference over others in a competitive marketplace." Often, a single-sourcing strategy is motivated by cost. Some examples include office supplies, travel planning, a p-card provider, or a bank. Generally, the products and services are fairly generic, and the choices are often predicated on cost and contract terms. In some cases, the single-sourcing decision is based on a preferred relationship or product, such as a Mac over a PC. Whatever the reason, if the source disappeared, you could choose another supplier relatively quickly. The risk of a supply disruption is fairly small and the potential damage caused is comparatively minor with single-source suppliers. The risk to a company's bottom line also is relatively minor.

Mitigating the Risk of Single-Sourcing can be performed by having a second source play a minor role in your supply chain, which can help ease some of the pain if the single-source supplier goes out of business or if quality issues occur. If your organization has a single source for office supplies, consider using another office supply company consistently for one or two commodities, such as paper or boxes. In a manufacturing company, for example, use a second foundry to cast a specific line of valves or brass castings only. By having a backup supplier waiting in the wings, a transition, if needed, will be much smoother at a company you have have previously done business with. In other words, risk mitigation is important when single sourcing.

Sole Sourcing is defined by the *ISM Glossary of Key Supply Management Terms* as "the use of one source when that source is the only available supplier possessing the ability to fulfill the firm's procurement needs." Although organizations try to avoid sole-source situations, some are unavoidable. There are several cases when an organization would use a sole source and they include conditions when:

1. A supplier holds the patent on a part or product the procuring company needs.

2. Only one company is licensed to produce a certain item or holds the intellectual property rights to a needed product or service.

3. A custom part is needed by a company and the tooling costs for the custom part are very expensive. In this case if the buyer chooses to purchase the tooling then the sole source could become a single source if other suppliers can make the item.

4. Only one company has the most efficient process to produce a product, making it significantly less expensive than any alternative.

5. Your company holds patent rights and intellectual property that need to be carefully guarded. In this case, the supply management organization chooses one supplier to produce the item to avoid sharing sensitive information with a variety of suppliers. In this type of scenario, supply management professionals must first lock down security provisions in a detailed contract.

As is illustrated above, in cases 3, 4, and 5 other suppliers are available making the "sole" supplier designation less firm. Software is a classic example of the above conditions. Though it is possible to make a change if your software provider goes out of business, it can be expensive and time-consuming. Unfortunately, sole sourcing opens your company to a greater risk of supply disruption.

Mitigating risk with a sole-source supplier can be broken down into three areas of (1) Risk identification; (2) Risk assessment; and (3) Contingency planning.

Risk identification. When trying to identify risk in a sole-source supplier, don't discount on-site and firsthand information from those in the field. Site visits, for example, can highlight signs of stress in a company—employee turnover, unkempt plants, and idle machinery. Often local industry sources have their ears to the ground and can tell if a certain company is stretching out its accounts payable or has missed a payroll run. Companies usually don't get into serious financial trouble overnight. Supply management professionals should be able to spot trouble months ahead of a breakdown and have time to assist the supplier or move on.

Risk assessment. Assessing risk involves analyzing the supplier's challenges to determine if the procuring company is a cause of the problem or if it can help resolve the situation. Helping out a sole-source supplier can be as simple as shortening payment terms from 90 to 30 days.

One buyer's company that negotiated the price of circuit board assemblies (PCBA) so low that the supplier actually went bankrupt because it had not figured its costs correctly, and by the time it did, the front doors were locked. By not assessing the supplier's risk or understanding the gravity of the low price negotiation this company spent almost a year finding a new supplier that met specifications. In hindsight, paying a little more for each PCBA would have produced a lower cost solution.

Contingency planning. Supply management professionals should have contingency plans in place to lessen the impact of a supply disruption if a sole-source supplier goes out of business or fails to live up to expectations. Whether it's maintaining an inventory buffer to absorb short-term supply shocks or staying abreast and tracking potential back-up suppliers. Having a plan will save much time when and if an actual problem occurs.

Adapted from: "Evaluate Risks, Challenges of Sole, Single Sourcing" Terry Volpel, CPSM, C.P.M., SCMP, *Inside Supply Management*, June/July 2013, pp.12–13.

purchasing newsletters, or the development of a comprehensive database containing information about potential supply sources. Internal sources, even those from diverse business units, can provide a great deal of information about potential supply sources and their experiences in using the particular supplier.

Determine Sourcing Strategy

No single sourcing strategy approach will satisfy the requirements of all supply managers. Because of this, the purchasing strategy adopted for a particular item or service will influence the approach taken during the supplier evaluation and selection process. In this chapter, we will not go into the detail on the processes used to develop a commodity strategy. Chapter 6 covers this subject in detail. There are many decisions that a purchaser initially makes when developing a sourcing strategy. However, these often change as a result of market conditions, user preferences, and corporate objectives. The considerations developed during the strategy phase need to be reevaluated during the selection process and will be affected by the quality of the search for potential suppliers. For example, if only one source is found to satisfy the requirement, then the sourcing strategy will be quite different from a search where multiple capable suppliers are identified. Thus the supplier selection and evaluation process and the chosen strategy are very much intertwined. In developing a sourcing strategy the purchaser must consider his/her sourcing alternatives as well as critical sourcing issues.

Consider Sourcing Alternatives

Once the list of potential and current suppliers is put into a database, it is further refined, considering the type of supplier a firm may wish to deal with based on the initial sourcing strategy. Major sourcing alternatives include whether to purchase from a (1) manufacturer or distributor; (2) local or national or international source; (3) large or small suppliers; and (4) multiple, single or sole supplier(s) for the item, commodity, or service.

Manufacturer vs. Distributor

The choice of buying directly versus from a distributor is usually based on four criteria: (1) the size of the purchase; (2) the manufacturer's policies regarding direct sales; (3) the storage space available at the purchaser's facility; and (4) the extent of services required.

Economically speaking, if all else is equal, the lowest unit price will be available from the OEM. The distributor buys from the OEM and resells, therefore incurring a transaction cost, and it must make a profit. Despite the exchange cost, recent trends have increased the role of distributors in providing the purchaser a low-cost solution. First, many OEMs cannot handle, or choose not to handle, the large volume of transactions required to sell directly. Second, buyers are requiring more services from their suppliers and distributors have stepped in to fill this need. **Supplier Managed Inventory** is a program that distributors market to manage their customer's inventory for them. Several organizations are using **integrated supply** where a distributor is awarded a longer-term contract. Integrated suppliers are given access to the purchaser's demand data and are expected to maintain certain levels of inventory and customer service on the contracted items.

Local or National or International Suppliers

International and national suppliers may be able to offer the best price and superior technical service. Alternatively, local suppliers are more responsive to the buying firm's changing needs and can economically make frequent smaller deliveries. The popularity of just-in-time (JIT) and quick-replenishment systems favor using more local suppliers. Local suppliers also allow the buying firm to build a degree of community goodwill through enhancing local economic activity. International suppliers provide opportunities to attain dramatic price savings. These savings must be evaluated against the additional inventory, communication, and logistics costs (see Chapter 10 for a complete discussion).

Large or Small Suppliers

All suppliers were at one time small suppliers. Growth over time is because of their ability to provide superior price, quality, and service compared to their competitors. Many purchasers prefer to focus on "capability to do the job" regardless of size. Size does become a factor when one firm decides to leverage its purchases from one or a few suppliers. In addition, the smaller supplier may not have the necessary capacity to meet the buyer's total needs. Leveraging also means that the supplier must have wide variety in its product or service offerings as well as the ability to service multiple geographic locations (in some cases worldwide locations).

Often the buying firm does not want the seller to become dependent on its business. To remedy this concern, many purchasers would limit their total expenditures with a supplier to a certain percentage (e.g., 35–45 percent) of the supplier's total sales revenue. Finally, supply departments that are building diversity into their supply base will often deal with an increased number of small suppliers.

Categorizing Suppliers for Multiple or Single or Sole Sourcing

Prior to deciding whether to use multiple or single sourcing the purchaser reviews the categories of suppliers available to meet the needed purchase requirement. Unlike purchasing for our individual needs, professional buyers only place business with suppliers who they have **prequalified or approved**. A pre-qualified/approved supplier has met the purchaser's initial screening and is deemed worthy of being considered for business. Becoming pre-qualified/approved may require a supplier visit and this is discussed later in the chapter.

As discussed earlier, a **preferred supplier** is one that consistently satisfies the performance and service standards defined by the buyer and responds to unexpected changes. **Certified suppliers** have had their quality systems extensively audited by the buying firm and are capable of consistently meeting or exceeding the buyer's quality needs. Parts from certified suppliers bypass the buyer's incoming inspection. **Partnered suppliers** are limited to a select group of suppliers who provide critical high value items to the firm. Partnership does not imply a legal relationship, but one that is built on close relationships between the buying and selling organizations and is usually viewed from a longer-term perspective. Finally, **disqualified suppliers** consist of suppliers who no longer meet the buying organization's standards and will not be considered for future business until their problems are corrected.

After a review of the supplier categories within a specific service or product buy a decision on the optimal number of suppliers must be made. For example, if the buying category is critical, then a partnered supplier may be chosen as a single source. Alternatively, if the buying category contains only pre-qualified/approved suppliers, then the decision may be made to use multiple sources. In cases where a firm's management or technical personnel specify one and only one supplier, the purchaser is left in a **sole supplier** situation. Sole supplier means there are no other approved suppliers of the product or service that the firm will accept. In this case the purchaser has little power and is often at the mercy of the supplier.

Though there is a trend to reduce the overall number of suppliers, risks of supply disruptions are causing buyers to review these strategies. *Single sourcing* provides numerous benefits including: (1) optimum leverage and power over the supplier; (2) the ability to develop closer relationships; and (3) the development of value adding programs such as supplier stocking, process improvement and so on. Alternatively, *multiple sourcing*

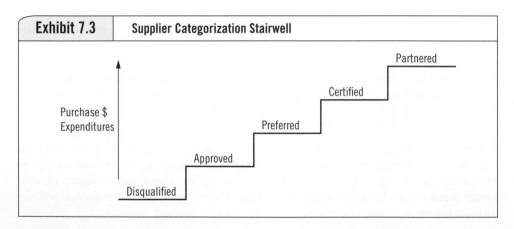

| **Exhibit 7.3** | **Supplier Categorization Stairwell** |

provides: (1) improved assurance of supply; (2) a check against price increases; (3) active competition that motivates the suppliers to perform effectively. Supply managers must assess these advantages as there is no one right solution that fits all situations. The decision to single or multiple source a buying category is very situation specific and changes with the supplier composition and economic conditions.

Evaluate Critical Issues

Each of these sourcing alternatives will generate specific critical issues that must be addressed to achieve an effective source selection process. Though each selection decision will generate its own specific critical issues, five important ones include: (1) size relationships; (2) risk/reward issues; (3) sustainability and diversity objectives; (4) competitors as suppliers; and (5) offshore suppliers & countertrade.

Size Relationship

A purchaser may decide to select suppliers over which it has a relative size advantage. A buyer may simply have greater influence when it has a relative size advantage over the supplier or represents a larger share of the supplier's total business. Some buyers track the annual dollar amount of their purchases divided by the supplier's total sales revenue, and this is a factor in source selection. One firm expects this ratio to be less than or equal to 40 percent.

Alternatively, when a buyer is only a small part of a supplier's business, he/she may get less attention. For example, Allen-Edmonds Shoe Corporation, a maker of premium shoes, tried unsuccessfully to implement JIT methods to speed production, boost customer satisfaction, and save money. Unfortunately, Allen-Edmonds had difficulty getting suppliers to agree to the just-in-time requirement of matching delivery to production needs. Although domestic suppliers of leather soles agreed to make weekly instead of monthly deliveries, European tanneries supplying calfskin hides refused to cooperate. The reason? Allen-Edmonds was not a large enough customer to wield any leverage with those suppliers.

Risk/Reward Issues

Purchasers always want to select suppliers who are profitable and growing. However, the supplier world is not created equally. Certain suppliers who may present the lowest price may also present greater risks. For example, a small supplier with a very competitive price/cost proposal may not have the ability to scale their business quickly enough to satisfy the purchaser's growing requirements. They may also be dependent on a few large customers for the majority of their business. Assessing risk is a key element of the purchaser's job and must be considered during the selection process. With the increase in supply disruptions created by longer supply chains (i.e., global sourcing), reduced inventory (i.e., JIT), increased natural disasters (e.g., 2011 Japanese tsunami) and anemic economic growth there is a concerted effort by upper management to monitor risk.

There are several third-party providers who can provide data to collaborate or dispute the purchaser's assumptions about the future of the supplier. Traditionally, purchasing has been risk averse; progressive purchasers understand the risk/reward tradeoff and are prepared to manage it better to attain overall lower costs. The sourcing snapshot discusses how to begin develop a critical supplier list monitoring manage risk in the supply base.

Sustainability and Diversity Objectives

Most purchasers are attempting to diversify their supply base by increasing purchases from traditionally disadvantaged suppliers. These include minority, female, veteran, or handicapped owned businesses. Several organizations are available to assist the buyer in finding and certifying diverse sources. These include the Small Business Administration, (SBA) http://www.sba.gov/, National Minority Supplier Development Council (NMSDC) http://www.nmsdc.org/nmsdc/ and the Women's Business Enterprise National Council (WBNEC) http://www.wbenc.org/

Buyers may also want to conduct business with suppliers that commit to improving sustainable practices (e.g., see P&G sourcing snapshot). Many buyers now require suppliers to be ISO 14000 certified to insure they have implemented sustainable practices versus only talking about them.

Competitors as Suppliers

Another important issue is the degree to which a buyer is willing to purchase directly from a competitor. Purchasing from competitors may limit information sharing between the parties. The purchase transaction is usually straightforward, and the buyer and seller may not develop a working relationship characterized by mutual commitment and confidential information sharing.

International Suppliers and Countertrade

The decision to select an international supplier can have important implications during the supplier evaluation and selection process. For one, international sourcing is generally more complex than domestic buying. As a result, the evaluation and selection process can take on added complexity. It may be difficult to implement JIT with international suppliers, as lead times are frequently twice or even three times as long as lead times for domestic suppliers. Generally, higher levels of inventories will be required when selecting an offshore supplier.

Countertrade requirements appear in many international sales contracts. Countertrade requires the purchaser to source goods in that country as a condition for selling in that country. Boeing, a producer of commercial aircraft, purchases a portion of its production requirements in markets where it hopes to do business. An organization involved in extensive worldwide marketing may have to contend with countertrade requirements before it can sell to international customers, which can have a direct impact on the supplier evaluation and selection process. Chapter 10 addresses international purchasing and countertrade.

Limit Suppliers in Selection Pool

Once the information has been gathered and the sourcing alternatives and critical issues assessed, the purchaser may have many potential sources from which to choose. Unfortunately, the performance capabilities of suppliers vary widely. Limited resources also preclude an in-depth evaluation of all potential supply sources. Purchasers often perform a first cut or preliminary evaluation of potential suppliers to narrow the list before conducting an in-depth formal evaluation. Several criteria may support the narrowing of the supplier list.

Supplier Risk Management

Anytime a purchase order is placed or contract awarded there will be a degree of risk to the purchaser. **Risk management** is the process of identifying potential negative events, assessing the likelihood of their occurrence, heading off these events before they occur or reducing the probability they will occur and making contingency plans to mitigate the consequences if they do occur.[3] Though risk can emanate from many places at the selection stage we will focus on two major risks *financial* and *operational*.

Financial risk management is defined as the continual monitoring of the strength of suppliers' financial condition to insure their ability to meet the purchaser's performance requirements for products or services. Most purchasers perform at least a cursory financial analysis of prospective suppliers. Although financial condition is not the sole criterion to evaluate a supplier, poor financial condition can indicate serious problems. A financial analysis performed during this phase of the process is much less comprehensive than the one performed during final supplier evaluation. During this phase, a purchaser is trying to get an indication of the overall financial health of the supplier. Buyers often consult external sources of information such as annual reports, 10K reports (available at www.sec.gov), and Dun & Bradstreet (D&B) reports to support the evaluation. Once a supplier is selected, several third-party providers can keep the buyer apprised of any problematic financial changes that would pose a disruption to supply.

Operational risk management focuses on the continued ability of the supplier's human, intellectual and physical capital to meet the buying firm's requirements with respect to quality and delivery. In the long term, it involves meeting demand fluctuations, new-product needs and providing continually improved products and services. For example, one firm in the high tech industry requires it suppliers to ramp-up volume for new-product introductions as well as meeting seasonal demands. The firm expects its suppliers to have the necessary operational capability and flexibility.

In one example, the supply manager noticed that supplier delivery promises were being missed from a previously excellent mid-sized supplier. When the sourcing team visited the supplier facility they noticed a sizable drop in the number of employees from their previous visit a year ago. Discussions with the key managers revealed this supplier lost a major contract with a key customer. As a result, the firm offered early retirements to senior employees and then laid off many younger employees. The result was a significant "brain drain" and reduced capacity, leading to longer lead times and reduced flexibility in operations.

Sourcing Snapshot

An Introduction to Evaluating Supplier Risk

Supplier risk can emanate from many points in the environment (e.g. natural disasters) or within the supplier's organization. The intent of this snapshot is to provide a framework to develop and monitor supplier risk through first developing a critical supplier list and then monitoring suppliers on that list to identify potential risks prior to a critical event that would disrupt supply and create customer problems.

Developing Critical Supplier List

Of the thousands of suppliers a company has, only a relatively few fall into the critical category. A *critical supplier* is one whose failure will greatly impact the buying company. Deciding which suppliers fit this description will vary from firm to firm. However some of the key criteria used to identify critical suppliers includes:

- Strategic suppliers
- Single suppliers
- Sole suppliers
- Suppliers with parts/services in many product lines or programs
- Suppliers with a high-dollar value of company owned tooling
- Suppliers with long qualification times
- Suppliers with a high percentage of business with the company
- Key disadvantaged suppliers

Ultimately each buying company determines which suppliers are to be included on the critical supplier list. For example, one organization's rule was simply "we want all of our direct material suppliers with expenditures of over $10 million on the list." However, such a rule will usually result in too many suppliers on the critical list, so a second or third round of evaluation will be needed to get the list to a manageable number of truly critical suppliers. Whatever method is used to create the critical supply list, the list will have to be periodically updated as the supply base changes.

Monitoring Suppliers

Once the critical supplier list is developed there is a need to monitor these critical suppliers. Every company has a number of suppliers that, if they should fail, would significantly impact the business. A key step in supplier risk management is identifying those relatively few suppliers who pose a high risk to the company. The challenge is to identify and monitor the high-risk suppliers. Identifying high-risk suppliers is best accomplished by a series of screens that successively reduce the number of suppliers to be monitored. (See Figure below.) The first screen identifies the critical suppliers, the second screen identifies critical suppliers with a high probability of financial or operational distress, and the last screen identifies the stressed suppliers that need intervention or mitigation.

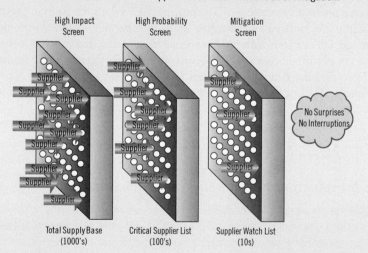

The decision to use an outside resource to help screen and monitor the supplier base is one of the most important decisions the risk management team will make. Engaging a third-party provider of risk management services (3PR) will significantly impact the risk management process and the overall cost of the program.

Adopted from "Supplier Financial and Operational Risk Management" by P.L. Carter & L.C. Giunipero, CAPS Research Study 2011 Tempe, AZ 70 pp.

Evaluation of Supplier Performance

A prospective supplier may have an established performance record with a purchaser. A purchaser may have used a supplier for a previous purchase requirement, or a supplier may currently provide material to another part of the organization. A supplier may also have provided other types of commodities or services to the purchaser than those under consideration. Based on prior experience, a purchasing manager may consider that supplier for a different type of commodity or service. Chapter 9 covers various methods of evaluating a supplier to monitor their performance once a contract has been issued.

Evaluation of Supplier-Provided Information

Buyers often request specific information directly from potential suppliers. Requests for information involve sending a preliminary survey to suppliers. The buyer uses this information to screen each supplier and to determine if the supplier's capabilities match the buyer's requirements. Buyers can request information on a supplier's cost structure, process technology, market share data, quality performance, or any other area important to the purchase decision.

A major U.S. chemical producer mandates that suppliers complete requests for information (which it calls presurvey questionnaires) before conducting more detailed supplier surveys. Besides ownership, financial information, and type of business, this company attempts to determine how sophisticated the supplier's current practices are and how far along it is toward achieving continual quality improvement.

Before committing time to evaluate a supplier further, suppliers should satisfy certain entry qualifiers. **Entry qualifiers** are the basic components that suppliers must possess before they proceed to the next phase of the evaluation and selection process. Typical qualifiers include: (1) *financial strength*; (2) *proven manufacturing or service capability*; (3) *capable and supportive management*; (4) *adequate facilities;* and a (5) *skilled professional and technical staff.* The time and cost associated with evaluating suppliers makes it necessary to limit suppliers in the selection pool to those that meet these qualifiers.

Determine the Method of Supplier Evaluation and Selection

Once an initial cut has eliminated suppliers that are not capable, the buyer or commodity team must decide how to evaluate the remaining suppliers, which may appear to be equally qualified. This requires a finer level of evaluation detail than that used in the initial process. There are a number of ways to evaluate and select suppliers from the remaining companies in the pool. These include evaluating supplier-provided information, conducting supplier visits, and using preferred, certified or partnered suppliers.

Supplier-Provided Information

As discussed on the previous page, buyers often receive and evaluate detailed information directly from potential suppliers for the purpose of awarding a purchase contract. This information may come from requests for quotes or requests for proposals. Increasingly, companies are also requesting that suppliers provide a detailed cost breakdown of their quoted price in their response to a request for quote, including details on cost composition, cost drivers, and justification of fuel surcharges or other added costs.

Supplier Visits

A team of cross-functional experts may visit potential suppliers. The next section discusses the criteria often used by cross-functional teams during supplier visits. Although many sources exist to discover information about a potential supplier, visiting the actual facility provides the most complete way to ensure an accurate assessment of the supplier.

Site visits are expensive and require buyer time in travel and information collection. They require at least a day and often several days, to complete. When factoring in travel time and post-visit reviews, it becomes clear that an organization must carefully select those suppliers it plans on evaluating. In many cases, a cross-functional team will perform the evaluation, which allows team members with different knowledge to ask different questions.

Purchasers often notify suppliers beforehand of any documentation required during the initial evaluation. For example, if a purchaser has no previous experience with a supplier, the reviewer might require a supplier to provide documentation of performance capability.

The purchaser needs to be alert and gather all necessary information along with being sensitive to the supplier's limitations on restricted information. Exhibit 7.4 provides a checklist of the key evaluation criteria that should be noted during the site visit. Key personal contacts in management, operations, and marketing may be useful resources in the later stages of the selection process.

Regardless of whether the supplier is a potential or existing supplier, the purchaser should compile this data into a report that is maintained in a data warehouse or on file for easy retrieval by members of the cross-functional team. The evaluation criteria listed in Exhibit 7.4 are covered in detail in the *Key Supplier Evaluation* section of this chapter.

The use of teams for supplier evaluation and selection is increasing, particularly among larger organizations that have the resources to commit to this approach.

Exhibit 7.4	Key Evaluation Criteria to Be Noted During a Supplier Visit

- Management capability
- Total quality management
- Technical capability
- Operations and scheduling capability
- Financial strength
- Personnel relations
- E-systems capabilities
- Technological sophistication and efficiency of the equipment
- ISO certifications
- Caliber of the supervision and inspection personnel
- Evidence of good management and housekeeping practices
- Types of inventory systems
- Nature of the receiving, storeroom, and shipping areas
- Quality control philosophy
- Environmental practices
- Representation of white- and blue-collar staffs
- Employee contract expiration dates
- Names and contact information of key decision makers

The advantage to the team approach is that each team member contributes unique insight into the overall supplier evaluation. Members may have expertise in quality, engineering capabilities, or manufacturing techniques, and they may be qualified to assess suppliers in these areas.

Use of Preferred Certified and Partnered Suppliers

As discussed earlier, purchasers often reward their best suppliers in the *preferred, certified, or partnered* categories. Using these highly capable suppliers can simplify the evaluation and selection process. A buyer can refer to the purchasing database to determine if there is a current supplier that can satisfy the purchase requirement. This eliminates the need to perform a time-consuming evaluation. Buyers can also use their category list of suppliers as an incentive to improve the performance of existing approved suppliers. Only the best suppliers are awarded preferred, certified, or partnered status.

Sourcing Snapshot

The Apple iPad: Supplier Selection Produces Familiar Names

Looking inside Apple Inc.'s iPad indicates more business for some familiar component suppliers, according to firms who specialize in disassembling and analyzing electronic hardware. The companies, which include iFixit Inc. and UBM TechInsights, took iPads apart.

Apple's iPad tablet-style computer was built on technologies it used in the design of the popular iPhone and iPod Touch. The company also relied on some of the same suppliers. Apple has used the Korean company and Toshiba Corp. of Japan as its main suppliers of flash memory. Samsung supplied the flash chips found in the iPad, which is one of the most costly parts of the system.

Apple had used Samsung micro-processors, which were based on a design popularized by ARM Holdings PLC to provide the primary calculating engines in the iPhone and iPod Touch. For the iPad, Apple stayed internal and for the first time designed its own ARM-based chip, called the A4. The A4 chip comes stacked with another variety of memory chips from Samsung, according to iFixit. These memory chips are called DRAM, for dynamic random-access memory. The proximity of the chips suggests that Samsung also manufactured the A4 for Apple, said Kyle Wiens, iFixit's chief executive.

David Carey, vice president of technical intelligence at UBM TechInsights, said the DRAMs used in the iPad read and write data in 64-bit chunks, one potential reason why reviewers have called the iPad surprisingly fast. "That helps it move a lot of data a lot faster," Mr. Carey said.

Similar to Apple's MacBook Pro, much of the iPad is machined from a solid block of aluminum, which increases weight slightly but makes the device more rigid than many laptops, Mr. Wiens said. Apple also used more epoxy to glue chips to circuit boards than in most other devices, adding to the iPad's durability, he said.

The iPad's battery is another reason for its 1.5 pound weight, which is less than conventional laptops but more than some e-readers like Amazon.com Inc.'s Kindle. But some reviewers have praised the iPad battery for lasting longer on a charge than the 10 hours Apple claims. Mr. Wiens said the device actually uses two batteries wired in parallel, giving the device 5.5 times the capacity of the battery in the iPhone. The battery supplier is Amperex Technology Ltd., a Hong Kong-based company that is a unit of Japan's TDK Corp., Mr. Carey said.

Other component suppliers for the iPad, Mr. Carey said, include Broadcom Corp., which supplied chips that help manage the machine's touch screen as well as allowing it to communicate using Wi-Fi and BlueTooth technology; Texas Instruments Inc., which supplied another chip associated with the touch screen; and Cirrus Logic Inc., which supplied a chip for managing audio in the device.

Source: Adapted from: Clark, D. (2010. April 5), "iPad Taps Familiar Suppliers," *Wall Street Journal,* B4.

Third-Party Information

Mattel Corporation's problems with lead paint in toys manufactured in China and building collapses in Bangladesh have resulted in other firms asking for third-party quality audits during the evaluation phase to improve assurances of quality.[4,5] Dun & Bradstreet's *D&B's Supplier Qualifier Report* provides purchasers with a web-based tool to help evaluate suppliers and potential suppliers according to risk, financial stability, and business performance. In the apparel industry several buyers are using third-party certification sources. Information can be a timely and effective way to gain insight into potential suppliers. For example, PVH, a German retailer and parent company of Tommy Hilfiger and Calvin Klein called for independent inspections of buildings to insure safety.[6]

Select Supplier and Reach Agreement

The final step of the evaluation and selection process is to select the supplier(s) and reach a contract agreement. The activities associated with this step can vary widely depending on the purchase item under consideration. For routine items, this may simply require notifying and awarding a basic purchase contract to a supplier. For a major purchase, the process can become more complex. The buyer and seller may have to conduct detailed negotiations to agree upon the specific details of a purchase agreement. Once the agreement is reached, the contract will have to be managed and this is covered in Chapter 14.

Key Supplier Evaluation Criteria

Purchasers usually evaluate potential suppliers across multiple categories using their own selection criteria with assigned weights. Purchasers that need consistent delivery performance with short lead times to support a just-in-time production system might emphasize a supplier's scheduling and production systems. A high-technology buyer might emphasize a supplier's process and technological capabilities or commitment to research and development. The selection process for a distributor or service provider will emphasize a different set of criteria.

Most evaluations rate suppliers on three primary criteria: (1) cost or price, (2) quality, and (3) delivery. These three elements of performance are generally the most obvious and most critical areas that affect the purchaser. For critical items needing an in-depth analysis of the supplier's capabilities, a more detailed supplier evaluation study is required. The following presents the wide range of criteria that a purchaser might consider during supplier evaluation and selection. These areas should be incorporated and covered in depth during supplier visits.

Management Capability

It is important for a buyer to evaluate a supplier's management capability. After all, management runs the business and makes the decisions that affect the competitiveness of the supplier. A buyer should ask many questions when evaluating a supplier's management capability:

- What is the top management's vision, strategy, and plan for the business?
- Has management committed the supplier to total quality management (TQM) and continuous improvement?
- Is turnover high among managers?
- What is the professional experience and educational background of the key managers?
- Is management customer focused?
- What is the history of labor/management relations?
- Is management making the necessary investments in people, equipment, and technology that are required to sustain and grow the business?
- Has management prepared the company to face future competitive challenges, including providing employee training and development?
- Does management put a priority on supply chain management?

It may be a challenge to identify the true state of affairs during a brief visit or by analyzing data from a questionnaire. Nevertheless, asking these questions can help the purchasing manager to develop a feeling for the professional capabilities of the managers in the supplying organization. When interviewing managers, it is important to meet as many of the executive team as possible to obtain a true picture of management capabilities.

Employee Capabilities

This part of the evaluation process requires an assessment of nonmanagement personnel. Do not underestimate the benefit that a highly trained, stable, and motivated workforce provides, particularly during periods of labor shortages. A purchaser should consider these points:

- The degree to which employees are committed to quality and continuous improvement
- The overall skills and abilities of the workforce
- Employee-management relations
- The frequency of work stoppages because of strikes or walkouts
- Worker flexibility
- Employee morale
- Workforce turnover
- Willingness of employees to contribute to improved operations

A buyer should also gather information about the history of strikes and labor disputes. Good management-employee relations provide the fundamental basis for determining how dedicated the supplier's employees are to producing products or services that will meet or exceed the buyer's expectations.

Cost Structure

Evaluating a supplier's cost structure requires an in-depth understanding of a supplier's total costs, including direct labor costs, indirect labor costs, material costs, manufacturing or process operating costs, and general overhead costs. Understanding a supplier's cost structure helps a buyer determine how efficiently a supplier can produce an item. A cost analysis also helps identify potential areas of cost improvement.

Collecting this information can be a challenge. A supplier may not have a detailed understanding of its own costs. Many suppliers do not have a sophisticated cost accounting system and are unable to assign overhead costs to products or processes. Furthermore, some suppliers view cost data as highly proprietary. They may fear that the release of cost information will undermine its pricing strategy or that competitors will gain access to its cost data, which could provide insight into a supplier's competitive advantage. Because of these concerns, buyers will often develop reverse pricing models that provide estimates of the supplier's cost structure during the initial supplier evaluation.

Total Quality Performance, Systems, and Philosophy

A major part of the evaluation process addresses a supplier's quality management processes, systems, and philosophy. Buyers evaluate not only the obvious topics associated with supplier quality (management commitment, statistical process control, defects) but also safety, training, and facilities and equipment maintenance. Alcoa defines its supplier quality requirements in four broad areas: management, quality measurement, safety and training, and facilities. Many purchasers are expecting potential suppliers to have adopted quality systems based on the Malcolm Baldrige National Quality Award (MBNQA) or International Organization for Standardization (ISO) 9000 criteria. The wide distribution of these guidelines has exposed many suppliers to the Baldrige and ISO definitions of quality.

Process and Technological Capability

Supplier evaluation teams often include a member from the engineering or technical staff to evaluate a supplier's process and technological capability. Process consists of the technology, design, methods, and equipment used to manufacture a product or deliver a service. A supplier's selection of a production process helps define its required technology, human resource skills, and capital equipment requirements.

The evaluation should include both the supplier's current and future process and technological capabilities. Assessing a supplier's future process and technological capability involves reviewing capital equipment plans and strategy. In addition, a purchaser should evaluate the resources that a supplier is committing to research and development. For service providers it is important to understand the specific supplier process and the extent to which technology is utilized to produce the service efficiently.

A purchaser may also assess a supplier's design capability. One way to reduce the time required to develop new products involves using qualified suppliers that are able to support product design activities. The trend toward the increased use of supplier design capabilities makes this area an integral part of the supplier evaluation and selection process.

Sustainability and Environmental Compliance

According to P&G, **sustainability** is about ensuring a better quality of life now and for generations to come, and it encompasses both social and environmental responsibility. It encompasses the entire supply chain from suppliers through manufacturing and to the end consumer.[7] As is illustrated in the following sourcing snapshot, P&G has launched a "sustainable supplier scorecard" to track improvements made by its suppliers, in line with the **triple bottom line (3BL)** philosophy of people, planet, and profit. "The triple bottom line (TBL) focuses corporations not just on the economic value they add, but also on the environmental and social value they add—and destroy."[8] Sustainability can be beneficial to an organization's bottom line by treating employees well and minimizing the impact on the environment. Recent research incorporated these by defining **sustainable supply management (SSM)** as the extent to which supply management incorporates environmental, social, and economic value into the selection, evaluation and management of its supply base.[9]

Many twenty-first-century firms are embracing the 3BL philosophy. A review of the Knight's 100 most sustainable Global firms shows four U.S. based firms Biogen, Intel, Cisco, Agilent Technologies in the top 25.[10] Voluntary adoption of sustainability is much different than the legislatively mandated era of the late 1980s and early 1990s in which environmental rules were compliance driven. For example, the Clean Air Act of 1990 imposed large fines on producers of ozone-depleting substances and foul-smelling gases. In selecting suppliers, purchasers certainly do not want to be associated with known environmental polluters from a public relations or potential liability standpoint.

Commonly used environmental performance criteria used when evaluating a supplier's performance include the following:

- Ongoing sustainability practices and top management support for sustainable practices, including a Corporate Responsibility Report
- The company's current and projected CO_2 emissions
- Attainment of ISO 14000 certification
- Evidence of measuring or requiring sustainable practices by their suppliers
- Formal hazardous and toxic waste reduction programs exist
- Purchasing recycled materials and implementation of practices encouraging recycling and reuse in internal operations
- Disclosure of any environmental infractions
- Programs to control or eliminate ozone-depleting substances

Intel's corporate responsibility report lists *supply chain responsibility* as one of the major areas of corporate social responsibility. It is evident from the report that suppliers are a key part of Intel's efforts. "We set clear expectations, provide tools and training to help suppliers measure and improve their social and environmental performance, and share our best practices across the industry. Audits and assessments enable us to identify issues and provide appropriate education and system-level solutions."

Intel is also a leader in addressing the issue of "conflict minerals" in the electronics supply chain. They have achieved their goal to manufacture a microprocessor that has been verified as "conflict-free" for the metal tantalum. (See Chapter 10 for definition of conflict minerals.)[11]

Sustainable carbon footprint reductions are being measured at both product and service suppliers. For example, SAP, one of the leading Enterprise Resource Planning

(ERP) software providers, reported that worldwide CO2 emissions for 2011 totaled 490 kilotons, an 18 percent decrease from the 2007 levels. This equates to a monetary savings of approximately 190 million euros in accumulated cost avoidance. Power usage was 80% of that in 2007. Additionally, renewable energy sources now account for 47% of total energy usage.[12]

Sourcing Snapshot

P&G Develops a Supplier Environmental Sustainability Scorecard

Procter & Gamble (P&G) Company uses a Supplier Environmental Sustainability Scorecard and rating process to measure and improve the environmental performance of its key suppliers. The scorecard assesses P&G suppliers' environmental footprint and encourages continued improvement by measuring energy use, water use, waste disposal, and greenhouse gas emissions on a year-to-year basis.

It is hoped that this work will lay the foundation for an industry standard and the scorecard will be an "open code" for use by any organization to help promote a working discussion and determine a common supply chain evaluation processes across all industries.

"The launch of the Supplier Environmental Sustainability Scorecard represents the next step in P&G's commitment to environmental sustainability and reflects the company's holistic, end-to-end supply chain strategy," says Bob McDonald, P&G's chairman, president and CEO.

P&G's new supplier scorecard is the result of 18 months of work and close collaboration with the organization's Supplier Sustainability Board, which includes more than 20 supplier representatives from P&G's global supply chain. The scorecard relies on global measurement standards, including protocols from the World Resources Institute, the World Business Council for Sustainable Development and the Carbon Disclosure Project, so as to minimize redundant efforts and build on existing best practices. P&G's goal in deploying the scorecard is to enhance supply chain collaboration, measure and improve key environmental sustainability indicators, and encourage the sharing of ideas and capabilities to deliver more sustainable products and services for its consumers.

"We worked closely with a global team of P&G personnel, suppliers and supply chain experts to determine the most effective way to measure the environmental performance of our diverse global supplier base," says Rick Hughes, P&G global purchasing officer. "Our suppliers wanted a tool that was flexible yet grounded in existing measurement standards, and by working together, we developed a framework that will help drive real improvement across all industries."

The scorecard is specifically designed to focus on, and encourage, year-on-year improvement—regardless of a supplier's total size or the current stage of its sustainability program. Roll-out beyond P&G's key suppliers will be determined once learnings from the first phase of deployment are incorporated. Suppliers will have a full year to prepare to report their data before the rating can adversely impact their supplier rating with P&G. In the future, P&G will use the scorecard to determine each supplier's sustainability rating as part of its annual supplier performance measurement process.

As part of its effort to create an initiative that can have a far reaching cross-industry impact, P&G suppliers are also encouraged to use the scorecard within their own supply chains. The scorecard is available at: http://www.pgsupplier.com/environmental-sustainability-scorecard.

Source:_____ _____ (2010. May 13), "P&G Launches Supplier Environmental Sustainability Scorecard," *Logistics Today*.

Financial Stability

An assessment of a potential supplier's financial condition should occur during the initial evaluation process. Some purchasers view the financial assessment as a screening process or preliminary condition that the supplier must pass before a detailed evaluation can begin. An organization may use a financial rating service to help analyze a supplier's financial condition.

Selecting a supplier in poor financial condition presents a number of risks. First, there is the risk that the supplier will go out of business. Second, suppliers that are in poor financial condition may not have the resources to invest in plant, equipment, or research that is necessary for longer-term technological or other performance improvements. Third, the supplier may become too financially dependent on the purchaser. A final risk is that financial weakness is usually an indication of other underlying problems. Is financial weakness a result of poor quality or delivery performance causing customers to change suppliers and cancel orders? Alternatively, is it a result of wasteful spending by management? Or has the supplier made poor financial decisions and taken on too much debt?

There may be circumstances that support selecting a supplier in a weaker financial condition. A supplier may be developing but has not yet marketed a leading-edge technology that can provide an advantage to the purchaser. A supplier may also be in a weaker financial condition because of uncontrollable or nonrepeating circumstances. Many small suppliers continually face cash flow issues because of their lack of access to capital or inability to collect accounts receivable in a timely manner. Additionally, the loss of a key customer can have dire consequences for a small business's total revenue. Thus, the purchaser must continually assess the small suppliers' financial condition.

If the supplier is publicly traded, specific financial ratios can be obtained from a variety of websites providing detailed financial ratios and industry averages to compare these ratios against. Some common ratios used to assess supplier financial health appear in Exhibit 7.5.

A sampling of websites available to obtain financial information include the following:

- Yahoo! Financial section (http://biz.yahoo.com/ne.html)
- Google Financial section (http://www.google.com/finance)
- Morningstar (http://www.morningstar.com)
- Marketwatch (http://www.marketwatch.com)
- The Securities and Exchange Commission (http://www.sec.gov)
- Dun & Bradstreet (http://www.dnb.com)

Professional purchasers should become familiar with financial ratios because they can provide quick and valuable insights into a supplier's financial health. Moreover, purchasing managers should track such ratios for possible red flags that may signify potential financial difficulty.

Scheduling and Control Systems

Scheduling includes those systems that release, plan, and control a supplier's production or service process. Does the supplier use a requirements planning system as part of an ERP system to ensure the availability of required components or meet service requests on a timely basis? Does the supplier track material and product and or service cycle time and compare this against a performance objective or standard? Does the supplier's scheduling system support a purchaser's delivery requirements? What lead time does the supplier's

Exhibit 7.5	Interpreting Key Financial Ratios

RATIOS	INTERPRETATION
LIQUIDITY	
Current ratio = Current assets/Current liabilities	Should be over 1.0, but look at industry average; high—may mean poor asset management.
Quick ratio = (Cash + Receivables)/Current liabilities	At least 0.8 if supplier sells on credit; low—may mean cash flow problems; high—may mean poor asset management.
Note: Calculation includes marketable securities	
ACTIVITY	
Inventory turnover = Costs of goods sold/Inventory	Compare industry average; low—problems with slow inventory, which may hurt cash flow.
Fixed asset turnover = Sales/Fixed assets	Compare industry average; too low may mean supplier is not using fixed assets efficiently or effectively.
Total asset turnover = Sales/Total assets	Compare industry average; too low may mean supplier is not using its total assets efficiently or effectively.
Days sales outstanding = (Receivables × 365)/Sales	Compare industry average, or a value of 45–50 if company sells on net 30; too high hurts cash flow; too low may mean credit policies to customers are too restrictive.
PROFITABILITY	
Net profit margin = Profit after taxes/Sales	Represents after-tax return; compare industry average.
Return on assets = Profit after taxes/Total assets	Compare industry average; represents the return the company earns on everything it owns.
Return on equity = Profit after taxes/Equity	The higher the better; the return on the shareholders' investment in the business.
DEBT	
Debt to equity = Total liabilities/Equity	Compare industry average; over 3 means highly leveraged.
Current debt to equity = Current liabilities/Equity	Over 1 is risky unless industry average is over 1; when ratio is high, supplier may be unable to pay lenders.
Interest coverage = (Pretax Inc. + Int. Exp.)/Int. Exp.	Should be over 3; higher is better; low may mean supplier is having difficulty paying creditors.

scheduling and control system require? What is the supplier's on-time delivery performance history? The purpose behind evaluating the scheduling and control system is to identify the degree of control the supplier has over its scheduling and processes to meet or reduce total cycle times.

Product suppliers can formally certify the quality of their production system by meeting the requirements of ISO 9000 once they have undergone a formal review of their system by a professional external auditor who has verified that the requisite process criteria are satisfied. (See Chapter 8 for further discussion.) Companies that are considering sourcing high volumes of product with a supplier will also want to consider whether the supplier has adequate capacity.

E-Commerce Capability

The ability to communicate electronically between a buyer and seller is now becoming a requirement during supplier selection. Firms decide how this electronic linkage will be implemented. Three major alternatives are: (1) Internet based software platforms;

(2) electronic data interchange (EDI); or (3) a combination of EDI and Internet based software. EDI was the first efficient way to communicate electronically and is still favored by many large organizations such as Walmart and Target. However, more and more companies are moving to web-based business-to-business (B2B) platforms for their transactions. IBM now states that the majority of its purchases (by dollar spent) occur via the Internet. However, such statements entail that suppliers have the required ability to adopt an e-commerce approach. Besides the efficiencies that B2B e-commerce provides, these systems support closer relationships and the exchange of all kinds of information.

Purchasing managers should also evaluate other dimensions of the supplier's information technology (IT). Does the supplier have computer-aided design (CAD) capability? Does the supplier have bar coding capability or radio frequency identification (RFID) technology? Can the supplier send advance-shipping notices or accept payment by electronic funds transfer? Does the supplier communicate primarily via e-mail? Do suppliers use social media for business purposes? What safeguards are in place to protect the confidentiality of electronic transfers? Evidence that the supplier is using these technologies can provide reasonable assurance that the supplier is current with e-commerce technologies.

Supplier's Sourcing Strategies, Policies, and Techniques

The concept of understanding a supplier's suppliers is part of integrated supply chain management. Unfortunately, organizations do not have the resources or personnel to investigate all of the suppliers within their supply chain. However, there are ways to obtain information on the performance capabilities of Tier 2 and even Tier 3 suppliers.

It is possible for a purchaser to develop an understanding of the purchasing approaches and techniques of suppliers that are three tiers or levels from the primary buyer. Assume that during the supplier selection process, a purchaser evaluates the sourcing strategies, approaches, and techniques of its first-tier supplier. Through discussions with the purchasing department of the first-tier supplier, the purchaser can gain insight about its second-tier suppliers. If the first-tier supplier also evaluates the sourcing strategies, approaches, and techniques of its first-tier suppliers (second-tier suppliers to the purchaser), then it can provide information about third-tier suppliers. Evaluating a potential supplier's sourcing strategies, approaches, and techniques is one way to gain greater insight and understanding of the supply chain. Because few purchasers understand their second- and third-tier suppliers, those that do can gain an important advantage over competitors.

Longer-Term Relationship Potential

A supplier's willingness to move beyond a traditional purchasing relationship should be part of the evaluation process for items and services where a longer-term relationship might be beneficial. Twenty-five years of research indicates that emphasizing supplier efficiency, quality, price, and delivery are acceptable for more transactional short-term relationships. Successful longer-term relationships require asking much deeper questions. These include:

- Has the supplier indicated a willingness or commitment to a longer-term relationship?
- Is the supplier willing to commit resources specific to this relationship?
- Does the supplier have the technical expertise to contribute to the relationship?
- What does the supplier bring that is unique?

- Will the supplier engage in joint problem solving and improvement efforts?
- Will there be free and open exchange of information across the two companies?
- How much future planning is the supplier willing to share?
- Is the need for confidential treatment of information taken seriously?
- Is the corporate culture similar between the two parties?
- How well does the supplier know our industry and business?
- Will the supplier share cost data?
- Is the supplier willing to come to us first with innovations?
- Is the supplier willing to commit capacity exclusively to our needs?
- Do both parties share a commitment to understanding each other's problems and concerns?[13]

This starter list of questions allows the supply manager to evaluate the possibility of a longer-term relationship and provides a framework to discuss future issues that are important. A numerical scale to quantify these questions for and overall score can be created.

Developing a Supplier Evaluation and Selection Survey

Supplier evaluation often follows a rigorous, structured approach using formal surveys. An effective supplier survey should have certain characteristics. First, the survey should include the performance categories considered important to the evaluation and selection process. Second, the survey process should be as objective as possible. This requires the use of a scoring system that defines the meaning of each value on a measurement scale.

A third characteristic is that the items and the measurement scales are reliable. This refers to the degree to which different individuals or groups reviewing the same items and measurement scales will arrive at the same conclusion. Reliable evaluations require well-defined measures and well-understood items.

A fourth characteristic of a sound supplier survey is flexibility. Although an organization should maintain a structure to its supplier survey, the format of the evaluation should provide some flexibility across different types of purchase requirements. The easiest way to make the process flexible is to adjust the performance categories and weights assigned to each category. The most important categories will receive a higher weight within the total evaluation score.

A final characteristic of an effective survey is that it is mathematically straightforward. The use of weights and points should be simple enough that each individual involved in the evaluation understands the mechanics of the scoring and selection process. To ensure that a supplier survey has the right characteristics, we recommend the use of a step-by-step process when creating this tool. Exhibit 7.6 presents the steps to follow when developing such a system. The following section discusses this framework and develops a sample evaluation survey.

Step 1: Identify Supplier Evaluation Categories

Perhaps the first step when developing a supplier survey is deciding the categories to include. As discussed earlier, there are many evaluation categories. For illustrative purposes, assume that a purchaser selects quality, management capability, financial condition, supplier cost structure, expected delivery performance, technological capability, systems

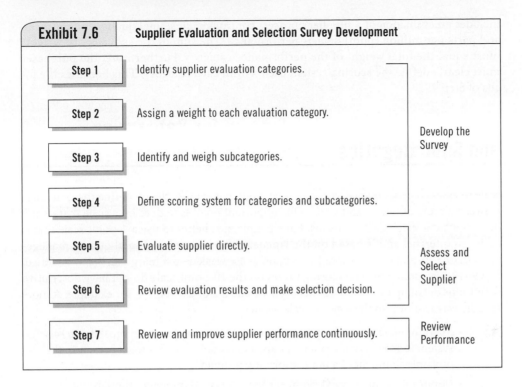

Exhibit 7.6 | Supplier Evaluation and Selection Survey Development

Step 1	Identify supplier evaluation categories.
Step 2	Assign a weight to each evaluation category.
Step 3	Identify and weigh subcategories.
Step 4	Define scoring system for categories and subcategories.

Develop the Survey

| Step 5 | Evaluate supplier directly. |
| Step 6 | Review evaluation results and make selection decision. |

Assess and Select Supplier

| Step 7 | Review and improve supplier performance continuously. |

Review Performance

capability, and a general category of miscellaneous performance factors as the categories to include in the evaluation. These categories would reveal the performance areas that the purchaser considers most important.

Step 2: Assign a Weight to Each Evaluation Category

The performance categories usually receive a weight that reflects the relative importance of that category. The assigned weights reflect the relative importance of each category. The total of the combined weights must equal 1.0.

Exhibit 7.6 shows the weight assigned to each selected performance category in our sample survey. Notice that the quality systems category receives 20 percent of the total evaluation, whereas systems capability receives 5 percent; this simply reflects the difference in relative importance to the purchaser between the two performance categories. Recall that an important characteristic of an effective evaluation system is flexibility. One way that management achieves this flexibility is by assigning different weights or adding or deleting performance categories as required.

Step 3: Identify and Weigh Subcategories

Step 2 specified broad performance categories included within our sample evaluation. Step 3 of this process requires identifying any performance subcategories, if they exist, within each broader performance category. For example, the quality systems category may require the identification of separate subcategories (such as those described in the Malcolm Baldrige Award criteria). If this is the case, the supplier evaluation should include any subcategories or items that make up the quality systems category.

Equally important, the purchaser must decide how to weigh each subcategory within the broader performance evaluation category. In Exhibit 7.7, the quality category includes an evaluation of a supplier's process control systems, total quality commitment, and parts per million (ppm) defects performance. The sum of the subcategory weights must equal the total weight of the performance category. Furthermore, the purchaser must clearly define the scoring system used within each category. This becomes the focus of Step 4.

Step 4: Define a Scoring System for Categories and Subcategories

Step 4 defines each score within a performance category. If an evaluation uses a 5-point scale to assess a performance category, then a purchaser must clearly define the difference between a score of 5, 4, 3, and so on. One important point is to develop a scale that clearly defines what a specific score means. For example, it is better to use a 4-point scale that is easier to interpret and is based on the language and principles of total quality management than a 10-point scale where 1–2 = poor, 3–4 = weak, 5–6 = marginal, 7–8 = qualified, and 9–10 = outstanding. The scoring values on the 10-point scale do not have descriptive definitions detailing the difference between a 1 and a 2 or a 3 and a 4, for example. A more specific way is shown in the 4-point scale below:

- Major nonconformity (0 points earned): The absence or total breakdown of a system to meet a requirement, or any noncompliance that would result in the probable shipment of a nonconforming product.

- Minor nonconformity (1 point earned): A noncompliance (though not major) that judgment and experience indicate is likely to result in the failure of the quality system or reduce its ability to ensure controlled processes or products.

- Conformity (2 points earned): No major or minor nonconformities were noted during the evaluation.

- Adequacy (3 points earned): Specific supplier performance or documentation meets or exceeds requirements given the scope of the supplier's operations.

- Major conformity (4 points earned): Documentation exceeds the buyer's requirements, internal process monitoring system in place to guard against major systems breakdowns, and total quality management system insures that only good parts will be made and shipped.

A well-defined scoring system takes criteria that may be highly subjective and develops a quantitative scale for measurement. Effective metrics allow different individuals to interpret and score similarly the same performance categories under review. A scoring system that is too broad, ambiguous, or poorly defined increases the probability of arriving at widely different assessments or conclusions.

Step 5: Evaluate Supplier Directly

This step requires that the reviewer visit a supplier's facilities to perform the evaluation. The specifics of supplier visits were covered in detail earlier in the chapter.

In our example below, the supplier will have to present evidence in the areas of process control systems, total quality commitment, and part per million defectives or delivery performance.

The following explains the calculation for the quality category in Exhibit 7.6: Quality Systems Performance Category (Weight = 20 percent of total evaluation).

Exhibit 7.7	Initial Supplier Evaluation

CATEGORY	WEIGHT	SUBWEIGHT	SCORE (5 PT. SCALE)	WEIGHTED SCORE	
Supplier: Advanced Micro Systems	20				
1. Quality Systems		5	4	4.0	
Process control systems		8	4	6.4	
Total quality commitment		7	5	7.0	
Parts-per-million defect performance					17.4
2. Management Capability	10				
Management/labor relations		5	4	4.0	
Management capability		5	4	4.0	
					8.0
3. Financial Condition	10				
Debt structure		5	3	3.0	
Turnover ratios		5	4	4.0	
					7.0
4. Cost Structure	15				
Costs relative to industry		5	5	5.0	
Understanding of costs		5	4	4.0	
Cost control/reduction efforts		5	5	5.0	
					14.0
5. Delivery Performance	15				
Performance to promise		5	3	3.0	
Lead-time requirements		5	3	3.0	
Responsiveness		5	3	3.0	
					9.0
6. Technical/Process Capability	15				
Product innovation		5	4	4.0	
Process innovation		5	5	5.0	
Research and development		5	5	5.0	
					14.0
7. Information Systems Capability	5				
EDI capability		3	5	3.0	
CAD/CAM		2	0	0	
					3.0
8. General	10				
Support of minority suppliers		2	3	1.2	
Environmental compliance		3	5	3.0	
Supplier's supply base management		5	4	4.0	
					8.2

Max Total Points = 100   Total Weighted Score   80.6
5 point rating scale
"0" = Lowest; "5" Highest

Subcategories are the following:

- *Process control systems* (4 points out of 5 possible points equals 80 percent) or 0.8×5 sub-weight = 4.0 points
- *Total quality commitment* (4 points out of 5 possible points) = 0.8×8 sub-weight = 6.4 points
- *PPM defect performance* (5 points out of 5 possible points) = 1.0×7 sub-weight = 7.0 points
- Total for category = 17.4 points or 87 percent of total possible points (17.4/20)

As shown in Exhibit 7.7, Advanced Micro Systems received a total overall evaluation of 80.6 percent. If the selection set a minimum score of 80 for consideration then Advanced Micro may be judged to close to qualify at this time for further purchase consideration. Purchasers should set minimum acceptable performance requirements for a supplier to meet before they become part of the supply base. In this example, the supplier performs acceptably in most major categories except delivery performance (9 out of 15 possible points). The reviewer must decide if the shortcomings in this category are correctable or if the supplier simply lacks the ability to perform.

Step 6: Review Evaluation Results and Make Selection Decision

At some point, a reviewer must decide whether to recommend or reject a supplier as a source. A purchaser may review a supplier for consideration for expected future business and not a specific contract. Evaluating suppliers before there is an actual purchase requirement can provide a great deal of flexibility to a purchaser. Once an actual need materializes, the purchaser is in a position to move quickly because it has prequalified the supplier.

It is important to determine the seriousness of any supplier shortcomings noted during the evaluation and assess the degree to which these shortcomings might affect performance. Evaluation scales should differentiate among various degrees of supplier shortcomings. One organization, explicitly defines the difference between a performance problem and a deficiency. A **performance problem** is "a discrepancy, nonconformance, or missing requirement that will have a significant negative impact on an important area of concern in an audit statement." A **deficiency** is "a minor departure from an intended level of performance or a nonconformance that is easily resolved and does not materially affect the required output."

The primary output from this step is a recommendation about whether to accept a supplier for a purchase contract. Exhibit 7.8 illustrates a simple recommendation form issued after a supplier evaluation visit conducted by a commodity team. An important outcome of any evaluation is the identification of improvement opportunities on the part of the supplier.

A purchaser may evaluate several suppliers that might be competing for the same contract. The initial evaluation provides an objective way to compare suppliers side by side before making a final selection decision. A purchaser may decide to use more than one supplier based on the results of the supplier survey.

The authority to decide the final selection varies from organization to organization. The reviewer or team who evaluated the supplier may have the authority to make the supplier selection decision. In other cases, the buyer or team may present or justify the supplier selection decision or findings to a committee or a manager who has final authority.

Exhibit 7.8	Sample Recommendation Form

Type of Supplier: _____Mfg._____

Qualification Survey Summary

Company Name	Foster Industries	Surveyed By:	Manufacturing Commodity Team
Address	PO Box 1256	Accompanied By:	Quality
City, State, Zip	Stroudsburg, PA 18370	(Initial Survey)	Resurvey
Phone	570-619-5411	Survey Date:	9/14/2013
Supplier Code	Foster	Contact:	Robert Jones
Supplier Score	80.8	**Minimum Required Score: 65**	

Recommendations

Supplier has potential to become a critical partner. However, limited design/development capability prevents continued growth. Foster will embark on implementing and upgrading design/development function for our business.

ACTION PLAN IS DUE BY: _____2/1/2014_____

Supplier Acknowledgment:

John Weaver   9/15/2013
                                              Date

Source: Adapted from Przirembel, J. (1997), *How to Conduct Supplier Surveys and Audits*, West Palm Beach, FL: PT Publications, 76.

Step 7: Review and Improve Supplier Performance Continuously

The supplier survey or visit is only the first step of the evaluation process. If a purchaser decides to select a supplier, the supplier must then perform according to the purchaser's requirements. The emphasis shifts from the initial evaluation and selection of suppliers to evidence of continuous performance improvement by suppliers. Chapter 9 addresses the management of a world-class supply base.

Reducing Supplier Evaluation and Selection Cycle Time

Across almost all business applications, competitive and customer pressures are forcing reductions in the time it takes to perform a task or carry out a process. These pressures are also affecting the time available to evaluate and select suppliers. Purchasing must increasingly be proactive and anticipate supplier selection requirements rather than react when a need arises.

Consider the stream of products introduced by Apple. In the past 10 years it reinvented the telephone, music players, the way we consume music, and mobile computing using the iPad. Even if it has nothing more in the coming years than new iterations of its existing products it operates at a fast pace. Consider the I-Phone 4, 4s, 5, and 5s were all released within on one year cycles. Time to market is key for not only Apple but firms in all categories.[14]

These processes that support new-product development, such as supplier evaluation and selection, must also shorten accordingly. The following presents a set of tools to reduce evaluation and selection time.

Map the Current Supplier Evaluation and Selection Process

Process mapping involves the identification of the steps, activities, time, and costs involved in a process. Once the current evaluation and selection process is understood, opportunities for improvement should become evident. Supply managers should measure process cycle times to identify rates of improvement against pre-established performance targets. Process mapping should be the first step in the improvement process.

Integrate with Internal Customers

The need to anticipate rather than react to supplier evaluation and selection decisions requires closer involvement with internal customers, which can be achieved in a variety of ways. Purchasing can colocate physically with marketing, engineering, and operations to gain early insight into expected supply requirements. Involvement on new-product development teams is also an ideal way to integrate with internal customers. Allowing internal customers to forward their requirements to purchasing, perhaps through an online requisition system, can also be an effective way to integrate with internal customers, particularly for routine purchase requirements. For example, IBM is now analyzing employee travel patterns and blocks of tickets for city parings prior to actual travel to secure better on-line pricing.[15]

Data Warehouse Software with Supplier Information

A data warehouse consists of easy-to-access supplier data and information. The data warehouse can include information about potential suppliers, performance history of current suppliers, details of current contracts, expiration dates of supply contracts, expected forecasts for purchased items, and any other information that supports a faster selection process.

Third-Party Support

Third-party support can range from consultants, to sourcing software providers or knowledge providers. For example, in the area of risk management there are several providers who can help when purchasers are doing their due diligence to qualify a new supplier or check the financial health of an existing supplier prior to the selection decision (e.g., rapid rating.com, equifax.com, and the like). Dun & Bradstreet and its subsidiary DnBi provide financial ratio data, the business background of the supplier's management team, payment trends, and an overall supplier risk score. Internet searches can produce a full list of third-party supplier information, including online directories of potential suppliers.

Integrating Technology into Organizational Design

Commodity teams have become a popular way to manage important purchase requirements. Once established, these teams can communicate virtually via mobile devices on company intranets. These cross-functional teams are responsible for understanding in depth entire families or groups of purchased goods and services. The teams are usually responsible for achieving improvements within their commodity, which may involve site visits to evaluate suppliers. They can communicate 24/7 anywhere in the world with mobile devices and company intranets.

Supplier Categorization

Many firms create a list of their highest-performing suppliers. These suppliers earn their place as preferred, certified, or partnered by consistently providing the best services and products to the buyer. A supplier categorization list can provide dramatic reductions in selection time because a buyer already knows the best suppliers to consider and the relationship is already established.

Electronic Tools

There are several software providers who offer either full suites of products for supply management or stand-alone tools, such as reverse auctions, eRFQs, spend management, and others. These tools can reduce supplier selection and evaluation cycle time. Two organizations that have developed full suites of electronic tools to improve the evaluation and selection process are IBM/Emptoris—Strategic Supply Management Solutions (http://www-01.ibm.com/software/procurement-solutions/emptoris/) and Ariba (www.ariba.com). Bravo Solutions (www.bravo.com) and CombineNet (www.combinenet.com) provide additional solutions. The capabilities of these electronic tools are discussed in Chapter 18.

Predefined Contract Language and Shorter Contracts

Most contracts address areas that are similar. Progressive supply managers work with their legal group to develop pre-established contract language that can be cut and pasted during a supplier negotiation. The role of the legal department is to review any changes from the pre-established language or approve areas the standard language does not cover. Progressive firms are also working to shorten the length of their contracts.

| **Good Practice Example** | *Improving Supplier Performance through SRM* |

The importance of being a good customer cannot be overstated, and asking for candid feedback can make a tremendous, positive difference in supplier relationships. How would you rate your relationships with your suppliers? Are there mutual expectations and commitments? Do your suppliers regard you as a customer of choice worthy of sharing in new innovations? Depending on the answers, it may be time to re-evaluate how you and your suppliers perceive each other and improve your supplier relationship management program (SRM)

For one company, that evaluation revealed a great deal about where it stood and where it wanted to excel. Alkermes plc, a global biopharmaceutical company based in Dublin, Ireland, recently recognized potential issues in its relationships with strategic suppliers. Within the past year, the company confronted the situation directly by approaching its suppliers through a confidential survey to find out how it could be a better customer.

The company found that supplier performance as well as responsiveness was waning. Deliveries were taking longer than usual, and suppliers were not providing immediate answers to questions as they had in the past. "We were concerned how we were perceived by our suppliers and if, perhaps, they were diverting resources to other customers," shares Christopher Silva, associate director of strategic purchasing at Alkermes. The supply management team held general key performance indicator (KPI) meetings with its suppliers, but feedback wasn't particularly helpful because suppliers reported everything as being "good." It was unlikely, given the lowered supplier performance levels, that all of Alkermes' supplier relationships were "good," says Silva. There was a need for more honest, frank answers. But to get that information, the supply management team knew it would have to significantly alter its approach.

However, gathering constructive input from suppliers is a fundamental challenge. "From the sales perspective, it's always harder to acquire a new customer than to retain an existing one, so suppliers will often tell buyers what they think they want to hear." "This is especially true in arms-length, price-driven relationships. The seller is afraid to rock the boat, as it fears the consequences might be lost business. Thus, being open and honest can be difficult when they are always worried about their standing on the next order," he stated.

Identify Areas for Improvement. Alkermes accepted the challenge that came with asking suppliers candid questions, and initiated its confidential survey with approximately 120 of its top suppliers. Recognizing that confidentiality was crucial to the survey process, Silva and his team chose a third-party survey tool, ensuring responses were anonymous. The tool also made it easy to collect feedback from a broader set of suppliers than they could manage with current staff. Thanks to the anonymity and ease of replying, nearly 40 percent of suppliers responded. This was more than sufficient to generate valuable information for Alkermes to use in its efforts to target areas for further discussion with suppliers.

"The goal of the survey was twofold," says Silva. "First, we sought to simply listen to our suppliers and find out what they thought about doing business with Alkermes. If we were such a 'good' customer when we spoke in the KPI meetings, why were we seeing diminished performance from our suppliers?" For instance, Silva's team wanted to find out if supplier performance was directly related to Alkermes' business practices. Were there things the company could or should be doing to help suppliers meet Alkermes' needs? "Secondly, we wanted to identify the key concepts in supplier relationship-building that we could provide to our internal management team, empowering them to improve supplier relationships and realize business results." Though Alkermes could see specific responses and detail, such data did not reveal the identity of the person or supplier that completed the survey. Data were aggregated to identify trends/areas for improvement that were, in turn, presented back to suppliers for more specific discussion.

The following are two sample questions from Alkermes' survey:

- "Compared to your other customers, how receptive is Alkermes to your ideas for streamlining the business process, improving cost, quality, or delivery in support of the relationship?" Silva says response options for this question ranged from "poor" to "leader."

- "Comment on what you consider to be Alkermes' greatest strengths and weaknesses in doing business with your company." This was an open-ended question in a free-form text field, allowing suppliers to elaborate as much or as little as they preferred in their responses.

Silva says the most valued responses came from the outliers. "These types of responses keyed us in on our strengths and also highlighted areas to focus on for improvement." He believes that using the survey approach depersonalized the issues so information was able to flow more freely from the respondents.

Because individual responses to the survey were anonymous, there was no need for sales people to be defensive. We presented the summarized survey results, and this became a means to initiate deeper conversations that had been missing from the individual relationships previously."

The key is to listen and remain open-minded throughout deeper conversations. In one situation, a discussion with a supplier led both parties to identify some possible root causes to an ongoing issue. In this particular case, the issue was all parties believed the supplier's process constraints were such that lead times were long, which resulted in Alkermes carrying higher inventory levels, according to Silva. Only by digging deeper into the supplier's organization, all the way down to the shop floor, did both the supplier and Alkermes teams discover areas for improvement by involving those people who physically produce the product. These deeper-level discussions ultimately led to improved lead times and inventory reductions with that supplier.

"It's only through the creation of a nonthreatening and improvement-driven culture that this can work," he says. "When a purchasing entity makes adjustments to improve the overall relationship, it opens things up to a higher level of trust and cooperation." "It's an ongoing process for the supply management team to provide internal stakeholders with the insight and tools to better assess suppliers and our existing relationships, and to identify ways we can continue to improve these relationships," he notes.

Silva believes that too often, people tend to put what they themselves value and can use, but those same things may not have value on the other side of the relationship. This can cause considerable frustration and confusion. "Thus, we have tried to overcome this common relationship trap with our new approach. So far, we are seeing excellent results."

Source: Adapted from "Lessons in Supplier Relationship Management", by Lisa Arnseth March 2012, *Inside Supply Management*® Vol. 23, No. 2, pp. 24–27.

CONCLUSION

The evaluation and selection of suppliers is one of the most important functions of business. When a purchaser performs these activities well, it establishes the foundation on which to further develop and improve supplier performance. In his book *Purchasing in the 21st Century*, John Schorr maintains that a buyer should look for certain characteristics when evaluating and selecting suppliers.[16] A good supplier does the following:

- Builds quality into the product, aiming for zero-defect production
- Makes delivery performance a priority, including a willingness to make short and frequent deliveries to point-of-use areas at a purchaser's facility
- Demonstrates responsiveness to a purchaser's needs by ensuring that qualified and accessible people are in charge of servicing the purchasers account
- Works with a purchaser to reduce lead times as much as possible. Long lead times make it difficult to plan and drive up supply chain costs.
- Provides a purchaser with information regarding capability and workload
- Creates the future rather than fears the future
- Reinvests part of its profits in R&D, takes a long-term view, and is willing to spend for tomorrow
- Meets the stringent financial stability criteria used when evaluating potential new customers for credit

Selection goals also consider the impact of *supplier diversity* and *sustainability* in the decision process. A focus on selecting only the best suppliers possible will make a major contribution to the competitiveness of the entire organization. The ability to make this contribution requires careful evaluation and selection of the suppliers that provide the goods and services that help satisfy the needs of an organization's final customers.

KEY TERMS

certified supplier, 256

deficiency, 276

disqualified supplier, 256

entry qualifiers, 261

financial risk management, 259

integrated supply, 255

operational risk management, 259

partnered supplier, 256

performance problem, 276

preferred supplier, 250

prequalified or approved supplier, 256

risk management, 259

sole supplier, 256

supplier managed inventory, 255

sustainability, 267

sustainable supply management, 267

triple bottom line (3BL), 267

DISCUSSION QUESTIONS

1. Why do organizations commit the resources and time to evaluate suppliers before making a supplier selection decision?

2. Discuss why purchasers have both distributors and manufacturers in their supply base.

3. Discuss the various sources of information buyers can utilize when seeking potential sources of supply.

4. Why are supplier-managed inventory and integrated supplier programs becoming more popular with buyers when selecting a supplier?

5. What are some possible indicators on a supplier visit that might determine whether the managers in a company are forward looking and or whether the company is capable of becoming a best-in-class supplier?

6. Discuss the pros and cons of sole, single, and multiple sourcing and the various risks associated with each of these buying strategies.

7. Discuss the reasons why suppliers are sometimes reluctant to share cost information with buyers, particularly during the early stage of a buyer-seller relationship.

8. Assume you are the Chief Purchasing Officer at a manufacturer of mobile cellular devices; develop a plan to manage the risks in your supply base.

9. What are the issues or questions purchasing needs to address when evaluating whether a supplier is a candidate for a longer-term relationship?

10. Define sustainability and discuss why it is becoming more important in supplier selection and evaluation.

11. Go to at least three of the financial websites listed under the "Financial Stability" section of this chapter and discuss their strengths and weaknesses.

12. What are the advantages of assigning numerical scores to the categories and subcategories included in a supplier survey?

13. Why is it important to discuss promptly the results of a supplier visit or survey with the supplier? If a supplier has a weak area, under what conditions would supplier development be appropriate?

14. Discuss a situation in which a purchaser might select a supplier that is having financial difficulties.

15. Why must the time it takes to evaluate and select suppliers decrease? What three methods would you think have the largest impact on reducing supplier selection time?

ADDITIONAL READINGS

Choi, T. Y., and Hartley, J. L. (1996), "An Exploration of Supplier Selection Practices across the Supply Chain," *Journal of Operations Management*, 14, 333–343.

Dwyer, R. F., Schurr, P. H., and Oh, S. (1987), "Developing Buyer-Seller Relationships," *Journal of Marketing*, 51, 11–25.

Giunipero, L., Hooker, R., and Denslow, D. (2012, December), "Purchasing and Supply Management Sustainability: Drivers and Barriers," *Journal of Purchasing and Supply Management*, 18(4), 258–269.

Gottfredson, M., Puryear, R., and Phillips, S. (2005), "Strategic Sourcing: From Periphery to the Core," *Harvard Business Review*, 83(2), 132–139.

Kannan, V. R., and Tan, K. C. (2003), "Attitudes of U.S. and European Managers to Suppliers Selection and Assessment and Implications for Business Performance," *Benchmarking: An International Journal*, 10(5), 472–489.

Lin, P., and Lee, C., (2009), "How Online Vendors Select Parcel Delivery Carriers," *Transportation Journal*, 48(3), 20–32.

Merritt, L. (2010, March), "Drop in the Bucket-Sourcing Plastic Containers," *Packaging Digest*, 47(3), 49–52.

Ng, E. (2010), "Understanding B2B Supplier Selection Relationships: The Case of Taiwan Agribusinesses," *Journal of Business to Business Marketing*, 17(2), 149–172.

Przirembel, J. L. (1997), *How to Conduct Supplier Surveys and Audits*, West Palm Beach, FL: PT Publications.

Schorr, J. (1998), *Purchasing in the 21st Century*, New York: John Wiley & Sons.

Seegers, L., Handfield, R., and Melynk, S. (2007), "Green Movement Turns Mainstream for Corporate America", *Environmental Leader*, Retrieved from http://www.environmentatlleader.com

Siguaw, J. A., and Simpson, P. M. (2004), "Toward Assessing Supplier Value: Usage and Importance of Supplier Selection, Retention, and Value-added Criteria," *Journal of Marketing Channels*, 11(2/3), 3–31.

ENDNOTES

1. ____, ____Retrieved from http://www-935.ibm.com/services/us/en/it-services/supply-chain-management-outsourcing.html?csr=agus_gpsscm-20120411&cm=k&cr=google&ct=USB RK001&S_TACT=USBRK001&ck=ibm_procurement&cmp=USBRK&mkwid=s1IvVyCPp-dc_32628361897_4327s716358 September 2013

2. Retrieved from AT&T website http://www.att.com/gen/press-room?pid=24206&cdvn=news&newsarticl eid=36441 September 2013

3. Carter, P. L., and Giunipero, L., (2011), *Supplier Financial and Operational Risk Management*, Tempe, AZ: CAPS Research, 70 pages.

4. Casey, N., Zamiska, N., and Pasztor, A. (2007, September 22, 23), "Mattel Seeks to Placate China with Apology on Toys," *Wall Street Journal*, pp. Al, A7.

5. Greenhouse, S. (2013, April 30), "Retailers Split on Contrition after Collapse of Factories" *New York Times*.

6. Ibid.

7. _____, ____ Retrieved from P&G website: http://www.pg.com/en_US/sustainability/environmental_sustainability/operations_suppliers/supplier_engagement.shtml)

8. Elkington, J. (1998), "Partnerships from Cannibals with Forks: The Triple Bottomline of 21st-Century Business," *Environmental Quality Management*, 8(1), 37–51.

9. Giunipero, L., Hooker, R., and Denslow, D. "Purchasing and Supply Management Sustainability: Drivers and Barriers," *Journal of Purchasing & Supply Management*, 18(4), 258–269.

10. ____, ____ Retrieved from Knight's Global 100 website: http://www.global100.org/annual-lists/2013-global-100-list.html

11. ___, ____ Retrieved from Intel website: http://csrreportbuilder.intel.com/PDFFiles/CSR_2012_Exe-Summary.pdf

12. ____, ____ *SAP AG: Driving Business Value from Sustainability Source*, Retrieved from www54.sap.com/bin/sapcom/downloadasset.sap-17-pdf.html

13. Spekman, R.E. (1988) "Strategic Supplier Selection: Understanding Long Term Buyer Relationships" Business Horizons 80–81.

14. Pallotta, D. (2013, January 16), "The Market Wants Apple to Unveil a Time Machine," *HBR Blog Network*, Retrieved from http://blogs.hbr.org/2013/01/the-market-wants-apple-to-unve/

15. Arnseth, L. (2013, May), "Services Reveals Strategic Opportunities," *Inside Supply Management*, pp. 29–31.

16. Schorr, J. (1998), *Purchasing in the 21st Century: A Guide to State-of-the-Art Techniques and Strategies*, New York: John Wiley Publishers.

Supplier Quality Management

Learning Objectives

After completing this chapter, you should be able to

- Provide a working definition of supplier quality management.

- Recognize and understand those critical to quality factors that influence supply management's role in managing supplier quality.

- Link the principles of total quality management to supplier management best practices.

- Understand the basic principles of Deming's 14 Points, Six Sigma quality, and the cost of quality.

- Understand how quality management programs, such as the Malcolm Baldrige National Quality Award (MBNQA), ISO 9001:2008, and ISO 14001:2004, can help assess and improve supplier quality management systems and performance.

- Develop the elements of a basic supplier quality manual.

Chapter Outline

Improving the Quality of Chinese Suppliers

Over the past several years, even the most casual observer will have seen a number of media articles and telecasts decrying significant quality failures stemming from Chinese-made goods-toys decorated with lead-based paint, milk products tainted with melamine, contaminated pet food, poorly made counterfeit knockoff products, defective drywall, and many others. For every significant Chinese quality failure reported in the media, how many more are overlooked, ignored, or not even recognized? Kreg Kukor, director of global quality systems for Cequent Transportation Accessories, states the problem this way, "Quality is clearly the top threat to Chinese ventures as evidenced by the ongoing threat of brand destruction, poor consumer confidence, and the rapid erosion of profits experienced by many U.S. manufacturers."

How do these situations come about? Like their domestic counterparts, many Chinese suppliers have long been tempted to ignore quality-related issues unless they are required to address them by their foreign customers. Chinese suppliers face the same severe pressures for cost reduction and ever-increasing product performance in terms of quality, lead times, and delivery. Ask a senior manager from a typical Chinese supplier about these quality failures, and you are likely to hear how well-meaning, but overly aggressive, overseas buyers continue to unrealistically demand ever lower and lower prices while simultaneously seeking even quicker turnaround times. These suppliers often feel like they have to say "yes" to these demands to keep their factories loaded. If affected workers feel like their employer is facing a potential cutback because of fewer orders, they may leave for another company where they can receive a steady paycheck.

Because of this pressure, there can be a substantial bullwhip effect that develops within the typical Chinese supply chain. For example, if a Chinese OEM is facing severe cost pressures from its overseas customers, then it has to pass along those demands for ever lower prices back through its supply chain, or else it will eventually become unprofitable and go out of business. At some point, one or more suppliers in the supply chain will be unable to meet these lower cost targets without making some kind of shortcut in terms of the quality of purchased materials or product specification reduction. When one link somewhere in the supply chain is unable to perform satisfactorily, then the entire supply chain is usually affected adversely.

Paul Midler, author of *Poorly Made in China: An Insider's Account of the China Production Game*, indicates that part of the problem often stems from miscommunication between the buying and supplying companies in terms of each company's expectations and requirements. Chinese suppliers are under the gun to reduce costs by reducing quality, whereas overseas buyers are striving for higher levels of quality at "fire sale" prices. He also implies that these quality failures may originate from this asymmetry in expectations. Chinese suppliers often understand the quality ramifications of the severe cost pressures placed on them but may be unwilling to pass along this information to their foreign customers.

Without good data and accurate information, the astute buyer must assume that there are significant potential risks to product quality but can only surmise where the corners are being cut. On occasion, Chinese factories have been known to make specification changes on their own, sometimes known as "quality fade," without sharing this knowledge with their foreign customers. As a precaution, a number of importers of Chinese-made goods have adopted the time-worn slogan *"caveat emptor"* and taken a more proactive stance to improve the visibility of the Chinese suppliers' production processes.

How can supply managers prevent future such occurrences? One U.S.-based buyer of Chinese components, Cequent Transportation Accessories, a Michigan-based division of TriMas Corporation and a leading manufacturer of vehicle accessories, has deployed a formal global quality management system to deal with potential quality issues from its Chinese supply base. The company has determined that many of its Chinese component suppliers have not had a longstanding history of effective quality and process management, so it has implemented its domestic quality compliance program into China.

The Cequent quality management program requires its Chinese suppliers to provide real-time evidence that they monitor and check for appropriate quality characteristics at key points during the process, not just after the component is completed. The software that Cequent uses provides a structure that also allows the use of failure effects mode analysis (FMEA) as well as the relevant control and inspection plans to collect and analyze this data. Cequent can now have total visibility into a supplier's process quality data on a real-time basis. If a quality problem is detected, then Cequent deploys a quality expert to work with the supplier plant to address the problem and to prevent future quality and process problems. By focusing strictly on the quality data derived, both Cequent and the Chinese supplier can work through linguistic and cultural barriers to jointly develop key performance criteria and metrics, as well as an effective corrective action plan.

In the twelve months following deployment of Cequent's global quality management system, overall monthly supplier defects parts-per-million decreased from 33,555 to less than 200, saving a total of $7.9 million. Additionally, more than 97 percent of Chinese products now move through originating plants without rework. Cequent has also developed the ability to implement supplier scorecards and deploy a dock-to-stock program to reduce costs.

Sources: Gipp, L. (2008, December 19), "Cequent Group: Improving Chinese Supplier Quality," *Supply & Demand Chain Executive.* Retrieved from http://www.sdcexec.com
Goss, J. (2007, August 31). "Unrealistic foreign buyers created Chinese product 'quality problem'," *China Daily.* Retrieved from http://www.chinadaily.com
Palmer, K. (2009, April 23), "Explaining China's Quality Control Problems," *USNews.com.* Retrieved from http://www.usnews.com/money

Introduction

This chapter approaches the management of supplier quality from several perspectives and provides a basic understanding of generally accepted quality principles, tools, and techniques. The first section presents a broad overview of supplier quality management. The second section investigates the various factors that affect supply management's role in managing supplier quality. Next, we present basic principles of total quality management and relate them to supplier quality management. Fourth, we define Six Sigma quality and discuss how it relates to purchasing and supply chain management. The chapter concludes with a discussion of ISO 9001:2008, ISO 14001:2004, and the Malcolm Baldrige National Quality Award (MBNQA) and how they can be used to more effectively manage supplier quality, including the elements of an effective supply quality manual.

Overview of Supplier Quality Management

What Is Supplier Quality?

Before discussing how to manage supplier quality, we should define the generic term "quality." One renowned quality expert, Dr. Armand Feigenbaum, defined **quality** as "the total composite of product and service characteristics of marketing, engineering, manufacturing, and maintenance through which the product or service in use will meet or exceed the expectations of the customer."[1] Joseph Juran, considered by many as perhaps the foremost expert on quality, defined quality simply as "fitness for use." Philip Crosby, another well-known total quality expert, defined quality as "conformance to requirements." In recent years, the concept of quality has changed radically from simply meeting customer requirements or expectations to consistently exceeding them. However, many organizations have traditionally viewed quality management merely as only a voluntary or nonessential expenditure; one that often goes by the wayside when facing financial difficulties like those encountered during the Great Recession of 2008 or with increasingly shorter lead times. Instead, quality should be viewed as a fundamental principle of sound business management in all aspects of the organization.

In addition, customer expectations are dynamic and constantly shifting. The challenge to effectively managing downstream customer expectations is the company's ability to succinctly and specifically define those expectations and then translate them into desirable product characteristics in goods and services, including back upstream throughout its supply chain.

Considering these quality perspectives, we can now more clearly define what we mean by supplier quality. **Supplier quality** represents the ability to meet or exceed current and future customer (i.e., buyer and eventually end customer) expectations or requirements within critical performance areas on a consistent basis. There are three major parts to this definition:

1. *The ability to meet or exceed.* This means that suppliers must satisfy or surpass buyer expectations or requirements each and every time. Inconsistent supplier quality performance, whether in physical product quality, related services, or on-time delivery, cannot be a characteristic of a quality supplier.

2. *Current and future customer expectations or requirements.* Suppliers must meet or exceed today's demanding requirements and should also possess the ability to anticipate and satisfy future customer requirements. Suppliers must also be capable of demonstrating and maintaining continuous performance improvement over time. A supplier that can only satisfy today's requirements but cannot keep pace with expected future requirements is not a quality supplier.

3. *Within critical performance areas on a consistent basis.* Supplier quality does not apply only to the physical attributes of a product. Quality suppliers must satisfy a discerning buyer's expectations or requirements in many areas, including product or service delivery, conformance to specifications, after-sale service and support, current technology and features, research and development, and total cost management.

Supply management's evaluation of a supplier's ongoing quality performance should include more than just direct, out-of-pocket purchase price, level of defects, and on-time delivery performance. It must also provide for the analysis of related indirect costs; i.e., transaction costs, communication, joint problem resolution efforts, buyer administrative oversight, accompanying services, cost of quality, and switching costs. In addition, the buyer must also evaluate the supplier's delivery consistency and reliability because higher levels of inventory will be necessary to cover inconsistent delivery and quality performance by a supplier.

Within its supply chains, supply management does not merely buy parts or services from suppliers—it buys (and sometimes must help manage and improve) current and anticipated supplier capabilities that will result in quality products and services. Buyers should focus not only on a supplier's physical output (the end result) but also on the supporting inputs, systems, and processes that create that output. This includes the supplier's expertise and capabilities in logistics, engineering, cost management, research and development, and supply chain management.

Part of supply management's role in supplier quality management involves being a good customer to its suppliers. It is difficult to maintain a trusting and collaborative relationship and receive quality goods and services when suppliers do not enjoy working with the buying organization. For this reason, supplier quality performance requires that a buyer learn how to become a preferred customer by understanding and adapting to what suppliers need, expect, and appreciate in the modern buyer-seller relationship. Trust is a two-way street.

Some of the expectations that suppliers may have of a buyer within a supply chain relationship include minimizing product design changes once production begins, providing visibility to future purchase volume requirements, and sharing early access and visibility to its new-product requirements. Suppliers also value reasonable production lead times, fair and ethical treatment, access to new technology, and accurate and timely payment of invoices. Therefore, whenever possible, buyers should also strive for minimizing changes to purchase orders after sending material releases to suppliers to alleviate supply disruptions and ultimately higher costs.

A buyer cannot realistically expect the highest levels of supplier performance when the supplier must respond to frequent or short lead time changes. Order stability allows a supplier to minimize its costs and more effectively plan its operations on the basis of accurate, timely, and consistent buyer order information. Frequent order quantity and specification changes limit a supplier's ability to meet the buyer's expectations, including its quality requirements, as well as increasing the supplier's costs and eventually the purchase price. Supply management plays a central role in helping to ensure that its suppliers consistently perform in a defect-free manner.

Why Be Concerned with Supplier Quality?

Lapses in managing supplier quality can quickly tarnish the hard-earned reputation of even the world's best companies and brands. As the opening vignette makes clear, any buying firm that does not effectively and consistently manage quality throughout its supply chain is risking long-term customer dissatisfaction, lower profitability, reduced market share, and increased costs, as well as potentially negative public relations. It is a competitive necessity to routinely assess actual supplier performance to make sure it aligns with expected supplier performance standards.

Supplier Impact on Quality

The late quality expert Philip Crosby estimated that external suppliers are responsible for about half of a firm's product-related quality problems. Furthermore, the average North American manufacturing firm spends more than 55 percent of its cost of goods sold on purchased goods and services; some manufacturers spend even more, some with purchased content approaching 100 percent. A firm that focuses only on its own internal quality issues will usually fail to recognize and take appropriate action on the true underlying root causes of many of its quality-related problems. Poor supplier quality performance can quickly undermine a firm's total quality improvement effort.

Continuous Improvement Requirements

Most firms seek to achieve continuous quality improvements in all aspects of their business. One way to do this is through the proactive management of supplier quality. Quality improvement requirements are a function of a company's industry along with how well its performance compares vis-à-vis its competitors. Companies in dynamic, high-technology industries, such as Honda, Boeing, Apple, and Philips, face intense competitive pressure to achieve quality levels that approach perfection while responding to rapid change in the marketplace. Other industries, such as furniture manufacturing, typically experience a slower and less dramatic rate of change. Regardless, it is safe to say that nearly all industries experience at least some pressure from customers to achieve continuous quality improvement while adapting to shifting customer tastes.

Outsourcing of Purchase Requirements

Reliance on a firm's suppliers for raw materials, components, subassemblies, and even finished products is steadily increasing. It is no longer a competitive advantage in some industries for firms to make most of the components of a product or to provide their own services. Therefore, progressive buyers are relying on world-class suppliers that can provide significant design and build capabilities, even for highly technical or complex part requirements. For example, Dell Computer is primarily an assembly operation that purchases most of its PC componentry (monitor, hard drive, keyboard, microprocessors, power unit, and so on) from external suppliers. The larger the proportion of the final product that a supply base provides, the greater the impact it will have on overall product cost and quality.

Factors Affecting Supply Management's Role in Managing Supplier Quality

Supply management must assume primary organizational leadership for managing the quality of its external suppliers. A number of factors influence how much attention supply management should commit to managing supplier quality:

- The ability of a supplier to affect a buyer's total quality. Certain suppliers provide high-value or key components and materials that are critical to a firm's success. Supply management must manage the suppliers of these critical items far more closely than those providing lower-value, standardized, or otherwise easy-to-obtain items or commodities. Recall our previous discussion of the Strategy Portfolio Matrix for Category Management in Chapter 6.

- The internal resources available to support ongoing supplier quality management and improvement. Firms with limited resources and/or minimal expertise in quality management and supplier improvement must carefully choose where to budget and apply those scarce resources. Attentive resource execution will greatly influence the overall scope of the firm's quality management efforts. These resources typically include personnel, budget, time, and information technology.

- The ability of a buying firm to practice world-class quality. A buying firm can help its suppliers apply and use quality concepts, tools, and techniques only after the buying firm itself understands and correctly applies these concepts, tools, and techniques internally. You can't expect someone else to do what you are unable or unwilling to do yourself.

- A supplier's willingness to work jointly to improve quality. Not all suppliers are inclined to work closely and collaboratively with a buyer. Instead, some suppliers may prefer a traditional, arm's-length purchase arrangement characterized by limited buyer involvement with a more hand's-off or laissez-faire management style. Others will enthusiastically embrace long-term, collaborative partnerships because they recognize the benefits of doing so.

- A supplier's current quality levels. A supplier's current performance level influences the amount and type of attention required from a buying firm. World-class suppliers will require less attention from the buyer, whereas suppliers providing marginal or less-than-desirable quality performance will require greater attention. Chapter 9 will discuss the concepts of supply base rationalization and optimization as well as supplier development.

- A buyer's ability to collect and analyze quality-related data. Supply management must utilize an effective supplier performance measurement system that utilizes properly designed metrics to track how well a supplier is meeting its quality performance expectations. For most firms, this means developing and employing a real-time research and tracking system that collects and distributes supplier-related quality data on a timely and cost-effective basis that can be shared throughout the buyer's entire organization.

Sourcing Snapshot

Intel's Supplier Continuous Quality Improvement Program (SCQI)

The vision of Intel's Supplier Continuous Quality Improvement Program (SCQI) is to "establish and develop long-term business relationships with a select group of key suppliers who provide the highest quality materials, equipment, and services with commitment to continuous improvement." SCQI is an enterprise-wide program designed to improve the quality performance of key suppliers while minimizing the time and cost of incoming inspection. Each supplier receives a quarterly report card that measures availability, cost, customer satisfaction, quality, strategic contribution, and technology.

The SCQI program is Intel's highest level of public supplier recognition and establishes aligned goals, indicators, and metrics by evaluating a supplier's total capabilities. Encouraging continuous improvement, it also promotes collaborative relationships, team problem-solving, and two-way continuous learning between buyer and supplier.

Utilizing the Intel SCQI Roadmap, the first level of recognition is the Certified Supplier Award (CSA), which covers stipulated outstanding supplier quality performance over two consecutive quarters, according to a series of objective criteria. The next level of recognition is the Preferred Quality Supplier (PQS) Award, which requires a minimum of one full calendar year of outstanding supplier quality performance over the same criteria. The top level, the Supplier Continuous Quality Improvement Award, extends the PQS Award to even greater performance, again using higher levels of the same criteria.

PQS and SCQI winners are announced at Intel's annual Supplier Day and are recognized in a *Wall Street Journal* advertisement as well. They are also allowed to publicize their Intel achievements from one (PQS only) to three years (SCQI only).

Sources: *Supplier Continuous Quality Improvement Program*, (2008) Santa Clara, CA: Intel, Retrieved from https://supplier.intel.com and Roos, G, "INTEL CORP.: It takes quality to be preferred by world's biggest chipmaker" Retrieved from http://www.purchasing.com

Supplier Quality Management Using a Total Quality Management Perspective

Supply management professionals at all levels must fully understand and commit themselves to the principles of total quality management (TQM) if they expect to create upstream value in the supply chain that benefits downstream customers. Applying these principles to supplier quality management becomes critical if firms want to avoid embarrassing and costly public relations nightmares in the marketplace.

The various principles that comprise TQM frame perhaps the most robust and powerful business philosophy ever developed. Unfortunately, merely reciting these principles is far easier than actually embracing and effectively practicing them on a day-to-day basis. Although external suppliers provide more than half the inputs required within a typical supply chain, a bona fide commitment to TQM in the supply base is often lacking by the buyer. If supplier quality is so important, why do many supply management departments lack the necessary performance measurement and visibility systems that can provide timely and objective information about what a supplier actually does? Why do many buyers make critical supplier selection decisions without fully analyzing and understanding a supplier's production and supporting processes?

Exhibit 8.1 presents an integrated set of key quality principles based on the thinking of W. Edwards Deming, Philip Crosby, and Joseph Juran.[2] The following sections present each principle along with a selected (but certainly not comprehensive) set of activities that, if fully put into place, will help ensure that buying firms truly practice TQM in their pursuit of superior supplier quality.

Defining Quality in Terms of Customers and Their Requirements

In a buyer-seller relationship, the buyer is the supplier's direct customer in the supply chain. One of the primary causes of nonconforming supplier quality involves inconsistent communication and the resultant misunderstanding of specifications, expectations, and requirements between supply chain members. Supply managers, working closely with their design and process engineers and other internal customers, must provide suppliers with clear specifications and unambiguous performance requirements regarding the design and function of a product, as well as any other relevant information that may ultimately affect the quality or delivery of a purchased input. Another important form of buyer communication is sharing of final product requirements, which at times can be broad or incomplete.

Exhibit 8.1	Eight Key Principles of Total Quality Management

- Define quality in terms of customers and their requirements.
- Pursue quality at the source.
- Stress objective rather than subjective analysis.
- Emphasize prevention rather than detection of defects.
- Focus on process rather than output.
- Strive for zero defects.
- Establish continuous improvement as a way of life.
- Make quality everyone's responsibility.

Source: Adapted from Trent, R.J. "Linking TQM to SCM," *Supply Chain Management Review*, 2001, 5(3), 71.

In this case, the process for determining final requirements must be established and mutually agreed on between buyer and supplier prior to purchase. Keki Bhote, a leading quality expert, correctly argues that the incomplete or inaccurate development and communication of product specifications has a disproportionate effect on supplier quality.

Many of the quality problems originating between customer [i.e., the buyer] and supplier are caused by poor product and performance specifications, for which the buying company is largely responsible. Most product or service specifications provided to suppliers tend to be vague or arbitrary. They are generally determined unilaterally by engineers, who may lift them from a volume of engineering standards and then embellish them with excessive safety factors to account for unknown liability risks. When bids are extended, the targeted suppliers are seldom consulted on specifications, and many are hesitant to challenge excessive specifications for fear of losing the bid. So the first cure for poor supplier quality is to eliminate the tyranny of capricious specifications.[3]

Developing a clear understanding of expectations and actual requirements has two dimensions. The first is the ability of the buyer to succinctly identify, define, quantify, or specify its technical and sourcing requirements. The second dimension is the buyer's ability to effectively communicate these requirements to suppliers, including change orders, which means that both parties fully understand the requirements and processes to be used in modifying them over time. Buyers must take the initiative to clearly communicate their requirements through detailed requests for proposals (RFPs), the contract negotiation process, and regular performance feedback sessions, using measurement systems that accurately quantify supplier performance.

The ability of a supplier to successfully fulfill product requirements is largely a function of the buyer explicitly informing the supplier about what is expected.

Deming's 14 Points

Dr. W. Edwards Deming, often considered to be the father of the modern quality movement, developed his comprehensive 14-point management philosophy as the basis for his views on achieving excellence and customer satisfaction in the modern organization, which is applicable to manufacturing and service industries alike, as well as government, not-for-profit, and educational organizations. However, Deming's quality philosophy has often been criticized because it does not prescribe specific firm-level actions and programs for management to follow. One of the unique features of the Deming philosophy, as outlined in Exhibit 8.2, is that these 14 points do not constitute an à la carte menu of quality

Exhibit 8.2	Unique Features of Deming's Philosophy

- Variation is the primary source of quality nonconformance.
- To reduce variation, the search for improved quality is a never-ending cycle of design, production, and delivery, followed by surveying customers—then starting all over again.
- Although quality is everyone's responsibility, senior management has the ultimate responsibility for quality improvement.
- Interacting parts of a system must be managed together as a whole, not separately.
- Psychology helps managers understand their employees and customers, as well as interactions between people.
- Intrinsic motivation is more powerful than extrinsic motivation.
- Predictions must be grounded in theory that helps to understand cause-and-effect relationships.

Source: Adapted from Evans, J.R. and Lindsay, W.M. *Managing for Quality and Performance Excellence* (8th ed.), Mason, OH: South-Western Cengage Learning, 2011, 91–99.

improvement activities, from which a company can pick and choose only those with which they agree. His quality philosophy dictates that all 14 points are complementary and equally necessary to successfully implement a TQM culture in an organization.[4]

Point 1: Create a Vision and Demonstrate Commitment

The top managers and executives in an organization are responsible for delineating its future strategic direction: mission, vision, and values. Not only do businesses exist to make a profit for their shareholders and owners, but they must also consider and be good stewards of the overall social and physical environment in which they operate. This requires a long-term view and commitment of sufficient resources by the organization: personnel, time, money, and effort.

Point 2: Learn the New Philosophy

Quality must be learned (and relearned continually) by everyone in the organization, which serves as the pervasive thread woven throughout everything the organization does. The focal point of the Deming philosophy is that the entire organization should be focused on satisfying customer needs, whether the customer is internal or external. Quality is no longer just for manufacturing.

Point 3: Understand Inspection

Since the Industrial Revolution, inspecting for defects has been the traditional method of controlling quality. The underlying consideration is that an organization recognizes that defects are inevitable and therefore must be inspected out of the process output. Deming indicates that the only proper way to deal with defects is to design and operate the process so that defects will never occur. This point requires that everyone, from the production line worker all the way up through the executive suite, understands the concept of process variation and how it affects every production process. Rework and disposal efforts (also known as the "hidden factory") increase cost and decrease productivity.

Point 4: Stop Making Decisions Purely on the Basis of Price

The lowest purchase price of an item may be important in the short run for supply management but may cause increased costs somewhere else in the production system over the long run: excessive scrap and rework, defective products, greater warranty claims, and so on. Enlightened supply management has embraced this point through its supply base optimization and rationalization initiatives as discussed in Chapter 9. The focus should always be on reducing total system costs, not just minimizing purchase price. Working with fewer suppliers allows the supply manager to concentrate on building trusting, collaborative relationships and supplier loyalty while improving quality in purchased goods and services. Communication between buyer and supplier is also enhanced.

Point 5: Improve Constantly and Forever

The quality-oriented organization must intimately understand its customers' evolving needs and wants. If the firm remains static in its quality performance, its competition will continue to improve and eventually bypass it. Continuous improvement, or **kaizen**, must be built into every single process in the organization. There is always room for improvement whether the organization is a market leader or a market laggard. In addition to maintaining continuous communication with its customers, the TQM-focused organization must also look at reducing process variation and seeking innovation in both product and process.

Point 6: Institute Training

It is very important that management provide its employees and suppliers with the necessary knowledge, skills, and tools to do their jobs efficiently and effectively. Well-developed and specifically targeted training and development programs can enhance product and service quality and worker productivity, as well as improve morale. Quality-wise, effective training should address performance measurement, diagnostic and analytical tools, problem-solving, and decision making

Point 7: Institute Leadership

There is a significant gap between real leadership and what we traditionally think of as management or supervision. For example, managers and supervisors are more involved in the day-to-day oversight, direction, and evaluation of workers. Leadership goes well beyond management and supervision by guiding and coaching employees to improve their skills and abilities with a greater focus on becoming more productive and delivering higher quality.

Point 8: Drive Out Fear

In the workplace, fear is obvious in a variety of ways. Employees may be fearful of making a mistake and facing a reprimand. Most people are risk-averse, so they do not want to try anything new or different for fear of failure. They are also creatures of habit and do not like to make changes in their routines. Middle managers may be fearful of letting go of their traditional power based on command and control. Departments may not seek to collaborate with other departments. Fear-free organizations are extremely rare as it takes a long time to develop and maintain an organizational culture that promotes risk taking and change. Eliminating fear encourages employee and supplier trial-and-error experimentation, which can lead to greater productivity and higher-quality processes over the long term.

Point 9: Optimize the Efforts of Teams

Teams are becoming more and more a part of day-to-day organizational life. When designed, implemented, and operated correctly, teams can be useful in eliminating cross-functional barriers by taking people from different disciplines and having them work together on a common task or project. However, dysfunctional teams can have the opposite effect; they may actually create additional barriers and reinforce existing ones. One of the greatest barriers in Western companies that restrict the potential value of teams is the mutual animosity and distrust extant between unions and management that impedes effective communication.

Point 10: Eliminate Exhortations

Slogans, signs, and posters are well-meaning and intended to effect change in people's behavior. However, they are seldom effective because they assume that most, if not all, quality problems are because of human behavior. Phrases such as "Do it right the first time," "Work smarter, not harder," and "Zero defects" are catchy motivational sayings and make great copy, but they do not help individual workers know what to do or how to do it better, let alone make changes to the process. Most quality deficiencies are based on the inherent design and operation of the processes and systems that create goods and services, not on workers' motivation. Designed-in systemic process variation is a managerial concern, not a labor issue.

Point 11: Eliminate Numerical Quotas and Measurement by Objective

Workers may game the system to make their individual production and output goals. These goals do not provide the necessary incentives for workers or suppliers to improve quality in the long run. Hard and fast output standards short-circuit TQM improvements and other quality initiatives. Why would workers stop to fix or adjust a piece of equipment if it meant that they would not make their production quotas or reach minimum piecework standards? In addition, many numerical based goals and objectives are often developed arbitrarily and far beyond the control of the individual worker. Goals should be developed jointly in conjunction with managers providing workers and suppliers with the skills and means to achieve them. Lastly, goals are often short-term in their focus, whereas quality improvement, by definition, must take a longer-term perspective.

Point 12: Remove Barriers to Pride in Workmanship

Too often, workers are treated as a simple commodity—interchangeable with each other with no uniqueness or consideration. Managers are often treated in the same manner when they are required to routinely work longer hours without overtime compensation. The performance appraisal systems in most organizations create real barriers to pride in workmanship as they promote competitive behavior and reward quantity over work over quality. When given the proper environment in which to work, most people want to do a good job. Unfortunately, the evaluation, reward, and compensation systems in many companies do not stimulate the right kind of culture to allow the workers to take pride in their efforts. For example, we assign people to work in teams but typically appraise and pay them as individuals.

Point 13: Encourage Education and Self-Improvement

Unlike training, which is geared primarily toward learning specific task-related skills, education and personal self-improvement are much broader in nature and focus on improving the quality of life for individuals by teaching them new skills and building higher levels of self-worth. Organizations that invest in education and self-improvement initiatives often find that their employees are more highly motivated and bring additional benefits to both the organization and the individual in terms of job satisfaction, productivity, and overall job performance.

Point 14: Take Action

Top management must initiate and invest in those activities that will result in improved product quality, job productivity, and quality of work life. A grassroots TQM effort that emanates from the lower levels of the organization is doomed to failure without active and visible top management commitment and support. Appropriate support may include time and monetary investments in process design, education, and training; new evaluation, reward, and compensation systems; and a changed organization culture. The key for success is to maintain the momentum of continuous quality improvement over the long term.

Pursuing Quality at the Source

Quality at the source occurs whenever value is added to a product or service as it moves through transformation processes in the supply chain. The value-adding activities in a process, however, represent potential creation of defects that require careful management and attention to detail to identify, mitigate, or correct. Perhaps more than any other group, supply management has the means to affect quality at the source with its suppliers because of its ability to determine and manage the external sources of many supply chain inputs.

Because suppliers themselves are a key source of supply chain quality, it makes intuitive sense that the firm's supplier selection process would be a primary vehicle through which to operationalize this principle. Although the costs of making international supplier site visits can be quite substantial, the costs of making a poor supplier selection decision can be significantly higher. Skilled and experienced cross-functional teams (CFTs) should visit and evaluate a potential strategic supplier on site, regardless of location, to determine its financial condition, operating environment, global capacity, logistical networks, supply management practices, process capability, willingness to work with the buyer, research and development, and technology innovation before making a strategic sourcing selection decision that will be difficult to reverse once made. Review Chapter 7 for a more in-depth discussion of supplier evaluation and selection.

A second major area that defines supplier quality is in product and process design. Progressive companies involve suppliers in both product and process development at a much earlier stage than has traditionally been the case. Allowing a supplier to apply its own experience and expertise to a buyer's new-product development project, known as early supplier design involvement (ESDI), often leads to better quality and product design because the knowledge and experience of the supplier is applied during the initial development of the customer's requirements, well before final specifications and ultimate cost structure are locked in. Suppliers can provide meaningful suggestions about how to simplify a product or process, anticipate and begin preproduction work, and collaborate with the buyer's design and process engineers to establish reasonable tolerances that more closely match the supplier's capabilities while meeting customer requirements and improving product quality and manufacturability.

Although the logic behind ESDI is relatively straightforward, making it work effectively on a day-to-day basis is often more difficult. Many firms struggle with sharing their proprietary information or trade secrets with outside entities. In addition, some firms simply do not know how to manage this delicate and sensitive sharing process. The mere presence of such constraints, however, does not mean that firms should not actively pursue early design involvement with carefully selected, strategic suppliers. Both the buyer and supplier will be better off by working together collaboratively in the design phase of new-product development or through value analysis and value engineering initiatives.

Sourcing Snapshot

Pallets

Sometimes, it is not only the product itself that causes a quality concern. A product's quality problem can originate from the packaging, handling, or other ancillary components of a product. For example, McNeil Consumer Healthcare's Tylenol brand had to recall several lots of its Arthritis Pain Caplet 100-count bottles and other products in late 2009 because of packaging materials used at its Puerto Rico plant being stored on tainted wooden pallets apparently containing the chemical 2,4,6-tribromoanisole (TBA). This chemical caused a musty, moldy odor to invade these packaging materials resulting in nausea, vomiting, stomach discomfort, and diarrhea to those who eventually purchased these products from the identified production lots. Tylenol surmises that the lumber for the pallets was treated with the fungicide TBP, which contained the suspect chemical TBA. When the TBP dried, it crystallized and became embedded into the wood pallets, which were likely sourced from the Dominican Republic. When the pallet containing this chemical got wet again, it released the 2, 4, 6-tribromoanisole, causing the odor to reoccur.

Various consumer goods companies are now requiring their pallet suppliers to provide additional certification that the wood used to make the pallets has not been contaminated with TBA. However, this has proven problematic, particular when the product is shipped on used or recycled pallets. In addition, use of wood pallets may also be problematic to food shipments in that they may have been made with wood that contains urea formaldehyde. These chemicals are often applied to prevent insect infestation.

Whatever the source of the contamination, it is ultimately the responsibility of the OEM to ensure that all materials used to produce and ship its products are of appropriate quality.

Sources: Lacefield, S.K. (2010, January 22), "Pallets Cause of Recent Tylenol Recall?" *DC Velocity.* Retrieved from http://www.dcvelocity.com
Rogers, L.K. (2010, February 5), "Supply Chain: Wood Pallets Cited as Cause for McNeil Consumer Healthcare's Tylenol Recall," *Logistics Management.* Retrieved from http://www.logisticsmanagement.com
"The Facts about Tylenol Recall and Relationship to Wood Pallets" (2010), Retrieved from http://www.nwpca.com

Stressing Objective Rather Than Subjective Measurement and Analysis

An executive responsible for coordinating Xerox's successful drive for the Malcolm Baldrige National Quality Award once stated that one of the keys to achieving total quality is recognizing that facts, rather than subjective judgment, must predominate.[5] Hence, if facts must drive decision making, the need for fact-based measurement and decision making becomes increasingly evident.

However, many organizations, large and small, have not sufficiently developed objective or rigorous supplier measurement systems, during either the supplier selection process or in post-selection performance measurement and evaluation. Although there are many reasons for this, a primary one is that some executives have not yet truly grasped the importance of external suppliers on the buying organization's performance. Even today, there are wide differences in the breadth and capability of supply chain performance measurement.

Why is measurement so important to supplier quality? Collecting and analyzing performance data allows supply managers to develop a preferred supplier list for awarding future business, identify continuous performance improvement opportunities, provide feedback that supports corrective action or future development, and track the results from improvement initiatives. Effective supplier performance measurement systems are also an excellent way to communicate a buyer's quality and performance expectations to suppliers.

Emphasizing Prevention Rather Than Detection of Defects

Prevention is the avoidance of nonconformance in products and services by not allowing errors or defects to occur in the first place. Although preventive activities can take many forms, each stresses the need for predictable consistency and reduced process variation.

Sourcing Snapshot

Quality Dashboard

Recognizing and understanding supplier quality upstream in the supply chain is imperative to satisfying customer demands and requirements downstream in the supply chain. Many companies now utilize supplier measurement and visibility systems, such as quality dashboards and supplier scorecards, to measure supplier performance and identify the real costs related to suppliers with poor quality performance. The information generated can also be effectively utilized in future supplier negotiations.

Graham Packaging Company has installed a quality dashboard and supplier scorecard system to ensure that it is able to satisfy its world-class customers, such as Coca-Cola, Pepsico, Heinz, and Unilever. Prior to the installation, the data necessary to effectively measure and evaluate supplier performance was spread throughout the company in SAP modules, various informal systems, and disconnected spreadsheets from all 81 of its plants, requiring substantial offline effort to aggregate this data to manage its supply base. For example, Graham's system of spreadsheets resulted in significant time delays, data errors, and inconsistencies in data collection.

Using a third-party provider, arcplan Information Services GmbH, Graham developed a standardized method of consolidating data that allowed the company to "identify sub-par vendors and see the actual cost of suppliers' products, considering both the initial price and the cost of re-work or identified quality defects." Data was captured by SAP, but the company needed to be able to effectively and efficiently extract and view supplier quality and cost data. The arcplan-powered Supplier Quality Dashboard and Scorecard complemented the existing SAP system and provided several benefits, such as fact-based cost negotiations, rationalization of the supply base, and improved quality.

Sources: "Quality Dashboard and Supplier Scorecard Eliminate Cost and Drive Quality at Graham Packaging," (2009). Retrieved from http://www.arcplan.com/gp.cfm?l=graham_packaging accessed May 15, 2010.

A thorough emphasis on defect prevention reduces reliance on appraisal, inspection, and other non-value-adding detection activities. A rigorous and structured approach to supplier evaluation and selection, for example, is an ideal way to ensure that selected suppliers have the requisite systems, processes, and methods in place to prevent defects.

A supplier certification program, another prime way to prevent defects, is the formal process of verifying, usually through an intensive cross-functional on-site audit, that a supplier's processes and methods actually produce consistent and conforming quality. Certification demands that suppliers continuously demonstrate process capability, use of statistical process control, and conformance to other accepted TQM practices, such as Six Sigma. The objective of supplier certification is to ensure that nonconforming items are not created or do not leave a supplier's facility. Supplier certification usually applies only to a specific part, process, or site rather than an entire company or product.

The extensive use of corrective action requests also supports prevention of nonconforming defects. For example, FedEx, a Malcolm Baldrige National Quality Award winner, uses a corrective action request system to protect the physical appearance of its brand. When FedEx or a supplier discovers a critical defect with printed shipping forms, the supplier must immediately investigate and remove the source of the error to prevent future defects. The supplier is also required to sort and inspect its current production, remove all defective units, and examine ten boxes of stock below and ten boxes above the discovered defect. Finally, the supplier must submit a full written explanation and corrective plan to FedEx for resolving the defect (root cause analysis) along with a continuous-improvement plan.[6] Although corrective action requests do not prevent the initial problem (they are forwarded to suppliers in response to an identified problem), their timely use helps prevent further problems. Exhibit 8.3 on p. 269 presents a sample corrective action template.

Focusing on Process Rather Than Output

Perhaps the most dramatic difference between traditional quality control methods and total quality management thinking involves a shift from a product orientation to a process orientation. TQM puts the focus on those value-adding processes that generate an output rather than on the output itself. Because quality processes are expected to create quality output, a logical focus is on the process of creation rather than the result. It is far less expensive and more efficient in the long run to avoid generating the defect in the first place than it is to inspect for it once it is created.

Assume that an organization evaluates and awards business primarily on the basis of competitive bidding and supplier prototypes or samples. At best, suppliers will provide only one or two prototypes or samples to the buyer for detailed analysis and acceptance. The following questions highlight the risk of focusing strictly on inspected output rather than the underlying process that created the output:

- What supplier would knowingly submit a poor sample for evaluation?
- How many parts did the supplier have to produce before it was able to get an acceptable sample?
- Are the samples truly representative of the production process operating under normal operating conditions?
- Did the supplier use the same process, methods, personnel, and materials that it will use during normal production, or was the prototype made under strictly controlled laboratory conditions?
- Did the supplier itself or a subcontractor actually produce the sample?
- Do the submitted samples give the buyer enough information about the supplier's real capacity or process capability?

An emphasis on process rather than finished product demands that a supplier provide evidence of its process capability (addressed in the next section) to the buyer on an ongoing, regular basis. Furthermore, every time a supplier modifies a process, a new process capability study should be instigated and analyzed. Focusing on the underlying process means minimizing over-reliance on samples unless there is a timely and comprehensive method of validating sample conformance to the buyer's requirements.

Perhaps the best way to implement and maintain a process focus involves developing a structured company-wide supplier evaluation and selection system, which itself represents a process. A well-defined supplier evaluation and selection process supports the development of best practices, reduces duplication across units, supports the transfer of knowledge across teams or units, and recognizes the critical link between the supplier selection decision and supply chain quality. Leading-edge firms make their supplier evaluation and selection process, along with any supporting tools and templates, available through their company's intranets for easy access and widespread availability.

Exhibit 8.3	Supplier Corrective Action form

Supplier Corrective Action Request

Section A: To be completed by buyer

Corrective action request log #:

Date:

To:

Subject:

From:

Type of defect / nonconformance:

Description of defect / nonconformance:

Estimated total cost of defect / nonconformance:

Charge to supplier?   ☐ Yes   ☐ No

If yes, indicate amount: _____

Section B: To be completed by supplier

Supplier corrective action response: (Please use back of page if additional space is required.)

Date corrective action response will be fully implemented:

Buyer sign-off: _____   Supplier sign-off: _____

Date: _____   Date: _____

Basics of Process Capability

Process capability is the ability of a process to generate outputs that meet engineering specifications and/or customer requirements and "refers to the normal behavior of a process when operating in a state of statistical control."[7] A state of statistical control exists when only common causes of variation are present; meaning, variation that occurs naturally and randomly from how the process was designed. If the process is not in statistical control, special causes of variation not designed into the process are present. This variation can be identified and rectified, thereby returning the process back to into a state of predictable statistical control.

To be considered capable, the outputs from a process must fall between stated upper and lower specification limits. We assume here that the distribution of output from the process is normally distributed. One property of normally distributed data is that 99.7 percent of all possible observations of process output occur within plus-or-minus three standard deviations of the process mean. A process that is stable and in control (i.e., no special and correctable causes of variation) can be expected to produce virtually all of its output within these natural tolerance limits. If the natural tolerance limits fall within the product's engineering specifications as defined by the upper and lower specification limits, then the process is deemed to be capable.

Two process capability indices are typically used to measure a process's capability: C_p and C_{pk}. To calculate these indices, the process under study must be in statistical control with only common causes of variation being present. The C_p process capability index quantifies the relationship between the process's natural tolerance limits and the product's specifications using a two-sided approach, regardless of process centering. It is calculated by subtracting the lower specification limit from the upper specification limit and dividing by six standard deviations. In general, quality practitioners suggest a relatively safe C_p index value of 1.5 or higher. Many customer companies require an even higher C_p value of 1.66 or higher for added assurance that the output will conform to product specifications.[8] This level allows the process to drift slightly because of special cause variation and still be able to meet established specifications.

However, the C_p index does not adequately account for situations where the process is not closely centered on the nominal specification target value. For situations where the natural process mean is not centered on the specification average, the C_{pk} index must be used. The C_{pk} index provides a conservative adjustment to the C_p index that takes into account how far the process mean actually varies from the target value of the specification. Hence, the C_{pk} value is always smaller than the C_p index.[9]

A process capability study is designed to provide information about the performance of the process under stable operating conditions; i.e., when no special causes of variation are present. The process capability study can provide information for the following actions:

1. Determine the operating baseline of a process.
2. Prioritize potential quality improvement projects.
3. Provide evidence of process performance to a customer.

Striving for Zero Defects

Philip Crosby argued that the only true performance standard that defines total quality is **zero defects**, which he defined as conformance to requirements. Genichi Taguchi further argued that any deviation from a target value carries with it some level of opportunity loss because of scrap, rework, and customer dissatisfaction.[10] We can operationalize the pursuit of zero defects, however defined, in several important ways. Each method recognizes the importance of eliminating product and process variability.

As mentioned previously, a well-designed and rigorous supplier evaluation and selection process is one way to identify and only work with suppliers that strive for zero defects.

Measurement systems using key performance metrics also help identify supplier improvement opportunities and progress toward meeting them. Another major approach, and one of the fastest and most effective ways to improve supply chain quality, is through supply base rationalization.

Supply base rationalization or **optimization**, as presented in detail in Chapter 9, is the process of determining the right mix and number of suppliers to maintain for a given purchase category or commodity. Almost half of the companies participating in a recent survey reduced their supply bases by 20 percent, and nearly 15 percent reduced their supply bases between 20 and 60 percent. Furthermore, three quarters of the firms indicated that they now commit 80 percent of their total purchase dollars with fewer than 100 suppliers.[11] Supply base optimization is, and must continue to be, a continuous, ongoing activity.

The supply base rationalization and optimization process is critical to improving supplier quality. Effective use of more advanced strategic sourcing approaches, such as early supplier design involvement and supply chain alliances, also require a reduced supply base. Furthermore, if a firm rationalizes and optimizes its supply base properly, the remaining suppliers should only include those that are the most capable of providing consistent goods and services. Inconsistency is the enemy of total quality. Few supply managers will knowingly eliminate their best suppliers. By definition, average supplier quality will increase as lower performers are eliminated.

Cost of Quality[12]

Although the concept of the **cost of quality** was initially developed in the 1950s, many companies have not yet fully embraced this concept to improve their processes and operations. In many respects, the cost of quality should actually be considered as the cost of "poor quality." Because of the nature of many cost accounting systems, quality costs are often aggregated into various overhead accounts, which mask their real impact on the finances and operations of an organization.

Quality has two primary impacts on the costs of a company: the costs because of non-conforming quality and the costs related to improving quality or avoiding poor quality. Because the language of executive management is quantified in dollars, it is important to measure and track how a firm's funds are actually spent in terms of quality. Within this broader viewpoint, the cost of quality can be subcategorized into three classifications: appraisal, failure, and prevention costs. Note that the cost of quality is a highly complex issue, not only incorporating the costs associated with poor quality but also the costs of designing and ensuring good quality.

Appraisal costs include the direct, out-of-pocket costs of measuring quality, specifically checking for possible defects. Areas of appraisal-related expense include laboratory testing of prototypes and samples, production inspection activities, supplier quality audits, incoming material inspections, and other forms of product monitoring.

Failure costs are further divided into internal and external elements. Internal failure costs occur before the product or service is provided to the customer, whereas external failure costs are those incurred following production or after the customer takes possession. Examples of internal failure costs include process troubleshooting, re-inspection following detection of a defect, production downtime caused by defects, scrap, and process waste. Examples of external failure costs include warranty costs, replacement of defective products to customers, liability lawsuits, and loss of customer goodwill, i.e. customer complaints.

Prevention costs are those costs incurred when production processes are designed or modified to prevent defects from occurring in the first place. Examples include design for quality, quality planning, equipment calibration, quality training, development of a quality manual, and maintenance of a quality management system.

Many traditional cost accounting systems are notorious for their failure to provide clear and concise information on just where funds are spent on quality-related expenses. These expenses are often incurred throughout various departments in the organization and not always under the control of personnel with specific quality responsibilities. In addition, many quality-related costs, such as training, are somewhat subjective in nature and seldom easily identified.

The Seven Wastes[13]

Honda's BP process is a well-known continuous-improvement process that focuses on eliminating waste from its production and support activity processes. The BP initiative, which stems from the terms Best Position, Best Product, Best Price, and Best Partners, outlines Honda's philosophy of doing business using continuous improvement as its foundation.

In the Honda BP process, there is an intense focus on identifying and eliminating common causes of waste that add cost, time, and effort to the product or service while not adding value to the customer. Common causes of waste can include any combination of the following:

- Inadequate processes
- Inadequate tools/equipment
- Inefficient layouts
- Lack of training
- Inadequate suppliers
- Lack of standardization
- Poor management decisions
- Mistakes by operators
- Inadequate scheduling

These seven wastes, as identified by the BP process, stem from these common causes listed above and include the following:

- Overproduction
- Idle time
- Delivery
- Waste in the work itself
- Inventory
- Wasted operator motion
- Waste from rejected parts

It is easy to see how overproduction results in waste. It takes time, resources, labor, and money to make products and/or deliver services. When a process is creating more output than is required to meet actual and forecasted sales levels, these scarce resources are wasted, and the process cannot make other products, which may be needed while it is overproducing.

Idle time results in waste because a valuable equipment or labor resource is not producing output. Time cannot be recovered once it passes. Also, when an operator stands by and watches a process being run, he or she is not productively engaged.

All delivery activities in a process can be considered wasteful. Why? Delivery merely adds to cost without creating corresponding customer value. If the various parts of a process are stretched out too far or are not located in close vicinity to one another, someone or something will be required to move the output between work stations. Moving elements of the process closer together often eliminates the need for additional material handling and allows for smaller, more frequent production lot sizes, which help to minimize overproduction as well.

Sometimes, work processes have waste already designed in. For example, equipment setups and product changeovers often take longer than necessary because all of the required tools, parts, and components may not be located near to where the setup or changeover takes place. Again, the excess time needed to perform the equipment setup or product changeover is lost forever and cannot be recovered. Consider how long a NASCAR pit stop might take if the pit crew had to go and locate all of the materials and tools necessary to service the race car each time it pulled into the pits.

Much like overproduction, excessive inventory is always a waste. Excessive inventory just sits around waiting to be used. While inventory is in storage, almost everything that can happen to the inventory is bad—obsolescence, deterioration, damage, misplacement, and theft. In addition, there are a number of other carrying costs involved with holding the inventory itself—insurance, a larger warehouse facility, cycle counting, information technology support, property taxes, administrative overhead, equipment, extra labor, and the like. All inventories, including raw materials, work-in-process, and finished goods, as well as MRO items, should be subjected to careful and rigorous inventory control methods as discussed in Chapter 16. Therefore, the supply manager should also carefully consider appropriate inventory policies and related activities several tiers back up the supply chain.

Inefficient operator movement also results in waste as it occupies otherwise productive time that could be better utilized in performing activities that do add value to the customer. The supply manager should be prepared to ask the supplier how any given activity adds value and whether it can be eliminated, simplified, or combined with another activity.

Lastly, waste occurs when nonconforming parts, components, and finished goods are made and then rejected. Much like the waste of overproduction, it takes scarce time, space, resources, labor, and money to make nonconforming products and services. In addition, replacement parts, components, and finished goods must then be created to replace those items that have been rejected, oftentimes with higher labor costs as a result of overtime or higher transportation costs because of short response times and use of premium transportation to replace the rejected materials in a timely manner.

Establishing Continuous Improvement as a Way of Life

The pressure for continuous improvement, or "kaizen," should be severe and relentless. Fortunately, there are a variety of ways to make supplier improvement part of the prevailing organizational culture. One approach involves using a supplier measurement system to shift performance targets. The upward shifting of performance targets takes effect once a supplier demonstrates that it can achieve current performance expectations and is willing to improve. Ideally, supplier performance improves at a rate faster than what the buyer's competitors are realizing from their supply chains.

Value analysis/value engineering (VA/VE), as presented in Chapter 12, is another approach for pursuing continuous improvement. VA/VE is the organized and systematic study of every element of cost in a part, material, process, or service to ensure that it fulfills its intended design and operational functions at the lowest possible total cost. Suppliers that are an intimate part of the buyer's VA/VE process actively review customer specifications, submit ideas on design, materials, and process improvements, and work with the buyer to identify, mitigate, and/or remove nonconformance costs. This approach represents one of the better ways of institutionalizing continuous improvement in the supply base.

Perhaps one of the most substantial changes over the last several years involves an increased willingness by larger firms to help improve supplier performance or develop supplier capabilities, a major topic in Chapter 9. Many activities can qualify as supplier development initiatives. Buyers, for example, are increasingly willing to offer Six Sigma quality training to suppliers. These buyers expect their Tier 1 suppliers to support the quality efforts of Tier 2 suppliers, and so on back through the supply chain.

If a firm has rationalized and optimized its supply base to a manageable level, and if the remaining suppliers receive longer-term, higher-volume contracts, it then becomes clear that switching suppliers will become increasingly difficult and costly. Once a firm fully rationalizes and optimizes its supply base, improvement will occur primarily by developing the capabilities of existing suppliers rather than by switching suppliers on a large scale.

A buyer can also offer inducements to encourage a supplier's continuous-improvement efforts. In fact, most supply managers have at their disposal some very powerful incentives and rewards to positively influence supplier behavior. Offering performance-related rewards to suppliers recognizes that there is a direct link between the reward and performance improvement. Traditionally, buyers demanded supplier improvement but were reluctant to share the resulting benefit, which encouraged self-promoting behavior by suppliers. Exhibit 8.4 highlights the various rewards that are available to encourage continuous supplier improvement.

Making Quality Everyone's Responsibility

This principle requires that buyers and suppliers assume ownership for total quality across the supply chain. The issue then becomes—how can buyers align their vision of, and need for, supplier quality improvement?

Exhibit 8.4	**Providing Incentives for Supplier Quality Improvement**

- Award longer-term purchase contracts.
- Offer a greater share of the purchaser's total volume to superior performers.
- Publicly recognize superior suppliers, including "supplier of the year" awards.
- Share the cost savings resulting from supplier-initiated improvements.
- Provide suppliers with access to new technology.
- Provide early insight into new business opportunities and product development plans.
- Invite suppliers to participate early in new-product and process development projects.
- Allow suppliers to use the purchaser's supply agreements to obtain favorable pricing.
- Invite suppliers to participate in executive buyer-supplier councils.
- Create a preferred list of suppliers that are offered first opportunity for new business.

Source: Adapted from Trent, R.J. (2001) "Linking TQM to SCM," *Supply Chain Management Review*, 5(3), 73.

Physically co-locating with suppliers is a powerful way to make quality everyone's responsibility and improve buyer-supplier communication. There are a number of ways to create physical coexistence with suppliers. For example, Johnson Controls shares a 225,000-square-foot facility with its plastic molding supplier, Becker Group L.L.C.[14] Plastic door panels produced by the supplier flow directly into Johnson Control's assembly process, allowing immediate quality feedback and eliminating the possibility of in-transit damage. Likewise, Volkswagen built a truck assembly plant in Brazil with seven suppliers physically located within the assembly facility. These suppliers produce components and subassemblies in the VW facility using their own equipment and with their own labor actually assembling those items into finished trucks and buses.

Progressive organizations are forming executive-level buyer-supplier councils as a means of aligning and creating partnerships with carefully selected key suppliers. As discussed in Chapter 5, these councils meet on a regular basis to coordinate longer-term product, process, and technology requirements; identify projects that buyers and suppliers can work on jointly; and promote closer and more collaborative supply chain relationships. Making quality each participant's responsibility is essential for total supply chain quality.

Sourcing Snapshot

Do Cost Reduction Pressures Affect Supplier Quality?

In 2001, a survey reported that automotive suppliers were cutting corners in response to OEM demands for price reductions. Only 20 percent of 261 reporting suppliers indicated that they were improving quality. Unfortunately, tragedies, such as the widespread failure of Firestone tires installed on Ford Explorers, provide substantial evidence that something is awry. The resulting charges and countercharges between the two companies raised serious concerns about the quality and safety of two of America's oldest brands.

Cost reductions alone do not necessarily signify lower quality. According to *Industry Weeks'* 2000 Census of Manufacturers, which surveyed 3,000 companies, manufacturers that were able to reduce their scrap and waste showed more improvement in quality than those whose costs increased. Although taking out waste is good, trimming into the bone is not. When buyers demand deep price cuts from suppliers that are already operating with razor-thin margins, it should come as no surprise that attention to quality might suffer as a result. The rampant cost cutting over the last two decades has caused some producers to question what level of durability and material quality they are willing to design into their products.

Some companies truly understand how to effectively manage cost reductions while achieving continuous quality improvements. Toyota, for example, expects a 3 percent reduction in costs each year from its suppliers. Even with these year-after-year price reductions from suppliers, how does Toyota maintain its reputation for product quality? The company's willingness to work collaboratively with suppliers to identify ways to jointly reduce costs is in stark contrast to simply mandating reductions, reductions that could lead to decreases in product quality and safety.

Sources: Adapted from R. D. Reid, "Purchaser and Supplier Quality," *Quality Progress,* August 2002; and D. Bartholomew, "Cost vs. Quality," *Industry Week,* 250(12), September 1, 2001, pp. 34-36, 40-41.

Pursuing Six Sigma Supplier Quality

The total quality principles just discussed work only if firms are able to operationalize them and demonstrate tangible results over time. When total quality was first popularized in the 1980s, too many firms educated their employees in the principles of TQM without committing the resources or time necessary to change a culture that believed "close enough is good enough." It is not surprising that many firms failed to achieve the dramatic kinds of performance improvement that they envisioned from their extensive TQM efforts. As a result, many participants became cynical about all total quality efforts, calling total quality "the management 'flavor' of the month." "If we just wait another few months," many said, "management will move on to another 'silver bullet.'" In addition, few buying organizations extended their internal total quality efforts out to their suppliers.

The fact that many firms became disillusioned with their total quality programs does not eliminate the competitive need to seek total quality improvement. **Six Sigma** can be considered as an updated version of total quality management. It focuses on quantitative results to the bottom line through a disciplined application of statistical tools for management decision making and problem-solving, as well as creating a sustainable infrastructure that positively affects the organizational culture.

Thomas Pyzdek, a noted Six Sigma author and consultant, explained the importance of Six Sigma this way:

"Six Sigma is a rigorous, focused and highly effective implementation of proven quality principles and techniques. Incorporating elements from the work of many quality pioneers, Six Sigma aims for virtually error free business performance. Sigma, σ, is a letter in the Greek alphabet used by statisticians to measure the variability in a process. A company's performance is measured by the sigma level of their business processes. Traditionally companies accepted three or four sigma performance levels as the norm, despite the fact that these processes created between 6,200 and 67,000 problems per million opportunities! The Six Sigma standard of 3.4 problems per million opportunities is a response to the increasing expectations of customers and the increased complexity of modern products and processes."[15]

"Six Sigma focuses on improving quality (i.e., reduce waste) by helping organizations produce products and services better, faster and cheaper. In more traditional terms, Six Sigma focuses on defect prevention, cycle time reduction, and cost savings. Unlike mindless cost-cutting programs, which reduce value and quality, Six Sigma identifies and eliminates costs that provide no value to customers, waste costs."[16]

Six Sigma reduces much of the complexity characterized by early TQM efforts. One expert estimated that TQM includes more than 400 different quality tools and techniques. Six Sigma relies on a smaller set of proven methods and trains individuals known as Black Belts to apply these sometimes sophisticated quality management tools and approaches.[17] Design of experiments (DoE) is an example of a quality improvement approach applied by Black Belts to find and eliminate defects before the final design is specified and costs become fixed. Many observers credit Motorola with coining the term "Six Sigma" and relating it to 3.4 defects per million opportunities (DPMO).

Six Sigma relates to supplier quality management in several ways. First, suppliers that operate at only three or four sigma quality typically spend between 25 and 40 percent of their sales revenues finding and solving problems. In an era of relentless cost-reduction pressures, this level of quality does not support longer-term competitive success. Suppliers that operate at Six Sigma quality levels, on the other hand, typically spend less than five

Exhibit 8.5	Six Sigma Performance Improvement Model

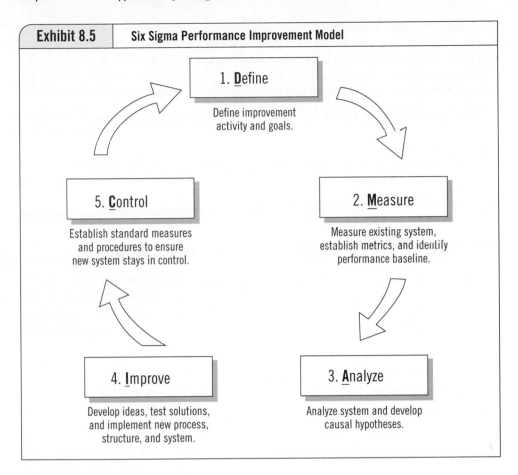

percent of their sales revenues addressing problems.[18] Second, quality management is not only about managing internal quality. Market success demands that buyer firms identify waste upstream in the supply chain through their Tier 1, Tier 2, and sometimes even Tier 3 suppliers. Many supplier development programs use experts from the buyer company to help their smaller, less capable suppliers achieve Six Sigma quality, as well as other productivity and cost improvements.

One aspect of helping suppliers improve involves educating them on the Six Sigma performance improvement model. Suppliers that apply this model should accelerate their rate of quality improvement as compared to those that do not. They should also make quality improvement a systematic part of their operations. Exhibit 8.5 outlines the various parts of this model, which is also known as the DMAIC model: D(efine), M(easure), A(nalyze), I(mprove), and C(ontrol).

Using ISO Standards and MBNQA Criteria to Assess Supplier Quality Systems

In general, quality standards, such as ISO 9001:2008 and ISO 14001:2004, are designed to create and maintain process consistency in the production of goods and services. In turn, these standards can provide the user or customer with greater confidence that purchased goods and services will satisfactorily meet its requirements. For the supplier, these standards provide added assurance that the goods and services sold will be predictable and uniform.

Within the United States, relatively few companies have applied a uniform set of quality standards to their supplier certification processes, often resulting in duplication of effort and other operating inefficiencies. When measuring and assessing their suppliers' quality management systems, supply managers are increasingly turning to established quality auditing and measurement systems to help drive supplier performance improvement.

Three widely accepted quality management frameworks are **ISO 9001:2008, ISO 14001:2004, and the Malcolm Baldrige National Quality Award (MBNQA)**. Companies that are unable to commit the necessary resources to assess or certify supplier quality on their own often accept ISO 9001:2008 registration as proxy evidence of a supplier's quality management capability. Other companies have used basic ISO 9001:2008, ISO 14001:2004, and MBNQA quality criteria to develop their own supplier assessment or certification processes. For these reasons, it is important for the buyer to have a working knowledge and understanding of all three programs.

ISO 9001:2008 Standards

A quality management process gaining widespread acceptance throughout the world is the ISO 9001 series of quality management system standards. Developed initially in 1987 to standardize quality requirements in Europe, ISO 9001 standards originally consisted of a series of process quality standards—but not product standards—recognizing that product quality will be a direct result of a quality process. Meeting these standards is not an easy task, although it is often perceived as a minimum requirement for competing globally. It is estimated that more than one million certificates have been issued to organizations in more than 150 countries. These standards do not specifically dictate how a business is to be operated but are more useful in how they can be used as the basis for improving operations.

The International Organization for Standardization, headquartered in Geneva, Switzerland, has released its 4th edition of ISO 9001 standards, identified as ISO 9001:2008, which provides continuous improvement from the 3rd edition, previously updated in 2000. The language in the new ISO 9001:2008 standards has been simplified; the text follows an outline format rather than paragraph form; and ISO 9002 and ISO 9003 registrations no longer exist. ISO 9004:2008 remains a key document that offers guidelines for performance improvements above the basic requirements of ISO 9001:2008. To remain current registration, the registration must be accomplished every three years.

There are five main sections contained in the ISO 9001:2008 standards. As ISO 9001:2008 standards are meant to be applied to any organization across any industry, the requirements are comprehensive and difficult to understand.

1. **Quality management system (QMS)**
2. Management responsibility
3. Resource management
4. Product realization
5. Measurement, analysis, and improvement

The first section on QMS covers the activities and steps required to implement ISO 9001:2008. Essentially, this section requires the applicant to clearly delineate and document its processes and related activities to create the quality management system; the process and activity interaction and sequencing; how the processes are operated and controlled; how supporting information is generated and disseminated; and how measurements and process analysis are conducted. The QMS consists of a quality manual, related procedures, and work instructions. Common templates are widely available that can guide the organization through its documentation process.

The second section, regarding management's responsibility for quality, contains information on the organization's overall quality policy and its quality-related objectives. Senior management must demonstrate that it has established quality responsibility and authority throughout the organization. It is an excellent idea to create standardized formats for job descriptions that contain common quality-oriented language. There should also be a senior-level manager who is specifically designated with the necessary authority and responsibility for overseeing quality within the organization.

Section 3 discusses and spells out how the organization should identify and make available the requisite resources to implement, maintain, and improve the organization's QMS. The organization should also address human resource needs and customer satisfaction in the allocation of its resources toward quality improvement, including training and personnel development needs.

The fourth section addresses how an organization designs and delivers its goods and services. ISO 9001:2008 defines product realization as "that sequence of processes and sub processes required to achieve the product."[19] Essentially, this refers to how the organization's products are designed, produced, evaluated, handled, and shipped. Because of the general nature of ISO 9001:2008, these generic activities can also apply to service delivery systems. Special emphasis is made on how the organization seeks to understand, communicate, and meet customer requirements in providing its goods and services. Organizations prepare work instructions and work flow process charts here to document how this is accomplished.

The final section outlines requirements for how organizations should develop metrics, measurements, and monitoring processes such that it can take timely corrective action as required. Measurement and monitoring activities should include internal audit procedures, external supplier audits, and how to effectively garner customer feedback and perception. All relevant measurement and monitoring activities need to be clearly defined, planned, and implemented, which allows the organization to manage by fact, not by managerial conjecture. This section is probably the most important and should be strongly emphasized in the organization's pursuit of ISO 9001:2008 registration.

The revised ISO 9001:2008 standards are based on the following eight generally accepted quality management principles:

- Customer focus
- Leadership
- Involvement of people
- Process approach
- System approach to management
- Continual improvement
- Factual approach to decision making
- Mutually beneficial supplier relationships

ISO 9001:2008 follows a process-based approach to quality management that stresses planning, acting, analyzing results, and making improvements. It is in the best interests of suppliers to pursue ISO 9001:2008 quality registration, particularly if their customers (i.e., buyers) value the process. In addition, suppliers receive many benefits from pursuing independent third-party ISO registration. For example, buyers have immediate confirmation that a supplier has achieved registration according to internationally accepted quality process standards. Furthermore, buyers may be willing to recognize ISO 9001:2008 registration in place of individual certification programs, resulting in lower costs for both the buyer and the supplier.

Each supplier that earns ISO 9001:2008 registration is included on a master list of companies satisfying the ISO standard. Inclusion on this list can lead to additional buying interest from other potential customers wanting to do business with ISO-registered companies. Suppliers that earn ISO 9001:2008 registration will also be in a stronger position to satisfy corresponding U.S. American National Standards Institute (ANSI) standards as well.

Buying firms also benefit from suppliers achieving ISO 9001:2008 registration. First, few buying firms have sufficient size or resources to independently develop and implement their own comprehensive supplier certification audits. Third party registration may also provide insight into a supplier's quality system conformance that a buyer may otherwise lack. The buying firm receives the benefit of a supplier quality certification without actually having to conduct its own quality certification audits.

Another potential benefit for buyers is that the supplier assumes responsibility for meeting the ISO standards and paying its own registration fees. With individual supplier certification programs, the buying firm assumes most, if not all, of the direct expenses related to supplier certification. ISO 9001:2008 registration requires suppliers to contract with a recognized independent registrar that is certified to perform ISO 9001:2008 audits.

Perhaps most importantly, suppliers that earn ISO 9001:2008 registration typically demonstrate higher levels of product and service quality than those suppliers that are not registered. Therefore, the buyer can have higher confidence in the supplier's ability to meet or exceed the buyer's quality expectations and requirements.

ISO 14001:2004 Standards

The concept of green and sustainable operations continues to grow in importance in the global marketplace. The ISO 14001:2004 series of standards, originally established in 1993, is designed to promote environmental awareness and protection as well as pollution prevention. It is an excellent way for a buyer to analyze and document a supplier's ability to proactively manage its environmental impact, sustainability, and carbon footprint. As with ISO 9001:2008, ISO 14001:2004 is intentionally broad and general in nature, but it does not, however, require specific levels of environmental performance.

The standards cover a broad perspective of environmental disciplines, ranging from the organization's **environmental management system (EMS)** to addressing "labeling, performance evaluation, life cycle analysis, communication, and auditing."[20] Benefits achieved through the ISO 14001:2004 certification process include fewer pollutants generated, reduced liability, improved regulatory compliance, better public and community relations, and lowered insurance premiums.[21] Under ISO 14001:2004, an organization's EMS should include guidance on how to evaluate its environmental impact, improve its environmental performance, and implement a systematic approach to address environmental issues, including monitoring and measurement.

Another primary outcome of pursuing and achieving ISO 14001:2004 certification is enhanced profitability through improved resource management and reduced waste generation. ISO 14001:2004 is a set of voluntary standards and consists of two general classifications: process-oriented and product-oriented standards. However, it does not build on existing governmental regulations, establish emissions and pollution levels, or detail any specific testing methods.[22]

Many buying firms now require suppliers to become ISO 14001:2004 certified in addition to earning ISO 9001:2008 registration. To do so, suppliers must publish an organizational environmental policy, develop a comprehensive EMS, implement an effective internal auditing system, and use corrective action plans to address unfavorable audit results.

The Malcolm Baldrige National Quality Award[23]

In 1987, U.S. President Ronald Reagan signed the Malcolm Baldrige National Quality Improvement Act, which established a national award, under the auspices of the National Institute of Standards and Technology (NIST) of the U.S. Department of Commerce, to recognize quality improvement among manufacturing, service, and small business organizations in the United States. More recent additions to MBNQA eligibility have included education, healthcare, and government and nonprofit organizations. Note that MBNQA winners are required to disseminate relevant information on their quality performance and strategies to other U.S. organizations and businesses. However, they are not required to share any proprietary information, regardless of whether or not it was included on their original applications.

The Baldrige criteria start with basic core values and concepts that make up the first six criteria categories related to systematic processes that are expected to yield improved performance results as shown in the seventh criteria category. Similar in many respects to ISO 9001:2008's generally accepted quality principles, the seven Baldrige criteria categories are as follows:

- Leadership
- Strategic planning
- Customer focus
- Measurement, analysis, and knowledge management
- Workforce focus
- Operations focus
- Results

A group of generally recognized quality professionals, including Dr. Joseph M. Juran, developed the initial award criteria. Since then, the criteria have become a de facto definition of TQM, and wide dissemination of the application guidelines has exposed many organizations and managers to the broad Baldrige definition of TQM. For example, a number of organizations have successfully used the MBNQA criteria as a template for developing and maintaining comprehensive quality management systems, and one of the more important outputs of the award has been the widespread dissemination of useful TQM practices.

Some managers believe the MBNQA provides a more comprehensive set of quality-related criteria for North American-based firms than does ISO 9001:2008. As such, the MBNQA is a competition and implies that a winning organization excels not only in quality management but also in quality achievement. The application for the MBNQA provides a broad framework for implementing a quality program and establishes benchmarks suitable for monitoring quality progress. Although the federal government has distributed thousands of MBNQA award applications over the years, the number of companies actively pursuing the award has actually decreased. Many current applications of MBNQA criteria are intended solely for internal use as a quality management tool and not just for award purposes. Even if an organization applies for but does not receive a MBNQA, it will receive a detailed examiner report providing feedback based on the rigorous scrutiny of trained quality experts who reviewed the organization's application materials.

It can take a company eight to ten years to adequately develop a quality management system that will be competitive for the award.[24] The MBNQA is composed of seven weighted categories, together worth a total of 1,000 points. These categories are outlined in Exhibit 8.6. Higher-performing companies, i.e., those with MBNQA scores of 700 or more, demonstrate balanced and outstanding performance across each of these categories.

Exhibit 8.6 | **Continuous Improvement in the Malcolm Baldrige National Quality Award**

Score Summary Worksheet — Business Criteria

Examiner Name _____   Application Number _____

Summary of Criteria Items	Total Points Possible **A**	Percent Score 0–100% (Stage 1–10% Units) **B**	Score (A × B) **C**
1 Leadership			
1.1 Organizational leadership	85	_____ %	_____
1.2 Public responsibility and citizenship	40	_____ %	_____
Category Total	125		_____ SUM C
2 Strategic Planning			
2.1 Strategy development	40	_____ %	_____
2.2 Strategy deployment	45	_____ %	_____
Category Total	85		_____ SUM C
3 Customer and Market Focus			
3.1 Customer and market knowledge	40	_____ %	_____
3.2 Customer satisfaction and relationships	45	_____ %	_____
Category Total	85		_____ SUM C
4 Information and Analysis			
4.1 Measurement of organizational performance	40	_____ %	_____
4.2 Analysis of organizational performance	45	_____ %	_____
Category Total	85		_____ SUM C
5 Human Resource Focus			
5.1 Work systems	35	_____ %	_____
5.2 Employee education, training, and development	25	_____ %	_____
5.3 Employee well-being and satisfaction	25	_____ %	_____
Category Total	85		_____ SUM C
6 Process Management			
6.1 Product and service processes	55	_____ %	_____
6.2 Support processes	15	_____ %	_____
6.3 Supplier and partnering processes	15	_____ %	_____
Category Total	85		_____ SUM C
7 Business Results			
7.1 Customer-focused results	115	_____ %	_____
7.2 Financial and market results	115	_____ %	_____
7.3 Human resource results	80	_____ %	_____
7.4 Supplier and partner results	25	_____ %	_____
7.5 Organizational effectiveness results	115	_____ %	_____
Category Total	450		_____ SUM C
GRAND TOTAL (D)	1000		_____ D

Source: U.S. Department of Commerce, National Institute of Standards and Technology, Retrieved from http://www.quality.nist.gov

Continuous improvement is the most basic and important tenet of the MBNQA criteria. In each of the major categories, companies must demonstrate how they plan to improve deficiencies in that area. The MBNQA criteria are both process- and results-oriented, addressing operations, processes, strategies, and requirements.

Just what does the MBNQA have to do with supplier quality? Many leading companies are now effectively using MBNQA criteria when designing their internal assessment systems for supplier quality performance. For example, companies such as Cummins Engine, Motorola, Pacific Bell, Alcatel, and Honeywell all use modified versions of MBNQA criteria to conduct in-depth studies of their major suppliers' quality management systems. They use similar scoring systems, and trained quality assessors typically spend several days visiting the supplier's facilities to rate their continuous-improvement efforts. Progressive companies such as these fully understand the logic behind applying well-established quality principles and guidelines to their total supply chain quality efforts.

Basic Contents of a Supplier Quality Manual

As discussed in the opening vignette, it is often far too common for the supplier and the buyer to poorly communicate their respective requirements and needs, often leading to misunderstandings and conflict, particularly if they are separated by substantial physical distance. One of the more effective tools to address potential miscommunications is to prepare a thorough **supplier quality manual** that outlines and discusses the buyer's relevant policies, quality requirements, and vocabulary. In addition, having a well-thought-out and complete supplier quality manual available whenever a new supplier is selected or when an existing supplier requires assistance in improving its performance, the buyer can standardize its procedures without having to reinvent the wheel each time.

What should an effective supplier quality manual contain? Although by its very nature such a manual has to be somewhat general, it should include, at a minimum, various quality control and process management procedures, metrics and measurement protocols, testing and acceptance procedures, definitions, and documentation control. Additionally, the supplier quality manual should spell out the basic responsibilities of both the supplier and the buyer. It may also delineate the minimum process required for the supplier regarding inspections, use of statistical process control, continuous improvement, testing, sample evaluations, performance improvement, and the like. Another key element of the effective supplier quality manual is to delineate the communication process to be followed whenever a quality incident occurs. Part of this communication process is to keep the various contacts at the supplier's company up to date.

A comprehensive supplier quality manual should also describe the supplier selection and evaluation processes (as discussed in Chapter 7), as well as how the buyer's audits are to be conducted. Coupled with this process description would be a discussion of the various quality improvement programs and activities that the buyer may have in place, such as supplier certification and supplier development. Copies of any relevant forms should also be included along with the requisite instructions needed to complete them. Any requirements and procedures for the control of proprietary information, including nondisclosure agreements, should also be explained.

Many companies also include a description of their production parts approval process and/or sample acceptance procedures designed to authenticate that supplier products will meet the buyer's specifications and any related engineering requirements. The supplier quality manual should also explain the process for submitting and approving engineering change orders when specifications and engineering requirements need to be changed.

For those goods requiring a supplier process capability evaluation, the manual should describe how the process capability study will be conducted—from both the buyer's and the supplier's perspectives. Any product, prototype, or sample testing and evaluation activities conducted by the buyer should also be listed and described to help prevent any misunderstandings or surprises to either party. Should a quality incident occur, the supplier quality manual should describe the relative responsibilities, in terms of cost, timing, and resources allocated, for both the buyer and the supplier. Related to this is the need for a well-defined process of how nonconforming products are to be handled and stored pending final resolution. Claims procedures should also be clearly defined, along with how to develop and submit corrective action plans to prevent future occurrences of nonconforming products.

If the buyer has established levels of supplier categories, these should be clearly defined as well as the procedures to be followed by the supplier to achieve higher category levels, such as preferred supplier, and the like. The supplier quality manual also needs to spell out any specific marking, packaging, and material handling requirements for various categories of products.

Good Practice Example

Collaborative Problem-Solving with a Supplier

Warren/Amplex Superabrasives, located in Olyphant, Pennsylvania, is a manufacturing division of Saint-Gobain Ceramics and Plastics, a French company that is the world's largest building materials company. An Asian customer, a high-volume data storage device manufacturer, reported a problem with one of the products that it purchased from Warren/Amplex. The product, a polycrystalline diamond slurry, was clogging the customer's filtering processes in its disk manufacturing plant. In addition, an unknown film was found after the clean-up step in the texturing process.

Ron Abramshe, product and technical sales manager for Warren/Amplex, quickly called together a quality control team to address the emerging quality situation. Fortunately, the supplier had previously developed a formal troubleshooting approach containing a structured line of questioning and a list of review procedures to address such a quality issue. In this case, the troubleshooting process consisted of the following questions.

- When was the problem first noticed?
- What was the lot number?
- What shift was working?
- Were the operators new or experienced?
- Have the filters been analyzed?
- Can we (Warren/Amplex) have a bottle of slurry sent back for analysis?
- Was anything added to the slurry?

The problem originated with the last shipment of polycrystalline diamond slurry, but the customer was unable to return samples as the situation was deemed critical. An emergency replacement shipment of slurry was required immediately as there was only three days' inventory in stock. When this inventory was depleted, the customer would be forced to shut down its production line, an unacceptable condition in the disk drive industry as there was a substantial penalty for missed shipment deadlines.

Texturing of the data disks involved placing a texturing pattern on the disk in a uniform pattern in width and depth. The textured patterns could then be encoded so that the read-write head could place and retrieve binary code information. After texturing, the disks are cleaned and moved to the next step in the process.

Initially, the supplier was unaware that the disk manufacturer was filtering the polycrystalline diamond slurry. Once this was known, the quality control team investigated the particle size in the slurry. Another Warren division provided insight that the presence of bacteria was likely causing a contaminated condition. Using a rapid technique to circumvent the normal petri dish method of testing for growing bacteria, Warren/Amplex was able to determine that there were indeed bacteria in the slurry. Because of the short time frame to provide replacement slurry to the Asian customer, the solution was to pasteurize the slurry at 80°C for ten minutes. An additional test showed that the bacteria were killed, allowing Warren/Amplex to manufacture a replacement batch of the polycrystalline slurry for the customer so that it could maintain its critical production schedule.

On further review, Warren/Amplex determined that the customer's modified processing requirements to meet new specifications for higher density disk drives were the cause of the bacteria growth, the ramifications of which neither party fully appreciated at the time the change was made.

Warren/Amplex's ability to rapidly work through this critical quality failure shows the value of selecting suppliers with greater capabilities than merely meeting production and shipment schedules. The importance of collaborative teamwork in problem-solving between buyer and supplier cannot be overemphasized. A buyer often buys more than a product or service; it often needs to evaluate other supplier capabilities as well.

Sources: Abramshe, R. "The Bug and the Slurry: Bacterial Control in Aqueous Products" (2007), Milwaukee, WI: American Society for Quality Retrieved from http://www.asq.org

CONCLUSION

The battleground for global competitive advantage has entered the domain of supply chain management. Although other competitive factors, such as mass customization and flexibility, will increasingly become order-winning market characteristics, the ability to design, produce, and sell high-quality products and services will always remain a primary market qualifier. Without thoroughly embracing TQM, however, a supplier should not expect serious consideration from potential customers.

Improving supplier quality involves much more than providing clear specifications and maintaining open communication between buyer and supplier. Supply management, aggressively pursuing the principles of TQM, can effectively improve supplier quality practices and set a high standard for sustained excellence. Supplier quality excellence can be achieved by being a good customer to suppliers, routinely measuring supplier performance and eliminating or developing poor performers, providing timely and accurate performance feedback, certifying and rewarding Six Sigma supplier performance, and helping suppliers reach mutual continuous-improvement goals. To achieve total quality, supply management must have skilled personnel who understand the principles and tools of TQM, including Six Sigma, ISO 9001:2008, ISO 14001:2004, the MBNQA, and can work effectively with suppliers to ensure that zero defects is the norm rather than the exception.

KEY TERMS

cost of quality, 303

Deming's 14 Points, 293

environmental management system (EMS), 312

ISO 9001:2008, 310

ISO 14001:2004, 310

kaizen, 294

Malcolm Baldrige National Quality Award (MBNQA), 310

Prevention, 298

Process capability, 301

quality, 287

Quality at the source, 296

Quality management system (QMS), 310

Six Sigma, 308

Supplier quality, 288

Supply base rationalization or optimization, 303

supplier quality manual, 315

zero defects, 302

DISCUSSION QUESTIONS

1. Why should a buyer be concerned with monitoring and managing supplier quality performance?

2. Discuss the following statement: Supply management not only buys parts or services from suppliers—it often buys a supplier's current and future performance capability.

3. Do all suppliers have an equal impact on product quality? Discuss the conditions under which one supplier may have a greater impact on a firm's final product quality as compared to another supplier.

4. Why is it important for a buyer to be a good customer? How can a buyer become a good customer to a supplier?

5. How can early supplier design involvement efforts contribute to higher levels of product quality?

6. Discuss the benefits to a supplier of achieving ISO 9001:2008 registration.

7. Some supply management experts argue that suppliers should not receive rewards for doing something that is already expected (e.g., continuously improving quality). Do you agree with this position? What are some common examples of rewards that a supplier might expect to receive?

8. Discuss the benefits to a buying company of certifying its suppliers. Describe the benefits to a supplier of being certified—to the buyer and to the supplier.

9. Why did many total quality management efforts in North America not succeed as expected during the 1980s?

10. What are the differences between TQM and Six Sigma quality approaches?

11. What principles of TQM does a well-developed supplier evaluation and selection process satisfy?

12. What principles of total quality management do supplier measurement systems satisfy?

13. Discuss the role of Deming's 14 Points in managing supplier quality.

14. Describe the various classifications of the cost of quality.

15. How can a buyer utilize ISO 14001:2004 to improve supplier environmental performance?

16. How can a buyer utilize MBNQA criteria as a basis for improving supplier quality?

ADDITIONAL READINGS

Baldrige 20/20: An Executive's Guide to the Criteria for Performance Excellence, (2011), Gaithersburg, MD: U.S. Department of Commerce, National Institute of Standards and Technology.

Baldrige National Quality Program: 2013–2014 Criteria for Performance Excellence, (2013), Gaithersburg, MD: U.S. Department of Commerce, National Institute of Standards and Technology.

Carton, T. J., and Jacoby, D. J. (1997), *A Review of Managing Quality and a Primer for the Certified Quality Manager Exam*, Milwaukee, WI: ASQ Quality Press.

Columbus, L. (2007), "Quality Partnerships with Your Customers," *Quality Digest*, 27(8), 44–48.

Dasgupta, T. (2003), "Using the Six-Sigma Metric to Improve the Performance of a Supply Chain," *Total Quality Management and Business Excellence*, 14(3), 355–366.

Duncan, W. L. (1995), *Total Quality: Key Terms and Concepts*, New York: AMACOM.

Evans, J. R., and Lindsay, W. M. (2011), *Managing for Quality and Performance Excellence* (8th ed.), Mason, OH: South-Western Cengage Learning.

Fernandez, R. R. (1995), *Total Quality in Purchasing and Supplier Management*, Delray Beach, FL: St. Lucie Press.

Foster, S. T. (2007), *Managing Quality: Integrating the Supply Chain* (3rd ed.), Upper Saddle River, NJ: Pearson.

Garvin, D. A. (1988), *Managing Quality: The Strategic and Competitive Edge*, New York: Free Press.

Gould, R. A., Arter, D. R., Ball-Brown, P., Creinin, D., Howe Garriz, L, Schoenfelt, T. I., and Van Arsdale, T. (2006), "Quality Management," in *The Supply Management Handbook*, J. L. Cavinato, A. E. Flynn, and R. G. Kauffman (Eds.), New York: McGraw-Hill, pp. 565–586.

Ishikawa, K. (translated by D. J. Lu) (1985), *What Is Total Quality Control? The Japanese Way*, Englewood Cliffs, NJ: Prentice Hall.

Juran, J. M. (1988), *Juran on Planning for Quality*, New York: Free Press.

Juran, J. M. (Ed.) (1999), *Juran's Quality Handbook* (5th ed.), New York: McGraw-Hill.

Jutras, C. (2009), *Taking Lean Six Sigma Beyond Manufacturing: The Journey to Business Improvement*, Boston: Aberdeen Group.

Maass, R., Brown, J. O., and Bossert, J. L. (1999), *Supplier Certification: A Continuous Improvement Strategy*, Milwaukee, WI: ASQ Quality Press.

Merrill, P. (1997), Do It Right the Second Time: Benchmarking Best Practices in the Quality Change Process, Portland, OR: Productivity Press.

Minahan, T. (1998), "Purchasing Needs to Do More Than Measure," *Purchasing*, 124(1), 59–61.

Nelson, D., Mayo, R., and Moody, P. E. (1998), *Powered by Honda: Developing Excellence in the Global Enterprise*, New York: John Wiley & Sons.

Newman, R. G. (1988), "Insuring Quality: Purchasing's Role," *International Journal of Purchasing and Materials Management*, 24(3), 14–21.

Pande, P. S., Neuman, R. P., and Cavanaugh, R. R. (2000), *The Six Sigma Way. How GE, Motorola, and Other Top Companies Are Honing Their Performance*, New York: McGraw-Hill.

Reid, D. R. (2002), "Purchaser and Supplier Quality," *Quality Progress*, 35(8), 81–85.

Smith, B. (2003), "Lean and Six Sigma—A One-Two Punch," *Quality Progress*, 36(4), 37–42.

Smith, G. F. (1995), *Quality Problem Solving*, Milwaukee, WI: ASQ Quality Press.

Smith, L. (2006), "Quality around the World," *Quality Digest*, 26(6), 41–47.

Statistical Process Control (SPC) Reference Manual, (1995), Detroit, MI: Automotive Industry Action Group.

Small, B. (Ed.) (1956), *Statistical Quality Control Handbook*, Indianapolis, IN: AT&T Technologies.

Stundza, T. (2007), "Assured Quality Critical in Global Sourcing," *Purchasing*, 136(11), 32.

Trent, R. J. (1999), "Achieving World-Class Supplier Quality," *Total Quality Management*, 10(6), 927–939.

Wesner, J. W., Hiatt, J. M., and Trimble, D. C. (1995), *Winning with Quality: Applying Quality Principles in Product Development*, Reading, MA: Addison-Wesley.

Zhu, K., Zhang, R. Q., and Tsung, F. (2007), "Pushing Quality Improvement along Supply Chains," *Management Science*, 53(3), 421–436.

ENDNOTES

1. Feigenbaum, A. V. (1983), *Total Quality Control* (3rd ed.), New York: McGraw-Hill, p. 7.

2. For a more complete discussion of Deming, Crosby, and Juran, see Walton, M. (1990), *Deming Management at Work*, New York: Putnam; Crosby, P. B. (1996), *Quality Is Still Free: Making Quality Certain in Uncertain Times*, New York: McGraw-Hill; and Juran, J. M. (1992), *Juran on Quality by Design: The New Steps for Planning Quality into Goods and Services*, New York: Free Press.

3. Bhote, K. (1987), *Supply Management: How to Make U.S. Suppliers Competitive*, New York: American Management Association, p. 87.

4. Evans, J. R., and Lindsay, W. M. (2011), *Managing for Quality and Performance Excellence* (8th ed.), Mason, OH: South-Western Cengage Learning, pp. 99–104.

5. From a presentation made by Jim Sierk at the Michigan State University Purchasing and Supply Chain Management Executive Seminar during the mid-1990s.

6. Used with permission from FedEx Quality Assurance. The five key performance attributes for printed forms are (1) dimension of label, (2) position of the die cut, (3) clarity of print, (4) test line of direct strike, and (5) color quality. A sixth category, called "other," allows additional requirements for specific items.

7. Small, B. (Ed.), (1956), *Statistical Quality Control Handbook*, Indianapolis, IN: AT&T Technologies, p. 45.

8. Evans and Lindsay, p. 636.

9. Evans and Lindsay, pp. 634–637.

10. Taguchi, G., and Clausing, D. (1995), "Robust Quality," in *Manufacturing Renaissance*, Cambridge, MA: Harvard Business Review Books, pp. 173–188.

11. Reese, A. (2000), "eProcurement Takes on the Untamed Supply Chain," *iSource*, November, p. 108.

12. Foster, S. T. (2007), *Managing Quality: Integrating the Supply Chain* (3rd ed.), Upper Saddle River, NJ: Pearson Prentice Hall, pp. 115–116.

13. Nelson, D., Mayo, R., and Moody, P. E. (1998), *Powered by Honda: Developing Excellence in the Global Enterprise*, New York: John Wiley & Sons, pp. 160–168.

14. "Johnson Controls to Share New Plant with Becker Group," (2000), *Coin's Detroit Business*, June, p. 2.

15. Pyzdek, T. (2000), *The Six Sigma Revolution*, Retrieved from http://www.pyzdek.com/six-sigma-revolution.htm

16. Pyzdek.

17. Pyzdek.

18. Pyzdek.

19. "What Is ISO 9001?" (2009), *Quality Information on ISO 9001*, Retrieved from http://www.iso9001council.org

20. *ISO 14001 Essentials*, (2009), Geneva, Switzerland: International Organization for Standardization. Retrieved from http://www.iso.org/iso/iso_14001_essentials

21. Swift, J. A., Ross, J. E., and Omachonu, V. K. (1998), *Principles of Total Quality* (2nd ed.), Boca Raton, FL: St. Lucie Press, pp. 369–373.

22. Summers, D. C. S. (2003), *Quality* (3rd ed.), Upper Saddle River, NJ: Prentice Hall, pp. 612–614.

23. *Baldrige National Quality Program: 2013–2014 Criteria for Performance Excellence*, (2013), Gaithersburg, MD: U.S. Department of Commerce, National Institute of Standards and Technology.

24. Handfield, R., and Ghosh, S. (1994), "Creating a Total Quality Culture through Organizational Change: A Case Analysis," *Journal of International Marketing*, 2(4), 15–30.

Supplier Management and Development: Creating a World-Class Supply Base

CHAPTER 9

Learning Objectives

After completing this chapter, you should be able to

- Recognize that supply base management and supplier development includes a broad range of activities intended to improve supplier performance

- Appreciate the relationship between supplier measurement and supplier management

- Understand how to develop different types of supplier measurement tools

- Understand the importance of a rationalized supply base in terms of size and quality

- Know when and how to apply supplier development tools, techniques, and approaches

- Recognize the various forms of supply base risk and understand how to manage and/or mitigate them effectively

- Understand the importance of managing for sustainability in the supply base

Chapter Outline

Introduction

Supplier Performance Measurement

    Supplier Measurement Decisions

    Types of Supplier Measurement Techniques

Rationalization and Optimization: Creating a Manageable Supply Base

    Advantages of a Rationalized and Optimized Supply Base

    Possible Risks of Maintaining Fewer Suppliers

    Formal Approaches to Supply Base Rationalization

    Summary of Supplier Rationalization and Optimization

Supplier Development: A Strategy for Improvement

    A Process Map for Supplier Development

    Supplier Development Efforts That Sometimes Do Not Work

Overcoming the Barriers to Supplier Development

    Buyer-Specific Barriers

    Buyer-Supplier Interface Barriers

    Supplier-Specific Barriers

    Lessons Learned from Supplier Development

Managing Supply Base Risk

Managing Sustainability in the Supply Base

Good Practice Example: Sonoco Builds a Reputation of Excellence in Sustainability

Conclusion

Key Terms

Discussion Questions

Additional Readings

Endnotes

The Importance of Supplier Management and Measurement

Sometimes, it is not enough to merely have a supplier performance measurement system in place. The buyer must also ensure that the performance data is accurate and all-encompassing. Any given supplier may be able to manipulate or falsify the product performance data that it provides to its customers. For example, Koito Industries Ltd., a Japanese aircraft seat supplier based in Yokohama, admitted to irregularities in certain safety testing data regarding approximately 150,000 aircraft passenger seats that it supplied to Airbus SAS and Boeing Co., ultimately impacting some 32 air carriers worldwide.

Because of growing demand for its aircraft passenger seats that had resulted in extremely tight production schedules, Koito utilized a computer program that created false safety data to meet standards regarding seat safety strength. In addition, some safety tests were omitted in their entirety, and in other cases safety data came from tests conducted on different production lots. The Japanese Transport Ministry determined that Koito altered its computer testing programs so that seat shock levels would read higher than they actually were. Additionally, some aircraft seat designs were unilaterally modified without proper notification. This erroneous safety data was revealed only when a whistle-blower made the information available publicly.

As a result of this scandal, which erupted in late 2009, the president of Koito Industries, Takashi Kakegawa, made a public apology in early 2010 and promised to retest all of the aircraft seats in question, repairing or replacing by the end of the year those that did not meet safety requirements. In addition, he admitted that falsification activities had dated back to the mid-1990s and had been an ongoing "organizational practice" emanating from the department, which oversaw the testing.

The European Aviation Safety Industry (EASA) pulled its approval for Koito seats in September 2009 and contemplated issuing an airworthiness directive (AD). The net effect was that Airbus was unable to meet delivery dates for certain aircraft equipped with Koito-sourced seats. For example, Airbus had to delay delivery of Singapore Airlines' 11th A-380 and indicated that about 2 percent of the global Airbus fleet were equipped with Koito-sourced seats. In addition, delivery of Boeing aircraft, such as the 777-300ER, was affected as well. Some of the other airlines affected included: Japan Airlines, Air Canada, KLM, All Nippon Airways, Thai Airways International, and Scandinavian Airlines. In addition to affecting new aircraft production, substantial delays in retrofitting and updating existing aircraft have also occurred.

Because of its larger number of affected aircraft, including Koito seats installed in first, business, premium-economy, and economy classes, Boeing was affected more severely than was Airbus. Therefore, Boeing sent a supplier development team to Koito to assist in reviewing and redeploying its quality management system. In addition, Boeing had to work individually with each of its affected airline customers to ensure that no safety of flight issues existed.

Sources: Wakabayashi, D. (2010, February 10), "Airplane Seat Maker Faked Data on Safety," *The Wall Street Journal,* B2.
Kirby, M. (2010, February 11), "EASA Bit Ruling Out AD after Koito Falsified Seat Test Results," Retrieved from www.flightglobal.com
Sasaki, M. (2010, February 9) "Plane Seat Maker Faked Safety Tests." Retrieved from www.asahi.com

Introduction

As the opening vignette illustrates, progressive firms need to meet the growing challenge of managing and improving supplier performance seriously. Gone are the days when vertically integrated companies mass-produced products with lengthy, slowly changing product life cycles. With rapidly growing global competition, companies increasingly rely on expansive networks of capable and dedicated suppliers to meet their business objectives. Businesses across every industry realize that marketplace success requires them to organize and manage resources and processes across a network of supply chain partners that has been designed on purpose, not in a haphazard manner.[1]

Effective supplier management and development include a broad array of activities taken to manage and improve a worldwide network of carefully screened and selected suppliers. The primary objective of these future-oriented supply base management and supplier development processes is the continuous improvement and growth of supplier capabilities. Supplier performance that is just sufficient today will not be competitive in the marketplace of tomorrow. History shows that, unless buyer companies are able to bring their supply base performance closer to world-class levels, they will be at the mercy of agile and progressive competitors that take their supplier performance improvement efforts far more seriously.

This chapter focuses on various ways organizations can more effectively manage the performance of their supply chains. Although a number of supplier management approaches exist, most will fall into the broad sets of activities described in this chapter. The first section discusses the important relationship between supplier measurement and effective supplier management. The next section describes **supply base rationalization and optimization**; for example, the process of identifying the proper mix and number of suppliers to support the organization's activities. The third section outlines how supplier development can be used as a strategy for supply base performance improvement. In the fourth section, we portray some of the barriers faced by organizations as they attempt to improve supply base performance through supplier development. The fifth section describes the growing importance of effectively managing supply base risk and sustainability in the supply chain. Finally, we conclude with a Good Practice Example of how a company uses sustainability management as a basis to build its competitive advantage.

Supplier Performance Measurement

An important part of supplier management involves continuous monitoring, measurement, evaluation, and analysis of supplier performance metrics. An organization must have the proper tools in place to oversee the performance of its supply base. Without an effective measurement system to record and evaluate supply base performance, how can buyers really know how well suppliers are satisfying contractual obligations? **Supplier performance measurement** includes the requisite methods and systems to collect and provide information to measure, rate, or rank supplier performance on an ongoing basis. The supplier measurement system is a critical part of the sourcing process—essentially serving as a supplier's report card. Note that supplier performance measurement differs somewhat from the process used to initially evaluate and select a supplier as it is a continuous process as opposed to a unique, one-time event.

Supplier Measurement Decisions

When formulating a supplier measurement system, organizations face several key decisions that are critical to the final design, implementation, and effectiveness of the system. According to Sherry Gordon, president of the Value Chain Group, prior to implementing a supplier measurement program, several key issues must be addressed. An effective supplier measurement system must consider the business unit's goals, objectives, and strategies and then construct supply management's corresponding goals, objectives, and strategies to support those of the business unit.

Secondly, supply management must develop its supplier evaluation strategy; for example, which supplier segments or groups need to be evaluated? Not all suppliers need to be evaluated in the same way. This activity will drive the sources and types of information that are generated from the supplier measurement system. Supplier segmentation must consider supply base risk levels, category spend amounts, and switching costs. Finalizing the supplier evaluation strategy requires the supply manager to understand the types of information required, how they will be deployed, the methods needed to obtain the information in a timely and cost-effective manner, and what resources will be required in the collection of this information.[2]

Additionally, many of the key supplier evaluation and selection criteria discussed in Chapter 7 can also be used as a beginning point for designing a capable and effective supplier measurement system.

What to Measure

Central to the design of all supplier measurement systems is the decision about what to measure and how to weight various performance categories. An organization must decide which performance criteria are objective (quantitative) and which are subjective (qualitative), as the metrics and methods used will be different between the two. Most of the objective, quantitative variables will lie within the following three categories:

- *Delivery performance:* Purchase orders or material releases sent to a supplier have a quantity and a delivery due date. Therefore, a buyer can readily assess how well a supplier satisfies its quantity and delivery due-date commitments. Quantity, lead time requirements, and due-date compliance are all part of a supplier's overall delivery performance. Note that Chapter 17 provides additional discussion regarding the effective management of sourcing transportation and related services.

- *Quality performance:* Virtually all supplier measurement systems include quality performance as a critical component. A buyer can evaluate a supplier's quality performance against previously specified objectives, track trends and improvement rates, and compare similar suppliers. A well-designed measurement system also helps define a buyer's quality requirements and more effectively communicate them to its suppliers. Refer to Chapter 8 for a more in-depth discussion of supplier quality management.

- *Cost reduction:* Buyers frequently rely on suppliers for cost-reduction assistance, which can be measured in a number of ways. One common method is to track a supplier's real cost after adjusting for inflation. Other accepted techniques involve comparing a supplier's cost against other suppliers within the same industry or against a baseline or target price. Some leading companies use the last price paid in the current year as the baseline price for comparisons during the next year. See Chapter 11 for additional discussion of strategic cost management.

In addition, a supplier measurement system must be compared against preestablished standards or goals, so that actual supplier performance can be evaluated with minimal bias. These standards or goals must be attainable, readily measurable, appropriate to the supplier being measured, routinely communicated to the supplier, and actionable.[3] For a goal to be considered actionable, it must be able to be acted upon; for example, corrective action can be taken.

Buyers can also use a number of qualitative factors to assess supplier performance. Exhibit 9.1 details some of the qualitative service factors available to buyers. Although

Exhibit 9.1	Qualitative Service Factors

FACTOR	DESCRIPTION
Problem resolution ability	Supplier's attentiveness to problem resolution
Technical ability	Supplier's manufacturing ability compared with other industry suppliers
Ongoing progress reporting	Supplier's ongoing reporting of existing problems or recognizing and communicating a potential problem
Corrective action response	Supplier's solutions and timely response to requests for corrective actions, including a supplier's response to engineering change requests
Supplier cost-reduction ideas	Supplier's willingness to help find ways to reduce purchase cost
Supplier new-product support	Supplier's ability to help reduce new-product development cycle time or to help with product design
Buyer/seller compatibility	Subjective rating concerning how well a buying firm and a supplier work together (also known as "wavelength")

these factors are largely subjective, a buyer can still assign a score or performance rating to each factor. For example, a buyer might evaluate four different qualitative factors (assume equal weighting for simplicity) along a five-point scale. The system adds the four scores and divides by the total points possible to arrive at a percentage of total points, so that a buyer can then rank suppliers by the percentage of total possible points earned.

Measurement and Reporting Frequency

Two important issues relate to the regularity of measurement: reporting frequency to the buyer and reporting frequency to the supplier. A buyer (or someone responsible for the day-to-day management of suppliers) should receive a daily report summarizing the previous day's activities. This report allows the buyer to scan incoming receipt activity and should highlight any past-due supplier receipts. A buyer can also receive additional reports summarizing supplier performance on a weekly, monthly, quarterly, and/or annual basis as needed.

Routine reporting of supplier performance relative to previously established goals and objectives should occur monthly or quarterly. Buyers should also meet with their major suppliers on at least an annual basis to review actual performance results and identify improvement opportunities. Note that more critical suppliers should meet with the buyers on a more frequent basis. However, a buyer should never delay reporting a supplier's poor performance, particularly when it adversely affects day-to-day operations. Poor performance must be addressed as soon as it is recognized to avoid or mitigate financial or operational repercussions.

Uses of Measurement Data

A supply manager can use the data gathered from the organization's supplier measurement system in a number of ways. This data can help identify those suppliers that are not performing at expected levels so that appropriate remedial or developmental actions can be taken to get their performance back to acceptable levels or to find a new supplier if they cannot. A measurement system also helps identify those highly capable suppliers that may qualify for consideration of longer-term partnerships or designation as preferred suppliers because of their exemplary performance.

Measurement data also support supply base rationalization and optimization efforts. If suppliers do not maintain performance to minimum acceptable levels, they are not likely to remain part of the supply base over the long term. Another use of supplier performance data includes determining a supplier's future purchase volume based on its past performance ratings. Some companies periodically adjust their purchase volume allocations and reward better-performing suppliers with a higher share of future purchase requirements. Adjusting volumes among suppliers also provides a financial incentive for a supplier to meet or exceed the buyer's performance expectations.

A major benefit from supplier measurement is that performance data allow the buying organization to identify those operational areas requiring improvement. Buyers can also use the data when making sourcing decisions. These differences in supplier performance become clearer when a buyer has a reliable measurement system that consistently rates and ranks a supplier's performance against that of other suppliers or preestablished performance standards.

Types of Supplier Measurement Techniques

Note that all supplier measurement systems have some element of subjectivity. Even the implementation of a computerized measurement system displays some level of subjectivity. What data to analyze, when to collect the data, what metrics to use, what performance categories to include, how to weight different categories, how often to generate performance reports, and how to use the performance data are all subjective to some degree. Moreover, there are no hard and fast rules regarding the specific categories to include in supplier measurement systems; that choice will depend on what is strategically important to the buyer.

Organizations typically use three common types of measurement techniques or systems when evaluating supplier performance. Each technique differs in its ease of use, level of decision subjectivity, required system resources, and implementation cost. Exhibit 9.2 compares the advantages and disadvantages of the three types.

Exhibit 9.2	**Comparison of Supplier Measurement and Evaluation Systems**		
SYSTEM	**ADVANTAGES**	**DISADVANTAGES**	**USERS**
Categorical	Easy to implement Requires minimal data Different personnel can contribute Good for firms with limited resources Low-cost system	Least reliable Less frequent generation of evaluations Most subjective Usually manual	Smaller firms Firms in the process of developing an evaluation system
Weighted-Point	Flexible system Supplier ranking allowed Moderate implementation costs Quantitative and qualitative factors combined into a single system	Tends to focus on unit price Requires some computer support	Most firms can use this approach
Cost-Based	Total cost approach Specific areas of supplier nonperformance identified Objective supplier ranking Greatest potential for long-range improvement	Cost accounting system required Most complex, so implementation costs high Computer resources required	Larger firms Firms with a large supply base

Categorical System

A **categorical system** is the easiest and most basic measurement system to put in place, but it is also the most subjective in measuring supplier performance. This system simply requires the assignment of a subjective rating score for each performance category. Categorical rating examples typically include categories such as: excellent, good, fair, and poor. These subjective evaluations can be completed by the buyer, other internal users, or a combination of both.

The categorical approach is commonly used by smaller organizations because it is both easy and relatively inexpensive to implement. Although the categorical approach provides some structure to the supplier measurement process, it does not provide sufficiently detailed insight into a supplier's true performance as the categories are usually ill-defined and subject to interpretation. Furthermore, because categorical systems often rely on manually collected data, a buying organization generates supplier performance reports less frequently than if an automated data collection system existed. The reliability of the categorical method is the lowest of the three measurement systems discussed here, which severely limits the value of this approach when assessing supplier performance. There is often significant variance in subjective ratings depending on who actually creates the ratings.

Weighted-Point System

This approach overcomes some of the subjectivity inherent in a categorical measurement system. A **weighted-point system** weighs and quantifies relative scores across different performance categories. This approach usually features higher reliability and moderate implementation costs.

Weighted-point systems are also flexible—users can change the weights assigned to each performance category or the actual performance categories themselves, depending on what is currently most important to the buyer. For example, the performance categories and associated weights for an MRO (Maintenance, Repair, and Operating) parts distributor would likely differ from those for a supplier furnishing critical production components.

Several important issues must be understood regarding the use of weighted-point systems. First, users must carefully consider and select which key performance categories to measure. Second, an organization must decide how to weigh the importance of each performance category. Although assigning relative weights is subjective, an organization can reach consensus on this through careful planning and involvement from different functional areas. Third, a set of clear and concise decision rules must be in place to compare a supplier's performance against a predetermined objective to develop a score for each category.

Exhibit 9.3 illustrates a sample weighted-point system based on a five-point scale, where five is the highest possible score here. The weighted-point plan should provide a higher level of objectivity for most performance categories and evaluate supplier performance in more detail compared with the categorical approach. (Note that actual rating scales will be much more detailed than the one summarized here.)

Cost-Based System

The most thorough and least subjective of the three supplier performance measurement systems is the **cost-based system**. This approach seeks to identify and quantify the total cost of

Exhibit 9.3	Weighted-Point Supplier Measurement and Evaluation of Davis Industries for Third Quarter 2015		
PERFORMANCE CATEGORY	**WEIGHT**	**SCORE**	**WEIGHTED SCORE**
Delivery			
On time	.10	4	.40
Quantity	.10	3	.30
Quality			
Inbound shipment quality	.25	4	1.00
Quality improvement	.10	4	.40
Cost Competitiveness			
Comparison with other suppliers	.15	2	.30
Cost-reduction ideas submitted	.10	3	.30
Service Factors			
Problem resolution ability	.05	4	.20
Technical ability	.05	5	.25
Corrective action response	.05	3	.15
New-product development support	.05	5	.25
Total Rating			3.55
1 = Poor, 3 = Average, 5 = Excellent			

doing business with a given supplier, as the lowest purchase price may not always result in the lowest total cost for an item or service.

Companies with highly capable information systems can readily implement a cost-based supplier measurement system. The major challenge involves identifying and recording those appropriate costs that are incurred whenever a supplier fails to perform as expected. To use such a system, an organization must estimate or calculate the additional costs that result whenever a supplier underperforms. The basic logic of the system is built around the calculation of a **supplier performance index** (SPI). This index, where a base value of 1.0 represents satisfactory performance, is a total cost index calculated for each major item or key commodity provided by a supplier:

$$SPI = (Total\ Purchases + Nonperformance\ Costs) / Total\ Purchases$$

Exhibit 9.4 illustrates a simple cost-based example of supplier performance measurement. The cost-based approach can also include an assessment of qualitative service factors to provide a more complete picture of overall supplier performance. This example compares the total cost of ownership (TCO) for each supplier of two items in the integrated circuit category. It also compares suppliers on the basis of their service factor ratings. Note that the lowest-price supplier, BC Techtronics, is not the lowest-total-cost supplier when the added costs of nonperformance are included. For both parts, Advanced Systems is the lowest-total-cost supplier, although it does not have the lowest purchase price. This is because BC Techtronics has a lower service rating score as compared with the other two suppliers.

Exhibit 9.5 summarizes supplier performance for a group of items comprising a single commodity. It details the total number of nonconformance occurrences, the cost of each event as identified by the buyer, and the total nonconformance cost for the quarter.

Exhibit 9.4	Supplier Performance Comparison through First Quarter 2015

COMMODITY: INTEGRATED CIRCUIT

PART NUMBER	SUPPLIER	UNIT PRICE	SPI	TOTAL COST
IC-04279884	Advanced Systems	$3.12	1.20	$3.74*
	BC Techtronics	$3.01	1.45	$4.36
	Micro Circuit	$3.10	1.30	$4.03
IC-04341998	Advanced Systems	$5.75	1.20	$6.90*
	BC Techtronics	$5.40	1.45	$7.83
	Micro Circuit	$5.55	1.30	$7.21

Service Factor Ratings:

Advanced Systems	78%
BC Techtronics	76%
Micro Circuit	87%

*Lowest-total-cost supplier for item (Unit price × SPI = Total cost).
Source: Monczka, R.M., and Trecha, S.J. (1988, Spring), "Cost-Based Supplier Performance Evaluation," *Journal of Purchasing and Materials Management*, 24(1) 1–4.

Exhibit 9.5	Supplier Performance Report for First Quarter 2015

Supplier: Advanced Systems
Commodity: Integrated circuit
Total part numbers in commodity: 2

A. Total purchase dollars this quarter: $5,232

NONPERFORMANCE COSTS

EVENT	NUMBER OF OCCURRENCES	AVERAGE COST PER OCCURRENCE	EXTENDED COST
Late delivery	5	$150	$750
Return to supplier	2	$45	$90
Scrap labor costs	3	$30	$90
Material rework cost	1	$100	$100
B. Total nonperformance costs			$1,030
C. Purchase nonperformance cost	(Line B)		$6,262
D. Supplier performance index	(Line C/A)		1.20
E. Service factor rating			78%

Lines C and D include the figures required for the SPI calculation. Line E is the ratio of points earned to the total possible points for the qualitative or service factors.

In many cases, the actual cost per nonconformance event may be difficult to estimate or calculate, as many traditional cost accounting systems are not designed to identify and capture such data. Refer back to Chapter 8 regarding a discussion of the cost of quality. For instance, the average cost of a late delivery may vary widely, depending on its impact to the customer, potential lost sales, line shutdown costs, and so on. Therefore, many organizations work around this limitation by assigning a standard cost charge each time a nonconformance event occurs.

However, the SPI can sometimes provide an incomplete or misleading assessment of supplier performance. For example, consider a supplier that delivers $100,000 of material, with one late delivery charged at $5,000. That supplier will have an SPI of ($100,000 + $5,000) / $100,000, or 1.05. This SPI appears more favorable than that of a supplier that delivers only $30,000 of material and has one late delivery, also charged at $5,000. The second supplier has an SPI of ($30,000 + $5,000) / $30,000, or 1.17. Although both suppliers committed the same infraction, the lower volume supplier received a comparatively more severe penalty relative to its purchase volume. A normalization adjustment (Q) can be used to eliminate this bias that favors higher-dollar-volume suppliers. Exhibit 9.6 illustrates how to calculate an SPI with the Q adjustment factor, which allows an "apples-to-apples" comparison between suppliers.

Management has many uses for the data derived from a comprehensive cost-based supplier measurement system. Such a system provides the necessary information that allows a buyer to justify buying from a preferred supplier despite a higher unit price. The system also allows a buyer to communicate the cost of specific nonconformance events to the originating supplier, which then helps it to identify improvement opportunities. Quantifying

Exhibit 9.6	Supplier Performance Index Calculation with Q Adjustment Factor		

Q is a normalization factor that eliminates high-dollar lot bias.

Q=(Average cost of a lot of material for an individual supplier)/(Average cost of a lot of material for all suppliers)

Consider the following information for Suppliers A, B, and C, each with a single late delivery nonconformance calculated at $4,000.

Assume the average cost of all lots for suppliers of this commodity is $2,500.

	SUPPLIER A	SUPPLIER B	SUPPLIER C
3rd quarter shipments	20 lots @ $500 each	20 lots @ $1,000 each	20 lots @ $10,000 each
Total value of shipments	$10,000	$20,000	$200,000
Average lot cost	$500	$1,000	$10,000
Nonconformance charges	Late delivery @ $4,000	Late delivery @ $4,000	Late delivery @ $4,000
3rd Quarter SPI	**($10,000 + $4,000) / $10,000 = 1.40**	**($20,000 + $4,000) / $20,000 = 1.20**	**($200,000 + $4,000) / $200,000 = 1.02**
Average cost of a lot from all suppliers	$2,500	$2,500	$2,500
Q calculation	$500/$2,500 = .2	$1,000/$2,500 = .4	$10,000/$2,500 = 4

Notice how different the SPI values are for the three suppliers, even though they each committed the same single incident of nonconformance. Supplier C, because of the high lot bias, has the lowest SPI.

SPI calculation with Q adjustment = Cost of material + (Nonconformance costs Q factor)/Cost of material

Supplier A: $10,000 + ($4,000 × .2)/$10,000 = 1.08

Supplier B: $20,000 + ($4,000 × .4)/$20,000 = 1.08

Supplier C: $200,000 + ($4,000 × 4)/$200,000 = 1.08

Applying the Q adjustment now allows a consistent and fair comparison across suppliers.

nonconformance costs can also result in a chargeback to the offending supplier for unplanned costs. Finally, a buyer can use this data to identify longer-term sources of supply based on a supplier's total cost performance history.

Each of the three types of measurement approaches featured in this chapter, although differing in their complexity and scope of use, raises a buyer's awareness about supply base performance. Supplier measurement is a powerful tool for managing and increasing the capabilities of the supply base.

Rationalization and Optimization: Creating a Manageable Supply Base

Effective supply base management and supplier development begins by determining the optimal number of suppliers that an organization should maintain. Supply base rationalization is the process of identifying how many and which suppliers a buyer will maintain. Supply base optimization involves a detailed analysis of the supply base to ensure that only the most capable and highest performing suppliers are kept in the supply base once rationalized. It often involves eliminating those suppliers that are unwilling to achieve (or are incapable of achieving) supply management performance objectives, either currently or expected in the future.

Supply base rationalization and optimization must be a continuous process. The elimination of both marginal and small-purchase-volume suppliers is usually the first phase of the rationalization process. Subsequent optimization requires the replacement of good suppliers with better-performing suppliers or initiating supplier development projects with existing suppliers to improve their performance. Organizations must develop effective supplier evaluation and measurement systems to identify the best-performing suppliers and then develop stronger business relationships with those suppliers. Oftentimes, companies must search worldwide for the best suppliers.

During the early phases of supply base rationalization and optimization, the process usually results in an absolute reduction in the total number of suppliers. Reduction, however, may not always be the result for each family or group of purchased items. The key is to determine the right number of suppliers to maintain in the supply base, not just arbitrarily cut down the number. For example, a U.S. truck assembly plant formerly received tires and wheels separately from different suppliers. OEM employees mounted and balanced the tires on the wheels inside the assembly plant in a labor- and space-intensive operation. The buyer established a new supplier location near the assembly plant that then received both the tires and wheels from their respective suppliers, assembling, balancing, and storing the finished wheel assemblies until shipping them to the assembly plant on a just-in-time basis. Although the company added an additional supplier to its supply base, overall system efficiency increased, and total cost actually declined. In this example, the optimization process resulted in the net addition of a supplier.

Advantages of a Rationalized and Optimized Supply Base

Supply base rationalization and optimization should result in real improvements in cost, quality, delivery, and information sharing between buyer and supplier. Because the process identifies the best suppliers in terms of number and quality, the remaining suppliers are often capable of performing additional tasks or providing other products and services that add value to the buyer-supplier relationship. Suppliers in an optimized supply base often develop longer-term relationships with buyers, which can lead to collaboration in further joint improvement efforts.

Buying from World-Class Suppliers

Because of the strong correlation between supplier performance and supply chain success, it is not difficult to see why choosing and maintaining only the best suppliers supports higher performance throughout the supply chain. Instead of being responsible for literally hundreds or thousands of suppliers, supply management can concentrate on developing closer relationships with a smaller core group of exceedingly capable suppliers. The benefits of doing business with higher performing, world-class suppliers include fewer quality and delivery problems, access to leading-edge technology, opportunities to develop collaborative relationships, and a lower total product cost as supply management and engineering gain key supplier input during new-product development.

Use of Full-Service Suppliers

The remaining suppliers in a rationalized and optimized supply base are often larger on average and more capable of offering a broader range of value-adding services. When a buyer uses a full-service supplier, it expects to reap substantial benefits in the form of access to the supplier's engineering, research and development, design, testing, production, service, and tooling capabilities. The full-service supplier approach places a greater burden on a supplier to manage an entire system of components, activities, and services, as well as to manage its own supply base effectively. The full-service supplier can also perform complete design and build work instead of the buyer performing the work internally or using several different suppliers in a loosely coordinated effort.

The automobile industry provides many examples of how full-service suppliers can provide these benefits. For example, all motor vehicles have extensive electrical wiring systems. Traditionally, automobile manufacturers designed each individual wiring harness internally and sent the design specifications to suppliers through a competitive bidding process. It was not uncommon to have ten different suppliers working on wiring systems for final assembly into a vehicle. Now, a single supplier, or only a few suppliers, might design and produce the entire wiring system for a new vehicle throughout the entire model life cycle. The result is lower cost, improved quality, and reduced product development time. Because of its expertise, a supplier can design the wiring systems concurrently with the overall design of the car, reducing concept-to-customer cycle time.

Reduction of Supply Base Risk

At first glance, it seems illogical that using fewer suppliers can result in reduced supply base risk. Here, risk can be defined as the magnitude of exposure to financial loss or operational disruption and stems from uncertainty. What if a single or sole source supplier for a critical item goes out on strike or has a debilitating fire at its production facility, disrupting its production process and ability to maintain an uninterrupted flow of materials? Historically, the risk of supply disruption has been the primary argument against supply base reduction or single-sourcing of purchased items.

However, many buyers have now concluded that, if they select suppliers carefully and develop close and collaborative working relationships with fewer suppliers, supply risk can actually decrease. Risk does not include only supply disruption. Other supply risks include poor supplier quality, poor delivery performance, or overpaying for items because of a noncompetitive sourcing situation. However, maintaining multiple suppliers for each item can actually increase the probability and level of risk. Having more suppliers for individual items creates the opportunity for increased variability or inconsistent quality in the purchased product.

Lower Supply Base Administrative Costs

Buyers routinely interact with their suppliers in many ways. Examples could include the following:

- Contacting suppliers about design and material specifications
- Communicating quality and other performance requirements
- Negotiating purchase contracts
- Visiting, auditing, and evaluating supplier facilities and processes
- Providing feedback about supplier performance
- Collaborating with suppliers when problems occur
- Requesting supplier input about product design
- Contacting suppliers regarding engineering change orders
- Transmitting material releases

These activities all have associated real costs in terms of time, effort, and potential for miscommunication. For example, the administrative cost of maintaining 5,000 suppliers will be dramatically higher than the cost of maintaining a core group of 500 highly qualified suppliers. Furthermore, highly qualified suppliers often require fewer problem-related interactions with the buyer. The best contacts between a buyer and seller are those that add value to the relationship rather than merely resolve problems.

Lower Total Product Cost

During the 1980s, buyers began to recognize the real costs of maintaining multiple suppliers for each item procured. Acquisition and operating costs increased as a result of greater variability in product quality and delivery and smaller production volumes offered by each supplier, which did nothing to spread out the supplier's fixed costs over greater output levels. Short-term purchase contracts that awarded small volumes of business to multiple suppliers only increased production costs and provided no incentive for individual supplier investments in process improvement. It became evident that, if fewer suppliers received larger-volume contracts, the resulting economies of scale could lower both production and distribution costs. Supply base rationalization and optimization provides the opportunity to achieve lower total product costs by awarding larger volumes to fewer, more capable suppliers.

Ability to Pursue Complex Supply Management Strategies

Implementing complex supply management strategies requires a rationalized and optimized supply base. The need for more complicated collaboration and interaction with suppliers requires a smaller supply base because of higher levels of two-way interactions between a buyer and seller on both tactical and strategic issues. Examples of complex supply management strategies include supplier development, early supplier design involvement, just-in-time sourcing, and the development of cost-based pricing agreements with suppliers.

Possible Risks of Maintaining Fewer Suppliers

Few supply management executives would argue in favor of maintaining multiple suppliers for every purchased item. Currently, the debate centers on maintaining a limited number of qualified suppliers for major items versus using a single source. Some organizations believe that using several suppliers for a purchased item promotes and maintains a healthy level of competition between suppliers. Others, however, believe that a single source can still deliver cost and quality improvements over the life of a contract if a buyer manages that supplier effectively. Although most buyers recognize the benefits of supply base rationalization and optimization, there are still potential risks from reliance on a smaller supply base.

Supplier Dependency

Some buyers fear that a supplier can become too dependent on the buyer for its economic survival. This situation can easily occur if a buyer combines its total purchase volume for an item with a single supplier. A smaller supplier with limited capacity for growth may need to eliminate some existing customers to meet the increased requirements of its now much larger customer. As a result, the supplier may become too dependent on a buyer for its financial viability. If, for some reason, the buyer no longer requires a particular item, the overly dependent supplier may no longer be financially solvent if that volume is taken away. Although supply base optimization can lead to a beneficial mutual commitment between buyer and seller, it can also result in an unhealthy dependence of one party on the other.

Absence of Competition

By relying on only one or a limited number of suppliers, some buyers fear losing the pricing advantages of a competitive marketplace. A supplier may hold the buyer hostage by unduly raising its prices without justification or becoming too complacent. The more difficult and expensive it is to change suppliers (e.g., higher switching costs), the more likely this scenario becomes. However, organizations with substantial supply base optimization experience argue that careful supplier selection and the development of mutually beneficial contracts that address continuous improvement requirements should prevent an over-reliance on suppliers that try to take advantage of a single-source situation.

Supply Disruption

Supply disruption is a potential risk when sourcing from a single-location supplier, or even multiple source suppliers if they are located in near proximity to one another. In 2011, the Tōhoku earthquake and resultant tsunami in Japan disrupted the supply of electronic components, which supported the global automotive industry. Electronic component plants were shut down for weeks and normal levels of output were curtailed for several additional months. Automakers throughout the globe reacted by hoarding electronic component inventories and reducing their production of finished goods. Suppliers outside Japan not affected by the quake increased their prices, resulting in a ripple effect throughout the automotive industry.

Likewise, labor strikes, facility fires, acts of nature, production or quality problems, or disruption within the supplier's own supply base can disrupt the smooth flow of materials through a supply chain. Buyers can minimize this risk by sourcing from a single supplier with multiple production facilities. For example, Dell Computer utilizes multiple sourcing for many of the key components that go into its notebook computers manufactured in Asia. If a disruption or lack of capacity occurs at one supplier's facility, Dell can quickly shift its sourcing to another qualified facility from the same supplier or even to a different supplier as needed to support its operations.[4]

Another method for minimizing supply disruption risk is to select suppliers with multiple capabilities—the practice of cross-sourcing. Here, a buyer selects or develops suppliers with multiple or redundant capabilities. If problems occur with a primary source of supply for an item, the secondary supplier, which is the supplier for another purchased item, then assumes the volume for that item. This approach requires identifying suppliers capable of producing different items or performing multiple functions throughout the production process.

Overaggressive Supply Reduction

However, buyers can move too aggressively when reducing the supply base. If this occurs, the suppliers remaining in the supply base may not have sufficient capacity or capability to meet additional purchase requirements if demand increases substantially. This happened when a major producer of hand tools developed a wide array of products that used rechargeable nickel-cadmium batteries. The supplier found that it did not have adequate manufacturing capacity to support new-product requirements for these batteries. In this case, the supply base optimization process required the buyer to identify and qualify new sources rather quickly. As part of the supply base optimization process, the buyer must ensure that it carefully evaluates the remaining suppliers' capacities and capabilities to produce larger volumes or develops other suppliers to cover the increased volumes.

Formal Approaches to Supply Base Rationalization

In his discussion of strategic supply management, Keki Bhote offers several possible supply base reduction methods.[5] Bhote's framework contains three primary elements: (1) phasing out current suppliers, (2) selection of finalist suppliers, and (3) selection of partnership suppliers. This section focuses on several methods commonly used to rationalize the supply base.

Twenty/Eighty Rule

This approach identifies those 20 percent of suppliers receiving the bulk of purchase spend or that minority of suppliers that cause the most quality problems. Level of spend and supplier quality are two possible decision criteria used to identify suppliers for reevaluation and/or elimination. Organizations often use this approach when they require a rapid reduction in the number of suppliers. A disadvantage to the 20/80 approach is the possible elimination of otherwise capable suppliers simply because they received fewer purchase dollars. This approach assumes the best suppliers receive the majority of the purchase dollars, which may or may not necessarily be true. In addition, the buyer may inadvertently exclude suppliers that have needed capabilities that are not currently being utilized by the buyer.

"Improve or Else" Approach

This approach provides all suppliers, regardless of their performance history, a chance to remain in the supply base. It involves notifying suppliers that they have a specified period of time in which to meet new, more rigorous performance requirements—ranging from improved quality levels and delivery performance, shorter lead times, cost reductions, or any other key performance indicators (KPIs). Suppliers that fall short of these new expectations may soon become ex-suppliers. Although this approach has the potential for driving dramatic performance improvement in the supply base in a short period of time, it can also be a heavy-handed way of dealing with suppliers. For example, this was the approach that the chief purchasing officer of General Motors, J. Ignacio Lopez de Arriortua, used in 1992 by demanding that GM's suppliers reduce their prices by 3 to 22 percent or risk losing their existing supply contracts.[6] However, this approach proved largely ineffective and caused long-term, substantial disruptions in the GM supply base.

Triage Approach

This approach requires the systematic evaluation of the performance of individual suppliers and ultimate placement into one of three categories. The first category, and most likely the largest, includes those suppliers that are marginal performers or otherwise incapable of meeting purchase performance requirements, either currently or in the future. The buyer then targets these suppliers for immediate removal from the supply base. The second category includes those suppliers that have not consistently met the buyer's requirements in all areas but have demonstrated sufficient improvement potential. The most promising of these suppliers are often targeted for supplier assistance and development. The third category includes those high-quality, capable suppliers requiring no improvement assistance. These suppliers are candidates for more collaborative buyer-seller relationships, which may include offering longer-term contracts in exchange for continuous improvement, as well as being considered for an alliance. The distribution of suppliers across these categories may vary across industries.

Exhibit 9.7 illustrates one company's triage approach to supplier reduction. This company compares suppliers against various performance criteria and segments the supply base into three groups: unacceptable performers, suppliers that meet minimum requirements but are not world-class, and world-class performers worthy of closer, more collaborative relationships.

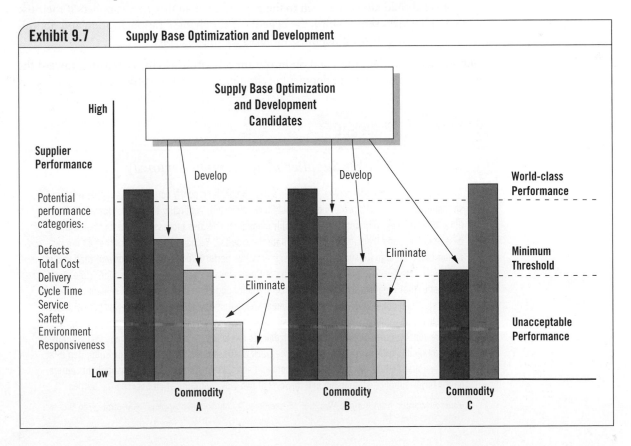

Exhibit 9.7 | **Supply Base Optimization and Development**

Competency Staircase Approach

This method requires suppliers to successfully navigate a succession of performance milestone improvements to remain in the supply base. Suppliers must pass a series of hurdles, which is analogous to climbing a staircase. First, all suppliers must meet a buyer's basic quality standards for consideration as potential suppliers. Each hurdle successfully navigated brings the supplier one step closer to its ultimate goal of remaining in the buyer's supply base.

The next set of hurdles may include a supplier's ability to meet a buyer's technical specifications and product performance requirements. Subsequent hurdles can include demonstrating sustained production competency, enhanced delivery capability (such as just-in-time requirements), growth capability, willingness to share information, supplier size, sustainability, and physical proximity to the buyer. Note that different purchase requirements will present varying sets of hurdles. Each hurdle results in fewer and fewer suppliers remaining in the supply base. The result is a strong and flexible supply base comprised of highly capable and motivated suppliers with demonstrated performance.

Summary of Supplier Rationalization and Optimization

Several conclusions about supplier rationalization and optimization can now be made. First, there are a variety of approaches to supply base rationalization and optimization. This chapter provides only a select sample of those approaches. Furthermore, an organization can combine more than one approach to meet its supply base reduction goals. Organizations may also decide to use varying approaches for different procurement requirements. Second, we do not have to limit our evaluation only to suppliers currently in the supply base. A buyer should always be open to the possibility of adding new suppliers if their use makes good business sense. Third, the benefits of supply base rationalization and optimization are real, whereas the potential drawbacks are manageable.

Supply base rationalization and optimization constitute a critical first step toward the effective management and development of the supply base. It is difficult to manage many

Sourcing Snapshot

McDonald's Takes Supplier Measurement Seriously

To measure supplier performance, McDonald's (Oak Brook, IL) recently employed a supplier relationship management (SRM) process to its global technology buy. According to Joseph Youssef, McDonald's SRM strategy "requires dedicated supply managers, effective processes to create standardized best practices, and tools to track and evaluate the results." Youssef also indicates that an organization must manage its supply base through effective performance measurement and then make supplier-related decisions using the outputs of those measurements. He outlines four prime measurements that organizations should consider in their supplier performance management systems. The first area includes day-to-day tactical measurements such as quality, service, responsiveness, and delivery performance. The second measurement focuses on contract management: making sure that previously agreed-to contractual arrangements are followed. The third area measured is financial management. Measurements in this area track to see that accurate invoices are submitted in a timely manner and for the agreed-on products and services. Lastly, the fourth measurement centers on the buyer-supplier relationship and the level of two-way communication between the parties.

Source: Adapted from Forrest, W. (2006, September 7) "McDonald's Applies SRM Strategy to Global Technology Buy," 16.

suppliers as efficiently as a small core group of suppliers, just as it is challenging to pursue progressive supply management strategies with too many suppliers. A large supply base also means the duplication of a wide range of supply management activities, adding to acquisition cost without a corresponding increase in value added to the customer. Finally, supplier rationalization and optimization should be a continuing activity with ongoing review and modification as needed.

Supplier Development: A Strategy for Improvement

The first documented applications of **supplier development** came from Toyota, Nissan, and Honda, with some of these applications dating back to pre-World War II. For example, Toyota's 1939 *Purchasing Rules* discussed the need to treat its suppliers as an integral part of the enterprise and to work together to improve their collective performance. Nissan implemented its first supplier development efforts in 1963, with Honda joining the club as a result of the first Arab oil embargo in 1973.[7] However, the rest of the world has often been hesitant to take up the supplier development banner.[8] Even the United Nations has recognized the need for supplier development; its *Guide to Supplier Development* is designed to improve the skills, capacities, and competitiveness of global industrial subcontracting and partnership exchanges.[9]

Although the concept was mentioned in several early purchasing books, early North American writings on supplier development began in earnest with researcher Michiel Leenders.[10] Broadly defined, supplier development is any activity undertaken by a buyer to improve a supplier's performance or capabilities to meet the buyer's short- and long-term supply needs. Organizations can rely on a variety of development activities to improve supplier performance, including sharing technology, providing incentives to suppliers for improved performance, promoting competition among suppliers, providing necessary capital, and directly involving its personnel with suppliers through activities such as training and process improvement.[11]

Direct involvement in a supplier's operations by buyer personnel is undoubtedly the most challenging part of any supplier development process. Not only must the buyer's management and employees be convinced that investing scarce company resources in an outside supplier's operations is a worthwhile risk, but the supplier likewise must be convinced that it is in the supplier's own best interest to accept the buyer's direction and technical assistance. Too often, the supplier is convinced that the only reason a buyer wants to engage in supplier development is to pressure the supplier to pass along all of the savings generated through price concessions or shrinkage of its profits margins. Even if a mutual understanding of the importance of supplier development is reached, there is still the matter of implementation and allocation of requisite resources by both parties, as well as ensuring that the impetus of the changes is maintained over time. Effective supplier development requires the often substantial commitment of financial capital and human resources, skilled personnel, timely and accurate information sharing, and performance measurement.

A Process Map for Supplier Development

After reviewing the strategies of more than 60 organizations, we have developed a generic process map for deploying a supplier development initiative, as shown in Exhibit 9.8.[12] Although many organizations have successfully deployed the first four stages of the process, some have been less successful in implementing the latter four stages.

Step 1—Identify Critical Commodities for Development

Not all organizations need to pursue supplier development. An organization may already be sourcing from world-class suppliers because of its existing strategic supplier selection processes, or it may be buying external inputs only in a small proportion to the total

Exhibit 9.8	Process for Implementation of Supplier Development Strategy

1. Identify critical commodities for development.

2. Identify critical suppliers for development.
- Benchmark
- Pareto analysis

3. Form cross-functional development team.
- Purchasing
- Engineering
- Quality

4. Meet with supplier's top management team.

5. Identify opportunities and probability for improvement.

6. Define key metrics and cost-sharing mechanisms.

7. Reach agreement on key projects and joint resource requirements.

8. Monitor status of projects and modify strategies as appropriate.

Source: Adapted from Handfield, R., Krause, D. Scannell, T, and Monczka, R. (1998, December), "An Empirical Investigation of Supplier Development Reactive and Strategic Process," *Journal of Operational Management*, 17(1), 39–58.

cost of goods sold. Therefore, supply managers must analyze their own individual sourcing situations to determine if a particular supplier's level of performance warrants development, and if so, which specific commodities and services will require attention.

Senior supply managers should thoroughly consider the following questions to determine if a given supplier warrants development effort.[13] A "Yes" response to a majority of these questions suggests a need for supplier development.

- Do externally purchased products and services account for more than 50 percent of product or service value?
- Is the supplier an existing or potential source of competitive advantage?
- Do you currently purchase or plan to purchase on the basis of total cost versus initial purchase price?
- Can existing suppliers meet your competitive needs five years from now?
- Do you need suppliers to be more responsive to your needs?
- Are you willing and able to become more responsive to your suppliers' needs?
- Do you plan to treat suppliers as partners in your business?
- Do you plan to develop and maintain open and trusting relations with your suppliers?

A corporate-level executive steering committee should then be formed to develop an assessment and spend analysis of the relative importance of all purchased goods and services to identify where to focus supplier development efforts. Review Chapter 6 for a description of how to conduct a spend analysis. The result of this assessment is a portfolio analysis of those critical products or services that are essential for marketplace success. This discussion is an extension of the company's overall corporate-level strategic planning process and must include participants from other critical functions affected by sourcing decisions, including finance, sales and marketing, quality, information technology, accounting, engineering, manufacturing and operations, and design.

Step 2—Identify Critical Suppliers for Development

The supply base performance assessment system helps identify those suppliers within a commodity group that could be targeted for development. A common approach involves a routine analysis of current supplier performance. As shown in Exhibit 9.7, leading companies regularly monitor supplier performance on a facility-by-facility basis and rank suppliers from best to worst. Suppliers failing to meet predetermined minimum performance standards in quality, delivery, cycle time, late deliveries, total cost, service, safety, sustainability, and/or environmental compliance are potential candidates for elimination from the supply base. If the supplier's product or service is deemed essential to the buyer, it should then be considered for supplier development. Those suppliers that currently meet minimum requirements but do not yet provide world-class performance are the most likely candidates for development efforts. Benchmarking and Pareto analysis are two sourcing tools that can assist in the identification of possible supplier development targets.

Step 3—Form Cross-Functional Development Team

Before approaching suppliers and asking for improved performance, it is critical to develop cross-functional consensus and support internally for the initiative. Supply management executives continually emphasize that supply base improvement begins from within through buyer-focused activities—that is, the buying company must have its own house in order before expecting commitment and cooperation from suppliers in developing their capabilities. Development teams typically include members from engineering, operations, quality, cost management, and supply management. At this point, a team charter (or mission statement) is created that describes the scope and detail of the supplier development project.

Step 4—Meet with Supplier's Top Management Team

Once the development team's charter has been established and an appropriate supplier candidate has been identified for improvement, the team should approach the supplier's top management team and establish three relational building blocks for seeking supplier improvement: strategic alignment, measurement, and professionalism. Strategic alignment requires business and technology alignment between the companies. It also requires alignment about key customer needs throughout the supply chain. Measurement requires an objective means of accurately assessing development results and progress in a timely manner. By approaching the supplier's top management with a solid and mutually beneficial business case for improvement, the demonstrated professionalism of all parties helps to establish a positive tone, reinforce collaboration, foster two-way communication, and develop mutual trust and commitment.

Step 5—Identify Opportunities and Probability for Improvement

At these meetings with the supplier's senior management, supply management executives should identify key areas earmarked for improvement. Companies adopting a strategic approach to supply base development can usually agree on the areas for improvement. Oftentimes, such improvement areas are driven by final customer requirements and expectations. However, only those projects identified as having a high probability of sustainable success should be initiated.

Step 6—Define Key Metrics and Cost-Sharing Mechanisms

Development opportunities, although not necessarily specific improvement projects, are evaluated next in terms of project feasibility and potential return on investment. The parties jointly determine if the opportunities for improvement are realistic and achievable and, if so, then establish measures and improvement goals. The buyer and seller must also agree on how to divide or share the costs and benefits from the development project. A common sharing arrangement is 50/50, but the actual cost/benefit sharing must take each party's level of resource investment and effort into consideration.

Step 7—Reach Agreement on Key Projects and Joint Resource Requirements

After identifying specific improvement projects to implement, the parties must identify the resources necessary to carry out the project or development effort and make the commitment to employ them. The parties also need to reach agreement regarding the specific measures and metrics that demonstrate project success. These measures may include a defined percentage improvement in cost savings, quality, delivery, or cycle time, or any other area relevant to supply chain performance. The most critical component of supplier development is that it must contain realistic and visible milestones, as well as specified time horizons to reach improvement. What gets measured is usually what gets accomplished. The agreement should also specify the role of each party, who is responsible for the outcomes of the project, and the manner and timing for deploying already agreed-on resources.

Step 8—Monitor Status of Projects and Modify Strategies as Appropriate

Progress must be routinely monitored after initiating a supplier development project. Moreover, an open, ongoing, and two-way exchange of information is needed to maintain a project's momentum. This can be achieved by creating visible milestones for objectives, posting progress, and creating new or revised objectives based on actual progress. Ongoing project management may require modifying the original plan, applying additional resources, developing new information, or refocusing priorities, depending on information uncovered in the course of the project.

Supplier Development Efforts That Sometimes Do Not Work

Evidence indicates that supplier development projects work—at least some of the time. Exhibit 9.9 presents the results of a comprehensive study of supplier development efforts and clearly indicates that, although there is no guarantee that comparable supplier

Exhibit 9.9	**Supplier Development Results**		
CRITERIA		BEFORE SUPPLIER DEVELOPMENT	AFTER SUPPLIER DEVELOPMENT
Incoming defects		11.65%	5.45%
% on-time delivery		79.85%	91.02%
Cycle time (from order placement to receipt, inclusively)		35.74 days	23.44 days
% orders received complete		85.47%	93.33%

Source: Krause, D. R., and Ellram, L. M. (1997), "Success factors in supplier development," *International Journal of Physical Distribution & Logistics Management,* 27(1), 39–52.

development efforts will be equally successful, on average the development process does produce substantial results. This does not mean that there are no barriers and challenges to successful supplier development. In fact, other studies have found these barriers to be substantial and very real. The next section describes some of the proven techniques and tools used by leading-edge companies to address the problems or barriers that may contribute to less-than-desirable supplier development effectiveness.

Overcoming the Barriers to Supplier Development

Barriers to effective supplier development typically fall into three classifications: (1) buyer-specific barriers, (2) buyer-supplier interface barriers, and (3) supplier-specific barriers. Companies can use a variety of approaches to overcome barriers to supplier development. In general, these approaches fall into one of three categories:

- *Direct-involvement activities (hands-on):* Companies often send their own experts to assist suppliers. These efforts are characterized as hands-on activities, where the buyer's representatives are directly involved in correcting supplier problems and increasing capabilities. An example would be the buyer assigning one of its process engineers to a supplier's facility to assist in physically rearranging its equipment to be more efficient.

- *Incentives and rewards (e.g., the "carrot"):* Companies can also use incentives to encourage suppliers to improve, largely by means of their own internal efforts. For example, a buyer might agree to increase future order volumes if the desired performance improvement takes place within a specific time, or it could hold an annual award ceremony to publicly recognize the best suppliers.

- *Warnings and penalties (e.g., the "stick"):* In some cases, companies may pull back current business or withhold potential future business if a supplier's performance is deemed unacceptable or if a lack of improvement is evident. Buyers may also use a competitive marketplace and rebid current contracts to provide a viable threat or incentive to a poorly performing supplier.

In many cases, organizations employ a combination of these three strategies to drive supplier improvement as quickly as possible, applying them judiciously in response to a particular supplier's capabilities and needs. The following sections address barriers to supplier development that are internal, external, or interface based, and provide examples of how leading companies overcome these barriers.

Buyer-Specific Barriers

A buying company should not engage in supplier development unless senior management recognizes the need for, or the benefits to be gained from, an investment in supplier development. Moreover, if supply management personnel have not already rationalized and optimized its supply base as discussed above, the volume of purchases with any particular supplier may not justify the joint investment. In addition, there may be a lack of top-level support for financing supplier development efforts in terms of both dollars and time.

Barrier: The Buying Company's Purchase Volume from the Supplier Does Not Justify Development Investment

Solution: Standardization and single-sourcing. Parts standardization across several product lines is a way to increase total order volumes with suppliers, which may justify a development investment. If buyer's personnel believe that using customized components will provide a market advantage, they will continue to use them. However, component standardization remains an important way to leverage worldwide purchase volume and shorten new-product development cycles.

Concurrent with component standardization, many supply managers also plan to rationalize their supply bases, wherever possible, to achieve economies of scope and scale. Some companies use single-sourcing wherever possible, relying on two or more suppliers only in situations with high potential for labor disputes.

Barrier: No Immediate Benefit to Supplier Development Is Evident to the Buying Organization

Solution: Pursue small wins. Varity Perkins, a producer of diesel engines used in automotive and construction vehicles, found its initial supplier development efforts to be relatively unsuccessful. This resulted in lowered internal expectations and dampened enthusiasm for future development efforts. However, Varity personnel realized that part of the problem was that they were trying to accomplish too much. Thus, the company focused on a smaller group of suppliers for kaizen (or continuous improvement) efforts to gain a series of small wins and build momentum. The kaizen approach achieved incremental improvements that ultimately gained renewed internal commitment for the supplier development process.

Barrier: Importance of Purchased Item Does Not Justify Development Efforts

Solution: Take a longer-term focus. Solectron, a contract manufacturer in the computer industry, has a competitive strategy that relies heavily on its supply chain management competencies. The company looks beyond the price of purchased inputs and examines how its most important suppliers affect the quality and technology of its products. Solectron expects its suppliers to provide designs offering integrated solutions that Solectron engineers can use in future product designs. Total cost and long-term strategic impact help justify ongoing investment in suppliers.

Barrier: Lack of Executive Support within the Buying Organization for Supplier Development

Solution: Prove the benefits. Support for supplier development is gained when management becomes convinced that the company can improve if supplier performance improves. For companies spending nearly 80 percent of their cost of goods sold on purchased inputs, such an argument is easy to make. For companies with lower percentages of purchased content, the argument may be more difficult. Proving a direct relationship between supplier improvement and increased profits can be problematic; someone within the supply management organization must document the outcomes. Managers also note that efforts to optimize their companies' supply bases, combined with part standardization, can help free up scarce resources over the long term, making supplier development more palatable to internal skeptics. In addition, the total cost approach to supplier performance measurement should also prove to be an effective communication tool for demonstrating the deleterious effects of poor supplier performance. However, many companies still view supplier development resources simply as additional overhead costs rather than a necessary investment in improving supply chain performance.

Buyer-Supplier Interface Barriers

Barriers to supplier development may also originate in the interface between the buyer and supplier in areas such as open communication, information sharing, alignment of organizational cultures, mutual goals and objectives, and trust. A reluctance to share sensitive or proprietary information about costs and processes on the part of either buyer or supplier is one of the more significant interface barriers.

Barrier: Supplier Is Reluctant to Share Information on Costs or Processes

Solution: Create a supplier ombudsman. Honda of America Manufacturing has supplier ombudsmen who deal with the "soft side" of the business—primarily human resource issues not usually associated with cost, quality, or delivery. Because the supplier ombudsman is not directly involved in sourcing contract negotiations, suppliers are often much more willing to talk openly and honestly with the ombudsman, who can then act as a liaison between the two companies. One ombudsman emphasized that it takes time to build trust with suppliers, and trust building varies by supplier. If a supplier approaches the ombudsman with a problem that is the result of poor communication or misunderstanding between Honda and the supplier, the ombudsman communicates the supplier's perspective to Honda and maintains as much confidentiality as possible. Over time, suppliers come to trust the ombudsman and appear to be more willing to share proprietary information with the company.

Barrier: Confidentiality Inhibits Information Sharing

Solution: Establish confidentiality agreements. Perhaps one of the biggest challenges in developing suppliers is sharing confidential information, especially when dealing with high-tech suppliers. Thus, many companies require nondisclosure or exclusivity agreements (e.g., the supplier provides a specific product to only one buyer) in development efforts, especially when dealing with technologically advanced products that contribute significantly to the buyer's competitiveness. However, nondisclosure agreements can benefit both parties. Ethical behavior on the part of the buyer will also support more open sharing of information with suppliers.

Barrier: Supplier Does Not Trust the Buying Organization

Solution: Spell it out. The driving forces behind kaizen events at Varity Perkins indicate that the company will not run an event without a properly executed written agreement between the parties. Although some supply management personnel at Varity Perkins prefer a "gentlemen's agreement," kaizen leaders believe the only way to gain a supplier's trust is to have the terms specifically written out and signed, especially when conducting the initial supplier development event at a supplier. In one instance, it took Varity Perkins eight months to convince a supplier to consider a kaizen workshop because the supplier felt that a similar event with a different company previously failed to yield any improvements. The trust problem was compounded further because of Varity Perkins' previous reputation for arm's-length relationships with suppliers, manifested by frequent switching of suppliers based solely on price. The company has moved aggressively to reverse this perception by implementing and publicizing a new supply management philosophy emphasizing collaborative relationships with its suppliers.

Barrier: Organizational Cultures Are Poorly Aligned

Solution: Adapt a new approach to local conditions. When setting up its U.S. auto assembly plant in South Carolina, BMW quickly realized it would have to change its supplier development approach to conform to the North American supply market. BMW uses a process consulting approach to supplier development in Germany, which involves analyzing suppliers' processes and telling them what is wrong. This approach works well in a mature buyer-supplier relationship, where the supplier intuitively understands what the customer wants because the parties have worked together over time. In the United States, however, it became obvious that a very different approach was required because those long-term relationships simply did not exist to the same extent.

When BMW started U.S. production, its local suppliers frequently had difficulty understanding what was required in terms of quality and continuous improvement, often resulting in strained relationships. Consequently, BMW spent a great deal of time explaining and communicating its performance expectations to suppliers. Eventually, BMW published a *Supplier Partnership Manual* that clearly delineated supplier responsibilities, as well as its own expectations. The company also held supplier seminars to present its "Roadmap to Quality." These efforts have helped align buyer-supplier expectations and create a shared culture toward improvement.

Barrier: Not Enough Inducements to Participate Are Provided to the Supplier

Solution: Designed-in motivation. Although Solectron is now generally able to offer large order volumes to suppliers, that was not always the case. To gain supplier cooperation in the low-volume years, Solectron emphasized that a supplier's products could become designed into its products and thus have a greater potential for future business.

Solution: Financial incentives. Hyundai Motor Company uses financial incentives as one motivational tool for supplier improvement. The company rates supplier performance from 1 (highest) to 4 (lowest). Class 1 suppliers receive cash immediately on their invoices; Class 2 suppliers receive payment in 30 days; Class 3 suppliers receive payment in 60 days; and Class 4 suppliers receive no new business. Because all suppliers know how Hyundai evaluates their performance, they can take the steps necessary to achieve higher levels of performance.

Supplier-Specific Barriers

Just as buyers sometimes fail to recognize the potential benefits accruing from supplier development, a lack of recognition by targeted suppliers may also keep their top management from fully committing to the joint effort. This lack of commitment may result in a failure to implement improvement ideas or to provide the technical and human resources necessary to support the development process. In addition, appropriate supplier follow-up may not take place once the development project has been completed, and the supplier's performance may revert back to its previous level.

Barrier: Lack of Commitment on the Part of Supplier's Management

Solution: Implement after commitment. Deere & Company's supplier development managers state that they will not engage in a supplier development project with a supplier unless the supplier's management demonstrates its full commitment to the process. This involves a joint examination of the proposed improvement project and determination of the potential costs and benefits. To do so, a supply base manager from Deere arranges an initial contact meeting with the supplier's top local management to obtain its commitment and involvement. To secure this, Deere's supplier development engineers educate the supplier's management about the scope and impact of the desired improvement efforts. Once the supplier's senior management agrees in principle to participate, the supplier development engineer conducts process mapping, establishes the base case situation, and delineates the expected benefits hand in hand with corresponding supplier personnel. Once Deere and the supplier agree to the goals and objectives of the intended project, the next step is to determine how to fairly share the costs and benefits. Deere typically allows the supplier to recover up front any capital-related costs required to implement the project and then splits the resulting savings 50/50 with the supplier, generally through a price decrease on future volume. By equitably sharing the resulting savings with the supplier, the supplier is more willing to engage in future development projects. In addition, success stories are shared with other possible supplier development targets to demonstrate the viability of the development process.

Barrier: Supplier's Management Agrees to Improvements but Fails to Implement the Proposals

Solution: Supplier champions. JCI Corporation, a first-tier supplier to the automotive industry, has instituted a Supplier Champions Program (SCP) designed to ensure suppliers are proficient in areas that are important to JCI's customers. The program was initiated because many of the suppliers that had attended JCI's training sessions failed to implement the tools and techniques that JCI provided. The SCP identifies what supplier personnel need to implement after they return from training. The program designates a Supplier Champion, a key supplier employee who understands JCI's expectations and demonstrates a high level of competence and credibility. The certification process requires that the Supplier Champion submit those actions to JCI that the supplier has identified for improvement. Such actions might include process mapping, failure mode effects analysis, quality control planning, best-practices benchmarking, and process auditing.

Barrier: Supplier Lacks Engineering Resources to Implement Solutions

Solution: Direct support. Honda of America Manufacturing has invested a significant amount of resources in its supplier support infrastructure. Of the more than 300 people then in Honda's supply management department, 50 were supplier development engineers who worked exclusively with suppliers. In one case, a small supplier did not have the capacity to keep up with requested volume, resulting in quality deterioration. Honda stationed four of its personnel at the supplier for 10 months at no charge, with additional services offered on an as-needed basis. As a result, the supplier improved its performance and now is a well-established Honda supplier.

Barrier: Supplier Lacks Required Information Systems

Solution: Direct electronic data interchange (EDI) support. At NCR Corporation, a manufacturer of ATMs, managers noted that access to timely and accurate information is critical to decision making and ultimately to improved performance. An important focus of NCR's supplier development program has been to get its suppliers to invest in EDI. NCR also provides direct assistance to those suppliers producing lower-level components that do not have sufficient resources to get online. In addition, NCR provides training for suppliers and recommendations on hardware and software purchases.

Barrier: Suppliers Are Not Convinced Development Will Provide Benefits to Them

Solution: Let suppliers know where they stand. Varity Perkins revamped its supplier evaluation system to show suppliers areas of potential improvement. Previously, the company sent a quarterly report to suppliers assessing quality, delivery, and price competitiveness performance. Perkins did not use the data in any manner, and as a result, suppliers did not take the assessments seriously. When revamping the system, the measures were changed to capture the impact of supplier performance on daily operations.

Varity Perkins measured supplier delivery performance using a weekly time bucket, and on-time performance averaged 90 to 95 percent. With a daily time bucket, on-time performance dropped to 26 percent on time. Since the daily measure was implemented, on-time delivery has improved to 90 percent. The supplier's history, its performance relative to Varity's other suppliers, and its deviation from the mean in each evaluated area all appear on the modified report. The report also uses more graphics to make the data more meaningful.

This measurement system has become the foundation for the company's supplier development program. By allowing suppliers to view their performance relative to competitors' performance, the company expects that suppliers will see the potential benefits of participating in supplier development activities as discussed earlier in the chapter.

Barrier: Supplier Lacks Employee Skill Base to Implement Solutions

Solution: Establish training centers. JCI Corporation realized that some suppliers, particularly smaller ones, lacked the internal skills required to implement improvement ideas. With this in mind, JCI built a facility dedicated to providing training to internal stakeholders, suppliers, and customers. Likewise, Hyundai also established a domestic training center to provide supplier personnel with training in key performance areas, such as specialized welding. The suppliers and Hyundai share this cost. The South Korean government also supports this training center by providing tax benefits for building costs and making the joint training costs tax deductible.

Solution: Provide human resource support. Hyundai Corporation recognizes that smaller suppliers with limited resources cannot consistently recruit and retain highly skilled engineers and other critical employees. Therefore, the majority of Hyundai's improvement efforts focus on smaller suppliers. Hyundai selects engineers from its own shops to spend time at supplier facilities. The engineers are co-located with their supplier counterparts, performing time/motion studies, teaching layout design, and improving productivity. Suppliers are consistently encouraged to learn, apply, and eventually teach the transferred knowledge to other internal stakeholders and second-tier suppliers, a train-the-trainer approach.

Lessons Learned from Supplier Development

An underlying theme from these examples is that many of the barriers to supplier development are interrelated. It appears that, as companies work toward resolving one barrier, they make concurrent progress toward resolving others. Therefore, we can discern several lessons from studying supplier development successes and failures.

1. *Managerial attitude is a common and difficult barrier to overcome.* A supply management executive at Honda of America Manufacturing noted that, although quality problems always have a solution, the attitudes of supplier management must be right before a problem can be truly resolved. Suppliers are sometimes not willing to accept outside help in the form of supplier development, either because they are too proud to accept help or because they do not see the value in improving quality or delivery performance. Management attitudes significantly affect the success of supplier development efforts. Oftentimes, suppliers feel that

the resources required for improvement come at the expense of other critical business needs. The savings must be real and readily achievable to get the supplier to sign on.

2. *Realizing a competitive advantage from the supply chain requires a strategic orientation toward supply chain management and the alignment of supply management objectives with business unit goals.* Supplier development plays a major role in helping to create sustainable competitive advantage along with aligning supply management and organizational goals. A strong supply management mission statement helps promote this strategic emphasis and alignment. Consider the following supply management mission statement from a European auto parts manufacturer: "We are committed to procure goods and services in a way that delivers our aims and objectives of becoming the most successful auto parts business in the world."

   The company pursues this mission through: (1) development of a world-class supplier base; (2) obtaining the highest-quality, most cost-effective goods and services in a timely manner; and (3) establishing long-term relationships with suppliers that strive for continuous improvement in all areas.

3. *Relationship management is critical to supplier development success.* Buyers can strengthen relationships with suppliers through focused supplier development activities. Besides developing mutual trust, the participants within a supply chain can begin to truly understand each other's needs and requirements, thereby making the entire supply chain more robust, agile, and competitive. Ideally, supplier development will lead to the recognition that there is a strong co-destiny between buyer and supplier. Successful supplier development requires a strong, collaborative relationship and mutual commitment between the parties.

Pursuing supplier development activities directly with suppliers is neither quick nor easy. It requires mutual vision, commitment, open communication, and equitable sharing of costs and benefits to work effectively. The long-term objective, of course, is to transform suppliers in such a way that continuous improvement becomes an integral part of each supplier's culture and DNA. Such joint accomplishments are achieved longitudinally and only by those companies that are patient and tenacious enough to make supplier development an important part of their supplier management processes.

Managing Supply Base Risk

With the growing complexity of managing worldwide supply chains, coupled with significant pressures to reduce cost at the firm level, supply managers must learn to manage the inherent risks of global sourcing effectively and efficiently.[14] The question of supply chain risk management is twofold: (1) What are the common sources of risk? and (2) How can they be mitigated and/or managed effectively? For the supply manager, all risks must be evaluated relative to their cost exposure and probability of occurrence.

Risk is inherent in all sourcing decisions, especially those concerning wide-ranging global supply chains. Supply chain risk, complexity, and uncertainty increase exponentially when sourcing from suppliers in foreign countries, especially those located in emerging markets, for example, third world or newly industrialized countries. There is, however, no "magic list" of all the various sources of risk that must be managed in each supply base. Every sourcing decision will be different and must be carefully evaluated regarding its own particular situation. The supply manager must consider where his/her organization's supply chain might be vulnerable and evaluate what options are available to address or mitigate those vulnerabilities.

Note that risk and uncertainty are not synonyms for one another. Uncertainty is related to not being able to accurately anticipate or predict future events and market conditions, whereas risk is concerned with how uncertainty will negatively impact the organization and its economic, sustainability, and social responsibility performance.

The buying organization intent on minimizing and/or mitigating its risk exposure must speak to several considerations. The bottom line is that the buyer should perform his/her "due diligence" before a risk event occurs, not afterward. One only has to recall BP's ongoing issues from its 2010 oil platform accident in the Gulf of Mexico to realize how events can negatively impact organizational profitability and public relations. However, once a risk event has actually taken place, it is usually too late to address it effectively; reactive damage control and crisis management then become the norm. Exhibit 9.10 outlines important questions that can help to guide the supply manager's risk assessment activities.

Merely ignoring supply base risk or not preparing for it proactively will dramatically increase the potential, likelihood, and negative impact of future economic losses and/ or operational disruptions. Experience tells us that risk recovery is very expensive in terms of time, effort, and money consumed in the process. Additional qualitative factors need to be considered and may include: negative public relations and loss of customer confidence, resulting in lost sales and reduced profitability. For example, recent use of cadmium plating, a known carcinogen, by various Chinese suppliers of children's jewelry to U.S. retailers created substantial problems for Walmart and others. However, there are substantial paybacks for those organizations that learn to conduct risk management well. Effective supply chain risk management can actually result in a competitive advantage vis-à-vis competitors.

Supply base risk can be grouped into several general categories that are summarized in Exhibit 9.11. The first is **political risk**. Political risk consists of such factors as: country stability, regional stability, political and governmental stability, levels of official corruption,

Exhibit 9.10	Supply Chain Risk Management Questions

- Where is the organization vulnerable to potential risk?
- Why is the organization vulnerable?
- How will this risk affect the organization if it happens?
- How will this risk affect the organization's customers? Suppliers? Stakeholders?
- What are the causes of the risk?
- What should the organization do if, and when, the risk occurs?

Exhibit 9.11	General Categories of Risk

- Political risk
- Market risk
- Sourcing risk
- Financial risk
- Supplier company risk

dissimilarities regarding contract law and intellectual property rights, elections, military actions, civil disturbances, terrorism, foreign trade balance issues, and customs duties and tariffs.

Regional political risk can affect country political risk, even if the buyer is conducting business with a supplier located in a relatively stable country but in an unstable region. A prime example here is the potentially disruptive activities and unpredictability of North Korea located alongside South Korea. Likewise, political elections, coup d'etats, wars, and civil disturbances can all negatively affect the buyer's ability to maintain supply continuity. For example, if the buyer had a key parts supplier located in either Thailand or Greece during 2010, it is conceivable that the flow of those sourced parts would be disrupted because of rioting.

There are also different types of legal systems that will affect the level of supply chain risk, such as English common law, the Napoleonic Code, and Islamic law. Differences between these legal systems demonstrate disparate perspectives on intellectual property rights, contract law, agency law, and jurisprudence systems. Unfavorable trade balances between countries can negatively influence trade or raise costs through imposition of retaliatory duties and tariffs, an inability to repatriate profits, and dealing with increasingly onerous administrative rules governing importing and exporting activities. There is a burgeoning growth of a "new nationalism," characterized by foreign governments reasserting themselves into various facets of life and commerce, which could severely restrict or limit an organization's ability to import and/or export goods.

The second major source of supply base risk deals with **market risk**. One of the issues with which a buyer must be concerned would be the number of buyers that are competing for the same goods or source of supply. In addition, a buyer must be prepared to deal with increasingly shorter product life cycles, which will require the supplier to attempt to recover its specific investments in plant and equipment, technology, production capacity, and capability even more quickly. There is also the threat of emerging, often disruptive, technologies that can affect contract length. A buyer could easily be locked into an existing technology whereas its competitors have access to newer, more efficient, technologies. A prime example here is the level and rate of technological change in the smart phone and tablet industry. Lastly, the buyer can face significant risk in trying to protect or maintain its trade secrets and intellectual properties from misuse or misappropriation by suppliers, particularly those located overseas. Loss of proprietary information can cause a buyer to lose its competitive advantage or even potentially create a new competitor.

A third general area of supply base risk can best be described as **sourcing risk**. For global supply chains, there is a strong correlation between longer supply pipelines and greater exposure to risk. The buyer must determine the potential for supply disruption in these extensive supply chains and create a supply network that would allow some redundancy and flexibility whenever disruptions occur. The level of supplier competition in the supply market will also determine the level of risk exposure. When there are fewer suppliers or significant switching costs, there is a greater risk of being held hostage by a supplier who understands the difficulty or cost that the buyer would incur if it decided to change suppliers. The longer and more complex the supply chain, the more difficult it is to effectively coordinate inventories and forecasts between supply chain members. In a global supply chain, there are also issues with language, communication, and time differences. Even speaking the same language from different cultural backgrounds and perspectives can be challenging. For example, what does "a.s.a.p." mean to an Asian supplier as compared to a North American buyer? Having a common supplier shared with a buyer's direct competitors can also cause issues of limited access to new technology and capacity, as well as not being considered a preferred customer when supplies get tight.

The fourth area of supply base risk is **financial risk**. When shipping pipelines are lengthened, inventory carrying costs become greater, for example, inventory investment, storage and warehousing costs, material handling, loss and damage, taxes, obsolescence, and lost opportunity costs. Effective management of currency exchange rates is always problematic, particularly when buying from a third world supplier. There is also the related issue of "soft" versus "hard" currencies to be considered. For all cross-border shipments, the buyer must be familiar with international terms of sale, or INCOTERMS, that determine which party (buyer or supplier) is responsible for the various costs involved in a global transaction: local freight at both the starting and ending points of the shipment, in-transit storage and warehousing, export packaging, certifications, freight forwarders' fees, insurance, customs duties and tariffs, line haul freight, and letters of credit, as well as vessel/vehicle loading and unloading. See Chapter 10 for additional information on INCOTERMS.

The final area of supply base risk occurs at the supplier company level. Here, the buyer should be concerned with the supplier's current financial stability and future viability. It is always difficult to get an accurate picture of any given supplier's financial health, particularly for those located in another country. Only relatively recently have commercial companies, such as Dun & Bradstreet and Standard and Poor's, introduced supplier and customer financial evaluation services for overseas importers and exporters.

The importance of a supplier's financial stability has been particularly acute during the recent recession. It is expensive and time-consuming for a buyer to locate, evaluate, and learn to conduct business with new or replacement suppliers overseas, particularly in emerging markets. Because of all of the complex issues and potential problems involved in global sourcing, buyers should question whether or not it is wise to procure goods internationally, particularly in the short term. The buyer also needs to evaluate the supplier firm's capabilities, such as its knowledge, skills, and abilities (KSAs), the need for performance improvement, and its ability to handle customer engineering change orders and volume fluctuations. However, a foreign supplier's own supply chain can be relatively invisible to a buyer in another country. Lastly, a supplier may be the subject of a merger or acquisition that can change the inherent nature of a buyer-supplier relationship. The supplier in question could join forces with a buyer's competitor, causing a potentially untenable situation.

How then does a prudent buyer obtain the necessary information to determine his/her supply base risk, particularly regarding foreign suppliers? In no particular order, a number of quality sources exist, including PricewaterhouseCoopers, U.S. Central Intelligence Agency, International Monetary Fund, Economist Intelligence Unit, Federation of International Trade, U.S. Library of Congress, Transparency International, International Trade Centre, Global Risk Group, Kurtzman Group, Global Corruption Report, World Bank Institute, Brookings Institute, Milken Institute, Organization for Economic Cooperation and Development, and the regional development banks, for example, Asian Development Bank, African Development Bank, and the Inter-American Development Bank. Note that some of these sources are free, whereas others are available only on a subscription basis. Which source to use will be contingent on the kind of risk being assessed and what information is required. It is important to triangulate or verify the information from several competing sources if possible.

Although many senior executives have indicated that their companies do not yet have a formal risk management process in place, more and more companies are starting to implement them.[15] There are a number of contingency management tools that can be effectively

Exhibit 9.12	Common Contingency Management Tools

- Inventory
- Multiple sourcing
- Use of third party intermediaries
- Scenario analysis
- Currency hedging
- Insurance
- Automated visibility and early warning systems

utilized at the tactical level to assist the supply manager to identify, analyze, reduce, and monitor supply base risk and are shown in Exhibit 9.12. The specific tools to be applied will be dictated by the supply manager's risk analysis. Increasingly, heavy deployment of sophisticated information technology is taking place to automate the monitoring and analysis of an organization's supply base.

Maintaining copious quantities of inventory has been the traditional method of dealing with supply base risk. As such, it is an expensive method of managing and mitigating risk. The purpose of inventory is to act as a buffer between buyer and supplier to guard against unforeseen supply disruptions, demand variability, and order cycle variability. The question is always whether the correct materials are in inventory. In many cases, inventory could actually increase the organization's risk exposure through greater inventory carrying costs and investment, obsolescence and deterioration, loss and damage (shrinkage), and excessive monitoring and handling. Inventory normally has a very short-term and reactive focus, but it can be used effectively with a new supplier until most of the start-up difficulties and problems are satisfactorily resolved.

Another traditional method of dealing with supply base risk is through the use of multiple sourcing. Having multiple suppliers for the same item may result in a more competitive marketplace and provides the buyer with alternative sources of supply in the event that a supplier is unable to fulfill its contractual performance obligations. The presence of multiple suppliers also allows upside volume potential if the buyer's needs increase dramatically, something that a single source supplier may not be able to handle. However, multiple sourcing can add quality variability to the sourced product because of the use of different materials, manufacturing techniques, and processes. It also restricts the buyer's ability to employ more complex sourcing strategies, such as supply base rationalization and optimization and early supplier design involvement. Deciding whether to use a multiple sourcing strategy to mitigate supply chain risk requires the buyer to apply a total cost of ownership approach.

Use of third party intermediaries, such as international freight forwarders, non-vessel operating common carriers, export management companies, export packers, goods surveyors, customs brokers, and export trading companies, can also help the buyer minimize his/her supply base risk. In many instances, the buying organization may not possess the requisite internal expertise and/or experience to effectively manage import transactions. Therefore, a third party intermediary may be required to supplement or replace the skills and abilities within the buying organization.

Scenario analysis in business dates back to its use by Royal Dutch/Shell prior to the Arab oil crises of the 1970s. This established technique allows a buying organization to react more quickly when supply chain risk events occur by already having previously prepared plans and proposed responses in place in advance of the actual risk event. It is sometimes commonly referred to as "what if" planning or "rehearsing the future." Although scenario planning is technically not considered a forecasting technique, it does attempt to explore and prepare for possible future scenarios that may have a significant negative impact on the costs and operations of an organization. Once a risk scenario is identified and vetted, using various sources of information as described earlier, contingency plans are created, reviewed, and approved by top management in the event that the risk event may actually occur.

In one sense, scenario planning is a form of brainstorming that requires managers to identify and consider the likelihood and impact of potential supply chain risk events and then create appropriate responses without the attendant time pressures, negative public perceptions, and "heat of battle" emotions that would likely exist without being adequately prepared beforehand, such as those conditions that worldwide automakers faced following the earthquake and resultant tsunami that idled much of the auto electronics manufacturer facilities in Japan during 2011. However, one of the criticisms of scenario planning is that, once the possible responses to a given scenario have been formulated, they are filed away until needed. However, these plans should be reevaluated periodically as the previous market conditions and environmental circumstances may have changed substantially since they were considered and developed. Exhibit 9.13 summarizes the steps involved in performing a scenario analysis.

Scenario analysis begins with the identification of a specific issue or situation, which, if encountered, would constitute a real-world challenge to the organization. Additionally, management needs to determine who in the organization would be impacted by the decision and how they might be affected. Secondly, to determine possible future ramifications and related activities that might be required, the baseline case must be established. During this phase, the organization should identify the relevant driving forces and constraints underlying the scenario under evaluation.

Next, the organization should classify these potential risk scenarios as to their severity and likely disruptive impact on operations. In this classification process, different possible responses to the scenario should be determined and evaluated as to their likely effectiveness and appropriateness to the situation. To be accepted by organizational decision makers, the risk scenarios being evaluated must be understandable, feasible, and internally consistent. These risk scenarios must also be evaluated, analyzed, and interpreted within the context of the difficulties that would have to be addressed and the operational decisions that would have to be made by management should they be encountered.

Once a risk scenario has been classified and analyzed, the organization's managers need to create viable working strategies and plans that would allow them (or their

Exhibit 9.13	Steps in Performing a Scenario Analysis

- Identification of a specific issue or situation that would negatively impact the organization
- Consideration of stakeholders impacted should a risk scenario occur
- Establishment of base line conditions
- Classification and analysis of potential risk scenarios as to severity and disruptive impact
- Creation of viable working strategies and plans to allow for quick response
- Identification and monitoring of key risk event "triggers" on an ongoing basis
- Periodic review of risk scenarios and corresponding contingency plans

successors) to respond quickly in the event that a specific risk scenario should actually come about. This way, the organization does not have to start from scratch on the fly under less-than-ideal working conditions, tight time constraints, and intense public scrutiny. Lastly, after appropriate contingency plans have been developed and thoroughly vetted, scenario planners must identify and implement those key risk event "triggers" that can be monitored on an ongoing basis and would act as an early warning system to detect when the risk event is likely to be encountered. Additionally, the organization should periodically review its risk scenarios and their corresponding contingency plans to re-verify their appropriateness and viability as the environmental and marketplace conditions may have changed since the risk scenarios were first identified and corresponding contingency plans prepared.

One major source of supply base risk stems from currency-related issues in global sourcing. The relative value of currencies used in foreign trade can fluctuate dramatically with other currencies, thereby changing the underlying cost structure and expected profitability of a long-term procurement arrangement. A common tool to address such risk is **currency hedging**, also known as managing transaction exposure. In essence, currency hedging protects the dollar value of a future foreign currency cash flow. The prime reason for hedging is to protect the buyer against major swings in the value of a future purchase. This is a highly technical process that should be closely coordinated with the buying organization's treasury department and international banking institutions.

The initial choice to be made in setting a currency hedge is to decide in which currency that the transaction will be valued, the buyer's home currency, the supplier's home currency, or a third country's currency. If the buyer's currency is utilized, the supplier bears the currency risk and is likely to build in additional contingency costs to cover its unknown risk. If the supplier's currency is selected, then the buyer accepts the currency risk and needs to take steps to ensure that it is protected should currency exchange rates turn unfavorable. Future contracts and forward exchange contracts can be utilized effectively to minimize currency exchange risk. See Chapter 10 for additional discussion of futures and forward exchange contracts.

Currency options, although expensive, can also be utilized to minimize the negative impact of shifts in currency exchange rates. Essentially, options are the equivalent to remaining unhedged, for example, retaining the currency risk, with the buyer firm purchasing an insurance policy to protect itself against unfavorable future exchange rate fluctuations. Nothing happens unless the organization exercises a currency option to purchase the currency in the future. However, the buyer is encouraged not to engage in currency hedging activities unless he/she has significant experience. It is usually prudent to call in currency experts to deal with futures contracts, forward exchange contracts, and currency hedging. One misstep on the part of an inexperienced buyer can result in significant losses not directly related to the actual purchase agreement itself.

Nearly every international shipment of merchandise requires insurance coverage with few exceptions. The cost of risk elimination is the cost of the insurance premium itself. Adequate insurance coverage is important in that it is a matter of *when* a loss occurs, not *if* a loss occurs in an international transaction. Note that the sole purpose of insurance in this sense is to redistribute economic loss and minimize risk by managing the probabilities of a loss. Goods in international trade are generally subjected to far greater risk of loss and damage exposure because of longer transportation pipelines and a greater number of handlings. Oftentimes, insufficient insurance coverage is discovered only after a loss actually occurs, because of the complexity of insurance and shipping terms for international movement of goods.

Sometimes, not every loss is fully covered or sometimes not even at all. Some losses are explicitly excluded from coverage unless a supplementary insurance rider is purchased for an additional premium. For example, certain risks, such as those arising from war, piracy, and losses attributable to delays in transit, are generally not covered by standard insurance policies. In addition, premiums for international shipments can change significantly on short notice because of rapidly changing risk conditions. The buyer needs to pay particular attention to the negotiated INCOTERMS, as discussed in Chapter 10, as to which party pays the premium for insurance coverage. Even if insurance is provided by the supplier, it generally only represents the minimum level of insurance coverage and serves more to protect the supplier's interests as opposed to the buyer's interests. If the buyer wants other risks to be covered by insurance, over and above the minimum amounts, he/she will need to ensure that the necessary supplementary policy riders are included and premiums paid. Note that international carriers generally offer only minimal insurance coverage under various international liability conventions.

Global **supply chain risk management** (SCRM) can be defined as how supply chain members communicate and collaborate regarding sources of risk, utilizing risk management tools to mitigate and minimize risk and uncertainty across the supply chain. SCRM is a systems approach that helps the organization to identify, assess, and develop appropriate risk responses designed to avoid or minimize potential disruptions to operations. In a 2008 study, Kinaxis discussed the capabilities required to successfully enable supply chain risk management.[16] The first SCRM capability is visibility, which allows an organization to recognize and assess risk across the supply chain. Therefore, SCRM must be capable of integrating with and deploying analytics garnered from a variety of ERP systems. The second SCRM capability is an event recognition and early warning system that will allow the organization to react more effectively during the early stages of an unfolding risk event. Thirdly, a SCRM system must contain a broad mix of real-time supply chain analytics so that the risk event can be better understood for decision making purposes. SCRM tools must also be capable of simulating models of risk events, suggesting risk mitigation strategies, and evaluating different risk responses. As risk response teams may be located in disparate locations across the globe, SCRM needs to provide the capability of collaborating with the right personnel across time and distance. Lastly, SCRM tools must be capable of critically evaluating various competing scenario responses to determine which approach best addresses the problem. Exhibit 9.14 summarizes the capabilities of an effective SCRM system.

The International Organization for Standardization has developed a risk management standard, ISO 31000:2009, which is intended to assist all types of organizations in managing their risk management efforts more effectively. "ISO 31000 provides principles, a framework and a process for managing any form of risk in a transparent, systematic and credible manner within any scope or context. It recommends that organizations develop,

Exhibit 9.14	Supply Chain Risk Management System Capabilities

- Real-time visibility of the supply chain
- Event recognition and early warning of a risk event
- Broad collection of real-time supply chain analytics
- Simulation models of risk events suggesting risk mitigation strategies and evaluating different risk responses

implement and continuously improve a risk management framework as an integral part of their management system."[17] Although not intended for use as a certification standard, ISO 31000:2009 provides benchmarking information useful for conducting supplier risk audits, as well as for internal use.

Managing Sustainability in the Supply Base

Greater numbers of buying organizations now recognize the importance of managing **sustainability** throughout the supply chain. Sustainability does not only reflect the importance of strategic environmental practices of an organization's suppliers but also the management of **social responsibility** in the supply base as well. To reflect this growing trend, the Institute for Supply Management (ISM) published its *ISM Principles of Sustainability and Social Responsibility with a Guide to Adoption and Implementation* in 2008. According to Paul Novak, then chief executive officer of ISM, this document is designed to provide "direction to supply professionals on how their companies and suppliers can develop and integrate sustainability and social responsibility practices and strategies into the business and the supply chain."[18]

In addition, a study by A. T. Kearney for the Carbon Disclosure Project indicates "that companies that demonstrated a true commitment to sustainability over the course of the recession appear to have outperformed their industry peers in the financial markets."[19] In this study, findings indicate that the financial markets may have rewarded truly sustainability-focused companies because they concentrated on long-term issues, provided strong corporate governance, engaged in sound risk management activities, and demonstrated investment in carbon emissions reduction. ISO 26000:2010 is another recent standard published by the International Organization for Standardization that is intended to assist organizations in pursuing higher levels of social responsibility. Like ISO 31000:2009, ISO 26000:2010 is not a certification standard; it is a set of voluntary guidelines for developing, implementing, and improving an organization's social responsibility initiatives.

According to ISM, sustainability is defined as "the ability to meet current needs without hindering the ability to meet the needs of future generations in terms of economic, environmental, and social challenges."[20] The organization also defines social responsibility as "a framework of measurable corporate policies and procedures and resulting behavior designed to benefit the workplace and, by extension, the individual, the organization and the community in the following areas: community, diversity and inclusiveness-supply base, diversity and inclusiveness-workforce, environment, ethics, financial responsibility, human rights, health and safety, and sustainability."[21] In its preamble, ISM expresses its belief that, because of their distinctive position within global supply chains, supply management professionals can be strategic contributors in developing and implementing sustainability and social responsibility initiatives. ISM also indicates that "[t]he development and implementation of metrics and performance criteria is important to the success of sustainability and social responsibility programs."[22] To that end, ISM maintains a series of sustainability and social responsibility metrics on its website at www.ism.ws/sr.

Supply managers are increasingly becoming involved in a wide variety of sustainable and environmental activities and practices in their supply chains. These include material-related, climate and energy, procurement-specific, and transportation and logistics activities and practices, as well as related metrics and measures.[23]

Material-related activities include the procurement of more environment-friendly materials replacing less "green" ones. Overall reduction in material usage and disposal can be accomplished through engineering design changes and reuse and recycle programs.

Material-related practices also concentrate on appropriate disposition activities for scrap, obsolete materials, and unused capital equipment.

Climate and energy activities center on conserving or reducing energy consumption, as well as reducing harmful atmospheric emissions, while procurement-specific activities seek to purchase environmentally-friendly packaging, materials, and components, including consideration of the methods and processes by which they are produced. Transportation and logistics activities focus on such sustainable practices as packaging, product, and vehicle tare weight reduction, improved routing of vehicles, reduced vehicle idling, vehicle fuel mileage improvements, and vehicle aerodynamics.

Supply managers can develop and include sustainable metrics and measurements into their supply contracts by incorporating appropriate contractual terms addressing these issues. In addition, the buying organization can include sustainability- and social responsibility-related goals and objectives in supply managers' individual performance appraisals. Tools to assist these activities include product life cycle analysis and environmental compliance auditing. Supply managers can also require ISO 14000 experience and/or compliance when identifying and selecting new suppliers, as well as encouraging or requiring existing suppliers to obtain ISO 14000 certification or closely follow its principles. Refer to Chapter 8 for a more detailed discussion of ISO 14000.

Sourcing Snapshot

Ford's Blueprint for Sustainability

Global automobile manufacturer and assembler Ford Motor Company has implemented its comprehensive *Blueprint for Sustainability* to guide its employees and suppliers in promoting and maintaining sustainability-related programs and activities over the near-, mid-, and long-term. For example, one of Ford's major sustainability goals is to reduce CO_2 emissions from U.S. and European new vehicles by 30 percent by 2020, using 2006 as the baseline case. In addition, it has accelerated development in battery-powered electric vehicles, committed the company to create new vehicles that will be best-in-class or among best-in-class in fuel economy, and introduced new engine technologies, such as EcoBoost™, which utilizes engine turbocharging to achieve 20 percent better fuel economy, 15 percent lower CO_2 emissions, and greater horsepower when compared to larger sized engines.

In addition to sustainability, Ford's *Blueprint for Sustainability* also addresses a variety of mobility, human rights, and vehicle safety issues. For example, Ford has provided substantial effort focused on human rights through its Aligned Business Framework program. "The primary focus of [its] supply chain human rights program is building capability among [its] suppliers to responsibly manage working conditions, including legal requirements and Ford expectations." It has also joined the United Nations Global Compact, which directs companies to align their operations and strategies with ten widely accepted quality of life principles in human rights, labor, the environment, and reduction of corruption.

Sources: Blueprint for Sustainability: Our Future Works (2009), Dearborn, MI: Ford Motor Company. "Ford Aims to Help Reduce the Carbon Footprint of Its Global Supply Chain" (2010). Retrieved from http://www.sdc.com/online/printer.jsp?id=12419

Good Practice Example	*Sonoco Builds a Reputation of Excellence in Sustainability*

Recognizing the growing importance of sustainability, Sonoco, a global leader in sustainable packaging, has established a Corporate Sustainability Council, reporting directly to Harris De-Loach, Jr., the chairman, president, and chief executive officer, who describes the substance of Sonoco's strategic intent in this way: "By balancing and integrating environmental stewardship, social responsibility and economic performance within our business strategy and culture, Sonoco is becoming more competitive and better prepared to meet the challenges of the future." According to the company's *2009 Sustainability Annual Report,* "The purpose of the Sonoco Corporate Sustainability Council is to provide oversight, guidance and direction on social, community and environmental issues that have potential impact on the reputation and long-term economic viability of the Company and our stakeholders." The Sonoco approach can best be described as a triple bottom line approach, consisting of a company's economic, environmental, and social performance. The Sustainability Council, chaired by a senior vice president and consisting of nine additional vice presidents and directors, provides periodic sustainability performance reports to the company's board of directors. These reports provide information about Sonoco's progress toward its corporate goals in environmental, social, and economic performance.

Some of the initiatives that Sonoco has undertaken include reduction in greenhouse gas emissions, energy usage, air emissions, water consumption, and waste in landfills. In setting up its sustainability program, Sonoco used 2008 as a base year. For example, the company has committed to reducing its greenhouse gas emissions by 15 percent through 2013. In addition, the company seeks to reduce energy usage at several of its recycled paperboard mills through increased capital investment. Also underway is the conversion of process steam production to include renewable and/or lower carbon-intensive fuel sources. It has extended its domestic North American sustainability goals to include its foreign manufacturing operations as well.

In recognition of Sonoco's ongoing sustainability efforts, it was named #27 on *Corporate Responsibility Office* magazine's 2009 "100 Best Corporate Citizens List." This list included only one other packaging manufacturing company. It has also been included on the *Dow Jones Sustainability World Index* that tracks world-class corporations in their sustainability efforts, one of only three packaging companies so designated.

As a supplier, Sonoco has directed its packaging designers, engineers, and material scientists to address its customers' performance, cost, and sustainability requirements as well. To achieve these ends, it has developed a proprietary sustainability packaging design software program intended to improve product recyclability by reducing packaging weight, eliminating materials, reducing packaging structure thickness, and simplifying package designs. Sonoco has also worked closely with its customer base to improve their package recovery and recyclability processes, as well as to reduce the generation of landfill waste from their manufacturing, distribution, and retail facilities. It has also achieved ISO 14001 certification at several of its European facilities. Corporate spending with women- and minority-owned suppliers increased 14 percent in 2009.

Sources: Sonoco 2009 Sustainability Annual Report (2009), Hartsville, SC: Sonoco Corporate Headquarters. Retrieved from http://www.sonoco.com/sustainability; Ashenbaum, B. (2008), "Green Corporate Strategies: Issues and Implementation from the Supply Management Perspective," *Critical Issues Report,* Tempe, AZ: CAPS Research. Retrieved from http://www.capsresearch.org

CONCLUSION

Effectively managing and improving supplier performance is a primary supply management and business function. Effective supplier management and development constitute the new model of supply management. No longer does a buyer simply purchase parts from the lowest-priced source. The activities that best describe today's enlightened buyer include planning, coordinating, managing, developing, and improving performance capabilities and compliance throughout the supply base. For many items, buyers no longer just buy parts from suppliers; they manage supplier relationships and capabilities.

Therefore, supply management must carefully select and manage a proper mix of suppliers. To accomplish this, the buying organization must invest the requisite resources for effective supplier management, including a broad-based supplier performance measurement system, contracts with preferred or certified suppliers, and a wide range of supplier development tools and techniques. An effective supplier management program helps maximize the contribution received from suppliers, lowering costs, increasing quality, and developing future capabilities.

KEY TERMS

categorical system, 328

cost-based system, 328

currency hedging, 355

currency options, 355

financial risk, 352

kaizen, 344

market risk, 351

political risk, 350

risk, 333

scenario analysis, 353

social responsibility, 357

sourcing risk, 351

supplier development, 339

supplier performance index, 329

supplier performance measurement, 324

supply base rationalization and optimization, 324

supply chain risk management, 356

sustainability, 357

weighted-point system, 328

DISCUSSION QUESTIONS

1. Provide reasons why most firms do not have an adequate supplier measurement system.

2. Your manager at the medium-sized company where you work has just called you in and asked you to explain why the company should spend its limited financial resources to develop a supplier measurement system. What do you tell her?

3. Why is it critical to have a smaller supply base before committing to a supplier management and development program?

4. Discuss the advantages and disadvantages of an optimized supply base. How can a buyer overcome the disadvantages?

5. Discuss the logic behind maintaining multiple suppliers for each purchased item.

6. Discuss the logic behind maintaining a reduced number of suppliers for each item.

7. What is a full-service supplier? What are the benefits of using full-service suppliers?

8. Why is the Honda approach to supplier development and improvement not widespread among U.S. firms?

9. Many companies are now using the World Wide Web to share performance information with suppliers, thereby allowing suppliers to compare their performance to other suppliers' within the buying company's supply base. Discuss the benefits of this strategy to both buyers and suppliers.

10. Discuss the different types of supplier development and support that a firm can offer. Which are the most common? Why?

11. Research has revealed that no single approach to supplier development is effective in achieving performance goals. Rather, a mix of the carrot, stick, and hands-on approaches seems to work best. Explain why you think this is the case.

12. A common statement made in some supply management organizations is, "We can't be spending money on supplier development—we're not in business to train suppliers and do their job for them!" What type of barrier does this statement represent? How would you respond to such a statement?

13. Of the barriers to supplier development mentioned in this chapter, which ones, in your opinion, are the most difficult to overcome?

14. A Chrysler executive once made the following statement: "Only about one in five supplier development efforts are truly 100 percent successful." Why do you think this is the case? What makes supplier development such a challenging effort for the buyer? For the supplier?

15. Discuss the reasons why top-management commitment is essential to the success of supplier management and development.

16. What are the advantages of calculating a Supplier Performance Index? What are the challenges associated with developing a measurement system that uses SPI?

17. What is the role of the Q adjustment factor in the SPI calculation?

18. Describe the major sources of supply base risk. What are some of the supply chain risk management tools available to avoid or mitigate supply chain risk?

19. Describe why companies are engaging in sustainability and social responsibility practices.

ADDITIONAL READINGS

Ashenbaum, B. (2008), "'Green' Corporate Strategies: Issues and Implementation from the Supply Management Perspective," *Critical Issues Report*, Tempe, AZ: CAPS Research.

Bolstorff, P., and Rosenbaum, R. (2007), *Supply Chain Excellence: A Handbook for Dramatic Improvement Using the SCOR Model* (2nd ed.), New York: AMACOM.

Butterfield, B. (2000), "Mentoring for Advantage," *Purchasing Today*, 11(3), 14.

Davenport, T. H., and Harris, J. G. (2007), *Competing on Analytics: The New Science of Winning*, Boston: Harvard Business School Press.

David, P., and Stewart, R. (2008), "Chapter Ten: International Insurance," *International Logistics: The Management of International Trade Operations*, Mason, OH: Thomson, 207–245.

de Crombrugghe, A., and Le Coq, G. (2003), *Guide to Supplier Development: For Programmes To Be Implemented by Industrial Subcontracting and Partnership Exchanges (SPXs)*, Vienna: United Nations Industrial Development Organization.

Dunn, S. C., and Young, R. R. (2004), "Supplier Assistance Within Supplier Development Initiatives," *Journal of Supply Chain Management*, 40(3), 19–29.

Forker, L. B., Ruch, W. A., and Hershauer, J. C. (1999), "Examining Supplier Improvement Efforts from Both Sides," *Journal of Supply Chain Management*, 35(3), 40–50.

Forrest, W. (2006), "McDonald's Applies SRM Strategy to Global Technology Buy," *Purchasing*, 135(12), 16–17.

Gattiker, T. F., Tate, W., and Carter, C. R. (2008), *Supply Management's Strategic Role in Environmental Practices*, Tempe, AZ: CAPS Research.

Gordon, S. (2008), *Supplier Evaluation and Performance Excellence: A Guide to Meaningful Metrics and Successful Results*, Ft. Lauderdale, FL: J. Ross Publishing.

Handfield, R. B., Krause, D. R., Scannell, T. V., and Monczka, R. M. (2000), "Avoid the Pitfalls in Supplier Development," *Sloan Management Review*, 41(2), 37–49.

Handfield, R. B., and McCormack, K. (Eds.), (2008), *Supply Chain Risk Management: Minimizing Disruptions in Global Sourcing*, Boca Raton, FL: Auerbach Publications.

Hershauer, J. (2008), "Process Guide for Supply Management Environmental Sustainability," *Critical Issues Report*, Tempe, AZ: CAPS Research.

Humphreys, P. K., Li, W. L., and Chan, L. Y. (2004), "The Impact of Supplier Development on Buyer-Supplier Performance," *Omega: The International Journal of Management Science*, 32(2), 131–143.

ISM Principles of Sustainability and Social Responsibility with a Guide to Adoption and Implementation, (2008), Tempe, AZ: Institute for Supply Management.

Kerr, J. (2006), "The Changing Complexion of Supplier Diversity," *Supply Chain Management Review*, 10(2), 38–45.

Krause, D. R., Handfield, R. B., and Tyler, B. B. (2007), "The Relationship Between Supplier Development, Commitment, Social Capital Accumulation and Performance Improvement," *Journal of Operations Management*, 25(2), 528–545.

Krause, D. R., and Scannell, T. V. (2002), "Supplier Development Practices: Product and Service Based Industry Comparisons," *Journal of Supply Chain Management*, 38(2), 13–22.

Li, W. L., Humphreys, P., Chan, L. Y., and Kumaraswamy, M. (2003), "Predicting Purchasing Performance: The Role of Supplier Development Programs," *Journal of Materials Processing Technology*, 138(1–3), 243–249.

Liker, J. K., and Choi, T. Y. (2004), "Building Deep Supplier Relationships," *Harvard Business Review*, 83(1), 104–113.

Nelson, D., Moody, P. E., and Stegner, J. R. (2005), *The Incredible Payback: Innovative Solutions That Deliver Extraordinary Results*, New York: AMACOM.

Nix, N. W., Lusch, R. F., Zacharia, Z. G., and Bridges, W. (2007, October 27–28), "The Hand That Feeds You: What Makes Some Collaborations with Suppliers Succeed, When So Many Fail?" *Wall Street Journal*, R8.

Patterson, J. L., and Nelson, J. D. (1999), "OEM Cycle Time Reduction Through Supplier Development," *Practix: Best Practices in Purchasing and Supply Chain Management*, 2(3), 1–5.

Prokopets, L., and Tabibzadeh, R. (2006), *Supplier Relationship Management: Maximizing the Value of Your Supply Base*, Stamford, CT: Archstone Consulting.

"Q&A Performance Measurement: Why It's Important to Measure Suppliers Well," (2000), *Purchasing*, 128(7), 36–39.

Robitaille, D. (2007), *Managing Supplier-Related Processes*, Chico, CA: Paton Professional.

Rogers, P. A. (2005), "Optimising Supplier Management and Why Co-Dependency Equals Mutual Success," *Journal of Facilities Management*, 4(1), 40–50.

Sako, M. (2004), "Supplier Development at Honda, Nissan and Toyota: Comparative Case Studies of Organizational Capability Enhancement," *Industrial and Corporate Change*, 13(2), 281–308.

Sanchez-Rodriguez, C., Hemsworth, D., and Martinez-Lorente, A. R. (2005), "The Effect of Supplier Development Initiatives on Purchasing Performance: A Structural Model," *Supply Chain Management*, 10(3–4), 289–301.

Supply Chain Report 2010, (2010), London: Carbon Disclosure Project and A. T. Kearney.

Teague, P. E. (2007), "How to Improve Supplier Performance," *Purchasing*, 136(4), 31–32.

Theodorakioglou, Y., Gotzamani, K., and Tsiolvas, G. (2006), "Supplier Management and Its Relationship to Buyers' Quality Management," *Supply Chain Management*, 11(2), 148–159.

Wagner, S. M. (2006), "Supplier Development Practices: An Exploratory Study," *European Journal of Marketing*, 40(5–6), 554–571.

ENDNOTES

1. Minahan, T., and Vigoroso, M. (2002), *The Supplier Performance Measurement Benchmarking Report,* Retrieved from http://www.aberdeen.com, accessed January 2, 2008.

2. Gordon, S. R. (2008), "Best Practices to Develop Supplier Scorecards and KPIs," in *ISM 93rd Annual Supply Management Conference Proceedings*, St. Louis, MO: Institute for Supply Management.

3. Ibid.

4. Friedman, T. L. (2006), *The World Is Flat, Release 2.0*, New York: Farrar, Straus, and Giroux, 517.

5. Bhote, K. R. (1989), *Strategic Supply Management: A Blueprint for Revitalizing the Manufacturer-Supplier Partnership*, New York: AMACOM, 75–78.

6. Greenwald, J. (1992), "What Went Wrong? Everything at Once," *Time*, Retrieved from http://www.time.com/time/magazine/article/0,9171,976990-6,00.html

7. Sako, M. (2004), "Supplier Development at Honda, Nissan and Toyota: Comparative Case Studies of Organizational Capability Enhancement," *Industrial and Corporate Change*, 13(2), 281–308.

8. Lamming, R. (1993), *Beyond Partnership: Strategies for Innovation and Lean Supply*, Hertfordshire, UK: Prentice Hall International, 215–216.

9. de Crombrugghe, A., and Le Coq, G. (2003), *Guide to Supplier Development*, Vienna: United Nations Industrial Development Organization.

10. See Leenders, M. R. (1965), *Improving Purchasing Effectiveness through Supplier Development*, Boston: Harvard University Press; and Leenders, M. R., and Blenkhorn, D. L. (1988), *Reverse Marketing: The New Buyer-Supplier Relationship*, New York: Free Press.

11. Krause, D. R., and Wagner, S. M. (2008), "An Investigation of Supplier Development and Its Role in New Product Development," *Focus Study*, Tempe, AZ: CAPS Research, 6.

12. Handfield, R., Krause, D., Scannell, T., and Monczka, R. (1998), "An Empirical Investigation of Supplier Development: Reactive and Strategic Processes," *Journal of Operations Management*, 17(1), 39–58.

13. Hahn, C. K., Watts, C. A., and Kim, K. Y. (1990), "The Supplier Development Program: A Conceptual Model," *International Journal of Purchasing and Materials Management*, 26(2), 2–7.

14. Patterson, J. L. (2007), "Supply Base Risk Assessment and Contingency Planning in Emerging Markets," in *Global Issues: Supply Chain Management, Electrical Insulation Conference Proceedings*, Nashville, TN: The Electrical Manufacturing & Coil Winding Association.

15. *Heeding Lessons from Economic Downturn, Majority of Corporate Executives Report Need to Overhaul Their Approach to Risk-Management, Accenture Study Finds* (2009), Washington, DC: Accenture, Retrieved from http://newsroom.accenture.com/article_print.cfm?article_id-4848

16. *Essential Characteristics of a Supply Chain Risk Management Strategy*, (2009), Ottawa, ON: Kinaxis, Retrieved from http://www/kinaxis.com

17. *ISM Principles of Sustainability and Social Responsibility with a Guide to Adoption and Implementation*, (2008), Tempe, AZ: Institute for Supply Management, Retrieved from http://www.ism.ws.sr

18. Lazarte, M., and Tranchard, S. (2010), *The Risk Management Toolbox*, International Organization for Standardization, Retrieved from http://www.iso.org/iso/home/news_index/news_archive/news.htm?

19. *Supply Chain Report 2010*, (2010), London: Carbon Disclosure Project and A. T. Kearney, 1.

20. *ISM Principles of Sustainability and Social Responsibility with a Guide to Adoption and Implementation*, (2008), Tempe, AZ: Institute for Supply Management. Retrieved from http://www.ism.ws.sr

21. Ibid, 3.

22. Ibid, 8.

23. Gattiker, T. F., Tate, W., and Carter, C. R. (2008), *Supply Management's Strategic Role in Environmental Practices*, Tempe, AZ: CAPS Research, 10.

Worldwide Sourcing

Learning Objectives

After completing this chapter, you should be able to

- Identify the differences between international purchasing and global sourcing
- Understand the concepts of offshoring, re-shoring and nearshoring
- Understand the reasons why firms pursue worldwide sourcing
- Identify the total costs associated with worldwide sourcing
- Become familiar with the problems and obstacles hindering global sourcing efforts
- Understand the advantages of using a foreign trade zone in worldwide sourcing
- Understand the key drivers needed for successful global sourcing efforts

Chapter Outline

Honeywell: Making Global Sourcing Cost Effective and Responsive

Darin Harvey is the Vice President of Global Sourcing for Honeywell Process Solutions, a business unit of Honeywell International located in Houston, Texas. This former Florida State University supply chain graduate has held a number of supply management jobs in very different environments; from being Director of Supply Management at a high-volume producer of quality hand tools, Director of Procurement with a leading engineering and construction company for large capital industrial projects, to now directing a Honeywell business that is "low volume, high variability" for automated control systems. In his current role, Darin oversees the procurement for all items that are used directly in manufacturing or that support Honeywell's line of process solutions that competes globally for business.

The global nature extends to both the buying and selling sides of the business. Harvey's task is further complicated by the wide reach of Honeywell's automated controls. He indicates, "We have three procurement functions in our business: (1) Project specific third-party sourcing; (2) indirect purchases; and (3) direct factory material, making us one of the more complex supply chains in Honeywell."

Global project sourcing is involved in procuring third-party material and services for *Process and Automation Solutions* used in oil refineries, chemical plants, upstream/midstream oil and gas, pulp and paper plants, and so on. anywhere in the world. "We buy for these projects to support the project operations personnel and then handle the service agreements once the project is completed," said Mr. Harvey. Many of these buys have "local content" requirements in the country in which the project is being performed. "There are a myriad of local sourcing rules in many of the countries in which we participate. These rules require the procurement team to find quality local sources that meet these local content rules," says Darin. There are times when the project team will consider local, regional, or global category agreements that are negotiated within Honeywell to gain price, cost of ownership, and/or delivery advantages on these projects.

Indirect buying involves all the expenditures necessary to support the business unit's own internal projects and factories. These include a diverse set of purchases from maintenance to consultants to travel and lodging for company employees. According to Darin, "The global spend in these categories varies greatly by item and type of good or service purchased." Many of these items are country or location unique, whereas others such as travel can be leveraged much more easily on a global basis.

Factory spend is the third category and the one that is most suitable for global sourcing strategies. Mr. Harvey describes the Honeywell approach to global sourcing as a "collaborative cross functional" approach that centers on achieving the "lowest total cost of ownership" for 20 manufacturing locations worldwide.

Contracts on factory spend can be negotiated locally, regionally, or globally. Global commodity managers are usually located in one of three regions: (1) the Americas; (2) Asia Pacific; or (3) Europe and Middle East. They scan their respective regions for the best sources and then present their findings to Mr. Harvey's cross-functional team composed of himself and his leaders, the VP of Integrated Supply Chain, the VP of Quality, various factory stakeholders, and business leaders. The outcome of these deliberations is a sourcing strategy to support the factories worldwide for a wide range of commodities such as circuit boards and electronics, stampings, castings, forgings, machining, computer hardware and software, and so on.

Depending on the total cost of ownership, an item may be sourced in China for all plants. "Our evaluations also include the relative level of risk of single source, so we might, for example, opt for dual sourcing to reduce that risk by placing 50 percent of the requirements in China and 50 percent in Eastern Europe," says Darin. "Our factories are quite active in giving their input, and sometimes we can do better overall by utilizing a dual sourcing strategy," he states.

The global sourcing managers are located in each of the three major regions and their location allows them to do a good job of locating and qualifying new sources. "Nothing beats having boots on the ground to assure that we are sourcing from a highly capable supplier with a robust quality control process to ensure defects are limited and do not make it out of the supplier's facility," states Mr. Harvey. "With the concern over emerging regions' quality, we have a supplier qualification and development team that performs comprehensive assessments and development activities with current and potential suppliers," says Darin.

Global sourcing changing to be highly responsive. Honeywell's philosophy on global sourcing has changed from one focused on a "low price" to "total cost of ownership" to now evaluating "revenue or business margin" impact. "I would say, early on we focused on getting the lowest price, and then we progressed to taking a deeper look at inventory, logistics, cost of poor quality, and voice of the customer. Now we are including response time and supplier flexibility in our evaluations."

This shift from a cost focus to revenue focus involves considering the impact of the sourcing decision on lost business and/or reduced margins on that business. "If we can't ship an order because our supplier can't respond fast enough or if we lose customer business because we quote longer lead times then low cost hasn't helped us," says Mr. Harvey. One of Honeywell's biggest challenges with global sourcing is demand planning. To address this issue, Honeywell is adopting a new demand flow process focused on providing information faster and more accurately from the customer to the suppliers. "While we are in the market to order business, this software gives us information visibility similar to what Walmart has on the retail side," says Darin.

In support of this strategy, the performance metrics and evaluations of global sourcing are also changing. There are currently four major categories in the global sourcing evaluation. They include: (1) Productivity / Cost Savings; (2) Working Capital: (3) Lead time, which includes responsiveness to Honeywell requests; and (4) Quality as measured on a part per million (PPM) basis. Though cost savings still carry the heaviest weight in the evaluation, changes are evident. "Many suppliers feel they received the business because of their low price and are hesitant to upgrade talent or add people to improve processes that are required to pursue lean practices and improve their businesses," states Mr. Harvey. "We have our work cut out for us in educating and implementing these value-enhancing practices across our global supply base," stated Darin. Honeywell's goal is to continue to develop a cost-competitive and responsive global supply base. Pursuing that goal keeps Mr. Harvey's days full of interesting and exciting challenges. "I take so many trips abroad visiting our supply base and internal customers that when I take a vacation, I like it close to home!" he stated.

Source: L. Giunipero interview Darin Harvey July, 2013

Globalization—Changing Supply Strategy in a Dynamic World Economy

The opening vignette illustrates Honeywell's global view of their business and supply base and how to best manage those challenges. Globalization is dramatically changing interactions among the world's economies through increasing interdependencies. The global banking collapse of 2008 is a perfect example of how intertwined the world's major economies have become.[1] Included in several definitions of **globalization** are the terms "interdependence," "connectivity," and "integration of economies" in social, technical, and political spheres. This trend toward seamless boundaries is explored in depth by Thomas Friedman in his best seller *The World Is Flat.*[2] Information now circles the globe with such ease that 245,000 employees located in India are housed in call centers scheduling airline flights, soliciting credit card customers, and answering questions about mortgages and insurance policies.[3] Technology will also accelerate globalization. For example, mobility in social platforms crosses borders seamlessly, robotics are replacing people in jobs such as receptionists, and 3D printing will reshape production.[4]

Globalization in developing economies such as China and India represents opportunities for cost savings on the buying side and new markets on the selling side. On the selling side, more affluent consumers are demanding higher-level brands. The well-known French cosmetics firm L'Oréal failed to make a profit competing in India's low-priced shampoo market. However, when it shifted its focus and advertising strategy to the emerging middle class, with products selling for 3 to 20 times the price of those of its rivals, profits followed. The 200-million-person Indian middle class desires many offshore brands, from Tommy Hilfiger jeans to Absolut vodka.[5]

In supply management, the *cost/price* benefits associated with sourcing in developing countries are a significant motivation for remaining competitive in an increasingly global environment. Several studies have indicated that *cost/price savings* are the number one reason for global sourcing. Other important benefits realized are *availability, quality,* and (to a lesser extent) *innovation.* Once a firm establishes sourcing roots in these countries, it facilitates entry to marketing and selling opportunities. Many larger multinationals take a more global perspective by seeking to supply their worldwide operations with common sources of supply at the lowest worldwide cost, and they are developing centralized and globally coordinated supply organizations to support these efforts.

One indicator of this increased international sourcing is the large U.S. merchandise trade deficit, which according to the U.S. Bureau of Economic Analysis, totaled more than $741 billion in 2012. Meanwhile, the balance of services was positive $207 billion, leaving a total deficit in both merchandise and services of $535 billion. Much of the focus on the increasing deficit is directed toward China. The merchandise trade deficit with China in 2012 was $315 billion (over 40% of the total merchandise trade deficit). Despite the consistent trade deficits with China and persistent pressure by the US government to lower its value, the currency dropped only 25 percent from its fixed 8 yuan per dollar in January 2005 to its recent (July 2013) value of 6.15 yuan per dollar.

This pressure on forcing the Chinese to allow their currency to fluctuate in the marketplace is justified. An analysis of the top U.S. trading partners reveals that Canada leads with China second, followed by Mexico, Japan, Germany, U.K., South Korea, Brazil, Saudi Arabia, and France. The figures for total merchandise trade (exports and imports) are shown in Exhibit 10.1. The dominance of the first three partners is evident as they account for 51 percent of total U.S. merchandise trade. Two of our three largest trading partners (Canada and Mexico) are part of the North American Free Trade Agreement.

Changing Global Dynamics Create Challenges

Globalization is changing the structure of many marketplaces as global companies extend their reach into all markets. Often the acquiring firm is not based in the United States. In the agribusiness industry, China's Shuanghai International Holdings has proposed to purchase Smithfield Farms one of the U.S.'s biggest pork producers for $4.7 billion ($7.1 billion including debt). This is the largest Chinese acquisition of a U.S. company to date and prompted concerns from Congress and food safety groups.[6]

In 2011, Chinese health inspectors discovered clenbuterol—a food additive banned in China and the United States—in pork products from Shuanghui International Holdings.

Exhibit 10.1	U.S. Trading Partners, 2012

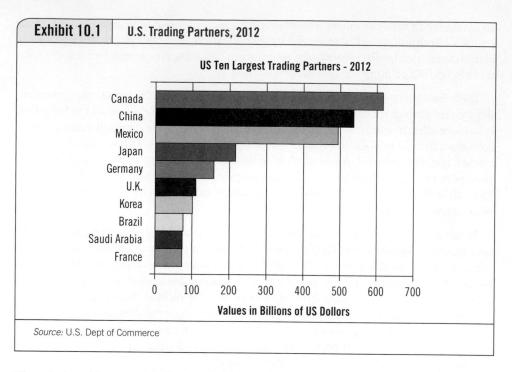

Source: U.S. Dept of Commerce

Though the additive speeds muscle growth in pigs, it can cause headaches and nausea and irregular heartbeats in humans.[7] Earlier in the year Brazil's 3G capital group in conjunction with Warren Buffett purchased H.J. Heinz an American icon.

Supply managers must remain vigilant to how globalization affects their sourcing efforts. **Outsourcing** involves contracting with independent suppliers outside the organization (domestic or foreign) to provide products or services that were performed inside the organization;whereas **offshoring** involves contracting with independent suppliers located outside geographic boundaries of the United States for these goods and services. However, trends and events in this ever evolving world of cost dynamics are also changing where supply managers position their supply base. The question that 21st century purchasers face is where in the world do I position my supply base for maximum effectiveness in supporting my organization's goals and strategies?

Driven by changing economics, quality and culture issues there has been a new term added to the supply management strategy kit called **re-shoring**. This concept is gaining favor with certain industries. For example, GE CEO Jeff Immelt has stated that offshoring is dead. He backed this up with and investment of $800 million in Appliance Park in Louisville, Kentucky and is moving some appliance manufacturing back to the U.S. from China.[8] We will talk more about this phenomena later in the Chapter.

Though some firms pursue re-shoring others have chosen to near-shore. **Nearshoring** is relocating sourcing to countries geographically closer to the United States. For example, if a firm moves sourcing of corrugated boxes from China to a source in Mexico or Brazil for shipping containers used in its North American facilities. The degree of globalization varies within organizations, therefore worldwide sourcing will be covered from the basic to the complex.

This chapter focuses on how supply managers can capture the benefits of globalization through international purchasing and global sourcing. **International purchasing** relates to a commercial purchase transaction between a buyer and a supplier located in different countries. This type of purchase is typically more complex than a domestic purchase. Organizations must contend with *lengthened lead times, increased rules and regulations, currency fluctuations, customs requirements*, and a host of other variables such as *language* and *time differences*.

Global sourcing, which differs from international purchasing in scope and complexity, involves proactively integrating and coordinating common items and materials, processes, designs, technologies, and suppliers across worldwide purchasing, engineering, and operating locations. Effectively implementing effective global sourcing requires continually assessing the proper location of the supply base. Thus effective global sourcing will require consideration of three major strategies *offshoring, re-shoring, and nearshoring*. Effective implementation of these strategies should align with and support the organizational goals.

Because of the differences between international buying and global sourcing, we will use the term **worldwide sourcing** for general discussions of the process of purchasing from other countries. We will also use the terms **foreign, offshore, or global** interchangeably when referring to suppliers in countries outside the geographic borders of the organization's home country in which they are headquartered.

This chapter contains three major sections. The first section presents an overview of worldwide sourcing, including the most common reasons why companies source worldwide. The second section identifies the areas that need to be addressed to develop a successful worldwide sourcing program. The final section presents those factors that drive successful global sourcing efforts.

Worldwide Sourcing Timeline

From a historical perspective, the oil embargo of the 1970s, coupled with shortages of other basic materials, forced supply managers to search overseas for suppliers. Many offshore producers were also becoming quality and cost leaders across a number of industries. During the mid 1970s purchasers were buying production machinery and equipment, chemicals, and mechanical and electrical components from offshore suppliers. These sourcing efforts were focused mainly on transactions with other developed nations such as Western Europe, Japan, and Canada.

During the mid-1980s, the value of the U.S. dollar increased dramatically against other currencies. U.S. imports became less expensive, and U.S. firms found it difficult to export and compete in world markets.

In 1987, the end of the Cold War led to the opening of trade with emerging markets in Russia, Eastern Europe, and China, which in turn led to the development of new markets and new sources of supply. Furthermore, import and export restrictions have been lessening, partly as a function of the General Agreements on Tariffs and Trade (GATT) agreement. GATT was originally termed the G7 and represented the world's largest economies, including those of the United States, Japan, Canada, and Western Europe. GATT gave way to the World Trade Organization (WTO), which encompasses many more nations.

The North American Free Trade Agreement, passed in 1993, has also resulted in a dramatic increase in trade among the United States, Canada, and Mexico. As previously shown, Canada and Mexico rank one and three respectively in terms of total trade with the United States. Trade talks between the United States and other countries, such as Japan and China, also reduced trade restrictions.

Sourcing Snapshot

The Global Outsourcing Phenomena—TVs to Engineers

Many news articles in the United States chastise outsourcing and the loss of domestic jobs that often accompany this phenomenon of the twenty-first century. In reality, it is really a process that illustrates globalization and extends beyond the borders of the United States as all companies, regardless of country, seek competitive advantage. Described below are two examples, one in the TV industry and the other involving automotive design centers.

Since its founding in 1910, Hitachi's overarching corporate philosophy is to contribute to society through advancing technology. However, in 2009 the company incurred the largest annual loss in history by a Japanese manufacturer. Hitachi responded to this $8.5 billion dollar loss by spinning off its consumer electronics business into a new company called Hitachi Consumer Electronics Co. The television unit of the digital products division accounted for most of the $1 billion dollar loss.

As a result, dramatic changes in the way Hitachi televisions will be sourced and built are being undertaken. These actions put Hitachi's supply mangers at the center of the strategy. The company is outsourcing more of its manufacturing and procuring key components from outside suppliers. Historically, the firm differentiated its products by using in-house production and using Hitachi-made components. Major changes are in the works to accomplish the outsourcing goal. Two major TV assembly plants in Mexico are up for sale. Both these facilities supplied the U.S. market with Hitachi TVs. An assembly plant in the Czech Republic, which supplies much of the European market, will be leased to an electronics company. Clearly, Hitachi's future strategy will depend much more on contract manufacturers coupled with component suppliers to provide its large U.S. and European markets with the latest LCD and plasma display TVs. The only market in which it will currently continue full production is its home market of Japan. Hitachi views outsourcing as a way to regain its profitability in the TV sector.

Although products and customer service activities were initial targets for outsourcing, innovation and research typically remained inside the organization. Companies are now challenging these traditional models and moving research to lower cost regions—for example, Nissan Motors. Nissan Motors recently began viewing Vietnam as a location to dramatically reduce the cost of developing cars. Although it is not uncommon to see assembly plants in low-cost countries such as Russia, Turkey, and Brazil, design and engineering centers have largely remained in United States, Germany, and Japan. As automakers seek lower costs in the design process and be more receptive to local market preferences design centers are moving to these regions. General Motors has begun designing interiors in China for Buicks it will sell in the United States. Also, according to Alan Taub, GM's director of Research and Development, locating in China has uncovered local preferences. For example, Chinese drivers want their rear seats more spacious and comfortable than U.S. consumers do, because many Chinese buyers have chauffeurs.

Nissan has 700 Vietnamese engineers located in Hanoi, designing basic auto parts such as fuel pipes and nozzles at one-tenth of the cost of doing the work in its main engineering facility in Japan. Vietnamese engineers are paid about $200 per month by the company. Other development projects are underway in India where Nissan and Renault are building an engineering center to develop a car that can be sold for less than $3000 in developing countries.

Carlos Ghosn, Nissan's president and CEO, does not believe the outsourcing trend will result in lost engineering jobs in Japan and the United States. He does feel the number of engineering jobs in the industrialized countries will grow much more slowly than in the past. The risk in outsourcing of design is the lack of experience in the new college graduates. Computer-aided design tools help, but the knowledge gap can translate into quality problems on the manufacturing floor. One strategy to close this gap is to put the design center in a country that already has an assembly plant. Outsourcing design is another indication of the globalization trend at work worldwide.

Source: Yamaguchi, Y., and Wakabayashi, D. (2009, July 10), "Hitachi to Outsource TV Manufacture," *The Wall Street Journal*, B3.
Shirouzu, N. (2008, February 7), "Engineering Jobs Become Car Makers New Export," *The Wall Street Journal*, B1, B2.

In the new millennium the impact of technology further flattened the world by making distance less relevant when contracting with offshore sources. As discussed earlier, many U.S.-based firms outsource noncritical functions to other countries and this is termed offshoring. Offshoring results when a process is moved from one country (usually a developed country) to another that has lower costs (a developing country). Early offshoring contracts were targeted to low-cost countries such as India, the Philippines, or China. When some companies had unfavorable experiences and moved the offshored operations back to the United States, the term *insourcing* was born. Meanwhile, other companies chose to locate their off-shoring efforts closer to the United States. These outsourcing contracts were termed "**nearshoring**" and included using Mexico and Central and South America as destinations. Starting in around 2011, the term **re-shoring** started to appear in business publications. Re-shoring defined as bringing offshored products, goods or services back to the country of origin.

Each company will pursue a slightly different global sourcing strategy. Exhibit 10.2 highlights the key evaluation criteria that can affect the decision offshore, nearshore or re-shore. As discussed above, offshoring provides cost savings through lower prices and was the reason many firms moved sourcing offshore. However recently with increasing wage rates, particularly in China, are causing firms rethink their outsourcing programs. Besides rapid wage increases the extended supply chains creates potential for increased as risk of loss damage, additional logistics costs, loss of flexibility to meet changes in customer demands, and the additional coordination costs. *Re-shoring* can reduce some of these concerns, and though there have been some exceptions it will require paying higher prices. *Nearshoring* offers an intermediate strategy of a closer physically located supply base along with enjoying some of the savings benefits. The important lesson from this brief discussion is that supply managers must continually reevaluate their major supply strategies with an emphasis on how the strategy impacts company revenues based on looking total cost of ownership.

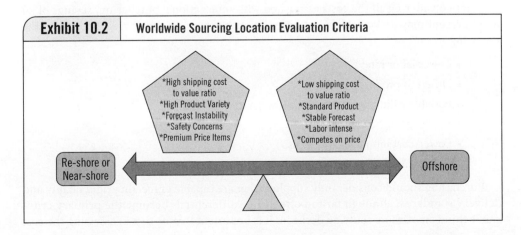

Exhibit 10.2   **Worldwide Sourcing Location Evaluation Criteria**

*High shipping cost to value ratio
*High Product Variety
*Forecast Instability
*Safety Concerns
*Premium Price Items

*Low shipping cost to value ratio
*Standard Product
*Stable Forecast
*Labor intense
*Competes on price

Re-shore or Near-shore

Offshore

Exhibit 10.3	Benefits of Worldwide Sourcing

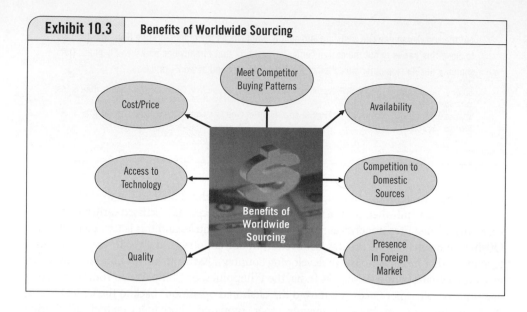

Exhibit 10.2 highlights several key characteristics of a purchased item or group of items and what factors tip the scale to nearshoring, re-shoring or offshoring. Favorable candidates for offshoring possess certain characteristics and include items that: are labor intensive standard products; have a low shipping cost to value ratio; and are sold in very competitive price driven markets. Candidates for nearshoring or re-shoring are those items that: require flexibility of output because of schedule uncertainty; need to have assurances regarding product safety; can be sold at premium prices and; have a high shipping cost to value ratio. Certainly there are other characteristics that will tip the scale in unique circumstances the choice set described above provides a good starting point.

Why Source Worldwide?

Although the previous discussion provided some reasons for purchasing internationally, let us discuss formally the more important reasons why companies pursue worldwide sourcing. Exhibit 10.2 highlights some of the major advantages of worldwide sourcing.

Cost/Price Benefits

After considering all the costs associated with international purchasing, savings of 20 to 30 percent may be available. Cost differentials between countries arise because of the following:

- Lower labor rates
- Different productivity levels
- Possible willingness to accept a lower profit margin
- Exchange rate differences
- Lower-cost inputs for materials
- Government subsidies

Purchasing should consider only suppliers that are capable of meeting rigid quality and delivery standards, although far too often price differentials become the primary criterion behind an offshore sourcing decision. It is important to note that in assessing the cost benefits of sourcing internationally, purchasers should include all of the relevant costs associated with sourcing items beyond piece price, which a later section discusses.

Access to Product and Process Technology

The United States is no longer the undisputed product and process technology leader in the world. Other countries have developed leading-edge technologies in a number of areas, such as electronic components. Purchasers that require these components know that Asian suppliers are technology leaders. Gaining access to the most current technology leaves many companies with little choice except to pursue worldwide sourcing.

Quality

Some countries, such as Japan and Germany, are obsessed with product quality. Producers in these countries have been able to capture an increasing share of world markets across a range of industries. U.S. purchasers stuck with domestic suppliers that produce poor quality often begin to source offshore components with the hope of improving end-product quality. The combination of consistently high quality and lower overall price has been a major contributor to the growth of U.S. companies buying internationally.

Access to the Only Source Available

Economic recessions, mergers, and government-imposed environmental regulations often result in suppliers exiting certain lines of business because of higher costs, loss of business volume, or both. This capacity reduction makes it increasingly difficult for U.S. buyers to source domestically. For example, although copper producers today are enjoying the benefits of high prices and tight capacity, this was not always the case. During the early- and mid-1980s, U.S. copper producers closed many mines because of low copper prices and inefficient process technology. As a result, some copper buyers turned to overseas producers to meet their requirements. A loss of supplier capability and availability in the automotive, machine tool, and electronics industries often left domestic buyers with no viable supply alternative except international sources.

Introduce Competition to Domestic Suppliers

Companies that rely on competitive forces to maintain price and service levels within their industry sometimes use worldwide sourcing to introduce competition to the domestic supply base. In industries characterized by limited domestic competition, this can diminish a supplier's power and break certain practices unfavorable to purchasers. For example, one electronic company historically sourced many chemical products with a single large U.S. supplier. However, this firm is now qualifying suppliers in emerging countries as a way to counteract the domestic supplier's pricing power. A more competitive supply market will shift power away from U.S. suppliers as well as shift power from sellers to buyers.

React to Buying Patterns of Competitors

This is probably the least-mentioned reason for worldwide sourcing, because most firms do not want to admit that they are reacting to the practices of competitors. Imitating the action of competitors is the "fashion and fear" motive. A purchaser may try to duplicate the factors that provide an advantage to a competitor, which may mean sourcing from the same suppliers or regions of the world that a competitor uses. There may be a belief that not sourcing in the same region(s) may create a competitive disadvantage. Many firms believe they must source in China or other low-cost countries or risk being at a cost disadvantage.

Establish a Market Presence in Another Country

Virtually the whole world is a potential market for goods and services from the United States, so it makes good economic and political sense to buy in those markets when planning to sell there. One way to develop goodwill in the country to assist in gaining product or service acceptance is through business relationships that will help support an expanded marketing presence.

Although the exact reasons each company sources internationally will vary, they surely include some of those discussed here. Without access to worldwide sources of supply, companies may not remain competitive. A domestic company that purchases a portion of its material requirements worldwide is better than a domestic company that is no longer in business as a result of its inability be globally competitive.

Barriers to Worldwide Sourcing

Companies with little or no international experience often face obstacles or barriers when beginning worldwide sourcing. These barriers include: (1) lack of knowledge and skills concerning global sourcing; (2) resistance to change; (3) longer lead times; (4) different business customs, language, and culture; (5) currency fluctuations and (6) increased supply risk (see Exhibit 10.4).

The lack of *knowledge and skills* pertaining to the intricacies of global sourcing inhibits a company from considering global sources. These shortcomings include a basic lack of knowledge about potential sources of supply or a lack of familiarity with the additional documentation required for international purchasing. International documentation requirements include:

- Letters of credit
- Multiple bills of lading
- Dock receipts
- Import licenses
- Certificates of origin

Exhibit 10.4	Barriers to Worldwide Sourcing

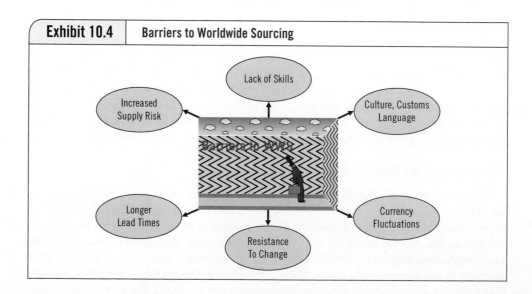

- Inspection certificates
- Certificates of insurance coverage
- Packing lists
- Commercial invoices

Resistance to change from an established, routine procedure or shifting from a long-standing supplier are also major barriers. It is natural to resist changes that represent a radical departure from existing ways of doing business. Domestic market nationalism has also presented itself as a barrier sometimes. Buyers are sometimes reluctant to shift business from domestic sources to unknown offshore sources. Home market nationalism, although not the obstacle it was years ago, can still be an issue.

Another barrier involves managing *longer lead times* and extended material pipelines. With longer lead times, accurate materials forecasts over extended periods become critical. Buyers must manage delivery dates closely because of the possibility of transit or customs delays. International sourcing also introduces an additional degree of logistical, political, and financial risk.

Other barriers relate to a lack of knowledge about *offshore business practices, language, and culture.* Negotiations with offshore suppliers can be more difficult, and simple engineering or delivery change requests can become frustrating experiences. Meetings and negotiations with international suppliers require knowledge of the customs and culture associated with the particular country. Lack of understanding of customs can lead to serious problems in making significant progress in negotiations and in building relationships with the supplier.

Currency fluctuations can have a significant impact on the price paid for the item. Major currencies fluctuate daily; therefore it is important for the buyer to understand the options to minimize this significant risk. Specific currency fluctuation strategies are discussed later in this chapter.

A critical assessment of the increased supply risks associated with offshore sources must be made prior to contracting, not after a commitment is made. Otherwise, the organization will increase the probability of experiencing supply disruptions. The type of risks vary with the sourcing country. For example, sourcing in Western Europe creates risks of currency exposure and longer lead times, but the purchaser is dealing in developed countries with similar business philosophies and a long trading history. Sourcing in China and other developing nations creates a broader set of problems that pose risks to the supply chain. These include quality, logistics, culture, and government issues. Risk assessments need to be considered prior to sourcing, and the purchaser should not be enamored with only the initial price savings. Leading companies are actively managing these potential risks through proactive initiatives. For example, McDonald's controls the paint supply of its toys manufactured in China, to insure that all items are free of lead paint.

Overcoming Barriers to Worldwide Sourcing

The most common method for overcoming these barriers involves *education and training*, which can generate support for the process as well as help overcome the anxiety associated with change. *Publicizing success stories* can also show the performance benefits that worldwide purchasing provides. Deploying various *technologies* such as globally linked computer-aided design systems, e-mail, RFID tags, and bar code systems that help track material through international pipelines have helped reduce the communication barriers surrounding worldwide sourcing. Some companies also insist on only working with those offshore suppliers that have *U.S.-based support personnel.*

Measurement and reward systems can encourage sourcing from the best suppliers worldwide. These firms measure and reward buyers on the basis of their ability to realize performance benefits from the selected use of international sources. The use of *third-party or external agents* can also help overcome barriers to international purchasing, particularly when first starting out. The use of brokers can be an efficient way to begin a worldwide sourcing program.

Regardless of the technique used to overcome worldwide sourcing barriers, the effort will fail unless *top management* supports worldwide sourcing. Management must send the message that going international is a means to remain competitive by using the most competitive suppliers and does not represent an effort to force domestic suppliers out of business.

Sourcing Snapshot

The Re-shoring Trend and Vernon's Life Cycle Theory

The Re-shoring Trend and Vernon's Life Cycle Theory

It seems that the re-shoring trend is challenging a major business theory. Vernon's life cycle theory developed in the 1960s was used to explain why the location of manufacturing moves. The theory suggests that early in a product's life cycle all the parts and labor associated with that product come from the area in which it was invented.This proximity enables quick feedback, allowing manufacturers to tweak product design and manufacture appropriately. As the market grows, and the product becomes standardized, production would spread to other rich nations, and competitors would arise. Eventually, as the product fully matured, its manufacturing would shift from rich countries to low-wage countries. The original country that developed the product may then even import the product from these low-wage countries.[1] However, the three examples below that highlight the re-shoring phenomena would contradict this theory.

In February 2012, GE re-shored the manufacturing of cutting-edge, low-energy water heaters to Appliance Park in Louisville Kentucky from a Chinese contract factory. This occurred 4 years after GE CEO Jeffrey Immelt had attempted to sell Appliance Park believing its time had passed. This was the first new assembly line at Appliance Park in 55 years. In March, a second new assembly line, to make new high-tech French-door refrigerators was opened. The top-end model can sense the size of the container you place beneath its purified-water spigot and shuts the spigot off automatically when the container is full. These refrigerators had been made in Mexico. Other additions include a new stainless-steel dishwasher line and another line will assemble the trendy front-loading washers and matching dryers. All told GE plans to spend $800 million to upgrade Appliance Park.[2]

In another stable product line Stanley Furniture Company has moved the production of baby cribs to a plant in Robbinsville, North Carolina from China despite having a labor intensive product and steep wage differentials. For example, the hourly rate of pay for one sanding operation in China is 63 cents per hour compared to $10/hour in North Carolina. Stanley cribs sell for about $700 compared to identical imports at $400. Stanley's marketing officials claim there are a number of trends that justify the differential. First and foremost is product safety. "We let people imagine this is American made versus made in China," stated Stanley's CEO. Secondly is product variety of 85 colors. Thirdly, is that grandparents are often willing to help their children and will pay extra for the sturdiness, durability, and quality. Finally, Stanley is able to meet the variety of their customer demands quickly and without mountains of additional inventory.[3]

In the Detroit suburb of Canton, workers are assembling large flat screen televisions. Currently, there is only one U.S.-based manufacturer of televisions. The California-based firm makes water-proof units for outdoor use. Flat screens are light and compact and domestic production avoids the 5 percent duty, saving about $27 per 46 inch television. This differential accounts for the wage differential. Lean production methods and a reduction in the number of parts required in assembly produce additional savings. Problems of sustaining this model include Mexican assembled televisions made with Chinese parts and the lack of competitive domestic component suppliers.

Potential explanations as to why these trends don't completely invalidate Vernon's theory include that it did not extend outside of the product life cycle and was used to explain international trade patterns. Secondly, many of the offshoring changes involve nearshoring as supply managers re-evaluate their global sourcing strategies. Nearshoring supports Vernon's theory. Finally, the movement to "regionalization" or "global localization ," by making products closer to where they are sold would also provide support for the theory.[4]

Sources:
[1] Hill, C. (2007), International Business Competing in the Global Marketplace 6th edition, McGraw-Hill p. 168.
[2] Fishman, Charles, (2012, December) "The Insourcing Boom," *The Atlantic*, pp. 22–25
[3] Aeppel, T. (2012, May 22), "A Crib for Baby: Made in China or Made in U.S.A.?," Wall Street Journal, B1,B2.
[4] Aeppel, T. (2012, May 23), "Detroit's Wages Take on China" Wall Street Journal, B1,B2.

Developing a Worldwide Sourcing Program

An organization progresses (often reactively) from domestic buying to worldwide sourcing for a multitude of reasons. For example, it may confront a situation for which no suitable domestic supplier exists, or because competitors are gaining an advantage because of their worldwide sourcing. The first-time buyer, considering worldwide sourcing, faces many additional issues that were not considerations in the domestic sourcing decision.

Information about Worldwide Sources

After identifying items to purchase internationally, a firm must gather and evaluate information on potential suppliers or identify intermediaries capable of that task. This can prove challenging if a company is inexperienced or has limited outside contacts or sources of information. Much information is available on the Internet. A good source of general information on international trade is Stat-USA/Internet. Stat-USA is a service of the U.S. Department of Commerce, and a single point of access to authoritative business, trade, and economic information. (http://www.stat-usa.gov). Part of the site has a link to Globus & NTDB, which is a fee subscription service that contains over 200,000 current and historical trade-related releases, international market research, country analysis, and trade and procurement leads.

Finally, social networking sites such as LinkedIn (www.linkedin.com) has several groups dedicated to global sourcing. The "Retail Global Sourcing and Buying" group started in 2008 has almost 43,000 members. The "Global Sourcing" group has 39,900 members and is an open group to all interested in global trade, sourcing and buying. Meanwhile the "Global Sourcing Council" with 7500 members that enables public, private and academic participants to interact with each other on current worldwide sourcing issues. The following sections provide information on identifying potential suppliers, trade intermediaries, and organizational issues in worldwide sourcing.

Worldwide Sourcing Directories

Directories, which are available in CD-ROM format or through the Internet, are a major source of information about suppliers by industry or region of the world. Hundreds of directories are available that identify potential international contacts. Here are some examples:

- *Principal International Businesses* (http://www.loc.gov/rr/business/duns/duns22.html)is a world marketing directory listing approximately 50,000 leading enterprises in 140 countries that are the largest employers worldwide It is published by Dun & Bradstreet.
- *Taiwan & China Products Online* (http://www.manufacture.com.tw/) is an online portal with manufacturers and suppliers from Asia, mainly in Taiwan and China.
- *Taiwan Products Online* http://www.taiwanproducts.com.cn/index.html is an online portal with manufacturers and suppliers from in Taiwan.
- *Zycon Industrial Directory of Manufacturing Companies* (http://www.zycon.com) is an international directory of industrial companies, manufacturers, distributors, and service providers.
- *www.globalsources.com* Global sources specializes in sourcing in China. Their website states that they create, manage, and deliver the information that trading partners need to meet and do business.

Trade Shows

Trade shows are often one of the best ways to gather information on many suppliers at one time. These industrial shows occur throughout the world for practically every industry. Most business libraries have a directory that lists worldwide trade shows. Internet searches will also reveal the time and place of industrial trade shows, including how to register. One major trade show is the International Manufacturing Technology Show (IMTS); manufacturing industry professionals from the United States and 102 other countries attend this show held every two years. The theme of the IMTS show is "connecting global technology." In 2012, 100,200 buyers, sellers, engineers, and managers were able to visit 1,909 exhibitors who displayed their latest manufacturing technology. Some $35 billion dollars in formal quotes were issued to buyers, 65 percent of whom planned to make a purchase decision within a year.[9]

Types of Intermediaries and Organization for Worldwide Sourcing
Trading Companies

Trading companies offer a full range of services to assist purchasers. These companies will issue letters of credit and pay brokers, customs charges, dock fees, insurance, and ocean carrier and inland freight bills. Clients usually receive one itemized invoice for the total services performed. One U.S.-based trading company offers more than 20 services, including

- Finding qualified sources
- Performing product quality audits
- Evaluating suppliers
- Negotiating contracts
- Managing logistics
- Inspecting shipments
- Expediting
- Performing duty classifications

The use of a full-service trading company may actually result in a lower total cost for international purchases compared with performing each activity individually. Countries such as Japan and South Korea have trading companies located in major U.S. cities. KOTRA, a Korean-based, government-directed trading company, is committed to promoting mutual prosperity between Korea and its trading partners through international commerce and investment.[10] Foreign trading companies offer one-stop shopping for buyers interested in the goods and services of a particular country. They will locate the sources, quote the prices, insure quality, and handle all the export and import documentation. The Kotra seal of excellence certifies a Korean supplier has passed the necessary quality tests and indicates the supplier is also trustworthy.[11]

Third-Party Support

Experts are available to provide international sourcing assistance. Independent agents, working on commission, will act as purchasing representatives in a foreign country. They locate sources of supply, evaluate the source, and handle the required paperwork and documentation. Some agents also provide, or can arrange for, full-service capability.

Agents and brokers are an option when a company lacks global expertise or a presence in a foreign market. They help locate foreign suppliers and act as intermediaries between the buyer and seller. Direct manufacturer representatives or sales representatives can also be a source of valuable information. Such individuals work directly for sellers as their representatives in a country. Finally, different state and federal agencies encourage and promote international trade. Services provided by these agencies are usually reasonably priced.

Trade Consulates

Purchasers can contact foreign trade consulates located in major cities across the United States for information. Almost all consulates have trade experts who are eager to do business with American buyers. Purchasers can also contact U.S. embassies located overseas to inquire about suppliers located in a particular country. The U.S. Department of Commerce also has offices staffed by trade specialists that offer several good services at a nominal fee.

Foreign Nationals

Foreign nationals are citizens (local residents) of the targeted sourcing country or region. In larger organizations these nationals are hired as full-time employees of the firm and assigned to source in their country or region. Because they are familiar with the country, its language, customs, and business practices, they can contribute quickly to developing a sourcing base in the specific country. However, utmost care must be taken when selecting offshore nationals. They become the representative of the company "on the ground" in the particular country and essentially create the image of the firm in that country. Where they are not hired full-time, sourcing experts who are offshore nationals will work on a "contract" basis in finding and contracting with suppliers in that specific country.

Organizational Issues-IPOs

The ultimate investment and commitment to worldwide sourcing is exhibited when an organization establishes International Purchasing Offices (IPOs) in selected areas around the world. Employees of these IPOs usually consist of a mix of home country (e.g., United States) employees and offshore nationals. Most IPOs fall under the control of a centralized corporate procurement office. This reporting relationship allows the IPO to support the sourcing needs of the entire organization. Larger firms are more likely than smaller ones to have international purchasing offices. Exhibit 10.5 identifies several major functions of IPOs.

A research study on global sourcing indicated that the growth in IPOs corresponded to an increase in higher-level global sourcing. Firms were using their IPOs to provide operational support from the development phase through contract management of the global agreement. Specific IPO activities included facilitating import and export requirements, resolving quality and delivery performance problems, and measuring supplier performance.[12]

Though there are many advantages of having IPOs, a firm needs to consider the risks. First, they are expensive to operate because they require additional personnel, facilities, and equipment. Second, care must be taken as to where to place the overseas IPOs because it will result in favoring sourcing out of these countries. Finally, IPOs will have to develop logistics expertise required to import goods. Some IPOs are able to recover their costs by marketing their services outside the organization to other mid-sized or smaller firms.

Exhibit 10.5	**Role of International Purchasing Offices**

Identify potential suppliers.

Solicit quotes or proposals.

Expedite and trace shipments.

Negotiate supply contracts.

Obtain product samples.

Manage technical and commercial concerns.

Represent the buying firm to suppliers.

Manage countertrade requirements.

Perform supplier site visits.

North America

South America

Europe

Asia Pacific

The *amount and type of information* required is partly a function of how a purchaser chooses to handle the offshore purchase. Purchasers that use intermediaries, such as trading companies and external agents, must search for information that identifies the best intermediaries. Purchasers that go more directly to the supplier must obtain information about suppliers from foreign nationals, trade directories, trade shows, embassies, supplier representatives, and other sources of international information. Finally, those firms willing to make major investments in worldwide sourcing establish IPOs.

Supplier Qualification and Selection Issues

Whether the purchaser or an external agent coordinates the international purchase, offshore suppliers must be subject to the same, or in some cases more rigorous, performance evaluation and standards as domestic suppliers. Never assume an offshore company can automatically satisfy a buyer's performance requirements or expectations. Here are some questions to ask when evaluating offshore sources:

- Does a significant total cost difference exist between the domestic and the offshore source after factoring in additional cost elements?
- Will the offshore supplier maintain any price differences over time?
- What is the effect of longer material pipelines and increased average inventory levels?
- What are the supplier's technical and quality capabilities?
- Can the supplier assist with new designs?
- What is the supplier's quality performance? What types of quality systems does it have in place?
- Is the supplier capable of consistent delivery schedules?
- How much lead time does the supplier require?
- Can we develop a longer-term relationship with this supplier?
- Are patents and proprietary technology safe with this supplier? Is the supplier trustworthy? What legal system does the supplier expect to follow?
- What are the supplier's payment terms?
- How does the supplier manage currency exchange issues?

At times buyers use trial orders to evaluate offshore sources. Purchasers may initially not be willing to rely on an offshore source for an entire purchase requirement. A buyer can use smaller or trial orders to begin to establish a supplier's performance record.

Understanding Cultural Issues

Perhaps one of the biggest barriers to worldwide sourcing involves the cultural differences that arise when doing business with other countries. **Culture** is the sum of the understandings that govern human interaction in a society. Culture is a multidimensional concept composed of several elements, including: (1) language, (2) religion, (3) values and attitudes, (4) customs, (5) social institutions, and (6) education. Two very important differences in culture that can affect the supply manager are values and behavior. **Values** are shared beliefs or group norms that are internalized; they affect the way people think. **Behavior** is based on values and attitudes; it affects the way people act. Understanding cultural differences will improve a purchaser's comfort and effectiveness when conducting business internationally. A major complaint about Americans is our ignorance of other cultures.

Cultural differences between countries can result in some unwelcome surprises when buying internationally. For instance, the standard procedures for negotiation and contracting are distinctly different in Asia, Europe, and the United States. Dealing with these issues requires purchasing personnel and organizations to manage different beliefs about contracting.

Many cultures place a premium on maintaining harmonious and smooth relationships. Thais and Indonesians, for example, will frequently say "yes" merely to be polite. It is a way of indicating that they are listening to you. "Yes" does not necessarily mean that they agree with what you are saying. Furthermore, they will often express their own position in the most ambiguous terms.[13] This is also true of the Chinese. Buyers in China have to be mindful of the importance to their Chinese counterparts of saving face, first and foremost. The concern is so great for Chinese companies it can result in suppliers saying they understand a buyer's requirements when in reality they do not. The Chinese suppliers then proceed to try to figure out the requirements on their own, sometimes with disastrous results. For example, according to Greg Toporcer of Global Discovery, "There can be difficulties in translating specs. . . . Additionally, Chinese standards may differ from American standards for the same material." The nickel content in Type 301 stainless in the United States could be different from the nickel content in Type 301 Chinese stainless steel. The best way to solve communications and standards problems is to have feet on the ground constantly monitoring suppliers, Toporcer says.[14]

Finally, beliefs in developing countries about ethical issues, such as bribery, differ widely from U.S. practices. What is an illegal activity in the United States (providing bribes) is often an accepted business practice in many other regions.

Language and Communication Differences

A major part of the supply manager's role is communicating requirements clearly and effectively to suppliers. Language differences can sometimes interfere with the effective communication of requirements. Not everyone understands English, and Americans will likely not understand the seller's native language.

The largest differences in communication styles across countries are message speed and level of content. Americans tend to give fast messages with the conclusions expressed first. This style is not appropriate in many countries, particularly in Europe.[15]

Dick Locke, a procurement manager who has handled buying operations in Tokyo, Europe, Mexico, and the Middle East, offers this advice about language and communication:[16]

- If a supplier is using English as a second language, the buyer should be responsible for preventing communication problems.
- To aid in communication, speak slowly, use more communication graphics, and eliminate jargon, slang, and sports and military metaphors from your language.
- Bring an interpreter to all but the most informal meetings. Allow an extra day to educate interpreters on your issues and vocabulary.
- Document, in writing, the conclusions and decisions made in a meeting before adjourning.

Logistical Considerations

Buyers should not underestimate the potential effects of extended distances on their ability to plan and manage a worldwide supply chain. Although advanced industrial countries have a developed infrastructure, many offshore countries do not, making shipping delays a real possibility.[17] Realizing this need for infrastructure between 2011 and 2015 China plans to spend $950 billion on roads bridges and ports. Currently, only 3 percent of Chinese people own a car, making mass transit a necessity.[18] China is also expanding its airline system with plans to build 97 new airports in the next 12 years.[19]

Though China is quickly trying to upgrade its infrastructure, India's efforts currently are lagging. India's supply chains are built on slow transit networks fed by poor roads, ineffective ports, and little distribution infrastructure. The National Highways constitute only 1.7 percent of the road network, but carry 40 percent of the total road traffic. Yet only 24 percent of the country's national highways are four-lane and meet the required standards. The main issues faced by ports include the level of containerization, custom procedures and insufficient connectivity to their hinterlands.[20]

Logistics infrastructure is severely limiting the country's growth, and costs are extremely high as a result. Earlier estimates indicated logistics costs are around 13 percent of GDP in India versus 10 percent in the United States.[21] In other developing countries, this ratio can be as high as 25 percent of total gross domestic product.[22]

Poor infrastructure becomes a factor when calculating the total landed cost for offshore goods. These additional logistics costs must be added to the purchase price in arriving at a final cost. Slower logistics responses also mean that the costs carrying extra inventories need to be added to final cost calculations. As China, India, and other developing countries add logistics infrastructure, these logistics differences will narrow. In preparation for this, U.S. ports are increasing their capacity and increasing their intermodal operations capabilities to increase their ability to handle larger vessels as a result of the widening of the Panama canal scheduled for completion in 2015.[23] (See Snapshot for more details.)

Incoterms-Moving International Shipments

Incoterms are internationally recognized commercial terms that describe the responsibilities of the buyer and seller in the arrangement of transportation. Delivery occurs (and risk of loss transfers) at the point designated by the term selected, however transfer of *title/ownwership* is NOT covered by any of the Incoterms and must be specified separately by the parties. They are used in conjunction with a sales agreement or other method of transacting the sale. The buyer and seller have an array of terms from which to choose, depending on the extent to which each party wants to be involved with the transportation and insurance. One of the complications is the modes by which an international shipment will move. Typically there will be more than one mode of transportation involved. Incoterms 2010 were developed to take account of the spread of customs-free zones, the increase in use of electronic communications, concerns about security following 9/11 and latest developments in trade and have replaced the 2000 version. (See Exhibit 10.6 for Incoterms 2010.)

Exhibit 10.6 highlights the 11 standard Incoterms 2010. EXW, CPT, CIP, DAT, DAP, DDP and FCA are commonly used for any mode of transportation. In EXW (ex-works), the seller prepares the goods at their location and prepares them for pickup. The buyer arranges for pickup at the seller's plant, then handles all the other arrangements and costs associated with getting the goods from the seller to the buyer's place of business. Buyers using EXW are either very experienced in the area of international freight and customs or

Exhibit 10.6 — Incoterms 2010

Location/Freight Responsibility	Seller Premise	Export Formalities	Named Place of Terminal	Loading Port of Shipment	OnBoard Ship/Rail/Plane	Discharge Port of Arrival	Named Place or Terminal	Import Formalities	Buyer Premise
Ex Works (EXW)	Seller ⚠	Buyer	Buyer	Buyer	Buyer	Buyer	Buyer	Buyer	Buyer
Free Carrier (FCA)[1]	Seller ⚠	Seller	Seller ⚠	Buyer	Buyer	Buyer	Buyer	Buyer	Buyer
Freight Alongside Ship (FAS)	Seller	Seller	Seller	Seller ⚠	Buyer	Buyer	Buyer	Buyer	Buyer
Free on Board (FOB)	Seller	Seller	Seller	Seller	Buyer ⚠	Buyer	Buyer	Buyer	Buyer
Cost & Freight (CFR)	Seller	Seller	Seller	Seller	Buyer ⚠	Buyer	Buyer	Buyer	Buyer
Cost Insurance & Freight (CIF)	Seller	Seller	Seller	Seller	Buyer ⚠	Buyer	Buyer	Buyer	Buyer
Carriage Paid To (CPT)[2]	Seller ⚠	Seller	Buyer	Buyer	Buyer	Buyer	Buyer	Buyer	Buyer
Carriage & Insurance to (CIP)[2]	Seller ⚠	Seller	Buyer	Buyer	Buyer	Buyer	Buyer	Buyer	Buyer
Delivered at Terminal (DAT)	Seller	Seller	Seller	Seller	Seller	Seller ⚠	Buyer	Buyer	Buyer
Delivered at place (DAP)	Seller	Seller	Seller	Seller	Seller	Seller	Seller ⚠	Buyer	Buyer
Delivered Duty paid (DDP)	Seller	Seller	Seller	Seller	Seller	Seller	Seller	Seller	Seller ⚠

⚠ Where risk passes

[1] Delivery can occur at seller premise or place of departure
[2] risk passes from seller to buyer when the goods are delivered to the first carrier

have hired a 3PL (third-party logistics) firm or another intermediary to handle the freight details. Under EXW the buyer has maximum liability for shipment and bears all the costs of the transportation, customs, and the like. Alternatively, under DDP (delivery duty paid named place of destination) the seller has maximum freight responsibility. The seller is responsible for handling all of the details of the shipment, including getting it through customs in the United States and getting it to the buyer's facility or other named destination.

FAS, FOB, CFR and CIF are used for sea and inland waterway modes of shipment. FAS (free alongside ship) is a popular Incoterm in contracts for heavy lift or bulk cargo. Under FAS the seller is responsible to clear the goods for export, deliver the goods and place them alongside the vessel at the named port of shipment. The buyer has to bear all costs and risks of loss of, or damage to, the goods once they are put alongside the vessel by the seller.

Legal Systems

Legal systems differ from country to country. Most buyer-seller contracts in the United States use either the Uniform Commercial Code or common law. Given the litigious nature of the U.S. system, parties seek to protect their interests, and this results in longer and more detailed contracts. For example, before one large firm redesigned its purchasing process, it was common for purchase contracts to be more than 40 pages in length. A redesign effort reduced this to around six pages.

Depending on the status of the legal system in other countries, much shorter contracts may be the norm, particularly in those countries using code or civil law. Developing countries often rely on personal relations and trust to cover many legal issues because of an inadequate legal system. As a result, many offshore organizations do not like to deal with the U.S. legal system and long contracts.

Developed countries have legal systems that provide the buyer protection and fair treatment. Often, developing countries offer no effective protection against the piracy of intellectual property. It is necessary, therefore, to perform a thorough check of prospective suppliers before releasing designs or other proprietary information.

International contracts can be used if the country the buyer is doing business with follows the **United Nations Convention on Contracts for the International Sale of Goods (CISG)** CISG took effect on January 1, 1988. The purpose was to facilitate international trade by removing legal barriers. Unless the parties have specified to the contrary, the CISG applies to sales of goods covering contracts between parties with places of business in the "Contracting States." Contracting States are those countries that have ratified the CISG.

Countries that are part of the World Trade Organization are expected to follow certain international trade practices and protect intellectual property. Buyers and sellers doing business across boundaries should agree, preferably in a contract, about what laws will cover the business transaction.

U.S. buyers firms must mindful of their conduct in dealings with foreign government officials. **The Foreign Corrupt Practices Act (FCPA)** was passed by Congress in 1977 to prevent companies from making questionable or illegal payments to foreign government officials, politicians, and political parties. The law prohibits U.S. citizens or their agents from making payments to foreign officials to secure or retain business, and it requires accurate record keeping and adequate controls for company transactions. Since 1998, these practices apply to foreign firms and persons who make such corrupt payments while in the United States. There is no dollar threshold on the act, making it illegal to offer even a dollar as a bribe. Enforcement focuses on the intent of the bribery more than the amount.

Sourcing Snapshot

Conflict Minerals Raise Supply Chain Traceability Issues

Conflict Minerals Raise Supply Chain Traceability Issues

Section 1502 Dodd-Frank Wall Street Reform and Consumer Protection Act of 2010 includes a section relating to Conflict Minerals. Conflict minerals are those minerals that are mined under conditions of armed force and trample human rights. The groups are often affiliated with rebel groups or with the Congolese National Army, but both use rape and violence to control the local population. Most of these violations are occurring in the Democratic Republic of the Congo (DRC).[1]

Section 1502 applies broadly to many individuals involved in supply chain activities. The goal of the bill is to curb the funding of militias in the DRC and the surrounding region who have used these minerals to exploit both the general population and extract wealth for themselves. Mines in eastern Congo are often located far from populated areas in remote and dangerous regions. One study indicated that armed groups are present at more than 50 percent of mining sites. At many sites, armed groups illegally tax, extort, and coerce civilians to work. Miners, including children, work in up to 48-hour shifts amidst mudslides and tunnel collapses that kill many.

If applicable, Section 1502 requires companies reporting to the Securities and Exchange Commission (SEC) that use these products to declare the status of their materials as "DRC conflict free." The four metals currently on the list find their way into many products used in our modern economies. These metals and their brief description are:

1) cassiterite, which is the chief ore needed to produce tin. Tin can be found in the production of tin cans and solder on the circuit boards of electronic equipment, and in certain chemicals.
2) columbite-tantalite, the metal ore from which the element tantalum is extracted. Tantalum is used primarily for the production of capacitors, which go into a wide variety of products such as airbags, laptop computers, digital cameras, and so on.
3) wolframite is an important source of the element tungsten. Tungsten is a very dense metal possessing hardness and resistance properties and is frequently used for metalworking tools, drill bits and milling, and golf club heads.
4) gold is a commodity that is widely used in coins, jewelry, and electronics.

Given the fact that many companies or their customers use products that contain tin, tantalum, tungsten, or gold, it is important for supply managers to determine if any of their products contain these metals. If it is determined that they do use any of these metals, the next step is to determine their origin. A detailed map of the supply chain is necessary to begin to trace the sources of the materials. An important element in traceability is to find out if tier 1 and tier 2 suppliers have their own conflict-free sourcing policies. Tracing the supply chain back to the original source will require the cooperation of several tiers eventually leading back to metal smelters The process of tracing a supply chain is complex and requires significant research. However, by performing this analysis supply managers develop a deeper understanding of their supply chains in a critical area. Further, they will determine their level of compliance in these conflict minerals.

Source: (1) Polgreen, Lydia (November 15, 2008). "Congo's Riches, Looted by Renegade Troops." The New York Times

Countertrade Requirements

A specialized form of international trade that has increased over the last 25 years is **countertrade**. This broad term refers to all international and domestic trade where buyer and seller have at least a partial exchange of goods for goods. This exchange can involve a complete trade of goods for goods or some partial payment to a firm in cash.

Although many companies have established a countertrade office or department, purchasing is sometimes involved in negotiating and managing countertrade agreements, including determining the market or sales value of countertrade deals or selecting appropriate products to fulfill countertrade requirements.

A country imposes countertrade demands for a number of reasons. First, some countries simply lack the hard currency to purchase imported goods. Developing nations often require Western multinationals to accept goods as at least partial payment for sales within their country. Another reason for countertrade requirements is that countertrade provides a means of selling products in markets to which a company may have otherwise lacked access. Sourcing in a particular country expedites the sales by the company into that specific country.

Countertrade demands often arise when several factors are present. Items involving large dollar amounts, such as military contracts, are prime candidates for countertrade. Companies can also expect countertrade demands from a country when that country's goods have a low or nondifferentiated perception in the world marketplace. This may include items that are available from many sources, commodity-type items, or items not perceived as technologically superior or having higher quality compared with other available products. Highly valued items or those sought after by the buying country are less susceptible to countertrade demands.

Types of Countertrade

Several different forms have evolved. The five predominant types of countertrade arrangements are (1) barter, (2) counterpurchase, (3) offset, (4) buy-back, and (5) switch trading (see Exhibit 10.7).

Barter

The oldest and most basic form of trading is **barter**, a process that involves the straight exchange of goods for goods with no exchange of currency. It requires trading parties to

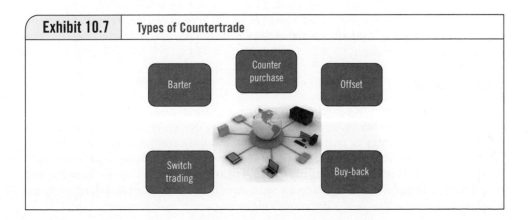

Exhibit 10.7	Types of Countertrade

enter into a single contract to fulfill trading requirements. Despite its apparent simplicity, barter is one of the least-practiced forms of countertrade today.

Barter differs from other forms of countertrade in several ways. Barter involves no exchange of money between parties. Next, a single contract formalizes a barter transaction, whereas other forms of countertrade require two or more contracts. Finally, barter arrangements usually relate to a specific transaction and cover a period of time shorter than that covered by other arrangements.

Counterpurchase

Counterpurchase requires a selling firm to purchase a specified amount of goods from the country that purchased its products. The amount of counterpurchase is a percentage of the amount of the original sale. This requirement usually ranges from 5 to 80 percent of the total value of the transaction but can actually exceed 100 percent under some circumstances.

This form of countertrade requires a company to fulfill its countertrade requirement by purchasing products within a country unrelated to its primary business. The counter-trading company identifies a list of possible purchase items that will fulfill the countertrade requirement. The purchaser must market the unrelated goods or use a third party to assume those duties, which introduces increased complexity and cost into the transaction.

Offset

Offset agreements, which are closely related to counterpurchase, also require the seller to purchase some agreed-upon percentage of goods from a country over a specified period. However, offset agreements allow a company to fulfill its countertrade requirement with any company or industry in the country. The selling firm can purchase items related directly to its business requirements, which offers the purchaser greater flexibility. An example of an offset purchase is a U.S. aircraft manufacturer that obtains a contract to sell planes in Spain and agrees to purchase products worth 100 percent of the contract value in Spain.

Buy-Back

Some countertrade authorities also refer to this type of countertrade as **compensation trading**. **Buy-back** occurs when a firm physically builds a plant in another country or provides a service, equipment, or technology to support the plant. The firm then agrees to take a portion of the plant's output as payment. Countries lacking foreign exchange for payment but rich in natural resources can benefit from this type of countertrade arrangement. Opportunities exist for Western companies to provide the plant, equipment, and expertise to bring resources to market.

Switch Trading

This form of countertrade involves the use of a third-party trader to sell earned counterpurchase credits. **Switch trading** occurs when a selling company agrees to accept goods from the buying country as partial payment. If the selling company does not want the goods from the country, it can sell, at a discount, the credits for these goods to a third-party trader, which sells or markets the goods. The trader charges a fee for handling the transaction. The original selling company must consider the discount and third-party fee when evaluating the total cost of a countertrade arrangement with a country.

Purchasing's role in countertrade will not be as visible as marketing's role. Purchasing is usually a reactive participant that must identify supply sources that will help satisfy any countertrade requirements that a company has incurred through the sale of its product.

Use of Foreign Trade Zones in Supply Management

In the United States, a **foreign-trade zone (FTZ)** is a secure location approved by the appropriate U.S. Customs and Border Protection (CBP) office. FTZs were originally authorized by the Foreign-Trade Zones Act of 1934. FTZs allow an importing company to delay, eliminate, or decrease its duty payments on foreign-sourced goods that enter the zone site. According the CBP Foreign-Trade Zone Manual, "FTZs are considered to be outside of the Customs territory of the United States for the purposes of payment of duty."[24] Only when foreign-sourced goods are withdrawn from a FTZ are they subject to duty payment.

The overarching purposes of FTZs are to attract foreign business and investment into the United States and to increase domestic economic development primarily through adding jobs to the U.S. economy. There are currently more than 750 FTZs in the United States, including 250 *general-purpose zones* and more than 500 *subzones* approved by the FTZ Board.

The general-purpose zone, is typically housed in a port or an industrial park and is available to multiple companies. A *subzone*, or usage-driven site, on the other hand, can be approved for a specific use or a specific company. "FTZ subzone status is focused on a particular site or a particular inventory. What that means is that a specific distribution center or manufacturing site may have [a] FTZ designation, or a portion of the facility (and the inventory within that area) may be a part of an FTZ."[25]

Advantages of Using an FTZ

Common advantages of using a FTZ in supply management include: duty exemption, duty deferral, inverted tariff, streamlined customs procedures, and a reduction in taxes. *Duty exemption* means that no duties or quota charges will be placed on goods that are reexported from the FTZ. *Duty deferral* allows the importer to improve cash flow by postponing payment of duties and tariffs until the imported goods are withdrawn from the FTZ. *Inverted tariffs* occurs when goods produced in a FTZ have a lower duty rate than the duty rates on the imported components that comprised the finished goods. In this case, the finished product may be subject to the lower duty rate when withdrawn from the FTZ. Inverted tariff status must receive prior approval to receive the lower rate. The ability of an FTZ company to file a single Customs entry for all its FTZ transactions in one week is an example of a *streamlined customs procedure*. A reduction of *state and/or local inventory taxes* on foreign-sourced goods and domestic goods destined for export that are held within the FTZ can provide a tax savings to the FTZ company.

Under the FTZ Act, goods brought into a zone can be stored, sold, exhibited, broken up, repacked, assembled, distributed, sorted, graded, cleaned, mixed with foreign or domestic merchandise, or otherwise manipulated, or be manufactured except as set forth in the FTZ Act, and be exported, destroyed, or sent into the Customs territory of the United States therefrom in the original package or otherwise (19 U.S.C. §81c)."[26] Any manufacturing and production activities must be specifically authorized by the FTZ Board. Two major restrictions on goods allowable in a FTZ include, merchandise or article whose importation is prohibited and any retail activities.[27]

If a buying company in the U.S. (or its U.S.-based suppliers) imports a substantial amount of parts, components, and/or finished goods from overseas suppliers a feasibility analysis of the costs associated with setting up and maintaining a FTZ site.

A few of the key costs that require evaluation include:

- Total annual value and volume of imported (dutiable) merchandise
- Number of Customs entries made annually
- Weighted average duty rate of imported merchandise
- Percentage and/or value of foreign (dutiable) reexports for the previous year
- Total annual value of imported merchandise shipped directly to the customer (drop shipments)
- Annual dollar amount of duty drawbacks for the previous year
- Annual value and volume of dual sourced merchandise (i.e., sourced both overseas and domestically)
- Forecast of annual growth of dutiable imports over the next 3 years
- Approximation of US value-added as a percent of finished products value (if manufacturing occurs)

Evaluating Costs Associated with International Purchasing

Purchasers must examine the additional costs associated with international purchasing. Whether the purchase transaction is with a domestic or offshore producer, there are certain common costs. The difference between domestic and foreign purchasing, however, is that foreign purchasing must include the additional costs associated with conducting overseas transactions. If price is a major factor, then a buyer must compare the total cost of the offshore purchase to the total cost of the domestic purchase. Exhibit 10.8 summarizes the various charges often associated with international purchasing and logistics.

Exhibit 10.8	Elements of Total Cost for Worldwide Sourcing

Base Price
- Ascertain quantity breaks, minimum buys for shipping efficiency, and any surcharges.
- Determine price for rush shipments of smaller-than-planned quantities, which are often more.

Tooling
- Ideally, the purchaser should own the tooling and pay for it only once.
- Consider shipping tooling from a domestic source if transferable.

Packaging
- This is a hidden cost (may be expensive for long distances and multiple handlings).
- Consult a packaging supplier or internal engineer for methods to minimize cost on international shipments.

Escalation
- Determine for how long the quoted price is firm.
- Determine components of escalation (i.e., ensure that price increases are not hidden in other costs).

(continued)

Exhibit 10.8	Elements of Total Cost for Worldwide Sourcing (continued)

Transportation

- Obtain assistance from logistics personnel who have expertise in international transportation.
- Consider consolidation of shipments with other corporations from the same geographical area.
- Use multinational carriers or freight brokers to manage shipments and cost where required.
- Consult the offshore supplier as a source of information regarding freight sources.

Customs Duty

- Duties paid any time a shipment crosses international lines can vary widely over a range of goods, and often change on short notice.
- Provided by U.S. Published Tariff Schedules.
- Items may fall into more than one classification.
- May be best to discuss this with a customs agent/broker.

Insurance Premiums

- These are not typically included in an ocean shipment price (need marine insurance).
- Do not pay for extra coverage that your company may already carry for international transactions.

Payment Terms

- Offshore suppliers often grant longer payment terms such as net 60.
- If dealing with intermediaries, the payment may be requested on shipment.

Additional Fees and Commissions

- Ask supplier, customs broker, and transportation personnel if other costs may be incurred, and who is responsible for these costs.
- If your shipment is held at the port of entry because of a lack of documentation and customs officials place it in storage, a storage fee will be billed to the customer. (Who will pay for this?)

Port Terminal and Handling Fees

- U.S. port and handling charges include unloading cargo, administrative services of port personnel, and use of port.

Customs Broker Fees

- There is a flat charge per transaction.

Taxes

- Consider any additional taxes that may be paid.

Communication Costs

- There will be higher phone, travel, mailing, telex, fax, and e-mail charges.

Payment and Currency Fees

- Bank transfers, bills of exchange, hedging, and forward contracts all incur fees.

Inventory Carrying Costs

- Higher levels of inventory will have to be held because of longer lead times.
- Costs include the interest rate forgone by investing funds, insurance, property taxes, storage, and obsolescence (check with controller).

Source: Adapted from Monczka, R. M., and L. C. Giunipero (1990), *Purchasing Internationally: Concepts and Principles* Chelsea, MI: Bookcrafters.

Comparable Costs

Certain costs are comparable between the domestic and offshore purchasing. These include the unit purchase price quoted by a supplier, tooling charges, and transportation from the supplier (comparable cost does not mean the costs are equal). Unit price evaluation must consider the effect of quantity discounts, minimum buys necessary for shipping efficiency, the effect on price because of expedited shipments, and any supplier-specified surcharges or extras.

Transportation costs also require critical evaluation. For example, what is the effect on transportation costs if the purchaser controls a shipment directly from the supplier instead of having the supplier arrange shipment? What is the effect on transportation costs because of longer distances? International transportation often requires assistance from personnel with special expertise. Transportation experts can review carrier quotations, evaluate shipping alternatives, and recommend the most efficient course of action, which may include combining international shipments with those of other purchasers to obtain favorable freight rates.

Sourcing Snapshot

Panama Canal Expansion Will Change Global Supply Chains

Panama Canal Expansion Will Change Global Supply Chains

The expansion of the Panama Canal to accommodate vessels capable of carrying up to 12,500 containers per vessel will alter global trade routes. The following highlights a report prepared by Colliers International that focusses on the actions taken to prepare for these large vessels called Panamax in this snapshot.

Paramax Ready Port Criteria. A port is considered post-Panamax ready when it has met three key criteria: (1) channel depth of 50 feet with sufficient channel width and turning basin size; (2) cranes capable of loading and unloading Panamax ships; and (3) docks engineered to handle the new bigger cranes.

North American Port Capacity. Port capacity is measured by TEUs (twenty foot equivalent units) an intermodal container. This container is a metal box, which contains imported cargo. Intermodal containers can be easily transferred between various modes of transportation, such as ships, trains, and trucks. All but four of North America's top twenty ports as ranked by container traffic are in the U.S. The remaining two are in Canada and Mexico. Los Angeles and Long Beach are the busiest North American container ports, followed by New York/New Jersey, Savannah, and Vancouver. 13 of the top 20 North American ports handle more than one million annual TEUs. The top 50 U.S. ports handle 32.5 million TEUs.

Canada's leading 5 ports handle 4.8 million TEUs and Mexico's top 10 ports handle 4.2 million TEUs.

Impact on Ports & Supply Chains. The canal expansion will alter global trade routes and the expansion will impact not only shipping companies, but retailers, manufacturers, and commodity traders will each feel the effects of new access to eastern ports on their supply chains. Data from the Port Import/Export Reporting Service (PIERS) shows that, for the first time since World War II, the East Coast surpassed the West in container traffic growth. Eastern ports saw traffic grow by 5.5 percent in Q1 2012 over the same quarter in 2011, as compared with 3.0 percent in the western ports. Eastern traffic growth will accelerate further after 2015. Part of this growth will be fueled by new manufacturing operations from Airbus (Mobile), Boeing (Charleston) and Caterpillar (Athens, Georgia), and a new commitment from Disney to exclusively use the port of Jacksonville for all imports bound to the Magic Kingdom in Orlando.

U.S. Infrastructure Improvements Needed. According to a recent U.S. Army Corps of Engineers report ("U.S. Port and Inland Waterways Modernization: Preparing for Post-Panamax Vessels") post-Panamax vessels will make up 62 percent of total container ship capacity by 2030. North American ports will need to spend billions to participate in this global trade opportunity. But the U.S. may be lagging behind—the nation ranks 23rd globally in infrastructure competitiveness, according to the World Economic Forum.

Source: Conway, K.C., (2012, August), "North American Port Analysis-Preparing for the PANMAX Decade" Collier's International 13 pages.

International Transaction Costs

International purchasing creates additional costs that are not part of domestic purchasing. Failure to include these costs in a total cost analysis can lead to a miscalculation of the total cost of the purchase.

For a first-time purchase, the seller may request a **letter of credit**. Letters of credit are issued by the purchaser's bank in conjunction with an affiliate bank in the seller's country. It assures the seller that the funds are in the bank. The supplier can draw against the letter of credit on presentation of the required documents. There are two basic types of letters of credit: revocable and irrevocable. The revocable type can be changed or canceled at any time by the buyer without the seller's consent and therefore is seldom used. The irrevocable type can only be changed or canceled with the agreement of all parties.

Packaging requirements and costs are usually higher with offshore purchases because of the longer distances traveled and increased handling of shipments. Each item entering a country is also subject to a *customs duty or tariff*. Duty rates vary widely over seemingly small differences between items. A knowledgeable customs broker may lower duty costs as well as expedite the shipment through customs. Total cost analysis must include duty and broker fees incurred during the international transaction.

International shipments often require *insurance* protection. This issue is important, because unlike domestic transportation, oceangoing carrier liability is generally limited. Insurance is usually required when a third party is financing the inventory or shipment, and is provided by large firms such as Lloyd's of London.

Other costs include port terminal and handling fees. Depending on the exact terms of the purchase contract, a purchaser can expect charges for unloading of cargo, administrative services of port authority personnel, and general use of the port; these are U.S. port terminal and handling charges. Even if a purchaser uses a third party to manage this part of the process and receives a single invoice, these cost elements are still part of the single involved charge. Someone had to pay these charges.

A critical factor during international purchasing is keeping to a minimum the surprises that affect total cost and customer service. For example, if a shipment arrives in Long Beach, CA, without proper documentation, customs will place the shipment in warehouse storage awaiting documentation. Whether the buyer or the seller pays the storage charges should be clear in the event this issue arises.

Managing Currency Risks

A major concern with international purchasing is managing the risk associated with international currency fluctuations. Because of this risk, companies often take steps to reduce the uncertainty associated with fluctuating currencies.

The following example illustrates the principle of currency fluctuation and risk. Suppose a U.S. company purchased a machine from Canada in June. The purchase is denominated in Canadian dollars at $100,000 paid on delivery in November. For simplicity, assume the exchange rate in June is $1 U.S. equals $1 Canadian. By November, however, the Canadian dollar has strengthened to the point where $1 U.S. equals $0.90 Canadian (it now takes less than one Canadian dollar to purchase a U.S. dollar;

the Canadian currency has appreciated vis-à-vis the U.S. dollar). Now, $100,000 U.S. equals only $90,000 Canadian. This U.S. firm needs $100,000 Canadian to pay for the machine, or $100,000 U.S./0.9 exchange rate = $111,111 U.S. If the purchaser does not protect itself from fluctuating currencies, the machine would cost $11,111 more than originally planned. On the other hand, if the U.S. dollar strengthened against the Canadian dollar during this period, the purchase would require fewer U.S. dollars in November to buy $100,000 Canadian dollars.

Companies use a variety of measures to address the risk associated with currency fluctuations. These range from very basic measures to the sophisticated management of international currencies involving the corporate finance department.

Purchase in U.S. Dollars

Buyers who prefer to pay for international purchases in U.S. dollars are attempting to eliminate currency fluctuations as a source of risk by shifting the risk to the seller. Although this appears to be an easy method of risk management, it is not always the best or most feasible approach. The offshore supplier, which is also aware of currency risks, may be unwilling to accept the risk of currency fluctuations by itself. Also, many offshore suppliers anticipate exchange rate fluctuations by incorporating a risk factor into their price. A purchaser willing to accept some of the currency risk may obtain a more favorable price.

Sharing Currency Fluctuation Risk

Equal sharing of risk permits a selling firm to price its product without having to factor in the acceptance of risk costs. Sharing of risk requires equal division of a change in an agreed-upon price because of currency fluctuation. In the Canadian machine example, the U.S. firm realized over $11,000 in additional costs because of currency fluctuations. With equal risk sharing, the Canadian and U.S. firms would evenly divide the additional cost. This technique works best on items that have a set delivery date, such as capital equipment.

Currency Adjustment Contract Clauses

With currency adjustment clauses, both parties agree that payment occurs as long as exchange rates do not fluctuate outside an agreed-upon range or band. If exchange rates move outside the agreed-upon range, the parties can renegotiate or review the contract. This provides a mutual degree of protection because firms do not know with certainty in which direction exchange rates will fluctuate.

Purchase contracts often contain one of two types of currency adjustment clauses: *delivery-triggered clauses* and *time-triggered clauses*. Delivery-triggered clauses stipulate that the parties will review an exchange before delivery to verify that the rate is still within the agreed-upon range. If the rate falls outside the range, the buyer or seller can ask to renegotiate the contract price. Time-triggered clauses stipulate that both parties will review a contract at specified time intervals to evaluate the impact of fluctuating exchange rates. The parties review the exchange rate at scheduled intervals, and a new contract is established if the rate falls outside the agreed-upon range.

Currency Hedging

Hedging involves the simultaneous purchase and sale of currency contracts in two markets. The expected result is that a gain realized on one contract will be offset by a loss on the other. Hedging is a form of risk insurance that can protect both parties from currency fluctuations. The motivation for using hedging is risk aversion, not monetary gain. If the purpose of buying currency contracts is to realize a net gain, then the purchaser is speculating and not hedging.

Buyers and sellers trade futures exchange contracts (also referred to as "futures contracts") on commodity exchanges open to anyone needing to hedge or with speculative risk capital. In fact, the exchanges encourage speculation because speculators help create markets for buyers and sellers of futures contracts. Futures traders sell futures contracts in fixed currency amounts with fixed contract lengths. **Options** to buy or sell a currency at a certain exchange rate are also available to buyers. Options may be used to lock in favorable rates during negotiations or anytime a purchaser is anticipating the purchase of an item from a specific country. The buyer pays a small premium to have the right to buy the currency at a later date.

Forward exchange contracts have a different focus than futures exchange contracts. Issued by major banks, these contracts are agreements by which a purchaser pays a pre-established rate for a currency in the future (as well as a fee to the bank). Trading participants include banks, brokers, and multinational companies. The use of forward exchange contracts discourages speculation. Forward exchange contracts meet the needs of an individual purchaser in terms of dollar amount and time limit.

Finance Department Expertise

Companies with extensive international experience usually have a finance or treasury department that can support international currency requirements. Finance can identify the currency a firm should use for payment based on projections of currency fluctuations. The finance department can also provide advice about hedging and currency forecasts, and whether to seek a new contract or renegotiate an existing one because of currency changes; it can also act as a clearinghouse for offshore currencies to make payment for offshore purchases.

Tracking Currency Movements

Purchasing managers should track the movement of currencies against the dollar over time to identify longer-term changes and sourcing opportunities because of changing economics. The dollar has strengthened moderated to the Euro over the 2008–2013 period making imports from Europe relatively attractive. Part of this could be attributed to the financial crisis in Greece and weak economies in Italy Portugal and Spain. During the 2008–2013 time period the Euro ranged from .63/USD to .84/USD and is now around .76/USD. The Euro's to Dollar range for 2012 was .74/USD to .82/USD or a 10.5 percent variation from high to low.

Meanwhile, China during the same period allowed the yuan appreciated almost 12 percent versus the dollar meaning imports from China would be higher on currency conversion alone. China has been criticized in the international community for holding down the value of the yuan, making their exports more competitive in other markets.

In any event, the more volatility experienced by a currency, the more purchasers need to build in currency adjustment clauses or take actions to hedge against currency fluctuation risks.

Moving to a Global Sourcing Philosophy

At some point, many companies determine that moving beyond basic international purchasing might yield new and untapped benefits. Exhibit 10.9 presents international purchasing and global sourcing as a series of evolving levels or steps along a continuum. An internationalization of the sourcing process takes place as firms evolve or progress first from domestic purchasing to international purchasing, and then to the global coordination and integration of common items, processes, designs, technologies, and suppliers across worldwide locations. Level I includes those firms that only purchase domestically. Sourcing domestically could result in purchases from international suppliers that have facilities in the United States.

Referring to Exhibit 10.9, Level II represents basic international purchasing that is usually reactive and uncoordinated between buying locations or units. Moving forward, strategies and approaches developed in Level III begin to recognize that a properly executed worldwide sourcing strategy can result in major improvements. However, strategies at this level are not well coordinated across worldwide buying locations, operating centers, functional groups, or business units.

Level IV, which represents the integration and coordination of sourcing strategies across worldwide buying locations, represents a sophisticated level of strategy development. Operating at this level requires

- Worldwide information systems
- Personnel with sophisticated knowledge and skills
- Extensive coordination and communication mechanisms
- An organizational structure that promotes central coordination of global activities
- Leadership that endorses a global approach to sourcing

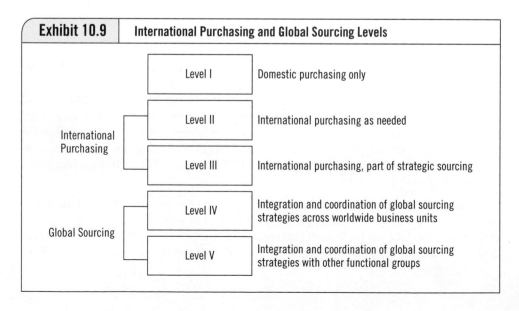

| Exhibit 10.9 | International Purchasing and Global Sourcing Levels |

	Level I	Domestic purchasing only
International Purchasing	Level II	International purchasing as needed
	Level III	International purchasing, part of strategic sourcing
Global Sourcing	Level IV	Integration and coordination of global sourcing strategies across worldwide business units
	Level V	Integration and coordination of global sourcing strategies with other functional groups

Although worldwide integration occurs in Level IV, which is not the case with Level III, the integration is primarily cross-locational rather than cross-functional.

Organizations that operate at Level V have achieved the cross-locational integration that firms operating at the fourth level have achieved. The primary distinction is that Level V participants integrate and coordinate common items, processes, designs, technologies, and suppliers across worldwide purchasing centers and with other functional groups, particularly engineering. This integration occurs during new-product development as well as during the sourcing of items or services to fulfill continuous demand or aftermarket requirements.

Only those firms that have worldwide design, development, production, logistics, and procurement capabilities can progress to this level. Although many firms expect to advance to Level V, the reality is that many lack the understanding or the willingness to achieve this level of sophistication.

Factors Driving Successful Global Sourcing Programs

A major research project on global sourcing, with 167 companies, identified a set of factors that drove global sourcing performance. These factors were (1) a defined process to support global sourcing, (2) centrally coordinated and centrally led decision making, (3) site-based control of operational activities, (4) real-time communication tools, (5) information sharing with suppliers, (6) availability of critical resources, (7) sourcing and contracting systems, and (8) international purchasing office support.[28] Exhibit 10.10 highlights these success factors, which are explained in more detail in the following section.

Defined Process to Support Global Sourcing

The development of a rigorous and well-defined approach or process is critical to global sourcing success. Some organizations have taken their commodity or regional strategy process and adapted it for global sourcing. When this occurs, the global process will likely weight certain factors differently. For example, more emphasis placed on risk factors and total landed cost. The a recent dual trends to evaluating revenue impact and the desire to minimize risk has lead to more nearshoring leading to a global sourcing strategy that positions the supply base regionally with central oversight. (see the opening snapshot)

A defined process helps overcome many of the differences inherent in global sourcing. Social culture and laws, personnel skills and abilities, and business culture are three areas

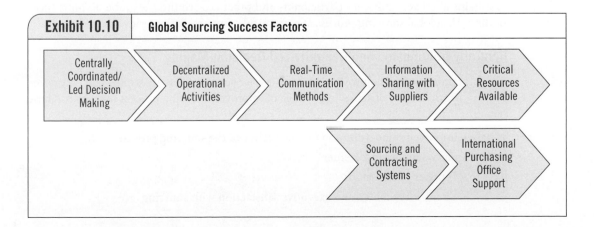

Exhibit 10.10   Global Sourcing Success Factors

Centrally Coordinated/Led Decision Making → Decentralized Operational Activities → Real-Time Communication Methods → Information Sharing with Suppliers → Critical Resources Available

Sourcing and Contracting Systems → International Purchasing Office Support

---

Exhibit 10.11 | **A U.S. Chemical Company's Global Sourcing Process**

Step 1: Identify Global Sourcing Opportunities

When identifying specific opportunities, an executive steering committee and globalization manager consider:

- What business units require the largest cost reductions?
- What does the company currently buy?
- How is the commodity currently specified?
- How much effort will it take to create a worldwide set of specifications?

Step 2: Establish Global Sourcing Development Teams

The executive steering committee forms cross-functional/cross-locational (CF/CL) teams with worldwide members to pursue global opportunities.

Step 3: Propose Global Strategy

A team charter provides project teams with responsibility for proposing a global strategy. Teams validate the original assumptions underlying the project, verify current volumes and expected savings, determine if global suppliers exist, evaluate the current set of specifications between design centers, and propose a global strategy.

Step 4: Develop Request for Proposal (RFP) Specifications

Teams are responsible for developing the request for proposal (RFP) that suppliers receive. This step consumes a large portion of the global sourcing process time.

Step 5: Release RFPs to Suppliers

On average, six suppliers receive an RFP during a global project. Project teams are responsible for following up with suppliers and answering any questions.

Step 6: Evaluate Bids or Proposals

A commercial and technical evaluation of supplier proposals occurs. Project teams will ask suppliers for their best and final offer and conduct site visits as required. Face-to-face negotiation occurs after analyzing the RFPs returned from suppliers.

Step 7: Negotiate with Suppliers

A smaller team negotiates with suppliers to finalize contract details. All negotiations are conducted at the buying company's U.S. headquarters and can last up to three days. The negotiation process lengthens if the buying company does not achieve its price and service targets.

Step 8: Award Contract(s)

Information concerning the awarded contract is communicated throughout the company via e-mail. The steering committee calculates expected savings and maintains the agreements in a corporate database.

Step 9: Implement Contract and Manage Supplier(s)

This step involves loading global agreements into the appropriate corporate systems. It also involves managing the transition to new suppliers and/or part numbers.

---

where differences are the greatest across different geographic units. A global sourcing process helps align very different participants and practices around the globe. Exhibit 10.11 outlines the global sourcing process at a chemical company with worldwide operations.

Centrally Coordinated and Centrally Led Decision Making

Maintaining central control and leadership over activities that are strategic in nature enhances the probability of achieving a range of improved sourcing process outcomes. These benefits include

- Improved standardization or consistency of the sourcing process
- Early supplier involvement
- Supplier relationships
- Client, stakeholder, and executive satisfaction with sourcing

Site-Based and Decentralized Control of Operational Activities

Firms that also decentralize operational activities during global sourcing are likely to realize lower total cost of ownership, better inventory management, and improved performance to external customers. Operational activities at a decentralized level include

- Issuing material releases to suppliers
- Expediting orders when necessary
- Resolving performance problems
- Planning inventory levels
- Developing logistics plans

Real-Time Communication Tools

Communication intricacies makes global sourcing more complex compared with domestic or regional sourcing. Global sourcing participants are often located around the world, making real-time and face-to-face communication difficult. Furthermore, participants may speak several languages while adhering to different business practices, social cultures, and laws.

Many communication and coordination approaches support global sourcing efforts. Examples include regular review meetings, joint training sessions involving worldwide team members, regularly reported project updates through the company intranet, and co-location of functional personnel.

A common approach for coordinating work efforts is to rely on audio conferencing or skype type visual meeting at scheduled time intervals. Participants have more access to a number of web-based communication tools, such as Go to Meeting, NetMeeting, Skype, Centra, and so on. One conclusion is clear: Successful global sourcing efforts feature well-established communication methods to help overcome the inherent complexities of the process.

It is hard to imagine a successful global sourcing effort without access to reliable and timely information. Examples of such information include a listing of existing contracts and suppliers, reports on supplier capabilities and performance, worldwide volumes by purchase type and location, and information about potential new suppliers. The ability to provide the data and information that global sourcing requires demands the development of global information technology systems and data warehouses.

Although access to a common coding system and real-time data is a major facilitator, the reality is that many firms lack essential IT capabilities. Many companies have historically grouped their procurement and engineering centers by region, whereas other companies that are the result of mergers and acquisitions usually feature different legacy systems, processes, and part numbers across locations. This forces firms to spend time and money to standardize and commonize their systems and coding schemes. Part number and commodity coding schemes have the second-lowest level of similarity from a list of 20 items when looking across all company-wide locations.

Information Sharing with Suppliers

Successful global sourcing requires both access to a range of critical information and the willingness to share that information with important suppliers on a worldwide basis. Firms that share performance information with their most important worldwide suppliers realize lower purchase price and cost. Shared performance information includes details about supplier quality, delivery, cycle time, and flexibility. A second type of information sharing relates to broader outcomes. This includes assessment of the supplier's technological sophistication, future capital plans, and product variety data.

Availability of Critical Resources

Resources that affect global success include budget support for travel, access to qualified personnel, time for personnel to develop global strategies, and the availability of required information and data. The availability of time was correlated highly with team effectiveness. Teams that had the time to pursue their agenda were more effective than those that did not have the time. This is very important given the fact that most organizations use teams to coordinate their global efforts.

Sourcing and Contracting Systems

The most important way to ensure access to information is to develop technology systems that make critical information available on a worldwide basis. Firms that have systems that provide access to relevant information are more likely to report lower total costs of ownership and improved sourcing process outcomes from global sourcing. Examples of these features and the information they provide include a worldwide database of purchased goods and services; common part coding schemes; contract management modules; and systems for measuring contract compliance, worldwide goods and services usage by location, and purchase price paid by location.

International Purchasing Office Support

As previously mentioned, IPOs support a higher level of global sourcing through greater access to product and process technology, reduced cycle times, and increased responsiveness. Additionally, the IPOs have the capabilities to provide operational support from initial negotiations through the contract management phase of the supplier selection cycle. The increasing movement to global sourcing has been enhanced by the growth of IPOs over the past five years.

Future Global Sourcing Trends

Globalization is a continuous journey of development and improvement. Foremost in this journey is the need to develop or obtain supply management skill sets that encourage evaluating the supply network from a worldwide perspective. Other developments include the need to agree on global performance measures and to establish integrated systems among worldwide units and with suppliers. Doing this requires the continued development and refinement of integrated and coordinated global sourcing strategies across the functional organization. Greater integration among marketing, engineering, and sourcing groups should occur as firms evolve toward higher globalization levels.

This increased integration has resulted in a trend toward doing business with suppliers that have global capabilities. In addition, the focus of global sourcing will shift from part (i.e., component) sourcing to subsystems, systems, and services. Cost reduction pressures will also provide a continuation of sourcing in low-cost emerging supply markets, such as China, India, Brazil and Eastern Europe. Although very attractive from a price standpoint, these markets have hidden costs that must be identified. The ability to manage these changes will begin to separate leading companies from average ones.

Companies that produce and sell worldwide should now view global sourcing as a part of their overall sourcing strategy. The pursuit of a competitive advantage requires the development of global processes and strategies that become an integral part of a firm's supply management efforts. Understanding the critical differences between transactional international purchasing and integrated global sourcing is essential before managers can begin to realize the benefits that global sourcing can offer an organization.

Good Practice Example	*Worldwide Sourcing at Selex*

Selex, a U.S.-based electronics company with $2 billion in annual sales, is a company in transition. Selex experienced eroding profit margins because of intense global competition and mature product lines (with some of its products being 20 to 25 years old), making it vulnerable to cost-reduction pressure and lower profit margins.

The company suffered through several costly product failures and lost market share as new competitors and technologies encroached on core markets. With much difficulty, the company was forced to change its culture to respond to the demands of a new marketplace. Selex has had to change from being a technology-driven company to a flexible, market-focused company.

Selex organizes supply management into three distinct groups: indirect purchasing, raw materials purchasing (any material that is required for production), and contract or finished goods purchasing (outsourced finished goods). Each group has pursued innovative approaches to worldwide sourcing.

Indirect Purchasing

Previous efforts at managing indirect purchases were U.S. focused, even though Selex has a manufacturing presence in the United Kingdom, Mexico, the United States, Japan, and China. A major corporate initiative at Selex has involved the development of a global sourcing process called Sourcing Vision. Using this process, project teams systematically review Selex's worldwide indirect spend with the goal of achieving cost savings of 7 to 15 percent annually.

An executive steering committee oversees the Sourcing Vision process. This committee consists of the vice president of research, the vice president of supply chain management, the vice president of marketing and sales, the vice president of information technology, and the corporate controller. Each member is at the executive vice president level, and each champions a specific global project.

Cross-functional project teams are an integral part of Sourcing Vision. Project teams engage in the following activities:

- Analyzing the industry and identifying buyer and seller strengths and weaknesses
- Defining improvement goals
- Identifying potential suppliers
- Forwarding and analyzing supplier proposals
- Determining the criteria for supplier selection
- Developing a sourcing strategy
- Making supplier selection decisions

Raw Materials Purchasing

The second major procurement group is raw materials purchasing (which most companies call direct materials). As part of its global procurement strategy, the raw materials group has focused on (1) identifying and qualifying sources worldwide and (2) aggregating volumes with leveraged agreements. This group also has responsibility for finished goods planning (which includes aggregate product planning).

A major change in raw materials procurement involves technical personnel, operations, and procurement working together worldwide to refine component materials specifications. This cross-functional approach, which is coordinated at the corporate level, examines systems tradeoffs to arrive at an expected lowest total component cost. A second major change emphasized a commodity approach to global strategy development, with leadership roles assumed by personnel from different sites. Selex has also established lead buyers at sites for items that are not part of the coordinated commodity approach. One individual at each plant is responsible for a procurement area and becomes Selex's resident expert.

Contract Purchasing

The global outsourcing of finished products at Selex is a result of the realization that vertical integration could not support 20 to 40 new product launches a year. Most Selex products use self-contained electronic components, which the company refers to as media. The physical housing of the product is the hardware. Selex insources media and outsources hardware because most of the innovation that customers value occurs within media rather than hardware.

Selex formed a contract manufacturing organization with primary responsibility for hardware outsourcing. This group now has responsibility for identifying and qualifying outsource partners, assessing product quality, and working with contract manufacturers during new-product development. As part of the contract manufacturing organization, the outsourcing director also has responsibility for two international purchasing offices (IPOs). The IPOs identify potential contract manufacturers or identify available suppliers for a specific application. The IPOs also support the indirect and raw materials purchasing groups discussed earlier.

Selex illustrates how a major corporation, faced with new competitive threats and declining markets, transformed itself from a slow, functionally driven organization into a responsive, market-driven, cross-functional enterprise. It also illustrates how three procurement groups, each taking very different approaches, have endorsed worldwide sourcing as a way to help achieve corporate objectives.

Source: Interviews with company managers. The corporate name was changed at the request of the company.

CONCLUSION

Worldwide sourcing of raw materials, components, finished goods, and services will continue to increase. Because of this, supply management personnel at all levels must become familiar with the nuances of worldwide sourcing. Although most organizations would prefer to purchase from suppliers that are geographically close, this is not always possible. Firms operating in competitive industries must purchase from the best available sources worldwide. Developing these sources requires continual monitoring of both supply market and country trends. As the risks and costs mount with China and developing country sourcing firms are considering implementing re-shoring and nearshoring into their global sourcing strategies. For the U.S.-based buyers this means increased sourcing in Mexico and South America. For those in Europe it can mean more Eastern European sourcing. Globalization will continue to be a major force that needs to be assessed on a company-by-company basis. Once the assessment is made, then supply management must respond with an effective global strategy.

KEY TERMS

barter, 387

behavior, 381

Buy-back, 388

compensation trading, 388

counterpurchase, 388

countertrade, 387

culture, 381

Foreign Corrupt Practices Act (FCPA), 385

foreign, offshore, or global, 369

foreign-trade zones, 389

forward exchange contracts, 395

global sourcing, 369

globalization, 366

hedging, 395

Incoterms, 383

international purchasing, 368

letter of credit, 393

nearshoring, 368

offset, 388

offshoring, 368

outsourcing, 368

options, 395

re-shoring, 368

switch trading, 388

United Nations Convention on Contracts for the International Sale of Goods (CISG), 385

values, 381

worldwide sourcing, 369

DISCUSSION QUESTIONS

1. Discuss whether globalization and the subsequent growth in worldwide sourcing will have a positive or negative effect over the long run in the United States. Why? What are the alternatives to worldwide sourcing?

2. China, India, Eastern Europe, and other developing countries have been sourcing hot spots. Explain why and also discuss any problems you see in sourcing from these low-cost countries.

3. What factors are making re-shoring and nearshoring more attractive as part of an organization's worldwide sourcing strategies.

4. What are the most important reasons for pursuing worldwide sourcing today?

5. What are the advantages of establishing an international purchasing office? What services do these offices provide?

6. Discuss the reasons why a firm would use a third-party external agent for worldwide sourcing.

7. Discuss some of the sources of information a buyer can use to identify potential offshore sources of supply.

8. How do international purchasing and global sourcing differ? Do you think the differences are meaningful? Why?

9. How do outsourcing, nearshoring and offshoring and re-shoring differ? What characteristics determine if a firm chooses to offshore and/or nearshore, and why?

10. Many U.S. firms begin worldwide sourcing on a reactive basis. What does this mean? What might cause a firm to shift from reactive worldwide sourcing to a proactive approach to worldwide sourcing?

11. What are the factors that drive successful global sourcing programs, and what do you feel are the biggest obstacles to global sourcing?

12. Refer to the barriers to worldwide sourcing that confront firms. For each barrier, discuss one or more ways that a company can overcome the barrier.

13. What form of countertrade appears to offer the most purchase flexibility? Why?

14. Discuss how foreign trade zones (FTZ) can improve on the advantages gained from worldwide sourcing. Next find the FTZ closest to you.

15. 15.Take a pro or con position on the issue of "conflict minerals" reporting requirements discussed in the sourcing snapshot.

ADDITIONAL READINGS

Den Butter, F. A. G., and Linse, K. A. (2008 Fall), "Rethinking Procurement in the Era of Globalization," *MIT Sloan Management Review*, 50(1), 76.

Bozarth, C., Handfield, R., and Das, A. (1998), "Stages of Global Sourcing Evolution: An Exploratory Study," *Journal of Operations Management*, 16, 241–255.

Das, A., and Handfield, R. B. (1997), "Just-in-Time and Logistics in Global Sourcing: An Empirical Study," *International Journal of Physical Distribution and Logistics Management*, 27(3–4), 244–259.

Fraering, M., and Prasad, S. (1999), "International Sourcing and Logistics: An Integrated Model," *Logistics Information Management*, 12(6), 451.

Giunipero, L., and Monczka, R. M. (1997), "Organizational Approaches to Managing International Sourcing," *International Journal of Physical Distribution and Logistics Management*, 27(5–6), 321–336.

Gray, J. V., Skowronski, K., Esenduran, G., and Rungtusanatham, M. J. (2013), "The Reshoring Phenomenon: What Supply Chain Academics Ought to Know and Should Do," *Journal of Supply Chain Management*, April, 27–33.

Kvedaraviciene, G. (2008), "Development of Nearshoring in the Global Outsourcing Market," *Economics and Management*, pp. 563–569.

Locke, D. (1996), *Global Supply Management*, Boston: McGraw-Hill.

Murray, J. Y. (2001), "Strategic Alliance-Based Global Sourcing Strategy for Competitive Advantage: A Conceptual Framework and Research Propositions," *Journal of International Marketing*, 9(4), 30–58.

Petersen, K. J., Frayer, D. J., and Scannel, T. V. (2006), "An Empirical Investigation of Global Sourcing Strategy Effectiveness," *Journal of Supply Chain Management*, 36(2), 29–38.

Porter, M., and Rivkin, J. V. (2012), "Choosing the United States," *Harvard Business Review*, March, 81–92.

Samli, A. C., Browning, J. M., and Busbia, C. (1998), "The Status of Global Sourcing as a Critical Tool of Strategic Planning," *Journal of Business Research*, 43(3), 177–187.

Trent, R. J., and Monczka, R. M. (2007), "Achieving Excellence in Global Sourcing," *Sloan Management Review*, Fall, 24–32.

ENDNOTES

1. Dunne, P., and Henwood, D. (2008, October 1), "The Banking Crisis Around the World," The Liscio Report on the Economy.

2. Friedman, T. L. (2005), The World Is Flat, New York: Farrar, Straus and Giroux.

3. Friedman, pp. 24, 25.

4. Cassandra, A. (2012, November 26), "Global Trends 2013-A Top Ten for Business Leaders," *Economist*. Retrieved from http://www.economist.com/blogs/theworldin2013/2012/11/global-trends-2013

5. Passariello, C. (2007, July 13), "Behind L'Oreal's Makeover in India: Going Upscale," *Wall Street Journal*, pp. A1, A4.

6. Mattoili, R., Cimilluca, D., and Kesmodel, D. (2013, May 30), "China Makes Biggest U.S. Play—Asian Meat Giant Strikes $4.7 Billion Deal for Virginia's Smithfield Foods," *Wall Street Journal*, p. A1.

7. Cameron, D. (2013, June 27), "Senate Panel to Examine Smithfield Foods Deal," *Wall Street Journal*, p. B2.

8. Fishman, C. (2012, December), "The Insourcing Boom," *The Atlantic*, pp. 22–25.

9. _____, _____ (2012, September 10), *IMTS Press Release*, Retrieved from website http://www.imts.com/media/imts_releases/20120919.html, accessed August 2013.

10. ____, ___ (2013, August), *Kotra*, Retrieved from http://www.buykorea.or.kr/main/BKBKMA010M.html

11. _____, _____ (2013, August), *Kotra seal*, Retrieved from http://kotraseal.en.ec21.com/

12. Monczka, R. M., Trent, R. J., and Peterson, K. J. (2006), *Effective Global Sourcing and Supply for Superior Results*, Tempe, AZ: CAPS Research, p. 13.

13. Kubin, M. (1997), "Developing Your Cross Cultural Communication Skills," 79th ISM International Conference Proceedings, Atlanta GA. Retrieved from http://www.ism.ws/pubs/Proceedings/confproceedingsdetail. cfm?ItemNumber=5206

14. Kubin. (2009, June 18), "ISM 2009—Best Practices Abound," *Purchasing*, 138(6), 1, 19.

15. Locke, D. (1996), *Global Supply Management*, Boston: McGraw-Hill, Irwin p. 46.

16. Locke, p. 51.

17. Hickey, K. (2003, September 15), "Chinese Puzzle," *Traffic World*, p. 16.

18. O'Reilly, J. (2008, September), "China's Port Boom Swings Full Speed Ahead," Retrieved from www.InbourndLogis tics.com, accessed September 2008.

19. O'Reilly. (2010, February), "China's Stimulus Wise or Wasteful," *RSS*, p. 1.

20. Agarwal, A. (2012), "India Infrastructure Summit 2012," Ernst and Young Report Retrieved from http://www.ey.com/Publication/vwLUAssets/FICCI_Infra_report_final/$FILE/FICCI_Infra_report_final.pdf)

21. Kilgore, M., Joseph, A., and Motersky, J. (2007, October 1), "Logistics Infrastructure Will Slow India's Progress," *Supply Chain Management Review*, p. 12.

22. Moradian, R. (2004, July), "The Logistics of Doing Business in China," *Inbound Logistics*. Retrieved from http://www.inboundlogistics.com/articles/3plline/3plline0704.shtml

23. Conway, K. C. (2012, August), "North American Port Analysis-Preparing for the PANMAX Decade," *Collier's International*, p. 2.

24. ____,____ (2011), *Foreign-Trade Zone Manual*, Washington, DC: U.S. Customs and Border Protection, p. 16.

25. Trunick, P. A. (2013), "Is an FTZ for You?" *World Trade 100*, 26(1), 23.

26. Foreign Trade Zone Manual, p. 100.

27. Ibid., pp. 164, 165.

28. Monczka et.al., pp. 24–26.

Strategic Sourcing Process

Strategic Cost Management

CHAPTER 11

Learning Objectives

After completing this chapter, you should be able to

- Understand the impact of cost management on the supply chain
- Understand the fundamental approaches to price management
- Understand approaches for reducing supplier costs of production and delivery
- Understand the concept of total cost of ownership
- Identify collaborative approaches to cost management

Chapter Outline

Honda of America's Emphasis on Strategic Cost Management Permeates Every Part of Its Business

Honda was built upon a cost management culture from the time the company began. The company founder sought to move into the automotive industry from a motorcycle base, despite government blockades, and found that the automotive supply base in Japan was unwilling to support his business. As such, he developed his motorcycle component suppliers into automotive component suppliers through supplier development, financial support, and most importantly, relationships and trust. This loyalty to suppliers, under any circumstances, still exists today. Honda will not "fire" a supplier unless the supplier requests them to do so. They will support and invest in suppliers who are going through difficult periods, but expect the same leeway when economic times become difficult in the automotive industry. This long-term view toward co-destiny has paid off. Moreover, like a strict but loving parent, Honda demands a lot from their suppliers, including multiple visits to their site to drive improvement with a refusal to take "no" as an answer. This concept of supplier development, integration, and ongoing socialization and trust is a core and integral component of the Honda business model.

Honda's business model has always been focused around a six-year plan, which is highly dependent on a small group of committed suppliers who are involved upfront for the entire six years. The second component of their model is 100 percent understanding of all components of product cost, with a high level of precision. The third component of their model concerns lean supplier development engineering, with a large population of field engineers working closely with key suppliers on every aspect of their production process. The fourth component is based on flawless new product launch. Honda is a firm believer in extreme attention to detail in every aspect of component, subsystem, and system development. The "Same Part, Same Place, Same Process" mentality emphasizes that multiple visits and meetings take place with a supplier during prototype development and ramp-up, to ensure that products coming off of a supplier's line are of "first product" quality and ready to go to market when production conditions occur. Finally, one of the most important components of Honda's business model is *communications.* The quality, frequency, and content of every communication that takes place between Honda and its dealers, suppliers, and stakeholders is reviewed, and is systematically controlled for in every aspect of their business model. Communications are the foundation for inter-organizational relationships.

Measurement systems support all cost management decisions. Initial metrics in the design include the price that the final product could be introduced at in the market. The price/value relationship for Honda's customer is a focal point of debate and discussion. What price level at the retail level can provide the required profit at the manufacturing level? A production cost is established at a high level as a target, and then R&D, manufacturing, and supply chain work on how to achieve it, separating manufacturing and supply cost to make that unit. They then break it down component by component, on how to build up to the target price. Certain types of quality characteristics are set in stone (five-star crash ratings, eight airbags, and so forth). There is then an ongoing effort by suppliers and supply management to share ideas and innovation with R&D teams early on to discover how to reduce expense, along with adding more value and features. Price is the first differentiator, followed by quality. Target cost elements are based on Activity Based Costing procedures, derived from historical analysis conducted by key R&D groups who are capable of estimating realistic manufacturing and supplier expenses. These are broken down into budgets developed by category teams. Tradeoffs are always a point of discussion at category team meetings. This is a stressful and rigorous process, as multiple teams each work on their own target costs, all seeking to meet the market price.

Cost engineers (procurement) at Honda are aligned by the specific types of suppliers they work with, and are dedicated to this role with the objective of becoming global experts. For example, a cost engineer can visit any given supplier of stampings, and produce a lengthy report documenting the level of capability associated with that supplier, based on one visit. There is a high level of capability and knowledge regarding what to look for, which is designed into the culture.

On a regular basis, all of the procurement groups meet at a quarterly meeting to discuss integrated global supply management strategy. At this meeting, the discussion focuses on opportunities for commonality and standardization, coordination with marketing's export strategy, new product planning, cost management, and technology transfer issues within the supply base.

An important part of this strategy meeting also focuses on development of a truly "global" supply base. All divisions and business units come together on a regular basis to discuss and share global platform development, common supply strategies, and ongoing cost management objectives. Opportunities for learning and identification of lessons learned are a major part of this effort. Honda continues to measure cost against attributes such as customer value, ensuring that its new vehicle costs do not rise even though global material costs are rising, and also to add features that ensure customers have a safe, innovative, and fulfilling driving experience.

Source: Handfield, R., and Edwards, S. (2009, July), "Cost Leadership Best Practices," White Paper, Supply Chain Resource Cooperative, NC State University.

Introduction

In today's economy, the driving force behind global competition can be summarized in a single equation:

$$\text{Value} = (\text{Quality} + \text{Technology} + \text{Service} + \text{Cycle Time})/\text{Price}$$

Although supply management has a major impact on all of the variables in the numerator in this equation, this chapter focuses on the denominator: price and its primary driver, cost. A major responsibility of supply management is to ensure that the price paid for an item is fair and reasonable. The price paid for purchased products and services will have a direct impact on the end customer's perception of value provided by the organization, thereby leading to a competitive advantage in the marketplace. By delivering value through continued progress in reducing costs, and thereby improving profit margins and return on assets for enterprises, supply management is truly becoming a force of its own within the executive boardroom.

Evaluation of a supplier's actual cost to provide the product or service, versus the actual purchase price paid is an ongoing challenge within all industries. In many situations, the need to control costs requires a focus on the costs associated with producing an item or service, versus simply analyzing final price. In these cases, innovative pricing approaches involve cost identification as a process leading to agreement on a final price. In other cases, however, supply management may not need to spend much effort understanding costs, and will focus instead on whether the price is fair given competitive market conditions.

Supply management and supply chain specialists must understand the principles of price and cost analysis. **Price analysis** refers to the process of comparing supplier prices against external price benchmarks, without direct knowledge of the supplier's costs. Price analysis focuses simply on a seller's price with little or no consideration given to the actual cost of production. In contrast, **cost analysis** is the process of analyzing each individual cost element (i.e., material, labor hours and rates, overhead, general and administrative costs, and profit) that together add up to the final price. Ideally, this analysis identifies the actual cost to produce an item, so the parties to a contract can determine a fair and reasonable price and develop plans to achieve future cost reductions. Finally, **total cost analysis** applies the price/cost equation across multiple processes that span two or more organizations across a supply chain. For example, the total cost of shipping a good manufactured from China into the United States may include shipping, tariffs, inventory, quality, and other costs that are over and above the actual price paid to the Chinese manufacturer. Total cost decisions may also extend to the cost of poor quality, or environmental risk. For example, consider the total cost of the decision to use a less expensive drilling pipe on the deepwater rig Horizon, versus the total cleanup cost resulting from the oil spill (see Sourcing Snapshot on p. 416).

This chapter presents a traditional discussion of price and cost fundamentals along with a number of innovative price and cost management tools that can be applied using available information on the Internet and simple spreadsheet analysis. Some of these tools are price analysis, reverse price analysis, and total cost analysis. By applying such tools, purchasers can evolve toward a system of strategic cost management that seeks to reduce costs across the entire supply chain. Although not all of these tools are appropriate for every situation, supply managers must learn to recognize when and how such tools can be applied.

A Structured Approach to Cost Reduction

Managers are increasingly considering the implications of price and cost management from a total supply chain perspective, as shown in Exhibit 11.1. In the past, many companies focused their cost efforts on internal cost management initiatives. These included approaches such as value analysis, process improvements, standardization, improvements in efficiency by utilizing technology, and others. Although these approaches are still relevant, the impact that they have on the majority of costs is not as great as in the past. Why? With the increased amount of outsourcing occurring in every global company today, the majority of the cost of goods sold is driven by suppliers, which are outside the four walls of an organization. In this environment, organizations wanting to fully capture the benefits of cost-reduction initiatives must implement approaches that include both upstream and downstream members of their supply chains. Such a change requires a fundamental shift in thinking in the minds of managers and employees.

This new generation of cost management initiatives requires that supply management and logistics executives adopt a series of new initiatives that can deliver results to the bottom line. As shown in Exhibit 11.2 on p. 414, strategic cost management approaches typically involve at least two supply chain partners working together to identify process improvements that reduce costs across the supply chain. Examples include team-based value-engineering efforts, supplier development and kaizen events, cross-enterprise cost-reduction projects, joint brainstorming efforts on new products, supplier suggestion programs, and supply chain redesign efforts. These types of efforts require that both parties commit to achieving cost-reduction strategies that go beyond simple haggling over prices.

Exhibit 11.1	Cost Management Approaches

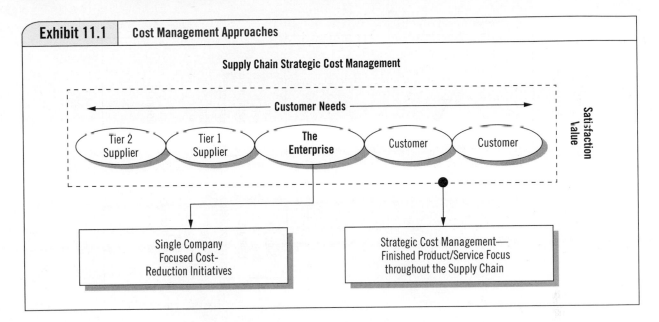

Supply Chain Strategic Cost Management

Strategic cost management approaches will vary according to the stage of the product life cycle. As shown in Exhibit 11.3 on p. 415, various approaches are appropriate at different product life cycle stages. In the initial concept and development stage, supply management will often act proactively to establish cost targets. Target costing/target pricing is a technique developed originally in Japanese organizations in the 1980s to combat the inflation of the yen against other currencies. Target pricing, quality function deployment, and technology sharing are all effective approaches for cost reduction used at this stage.

As a product or service enters the design and launch stages, supplier integration, standardization, value engineering, and design for manufacturing can improve the opportunity to use standard parts and techniques, leverage volumes, and create opportunities for cost savings. During the product or service launch, supply management will adopt more traditional cost-reduction approaches, including competitive bidding, negotiation, value analysis, volume leveraging, service contracts focusing on savings, and linking longer-term pricing to extended contracts. As a product reaches its end of life, supply management cannot ignore the potential value of environmental initiatives to remanufacture, recycle, or refurbish products that are becoming obsolete. As an example of this, print cartridge manufacturers have developed innovative technologies that allow customers to recycle laser toner cartridges, which are subsequently refurbished and used again, eliminating landfill costs.

The major benefits from cost-reduction efforts occur when supply management is involved early in the new-product/service development cycle. When sourcing decisions are made early in the product life cycle, the full effects of a sourcing decision over the product's life can be considered. When supply management is involved later in the product development cycle, efforts to reduce costs have a minimal impact because the major decisions regarding types of materials, labor rates, and choice of suppliers have already been made. A manager in a major automotive company described this situation as follows: "In the past, we allowed engineering to determine the specifications, the materials, and the supplier. In fact, the supplier already produced the first prototype. That is when they decided to call in supply management to develop the contract. How much leverage do you have in convincing

Exhibit 11.2   Supply Chain Cross-Enterprise Focus

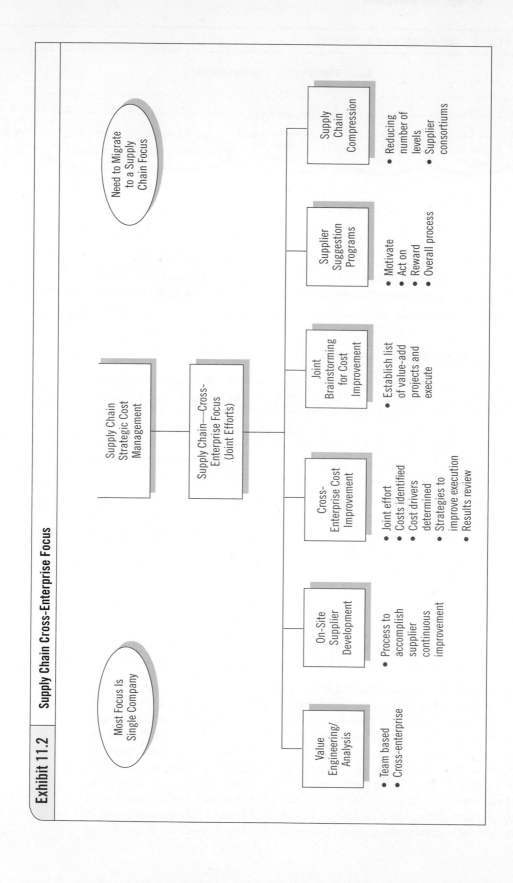

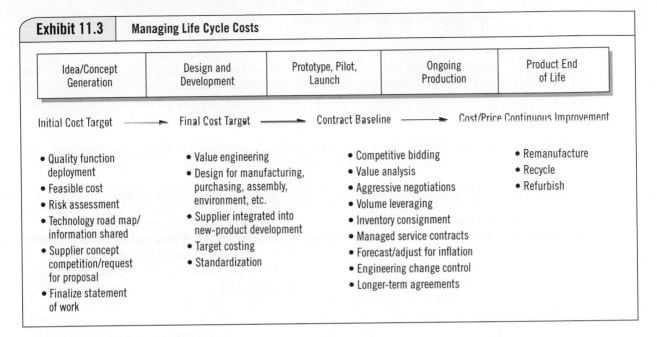

Exhibit 11.3	Managing Life Cycle Costs

Idea/Concept Generation	Design and Development	Prototype, Pilot, Launch	Ongoing Production	Product End of Life

Initial Cost Target ⟶ Final Cost Target ⟶ Contract Baseline ⟶ Cost/Price Continuous Improvement

- Quality function deployment
- Feasible cost
- Risk assessment
- Technology road map/ information shared
- Supplier concept competition/request for proposal
- Finalize statement of work

- Value engineering
- Design for manufacturing, purchasing, assembly, environment, etc.
- Supplier integrated into new-product development
- Target costing
- Standardization

- Competitive bidding
- Value analysis
- Aggressive negotiations
- Volume leveraging
- Inventory consignment
- Managed service contracts
- Forecast/adjust for inflation
- Engineering change control
- Longer-term agreements

- Remanufacture
- Recycle
- Refurbish

Exhibit 11.4	Framework for Strategic Cost Management

VALUE

High

Critical Products

Strategies:
- Cost analysis
- Collaborative cost-reduction efforts focused on total cost

Commodities

Strategies:
- Leverage preferred suppliers
- Price analysis using market forces

Low

Unique Products

Strategies:
- Cost Analysis & Reverse Price Analysis
- Standardize requirements

Generics

Strategies:
- Total delivered cost
- Automate to reduce purchasing involvement

Low   High

NUMBER OF AVAILABLE SUPPLIERS

the supplier to reduce costs when the supplier already knows they are guaranteed the business, and they have already sunk money into a fixed design and tooling for the product?"[1]

When prioritizing efforts to reduce costs, companies often apply a structured framework for cost reduction similar to the one illustrated in Exhibit 11.4. This framework is consistent with the portfolio analysis framework developed in Chapter 6 and should be integrated into an organization's category strategy development process. As shown in Exhibit 11.4, each approach requires a different strategic focus in terms of price versus cost. In general, low-value generics in which a competitive market with many potential suppliers exists should emphasize total delivered price. There is no need to spend time conducting a detailed cost analysis for low-value items that do not produce significant returns. Greater returns can be obtained by having users order these products or services directly through supplier catalogs, procurement cards, or other e-procurement technologies. Commodities are high-value products or services that also have a competitive market situation; for example, computers and technology are certainly in this category (as discussed in the opening vignette). These types of products and services can be sourced through traditional bidding approaches that require price analysis using market forces to do the work and identify what is a competitive price. With greater standardization being introduced in many industries, products once considered as critical are being moved into the commodities quadrant.

Unique products present a different challenge: Companies must strive to reduce costs for products with few available suppliers, yet that are still low value. Examples include suppliers of unique fasteners, specialty papers, and specialty MRO items. For such items, purchasers will want to identify suppliers that are charging too high a price. Further analysis of their pricing through a technique known as "reverse price analysis" (discussed later in the chapter) may identify price discrepancies that can be reduced through greater standardization of user requirements or ongoing negotiations with problematic suppliers. In effect, this may mean transitioning a product or service from the unique quadrant to the generics quadrant. Many of the commodities previously thought to belong in the generics quadrant are shifting to strategic, based on global capacity and demand forecasts for 2011 onward.

Sourcing Snapshot

Building a Cost Model to Control Complexity in Aftermarket Parts for a Large Truck Manufacturer

A large truck manufacturing company based originally in Europe has expanded its presence in North America, and has developed a strong brand reputation as a top tier service provider, with strong after-market support and parts availability on all its truck models. With this expansion, there has also been an increase in the number of new features and components on new product models, resulting in a challenging environment. On the one hand, there is a need to continue to meet customer requirements for new features, customized trucks, and features preferences, but on the other, there is a competing need to control cost. Specifically, the introduction of an increasing number of parts to support has significantly increased the logistics and material handling costs associated with providing the same level of after-market customer support that customers have grown used to and which is associated with the brand.

Several statistics suggest the speed at which the growth in part complexity is occurring:

- One truck brand has moved from 66 to 84 models
- The second truck brand has moved from 38 to 60
- The number of new parts is growing at a rate of 25 percent.
- Each brand has 15,000 to 25,000 possible different variants that customers can choose from. Few customer adaptation parts are being removed once produced, and many will never be utilized again.
- The total number of kitted part numbers was has tripled to 3100 kits in 2013 in two years.

- Total factory space dedicated to kitting activity has increased by 65,000 square feet from 2010 to 2013.
- The estimated cost of parts maintenance, including logistics, engineering, product development, and scrap, has risen to approximately $10,500 per part number in 2012.

These data suggest that the number of models and part numbers is rapidly increasing. However, there is little data that provides any tangible evidence of the ROI associated with this increase in complexity costs incurred. In reviewing the actual usage of new model variants for one model, it was found that the stream of revenue for the 20 new variants for that model accounted for less than one percent of incremental revenue. There is also a renewed interest in controlling logistics costs coming from other influences within the company's manufacturing and customer environment. Although there have been historical efforts to cancel old parts as new parts come in at roughly a one to one ratio, this ratio has not increased to the point where future business opportunities (that may or may not be realized) is being applied as the reason for the increase in this ratio.

Management recognizes a need to create a more systematic decision-making process for adding new parts to evaluate the benefits of this increased logistics complexity. This approach will provide various decision filters to bring a strong fact-based business case for adding new components or eliminating old ones, and rationalize the evolution of new products and parts going into the marketplace. This approach will enable the company not only to control logistics costs, but could also bring additional insight that would bring increased revenue to the business, and provide greater clarity for the commercial team's decisions and their impact to the business. The approach should encourage collaboration between commercial and supply chain groups to agree on product development resource allocation, based on resource man hours, fully burdened overhead rates, or testing costs balanced against the potential commercial revenue lift created by adding a model.

This decision filter will take the form of a cost model that will recognize the full logistics and material handling costs that are impacted by different types of model change decisions, and assign these expenses using a more direct cost allocation approach.

The focus of the costs would be primarily on the following parameters:

- kitting
- floor space
- transportation models
- sequencing
- lead time
- receiving quality
- throughput velocity
- warranty

The costs associated with the approach will be factored into budgeting decisions as well, especially as projected budgets are setting productivity improvement goals of 6 percent or more. The decision process can be made more insightful and holistic relative to the many parameters that are changing in this approach.

Source: Handfield, Robert, Interviews with truck manufacturer, 2013.

The major focus of a purchaser's efforts to reduce costs should be on critical products where relatively few suppliers exist but the items are higher value. Managers should commit time to exploring opportunities for value analysis/engineering, cost-savings sharing, collaborative efforts focused on identifying cost drivers, and supplier integration early in the product development cycle. Cost analysis involves breaking down a supplier's price into its cost elements to uncover potential cost savings and, hence, price reductions.

The remainder of this chapter presents a discussion of price analysis (commodities and generics quadrants), cost analysis (unique and critical quadrants), and total cost analysis (all four quadrants) that can be applied to help control the costs associated with these different purchased goods and services.

Price Analysis

To understand the factors affecting pricing levels in a given market, it is crucial to employ a market analysis—an analytical tool that identifies the primary external forces that are causing prices to either increase or decrease. As shown in Exhibit 11.5, prices are driven to a large extent by the degree of competition in a market, as well as by conditions of supply and demand. The resulting market prices are indicated by a heavier line, depending on the volume of supply in a given situation.

When demand exceeds supply, a seller's market exists, and prices generally increase. The reverse situation, a buyer's market, occurs when supply exceeds demand, and prices generally move downward. There should be an appreciation for the variety of variables that directly and indirectly influence an item's price.

Market Structure

Although it is clear that the supplier's market condition has a major influence on price, the factors affecting market conditions are not always easy to predict. Market environment is often driven by the number of competitors in an industry, the relative similarity (or lack thereof) of their products, and any existing barriers to entry for new competitors. At one end of the scale, there may exist a monopoly, where only one supplier can provide a given product or service. A good example of this condition exists in the pharmaceutical industry, where the company first to market with a new patented drug has exclusive rights to sell the product for seven years. (At the end of this period, generics that copy the drug's formulation enter the market, thereby driving down the cost of the drug.)

At the other end of the spectrum is perfect competition, in which there exist identical products with minimal barriers for new suppliers to enter the market. Price is solely a

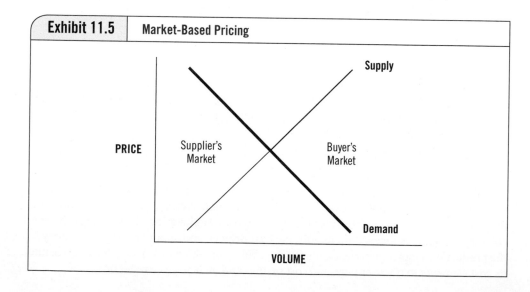

Exhibit 11.5 | **Market-Based Pricing**

function of the forces of supply and demand. No single seller or producer controls enough of the market to affect the market price. Of course, a seller could reduce its price with the hope of selling additional products. In the long run, however, this simply results in lost revenue.

An industry with only a few large competitors is classified as oligopolistic. The market and pricing strategies of one competitor directly influence others within the industry. Examples of oligopolies in the United States historically include the steel, automobile, and appliance industries. Within an oligopolistic industry, a firm may assume the role of a price leader and raise or lower prices, which can result in all other firms changing their prices or choosing to maintain existing price levels. If others do not follow, the initiating firm might be forced to reverse the change. The growth of international trade and competition has created additional choices in many industries, shifting market power away from the producer and toward the purchaser.

Economic Conditions

Economic conditions often determine whether a market is favorable to the seller or to the purchaser. When capacity utilization at producers is high (supply is tight) and demand for output is strong, supply and demand factors combine to create pricing conditions favorable to the seller. When this occurs, buyers often attempt to keep prices or price increases below the industry average. When an industry is in a decline, purchasers can take advantage of this to negotiate favorable supply arrangements.

Global markets influence prices; for example, interest rate levels influence the internal rate of return at a supplier—the overall cost of capital, which drives productive investment. Even the level of the dollar in relation to other currencies influences price, particularly for international supply management. Also, tight labor markets can create cost increases, resulting in higher purchase prices.

Knowledge of economic conditions is helpful when identifying the market factors affecting the supply and demand for a product or commodity. Awareness of current and forecasted economic conditions assists in the development of purchase budgets and material forecasts, and also provides valuable insights when developing future price negotiating strategies. One good source of information is the website for Bureau of Labor Statistics, http://www.bls.gov/ppi/, which presents key data on pricing trends for a variety of commodities. Other sources of pricing trends in commodity markets are shown in Exhibit 11.6 below.

Exhibit 11.6	**Sample Category Specific Pricing/Production Indicators**

Category	Index Name	Index Link
Semiconductors	SIA Integrated Circuit Wafer - Fab Capacity and Utilization	http://www.sia-online.org/pre statistics.cfm
Printed Circuit Boards	IPC N. American PCB Book-To-Bill Ratio	http://www.ipc.ora
Aluminum, Copper, Lead, Nickel, Tin, Zinc	London Metal Exchange	http://www.lme.com/dataprices monthlyaverages.asp
Steel Sheet & Steel Scrap	American Metal Market	http://www.amm.com
Corrugated & Boxboard	Pulp & Paper Week	www.paperloop.com
Durable Goods Orders Values and Construction Spending	US Census Bureau	www.census.gov
Machinery Producer Price Index	Machinery Producer Price Index	http://data.bls.gov
Computers	Manufacturers' Shipments, Inventories, and Orders (M3)	http://www.census.gov/indicator/www/m3/
Plastic Resins	Plastics Technology Magazine	www.plasticstechnoloav.com
Plastic Resins	Plastics News	www.plasticsnews.com
Crude Oil & Natural Gas Futures	NYMEX	www.nymex.com
Benzene, Ethylene, and Propylene	Chemical Market Reporter	www.chemicalmarketreporter.com
PPI	PPI Data for Food, Manufacturing, Textiles, etc.	http://www.bls.aov/ppi/home.htm
Fuel	Dept of Energy Fuel Index	http://tonto.eia.doe.aov/ooa/info/adu/aasdiesel.asp
Freight	Bureau of Transportation Statistics	http://www.bts.aov/xml/tsi/src/index.xml
Freight	Cass Freight Index	http://www.cassinfo.com/frtindex.html
Labor	US Department of Labor	http://www.dol.aov/
Labor	Manpower	http://www.manpower.com

Pricing Strategy of the Seller

Sellers pursue different strategies or approaches that affect the pricing of their products or services. Some sellers rely on a detailed analysis of internal cost structures to establish price, whereas others simply price at a level comparable to the competition.

The pricing strategy of the seller has a direct impact on quoted prices. To remain in business, suppliers must cover their costs and earn an overall profit to meet their corporate objectives. In many cases, however, the price charged by a seller may have little or no relationship to actual costs. As strange as this seems, pricing strategies are often based on other factors that are important to the seller. A seller may quote an unusually low price to secure a purchase contract, with the intention of raising the price once it drives competition from the marketplace. In other cases, the seller may exploit its position when he or she senses it has the purchaser over a barrel by charging an excessive price. In still other cases, the seller may simply not understand its own costs.

Several questions should be asked when analyzing a seller's pricing strategy. These include the following:

- Does the seller have a long-term pricing strategy, or is it short-term in nature?
- Is the seller a price leader (sets new pricing levels in the market), or a price follower (only matches price increases/decreases when the competition does so)?
- Is the seller attempting to establish entry barriers to other competitors by establishing a low price initially, then preparing to raise prices in the future?
- Is the seller using a cost-based pricing approach, which develops price as a function of true costs, or a market-based pricing approach? If a market-based pricing approach is being used, there may be little need for conducting a detailed cost analysis, as the price charged may be unrelated to any elements of cost.

The elements that make up the price charged by a supplier are shown in Exhibit 11.7. Essentially, the supplier's costs include materials and labor (which together make up manufacturing cost), plus overhead and sales, general and administrative expenses (which

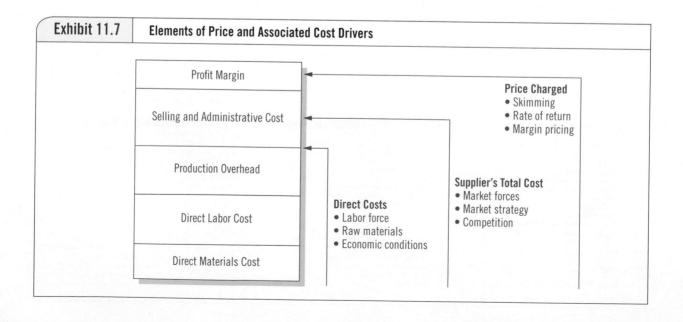

Exhibit 11.7   Elements of Price and Associated Cost Drivers

cumulatively establish the supplier's total cost), plus margin, which then equates to the price charged. Based on the interplay among these different elements, which may vary depending on the supplier's pricing model, the price charged to a buyer can vary significantly. Seller pricing strategies can be grouped into two categories: market-driven models and cost-based models. As we noted earlier, price analysis involves having the supply manager gauge the pricing strategy used by the supplier, without going into the details of how its detailed cost elements are established. We will cover market-driven pricing models first and then cover cost analysis techniques later in the chapter.

Market-Driven Pricing Models[2]

Price Volume Model

In the price volume model, the supplier analyzes the market to find the combination of price per unit and quantity of sales that maximizes its profit on the assumption that (1) lowering the price will result in more units being sold, and (2) greater volume will spread the indirect cost over more units, therefore maintaining or even increasing the profit as it relates to the price. The most basic example of this model is the suppliers offering quantity price breaks to induce the buyer to purchase in larger quantities (a core approach adopted by Sam's Club and Costco stores). Strategic sourcing initiatives should always engage a thorough analysis of the relationship between price and quantity in different marketplaces.

Combining purchase requirements across separate operating units can yield savings in tooling, setup, and operating efficiencies. A major benefit of reduced or single sourcing is a lower price that results from the higher volumes offered to a supplier. In return for a purchase contract with higher volumes, a buyer expects favorable pricing because a supplier should realize lower per-unit costs. The willingness of a supplier to offer quantity discounts also affects the final selling price.

Although a quantity discount has a positive effect on the purchase price, a purchaser must be cautious about the net impact on the total cost of the item. Buying in larger-than-normal quantities requires additional storage of purchased goods. At a time when most firms are reducing or even eliminating inventory, the additional inventory-carrying costs must be evaluated against the benefit of the quantity discount.

Market-Share Model

In the market-share model, pricing is based on the assumption that long-run profitability depends on the market share obtained by the supplier. This approach, also referred to as "penetration pricing," is an aggressive pricing approach for efficient producers because price is a direct function of cost. Penetration pricing can lead to faster market penetration for a product because of the lower profit margins a seller is willing to accept. Generally speaking, the seller is willing to take a lower price because of the potential mass market appeal of the product, resulting in substantially higher sales volumes. In the initial stages of this model, the supplier may even accept losses, but as its volume increases, the cost per unit decreases and long-term profits are achieved. A word of caution is in order here: Purchasers should question whether the seller is the most efficient producer willing to accept lower margins to win market share, or is the real intention to drive competition from the marketplace and later raise prices to exorbitant levels?

Sourcing Snapshot

When Should Companies Use Price Hedging

The last few years have witnessed a remarkable volatility in prices. The following snapshot written by Robert Rudzki provides some insights into how supply managers can manage price risks, and avoid getting into trouble.

Rudzki provides insights into what he calls "financial risk management" or as it is more generally termed—hedging. A common way for companies to begin to focus on the subject of commodity price risk-and to gain an unpleasant first experience-is to experience a massive run up in commodity prices. This event typically results in two unpleasant outcomes. The first is that it creates an unfavorable financial variance to a business plan that attracts top management's attention.

The second unpleasant experience results from the reaction to the first: it often spurs those companies to begin hedging right away, often at (in hindsight) what turns out to be the peak of commodity prices. Inevitably, in a short period of time they see their hedging programs begin to report unfavorable variances to market prices as commodity prices retreat away from their recent peaks. At that point, if it has not occurred sooner, the finger-pointing begins.

Successful risk management starts with proactively identifying and managing risks with a focus on minimizing the potential financial impact on the corporation. For each corporation, there is some level of risk, which that corporation is willing and capable of assuming (sometimes referred to as the corporate risk retention level). The capability of the corporation to assume risk is heavily influenced by its capital structure, liquidity, and business outlook. An investment grade company that has strong earnings and cash flow can retain much more risk than a below-investment grade company having poor liquidity and marginal earnings performance.

Companies that jump to a narrow implementation of hedging tools, without the benefit of strategically considering their earnings at risk "Value at Risk (VAR)" may face challenges in the future. Unexpected events and disappointing results may follow.

Let us assume that the high-level thought process described in the prior paragraph has occurred. It is probably appropriate for every corporation, regardless of financial condition, to do certain amounts and types of financial risk management to reduce risks and to add value. Hedging represents a way to reduce risk as well as to add value. Hedging should play a prominent role in financial risk management, especially in the areas of interest rate exposures, commodity price exposures, and foreign currency exposures.

Hedging is a strategy used to offset (and thereby reduce) risk, generally accomplished with options (caps), swaps, or costless collars. The principal attributes of these hedging tools appear in the figure below. A perfect hedge is one that eliminates the possibility of future (additional) gain or loss by exactly offsetting the exposure being hedged. Most hedges are imperfect to varying degrees.

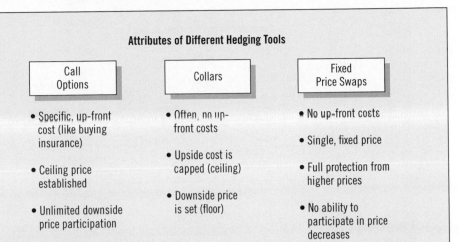

Attributes of Different Hedging Tools

Call Options	Collars	Fixed Price Swaps
• Specific, up-front cost (like buying insurance)	• Often, no up-front costs	• No up-front costs
• Ceiling price established	• Upside cost is capped (ceiling)	• Single, fixed price
• Unlimited downside price participation	• Downside price is set (floor)	• Full protection from higher prices
		• No ability to participate in price decreases

When a customer buys a fixed-price swap (figure above), they lock in a known price regardless of what happens to the market price. When a customer buys a call option (see figure above), they buy a "ceiling" beyond which their price will not rise. If the market price falls, they participate fully in that price drop. The difference between the price paid and the market price reflects the premium paid to have the "insurance" protection of the call option. If a customer is mainly interested in ensuring that the price paid falls within a price "band," a zero-cost collar merits consideration (see figure below).

Customer Buys a Fixed-Price Swap

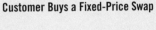
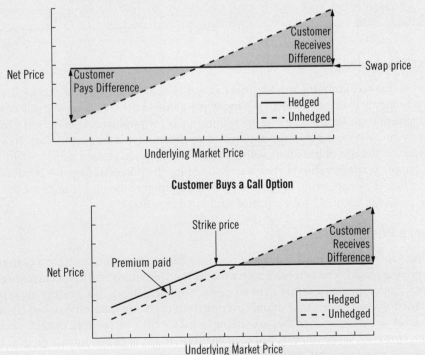

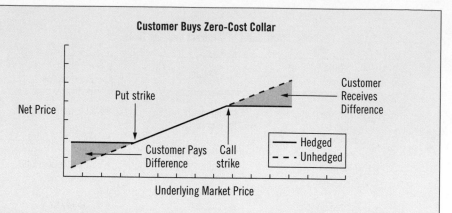

Customer Buys Zero-Cost Collar

Net Price

Put strike

Customer Receives Difference

Customer Pays Difference

Call strike

—— Hedged
- - - Unhedged

Underlying Market Price

It should be noted that the use of "excess inventories" to *physically hedge* a future price exposure is often an option, though not the focus of this discussion. In the case of physical hedges, an analysis of the holding costs associated with the physical hedge must be considered. In addition, there may be practical limitations to the extent of physical hedging possible. The market's ability to allow you to acquire the desired amount of physical inventory in a short time span may severely limit the usefulness of a physical hedging program. Space limitations at the manufacturing plant may make it impractical to achieve a desired six- to twelve-month hedge for a critical material. Thus, financial hedges, which are not space-limited (but may be limited by your credit capacity), may be a more flexible way to proceed.

Source: Portions of these columns are excerpted with from Chapter 19 of the book *Straight to the Bottom Line*® (Rudzki, Smock, Katzorke, Stewart). "Straight to the Bottom Line" is a registered trademark of Greybeard Advisors LLC.

Market Skimming Model

In the market skimming model, prices are set to achieve a high profit on each unit by selling to supply managers who are willing to pay a higher price because of a lack of supply management sophistication or who are willing to pay for products or services of perceived higher value. An example of the application of this model is frequently seen by supply managers in the use of backdoor selling to non-supply management professionals in the firm. Supply managers should always seek to reduce the potential negative impact of this pricing model by cost, price, or value analysis to ensure that the higher price for the product or service is justified by the reported additional benefits.

Revenue Pricing Model

When downturns in market demand occur, suppliers often must resort to a current revenue pricing model. The emphasis of this model is on obtaining sufficient current revenue to pay for operating cost rather than on profit. Suppliers using this strategy are typically concerned about capacity utilization, covering fixed costs, and retaining skilled labor during market slowdowns, when they are willing to reduce their prices until market conditions change. However, supply managers should be on guard for negative impacts on quality and service resulting from cost cutting on the part of the supplier.

Promotional Pricing Model

The promotional pricing model presents pricing for individual products and services that is set to enhance the sales of the overall product line rather than to ensure the profitability of each product. Current examples of this are the sale of cell phones at below cost to induce consumers to buy the annual service contract, or the use of extremely low prices for printers that require the use of the supplier's highly profitable ink cartridges. Total cost of ownership (TCO) analysis (discussed later in the chapter) should be used to avoid surprising and unfavorable financial impacts that can result from dealings with suppliers using this model.

Competition Pricing Model

The competition pricing model focuses on pricing actions or reactions to pricing proposals offered or expected to be offered by the supplier's competitors. The pricing strategy is based on determining the highest price that can be offered to the supply manager that will still be lower than the price offered by competitors. An excellent example of this model is the reverse auction process.

Cash Discounts

The practice in most industries is to offer incentives to pay invoices promptly. One way to encourage this is to offer cash discounts for payment within a certain period of time. For example, a seller may offer a discount of 2 percent for invoice payment within 10 days of receipt. The seller usually expects full payment within 30 days. (This is often expressed as "2 percent 10/net 30.")

Unlike quantity discounts, it is usually worthwhile to take advantage of cash discounts. Purchasers can rarely earn the equivalent return within a 10-day period of transactions offered with a cash discount. The opportunity cost of not taking the discount is almost always higher than the opportunity cost of taking the discount. Well-managed firms take advantage of cash discounts and arrange payment within the specified time frame.

Understanding the pricing model used by suppliers can provide supply managers with significant insights into the strategies needed to generate cost savings for their firm.

Using the Producer Price Index to Manage Price

As noted earlier, price analysis is appropriate for certain types of commodities. Specifically, monitoring price instead of cost is appropriate for market-based products where pricing is largely a function of supply and demand. Examples include steel, paper, plastic, and other types of bulk commodities. When assessing whether the price charged is fair compared with the market, managers can compare price changes for a purchase family to an external index. An important factor when conducting a price analysis is the Producer Price Index (PPI), which is maintained by the U.S. Bureau of Labor Statistics.

This information can easily be downloaded from the Bureau of Labor Statistics web page (www.bls.gov/ppi). The index tracks material price movements from quarter to quarter. It is scaled to a base year (1988) and tracks the percentage increase in material commodity prices based on a sample of industrial purchasers. By converting price increases paid from quarter to quarter into a percentage increase, and comparing the changes to the PPI for a similar type of material, the purchaser can determine whether the price increases paid to the supplier of that material are reasonable.

To use this tool, users will first need to identify the supplier's standard industrial code (SIC). This can be found at www.FreeEDGAR.com. Next, look at the price index for the SIC and product that you are interested in. Consider the following example for iron castings. The PPI for iron castings is shown in Exhibit 11.8.

Price paid to supplier on March 30, 2014: $52.50/unit

Price paid to supplier on June 30, 2014: $53.20/unit

Exhibit 11.8 — Example of Iron Castings PPI Data

SERIES ID: PCU3321#4 (N)
INDUSTRY: GRAY IRON FOUNDRIES
PRODUCT: OTHER GRAY IRON CASTINGS
BASE DATE: 8606

YEAR	JAN	FEB	MAR	APR	MAY	JUN	JUL	AUG	SEP	OCT	NOV	DEC	ANNUAL
2001	111.1	111.5	111.5	111.6	111.8	111.7	111.8	111.6	111.4	111.4	112.0	112.3	111.6
2002	112.4	112.5	112.7	113.2	113.5	113.7	113.8	114.0	115.1	115.2	115.6	115.7	114.0
2003	116.8	118.5	118.7	118.7	118.7	118.7	119.4	120.6	120.8	121.2	121.3	121.6	119.6
2004	122.5	122.8	122.9	122.9	122.8	122.9	122.9	123.1	122.5	123.3	123.4	123.3	122.9
2005	123.3	123.1	123.2	123.1	123.2	123.2	123.3	123.0	123.5	123.5	123.1	123.2	123.2
2006	123.3	123.6	123.5	123.6	123.6	123.7	123.7	123.7	124.3	124.2	123.9	124.7	123.8
2007	124.6	124.7	124.7	124.6	124.7	124.7	124.7	124.8	124.8	124.8	124.4	124.4	124.7
2008	126.0	126.0	126.1	126.1	126.3	126.4	126.3	126.2	126.3	126.2	126.1	126.1	126.2
2009	126.0	125.9	126.0	126.0	126.0	126.0	126.0	126.0	126.2	126.1	126.2	126.1	126.0
2010	126.1	126.1	126.2	126.4	126.7	126.7	126.8	126.8	127.3	127.4	127.2	127.2	126.7
2011	127.1	127.2	127.2	126.8	126.8	127.5	127.7(P)	127.6(P)	127.6(P)	127.7(P)			

N: NAICS replaces SIC with PPI data for January 2004. See http://www.bls.gov/ppi/ppinaics.htm. P: Preliminary. All indexes are subject to revision four months after original publication.

Percentage price increase = ($53.20 − $52.50)/$52.50 = 1.33%

Steel castings PPI (March 30, 2014) = 127.2

Steel castings PPI (June 30, 2014) = 127.5

Percentage inflation for steel castings = (127.5 − 127.2)/127.2 = 0.2%

In this case, the price increase paid by the purchaser is over five times as much as the increase in the PPI for iron castings—surely an unreasonable increase. The purchaser should definitely question the supplier about this recent price increase, and negotiate a better price.

In addition to PPI data, the Bureau of Labor Statistics website also contains information on labor rates in different regions of the country, and updates on pricing and market conditions. Information on employment cost data is also available in Supply management magazine's "Buying Strategy Forecast," a semimonthly newsletter, and the Direct-ICE report prepared by Thinking Cap Solutions (www.ice-alert.com). Other sources of commodity price information are the "Pink Sheets" published by the World Bank (www.worldbank .org/prospects).

Some companies set an objective of consistently bettering price inflation with suppliers. That is, they expect that performance should be better than the market.

As shown in Exhibit 11.9, this can provide the company with a relative competitive advantage in terms of pricing. Caution should be used when applying PPI data that match the commodity being purchased. The buyer should carefully study the history of the index to ensure that it has a strong correlation with the price history of the commodity being purchased. Several questions should be asked in this situation:

- How did the supply management situation affect the price fairness and reasonableness at the time?
- How have conditions (e.g., delivery requirements) changed?

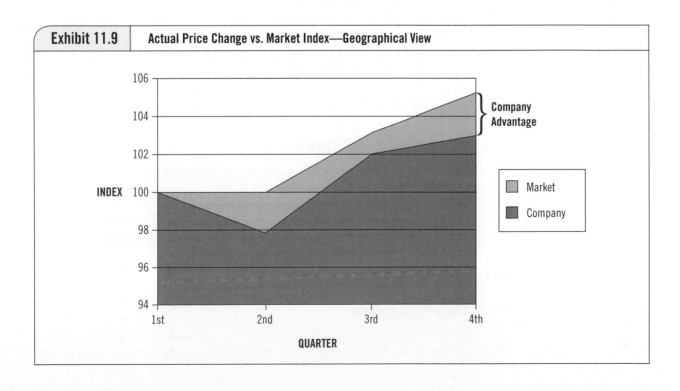

Exhibit 11.9 | **Actual Price Change vs. Market Index—Geographical View**

Exhibit 11.10		Actual to PPI Comparison				
	PPI 9/10	PPI 9/11	% CHANGE	ACTUAL 9/10	ACTUAL 9/11	% CHANGE
Gasoline	90.3	109.9	21.7	100.0	115.0	15.0
Lumber	169.9	184.5	8.6	100.0	110.0	10.0
Paper	186.8	190.7	2.0	100.0	102.0	2.0

Source: PPI data from U.S. Bureau of Labor Statistics, http://stats.bls.gov/ppihome.htm

- What is the effect on price of changes in the quantity of a material or service purchased?
- Was the supply management situation a sole source or competitive source?
- Are the index comparisons driving supply management strategies?

A real benefit of using this price analysis approach is to track price changes across different commodities and compare performance. For example, consider the following.

Three sourcing teams are discussing their cost results for the past year:

Gasoline team: 15 percent cost increase

Lumber team: 10 percent cost increase

Paper team: 2 percent increase

Which team has been most effective at managing costs for the year?

At first glance, it would appear that the paper team is doing the best because they have the lowest cost increases (2 percent). However, in comparing the results with the PPI data shown in Exhibit 11.10, the picture is markedly different. The lumber team has failed to capture savings in a market that has seen prices increase by only 8.6 percent, whereas the paper team has limited price increases to 2 percent, which is only par for the course in terms of what is happening in the market. The gasoline team, however, has been able to contain price increases to 15 percent in the face of a market that has seen gas prices increase by more than 21 percent, largely because of speculation associated with the Iraq war during this period. This analysis can help identify different price changes in markets where a fair and open market is present.

Cost Analysis Techniques

As noted earlier, more and more organizations are shifting their attention away from price management and toward cost management. In so doing, there may be opportunities to reduce costs that are not available when the discussion focuses only on price. In cost analysis, the supply manager performs a detailed analysis of the different elements of costs shown earlier in Exhibit 11.6 and identifies what is driving the different elements.

Cost-Based Pricing Models[3]

Cost Markup Pricing Model

In this model, the supplier simply takes its estimate of costs and adds a markup percentage to obtain the desired profit. This markup percentage could be added to the product cost only (usually direct materials plus direct labor plus production overhead), in which case the markup would have to provide for profit, plus all other indirect costs of operating the business. However, if the markup is applied to the total cost (product cost plus general, administrative, and sales expenses), then the markup is solely profit to the supplier. For example, a supplier that wanted a 20 percent markup over its total cost of $50 would quote a price of $60 ($50 + (20% of $50) = $60), which would leave a profit of $10.

Margin Pricing Model

In the margin pricing model, the supplier is still attempting to obtain a profit related to its costs, but instead of adding a markup to cost, the supplier establishes a price that will provide a profit margin that is a predetermined percentage of the quoted price (i.e., not a percentage of cost, as in markup pricing). For example, the supplier discovered that last year its margin as a percentage of sales was 1 percent, and this year the supplier would like it to be 20 percent. Using the same total cost of $50 as above would result in the supplier quoting a price of $62.50 to obtain the margin of 20 percent. This is calculated using the new equation for margin pricing:

$$\text{Cost} + (\text{Margin Rate} \times \text{Unit Selling Price}) = \text{Unit Selling Price}$$

Using simple algebra, solving the equation for unit selling price results in the formula:

$$\text{Cost}/(1 - \text{Margin Rate}) = \text{Unit Selling Price}$$

or

$$(\$50)/(1 - 20\%) = \text{Unit Selling Price}$$

As in cost markup pricing, the supply manager must be aware if the margin pricing is based on product cost only or if it is based on total cost.

Rate-of-Return Pricing Model

A third common model in the cost-based category is the rate-of-return pricing model, wherein the desired profit is added to the estimated cost. In this model, the supplier bases the profit on the objective of a specific desired return on the financial investment, rather than on the estimated cost. For example, if the supplier wanted a 20 percent return on its investment of $300,000 (which might include R&D, equipment, engineering, or other elements), to make 4,000 parts with a total cost of $50 each, the quoted price would be $65, using the following approach:

$$\text{Unit Cost} + \text{Unit Profit} = \text{Unit Selling Price}$$
$$\$50 + ((20\% \times 300,000)/4,000) = \$65$$

Product Specifications

Whether they realize it or not, purchasers impact price at the time they set the specifications for the product or service. Specifying products or services requiring custom design and tooling affects a seller's price, which is one of the reasons purchasers try to specify industry-standard parts whenever possible. Cost (and hence price) becomes higher as firms increase the value-added requirements for an item through design, tooling, or engineering requirements. Purchasers should specify industry-accepted standard parts for as much of their component requirements as possible and rely on customized items when they provide a competitive product advantage or help differentiate a product in the marketplace.

The ability to perform a cost analysis is a direct function of the quality and availability of information. If a purchaser and seller maintain a distant relationship, cost data will be more difficult to identify because of the lack of support from the seller. An obvious approach that can help in obtaining necessary cost data is to require a detailed production cost breakdown when a seller submits a purchase quotation. The reliability of self-reported cost data must be considered. Another approach or option involves the joint sharing of cost information. A cross-functional team composed of engineers and manufacturing personnel from both companies may meet to identify potential areas of the supplier's process (or the purchaser's requirements) that can potentially reduce costs. One of the benefits of developing closer relations with key suppliers is the increased visibility of supplier cost data. The following section details some techniques that focus on cost.

Estimating Supplier Costs Using Reverse Price Analysis

Often suppliers will not be forthcoming in sharing cost data. In these situations, the purchaser must resort to a different type of analytical approach called "reverse price analysis" (also known as "should cost" analysis). A seller's cost structure affects price because, in the long run, the seller must price at a level that covers all variable costs of production, contributes to some portion of fixed costs, and contributes to some level of profit. As discussed later in the chapter, many suppliers are reluctant to share internal cost information. This information, however, is valuable to a purchaser, particularly when evaluating whether a supplier's price is justifiable and reasonable. In the absence of specific cost data, a supplier's overall cost structure must be estimated using a cost analysis—meaning that if the supplier is assigning costs in an appropriate manner, what should the product cost based on these calculations?

Information about a specific product or product line is often difficult to identify. A purchaser may have to use internal engineering estimates about what it costs to produce an item, rely on historical experience and judgment to estimate costs, or review public financial documents to identify key cost data about the seller. The latter approach works best with publicly traded small suppliers producing limited product lines. Financial documents allow estimation of a supplier's overall cost structure. The drawback is that these documents do not provide much information about a specific breakdown of cost by product or product line. Also, if a supplier is a privately held company, cost data become difficult to obtain or estimate.

Despite these difficulties, there are tools available that can be used to estimate a supplier's cost using some publicly available information. When evaluating a supplier's costs, the major determinants of a supplier's total cost structure must be taken into consideration. Let's assume a supply management manager is buying a product or service for the first time without experience of what fair pricing might be. Because they do not have the tools at hand, or because they are too busy, many purchasers' usual technique is to go with their gut feel or to evaluate competitive bids. It may be worth the time and effort, however, to perform some additional research using data from an income statement or from Internet sites. In doing so, the purchaser may perform a reverse price analysis— which essentially means breaking down the price into its components of material, labor, overhead, and profit.

Let's start the process with a supplier-provided price of $20 per unit. The first component to consider is the price contribution toward profit, and sales, general, and administrative (SGA) expenses. For publicly traded companies, this can be estimated by looking at a variety of websites that provide information on financial reports, including balance sheets, income statements, cash flow statements, and annual reports shown in Exhibit 11.11 under the "Financial Reports" section.

Exhibit 11.11 provides a list of available data sources for other components of cost. For this example, assume the purchaser determined that the supplier is a privately held company. This is still not a problem, assuming the buyer can look up the supplier's SIC code (www.FreeEDGAR.com). Another useful resource is Robert Morris Association (www. rmahq.org), which publishes the gross profit margin for this SIC overall, as well as before-tax profit percentages. Although this is a rough estimate, it does offer a good starting point. In Exhibit 11.12, the gross profit and SGA expense percentage for this supplier's SIC code is 15 percent. Thus, on a price of $20, the estimated profit is $3. Next, the purchaser will need to understand the labor and material cost components of price.

Material costs can often be estimated by consulting with internal engineers. Using an estimate of required material, as well as external information on current pricing of these materials (as shown in the previous section), a rough estimate can be made of the amount of material in the product. In our example, we discovered that an approximation of the amount of material included is 20 percent of the price, or $4.

Exhibit 11.11	Data Sources

- Labor: Annual Survey of Manufacturers-total direct labor and material for SIC codes
- Overhead: 150% for labor intensive, as high as 600% for capital intensive
- Materials and Profit: Robert Morris Associates data broken out by SICs including the following:

    Income sources
    Gross profit margins
    Percentages for operating expenses
    Percentages for all other expenses
    Before-tax profit percentages

Other Sources of Data

Financial reports (profit and SGA estimates):

- Ward's Industrial Directory Census of Manufacturers
- Yahoo! financial section (biz.yahoo.com)
- Morningstar (www.morningstar.com)
- Marketwatch (cbs.marketwatch.com) 411Stocks (www.411stocks.com)
- The Street (www.thestreet.com)
- Thinking Cap Solutions (www.ice-alert.com)

Exhibit 11.12	Reverse Price Analysis

Hypothetical price	$20
Profit/SG&A allowance (15%)	−$ 3
Subtotal	$17
Direct material	−$ 4
Subtotal	$13
Direct labor	−$ 3
Manufacturing burden	=$10

To find out how much labor is included, the best place to look is the Annual Survey of Manufacturers, published by the U.S. Department of Commerce and available at http://www.census.gov/prod/www/abs/industry.html. This site allows the purchaser to download information on total direct-labor costs and total material costs for any SIC number. This information allows the purchaser to calculate a materials-to-labor ratio. For the analysis shown in Exhibit 11.12, suppose that the purchaser discovered that the ratio of materials to labor based on the SIC code was 1.333. Thus, if material costs were previously estimated at $4, then direct-labor costs should be approximately $3 (4/1.333).

After subtracting the estimates for profit/SGA, materials, and labor from the price, the remaining portion of cost is considered manufacturing burden or overhead. At this point, the purchaser must determine whether $10 per unit paid on a price of $20 per unit is a reasonable amount for overhead costs. Typically, overhead is expressed as a percentage of labor costs. For labor-intensive industries, the ratio could be as low as 150 percent. For capital-intensive industries, it could be as high as 600 percent. In our example, the overhead rate is 333 percent of labor ($10/$3). Using other data from Robert Morris Associates, the purchaser can also estimate the percentages for operating expenses and for all other expenses. With this cost estimate in hand, the purchaser should now be able to approach the supplier in a negotiation and initiate a discussion that addresses price and cost. Although these estimates may not be 100 percent accurate, they provide a baseline for discussion of the supplier's cost structure.

Labor cost will be an increasing factor in many cost estimates. The period from 2010 to 2015 will see the next impact of the baby boomer population on society. This impact will be in terms of a large number of people from this group retiring and leaving the work force. The number of retirees from multiple industries is expected to reach levels that have never been seen previously.

At the same time, the U.S. economy will continue to grow, and the demand for labor will escalate proportionately. Given the movement toward the service economy, the need for labor in selected industries is expected to grow significantly. Experts believe that services will be most affected, with a 29 percent growth rate. Transportation, retail trade, construction, and wholesale trade labor demand will also increase by double digits during this period. In construction alone, demand for drilling, specialty trades, and refining positions will increase by 17 to 18 percent during this period.

In discussing the supplier's cost structure with the supplier and how it applies to the price paid, the purchaser should attempt to initiate discussion in the following areas to discover opportunities for cost reductions.

- *Plant utilization.* The cost impact of additional business on the operating efficiency of a supplier should be evaluated. Is a supplier currently operating at capacity?

  Will additional volume actually create higher costs through overtime? Or will a supplier be able to reduce its cost structure through additional volume? The utilization rate of productive assets contributes directly to a supplier's cost structure.

- *Process capability.* The purchaser should also consider if projected volume requirements match a supplier's process capability. It may be inefficient to source smaller lot sizes with a supplier that requires long runs to minimize costs. On the other hand, suppliers specializing in smaller batches cannot efficiently accommodate volumes requiring longer production runs. A supplier's production processes should match a purchaser's production requirements. Supply management should also evaluate production processes to determine if they are state-of-the-art or rely on outdated technology. Production and process capability influences operating efficiencies, quality, and the overall cost structure of a seller.

- *Learning-curve effect.* Learning-curve analysis indicates whether a seller can lower its cost as a result of the repetitive production of an item.

- *The supplier's workforce.* A supplier's labor force affects the cost structure. Issues such as unionized versus nonunionized, motivated versus unmotivated, and the quality awareness and commitment of employees all combine to add another component to the cost structure. When visiting a supplier's facility, representatives from the purchaser should take the time to talk with employees about quality and other work-related items. Meeting with employees provides valuable insight about a supplier's operation. In recent years, the cost of labor in the workforce has gone up dramatically.

- *Management capability.* Management affects costs by directing the workforce in the most efficient manner, committing resources for longer-term productivity improvements, defining a firm's quality requirements, managing technology, and assigning financial resources in an optimal manner. Management efficiency and capability have both a tangible and intangible impact on a firm's cost structure. In the end, every cost component is a direct result of management action taken at some point in time.

- *Supply management efficiency.* How well suppliers purchase their goods and services has a direct impact on purchase price. Suppliers face many of the same uncertainties and forces in their supply markets that purchasers face. Supplier visits and evaluations should evaluate the tools and techniques suppliers use to meet their material requirements.

Break-Even Analysis

Break-even analysis includes both cost and revenue data for an item to identify the point where revenue equals cost, and the expected profit or loss at different production volumes.

Firms perform break-even analysis at different organizational levels. At the highest levels, top management uses this technique as a strategic planning tool. For example, an automobile manufacturer can use the tool to estimate expected profit or loss over a range of automobile sales. If the analysis indicates that the break-even point in units has risen over previous estimates, cost-cutting strategies can be put in place. Divisions or business units can use the technique to estimate the break-even point for a new product line.

Supply management and supply chain specialists use break-even analysis to develop the following insights:

- Identify if a target purchase price provides a reasonable profit to a supplier given the supplier's cost structure.

- Analyze a supplier's cost structure. Break-even analysis requires detailed analysis or estimation of the costs to produce an item.

- Perform sensitivity (what-if) analysis by evaluating the impact on a supplier of different mixes of purchase volumes and target purchase prices.

- Prepare for negotiation. Break-even analysis allows a purchaser to anticipate a seller's pricing strategy during negotiations. Research indicates that a direct relationship exists between preparation and negotiating effectiveness.

Sourcing Snapshot

A Total Cost of Ownership Perspective on the Paperless Office

In today's cost-cutting environment, many procurement and category management teams are sharpening their pencils and looking at ways to reduce indirect spend in areas such as printing, document management, and paper. In addition, the push to become more sustainable is also driving people to think about printing less, and saving trees. These two distinct elements are causing supply management teams to explore what is happening in the printing space.

Many readers will recall that when inkjet printing entered the market, everyone could now cheaply print documents. If you found a couple of typos in your document, you didn't bring out the white-out; you just made the corrections and printed out the entire document. The old one? Into the trash (or perhaps the blue bin…) In today's environment, the need for cost-cutting is driving managers to consider print costs, within the large scope of the expanding IT platform control issue.

There are two distinct lines of thinking on the paperless office. One is the environmental initiatives and sustainability initiatives. Then there is the cost management / IT/infrastructure piece and what that is producing. Managers recently interviewed note that there is definitely a shift in enterprise IT initiatives away from individual inkjet printers. Not only because of the economy driving challenges—but a shift toward centralized laser printers. Laser printing is seeing increased placement in many office settings. A lot of small to medium businesses are moving to, a high end laser jet printers (for example, HP's Office Jet product—rather than a low end laser. The growth is not necessarily in the top high-end range multi-color printers, but rather the mid-range multifunction color machine where there is growth on the order of 20 percent per annum.

Cost of ownership is part of the business case that explains this trend. Lasers like the Office Jet have good cost per page and a lower cost of ownership but this may also depend on how much people are printing. A low-end laser has lots of color but it is hard may not have the lowest cost per page. Ink does have a lower cost per page in general, but it won't always be the case in every situation. If you are printing full color marketing collateral, you will get a better cost per page in a laser than an ink for that type. However, end users probably do not do that level of purchase decision. For example, a home user with a black and white laser who wants to get into color may think that color laser is expensive, and will upgrade from a mono laser to color ink product, even though they won't use a lot of color.

Large companies interviewed are pushing the "electronification of paper" (not a real word…). This is a program to reduce the amount of paper used. That happens through encouraging associates not to print. With centralized print, companies can track metrics such as paper usage and toner usage and put out a report for each employee on how much they have printed. Having this data shown to people in many cases will cause them to re-think whether they need to really print out everything!

Another interesting variable at play is the reduction in number of people who work in an office, combined with the growth of remote working programs. As people are working from home and have to order their own toner or decide not to buy a printer from the company they work for and print at their own expense, they are moving away from print cartridges. When people can work two days from home, they have to carry all their work with them—and as such are incentivized not to carry paper! In the words of one associate, "I never print anything anymore! I need to have it all on my computer and can work from home."

That leads us to ask the question—are we moving toward a paperless office, as prophesized by management gurus in the past? The short answer, in the words of a senior print sales account manager, is "not one iota!" Even re-manufactured toner cartridges are not seeing a huge growth, because in many cases the print quality is not as good, and the life of these cartridges are not as long for the money paid. With the exception of state and local governments that are cutting budgets and driving sustainability to reduce print, most companies are seeing continued growth in print spending. IT departments are controlling what printers people can use and moving toward centralized print, but the current generation (myself included) refuses to do away with their need for tactile manipulation, and continue to print away! Perhaps the next generation will print less, but in the end, I still love the feel of a crisp sheet of paper in my hand to scribble on in blue ink!

Source: Handfield, Robert, Blog, "The Paperless Office: Pipedream, procurement mandate, or sustainability boondoggle?" May 17, 2012, http://scm.ncsu.edu/blog.

Sourcing Snapshot

Measuring Supply Management's Cost Savings at a Large Consumer Packaged Goods Company

A CPG company has $12B in controlled spend. Within this organization, however, there were several "rifts" that were occurring. Procurement had no credibility with senior management, because of the fact that the savings the team claimed to achieve were not credible and were not "believed" by other business stakeholders. Although Supply Management had indeed generated savings, these savings were being measured using Purchase Price Variance (PPV)-which simply measured the change in prices paid on an annual basis. PPV savings varied widely, based on market volatility and changes in market prices and, as a result, the Chief Financial Officer (CFO) challenged these savings as being invalid. The Chief Procurement Officer (CPO) felt that his team was generating benefits, but finance did not have a proper understanding of market volatility. Further, finance was not seen as a partner to procurement, and the CPO emphasized that the CFO did not understand long-term contracts.

In fact, the real problem in this case was the PPV metric, which was ineffective, unreliable, and could not be well communicated and translated to stakeholders. The metric drove questions such as "Did we overpay last year?" "Should we have saved 30 percent instead of 10 percent?" and the like. And no one was sure of how to better align financial budgets to market realities. At this stage, the CEO became involved, as he possessed some procurement experience. His analogy to the PPV metric went something like this: "Investors have a portfolio, and our company is measured by our stock price relative to other companies in that portfolio. If it goes up 5 percent relative to a market that goes up by 10 percent, that is not good. But if the market shrinks by 10 percent and our share price is only down by 5 percent, analysts will buy our stock. So why can't we establish a similar set of measurements for supply management performance? Can we create a portfolio to measure supply management price performance?" The CEO recommended moving to a market benchmarking basis where procurement had a Purchase Price Index that was measured against market indicators.

The next battle was how to measure market pricing? Benchmarking some categories such as true commodities was easy, as indicators existed for those items (e.g., paper, resin, and so forth). But there were also special commodities whose price behavior was more erratic. For this situation, the company hired a third-party market research provider, Beroe, to create a true commodity baseline and historical relationship, and then calculate an offset. For a finished product, Beroe created a cost driver model that calibrated company spend to market costs, and used market trends to define benchmarks. Savings performance moved from a project focus to a portfolio focus.

The next challenge? Procurement is also being asked to continue to monitor supplier financial risk and carbon footprint, and ensure integration with stakeholders. As procurement plays a more important role in the strategic planning of this organization, they are being tasked to become more creative in understanding risks and opportunities in the supply chain, and communicating these to stakeholders.

Source: Bucci, M. B. (December, 2009) Sales Director, Beroe, Inc., presentation, Supply Chain Resource Cooperative.

Break-even analysis requires the purchaser to identify the important costs and revenues associated with a product or product line. Graphing the data presents a visual representation of the expected loss or profit at various production levels. Cost equations also express the expected relationship between cost, volume, and profit. When using breakeven analysis, certain common assumptions are typically used:[4]

1. Fixed costs remain constant over the period and volumes considered.

2. Variable costs fluctuate in a linear fashion, although this may not always be the case.

3. Revenues vary directly with volume. This is represented graphically by an upward-sloping total revenue line beginning at the origin.

4. The fixed and variable costs include the semivariable costs. Thus no semivariable cost line exists.

5. Break-even analysis considers total costs rather than average costs. However, the technique often uses the average selling price for an item to calculate the total revenue line.

6. Significant joint (i.e., shared) costs among departments or products limits the use of this technique if these costs cannot be reasonably apportioned among users. If shared costs cannot be apportioned, then break-even analysis is best suited for the entire operation versus individual departments, products, or product lines.

7. This technique considers only quantitative factors. If qualitative factors are important, management must consider these before making any decisions based on the break-even analysis.

Break-Even Analysis Example

The following example assumes that fixed costs, variable costs, and target purchase price for a single item are reasonably accurate. The construction of a break-even graph requires these three pieces of information.

Exhibit 11.13 shows the required cost and volume data along with the break-even graph for this example. Because a buyer is estimating the break-even analysis for a supplier, the price is a target purchase price established by the purchaser. A range of prices can be analyzed to estimate a supplier's expected profit or loss given the fixed and variable costs.

In this example, the purchaser wants to determine if the anticipated volume of 9,000 units provides an adequate profit for the supplier at the target purchase price.

| Exhibit 11.13 | Break-Even Analysis for Supplier XYZ |

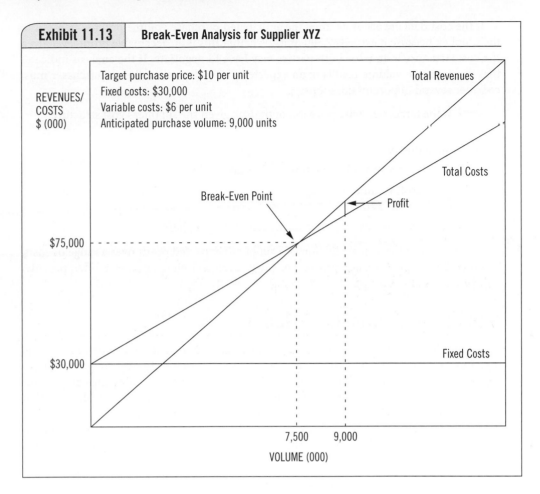

Target purchase price: $10 per unit
Fixed costs: $30,000
Variable costs: $6 per unit
Anticipated purchase volume: 9,000 units

Exhibit 11.13 indicates that the supplier requires at least 7,500 units to avoid a loss with this cost structure and target purchase price. The following equation identifies the profit or loss associated with a given volume:

$$\text{Net Income or Loss} = (P)(X) - (VC)(X) - (FC)$$

where P = average purchase price, X = units produced, VC = variable cost per unit of production, and FC = fixed cost of production for an item.

The supplier's expected profit for the anticipated 9,000 units is calculated as follows, using $10 per unit as the average purchase price:

$$\text{Net Income} = (\$10)(9{,}000) - (\$6)(9{,}000) - (\$30{,}000) = \$60000 \text{ Profit}$$

We can also calculate the number of units the supplier needs to produce to break even (i.e., cover fixed costs). This is calculated as follows:

$$\text{Total Revenue} = \text{Variable Cost} + \text{Fixed Cost}$$
$$\$10(X) = \$6(X) + \$30{,}000$$
$$\$4(X) = \$30{,}000$$
$$X = 75000 \text{ units}$$

If the cost data are accurate, then the anticipated purchase volume provides a profit to the supplier, because it exceeds 7,500 units. Whether this is an acceptable profit level given the cost structure is an issue both parties may have to negotiate. If the analysis indicates that the purchase volume results in an expected loss to the seller, then a purchaser must consider several important questions:

- Is the target purchase price too optimistic given the supplier's cost structure?
- Are the supplier's production costs reasonable compared with other producers in the industry?
- Are the cost and volume estimates accurate?
- If the cost, volume, and target price are reasonable, is this the right supplier to produce this item?
- Will direct assistance help reduce costs at the supplier?

This method allows an evaluation of a supplier's expected profit over a range of costs, volumes, and target purchase prices. The break-even technique, however, often provides only broad insight into a purchase decision.

Building a Should-Cost Model

A "should cost" model is an approach to estimating the different components that make up the supplier's per unit price per unit of product or service, (e.g., "what the product or service SHOULD cost in a theoretical world. Understanding the components of cost that make up price is an important step in understanding the cost "drivers" that account for increases in price. It can also lead the procurement manager to better understand elements of overhead, mark-ups on non-value-added costs, and other components that can undermine price inflation. The fundamental equation in the price of a product is:

$$PRICE = COST + PROFIT$$

Or

$$COST = PRICE - PROFIT$$

In many cases, price is set by the market, or through negotiations. Profit is the margin the company needs to be able to continue to re-invest in the business and be competitive. Cost comprises the financial resources required to meet customer functional requirements including delivery and quality. In effect, cost is the only element that can be impacted by the procurement organization in a negotiation.

Costs are impacted by a number of underlying decisions that are called "cost drivers." A cost driver is a specific dimension of cost that is attributable for a significant portion of the overall pattern of cost increases or reduction. Examples of cost drivers include the following:

Materials: Commodity fluctuations, handling difficulties, tolerances, lead times, design limitations, managed flow, cost of poor quality

Labour: Production method: complexity, awkward, safety concern, scrap, efficiencies, turnover, correction, cost of poor quality

Overheads: Machines / tools: complexity, uniqueness, indirect labour, maintenance, transactional costs, governmental constraints.

Value Chain Map Guides Understanding of Overall Cost Elements

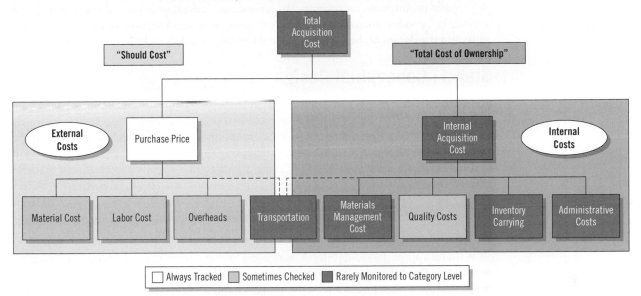

- Where no data is available, industry benchmarking or other research is required

The figure above provides a good starting place to begin the discussion on building a "should cost" model. The first step is to begin to estimate the high-level cost elements that make up the purchase price, and then begin to estimate all of the other internal acquisition costs associated with doing business with a given supplier. The left-side of this equation refers to the "should-cost" making up the purchase price, and the right side of this diagram, when added to the purchase price, provides the "total cost of ownership" used to assess the relationship cost. Depending on the industry, geography, and type of supplier, different elements of this cost model can be emphasized more, and may require more detailed levels of analysis.

A general approach that can be used to complete a cost model is an important tool for building world-class category management strategies. The approach documented here may vary based on the specific attributes of the geography, economic conditions, and others elements, but provides a high-level set of guidelines to follow.

Some basic definitions are in order first:

Net Sales = Gross Sales − Returns & Discounts
Cost of Goods Sold = Material + Direct Labor + Factory Overhead
Gross Profit = Net Sales − Cost of Goods Sold
Operating Expenses = Interest, Misc. Expenses, and other non-operating expenses
Profit Before Taxes = Gross profit − Operating & other expenses

There are several steps to think about when building a should-cost model. Getting started is often the biggest challenge, as it might seem like there is no clear place to start. With that in mind, a good idea is simply to put together a team of subject matter experts, call a meeting, and start wherever it makes sense! Here it is important to think about the right people for the team. For example, one company has a production plant in Mexico that builds many of the same types of products that are also sourced from suppliers. In this case, a cost model for a supplier should include individuals familiar with production costs and processes at this facility, as they would have first hand knowledge of typical costs for this type of production environment. In other cases, including industrial engineering, cost accounting, product managers, material handlers, or other experts who can contribute insight into the design of the cost model would be important to include.

Step 1: Conceptual Design

In the first step, the central question should cover the issue of "What are we attempting to model?" as well as "what suppliers are we attempting to model?" The best cost models are generally the brainchild of strong cross-functional team members, so addressing the clarity of purpose around "what" we are attempting to model is a first priority. This will of course lead to the natural question of "What information is required to create the model?" This session should be allowed to wander a bit to ensure that outside influences or uncertainties are incorporated into the model to assess risks. To facilitate this meeting, the team leader should identify and collect all potential issues or concerns regarding the business or decision the team is looking to model.

A useful approach is to develop a "rough-cut" value stream map, and based on this map, brainstorm the different cost elements that can be derived from the map. The value stream map provides a high level view of the supply chain, and then the supplier's primary cost elements are broken down into material, labor, overhead, transportation freight, inventory cost, maintenance costs, and others. The team has also begun to identify some of the cost drivers that may be influencing the cost. A cost driver is very simply an element of cost that when changed can result in an increase or decrease in that cost factor. In this case, supplier location, supplier lead time, transportation mode, and order size may be cost drivers that could influence the cost category of Freight Cost.

Note at this phase of the model, it is not important to worry about where the data is going to come from to estimate elements of the model. It is more important to be as inclusive as possible to identify all potential sources of costs that might influence the overall price or total cost of ownership. The team can also begin to use arrows in an influence diagram to show hypothesized relationships that might exist between different elements of cost.

Step 2: Refine and Derive Elements of the Cost Model

In the next phase, the team should begin to collect additional data. For example, the team may decide to visit a supplier's facility, and see for themselves if the value stream map they developed is valid, or if critical steps are missing from the supply chain. The team should also begin to develop more granular understanding of the process, including elements such as types of equipment (automated vs. manual), processing times, scrap rates, etc. This exercise can begin to provide insights into the different elements of the model, and should also result in a set of specific questions related to the cost model components. Examples of specific questions that might emerge include the following:

- What is the labor rate for machinists in different regions?
- What are productivity factors for automated vs. semi-automated equipment?
- What are the major material elements that go into this product?
- What is the cost difference for shipping from overseas vs. from Mexico to the US facility? What are differences for regular vs. premium shipping? What are import quotas, fees, or other costs we haven't included?
- How are overhead rates, profit, and SG&A derived for different suppliers?

Note that these questions are beginning to guide the user toward specific data that need to be collected. We haven't yet identified WHERE to obtain this data, but understanding the key questions is important before we go on a wild goose chase!

Step 3: Design and Construction of Cost Model

Finally, the team is ready to begin construction of the cost model, and to begin populating the model with data. With the influence diagram, value stream map, and questions identified, cost model development is the next step. In most cases, managers will use Microsoft Excel as a flexible tool for cost modeling, but there is nevertheless the need for a well-defined architectural structure with a clear and logical flow, and which can be audited.[1]

There are certain best practices that should be followed in constructing a cost model, and some consistent elements that need to be utilized when building the architecture of the cost model. The first is Usability. If the user interface for the cost modeling tool is overly complex, it may deter people from using it. For example, the designer should create a single tab (i.e. single spreadsheet in a workbook) for the user interface. The components in this tab include ALL variables that you wish to manipulate or adjust. Typically these variables are separated into "assumption variables" and "decision variables." Assumption variables are any components NOT under the direct control of the buying or supplying company but those that have a significant influence on the outcome being modeled. Examples might include currency fluctuations, interest rates, import duties, and commodity prices. Decision variables include those components the company has direct control or influence over, including elements such as make-or-buy, transportation mode, production volume, and price point. Both assumption and decision variables should be located on the same tab of the dashboard/user interface worksheet, but should reside in separate, clearly labeled areas of the sheet. This will allow the user to conduct scenario testing based on assumption and decision variables together and independently.

A second important component of design is Auditability, which refers to the integrity and transparency of the cost model created. Cost models should have clearly documented logic that can be replicated; therefore it is important that the designer adequately document the model, so anyone trying to use it can immediately understand the logic and sources of data. A few simple rules prevail. First, avoid references and links to outside workbooks, spreadsheets, and files. Links to outside workbooks are difficult to follow, and if cell references change, the model is rendered useless. Second, always reference cells in a spreadsheet by an assigned name (e.g., "Material"), NOT by their cell address location (e.g., C43). Use a consistent format that allows you to distinguish assumption variables, decision variables, and calculated fields. This allows users to easily understand the formulas present in the model. Third, do not "hard code" values into formulas for formulation purposes. Make the hard-coded value an input into your user interface (either as an assumption or decision variable). For example, instead of using 0.07 in your formula, reference the "Interest rate" named range of your input template that has the value of 7 percent in it. Lastly, work to keep all calculations in the model on a single tab in the workbook, which can improve visibility into the inner workings of the cost model.

Another important element making the model easy to navigate is to include an additional tab within the workbook that shows the overall influence diagram, any formatting conventions utilized, the version of the model, the model designer's name, and the latest revision date. This could be a simple box and arrow diagram that shows the dashboard, input parameters, output, and charts produced.

[1] Sower, Victor, and Sower, Christopher, "Better Business Decisions Using Cost Modeling", New York: Better Business Expert Press, 2011.

The last element of architecture is fitness for purpose. This refers to the model's ability to provide output necessary to assist in decision-making. Once the model is constructed, it is ready to enter inputs, and the calculations have been tested and shown to work as designed. The output of the model must then be represented in a fashion that is easy to understand and translate. The best scenario is to keep the output on the same tab of the spreadsheet, so that the user has a "dashboard" feel for the tool. The dashboard should

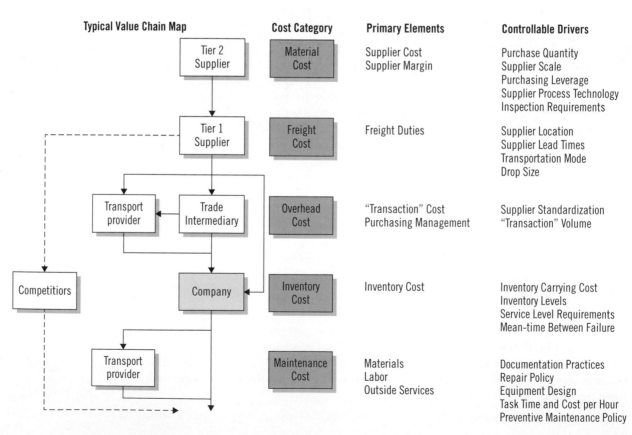

Product Cost Models

Scope	Develop Detailed Supply Chain Model	Identify Data Sources	Finalize Model

• Identify the supplier we are modeling
• Identify the product(s) we are modeling
• Identify the locations of facilities
	• Work with site teams (i.e. buyer's site) to develop process maps
	• Conduct a site visit of facility for deeper granularity on operations/processes
	• Finalize process maps and identify critical cost points
		• Pinpoint the critical costs in the supply chain
		• Identify credible data sources to begin populating the model
		• Begin to add data points to the template (i.e. raw materials, direct labor, expenses, etc.)
			• Add data points to the template
			  • raw materials
			  • direct labor
			  • expenses
			  • OH
			  • etc.

Typical Value Chain Map	Cost Category	Primary Elements	Controllable Drivers
Tier 2 Supplier	Material Cost	Supplier Cost Supplier Margin	Purchase Quantity Supplier Scale Purchasing Leverage Supplier Process Technology Inspection Requirements
Tier 1 Supplier	Freight Cost	Freight Duties	Supplier Location Supplier Lead Times Transportation Mode Drop Size
Transport provider / Trade Intermediary	Overhead Cost	"Transaction" Cost Purchasing Management	Supplier Standardization "Transaction" Volume
Competitiors / Company	Inventory Cost	Inventory Cost	Inventory Carrying Cost Inventory Levels Service Level Requirements Mean-time Between Failure
Transport provider	Maintenance Cost	Materials Labor Outside Services	Documentation Practices Repair Policy Equipment Design Task Time and Cost per Hour Preventive Maintenance Policy

update automatically as changes are made to the assumption and decision variables, and charts/pivot tables should also be updated. The dashboard should provide output that meets management needs for decision-making input.

In sum, the output of the cost model should be of sufficient detail, so that not only can the team make a recommendation to the category team, but also the impact of different cost inputs and assumptions can be seen.

Step 4: Identify Data Sources for the Model

As every programmer knows, "garbage in garbage out" is a key principle that equally applies to cost modeling. To develop good model insights, the data must be valid, reliable, and of sufficient detail. As such, data sources must be reputable, and must be referenced within your model as key assumptions where appropriate. Even the best model will be easily dismissed if the data that goes into it is not valid. There are several sources of data to explore as inputs.

Internal Data

Some of the data needed for cost modeling can come directly from your own information systems, whether these be ERP systems, accounting system, or MRP system. HRM systems can also be leveraged if there are hours and wages as important inputs to your model. Finally, don't forget to include "hidden" costs like transfer prices, material handling, inspection costs, and other costs that may not be apparent to you but are obvious to internal operations people. In other cases, there may be plants that are producing a similar type of product within your organizational network (if you happen to work for a conglomerate) that could also help you understand plant level production data.

US Publicly Available ▾	International Publicly Available ▾	Subscriptions ▾
Economic census	World Bank	Hoovers
2011 economic census & surveys	NationMaster	Dunn & Bradstreet
Annual survey of manufacturers	UK Office of National Statistics	RMA Annual Statement Studies
Bureal of Labor Statistics	Statistics Norway	Financial Rations
Producer price indices	China	Ratios
Wages by area & occupation	Japan Statistics Bureau & Statistics Center	Bloomberg
Earnings by industry	Australian Bureau of Statistics	
Labor and productivity costs	European Statistical Office	
International labor comparisons	Statistics Canada	
International prices indices	Statistics South Africa	
International productivity	Statistics New Zealand	
IRS tax statistics		
Federal Reserve Board		
Bureau of Economic Analysis		
Department of Energy		
Bureau of Transportation Statistics		
Federal Motor Carrier Safety Admin		
EDGAR Online		
Salary.com		
Various trade associations		

Supplier Provided Data

Supply management professionals working with suppliers know how valuable their information can be. This is certainly the case in cost models. If you have a good relationship with your supplier, he/she will be happy to pass on cost data that can help you to validate your inputs. This is not always likely however, particularly in North American supplier relationships, so professionals generally collect cost details by making its inclusion mandatory as part of a request for information (RFI) or request for proposal (RFP). Many companies include a detailed workshop that asks for various cost model inputs, including material, handling, labor, scrap, inspection, run rates, setup times, etc. Understanding all of these cost components improves when multiple suppliers are providing the same information, as the data can be compared to identify "best-in-class" cost elements, leading to a "theoretical" lowest possible cost when all elements are combined. The value of supplier site visits to "see for yourself" cannot be overemphasized here. If this is not possible, visiting the supplier websites, annual reports, or other sources should be considered at a minimum.

Finally, external (third party) data sources can be utilized in defining assumption variables, such as currency, commodity prices, interest rates, etc. Examples of some potential sources are shown in the table at the bottom of page 443.

Total Cost of Ownership

Total cost of ownership (TCO) requires a purchaser to identify and measure costs beyond the standard unit price, transportation, and tooling when evaluating purchase proposals or supplier performance. Formally, **total cost of ownership** is defined as the present value of all costs associated with a product, service, or capital equipment that are incurred over its expected life.

Most large firms base purchase decisions and evaluate suppliers on cost elements beyond unit price, transportation, and tooling. Research indicates, however, that companies differ widely about what cost components to include in a total cost analysis.

Typically these costs can be broken into four broad categories:[5]

- *Purchase price.* The amount paid to the supplier for the product, service, or capital equipment.
- *Acquisition costs.* All costs associated with bringing the product, service, or capital equipment to the customer's location. Examples of acquisition costs are sourcing, administration, freight, and taxes.
- *Usage costs.* In the case of a product, usage costs are all costs associated with converting the purchased part/material into the finished product and supporting it through its usable life. In the case of a service, all costs associated with the performance of the service that are NOT included in the purchase price are usage costs. In the case of capital equipment, all costs associated with operating the equipment through its life are usage costs. Examples of usage costs are inventory, conversion, scrap, warranty, installation, training, downtime, and opportunity costs.
- *End-of-life costs.* All costs incurred when a product, service, or capital equipment reaches the end of its usable life, net of amounts received from the sale of remaining product or the equipment (salvage value) as the case may be. Examples of end-of-life costs are obsolescence, disposal, clean-up, and project termination costs.

Building a Total Cost of Ownership Model

Building a TCO model is not an easy task. It requires input from different parts of the organization and a thorough understanding of the process through the entire life cycle. The following steps must be taken to ensure that all costs are captured correctly:

Step 1. Map the process and develop TCO categories. Construct a process map from the time a need for the product, service, or capital equipment is identified all the way through the life cycle. The activities that you identify will help to develop broad TCO categories.

Step 2. Determine cost elements for each category. Using the process map as a guide, identify the subcost elements that make up each TCO category.

Step 3. Determine how each cost element is to be measured. This is a critical step. The metrics must be determined to quantify each of the cost elements identified in Step 2. For example, to quantify the costs of sourcing labor, the hourly rate of the individuals performing the sourcing activity and the amount of time they spend or will spend doing it will need to be known.

Step 4. Gather data and quantify costs. This is the most difficult and time-consuming step. In this step, gather data for each of the metrics identified in Step 3 and quantify the respective costs. This requires information from various sources including interviews, surveys, the A/P system, and other internal databases. If information from internal databases is used, make sure to validate the numbers. Input errors can sometimes cause the numbers generated by these databases to be significantly inaccurate.

Step 5. Develop a cost timeline. Construct a cost timeline for the length of the life cycle. Place each cost element quantified in Step 4 in the appropriate time period. Then calculate totals for each time period as shown in the example.

Step 6. Bring costs to present value. Computing the present value allows decisions to be made based on present dollars. This is important because a dollar spent one year from now is not worth the same as a dollar spent now. The value of money spent any time in the future will depend on the organization's cost of capital. To calculate the present value, therefore, obtain the organization's cost of capital from its finance department. Then calculate the present value of each total in the cost timeline by using a present value table or a financial calculator. The sum of present values for each time period represents the total cost of ownership.

The Importance of Opportunity Costs

When considering usage costs, make sure to identify opportunity costs, if any. An **opportunity cost** is defined as the cost of the next best alternative. Typical opportunity costs include lost sales, lost productivity, and downtime. The absence of these costs in an analysis could lead to an entirely different decision and, possibly, a wrong one, as illustrated below.

A supply manager looking to purchase a machine was evaluating two alternatives. Alternative A was priced at $100,000, and B was priced at $125,000. The delivery lead time for Machine A was 90 days, and for Machine B it was 30 days. When determining usage costs for A, it was important to add the lost revenue that would have been generated during the 60 days (90 − 30 = 60) had machine B been installed. By including the cost of lost revenue, B became the better alternative even though it was priced higher.

In another case, a supply manager made the decision, based primarily on price, to purchase Machine Y instead of Machine X. His analysis, however, omitted the opportunity cost from the difference in production capacity between the two machines. Machine X was capable of producing 10 percent more units than Machine Y. In a market upswing, sales potential increased by 10 percent. Machine Y was unable to handle the increase, and a new machine had to be purchased. Had the supply manager selected Machine X, the purchase of a new machine could have been deferred, thereby saving hundreds of thousands of dollars. Mistakes like this can easily be avoided by ensuring that all costs, especially opportunity costs, are captured in the TCO.

Sourcing Snapshot

Xerox Product Cost Management

Xerox has two product areas: production systems and office machines. Production systems are the products manufactured for companies that generate revenue with Xerox's large systems. Examples include print shops, insurance companies, and banks that run millions of print documents every month. In this environment, the goal is to deliver business solutions for a total cost decision, where the price of the unit is not an important parameter, but rather the solution that delivers more print per hour is more competitive, and the service package wrapped around that solution. The profit drivers in this case are in the consumables down the road, and the reliability of the machine is the number one cost driver. Costs will not be traded off for reliability in any new product design.

Office machines are all the multi-functional copiers, printers, and devices utilized in office environments. In this business, lowest price possible is the singular parameter driving customer sales. However, cost competitiveness is critical to drive down selling price, and profit is made from the consumables and service that is provided to the business.

At Xerox, cost management is acknowledge to be the #1 driver for all new product introduction activity, as well as the #1 driver for business plans and all sourcing activities around target cost.

Xerox has established their own internal systems group, called product cost engineering that conducts competitive teardowns, cost analysis, and best of breed modeling on an ongoing basis. The team regularly meets to identify the best elements from new competing products to derive a best of breed product and a target price to work toward. Working in parallel with the business teams, they will then work to develop a cost target based on the business's model and marketing plan.

These two elements—the business plan and the cost target combined with best of breed pricing, forms the underlying basis for all worldwide sourcing activity.

There is an understanding that not all target prices will be hit, although Xerox will be very close on some. A best of breed profile is provided, whereby directives such as "you will find stampings in the Czech republic, and assembly in Mexico," and so forth are found. However, this provides a mechanism for negotiating terms other than bottom line price. The PC (Product Cost) group provides a full cost breakdown, with labor estimation, profit, and overhead estimation, with the objective of getting key suppliers to share that same data. If a cost estimate is off, based on APO (Accounts Payable Organization) data validation, it can be a PC education. There are many different negotiations and cost elements that go into each one.

To support PC, investments in software were made early on. This is a proprietary application developed at Xerox that allows PC's to conduct their analysis. This is well-established on the direct side, but there is an opportunity to better utilize this capability on the indirect side. A PC can tell you how much a pound of resin should cost, but is not able to break down the cost drivers for toner. This was a labor intensive process on the front end to collect the data. However, the system now allows product cost engineers to input design concept data, go through a series of process steps, pick and choose options, which drives specific data such as sheet metal parts, the machine hours for that region, and the labor hours. The PC essentially identifies the part, inputs the process, and identifies the correct parameters to build up the cost model.

Advanced Manufacturing Engineers (AMEs) with expertise in processes are employed in the early stages of product concept design, and suppliers are invited to send major representatives to work with the design group. At these meetings, the team reviews individual parts, look for design changes that can be made for ease of manufacture, and focus primarily on the high cost complex parts, using Design for Six Sigma approaches. The AMEs have a strong background in plastics, sheet metal, electronics, and the like, and understand best practices in the technology, which helps them to work with the design community and guide them in the right decision.

Xerox utilized a contract manufacturer (CM), and this relationship is driven around a total landed cost model. The CM does almost the entire printer manufacturing for the office market, and will ship the completed printer to Xerox. Their logistics group is also involved in supply chain modeling to enable amortization of shipping costs, understand where parts are coming from, going to, and what the resulting chain will look like when the design is executed. This may further drive moving business to different suppliers when transportation costs drive this decision.

Source: Handfield, R., and Edwards, S. (2009, July), "Cost Leadership Best Practices," White Paper, Supply Chain Resource Cooperative, NC State University.

Important Factors to Consider When Building a TCO Model

- Building a TCO can be a costly and time-intensive activity. Use it for evaluating larger purchases.

- Make sure to obtain senior management buy-in before embarking on a full-fledged TCO. It will make data gathering much easier, especially if several people from different parts of the organization have to be interviewed.

- Work in a team. This will greatly reduce the time required for data collection activities, which can be distributed among team members.

- Focus on the big costs first. Spending extended periods of time quantifying small cost elements will only delay the decision, which in most cases will not be impacted by them.

- Make sure to obtain a realistic estimate of the life cycle. A life cycle that is too short or too long could result in a wrong decision.

- Whether evaluating a purchase option or making an outsourcing decision, a TCO model will ensure that the right decision is made, at least from a cost perspective.

- When considering global sourcing, consider all of the relevant labor, quality, logistics, and import costs associated with the total supply chain.

Example of a TCO Model

Supply manager Joe Smith was considering the purchase of 1,000 desktop PCs for his organization. The life cycle was three years, and the organization's cost of capital was 12 percent. He calculated the TCO for one of the purchase options as shown in Exhibit 11.14.

Using these elements, the total cost of ownership for each of these decisions was calculated as shown in Exhibit 11.15.

Exhibit 11.14	TCO Calculation for One Purchase Option
COST ELEMENTS	**COST MEASURES**
Purchase Price (Step 1):	
• Equipment (Step 2)	Supplier quote: $1,200 per PC (Steps 3 and 4)
• Software License A	Supplier quote: $300 per PC
• Software License B	Supplier quote: $100 per PC
• Software License C	Supplier quote: $50 per PC
Acquisition Cost:	
• Sourcing	2 FTE @ $85K and $170K for 2 months
• Administration	1 PO @ $150, 12 invoices @ $40 each
Usage Costs:	
• Installation	$700 per PC (PC move, install, network)
• Equipment Support	$120 per month per PC—supplier quote
• Network Support	$100 per month—supplier quote
• Warranty	$120 per PC for a 3-year warranty
• Opportunity Cost-Lost Productivity	Downtime 15 hours per PC per year @ $30 per hour
End of Life:	
• Salvage Value	$36 per PC

Exhibit 11.15	Total Cost of Ownership Calculation			
COST ELEMENTS	**PRESENT**	**YEAR 1 (STEP 5)**	**YEAR 2**	**YEAR 3**
Purchase Price:				
Equipment	$1,200,000			
Software License A	$ 300,000			
Software License B	$ 100,000			
Software License C	$ 50,000			
Acquisition Cost:				
Sourcing	$ 42,500			
Administration	$ 150	$ 480	$ 480	$ 480
Usage Costs:				
Opportunity Cost—Lost Productivity		$ 50,000	$450,000	$ 450,000
Installation	$ 700,000			
Equipment Support		$1,440,000	$1,440,000	$1,440,000
Network Support		$1,200,000	$1,200,000	$1,200,000
Warranty	$ 120,000			
End of Life Costs:				
Salvage Value				($6,000)
TOTAL	$2,512,650	$3,090,480	$3,090,480	$3,054,480
Present Values @ 12%	$2,512,650	$2,759,799	$2,463,113 (Step 6)	$2,174,790

On the basis of this model, the supply manager should explore the possibilities of reducing service costs such as equipment support and network support—these appear to be the highest value, and contribute most to costs. This is also typically the most profitable area for the supplier, as services are often not audited.

Collaborative Approaches to Cost Management

Progressive supply management departments across multiple industries such as automotive, electronics, and pharmaceutical have learned the hard way that the most effective way to reduce costs for strategic commodities is not through price haggling, but through effective collaboration. When supply management, engineering, and suppliers put their heads together to find innovative ways to reduce costs, the outcome is generally mutually beneficial for both parties: The buying company gets a lower price, and in many cases, the supplier benefits from a higher margin and a guarantee of future business. Two of the most common approaches to collaborative cost management include target pricing and cost-savings sharing.

Target Pricing Defined

Target pricing is an innovative approach used in the initial stages of the new-product development (NPD) cycle to establish a contract price between a buyer and seller. Japanese manufacturers, in an effort to motivate engineers to select designs that could be produced at a low cost, originally developed target pricing methodologies during the 1980s to battle the rising yen versus the U.S. dollar. These innovators came up with a simple concept to apply in new-product development: The cost of a new product is no longer an outcome of the product design process; rather, it is an input to the process. The challenge is to design a product with the required functionality and quality at a cost that provides a reasonable profit. In a new car, for example, the development team may work with marketing to determine the target price of the vehicle for the product's market segment. Using final price as a basis, the product is disaggregated into major systems, such as the engine and power train. Each major system has a target cost. At the component level (which represents a further disaggregation from the system level), the target cost is the price that a purchaser hopes to attain from a supplier (if the item is externally sourced).

With target pricing, a product's allowable cost is strictly a function of what a market segment is willing to pay less the profit goals for the product. Under traditional pricing approaches, however, product cost + profit = selling price. Using a target pricing approach, the selling price – profit = the allowable product cost. Generally speaking, the target cost is not always achievable by the supplier in early negotiations. Moreover, the supplier's current price to provide a product or service today is probably greater than the target price set forth by the buying company.

The difference between the supplier's price and the target cost becomes the strategic cost-reduction objective. This gap must be reduced by both parties in a collaborative effort through such methods as value engineering, quality function deployment, design for manufacturing/assembly, and standardization. Setting product level target costs that are too aggressive may result in unachievable target costs. Setting too low a strategic cost-reduction challenge leads to easily achieved target costs but a loss of competitive position. In setting target prices and target costs, the new-product development team should bear in mind the cardinal rule of target costing: The target cost can never be violated. Moreover, even if engineers find a way to improve the functionality of the product, they cannot make the improvement unless they can offset the additional cost.

One of the pioneers and industry leaders in target pricing is Honda of America Manufacturing (described in the opening paragraph to this chapter). The company breaks product costs down to the component level. Suppliers are asked to provide a detailed breakdown of their costs, including raw materials, labor, tooling, and required packaging as well as delivery, administrative, and other expenses. The breakdown of costs is helpful in suggesting ways that suppliers can seek to improve and thereby reduce costs. Cost tables are jointly developed with suppliers and used to find differences (line by line) across all elements of cost. A potential area of disagreement involves the supplier's profits and overhead. A fair profit is required but may be dependent on the level of investment. No fixed profit level is used in negotiations. Supply management must then aggregate the parts costs and compare them with the target costs. If total costs exceed target costs, the design must change or costs must be reduced. Although the supplier's profit margins might be an easy place to look for cost savings, Honda realizes that doing so would squander the trust it worked hard to develop with suppliers.[6]

Once a purchaser has established a target price with a supplier for the first year of a contract, additional cost reductions over the life of the product can be made through an ongoing effort to drive down costs year over year. This can be achieved through a technique known as cost-savings sharing.

Cost-Savings Sharing Pricing Defined

Cost-savings sharing differs from traditional market-based pricing in several ways. First, cost-sharing approaches require joint identification of the full cost to produce an item, which is not the case with market-based pricing (where the buyer has little or no knowledge of the supplier's costs). Second, profit is a function of the productive investment committed to the purchased item and a supplier's asset return requirements (i.e., return on investment). Profit is not a direct function of cost (which is usually the practice with market-driven prices). The cost-based approach provides a supplier with incentives to pursue continuous performance improvement to realize shared cost savings and invest in productive assets. A later example illustrates these concepts.

An important feature of cost-savings sharing is the financial incentives offered to a seller for performance improvements above and beyond the improvements agreed to in the purchase contract. This differs from the traditional market-based pricing approach where one party (usually the purchaser) seeks to capture all cost savings resulting from a supplier's improvement effort. Traditional pricing practices have been a deterrent to cooperative efforts to make design, product, and process improvements. A cost-savings sharing approach recognizes the need to provide financial incentives to a supplier along with enhancing closer relationships.

Prerequisites for Successful Target and Cost-Based Pricing

For target and cost-based pricing to occur, there must be joint agreement on a supplier's full cost to produce an item. Identification of all costs provides the basis for establishing joint improvement targets. The total cost to produce an item includes labor, materials, other direct costs, any costs because of start-up and production, and administrative, selling, and other related expenses.

Besides total cost components, the parties must jointly identify and agree upon product volumes, target product costs at various points in time, and quantifiable productivity and quality improvement projections. Each firm must also agree on the asset base and return requirement at the supplier that determines an item's profit.

There must also be agreement on the point in time when mutual sharing of cost savings takes place, as well as the formula used to share the rewards. Mutual sharing of rewards usually occurs for savings above and beyond the performance improvement targets agreed to in the purchase contract, and savings on any items incidental to joint performance improvement targets.

This approach requires a high degree of trust, information sharing, and joint problem solving. This process will fail if one firm takes advantage of the other or violates confidentiality of information sharing. There must also be a willingness to provide the resources necessary to resolve problems affecting overall success.

The ability to manage the risks associated with target pricing is another key prerequisite. Perhaps the main risk concerns volume variability. Because volume affects cost levels, both parties must carefully consider and manage the impact of changes from planned volume projections. Higher-than-projected volumes will result in a supplier achieving greater economies and lower per-unit costs. These lower costs, however, are not the result of a supplier's performance improvement. Conversely, lower-than-projected volumes may raise a supplier's average costs. Contractually, the parties must determine how to manage changes from the buying plan.

When to Use Collaborative Cost Management Approaches

A cost-based approach to determining price is clearly not appropriate for all purchased items. Many items do not warrant cost analysis, or the marketplace determines price. Based on the cost management portfolio matrix discussed earlier in the chapter, it is obvious that products that are readily available from multiple sources, standardized instead of customized, and heavily influenced by the market forces of supply and demand do not fit the profile of items appropriate for cost-based pricing.

What types of items are feasible for a cost-based cooperative approach? A cost-based approach is feasible when the seller contributes high added value to an item through direct or indirect labor and specialized expertise. This approach is particularly appropriate for complex items customized to specific requirements. Also, products requiring a conversion from raw material through value-added designs at a supplier are possible candidates. Examples of such items include a specially designed antilock brake system or a dashboard for an automobile. These items require a high value-added conversion from raw materials into a semifinished product. The supplier also likely contributes design and engineering support.

An Example of Target Pricing and Cost-Savings Sharing

Although actual target and cost-savings sharing agreements can be lengthy and complex, the following example demonstrates the fundamental principles of this strategic cost management approach. This example is based on an actual situation that occurred between an automotive OEM and a first-tier supplier.

Exhibit 11.16	Key Data for the Cost-Based Pricing Example

First-Year Target Price: $61.00
Negotiated/Analyzed Cost Structure

Material	$20 per unit
Labor rate	$8.50 per unit
Burden rate*	200% of direct labor
Scrap rate	10%
Selling, general, and administrative expense rate	10% of manufacturing cost
Effective volume range	125,000 units per year ± 10%
Projected product life	2 years
Return on investment agreed to	30%

	YEAR 1	YEAR 2
Supplier investment	$3 million	$2 million
Total supplier investment	$5 million	
Supplier improvement commitment		
Direct labor	10% reduction annually	
Scrap rate	50% reduction annually	

Improvements incidental to agreed-upon performance improvements: Shared 50/50

*Burden is a term used in accounting to describe costs of manufacture or production not directly identifiable with an exact product or unit of production. They are indirect or apportionable costs

A purchaser seeks to purchase a designed component that is part of a final end product. The final selling price of the product has been determined through discussions with marketing, and this figure has been rolled down (or disaggregated) to the component level. As such, both parties have agreed to target a purchase (or selling) price of $61 for the component for the first year. The purchaser has targeted this price as one that will support meeting the overall target price of the final end product.

Cost-savings sharing assumes that the buyer and seller will collaborate to identify the most efficient processes to produce a product as the basis for the cost structure. This approach does not reward inefficient processes or practices, and also assumes that engineers at the buying organization are flexible and willing to modify product specifications to align with the supplier's processes. Throughout this example the supplier's costs and return requirements serve as the basis for determining a fair and competitive price. Both parties agree to a negotiated cost-based approach because the parties have developed a close working relationship, supporting the sharing of detailed cost data, and because the supplier's cost structure is relatively efficient.

Exhibit 11.16 details the costs and investment data needed to develop a cost-based purchase contract.

Both firms must identify the costs and supplier investment associated with the purchased component, identify and agree on the supplier's asset return requirements, and identify supplier commitments to annual performance improvement targets.

These exhibits provide the basis for evaluating cost and price throughout the life of the contract.

Exhibit 11.17 details the cost breakdown and subsequent price of the component for each year of this contract. Data for year one include the negotiated/analyzed information

Exhibit 11.17	Cost and Profit Breakdown for the Cost-Based Pricing Example		
	YEAR 1	**YEAR 2**	
Materials	$20.00	$19.24	Materials reduction of $1.50 plus an overall materials increase of 4% (($20.00 − $1.50) × 1.04)
Labor	8.50	7.88	Reduction of 10% - Contractual target improvement plus 3% increase ($8.50 × .9 × 1.03)
Burden (200% labor)	17.00	15.76	
Total materials, labor, burden	$45.50	$42.88	
Scrap (10%)	4.55	2.14	Scrap reduced from 10% to 5% − Contractual target ($42.88 × .05)
Manufacturing cost	$50.05	45.02	
Selling and administrative expenses (10%)	5.00	4.50	
Total cost	$55.05	$49.52	
Profit*	6.00	6.75	Includes $.75 share for joint material reduction ($6 + ($1.50/2))
Selling price	$61.50	$56.27	New selling price after year 1 events

*Profit is based on the 30% return on the investment figure agreed to between buyer and seller. Profit = ($5 million total two-year investment × 0.3)/250,000 total units = $6.00 Profit

presented in Exhibit 11.16. During the first year, the following events affected the selling price at the start of year two:

- Overall material costs rise by 4 percent because raw material cost increases.
- A joint value analysis team identifies a substitute material that reduces material costs by $1.50 per unit.
- Labor rates increase by 3 percent per unit because of a scheduled contractual increase at the supplier.
- The supplier meets the agreed productivity improvement targets for reduced scrap and improved labor productivity.

Year Two data include these events:

- The supplier receives 50 percent of the $1.50 material reduction identified by the value analysis team.
- The profit figure for year two includes the supplier's share of the material reduction.
- The selling price at the start of year two becomes $56.27.

By focusing on joint and continuous performance improvement, the purchase price was reduced at a time when material and labor costs actually increased. This example illustrates the potential for improvement that can occur through joint price/cost analysis.

Establishing agreement on cost and price early in design and development supports the reduction of material costs through cooperative efforts. The use of cost savings sharing can induce both parties to work together to achieve mutual goals. The purchaser reduces its cost curve for purchased items and also establishes a basis for continuous cost-improvement initiatives. The supplier benefits from longer-term contracts, a fair profit based on its asset investment, and increased competitiveness thanks to improvements occurring because of the purchaser's insights and contributions.

Good Practice Example

Best Practices in Strategic Cost Management Leadership

A recent benchmarking study carried out interviews with 13 organizations in a variety of industries to identify current practices in strategic cost management. The population of companies was segmented based on whether their cost management practices were considered "Basic," "Moderately Advanced," "Advanced," or "Most Advanced." The key differences and transitional elements noted for firms in each category were documented and are highlighted in this executive summary. We focus here on the key steps required to progress from a "Basic" level of cost management, through different stages of maturity, and the core capabilities that must be developed through this evolution

Moving from Basic to Moderately Advanced

Firms in the "Basic" category seeking to move to the next level were generally focused on "establishing the foundation," through a focus on getting back to the basics of spend analysis, data cleansing, and establishing simple governance structures for cost management. This includes the following actions:

- **Governance**—Establish a Demand Management program to drive business unit leaders to create realistic budgets for spending, new product introductions, and forecasting of requirements to enforce a discipline of cost budgeting.
- **Systems**—Initiate a corporate-wide cost systems effort focused on data cleansing of all historical pricing, spend AP data, and labor rates to establish the backbone of a cost management support system.
- **Supply Base Management**—Establish a program for supply base consolidation, with specific targets defined by business, by category, and by platform.
- **Leadership and Planning**—Establish a corporate champion for cost leadership as a priority for competitive success across all key functional lines of business, with a governance committee to drive oversight and support.
- **Metrics**—Establish Key Performance Indicators for cost management alignments with financial projections, profit targets, line of business NPI projects, and market growth targets.
- **Talent**—Establish a network of key subject matter experts from across the organization with the requisite talent and skills, to build a cost management organization to provide decision-support to NPI, sourcing, and make or buy projects.
- **NPI**—Conduct a major audit of NPI processes to ensure that cost targets are tied product design outcomes, with accountability for cost established for the NPI team.

Moving From Moderately to Most Advanced

Firms in the Moderately Advanced category have established the core foundational elements required to build a cost management culture and system and should seek to establish the next level of cost capability through the following activities:

- **Governance**—Organizational realignment to ensure cost engineers are aligned by material or process globally, with specific roles, responsibilities, and accountability to business. Realignment to also create a joint material handling, packaging, procurement and logistics costing team tasked with building total cost models for all major point to point sourcing movements for major shipments around the globe.
- **Systems**—Accurate spend analytics database with updated and historical spend by category, by part family, by supplier, and by business accessible by all relevant functional teams.
- **Supply Base Management**—Segmented supply base with strategic approved suppliers (established quality, cost, and technology), approved suppliers, and emerging suppliers.

- **Leadership and Planning**—NPI planning team to establish projected key capacity bottlenecks and supplier cost overruns, based on NPI new product forecasted projections, data collected from impacted facilities, cost engineering leads, cost management team associates, and global sourcing category leads. This team should have a rolling five-year view on all upcoming new projects; highlight impacted areas, and key areas of immediate and pending concern.
- **Metrics**—Documented internal labor and material cost histories for all major facilities and product lines established and available through efforts of IT/team.
- **Talent**—Talent development efforts to establish key engineering cost manager roles in procurement, including competitor teardown and should-cost modeling, cost target objective setting, VA/VE, material and labor costing, and collaborative design.
- **NPI**—Initial engagement of strategic suppliers to attend NPI team meetings, with the objective of establishing consistent input and feedback for achieving cost targets.

Moving Froam Advanced to Most Advanced

Firms in the Advanced category have established a cost leadership organization, processes, systems for supporting cost decisions, and key performance indicators and are poised to engage on the next level of key activities to establish cost leadership in their industry:

- **Governance**—Global sourcing offices staffed with multilingual expats and local sourcing professionals aligned with NPI product requirements for supplier engagement in emerging countries.
- **Systems**—Cost management systems that drive part commonality, re-use, preferred suppliers, cost histories, and regular updates available to all NPI, sourcing, and manufacturing/engineering teams across the globe.
- **Supply Base Management**—A set of long-term supplier partnerships with active involvement on all NPI teams, engaged in on-site technical and material management support for cost management in NPI and production.
- **Leadership and Planning**—A documented category strategy and cost improvement plan for every part currently in production or going into production.
- **Metrics**—Detailed cost breakdowns, pricing histories, commodity and labor forecasts on all preferred suppliers with cost containment strategies available on a rolling three-year basis.
- **Talent**—Clear career path and leadership plan to attract the most highly talented individuals into the cost engineering roles.
- **NPI**—Development of Advanced Manufacturing Engineering teams that work in the supplier and technology community to track new developments, cost trends, and emerging technologies that need to be identified and nurtured for development. Active supplier development teams working at supplier locations through major NPI product ramp-up, launch, and post-launch.

Questions

1. Is the transformation of an organization to cost leadership a procurement responsibility, or a shared responsibility?
2. What is the role of change management and cultural changes in driving cost leadership?
3. Discuss the key elements that are required to transform an organization, which is just beginning this journey? What do you think is the critical success factor?

Source: Handfield, R., and Edwards, S. (2009, July), "Cost Leadership Best Practices," White Paper, Supply Chain Resource Cooperative, NC State University.

CONCLUSION

An awareness of cost fundamentals, cost analysis techniques, and innovative approaches to product costing is simply another area for the supply management and supply chain professional to master. Buyers and supply chain specialists involved with nonstandard, technically complex items must have the ability to evaluate a supplier's cost structure and match supplier capabilities and product requirements from a cost perspective.

The ability to practice price and cost analysis techniques, such as those outlined in this chapter, can make the difference between creating value and creating waste.

KEY TERMS

cost analysis, 412

opportunity cost, 445

Price analysis, 411

total cost analysis, 412

total cost of ownership, 444

DISCUSSION QUESTIONS

1. Why should a purchaser evaluate the cost of making an item instead of simply evaluating the purchase price? Is this true for all types of products? Why or why not?

2. List some of the reasons suppliers are reluctant to share detailed cost information. What can purchasers do to convince suppliers that shared cost data will not be exploited?

3. Is global sourcing always the lowest-cost option on account of the low labor rates? What other types of data have to go into this decision?

4. What is the difference among a fixed cost, a semivariable cost, and a variable cost?

5. Discuss the different pricing strategies a seller can use along with the key features of each. Provide examples of current marketplaces where these types of pricing arrangements are shifting dramatically.

6. Can you provide examples of suppliers or industries that are currently utilizing a price volume model, market share model, competition pricing model, and revenue pricing model?

7. What types of cost information are available on the Internet? What types of price information are available on the Internet? Is this information reliable?

8. Under what conditions does a buyer have the most supply management leverage over a seller?

9. When does a seller have the most leverage over a buyer?

10. What is the total cost of ownership concept? What are some of the challenges that must be overcome when implementing a total cost measurement system?

11. What are the benefits from measuring the total cost of ownership for a purchased item? Are there any potential disadvantages of this approach? If so, what are they?

12. How is the price of an item established in a target pricing contract? What makes target pricing attractive to a buyer and seller?

13. Can a company use a target pricing model without a follow-on cost-savings sharing agreement? Why or why not?

14. If a buyer and seller do not have a close working relationship, how can a buyer obtain cost data to perform a cost analysis for a supplier before awarding a purchase contract?

15. What happens if a supplier cannot meet a purchaser's initial target price? How is this issue resolved?

ADDITIONAL READINGS

Bendorf, R. (2002, May), "Supplier Pricing Models," *Inside Supply Management*, pp. 18–19.

Chen, C. C., Yeh, T. M., and Yang, C. C. (2006). "The Establishment of Project-Oriented and Cost-Based NPD Performance Evaluation," *Human Systems Management*, 25(3), 185–196.

Cooper, R. (1995). *When Lean Enterprises Collide: Competing Through Confrontation*, Boston: Harvard Business School Press.

Cooper, R., and Slagmulder, R. (1997). *Target Costing and Value Engineering*, Portland, OR; Montvale, NJ: Productivity Press; IMA Foundation for Applied Research.

Cooper, R., and Slagmulder, R. (1999). "Develop Profitable New Products with Target Costing," *Sloan Management Review*, 40(4), 23–33.

Cooper, R., and Slagmulder, R. (1999). "Integrating Activity-Based Costing and Economic Value Added," *Management Accounting: Official Magazine of Institute of Management Accountants*, 80(7), 16.

Cooper, R., and Slagmulder, R. (1999). *Supply Chain Development for the Lean Enterprise: Interorganizational Cost Management*, Portland, OR; Montvale, NJ: Productivity Press; IMA Foundation for Applied Research.

Cooper, R., and Yoshikawa, T. (1994). "Inter-Organizational Cost Management Systems: The Case of the Tokyo-Yokohama-Kamakura Supplier Chain," *International Journal of Production Economics*, 37(1), 51–62.

Degraeve, Z., and Roodhooft, F. (1999), "Effectively Selecting Suppliers Using Total Cost of Ownership," *Journal of Supply Chain Management*, 35(1), 5.

Dubois, A. (2003), *Strategic Cost Management across Boundaries of Firms*, Industrial Marketing Management.

Ellram, L. (1993), *Total Cost of Ownership*, Tempe, AZ: Center for Advanced Supply Management Studies.

Ellram, L. (1996), "A Structured Method for Applying Supply management Cost Management Tools," *International Journal of Supply Management and Materials Management*, 32(1), 11–19.

Ellram, L. (2002), *Strategic Cost Management*, Tempe, AZ: Center for Advanced Supply Management Studies.

Ellram, L. (2002), "Supply Management's Involvement in the Target Costing Process," *European Journal of Purchasing and Supply Management*, 8(4), 235–244.

Ferrin, B., and Plank, R. E. (2002), "Total Cost of Ownership Models: An Exploration Study," *Journal of Supply Chain Management*, 38(3), 18–21.

Kaplan, R. S., and Cooper, R. (1998). *Cost & Effect: Using Integrated Cost Systems to Drive Profitability and Performance*, Boston: Harvard Business School Press.

Lockamy, A., III, and Smith, W. I. (2000), "Target Costing for Supply Chain Management: Criteria and Selection," *Industrial Management and Data Systems*, 100(5), 210–218.

Monczka, R., and Trecha, S. (1988), "Cost-Based Supplier Performance Evaluation," *International Journal of Supply Management and Materials Management*, 45, 12–18.

McNair, C. J., Polutnik, L., and Silvi, R. (2001). "Cost Management and Value Creation: The Missing Link," *European Accounting Review*, 10(1), 33–50.

Ness, J. A., Schroeck, M. J., Letendre, R. A., and Douglas, W. J. (2001). "The Role of ABM in Measuring Customer Value." Part One. *Strategic Finance*, 82(9), 32–37.

Ness, J. A., Schroeck, M. J., Letendre, R. A., and Douglas, W. J. (2001). "The Role of ABM in Measuring Customer Value." Part Two. *Strategic Finance*, 82(10), 44–49.

Newman, R., and McKeller, J. R. (1995), "Target Pricing: A Challenge for Supply Management," *International Journal of Supply Management and Materials Management*, 31(3), 12–20.

Shank, J. K. (1999), "Case Study: Target Costing as a Strategic Tool," *Sloan Management Review*, 41(1), 73–83.

Shank, J., and Govindarajan, V. (1993), *Strategic Cost Management: The New Tool for Competitive Advantage*, New York: Free Press.

Sower, V., and Sower, C. (2011), *Better Business Decisions Using Cost Modeling*, New York: Better Business Expert Press.

Stundza, T. (2000, March 2), "Focus Is on Total Cost of Ownership," *Inside Supply Management*, p. 34.

Toomey, J. W. (1994). "Adjusting Cost Management Systems to Lean Manufacturing Environments," *Production & Inventory Management Journal*, 35(3), 82–85.

"Understanding Total Cost of Ownership," (2000), *NAPM InfoEdge*, 5(3), 22.

ENDNOTES

1. Based on Bendorf, R. (2002, May), "Supplier Pricing Models," *Inside Supply Management*, pp. 18–19.

2. Based on Bendorf.

3. Schmidgall, R. S. (1986), *Managerial Accounting*, Educational Institute, pp. 271–272.

4. This section is based on Menezes, S. (2001, January), *Supply Management Today*, pp. 28–32.

5. Adapted from Krause, D., and Handfield, R. (1999), *Developing a World Class Supply Base*, Center for Advanced Supply Management Studies.

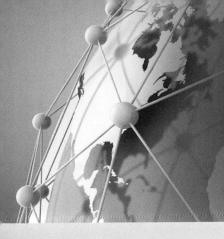

Purchasing and Supply Chain Analysis: Tools and Techniques

CHAPTER 12

Learning Objectives

After completing this chapter, you should be able to

- Understand fundamentals of project management tools
- Understand how to calculate the effect of learning curves on supplier costs
- Develop a basic understanding of the value analysis process
- Develop basic skills in process analysis and value stream mapping in a supply chain

Chapter Outline

Improving the Bottom Line through Supply Chain Processes at Harris Corporation

Neal Serven has made a career for himself in the world of government contracting, specifically in the areas of subcontract management and supply chain management. This senior subcontracts manager has close to 30 years experience in the field. After graduating from Florida State University with a double major in Purchasing/Supply Management and Management Information Systems, Neal accepted a position at Harris Corporation. During his time at Harris, Mr. Serven has held numerous positions including all areas within Supply Chain (Procurement, Material Planning, Pricing and Subcontracts), Program Management and Business Development.

Harris Corporation is an international communications and information technology company serving government and commercial markets in more than 125 countries. Headquartered in Melbourne, Florida, the company has approximately $5 billion of annual revenue and about 14,000 employees—including 6,000 engineers and scientists. Harris is dedicated to developing best-in-class *assured communications®* products, systems and services. Mr. Serven works in the Government Communications Systems (GCS) segment at Harris. GCS is a $1.8 billion business. These revenue figures are representative of the most current Harris fiscal year (HFY) 2013 performance. Harris' fiscal year runs from July 1st to June 30th. The other two Harris segments are RF Communications (producer of two way radios), and Integrated Network Solutions that provides network systems and services in government, healthcare, energy and maritime markets.

Anyone involved with government sector knows the roller coaster environment created by budget expansions then budget cuts. Currently the environment is one of budget cuts. Harris has responded to this by using many proven techniques such as lean initiatives and Six Sigma. According to Neal, "We are facing a difficult budget environment and market headwinds that make revenue growth challenging, so one major focus is to streamline internal operations." To that end the company launched Harris Business Excellence (HBX) in HFY 2013.

HBX is the new operational excellence platform helping to transform the way Harris does business. HBX taps in to the power of every employee to drive continuous improvement in business performance and customer satisfaction. These improvement efforts are directly linked to company-wide objectives, and are measured against targets to ensure progress is being driven in every business area. HBX is an advanced operating system upon which all processes and procedures are being built. It is a platform of industry-proven processes and tools that will serve as the foundation for the way Harris runs its business. The tools are based on Lean /Six Sigma principles and include value stream mapping, root cause analysis, mistake proofing, and waste elimination, among others. The transformation to a true HBX culture is a journey that is never really complete. In a short time HBX has produced significant results through increased productivity, waste reduction and optimized processes. Customers have responded positively and more than $75 million of savings from HBX-related productivity improvements were either returned to shareholders or re-invested in the company in HFY 2013.

Applying HBX in Supply Chain, specifically in the areas of subcontracting and procurement, has led Mr. Serven and the Harris Supply Chain team to employ a number of creative strategies and techniques focused on obtaining the products and services that Harris buys at the most economical price available. One of the key strategies being utilized is combining the talents of Harris' Engineering organization with that of the Supply Chain group to improve the overall requirements development process so that the majority of the items that Harris buys are competed amongst qualified bidders. Serven states that, "in both the government and commercial markets, nothing drives down supply chain costs better than healthy competition."

It is a given in the high tech sector that many buys are unique, hard to find or involve technologies where competitive sources may not be available. To address this problem Neal has found that a partnership between the Engineering and Supply Chain functions is critical. Serven's efforts in this partnership focus on requirements management. He states, "We want to prevent over specification of our requirements." Understanding products from a technical standpoint helps Harris purchasers to be more thoroughly prepared for meaningful supplier negotiations. To this end, Mr. Serven's organization has developed techniques and tools to assist in fact-finding supplier proposals to help Harris identify the key areas to address during negotiations.

Some of the other areas where the collaborative efforts between Engineering and Supply Chain are beginning to help reduce costs are Parts Standardization and Design to Cost/Design for Manufacturability (DTC/DFM). GCS's business is extremely diverse, supporting a wide variety of government, commercial and international customers. The products and systems produced to meet their customers' needs are diverse as well. Therefore, standardizing on common components and hardware across the enterprise enables Supply Chain to obtain the lowest possible prices for these products. DTC/DFM is a set of engineering processes that treat product cost and manufacturing requirements with equal weighting to the products technical requirements such as size, weight, power, electrical performance, etc. DTC/DFM significantly increases the probability that Harris will be able to produce a product or system within predetermined project cost budgets and schedule.

Finally, Harris is investing in Supply Chain automation. The company continues to augment its internally developed Supply Chain Portal known as *EXPO*. This web-based portal provides an extensive suite of on-line, automated tools and capabilities that include:

- Supplier Insight and Management
- Spend Management and Analytics
- Procurement Excellence
- Product Life-Cycle Management
- Engineering Collaboration and Discovery

EXPO provides Harris with the following key business benefits:

- Standardized platform that supports integrated communication
- Unified view of data—reduced cost and complexity through visibility
- Collaborative, self-service order management—reduced transactional costs
- Supplier performance management—scorecards reflecting key performance metrics
- Enables collaborative planning and forecasting

And beyond *EXPO*, GCS continues to innovate. The Supply Chain team recently rolled out a new capability called "Buy Smart". This new capability enables design engineering to directly identify, select and procure (on-line) low cost, standard, commercially available electronic components and accessories to streamline the early stages of the design process.

It is through these process innovations in automation and collaboration that Harris plans to counter its market and budgetary headwinds and contribute to improvements to the company's bottom line.

Source: L. Giunipero interview Neal Serven, Harris Corporation October 2013

Introduction

Having the right tools and applying the right techniques is an essential part of supply chain management. As the opening vignette illustrates, the commitment to continually improve profits can lead to higher profits. The Harris Business Excellence program (HBX) is based on the principles of Lean /Six Sigma and include value stream mapping, root cause analysis, mistake proofing, and waste elimination. Much of Harris's business is based on high technology government contracts. Supply managers at Harris involved with the Harris Business Excellence program (HBX) perform a variety of duties that are covered in this chapter. They: (1) manage projects; (2) assess costs associated with work done by suppliers/subcontractors; (3) consider the learning-curve effect on ultimate price; (4) apply value engineering/value analysis to insure that items are not over-specified; (5) insure that purchased materials receive maximum discounts in the appropriate quantities; and (6) engage in value stream mapping in both internal processes and where possible external supplier processes to identify waste.

To effectively accomplish many of their assignments, supply managers must be project managers. They must be skilled in managing team assignments involving multiple tasks and team members. Buyers must understand how to take advantage of learning improvements that occur at a supplier or subcontractor. These improvements should be shared and lead to lower costs for both parties. Process mapping helps identify and eliminate waste throughout the supply chain. Value analysis (VA) supports continuous quality improvement. All of these tools are important for purchasers to be effective in driving competitive success for their organization.

This chapter presents a set of tools and techniques that support effective purchasing and supply chain management. The tools discussed include project management, learning-curve analysis, value engineering/value analysis, quantity discount analysis (QDA), and process mapping.

Project Management

Project management is a valuable skill for supply chain managers to have because more and more work is being structured as projects. According to the Project Management Institute (PMI), **project management** is "the application of knowledge, skills, tools, and techniques to a broad range of activities to meet the requirements of a particular project."[1] Projects have certain characteristics that make them unique compared with other forms of work.

A **project** is a series of tasks that requires the completion of specific objectives within a certain time frame; has defined start and stop dates; consumes resources, particularly time, personnel, and budget; and operates with limited resources. Examples of projects involving purchasing and supply chain personnel include: (1) working with research personnel or engineers to develop new products; (2) working with information technology to procure new software and hardware; (3) lowering costs through value analysis team programs; (4) developing sourcing strategies; and (5) initiating performance improvement plans at a supplier.

Project management can be crucial in applications that span several organizations. They range from implementing Enterprise Resource Planning (ERP) systems to capital equipment acquisitions and construction projects to developing a marketing plan and modifying the website.

Defining Project Success

The project manager is asked to manage three sometimes conflicting issues in his/her quest to get the project done on time and within budget. First, all projects have a defined *scope,* which consists of the project overview and agreed-upon tasks, responsibilities, and

Sourcing Snapshot

China: Calling All Project Managers

The economic growth in China has created a need for talented project managers. Greg Balestrero, CEO of the Project Management Institute (PMI), the world's leading provider of project management training and standards, discusses how the need for project management professionals has grown. PMI has 225,000 members in 160 countries.

Q: Projects have been around since the Pyramids; why are project managers so important now?

A: There is the issue of assurance of repeatable success in projects, being able to predict a result and repeat it. This is particularly the case when you're talking about short life cycles, for example, fourth- or fifth-generation products that have a life cycle of less than 12 months. Aligning project skills with product development skills is one of the most important things. Then there is an obsessive demand for return on value earlier and earlier. Even if you're not in product delivery but putting in an IT system in a new facility, the era of the five-year project is long gone. Companies need the IT installation now, and within 12 months it needs to be generating the value that it was set out to do. So there is this increase in shortness.

Q: How has globalization affected project management?

A: Globalization—for good, bad, or however you look at it—has created a demand for multicultural projects. Look at the Airbus A380: It required 1,500 suppliers and 2,400 projects across 30 countries. That is pretty complex. Everyone thought the BMW Z4 was pure German. But only about 18 percent of the products are manufactured in Germany; 82 percent are manufactured in 30 other countries. When you are managing projects across cultural lines and national borders, you must put in place a standard that is a common language, a common approach, so everyone can answer the question "Is it on budget?" You need an answer that is accurate and understandable to everyone.

Q: Is there a shortage of people who can manage projects?

A: There's a shortage of project managers worldwide. And we are working 24/7 to provide education and certification worldwide. There is no lack of demand for certified professionals in project management, so they can command good salaries worldwide.

Q: What is your focus in training project management professionals in China?

A: Our real focus in China is ensuring professionals recognize that our standards and our certification are the two most important things to them. Since 2001 we've had 22,000 certified professionals here in China; we call them Project Management Professionals-and the growth rate is getting close to 50 to 60 percent a year.

Q: How many project managers does the country need?

A: An independent UN study predicted China would need more than 100,000 trained, certified, qualified project managers over the next five years. The 11th Five-Year Plan has shown the need to move infrastructure out into central China and—whether it's power generation, roads, transportation, fresh drinking water, health care, education—it's all project-related.

Source: Adapted from "China: Calling All Project Managers" (2007, April 18), *BusinessWeek* Online, Retrieved from http://www.businessweek.com/globalbiz/content/apr2007/gb20070418_435349.htm

deliverables. All projects have a *time frame* consisting of a starting and ending point. Finally, the *cost* dimension, which is very visible and if not well managed, can start to generate cost overruns, tarnishing the success of the overall project. Given these three rather concrete dimensions, it is often easier to measure project success as compared with other types of work.

For example regarding scope, did a supplier quality improvement project improve supplier quality by the intended amount? Was a new product developed within the time and budget constraints? Did the new product achieve its initial sales goals? Though the major project criteria as mentioned above are scope, time, and budget/cost, other general success factors include measures that address whether the project was *completed* within the following constraints:

- Within the allocated time period and budget
- At the proper performance or specification level as determined by the stated goals and objectives of the project
- At a level accepted by the customer, user, or management
- With minimal or only mutually agreed-upon changes
- Without disturbing the main work flow of the organization

Before *initiating* a project, supply managers should consider the following points:[2]

- Make sure the objectives and outcomes are championed by senior executive management
- Place the program under the leadership of people with skill, credentials, and credibility
- Establish an effective governance process with a cross-functional team
- Maintain active participation from team members (e.g., use their talents)
- Break down the project into phased deliverables
- Manage expectations continuously and consistently
- Measure objectively
- Ensure rapid problem escalation and resolution

Project Phases

Projects move through various phases from conception to completion. Exhibit 12.1 summarizes six phases, along with the characteristics defining the activities that make up each phase. The phases become increasingly detailed as projects progress from concept through completion. For maximum project effectiveness, it is important for the supply manager to be involved and participate at this stage.

Concept

Early in the project management process, project planners must develop a broad concept or definition of the project. A broad project objective may include developing a new product for a certain market within a specified time and budget. Project planners also identify any broad constraints facing the project. Budget estimates made during the concept phase vary considerable in accuracy. Generally those estimates that fall within 30 percent of final budget targets are considered acceptable.

Project Definition

If a project is initially feasible, it proceeds to the definition phase. This phase requires the development of a project description that provides greater detail than the concept phase. The project description identifies how to accomplish the work, how to organize for the project, the personnel required to support the project, tentative timing schedules,

---

Exhibit 12.1 | **Project Phases and Characteristics**

Concept
- Initiate broad discussion of project.

Project Definition
- Develop project description.
- Describe how to accomplish the work.
- Determine tentative timing.
- Identify broad budget, personnel, and resource requirements.

Planning
- Develop detailed plans identifying tasks, timing, budgets, and resources.
- Create organization to manage the project.

Preliminary Studies
- Validate the assumptions made in the project plan through interviews, data collection, literature search, and experience.

Performance
- Execute the project plan and perform work.
- Use project control tools and techniques here.

Post-completion
- Confirm project results.
- Reassign personnel.
- Restore equipment and facilities.
- Document project files for future reference.

---

and tentative budget requirements. Budget estimates begin to become more exact, with a target of approximately 5 to 10 percent of the actual final budget.

Planning

Planning involves preparing detailed plans that identify the tasks, timing milestones and determining budgets and resources required to support each task. This phase also includes creating the organization that will carry out the project, often through the use of project teams. The planning phase is particularly critical because there is a strong correlation between effective planning and successful project outcomes.

The project plan developed during the concept or project definition phase is usually not detailed enough to provide guidance during project implementation. Detailed planning provides an opportunity for discussing each person's role and responsibilities throughout the project. An organization must also define how the different tasks and activities comprising the project will come together to complete the project.

Preliminary Studies

A final phase before actually executing the project involves verifying the assumptions in the project plan, including performing literature searches, conducting field interviews, and gathering any required data. This phase confirms the planning work performed (or not performed) to date. Once the project manager or team confirms the assumptions made during detailed planning, then the actual performance of the project begins.

Performance

The performance phase involves executing the project's plan, controlling the project via periodic monitoring, and reporting the work results on a continuous basis to management or customers. Effective planning increases the likelihood that actual performance outcomes will meet expectations. Project managers play a particularly important role here in coordinating and directing the work effort. Depending on the type of project, this may be the longest of the six phases in terms of time and resources consumed.

Sourcing Snapshot

Project Management Does It Better, Faster, and Cheaper

According to a seasoned professional, project managers must constantly clarify the requirements in the faster-cheaper-better mandate and negotiate their relative importance to the project. Project Scope Statement: *Build a 2,000-square-foot, three-bedroom, two-bathroom house.*

The Project Scope does not address many parameters of the project. What is the most important criterion for this project? Faster? Cheaper? Better? Better implies higher quality and materials and labor make a huge difference. Better can usually be achieved by sacrificing cheaper or faster.

Faster is dependent on lots of things. These include: (1) the weather; (2) worker availability; (3) building permits; (4) financing; (5) material availability, etc. There are literally hundreds of things that can slow down or stop this project. How important is faster? Are you living in a one-bedroom apartment with your family of four, ready to have a mental breakdown if you do not get some space soon? Or do you have time and want to build the house well at a reasonable cost, without any concern about common delays?

Lower price is a factor in most home-building projects because most people live on a limited income. Spending to much of one's disposable income on a house reduces the quality of life in other areas.

There is a documentary about a competition between builders in San Diego, California. The rules were simple. Build a 2000-square-foot, three-bedroom, two-bath home that must pass code and meet design specifications, as fast as you can. This home had to be complete and ready to move into. Unlimited resources could be applied to the project and there was no limit on the time needed to plan for the build. The ultimate project management job was started.

How much time do you think the winning team took to build the house? Weeks? Days? The name of the documentary is "Four-Hour House." The winning team actually built the home, to code and specifications, in a little more than three hours. Each team brought more than 300 workers to the site and every kind of equipment imaginable. The project plan was in minutes, with tasks performed simultaneously. For example, the holes were drilled in walls for electrical wire while the walls were being built. The roof was being built off to the side of the house so it could be craned into place when the structure was ready. The foundation used chemicals to quick-cure the cement so building could occur immediately after pouring the cement. The coordination and enthusiasm of the teams was amazing as they performed what most would consider impossible. It also demonstrated that months of planning were required to execute a project like this in three hours.

After taking preferences into account, the final Revised Project Scope Statement reads: *Within six months, and within a budget of $250,000, build a 2,000-square-foot, two-story home to the attached design specifications. The owner must approve in writing any changes to materials, costs, or building schedule.*

Source: Adapted from Cretsinger, D. (2006, December 14), "Faster, Cheaper, Better," Retrieved from http://www.projectsatwork.com/content/articles/234376.cfm

Post-completion

Project managers or teams perform several important tasks during the post-completion phase:

- Confirm that the final project meets the expectations of management or customers. This usually involves a comparison of the project performance outcome compared with the expected outcome established during earlier planning.

- Conduct a post-implementation meeting to discuss the strengths and weaknesses of the project. An effective organization learns from the experiences of its project teams. Any lessons learned should be communicated to other project teams.

- Reassign project personnel to other positions or other projects. One of the primary characteristics of projects as a form of work is the movement of personnel from project to project.

- Restore any used equipment or facilities to their original status. Also, make sure all files are in good order and are available for future reference.

Project Planning and Control Techniques

Various tools and techniques are available to plan, control, and coordinate work activities. These tools allow a project manager to track what requires completion, by whom, and by when, as specified in the project plan. These tools also allow performance tracking over time, particularly in the areas of time and budget. Two popular planning and control techniques are Gantt charts and project networking tools such as Critical Path Method (CPM) and Program Evaluation and Review Technique (PERT).

Gantt Charts

A **Gantt chart** visually displays the tasks and times associated with a project. Named after Henry Gantt, a mechanical engineer, the chart is a horizontal bar chart with activities listed vertically and times or dates displayed horizontally. The advantage of Gantt charts is that they are relatively inexpensive to develop and use and can convey a great deal of information. The primary disadvantage is that for larger projects, they become increasingly difficult to use or to keep up to date. In such cases, project management techniques such as CPM and PERT are recommended. Exhibit 12.2 illustrates a Gantt chart for a project involving the transfer of equipment to a supplier during an outsourcing project.

CPM/PERT

Critical Path Method (CPM) and **Program Evaluation and Review Technique (PERT)** are two popular project control techniques, particularly for projects that are complex or involve many activities or tasks. These techniques require the user to identify the activities or tasks that make up a project and to determine the sequence of those activities.

Users apply CPM to projects where there is a single known time (referred to as a deterministic time) for each activity with no variance. PERT applies to projects where time estimates are variable or uncertain. Each activity in PERT has three time estimates: (1) most likely, (2) pessimistic, and (3) optimistic. Project managers combine these estimates to arrive at a single estimate of the expected activity time for each activity within the network.

Project control techniques allow project managers to monitor progress over time along with managing costs across all activities. Users can also determine the probability of completing projects by certain target dates using normal distribution statistics.

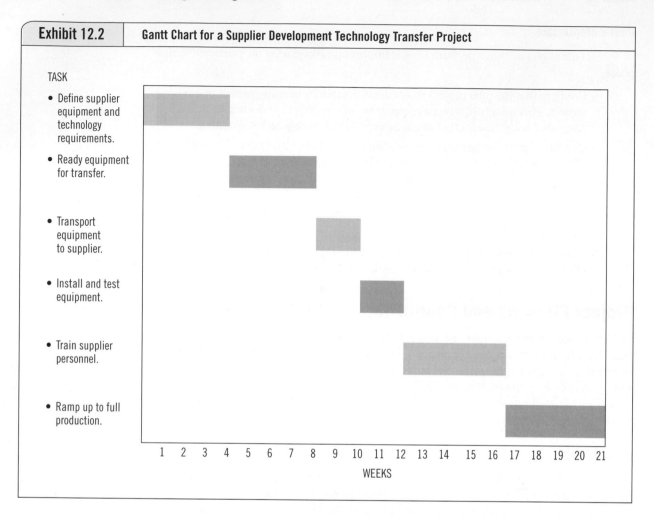

Exhibit 12.2 | **Gantt Chart for a Supplier Development Technology Transfer Project**

TASK

- Define supplier equipment and technology requirements.
- Ready equipment for transfer.
- Transport equipment to supplier.
- Install and test equipment.
- Train supplier personnel.
- Ramp up to full production.

1 2 3 4 5 6 7 8 9 10 11 12 13 14 15 16 17 18 19 20 21

WEEKS

Readers requiring in-depth detail of probability analysis or time/cost tradeoffs are urged to consult an operations research or project management textbook.

Rules for Constructing a Project Management Network

A graphical network can be used to represent each PERT or CPM project. A network is a graphical representation that shows how each individual activity relates in time and sequence to all other activities. Network illustrations are powerful because they show how separate activities come together to form an entire project. The construction of CPM and PERT project networks follows generally accepted rules or conventions, shown in Exhibit 12.3 on p. 469.

Later in this section we will use a purchasing project example to demonstrate the use of these rules, which apply only to constructing the network and do not yet involve the use of time estimates.

Project Management Example: Sourcing Strategy

A cross-functional team is responsible for developing a sourcing strategy, which will involve selecting a supplier follow-on systems development. The project has three primary objectives: (1) develop a set of performance criteria along with the evaluation system to assess potential supplier performance; (2) identify, evaluate, and select suppliers for a critical commodity; and (3) develop an information technology system that will evaluate the performance of selected suppliers on a continuous basis.

The project manager has identified the unique tasks that are required to meet the primary objectives of this project. (The letters refer to the sequence of activities shown in Exhibit 12.4)

Exhibit 12.4 illustrates the network for this project. There are three paths of activities through this project: A–B–E–F–G–K; A–C–D–F–G–K; and A–H–I–J. (A path is a continuous or connected flow of activities from project start to finish.) The project manager must

---

Exhibit 12.3	**Network Rules**

1. Identify each unique activity within a project by a capital letter that corresponds only to that activity.
2. A unique branch or arrow represents each activity in the project. Circles or nodes represent events. For example:

   This is the branch for activity A. Sometimes we also number the events, which represent points in time. The events associated with this activity (the circles) represent the start and completion of this activity. This diagram means only that B cannot start until A is complete. Branches show only the relationships among different activities; the length of the branches has no significance.
3. The sequence of the branches, however, is important.

4. Branch direction indicates the general progression in time from left to right.
5. When a number of activities end at one event, no activity starting at that event may begin before all activities ending at that event are complete.

   Activity D can start only after all activities preceding it in the network are complete. In this example, activities B and C must both be complete before beginning D. Activities B and C are predecessors of D (activities that must be complete before work on D can begin).
6. Two or more activities cannot share graphically the same beginning and ending events.
   Not allowed:

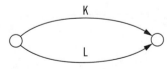

   Allowed:

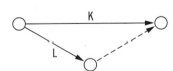

   This rule may require the use of a dummy activity, which is simply an extension of the activity that precedes it. In this case, the dummy activity is an extension of activity L. Dummy activities have no expected activity time—they simply carry forward the time from the preceding activity.

Exhibit 12.3 | Network Rules (Continued)

7. Networks start and finish at only a single event.

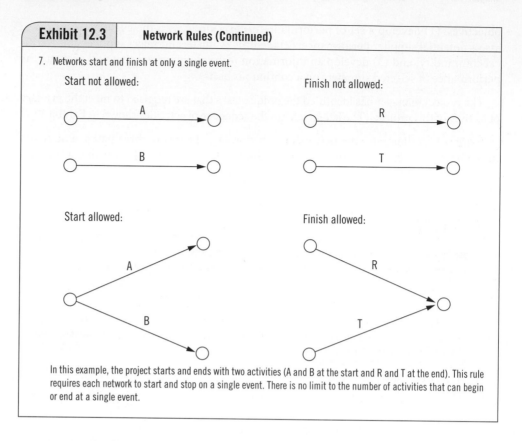

Start not allowed:

Finish not allowed:

Start allowed:

Finish allowed:

In this example, the project starts and ends with two activities (A and B at the start and R and T at the end). This rule requires each network to start and stop on a single event. There is no limit to the number of activities that can begin or end at a single event.

evaluate the progress of all three paths to ensure meeting the original project objectives. After reviewing Exhibit 12.4, one of the primary benefits of networking should become clear: the ability to see the relationships among all the tasks in a project.

Three observations are important at this point. First, the project manager has not identified the time associated with each task, only the tasks and their sequence. The manager

Exhibit 12.4 | Project Network Illustration for the Supplier Selection Project

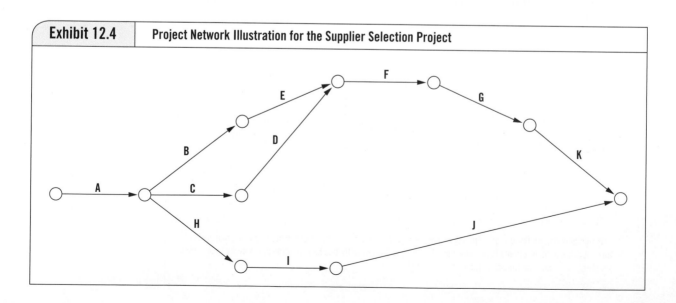

ACTIVITY	DESIGNATION	PRECEDING ACTIVITY
Assemble project team	A	
Identify potential commodity suppliers	B	A
Develop supplier evaluation criteria	C	A
Develop supplier audit form	D	C
Perform preliminary supplier financial analysis	E	B
Conduct supplier site visits	F	E, D
Compile results from site visits	G	F
Identify requirements for computerized supplier performance system	H	A
Perform detailed systems analysis and programming	I	H
Test computerized system	J	I
Select final suppliers	K	G

does not yet know which set of activities will make up the longest path (the critical path) within the project. Second, projects continuously change over time. As the project team progresses on its assignments, it must update the network to reflect that progress. The network looks like it does in Exhibit 12.4 only at the beginning of the project. PERT and CPM require regular updating with the most current information available. Third, computer software, such as Microsoft Project, is available that will construct the network and allow the user to perform various analyses. The most challenging part of project management is defining the activities that make up a project, the relationship among those activities, and the time and budget required for completing the activities.

Project Management with Time Estimates

The following steps describe how to develop a PERT network with variable time estimates:

1. Identify each activity requiring completion during the project and the relationship between those activities. This is a critical step. The activities should not be too broad or too narrow in scope. They must be definable tasks with a start and stop point whose completion supports the objectives of the project.

2. Construct the network reflecting the proper precedence relationships using the rules discussed earlier.

3. Determine the three time estimates for each activity (optimistic = a, pessimistic = b, and most likely = m). The optimistic and pessimistic estimates should reflect the end points on the time estimate continuum. These times should have only a 10 to 20 percent chance of actually occurring. Accurate time estimates are critical. Inaccurate time estimates or those with a great deal of variability will lessen the validity of the control process.

4. Calculate the expected activity time for each activity using the following formula:

$$\text{Expected Activity Time} = (a + 4m + b)/6$$

If activity G has an optimistic time of 5 weeks, a most-likely time of 6 weeks, and a pessimistic time of 13 weeks, then its expected activity time is $(5 + 24 + 13)/6 = 7$.

G
7

5. Place the expected activity times on the network under their respective activity branches and identify the critical path. The critical path is the longest (in time) path of continuous activities through the network. Any delay for activities on the critical path will delay the entire project. There can be more than one critical path in a project.

6. Identify the early start (ES), late start (LS), early finish (EF), and late finish (LF) times. These times also appear on the activity branch and provide a great deal of information to the project manager:

- *Early start.* The earliest point in time an activity can begin.
- *Late start.* The latest point in time an activity can begin without delaying the entire project.
- *Early finish.* The earliest time a project can finish given the expected activity time. Early finish time equals ES + expected activity time.
- *Late finish.* The latest time an activity can finish without delaying the entire project. Latest finish time equals LS + expected activity time.

Project Management Example with Time Estimates

Using the project presented earlier, we can now include time estimates (in weeks) and calculate the expected time for each activity. Project planners calculate these estimates

TASK	OPTIMISTIC	MOST LIKELY	PESSIMISTIC	EXPECTED ACTIVITY TIME
Assemble project team (A)	1	2	3	2
Identify potential commodity suppliers (B)	3	6	9	6
Develop supplier evaluation criteria (C)	2	4	5	3.8
Develop supplier audit form (D)	2	3	4	3
Perform preliminary supplier financial analysis (E)	1	2	4	2.2
Conduct supplier site visits (F)	4	8	12	8
Compile results from site visits (G)	2	5	8	5
Identify requirements for computerized supplier performance system (H)	2	4	8	4.3
Perform detailed systems analysis and programming (I)	8	10	16	10.7
Test computerized system (J)	2	3	5	3.2
Select final suppliers (K)	1	2	3	2

Exhibit 12.5 shows this project with all times displayed. When calculating times, the user always completes the early start (ES) and early finish (EF) times, moving left to right across the top of the network. Next, the user completes the bottom half of the network, which includes the late finish (LF) and late start (LS) times, by moving right to left through the network. Notice that all projects start at time 0, not time 1.

Activities E and D converge at the same event, which means that activity F, in this case, requires the completion of both E and D before it can begin. It is common for two or more activities to conclude at the same event. When this happens, the early start (ES)

Exhibit 12.5	Project Network Illustration for the Supplier Selection Project with All Times Displayed

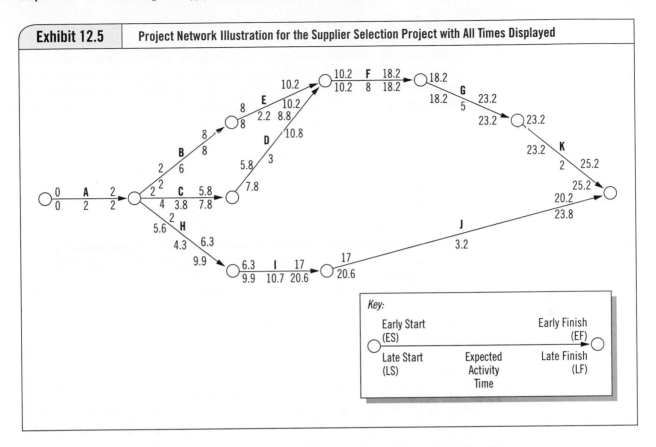

time for the next activity (activity F) is the larger of the early finish (EF) times for the preceding activities. This makes sense because the subsequent activity cannot start until all preceding activities are complete. Working right to left to arrive at the late finish and late start times on the bottom half of the network, we notice that three activities (B, C, and H) originate from the same event. In this case, the smaller of the late start (LS) times becomes the late finish (LF) time for activity A. In this case, two weeks is the late finish time for activity A.

The longest path (in time) through the network is the critical path. It is also the path on which the connected activities each have no slack. In our example, the critical path of this project consists of activities A–B–E–F–G–K. Any delay beyond the estimated times for each activity will result in a delay to the entire project. Project managers must always be aware of the status of critical path activities because they have no time slack.

Sourcing Snapshot

Learning Curves Applied to Professional Services

The majority of research on learning curves has been applied to the production of goods. How-ever, the services sector is growing and more services are being outsourced. The following research based on seven years of data collected from an architectural engineering (A/E) firm shows that professional services exhibit learning.

Professional services are different from other manufacturing or services in that they provide customized solutions to their clients using highly trained labor. However, business solutions proposed by service firms are not recreated anew, but rather, they are generated using previous experiences. The learning effect is not gained from direct repetition but rather through insights generated from prior projects.

Learning gains in professional services depend on technologies that codify and map this collective experience and on the ability of highly trained professionals to locate, interpret, partially reuse, or adapt prior solutions. For example, firms could establish a set of rules to complete a task or techniques, methods, and templates that can be reused. Professional services are by nature very labor intensive. In professional services, the overall volumes are low, which may lessen the amount of learning gains.

Another area for learning gains in services is their communication and knowledge management systems. Learning gains can result from better communication among the professional workers, helping project teams find colleagues within or outside the organization to solve problems. Facilitating communication, by developing formal routines that synthesize insights from past projects will create "new" knowledge that can then be codified and used in anticipation of future service requests. Gains in "knowledge management" systems have made it easier for professional service firms to access such information and improve learning.

Past studies that indicate depreciation also occurs in learning. Researchers, have computed the rate at which the knowledge stock erodes in a variety of businesses such as aircraft, shipbuilding, and automotive. Results vary widely, but they all experienced **learning depreciation**. Specialization of work, motivation of workers, turnover, etc. were possible explanations for depreciation.

Alternatively, professional service workers share a common body of knowledge through formal education and training. There are mandated and well-documented standards, protocols, and procedures followed for service delivery. For example, an electrical engineer must comply with local and state codes, and design of electrical circuits should conform to well-established design principles. Firms also encourage their workers to be certified (e.g., bar exam, CPA, professional engineer, etc.) and take continuing education hours to remain current. This specialized knowledge and its continued use in ongoing project work make the professional worker resistant to knowledge depreciation. Meanwhile, turnover may act to increase knowledge depreciation as new workers must be trained and learn new jobs and routines; thus experience is a factor in the rate of learning.

The three key findings are: (1) that professional services exhibit learning curves, (2) services exhibit virtually no depreciation of knowledge, and (3) the rate of learning accelerates with experience. All of these are important lessons for supply managers to keep in mind when evaluating service offerings.

Source: Boone, T., Ganeshan, R., and Hicks, R.L. (2008, July), "Learning and Knowledge Depreciation in Professional Services," Management Science, 54(7), 1231(6).

The difference between the late start and early start (LS − ES) or the late finish and early finish (LF − EF) times is slack—the maximum amount of leeway in an activity that will not delay the entire project. Activities without any slack (activities A, B, E, F, G, and K) are by definition on the critical path. Activities not on the critical path will have slack.

Of special interest to project managers is a project's path slack—the amount of time that activities along the path can be delayed without delaying the entire project.

Notice in our example there are three continuous paths throughout the project. Exhibit 12.5 details the paths and their total time. Of the three paths, A–B–E–F–G–K is the longest path at 25.2 weeks. None of the activities on this path have any slack.

The length of the path equals the sum of the expected activity times for each activity on that particular path. Note that the length of path A–C–D–F–G–K is 23.8 weeks. We must further notice that the slack for this path resides in only two activities—C and D each have two weeks of slack. However, this does not mean there are a total of four weeks of slack. There are only two weeks between the two activities. If activity C finishes at week 7.8 instead of 5.8, then activity D no longer has any slack because it now cannot start until week 7.8.

Project management tools are critical when managing large-scale projects, such as the example discussed in the opening vignette. Purchasing professionals are managing an increasing number of projects involving more than one functional area and large amounts of resources. To do this effectively, they must have an understanding of project management control tools and techniques.

Learning-Curve Analysis

Learning curves establish the rate of improvement because of learning as producers realize direct-labor cost improvements as production volumes increase. When referring to learning improvement, the learning rate represents a reduction in the cumulative average number of labor hours as production doubles from a previous level. For example, with an 85 percent learning rate, the average amount of direct labor required to produce a single unit declines by 15 percent each time production doubles.

With a 90 percent rate, direct-labor requirements decrease by 10 percent each time production doubles. The fundamental principle of the learning curve is that as production doubles, direct-labor requirements decline by an observed and predictable rate. The rate of improvement varies directly with the degree of learning and is project specific.

Why should purchasers be concerned with learning curves? If learning occurs at a supplier during the performance of a purchase contract, and the buyer does not take that into account, then the supplier will reap the financial benefits that result from learning. If learning occurs, the benefits must go somewhere—either into increased supplier profits or to the buyer as a cost savings! In collaborative relationships, buyers and suppliers can work together to mutually share the benefits of learning curves and productivity improvements.

Learning curves apply to the average direct labor hours required to produce a unit of output. The labor component is usually the easiest data to gather because companies assign direct-labor hours to specific items or projects. Historically, the term "learning curve" refers to the reduced direct-labor requirement per unit of output because of the effects of learning. This empirically derived concept was first noted by Boeing Corporation, which noticed that the amount of time required to build the same model aircraft decreased over time. The term "experience curve" refers to the longer-term factors of production that systematically reduce production costs. These factors include the shorter-term labor component along with longer-term product and process modifications. As is shown in the Sourcing Snapshot on page 473, the learning curve has applicability to services as well as goods. Services exhibit virtually no depreciation of knowledge and the rate of learning accelerates with experience.

Components of the Learning or Experience Curve

What drives the expected cost reductions, which are the basis of the learning curve and the broader experience curve? Different factors combine to produce a learning effect. The first factor is the *work force*. This includes the ability of the worker on the job to learn and improve through repetitive effort and increased efficiency, and the effort by management to pursue productivity gains. In the area of professional services, learning is gained from insights gained through previous projects.

The next factor includes modifications to the production process. Because labor improvements quickly reach the point of smaller and smaller returns, management often relies on *process changes to* realize continuous improvement. Management may introduce new production methods, substitute increased automation for labor, or pursue vertical integration that results in greater cost control. Some firms also update their process technology during the life of a product to take advantage of improvements offered with newer equipment. Offering a supplier a longer-term contract with guaranteed volumes, for example, encourages investment in equipment that results in lower production costs. In professional services technologies such as "knowledge management," systems facilitate process improvements and hence learning efficiencies.

When to Use the Learning Curve

Not all processes or items benefit from, or exhibit improvement from, learning. In fact, when used incorrectly, this approach can result in a significant underestimation of true production costs. The learning-curve approach applies when certain operating conditions are present.

Learning-curve analysis is appropriate when a supplier uses a new production process or produces an item for the first time. Production efficiency usually increases as a supplier's workforce becomes familiar with a new process. The learning curve is also appropriate when a supplier produces a technically complex item for the first time. The approach is also appropriate when an item has high direct-labor content.

The human factors present at the beginning of production must remain fairly constant over time to apply the learning curve. If an organization experiences high turnover, then the workforce may not demonstrate the anticipated rate of learning. Using one classical example, the Douglas Aircraft Company (now part of Boeing) experienced high turnover because of a tight labor market during the initial production of its DC-9. The company was unable to realize the labor efficiencies it had factored into the sales price of the aircraft. The resulting higher-than-planned costs created a financial strain on the company. More recently, part of the additional costs and quality problems incurred on the Boeing Dreamliner resulted from moving production of certain components from Seattle to South Carolina. The learning curves for these components were longer than Boeing originally anticipated.

Learning curves require the accurate collection of cost and labor data, particularly during the early stages of production. A buyer must have confidence that learning occurs at a uniform rate and that any improvements result from employee learning. Initial production data often provide the basis for negotiation regarding expected improvement rates and scheduled price reductions.

Learning Curve Illustrated

Exhibit 12.6 provides direct-labor data for a purchased item over increasing levels of output. Learning-curve examples can become quite complex, especially when using logarithmic scales to show the relationship between units produced and labor requirements.

Exhibit 12.6	Supplier Learning-Curve Data		
(A) UNITS	(B) TOTAL LABOR HOURS	(C) AVERAGE LABOR HOURS PER UNIT	(D) LEARNING RATE
1	20	20.0	—
2	34	17.0	15.0%
4	58	14.5	14.7%
8	100	12.5	14.8%
16	168	10.5	16.0%
32	288	9.0	14.3%
64	493	7.7	14.4%
Average improvement rate: 15% or 85% learning curve			

This simple example illustrates the effect on the average labor requirement because of a fairly consistent rate of learning.

Each column in Exhibit 12.6 provides data needed to estimate the cumulative learning rate for this supplier:

- Column A: The total units produced over a period of time. In this example, a total of 64 units were produced.
- Column B: The cumulative total labor hours (TLH) required to produce a given level of units. This supplier used 288 total labor hours to produce 32 total units but only 493 total labor hours to double production to 64 total units.
- Column C: The total labor hours for a given level of output divided by the units produced. The figure represents the cumulative average labor per unit of output.
- Column D: The associated learning rate for each doubling of production. The learning rate from one to two units of production equals (20 LH/unit–17 LH/unit)/(20 LH/unit) = 0.15 or 15 percent. Note that LH/unit is the average labor hours per unit and is calculated by dividing the total labor hours (column B) by the number of units (column A). The learning rate from two to four units equals

$$(17 \text{ LH} = \text{unit} - 14{:}5 - \text{LH} = \text{unit}) = (17 \text{ LH} = \text{unit}) = 0{:}147 \text{ or } 14{:}7\%$$

Each level can be calculated in a similar way.

This analysis reveals that the supplier has an approximately 85 percent learning curve for this item, which means that as production doubles, the direct labor required to produce a unit should decrease 15 percent on average. A producer realizes the most dramatic learning improvements over early volumes when the effect from learning is the greatest.

The successful use of the learning curve requires knowing when and how to apply the technique. A buyer's objective must be to use the tool to identify anticipated labor costs for increasingly larger production volumes. An analyst often cannot identify a learning rate until some preliminary production data are available. If data are not available, one approach is to rely on historical learning rates or previously observed rates at a supplier.

Learning-Curve Problem

A buyer does business with a supplier that uses a production process that historically demonstrates an 80 percent learning curve; that is, as production rates double, there is a 20 percent reduction in the average direct-labor hours required to produce a unit.

Given this learning rate, a buyer hopes to capture this reduced labor requirement through a lower purchase price.

Exhibit 12.7 outlines one use of the learning curve in purchasing. In this example, the buyer expects the per-unit price on a 600-unit order to lower from $228 to $170 because of learning. Whether the buyer actually receives a $170 unit price will probably be subject to negotiation. The supplier may argue that overhead did not change since the original order and should remain at $50 per unit. The supplier's profit is affected as both direct and overhead costs decline and profit remains at 20 percent of total costs. The buyer may counter that material costs should decline because of larger volumes. The key point is that the buyer now has a price range for negotiation with the supplier.

Exhibit 12.7	Learning-Curve Problem

XYZ Corporation is buying a new item produced by a process that historically demonstrates an 80 percent learning curve. A buyer has placed an order for 200 pieces and receives a quote of $228 per unit. The buyer has accumulated the following per-unit cost data:

Material	$ 90	(Five hours on average per unit at $10 per hour) (Assume 100 percent of direct labor)
Direct labor	$ 50	
Overhead	$ 50	
Total costs	$190	(Difference between per-unit price and total costs, which equals 20 percent of total costs)
Profit	$ 38	
Total per unit	$228	(Quoted price)

The buyer wants to place a second order for an additional 600 pieces, or a combined total order of 800. How much should the buyer expect to pay per unit given the expected benefit of the learning curve (which affects direct-labor requirements)?

1. Calculate the average labor hours for the entire combined order of 800 units: From the first order, 200 units required an average of 5 hours labor per unit. Therefore, 400 units should require only 80 percent as much as the original 200, or an average of 4 hours of labor per unit, given an 80 percent learning rate. 800 units should require an average of 3.2 hours of labor per unit (80 percent of 4 hours is 3.2 hours). One of the guidelines of learning curve is that labor costs decrease by a predictable rate each time production doubles.

2. Calculate the hours required for the total combined order of 800 units less the labor incurred for the original 200-piece order:

   800 units × 3.2 average hours = unit = 2,560 total hours

Less:

   200 units × 5 average hours per unit = 1,000 (direct labor required for original 200-piece order)
   1,560 total labor hours required for the next 600 units

3. Calculate the additional total and per-unit labor cost for the additional 600-unit order:

   1,560 hours × $10 per direct-labor hour = $15,600 total additional labor cost
   $15,600/600 units = $26 per unit

4. Calculate the expected new per-unit price for the additional 600-piece order:

   Additional 600 pieces per-unit cost

Material	$ 90	(Remains unchanged, although higher quantities may reduce the per-unit material cost)
Direct labor	$ 26	
Overhead	$ 26	(Assume 100 percent of direct labor)
Total costs	$142	
Profit (20%) of total costs	$ 28.40	
Total per unit	$170.40	

Learning-curve analysis highlights a key reason why many purchasers consolidate purchase volumes with fewer suppliers. Astute buyers know that an even lower purchase price may be obtained if the buyer correctly factors in the effects of learning as production volumes increase.

Value Analysis/Value Engineering

Value analysis involves examining all elements of a component, assembly, end product, or service to make sure it fulfills its intended function at the lowest total cost. Value analysis techniques are primarily applied to existing products and services. In contrast, **value engineering (VE)** is the application of value principles during product or service design. VE is a much more proactive approach to embracing value concepts. Larry Miles is said to have started using the technique at General Electric in the late 1940s and is considered the father of VA/VE.

The basic component of VA and VE is value—the lowest total cost at which an item, product, or service achieves its primary function along with satisfying the time, place, and quality requirements of customers. Although value analysis traditionally applies to tangible products, there is no reason that companies cannot apply VA techniques to services.

The primary objective of value analysis is to increase the value of an item or service at the lowest cost without sacrificing quality. In equation form, value is the relationship between the function of a product or service and its cost:

$$\text{Value} = \text{Function}/\text{Cost}$$

Using this formula to identify candidates for value analysis projects would result in targeting either those with Low Function and High Cost or those with High Function and High Cost. In the case of Low Function and High Cost items, the goal is to reduce the cost. These projects can produce significant savings and propel a value analysis program forward. In the case of High Function and High Cost, gains would be targeted to reducing costs but maintaining functionality desired by the customer.

However, there are many variations of function and cost that will increase the value of a product or service. The most obvious ways to increase value include: increasing the functionality or use of a product or service while holding cost constant, reducing cost while not reducing functionality, and increasing functionality more than increasing cost. For example, offering a five-year warranty versus a two-year warranty with no price increase raises the value of a product to the customer.

Value analysis is a way to achieve continuous performance improvement in an item, product, or service. It is not a technique for cheapening a product or service by lowering quality or other performance attributes below what customers expect. Many firms realize that VA is a powerful technique that can help a firm achieve its continuous cost and quality improvement targets.

Who Is Involved in Value Analysis?

Value analysis, certainly not exclusively a purchasing tool, involves many organizational functions. However, because most products and services require major inputs from suppliers, purchasing should take an active role in coordinating value analysis activities.

A common approach for using value analysis involves creating a VA team composed of professionals with knowledge about a product or service. Many functional groups can contribute to the value analysis team:

- *Executive management.* Executive management provides overall guidance and support for the VA process and allocates the time, budget, and personnel to work actively on VA projects.

- *Suppliers.* Because much of what value analysis examines involves the cost and design of component parts, it is logical to request input from suppliers, a group that can propose alternative materials, provide insights into what other firms are doing, and identify lower-cost production methods.

- *Purchasing.* Purchasing often takes a primary role in organizing the VA effort by coordinating and disseminating relevant information.

- *Design engineering.* Design engineers evaluate any proposed changes to the design of an item. They also help define product function, establish quality and engineering standards, and evaluate the effect of VA changes on other parts within the product.

- *Marketing.* The marketing group provides insight about the impact that VA changes may have on customers.

- *Production.* The production group has the responsibility of producing final items or products, and it can also propose better ways to produce an item or service to achieve higher quality or lower total cost. It is essential that this group be informed about any changes proposed by other functional groups.

- *Industrial/process engineering.* This group can contribute extensively, particularly when discussing methods of producing and delivering a product or service. Industrial/process engineers can evaluate proposed manufacturing methods, material handling and flow, the effect of alternative materials on the production process, and packaging requirements.

- *Quality control.* Quality control can evaluate the impact on quality that proposed changes may have. Quality control can also establish how and where to evaluate quality performance levels for a proposed production method. This group can work with purchasing to support quality control efforts at suppliers as well.

Tests for Determining Value in a Product or Service

Value analysis teams ask a number of questions to determine if opportunities exist for item, product, or service improvement:

1. Does the use of this product contribute value to our customers?
2. Is the cost of the final product proportionate to its usefulness?
3. Are there additional uses for this product?
4. Does the product need all its features or internal parts?
5. Are product weight reductions possible?
6. Is there anything else available to our customers given the intended use of the product?
7. Is there a better production method to produce the item or product?
8. Can a lower-cost standard part replace a customized part?
9. Are we using the proper tooling considering the quantities required?

10. Will another, dependable supplier provide material, components, or subassemblies for less?

11. Is anyone currently purchasing required materials, components, or subassemblies for less?

12. Are there equally effective but lower-cost materials available?

13. Do material, labor, overhead, and profit equal the product's cost?

14. Are packaging cost reductions possible?

15. Is the item properly classified for shipping purposes to receive the lowest transportation rates?

16. Are design or quality specifications too tight given customer requirements?

17. If we are making an item now, can we buy it for less (and vice versa)?

The most likely VA improvement areas include modifying product design and material specifications, using standardized components in place of custom components, substituting lower-cost for higher-cost materials, reducing the number of parts that a product contains, and developing better production or assembly methods.

The Value Analysis Process

Value analysis projects follow a systematic approach consisting of five stages:

1. Gather information

2. Speculate

3. Analyze

4. Recommend and execute

5. Summarize and follow up

These stages occur after identifying an item or product as a VA candidate.

Gather Information

The first stage for any value analysis project requires agreement about an item or product's primary and secondary functions for customers. VA participants should ask, "What does this product do for the customer?" and "Why does a customer buy this product?" It is important to understand a product's primary and secondary functions. Value analysis experts recommend naming each function of an item or product with two words—a verb and a noun. After this is complete, the team must agree on which functions are primary versus secondary. For example, the primary function of an industrial pump may be to move fluids at a rate required by the customer. A secondary function may be to minimize noise in the customer's facility. In this case, the VA team must recognize that moving fluids is the primary function of the industrial pump. Minimizing noise, a secondary consideration for industrial pumps, still must receive attention during analysis.

During this stage, detailed information about the item or product is collected. This includes sales trends, supplier performance data, costs to make and sell, design drawings, quantity estimates, and production method analyses.

Speculate

This stage calls for wide-open or creative thinking on the part of the VA team. Brainstorming is ideal as the team evaluates an item or product against the various tests or questions presented earlier. The primary objective of this phase is to develop as many improvement ideas as possible by withholding judgment on any of the proposed alternatives. This is why non-evaluative brainstorming is used during this phase. *Brainstorming* is a technique where individuals throw out ideas without any comments as to the feasibility or usefulness of the idea. The intent is to generate a broad list of ideas and later evaluate those ideas. A VA team moves to the analysis stage after it exhausts its ideas about how to improve a particular item or product.

Analyze

This stage critically evaluates the different ideas put forth during the speculation phase. Analysis can include cost/benefit calculations or assessment of the feasibility of implementing an idea. The result is a set of ideas that satisfy the original goals and objectives of the VA effort. This phase is very specific and no longer involves generalities.

Recommend and Execute

Up to this point the VA process has generated only a prioritized list of ideas. The team may have to present its proposals to executive management for approval. Moving an idea from the team to the organization requires the ability to: (1) motivate others; (2) be creative; (3) utilize good communication skills; (4) think analytically; and (5) possess solid product knowledge, commitment, and salesmanship.

Once a team receives approval, it must implement its ideas. Some ideas will be quite simple to carry out, whereas others will be more complex. The team must develop a project plan with timings, budget requirements, and responsibilities. The team often has to generate support outside the team for its proposals and help during implementation.

Summarize and Follow Up

This step is common during the implementation of any idea or plan. It may be the responsibility of the VA team or group to follow up and track implementation progress. The team may also track the gains achieved by the VA effort.

Quantity Discount Analysis

Quantity discount analysis (QDA) is a technique used to examine the incremental changes in cost between quantities within a supplier's price quotation. This tool allows the user to verify that quantity discounts are reasonable. Using this technique, a buyer may be able to negotiate price improvements through a better understanding of incremental unit costs.

There are two primary types of quantity discount analyses. The first involves prices at specific quantities, whereas the second examines discounts over quantity ranges.

Quantity Discount Analysis Illustrated

Exhibit 12.8 on p. 483 demonstrates how to use QDA when a buyer has price breaks at specific quantities. Exhibit 12.9 on p. 484 illustrates how to use QDA when a buyer has price breaks in ranges of quantities. The exhibits explain how to perform the appropriate calculations.

When using quantity discount analysis, the key calculation is the incremental cost of each additional unit at different quantity levels. In Exhibit 12.8, even though the original

Exhibit 12.8	Quantity Discount Analysis (Price Breaks at Specific Quantities)

1. Quotation from Avco at Specific Quantities

1 unit @ $85 each

3 units @ $80 each

6 units @ $70 each

10 units @ $69 each

2. Instructions:

Line 1: Place specific quantities from the quotation on line 1 in the appropriate column. Each column represents a specific quantity. Assume that ordering 0 is an option. This will support the quantity discount calculation.

Line 2: Place the quoted price from the supplier for each specific quantity on line 2 in the appropriate column.

Line 3: Multiply line 1 by line 2 for each column to arrive at a total price per order.

Line 4: Take the difference between the total price per order (line 3) and each successive order. For column A, it is the difference between $85 and ordering zero pieces, or $0.00. For column B, it is the difference between column B/line 3 and column A/line 3, or $240 minus $85 ¼ $155.

Line 5: This is the difference between each quantity break specified on line 1.

Line 6: This equals line 4 divided by line 5 for each column.

3. Price Breaks at Specific Quantities

Supplier Avco Part Name & No. Compressor 04273999 Date 12/14/10

		A	B	C	D	E	F	G	H
1. Number of units per order	0	1	3	6	10				
2. Price per unit (quoted price)	0	85	80	70	69				
3. Total price per order	0	85	240	420	690				
4. Price difference between orders		85	155	180	270				
5. Quantity difference between orders		1	2	3	4				
6. Price per unit per order quantity difference		$85	$77.50	$60	$67.50				

4. Quantity Discount Analysis

QUANTITY	TOTAL COST	INCREMENTAL QUANTITY	INCREMENTAL COST
1	$ 85	1	$85
		2	$77.50
3	$240	3	$77.50
		4	$60
		5	$60
6	$420	6	$60
		7	$67.50
		8	$67.50
		9	$67.50
10	$690	10	$67.50

quote at the three quantity levels moves lower on a per-unit basis, the incremental cost for units 7–10 ($67.50) is actually higher than for units 4–6 ($60). The same type of situation occurs in Exhibit 12.9. A buyer faced with this quote would want to know why incremental unit costs increase rather than decrease. Often, the supplier is unaware of why the incremental costs are higher.

Exhibit 12.9	Quantity Discount Analysis (Price Breaks in Ranges of Quantities)

1. Quotation from Dynamic Industries at Ranges of Quantities

RANGE	PRICE PER UNIT IN RANGE	RANGE	PRICE PER UNIT IN RANGE
1–5	$10.00 each	21–100	$7.60 each
6–10	$8.00 each	101–499	$7.00 each
11–20	$7.80 each	500+	$6.90 each

2. Instructions

Line 1: Place specific quantity ranges from the supplier quotation on line 1 in the appropriate column. Each column represents a specific quantity range provided by the supplier.

Line 2: Place the price per unit within each quantity range in the appropriate column. This is information provided by the supplier on the quote.

Line 3: "Total price per order" equals the lowest quantity in a range from line 1 times the "price per unit" in line 2 for each column. For example, for column C (quantity range 11-20), "total price per order" equals 11 times $7.80 = $85.80.

Line 4: Take the "total price per order" from the next-highest quantity range (line 3) and divide this by "price per unit" for the column being calculated. For example, for column A, the maximum units to order equals 48/10 equals 4.8. For column B, the maximum units to order equals 85.80/8 = 10.7, and so on. Round down to the nearest whole number.

Line 5: This equals line 2 times line 4 for each column.

Line 6: Calculate the difference between the "total price maximum order" for successive quantity ranges. For example, the "total price per maximum order" for column B (6-10 quantity range) is $80, whereas the "total price per order" for column A (1-5 quantity range) is $40. The difference is $40, which appears in column A on line 6. Calculate all other columns on line 6 accordingly.

Line 7: This is the difference between line 4 and the preceding column value on line 4. It is the difference between the maximum units to order from one quantity range to the next.

Line 8: This equals line 6 divided by line 7 for each column. It represents the incremental cost for each unit within that quantity range.

3. Price Breaks in Ranges of Quantities

Supplier Dynamic Industries Part Name & No. Wedge 04336280 Date 11/14/10

		A	B	C	D	E	F	G	H
1. Number of units per order	0	1–5	6–10	11–20	21–100	101–500	500+		
2. Price per unit (quoted price)	0	10	8	7.80	7.60	7.00	6.90		
3. Total price per order (use minimum quantity)	0	10	48	85.80	159.60	707	3,450		
4. Maximum units to order	0	4	10	20	93	492	—		
5. Total price per maximum order		40	80	156	706.80	3,444	—		
6. Price difference between maximum order		40	40	76	550.80	2,737.20	—		
7. Quantity difference between maximum units to order		4	6	10	73	399	—		
8. Price per unit per order quantity difference		$10	$6.67	$7.60	$7.54	$6.86			

4. Quantity Discount Analysis

QUANTITY	QUOTED PRICE	QUANTITY RANGE	INCREMENTAL COST
1–5	$10.00	First 5 units	$10.00 each
6–10	$8.00	Next 5 units	$6.67 each
11–20	$7.80	Next 10 units	$7.60 each
21–100	$7.60	Next 80 units	$7.54 each
101–500	$7.00	Next 400 units	$6.86 each
500+	$6.90	——	

QDA provides the buyer with information for questioning and negotiating improvements in the discount schedule. The analysis often reveals an up-and-down roller-coaster effect between incremental price differences. Questions asked because of a QDA often produce additional discounts and a better understanding of the quotation by the buyer and seller. The buyer should not accept a quote that features higher incremental costs as volumes increase unless the supplier can provide a valid explanation.

Process Mapping

Process mapping is a tool that reduces processes to their component parts or activities and helps identify and then eliminate non-value-added activities (waste) or delays within a process. Process mapping is valuable in purchasing, for example, when attempting to streamline the flow of material or information between suppliers and a purchaser.

Organizations have many processes that, when taken together, define the organization's primary work. A process is essentially an outcome composed of a set of tasks, activities, or steps. How well an organization performs these tasks determines how efficient and effective it is at that process. As you can see from the initial opening snapshot Harris Corporation uses process mapping extensively. The following supply chain processes are among those that most businesses perform:

- Supplier evaluation and selection
- Supply-base management
- New-product design and development
- Accounts receivable/accounts payable
- Inventory control and management
- Customer service support
- Training and education
- Inbound logistics
- Outbound logistics and physical distribution
- Research and development
- Customer order fulfillment

Most processes cross more than one functional boundary. When this happens, there is a risk that no one actually owns or takes responsibility for the entire process. In fact, some departments may actually have goals that are in conflict with one another. A transportation department evaluated on cost may use the least expensive method possible, such as rail. Customer service, on the other hand, may want to make material available to customers as soon as possible, which implies speed. Rapid delivery will likely increase transportation costs. These two groups may thus have goals that conflict.

Organizations use process mapping to redesign or reengineer processes. There are two basic types of processes: sequential and concurrent. **Sequential processes** are those in which the set of steps or activities that make up the activity occur one after the other. As shown in the following diagram, Activity B does not begin until A is complete, whereas C does not begin until B is complete. When mapping processes, we may place time estimates of the activity along with the sequence of the activities. A primary goal of process mapping is to eliminate waste from a process. Activity times are important to this goal.

A   B   C

Concurrent processes consist of activities or steps performed concurrently during the main flow of work. For example, many organizations are attempting to develop new products concurrently rather than sequentially, which not only saves time and money but also allows agreement on major issues early in the process.

Sourcing Snapshot

A Day in the Life of a Procurement Project Manager

Carlton W. Bradshaw, C.P.M., a procurement project manager for Eaton Corp., arrives at the office between 7:00 and 8:00 a.m. and prepares for the day checking e-mail, voice mail, faxes, and so forth. Big question: Just how unusual or normal will today be?

It can be said that the day in the life of a project manager is never really typical, and for many that's what makes this specialized career exciting. Meetings, check-ups on progress, evaluation of project by key players, checking future needs for upcoming critical events, and much more-these elements keep project managers hopping. And here is what it looks like:

8:30 a.m.: It is Wednesday and time for the "core teams" meeting the people who are functional representatives of a project team. The meeting lasts an hour and a half, and several issues are reviewed. Each team member takes information back to his or her respective function.

10:00 a.m.: Next comes a meeting with Susan Whalen, engineering process development manager, whose responsibilities include engineering processes. Bradshaw and Whalen discuss how procurement will support engineering on various projects, and Bradshaw identifies any special needs that might arise. All this takes place on a high process level.

11:00 a.m.: Back in the office, Bradshaw does follow up and department management tasks.

1:00 p.m.: A subproject team that supports larger project teams in connection with materials in the pipeline and cost reduction meets. This is a detail-oriented working meeting. Engineering could have from 15 to 30 miniprojects going under the umbrella of a larger one, and this sub-team works out the details of these aspects. A weekly meeting establishing engineering priority also takes place. This focuses on the larger horizon of engineering marketing—where are the markets going further out? Bradshaw represents procurement at these meetings. They are typically two hours long and focus on three market segments, one per meeting.

3:00 p.m.: A weekly supplier-driven cost-reduction program meeting is held. Bradshaw leads a small team on this one. Ideas from suppliers are evaluated and fed to engineering.

4:45 p.m.: Bradshaw meets with staff within the procurement function of procurement project leaders to get caught up.

Source: Adapted from Lester, M. (1998, December). "Purchasing and Supply Meet Project Management," *Purchasing Today*, 9(12), 30–36.

Cross-functional teams often use process mapping. Because most processes move across functional boundaries, it is logical to have those groups connected with the process involved with mapping and improving the process. This involvement will help generate buy-in from different groups concerning any proposed changes while keeping all impacted groups informed of those changes.

Good process mapping is a key to value improvement and waste reduction. The following steps are critical to effective process mapping:

- Search for better ways and methods to perform the tasks comprising a process, which often involves using information technology to automate transactions within the process.

- Replace sequential activities with concurrent activities wherever possible.

- Identify those activities that contribute to waste or add minimal value to the process and target those for elimination.

- Identify the time associated with each part of a process and identify how much of that time is waste.

- Involve the functional groups that impact a process.

- Represent graphically the process so those involved have a clear understanding of the process steps.

Value Stream Mapping

Value stream mapping (VSM) is a process of visually presenting the flow of materials and information to identify wasted time and actions in a manufacturing or service process. VSM can be depicted broadly from the supplier to the focal firm and out to customer. Alternatively, VSM can be used for a specific operation or series of operations. By identifying unnecessary steps and resources VSM streamlines processes for greater efficiency. Visual depiction of the process enables analysts to highlight areas for improvement and get closer to what is termed the "ideal state."

Much of the history of VSM is attributed to Toyota Motor Corporation and Taiichi Ohno. Ohno states in his text, "All we are doing is looking at the time line from the moment the customer gives us an order to the point when we collect the cash. And we are reducing that time line by removing non-value added wastes."[3] There is some overlap between the terminology used in VSM and those termed lean techniques because both attempt to identify and eliminate waste. According to Ohno and Toyota, there are seven categories of waste. These are:

1. *Overproduction:* Producing items for which there are no orders.
2. *Waiting Time:* Employees standing about. Inventory at stand-still.
3. *Unnecessary Transport:* Moving material unnecessarily or long distances.
4. *Over-processing:* Using more steps to produce a product than necessary.
5. *Excess Inventory:* Retaining unnecessary inventory between process steps.
6. *Unnecessary Movement:* Any wasted motion by man or machine.
7. *Defect:* Making incorrect product.[4]

Value and Non value added activities   In VSM, value is from the customer's perspective, the customer being the person who uses the output. *Value adding* actions and resources are those which create value for the customer. *Non-value-adding* is everything done in the process, which contributes no value for the customer but which they are forced to pay for when they buy the product or service. *Necessary non-value-adding* are those actions in a process that must be done to make the product but create no value for the customer. Unnecessary non-value-adding is removed and necessary non-value-adding is minimized.[5]

Processing a part or writing a report is value adding activity. A person writing a report waiting for approval to finalize the report or obtain feedback from a colleague who needs to review a key technical part of the report would be categorized as non-value added. Meanwhile replacing a printer cartridge to print the final report is a necessary non-value adding activity.

VSM Process   The VSM begins with the team reaching agreement on the process to analyze and then establishing boundaries for the specific process. Next the actual process is observed from start to finish. The observer monitors and measures what happens within, and between, each process step. For each process step the following are recorded: (1) the variety of resources used in the step; (2) the quantity/amount of usage; and (3) the range of times each resource is in use. The measured variables are collected together in a '*variable block.*' The variation or spread, of the variables is recorded by lowest, average and highest times. The presence of variability offers great opportunity for improvement. Specific VSM dimensions recorded in the variable block can include: the people required; the cycle time; value-add time; throughput time; and so on.

High quality and believable VSM requires spending time in the workplace recording the details of people, product, equipment, and information movements. As mentioned above, it is necessary to record and time the range of variables that occur in each process step during the operation. It also requires viewing written records related to the process to record dates, quantities, delays, stoppages, breakdowns, operating decisions, absentees, etc. that impacted on the performance of the operation during the period being analyzed. The believability of the analysis is only as good as its completeness of its content and the truthfulness and honesty it contains. When there are provable facts extracted from documented evidence and recorded site observation there can be belief in the findings from the investigation.[6]

Next the information collected during data gathering the process is depicted in a flow diagram showing the times and resources used at each step and the time delay between each step. This diagram is called the **current state map** and is illustrated in Exhibit 12.10 depicts a broad VSM chart that extends from supplier to final customer. When viewing the *current state map* it shows how the information flow begins with an MRP report that includes weekly orders and is transmitted from the focal firm to the supplier. Based on the information contained in the MRP report the supplier manufactures the goods and ships on a weekly basis. The components are inspected and put into inventory then run through the oven and made into wafer boards or integrated circuits. These components are then placed on circuit boards are built then tested.

Final assembly testing is completed prior to customer shipment. The entire process takes 8.3 days and analysis of the *current state map* illustrates that only 8 minutes are value added. To better understand the logic of VSM Exhibit 12.11 shows the meaning of commonly used symbols in a VSM diagram.

Next, after analyzing the *current state map,* the team focuses on making process improvements to optimize the value and minimize the non-value added streams. This process leads to the development of **a future/ ideal state map**.

When developing proposals it is best if the users of the process are included in identifying the solutions so they take ownership for the future implementation. During the analysis phase simplifications in process steps are identified, procedural changes to stop wasted actions show themselves, and equipment and process modifications needed to increase throughput rates become evident. VSM makes use of statistical techniques such as: (1) Scatter plots; (2) Pareto charts; (3) pie diagrams; and (4) cause and effect diagrams

| Exhibit 12.10 | Current State Value Stream Mapping Diagram |

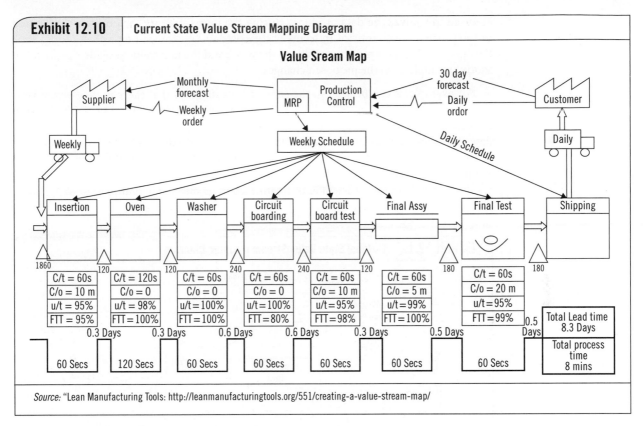

Value Sream Map

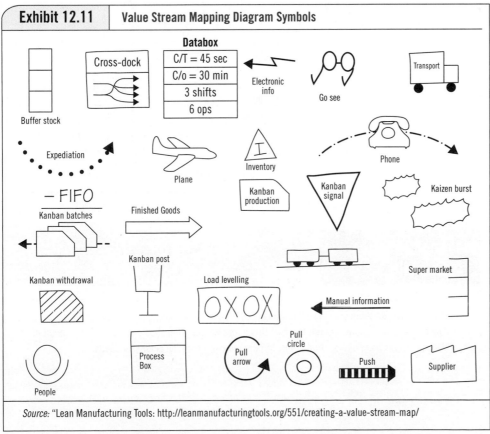

Data boxes:

Insertion	Oven	Washer	Circuit boarding	Circuit board test	Final Assy	Final Test
C/t = 60s	C/t = 120s	C/t = 60s	C/t = 60s	C/t = 60s	C/t = 60s	C/t = 60s
C/o = 10 m	C/o = 0	C/o = 0	C/o = 0	C/o = 10 m	C/o = 5 m	C/o = 20 m
u/t = 95%	u/t = 98%	u/t = 100%	u/t = 100%	u/t = 95%	u/t = 99%	u/t = 95%
FTT = 95%	FTT = 100%	FTT = 100%	FTT = 80%	FTT = 98%	FTT = 100%	FTT = 99%

Inventory triangles: 1860, 120, 120, 240, 240, 120, 180, 180

Timeline: 0.3 Days, 0.3 Days, 0.6 Days, 0.6 Days, 0.3 Days, 0.5 Days, 0.5 Days

60 Secs | 120 Secs | 60 Secs | 60 Secs | 60 Secs | 60 Secs | 60 Secs

Total Lead time 8.3 Days

Total process time 8 mins

Source: "Lean Manufacturing Tools: http://leanmanufacturingtools.org/551/creating-a-value-stream-map/"

| Exhibit 12.11 | Value Stream Mapping Diagram Symbols |

Databox

Buffer stock

Cross-dock

| C/T = 45 sec |
| C/o = 30 min |
| 3 shifts |
| 6 ops |

Electronic info

Go see

Transport

Expediation

Plane

Inventory

Phone

— FIFO

Kanban batches

Kanban production

Kanban signal

Kaizen burst

Kanban withdrawal

Finished Goods

Kanban post

Load levelling

OXOX

Manual information

Super market

People

Process Box

Pull arrow

Pull circle

Push

Supplier

Source: "Lean Manufacturing Tools: http://leanmanufacturingtools.org/551/creating-a-value-stream-map/"

are used to analyze the data produced during the investigation. The problems identified in the process are quantified in terms of the costs and customer-non-value-adding time they take. Assigning a monetary value to the waste and the non-value provides justification motive to implement the proposed changes.

For example, it can be seen in the *current state diagram* that there is excessive inventory caused by weekly supplier deliveries, a long cycle time, poor quality yields showing in the circuit board testing area and large lot sizes being processed. All these are candidates for improvement. In the *ideal state* VSM shown on Exhibit 12.12 the total lead time was slashed from 8 days to 1 day and the total process time improved from 8 minutes to 1 minute. The results of these changes allow the firm to be more responsive to its customers through being more efficient and streamlined in its internal operations.

Exhibit 12.12	Ideal State Value Stream Mapping Diagram

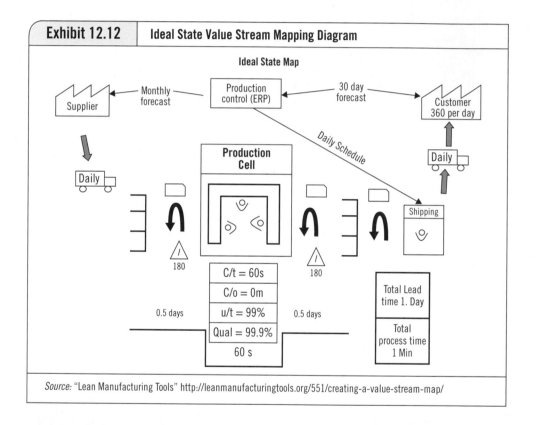

Source: "Lean Manufacturing Tools" http://leanmanufacturingtools.org/551/creating-a-value-stream-map/

Good Practice Example

Best Practice in Project Management- The Project Life Cycle

Dr. Rene G. Rendon, Associate Professor, and Dr. Keith F. Snider, Professor, are both at the Naval Postgraduate School in Monterey, California. What follows is a discussion on the *project life cycle* concept in project management. Much of this is drawn from their text entitled *"Management of Defense Acquisition Projects"* that covers large scale projects in the defense industry.

Projects are complex and the goal of project management is to effectively manage this complexity. Practitioners have many techniques to improve project management, but one of the best practices is the use of a project life cycle. Organizations use project life cycles to monitor and control the progression of the project activities. In the commercial world, one can formally define the project life cycle technique as a series of activities necessary to fulfill project goals or objectives. These activities include starting the project, organizing and preparing, then carrying out the work, and finally closing out the project.

In the world of military procurement the project life cycle focuses on the monitoring and controlling aspect. The United States Department of Defense (DoD) requires the use of a project life cycle for its major defense acquisition programs. To DoD "project life cycle" is the monitoring and controlling part of project management and is especially necessary in projects that involve the research, development, and production of high-technology products such as major defense weapon systems.

The project life cycle provides the project team with a defined management approach that establishes a road map for directing and monitoring the activities of the project. The road map reflects the sequential phases of the project, with each phase consisting of specific processes, work activities, and tools used by the project team. These monitoring techniques (control gates) provide the project manager and higher-level decision-makers with a tool for regulating and controlling the progress of the project. As the project progresses through each sequential phase, the completion of each phase should result in specific deliverables. The deliverables should be reviewed and evaluated to determine if the planned objectives of the project phase were achieved. Based on the results of each project-phase review, the project decision-making authority will determine if the project should progress into the next phase, remain in the current phase until satisfactory completion of the project-phase deliverables or outputs, or if the project should be terminated. Thus, the benefits of developing and using a project life cycle include a road map for sequencing project activities, as well as control gates for regulating the progress of the project.

An example of a project life cycle is illustrated in the figure below. This project life cycle contains five project phases 1) Need Development, 2) Concept Development, 3) Preliminary Design, 4) Detailed Design, and 5) Production, Deployment, Operations, Support and Disposal.

As reflected in the figure below, the project life cycle begins with the organization *determining its needs* and desired capabilities to be satisfied through the acquisition of a product or service. The need or desired capability is documented, reviewed, validated, and approved. A favorable Need Approval milestone decision by senior organization decision-makers begins the process of determining the most appropriate solution to satisfy that need.

The *Concept Development* phase entails studying and refining preferred concept(s) to satisfy the approved need. This phase often entails cost-benefit and trade-off analyses of various solutions, as well as development and assessment of technologies necessary to achieve those solutions. It culminates with the Preliminary Design Approval milestone decision. At this milestone, decision-makers review the "business case" for the preferred solution, that is, the match between the need and the resources (knowledge, time, workforce, money) necessary to acquire the preferred solution. Approval at this milestone decision approves proceeding with the design of the preferred solution.

The *Preliminary Design* phase entails the development and definition of specifications for the major subsystems, items, and components of the system solution. Development and testing of models and prototypes often characterize this phase, the objectives of which are usually accomplished when the design has stabilized. The milestone decision point, *Detailed Design Approval,* indicates that the contractor has determined that the design will meet customer requirements within cost and schedule constraints.

The Detailed Design phase entails the completion of design work and preparation for production. It is usually characterized by significant amounts of testing on all aspects of system performance, to include reliability and other support-oriented testing. It also involves demonstrations of production processes, capabilities, and capacities. The Production Approval milestone indicates that sufficient knowledge has been achieved to assure that the product can be produced within cost, schedule, and performance goals.

During the *Production, Deployment, Operations, Support, & Disposal* phase, the system is manufactured, deployed to the user, and supported in its operations. Testing may continue, and modifications may be undertaken, which may result in a new project to manage the modification(s). After some time, the continual process of Need Development will result in an assessment that the system is no longer adequate or necessary, and will perhaps also result in a new project for a replacement system or capability. Disposal may take several forms, from scrapping items to selling them to other nations.

It should be emphasized that the defense acquisition project life cycle is not intended as a rigid set of phases and decisions to be followed in "lock-step" fashion. Rather, it should be adapted or tailored to fit any project's particular requirements. This means that phases and decision points may be adjusted or eliminated if they are not needed. Allowing for tailoring of the project life cycle recognizes that each project is—by necessity and by design—unique.

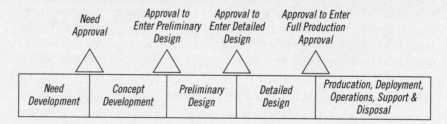

Sources: Rendon, R.G., & Snider, K.F. (Eds.). (2008). *Management of Defense Acquisition Projects.* American Institute of Aeronautics and Astronautics, Reston, Virginia.

Commercial Project Life Cycle definition downloaded from: http://www.uakron.edu/pmo/plc/
Interview: L. Giunipero with Rene Rendon November 2013

CONCLUSION

Purchasers and supply chain specialists rely on various tools and techniques to support and improve the purchasing and sourcing process. The need to routinely apply the techniques and tools presented in this chapter is critical to world-class purchasing and supply chain management. Wherever possible, decisions should be based on quantitative analysis rather than qualitative information.

KEY TERMS

concurrent processes, 486

Critical Path Method (CPM), 467

current state map, 488

Future/ideal state map, 488

Gantt chart, 467

learning curves, 475

learning depreciation, 474

Process mapping, 485

Program Evaluation and Review Technique (PERT), 467

project, 462

project management, 462

quantity discount analysis, 482

sequential processes, 485

value engineering, 479

value stream mapping, 487

DISCUSSION QUESTIONS

1. Why does the learning curve apply mainly to direct rather than indirect labor?

2. If each time production volume doubled and cumulative average direct-labor requirements decreased by 5 percent, what would be the appropriate learning rate?

3. Discuss why it is important for buyers to have knowledge of a supplier's learning rate when preparing to negotiate a purchase contract.

4. Do you feel learning is different in professional services firms versus manufacturing organizations? Explain why or why not.

5. Describe the concept of value as it relates to value analysis. Provide examples of how an organization can increase value to itself or to its customers.

6. Why do progressive firms actively practice value analysis?

7. Assume you are the leader of a value analysis team. Discuss how you would go about identifying value analysis opportunities.

8. What are the major differences in working on projects, as opposed to general work in most purchasing environments?

9. In general, do you believe the demands and responsibilities placed on project managers are making them more valuable to organizations? Why or why not?

10. When are users most likely to use Gantt charts for project management? When are they likely to use CPM or PERT?

11. What does it mean for a path to have three weeks of slack? Does each activity necessarily have three weeks of slack? Why or why not?

12. Discuss the information gained from flowcharting a process.

ADDITIONAL READINGS

Asher, H. (1956), *Cost-Quantity Relationships in the Airframe Industry*, Santa Monica, CA: RAND Corporation.

Budd, C., and Budd, C. (2010), *A Practical Guide to Earned Value Project Management: Management Concepts*, 2nd ed., London: Kogan Publishing.

Damelio, R. (2011), *The Basics of Process Mapping*, New York: Productivity Press.

Geiger, H. (2003), *Project Management Fundamentals*, New York: Element K.

Hartley, J. (2000), "Collaborative Value Analysis: Experiences from the Automotive Industry," *Journal of Supply Chain Management*, 36(4), 27–32.

Hill, G. M. (2010), *The Complete Project Management Methodology and Toolkit*, New York: CRC Press Division of Taylor & Francis Publishing.

Miles, L. (1972), *Techniques of Value Analysis*, New York: McGraw-Hill.

Sinclair, G. (1999), "Purchasing and the Learning Curve: A Case Study of a Specialty Chemicals Business Unit," *Journal of Supply Chain Management*, 35(2), 44–49.

Teplitz, C. J. (1991), *The Learning Curve Deskbook: A Reference Guide to Theory, Calculations, and Applications*, Westport, CT: Praeger Publishing.

Wysocki, R. K. (2010), *Effective Project Management: Traditional, Agile, Extreme*, 5th ed., Hoboken, NJ: Wiley.

_____,_____. (2013), *A Guide to the Project Management Body of Knowledge*, 4th ed., Newtown Square, PA: Project Management Institute.

ENDNOTES

1. Project Management Institute. (2008), *A Guide to the Project Management Body of Knowledge (PMBOK)*, 4th ed., Upper Darby, PA: Project Management Institute.

2. Campbell, P., and Pollard, W. (2002, June), "Applying Project Management Principles to Supplier Management," *Inside Supply Management*, pp. 48–52.

3. Ohno, T. (1988), *Toyota Production System: Beyond Large-Scale Production*, Portland, OR: Productivity Press, p. 12.

4. Ibid., p. 25.

5. *Source:* Mike Sondalini "How To Do Value Stream Mapping," Lifetime Reliability Solutions, Web: www .lifetime-reliability.com, accessed November 7, 2013.

6. **Ibid. www.lifetime-reliability.com**

Negotiation and Conflict Management

CHAPTER 13

Learning Objectives

After completing this chapter, you should be able to

- Understand when and why a buyer enters into a supply management negotiation
- Recognize the importance of effective planning within the negotiation process
- Appreciate the different sources of power that are present during negotiations
- Understand the characteristics of effective negotiators
- Comprehend the central role of concession management during negotiation
- Recognize the subtleties and complexities involved with global negotiation
- Understand how to effectively negotiate via electronic means

Chapter Outline

Basics of Negotiating in China

Because of the growing importance of commerce between businesses from the People's Republic of China and the rest of the world, it is important for Western supply managers to thoroughly understand the differences and subtleties involved when negotiating with their Chinese counterparts. The following discussion, garnered from a variety of sources, outlines some of the key differences in culture and business perspective that the Western supply manager must take into account when negotiating procurement contracts with a Chinese supplier.

A common misperception in Western companies is that China is a large, homogeneous market with a strong, centralized national government. The reality is that the Chinese marketplace is a broad collection of individual markets that can vary widely in their sophistication and economic makeup, coupled with local and provincial governments taking a leading role. In addition to the substantial economic opportunities provided by rapid economic and population growth in China, there are also substantial risks to be considered when entering into a Chinese business relationship. Therefore, the well-informed Western negotiator must take into account many different issues and concerns when preparing the negotiation plan, during the actual negotiation, and following up after the negotiation. In fact, much of the reason for failure in Western-Chinese negotiations comes from the Western negotiator's misunderstanding of the broader context of Chinese culture and values. Merely understanding basic etiquette will not maintain the business relationship over the long term.

At first blush, Western and Chinese negotiators' needs and wants appear to be incompatible and totally out of sync with each other. Breakdown in Western-Chinese negotiations is common when the Western counterpart is either underprepared, inexperienced, or naïve. For example, Western negotiators often assume that their Chinese counterparts are indirect and inefficient, perhaps even a bit dishonest. On the other hand, Chinese negotiators typically assume that their Western counterparts are overly-emotional, far too aggressive, and uninterested in the relationship. It is important to understand the underlying elements of Chinese culture that lead to these assumptions so that the Western negotiator can develop a mutual long-term relationship.

In China, negotiations and factory visits are typically choreographed with both the Western and Chinese parties having clearly defined roles, which are carefully planned beforehand. Therefore, the Western negotiator is expected to understand his/her role in the process whether or not he/ she understands Chinese culture. There are many cultural subtleties that can easily trip up negotiations. In addition, higher-level Chinese managers are usually the decision makers, so the higher up in the Chinese organization you can negotiate, the more likely you can reach an agreement. As in many negotiation scenarios, there is the cover story and the real, underlying story. The only way to uncover the real story is to ask many questions and take abundant notes. Too many Western negotiators are too trusting and take too much information at face value without digging down into the underlying issues driving the negotiation.

The prepared Western negotiator should always be ready to deal with one last issue that is tossed in at the final moment in the negotiation. Whereas the Western negotiator typically ends the negotiation at the end of the workday, the Chinese counterpart often continues the negotiation at dinner or during karaoke in the evening where any final details can be agreed upon in an informal setting. Another effective negotiating technique is to hold back something of the Western party's needs or wants. As in many Asian negotiations, it is wise not to corner the other party but offer a way out to save face. Note here that the ultimate goal is to develop cooperation.

Chinese negotiators are generally well-prepared and can use this knowledge to their advantage to browbeat the other party into submission. Therefore, the Western negotiator must know all of the details and numbers of the negotiation thoroughly. Abstract details and responses indicate a potential weakness that can be exploited. Additionally, the Western negotiator should learn to verify every single detail of the negotiation. Oftentimes, Western-Chinese negotiations are a zero-sum game, meaning that there are winners and losers, primarily because there is a lack of trust between the Chinese and foreigners.

A related negotiation phenomenon is that the Chinese negotiator has a great tolerance for patient waiting and using time to his/her advantage. The more the Western negotiator is stonewalled and forced to wait, the more likely he/she will give up a significant concession without receiving anything of value in return. The Western negotiator must learn that waiting a few days is not a long time in Chinese eyes. Learn to be patient.

For the Chinese negotiator, the written contract is only the beginning point, not the end point. The terms of the contract will typically not be referred to again unless the Western negotiator does so. What may seem to be a renegotiation is simply part of the process of signing the contract. However, the Western negotiator may want to periodically pull out the contract to remind his/her Chinese counterpart what the agreed-upon terms actually were. Also, the Western negotiator should never try to modify the contract once it is agreed upon. From the Chinese perspective, this allows them to open all clauses and subject all previous agreements to renegotiation. Ensure that the initial contract is comprehensive and addresses as many situations as possible to avoid opening up a Pandora's Box.

For supply managers seeking to negotiate an outsourcing agreement with a Chinese company, it is imperative to recognize that negotiating an effective agreement will take time, patience, understanding, and tolerance. Take your time to prepare and seek out the appropriate resources to assist you.

Sources: Adapted from Clayton, D. (2007, October 15), "Negotiating in China: Maintaining Your Advantage." Retrieved from www.GlobalSources.com., Graham, J. L. and Lam, N. M. (2003, October) "The Chinese Negotiation," *Harvard Business Review*, 82–91. Hoenig, J. (2007), "Wise companies prepare for—and minimize their exposure to—risks when investing in China." Retrieved from www.chinabusinessreview.com/public/0611/hoenig.html

Introduction

Everyone negotiates something every day, ranging from dealing with other drivers at a four-way intersection all the way to merging with or acquiring another company. As such, negotiation can be a highly complex and dynamic process and a soft skill that is essential to all supply managers. Many books and articles have been written on how to negotiate effectively in a variety of situations. This chapter highlights important topics that are typically part of any negotiation, especially those between buyers and suppliers. We begin this chapter by broadly defining the concept of negotiation. The second section presents negotiation in supply management as a five-phase process. Next, perhaps the most important, yet often neglected, part of any negotiation process—planning—appears in detail. The following sections present common sources of negotiation power, the effective use of concessions, negotiation strategies, and tactics, and the important topics of win-win negotiation, international negotiation, and the effect of electronic media on negotiation.

What Is Negotiation?

One of the most important activities performed by supply managers involves negotiating sourcing agreements or contracts with their suppliers. Although supply management is certainly not the only group in an organization that negotiates, negotiation is a vital part of every sourcing process. Negotiation supports the implementation of the supply management strategies and plans developed by a business unit. It is also often a critical means to convey the buyer's specific sourcing requirements and specifications to its supply base.

Negotiation has been defined in a variety of ways: "A negotiation is an interactive communication process that may take place whenever we want something from someone else or another person wants something from us."[1] "Negotiation is the process of communicating back and forth for the purpose of reaching a joint agreement about differing needs or ideas."[2] "Negotiation is a decision-making process by which two or more people agree how to allocate scarce resources."[3] "Negotiating is the end game of the sales process."[4]

For our purposes, we define **negotiation** as a process of formal communication, either face-to-face or via electronic means, where two or more people, groups, or organizations come together to seek mutual agreement about an issue or issues. The negotiation process involves the management of time, information, and power between individuals and organizations who are interdependent. Each party has a need for something that the other party has, yet recognizes that an interactive process of give-and-take, often through compromise or concession, is required to satisfy that need.

An important part of negotiation is realizing that the process involves relationships between people, not just organizations. An integral part of negotiation involves each party trying to persuade the other party to do something that is in its best interest. The process involves skills that individuals, with the proper training and experience, can learn and enhance. Good negotiators are not born; they must learn how to hone these necessary skills through planning, practice, observation, and constructive feedback.

Exhibit 13.1	Negotiation Definitions

- Negotiation
  - A process of formal communication, either face-to-face or via electronic means, where two or more people, groups, or organizations come together to seek mutual agreement about an issue or issues
- BATNA (Best Alternative to a Negotiated Agreement)
  - That point in the negotiation where is it most advantageous for the negotiator to walk away from the table and implement his or her next best option
- Position
  - His or her opening offer, which represents the optimistic (or ideal) value of the issue being negotiated
- Interest
  - The unspoken motivation or reason that underlies any given negotiation position
- Need
  - That negotiation outcome that the negotiator *must have* to reach a successful outcome to the negotiation
- Want
  - That negotiation outcome that a negotiator would *like to have*
- Fact
  - A reality or truth that the parties can state and successfully verify
- Issue
  - An item or topic to be resolved during the negotiation
- Strategy
  - The overall approach used to reach a mutually beneficial agreement with a supplier that holds different points of view from the buyer
- Power
  - The ability to influence another person or organization to do something
- Concession
  - A movement away from a negotiating position that offers something of value to the other party to gain something else of value
- Tactic
  - A short-term plan or action employed to execute a strategy, cause a conscious change in a counterpart's position, or influence others to achieve one's negotiation objectives

There are a number of terms with which all negotiators should be familiar: BATNA, positions, interests, needs, and wants. A negotiator's best alternative to a negotiated agreement (BATNA) is also known as the negotiator's bottom line or reservation point, that is, that point in the negotiation where it is most advantageous for the negotiator to walk away from the table and implement his or her next-best option.[5] A negotiator should take extra caution to ensure that his or her reservation point or BATNA is never revealed to the other party, because the final settlement is unlikely to vary much from that point.[6] In addition, all negotiation settlements must ultimately be judged in light of the other viable alternatives that existed *at the time of the agreement.*

A negotiator's position can be defined as his or her opening offer, which represents the optimistic (or ideal) value of the issue being negotiated. A position is the stated demand that is placed on the table by a negotiator. In contrast, the negotiator's interest is the unspoken motivation or reason that underlies any given negotiation position. In many negotiation scenarios, the negotiator's underlying interests are unlikely to be expressly stated or acknowledged, oftentimes because they may not be directly germane to the stated position or because they may be highly personal in nature. Sharing the underlying interests behind a position may cause a negotiator's power to shift toward the other party, ultimately resulting in a less than desired outcome. The negotiator must, in effect, play detective to try to discern the other party's interests through a series of open-ended, probing questions. To reach a negotiated agreement using principled negotiation, a negotiator should always attempt to focus on the other party's underlying interests, not his or her stated position.[7]

The astute negotiator must also be able to distinguish between the other party's needs and wants. Needs are considered to be those negotiated outcomes that the negotiator *must have* to reach a successful outcome to the negotiation. Wants on the other hand, refer to those negotiated outcomes that a negotiator would *like to have* as opposed to those outcomes that *must be* achieved. Wants can also be exchanged as concessions to the other party during a negotiation because they are not as critical to achieving a successful conclusion to the negotiation. When a negotiator is planning an upcoming negotiation, it is imperative to prioritize all of the potential issues to be negotiated into needs and wants, thereby knowing what must be achieved and what can be exchanged for something else of value.

A simple negotiation planning tool, called "Triangle Talk," can help the negotiator begin the initial preparation for an upcoming negotiation. This planning process, shown in Exhibit 13.2, consists of the following three steps: (1) know exactly what you want; (2) find out what they want and make them feel heard; and (3) propose action in such way that they can accept it.[8]

Step 1 in Triangle Talk involves determining and formalizing the negotiator's own specific goals and objectives for the upcoming negotiation. Being specific with one's expectations and writing them down helps the negotiator to remain focused on his or her predetermined priorities during the negotiation. Having them written down also allows the negotiator to refer back to them during the course of the negotiation, when it is often easy to be distracted by the other negotiator's tactics and the pace of the give-and-take process. The more clearly a negotiator can define his or her priorities, the more likely he or she is to obtain them in the final agreement.

Step 2 involves trying to discern what the negotiator's counterpart is likely to need or want from the negotiation. It is difficult to develop common ground in the negotiation without knowing what the other party is seeking. Ask yourself specifically, "What does the other party need or want?" Delve into the other party's likely positions and try to discern or estimate what the underlying interests are behind the positions. However, a negotiator

Exhibit 13.2	Triangle Talk

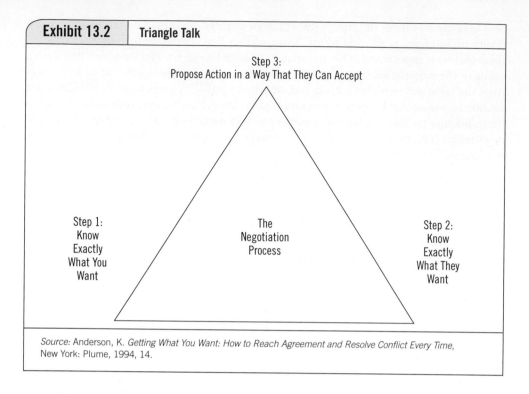

Step 3:
Propose Action in a Way That They Can Accept

Step 1:
Know
Exactly
What You
Want

The
Negotiation
Process

Step 2:
Know
Exactly
What They
Want

Source: Anderson, K. *Getting What You Want: How to Reach Agreement and Resolve Conflict Every Time,* New York: Plume, 1994, 14.

cannot automatically assume that the other party thinks the same way he or she does. During the negotiation, the negotiator should ask open-ended, probing questions to verify his or her preliminary analysis of the other party's needs and wants. If the negotiator determines that the other party's needs and wants differ from what was presumed, he/she will have to readjust his/her own goals and objectives to account for this change. In addition, the negotiator should develop a strategy and utilize appropriate accompanying tactics that will make the other party feel heard. This allows the third step in Triangle Talk to take place.

Step 3 involves the consideration and analysis of the negotiator's own needs and wants and the needs and wants of the other party. This way, proposals and counterproposals can be offered that take both sets of needs and wants into account and are framed in such a way as to make it easy for the other party to say "Yes." It is important to remain flexible, fair, and reasonable so that the parties can work out an agreement in which they are both better off. In addition to acknowledging (but not necessarily agreeing with) the other party's concerns, the negotiator can accomplish this by speaking to those needs first when framing his or her proposals.

The Negotiation Framework in Supply Management

Perhaps the best way to approach a buyer-supplier negotiation is by presenting it as an interactive, give-and-take process involving five major phases or sets of activities:

1. Identify or anticipate the sourcing requirement
2. Determine if negotiation or competitive bidding is required
3. Plan for the negotiation
4. Conduct the negotiation
5. Execute and follow up on the agreement

Exhibit 13.3	Five-Phase Negotiation Process

Identify or anticipate the sourcing requirement	Determine if negotiation or competitive bidding is required	Plan for the negotiation	Conduct the negotiation	Execute and follow up on the agreement
1	2	3	4	5
• Purchase requisitions • Inventory counts • Reorder point systems • New-product development • New facilities	• Is bid process inadequate? • Are many non-price issues involved? • Is contract large? • Are technical requirements complex? • Does contract involve plant and equipment? • Does contract involve a partnership? • Will supplier perform value-added activities? • Will there be high risk and uncertainty?	• Identify participants • Develop objectives • Analyze strengths and weaknesses • Gather information • Recognize counterpart's needs • Identify facts and issues • Establish positions • Develop strategies and tactics • Brief personnel • Practice the negotiation	• Perform fact finding • Recess or caucus as necessary • Work to narrow differences • Manage time pressures • Maintain informal atmosphere • Summarize progress periodically • Employ tactics • Keep relationships positive	• Provide performance feedback • Build on the success of the negotiation

Exhibit 13.3 summarizes the generic supply management negotiation process and lists points, questions, and activities falling into each phase.

Identify or Anticipate the Sourcing Requirement

Chapter 2 addresses how firms identify or anticipate sourcing requirements or what is typically referred to as the purchasing cycle or process. The purchasing cycle begins with identifying (or anticipating) a specific need or requirement for a part component, raw material, subassembly, service, piece of equipment, or finished good to be sourced to conduct or support organizational operations. Often, supply management can pre-identify these requirements during its involvement with new-product development in collaboration with its various internal customers within the buying organization, such as marketing, operations, engineering, design, and/or research and development, and in some instances with key suppliers through early supplier design involvement (see Chapter 8 for additional discussion of ESDI). For the procurement of many existing items, there may not be a need to identify a supplier because an existing sourcing agreement may already be in place. New sourcing requirements, however, often require supply management to identify, evaluate, and qualify new potential suppliers as described in Chapter 7.

Determine If Negotiation or Competitive Bidding Is Required

Not all purchase requirements require buyers and sellers to conduct a thorough, detailed, and time-consuming negotiation. For many items, competitive bidding will satisfy a buyer's purchase requirements, as may be the case for commodity-like items that are low value, widely available, or have preexisting standard specifications. Negotiation is more appropriate when other issues besides price are important or when competitive bidding will not satisfy the buyer's requirements on various issues. However, a buyer can still use a competitive bidding process to initially identify several potential sources of supply. After identifying a potential supplier through competitive bidding, the buyer may need to negotiate with the preferred supplier to resolve final price as well as other non-price issues affecting the sourcing agreement.

The following situations or issues may require supply management to negotiate with its suppliers:

- Identification of and agreement on a supplier's allowable or reimbursable costs
- Delivery schedules and lead time requirements
- Definition of expected product and service quality levels
- Performance metrics and how information is to be gathered, shared, and used
- Technological support and assistance
- Contract volumes and release timing
- Special packaging, handling, and shipping requirements
- Mode of transportation and responsibility for carrier selection, as well as filing freight and loss and damage claims
- Liability for loss and damage, including payment for insurance coverage
- Payment terms and currency exchange issues
- Progress payment schedules
- Product warranties and replacements
- Capacity commitments
- Nonperformance penalties or performance incentives
- Contract length and renewal mechanism
- Protection of proprietary information
- Ownership and use of intellectual property
- Resources related to developing closer relationships
- Performance improvement requirements in quality, delivery, lead time, cost, responsiveness, and so forth
- Contract dispute resolution mechanisms
- Spare parts, after-sales service, and operator or maintenance training support
- Access to technology

This list, although lengthy, is not exhaustive and represents merely a subset of all possible topics that buyer negotiators can address. Besides the need to agree on non-price issues, other reasons exist for negotiating with suppliers:

- *The total contract value or volume is large.* It is not unusual for supply managers to negotiate long-term, multi-year contracts worth millions of dollars. Supplier nonperformance on such large contracts can cause unusually severe problems and risks, such as an interruption in continuity of supply. The buyer should negotiate specific safeguards to make sure the supplier recognizes the importance of performing exactly as required.

- *The purchase involves complex technical requirements, perhaps even product and process requirements and specifications that are still evolving.* Under this condition, it is difficult for the parties to reach definitive agreement upfront on a purchase requirement, such as the widely disparate flight performance characteristics of the F-35 fighter variants being developed for the Air Force, Navy, and Marine Corps. However, a buyer may want the supplier to begin work to fulfill the contract even if final product requirements and specifications have not yet been established.

- *The purchase involves utilization of capital-intensive plant and equipment.* Suppliers often customize or dedicate capital-intensive assets, such as plant, equipment, and processes, to meet a buyer's specific needs.

- *The agreement involves a special or collaborative relationship.* Special or collaborative relationships must address issues far beyond a traditional or conventional purchase agreement. For example, the two parties may discuss the joint development of technology featuring the sharing or colocation of technical personnel, laboratories, and testing equipment, as well as risks and benefits.

- *The supplier will perform important or significant value-added activities.* Increasingly, buyers are asking suppliers to perform key activities such as product design, testing, distribution, or inventory management. These additional activities often require substantial discussion and negotiation to determine appropriate timing, compensation, performance standards, and performance metrics.

Another important question for the supply manager to consider is how much will the development of information technology systems, such as Internet-based reverse auctions and use of electronic-based communication media, change the need to negotiate face-to-face or have electronic interaction with suppliers? As will be discussed at the end of this chapter, the growing use of electronic media has reduced the need for face-to-face interaction or negotiation between buyers and sellers. However, it also likely that the type of items and services obtained through reverse auctions (e.g., standard commodities with a moderate total dollar spend) may not warrant higher-level negotiations in the first place. For items that are critical to the buyer or may involve many non-price issues, the likelihood that buyers and suppliers no longer need to engage in face-to-face negotiation is small.

Plan for the Negotiation

Negotiation planning involves a series of purposeful steps that strive to prepare the parties adequately for a pending negotiation. Many buyer-supplier negotiations are routine and relatively straightforward, often only requiring rudimentary preparation and planning. Other negotiations may be highly complex and require months of thorough and detailed data gathering and preparation. Regardless of the circumstances, supply managers who take the time necessary to adequately plan and prepare for an upcoming negotiation generally experience better outcomes than those negotiators who do not. Planning is so crucial to achieving desired negotiation outcomes that a later section in this chapter addresses this topic in greater detail.

New electronic communications technology may make face-to-face buyer-supplier negotiation, both for domestic and international requirements, far less important. Virtual

Sourcing Snapshot

American Airlines Knows the Importance of Negotiation

In a previous era, the sign of a good purchase negotiator was someone who could get a rock-bottom price from suppliers. Today, experienced negotiators realize that not all negotiations require a price focus or the same set of skills. "Low-level negotiations," says John MacLean, vice president of purchasing with American Airlines, "involve products or services that are competitive in the marketplace but are not strategically important to American Airlines." He points out that getting the best price is a good indicator of effectiveness for these types of items. MacLean also knows the importance of strategic negotiations when obtaining critical items and services. "Win/win negotiations," says MacLean, "are conducted in long-term relationships with suppliers. In these cases it is important that the supplier and American Airlines feel they are getting a good deal because the plan is to work together for a long while." At the most advanced level, the strategic compatibility of the companies involved may determine the success of a negotiation. Says MacLean, "Principle-based negotiating is used in a single-source situation or alliance where the two parties begin the negotiation by agreeing to certain principles, such as how the companies plan to grow together." American Airlines recognizes two important principles about negotiation. First, not all negotiations are equal in importance or require the same skill set. Second, negotiation is a fundamental part of the company's strategic supply plans.

Sources: Adapted from Ciancarelli, A. (1999, March 25), "Strategic Negotiating Goes Far beyond Best Price," *Purchasing*, 126, 4.

negotiations can be a very attractive alternative to expensive and time-consuming international travel as more organizations engage in global supply management, which creates a host of new negotiation challenges. It also substantially changes how a supply manager plans for and conducts the negotiation.

Highly advanced online communication and video-conferencing tools are becoming more readily available that feature the ability to negotiate issues beyond price with multiple suppliers, regardless of physical location. With these tools, e-procurement managers no longer have to spend hours traveling and then engaging in face-to-face meetings arguing over details with suppliers. A buyer simply fills out a predetermined request for proposal (RFP) or request for quotation (RFQ) template and then forwards the document electronically to a select group of qualified suppliers.[9] Suppliers can then more easily and quickly respond electronically with detailed online proposals outlining price, payment terms, shipping methods, and other issues that are relevant to the buyer. It is also much easier to make changes as the negotiation process progresses. These tools enable a buyer to negotiate simultaneously with more than one supplier during the process, which can lead to greater bidding efficiencies and lower prices through increased competition (similar to reverse auctions).

Conduct the Negotiation

Negotiations with a supplier should commence only when a buyer is confident about the level of planning and preparation put forth. However, note that negotiation planning is not an open-ended process; buyers must usually meet specific deadlines that satisfy the needs of their internal customers. Thus, the buyer faces pressure to initiate, conduct, and conclude the negotiation within a reasonable time, often on short notice. Effective planning also requires substantial emphasis to be placed on the following points:

- Defining the parties' issues, needs, and wants
- Assembling information about the issues, needs, and wants
- Defining the bargaining mix
- Estimating and defining the parties' interests
- Defining one's own objectives (targets and bottom lines) and opening offers (where to begin)
- Assessing the role of stakeholders and other constituents, as well as the social context in which the negotiation will occur
- Analyzing the other party (recall Step 2 in Triangle Talk)
- Planning issue presentations and defenses
- Defining process protocols: where and when the negotiation will occur, who will be there, what items will be on the agenda, and so on[10]

Deciding the physical location of where to negotiate can be an important part of any planning process. A home location can provide a substantial advantage to a negotiator, particularly during international negotiations. However, advances in electronic media technology now allow some negotiations to occur electronically rather than face-to-face. Most experts agree that the atmosphere surrounding a negotiation should be less formal wherever possible to help build trusting relationships and long-term commitment to the agreement.

Excessive formality can effectively constrain the parties and restrict the free exchange of ideas and solutions. Although negotiating in some cultures may require a more formal scenario. It is also a good idea to periodically summarize positions and points of previous agreement throughout the negotiation, which helps reduce misunderstanding along with helping track progress against the negotiation agenda. It may also help to have a dedicated note taker or scribe throughout the negotiation whose primary responsibility is to record what was said, who said it, what the other party's reaction was, and what the areas of agreement were.

It is during the course of give-and-take negotiation that the parties play out their strategy with tactics—e.g., the skill of employing available means to accomplish or achieve a desired end. Tactics are the action plans designed to help achieve a desired result. A later section reviews various common tactics that negotiators may employ or for which they should be prepared. Tactics can be either ethical or unethical, and the shrewd negotiator should be on the lookout for both types as they can adversely affect the negotiation process and outcomes.

An iterative sequence of four phases often characterizes both face-to-face and virtual negotiations. The first phase consists of fact finding and information sharing between the parties. This part of the process helps clarify or confirm initial positions and information provided by the buyer and seller. At the beginning of the second phase, the parties often take a recess after fact finding. This allows the parties the opportunity to reassess their relative strengths and weaknesses, review and revise objectives and positions if necessary, and reorganize the negotiation agenda. Next, the negotiating parties meet face-to-face, or electronically, in an attempt to narrow their differences on specific issues. This phase typically includes the offering of proposals and counterproposals and exchanging concessions. Finally, the parties seek an agreement and conclusion to the negotiation, as well as agreement on any follow-on activities.

Effective negotiators have been shown to display certain behaviors or characteristics when conducting a negotiation. They may be willing to compromise or revise their goals, particularly when irrefutable new information effectively challenges their predetermined positions. Effective negotiators may also view issues independently, without linking them in any particular sequence. Packaging issues together risks undermining an entire negotiation if the parties reach impasse on a single issue within the linked proposal. Effective negotiators should also establish lower and upper ranges for each major issue, as well as a most likely outcome, as opposed to a single, rigid position that may limit the number of viable options available and be more likely to create an impasse.

Highly effective or skilled negotiators also explore more viable options per issue than do average or less prepared negotiators. Furthermore, effective negotiators also build and focus on the common ground between the parties (rather than the differences) than do average negotiators. Finally, when compared with average negotiators, effective or skilled negotiators make fewer irritating comments about the other party, give fewer reasons for the arguments they advance (too many supporting reasons can dilute an argument), and make fewer counterproposals. However, effective negotiators are willing to make counterproposals, although not as many as an average negotiator. Making too many counterproposals generally means that a negotiator is compromising too much, offering too many concessions, or is unsure about his/her relative position and power. It may also indicate a lack of adequate planning and preparation or a sign of vulnerability.

Execute and Follow Up on the Agreement

Good negotiators know that reaching agreement is not the end of the negotiation process by any means. Rather, an agreement between the parties merely represents the beginning of performing or managing the contract's actual performance for the item, service, or activity covered by the agreement. An important part of executing and following through on a negotiated agreement is loading the agreement into a corporate contract system, so others throughout the organization can have visibility of the agreement and determine the impact of the contract on their respective spheres of responsibility.

During the life of an agreement, a buyer must let a supplier know in a timely manner if the supplier is performing adequately or not meeting its contractual requirements. If not, the buyer's legal remedies may be constrained. Conversely, it is also the supplier's responsibility to let the buyer know if the buyer is not meeting its responsibilities within the negotiated agreement. Both parties should work to build on the success of a negotiation through their contract management activities. Refer to Chapter 15 for more information regarding buyers' and sellers' rights under the Uniform Commercial Code. Executing and monitoring the agreement as agreed upon should reaffirm the commitment of all parties to work together in the future.

Negotiation Planning

Experts on negotiation generally agree that planning is perhaps the single most important part of the negotiation process. Unfortunately, many negotiators fail to prepare adequately before entering into a formal negotiation, oftentimes because of a very short timeframe in which to make a deal. A **plan** is a method or scheme devised for making or doing something to achieve a desired end. **Planning**, therefore, is the process of devising methods to achieve a desired end. Once negotiators develop their plan and an overall guiding strategy, they begin to develop the specific strategies, research, actions, and tactics necessary to carry out that plan. Negotiators frequently fall short of their goals or reach an impasse because they neglect the other party's problems, focus too much on price, focus on positions instead of interests, focus too much on common ground, neglect their BATNAs, or overadjust their perceptions during the actual negotiation.[11]

Most of the successful outcomes of any negotiation are determined by thorough and effective planning prior to the negotiation. Preparing at the last minute or just prior to walking into a negotiation is a surefire formula for disaster, especially when negotiating against someone who is far more skilled and/or prepared. Therefore, simply being quick and clever while thinking on one's feet is insufficient to ensure successful negotiation outcomes. Successful negotiation planning should be proactive, not reactive, and consists of the following nine steps, none of which should be omitted.

Develop Specific Objectives

The first step of the negotiation planning process involves developing specific goals, objectives, and desired outcomes to be achieved during the negotiation. An **objective** is an aspiration or vision to work toward in the future. For example, an obvious objective in a sourcing negotiation would be to reach an agreement that covers the purchase of a good or service. Neither a buyer nor a seller would commit scarce resources if the goal were to see a negotiation fail. Before actual negotiations begin, the parties need to believe realistically that they can reach an agreement. If the parties believed otherwise, they would not put forth the requisite time and effort to prepare for and conduct a successful negotiation.

An important objective during a sourcing negotiation is to reach agreement on a fair and reasonable price between a buyer and seller. Examples of buyer objectives could also include achieving an acceptable unit price, contract quantities, required delivery lead time, or improved supplier quality. The buyer may also want to persuade the supplier to collaborate at a level higher than that of competing suppliers. Not all objectives are equally important, so the buyer must begin to identify the relative importance of each one and prioritize them, depending on the negotiation at hand. Less important or critical objectives could be considered targets for future concessions. For example, leading companies typically separate their objectives into "must have" (needs) and "would like to have" (wants) categories. This begins to differentiate the importance of each objective should the negotiator need to compromise or offer concessions to reach agreement.

Analyze Each Party's Strengths and Weaknesses

Knowledgeable negotiators strive to understand their counterparts through research and experience. This means trying to understand what is important to the other party along with the personality, negotiation style, and history of the negotiator's opposite number. For example, when a buyer negotiates with a supplier for the first time, he/she must often commit substantial time and energy to additional research to more fully understand that particular supplier and its expected needs, wants, and priorities.

Analyzing the other party also requires a thorough assessment of the relative strengths and weaknesses of the parties, as well as the particulars for each individual issue to be negotiated. This due diligence process is often overlooked but can greatly influence the effectiveness of the strategy and tactics employed at the bargaining table. Buyers cannot automatically assume that they have power or influence over the supplier or vice versa. Many times a supplier holds a power position over the buyer because of its relative financial size or perhaps because the supplier does not have a great need for the contract. A later section details various sources of power that are part of the negotiation process.

Gather Relevant Information

The ability to critically analyze yourself and your negotiating counterpart requires sufficient, timely, and accurate information. This process need not be complex, particularly if the buyer and seller have worked together before. When this is the case, the buyer may have already answered a number of important questions. What happened between the parties? Were we satisfied with the previous outcome of the negotiation? Are we negotiating with the same people or with different negotiators? What were the important issues to this supplier? To us? What were the areas of disagreement? Is there anything about the conduct or protocol of the negotiation that we would like to change? What is relative power between the parties? Who has the most to lose? To gain?

Where does a buyer, who has no experience with a given supplier, gather the required information? One possible source may be contacting other buyers or organizations who have had experience with that supplier. Published sources of information may also be available. These sources include trade journals, other business publications, trade association data, government reports, annual reports, financial evaluations (such as Dun & Bradstreet reports), commercial databases, inquiries directly to personnel at the supplier, and information derived through quality sources over the Internet.

Recognize Your Counterpart's Needs

The buyer and seller in a sourcing negotiation are, in some ways, mirror images of each other. Each party wants to reach an agreement that is favorable to its longer-term success. As a buyer gathers information about a supplier, it is important to identify those key issues that are particularly critical to the supplier. For example, a supplier may want to maintain or grow its market share and volume in its industry. Therefore, receiving the entire purchase contract, rather than only a portion, may be an important objective to that supplier.

The issues that are most critical to a supplier are not likely to be those most critical to a buyer. When one party has a key issue or requirement that is relatively unimportant to the other, then the parties are more likely to reach agreement. For example, a supplier's production scheduling system may require the supplier to produce a buyer's requirement late in the day with delivery during the evening. If a buyer has an evening work crew that can easily receive late deliveries, the buyer can satisfy the supplier's requirement for off-hour deliveries. In return, the buyer may now expect the supplier to be more accommodating on another issue that is important to the buyer. Give-and-take here is essential to negotiation, and each party should not expect to prevail on all issues. This is why it is important for buyers to do their homework before the negotiation begins by identifying ranges of acceptable outcomes for each and every issue and setting priorities in the event that concessions or tradeoffs are required.

Identify Facts and Issues

Negotiation planning requires differentiating between facts and issues. The two parties will want to reach agreement early concerning what constitutes a fact versus an issue. A fact is a reality or truth that the parties can state and successfully verify. In negotiation, facts are not open to debate. For example, a buyer wants to purchase a piece of capital equipment. There is no negotiating with a supplier on whether the buyer actually needs that particular piece of equipment (although the specific type of equipment may be an unanswered question requiring interactive discussion).

Issues, on the other hand, are items or topics to be resolved during the negotiation. Issues that typically require resolution include purchase price, volume, quality, contract length, and delivery date. The parties to a negotiation can discuss and resolve many issues besides price, including quality, service, flexibility, performance metrics, and performance improvement. Part of the planning process requires identifying all of the critical issues and outcomes that each party seeks to resolve through the negotiation. As discussed earlier, the Triangle Talk technique can help negotiators determine not only the issues involved but also the range of acceptable outcomes for each issue.

Establish a Position on Each Issue

The parties to a negotiation should establish positions that offer agility and flexibility. Negotiators should therefore develop a range of positions—typically, a minimum acceptable position (or BATNA), a maximum or ideal outcome, and a most likely position located somewhere between the two extremes. If the issue is price, a seller may have a target price for which it wants to sell a product. Of course, the seller will take a higher price if the buyer is willing to offer one. The critical part of the range will be based on the seller's minimum acceptable price or resistance point. This is the lowest price at which the seller is willing to sell to a buyer. Any price, lower than the minimum, will result in no deal or an unacceptable outcome for the supplier. This area of overlapping positions among issues, when there is one, is termed the bargaining or settlement zone.[12] The bargaining zone represents the heart of the negotiation process, as any proposal or counterproposal offered outside of this range is likely to be rejected by the other party because it is not what he or she is willing to settle for.

Exhibit 13.4 demonstrates a settlement zone for a typical price-based negotiation. Looking at Example A, the parties will probably not reach mutual agreement unless one or both of the parties modify their original price range or position. The minimum selling position of the seller is far above the buyer's maximum position with no overlap. In Example B, there is an overlap between the two positions that should lead to an agreement. In this example, the buyer is willing to pay up to $11.45 per unit. The supplier is willing to sell as low as $11.15 per unit. Therefore, the two parties will likely reach an agreement somewhere between those two figures. As a bargaining tactic, the buyer may open with an offer to purchase at something less than $11.00 (that is, start out very low), whereas the supplier may open with an offer to sell at something above $11.50. However, if the buyer and the seller remain with their original positions, the negotiation will likely conclude within the overlap range.

Several factors will influence whether a party modifies or even abandons its original position(s). These include the desirability of the contract, the revelation of irrefutable information that challenges the accuracy and credibility of the party's original position, or a major concession that leads the other party to modify its position on another issue for the sake of reciprocation.

Develop the Negotiation Strategy and Accompanying Tactics

Negotiation strategy refers to the overall approach used to reach a mutually beneficial agreement with a supplier that holds different points of view from the buyer. A major part of the strategic planning process involves the application of tactics—the art or skill of employing available means to accomplish an end, objective, or strategy. They include the current set of action plans and activities adopted to achieve the negotiation objectives and strategy. A later section discusses the effective use of tactics in greater detail.

Exhibit 13.4	Developing Negotiating Ranges for a Purchase Price

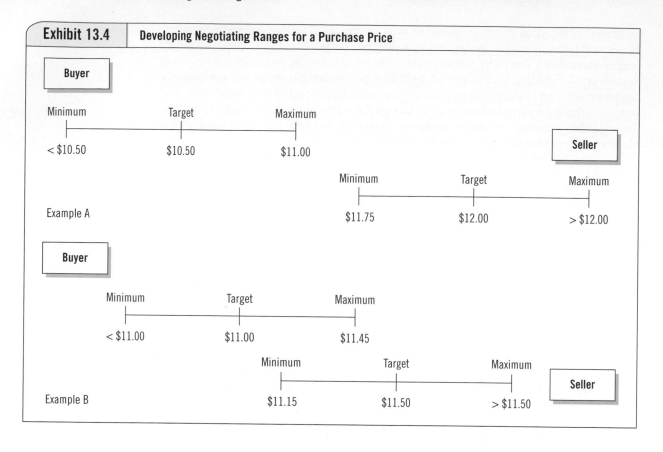

Strategic negotiation issues involve the broader questions regarding who, what, where, when, and how to negotiate. We can think of strategy and tactics as two dimensions of the same negotiation process. The ideal situation is to have a well-developed negotiation strategy with appropriate and ethical tactics that support that strategy. As an analogy, consider a military battle. The best-developed strategy will fail unless a commander has employed the requisite tactics and resources to implement that strategy in the field.

Brief Other Stakeholders

A procurement negotiation usually affects other stakeholders throughout the organization who have an interest in or will be affected by the negotiation outcomes. An individual or team conducting the negotiation should adequately brief these stakeholders ahead of time to ensure that they are aware of, and in agreement with, the desired objectives for the negotiation. This briefing should also address the major issues of the negotiation and the organization's initial positions on these issues, along with the rationale for each. Briefing stakeholders before a negotiation helps eliminate unwanted surprises during and following the actual negotiation when the stakeholder disagrees with the negotiated settlement. Oftentimes, it is important to garner prior stakeholder buy-in or support of the negotiation through this briefing process to ensure that the final outcomes are implemented as agreed upon at the bargaining table.

Practice the Negotiation

Experienced negotiators often practice or rehearse a complex negotiation before commencing the formal negotiation, especially if the negotiation involves a large dollar amount, covers a longer span of time, or is crucial to the success of the organization. One way to do this is to hold a mock or simulated negotiation. For instance, a marketing representative or salesperson might represent the supplier. The counterpart in a practice negotiation session may be able to raise questions and issues that the buyer had not originally anticipated but for which he or she can now more adequately prepare. When using simulation, it is important for each party to play its role as realistically as possible.

Another effective way to conduct a mock negotiation is for the buyer to role-play the negotiation from the supplier's side. This technique allows the buyer to empathize with the supplier and more fully understand how the supplier might approach the negotiation; it could also provide invaluable insight into the supplier's anticipated needs and wants. Here again, the use of Triangle Talk can play a valuable role in this key planning process.

Effective planning means that buyers achieve an agreement that is more creative and valuable than one that might be available to their competitors. It also means managing the buyer-supplier relationships that support future negotiation and cooperative interaction between the parties.

Power in Negotiation

An important part of the negotiation process involves the recognition and analysis of the relative power dimension that exists between parties. **Power** is defined here as the ability to influence another person or organization to do something. For example, party "A" has power over party "B" if "A" can get "B" to do something that directly benefits "A." Throughout human history, we have seen both positive and negative uses of power. Note, however, that power, in and of itself, possesses neither a positive nor a negative connotation; it is how that relative power is used or applied that gives it a particular undertone. In the negotiating process, the effective use of power can dramatically influence the actual outcome of a negotiation or even result in a stalemate or impasse.

Both individuals and organizations bring different sources of power to the negotiation table, and the consideration of the level and source(s) of power should be a part of any negotiation strategy. Use of some types of power can be detrimental to a continuing relationship, whereas others are the result of technical expertise or access to information. Therefore, negotiators must understand the advantages and disadvantages of using each source of power. They must also determine and understand the possible effects that using a particular source of power could have on the relationship between the parties.

Sources of Negotiation Power

Researchers have identified six generic types of power that can be exercised by individuals or organizations in a negotiation: (1) informational, (2) reward, (3) coercive, (4) legitimate, (5) expert, and (6) referent.[13]

Informational Power

Ready access to relevant and useful information is typically the most common application of power found in a negotiation. It relies on trying to influence the other party through the cogent presentation of facts, data, information, and persuasive arguments to support one's own positions and/or to mitigate or challenge the other party's positions. However, the effective use of information in a negotiation does not necessarily mean open and complete sharing. For example, one party may present only favorable information that supports its position, whereas the other side may present only negative information to refute a position. One party often manipulates information, as a source of power, to control or constrain the options available to the other party.[14]

Reward Power

Reward power means that one party is able to offer something of perceived value to the other party, such as a purchase contract or access to a new product or technology. Using rewards represents a direct attempt to exert active control over the negotiation, particularly when combined with the use of informational power, which relies more on persuasion. The basis of reward power is the belief that individuals respond and behave accordingly when valued rewards are available. However, a key risk in the use of reward power is that the negotiator's counterpart may eventually learn to respond positively only when offered rewards.

Coercive Power

Coercive and reward power are somewhat related; they are two sides of the same negotiation coin. If one party can offer the other party something of value (reward power), then the first party can also take it away (coercive power). Therefore, coercive power includes the ability to punish the other party—financially, physically, emotionally, or mentally. Note that repeated use of coercive power can have detrimental effects on future relationships because of the innate desire to get even with the other party. There is also a strong likelihood that retaliation or escalation will occur if the power structure shifts unfavorably in the future. For example, when supply markets begin to tighten during an economic recovery, suppliers may retaliate against the buyer by pursuing large price increases, reducing customer service to certain buyers, or even disrupting continuity of supply to the offending buyer.

Legitimate Power

The official job position or title that an individual holds, rather than the characteristics of the individual him/herself, is the basis of legitimate power. Parents, pastors, executives, and elected officeholders are all examples of individuals possessing legitimate power. In sourcing, a buyer may have legitimate power simply because he or she legally represents a prominent company and has the authority to buy. It is not necessarily the case that individuals with legitimate power have reward or coercive power (e.g., a church pastor); although the combination of different types of power holds some synergetic properties.

Expert Power

Expert power is a related and special form of informational power. Successful application of informational and expert power involves the development and maintenance of a useful body of knowledge. Informational power exists when someone has thoroughly researched and prepared for a negotiation. An expert is often recognized as having accumulated and mastered a high level of knowledge about a particular subject, often coupled with verifiable credentials and stature that document the mastery. Expert power can influence others in a negotiation by reducing the likelihood that another party will be able to refute the expert's position successfully. Furthermore, non-experts are less likely to challenge an expert because of the expert's perceived depth of knowledge and credibility. However, the other party must value the displayed expertise in order for it to be effective.

Referent Power

This source of power comes from interpersonal appeal based on socially acceptable individual qualities and attributes, such as one's personality or attractiveness. These qualities could be physical but can also include individual characteristics such as honesty, charisma, friendliness, empathy, or sensitivity. In this source of power, the power holder—the referent—has some attributes or interpersonal qualities that attract the other party or make him or her want to be like or respect the power holder. The basis of referent power is that the non-referent person wants the referent to look favorably upon him/her. Referent power is most successful in negotiation when the referents are aware that a counterpart identifies with or has an attraction to them.

Parties holding power differentials will likely apply all available types of power to their advantage during a negotiation. Negotiators must be careful not to abuse their power, or they risk damaging relationships, inviting retaliation, or diminishing the value of that power through overuse. In most commercial negotiations, the sources of power that are usually the most effective are legitimate, informational, and expert. They are usually the sources of power that allow the parties to maintain a positive relationship after reaching agreement. However, referent power can also synergistically interact with the other sources of power, making each stronger or more effective in the influence process.

Concessions

A fundamental part of every negotiation process involves the offering and exchange of **concessions**—movements away from a negotiating position that offer something of value to the other party to ultimately gain something else of value. For example, a buyer's willingness to offer $8.50 per unit instead of $8.25 is a concession that favors the supplier. However, by offering $8.50, the buyer should expect to get something of relatively equal or greater value in return, such as faster delivery, higher quality, or more favorable payment terms.

Effective negotiators quickly learn to offer concessions that have little value to themselves in exchange for concessions from the other party that do have perceived value. To make the concession process work, each party must recognize that give-and-take is a normal and necessary part of any negotiation. Buyers, however, will still want to minimize how much they concede on each point by getting corresponding or even greater value in return. The effective negotiator does not give away any concession without getting something of equal or greater value in return.

Without an effective concession strategy, most negotiations will result in deadlock or a failure to agree—an impasse. However, reaching a deadlock does not necessarily mean that the negotiation has failed. The parties to a negotiation could be so far apart in their positions that an agreement is not forthcoming. In such cases, it may actually be better not to agree and walk away from the negotiation than to accept a poor agreement. This is why it is very important for the negotiator to have adequately prepared and established a thoughtful BATNA for each issue before the negotiation begins. The negotiator must be aware of available options and understand that not reaching agreement may be preferable to making a bad deal.

The manner in which a negotiator approaches concession making is an important part of every successful negotiation strategy. A buyer who opens the negotiation with a low initial offer (on price, for example) followed by a relatively small concession is signaling a reluctance to be flexible. Conversely, a cooperative opening position or moderate offer followed by a relatively strong concession signals a willingness to be flexible and to reach mutual agreement. However, concessions should be made in decreasing increments, not increasing ones. With increasing concessions, it is in the other party's best interest to wait for additional future concessions rather than to agree now. The manner in which negotiators position their concessions will often affect the length and cost of the negotiation. It also affects the other party's expectations of the possible outcomes.

Hendon, Roy, and Ahmed offered the following 12 guidelines for making successful concessions.[15]

- Give yourself enough room to make concessions.
- Try to get the other party to start revealing his or her needs and objectives first.
- Be the first to concede on a minor issue but not the first to concede on a major issue.
- Make unimportant concessions and portray them as more valuable than they are.
- Make the other party work hard for every concession you make.
- Use tradeoffs to obtain something for every concession you make.
- Generally, concede slowly and give a little with each concession.

- Do not reveal your deadline to the other party.
- Occasionally say "no" to the other negotiator.
- Be careful trying to take back concessions, even in tentative negotiations.
- Keep a record of concessions made in the negotiation and try to identify a pattern.
- Do not concede too often, too soon, or too much.

Sourcing Snapshot

Will E-Procurement Change Negotiation?

As the number of people buying online continues to grow, certain changes are in store for supply management professionals who have traditionally prided themselves on their face-to-face people skills. Kevin Rohan, a purchasing specialist at JP Cannon Associates in New York, believes being a strong negotiator is not enough in today's market. Candidates need to continue to develop their skills and be familiar with the latest technology such as how to use the Internet, identify market changes, and perform strategic planning. However, the chances that e-procurement will completely replace one-on-one negotiation in the near future are slim. Emery J. Zobro, president of the John Michael Personnel Group in Chattanooga, TN, is confident that, though the characteristics of a successful supply management professional might change over time, certain qualities will survive e-procurement's infiltration of the industry. "In five years a person who hasn't established a track record with e-commerce and e-procurement will definitely be left behind," Zobro says. Nevertheless, he remains firm in the assessment that "buying things over the computer will never take the place of one-on-one negotiations."

Sources: Adapted from Francis, D. (2000, August 24), "The Decline of the Negotiator?" *Purchasing* 129(3), 160.

Although the use of concession-making is an important part of any negotiation process, a willingness to offer large concessions, particularly as described above, is usually not in the best interests of a buyer. The level of pre-negotiation planning and relative power of each party will influence how much, how often, and when each party should concede its positions during a negotiation.

Negotiation Tactics: Trying to Reach Agreement

Negotiation tactics are those short-term plans and actions employed to execute a strategy, cause a conscious change in a counterpart's position, or influence others to achieve one's negotiation objectives. Negotiators develop tactics ethically (and sometimes unethically) to persuade their counterparts to accept a certain position or agree to a preferred outcome. Furthermore, the savvy negotiator must learn to recognize and understand the type of tactics a counterpart is using, as well as how to counter them. An awareness of a counterpart's tactics usually mitigates the effectiveness of those tactics.

Some unethical tactics used by buyers and sellers are actually ploys or tricks to get the other party to agree to an issue or position without question or a thorough examination of the facts. However, this does not diminish the fact that there are many legitimate and ethical tactics that can be used to persuade the other party to accept a particular perspective. The following represents only a small subset of typical negotiation tactics that the astute and adequately prepared negotiator should be aware of and prepare for:

- *Low Ball.* This tactic involves one party, often the seller, offering an unusually low price to receive a buyer's business (e.g., getting one's foot in the door). Suppliers know that, once a buyer makes a commitment to a seller, it is often difficult for that buyer to switch to another supplier because of the consistency principle.

- *Honesty and Openness.* Parties with a close working relationship often have a high level of mutual trust that promotes free and open sharing of information. The objective of this tactic is to make each party aware of the relevant information needed to create a mutually acceptable agreement.

- *Questions.* Open-ended questions serve a dual purpose as a negotiation tactic. First, insightful questions can result in revealing new information about the interests underlying the other party's stated position. Second, questions provide a period of relief or reflection as the other party takes time to consider an answer. Questions seeking only a "yes or no" answer do not provide much additional information.

- *Caucus.* This tactic involves taking a time-out; negotiators might need to process new information, take a needed break, or take a recess if the negotiation is going poorly; negotiators might feel they are making too many concessions and need to break an unhealthy pattern of interaction.

- *Trial Balloon.* A negotiator using this tactic might ask, "What if I can persuade my manager to endorse this option? Would you go along?" Trial balloons are tests of acceptability. The other party's on-the-spot reaction to the idea influences whether the parties should pursue the idea further.

- *Price Increase.* Sellers sometimes argue that, if a buyer does not agree to a certain price or condition, the price will soon increase. A well-informed and adequately prepared negotiator can tell the difference between a real price change and a tactic used by the seller merely to make the sale.

- *High Ball.* This tactic involves taking an abnormally high initial position on an issue. For example, the seller may put forth an extremely high selling price. The underlying logic is that, once a party actually makes a concession from the extreme position, the new position may appear far more acceptable to the other party by contrast. It also attempts to shift the bargaining zone in one's favor.

- *Best and Final Offer.* This tactic often signals the end of a negotiation on a given issue. The caveat to this tactic is that the person making the best and final offer must be prepared to actually end the negotiation if the other party does not accept the offer. If a party rapidly amends a best and final offer, then this tactic quickly loses its effectiveness, and the negotiator loses credibility when the bluff is called.

- *Silence.* This tactic involves not immediately responding when the other party makes an offer in the hope that an awkward silence will encourage further offers or concessions from the other party. People routinely show the tendency to fill in the gaps when a discussion encounters silence so as to not offend the other party. Also, when the counterpart makes a point that weakens our position, it may be better to remain silent than to admit that the other party is correct. The other party may actually back away from its earlier position.

- *Planned Concessions.* This tactic uses concessions to influence the other party's behavior. The use of planned concessions signals that it is now the other party's turn to reciprocate and make a concession on an important issue. There is a natural tendency for an individual to respond in kind when receiving a concession.

- *Venue.* Some negotiators insist on negotiating in a location that is more favorable to them. One party may have to travel a great distance, face the sun, or sit in an uncomfortable chair in an effort to create stress. Also, the choice of venue can affect whether or not a negotiator can get up and leave the negotiation at a critical time.

According to Robert Cialdini, an expert on the psychology of negotiation and conflict resolution, we can cluster the literally hundreds of negotiation tactics that exist into six general categories, which represent fundamental social psychology principles that guide human behavior.[16]

- *Reciprocation.* Virtually every human society adheres to the principle of reciprocation, which means that people feel an obligation to give something back of equal or greater value to someone else after we have received something of perceived value from them. In a negotiation, this principle creates the obligation to return something in kind when the other party offers a concession. Effective negotiators understand the powerful influence that reciprocity has on most individuals. Negotiations have a definite pattern in the concession exchange process and can strongly influence the quality or level of concession offered by each party. However, it is often unnecessary to respond to a concession at the same or higher level of value if the concession being requested is important to you. In such a situation, the negotiator may break the pattern of reciprocity and offer a lesser concession. This can also signal that the conceding negotiator is getting close to his/her BATNA or reservation point.

- *Consistency.* This principle says that we prefer to be consistent in our beliefs and actions. In a negotiation, if we can get others to agree to something, then not following through on their part would be inconsistent and irrational, an uncomfortable behavior to be avoided. Also, skilled negotiators also understand that, after someone agrees to something, he or she feels better about that decision than before he or she agreed to it. Furthermore, once a small commitment is in place, it becomes easier to request larger commitments later. The consistency trap is a very powerful tactic and can be difficult to back away from.

- *Social Proof.* According to this principle, we look to the behavior of others to determine what is desirable, appropriate, and correct.[17] This principle often works against us in negotiations if we look to the other party to determine our behavior. For example, a seller may state that a well-respected company uses its product, thereby providing social proof of the value of the purchase to the buyer.

- *Liking.* This principle states that we work well and are more agreeable with people we like or who are like us. Effective negotiators, therefore, should take sufficient time to get to know their counterparts, knowing that achieving desired concessions is more likely when a favorable level of familiarity exists.

- *Authority.* This principle states that we are more likely to accept the positions, arguments, and direction from recognized authority figures, not unlike the impact of legitimate power described above. In a negotiation, a senior sales executive may be able to influence an inexperienced buyer substantially, simply because of his or her implied authority or formal position in the organization.

- *Scarcity.* Sellers learn early in their career the powerful influence that scarcity, or even the perception of potential scarcity, can have on a buyer. Who wants to close or disrupt a facility because supply will be short next month (unless the buyer acts now)? The same argument applies to price increases. If the product will be scarce at the new price, then the implication is that the buyer needs to act before the price increase takes effect.

A tactic used during one negotiation may not be successful or applicable to another negotiation, even with the same counterpart. When conducting a negotiation, effective negotiators must be willing to modify use of tactics that are not effective and prepare for responses to tactics that are likely to be used against them. Tactics are most effective when the other party is unprepared, stressed, under severe time pressure, inexperienced, fatigued, or disinterested. Be prepared, and do not react off-the-cuff without analyzing the tactic and its real, intended effects.

Win-Win Negotiation

Many traditional supply managers believe that the primary objective of a negotiation is to win at the expense of suppliers. We call this win-lose negotiation (also called competitive or distributive bargaining). **Win-lose negotiation** means that two or more parties are competing over a fixed sum value with the winner taking all or the larger share. It is also known as a zero-sum, or fixed-sum, game—if one party gains, it is only at the expense of the other party. Every increase in the purchase price benefits only the seller, and every decrease in price benefits only the buyer. There are no other possible outcomes. The level of competition in a win-lose purchase negotiation rarely makes a supplier anxious to cooperate with a buyer to provide advantages that are not available to other customers. There is no inherent advantage for the supplier to do so without receiving a corresponding concession.

Win-win negotiation (sometimes called integrative or collaborative bargaining) seeks to expand the value or resources of outcomes available to all parties through cooperative negotiation. The parties still negotiate, but they do so to determine how to equitably divide a bigger and expanded value pie through the use of creative proposals that seek to simultaneously meet both parties' needs and wants, obviously not an easy process. For example, increased value to the buyer may mean receiving a more favorable purchase price than a competitor's, a shorter order cycle time from the supplier, joint efforts to reduce duplication or waste between the parties, or assistance in developing new technology or product designs. On the supplier's side, increasing value may mean additional sales volume, preferential treatment for future business, or technical assistance provided by the buyer to help reduce its operating costs. Exhibit 13.5 contrasts the characteristics of win-lose and win-win negotiation.

Exhibit 13.5	Characteristics of Win-Lose and Win-Win Negotiations
CHARACTERISTICS OF WIN-LOSE NEGOTIATION (DISTRIBUTIVE BARGAINING)	**CHARACTERISTICS OF WIN-WIN NEGOTIATION (INTEGRATIVE BARGAINING)**
• Assume rigid negotiating positions. • Compete over a fixed amount of value. • Practice strict use of power by one party over another. • Pursue adversarial relationships.	• Understand each other's needs and wants. • Focus on common rather than personal interests. • Conduct joint efforts to solve problems and develop creative solutions that provide additional value. • Engage in open sharing of information.

The fundamental question of win-win negotiation is how the buyer and seller, through a collaborative negotiation process, can pursue integrative bargaining and increase the benefits available to both parties. Previous research has identified five different methods for pursuing integrative (win-win) agreements.[18]

- *Expand the Pie.* Working closely together, the parties identify new and creative ways to expand available resources or generate new value obtained through a negotiated agreement. For example, the seller that offers a buyer early access to new technology for inclusion in its own new products can help create new value. If the market embraces the new product, presumably sales will increase, and the supplier will receive larger future orders. Both parties become better off.

- *Logroll.* Successful logrolling requires the parties to identify more than one issue where disagreement exists. The parties agree to trade off these issues so that each party has one of its top-priority issues satisfied. This is a form of compromise in which each party gets more in those issues that are most important to him or her along with giving up more on those issues that are less critical yet are important to the other party.

- *Use Nonspecific Compensation.* With this approach, one party achieves his or her objective on an issue, whereas the other receives something else of value as a reward for going along. This approach works only when the compensating party knows what is valuable to the other party and makes a reasonable offer to make the other party whole for agreeing.

- *Cut the Costs for Compliance.* With cost cutting, one party (usually the buyer) gets a lower price as the parties work jointly to reduce the seller's costs or the joint transaction costs of doing business together. The buyer satisfies his or her objective of obtaining a competitive price, whereas the seller becomes more competitive in the marketplace or achieves a higher profit margin because of its new, reduced cost structure.

- *Find a Bridge Solution.* Bridging involves inventing new options that satisfy each party's needs. Although bridging solutions will likely not totally satisfy each party, they are usually satisfactory to each side. As in the third point of Triangle Talk (propose action in such a way that they can accept it), the negotiators seek to create solutions jointly that satisfy the interests and needs of both parties.

A win-win negotiation approach works best for items or services that are important to the buyer's products or business or when the item involves high-dollar items or services where cost control is critical. It is also appropriate when the supplier adds a high level of value to the product or service. When variables such as technology, cycle time, quality, and price/cost are important, win-win negotiating may also be the best approach to achieving mutual benefit between parties.

Good Practice Example	*Mack Trucks Uses Negotiation to Rev Up Its Sourcing Process*

Mack Trucks, which is part of a newly consolidated operation comprising the truck-making units of Volvo, Renault, and Mack, is facing intense pricing pressure from customers and competitors. The ability to meet its financial targets has presented a major challenge for the company. With limited ability to raise truck prices and declining demand, the alternatives facing Mack were to manage material costs better or absorb price increases through lower profit margins and profitability.

Even before Volvo assumed ownership of Mack Trucks and Renault, Mack and Renault sought to leverage the commonality between them on a global basis. Mack Trucks had concluded that procurement offered excellent opportunities for global synergy across Europe and North America. Mack Trucks, working jointly with Renault, had implemented a global sourcing process designed to leverage the volumes available through the combined truck units. Volvo Truck is now part of that process. A central part of this process features negotiation to help the three combined companies carry out their vision of global procurement.

Mack Truck's Global Sourcing Process

The global sourcing process at Volvo/Renault/Mack Trucks, originally developed by Mack, consists of nine steps. Part of the benefit from this process is the discipline concerning the completion of tasks built into each step. Cross-functional sourcing teams are responsible for following this process as they develop and negotiate global procurement contracts. The company uses the nine-step process even for contracts that the sourcing teams determine are regional rather than global.

Exhibit 13.6 describes the Volvo/Renault/Mack Trucks' nine-step global sourcing process. Steps 0–4 of the process involve strategy development, whereas Steps 5–8 involve strategy implementation.

Step 0: Select Global Sourcing Projects

An executive steering committee is responsible for selecting sourcing projects and identifying the cost savings expected from each project. The steering committee plays a vital role in maintaining the intensity of the global sourcing process. Step 0 is continuous because the agreements established early in the global process eventually come up for periodic review and/or renewal.

Step 1: Launch the Project

Perhaps the most important task associated with Step 1 is the formation of sourcing teams. The executive team selects team members based on their familiarity with the items under review. A formal team leader works with the team to develop time schedules, a list of deliverables, and expected milestones.

In Step 1, the teams validate the sourcing opportunity by collecting and analyzing data. Various tools are available to support each team's analysis. For example, the teams use a portfolio analysis approach with suggested tactics and strategies depending on the characteristics of the purchase requirement. This tool helps the team develop a sourcing strategy that best matches the actual purchasing need.

Step 2: Develop the Sourcing Project

Some managers believe this step to be the most critical, as the sourcing teams identify potential worldwide suppliers. From a list of potential suppliers, the teams sends a request for information, which is a generic questionnaire that asks about sales, production capacity, quality certification (such as ISO 9000), familiarity with the truck business, and major customers.

Step 2 requires a major work effort on the part of engineering. Engineers will examine drawings in an effort to standardize part specifications among Volvo, Renault, and Mack Trucks. Although a team may conclude that there is no global supplier, they may be able to standardize design specifications across the companies.

Step 3: Develop Requests for Proposals

Step 3 features the development, sending, and analysis of formal proposals to suppliers identified in Step 2. Suppliers typically require six weeks to analyze and return the RFPs. The sourcing teams are responsible for analyzing the details of the returned RFPs. The teams are empowered to determine the criteria and the evaluation weights used to analyze each supplier, but members must reach consensus in their choices about which suppliers to recommend.

A negotiation workshop occurs during this step at the Renault Learning Center in France. The purpose of this workshop is to review the tools that are necessary to support the global process and to improve negotiation skills. The first half of the meeting is committed to overall training. The second half helps individual teams develop their negotiation strategy. The teams will also select a negotiation leader. The decision of who should be the negotiation leader is based on discussion and consensus rather than voting. Of the first 27 global projects, fully one-third of the negotiation leaders were selected from outside the sourcing team.

Step 4: Recommend Strategy and Negotiate with Suppliers

Each sourcing team makes a strategy recommendation to an executive committee comprising the vice president of purchasing and the vice president of engineering from each of the three companies. Team recommendations include the selected supplier(s) to use with expected savings and timings identified.

All negotiation that occurs in Step 4 is face-to-face with suppliers. To date, half of the negotiations have occurred in the United States and half in Europe at company-owned sites. When suppliers arrive for a negotiation, they review the global sourcing process so they are aware that this step will only produce a recommendation.

Before suppliers arrive for negotiations, they receive feedback concerning their competitiveness, which allows them to revise their proposal before negotiations commence. A team may disqualify a supplier if the supplier is not competitive and chooses not to revise its proposal. The negotiation also serves as an opportunity to verify that new suppliers can meet technical or commercial requirements.

Once the lead negotiator takes over, the team leader's role begins to diminish (unless the team leader is the lead negotiator). The team leader usually remains part of the negotiating team. Negotiation sessions generally take about three hours. Although the team's objective is to achieve cost savings, the negotiations can discuss many kinds of issues.

Step 5: Certify Suppliers

During Step 5, the purchasing and engineering groups receive the global sourcing team's recommendation and results from the negotiation. Functional directors will begin budgeting expected savings in their financial plans. The output from Step 5 is a certification from affected functional groups of the recommended supplier. Step 5 represents a hand-off of a proposed and negotiated sourcing strategy from the global sourcing team to the purchasing, engineering, and quality groups.

Step 6: Formalize the Sourcing Contract

This step involves formalizing what transpired during contract negotiations. The negotiation leader remains with the process until the contract is complete. The legal department is also involved, but a buyer writes the contract using a predetermined template.

Global contracts, which are typically two to three years in duration, differ from traditional contracts. The global agreements include productivity improvement requirements to offset material cost increases and encourage technical advancements by the supplier. And, in a somewhat significant departure from previous contracting practices, incentives such as 50/50 improvement sharing are starting to appear.

Step 7: Sample Testing and Approval

This step assesses the samples provided by the selected supplier. The production facilities develop initial sample inspection reports, and the negotiation leader develops a production rollout plan.

Step 8: Production Readiness

Step 8 is the pilot production stage. The selected supplier may send a day's worth or a week's worth of supply for use and testing in actual production.

Exhibit 13.6	Nine-Step Global Sourcing Process

Step 0:	Select Global Sourcing Projects
Step 1:	Launch the Project
Step 2:	Develop the Sourcing Project
Step 3:	Develop Requests for Proposals
Step 4:	Recommend Strategy and Negotiate with Suppliers
Step 5:	Certify Suppliers
Step 6:	Formalize the Sourcing Contract
Step 7:	Testing Samples and Approval
Step 8:	Preparing Production Readiness

The Good Practice Example illustrates how one company used negotiation training and awareness to add value to its international sourcing process. Without highly skilled and well-trained negotiators, the development of complex global sourcing strategies, such as the one illustrated here, would not be possible. The magnitude and complexity of global agreements, which are usually longer term in length and address many non-price issues, demand face-to-face negotiation.

International Negotiation

With the burgeoning growth in international business, especially regarding outsourcing and global sourcing activities over the last twenty years, the need to negotiate effectively and efficiently across cultures has increased exponentially. Thomas Friedman gave us an exemplary sample of a truly global supply chain in his book, *The World Is Flat*, in which he describes how Dell sources components for and builds its notebook computers.[19] In the operation of its global supply chain, Dell utilizes multiple components suppliers located in a variety of countries for different parts and components. If a given Dell supplier is unable to meet current demand for a particular item, then Dell can shift its sourcing to another supplier with available capacity or to a different facility from that same supplier, regardless of physical location. For example, Dell can shift its sourcing of microprocessors from Intel factories located in the Philippines, Costa Rica, Malaysia, or China, depending on available capacity or anticipated risk conditions. Therefore, different or customized negotiation strategies may be needed to negotiate purchase agreements across diverse cultures.

Negotiations with suppliers located literally anywhere on the globe take on added complexity and challenge when the parties have different languages, customs, laws, and cultures. When preparing for a negotiation with a supplier located in another country, companies must invest in substantial extra time and effort in planning for the negotiation to accommodate new language translations, travel, modes of transportation, and other foreign business requirements. One of the more important considerations in negotiating a global sourcing agreement is culture shock.[20] **Culture shock** occurs as a result of negotiators being immersed in a place in which their established norms have been confronted and may no longer be applicable. The negotiator's preexisting values, beliefs, rules, and decision-making schema may not apply in the new situation. Emotions run higher, and negotiators may initially encounter substantial anxiety, disorientation, and confusion, thereby reducing the likelihood of successfully achieving their desired negotiation outcomes.

Various barriers may dramatically affect the conduct of international negotiations.[21] In order of importance, major obstacles to effective international negotiation include miscommunication because of language, time orientation, cultural differences, and limited on-the-ground authority of the international negotiator. Effective international negotiators also demonstrate certain personal characteristics that can help overcome these obstacles. These flexible characteristics include extreme patience, thorough knowledge of the contract agreement, an honest and polite attitude, and familiarity with foreign cultures and customs. See Sourcing Snapshot: FedEx Expert Shares His International Negotiating Insights for a look at how one company effectively considered the nuances and differences among cultures to negotiate more effectively.

Beyond the natural barriers of language differences, it is still possible to fail to understand and/or to be understood. What we consider as generally accepted words may have substantially different meanings in other countries, even among countries that speak the same language,

Sourcing Snapshot

FedEx Expert Shares His International Negotiating Insights

Mike Babineaux, senior business specialist at FedEx's Strategic Sourcing and Supply Center of Excellence, offers good advice for any American who negotiates internationally. "Every person who negotiates with other cultures must be aware of the serious and costly mistakes and misunderstandings in business practices that are caused by cultural differences," warns Babineaux. Although nations, on the surface, are changing every day in many ways, the fundamentals of culture evolve at a much slower pace.

In the area of communication, Babineaux says, "Americans tend to speak directly and openly. We want the truth, and we want it now. We are suspicious when we think someone is being evasive." Unfortunately, the American who proceeds in the direct American style in a negotiation will not be particularly effective in some countries. "He or she will be on a different wavelength than the foreigner because our style of communication is very different from others," he explains. An open person may be seen as weak, directness may come across as abrupt, and written contracts may imply that a person's word is not good. In the end, Babineaux explains, "Negotiators who have the greatest success in doing business around the world are those who have learned to have credible appreciation and understanding of those with whom they do business."

Sources: Adapted from Mazel, J. (2000, March 1), "5 Negotiation Experts Reveal Their Secrets to Supplier Management." Retrieved from http://www.ioma.com

because local culture and context play such a significant role in communication. For example, during an international negotiation, an interpreter might verbally communicate yet not fully convey the underlying significance of unspoken actions, signals, and customs that may be invisible to the foreign or nonnative negotiator. For example, what does "a.s.a.p." mean to a negotiator from a culture where punctuality is considered less important than in the United States or Western Europe? It may mean "when we get around to it" instead of immediately.

International negotiation requires substantial extra planning and upfront preparation to be successful. Not only must buyers perform their normal market and supplier analyses and fact finding, they must also strive to understand the subtleties of unfamiliar customs and traditions of their counterpart more fully. As buying and selling increases between organizations located in different countries, the need for higher-level global negotiation skills will also increase.

Selected Countries[22]

The following discussion presents a sample of stereotypical national characteristics when negotiating internationally, albeit from a strictly American perspective. However, understanding these generalities can prove beneficial when developing negotiation strategies and tactics. A negotiator must be aware, however, that there is a danger in stereotyping or oversimplifying the cultural characteristics of different countries or regions. There is always substantial interpersonal variation to consider within a single culture. However, there are certain general tendencies within the culture of which to be aware.

The following discussion outlines general observations and guidelines for several common business cultures (shown in alphabetical order) in which an American supply manager is likely to negotiate.

Brazil

Although Brazilians are receptive to discussing most subjects, home and family are private, personal matters and are not appropriate topics for casual acquaintances. Avoid conversations involving religion or politics. You may speak English or use an interpreter unless you are conversant in Portuguese. They are generally more analytical than other Latin American cultures and will look at the particulars of each situation rather than referring to rules or laws for guidance. They like to bargain and concede little by little. During negotiations, Brazilians tend to approach problems indirectly, allowing their feelings, passion, and enthusiasm to influence their decisions. Although the presentation of facts during a negotiation is acceptable, these facts usually will not overrule underlying subjective feelings. The image of the macho male is still prevalent, although to a lesser extent than in Mexico, for example, and Brazilian men expect women to be subordinate. There are also large numbers of German and Japanese descendants in Brazil, which may complicate the negotiation somewhat.

China

When negotiating with the Chinese, it is important to avoid slang or jargon and to use short, simple sentences with pauses to ensure your words are understood exactly. Never do anything that might embarrass your Chinese counterpart. A negotiator should expect to make presentations to many groups at various organizational levels. Because U.S. managers have a reputation for impatience, the Chinese will extend negotiations beyond the deadline to gain an advantage. Do not exaggerate your ability to deliver on your promises. Your counterparts will hold you to your commitments. They may even try to renegotiate previously agreed-upon issues on the last day, and they will continue to try for a better deal even after signing the agreement. However, you must be patient in your dealings with Chinese negotiators, who also prefer to deal with groups, not individuals. Use an interpreter, even if your Chinese counterpart speaks excellence English.

France

Given their highly formal and reserved nature, a casual attitude during business may alienate the French. Allow for sufficient time to conduct the negotiation, as decisions are made slowly and deliberately. During negotiations, arguments are made from a critical perspective with elegant wit and logic. The French enjoy engaging in debate, striving for effect rather than detail and facts. You should consider using a local agent to assist with the process. Although the French will accept information for the purpose of debate and may even change their minds, a desire to maintain a strong cultural heritage often prohibits them from accepting anything that is contrary to their cultural norm. Because the French are strongly individualistic with a centralized authority structure, negotiating with the proper individual can lead to quick decisions. Dress conservatively in well-made clothing.

Germany

Germans are not openly receptive to outside information. Their strict hierarchies and separation of units often prohibit the sharing of information even across the same organization. These hierarchies can also slow the making of business decisions. Germans rarely engage in humor during business activities. During a negotiation, objective facts form the basis of truth rather than subjective feelings, and Germans are highly analytical. Nowhere is punctuality more important than in Germany. Arriving just two or three minutes late to a negotiation can be insulting. During negotiations, Germans tend to be unemotional because of a high need for social and personal order. German contracts are often more detailed and specific than their counterparts in the United States, and documentation and clarity are both very important.

India

English is widely spoken in India among businesspeople and government officials; therefore, it is less necessary to obtain an interpreter or translate one's business cards. Be sensitive of the need to avoid personal questions and talking about religion, poverty, or politics. It is important to speak with the highest-ranking person possible, as decisions are made at the highest levels of the organization. Organizations in India tend to be very hierarchical and autocratic. In addition, Indian bureaucracy is very burdensome, whereas the pace of business tends to be leisurely. As a result, delays in the negotiation are to be expected. Vegetarian diets are typical, and business negotiations often occur in prominent hotels, not in restaurants. Titles are highly valued, so always address your counterparts by their official titles.

Japan

Japanese culture is vastly different from American culture. Despite such differences, the extra effort needed to develop mutually satisfying negotiations can result in an excellent relationship—Japanese firms are dependable and loyal suppliers. They will treat their customers like valuable family members. The negotiation process with Japanese companies is unique. For example, the Japanese are comfortable with extended silence, which is not true with Americans. As members of a collectivist society, they are loyal team players concerned with the well-being of their country and firm rather than themselves as individuals. Politeness is valued above all else. Instead of saying "No," the Japanese often say "Hai," which does not indicate agreement but merely that they hear or understand. The Japanese do not like surprises, and they typically reach decisions through a consensus process, which can often extend negotiations. When negotiating, keep in mind that it is necessary to convince the whole group rather than a single individual. Also, avoid placing the Japanese in a position in which they must admit failure or lose face. The Japanese do not like the appearance of having to make forced concessions. There is a strong emphasis on interpersonal relationships and less on formal contracts. Therefore, connections with intermediaries are important. Choose them wisely.

Mexico

As in Brazil, subjectivity is often the basis for decision making. Mexican negotiators enjoy the process of bargaining and exchange. The pace of business activity will be much slower than what Americans are used to. It is important to develop and maintain close personal friendships with the right people. Individual dignity is important, so be polite and avoid anything that might embarrass your Mexican counterpart. The foreign negotiator should emphasize the benefits of a proposal to the individual, his or her family, and pride. Financing is often an issue, so you need to be creative in offering financial solutions. It is customary for the oldest person to pick up the tab for a group meal, although it is typical to haggle over the check. It is important to recognize a person's title and position.

Russia

Russian negotiators are very patient, and compromise is considered a sign of weakness. However, they tend to make very extreme initial demands and wait for the foreign negotiator to concede. Final offers are seldom final during the initial stages of negotiation. Long-term interpersonal relationships are less important than in many other cultures. They expect you to walk away from the table and threaten that you cannot reach agreement with them. However, Russian negotiators often have limited authority to make decisions at the table and will refer to absentee third-party decision makers. You need to be aware that some negotiations are designed only to generate information, not to make a deal. End-of-negotiation demands are typical, even though you may assume that the deal is complete. Because of the inconvertibility of the ruble, financing may be difficult and require creative solutions such as countertrade or third-party financing.

Saudi Arabia

Saudi negotiators are considered astute and perceptive. They may stand very close to you and place a hand on your shoulder. Concession making is ritualistic and stems from extreme opening proposals. Decisions take time to materialize from extensive deliberation. Deadlines are made to be ignored. As in many other cultures, developing and maintaining a strong interpersonal relationship with your counterpart is important. Social life usually takes place during the day, as there is no nightlife as we might expect at home in the U.S. Saudi negotiators rely heavily on their religious beliefs to make decisions. Also, plan your trip so as not to conflict with religious holidays. "Yes" generally means "maybe."

South Korea

South Korean negotiators generally prefer one-on-one meetings to represent the company, and the astute negotiator will need to establish a strong interpersonal relationship with the Korean contact. As in most Asian environs, age and rank are important issues in South Korea. When negotiating in a team, senior people should enter the negotiation first, followed by more junior ones. It is important to be firm and consistent but not too aggressive. English is widely spoken, and written materials can be provided in English. Business breakfast meetings are rare, but it is common to meet for business dinners where there are likely to be large quantities of alcohol consumed amid multiple toasts. Avoid comparing Korean and Japanese culture as the two countries have a long, acrimonious history. Silence is a sign that your Korean counterpart may not have understood your last statement or proposal.

Vietnam

You will need to be patient and wait until your Vietnamese counterpart initiates the business discussion. Answers on many questions will be broad and not very specific. A nodding head does not mean "yes," merely that you are being heard or perhaps even that they disagree with you. Patience is very important and is often used to wear down the foreign negotiator into making unreciprocated concessions. Use of a skilled interpreter is vital as there are various nuances to the words chosen and gestures made. However, speak directly to the other party, not to the interpreter. Vietnamese typically negotiate in a group setting, not individually.

The Impact of Electronic Media on Negotiations

Use of electronic media such as e-mail, texting, and instant messaging can dramatically change the dynamics and effectiveness of a negotiation. One advantage of e-negotiating is that the negotiator can read and reflect on the e-mail communication before responding. However, it is more difficult to establish a cordial and cooperative relationship electronically. In addition, electronic means of negotiation, or e-negotiation, tend to equalize the interactions between the parties because normal visual cues and sources of power are not as evident.[23] Status differences are not as readily apparent, and social norms and behaviors are more difficult to discern. Parties may also behave differently when negotiating electronically than they do in person. Voice inflections and nonverbal cues, which often provide substantive meaning to the words used to communicate ideas, do not exist electronically. Devices as emoticons may be used in an attempt to provide some level of context, but they are not as effective as nonverbal communication. In addition, the negotiator at the other end of the electronic connection is relatively anonymous. Is the person with whom you think you are negotiating actually the one doing the negotiating?

According to Karrass,[24] research indicates that e-mail-based negotiations typically take longer to complete than those conducted face-to-face. The realized outcomes of electronic negotiations are also less satisfying to the e-negotiators and are perceived as less fair. Negotiations done electronically tend to be more impersonal and do not promote sufficient rapport between the parties. Because of the impersonal nature of e-negotiations, the interchange between parties is more aggressive and less diplomatic, resulting in messages and communication that are often misconstrued and taken out of context. The bottom line is that e-negotiations are more likely to end in impasse and create mistrust between the parties.

E-negotiators tend to engage in behaviors that indicate that they are communicating in real time even when they are not. The normal give-and-take in a face-to-face negotiation is not present, and the e-negotiators generally ask fewer questions and tend to make more assumptions during the negotiation. For example, what does silence mean when the negotiators are communicating electronically? If the other party does not respond quickly to a request or proposal, does this mean that they are ambivalent to it or just too busy to respond at the moment? Also, e-negotiators often feel less accountable for the outcomes because of a perceived disconnect with their counterparts in a different locale. They also tend to take on a more adversarial, "us-versus-them," mentality. The bottom line is that negotiators who interact face-to-face are more likely to reach agreement and avoid impasse than their e-negotiation counterparts.

Considering all of the challenges in negotiating electronically, it remains a business reality that some negotiations, particularly global negotiations, must be accomplished at a distance because of time constraints and substantial travel costs. One way to mitigate the negative effects of a distance-challenged negotiation is to hold an initial "let's get acquainted," face-to-face meeting prior to e-negotiations, even if no substantive negotiating actually takes place. This meeting helps to foster greater trust and can reduce uncertainty in future interactions that are conducted electronically. Many long-term sourcing agreements can be facilitated effectively in this manner, that is, after the initial physical meeting is followed by e-negotiation. If a face-to-face meeting is impractical, some of the same positive effects can be accomplished initially through the use of a telephone call or real-time videoconference, such as Skype or Face Time, between the parties, allowing for an informal period of sharing and getting to know your counterpart as a person.[25]

Other techniques and considerations can help bridge the challenges of e-negotiating. Although it is tempting to do so because of the speed of communication, negotiating e-mails should not be written quickly and fired off in haste without carefully contemplating the tone of the message and how it might be received or misconstrued. The astute negotiator would not do that in a face-to-face setting. Invariably, things are left out or stated poorly, resulting in confusion and the need for an additional communiqué. E-mails have a tendency to live forever, so be careful of what you say and how you say it. The e-negotiator must also realize that once the e-mail is sent, it is irretrievable and can be forwarded to unintended recipients. The e-negotiator also needs to verify the "To:" and "cc:" addresses carefully to ensure that the e-mail is being sent only to its intended recipient(s).

The e-negotiator should also understand how to use generally accepted e-mail protocols. Even though the use of e-mail tends to be very informal, it is still important to treat a negotiation e-mail as a far more formal document. The e-mail sender should use clear,

Effective E-Negotiating Practices[26]

- Use a blended negotiation, starting with an initial face-to-face meeting or a telephone call to build essential rapport with the other party; occasionally, a follow-up, face-to-face meeting or telephone call may be necessary to clarify information or smooth ruffled feathers.
- As part of the initial contact, share relevant personal information and begin to develop a personal relationship with the other negotiator.
- Establish common ground and interests to build mutual trust.
- Use "emoticons" to counter the lack of nonverbal awareness in an e-negotiation, but be careful where and how often they are used.
- Summarize agreements and concessions frequently to avoid misunderstandings.
- Include positive language that refers to the importance of the relationship.
- Maintain a folder of e-negotiation correspondence for a permanent record.
- Know when and how to reply to or forward e-negotiation correspondence; Do not do so without seriously considering the possible consequences of a hasty or ill-thought-out response.
- Proofread the entire message, including addressees, before sending the e-mail out; once it is sent, it is difficult, if not impossible, to retrieve or recover from.
- Recognize that it takes longer to successfully conclude an e-negotiation than it does a face-to-face one.

concise language but not use such social media conventions as all capital letters, excessive punctuation symbols, underlining, bolding, italics, or off-the-cuff comments. Use of these can be confusing and may be misconstrued as having an unintended meaning to the receiver. Also, avoid copying the other negotiator's boss or any other person who may be perceived to have influence over him/her. This practice is unprofessional and may send a strong signal that you do not trust them.

Good Practice Example	*Texas Instruments Provides Its Procurement Professionals with Comprehensive Global Negotiation Skills and Enhanced Cultural Understanding*[27]

Many U.S.-based companies have successfully demonstrated their negotiation and relationship skills in dealing with domestic suppliers. However, those same levels of negotiation skills and relationship management experience often prove inadequate when dealing with an increasingly global supply base. There are substantial caveats and challenges involved in negotiating with foreign suppliers, particularly in the initial stages of negotiating a sourcing contract. In 2003, Texas Instruments (TI) developed and implemented a comprehensive professional development program to more effectively prepare its procurement professionals and others within the company to comprehend, value, and appropriately act in response to those cultural differences they will face in foreign cultures where they conduct business.

TI introduced this cultural awareness program in response to a corporate strategy that focused on finding and utilizing suppliers in low-cost countries and regions, such as Eastern Europe and Asia. The program allows TI's procurement professionals to develop higher-level negotiation and relationship skills with suppliers located in these cultures. These professional development programs are delivered by internal personnel and can be tailored to TI employees operating throughout the world. Training can be specifically adapted to cultural differences encountered and for different industries, companies, and products.

Program deliverables include the ability to challenge personal expectations and assumptions from both the buyer and supplier perspectives, describe the buyer's expectations in clear and understandable terms, scrutinize and cultivate understanding of the supplier's assumptions, and bridge the differences encountered in the exchange process. The overall program objective is to prevent, preclude, or mitigate the difficulties and disruptions that would typically be encountered when negotiating with people from other cultures.

One of the prime benefits from this has been the ability of negotiators to understand why previous negotiations may not have gone as well as expected. Building on this expanded knowledge and cultural awareness, the outcomes from more recent negotiations have been more in line with company expectations. Those who have completed this training have been able to effectively break down negotiation and relationship barriers. It has proven important to understand the supplier's perspectives and values and take them into active consideration when planning and conducting a sourcing negotiation. The TI courses have also conditioned participants to be better prepared to deal with the extended time frames typically involved in negotiating with global suppliers because of the need for protracted relationship building. One additional benefit that does not relate to global negotiations is that the same skills have been applied to improving the performance of TI's global work teams.

CONCLUSION

An organization's commercial success is partly because of the skill of its negotiators, from both its buying and selling activities. Regardless of the industry, effective negotiators share common traits. They realize that they are not born with requisite negotiation knowledge and skills. Therefore, they must continuously study, practice, and train to become more effective negotiators. Research shows that skilled negotiators also have higher aspirations and pursue more aggressive goals than their less-effective counterparts, which are generally achieved. Finally, individuals who are skilled at negotiation are destined to be among an organization's most valued professionals.

Professional supply managers must become more effective negotiators by participating in training, simulations, and workshops that develop these critical negotiation skills. The difference between a good sourcing agreement and an excellent one is often more a function of the level of preparation and interpersonal and relationship-building skills of the negotiator or negotiating team.

KEY TERMS

bargaining, 509	**needs**, 499	**settlement zone**, 509
BATNA, 499	**negotiation**, 498	**strategy**, 509
concessions, 513	**objective**, 507	**tactics**, 505
culture shock, 522	**plan**, 506	**wants**, 499
fact, 508	**planning**, 506	**win-lose negotiation**, 517
interest, 499	**position**, 499	**win-win negotiation**, 517
issues, 509	**power**, 511	

DISCUSSION QUESTIONS

1. Why is negotiation such an important part of the purchasing process?

2. Discuss the resources necessary to support effective negotiation planning and execution.

3. The parties to a sourcing negotiation can discuss many issues besides price. Select five non-price issues over which a buyer and seller can reach agreement, and explain why each issue might be important to the buyer or seller.

4. Will electronic purchasing through the Internet increase or decrease the need for negotiation between buyers and sellers? Why?

5. Develop a profile of a skilled or effective negotiator.

6. Contrast a win-win negotiator with a win-lose negotiator.

7. Discuss different strengths and weaknesses that a buyer and seller might bring to the negotiating table.

8. What information should a buyer gather about a supplier before entering a negotiation?

9. What are likely to be the most important sources of power in a buyer-seller negotiation?

10. Why are concessions important during a sourcing negotiation? How do the parties to a negotiation demonstrate their willingness to compromise?

11. What is the risk of relying too heavily on the typical profiles of international negotiators? Is there a benefit to using these profiles?

12. Give examples of tactics practiced by a buyer or seller that might be considered unethical.

13. Discuss the concept of BATNA and explain how a negotiator can effectively use it to plan a negotiation.

14. Describe the technique of using Triangle Talk to plan a sourcing negotiation.

15. Explain how and when the negotiator can effectively use e-negotiation techniques.

ADDITIONAL READINGS

Acuff, R. L. (1997), *How to Negotiate Anything with Anyone Anywhere around the World*, New York: AMACOM.

Anderson, K. (1994), *Getting What You Want: How to Reach Agreement and Resolve Conflict Every Time*, New York: Plume.

Bazerman, M. H., and Neale, M. A. (1992), *Negotiating Rationally*, New York: Free Press.

Burr, A. M. (2001), "Ethics in Negotiation: Does Getting to Yes Require Candor?" *Dispute Resolution Journal*, 56(2), 8–15.

Camp, J. (2007), *No: The Only Negotiating System You Need for Work and Home*, New York: Crown Business.

Cellich, C., and Jain, S. C. (2004), *Global Business Negotiations: A Practical Guide*, Mason, OH: Thomson South-Western.

Cialdini, R. B. (2001), *Influence: Science and Practice* (4th ed.), Boston: Allyn and Bacon.

Corvette, B. A. B. (2007), *Conflict Management: A Practical Guide to Developing Negotiation Strategies*, Upper Saddle River, NJ: Pearson Prentice Hall.

Diamond, S. (2010), *Getting More: How to Negotiate to Achieve Your Goals in the Real World*, New York: Crown Business.

Fells, R. (1989), "Managing Deadlocks in Negotiation," *Management Decision*, 27(4), 135–141.

Fisher, R., Ury, W., and Patton, B. (2011), *Getting to Yes: Negotiating Agreement without Giving In* (revised ed.), New York: Penguin Books.

Fogg, R. W. (1985), "Dealing with Conflict: A Repertoire of Creative, Peaceful Approaches," *Journal of Conflict Resolution*, 29(2), 330–358.

Gelfand, M. J., and Brett, J. M. (Eds.). (2004), *The Handbook of Negotiation and Culture*, Palo Alto, CA: Stanford University Press.

Ghauri, P. N., and Usunier, J. C. (Eds.). (1996), *International Business Negotiations*, Tarrytown, NY: Pergamon.

Hendon, D. W., Hendon, R. A., and Herbig, P. (1998), "Negotiating across Cultures," *Security Management*, 42(11), 25–28.

Hunt, P. (2000, October 5), "Making a Good Deal," *Supply Management*, pp. 37–39.

Kublin, M. (1995), *International Negotiation: A Primer for American Business Professionals*, New York: International Business Press.

Lamming, R., Caldwell, N., Phillips, W., and Harrison, D. (2005), "Sharing Sensitive Information in Supply Relationships," *European Management Journal*, 23(5), 554–563.

Lax, D. A., and Sebenius, J. K. (2006), *3D Negotiation: Powerful Tools to Change the Game in Your Most Important Deals*, Boston: Harvard Business School Publishing.

Lewicki, R. J., Barry, B., and Saunders, D. M. (2009), *Negotiation* (6th ed.), New York: McGraw-Hill Irwin.

Lewicki, R. J., Saunders, D. M., and Barry, B. (2009), *Negotiation: Readings, Exercises, and Cases* (6th ed.), New York: McGraw-Hill Irwin.

Lytle, A. L, Brett, J. M., and Shapiro, D. L. (1999), "The Strategic Use of Interests, Rights, and Power to Resolve Disputes," *Negotiation Journal*, 15(1), 31–51.

McCormack, M. H. (1995), *On Negotiating*, Los Angeles: Dove Books.

McRae, B. (1998), *Negotiating and Influencing Skills: The Art of Creating and Claiming Value*, Thousand Oaks, CA: Sage.

Menard, R. (2004), *You're the Buyer: You Negotiate it!* Bloomington, IN: Author House.

Miller, P., and Kelle, P. (1998), "Quantitative Support for Buyer-Supplier Negotiation in Just-in-Time Purchasing," *International Journal of Purchasing and Materials Management*, 34(2), 25–31.

Mintu-Wimsatt, A. (2002), "Personality and Negotiation Style: The Moderating Effects of Cultural Content," *Thunderbird International Business Review*, 44(6), 729–748.

Moran, R. T. (1991), *Dynamics of Successful International Negotiation*, Houston: Gulf Publishing.

Morrison, T., Conaway, W. A., and Borden, G. A. (1994), *Kiss, Bow, or Shake Hands: How To Do Business in Sixty Countries*, Holbrooke, MA: Adams Media Corporation.

Mortensen, K. W. (2004), *Maximum Influence: The 12 Universal Laws of Power Persuasion*, New York: AMACOM.

Shell, G. R. (2006), *Bargaining for Advantage: Negotiation Strategies for Reasonable People* (2nd ed.), New York: Penguin Books.

Stark, P. B., and Flaherty, J. S. (2002), *Everyone Negotiates: 101 Winning Tactics*, San Diego: Bentley Press.

Thompson, L. (2012), *The Mind and Heart of the Negotiator* (5th ed.), Upper Saddle River, NJ: Prentice Hall.

Watkins, M. (2002), *Breakthrough Business Negotiations: A Toolbox for Managers*, San Francisco: Jossey-Bass.

Whipple, R. T. (2006), *Understanding E-Body Language: Building Trust Online*, Rochester, NY: Productivity Publications.

ENDNOTES

1. Shell, G. R. (2006), *Bargaining for Advantage: Negotiation Strategies for Reasonable People* (2nd ed.), New York: Penguin Books, p. 6.

2. Acuff, R. L. (1997), *How to Negotiate Anything with Anyone Anywhere around the World*, New York: AMACOM, p. 18.

3. Thompson, L. (2005), *The Mind and Heart of the Negotiator* (3rd ed.), Upper Saddle River, NJ: Pearson, p. 2.

4. McCormack, M. H. (1995), *On Negotiating*, Los Angeles: Dove Books, p. 7.

5. Fisher, R., Ury, W., and Patton, B. (2011), *Getting to Yes: Negotiating Agreement without Giving In*, New York: Penguin Books, pp. 101–103.

6. Thompson, p. 46.

7. Fisher and Ury, pp. 10–11.

8. Anderson, K. (1994), *Getting What You Want: How to Reach Agreement and Resolve Conflict Every Time*, New York: Plume, pp. 10–15.

9. Waxer, C. (2001, June), "E-Negotiations Are In, Price-Only E-Auctions Are Out," *ISource*, pp. 73–76.

10. Lewicki, R. J., Saunders, D. M., and Barry, B. (2006), *Negotiation* (5th ed.), New York: McGraw-Hill Irwin, p. 113.

11. Lewicki et al., p. 447.

12. Lewicki et al., p. 35.

13. Thompson, citing original work by French and Raven (1959), *The Bases of Social Power*, in *Studies in Social Power*, Ann Arbor: University of Michigan Press.

14. Lewicki et al., pp. 188–191.

15. Lewicki et al., p. 51, citing original work by Hendon, D. W., Roy, M. H., and Ahmed, Z. U. (2003), "Negotiation Concession Patterns: A Multicountry, Multiperiod Study," *American Business Review*, 21, 75–83.

16. Cialdini, R. B. (2001), *Influence: Science and Practice* (4th ed.), Boston: Allyn and Bacon.

17. Thompson, pp. 164–165.

18. Lewicki et al., pp. 83–86.

19. Friedman, T. L. (2006), *The World Is Flat: A Brief History of the Twenty-First Century Release 2.0*, New York: Farrar, Straus and Giroux, pp. 515–520.

20. Martin, D., Mayfield, J., Mayfield, M., and Herbig, P. (2003), "International Negotiations: An Entirely Different Animal," in R. J. Lewicki, D. M. Saunders, J. W. Minton, and B. Barry (Eds.), *Negotiation: Readings, Exercises, and Cases* (4th ed.), New York: McGraw-Hill Irwin, pp. 340–343.

21. Min, H., and Galle, W. (1993), "International Negotiation Strategies of U.S. Purchasing Professionals," *International Journal of Purchasing and Materials Management*, 29(3), 46.

22. Morrison, T., Conaway, W. A., and Borden, G. A. (1994), *Kiss, Bow, or Shake Hands: How To Do Business in Sixty Countries*, Holbrooke, MA: Adams Media Corporation; and Acuff.

23. Thompson, pp. 304–316.

24. Karrass, C. L. (2010), "Negotiating Via E-Mail?" *KARRASS Effective Negotiating® Tip*. Retrieved from http://www.karrass.com/kar_eng/tips_56.htm

25. Atkinson, W. (2007, August 16), "Texas Instruments Trains Buyers on Global Negotiating Skills," *Purchasing*, pp. 16–17.

26. Morris, M., Nadler, J., Kurtzberg, T., and Thompson, L. (2002), "Schmooze or Lose: Social Friction and Lubrication in E-Mail Negotiations," *Group Dynamics: Theory, Research, and Practice*, 6(1), 99.

27. Adapted from Karrass, and Knight, C. M. (1999), "Top 7 Ways to Get the Most from Negotiating Via Email," *Top7Business*. Retrieved from http://top7business.com/?cat=Negotiation

Contract Management

CHAPTER 14

Learning Objectives

After completing this chapter, you should be able to

- Understand the different types of contracts that exist
- Develop knowledge of long-term contracts and when they should be used
- Understand different types of contracts for nontraditional areas of spending
- Understand legal alternatives to contractual disputes that work

Chapter Outline

Managing Supplier Financial Risk in Difficult Economic Times

Although many people believe that contracts spell out how buyer-supplier relationships should function in any type of situation, the fact is that it is almost impossible to predict every single possibility at the outset of a contractual relationship. This was never truer than during the challenging economic recession that began in 2008 and is still underway as we write this book in 2010. One of the lessons learned by many firms during this period is the importance of moving beyond legal contractual guidelines to improve relationships with desired long-term suppliers and with those who supply critical and strategic items and services. Recent research based on procurement executive surveys collected during the 2008–2010 recession suggests two important findings: first, supply chain disruptions may be reduced when buyers focus on improving key supplier's financial health, and second, proactive contract renegotiation practices may also lead to reduction supply chain disruptions. When asked about what would be a probable impact of a supply chain disruption, 38.6 percent of procurement executives stated it would result reduction in revenue, 20.9 percent in worse customer service, 13 percent shutdown of operations and 27.5 percent felt that impact would impact two or more of these elements. The results of this study suggest that communication with suppliers is important but must be combined with a proactive approach for meaningful contract renegotiations, to improve access to credit, reduce payment terms, and provide easier access to needed working capital.

Note that this result makes sense, but the results suggest that this is not always taking place. Specifically, buying firms do not always take meaningful action when confronted by supplier financial duress. During the 2008–2009 global economic recession, only 50 percent of buying firms surveyed in North America were making any efforts to work with and assist suppliers deal with financial issues, and less than 20 percent were adjusting policies in accounts payables and receivable. Because suppliers are not always open to sharing financial problems, other indicators such as quality or delivery problems may be latent indicators of financial duress in a supplier's operations.

The important takeaway from this research is that firms must act to make a difference, and it is executive leadership's responsibility take the lead in promoting this attitude. An excellent example of such action was described by a CPO at a major Tier 1 automotive company, in March 2009:

> As we worked through many difficult situations in the past 3 years, proactive communication was the key to mitigating much of the inherent risk in the relationship. I chaired a weekly meeting with the global category managers to provide the visibility and escalation to ensure that we were working on the issues with all appropriate levels of management, engaging treasury when we needed to work with our suppliers CFO or even their banks when the concern level was heightened. Our buyers learned that there are many elements of the relationship that can be enhanced with great communication, which was a great transformation for many of them who for years were "price quoters." Traditionally we had the belief that all suppliers were basically disposable and as a result we had a "best in class" process for supplier crisis replacement. I changed that about 18 months ago with inception of a department focused on Proactive mitigation of supplier risk. Much of this process was based on getting early signals from buyer communications regarding strains or stresses in the relationship. We then used tools such as supplier development and some of our advanced financial analysis from our finance and cost managers to evaluate methods to stabilize and mitigate supplier risk by helping solve the problems that were driving them toward crisis.

It is thus important for organizations to develop a dynamic capability to monitor and manage supplier financial health and seek contract renegotiation to deal head on with these challenges. During the 2009–2009 recession, the Association of Financial Professionals (AFP) found that up to 63 percent of companies with under US$1B in revenues relied on secured and unsecured lines of credit for their short-term cash needs. Unfortunately, this is exactly the type of credit that is becoming less available. Buying organizations need to have more frequent updates on the state of supplier's financial condition, and no method is better than engaging in a direct dialogue with the supplier's management team, as shown in the example above.

A second and more prescriptive approach is the need for buying companies to create internal alignment on strategies to mitigate and manage supplier financial risk. Procurement needs to adopt a more formal and focused approach to management of supplier financial risk, with a long-term view of how to manage peaks and troughs that exist in the global economy. The move toward a global supply network necessitates an approach that considers how to align strategies, growth, and capacity and establish common objectives along these lines.

Source: Handfield, Robert, and Paolo, Marcos, Working Paper, Supply Chain Resource Cooperative, July, 2013.

Introduction

In global commerce, people make risky deals—and make promises they cannot keep. They sign a contract without reading it, and one they do not understand. They make risky assumptions, without noticing it, and make or accept unreasonable demands with or without knowing it. They assume that the terms of one market are acceptable in another and do not recognize cultural or legal landmines. All of these are major pitfalls in the current global economic environment.

The area of managing contracts in a global environment continues to be a major source of problems, misunderstanding, and poor execution for companies. Moreover, companies often fail to bring the required resources to bear in contractual discussions that fall outside of "normal" contractual guidelines that are traditionally accepted in Western settings. This is particularly true in Asia Pacific and Latin America, where there are significant differences in the perception of how to view and manage contractual relationships. Further, the ongoing commitment and relationship management often supersedes contractual terminology in these cultures. Many executives in international settings recognize that seeking legislative retribution for contract noncompliance is often a nonproductive outlet, especially given the uncertain and risk-laden environment for many judicial disputes. As such, many companies seek to resolve issues through a process known as "preventive contracting," which involves spending more time in the initial contracting stages to fully understand stakeholder requirements, expectations, and repeated communication of expectations, to gain a full understanding of elements. Another important element is the need for flexibility in contractual terms and clauses, to facilitate mutual benefit for the sustenance of the relationship, given highly volatile market input factors and uncertain factor demands.

These issues were reflected in a recent study[1] in which a number of interviews with key individuals discussed some of the challenges they had experienced in global contracting environments:

"Our global corporate culture demands ultimate flexibility from the supplier. We will give you no demand forecast, and we expect you to do it. We can also terminate at will and

will retain all of the IP rights—so all the flexibility is on our side. Strangely enough, suppliers see this as unreasonable. So when they see that, they will of course assign costs to this requirement. We are blind, as we force them to give us all the flexibility, as if there is NO COST to doing so! We need to have some flexibility in establishing price redetermination clauses, and have the ability to tie it into quantity discounts. However, we are unable to stick to any forecast or production curve, which presents a huge risk in the marketplace. We cannot give suppliers a forecast that they can depend on.

What we need to do is to be able to break the contract into three key chunks: (a) standard T's and C's with basic housekeeping elements, which we know we can get right, (b) commercial terms for this specific deal around quality and price determination, and (c) actual pricing structures, which reflect the changes in the marketplace. This is the biggest challenge for us on a global contractual basis."

In considering the challenges around contracts, Louis Brown, the father of preventive law, who wrote the now-famous Manual of Preventive Law,[2] noted the following:

"It usually costs less to avoid getting into trouble than to pay for getting out of trouble."

What this means is that contracts are a critical juncture for determining the success or failure of a commercial relationship. It is better to spend the time up front to discuss expectations, define specific language and terminology, and ensure 100 percent communication of potential contingencies than fight a lawsuit later on when things go wrong. Despite the obvious simplicity of this statement, firms continue to fight lawsuits at an escalating rate, and firms continue to expend extraordinary funds on legal dispute resolution and lawsuits. One executive noted the following:

"We have a legal counsel to avoid litigation. We will do everything possible to stay out of the court systems—because it always costs money to do so. We do not want to be involved in appearances of the big bad Fortune 100 company versus the little supplier. Ethically we seek to do the right thing. We will settle and go to extremes to stay out of the press. Disagreements around labor contracts with consultants and manpower people are one of our biggest headaches. Suppliers who are supplying IT labor to us seem to cause a big problem. We buy $12 billion of labor annually and a lot of this is with smaller companies. We have been proactive in leveraging of labor spend. We appear to use global suppliers, but in reality they will outsource and tier down to a second- or third-tier supplier. Unfortunately, if we push down to a supplier in their first year, $5 million worth of business, and they have no credit line, many are not able to handle the business, and default with their second-tier suppliers. We want to deal only with first tier from a leveraged standpoint, but the complaints still bubble up. And we end up having to resolve the conflicts and try to keep it out of court and out of the press."

Because supply professionals buy products and services as a career, it is not surprising that they deal regularly with contracts and complicated Tier 1 and Tier 2 supplier contracts. It is therefore critical for supply managers to understand the underlying legal aspects of business transactions and develop the skills to manage those contracts and agreements on a day-to-day basis. Once a contract has been negotiated and signed, the real work begins. From the moment of signing, it is the supply manager's responsibility to ensure that all of the terms and conditions of the agreement are fulfilled. If the terms and conditions of a contract are breached, purchasing is also responsible for resolving the conflict. In a perfect world, there would be no need for a contract, and all deals would be sealed with a handshake. However, contracts are an important part of managing buyer-supplier relationships, as they explicitly define the roles and responsibilities of both parties, as well as how conflicts will be resolved if they occur (which they almost always do!).

The importance of understanding contracts is even greater in the age of electronic commerce. In early 2000, President Clinton signed the Electronic Signatures in Global and National Commerce Act, which recognizes electronic signatures as equivalent to hard copies. However, there are important exceptions for noncommercial contracts such as divorce settlements, wills, and many other types of contracts where electronic signatures do not have legal parity with written signatures. This law facilitates the full integration of business transactions via the Internet and was a major stepping-stone to future developments in electronic commerce. However, the importance of understanding contracts and "reading the fine print" should not be overshadowed by this event. In fact, it makes the role of contracts even more important in the Internet age.

This chapter addresses contracting from several perspectives. The first sections address the core elements of a contract and how purchasing managers go about writing a contract. Then, the different types of contracts available to purchasing managers are described. The next section deals with an important type of contract being used more in purchasing scenarios: long-term contracts and alliance agreements. In the next section, we discuss a number of unique contracts, involving information systems deployment, minority business contracts, consulting, and construction. In the final section, we conclude with an important element: how to settle contractual disputes in a buyer-supplier relationship when they arise.

Elements of a Contract

Although there are significant differences in the specific wording and details of contracts employed by supply managers for sourcing products, processes, and services, the structures of contracts used in purchasing products and services are fairly standard and have a number of common attributes. In general, these attributes are established by a firm's legal counsel and then are modified for different types of suppliers, products, and services. The important point to remember is that contracts establish the terms and conditions by which two parties agree to conduct business. They define the type of relationship and pave the way for ensuring that both parties come away with mutual benefits. As such, it is always better to spend more time in negotiations to ensure that the right terminology, measures, and requirements are spelled out in detail and agreed to. If both parties are clear about their understanding of how they will work together, the likelihood that there will be problems and misunderstandings is reduced significantly. It is much more difficult to go back and negotiate what contractual terms actually mean once the contract has been signed and a period of time has passed. In this regard, contracts are sometimes compared to human relationships and nuptial vows; you'd better define your understanding of what the expectations will be early on, rather than try to define expectations after the marriage has taken place.

A contract typically begins with an introduction of the parties who will be engaged in the contract. For example, it might begin with the following:

THIS AGREEMENT IS MADE _____ this day of _____ 2010

BETWEEN

1. ABC COMPANY LIMITED, a company registered in England and having its registered office at 44 Downing Street, London (the "Buyer") and

2. XYZ, INC., a corporation duly organized under the laws of the State of Illinois and having its principal place of business at 123 Ridge Road, Chicago, Illinois 60014, U.S.A. (the "Supplier").

Following the introduction, there are several numbered sections (called "clauses") that describe the different sets of conditions that the parties agree to follow in their conduct of their business relationship. These clauses in the first part of the contract may also refer to a series of "schedules" that provide specific details behind the clauses. These schedules may provide additional information on the method of manufacture, the statement of work, how to calculate specific measures, health and safety requirements, pricing schedules, and other important details. The schedules (which are typically contained in the appendices at the end of the contract) are where the real "meat" of the negotiations has often taken place. It is in these schedule sections that supply managers should spend the bulk of their time determining the operational requirements for the relationship (e.g., price, quality, delivery, service) with specific metrics and deliverables identified. The clearer these schedules are in terms of providing details, specific formulas, websites for price indices, and so forth, the less likely that there will be a conflict. The following example of a specific contract between two companies (a large Fortune 500 company and a mid-sized service supplier) is used to illustrate typical contract structures with clauses and schedules. Bear in mind that there will be major variations in the details of a contract, but the contract structure that follows is fairly representative of what most supply management students will use in contract negotiations.

1. *Definitions.* This section defines all of the important terms contained within the contract and is important so everyone understands exactly what each term means. It is better to get this clear up front, to avoid confusion later on. Some of the typical terms might include the product or service definition and terms such as raw materials, purchase orders (POs), on-time delivery, and price. Although these might seem obvious to some people, if it is in writing, it is clear.

2. *Scope of Agreement.* This section defines what is in and out of scope. This might include the geographical limitations, the validity or invalidity of prior contracts, preferential treatment by the supplier, or other elements.

3. *Purchase Orders.* This section outlines the relationship between the Agreement and any other purchase orders issued by the company to the supplier. For example, it might state that "Any Purchase Order for Products submitted by a Buyer affiliate during the term of this Agreement shall be deemed to be on the terms and conditions set out in this Agreement." This also stipulates what happens if a purchase order is cancelled and what happens if terms conflict between the PO and the Agreement, and which document supersedes which.

4. *Supply and Delivery.* This clause specifies the terms for supply and delivery of the product or service. For instance, if there is a 10-day lead time stipulated between order placement and delivery, what happens if the supplier does not deliver in time? This clause may also reference an appendix that provides additional details on how delivery is measured, what is considered on-time delivery, what are the penalties for late delivery, and other details.

5. *Specifications, Quality, and Health, Safety, Environment.* This clause describes method of manufacture and quality requirements, and may include language specific to terms of quality (e.g., "The Products delivered under this Agreement shall be manufactured in conformity with any mandatory requirements of applicable law in the country of origin or supply and any international standards relevant to such Products."). Charges for delivery of off-specification products or services may also be identified in the appendix. For services, a Statement of Work contained in the appendix will provide details of the exact scope of work to be performed and the service quality expectations. Finally, elements associated with safety, health, and environmental standards are identified in terms of expectations from the supplier.

6. *Payment.* This section may specify terms such as "current price," "prior price," and other criteria that determine how or if prices will be adjusted over the course of the contract. Again, details of how often prices will change and any indices associated with pricing change agreements or related to cost-savings sharing are identified in a schedule in the appendix.

7. *Liability.* This can sometimes be a contentious clause and may often contain language such as "The Supplier shall assume entire responsibility for and shall defend, indemnify and hold Buyer and Buyer's Affiliates harmless against all losses, liabilities, costs and expenses arising directly or indirectly out of, or in connection with, this Agreement or any Purchase Order and arising from injury or damage to the property of the Supplier." The clause generally specifies who is responsible if there are injuries or damage, over the course of the contract, and any damages to be paid. This may also include insurance requirements and sub-supplier issues as they arise.

8. *Force Majeure.* This clause describes the course of events that occur if there are unforeseen calamities such as earthquakes or hurricanes that prevent a supplier from fulfilling its obligations to the buyer. Generally, this clause includes language such as "The party whose performance of this Agreement is so affected shall notify the other party as soon as is reasonably practicable giving the full relevant particulars and shall use its reasonable efforts to remedy the situation immediately."

9. *Effective Date and Termination.* This clause states when the contract becomes effective, when it terminates, and any agreements relating to conditions when the contract can be extended beyond the termination date. It also stipulates whether either party has the ability to terminate the contract at any time, and how much advance notice must be given.

10. *Intellectual Property.* This clause specifies conditions regarding who owns any intellectual property (IP) that comes out of the agreement, and who owns what IP going into the agreement. If an innovation comes out of the agreement, there may also be stipulations as to who owns the "residuals" of that IP.

11. *Assignment and Contracting.* This clause stipulates whether the supplier can assign its rights described in the agreement to another party, and whether subcontracting is permissible.

12. *Technology Improvements.* If the buyer becomes aware of any technology or cost improvements of other products in the market, this section may specify whether they can share this information with the supplier, and how the supplier should act on this information.

13. *Most Favored Customer.* This clause states whether the buyer can expect to receive preferential status over the supplier's other customers. This is not only difficult to measure, but also difficult to enforce, so it is not always used in practice.

14. *Confidentiality.* This clause ensures that all information, technology, and so on shared between the parties remains confidential and is not shared with other customers or suppliers.

15. *Statistics.* This clause provides guidelines regarding what type of reporting statistics and measures the supplier must provide to the buyer on a regular basis, defined clearly. Additional details may be in a schedule in the appendix.

16. *Key Performance Indicators and Compensation.* This clause provides specific details on how the supplier's performance will be measured and if any compensation will be awarded by the supplier to the buyer if these defined levels of performance are not maintained. For example, if delivery falls below 90 percent, there may be a penalty the supplier will need to pay.

17. *Notices.* This clause establishes where bills, invoices, notices, and other documents should be sent, as well as the key contact person at the buying and supplying company to whom to direct all questions and issues concerning the relationship.

18. *Severability.* This clause describes how an issue will be addressed if a portion of the agreement is void or unenforceable, and which court of law will resolve the difference.

19. *Third-Party Rights.* This clause stipulates that any benefits attributed to a third party (other than the buyer and supplier) identified in the contract must be enforced. For example, if there is a bank that handles transactions between the two and charges a fee, this fee must be paid by the parties according to the agreement.

20. *Free Trade Areas.* This clause identifies any free trade issues and benefits, and how to share the benefits.

21. *Minority- or Women-Owned Business Enterprises.* This clause stipulates that the supplier agrees to use its best efforts to support MWBE (Minority- and Women-Owned Business Enterprises) purchasing or that a certain percentage of its business must be awarded to MWBE enterprises.

22. *General.* Any other general business principles.

23. *Governing Law.* This clause stipulates the court of law where any disputes will be settled. This clause contains language such as "Mandatory application of local law or a statement to the contrary in the relevant Purchase Order, which is agreed upon by the Supplier, shall be exclusively governed by the laws of England." This clause may also stipulate the use of arbitration or other forms of conflict resolution (described later in this chapter).

24. *Signatures*

IN WITNESS WHEREOF this Agreement has been duly executed by the parties hereto, the day and year first above written.

ABC COMPANY LIMITED

By: _____

Name: _____

Title: _____

XYZ, INC.

By: _____

Name: _____

Title: _____

An example of schedules that may be used in the appendices include the following:

Schedule 1: Product/process/service specifications, statement of work, or scope of work

Schedule 2: Prices and price adjustment mechanisms

Schedule 3: Health, safety, and environmental guidelines and requirements

Schedule 4: Packaging materials

Schedule 5: Approved method of manufacture, delivery, or service deployment

Schedule 6: Delivery targets and lead times

Schedule 7: Supplier's hours of operation

Schedule 8: Storage and inventory control

Schedule 9: Quality assurance manual

Schedule 10: Loss allowance calculations and throughput allowances

Sourcing Snapshot

Was BP the Only One At Fault on the Spill?

It has become apparent that errors in judgment of workers on the Deepwater Horizon drilling plat-form probably caused the explosion that destroyed the rig and triggered a huge oil spill in the Gulf of Mexico.

But whose errors were they? Was BP, Transocean or Halliburton to blame?

BP informed congressional investigators that a "fundamental mistake" was the most likely cause of the gas blowout that destroyed the Deepwater Horizon. Workers on the rig continued with work to complete the well that gushed millions of barrels of oil into the Gulf despite clear warnings of a "very large abnormality" in pressure tests. These results signaled that cement sealing the well may have failed, and a dangerous gas bubble had built up in the wellbore. The workers who overlooked the warnings may have sealed the rig's fate.

After a month of obfuscation about what actually happened the night of the disaster, these are welcome revelations. But that's where the clarity ends. BP's testimony to Congress apparently did not identify who was responsible for making the decision to push ahead with the well despite the dangers, or why they chose that course of action.

So the finger-pointing continues.

BP argues that most of the drilling work on the rig was conducted by Transocean, with oversight from a handful of BP managers. The responsibility for cementing and completing the well lay with oil-services company Halliburton, BP says.

Meanwhile, Transocean and Halliburton say they were acting precisely in accordance with BP's in-structions. There is no question that BP is the party ultimately responsible for whatever happened on the rig, they say.

Until the U.S. authorities investigate and reach their own conclusions about what really happened the night of April 20, 2010, everything is speculation. But when light is finally shed on the incident, three key points will determine who will get the blame and pay the financial cost for an immense disaster.

First, why did the cement in the well fail, allowing a dangerous pocket of gas to build up? Was it a poorly executed cement job? Or was it a poorly designed well, as some industry observers are speculating?

Second, who decided to overlook the worrying results from pressure tests in the wellbore and allow a gas bubble to blast up to the surface and trigger a huge explosion that incinerated 11 men, destroyed the rig, and triggered one of the worst environmental disasters in U.S. history?

And, perhaps most important, why did they make this decision? Was it simple human error, or were there other factors that forced this tragic decision?

The answers to these questions will determine where, and how high, the blame for this disaster ultimately goes.

Source: Herron, J., (2010, May 24) "Errors in Judgment Probably Triggered BP Disaster—but Whose?" Wall Street Journal, A1.

An example of the importance of establishing roles and responsibilities for contractual duties and services is illustrated in the BP Deepwater Horizon snapshot shown above. Expectations and responsibility for safety issues is of particular importance in not just oil and gas contracts, but all contracts.

How to Negotiate and Write a Contract

In negotiating a contract, one would think that purchasers spend more time on the specific elements of performance, not the legal terms. Nothing could be further from the truth! Research by the International Association of Commercial and Contract Management shows that for all the talk about a changing environment, the Top Ten Frequently Negotiated Terms shows no sign that it has affected the behavior or attitudes of those charged with responsibility for setting policy or leading negotiations. True, most corporations continue to issue very mixed messages. They declare a strategic intent to differentiate, to partner, to add value. But at the same time, they send internal messages about control, cost reduction, standardization, and risk avoidance. They highlight the need to be flexible, adaptive, and agile, yet they introduce software tools and measurement systems that enforce compliance and inhibit change. And in their trading relationships, they offer the promise of a match made in heaven—until they introduce the prenuptial agreement and its administrators.

As a result, the value-reduction terms at the top of the "Top Ten Negotiated Items" list include limitations of liability, levels of indemnity, control of intellectual property, rights to terminate, liquidated damages for performance failure, and so on. These are often called "value-reduction" terms because they contribute little or nothing to the quality of the relationship, or the likelihood of its success. They distract from value-add relationships or eliminate the possibility for discussions that can lead to more productive relationships. And they tackle risk in only a very narrow sense—most of these terms are about allocating the consequences of failure. By undermining the framework for collaboration, they often increase the probability of failure.

Moreover, Tim Cummins, the CEO of IACCM, notes that "Companies continue to invest in resources and software systems that focus on control and compliance. Internal measurements are either insufficient or lacking when it comes to the quality or outputs of the contracting process; they do not encourage or prompt change or improvement. They do not require the custodians of terms and conditions to become more innovative or creative in their thinking, or to focus on wider issues of company performance and risk."[3]

One of the biggest problems faced by companies that results in contractual problems is the common habit of simply "reusing" prior contract templates without any material changes to the contract. Most commonly used contracts are developed from earlier contracts that are subsequently modified to fit the situation at hand. Although this procedure minimizes the amount of administrative effort required each time a purchase contract is written, there is a danger in blindly assuming that all past contracts will be appropriate, particularly in dynamic environments where technology changes occur rapidly or where there are few legal precedents. Purchasing managers should keep a contract file and refer to portions of previous contracts to create a contract that uniquely fits the situation at hand.

The most appropriate method of drafting a new contract is to start with a general form (or forms) and samples of past contracts for similar situations. Purchasing managers will often get advice from the legal department or appropriate counsel and create several different general forms for the various types of purchase situations that may be routinely encountered. Verifying the following information will help ensure that the contract is appropriate:[4]

- The contract identifies clearly what is being bought and the cost.
- The contract specifies how the purchased item is going to be shipped and delivered.
- The contract covers the question of how the items are to be installed (if installation is to be a part of the contract).
- The contract includes an acceptance provision detailing exactly how and when the purchaser will accept the products.
- The contract addresses the appropriate warranties.
- The contract spells out remedies including liquidated damages and clauses specifying the consequences for late performance.
- The contract does a good job on the "boilerplate," which includes the standard terms and conditions common to all contracts and purchase agreements. It is common among these clauses to include a force majeure clause that identifies the conditions under which performance is excused. Common items included in a force majeure clause are war, embargo, and changes in the law.

The purchasing manager should consider arbitration or other dispute resolution mechanisms for inclusion in the contract. The advantages of arbitration are important: Arbitration is fast and confidential, with less variance in outcome or damage awards, and it is not appealable. It is always a good idea to double-check all attachments to the contract, because many of the technical details are included there.

Technical sections of the contract are typically the greatest source of misinterpretation of terms and conditions. For instance, if the contract contains a clause that says, "This is the entire agreement," remember that this means exactly what it says; there are no other additions or modifications to the agreement that are enforceable. This is called an "integration clause" and should be located near the end of the contract.

In developing international contracts, purchasing managers should pay particular attention to the following details:[5]

- *Forum selection.* In the event of a dispute, where would the arbitration forum for resolving the dispute take place?
- *Choice of law.* The parties to an international contract should agree on the contract law that will govern the contract in the event of a dispute.
- *Payment.* What currency will be used to make payments under the contract?
- *Language.* The contract should specify the official language to be used in the contract, as translations are not exact.
- *Force majeure.* It is common in international contracts to excuse performance when events take place that make performance as called for in the contract impossible. Force majeure clauses typically excuse performance when war, natural disasters, or political upheaval occurs.

Types of Contracts

Purchasing contracts can be classified into different categories based on their characteristics and purpose. Almost all purchasing contracts are based on some form of pricing mechanism and can be categorized as a variation on two basic types: fixed-price and cost-based

Exhibit 14.1	Types of Contracts		
TYPE OF CONTRACT	**DESCRIPTION**	**BUYER RISK**	**SUPPLIER RISK**
Firm fixed price	Price stated in the agreement does not change, regardless of any type of environmental change.	Low	High
Fixed price with escalation/de-escalation	Base prices can increase or decrease based on specific identifiable changes in material prices.		
Fixed price with redetermination	Initial target price based on best-guess estimates of labor and materials, then renegotiated once a specific level or volume of production is reached.		
Fixed price with incentives	Initial target price based on best-guess estimates of labor and materials, then cost savings because of supplier initiatives are shared at a predetermined rate for a designated time period.		
Cost plus incentive fee	Base price is based on allowable supplier costs, and any cost savings are shared between the buyer and supplier based on a predetermined rate for a designated time period.		
Cost sharing	Actual allowable costs are shared between parties on a predetermined percentage basis and may include cost productivity improvement goals.		
Time and materials contract	Supplier is paid for all labor and materials according to a specified labor, overhead, profit, and material rate.		
Cost plus fixed fee	Supplier receives reimbursement for all allowable costs up to a predetermined amount, plus a fixed fee, which is a percentage of the targeted cost of the good or service.	High	Low

contracts. As described earlier, the general description of the type of price/cost mechanism is contained in the "Payment" clause, but the actual details describing the specific nature of the pricing formula, cost elements, pricing index, or other elements is typically described in a schedule in the appendices. If a specific formula-based pricing or costing model is going to be used, it is also a good idea to include an example in the schedule that shows how the price or cost should be calculated given the data that is available, so everyone clearly understands how the calculation occurs. The major types of contracts are shown in Exhibit 14.1.

Fixed-Price Contracts

Firm Fixed Price

The most basic contractual pricing mechanism is called a firm fixed price. In this type of purchase contract, the price stated in the agreement does not change, regardless of fluctuations in general overall economic conditions, industry competition, levels of supply, market prices, or other environmental changes. This contract price can be obtained through any number of pricing mechanisms: price quotations, supplier responses to the buying organization's requests for proposal, negotiations, or any other method. Fixed-price contracts are the simplest and easiest for purchasing to manage because there is no need for extensive auditing or additional input from the purchasing side.

If market prices for a purchased good or service rise above the stated contract price, the seller bears the brunt of the financial loss. However, if the market price falls below the stated contract price because of outside factors such as competition, changes in technology, or raw material prices, the purchaser assumes the risk or financial loss. If there is a high level of uncertainty from the supplying organization's point of view regarding its ability to make a reasonable profit under competitive fixed-price conditions, then the supplier may add to its price to cover potential increases in component, raw material, or labor prices. If the supplier increases its contract price in anticipation of rising costs, and the anticipated conditions do not occur, then the purchaser has paid too high a price for the good or service. For this reason, it is very important for the purchasing organization to adequately understand existing market conditions prior to signing a fixed-price contract to prevent contingency pricing from adversely affecting the total cost of the purchase over the life of the contract.

Fixed-Price Contract with Escalation

There are a number of variations on the basic firm fixed-price contract. If the item being purchased is to be supplied over a longer time period and there is a high probability that costs will increase, then the parties may choose to negotiate an escalation clause into the basic contract, resulting in a fixed-price contract with escalation. Escalation clauses allow either increases or decreases in the base price, depending on the circumstances. A greater degree of price protection is therefore provided for the supplier, whereas the purchaser enjoys potential price reductions. All price changes should be keyed to a third-party price index, preferably to a well-established, widely published index (such as the Producer Price Index for a specific material).

Fixed-Price Contract with Redetermination

In cases where the parties cannot accurately predict labor or material costs and quantities to be used prior to the execution of the purchase agreement (e.g., an unproven technology), a fixed-price contract with redetermination may be more appropriate. In this scenario, the buying and selling parties negotiate an initial target price based on best-guess estimates of the labor and materials to be used in manufacturing a new product. Once a contractually agreed-upon volume of production has been reached, the two parties review the production process and redetermine a revised firm price. Depending on the circumstances surrounding the contract, the redetermined price may be applied only to production following the redetermination, or it may be applied to all or part of the units previously produced. Care should be taken, though, because a contract that calls for an agreement to agree in the future is not enforceable.

Fixed-Price Contract with Incentives

A final type of fixed-price contract is the fixed-price contract with incentives. This contract is similar to the fixed-price contract with redetermination except that the terms and conditions of the contract allow cost-savings sharing with the supplier. As in the redetermination contract, it is difficult for the buying and selling parties to arrive at a firm price prior to actual production.

If the supplier can demonstrate actual cost savings through production efficiencies or substitution of materials, the resulting savings from the initial price targets are shared between the supplier and the purchaser at a predetermined rate. This type of purchase contract is typically utilized under conditions of high unit cost and relatively long lead times. The sharing of cost savings may be 50/50 (or some other split may be a negotiated part of the contract).

Cost-Based Contracts

Cost-based contracts are appropriate for situations in which there is a risk that a large contingency fee might be included using a fixed-price contract. Cost-based contracts typically represent a lower level of risk of economic loss for suppliers, but they can also result in lower overall costs to the purchaser through careful contract management. It is important for the purchaser to include contractual terms and conditions that require the supplier to carefully monitor and control costs. The two parties to the agreement must agree what costs are to be included in the calculation of the price of the goods or services procured.

Cost-based contracts are generally applicable when the goods or services procured are expensive, complex, and important to the purchasing party or when there is a high degree of uncertainty regarding labor and material costs. Cost-based contracts are generally less favorable to the purchasing party because the threat of financial risk is transferred from the seller to the buyer. There is also a low incentive for the supplier to strive to improve its operations and lower costs (and hence price) to the purchaser. In fact, there is an incentive, at least in the short run, for suppliers to be inefficient in cost-based contracts because they are rewarded with higher prices.

Cost Plus Incentive Fee

Another cost-based contract is the cost plus incentive fee contract. This contract is similar to the fixed-price plus incentive fee contract except that the base price depends on allowable supplier costs rather than on a fixed-price basis.

As before, if the supplier is able to improve efficiency or material usage as compared with the initial target cost, then the buying and selling parties will share any cost savings at a predetermined rate. This type of contract is appropriate for cases where both parties are relatively certain about the accuracy of the initial target cost estimates.

Cost-Sharing Contract

With pure cost-sharing contracts, allowable costs are shared between the parties on a predetermined percentage basis. The key to successful negotiation is the identification of a firm set of operating guidelines, goals, and objectives for the contract. When in doubt, the two parties to a cost-sharing contract need to spell out their expectations in as much detail as possible to avoid confusion and misunderstanding regarding their respective roles and responsibilities. Cost-sharing contracts are especially important during a period when raw material prices are increasing. The contract schedule detailing how both parties can share the expense of increasing input costs can prevent major problems and may also ensure that the supplier does not go bankrupt because of its inability to produce the product at a fixed price when the cost of materials is going up. The Sourcing Snapshot for Delphi illustrates the importance of on-going communication and continuous improvement as an important component of contracts, especially in times of financial difficulty. The snapshot on Honda shows the challenges in maintaining a fixed price contract when operating in China.

Time and Materials Contract

Another cost-based contract is the time and materials contract. This type of contract is generally used in plant and equipment maintenance agreements, where the supplier cannot determine accurate costs prior to the repair service. The contract should spell out the appropriate labor rate (generally computed on a per-hour basis), plus an overhead and profit percentage, resulting in a "not-to-exceed" total price. With these terms and conditions, the purchaser has little control over the estimated maximum price. Thus labor hours spent should be carefully audited over the life of the contract.

Sourcing Snapshot

Building Supplier Relationships in the Automotive Industry

Jon Steger served as the General Director of Global Purchasing at Delphi Corporation from 2005 to 2008, and encountered many challenges as the Tier 1 automotive company experienced significant economic challenges. In an interview, he emphasized the importance of communication and supplier relationship management that went beyond contracts as key to keeping the company's operations working. Jon noted,

"As we worked through many difficult situations at Delphi in the past three years, proactive communication was the key to mitigating much of the inherent risk in the relationship. I chaired a weekly meeting with the global category managers to provide the visibility and escalation to ensure that we were working on the issues with all appropriate levels of management, engaging treasury when we needed to work with our supplier's CFO or even their banks when the concern level was heightened. Our buyers learned that there are many elements of the relationship that can be enhanced with great communication, which was a great transformation for many of them who for years were price quotes. Traditionally GM (and Delphi) had the belief that all suppliers were basically disposable and as a result GM and Delphi had a "best in class" process for supplier crisis replacement. I changed that about 18 months ago with inception of a department focused on proactive mitigation of supplier risk. Much of this process was based on getting early signals from buyer communication regarding strains or stresses in the relationship. We then used tools such as supplier development and some of our advanced financial analysis from our finance and cost managers to evaluate methods to stabilize and mitigate supplier risk by helping solve the problems that were driving them toward crisis."

Source: Interview with Jon Stegner (December, 2009), Supply Chain Resource Cooperative meeting.

Cost Plus Fixed-Fee Contract

In a cost plus fixed-fee contract, the supplier receives reimbursement for all of its allowable costs up to a predetermined amount plus a fixed fee, which typically represents a percentage of the targeted cost of the good or service being procured. Although the supplier is guaranteed at least a minimal profit above its allowable costs, there is little motivation for the supplier to dramatically improve its costs over the life of the contract. The U.S. military has been highly criticized for using such contracts on a routine basis with suppliers, which are making above-normal profits for commonly used goods and services at the expense of taxpayers.

To be most effective, cost-based contracts should include cost productivity improvements to drive continuous cost reduction over the life of the contract.

Considerations When Selecting Contract Types

Among the more important factors to consider when negotiating with a supplier over contract type are the following (see Exhibit 14.2):

1. Component market uncertainty
2. Long-term agreements
3. Degree of trust between buyer and seller

Exhibit 14.2	Desirability of Using Contracts under Different Conditions

ENVIRONMENTAL CONDITION	FIXED-PRICE CONTRACT	INCENTIVE CONTRACT	COST-BASED CONTRACT
High component market uncertainty	Low	Desirability of use ←————————————→	High
Long-term agreements	Low	←————————————→	High
High degree of trust between buyer and seller	Low	←————————————→	High
High process/technology uncertainty	Low	←————————————→	High
Supplier's ability to affect costs	Low	←————————————→	High
High dollar value purchase	Low	←————————————→	High

4. Process or technology uncertainty

5. Supplier's ability to impact costs

6. Total dollar value of the purchase

The first of these factors, component market uncertainty, refers to the volatility of pricing conditions for major elements of the product, such as raw materials, purchased components, and labor. The more unstable the underlying factor market prices, either upward or downward, the less appropriate a fixed-price contract will be for the two parties. Increasing factor market prices will place more risk on the supplying organization, whereas decreasing such prices will shift the contract economic risk to the purchasing party. (This condition also applies in the case of unstable currency exchange rates in contracts with international suppliers.)

The length of the purchase agreement can also have a significant impact on the desirability of different contract types. The longer the term of the purchase agreement, the less likely firm fixed-price contracts will be acceptable to the supplier. For on-going purchase arrangements, suppliers will generally prefer to employ fixed price with escalation or any of the cost-based contracts, because they incur less economic risk for the selling party. Purchasing managers must therefore evaluate the economic risk of the different contract types and make a decision as to the acceptability of each type for the entire length of the agreement. For most short-term contracts and in conditions of stable component factor markets, firm fixed and fixed-price with redetermination contracts can safely be applied. The choice of contract type is also dependent on the nature of the buyer-seller relationship.

If the relationship has been mutually beneficial in the past and has existed for a considerable period of time, a greater degree of trust may have developed between buying and selling parties. In such cases, both buyer and supplier are more likely to cooperate in the determination of allowable costs, thereby preferring cost-based purchase agreements.

For products and services characterized by high process or technological uncertainty, fixed-price contracts are less desirable for the seller. However, if the purchaser has a reasonable estimate of the supplier's cost structure, then cost-based contracts may be preferable because they allow the price to be adjusted either upward or downward, depending on the efforts of the supplier. If the supplier can potentially reduce costs through continuous improvement, then an incentive-type contract may prove beneficial to both contracting parties.

As the total dollar value/unit cost of the contract increases, purchasers must spend more effort creating effective pricing mechanisms. The contracting parties must consider each of the factors in Exhibit 14.2 in detail, as well as the total impact of the contract over the lifetime of the agreement. It is important to remember that both parties in a contract must benefit (although not necessarily in the same proportion).

Long-Term Contracts in Alliances and Partnerships

A common method of classifying industrial buying contracts is based on the length of the contract term. **Spot contracts** are defined as those purchases that are made on a nonrecurring or limited basis with little or no intention of developing an ongoing relationship with the supplier. **Short-term contracts** are defined as contract purchases that are routinely made over a relatively limited time horizon, typically one year or less. **Long-term contracts** are contract purchases that are made on a continuing basis for a specified or indefinite period of time, typically exceeding one year. Because long-term contracts involve greater commitments into the future, the contractual terms and conditions must be carefully developed. In this section we focus primarily on long-term contracts, but a number of the considerations covered may apply to shorter-term agreements as well.

Benefits of Long-Term Contracts

Regardless of the terminology used, almost all buyer-seller relationships have a contract (even if it is implied) that govern them. Even when there is no contract, most transactions are covered by a "gap filler" known as the Uniform Commercial Code (UCC), covered in the next chapter. The contract itself is a formal symbol indicating that these joint responsibilities and expectations exist. Effective long-term contracts (with a duration of more than one year) generally have specific and measurable objectives clearly stated in them, including pricing mechanisms, delivery terms, quality standards and improvements, productivity improvements, cost-savings sharing, evergreen clauses, risk sharing, conflict and dispute resolution, and termination of the relationship. Because long-term contracts are increasingly being used in industry, it is worthwhile to discuss the attributes, advantages, and risks of this approach in detail.

Why would a buying organization consider a long-term contract with a supplier? In a general sense, the buyer usually expects a greater level of commitment from a supplier involved in a long-term contract. Long-term contracts can also result in an opportunity for creating joint value between the contracting parties. Joint value can be enhanced through the sharing of information, risk, schedules, costs, needs, and even resources. In addition, a long-term contract serves as a blueprint or guide for the relationship between the buyer and the supplier. It typically delineates initial price, mechanisms for price adjustments, cost-reduction expectations, intellectual properties such as patents and copyrights, and currency adjustment procedures, as well as any other responsibilities.

There are many reasons why both buyers and suppliers would want to consider a long-term contract (see Exhibit 14.3). These are discussed in more detail here.

Assurance of Supply

Perhaps the most compelling reason to consider a long-term contract, from the buyer's perspective, is that such contracts may reduce the level of risk incurred if shorter-term contracts are employed. By committing to a clearly defined, concise, and mutually beneficial long-term agreement, buyers can reasonably assure themselves of a continued source

Exhibit 14.3	Advantages and Disadvantages of Long-Term Contracts

POTENTIAL ADVANTAGES	POTENTIAL DISADVANTAGES
Assurance of supply	Supplier opportunism
Access to supplier technology	Selecting the wrong supplier
Access to cost/price information	Supplier volume uncertainty
Volume leveraging	Supplier forgoes other business
Supplier receives better information for planning	Buyer is unreasonable

of supply, particularly important if the material, product, part, or component being procured is subject to potentially severe supply disruptions or extreme variations in quality, price, availability, or delivery. "Most Favored Customer" clauses are especially important when committing to these types of agreements.

Access to Supplier Technology

Long-term contracts can help the buyer to gain exclusive access to proprietary supplier technology. Blocking competitor access to this supplier technology through a long-term exclusivity contract can result in at least a short-term competitive advantage for the buyer. Tying up a supplier in the initial introductory stage of a new or dramatically improved technology product life cycle either forces competitors to spend valuable time and effort searching for a comparable technology elsewhere, or it means they have to develop it internally. The buying firm therefore can reach the marketplace first and establish a "first mover" advantage. The potential risk here is that the buyer must be forward-looking enough to choose suppliers with the most promising or most marketable technology, at the peril of locking themselves into the wrong technology and losing their expected competitive advantage.

Access to Cost/Price Information

Agreeing to a long-term contract frequently allows the buyer to have access to more detailed cost and price information from the supplier in exchange for the extended contract term. Longer-term contracts create greater incentives for suppliers to improve or expand their processes through capital improvements because they are able to spread their fixed costs over a larger volume. Long-term contracts should be written to include incentive or cost-sharing arrangements (written into a schedule) that reward the supplier for making improvements in its processes along with passing some of the cost savings to the buyer. This additional supplier investment can also result in higher product quality as well as lower costs. Joint buyer-seller teams may work together to improve the supplier's process and divide the resulting savings. The cost-savings sharing terms should be explicitly negotiated and written into the contract (do not assume that the savings will automatically be divided 50/50).

Volume Leveraging

A final benefit of developing a long-term contract is that the buyer can leverage his or her enhanced position to drive the supplier toward a higher rate of performance improvement. Using the added leverage of a long-term, multiyear agreement with the supplier, the buyer can require the supplier to increase its rate of progress up the learning curve and pass along the savings to the buyer at an accelerated rate. This performance improvement can be driven by additional capital investment as described earlier, an accelerated learning curve effect, and a higher level of commitment on behalf of the supplier. Long-term contracts with incentives are based on the notion that as purchase volumes increase, cost structures change. Long-term agreements in cases of increasing volumes should establish productivity improvement goals and cost-savings sharing, where both buyer and seller share in cost reductions achieved. If suppliers are not forthcoming with labor and material cost data, cost models can be developed to improve the buyer's negotiating position using material/labor ratios available from industry databases (see Chapter 11).

Supplier Receives Better Information for Planning

A supplier may have several reasons for preferring a long-term contract. First, the supplier receives better scheduling information, which in turn helps the supplier's production area improve efficiency and materials planning. With less uncertainty in production schedules, the supplier's purchasing departments can buy material in larger quantities, thereby obtaining volume discounts. Second, detailed projections of volumes and delivery dates allow the supplier to better budget the flow of funds and investment stemming from the expectation of continued future volume. In turn, the supplier's organization lowers unit costs, because fixed costs are spread out over a larger number of units. Third, the supplier can realize lower administrative costs over the term of the contract. Less effort is required to seek out and develop replacement volume on an ongoing basis.

Risks of Long-Term Contracts

A buyer or seller must consider a number of risks when evaluating whether a long-term contract is necessary or even desirable. Three primary questions must be asked when developing a long-term contract and considering the risks:

1. What is the potential for opportunism? In other words, how likely is the supplier to take advantage of the purchaser (or vice versa)?
2. Is this the right supplier to engage in a long-term contract?
3. Is there a fair distribution of risk and gains between the parties involved?

Supplier Opportunism

From the buyer's perspective, there is a major risk that the supplier will become too complacent and lose motivation to maintain or improve performance as the contract progresses. Performance deterioration can be observed in a variety of ways: higher price, deteriorating quality and delivery, lagging technology, and increased cycle times. It is important for buyers to build appropriate incentive clauses into their long-term agreements that serve to motivate suppliers to adequately perform as expected over the term of the agreement.

Selecting the Wrong Supplier

An additional risk associated with long-term contracts is the possibility that the best available supplier may not be recognized or chosen to participate in the long-term agreement. It is the buyer's responsibility to conduct adequate research that documents the supplier's past performance, capabilities, financial health and stability, technology road map, and commitment to the relationship.

Once a long-term agreement with a given supplier has been executed, it is much more difficult (and expensive) to switch suppliers. To ensure a successful future relationship, sufficient time and effort must be invested prior to signing a long-term contract.

Supplier Volume Uncertainty

To be successful, a good long-term contract considers the needs of both parties. The buyer must consider a number of issues from the supplier's perspective. The first and foremost is volume uncertainty, particularly when dealing with a new product or a new customer. Although the prospective buyer may indicate to the supplier that a certain purchased volume level may be expected, there are many reasons why that volume might never be achieved. Possible reasons include overforecasting of requirements, lack of marketability of the end item, intense competition in the marketplace, and other environmental considerations such as government regulation. A related reason is that the item being supplied may be in the mature or decline phase of the product life cycle. A long-term contract that indicates volume growth under these circumstances is unlikely ever to be fully realized.

Supplier Forgoes Other Business

Agreeing to a long-term contract that limits the supplier's ability to service the buyer's competitors might lock the supplier out of several profitable business opportunities. Also, when companies agree to supply a particular customer's needs, this precludes them from taking on more profitable business with other customers later on because of a lack of available capacity. This is particularly true in industries that are approaching full capacity.

Buyer Is Unreasonable

Another risk that the supplier must consider is the likelihood of the buyer making extraordinary demands once the contract has been executed. Unforeseen customer demands typically result in higher costs that the supplier may or may not be able to recover under the terms of the agreement.

Contingency Elements of Long-Term Contracts

Effective long-term contracts contain a number of elements that allow for contingencies that may arise during the course of the contract.

Initial Price

A buyer must focus intently on determining an acceptable initial price because over the course of a long-term contract the price adjustment mechanism will use the initial price as the base for future adjustments. An initial price that is too high will cause all following prices to be too high. A buyer needs to be aware that some suppliers often front-load their initial price by including excess profits, which inflates all future prices. Likewise, if the initial price is too low, then the supplier may not be motivated to perform as expected because all future prices will be too low and unprofitable. In a long-term contract the relationship between the parties is immaterial unless both parties gain something during the course of the exchange.

Price-Adjustment Mechanisms

Selecting an appropriate price-adjustment mechanism is also a key consideration in a long-term contract. If future price adjustments are linked to an outside index or the price of a related product, then care should be taken in selecting which index or related product is to be used. Choice of the wrong index or related product can also result in higher prices over the term of the agreement.

Supplier Performance Improvements

Buyers should use long-term agreements to obtain specific supplier performance improvements over time. Again, this compels the buyer to conduct extensive research regarding the supplier's capabilities and past performance, as well as determining the types and levels of risk that might be associated with a particular long-term supply contract. Managers must decide whether the contract should be written for a specific period such as three or five years, or whether the contract should be a series of rolling contracts with an evergreen clause, which renews the agreement at the end of every period.

Evergreen, Penalty, and Escape Clauses

An evergreen clause assumes the contract will be renewed every year unless the supplier is otherwise notified that this is not the case. An effective evergreen clause should be based on a periodic joint review period, typically one year or shorter, and should incorporate a point system that rewards the supplier for acceptable performance. In cases when expectations are not met, the purchasing manager may request specific corrective action and may even charge back lost time and expenses to the supplier.

Associated with the evergreen clause is an escape clause, which allows the buyer (and possibly the supplier) to terminate the contract if either side fails to live up to contractual requirements. However, a long-term contract will usually contain terms and conditions that call for a corrective action process if the supplier continually fails to meet its contractual performance requirements. In such a scenario, the buyer must first notify the supplier within a particular time period if the supplier's performance has not met expectations. The supplier will have a specific time period to take corrective action to bring quality, delivery, and responsiveness to acceptable levels. If the supplier has not achieved contractually acceptable levels of performance within the specified time period, then the buyer can terminate the contract without recourse. Long-term contracts should also contain appropriate clauses covering conflict resolution, termination of the agreement, and handling of unanticipated requirements. Such contingency planning may prolong the contract negotiation period up front but may prove to be invaluable later on should problems occur.

Nontraditional Contracting

In addition to long-term contracts, companies must also create special types of contracts with information systems providers, consultants, minority business owners, and service providers. All of these purchases require unique contractual approaches.

IT Systems Contracts

Systems contracts, also known as systems outsourcing, are designed to provide access to expensive computer networks and software that single companies are unable to afford on their own. Examples of systems contractors include SAP, Oracle, IBM, and EDS.

Subcontracting information technology (IT) requirements to an outside service provider is a major contractual issue for companies. Both legal and purchasing executives from the company should bring their expertise to the table on issues that represent a major cost and commitment for the enterprise. Unfortunately, IT departments often enter into such agreements on the basis of technical evaluation without the benefit of input from purchasing or legal, and later pay in the form of higher costs or poor service requirements contained in the "fine print." Prior to committing to an outsourcing contract with such a service provider, a systems outsourcing team should consider the length of the proposed agreement, the role of company growth or downsizing, service provider defaults or contract amendments, data security, control of outsourcing costs, and control of information systems operations. A number of other issues pertain to IT systems contracting.

Systems Contracting Risks

One of the leading causes for failure of systems contracts is that purchasers get locked into price structures that do not adequately reflect changes that have occurred since the agreement was originally signed. Examples of such changes include dramatic shifts in user demand patterns, dramatically reduced costs for services provided, and quantum leaps in software and hardware technology.

Level of Service

The extent that a systems supplier becomes involved in the buying firm's operation is determined by three basic levels of service: (1) turnkey, (2) modular, and (3) shared. In the turnkey approach, the client company essentially turns over the entire outsourced service at a given point in time. The outsource service provider performs 100 percent of that function for the buying organization. In the modular approach, the outsource service provider takes on only two or three small functions from the client, using a stepping-stone approach. As the service provider and the client company become more at ease with each other and a higher level of trust develops, additional services are shifted from the client to the service provider. In the shared approach, the service provider and the client company share resources and operational control over the outsourced service. Under the best of conditions, outsourcing systems contracts remains a risky proposition because of the nature of uncertainty associated with the transaction. Purchaser negotiations should focus on price, performance, and procedures.

Price

Purchasers should consider negotiating a fixed, all-inclusive fee instead of relying on a flexible pricing system that may or may not accurately reflect changing business conditions. If future changes are anticipated, then the purchaser should carefully think how contract prices should be set to reflect those changes. Critical pricing issues include the payment method and timing, scheduling of work loads, and reporting. There should also be an auditing process to ensure that the work carried out was billed at the appropriate rate and that the right personnel associated with a work rate actually completed the work.

Performance Criteria

Performance considerations for a systems contract should, at a minimum, include specification of the overall business requirements required by the service provider. The acceptance test criteria should be specified before issuing the contract so that both parties completely understand how the outsourcing system is expected to perform. A primary concern for the purchaser is the development of a measurement system for evaluating the service provider over the course of system development.

A major concern with many outsourced system contracts today is that much of this work is going overseas to countries such as India. Programming, call centers, and software design are increasingly being performed by lower-cost workers in these countries. To ensure that the work is performed according to specific criteria, many enterprises are adopting the Software Capability Maturity Model developed by the Software Development Institute and Carnegie Mellon University. This model ensures that the provider complies with specific criteria measuring elements of software development performance.

The more specific the purchaser can be in providing clear goals and objectives for the service provider to meet, the less likely it is that misunderstandings and conflicts will result.

Procedures

In addition to acceptance criteria, systems contracts should also provide a complete conversion plan that details the steps to be taken in converting from an in-house system to the outsourced system. Again, the more specific the purchaser can be in providing this information, the less likely it is that serious problems will occur later. Also, the purchaser should be careful in specifying how to handle technological changes. Updates to the system may often be excessive, so language in the contract needs to be included that specifies the cost of such updates. It is the joint responsibility of the purchasing manager and the supplier to ensure that the technology provided remains current with future needs. Various types of information requirements planning techniques can be beneficial in the earliest systems-planning stages to make sure that the system will actually meet user needs.[6]

Other Service Outsourcing Contracts

The use of outsourcing contracts is not limited strictly to information processing. Other potential applications include the following:

- Facility management services
- Research and development
- Logistics and distribution
- Order entry and customer service operations
- Accounting and audit services

Minority- and Women-Owned Business Enterprise Contracts

There have been programs to stimulate growth of minority-owned businesses in the United States since the late 1960s. The term "minority-owned suppliers" is used by the U.S. government to describe a company that is at least 51 percent owned by minorities such as African Americans, Hispanic Americans, Native Americans, or Asian-Pacific Americans (at one time that status also applied to enterprises that were more than 50 percent owned by women).

Women-owned businesses and firms that are owned by physically disabled people are separate classes of firms with unique designations. The following federal actions were carried out to promote minority-owned businesses:

- Executive Order 11485 (1969): Established by the U.S. Office of Minority Business Enterprise within the Department of Commerce for the purpose of mobilizing federal resources to aid minorities in business.
- Executive Order 11625 (1971): Gives the secretary of commerce the authority to implement federal policy in support of minority business enterprise programs, to provide technical and management assistance to disadvantaged businesses, and to coordinate activities among all federal departments to aid in increasing minority business development.
- Executive Order 11246 (1965): Requires that all contractors that do more than $50,000 worth of business with the federal government must have affirmative

action programs for each job category that is under-represented by minorities. "Underrepresentation" is defined by the 4/5ths Rule, which is the ratio of minority job incumbents relative to their population in the relevant labor market, relative to the ratio of nonminorities relative to their population, for each job category. If that ratio falls below 0.8 (4/5ths), then the company must report to the government its plans for remedying the underrepresentation.

Consulting Contracts

A knowledgeable consultant can often provide an objective point of view and contribute to an analysis of a situation that is not biased in favor of a predetermined solution. An important factor to consider when hiring an outside consultant to perform contract services for a company is that such a person is the purchasing company's agent, not its employee. The distinction is critical because as an agent, the consultant will often maintain ownership of any intellectual properties developed during the consultation. As such, language must be specified in the contract that the intellectual property shared remains with the buyer. Another important element of discussion is regarding "residuals." A residual is new intellectual property (such as tools, methodologies, and knowledge) developed as the result of the interaction between the enterprise and the consulting company. Some companies (such as the Bank of America and others) have specific language in the contract that requires that any residuals created through the contract remain the property of the buyer. This prevents the consultant from taking this knowledge and selling it to a competitor, thereby eliminating the competitive advantage.

There is an automatic determination of copyright ownership unless the consultant and the client company execute an agreement specifically assigning the copyright to the client company. If the consultant were considered an employee, then the firm—not the individual, because of the "works made for hire" concept under U.S. copyright law—would own the copyright. One of the legal means to distinguish an independent contractor consultant from an employee is the presence of a written contract that describes the consultant's expected services and the ability to produce the results of the consultation. Also, if the company does not withhold income taxes, the consultant will normally be viewed as an independent contractor, not an employee.

Consultants will typically consider the following six goals when negotiating a consulting contract for their services:[7]

- Avoidance of misunderstanding
- Maintenance of working independence and freedom
- Assurance of work
- Assurance of payment
- Avoidance of liability
- Prevention of litigation

Perhaps the most important clause of a consulting contract is the assurance of payment.

Typical consulting contracts will demand a large down payment, perhaps as much as one third of the total amount. There are a range of options for payment of the balance due, including percentage of work accomplished and time elapsed. Because of the extensive litigative climate in the business world, contracts written by the consultant will seek to minimize the consultant's exposure to liability and subsequent potential litigation. Language in this section of the contract should spell out exactly what the consultant is, and is not, liable

Sourcing Snapshot

Increasing Labor Costs in China

Around China, foreign companies are overhauling their labor relations and improving benefits for workers as the continuing strike by local Honda Motor Co. employees raises fears of growing labor militancy in a tight job market. The strike and resulting increase in pay at Honda has spilled over, and affected bonuses and labor rates at Daimler AG, as well as to its white collar workers. A representative from Daimler noted, "We are faced with shortages of skilled workers in China, and it's a lot more competitive out there. We want the best people available." Other firms impacted include Copal Electronics, the world's largest contract manufacturer of notebook PCs, and Hon Hai Precision Industry, which produces electronics for Apple and Hewlett Packard. The *Wall Street Journal* reports that foreign companies have become easy targets in the current flare-up of labor unrest in China, even though they often set high standards for how to treat workers—one of the reasons the Chinese government has welcomed foreign investment. "It's always easier for workers [at foreign-owned plants] to gain support from the government, especially if they use nationalism as part of the reasons why they are dissatisfied with their workplace," says Mary Gallager, a professor of political science at the University of Michigan.

Source: Shirouzu, N., Chao, L, and Dean, J. (2010, June 15) "Foreign Firms Act on Labor in China," Wall Street Journal.

for. Consultants will try to identify those circumstances that may cause the project to fail and for which they will disavow any responsibility.

There are two general causes for litigation arising from a principal-client relationship. The first concerns belief on the purchaser's part that the consulting work was not completed in full, within a reasonable time, or properly. The second concern is when the consultant fails to receive the entire fee that he or she believes was due and proper. Consultants will typically avoid litigation whenever possible to avoid negative public relations. Payment clauses, down payments, and installment payments usually include the following terms and conditions:

- Payment on delivery of the final report
- Late-payment penalties
- A negotiable promissory note or a collateralized promissory note
- The inclusion of an arbitration agreement, so that disputes can be resolved quickly and expertly. Arbitrators are specialized, and a contract can call for selection of arbitrators among specialists. Arbitration agreements generally call for confidentiality and for rapid, nonappealable decisions, which can sometimes salvage a business relationship between the client-business and the consultant, whereas such a relationship is unlikely to survive protracted court litigation.

To summarize, it is critical that purchasing develop a standard contract template/format for all consulting/professional services and ensure that users comply with the use of this template. Adoption of a standard contract template provides visibility regarding a company's policy to all potential consultants. Some companies have an online format that can be downloaded from the company intranet, which ensures that all service-level agreements are built in. The entire scope of the project should be defined at this level, with emphasis on the various elements of the scope as independent clauses in the contract. These should include deliverables, deadlines, budget, and so on. If a company utilizes an incentive system to reward or penalize suppliers, it should also be built into the contract. Finally, the contract should allow for renegotiation in case of major scope changes.

Construction Contracts

Many construction contracts involve the owner/purchaser seeking bids from approximately four or five contractors. A typical sequence of events starts with the owner/purchaser determining a base of preferred contractor bidders. The bidders are then contacted prior to distribution of the bid package to ascertain if they are interested in preparing a competitive bid for the proposed construction project. Following the distribution of the bid requests, the purchaser usually holds a prebid meeting with interested bidders to answer any questions that they may have regarding the initial bid documents. All future questions are then submitted to the purchaser in writing to prevent any misunderstanding.

All final bid submissions should consider the stated completion period. The purchaser should require that all bid submissions break the total price into different costs by type, phase, or area. The purchaser should also provide guidance to the bidders regarding how the bidders' indirect costs are to be applied. Contractor overhead costs can be segregated into several categories based on the chosen method of cost allocation or recovery. The following are the most common categories:

- Payroll taxes and insurance premiums
- Field project overhead
- Home office overhead

Construction safety requirements are an important aspect of any construction contract. In selecting from a group of bidders who have already qualified because of past safety performance for the project, the following guidelines should be followed:[8]

1. Make a thorough review of each bidder's written construction safety plan.
2. Before the final selection is made, refer to each bidder's previous injury experience to determine if it is current and if any areas need improvement because of an excessive number of one type of injury from the same hazard. Check with government sources such as OSHA to see if there have been any recent citations of the bidder and what corrective measures are required. Calls to the state worker compensation authorities may be a good check to determine if there are any claims that have been filed against the contractor for failure to complete work in a timely manner.
3. Make a site visit to current projects on which bidders are working to see firsthand the day-to-day quality and functioning of each bidder's construction safety program. References from past clients should also be researched in detail.

In all of these cases, the purchaser is seeking to determine whether senior managers in the firm have established an accountability system under which supervisors at all levels are held accountable for their subordinates' accidents. Previous research about the effect of top management on safety in construction has found that safety had to be a goal of top management in order for others in the firm to take it seriously. A buyer of construction services who maintains a "hands-off" policy through the use of "hold-harmless" clauses is in for a surprise if an accident occurs; the only way to guarantee reduced liability for accidents is to ensure that fewer accidents occur.[9]

Once a construction contract has been completed, a monthly job cost summary can be used to identify the contractor's total costs. An actual cost system records the amounts actually expended, whereas a standard cost system estimates what the cost should be, based on known parameters. Any claims presented by the contractor must be carefully scrutinized, as the claimed costs may not actually be incurred costs.

Contractors must be able to substantiate their costs by producing records consistently maintained in the normal course of business.

Purchasers can minimize the likelihood of contractor claims through a number of actions. The first is the presence of a realistic timetable that takes into account foreseeable delays because of factors beyond the control of either the contractor or the purchaser. A second action involves setting clear specifications that define exactly what is to be constructed. Last, the design documents created by the architect should be complete and up to date, reflecting any and all changes as they occur. If the contractor presents a claim against the purchaser, the purchaser should insist on the following information, at a minimum, to help determine the accuracy and appropriateness of the contractor's actual costs in the claim:

- A breakdown of the claim by dollar amounts into the greatest possible number of components
- A detailed outline of the derivation of all hourly rates, equipment costs, overhead, and profit
- The underlying assumptions on which the claim is based to help ensure that the claim is not inflated

Contract administrators for construction projects may also wish to employ penalty clauses to avoid prolonged delays in the construction schedule. Technically, penalty clauses are called "liquidated damages clauses." If they are labeled "penalty" clauses, there is a long line of cases that says they are not enforceable. For instance, a liquidated damages fee of $100 to $1,000 per day for every day late can provide strong incentives to the construction firm to meet schedules.

Other Types of Contracts

Some of the other types of contracts that may be encountered by purchasers include the following:

Purchasing Agreements

One type of purchasing agreement groups similar items together for procurement help to reduce the amount of paperwork for numerous and repetitive small orders. Purchasing agreements also increase the buyer's negotiating clout with the supplier by leveraging its volume of business. There are a number of variations of purchasing agreements:

- Annual contracts: Generally run for a 12-month period and may or may not come up for renewal at the end of the year.
- National contracts: Specify that the purchaser will buy a certain amount of goods and services for the duration of the agreement.
- Corporate agreements: Specify that business units within a corporate organization must buy from specific suppliers during the term of the agreement.
- National buying agreements: Nonbinding on either the purchaser or the supplier; typically provide discounts to corporate buyers based on total volume for the corporation as a whole, not for any subunits individually.

- Blanket orders: Typically cover many different items that can be purchased under the same purchase order number, thereby minimizing repetitive paperwork in the purchasing department for relatively low-cost items (e.g., office supplies).
- Pricing agreements: Occur in situations in which a buyer is allowed to automatically discount the published purchase price by a negotiated percentage for all purchases from a given price list or catalog during the contract period.
- Open-ended orders: Similar to blanket orders but allow the addition of items not originally included in the blanket order; may also allow the original purchase order to be extended for a longer term.

Online Catalogs and E-Commerce Contracts

Coupled with the growing trend toward longer-term agreements and consolidated purchasing agreements, many firms have turned to electronic commerce to further reduce their administrative overhead. The use of automated online catalogs by major suppliers of MRO items such as Staples, Grainger, and OfficeMax allows users to buy directly from blanket orders and national contracts from their desktop.

Despite the recent laws validating electronic signatures on contracts, many firms are wary of using electronic contracts and related documents because of a perceived lack of control regarding who is authorized to represent the firm. There are four major issues that buyers and sellers need to be aware of with respect to e-commerce contract:[10]

1. Parity between electronic and paper records. Unless online agreements are enforced, little e-commerce will take place. The prospect of treating electronic records the same as paper records is opposed by many groups. "Record" is the legal term now used to replace "document" or "writing."

2. Enforceability of shrinkwrap, clickwrap, and boxtop agreements and licenses. In many situations, buyers are bound by agreements that are appended to the basic transaction (purchases of goods or transfers of computer software) that have significant legal effects that are not apparent to purchasers at the time of purchase.

3. Attribution procedures. With electronic (mouse-click) purchases, a vendor needs secure mechanisms to be assured that an order received is legitimate. The vendor also wants a procedure that legally points to an individual so that individual's credit card can be debited by the vendor. Accompanying concerns revolve around the conditions under which a vendor can sue a person for an order received online from a website visitor.

4. Digital signatures. With standard paper contracts, signatures have operated to uniquely identify parties to a contract. Recent legislation by Congress attempts to provide several acceptable substitutes for traditional signatures in electronic commerce, but not without some remaining concerns. Article 2 of the UCC is being revised to accommodate e-commerce issues.

Settling Contractual Disputes

All contracts, no matter how carefully worded and prepared, can be subject to some form of dispute or disagreement. It is virtually impossible to negotiate a contract that anticipates every potential source of disagreement between buyer and seller.

Generally speaking, the more complex the nature of the contract and the greater the dollar amounts involved, the more likely it is that a future dispute over interpretation of the terms and conditions will occur. Purchasing managers must therefore attempt to envision

Exhibit 14.4	Means of Settling Contractual Disputes

ACTION	DESCRIPTION
Legal action	File a lawsuit in a federal/state/local court
Nonlegal actions	
Arbitration	Use of an impartial third party to settle a contractual dispute
Mediation	Intervention by a third party to promote settlement, reconciliation, or compromise between parties involved in a contractual dispute
Minitrial	An exchange of information between managers in each organization, followed by negotiation between executives from each organization
Rent-a-judge	A neutral party conducts a "trial" between the parties and is responsible for the final judgment
Dispute prevention	A progressive schedule of negotiation, mediation, arbitration, and legal proceedings agreed to in the contract

the potential for such conflicts and prepare appropriate conflict-resolution mechanisms to deal with such problems should they arise (see Exhibit 14.4). Sourcing Snapshot: Online Dispute Resolution also describes a more recent application of e-commerce technology, where companies are beginning to use online dispute resolution websites to manage contractual conflicts.

The traditional mechanism for resolving contract disputes is grounded in commercial law, which provides a legal jurisdiction in which an impartial judge can hear the facts of the case at hand and render a decision in favor of one party or the other.

Because of the uncertainty, cost, and length of time required to settle a dispute in the U.S. legal system, most buyers and sellers prefer to avoid the problems associated with litigation and deal with the situation in other ways. Taking a dispute into the jurisprudence system should be viewed as a last resort, not an automatic step in resolving contractual disputes.

Legal Alternatives

New methods of settling buyer-seller disputes have evolved in the last several years. These techniques, although diverse in form and nature, have a number of similar characteristics:[11]

- They exist somewhere between the polar alternatives of doing nothing and escalating conflict.

- They are less formal and generally more private than ritualized court battles.

- They permit people with disputes to have more active participation and more control over the processes for solving their own problems than traditional methods of dealing with conflict.

- Almost all of the new methods have been developed in the private sector, although courts and administrative agencies have begun to borrow and adapt some of the more successful techniques.

Perhaps the simplest method of resolving a contractual disagreement involves straightforward, face-to-face negotiation between the two parties involved. Frequently, there are other factors surrounding the dispute that can be brought into consideration by the parties, even though these factors are not directly involved in the dispute at hand. For example, if the buying and selling parties to a contract disagree on the interpretation of the contract's

Sourcing Snapshot

Online Dispute Resolution

As with other aspects of the Internet, innovation in online dispute resolution (ODR) has been rapid. Cybersettle.com is an online mechanism for settling disputes, particularly those that involve insurance companies. Not surprisingly, there are other online vendors offering both mediation and arbitration services. For mediation, there is Online Mediation (www.onlineresolution.com) and MediationNow (www.mediationnow.com). Online arbitration services include Online Resolution-Arbitration (www.onlinesolution.com/index-ow.cfm). According to the latter's website, "Online Arbitration is similar to traditional arbitration, except that all communications take place online. The Online Arbitrator appointed for your case will be an experienced professional, who knows the subject area of your dispute." One advantage of ODR is that through use of the computer, rather than personal appearances, the costs of "attending" negotiations, mediation, and arbitration proceedings are lower. However, it is important to bear in mind that most mechanisms for resolving disputes online are unfamiliar to many businesses. For ODR to serve as an effective mechanism, both parties must agree to use ODR, even though parties unfamiliar with the process will be cautious in trying such a "new" procedure. In order for them to be enforceable, courts must accept ODR results. In at least one case, a federal district court refused to be bound by the results of a proceeding.

Source: Baumer, D.L., and Poindexter, J.C. (2004), *Legal Environment of Business in the Information Age,* New York: McGraw-Hill/Irwin.

terms and conditions regarding delivery, then perhaps they might be able to collaborate on other terms and conditions such as price or scheduling.

When this alternative is exhausted, both parties may become aware of the fact that it is not feasible to agree on suitable alternatives. In such cases, it may be virtually impossible for the parties to negotiate an acceptable resolution of the dispute on a good-faith basis without additional assistance from outside parties.

Arbitration

The use of an outside arbitrator, or third party, to help settle contractual disputes is the fastest-growing method of conflict resolution among contracting parties, both in the United States and overseas. Because of the parties' inability to reach a negotiated settlement, emotional reactions to the problem (frustration, disappointment, and anger) may prevent rational examination of the true underlying causes of the source of disagreement.

The only solution in such cases may be **arbitration**, which is defined as "the submission of a disagreement to one or more impartial persons with the understanding that the parties will abide by the arbitrator's decision."[12] If set up and handled properly, arbitration can serve to protect the interests of both parties to the dispute because it is relatively inexpensive, less time consuming, private, and typically a reasonable solution for all involved.

When writing and negotiating purchase contracts, many purchasing managers include an arbitration clause in the boilerplate terms and conditions. Such a clause typically spells out how the disputing parties will choose an appropriate arbitrator and the types of disputes for which arbitration will be considered. A good source for commercial arbitrators is the American Arbitration Association, which can also handle the administrative burden of the entire process from an impartial point of view. It is important to ensure that the arbitrator's opinion will be binding on both parties to the dispute. A key point to remember here is that adequate advance planning for potential disputes can prevent significant problems later, should an unforeseen conflict arise. Also, it is a good idea to spell out the location and method of conducting the arbitration hearings, particularly if the dispute involves companies or individuals from different states or countries.

When preparing the purchase contract or purchase order, contract managers should consider two factors (in conjunction with the organization's legal counsel), to ensure that the ruling of an arbitrator will be legally binding:

- State statutes must be reviewed to determine whether the state or states in question do, in fact, have such legal provisions allowing arbitration.

- Wording of the arbitration clause should be developed carefully in accordance with state law, federal law (the Federal Arbitration Act), and the guidelines published by the American Arbitration Association.

Purchasing managers wishing to take advantage of the process in their dealings with suppliers should understand several caveats regarding binding arbitration.

Purchasers cannot rely on an arbitration clause contained in their forms, particularly if the supplier's forms do not contain such a clause. If the supplier's forms contain an arbitration clause that is not in the buyer's forms, and the buyer does not want to follow it, the supplier cannot rely on the presence of such a clause. Finally, if both the buying and selling organizations' forms contain arbitration clauses, arbitration will become an enforceable part of the overall agreement.

Other Forms of Conflict Resolution

Along with the rising popularity of arbitration between buyers and sellers, a number of different forms of conflict resolution have been introduced. When people think of the arbitration process, the process that generally comes to mind is mediation—an intervention between conflicting parties to promote reconciliation, settlement, or compromise.

The mediator's responsibilities include listening to the facts presented by both parties, ruling on the appropriateness of documents and other evidence, and rendering judgment on a solution that reconciles the legitimate interests of both disputing parties. Mediation varies from arbitration in that arbitration is binding on both the parties. In the mediation process, however, the disputing parties preserve their right of final decision on the solution proffered by the mediator.

The second type of dispute resolution mechanism is called a minitrial, which is not actually a trial at all. The mini trial is a form of presentation, involving an exchange of information between managers from each organization involved in the dispute.

Once the executives hear both sides of the presentation, they then attempt to resolve the dispute through negotiation with their executive counterparts. Because mini trials are generally more complicated than other forms of negotiation, they are typically used when the dispute between the parties is significant and highly complex. One of the benefits of such a process is that it turns a potential legal conflict into a business decision and promotes a continuing relationship between the parties.

Another related conflict-resolution mechanism is the "rent-a-judge," which is a popular name given to the process by which a court refers a lawsuit pending between the parties to a private, neutral party. The neutral party (often a retired judge) conducts a "trial" as though it were conducted in a real court. If one or both of the parties is dissatisfied with the outcome of the rent-a-judge decision, then the verdict can be appealed through normal appellate channels. In this process, the parties agree to hire a private referee to hear the dispute. Unlike the binding arbitration process, rent-a-judge hearings are subject to legal precedents and rules of evidence.

A final alternative to dispute litigation and dispute resolution that is gaining popularity is dispute prevention, a key factor in the concept of collaborative business relationships such as long-term contracting, partnering, and strategic alliances. When contracting parties initially agree to dispute-prevention processes, a progressive schedule of negotiation, mediation, and arbitration followed by litigation as a last resort can be defined and delineated in the agreement. The "baring of souls" involved in this type of close, collaborative relationship dictates that the two parties fully recognize and agree upon the mechanisms for dispute resolution that are to be utilized under certain conditions.

There are a number of factors to consider when deciding which dispute-resolution mechanism to use. The first, and perhaps foremost, consideration is the status of the relationship between the parties in the dispute. In cases where the relationship between the parties is ongoing and expected to continue for the foreseeable future, the disagreeing parties will prefer to resolve the contract dispute through means that hopefully will preserve the relationship.

The choice of mechanism should also be based on the type of outcome desired by the purchaser. There may be a need to establish an appropriate precedent to govern the purchaser's actions in future disputes as well as the one at hand. Another consideration is whether the disputing parties need to be directly involved in generating the outcome or resolution. The presence of the disputing parties is important to resolving disputes successfully using techniques such as negotiation, arbitration, mediation, mini trials, and rent-a-judge proceedings. Active participation by all parties involved in a dispute generally results in a more equitable and harmonious resolution (as opposed to having third parties such as attorneys involved).

The level of emotion displayed by the principals is another important consideration. If emotions such as anger and frustration are high, the total cost of litigation, in terms of time, money, and management effort, may be more significant than originally anticipated. The following snapshot shows the importance of solid market intelligence when contracting futures for commodity markets, which takes the wind out of any opinions that may arise leading to a dispute.

Sourcing Snapshot

The Future of Contracting

Every year, the International Association of Commercial and Contract Manufacturing (IACCM.com) publishes an update called "the Future of Contracting," hich documents new information and challenges in contracting. IACCM is an organization dedicated to raising individual, organizational and institutional capabilities in contracting and commercial management, providing research, learning, certification, and benchmarking to a global audience. In the 2012 version of this publication, several key trends emerged, as noted below:

- The world's private and public sector leaders believe a rapid escalation of 'complexity' is the biggest challenge confronting them, which is expected to accelerate in the coming years.
- Enterprises today are not equipped to cope effectively with this complexity.

- Creativity is the single most important leadership competency for enterprises seeking a path through this complexity.

In addition, the study predicts several changes in the following years:

- 86% say there will be more international standards
- 78% say there will be a focus on plain language in contracting
- 69% say common law will maintain its dominance as the framework for international contracts
- 62% say there will be greater use of visual techniques such as pictures, graphs, and flowcharts embedded into contracts.

In addition, experts believe that several changes will occur in the relationships between buyers and sellers:

- Seven out of ten experts expect 'the relationship' will integrate more closely with 'the contract'
- The terms negotiated with the greatest frequency remain as Limitation of Liability, Indemnification, and Price Changes.
- During the post-award phase of contract performance, the top three terms, which are most frequently the object of a claim or dispute include Delivery/Acceptance, Price Changes, and Change management.
- Nine out of ten expect rapid growth in the impact of technology
- 71% believe there will be significant changes to performance undertakings and measurements.
- 85% believe the contracting process must become more holistics.

Clearly, this vision is one that promises to increase the importance and level of contract professionalism from its current state. Contracting is rapidly becoming one of the most important areas for procurement excellence.

Source: IACCM, "The Future of Contracting," www.iaccm.com.

Sourcing Snapshot

The Father of Collaborative Negotiation Contracting Passes Away. . . . But Leaves a Lasting Impact

Unless you happened to be reading the *NY Times obituary columns* on September 25, 2012, you wouldn't have noticed that one of the great supply chain innovators of the 20th century, Gerard I. Nierenberg, passed away with little notice. Nierenberg, a lawyer whose frustration with the adversarial nature of legal disputes led him to develop methods of negotiating contracts that he promoted in training seminars and popular books, including *The Art of Negotiating* and *How to Read a Person Like a Book*. He passed away in Manhattan at the ripe old age of 89.

The fact that a lawyer was the one to develop approaches that could avoid contractual disputes, which are so common in today's litigious environment, is an ultimate testimony to how far we have wandered away from the concept of collaboration contracting. What was so unique about Nierenberg was his views that negotiation and contracting was not about "tactics" (like so many negotiation seminars advertise), but about creation of mutual value. His specific message was that in a successful contract negotiation, "everyone wins."

As noted in the Times, Nierenberg had been running a real estate law practice in New York in the early 1960s when he came to the conclusion that he and many other people spent an enormous amount of time negotiating agreements at work and at home and yet had no formal training in how to do it. Too often, he found, negotiating meant trying to win at all costs.

"If you're going to try to make everyone else lose who plays with you, and you think life's a game, how far do you think you're going to get in life?" he said in an interview in 1983. "Everyone's going to try to beat you. And, boy, that makes a hell of a life." He wrote a book on the subject, and started the *Negotiation Institute* that is now run by his son George.

What is also so interesting about Nierenberg is the thinking behind what makes contract negotiation work, which he wrote about in his book. Much of his thinking on negotiating contracts was rooted in his interest in general semantics, a field within linguistics that views words as labels that distract attention from the things they represent. He was interested in "how we know what we know" and how that "locks us into self-limiting the kinds of choices we can make."

How many of the contractual supply chain disputes that we hear about are rooted in the limiting terminology of "indemnification" and "limits of liability," which ultimately locks buyers and sellers and customers into defeatist, obstructive behaviors that prevent the creation of value? How much of negotiation is about "winning," versus really identifying mutual risks and rewards that can be identified, shared, and discussed. How much of contract management is about legal positioning, versus problem-solving?

I think Gerard was probably a fair negotiator. As his wife Juliet noted to the Times, "I could always rely on reminding him, or he would remind me, about the principles of contract negotiation."

Source: Handfield, Robert, "The Father of Collaborative Relationship Management Passes Away," Supply Chain View from the Field, blog, http://scm.ncsu.edu/blog/2012/09/25/the-father-of-collaborative-relationships-passes-away/

The harsh experience of a prolonged court battle has convinced more than one set of potential litigants to consider less costly and more timely dispute-resolution alternatives.

The importance of speed in obtaining a resolution can be a factor determining whether to litigate, mediate, or arbitrate. In many instances the alternatives to court adjudication are quicker than litigation. Time pressures may force the disputing parties to be more creative and understanding in reaching an appropriate resolution short of meeting in court. There is a direct relationship between the time involved in settling a dispute and the cost involved. Quicker resolution is generally cheaper.

The information required to reach a settlement may dictate the mechanism preferred. The closer the parties come to having the courts settle their dispute, the more formal the information requirements. Strict rules of evidence in the courtroom may not be desirable to parties because of publicity. Companies involved in the dispute may not be willing to spread out their dirty linen or trade secrets in public. In addition, the credibility of experts and other witnesses may be more difficult to achieve or maintain in a trial. All of the conflict-resolution mechanisms or settlement options presented here allow a greater degree of privacy to the parties involved than that which can be attained in a court.

Good Practice Example
United Applies Clean Sheets to All Contract Negotiations

When Grace Puma arrived at United Airlines in 2009, she brought with her more than 20 years of experience leading global strategic sourcing organizations for companies such as Kraft Foods, Motorola, and Gillette. Because a major airline like United requires a variety of sourced products and services spanning many different potential contractual forms, she saw an opportunity to implement a standard sourcing process through category management teams focused on driving the lowest total cost of ownership (TCO) in supplier relationships. This occurred through improved alignment with strategic suppliers through collaborative development of relationships. "We set the expectation that our suppliers operate in a transparent and fact-based manner," explains Puma. "Specifically, we discuss opportunities to enhance service performance and drive out cost via supply chain inefficiencies and engage with key partners on driving innovative solutions to increase revenue and customer satisfaction." When it comes to offsetting costs with outside suppliers, one of the department's most valuable tools is its Clean Sheet model, which is a financial model to determine what a particular item "should cost." The team identifies the cost drivers in detail and uses industry research on those cost drivers to develop an estimate of what the item should cost, building in overhead and profit levels as well. This information is solely for internal use at United and is not shared with suppliers, but is used to create a common language template using the cost drivers derived from the Clean Sheet. Once supplier bids are received, the strategic sourcing team has detailed negotiations on each component of the pricing and focuses on areas where large variances exist between the Clean Sheet and the supplier bid. "The Clean Sheet allows us to have a very different kind of conversation with our suppliers about what United is willing to pay," notes Puma. It gives us better knowledge around the subcomponents of the cost, because we can discuss precisely why the supplier is much more expensive in a specific subcategory of the cost than what we have found in another bid. It could be that their accounting department has certain procedures, or we might be driving specific specifications that are more costly to them. These are fact-based discussions-much more intellectual than just the end-bid price. In addition, collaborative workshops with suppliers have opened up communication and trust between suppliers and United. The information gleaned from these sessions help the strategic sourcing team as it develops the Clean Sheets. These individual workshops occur prior to commencement of a competitive bid, and two or three known suppliers are invited. Suppliers are asked to provide specific "homework" two days prior to the meeting so that both teams are prepared for the discussion, which ranges from current market dynamics and trends to supplier cost structures. Typically, supplier participants are limited to technical, operational and financial/ contracting representatives, so that they do not turn into sales pitches. "Our approach to sourcing is really around supplier development, helping them to understand that our success is their success, and that they have an active accountability to ensure that our customers have a good experience on board our planes." says Puma.

Questions

1. How do you think suppliers feel about the use of "Clean Sheets" in negotiations?
2. Do you think that Clean Sheets will always drive the supplier's margins lower? Why or why not? Under what conditions might margins actually increase?
3. What is the fundamental element emphasized by Grace Puma as critical to using a TCO approach to contract negotiations? Is United applying this element?

Source: Aruseth, L. (2010. January), "Soaring to New Collaborative Heights," *Inside Supply Management*, 18–20.

CONCLUSION

This chapter provides an overview of the types of contracts used by purchasers, administration procedures applied, and methods of resolving contractual disputes.

Although it is impossible to cover all potential situations where a specific contract should be applied, the rules of thumb developed here should provide a reasonable set of guidelines. As a final point, it is interesting to note that many organizations are eliminating contracts altogether and are choosing to do business with suppliers on an informal basis. This type of arrangement requires the development of excellent supplier relationships and trust between the parties. It is highly unlikely, however, that contracts between buyers and sellers will ever disappear.

KEY TERMS

arbitration, 562

long-term contracts, 549

short-term contracts, 549

spot contracts, 549

DISCUSSION QUESTIONS

1. Where do you believe buyers spend most of their time in negotiations: on the upfront clauses or on the attached schedules?

2. What are some examples of price indices that might be used to track commodity prices such as steel or copper, and how should they be included in the schedule to minimize risk to both parties?

3. What are the risks to buyers associated with each of the different types of contracts (fixed-price, incentive, and cost-based contracts)?

4. What are the risks to suppliers associated with each of the different types of contracts (fixed-price, incentive, and cost-based contracts)?

5. Which types of firms are most suited to using turnkey systems contracts for their information system development?

6. Suppose you are a purchase manager who is the contract administrator for a major consulting firm installing a major enterprise resource planning system such as SAP or Oracle. What are some of the key elements that you would wish to include in the contract with the consulting company implementing this system?

7. Why do consultants typically want to avoid including detailed outcomes in their contracts? Is this ethical?

8. Under what conditions are short-term contracts preferable to long-term contracts?

9. Certain industries, such as the computer industry, are faced with constantly changing technologies, short product life cycles, many small-component suppliers, and demanding customers. Under these conditions, what type of contract would you recommend for a critical component supplier? What other measures would you include in this contract?

10. What are the implications for contract writing as a result of electronic signatures now being enforceable by law?

11. What are the dangers associated with taking an old contract and merely changing the name of the supplier for use in a new, three-year contract with a different supplier?

12. Why do many firms attempt to avoid litigation in settling contract disputes?

13. What are the different venues available for arbitration settlements?

14. What are the implications of e-commerce on enforcing contracts? Where do you think the venue for resolution should be if a conflict arises?

ADDITIONAL READINGS

Alston, F. M., Worthington, M. M., and Goldsman, L. P. (1992), *Contracting with the Federal Government*, New York: John Wiley & Sons.

Baumer, D. L, and Poindexter, J. C. (2004), *Legal Environment of Business in the Information Age*, New York: Irwin.

Behn, R. D. (1999, June), "Strategies for Avoiding Pitfalls of Performance Contracting," *Public Productivity and Management Review*, 470, 1–90.

Buvik, A. (1998, Fall), "The Effect of Manufacturing Technology on Purchase Contracts," *International Journal of Purchasing and Materials Management*, 21–28.

Carbonneau, T. E. (1989), *Alternative Dispute Resolution: Melting the Lances and Dismounting the Steeds*, Urbana: University of Illinois Press.

Coulson, R. (1982), *Business Arbitration: What You Need to Know* (2nd ed.), New York: American Arbitration Association.

Cummins, T. (2007, November), *Contracting Excellence*. Retrieved from www.iaccm.com/contracting excellence.php?id=67

Ellram, L., and Tate, W. (2004, August), "Managing and Controlling the Services Supply Chain at Intuit," *Practix*, CAPS Research. Retrieved from http://www.capsresearch.org/Research/Practix.aspx

Emiliani, M. L., and Stec, D. J. (2001). "Online Reverse Auction Purchasing Contracts," *Supply Chain Management*, 6(3–4), 101–105.

Fisher, R. X. (2000, March), "Checklist for a Good Contract for IT Purchases," *Health Management Technology*, pp. 14–17.

Gordon, S. B. (1998, August), "Performance Incentive Contracting: Using the Purchasing Process to Find Money Rather Than Spend It," *Government Finance Review*, pp. 33–37.

Hancock, W. A. (Ed.). (1987), *The Law of Purchasing* (2nd ed.), Chesterland, OH: Business Laws.

MacCollum, D. V. (1990), *Construction Safety Planning*, New York: Van Nostrand Reinhold.

Maughan, A. (2003), "Crash-Proof Contracts," *Supply Management*, 8(1), 37.

Murray, J. (2001), "Contract Modifications Can Lead to Problems," *Purchasing*, 130(5), 20–22.

Rohleder, S. (1999, September), "Contracting for the Best Results," *Government Executive*, p. 72.

Seide, K. (Ed.). (1970), *A Dictionary of Arbitration and Its Terms*, Dobbs Ferry, NY: Oceana Publishing.

Shenson, H. L. (1990), *The Contract and Fee-Setting Guide for Consultants and Professionals*, New York: John Wiley & Sons.

Singer, L. R. (1990), *Settling Disputes: Conflict Resolution in Business, Families, and the Legal System*, Boulder, CO: Westview Press.

Tepedino, F. J. (1991), *Contract Claims and Litigation Avoidance*, San Diego: Condor Group.

Turtle, A. (2001), "Becoming a Single Source," *Industrial Distribution*, 90(9), 47–49.

Werner, C. (1998, May), "Contract Compliance: A Double-Edged Sword for Most Suppliers," *Health Industry Today*, pp. 1–2.

ENDNOTES

1. Handfield, R. B. (2005), "Legal and Regulatory Requirements in the Emergent Global Supply Chain," White Paper, Supply Chain Resource Cooperative. Retrieved from http://scm.ncsu.edu

2. Brown, L. (1950), *Manual of Preventive Law*, New York: Prentice Hall.

3. Cummins, Tim, Blog, Retrieved from http://www.iaccm.org

4. Hancock, W. A. (Ed.). (1987), *The Law of Purchasing* (2nd ed.), Chesterland, OH: Business Laws, 68.02.

5. Baumer, D. L., and Poindexter, J. C. (2004), *Legal Environment of Business in the Information Age*, New York: McGraw-Irwin.

6. Wetherbe, J. C. (1991), "Executive Information Requirements: Getting It Right," *MIS Quarterly*, 15(1), 51–56.

7. Shenson, H. L. (1990), *The Contract and Fee-Setting Guide for Consultants and Professionals*, New York: John Wiley & Sons, pp. 131–134.

8. MacCollum, D. V. (1990), *Construction Safety Planning*, New York: Van Nostrand Reinhold.

9. Samelson, N. M., and Levitt, R. E. (1982, April), "Owner's Guidelines for Selecting Safe Contractors," *ASCE National Spring Convention Proceedings*, April 26–30, 617–623.

10. Baumer and Poindexter.

11. Singer, L. R. (1990), *Settling Disputes: Conflict Resolution in Business, Families, and the Legal System*, Boulder, CO: Westview Press, p. 5; Baumer and Poindexter.

12. Coulson, R. (1982), *Business Arbitration: What You Need to Know* (2nd ed.), New York: American Arbitration Association, p. 5.

Purchasing Law and Ethics

CHAPTER 15

Learning Objectives

After completing this chapter, you should be able to

- Understand the legal authority & liability of the purchasing manager
- Understand the essential elements of contract law in purchasing
- Understand the provisions of the Uniform Commercial Code in contracts
- Identify antitrust laws and legislation affecting global sourcing that impact purchasing
- Understand why it is so important for purchasing to act in an ethical manner, and identify the risks of unethical behavior
- Recognize the increased corporate awareness and supply management involvement in sustainability and social responsibility initiatives

Chapter Outline

Panama Canal Expansion Slowed by Contract Dispute

The Panama Canal is one of the world's major trade routes providing an efficient path for ocean vessels carrying cargo from the Far East to U.S. and European destinations as well as cargo to Asia from Western markets.

Brief History of the Canal

The canal opened with great fanfare in 1914 and was widely considered one of the engineering marvels of the world. Ships traveling in either direction could reach Asian and U.S. or Western European markets much faster. It also delayed an often treacherous journey around Cape Horn in South American and cut lead times dramatically.

Started by the French in 1881 with a goal of building a canal similar to the Suez Canal, completion of the Panama Canal was a long arduous task. After over 20 years and thousands of deaths from malaria the French gave up. It is often stated that the French rushed to begin work, with insufficient prior study of the geology and hydrology of the region, (similar to what we will see now) and the men who started and directed the project had little or no engineering training or experience. After failed attempts by the French, the U.S. became interested in the canal and was granted rights by the Columbian government. Rebels in the area wanted Panama to be independent from Columbia and hoped for U.S. support. U.S. President Theodore Roosevelt backed a U.S. naval blockade to restrict Columbian troops and then recognized Panama as an independent nation immediately in November of 1903. The U.S. then purchased all French equipment and proceeded with a 10-year project to finish the canal. During the decades of the 1950s, 1960s, and 1970s, U.S. ownership of the canal became a contentious issue with Panamanians. In 1977, the control of the canal was given to Panama with the provision that they would guarantee permanent neutrality over it. Effective December 31, 1999 Panama was given full control over the canal and the Panama Canal Authority (PCA) was the government body that was given the authority to manage the canal.

Larger Ocean Vessels Create Need for Widening

Having full control of the canal and realizing how important traffic through the canal was for the Panamanian economy, the government of Panama wanted to insure the canal operated to its potential. Studies in the middle 2000s indicated that the canal could not accommodate larger ocean vessels that were being built. These larger vessels now used Pacific Ocean ports located on the west coast of the U.S. and Canada. One typical logistics path for these larger vessels was to enter port of Long Beach and load their containers on rail cars bound for Mid-West and East coast destinations. The vessels would then reload with containers headed for the Far East and return across the Pacific.

The PCA determined that an extra set of wider locks was needed to handle the wider ships and accommodate increased traffic through the canal. The current capacity of the canal is 43 ships per day. It takes 8 to 10 hours to pass from Pacific to Atlantic, or vice-versa. At times, more than 100 ships have been waiting to enter the canal. The wait is lengthened when repairs to the locks are being made. If the wait is too long, a ship captain can decide if it's faster and cheaper to travel around South America, rather than lingering in the waters outside of Panama waiting for passage. This costs Panama a lot of money. The average toll to pass through the canal is roughly $50,000. Depending on the size and cargo of the ship, tolls have been as high as $375,000. In response to this port congestion and lost commerce, the Panamanian government in the fall of 2007 announced that it would spend $5.25 billion to widen and overhaul the Panama Canal.

The Contracting Process

The major expenditure for the canal widening project was comprised of building a third set of locks on both the Atlantic and Pacific entrances to the canal. The size and prestige of the project attracted many bidders several of whom were in consortiums. A European consortium called Grupo Unidos por el Canal (GUPC) won the bid for a price of $3.2 billion. The consortium was led by the Spanish construction company Sacyr and four other companies. The other firms in the consortium included: Impreglio of Italy, Spain's Vallehermoso, Jan De Nul of Belgium, and Constructora Urbana SA of Panama. GUPC's bid was considerably lower than its competitors. It was also lower than the internal in-house estimates prepared by the PCA.

While months behind original schedule, construction had been proceeding at a reasonable pace. In early January of 2014 GUPC approached the PCA claiming more than $1.5 billion in cost overruns and wanted to be paid for them. GUPC argued that the PCA provided poor geological studies, which has driven the final price tag for the work to rise much higher than the original contract price. These inadequate studies lead to unexpected problems with the quality of material supposed to be used to make cement and in effect was the major driver of the massive cost overruns.

The PCA immediately rejected the proposal. "There is no negotiation outside the contract," canal administrator Jorge Luis Quijano said. The following day after rejecting the GUPC proposal, the PCA stated that it would put an additional $183 million into the project to allow the consortium expanding the canal to continue work for several months until a permanent solution could be negotiated over the more than $1.5 billion in cost overruns. The PCA also wanted the consortium to put in $100 million. In response to the PCA's actions another consortium member company, (Italy's Impregilo) countered with a demand for $1 billion from the PCA.

Quijano said the PCA was sticking by its proposal for a joint injection of $283 million, moving the conflict closer to the January 20 deadline that the consortium has established for resolving the dispute or halting work. "We hope they're reasonable and let the work finish," he said. "But we have no qualms about working with another contractor."

If PCA agreed to all GUPC overrun cost demands then entire cost of the canal expansion project could exceed $7 billion. Panama had initially estimated that the entire project would cost $5.2 billion, with new wider locks and deeper channels providing passage for larger ships through the 50-mile waterway and also reducing the wait time for smaller vessels.

Settling the Contract Dispute

As is true in all contracts both parties have needs to be fulfilled. The PCA wants the canal expansion to be completed by 2015 and within budget. The contractor (GUPC) feels they encountered massive overruns because of poor specifications concerning the geological structure of the land in Panama. Threats have been made by both parties. The GUPC has said it will halt work that will delay completion of the canal expansion and result more lost revenue for PCA if a settlement is not reached in a reasonable time. The project is already 9 months behind schedule and projected to complete by the summer of 2015. PCA has threatened to abort the contract and use another contractor if GUPC doesn't honor the contract terms. Finding, qualifying, and contracting with another contractor could add more time for the completion.

As previously mentioned, after the threats subsided, PCA made a counterproposal to inject an additional $183 million into the project, assuming the contractor also shows good faith by ponying up an additional $100 million. PCA feels this would allow work to continue until a reasonable settlement could be reached. This indicates that PCA is willing to negotiate the original contract terms. However the $283 million joint financing package was less attractive for GUPC because it requires them to put up fresh cash while the authority would simply advance funds it would have paid anyway.

A counterproposal by GUPC was made for a $400 million dollar advance paid by the PCA. In response to this PCA countered with a plan that they and the consortium would each put up $100 million, while the PCA would give GUPC more time to repay $83 million that was advanced to them. The proposal was conditional on the GUPC withdrawing a threat to stop work on January 20 and to process its claim for $1.6 billion in cost overruns separately through agreed arbitration panels. Meanwhile Bechtel, a US based construction firm, which lost the original bid, could be an alternative source for PCA should negotiations fail. Finally, a review of the contract shows the following sequence of events. First, the parties would bargain in good faith. If negotiation fails to produce a solution, then the parties would have no choice but to pursue legal actions in court. This last action would prove most costly and least productive for all parties.

Sources: Adapted from following sources

1. _____,_____ "Panama Canal Talks Run Into Trouble over Money" ABC News http://abcnews .go.com/International/wireStory/panama-canal-talks-run-trouble-money-21471084 Accessed January 10, 2014
2. Lomi Kriel and Elida Moreno "Panama Canal, Consortium Closer to Deal to Keep Expansion Going" January 7, 2014 http://uk.reuters.com/article/2014/01/07/uk-sacyr-panama-financing-idUKBREA060VJ20140107
3. Jason Magolis "After six years and billions of dollars, the Panama Canal expansion may grind to a halt"PRI's The World (Public Radio International) January 10, 2014 http://www.pri.org /stories/2014-01-10/after-six-years-and-billions-dollars-panama-canal-expansion-may-grind-halt
4. JOC Staff Panama Canal Won't Negotiate Locks Contractor's Claims Outside Contract January 08, 2014 https://www.joc.com/port-news/panama-canal-news/panama-canal-won%E2%80%99t-negotiate-locks-contractor%E2%80%99s-claims-outside-contract_20140108.htm

Introduction

As illustrated in the Panama Canal expansion contract dispute, today's global business environment has made it more important than ever for purchasing managers to understand the changing nature of law at the international, federal, state, and regional levels. It also is critical that purchasers making contracting decisions act ethically and in the best interest of their organization. Purchasing activities are concerned with the laws regarding contracts and the laws regarding agency, the majority of which concern contract laws.

Contract law essentially determines the nature of agreements that are enforceable and create legal rights between the parties. The characteristics of offer and acceptance, satisfaction and nonperformance have all been clearly established by the law. Contracts between two or more parties allow the shifting of risk between the entities and constitute the foundation and fabric for every type of supply chain relationship.

Agency law, on the other hand, deals with the role of managers as individual representatives acting on behalf of their organization. It is important that purchasing managers understand the role they play as agents of their organization, so that they do not exceed the responsibilities bestowed upon them in this role. As agents of their organization, purchasing managers also wield a great deal of power in allocating the business of the company to their suppliers. They must be aware of the potential for ethical abuses of this power that may be encountered as well.

Although we cannot provide a comprehensive treatment of these issues here, this chapter will introduce some of the basic legal concerns that purchasing managers must be aware of in their profession. Specifically, we begin with a discussion of the roles and responsibilities of purchasing managers as individuals representing their organization and then discuss the major features of the Uniform Commercial Code (**UCC**). The major features of contract law are reviewed, as well as the important area of patents and intellectual property. Antitrust laws that affect purchasing are discussed next, followed by an overview of purchasing ethics and social responsibility.

Legal Authority and Personal Liability of the Purchasing Manager

Laws of Agency

The laws regarding agency are concerned with governing the relationship of principals and agents. An **agent** is a person or entity who has been authorized to act on behalf of some other person or entity. A *principal,* on the other hand, is the corresponding person or entity for whom agents carry out their authority. The purchasing manager/buyer is typically considered to be a *general agent* for the buying firm (the principal). That means that a supplier dealing with this manager/buyer has a right to rely on the individual's statements, both in written form and verbally. Conversely, the sales representative can also be considered to be an agent of the selling firm (also a principal). In most cases, the sales representative is a special agent who can only solicit orders but not change prices, terms, or conditions. Meanwhile, the purchasing agent is a *general agent* with *broad authority* to change prices, terms, and conditions.

Legal Authority

Purchasing managers generally have final authority over purchasing decisions within their firms. However, this final decision may be reached through the input provided by a cross-functional sourcing team. In the end, however, someone has to sign the contract, so the purchasing manager, as discussed above, is most often considered as the general agent. A general agent role merely implies that the guidelines provided by the employer for this individual are quite broad and general in nature. Because purchasing managers are responsible for a significant amount of expenditures, the employer's instructions to its purchasing managers should be expressed clearly and succinctly. The purchasing agency relationship is created between the employer and employee when the company hires an individual to perform the purchasing job. Typically, a job description provides the basis for an agreement between the employing firm and purchasing agent/manager regarding actual scope of authority.

Purchasing managers have the right to require clear and unequivocal instructions from their employers regarding the scope of their day-to-day job performance expectations. From a legal perspective, purchasing managers have a *fiduciary obligation* to act in the best interests of their employer. This means that if they carry out their duties in a faithful, ethical, and conscientious manner, then their obligations to the employers are fulfilled.

However, in agreeing to perform the purchasing duties for the employer, purchasing managers do not imply that they will never make mistakes.

Personal Liability

Certain individuals in many organizations have interpreted the statement "acting in the best interests of the employer" in radically different ways. There are a number of ways in which purchasing managers can be held personally liable in the conduct of their day-to-day activities, even if they were supposedly following these guidelines. Depending on the issue at hand, this personal liability can take the form of either a civil or criminal suit. The concept of "apparent versus actual authority" is the determining factor in such cases.

Actual authority stems from the instructions and granting of authority to the purchasing manager via the job description provided by the employer. These documents typically define the limits and parameters under which the purchasing manager is expected to operate. *Apparent authority,* on the other hand, is that level of authority perceived by the seller to be available to the purchasing manager. In most instances, apparent authority can be defined as the scope of authority possessed by other purchasing managers with similar positions in other organizations within the same industry. When a non-agent such as a maintenance supervisor, engineer or finance analyst makes a commitment with a supplier, this is termed *implied authority.* In such cases the non-agent will usually have to come to purchasing to get a purchase order issued "after the fact" since they have already made a commitment. Purchasing can put suppliers "on notice" that any commitments made by non-agents will not be honored. In lieu of this statement to suppliers and direct discussion with non-agents, implied authority exists.

If a purchasing manager, in carrying out normal procurement responsibilities, exceeds his or her actual but not apparent authority, then the employer is still responsible for performance of the resulting contract but could seek legal action against the purchasing manager personally. Exceeding both actual and apparent authority can have dire consequences; an individual may be held directly liable by the supplier or other third party (see Exhibit 15.1).

It is in the purchasing manager's own self-interest to ensure that all suppliers or other third parties are aware that his or her actions are on behalf of the employing firm. All contracts should be signed in a manner that demonstrates the agency relationship. The following illustrates two alternative types of language that might be used in a contract:[1]

[your name] on behalf of [your company]or [your company name] by [your name]

Purchasing managers can be held personally liable for their damaging and illegal activities if they perform them without the authority of their firm. This personal liability may occur even if the purchasing manager believes (incorrectly) that he or she actually possesses the authority. Any damaging acts performed outside of the manager's scope of authority (whether actual or apparent) can lead to personal liability, even though such acts were intended to benefit the employer. In essence, any act that causes damage to any other person could cause a legal liability to the purchasing manager who performs such an act.

Other areas of activity for the purchasing manager that could lead to personal liability include the following:[2]

- Deception for personal gain while acting as an agent for the principal firm (includes taking bribes)
- Violating the lawful protection of items owned by others, such as patent infringement

Exhibit 15.1	Laws of Agency

ACTUAL AUTHORITY
(what the agent is
authorized to buy)

	Within	Exceed
Within	OK	Employer responsible for performance of contract
Exceed	Not relevant	Purchasing manager liable (dire consequences)

APPARENT AUTHORITY
(what the seller perceives)

- (Mis)use of proprietary information
- Violation of antitrust laws
- Unlawful transportation of hazardous materials and toxic waste

These activities are related to another important aspect of purchasing law: ethical behavior. A good rule of thumb is to remember that purchasers must always act in the best interests of their employer. This includes maintaining loyalty, respecting confidential information, and avoiding compromising relationships that may lead to a conflict of interest, which will be discussed later in the Purchasing Ethics section. Understanding contract law is one way to ensure that purchasers will legally protect their employer's best interests.

Contract Law

Essential Elements of a Contract

Commercial law is defined as that "body of [the] law that refers to how business firms (parties) enter into contracts with each other, execute contracts, and remedy problems that arise in the process."[3] Two major topical areas of commercial law are of day-to-day interest to the purchasing professional: the laws regarding agency and the laws regarding contracts. We discussed agency law earlier in the chapter. Thus, we will turn our attention to the laws regarding contracts.

In its most basic form, a contract can be defined as an agreement between two or more parties that can be legally enforced. Note that people make agreements every day, but not every agreement can be considered a contract. A **contract** is a set of promises between two or more parties the performance of which the law expects, the breach of which the law provides remedies. The situation below represents a simple contract:

Shirley wants to go to the store to buy some potato chips, but she does not have a car. Shirley says to Rich, "I will pay you five dollars to take me to the store to buy some potato chips." Rich agrees and takes Shirley to the store.

The above statement can be characterized as a contract. Shirley agreed to do a specified thing (pay Rich five dollars) in exchange for another specified thing (take Shirley to the store). In legal thinking a contract has three essential elements:

- Offer
- Acceptance
- Consideration

If any one of these elements is lacking, then an enforceable contract does not exist. Let us take a closer look at these three elements.

Offer

An **offer** is a proposal or expression by one person that he or she is willing to do something for certain terms. For example:

Betsy goes into Mimi's Wholesale Video Store and says to Mimi, "I want to buy 500 DVDs of the Last Vegas movie from you. I will pay you $10 for each DVD."

Betsy has made a specific offer—to purchase a specific movie—in specific volumes (500)—at a specific price ($5,000). This constitutes a valid offer. Somewhat different is a conditional offer, which includes additional criteria for completion of the agreement.

For example:

Betsy goes into Mimi's Wholesale Video Store and says to Mimi, "I want to buy 500 DVDs of the Avatar movie from you. I will pay you $10 for each DVD If you deliver them to my place of business on February 1, 2015."

In this case, a deadline has been added to the offer. The offer is valid if the conditions are met.

Acceptance

The second important part of the contract is the *acceptance,* legally, a contract does not exist until the offer is formally accepted, either verbally or in written form. The offer and acceptance should generally match. However, this is not always the case. Under the Uniform Commercial Code (discussed later in the chapter), the offer and acceptance need not always match. An acceptance can have additional terms, which will become part of the contract unless the offeror objects within a reasonable amount of time.

Assuming the offer and acceptance match, there is an agreement leading up to a contract. If they do not, it is more like a negotiation: an offer, to which someone responds with a counteroffer rather than an acceptance, must be restated. This continues until both sides reach an agreement, or a so-called meeting of the minds. It is important to note that a contract exists only when there is an agreement resulting from both an offer and an acceptance. The agreement does not exist until the supplier accepts the offer, and a meeting of the minds occurs. An acceptance, as recognized by the Uniform Commercial Code, can be in "any manner and by any medium reasonable to the circumstances." In other words, the manner and medium of acceptance by the supplier can be met either through the promise of an acceptance or by the supplier's performance of the terms and conditions of the contract—that is, the actual delivery of the requested goods or services without prior verbal advance notice.

Many customer purchase orders typically contain a written copy that outlines the procedures for acknowledgment or acceptance by suppliers. However, suppliers frequently accept or acknowledge customer orders on their own form, which may contain language and terms different from the customer's original purchase order. UCC Section 2–207 covers additional terms. These additional terms will become part of the final contract unless:

1. The supplier's terms substantially or materially alter the original intent of the offer (purchase order).
2. The buyer has previously objected to the additional terms or now objects to the supplier's additional terms in writing within a reasonable time.
3. The purchase order explicitly states that no alteration of terms is acceptable.

If a contract is performed by "conduct," this means the parties are acting as if they have a contract. If the terms of the buyer's purchase order and the supplier's acceptance or acknowledgment conflict, and none of the conditions listed above are present, all of the terms of both the purchase order and the acceptance become part of the resulting contract except the conflicting terms and conditions. In effect, the conflicting terms and conditions are simply disregarded. The purchasing manager must therefore ensure that the terms and conditions of all supplier acceptance forms are carefully reviewed.

If the buyer wants to avoid any dispute over the terms and conditions of the contract, the purchase order should include a statement to the effect that "absolutely no deviation from the terms and conditions contained herein is permitted" or "these terms and conditions constitute the entire agreement."

Consideration

The third element of a contract is difficult to define. Consideration, which has nothing to do with being considerate or nice to people, is rather a form of "mutual obligation"— with each party bound to perform at certain levels and agreeing to carry out his or her responsibilities. Consideration is something of value in the formation of the contract that gives it legal validity. Consideration takes place when the offeree incurs a legal detriment in response to the offeror's offer. The offeree indicates a willingness to give up something of value to the offeror or a designated third party or give up something of value to him- or herself. In the business world, mutual promises in a contract of sale, whether express or implied, are generally sufficient consideration. For example, in the previous example, Betsy made an offer that Mimi accepted. There has also been consideration. Betsy's consideration is expressed: She promised to pay $10 per DVD. Mimi's consideration is implied: By saying "OK," she implied that she promised to sell Betsy 500 DVDs for $10 apiece.

Two other elements are important to consider in contract law: competent parties/ mutual assent and legal subject matter.

Competent Parties/Mutual Assent

The parties to a legally enforceable contract must have full contractual capacity through being either principals or qualified agents as described earlier. In addition, both the buyer and the seller must not have engaged in any fraudulent activities when formulating the agreement. The use of force or coercion to reach an agreement is not acceptable in signing a contract, because both parties must enter into the agreement of their own free will. Both parties must indicate a willingness to enter into the agreement and be bound by its terms.

Legal Subject Matter

If an agreement has been made regarding a purpose that is illegal, then the resulting contract is null and void. The performance of a party in regard to the contract must not be an unlawful act if the agreement is to be enforceable. However, if the primary purpose of a contract is legal, but some terms contained within the agreement are not, then the contract may or may not itself be illegal depending on the seriousness of the illegal terms and the degree to which the legal and illegal terms can be separated.

The Purchase Order—Is It a Contract?

In most instances, the contracting parties participate in a series of negotiation deliberations through which the various terms and conditions of the contract are discussed, outlined, and agreed upon. As shown in Exhibit 15.2, a process takes place before the purchase order develops. This is initiated by the request for quotation (RFQ), sent by the buyer to the supplier. The RFQ contains the following:

- Standard terms and conditions of the transaction
- Quantity/conditions of delivery
- Description, specifications, and end use of the item
- If customized, reviewed by legal counsel before the RFQ is submitted
- If a competitive bid, description of the manner and time period in which the bids will be evaluated
- Services

The RFQ is not an offer but a request for price and availability. The supplier will generally respond to the RFQ with a quote (an offer to sell), which may then initiate further

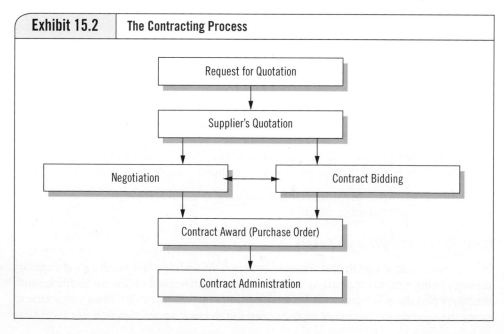

Exhibit 15.2 | **The Contracting Process**

Request for Quotation

↓

Supplier's Quotation

↓

Negotiation ↔ Contract Bidding

↓

Contract Award (Purchase Order)

↓

Contract Administration

discussion and negotiation between the purchasing commodity team and the supplier's team. Eventually, this leads to a contract, which documents all of the different offers and counteroffers. Most commercial contracts are comprised of similar sets of general terms and conditions. With the exception of a description of the parties involved, a description of the basic subject of the contract and statement of work including dates, and a clearly definable or determinable quantity, the UCC can be relied upon to supply all other terms.

A purchase order can be an offer, acceptance, or counteroffer, depending on the circumstances. It is an offer if it is sent without a quote or other conversation with the seller concerning terms of the order. It is a counteroffer if it is sent in response to a quote but changes one or more of the terms of the quote (e.g., delivery, quantity, or packaging). It would be an acceptance if it mirrors the seller's quote. Once accepted, a purchase order becomes a contract. The major parts of a purchase order include the following:

- Fixed prices and quantities (including taxes)
- Buyer's right of inspection and rejection
- Right to make specification/design changes
- Holding buyer harmless, patent infringement
- Supplier's right to assign contract to a third party
- Instructions regarding risk of loss
- Statement of credit and payment terms
- Identification
- Packing and preparation
- Statements of warranty
- Shipment quantities/dates
- Assignment of seller's rights
- Arbitration clause
- Right to cancel unshipped portion

Price

Of the terms listed above, the price term is perhaps the single most important element of the entire contract. Section 2–305 of the UCC, entitled "Open Price Term," indicates explicitly that the parties do not necessarily need to reach agreement on a price in order to have an enforceable contract. Section 2–305 states that absent a specified price, the price "shall be a reasonable" price at the time of delivery. In other words the supplier may not "price gouge."

Although the UCC allows for open price terms, quantity must be specified, so that there is a reasonably certain basis for determining damages in the event of a breach of contract. Although the "open price term" clause promotes flexibility in setting prices, the possibility of being charged an unacceptable price increases. If the contract indicates that the price is to be determined at some point in the future or by some other mechanism, two basic requirements must be satisfied per Section 2–305 of the UCC. First, both parties must intend to make a binding contract even though the price remains open. Second, there must be some reasonably certain basis for giving relief (or determining value). A purchasing manager who is in doubt as to whether an enforceable contract might have been reached without agreeing upon a price should indicate in correspondence with the supplier that no contract or agreement exists unless there is agreement on a specific price.

Boilerplate Contract Terms and Conditions

In addition to the negotiated terms of price determination, description of the goods, delivery, and quantity, a number of other standard terms and conditions (often referred to as "boilerplate") are typically included in most commercial contracts and purchase order agreements. Usually preprinted on the back of forms used by the purchaser (and the seller), these terms and conditions are intended to provide a measure of protection for the purchaser against undesirable actions by a supplier and require the supplier to conform to certain business practices and procedures.

Because boilerplate language and the wording of other preprinted purchase order and sales documents may often conflict, it is important to communicate clearly with suppliers exactly which terms are in effect. (If in doubt, do not sign it and assume that things can be worked out later!)

Oral vs. Written Contracts

Many purchase orders are placed over the telephone, in person, and increasingly, through the Internet; purchasing managers must thus be aware of the potential pitfalls of oral contracts. It is important to remember that a contract is a relationship—not a physical entity—between the parties involved.

When the contract is reduced to writing, the written document is not the actual contract but simply hard evidence of the existence of the underlying contractual relationship. Also, whenever a contract is reduced to writing, the written document supersedes all previous oral evidence. It is therefore important to ensure that all relevant negotiated data and warranty-related oral statements deemed to be part of the agreement are also reduced to writing in the contract. The **Statute of Frauds** is a law designed to prevent fraud or perjury by requiring certain contracts to be in writing. Under UCC this applies to contracts for goods worth more than $500 or any contract that cannot be fully performed in one year. The UCC under Section 2–201 specifies the following:[4]

- In order for a contract to exist, there must normally be some written (and signed) notation if the value of the order for the sale of goods is $500 or more. Exceptions where a verbal contract would be valid on orders over $500 are when the following conditions are met:
- The goods are made specifically for the buyer.
- There is proof to show the parties behaved as if a contract existed.
- The parties have always done business on a verbal basis.
- If the supplier provides a written confirmation memorandum that is not in accordance with the purchaser's understanding of an oral order, the purchaser must give a notice of objection to the supplier within 10 days of receipt of the memorandum.

A good example of this situation is when you are shopping for a used vehicle. The salesperson may exaggerate the virtues of a particular car while walking around the lot, yet when you sit down to review the contract, you may find that many of the "promises" are no longer in writing. In order to determine the true conditions of the sale, you should write down exactly what you have been told, and ask for the salesperson's written signature underneath your notes while still out on the lot.

One final issue is the doctrine of *Promissory Estoppel,* which holds that if one or more parties made a promise even orally, he or she cannot renege on that promise if the other party acted on reliance on the promise. Thus, a contract may be unenforceable under the "Statute of Frauds" because of the monetary amount, yet enforceable under Promissory Estoppel.

Cancellation of Orders and Breach of Contract

A good contract will protect the interests and rights of both buyer and seller. As a result, contractual obligations are equally binding upon both parties to the agreement.

People cannot go around arbitrarily canceling or defaulting on their contracts. In some instances, however, one of the parties to a contractual arrangement may seek to cancel the agreement after it has been made. In other cases, the supplier may simply fail to perform in the manner agreed to in the contract. Under these conditions, the buyer will always go back to the original contract to determine what the potential remedies are to these situations. If they are not spelled out in detail, the UCC once again provides some help.

Cancellation of Orders

Contract cancellations can generally be classified into three categories: (1) cancellation for default, (2) cancellation for convenience of the purchaser ("anticipatory breach"), or (3) cancellation by mutual consent.

Cancellation for default can be defined as failure of one of the parties to live up to the terms and conditions of the contract. Supplier actions that can result in this type of breach of contract include late deliveries, failing to meet product specifications, or otherwise failing to perform in accordance with contract provisions. The types of damages that might be awarded include production cost penalties, additional overtime, or expedited transportation costs. In actual practice, more effective settlements can be reached through negotiation with the supplier rather than through the litigation process.

Cancellation for the convenience of the purchaser, or anticipatory breach, makes the purchaser liable for any resulting injury to the supplier. A general rule here is that the supplier should not be called upon to incur any loss because of the purchaser's default.

Generally speaking, purchasers should stay away from this term altogether in their purchase contracts. The term is highly interpretable in court and can result in any number of negative actions.

Cancellation by mutual consent indicates that cancellation of a previously agreed-upon contract does not automatically lead to legal action. If both parties mutually agree to terminate the agreement, then they have, in effect, created another contract with the intent of nullifying the first agreement. If there is no potential loss, the supplier will often accept a purchaser's cancellation in good faith as a normal risk of doing business. Even when suppliers have purchased special components or materials in anticipation of fulfilling their responsibilities under the agreement, the parties can usually reach a mutually agreeable resolution through the process of negotiation rather than through litigation.

Breach of Contract

Under a commercial contract, the supplier is obligated to deliver the goods according to the contract's terms and conditions, and the purchaser is likewise obligated to accept and tender payment for the goods according to the terms of the agreement. A **breach of contract** occurs when either party fails to perform the obligations due under the contract (without a valid or legal justification). A breach may entitle the offended party to certain remedies or damages (discussed in greater detail in the next section).

For example:

Mimi's Wholesale Video Store and Betsy now have a valid contract. Betsy has promised to buy 500 DVDs for $10 apiece, and Mimi has promised to deliver them to Betsy's place of business on February 1. However, Mimi never shows up with the delivery.

Mimi may indeed be liable for breach of contract. However, one of the basic rules of the UCC is that each party to a contract must give the other party the total time agreed upon to complete his or her obligations under the contract.

Buyers should avoid the practice of routinely tolerating suppliers that breach purchase contracts. Doing so may result in the buyer forfeiting the right to legal action. If you, as the purchaser, have systematically accepted late deliveries from a supplier in the past and continue to accept late deliveries even though you must expedite late shipments, then you may have waived your right to pursue legal action for damages caused by the late shipments. For example:

A buyer and a supplier have been doing business for several years. During the past year, approximately one-third of the shipments from the supplier arrived a week or so late, but the buyer accepted them without serious complaints. In the eyes of the law, these acceptances by the buyer may well have set a precedent that waives the buyer's rights to timely delivery on future contracts.

To regain his or her legal rights, the buyer must give explicit written notice to the supplier and provide the supplier a reasonable period of time to ramp up to meet the new delivery requirements. The new contract should also include the minimal lead time required for design changes, and so on.

In major contracts, it is often apparent that a breach of contract may create major headaches for either the buyer or supplier; the level of damages in such cases is difficult to determine. To avoid this confusion, many organizations include an up-front termination or *liquidated damages* provision in the contract at the time of negotiation.

A liquidated damages provision stipulates the mechanism to be used in determining any costs and damages to the injured party in the event of a breach of contract. The specified amount must be a reasonable estimate and agreed to prior to contract signing. Being explicit about breach obligations prior to contract signing helps avoid confusion later.

Damages and Remedies

The concept of damages in the UCC is based on the remedy of a party being "made whole." In other words, a purchaser who is damaged by a breach of contract must receive damages that bring the purchaser back to the position where he or she would have been if the breach had not occurred. Damages include either actual damages (which include losses that are real or known, or can be reasonably estimated), as well as punitive damages (extra money over and above as "punishment" for the defendant's bad behavior). The UCC is quite clear on the point that punitive damages are not allowed, even if such a provision is contained in the contract. There are essentially three types of damages available to the purchaser:

- *Restitution.* Money the plaintiff actually paid to the defendant in connection with the contract.
- *Reliance.* Money the plaintiff lost because he or she was relying on the contract, depending on the defendant to live up to his or her obligations under the contract.
- *Expectancy.* Money the plaintiff was hoping to gain from the contract.

Back at Mimi's Wholesale Video Store, Mimi and Betsy had a valid contract. Betsy promised to buy 500 DVDs for $10 apiece, and Mimi promised to deliver them to Betsy's place of business. Betsy gave Mimi $2,000 as a down payment on the delivery. Betsy also spent $5,000 building new shelves in her retail video store to display and store the DVDs. Finally, Betsy expected to make a profit of $10,000 after expenses from selling or renting the DVDs to her customers. However, Mimi never delivered the DVDs, and Betsy sued for breach of contract. What damages is she entitled to?

Betsy can sue for $2,000 in restitution damages for loss of the down payment, $5,000 in reliance damages for the shelves, and $10,000 in expectancy damages. This is for the $10,000 in profits she expected to make (for a total of $2,000 + $5000 + $10000 = $17,000).

It should be noted, that in order for a firm to recover lost profits, the firm must produce credible evidence that it would have made such profits. In the above example, in real life it would indeed be rare for a party to recover $17,000 in a contract where the restitution and reliance damages are $7000. Why? Because the plaintiff in such a case could be asked, "Why didn't you go out on the market and *cover*?" meaning that the plaintiff would have an obligation to purchase alternative supplies and continue operations. The plaintiff cannot just passively sit back in the event of breach and reap possible profits without effort.

There are various methods of calculating damages. General damages are equal to the difference between the value of the purchased goods at the time of delivery and the goods' value at the time of specified delivery. Incidental damages include expenses reasonably incurred in inspection, receipt, transportation, and the care and custody of goods appropriately rejected by the purchaser.

Consequential damages are those expenses incurred by the purchaser because the goods were not delivered when expected or as specified. **Liquidated damages** are those that result if the terms of the contract are not fulfilled and, as discussed above under remedies, must be defined prior to the breach under the terms of the contract. To recover liquidated damages the buyer must include a "time is of the essence" clause and tie the losses to viable economic losses. For example, for every day the DVDs are shipped later than February 1st Betsy suffers losses of $100/day.

It should be noted that even though the UCC calls for full compensation for a party that is a victim of breach of contract, attorney fees are not recoverable. Also, *speculative damages* and lost time of executives are not generally recoverable. The bottom line is that a breach of contract lawsuit will rarely make the nonbreaching party completely whole again.

Acceptance and Rejection of Goods

The UCC allows the purchaser to accept part of the shipment and reject the remainder for cause, or to accept or reject the entire shipment. After the point of acceptance, the supplier's rights increase and the purchaser's rights decrease. Once the purchaser accepts the goods, there is only one recourse—to make a claim against the supplier.

The UCC specifies that the purchaser does not have the legal right to withhold payment from the supplier once acceptance has been made. The purchaser also does not have the right at this point to send the goods back unless the supplier consents to this action.

The legal concept of acceptance is closely related to the concept of inspection. Purchasers have a legitimate *right to inspect* contracted goods before accepting or rejecting them. The law is quite explicit when it states that the purchaser accept the goods within a reasonable time whether or not the goods are physically inspected.

Obvious defects must be discovered and rejected within this reasonable time frame, or the purchaser has no recourse against the seller. *Latent* defects are those that could not have been easily discovered during an inspection and do not fall under this rule. In certain limited situations, the purchaser is able to revoke an acceptance of delivered goods. A purchaser may revoke a prior acceptance if a problem is discovered that substantially impairs the value of the goods. Also, a purchaser can revoke a prior acceptance when a prior inspection could not take place for reasons not related to negligence on the part of the purchaser.

When the goods delivered by the supplier are actually rejected by the purchaser because of nonconformance, the purchaser must provide notice to the supplier within a reasonable period of time. The purchaser should be specific in notifying the supplier that he or she is in breach of contract. General statements about the problems at hand without stating that the supplier is considered in breach of contract are not adequate notification. The exact terms "breach of contract" must be used, or the purchaser stands to lose his or her right to recourse from the supplier. The seller has the right to *cure* (i.e., make the situation right) the defect before a breach can be declared. The seller has a reasonable time to cure the defect.

Once goods are accepted, there are two obligations that the purchaser must meet in order to recover his or her rights. First, the purchaser must carry the burden of proof that the goods did not conform to the terms and conditions of the contract. Second, the purchaser must, within a reasonable time after the breach is discovered, notify the supplier of that breach or lose the chance for remedy.

Acceptance of the contracted goods by the purchaser means that ownership of the goods has been transferred. There are no rituals or formalities required to make the transfer of ownership. Any words or acts by the purchaser that provide an indication of the purchaser's intention to transfer ownership are enough to effect the transfer.

Even though the goods may have been formally rejected by the purchaser, actions typifying ownership may indicate that acceptance has instead been accomplished. In order to prevent or mitigate problems arising from the acceptance or rejection of goods, a number of steps to manage the acceptance process can be implemented by the purchaser:[5]

- The receiving department should stamp all receipts of goods with a statement something to the effect of "Received subject to inspection, count, and testing."
- A thorough set of purchase order terms and conditions should indicate that all receipts from suppliers are subject to inspection, count, and testing.
- All delivered goods should be inspected as quickly as possible, and ideally, immediately upon delivery.
- Contracts for such items as production equipment should contain a clause stating that acceptance will not be made until the equipment has been installed and run satisfactorily for a certain period of time.
- For hardware- and software-related contracts, the purchaser should carefully define the acceptance criteria and notify the supplier of the specific processes or tests that the hardware and software will be subjected to.

Honest Mistakes

Sometimes, in spite of the best efforts of the purchaser and the supplier, *honest mistakes* occur when parties draw up a purchase agreement. In such instances, careful consideration of all the circumstances is necessary to determine whether the resulting contract is valid or invalid. Generally, honest mistakes by a single party to the contract will not void the contract. If the other party was truly unaware of the mistake, then the contract is still intact. Note that mistakes made by both parties also do not necessarily affect the validity of the contract.

Mistakes are not covered under the UCC. The parties must rely on traditional contract law to solve any dispute resulting from a mistake. "As a general rule, a party will not be given relief against a mistake induced by his own negligence. But the rule is not inflexible, and in many cases relief may be granted although the mistake involved some element of negligence, particularly when the other party has been in no way prejudiced."[6] The rules for determining whether or not a contract exists after a mistake has been made are the basic fairness rules. The judicial system will more than likely allow a supplier to be absolved from the contract because of a mistake if the supplier gave the purchaser notification of the mistake before the purchaser relied on the bid. All attempts should be made by the buyer to minimize the occurrence of contractual mistakes.

The Uniform Commercial Code

A History of the UCC

In today's society, we take for granted that there is a certain level of fairness and predictability in the legal system. This was not always the case. Laws differed from nation to nation, state to state, and city to city. In the United States, every state had, and still does have, the power to enact its own laws concerning business transactions.

Beginning in the 1950s, a national editorial board of legal scholars drafted the body of laws concerning business transactions, which was intended to make business transactions regular and predictable. The goal was to reduce the number of state-by-state variations. The resulting code was the federal **Uniform Commercial Code (UCC)**. In 1952, all of the states (with the exception of Louisiana) adopted the UCC.

It is important to note that the UCC does not apply in international contracts. For international contracts the **United Nations Convention on Contracts for the International Sale of Goods (CISG)** can be applied as it has been ratified in 80 countries. (CISG will be discussed later in the chapter)

A number of subsequent revisions to the UCC have kept its provisions more responsive to changing business conditions. The UCC that is in use today consists of the 10 articles. Section 2 pertains most directly to purchasers and section 7 to other supply chain participants. The 10 articles are the following:

1. General introductory provisions
2. Sales of goods and products
3. Transactions in commercial paper (bank checks, liability for endorsements)
4. Bank deposits and collections
5. Letters of credit (financial instruments issued by banks and other institutions)
6. Bank transfers
7. Warehouse receipts, bills of lading, and other documents of title to goods
8. Transfers in investment securities
9. Secured transactions
10. Technical matters

It is important to understand that the established common law of contracts discussed in the previous section may often be at odds with actual commercial practices that were favored by contracting parties for the flexibility and efficiency they offered. As such, the Uniform Commercial Code is not actually "the law" of commercial contracts. For the most part, the UCC is a "gap-filler" and is only pertinent if the parties themselves do not supply a contract term, or the term is left open. For example, if nothing is said in a sales contract about delivery, then under the UCC, the goods are considered delivered to the buyer when they are given to the buyer at the seller's establishment. In like fashion, under the UCC if nothing different is said in a sales contract, payment is due at the time of delivery of goods. In general, the "standard terms" as dictated by the UCC are applicable unless the parties agree to something else, which they generally do.[7]

The primary portion of the Uniform Commercial Code that concerns purchasing is Article 2, which deals with sales contracts. The UCC provides benefits to the buying firm in four ways:

1. If a seller makes an offer in writing, the seller has to live up to it for the period of time stated.

2. Verbal agreements, when confirmed in writing and if no objection is made, are valid.

3. The conflict between a buyer's purchase order terms and a seller's acknowledgment terms will generally be resolved according to the two firms' prior conduct. Specifically, a course of dealing (prior conduct) between parties and any usage of trade in the vocation or trade in which they are engaged give particular meaning or qualify terms of an agreement.

4. As far as warranties are concerned, the purchasing manager can legally rely on the supplier to provide the item needed to do the job.

The real effect of Article 2 is to support the buying firm's position in its commercial dealings with its suppliers. The UCC, as opposed to other laws such as the Uniform Sales Act, establishes each party's rights and obligations based on the concepts of fairness and reasonableness, which are founded on accepted business practices.

It should also be noted that the UCC applies to the sale of goods. Without proactive action by the buyer, the sale of services will be covered under common law (system of jurisprudence). Since many service contracts involve some "deliverable" (a product), if advantageous, the buyer can include a "UCC Applicability" clause. In these mixed cases where either the common law or the UCC may apply, the courts will look at either where the majority of funds are expended or where the dispute occurred. See the situation below: *Joe's heating/air contractor ($20,000 for service) is installing a new air handling system ($30,000 for the product) in XYZ's office building. After installation the system doesn't work.* In this case the UCC would apply as the majority of the funds were for the air handling system. Alternatively in case 2 *Joe's heating/air contractor ($20,000 for service) is installing a new air handling system ($30,000 for the product) in an XYZ's office building. After installation it is determined that Joe's improperly wired the units.* In this case common law would apply since the dispute was over the wiring, which is the service element of the contract.

One can also agree in a contract to override parts of the UCC—so it is important to read the fine print on contracts, being aware of the words "unless otherwise agreed." The most basic elements of Article 2 within the UCC involve the following four issues:

- Warranties
- Transportation terms and risk of loss

- Seller's rights
- Buyer's rights

Prior to discussing the basic elements of Article 2, we will briefly discuss the impact of the "information age" and "electronic" contracts.

Electronic Contracts and Signatures

Entering the 21ˢᵗ Century, the movement toward more electronic contracting led to efforts to build frameworks to govern these contracts. **The Electronic Signatures in Global and National Commerce Act ("E-Sign")** was signed into law in 2000. E-Sign does not amend existing laws but provides that a signature, contract or other record relating to a transaction may not be denied validity solely because it is in electronic form. It is a federal law that facilitates the use of electronic records and signatures in interstate and global commerce by ensuring the validity and legal effect of contracts entered into electronically. The first section of the law states that a contract or signature "may not be denied legal effect, validity, or enforceability solely because it is in electronic form."

Meanwhile, the National Conference of Commissioners on Uniform State Laws (NCCUSL) an organization that worked extensively in developing the UCC, drafted a stand-alone law entitled the **Uniform Electronic Transactions Act (UETA)** in 1999. Similar to E-Sign, UETA does not change existing contract law, but adapts existing "paper and pencil" concepts to the electronic age. In effect UETA makes electronic records equivalent to written documents and electronic signatures similar to handwritten signatures for legal purposes.

Section 2 of the law provides definitions. An *electronic record* is defined as a record created, generated, sent, communicated, received, or stored by electronic means. An *electronic signature* is defined as an electronic sound, symbol, or process attached to or logically associated with a record and executed or adopted by a person with the intent to sign the record. Forty-seven states, the District of Columbia, Puerto Rico, and the U.S. Virgin Islands have adopted UETA.[8]

Sourcing Snapshot

Contract Rights in a Declining Market

The decrease in market price of an item was the cause of a dispute involving an electronic contract manufacturer (ECM) that supplied the subassemblies to a first tier military contractor. The ECM purchased the components from a distributor of electronic components for a contract it had received on a major satellite project.

After receiving the subcontract on the satellite project, the ECM sent out bids on a number of components. The distributor was awarded a contract to supply integrated circuits (ICs) and other items on an "as needed" basis. In essence the ECM agreed to buy all of the integrated circuits needed during the contract period from the distributor.

After nine months the distributor noticed that the quantities of ICs had dropped dramatically. An e-mail was sent to the supply manager indicating that hardly any ICs had been purchased during the previous six weeks. The supply manager's e-mail reply was that "a competitor is supplying us ICs to the same specification at less than half of the price you charged us. If you can meet the price, fine. Otherwise we no longer need ICs from your firm." In her reply the distributor agreed that a new technology and lower demand had triggered lower market prices. However, the ECM had agreed to purchase all the ICs at a higher price earlier in the year. Subsequent meetings failed to produce a satisfactory agreement, and the parties agreed to binding arbitration.

In its arguments to the arbitrator, the ECM contended that the contract merely represented its agreement to purchase as few or as many ICs as it desired and that the distributor was obligated to supply the ICs as needed. Because the ECM was well stocked with ICs from the distributor's competitor it did not require additional ICs. The distributor argued that the ECM was committed to buying all ICs from it at the agreed-upon price. Any purchases from an outside source violated the spirit and terms of the contract.

Arbitrators Ruling

The arbitrator ruled that a mere price drop was not a reason to circumvent the terms of the contract. First, the contract was voluntarily made by competent parties. There was no indication of undue pressure nor was any party made to accept the terms. Thus the contract was not "unconscionable." Second, a needs contract should be given its literal interpretation. In this case the ECM must purchase any ICs it needs from the distributor named in the contract. Clearly it needed the ICs it purchased from the competitor. It is unfortunate for the buyer that the market price for the ICs dropped. However, if the price had risen, the distributor would have had to furnish the ICs at the lower price. These are hazards of the marketplace that are faced by both buyers and sellers. The ECM was directed to purchase the entire quantity of the ICs it had contracted for from the distributor and all future requirements needed over the remainder of the contract period.

Source: Adapted from Friedman, G. H. "Contract Challenge," *Electronic Buyer News*, August, 1992.

Warranties

Warranties ensure that a buyer can legally rely on a supplier to provide the item needed to do a job. In its most basic form, a warranty is defined as "a promise or representation made by the seller, which, if necessary, can be legally enforced."[9] There are two major types of warranties: express and implied.

Express Warranty

The UCC definition of an **express warranty** is, "Any affirmation of fact or promise made by the seller to the buyer which relates to the goods and becomes part of the basis of the bargain creates an express warranty that the goods shall conform to the affirmation or promise." Section 2–313 of the UCC indicates that use of a sample or a description of a good, which could include advertising, can create an express warranty. Warranties can be created in a variety of ways without being a written part of the contract.

Buyers must be aware that the legal system in the United States has repeatedly ruled that suppliers' sales representatives (i.e., special agents) have a natural tendency to promote the capabilities and performance of their products and services for the sole purpose of making a sale. In other words, it is not illegal for sellers to exaggerate the merits of their product during their sales pitch. Because sales personnel are considered special (not "general") agents, it is not illegal for them to exaggerate the merits of their product. In general, sellers are bound by representations of sales agents unless they indicate in the contract that they are not bound. However, the buyer should make notes on the perceived exaggerations and ask that the seller put it in writing; in effect, making the seller's claim an express warranty.

For example, consider the following:

Mike's Bakery needs flour, so Mike goes to Billy Bob's Flour Power Mill. Billy Bob says that he has a shipment of Grade A flour ready to sell. Billy Bob says that the shipment is all Grade A flour, and he gives a sample of the flour to Mike to inspect and provides a written statement describing the composition of the "Grade A flour." The sample of flour that Mike inspects meets the requirements for Grade A flour.

Mike buys the flour, pursuant to a contract of sale for "Grade A flour." However, when the shipment arrives at the bakery, it is not Grade A flour; it is spoiled and full of worms.

There is no doubt that Mike can sue Billy Bob for breach of an express warranty that the flour was Grade A flour. The contract said the shipment would be Grade A flour; Billy Bob made an affirmation of fact when he told Mike that the shipment was Grade A flour and, more importantly, provided a written statement describing the composition of Grade A flour. Further, the sample of flour was an express warranty that the rest of the flour would be as good as the sample.

Implied Warranty

The other form of warranty is the implied warranty, which deals with the concept of fitness for use and merchantability. These are also part of the contract even though they are not written, unless they are specifically disclaimed. The implied warranty of *fitness for use* (particular purpose) means when the seller at the time of contracting has reason to know of any particular purpose for which the goods are required, and the buyer is relying on the seller's skill or judgment to select or furnish suitable goods, there is (unless excluded or modified) an implied warranty that the goods shall be fit for such purpose. For example:

Mike goes to buy an industrial air-conditioning unit for his bakery. He goes to Joe's Air-Conditioning Supply Company. Mike describes the size of his bakery, the amount of heat produced by the machinery, how cool he wants to keep the facility, and so on. Joe recommends the NotSoHot 1000, and Mike buys it. The machinery turns out to be inadequate: It cannot keep the bakery cool, and it blows out after a few days.

In this case, Mike can sue Joe for breach of the implied warranty of fitness for a particular purpose, because Joe had reason to know that Mike was buying an air conditioner for a particular purpose and that Mike relied on Joe's skill and judgment to select a suitable machine. A warranty of merchantability means that the good being exchanged meets the standards of the trade and its quality is appropriate for ordinary use. This means that people who are in the business of selling certain products imply to their customers that the products are of "fair average quality." Another example:

Mike's Bakery sells 10,000 glazed doughnuts to Dot. Dot runs a retail business called Dot Donut Dollies, which sells coffee, doughnuts, and other breakfast items. The doughnuts turn out to have been mistakenly glazed with salt instead of sugar and, are inedible.

Dot can sue Mike for breach of an *implied warranty of merchantability*, because Mike's Bakery is a merchant with respect to doughnuts, and the doughnuts are not fit for the ordinary uses for which such products are used (i.e., enjoyable eating!).

Warranty of Title and Warranty of Infringement

The purchasing manager in day-to-day activities may occasionally encounter two other types of warranties: warranty of title and warranty of infringement. *Warranty of title* essentially indicates that the supplier warrants that it has title to the goods and that they are not stolen or subject to any security interest or liens. In our example, Billy Bob warrants that the flour is his to sell to Mike, and that it is not stolen property. When there are doubts as to the legitimacy of the title to the goods, purchasing managers will need to take additional steps to ensure proper transfer of title, and ensure that the supplier has the right to sell the product.

The *warranty of infringement* refers to the supplier's guarantee that the goods being exchanged do not illegally infringe on another party's patent protection. The costs and penalties for patent infringement are so severe that most standard purchasing agreements contain an appropriate patent indemnification clause. If patent infringement is determined, then the damaged party can sue for an injunction to prevent further use of that item, potentially disrupting a firm's sales of products containing the item in dispute. A simple warranty of infringement in the purchaser's contracts is not enough protection. A broader patent indemnification clause provides a greater level of safety for the buying organization. For example, if a firm provides design specifications that infringe on a third party's patent, the organization as well as the maker of that particular part may be subject to litigation. If the seller warrants that his goods do not infringe and the buyer obtains an indemnification clause, it means that the seller is liable to pay the legal expenses and court damages for a buyer sued by a third party for a patent infringement.

Patent infringement goes both ways and should be adequately protected against.

The following general suggestions can help purchasing managers to protect their organizations against warranty problems:[10]

- Write a complete purchase order (and order acceptance form)
- Build a file
- Write letters and save letters
- Use standard terms and conditions
- Consider calling the seller's attention to the warranties

Transportation Terms and Risk of Loss

Although very important, transportation documentation and delivery terms are frequently overlooked as a significant factor in many purchasing contracts. Transportation documents are used in domestic transportation to govern, direct, control, and provide information about a shipment.[11] Most of the laws governing movement of freight by truck or rail are enforced by the National Surface Transportation Board (NSTB).

The *bill of lading* is perhaps the most common and singularly important shipping document. It describes the origin of the shipment, provides specific directions for the carrier, delineates the transportation contract terms, and functions as a receipt for the shipment. In some circumstances, the bill of lading may also serve as a certificate of title for the shipment. The bill of lading contains the following information:

- The name and address of the consignor and consignee
- Routing instructions for the carrier
- A description of the goods being transported
- The number of items with corresponding commodity descriptions
- The freight class or rate for the commodity being shipped

The *freight bill* serves as the carrier's invoice for the freight charges involved in the movement of a particular shipment. As part of the freight bill, the NSTB regulations require that credit terms be listed to avoid potential price discrimination among shippers. Freight bills may be classified as either *prepaid* or *collect* to determine when the freight bill is to be tendered, regardless of whether the charges are paid in advance or not. On prepaid shipments, the freight bill is presented on the effective date of shipment. On collect shipments, the freight bill is presented on the effective date of delivery. Also, any adverse condition of the shipment should be noted here to facilitate any potential freight claims with the carrier.

Under the UCC, the risk of loss is with the seller until the title passes to the buyer.

However, the following conditions can apply:

- The buyer and seller can agree in their contract as to when in the transaction the risk of loss becomes the buyer's rather than the seller's.
- If the seller is to ship goods by a third-party carrier, but the seller is not required to deliver the goods to a specific place (just to take the goods to the carrier), the risk of loss becomes the buyer's when the goods are delivered to the carrier.
- If the seller is required to ship goods to a specific place, the risk of loss becomes the buyer's when the goods are delivered to the specific place.
- If the goods are held by a third party that is responsible for their storage, such as a commercial warehouse, the risk of loss becomes the buyer's when the buyer receives certain documents of title or the third party acknowledges the buyer's right to take the goods.
- If the goods are defective, the risk of loss does not become the buyer's unless the defects are fixed or the buyer agrees to accept the defective goods.

FOB Point

Delivery terms essentially describe who is responsible for the selection of a carrier, and payment of the freight bill, and the method in which the title of goods passes between the purchaser and the supplier. Unless the parties specify differently, the term "FOB" (free on board) delineates the point at which the supplier is responsible for freight charges and where the purchaser assumes title to the shipment. "FOB shipping point" (or "FOB origin") indicates that the purchaser is responsible for payment of transportation costs and assumes title of the goods at the supplier's shipping dock. "FOB destination" (or "FOB delivered") tells us that the supplier is responsible for transportation, and the purchaser assumes title of the goods at his or her own shipping dock. The FOB term also defines which party is responsible for filing any freight damage claims. Essentially, the party who possesses title to the goods is responsible for filing the claim.

In most cases, a loss results in a freight claim being filed with the carrier to recover payment as a result of shipment loss, damage, or delay. Such documents can also be filed with the carrier to recover overcharge premiums. In order to be valid, freight claims must be filed within nine months of the date of actual or reasonable date of delivery.

The carrier must respond with an acknowledgment of receipt of the claim within 30 days and then notify the claimant regarding whether or not the claim will be paid within 120 days. If the claim is not resolved within an additional 120 days, the carrier must notify the claimant of the reasons for not settling the claim each 60 days. If the carrier has refused to pay the claim, then the claimant has two years from the time the claim was disallowed to file for legal relief in the courts.

It is recommended that purchasing managers clearly specify delivery terms in the purchase contract to ensure that they receive the shipping and freight terms expected. It is important to signify these terms in as much detail as possible, even to the point of spelling out exact locations including street addresses and dock locations, if applicable. When in doubt, err on the side of increased detail. Unless otherwise specified in the purchase contract, the UCC recognizes FOB origin as the default delivery term.

Sellers' and Buyers' Rights

Sellers' Rights

Article 2 of the UCC is very specific about sellers' and buyers' rights. Specifically, sellers have the right to do the following:

- Sue the buyer for the purchase price of the goods if the buyer basically refuses to pay for them.
- Recover reasonable costs and expenses incurred if goods have to be resold.
- Receive compensation for additional costs and expenses incurred by reason of the buyer's wrongful conduct.

The right to sue for the purchase price of goods is basically a breach of contract lawsuit. However, if there are still goods in the seller's possession, the seller may be required to try to resell the goods for a fair price in order to offset what the buyer owes. This becomes especially important in end-of-life strategies. The buyer should let the seller know well in advance if a product is going to be discontinued to allow the seller to deplete existing inventories. If the goods are in the possession of the seller, the buyer cannot resell them.

Buyers Rights

According to the UCC, a buyer's rights include the right to do the following:

- Reject defective goods that the seller cannot repair within a reasonable time.
- Sue for breach of contract.
- Revoke acceptance of goods if the buyer discovers latent defects.
- Seek a court order forcing the seller to deliver the goods ("specific performance").
- Recover any extra expense incurred for having to purchase replacement goods from another seller.
- Retain the right to recover costs and expenses caused by a breach of warranty.

According to Article 2 of the UCC, a buyer can reject defective goods, but that right is waived once the buyer accepts the goods after having an opportunity to inspect. However, the buyer has responsibility with respect to seller's goods in the buyer's possession. When a buyer accepts delivery of goods from a supplier (including a pickup from the supplier's plant), the buyer is responsible if it does not catch the defects. This is an excellent argument for certifying suppliers' processes and not relying on inspection as a means to ensure quality. In most cases, a supplier will want to remedy the problem to avoid conflict, but not always. If absolutely necessary, a buyer can get a court order to force the seller to deliver the goods. This might occur in a capacity problem and is known as "specific performance." A buyer can also recover costs and expenses caused by a breach of warranty, including costs of inspection, storage, and return shipment.

Patents and Intellectual Property

As suppliers become increasingly integrated into new-product development, intellectual property agreements are becoming the norm. The U.S. Constitution provides the framework for the intellectual property legal system, including patent and copyright law, as we know it today, through Article 1, Section 8, Clause 8, which says that "Congress shall have the Power . . . to promote the Progress of Science and useful Arts, by securing for limited Times to Authors and Inventors the exclusive Right to their respective Writings and Discoveries."[12] There are three kinds of intellectual property in the United States: (1) **patents**, (2) **copyrights**, and (3) **trade secrets**. Patent law has been established in several federal patent statutes including the Patent Act of 1790, 35 U.S.C Section 1, and companion laws. Copyright law is founded in the federal statutes, particularly in the Copyright Act of 1976. Federal patent and copyright laws overrule any

Sourcing Snapshot

You Be the Judge

Scenario 1

The Mark Antony Pet Shop writes to Cleopatra, stating, "Dear Cleo: A once-in-a-lifetime opportunity for you. We just received a shipment of asps. They are healthy and friendly, love kids, and make great watch-snakes. As a preferred customer you can receive one for $50. The price includes fang removal. Please respond by fax only." Cleo sends a letter of acceptance by regular mail because the UCC allows acceptance by "any reasonable means." Is Cleo's acceptance valid?

Scenario 2

The Voyager Ports Steamship Line contracts to buy 50 of the 25-person-capacity lifeboats from Robinson Crusoe's Lifeboat Company. Crusoe ships the 15-person lifeboats instead of the 25-person ones. Could there be a contract under these conditions?

Scenario 3

Amanda, a buyer for ABC, orders 100,000 Read Only Memory (ROM) devices for delivery on June 1. On May 10, the seller advises Amanda there will be no shipment on June 1 because of production problems. What are Amanda's alternatives?

Answers
Scenario 1

Cleo's acceptance is not valid because Mark Anthony specifically and unambiguously asked for a fax. Although acceptance through any reasonable means is normally valid, offerors can restrict the acceptable means of acceptance as long as they do so unambiguously.

Scenario 2

There is a contract only if Voyager Ports Steamship accepts the nonconforming goods. This could occur in the following ways: (1) notifying Crusoe that it will take the boats even though they are nonconforming; (2) failing to inspect them after a reasonable time to do so; and (3) acting inconsistently with Crusoe's ownership (UCC Section 2–606), such as attaching the lifeboats to Voyager's ships.

Scenario 3

UCC Section 2–217 states that after a breach the buyer is entitled to cover by going into the market and buying the goods to replace those not forthcoming. The buyer must recover from the seller the difference between the contract price and the cover price. The buyer may also recover any incidental and consequential damages less any expenses saved as a result of the cover.

Source: Adapted from "UCC Article 2 Quiz," (1991, April), *Purchasing Management of Silicon Valley Newsletter*, 4.

contradictory state statutes. By contrast, trade secret law is grounded in common law and is intended to protect unique ideas that would not otherwise have legal protection under patent and copyright law. Because common law varies by state, there is some variance in actual statutes. However, most states have created laws that are very similar.

In its most basic form, a *patent* is an agreement between the inventor and the federal government. Successful patentees in the United States are now entitled to exclusive rights (to make, use, or sell) an invention for the life of the patent 20 years from the filing date with the U.S. Patent Office.

Although the inventor has exclusive rights (i.e., a monopoly) to the invention during the patent period, others gain that right to the benefits of the invention following expiration of the protection period, thereby providing public benefit. A U.S. patent is applicable only to the inventor's exclusive use within the borders of the United States. Inventors wishing to expand their patent protection to other countries must file appropriate patent applications in each country in which protection is desired.

Note that in some countries, such as China and India, copyrights and patents may not be recognized at all. In recent years, because of the entry of these countries into the World Trade Organization, both China and India recognize copyrights (at least verbally), but piracy remains a constant problem.

A firm needs to protect itself from inadvertent patent infringement whenever it purchases a product from a supplier. This can best be done by including a patent indemnification clause in all purchasing documents. This clause should consist of three parts:

1. An indemnification, which seeks the supplier's assurances that the goods being contracted for do not infringe on any other party's patents
2. The right to require the supplier to defend any patent infringement suit itself
3. The right to have the purchaser's own attorneys involved in defense of any lawsuit concerning patent infringement

The UCC provides minimal protection for the purchasers in defending themselves against legal actions stemming from patent infringement. Therefore, indemnification agreements should be included in contracts with suppliers whenever possible.

A copyright is designed to afford protection for persons who create original works such as books, software, songs, and films. A copyright on written material is generally good for the life of the author plus 50 years. Copyright law does not require a formal application, as does patent law. In addition, it is not necessary for the copyright originator to place any legend or indication on the protected material indicating that the material is copyrighted. Copyright is automatically assumed. However, most legal experts recommend that some sort of language in the form of a copyright notice be included on any works desired to be protected, along with the copyright symbol ©. This notice provides evidence that the creator of the article in question intends to maintain copyright privileges in the event of infringement. It should also be noted that registering copyrightable works and providing notice entitles copyright owners to much greater damages in the event of a copyright infringement suit.

A *trade secret* (also known as confidential information) is a very broad category of intellectual property. Virtually any information believed to be confidential and important to an organization can be deemed to be a trade secret or confidential information.

Resources as diverse as formulas, supplier and customer lists, procedures, and training programs could all be regarded as trade secrets. In order to receive trade secret protection under the law, the organization must take steps to minimize or preclude the distribution of its sensitive information. The information must also be deemed to possess the following three characteristics:

- It is economically valuable.
- It is not generally known.
- It is kept as a secret.

Trade secret protection becomes essentially self-serving through the actions of the organization itself. For instance, if information that could otherwise be considered trade secrets is not protected through devices such as limited access or other security precautions, then the courts have ruled that this information is not confidential and, therefore, not entitled to protection. This test of confidential information can also be applied to any information that suppliers provide to the purchasing firm through the normal course of business dealings. As before, however, the supplier must make it known that the information is proprietary and is to be kept confidential. As a precaution, any information given to a supplier should be accompanied by notification that the information is provided in confidence and should be treated as such by the supplier. This is typically known as a *nondisclosure agreement* (NDA). See Exhibit 15.3 for an example of a nondisclosure agreement.

Exhibit 15.3	Nondisclosure Agreement

Supplier's Name

Supplier's Address

City, State, Zip Code

Re: *Nondisclosure Agreement*

In conjunction with recent discussions, our Company has disclosed and it is anticipated in the future that our Company will disclose to your company or your company will observe, or come in contact with, certain confidential information that is the property of our Company. This information will include, without limitation, certain proprietary items related to our Company's know-how, processes, machinery, and manufacturing aspects of our Company's business.

In consideration thereof, it is our understanding that except as hereafter specifically authorized in writing by our Company, your company shall not disclose to any party: (a) the fact that it is assisting our Company in this matter; (b) any confidential information heretofore or hereafter disclosed by our Company to your company or that your company observes or comes in contact with, not in the possession of your company prior to the date of such disclosure, observance, or contact; or (c) any marketing, financial, or technical information developed or generated by your company for our Company at our request and direct or indirect expense. Your company shall neither use nor furnish to any party any equipment or material embodying or made by the use of such information, provided, however, that:

1. Should any of the aforesaid information be published or otherwise made available to the public through sources that are entitled to disclose the same, and should your company demonstrate to our Company that it has obtained said information from a source available to the public, then in that event your company shall be free with respect to this understanding to disclose said information to any party;
2. Your company understands that nothing herein shall be construed to grant any right or license under any industrial property rights (patents, trademarks, and copyrights) of our Company.

Will you please indicate your company's concurrence in the foregoing understanding by signing and returning to us the enclosed duplicate of this letter?

Very truly yours,

_____

(Name and title)

XXX: xxx

Accepted By: _____

Name: _____

Title: _____

Date: _____

Other Laws Affecting Purchasing

Antitrust and Unfair Trade Practice Laws

A number of federal laws deal with antitrust and competitive practices of interstate commerce. Each law seeks to promote the fair conduct of business and preserve competition in markets. Although most of these laws apply to the conduct of the seller, some provisions apply directly or indirectly to purchasers.

Sherman Antitrust Act (1890)

This law prohibits actions that are "in restraint of trade" or actions that attempt to monopolize a market or create a monopoly. Price fixing, dividing territories among competitors, and agreements that limit the supply of a commodity are violations of the Sherman Act. However, the law also prohibits reciprocity or reciprocal purchase agreements, where the effect of such agreements limits competition.

Federal Trade Commission Act (FTCA, 1914)

This act authorizes the Federal Trade Commission (FTC) to interpret trade legislation, including the provisions of the Sherman Antitrust Act that deal with restraint of trade. The FTCA also addresses unfair competition and unfair or deceptive trade practices. Unfair trade practices include: (1) those that allow large firms to gain advantage over smaller rivals; (2) predatory competition; (3) restraint of trade; and (4) misleading or deceptive practices such as false advertising.

Clayton Antitrust Act (1914)

This law, which broadened the Sherman Act, makes price discrimination illegal and prohibits sellers from exclusive arrangements with purchasers or product distributors. One of the most common exclusive agreements is a *tying agreement*, where a supplier makes the sale of one product contingent upon the sale of another product. Thus suppliers must make unbundled individual products available to buyers. Exclusive agreements are those where the buyer must purchase all requirements from one supplier. Price discrimination among different purchasers is prohibited if such discrimination substantially lessens competition or tends to create a monopoly in any line of commerce.

Robinson-Patman Act (1936)

This law strengthens the Clayton Act by clarifying the issue of price discrimination, particularly as it pertains to limiting the powers of large buyers. It prohibits sellers from offering a discriminatory price where the effect of discrimination may limit competition or create a monopoly. Price differences must be based on "economies of scale" because of lower costs. There is also a provision that prohibits purchasers from inducing a discriminatory price. Although a seller may legally lower a price as a concession during negotiations, the purchaser should not mislead or trick the seller, thus resulting in a price that is discriminatory to other "like size" buyers in the market. Robinson-Patman violations occur when different prices are charged to different buyers. Thus, most sellers develop uniform pricing policies that are subject to quantity discounts as a result of economic scale advantages for producing and selling larger quantities.

The law makes provision for price differences in certain situations. The first, as mentioned above, is for differences in costs of manufacturing or sale because of quantities and methods of production and distribution. The second is the good-faith attempt to meet a lower competitive price. The third is if the goods are perishable via deterioration, seasonality, or distress sales under court orders.

Laws Affecting Global Purchasing

Many laws—U.S., foreign, and international—affect global commerce. The following briefly summarizes some of the laws that can affect a purchaser's international business dealings.[13]

The United Nations Convention on Contracts for International Sale of Goods (CISG)

This is an attempt by the United Nations to facilitate international trade by removing legal barriers. Unless the parties have specified to the contrary, the CISG applies to the sale of goods between parties with places of business in the contracting states. Contracting states are countries that have ratified the CISG. As of August, 2010 76 countries had ratified the CISG. These 80 countries account for 75 percent of the world's trade. One of the key provisions to its success is the flexibility to take exception to specified articles of the code on a contract-by-contract basis.

Foreign Corrupt Practices Act

This law prohibits payments (such as bribes) that might benefit a foreign official personally. Such payments are not restricted to just monetary forms but may include anything of value. For example, a Marketing executive invites a Chinese executive to Las Vegas along with his/her spouse provides airfare, meals, lodging in a casino hotel the week before they meet to discuss the Chinese contract. The value of the package while not a direct bribe is something of "value" and therefore violates FCPA. Although the law usually pertains to sellers, purchasers should understand its provisions so they can recognize situations addressed by the act.

International Anti-Bribery Act

The law amends the Foreign Corrupt Practices Act by implementing the provisions of the Organization for Economic Cooperation and Development's Convention on Combating Bribery of Foreign Public Officials in International Business Transactions. The act makes it illegal for a citizen or corporation of the United States or a person or corporation acting within the United States to influence, bribe, or otherwise seek an advantage from a public official of another country.

Anti-Boycott Legislation

Various laws address doing business with countries that support the boycott of one nation against another. Examples include the boycott of Israel by Arab countries and the boycott of Taiwan by mainland China. These laws require reporting of any request to participate in a boycott, which purchasers often fail to do.

Homeland Security Presidential Directive (HSPD-12)

The primary intent of HSPD-12 is to enhance security, increase government efficiency, reduce identity fraud and support the fight against global terrorism. It establishes a mandatory, government-wide standard for verifying identity, and providing identification and badging credentials to its employees and contractors who work in federally controlled facilities or have access to federal information systems.

The Department of Homeland Security was created after the terrorist actions of September 11, 2001, and was established to create better transportation security systems to move people and cargo more securely and efficiently. DHS also strengthened border security and enforcement. Both the directive and DHS have implications for purchasers who are sourcing outside the United States, as incoming shipments will now receive much more scrutiny.[14]

Export Administration Act

Various laws and regulations govern, and sometimes even restrict, the export of goods, information, and services. Purchasers may not perceive that they are engaged in exporting. However, the law views certain types of drawings, specifications, and prototypes forwarded to a foreign entity as restricted exports of technology. Purchasers are urged to seek the advice of an expert when questions arise in this area.

U.S. Customs and Border Protection (CBP) Laws

Customs laws address the importation of goods into the United States. Customs brokers who are familiar with customs laws can be quite valuable in understanding the rules and regulations governing importation. With the increased awareness of terrorist threats to U.S. security, the U.S. Customs and Border Protection (CBP) was established as an agency of the Department of Homeland Security, merging functions of the former U.S. Customs Service, Immigration and Naturalization Service, Border Patrol, and Animal and Plant Health Inspection Service. The agency ensures that all imports and exports are legal and comply with U.S. laws and regulations, and collects revenues associated with the enforcement of those laws.

CBP has implemented a cargo security strategy designed to enhance national security while protecting the economic vitality of the United States. These efforts include: (1) the 24-hour Manifest Rule; (2) Container Security Initiative; (3) Customs-Trade Partnership Against Terrorism (C-TPAT); (4) Non-Intrusive Inspection Techniques; (5) Automated Targeting System; (5) the National Targeting Center and; (6) the Secure Freight Initiative.

The Secure Freight Initiative ("10+2" initiative) is intended to help reduce the risk of terrorism, by utilizing the latest tracking and tracing technology, current data capture methods, and communicating and reporting capabilities along with cooperation among trade partnerships and governments. The result is a much more detailed account of goods and materials entering the United States via maritime shipping containers. CBP's goal is to identify potential high-risk cargo movements while expediting processing of low-risk cargo, and improving the accuracy of cargo descriptions.[15]

Foreign Country and International Laws

In addition to the U.S. laws that apply to foreign transactions, the laws and regulations of other countries involved in a business transaction may also apply. These laws will likely address contract law, export control, currency control, and criminal law. Some transactions could be illegal if structured in a certain manner.

International laws may apply to business transactions that are not part of any specific country's laws and regulations. Maritime laws are a good example of international laws that affect international commerce. Several international documents are also pertinent to international transactions. These include International Contracting Terms and the CISG mentioned earlier.

The laws governing purchasing are complex and varied. Other laws address environmental and labor issues. This overview simply points out that today's purchaser must be aware of the laws and regulations governing domestic and international purchasing. A purchaser is urged to discuss with legal counsel any questions that arise during the performance of job responsibilities. Ignorance of the law is not a valid defense.

Purchasing Ethics

Ethics have their basis in the field of philosophy and identify common principles associated with appropriate versus inappropriate actions, moral duty, and obligation. Ethics are the set of moral principles or values guiding our behavior. In a business setting, ethical behavior is the use of recognized social principles involving justice and fairness throughout a business relationship. When interacting with suppliers, an ethical buyer treats them in a just, decent, fair, honest, and fitting manner. Being ethical means following a code viewed as fair by those within the profession as well as the community.[16] A study on purchasing education and training requirements indicated ethics was the number one knowledge requirement for purchasers now and in the future.[17]

Three rules are understood to be a part of ethical behavior. First, buyers must commit their attention and energies for the organization's benefit rather than personal enrichment at the expense of the organization. Ethical buyers do not accept outside gifts or favors that violate their firm's ethics policy. Ethical buyers are also not tempted or influenced by the unethical practices of salespeople and do not have personal financial arrangements with suppliers. Second, a buyer must act ethically toward suppliers or potential suppliers. This means treating each supplier professionally and with respect. Finally, buyers must uphold the ethical standards set forth by both their organization and the purchasing profession. A code or statement of professional ethics usually formalizes the set of ethical standards.

Purchasing managers, more than any other group within a firm, face pressure to act in unethical ways. This occurs for several reasons. First, purchasing has direct control over large sums of money. A buyer responsible for a multimillion-dollar contract may find sellers using any means available to secure a favorable position. Second, the very nature of purchasing means that a buyer must come in contact with outside, and occasionally unethical, sellers. A third reason is the pressure placed on many salespeople. A seller that must meet aggressive sales goals might resort to questionable sales practices.

Risks of Unethical Behavior

A buyer who performs an unethical act runs the risk that the act is also illegal. For example, a government buyer who accepts payment from a defense contractor has clearly committed an unethical and illegal act. If this payment becomes known, the buyer risks legal penalty as defined by the law. The buyer's firm also risks a legal penalty. At a minimum, the buyer will probably lose his or her job.

Unethical behavior also presents a personal risk to a buyer's professional reputation. Sellers quickly become aware of buyers who are open to offers "on the side." Once a buyer earns a reputation within an industry, it is difficult to change it. A buyer also runs a risk that management will discover his or her lack of ethics and terminate employment. A professional reputation is something a buyer carries throughout an entire career. If a buyer is found guilty of accepting a bribe, companies will not only terminate the buyer, but may often pursue litigation as well. Personal financial bankruptcy or even jail sentences can result for buyers who are found guilty of accepting large bribes.

A final risk of unethical behavior is the risk to a firm's reputation. A buyer who makes purchase decisions based on factors other than legitimate business criteria risks the reputation of the entire firm. For example, quality may suffer if a buyer accepts substandard performance from a supplier that offered outside inducements. A buyer's unethical behavior can jeopardize the livelihood of others dependent on a firm's success. World-class suppliers do not have to practice unethical behavior to win contracts.

To summarize the legal perspective, accepting a supplier's outside gifts and favors in exchange for special treatment is a form of corruption. The U.S. business environment does not treat unethical behavior lightly. Buyers who practice unethical behavior subject themselves and their firms to increased risk and diminish the integrity of the purchasing profession. Firms dealing with global sourcing sometimes encounter unethical behavior, particularly in developing countries, where bribery may be viewed as a routine source of extra income. However, global firms are increasingly adopting an unequivocal zero-tolerance stance toward any form of bribery, even if it means sacrificing short-term profitability to maintain a global reputation of integrity and honesty in its dealings with suppliers. Further, the main provisions of the Foreign Corrupt Practices Act make it illegal to offer gifts or payments to officials in foreign countries.

Types of Unethical Purchasing Behavior

Suppose a buyer at Firm XYZ has the highest moral and ethical values—the buyer has strong beliefs about what is proper behavior within the purchasing profession. Conflict can occur if a supervisor asks the buyer to do something the buyer feels is unethical. For example, a manager may ask a buyer to award a contract because of a personal friendship with a supplier. The buyer may feel this is unethical.

Does the buyer simply award the contract in compliance with the manager's instruction, and ignore his or her own personal and moral values? Or does the buyer refuse to award the contract, thereby challenging the authority of a manager and jeopardizing his or her career? Although a professional buyer should know the difference between right and wrong, organizational pressures can force a buyer to behave in ways that conflict with personal values, which creates a difficult situation for the individual. How should a person respond in this situation?

The definition of ethical behavior can differ from buyer to buyer or from firm to firm. Despite these possible differences, most professionals recognize certain behavior or actions as unethical. Most companies have established guidelines that reinforce that these behaviors are unethical and therefore unacceptable. Some of these behaviors are listed below.

Sharp Practices

A **sharp practice** is any misrepresentation by a buyer that falls just short of actual fraud.[18] Sharp practice occurs whenever a buyer plays games with a supplier and operates in an underhanded manner. The practice includes many different behaviors·

- Willful use of misinformation. When a buyer knowingly deceives a supplier to realize some advantage. For example, requesting quotes on inflated volumes and then placing smaller orders at the reduced price is a willful use of misinformation.

- Exaggerating problems. A buyer who exaggerates the size of a supplier-caused problem to extract a larger penalty or concession from a supplier is using a sharp practice.

- Requesting bids from unqualified suppliers for the sole purpose of driving a qualified supplier's price lower. A buyer should request bids from qualified suppliers only.

- Gaining information unfairly through deception.

- Sharing information on competitive quotations. The integrity of the competitive bid process requires confidentiality. Buyers who share supplier-quoted information violate the ethics of the bid process.

- Not compensating a supplier for design or other work. Buyers often request design and cost-savings assistance from suppliers. A supplier that helps a buyer should receive fair compensation for its efforts.

- Taking unfair advantage of a supplier's financial situation. A buyer who knowingly pressures a financially troubled supplier into providing a lower-than-normal price places the supplier in further financial jeopardy. Taking advantage of a financially susceptible supplier is an unethical business practice.

- Lying or misleading. Any instance of lying or misleading a seller is a sharp practice.

Accepting Supplier Favors

Accepting gifts and favors from a supplier is the most common ethical infraction involving buyers. These gifts and favors can affect a buyer's judgment to evaluate and select the most capable suppliers. The policy on supplier offerings is often a confusing issue. At what point does a supplier's gift or favor depart from a friendly showing of appreciation for a firm's business to an attempt to influence a buyer's purchase decisions? Accepting free items from potential suppliers is especially questionable. Here, a supplier does not even have a purchase contract. Most firms address this issue in their ethics policies under gifts and gratuities and specify exactly what a buyer may or may not accept from a supplier.

Reciprocity

This action involves giving preferential treatment to suppliers that are also customers of the buying organization.[19] In simple terms, it refers to a purchasing arrangement that dictates, "I'll buy from you if you buy from me." The Federal Trade Commission has taken an aggressive stance against reciprocal buying arrangements, ruling that it is illegal "to abusively use large buying power to restrict competitive market opportunities."

It is legal to buy from customers when such actions do not restrict competition. However, from a practical perspective, reciprocity can restrict competition among suppliers or potential suppliers since competing sellers know the business is "closed" to competition and that the favored "reciprocal" supplier will receive most of the business. Finally, the reciprocal supplier may become lax on quality and delivery knowing the business is "locked up."

Personal Buying

This occurs when a purchasing department purchases material for the personal needs of its employees. Some states have outlawed such practices with statutes called "trade diversion laws." These laws prohibit purchasing from engaging in personal buying for items not required during the normal course of business.

There are some exceptions to these laws. For example, a firm can purchase safety shoes, hats, gloves, or even special tools required by the employee. A purchasing department can use its knowledge to purchase products conforming to specific quality standards. Personal buying is a gray area for some purchasing departments. Some firms view personal buying as a fringe benefit and service to the employee. Other firms flatly prohibit the practice. A buyer confronted with a request for personal buying should first determine the legal status of the practice and then discuss the subject with management.

Financial Conflicts of Interest

When a buyer awards business to a supplier because the buyer, the buyer's family, or relatives of the buyer have a direct financial interest in a supplier, this is considered a major unethical practice. This behavior is one reason many companies require employees to detail any investments in companies. Direct financial interest does not imply that a buyer cannot invest in publically traded companies. In most cases the ownership percentage of a large firm with millions of shares outstanding would not be considered a conflict of interest.

Financial conflict of interest is much more likely in smaller firms where an investment could comprise a significant amount of the firm. In such a case the buyer's best course of action is to disclose the potential conflict and let management decide on whether it would be best to switch the commodity or service to another buyer.

Certainly, awarding a purchase contract to a company in which a buyer has a significant personal financial interest poses serious ethical issues. This action is similar to an executive buying or selling stock because of inside knowledge, which is an illegal act.

Personal Conflicts of Interest

Personal conflicts of interest arise in cases where the buyer is dealing with a company that employs a close relative or that the buyer has approached or been approached for future employment. For example, a supply manager contracts with a temporary services firm where his wife is the Director of Marketing. This would be a personal conflict of interest and should be reported to management for the appropriate decision. The key with personal conflicts of interest is disclosure and openness, since conflicts will occur through no fault of either party. Buyers must be clear to remove themselves from these conflicts to preserve their reputation.

Disclosure of Confidential/Proprietary Information

Purchasers are obligated to protect information given to them by suppliers. Certainly this applies when it is indicated the material is confidential. Giving such information to competitors violates the integrity of the buyer-seller process. Further it discourages suppliers from engaging in open dialogues that could improve the outcomes of both the buyer and seller. Sellers who share information with key customers expect buyers to keep this information confidential.

Influence and Ethics

Influence and attempts to influence decisions exist at several points in the supply chain. The Institute for Supply Management's (ISM's) Ethical Standards Committee addressed this important issue. Influence can be defined in several ways. Most frequently, **influence** is defined as the power to sway: "the power that somebody has to affect other people's thinking or actions by means of argument, example, or force of personality." Supply professionals regularly make decisions about what their organization buys, who they buy from, how much they buy, and how they buy it. Often, they also have input into the specifications and requirements surrounding the purchase. Suppliers regularly work to influence the decisions of supply professionals.[20]

Supply professionals must overcome the negative aspects of influence to ensure that they are objective in their decision making and that they are operating in an ethical manner. Positive and appropriate influences include: (1) suppliers sharing new ideas, methodologies, and technologies; (2) sharing data when being involved early in design issues; and (3) a cross-functional team being involved in a comparative analysis of competing suppliers; they add value to decision making, whereas other influences may detract from the quality of decisions. Negative sources of influence conflict with the goal of supply professionals and other leaders to manage their responsibilities according to ethical guidelines set forth by their organizations or ISM. Examples of negative influences include: (1) giving personal interests priority over employer interests; (2) inappropriate sharing of confidential or proprietary information with suppliers; and (3) accepting gifts, entertainment, or meals as a reward for a decision that could be made in favor of the supplier. These negative factors can have an unfavorable impact on an organization.[21]

An ethics survey by the ISM's Ethical Standards Committee (see Exhibit 15.4) showed that influence is a challenge for supply professionals. Survey results related to influence revealed that inappropriate preference for suppliers in sourcing decisions was a concern from 34 percent of the survey respondents, and politics inappropriately influencing sourcing decisions was a concern to 46 percent of respondents. Although only 6 to 7 percent of supply professionals were concerned about gifts, entertainment, and meals influencing sourcing decisions within their function, over 45 percent of the survey respondents indicated that individuals outside of their function received gifts, entertainment, or meals from suppliers.[22] It is important for supply professionals to be aware of the subtleties of influence so that they can better manage the potential impact on their decisions and behaviors. Regardless of the culture or continent, influence is a reality, and the goal of the supply professional is to appropriately manage it.

Exhibit 15.4		
ISM ETHICS SURVEY: INFLUENCE ISSUES	**NO INFLUENCE**	**INFLUENCE**
There are instances where your organization gave inappropriate preference to suppliers in sourcing decisions.	66%	34%
There are examples in your organization where politics inappropriately influenced sourcing decisions.	54%	46%
Gifts or entertainment inappropriately influenced sourcing decisions in your function.	93%	7%
Meals with suppliers influenced sourcing decisions in your function.	94%	6%
Others outside of your function have received gifts or entertainment from suppliers outside of your organization's policy.	55%	45%

Source: 2006 ISM Ethics Survey.

ISM Professional Code of Ethics

The Institute for Supply Management is the largest organization representing the purchasing profession. Since 1959, the *Standards of Conduct* serves as a guide for the ISM membership by imposing rules of conduct, particularly when a buyer's own company lacks a policy or statement of ethics. In the words of the code, "It is necessary for all of us to exercise a strict rule of personal conduct to insure that relations of a compromising nature, or even the appearance of such relations, be scrupulously avoided." The document reflects the ISM's commitment to ethical behavior and fair business dealings.

The Standards of Conduct specifies three guiding principles of purchasing practice: (1) loyalty to company, (2) justice to those with whom a buyer deals, and (3) faith in the purchasing profession. From these principles ISM derived its standards of purchasing practice, or Code of Ethics:

1. Consider, first, the interest of your company in all transactions and carry out and believe in its established policies.

2. Be receptive to competent counsel from your colleagues and be guided by such counsel without impairing the dignity and responsibility of your office.

3. Buy without prejudice, seeking to obtain the maximum value for each dollar of expenditure.

4. Strive consistently for knowledge of the materials and processes of manufacture and establish practical methods for the conduct of your office.

5. Subscribe to and work for honesty and truth in buying and selling, and denounce all forms and manifestations of commercial bribery.

6. Accord a prompt and courteous reception, so far as conditions will permit, to all who call on a legitimate business mission.

7. Respect your obligations and require that obligations to you and to your concern be respected, consistent with good business practice.

8. Avoid sharp practice.

9. Counsel and assist fellow purchasing managers in the performance of their duties, whenever the occasion permits.

10. Cooperate with all organizations and individuals engaged in activities designed to enhance the development and standing of purchasing.

These standards often help guide a firm's ethical code of conduct and policy.

The ISM standards specifically state that its members should maintain standards on an even higher plane than those accepted by society—what becomes the "true test of greatness." This is stated as follows in the code:

Nothing can undermine respect for the purchasing profession more than improper action on the part of its members with regard to gifts, gratuities, or favors. People engaged in purchasing should not accept from any supplier or prospective supplier any money, gift, or favor that might influence, or be suspected of influencing, their buying decisions. We must decline to accept or must return any such gift or favor offered us or members of our immediate family. The declination of these gifts or favors must be done discreetly and courteously. Possible embarrassment resulting from refusals does not constitute a basis for exception.

The ISM Standards of Conduct is a powerful document. It holds the purchasing profession to the highest levels of ethical conduct. Companies of all sizes from many industries have used the Code of Ethics as a guide when developing their own ethical policies.

Supporting Ethical Behavior

A firm can take many actions to make sure its employees conduct business in an ethical manner. The following sections summarize the actions a firm can take to enhance the ethical behavior of its purchasing personnel.

Developing a Statement of Ethics

Most research on purchasing ethics concludes that adopting a formal ethics policy helps define and deter potentially unethical purchasing behavior. An earlier study found that firms without formal ethical policies disclosed supplier bid prices to other suppliers at a much higher rate than firms with a formal policy prohibiting this practice.[23] Also, firms without a formal ethics policy were more likely to make discounted purchases for their employees, a questionable practice in some states. A formal ethics policy helps define the boundaries of ethical behavior.

Top-Management Commitment

Executive management sets the ethical code of behavior within a firm. Although the highest executive may not actually write a firm's purchasing or marketing code of ethics, the ethical behavior of top executives sends a message about whether or not unethical behavior is tolerated. Lower-level managers quickly recognize top management's commitment to ethical behavior and imitate the commitment, especially when other managers are fired because of their unethical behavior! (See the Good Practice Example on Eaton Corporation at the end of this chapter.)

Closer Buyer-Seller Relationships

Dealing with a smaller supply base or a single supplier for an item will probably do more for ethical purchasing behavior than any other recent trend or action. Firms are increasingly using buying teams to evaluate potential suppliers across different performance categories. Using a team approach to evaluate a supplier's capabilities limits the opportunity for unethical behavior. Unethical suppliers will find it tougher to influence a team of professionals.

Ethical Training

New buyers, usually at larger firms, often enter a training program before actually assuming their professional duties. One part of the training usually deals with purchasing ethics. Such a program is an opportunity to educate a new buyer about a firm's ethics policy. Firms often use role playing to help buyers learn how to identify different types of unethical behavior and how to confront and deal with these situations. Ethics training reinforces a firm's commitment to the highest ethical standards.

Developing Consistent Behavior

Confusion about proper ethical behavior can arise when marketing and purchasing have separate ethical standards. A firm that prohibits its purchasing personnel from accepting gifts from suppliers but allows its marketing department to distribute gifts to its customers is not acting consistently. When different standards of behavior exist within the same firm, it becomes easier for one group to rationalize or justify unethical behavior. How can it be ethical for one group (marketing) to provide gifts and favors but unethical for another group (purchasing) within the same firm to accept any items?

Internal Reporting of Unethical Behavior

Executive purchasing management should create an atmosphere that supports the reporting of unethical behavior. A buyer should be able to approach management about an ethical impropriety with confidence that management will correct the problem. A firm should also encourage suppliers to report instances of unethical behavior by anyone within the buying firm.

Preventive Measures (Commodity Rotation and Limits of Authority)

One common strategy is to rotate buyers among different items or commodities, which prevents a buyer from becoming too comfortable with any particular group of suppliers. Although a buyer should become familiar with purchased items and suppliers, it is often a good idea to rotate personnel between buying assignments. Rotation usually occurs every several years.

Another preventive measure is to limit a buyer's purchase authority without higher-level approval. For example, a firm's policy may limit a buyer's authority for awarding purchase contracts to amounts of $100,000 or less. Contracts greater than $100,000 then require a manager's signature. A buyer must justify the selection decision based on sound purchasing criteria before obtaining the final sign-off. This provides a system of checks and balances and reduces the possibility of unethical supplier selection.

Although there is a fine line between ethical and legal behavior, we believe that ethics should always come first. However, it is also important that a professional purchasing manager develop a detailed understanding of purchasing law. Having a good working knowledge of legal issues can have a positive impact on daily and long-term actions in the profession.

Corporate Social Responsibility

Corporate social responsibility is the idea that organizations and institutions have an obligation to society that extends beyond compliance with regulations in considering the broader effects of their actions. Social responsibility is becoming more accepted in twenty-first century corporations. ISM has developed a guide to assist supply managers in developing their socially responsible practices. The areas covered in the policy are (1) community, (2) diversity, (3) environment, (4) ethics, (5) financial responsibility, (6) human rights, and (7) safety. Many of these topics are covered in Chapters 7 and 8 on supplier strategies and selection. This chapter has discussed ethics and to a lesser extent community issues. We will focus on the environmental issues in the remainder of this chapter; ISM's Principles of Social Responsibility encourage buyers to be proactive with suppliers and customers in creating a culture of environmental responsibility (see Exhibit 15.5).

Environment & Sustainability

The environment and sustainability under the green movement is becoming a large initiative, as several major corporations have become aware of the need to reduce their impact on the environment. For example, OfficeMax has had success selling paper with higher recycled content (50 percent and 100 percent post-consumer content). Recycled paper has been among its fastest growing office-papers segments, and it is helping OfficeMax improve business with existing customers as well as acquire new accounts. The company says it is a leader in paper carrying third-party environmental certification.[24]

Dolphin Blue, a Dallas-based online supplier of recycled office products, supplies the U.S. Postal Service with envelopes made of recycled fiber that is chlorine free. It is also printed with soy inks and uses a latex gum self-seal closure. Dolphin Blue CEO Tom Kemper says that paper and paper packaging are two single largest-volume commodities entering the waste stream. "Using recycled office products saves energy, reduces emissions, and preserves the forests, so it makes sense to use them," he says.[25]

In another sustainability example, Dell Computer Corp unveiled its "Three Cs (cube, content and cushioning) of Smarter Packaging" initiative, with a goal to reduce the size of its boxes, increase its use of green materials in packaging and make much of its packaging recyclable. Dell looked into how its packaging can be less reliant on hardwoods and softwoods, which can take a long time to grow. Dell held brainstorming sessions on its Three C packaging initiative with suppliers. Unisource longtime Dell supplier, suggested bamboo, which, as a member of the grass family, grows back much faster than hardwoods, making it more environmentally friendly. A cost analysis showed bamboo would in fact reduce Dell's packaging costs. Unisource provided samples of the materials it would use and suggested supply sources for the raw bamboo. The process of turning bamboo into pulp is mechanical, according to Dell, and uses fewer chemicals than paper pulp.

Exhibit 15.5	ISM Principles of Sustainability and Social Responsibility Management

Sustainability is the ability to meet current needs without hindering the ability to meet the needs of future generations in terms of economic, environmental, and social challenges. *Social responsibility* is defined as a framework of measurable corporate policies and procedures and resulting behavior designed to benefit the workplace and, by extension, the individual, the organization, and the community. Listed below are the ten ISM principles of Sustainability and Social Responsibility; (in alphabetical order):

1. **Anti-Corruption**
   Corruption in all of its forms, including extortion and bribery, will not be tolerated.

2. **Diversity and Inclusiveness—Workforce and Supply Base**
   Workforce. Workforce diversity and inclusiveness is the attraction and retention of a workforce that reasonably represents the customer and communities in which the organization operates.
   Supply Base. Attraction and retention of a diverse supply base is the responsibility of each supply professional.

3. **Environment**
   Supply management promotes protection, preservation and vitality of the natural environment.

4. **Ethics and Business Conduct**
   Every supply management professional is responsible for behaving ethically and actively promoting ethical conduct throughout the supply chain.

5. **Financial Integrity and Transparency**
   Financially responsible supply management is characterized by integrity and transparency in all supply-related dealings and decisions.

6. **Global Citizenship**
   Global citizenship is the ethical and moral obligation to act for the benefit of society locally, globally, and virtually.

7. **Health and Safety**
   Health and safety is the condition of being protected or free from the occurrence of risk of injury, danger, failure, error, accident, harm, and loss of life.

8. **Human Rights**
   Human beings have universal and natural rights and status regardless of legal jurisdiction and local factors.

9. **Labor Rights**
   Supply management is committed to protecting and respecting labor rights globally.

10. **Sustainability**
    Sustainability is the ability to meet current needs without hindering the ability to meet the needs of future generations in terms of economic, environmental, and social challenges.

Source: "ISM Principles of Sustainability and Social Responsibility: With a Guide to Adaption and Implementation", Tempe, AZ., ISM, 2012. http://www.ism.ws/files/SR/PSSRwGuideBook.pdf

Currently, much of the corrugated packaging being used in Dell's China plants originates as recycled material from North America. Bamboo would actually have a smaller carbon footprint, since it would originate in China. There are more than 1,500 types of bamboo, and Dell had to verify that the type selected was not eaten by panda bears. Further, the sourcing region was important since Dell had to insure the bamboo was not taken within a certain distance of a panda habitat. Dell's total packaging volume through 2012 was down 12.1 percent from the previous year. Increasing content recyclability is another area of growth where efforts are being made to reduce petroleum based cushioning materials. A substitute is cotton hulls, rice hulls or wheat chaff being placed in a mold and injected with mushroom spawn. In 5–10 days the mushroom root structure completes its growth cycle providing a product as strong and protective as Styrofoam, but completely organic and compostable.[26]

While Dell is focusing on indirect spend General Mills made a bold statement indicating it would sustainably source its top 10 priority commodities by 2020. Doing this involves working with its partners. "Improving sustainability is a continuing process—one that General Mills does not undertake alone. Nearly two-thirds of General Mills' greenhouse gas emissions and 99 percent of water use occur outside the company's operations, primarily in agriculture. Therefore, the company believes it can have the greatest impact by working with industry partners and non-governmental agencies across the supply chain to identify new solutions." Representatives of the World Wildlife Fund praised General Mills efforts. "The company has an opportunity to take a leading role in the move toward global sustainable agriculture, while addressing critical issues like ecosystem health and water scarcity."[27]

Finally, green companies will also emphasize their commitment to sustainability by providing discounts to their employees. For example, may be a great source of talent and also. "Students are looking to work for companies that care about the environment," claims author Lindsey Pollak. "They are almost expecting greenness like they expect work-life balance, ethnic diversity, and globalization."[28] To attract students, corporations are advertising their environmental efforts. For example, Bank of America outlines its environmental initiatives on the back of its recruiting brochures.[29]

| Good Practice Example | *Increasing Asia's Sustainability Offers Substantial Savings* |

Chipmaker Intel sees many business advantages to going green. The motivation for going green was simple according to Sherry Boger, the General Manager of an Intel facility in Ho Chi Minh City in Vietnam. "It turns out, what's good for the environment is also good for business," said Boger. Intel's new $1 billion chip factory in Vietnam embraces environmental and sustainability measures that far exceed Vietnamese laws. First, the facility has Vietnam's largest operating solar energy system, and the water reclamation system will help reduce water consumption by 68 percent over a traditional facility. Second, the facility is waiting to receive the U.S. Green Building Council's LEED certification. LEED stands for Leadership in Energy and Environmental Design and the U.S. Green Building Council is recognized as one of the leading global certifiers.

According to the Council only about 300 manufacturing facilities in Asia are either currently LEED certified or awaiting certification. It is difficult to estimate exactly how much energy or money the average facility would save by investing in processes and implementing practices to achieve certification. However, experts suggest that with the enormous number of consumer goods and industrial manufacturing facilities in Asia, the saving could be significant. For example, one study compared a typical Vietnam shoe factory to a LEED certified one. Both the facilities produced shoes exclusively for Nike. The LEED certified facility used 18 percent less electricity, 18 percent less fuel, and 53 percent less water. According to its records, Intel has made $59 million worth of sustainability investments since 2008 and this has resulted in a payback of $111 million worth of energy savings. In terms of carbon footprint this savings would equate to the amount produced by 126,000 U.S. households annually. Intel's solar energy savings alone at the new chip facility mentioned above equates to a daily carbon footprint reduction equal to 500 of Vietnam's motorbikes.

In addition to Intel other global firms are recognizing a range of benefits from sustainability that include: (1) traditional energy savings; (2) compliance with corporate policies; and (3) risk reduction. A spokesperson for Colgate-Palmolive indicated the company's seven LEED certified factories have reduced construction waste as well as lowered water and energy use. Other Western multinationals push for LEED certification to comply with corporate policies that require sustainable building design. From a marketing perspective a LEED certified facility provides the company with security against "brand degradation." For example, the collapse in 2013 of a poorly built garment factory in Bangladesh, which killed 1100 workers, or chemical spills and other mishaps tarnish a firm's image. This "image tarnishing" moves at viral speeds today across social media sites and definitely affects sales.

In contrast, most Asian firms currently see sustainability as an energy saver. They see less benefit for the need to be certified and are instead focusing on the payback from energy savings. A director of a French energy consulting firm states that "90 percent of his clients were motivated by a desire to reduce energy costs rather than polish their corporate images or attain LEED certification." However, given the number of facilities in the region any sustainability efforts will result in a win-win for both the environment and the companies bottom line.

Questions

1. Why are Asian firms slower than U.S. or European firms to adapt sustainability initiatives?
2. As the Chief Executive Officer having read the above article, how would you convince the Board of Director's to adopt a sustainability and social responsibility policy?

Source: Adapted from Mike Ives, "Slowly, Asia's Factories Begin to Turn Green", *New York Times* January 8, 2014 p. B6.

CONCLUSION

The purchaser is the legal agent for the organization and has broad authority to enter into contracts. When dealing with suppliers in contract negotiations, contract management, breach of contracts, potential damages, and patent or trade secret disputes, purchasing managers must be sure to stipulate the appropriate terms and conditions. Nevertheless, many legal disputes are being handled through discussions with suppliers instead of being referred to legal departments. Both purchasing managers and suppliers also generally prefer using negotiation as an alternative to formal legal proceedings. In either case, purchasing managers must be aware of the potential pitfalls implicit in standard legal terminology and must seek to prevent the occurrence of such disputes. Knowing basic legal rights and placing them in the contract protects the purchaser's firm and assures remedies against supplier default. Beyond legality, purchasers must act ethically and consider social responsibility in selecting suppliers. Today, most organizations are very cognizant of the need to minimize their impact on the environment through implementing sustainable practices. Responsible purchasing practices can promote sustainability in the supply chain by selecting and encouraging socially responsible suppliers.

KEY TERMS

agent, 575

breach of contract, 583

commercial law, 577

consideration, 579

contract, 577

Contract for the International
Sale of Goods (CISG), 587

copyright, 595

corporate social
responsibility, 609

Electronic Signatures
in Global and National
Commerce "E-Sign", 589

express warranty, 590

implied warranty, 591

influence, 605

liquidated
damages, 585

offer, 578

patents, 595

reciprocity, 604

sharp practice, 603

Statute of Fraud, 582

trade secrets, 595

Uniform Commercial Code
UCC, 587

Uniform Electronic
Transactions Act
UETA, 589

DISCUSSION QUESTIONS

1. Why is it important for supply managers to understand legal issues? Isn't that the lawyer's job?

2. What is the relationship among contract law, the UCC, and commercial law?

3. What does the term "agent" mean? Under what conditions can purchasing agents be held personally responsible for abusing their position?

4. Suppose you arrive at a verbal agreement with someone on the price of purchasing his or her vehicle. Under what conditions have you reached an enforceable contract?

5. Suppose you sign a contract with a supplier for $50,000 worth of tablet computers. You tell the supplier that you are only authorized to sign contracts for $40,000 without approval from the supply manager of your company, but the supplier agrees anyway. A few days later, because of budget cutbacks you find out that you only need $30,000 worth of tablet computers. How many dollars of tablet computers are you legally bound to purchase from the supplier?

6. A seller verbally tells you that his cleaning product can remove any stain from the surface of your company vehicles. Your maintenance crew later finds out that this is not the case. In fact, you find that the cleaning product does not work very well at all in removing stains. Do you have a legal claim against this seller? What types of damages are you entitled to?

7. In the above case, the seller points to the fine print on the product, which states that the product can only be used in temperatures above 40 degrees Fahrenheit. Your employees were using it in temperatures of 35 degrees. Do you have a claim?

8. List the important items that should be included when entering into a long-term contract (e.g., more than one year) with a supplier?

9. Briefly, explain the Uniform Commercial Code. Is it enforceable in all 50 states of the United States?

10. You write a contract that contains specific language about transportation requirements, and the supplier agrees to it but later claims that it is not acceptable under the UCC. Who in your opinion has the upper hand in this case and why?

11. Suppose a supplier gives you a price on a contract and then later comes back and claims that he mistakenly wrote down the wrong price. Do you have the right to sue the supplier over breach of contract? What conditions are important here?

12. Discuss the concept of ethics. Why is the purchasing profession particularly sensitive to this topic?

13. Intellectual property and patent laws vary greatly in developing countries. How would you propose to protect your products in a developing country with a large population where the CEO of a generic pharmaceutical manufacturer states: "The U.S. would grant a patent on a piece of toilet paper. Just because the U.S. granted a patent doesn't mean it should be valid in our country."

14. Discuss the reasons why some issues that confront a buyer are often not clear from an ethical perspective.

15. What is the purpose of a professional code of purchasing ethics?

16. Why is it important for a firm to have a written ethics policy? What is the importance of top management's commitment to the policy?

17. Discuss why you would be more interested in working for an organization that supports environmentally friendly policies. Are there any negatives to working for an environmentally friendly organization?

18. You are a supply manager for a major distributor; the CEO has strongly encouraged that you buy lighting products for the new municipal stadium from a supplier that belongs to the CEO's country club. How would you handle this attempt to influence you?

19. You are the Chief Purchasing Officer for a large regional Bank, list some of the ways you could increase sustainable practices in your supply base.

ADDITIONAL READINGS

Carter, C. R. (1998), *Ethical Issues in Global Buyer-Supplier Relationships*, Tempe, AZ: Center for Advanced Purchasing Studies.

Cavinato, J. L., Flynn, A., and Kauffman, R. (2006), *The Supply Management Handbook*, New York: McGraw-Hill, pp. 643–675.

Crowder, M., and Brown, D. (1997), "Ethical Integrity and the Supply Chain," *Purchasing Today*, March, p. 37.

Gabriel, H. (1994), *Practitioner's Guide to the Convention on Contracts for the International Sale of Goods (CISC) and the Uniform Commercial Code (UCC)*, New York: Oceana Publishing.

Giunipero, L., Hooker, R., and Denslow, D. (2012, December 4), "Purchasing and Supply Management Sustainability-Drivers and Barriers," *Journal of Supply Management*, 18(4), 258–269.

Johnston, D. F. (1982), *Copyright Handbook*, New York: R. R. Bowker.

Murray, J. E., Jr. (2003), "When You Get What You Bargained For—But Don't," *Purchasing*, 132(4), 26–27.

Paulraj, A. (2011), "Understanding the Relationships Between Internal Resources and Capabilities, Sustainable Supply Management, and Organizational Sustainability," *Journal of Supply Chain Management*, 47(1), 19–37.

Schildhouse, J. (2005, March), "Corporate Ethics: Taking the High Road," *Inside Supply Management*, 30–31.

_____, _____(2006), "Social Responsibility and the Supply Management Professional: A Study of Drivers and Barriers to Ethical Practices," ISM Ethical Standards Committee, ISM Tempe, AZ, 8 pp.

ENDNOTES

1. Hancock, W. A. (2006), *The Law of Purchasing* (2nd ed.), New York: Business Laws Inc.-Thomson Reuters.

2. Cavinato, J. L. (1984), *Purchasing and Materials Management: Integrative Strategies*, St. Paul, MN: West Publishing, p. 146.

3. Scheuing, E. E. (1989), *Purchasing Management*, Englewood Cliffs, NJ: Prentice Hall, p. 55.

4. Hancock, 10.18–23.18.

5. Hancock, 22.05–22.06.

6. Hancock, 10.18–23.18.

7. Baumer, D. L., and Poindexter, J. C. (2004), *Legal Environment of Business in the Information Age*, New York: McGraw-Hill/Irwin.

8. Siegfried, S. H. (2011), *The E-Commerce Revolution: E-Sign and UETA*, July 28, Retrieved from https://web.archive.org/web/20110728165018/http://www.vsb.org/sections/rp/articles/ESign .siegfried.html

9. Stockton, J., and Miller, F. (1992), *Sales and Leases of Goods in a Nutshell* (3rd ed.), St. Paul, MN: West Publishing, pp. 84–87.

10. Hancock.

11. Coyle, J. J., Bardi, E. J., and Langley, C. J., Jr. (2003), *The Management of Business Logistics* (7th ed.), Mason, OH: South-Western Cengage Publishing, p. 360.

12. Kintner, E. W., and Lahr, J. L. (1975), *An Intellectual Property Law Primer*, New York: Macmillan, p. 6.

13. Cabarra, M. J., and Gabbard, E. (2000), "What's on the Books: Other Laws Affecting Purchasing and Supply," in *The Purchasing and Supply Yearbook*, Woods, J. A. (Ed.), New York: McGraw-Hill, pp. 332–339.

14. Handfield, R. B. (2008), *CPSM Study Guide Vol.1*, Tempe, AZ: Institute for Supply Management, pp. 58, 190.

15. Prantis, R. (2009, September), "Examining the 10+2 Rule," *Inside Supply Management*, 20(9), 12–13.

16. Haynes, P. J., and Helms, M. M. (1991), "An Ethical Framework for Purchasing Decisions," *Management Decision*, 29(1), 35; Page, H. (1986), "More on Ethics—Helping Your Buyers," *Purchasing World*, 30(12), 60.

17. Giunipero, L., and Handfield, R. (2004), *Purchasing Education and Training II*, Tempe, AZ: CAPS Research.

18. Haynes and Helms, p. 36.

19. Haynes and Helms, p. 36.

20. Adler, D., Baranowski, J., Kalin, L., Lallatin, C, Smiley, S., Turner, G., and Sturzl, S. (2007, May), "Ethical Behavior: Boundaries of Influence," 92nd ISM International Conference Proceedings.

21. Adler et al.

22. Adler et al.

23. Forker, L. B., and Janson, R. L. (1990), "Ethical Practices in Purchasing," *International Journal of Purchasing and Materials Management*, 26(1), 19–26.

24. ____,____ (2010, March 11), "Green Offices Are Growing," *Purchasing*, 139(3), 16–17.

25. ____,____ "Green Offices," 16.

26. ____,____ (2014, January 2), "The 3Cs of Packaging Innovation," Dell Corporation. Retrieved from http://www.dell.com/learn/us/en/uscorp1/corp-comm/earth-products-packaging

27. _____,_____ (2013, September 25), "General Mills Commits to Sustainably Source 10 Priority Ingredients by 2020" Retrieved from http://www.generalmills.com/en/ChannelG/NewsReleases/Library/2013/September/sourcing_10.aspx

28. Mattoli, D. (2007, November 13), "How Going Green Draws Talent, Cuts Costs," *Wall Street Journal*, p. BIO.

29. _____,_____ (2014), *Environmental Sustainability at Bank America*. Retrieved from http://about.bankofamerica.com/en-us/global-impact/environmental-sustainability.html#fbid=s4eR_P2RvvM

Critical Supply Chain Elements

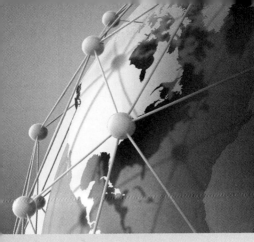

Lean Supply Chain Management

Learning Objectives

After completing this chapter, you should be able to

- Identify the different categories of inventory

- Identify the various costs associated with maintaining supply chain inventory

- Assess the financial impact of managing inventory more effectively

- Understand the right reasons for maintaining an investment in inventory

- Appreciate the challenges of creating a lean supply chain

- Identify ways to manage and improve inventory investment

- Recognize the important relationship between inventory management and delivering the perfect customer order

Chapter Outline

The Fragmentation of Global Logistics Channels in the Era of E-Commerce

A recent study was undertaken that involved interviews with over 60 Chief Supply Chain Officers as well as a survey of over 1400 supply chain executives in multiple countries, including the United States, Germany, China, India, Brazil, and Russia. The results point at the undeniable fact that organizations must build network capabilities to survive in the increasingly competitive environment being driven by the explosion of purchasing on the Internet. With the rise of e-commerce, there has been a rapid mergence of new channels with customers that are not well developed and that are interlinked with other channels. For example, consider the traditional retail apparel channel. The old formula for retail success in apparel markets was straightforward: give customers quality in-trend garments at the right price point, in an attractive store setting with helpful sales associates. The supply chain only had to deliver goods to the retail store. Today, however, bricks and mortar stores are only one of multiple channels. Others include outlet locations, e-commercial sites, social and mobile sites, catalogs, and other seasonal/single-use channels such as pop-up stores and flash sales. And with these new channels, supply chain managers must simultaneously accommodate and anticipate varying internal and external demands to meet time windows, keep costs low, ensure inventory can satisfy channels, and help fuel growth.

In a networked economy, enterprises are expected to have extreme levels of flexibility. Apparel retailers must grapple with how to fulfill different types of orders, and how to handle inventory behind the purchases, as customers are offered an array of different delivery mechanisms (ship to home, pick up at store, etc.). And e-commerce orders are typified by higher volume but smaller picked orders delivered to homes are more common. To complicate this, reverse logistics capabilities must be established to handle the high volume of exchanges, returns, and damaged goods as more websites cater to a guaranteed zero cost of return policy.

To cope with this environment, companies are seeking to outsource more technology design, inventory management, working capital investments, and planning execution to other partners in the supply chain. Some have warned that driving too much responsibility down the supply chain can result in significant risk and loss of control, and that control of the channel could become problematic if suppliers decide to integrate upstream toward customers. In such cases, the total cost of ownership (including such things as transportation and inventory management) become opaque to the Original Equipment Manufacturer, and the enterprise can lose leverage to reduce costs if they hand over an entire subsystem to a single supplier. This trend is offset by the other view in industry that logistics is all about cost savings and is often not recognized by many as a source of value-added capability.

An offshoot of this trend is the bundling of product and logistics solutions. Customers are requiring solutions to problems that they face, which means being able to not just have the physical movement of the product, but a combination of packaging, distribution, tracking, and responsiveness to requirements. This has been the case in the automotive industry for years, where JIT deliveries on an hourly basis based on real-time EDI transmissions are the norm. Increasingly, organizations don't wish to manage inventory, and are requiring suppliers to provide vendor managed inventory, real-time responsiveness to inventory tracking software, and technical support. Many companies are unable to provide these capabilities on their own, and are partnering with solution providers to develop combined product-service supply chain solutions.

> We are moving more toward systems solutions for our customers, not just chemical product shipments. We produce solutions with products that include third-party materials. In construction, we don't sell insulation; we sell square meters of insulated walls. We don't sell paint we sell a colored chassis. This is a whole new dimension of supply chain management, which is not just about order shipping, but how you can team up with others in the supply chain to bundle your product capabilities with theirs to deliver on time to the customer. This is 40 percent of our portfolio today, and we are reaching even further into the supply chain. [Chemical Executive]

Many of the companies interviewed recognize that they cannot "do it alone," but need to become experts at managing global relationships. This is particularly true in regions where sales are only starting out, and in many cases, companies need to figure out the "pieces of the puzzle" and what it means to operate regionally. To do so, partnerships are key, particularly for importing into regions. Many countries such as India and China have specific requirements for packaging, shipping, and other importation issues that require customization of logistics processes. Organizations need to develop specific packaging requirements inside these countries to meet government laws, and then set up processes to import products and customize to the local market. Shipping across boarders has an impact on the effectiveness of the channel, and so organizations need to carefully choose distributors and selling locations. A supply chain strategy involves making decisions: How do you distribute? Into your own warehouse structure or another? And how many distributors do you select for the territory? Top performing organizations are able to identify partners who can optimize and understand local legislation and conditions to effectively make these decisions.

Almost 80 percent of executives agreed that collaboration in the supply chain is to achieve improved coordination and increasing trust, as well as to improve synergies and increase innovation. These trends clearly suggest that organizations are seeking to develop new forms of logistics value and innovation, and an open and trusting dialogue where all parties can openly share ideas for improvement is the only way to do this. There are still many issues relative to identifying the right partners for long-term network relationships, but the study clearly supports a direction that is leaning toward a more cohesive and integrated set of relationships with fewer partners. Such relationships are built on identified synergies that create new capabilities, innovative supply chain solutions, and shared capacity and risk.

1. *Source:* Handfield, Robert, Straube, Frank, Pfohl, Hans-Christian, and Wieland, Andreas. *Trends and Strategies in Logistics and Supply Chain Management*, BVL International, 2014.

Introduction

If U.S. companies learned anything over the last 20 years, it is that managing inventory efficiently and effectively is central to remaining competitive. As shown in the opening vignette, inventory is important to diverse industries, including retail, logistics service providers, distributors, manufacturing, and healthcare. Inventory and order fulfillment processes have to adopt to increasing e-commerce orders through the Internet, and customer expectations for improved on-time delivery and service. Although service companies do not produce manufactured products, they still have to manage significant amounts of inventory, particularly in settings like hospitals and utilities that have to respond quickly to emergencies.

Although maintaining high levels of inventory was an accepted practice for many years, it resulted in high carrying costs, reduced profit, and diminished market share. Furthermore, high inventory levels often hid other problems such as poor material quality, inaccurate demand-forecasting systems, and unreliable supplier delivery. To avoid having to deal with these problems, it was often easier to increase safety stock levels or increase the amount ordered from suppliers.

Although the concept of "lean" is generally associated with "just-in-time" or "zero inventory," the concept is much broader in scope and has a major influence on management thinking in supply chains in the last five years. In his book "Learning to See," John Shook defined **lean** as "a philosophy that seeks to shorten the time between the customer order and the shipment to the customer by eliminating waste."[1] Womack and Jones, in their book *Lean Thinking,* argued that all activities associated with lean attempt to achieve three objectives: **flow, pull, and striving for excellence**.[2]

Flow means that inventory moves through the supply chain continuously with minimal queuing or non-value-added activity being performed. **Pull** means that customer orders start the work process, which ripples down through the supply chain. An upstream work center or operation will not create output unless a downstream center directly requests (i.e., pulls) that output. The downstream center needs and then consumes the output, leading to no inventory or waste. The third element, **striving for excellence**, means that supply chains must have perfect quality. Anything less than perfect quality leads to waste.

The primary objective of this chapter is to provide an understanding of the role of managing and controlling supply chain inventory in building lean supply chains. In the following sections, we present the types and costs of inventory, the right and wrong reasons for maintaining inventory, and the close ties between the concept of the lean supply chain and the just-in-time (JIT) philosophy. We also present powerful ways to manage inventory investment and discuss the concept of the perfect customer order. The chapter concludes with a Good Practice Example of how biopharmaceutical companies are using Lean Thinking to improve performance in the clinical trials supply chain, in a race to get their products through patent approval and capture the market for a particular therapy. Multiple examples of lean thinking are also discussed throughout the chapter, emphasizing how universal these approaches are to any industry.

Understanding Supply Chain Inventory

The best place to start our discussion of lean supply chains is to understand the basic principles of inventory management. This section discusses the different types of inventory, the costs associated with holding inventory, and the changing view of inventory as a financial and operating liability rather than an asset.

Types of Inventory

Inventory represents the largest single investment in assets for most manufacturers, wholesalers, and retailers. The five primary categories of inventory are (1) raw material and semifinished item inventory; (2) work-in-process (WIP) inventory; (3) finished-goods inventory; (4) maintenance, repair, and operating (MRO) supplies inventory; and (5) pipeline/in-transit inventory.

Raw Material and Semifinished Item Inventory

This inventory includes the items purchased from suppliers or produced internally to directly support production requirements. Raw materials include those items purchased in a bulk or unfinished condition. Bulk quantities of chemicals, resins, or petroleum are examples of purchased raw materials. Semifinished inventory includes those items and components used as inputs during the final production process. Every producer relies on some level of raw material or semifinished inventory to support final production requirements. This type of inventory is managed primarily by purchasing, a materials planning group, or supply chain managers.

Work-in-Process Inventory

At any given point in time, work-in-process is the sum total of inventory within all processing centers. Work-in-process is incomplete—it has not yet been transformed to a saleable finished good. This includes materials that are the following:

- Waiting to be moved to another process
- Currently being worked on at a work center
- Lining up at a processing center because of a capacity bottleneck or machine breakdown

If WIP increases over a certain level, this may indicate production bottlenecks or delays. One study found that in most facilities, 36 percent of WIP inventory is in line waiting for further work or processing. Another 27 percent is waiting on movement to another work area or center, 4 percent is in the process of being moved, and only 24 percent is actually in process.[3] If WIP builds up at a workstation, a scheduler may have to reroute the flow of material to another work center.

Finished-Goods Inventory

Finished-goods inventory includes completed items or products that are available for shipment or future customer orders. A firm that produces items in anticipation of customer orders should monitor its finished-goods inventory closely. A higher-than-anticipated level of finished goods may mean that a decrease in customer demand is occurring. A lower-than-anticipated finished-goods inventory level may indicate that customer demand is increasing. Either condition may also indicate that the forecasts of anticipated customer demand do not match current output levels.

When firms produce goods in anticipation of future customer orders, they are operating in a make-to-stock environment. They expect to hold finished inventory in anticipation of future demand. When firms produce goods in response to a customer order, they are operating in a make-to-order environment. Just-in-time firms usually operate in a make-to-order environment.

Maintenance, Repair, and Operating Supplies Inventory

MRO inventory includes the items used to support production and operations. These items are not physically part of a finished product but are critical for the continuous operation of plant, equipment, and offices. Examples of MRO inventory include office supplies, spare parts, tools, and computers.

Pipeline/In-Transit Inventory

This inventory is in transit to a customer or is located throughout distribution channels. Most consumable-goods inventory is either on trucks or on grocery store shelves. In fact, grocery stores only provide a shelf for the product; they do not own the inventory. The inventory is owned by the supplying company or distributor, which receives payment when the consumer buys the product.

Inventory-Related Costs

One of the drawbacks of holding excessive inventory is the effect this has on a firm's working capital. Working capital represents the funds committed to operating a business, including the purchase and holding of inventory. Excessive inventory consumes or ties up funds that a company could use more productively elsewhere. Ordering and carrying physical inventory involves a number of costs.

Unit Costs

The most basic and the easiest inventory-related cost to quantify and track is unit cost. We can view the calculation of unit costs in several ways. First, each item or good purchased from a supplier or another internal facility has a related unit cost, which is the price a firm pays. Second, a finished product has a unit cost. The calculation of this cost may be more complex. Besides the direct material used to manufacture the finished product, the product also has a labor cost and allocated overhead. Cost accountants are largely responsible for identifying and assigning these costs.

Ordering Costs

Ordering costs are a composite of the costs associated with the release of a material order. These costs may include the cost of generating and sending a material release, transportation costs, and any other cost connected with acquiring a good. If a firm produces an item or good itself, the ordering cost may also include machine setup costs.

Carrying Costs

Carrying costs consist of three separate components: (1) cost of capital; (2) cost of storage; and (3) the costs of obsolescence, deterioration, and loss. The dollar amount invested in physical inventory has an opportunity cost associated with it. Resources committed to inventory are not available for other economic uses. Therefore, committing financial resources to holding physical inventory creates an inventory carrying cost.

The physical storing of inventory creates costs, including any costs related to storage space, insurance costs, or the cost to maintain the inventory (such as performing cycle counts). Carrying costs vary with the level of inventory, which makes these costs variable. Fixed costs are not included as part of carrying costs because inventory levels typically have no effect on a fixed cost, at least in the short run.

Holding inventory also increases the risk of theft, damage, spoilage, and obsolescence. For example, obsolescence is a major issue in the computer industry, where inventory loses about 1.5 percent of its functionality a week as a result of rapidly changing technology, making the extended holding of any inventory financially risky.

For most industries, inventory costs typically range from 15 to 25 percent of the value of the inventory, depending on the company's cost of capital. As shown in Exhibit 16.1, a variety of costs makes up the total carrying cost. The calculation of an inventory carrying cost is as follows:

$$\text{Inventory Carrying Cost} = \text{Average Inventory in Units} \times \text{Unit Price} \times \text{Carrying Cost per Year}$$

Exhibit 16.1	Inventory Carrying Cost Components	
ELEMENT	**AVERAGE**	**RANGES**
Capital cost	15.00%	8–40%
Taxes	1.00%	0.5–2%
Insurance	0.05%	0–2%
Obsolescence	1.20%	0.5–2%
Storage	2.00%	0–4%
Total	19.25%	9–50%

Source: Bowersox, D.J., and Closs, D.J. (1996), *Logistical Management,* New York: McGraw-Hill, 255.

If a company averages 1,000 units in inventory, for which the unit price is $1.00 per unit, and the annual carrying cost is 25 percent, the total inventory carrying cost per year for inventory is $(1{,}000 \times \$1 \times 0.25) = \$250$.

Quality Costs

Quality costs include any cost associated with nonconforming items or goods. The total cost of inventory ownership is more than simply the unit, ordering, and carrying costs. Quantifying the cost of poor quality can help identify the causes of problems. Examples of additional costs because of defective inventory include field failure costs, rework, losses because of poor product yields, inspection, lost production, and warranty costs.

It is often difficult to quantify the total costs associated with ordering and carrying physical inventory. Part of this results from the historical neglect of calculating total inventory costs along with a lack of systems capable of identifying inventory-related costs. Most cost accounting systems are not capable of identifying and assigning the true costs related to maintaining physical inventory. However, activity-based costing accounting systems are increasingly able to quantify the distinct costs associated with holding inventory. New types of enterprise resource planning systems also help managers more accurately measure the actual level of inventory on hand, as opposed to "guesstimating."

Inventory Investment—Asset or Liability?

The opportunity to improve financial performance through effective inventory management practices is great and, at many firms, largely unrealized. For example, many companies in historically high-margin industries (such as energy, utilities, and pharmaceuticals) pay little attention to inventory, as it was always argued that the savings associated with inventory reduction outweighed the potential risk of a lost customer sale. This view has begun to change, as the full impact of inventory on the balance sheet and financial valuations on Wall Street reflect heightened awareness of inventory turnover as a key indicator of financial health.

This has not always been the case. From the financial accounting perspective, inventory has historically been considered a current asset (see Exhibit 16.2). When inventory resides in the same category as cash and marketable securities, one cannot help but get a feeling that there is actually something good associated with holding lots and lots of inventory. For many years, this was precisely how most U.S. managers viewed this special kind of asset. Only recently, financial analysts have begun to weigh in the impact that the funds committed to inventory have on cash flow, working capital requirements, and profitability, and are

Exhibit 16.2	Consolidated Balance Sheet		

		JUNE 30	
		2012 (IN THOUSANDS)	2013 (IN THOUSANDS)
Current Assets			
Cash and cash equivalents		$ 647,595	$ 408,378
Marketable securities		242,952	421,111
Receivables		638,974	632,870
Inventories		917,495	771,233
Prepaid expenses		84,588	70,211
Total current assets		2,531,604	2,303,803
Investments and Other Assets			
Investments in and advances to affiliates		205,835	160,455
Long-term marketable securities		770,808	813,631
Other assets		567,350	403,140
		1,033,378	1,014,400
Property, Plant, and Equipment			
Agricultural processing		2,275,016	1,724,460
Transportation		4,206,090	4,073,470
		26,956,250	21,318,070
		$62,606,070	$54,500,100

making stock-buying recommendations based on this factor. All of a sudden, senior leadership at firms are beginning to pay attention to this number in their analyst's calls.

Any discussion of inventory management should focus on the need to translate the impact that inventory management practices have on financial measures. A CEO of an industrial company is not likely to get overly excited when he or she hears that total inventory turns increased from seven to nine because of better inventory practices. Executive managers have not traditionally been concerned about the same set of key performance indicators as the typical supply chain manager. However, in recent years senior executives have begun to appreciate the importance of effective inventory management, once the relationship between the impact of increased turns on financial indicators has been elevated by Wall Street analysts.

Exhibit 16.3 illustrates one way to translate the impact that improved inventory turns (which is the visible outcome of inventory management turnover) has on an important performance indicator, return on investment. The two firms in this exhibit are identical in every way but two—Firm B has half the amount of inventory on its balance sheet as Firm A, and Firm B has a slightly higher profit margin than Firm A. It is reasonable to assume that Firm B will have a higher profit margin because of lower average carrying charges resulting from shorter periods of storage with less handling and reduced inventory maintenance requirements. Margins should also improve because of the elimination of non-value-adding activities.

This exhibit shows how better inventory management can affect return on investment. A doubling of inventory turns, combined with the benefit of lower inventory-related expenses that contribute to a higher profit margin, increases return on investment from 9.36 percent to 11.55 percent, an increase of almost 25 percent.

Identifying the impact of inventory management activities on return on investment is not the only way to demonstrate the value of such efforts. Supply chain and financial

Exhibit 16.3	Linking Inventory Management and Financial Performance	
	FIRM A	**FIRM B**
Sales ($M)	$200	$200
Profit Margin	6%	7%*
Assets		
Cash	$ 10	$ 10
Securities	$ 15	$ 15
Receivables	$ 8	$ 8
Inventories	$ 20	$ 10
Plant and equipment	$ 75	$ 75
Total Assets	$ 128	$ 118
Financial Formulas:		
Inventory Turns = Sales/Inventories	$200/$20 = 10 turns/year	$200/$10 = 20 turns/year
Asset Turnover = Sales/Total Assets	$200/$128 = 1.56 turns/year	$200/$118 = 1.69 turns/year
Return on Investment = Profit Margin × Asset Turnover	6% 1.56 = 9.36%	7% 1.69 = 11.55%
		Through efficient inventory management, Firm B has an ROI that is 23% higher than that of Firm A.

Note: All figures in millions of dollars.
*Assumes more efficient supply chain operations and less waste.

managers should work together to determine the impact of inventory management activities on earnings per share, economic value-add, return on assets, working capital, cash flow, and profit margin. The point here is that effective inventory management is critical for managing assets and controlling expenses. Translating inventory actions into their effect on higher-level performance indicators is essential for capturing executive management's attention. This was indeed the case when Amazon realized its inventory management practices were causing significant ripples on Wall Street, and turned around its inventory system in a matter of two years (see Sourcing Snapshot: Walmart vs. Amazon: Who has the leanest inventory system?).

Sourcing Snapshot

Walmart vs. Amazon: Who has the leanest inventory system?

For almost a decade, Walmart Stores Inc. has been boasting that it will dominate Internet retailing the way it dominates strip malls, toppling Amazon.com Inc. as the world's largest online merchant. And every year, those boasts have proved to be hollow. But this holiday shopping season, Walmart has started aiming at what it sees as Amazon's Achilles' heel: the costs and delays of shipping online purchases to buyers. Customers who buy some of the more than 1.5 million products on Walmart.com can have them shipped free to a local Walmart, where new service desks at the front of some stores make it easier for shoppers to retrieve their stuff. On the outskirts of Chicago, it is testing a radical new concept: a drive-through window, similar to those found at pharmacies and fast-food restaurants, where shoppers can pick up their Internet orders.

"There was a time when the online and offline businesses were viewed as being different," said Walmart.com Chief Executive Raul Vazquez. "Now we are realizing that we actually have a physical advantage thanks to our thousands of stores, and we can use it to become No. 1 online." Heading into Christmas, the company said 40 percent of its online orders are being delivered through stores.

Walmart.com now ranks among the top e-commerce sites in traffic according to comScore Inc.'s tracking service. But with just $1.7 billion in annual sales, according to estimates by trade publication *Internet Retailer*, it badly trails Amazon, which reported $19.17 billion in annual revenues last year.

Of course, store pickup of Internet purchases is not a totally new concept—consumer electronics retailers helped pioneer store pickups of online orders at the start of this decade, and other companies have been offering it for years. But Walmart and other old-school retailers are sharply increasing efforts to link stores and Web sales as a broad shift to Internet shopping and this is gaining momentum in the bad economy.

Though e-commerce represents less than 5 percent of American retail spending, merchants are finding that even technologically unsophisticated consumers start their shopping on computers or mobile phones, perusing product reviews and price comparison websites.

Walmart is marshaling its distribution might to help walmart.com better compete with online sellers. Amazon says that it does not see shipping as a weakness. "Shopping on Amazon means you don't have to fight the crowds. We bring the items to your doorstep. You don't have to fight through traffic or find a parking space," said spokesman Craig Berman.

Amazon has taken steps recently to speed delivery times, using lean concepts to improve distribution. It began offering same-day delivery in seven U.S. cities, at an extra cost to shoppers. By working with carriers and improving its own internal systems, Amazon has started offering second-day deliveries on Saturdays—shaving two days off some orders. "We know customers are not going to tell us one day that it is OK if you send me my stuff a little slower," said Mr. Berman.

Though the attention-grabbing moves are drawing Web and store traffic, Walmart is counting on its "site to store" free shipping program to increase online revenue. It allows the discounter to piggyback on its supply chain operations for deliveries, and lures online customers inside stores, where they can make add-on purchases.

Walmart is learning to exploit the long tail of Internet retailing by offering thousands of items online which it does not stock in its enormous superstores.

Source: Bustillo, M., and Flowers, G., (2009, December 15), "Wal-Mart Uses Its Stores to Get an Edge Online," *Wall Street Journal,* A1.

Exhibit 16.4	Amazon.com Financial Results-1997–2006		
YEAR	**NET SALES (MILLIONS)**	**INVENTORY**	**INVENTORY TURNS (DEC. 31, MILLIONS)**
1997	$ 148	$ 9	16.4
1998	$ 610	$ 30	20.3
1999	$ 1,640	$221	7.4
2000	$ 2,762	$175	15.8
2001	$ 3,122	$143	21.8
2002	$ 3,933	$202	19.5
2003	$ 5,264	$294	17.9
2004	$ 6,921	$480	14.4
2005	$ 8,490	$566	15.0
2006	$10,711	$877	12.2

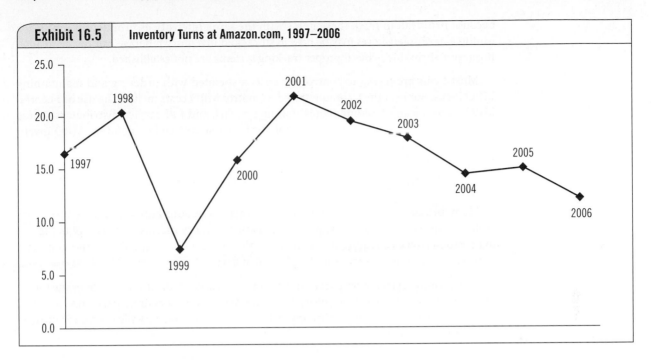

Exhibit 16.5   Inventory Turns at Amazon.com, 1997–2006

The Right Reasons for Investing in Inventory

Physical inventory plays an important role in all supply chains. Without inventory, companies cannot build products, provide customer service, or run their operations. When deciding whether to maintain an investment in inventory, a broad premise to follow is that inventory should be held only when the benefit of holding inventory exceeds the cost of holding inventory. The following section examines the proper reasons for carrying inventory.

Avoid Disruptions in Operational Performance

A major reason for maintaining an investment in inventory is to support production requirements and avoid any type of supply disruptions. Even in an era of just-in-time production, almost all firms hold some level of preproduction inventory, which may include bulk supplies of raw materials, semifinished goods, or materials to support the packaging and shipping of finished products.

Production inventory consumes a major portion of inventory investment. For this reason, firms emphasize the development of systems designed to control and reduce the amount of production-related inventory maintained at any given time. The reduction of production (particularly work-in-process) inventory results in reduced inventory costs. Although the need to support production requirements will always remain as a primary reason to hold physical inventory, it is not a reason to hold excessive inventory. Supply managers need to strike a delicate balance between avoiding any supply disruptions and holding excessive amounts of inventory that weigh down a firm's or business unit's balance sheet.

Support Operational Requirements

Nearly every organization carries MRO inventory—maintenance, repair, and operating supplies—to support operations. The true cost of MRO inventory often goes unnoticed because firms fail to track these items with the same intensity as production inventory. Multiple or obsolete items may be held in stock, and inventory pilferage can further lead to inventory-shrinking losses if proper tracking systems are not established.

Most firms are trying to control the costs associated with ordering and maintaining MRO items. Some of the techniques used to control MRO costs include the use of a central MRO stores location, online requisitioning systems, and full-service distributors. These distributors are responsible for managing the entire supply and demand for MRO inventory items and may charge an additional fee for their services.

Support Customer Service Requirements

Many products, such as computers, appliances, and automobiles, require service or replacement parts. A lack of adequate spare parts inventory increases the risk of not meeting customer service requirements. To avoid this possibility, companies often maintain a significant inventory of service and replacement parts.

Service and replacement parts can be a major source of inventory waste or customer dissatisfaction if incorrect inventory levels are maintained. Accurate parts forecasts and material control systems are critical for maintaining proper inventory levels for service and replacement parts.

Hedge against Marketplace Uncertainty

Supply chains are sensitive to changes in markets, including changes in the availability of material supply as well as price changes. When purchasers anticipate materials shortages or price increases, they often increase purchase quantities as a hedge against these uncertainties. Material hedging is a common response, for example, when a strike by a supplier appears likely. Another reason to hedge occurs when potential shortages in common commodities (e.g., lumber) appear imminent, with the knowledge that price increases are likely. In these situations, purchasers will carry out forward buys by ordering larger-than-normal quantities.

Increasing inventory levels in response to a legitimate threat of a shortage can be a good reason, at least in the short run, for holding additional material. One of the primary objectives of purchasing and supply chain management is to support continued and uninterrupted operations. If this requires increased inventory to avoid a materials shortage, then a purchaser should consider such an action, assuming that additional sources of supply are not readily available. However, firms should avoid taking undue and unnecessary hedging risks. The sourcing snapshot on UPS and the inventory situation in the days prior to December 25, 2013 illustrates the importance of inventory positioning.

Take Advantage of Order Quantity Discounts

Suppliers often offer quantity discounts to encourage larger orders from purchasers, which Chapter 12 discussed. A purchaser might consider ordering a two-month supply versus a one-month supply, for example, in exchange for a per-unit discount. At one time, most companies felt these discounts were worthwhile because they resulted in a lower average price. However, a lower purchase price does not necessarily translate into a lower total cost. Lower total costs result only if the benefit from reduced ordering costs (larger purchase quantities means ordering less frequently) and a lower per-unit price outweigh the cost of holding additional inventory. It sometimes makes economic sense from a total

Sourcing Snapshot

UPS Disappoints Christmas Customers

In the days before the Christmas season of 2013, many online retailers experienced a floor of customer orders, from individuals who had waited until the "last minute" before placing their orders. Although retailers such as Amazon, Zappos, and others had the inventory in their warehouse, they relied on providers such as United Parcel Service and Federal Express to be able to accommodate the rush of last minute orders. In fact, UPS did not have the physical equipment to move the inventory from the warehouses, through the logistics network, and to customers waiting on their packages in the waning days of December 22–25. As a result, many packages did not make it to their destination by Christmas, leading to many disappointed customers. This story illustrates the importance of positioning finished goods inventory in the logistics pipeline, and understanding the limitations that exist in the infrastructure to ship finished goods inventory.

Source: Handfield, Robert, based on executive interviews.

cost perspective to take advantage of the quantity discounts offered by suppliers and to hold larger amounts of inventory.

Each of the reasons presented here can result in holding some level of physical inventory. Regardless of the reason for holding inventory, supply chain managers must be aware of total inventory costs. The key is to minimize inventory investment wherever possible along with meeting competitive and customer requirements.

The Wrong Reasons for Investing in Inventory

Any discussion of inventory must differentiate between the good and bad reasons for carrying inventory. Unnecessary inventory usually results from one thing: uncertainty. Uncertainty results in not being able to adequately plan inventory requirements because of supply chain variability. It may be the consequence of variability in forecasting accuracy or inconsistent logistics, which usually results in greater amounts of safety stock. The following discussion considers the bad reasons for maintaining an investment in inventory. Some of the ideas presented in the later section titled "Approaches for Managing Inventory Investment" address these bad reasons directly.

Poor Quality and Material Yield

Poor quality and material yield have historically been major sources of unnecessary inventory investment. Unfortunately, it is easier to increase a material release by 10 percent or carry safety stock to cover supplier quality problems than to correct the root cause of a problem. It became a routine practice for many companies to order more than required to cover expected supplier inconsistency. A certain level of material defects was an accepted part of the transaction.

Variable material yield also may also contribute to unnecessary levels of inventory. Material yield is a term typically associated with raw materials. A purchaser who specifies a raw material at a particular grade expects to receive a shipment conforming to that specification. Poor quality affects material yields when a portion of the shipment is a lower grade or quality than what was specified, therefore providing less output than expected. When this happens, purchasers must often increase their purchase quantity to guarantee that their receipt yields the proper amount of usable material. This increase in inventory provides nothing of value in return.

Unreliable Supplier Delivery

Suppliers that cannot meet delivery schedules create delivery uncertainty. To compensate for unreliable delivery, supply chain managers usually increase safety stock levels or make ordering lead times longer. Delivery uncertainty is often the result of poor supplier scheduling or production systems and can be a problem when buying from small suppliers that do not have the resources or experience to develop sophisticated scheduling systems. It can also be the result of discrepancies and logistics problems. Missed shipments, delays at international customs points, bad weather, and many other unexpected problems can result in late deliveries.

Purchasers must also accept part of the blame for delivery uncertainty. Suppliers value a stable production schedule with reasonable production lead times. A purchaser who provides suppliers with short notice or requests frequent changes to a schedule increases the probability of delivery uncertainty. A major step toward eliminating delivery uncertainty is a commitment to stable release schedules with realistic (but not overly generous) supplier lead times.

Extended Order-Cycle Times from Global Sourcing

A major business objective today is to reduce the total time between the recognition of a purchase requirement and the physical receipt of material from a supplier—that is, the order-cycle time between purchaser and seller. As order-cycle times lengthen as a result of the extension of supply chains because of global sourcing agreements (which may require six-month lead times), a common practice has been to carry a higher level of inventory to compensate for greater uncertainty. The ability to plan material requirements accurately decreases as order-cycle time lengthens. Much more can happen to disrupt plans over a three-month ordering cycle than over a two-week ordering cycle.

Inaccurate or Uncertain Demand Forecasts

Inaccurate or uncertain demand forecasts are a common source of uncertainty affecting inventory levels, particularly for companies that produce products in anticipation of future orders. Companies often use increased safety stock levels to compensate for demand uncertainty or inaccurate forecasts. Some firms simply have poor forecasting systems.

Consider the case of an East Coast confectioner that forecasts monthly in a make-to-stock environment. The supply chain group at this company recently analyzed finished product forecasting error in its efforts to manage inventory investment more effectively.[4] The company found that its stock-keeping units (SKUs) had an average error of 45 percent when comparing actual and predicted monthly demand using the mean absolute deviation technique of error assessment. A closer investigation revealed some disturbing findings. Material planners believed that a four-week safety stock for all items would alleviate the impact of poor forecasting, thereby reducing the need to be concerned with forecast accuracy. Furthermore, no single manager or group was accountable for forecast integrity. Marketing, which technically had responsibility for generating monthly forecasts, admitted that forecasting was a "nuisance" and not the best use of their members' time. Finally, an analysis across the company's 900 SKUs found that inventory was sometimes severely misallocated across geographic locations and product lines, creating problems in meeting the delivery dates for key customer orders. As a result, this company has created a cross-functional sales and operations planning group to address product forecasting and finished-goods distribution.

Companies should periodically evaluate the accuracy of their forecasting systems by comparing forecasted demand to actual requirements. Forecasting systems should have a goal of minimizing the difference between a forecasted requirement and an actual requirement to avoid having to carry higher inventory levels as protection.

Specifying Custom Items for Standard Applications

Specifying custom items for standard applications is an area of debate between purchasing and engineering. Purchasers would like to buy industry-standard parts wherever possible along with meeting engineering's quality and design requirements. Specifying customized parts when standardized parts are available adversely affects material inventory because customized parts are usually more expensive. A supplier usually designs and creates specific tooling for each customized item. In addition, a supplier usually produces smaller batches of the item because of its custom specification. The smaller batches result in an increased piece-part cost. Customized parts, because of higher design and production costs, increase total unit and inventory-carrying costs.

Extended Material Pipelines

Long distances between supply chain members can result in higher inventory levels and costs. Distance increases delivery uncertainty, often for reasons outside the control of a supplier or buyer. Overseas shipments can experience a variety of delays at customs. Longer shipping distances also increase the potential for in-transit shipping damage, theft, or obsolescence. Furthermore, someone in the supply chain (the supplier, purchaser, or end customer) owns the inventory as it travels over great distances. This increases the risk and exposure to financial loss, if the inventory is damaged, is stolen, or simply disappears into one of the many "black holes" that exist in the global supply chains at distribution points, ports, shipping terminals, railway nodes, and other locations. Extended material pipelines are a major consideration when comparing the cost of domestic versus international purchasing. Many firms fail to consider the higher cost of inventory when they outsource their supply chain to Asia and do not take into account the impact of longer planning times, inventory obsolescence, and slower customer response associated with long global supply lead times.

Inefficient Manufacturing Processes

A producer whose manufacturing system is not efficient must hold higher-than-necessary inventory levels to compensate for poor quality or process yield. One indication of an inefficient scheduling or production system is a large amount of work-in-process inventory located behind each work center. Inefficient scheduling and productions often create congested work areas as inventory accumulates in production centers. This increases total inventory carrying costs because longer production times increase work-in-process inventory. Inefficient production processes also lead to higher costs through poorer yield or quality.

Sourcing Snapshot

Applying RFID and Lean Thinking to a University Hospital

When Jon Stegner, walked in to his first week at the University of Chicago Medical Center, one of the first places he visited was the Emergency Room, and the nearby supply room. What he saw there, was in his words, "disgusting."

Medical supplies were in boxes strewn in random piles. Many of the boxes contained medical supplies that were out of date or expired. The bins had dust bunnies, and "guck" in the bottom of them. Visits to other supply rooms in other parts of the hospital were equally as bad.

Jon came from a background in distribution, procurement, and logistics at Delphi and Honda, and knew that this was a perfect approach for building a lean supply system. He also wondered if it were possible to apply the principles of lean production and just-in-time to the healthcare environment.

Jon and his team started by putting together a plan for every part, and worked to create standard categories. For each category of part, the team mapped out what items were in the supply room, and which items were most frequently accessed. Like items were also grouped together in a standard layout facility. Each stockroom then applied the same functional layout, with the admitting supplies in the first column of bins, followed by ortho supplies, etc. That way, a clinician walking into any supply room would know exactly where to find the supplies—much like walking into a Lowes store!

Next, the team examined the average usage of parts, and established the reorder quantity for each part, as well as the average inventory that should be in each bin, with the objective of keeping no more than four days' worth of supply in each bin, and a one day resupply level. This seemed reasonable, and might mean different quantities based on usage.

Finally, his team sought to pull together a kanban system that would use a two-bin system. The two-bin system was quite simple. Each bin had two sections, with a separator in the middle. When one side of the bin was empty, the clinician would pull the "Low Stock" card, and place it in a card holder by the door. The card was actually an RFID card that contained the part number, the resupply level, the bin location, etc., and the card holder had an RFID reader on it which would automatically pick up the signal for a resupply. When the last item in the bin was used, the "Stock out" card was placed in the card holder.

All cards placed in the holder by 11 a.m. would be electronically updated into the inventory resupply system, sending a signal to the wholesaler Cardinal Health (in Waukegan, 45 minutes away). Cardinal employees pick and ship the required parts for all supply rooms in the hospital, grouped in a bag together in a tote designated for each supply room. That afternoon, when the totes arrived, an inventory planner would take the tote up to the room, resupply the bins, and replace the Low Stock RFID card back into the bin.

Each card holder also has an electronic panel that shows the number of stockouts, number of cards pulled etc. This allows regular monitoring of cards. The stockout indicator also provides an idea of what parts are stocking out. In most cases, this is happening because clinicians (often nurses) were not pulling the cards for a bin when they took material out. Jon keeps track of stockouts by nurse, and can also determine if there is a deviation in material pulled vs. cards pulled. He takes this list and goes to each nurse with the same message: "If you pull the material, pull the card. We will make sure it is there, I guarantee it. But if you don't pull the card, you will always stock out. So pull the card!" Now 35,000 items are all on the RFID two-bin system.

The implementation of this effort wasn't simple. It required cleaning up every room, organizing the parts, and throwing away massive amounts of expired product (over half a million dollars worth in the first 9 months, and over a million in the first 18 months). Much of this was material that no one was using, or overstock returns.

There is also a move today to place RFID tags on high value items, suck as stents, etc. These will be put into specialized cabinets, and pulled by physicians near operating rooms. This will provide a great deal of visibility.

Low value items are stocked in drawers, cabinets, etc., and are there for clinicians to use on the store. These items also use a form of kanban. The stocker goes to every floor with a cart that is full of material, and fills in every location, which has a standard configuration and quantity of items (cotton balls, disposable gowns, gloves, swabs, and other disposables). When he or she is finished replenishing these items on the floor, the cart is taken to the supply room for that floor, and replenished using the available stock. This allocates the stock used to that floor's inventory record, and kanban cards are pulled using a two-bin system for those items in the stockroom.

The hospital moved to a new state of the art facility, which had 30 percent more stock rooms. There used to be just one Operating room for case picking, and now have two. Inventory has dropped by $1M, out of $23M in inventory, and this will increase with the high value inventory items going onto RFID. With $500M in spend, this type of improvement is not only financially beneficial, but is creating major wins with nurses, administrators, and staff who now have a much better operating environment. The stock rooms now also have 5S layouts for larger items that are used on the floor, and also for linents, and other items used in the hospital. The application of lean, RFID, and common sense change management is making University of Chicago a poster child for lean deployment in healthcare, showing that lean isn't just for automotive anymore.

Source: Robert Handfield, "Supply Chain View from the Field," http://scm.ncsu.edu/blog.

Most inventory waste results from underlying problems that management has failed to correct. When inventory disguises operating inefficiencies, this accepts inefficiencies as part of conducting business. Failure to correct these underlying problems makes the inefficient producer vulnerable to challenges from cost-efficient producers. Whereas balance sheet accounting presents inventory as an asset, experienced supply chain managers recognize it is an asset worth controlling and, when necessary, even eliminating.

Creating the Lean Supply Chain[5]

Lean supply chains have their origin in the just-in-time philosophy, first adopted by many American and European firms in the late 1980s. This emerged early on as "Just-in-Time" when used primarily in a manufacturing setting, but has evolved to "lean thinking" to encompass many different types of supply chain functions beyond manufacturing.

Lean thinking is a way to understand value from the customer's perspective, and eliminate waste processes that do not add value. It is a process improvement methodology to eliminate waste as seen from the customer's perspective.

Lean thinking is based on the fundamental concepts of "Just-in-Time," that evolved from many of the early Japanese manufacturing techniques developed by companies such

Sourcing Snapshot

John Deere is Looking for Lean Suppliers

John Deere is a global provider of farming equipment and turf care products and is committing to building a strong portfolio of products for people who are "linked to the land." Its major growth objectives for 2014 include establishing profitable growth, improving asset performance, and disciplined execution of its Enterprise Product Delivery Process. The latter element has a strong emphasis on providing high-quality products, delivering on time, managing costs and assets effectively, and operating as highly aligned teams.

One of the important components of this strategy extends to building partnerships with key suppliers of their products. Deere is beginning to partner with key suppliers to not only produce components, but produce extensions to their existing product lines. Such partnerships are not entered into lightly, as they involve deploying the partnering process. This process involves extensive investigation into suppliers operations, culture, and philosophy, and determining whether it is aligned with Deere's path into the future. One of the important elements of this evaluation includes examining the supplier's past performance and current initiatives on deploying lean initiatives.

The ideal characteristics of a supplier integrated partner as it relates to Flexible and Predictable Delivery include the following:

- Lean Manufacturing Culture
- Continuous Improvement Culture
- Electronically Integrated ERP System
- Optimized line flow and inventory control
- Available capacity to meet demands

Typical Measures and Performance Levels:

1. E-Commerce Capability
2. Raw and WIP Inventory
3. Scrap and Material Obsolescence
4. Cycle Time reduction

As Deere moves forward with supplier partnerships, they require suppliers who embody and adopt their own thinking and principles around continuous improvement, effective inventory management, and reliable, predictable delivery capabilities.

Source: Simpson, G. R. (2005, November 22), "In Year of Disasters, Lean Emergency Materials Management Brings Order to the Chaos of Relief Operations," *Wall Street Journal* A1.

as Toyota, Honda, and others. Lean focuses on reducing lead times, inventory, eliminating bottlenecks, and elimination of non-value-added processes. Lean manufacturing (or lean production) involves applying a number of core principles to the manufacturing workplace, to attack problems such as long internal lead times, long changeover times between runs, excessive inventories, bottlenecks at critical processes, and long wait time for non-value added processes. Some of the tools used in lean include elements such as employee involvement, 5S visual management, pull systems, continuous flow and flexible manufacturing, and supplier partnerships.

Six Sigma

On the other hand, Six Sigma is focused on eliminating process variance, as well as improving processes that are not in control. Six sigma relies on statistical and problem-solving tools that are related to these elements, and provide a core set of philosophical underpinnings based in the broader principles of Total Quality Management, which evolved from the work of quality gurus such as William Deming and Joseph Juran. Six sigma approaches are often utilized to attack problems such as excessive process variance, too much rework, quality defects, processes that are unreliable and out of control, unexplained shifts in product specification outcomes, or excessive reliance on inspection as a form of quality control.

Generally speaking, today people group these techniques under the broader rubric of "Lean Six Sigma" or "Lean Sigma," referring to these components as a broad set of continuous improvement processes focused on improving quality and eliminating waste. Firms following the lean philosophy often experience remarkable improvements in their productivity (outputs/inputs), inventory levels, and quality. To understand why lean (then called JIT) made such an impact in the late 1980s, consider some eye-opening statistics from 1986, which compared performance at Toyota's Takaoka facility with that of GM's Framingham plant (Exhibit 16.6). Numbers such as these kicked off the JIT revolution in the American automotive industry during the late 1980s and early 1990s.

Notice how the Toyota plant needed fewer hours and much less inventory to do its job. This ability to do more with less led many people to refer to JIT as lean production. Similarly, the phrase "just-in-time" reflected the idea that the timing and level of inventory and production activities are closely matched to demand. With average inventory levels of only two hours, the Toyota plant was clearly "just" receiving parts and materials before they were needed.

The underlying emphases of lean—to eliminate all forms of uncertainty and waste—are relevant to all organizations, regardless of the specific planning and control tools that are used. Second, even though some techniques such as Just-in-time are not suitable in certain production and service environments, it is entirely possible that an organization can follow the lean philosophy. To summarize:

- The lean philosophy can be applied to a wide range of production and service environments. In fact, one could easily argue that there is no environment that would not benefit from adopting its core principles.

- Companies following the lean philosophy can and do use a wide range of planning and control techniques, not just just-in-time inventory management.

- Lean is closely aligned with total quality management and supplier management initiatives.

Exhibit 16.6	The Performance Advantage of a JIT Plant, Circa 1986	
	GM FRAMINGHAM	TOYOTA TAKAOKA
Assembly hours per vehicle	40.7 hours	16 hours
Defects per 100 vehicles	130 defects	45 defects
Average inventory levels	Two weeks	Two hours

The lean concept is based on several key principles:

- Maximize use of people—In this approach, people are considered productive, useful sources of innovation. Traditional manufacturing approaches relied more on Frederick Taylor's approach of timing people's actions, and driving them to become more efficient by forcing them to do repetitive work. The lean approach emphasized that workers were the best source of ideas on how to improve processes. Because people are working around the equipment and the process all day, they naturally become highly familiar with the strengths and weaknesses of the current systems. As such, lean approaches schedule time during each day for people to experiment with new work methods, new material handling approaches, and new processes, to continuously improve processes and make them more efficient and effective.

- Simplify first, and only then apply new technology—This is a simple but important lesson. It is always better to study existing processes and learn to improve them, before bringing in new technology. New technology not only takes time to implement and learn, but may present a whole new set of complicated issues to deal with. Once existing processes have been fully optimized, and it is determined that they cannot meet process requirements, then it makes sense to look at different, new technological improvements.

- Focus on gradual, but continuous, improvement—Gradual improvement implies making small, incremental improvements that over time, will take on great meaningful steps. The phrase "Rome wasn't built in a day" applies here. Continuous improvement involves small, daily improvements that ensure that the process is moving forward. This is also known as "kaizen" in Japanese terms.

- Minimize waste (including poor quality)—**Waste** refers to any type of activity that is not creating value, which includes wasted time, wasted effort, wasted movement, or anything else. Poor quality is one form of waste, but the key to lean production is to attack waste in any form, and be constantly vigilant about waste.

To put these forms of waste in context, suppose it takes an inspector at a manufacturing plant 15 minutes to inspect an incoming batch of material. The traditional perspective would be that inspections like these are a necessary and prudent business expense. But according to lean thinking, this is a waste of both time and personnel caused by defects. Services examples abound as well. If you have to wait even five minutes at the doctor's office before being seen, then waste has occurred. If this definition seems harsh, it is meant to be. The point is to get organizations thinking critically about the business processes they use to provide products and services, as well as the outcomes of these processes. As far as lean thinking is concerned, if there is any waste at all, there is room for improvement.

The Lean Perspective on Inventory

One hallmark of a lean environment is the strong emphasis placed on reducing raw material, work-in-process, and finished goods inventories throughout the system. This is because inventory is not only seen as a form of waste in and of itself, but also because inventory can cover up wasteful business practices. Under the lean philosophy, lowering inventory levels forces firms to address these poor practices.

To illustrate how inventory can hide problems, consider a simple facility consisting of three work centers (A, B, and C), shown in Exhibit 16.7.

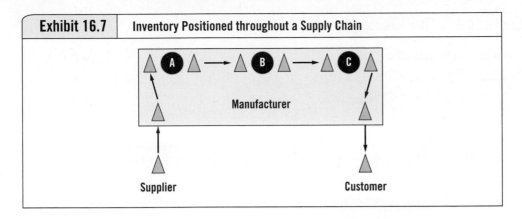

Exhibit 16.7 | **Inventory Positioned throughout a Supply Chain**

The triangles in the diagram represent inventory. In addition, between each work center is plenty of room for inventory. Take one of the work centers, say Center B, and consider what happens if it has an equipment breakdown that reduces its output. The answer is, in the short run, only Center B is affected. Because there is plenty of space for inventory between A and B, then Center A can continue to work. And because inventory exists between Center B and C, Center C can continue to work as long as the inventory lasts. Most importantly, the customer can continue to be served. The same result occurs regardless of the reason for any disruption in Center B, including worker absenteeism, poor quality levels, and so forth. Whatever the problem, inventory hides it (but at a cost).

Now let us take the same facility after a successful lean program has been put in place. The work centers have been moved closer together, eliminating wasted movement and space where inventory could pile up. Setup times have also been reduced, allowing the work centers to make only what is needed when it is needed. If we assume the program has been in place for a while, we can also assume that the inventory levels have been reduced dramatically, giving us a revised picture of the facility (see Exhibit 16.8).

Now, inventory has been reduced to the point where it shows up only in the customer facility. Under these conditions, what happens in the short run if the equipment at Center B breaks down? The answer this time is that everything stops, including shipments to the customer. Center A has to stop because there is no spot for it to put inventory, nor is there any demand for it. Center C has to stop because there is no inventory on which to work.

Inventory in the supply chain is often compared to water in a river. If the "water" is high enough, it will cover all the "rocks" (quality problems, absenteeism, equipment breakdowns, and so forth), and everything will appear to be running smoothly.

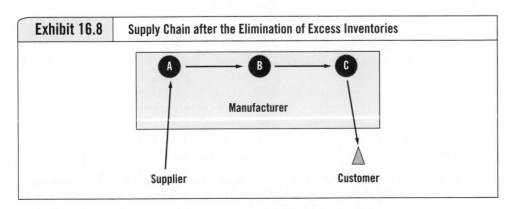

Exhibit 16.8 | **Supply Chain after the Elimination of Excess Inventories**

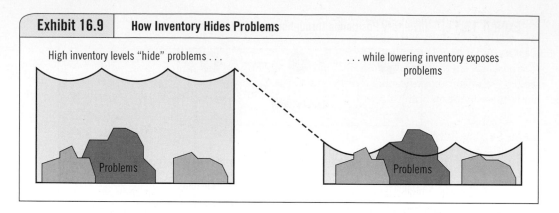

Exhibit 16.9 | How Inventory Hides Problems

High inventory levels "hide" problems . . .   . . . while lowering inventory exposes problems

Problems   Problems

In a lean environment, the approach is to gradually remove the "water" until the first "rock" is exposed, thereby establishing a priority as to the most important obstacle to work on. After resolving this problem, inventory levels are reduced further until another problem (and opportunity to eliminate waste) appears. This process continues indefinitely, or until all forms of waste and uncertainty have been eliminated (see Exhibit 16.9).

This is not an easy approach to implement. The implication is that every time a process is working smoothly, there may be too much inventory and more should be removed until the organization hits another "rock." That is certainly not a natural action for most people, and the performance evaluation system needs to be altered to reflect this type of activity.

Next, let us examine three of the primary elements of a lean supply chain: (1) Lean Supply, (2) Lean Transportation, and (3) just-in-time kanban systems.

Lean Supply

Implementing a lean supply system is the first major element of a lean supply chain. A lean supply system receives frequent receipts of material from suppliers to meet immediate requirements. The following features define a lean supply system:

- A commitment to zero defects by the buyer and seller
- Frequent shipment of small lot sizes according to strict quality and delivery performance standards
- Closer, even collaborative, buyer-seller relationships
- Stable production schedules sent to suppliers on a regular basis
- Extensive sharing of electronic information between supply chain members
- Electronic data interchange capability with suppliers

In creating the lean value chain, effective and detailed supply planning is a must. An ongoing requirement is to establish the financial health of all players, their ability to grow with the company, and most importantly, the ability to continuously improve. Supply management must be aware of the need to colocate supplier engineers and materials managers—and although many companies are not interested in managing their second tier, they must select first tiers who are effectively able to do so! This point is often overlooked in most companies.

An effective supply planning function begins and ends with thorough and well-developed commodity strategies. In fact, we have developed an entire learning module on this element. Every major spend area should have a document strategy that provides goals and strategic actions, and is monitored on an ongoing basis. Finally, a plan for continuous cost improvement throughout the supply chain by establishing critical cost drivers forms the basis for identifying the contribution of supply management to organizational profit goals. Organizations who partner with customer/suppliers to eliminate non-value added activities benefit on both sides of the relationship.

Lean Supply Barriers

Lean supply in Western companies has been slowed or even prohibited by a variety of barriers that are part of the Western business system and culture, although industries are affected differently.[6] Fortunately, some of these barriers are not as great as they were when JIT/Lean first became popular during the early and mid-1980s. Important barriers include the following:

- *Dispersed supply base.* Most purchasers have a geographically dispersed supply base. Because lean supply relies on frequent deliveries of smaller quantities from suppliers, it may be difficult to achieve a level of consistent delivery reliability from suppliers located 800 or even 8,000 miles away. The greater the distance between buyer and seller, the greater is the variability around delivery times.

- *Historic buyer-seller relationships.* Buyers and sellers often lack the cooperative relationship required to pursue lean supply. A true lean system requires mutual trust and respect between parties. Historically, the relationship between U.S. buyers and sellers has been closer to adversarial than cooperative.

- *Number of suppliers.* Some supply chains still have too many suppliers to support an efficient lean system. Like other progressive purchasing strategies, lean requires a drastically reduced supply base to minimize interaction and communication costs. It is nearly impossible to develop closer relationships with thousands of suppliers.

- *Supplier quality performance.* Some sellers simply have not achieved the levels of near-perfect quality required for lean supply. A total commitment to product and delivery quality is a prerequisite for a successful lean system.

Lean Transportation

Lean transportation, the second element of a lean supply chain, refers to the efficient movement of goods between the buyer and seller. This involves frequent deliveries of smaller quantities directly to the point of use at the purchaser. A lean transportation network relies on company-owned or contracted vehicles that pick up and deliver according to a regular and repeatable schedule. This repeatable schedule, also called a closed-loop system, moves goods from supplier to purchaser and then from purchaser back to supplier with return material, such as containers. Long-term dedicated contract carriage replaces commercial carriage as the primary mode of transportation in a closed-loop transportation system.

Exhibit 16.10 on p. 644 compares a traditional delivery system with a just-in-time delivery system. In a traditional system, the supplier and purchaser do not coordinate their material requirements or production schedules. Suppliers produce material and then store that material, awaiting an order from the purchaser. In a lean system, suppliers coordinate production schedules with customers' schedules. Production moves from the supplier's

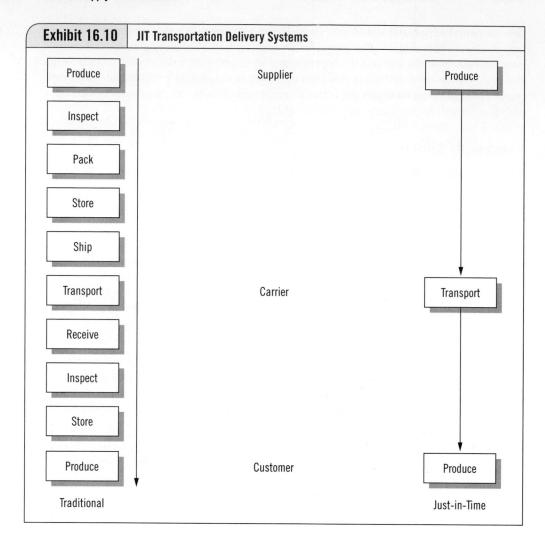

Exhibit 16.10 | JIT Transportation Delivery Systems

Supplier

Produce

Inspect

Pack

Store

Ship

Transport   Carrier

Receive

Inspect

Store

Produce   Customer

Traditional

Produce

Transport

Produce

Just-in-Time

work center to the carrier and directly to the purchaser. Designing a lean transportation network involves certain steps:

- Reduce the number of carriers. Reduce the number of carriers, perhaps even to one per region.

- Use longer-term contracts. Negotiate longer-term agreements with carriers that formalize the dedicated transportation network.

- Establish electric linkages. Establish GPS linkages and onboard mobile technology with suppliers and carriers to coordinate and control the movement of material through the network. The use of GPS systems combined with mobile technology allows transportation planners and drivers to better coordinate, reroute shipments, and avoid major traffic problems that can improve delivery performance.

- Implement a closed-loop system. Pick up all freight from suppliers and deliver on a regular schedule. Use returnable containers to eliminate waste. Even little things like planning a window for arrival that is not on a weekend can save driver time (and, thus, eliminate waste).

- Handle material efficiently. Use state-of-the-art material-handling equipment and technology. Lean transportation systems feature certain innovations that can further eliminate supply chain waste. The first includes specialized transportation vehicles that allow easy loading and unloading of smaller quantities. These trucks are smaller, more efficient, and more versatile. The second innovation includes the extensive use of returnable plastic or steel containers. As drivers pick up material from suppliers, they leave empty containers for reuse. A third innovation involves point-of-use doors at production facilities. Because excessive material handling and travel within a facility is wasteful, deliveries occur close to where the material is needed.

Just-in-Time Kanban Systems

Developed along with the lean movement, a JIT **kanban system** is a production control approach that uses containers, cards, or visual cues to control the production and movement of goods through the supply chain. These systems have several key characteristics:

- Kanban systems use simple signaling mechanisms such as a card, or even an empty space or container, to indicate when specific items should be produced or moved. Most kanban systems, in fact, do not require computerization.
- Kanban systems can be used to synchronize activities either within a plant or between different supply chain partners. As such, a kanban system can be an important part of both production activity control and supplier order management systems.
- Kanban systems are not planning tools. Rather, they are control mechanisms that are designed to pull parts or goods through the supply chain based on downstream demand. As a result, many firms use techniques such as material requirements planning (MRP) to anticipate requirements, but depend on their kanban systems to control the actual execution of production and movement activities.

As we noted before, cards are not the only signaling method used in a kanban system. Some other methods include the following:

- Single-card systems. The single card is the production card, and the empty container serves as the move signal.
- Color coding of containers.
- Designated storage spaces.
- Computerized bar coding systems.

Lean supply is a proven approach for improving bottom-line business results. By focusing on attributes of the manufacturing system that impact customers, it ensures that product and a process defect are reduced, and provides tools and methodologies to identify and fix root causes of problems. It eliminates process waste, variation, and defects that customers experience in products and service. However, it cannot occur in a vacuum.

First, management leadership MUST be committed and involved in deploying lean. Without top management support through dedicated resources, performance-based metrics tied to pay and incentives, and driving the vision throughout the company, lean efforts will always fail. Leaders need to believe that lean will work, and motivate the entire workforce to engage and participate in the changes that will inevitably occur.

Second, improvement activities must focus on elements of the process that directly impact business objectives such as profitability, market share, customer satisfaction, and so forth.

If lean manufacturing is done only because it is "the fad of the day," or because somebody in the upper echelons of the company suddenly took a fancy to the concept, it will fail.

Lean approaches take time, discipline, and effort. Management must be committed to assigning top people who are leaders, who are engaged and dedicated, and who will not give up to the effort to drive continuous improvement. These highly motivated individuals are required to drive change into the organization as the new approaches are implemented.

Lean production requires people to apply disciplined methodologies to first drive improvements, and then sustain them into the future. Some of these methodologies include value stream mapping, measurement of systems, action plans for improvement, implementation of changes, and measurement and continuous improvement of the process improvement. In a sense, improvements are NEVER finished, but become an inherent part of the management culture within the organization.

Finally, decisions must be based on facts and data, NOT opinions or preferences of influential individuals. People may often want to bury the facts, as they are uncomfortable admitting that current processes are broken and are not working as they should. This is part of the change that is required. People must be willing to accept the facts, not deny them, and once they accept them, become determined to change the picture and drive improvements to current processes.

Approaches for Managing Inventory Investment

The effective management of inventory investment should be a primary objective when searching for ways to manage costs, improve profitability, and enhance shareholder value. How managers view inventory can differ, depending on where one resides in the supply chain. Although financial planners view inventory in terms of dollars, as reported on the balance sheet, supply chain planners typically view inventory in terms of units. What is the right viewpoint if we expect to manage this investment? Actually, assuming multiple perspectives about inventory is a worthwhile way to approach this topic.

Companies that are serious about managing inventory must visualize how their practices and approaches will affect the three V's of inventory management—the volume, velocity, and value of inventory. Exhibit 16.11 highlights the "Three-V Model of Inventory Management," including key objectives, measures, and examples of activities that relate to each dimension.

Volume refers to the amount of inventory that a firm owns at any given time. Volume measures will relate to total units on hand, including safety stock levels. Velocity refers to how quickly raw material and work-in-process inventory transform into finished goods that the customer accepts. As the rate at which inventory moves from suppliers, through operations, and on to customers accelerates, the average amount of inventory on hand at any given time is reduced. Faster velocity requires a lower commitment of working capital and improves cash flow. Velocity measures include material throughput rates, inventory turns, and order-to-cash cycle times. Finally, value refers to the unit cost of the inventory. Key measures include standard costs and the total value of inventory, including raw materials, components, subassemblies, and finished goods.

Although certain actions can predominantly affect a specific variable (velocity, volume, or value), there is often interdependence among these variables. The point here is that organizations must pursue activities and approaches that positively affect the volume, value, and velocity of inventory through and across the supply chain. The following sections present some powerful ways to manage inventory investment.

| Exhibit 16.11 | Three-V Model of Inventory Management |

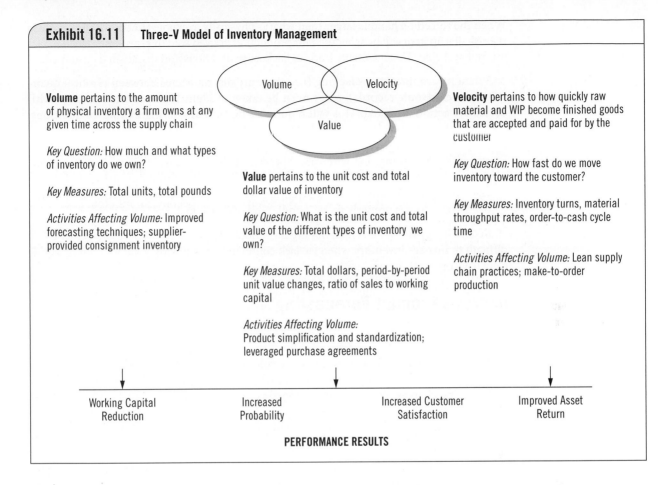

Volume pertains to the amount of physical inventory a firm owns at any given time across the supply chain

Key Question: How much and what types of inventory do we own?

Key Measures: Total units, total pounds

Activities Affecting Volume: Improved forecasting techniques; supplier-provided consignment inventory

Value pertains to the unit cost and total dollar value of inventory

Key Question: What is the unit cost and total value of the different types of inventory we own?

Key Measures: Total dollars, period-by-period unit value changes, ratio of sales to working capital

Activities Affecting Volume: Product simplification and standardization; leveraged purchase agreements

Velocity pertains to how quickly raw material and WIP become finished goods that are accepted and paid for by the customer

Key Question: How fast do we move inventory toward the customer?

Key Measures: Inventory turns, material throughput rates, order-to-cash cycle time

Activities Affecting Volume: Lean supply chain practices; make-to-order production

Working Capital Reduction   Increased Probability   Increased Customer Satisfaction   Improved Asset Return

PERFORMANCE RESULTS

Achieve Perfect Record Integrity

A logical place to begin when managing inventory investment is to make sure there is agreement between physical and electronic inventory. Firms often compensate for error and variability in supply chains with excess inventory, usually in the form of safety stock or safety lead times. This also applies when there is excessive error in record integrity systems. Perfect record integrity must become an important inventory management objective.

Record integrity is the result of various activities and procedures designed to ensure that the amount of physical material on hand (POH) is equal to the computerized record of material on hand (ROH). In short, record integrity exists when the physical inventory on hand equals the electronic record on hand (POH = ROH), regardless of the quantity of inventory. Any difference between POH and ROH represents error. This error can be the result of operationally mismanaging inventory, which affects the physical (POH) side of record integrity. Error can also result from systems-related sources, which affect the computerized side (ROH) of record integrity. Concern over managing the actual volume, velocity, and value of inventory should arise only after confidence in the integrity of inventory records has been established.

The effects of poor record integrity on supply chain operations can be severe. When physical inventory exceeds the amount the computerized system believes is available (POH > ROH), the physical inventory cannot be sold or used to satisfy customer demand.

When the record on hand is larger than what is physically available (ROH > POH), there is the risk that an item will be scheduled for production or even sold to a customer when in fact it is not available. This inevitably leads to backorder situations and dissatisfied customers.

When record integrity is lacking (i.e., there are discrepancies between physical quantities and electronic records), steps must be taken to identify the sources of error with corrective action expected. This will require asking and answering a range of questions. For example, are record errors displaying a random or systematic pattern across SKUs? How severe are the differences between physical stock and electronic records? Are proper receiving, stock-keeping, and withdrawal procedures and systems in place? Is theft a problem? Are suppliers shipping quantities that match their documentation? Are effective cycle-counting procedures used? Is inventory scrap and obsolescence accounted for correctly? Do employees properly move, handle, and disburse material?

Record integrity is an essential but often overlooked part of inventory management. It is difficult to manage inventory when we lack confidence in knowing what we own or physically have on hand.

Improve Product Forecasting

Perhaps the most important piece of information that moves across a supply chain is the forecast of end customer demand. Unfortunately, many companies fail to recognize the effect that inaccurate forecasting has on the volume and velocity at which inventory moves toward the customer. The downside of poor forecasting includes higher inventory volumes and carrying charges, poor customer service as inventory is misallocated across locations and products, and excessive safety stock levels. For companies that are serious about better inventory management, improving the quality of product forecasts, like improving record integrity, is an ideal place to start.

Longs Drug Stores illustrates the benefits of better forecasting and product placement.[7] This company has improved its ability to identify the best possible combination of when to order prescription drugs, how to ship them, and how much to carry in a retail outlet on any given day. The company worked with a third party to develop a system that pulls data each day from point-of-sale terminals at hundreds of stores. Then, using two years of historical data and a forecasting algorithm that includes 150 variables per product that effectively predicts consumer demand out to 91 days, the company determines finished goods requirements for its retail outlets on a daily basis. The system also determines the amount to order from upstream suppliers (the pharmaceutical companies).

What effect has improved forecasting had on inventory and capital requirements? Longs executives say that the new system has allowed a 26 percent reduction in system-wide inventory requirements, leading to $30 million in savings. This system has also freed up $60 million in working capital, which the company has used to acquire a 20-store drug chain. The results are so encouraging that Longs signed a five-year extension with its third-party forecaster and expects to extend the system to include nonprescription products in the front of its stores. This example illustrates the link among better forecasting, reduced inventory requirements, and improved financial performance.

Standardize and Simplify Product Design

Why be concerned with standardizing and simplifying designs? A simplified design usually requires fewer part numbers, resulting in fewer suppliers, reduced transactions to support the inventory, and lower inventory management costs. The elimination of unnecessary components also reduces product cost, which reduces the value of the inventory required to support customer demand and service requirements. In some cases, this approach to greater standardization may require a major cultural shift in the company and a strategic decision to move in a particular direction. In many cases, the product complexity decision is embedded in the very DNA of the organization and requires a fundamental shift driven by top leadership toward containing complexity and SKU proliferation. For example, a leading truck manufacturer was undergoing a major shift in company philosophy, in which the entire product line and product offering was undergoing a major transformation:

> *We are primarily engineered to order historically—but are moving more towards standardized options. We are making some components standard and are moving from 13 variations to 3 or 4 and are being pushed to do that by senior management. As it stands historically, if the customer wanted it, we would put it on. The move towards standardization is a senior management decision. We have some tools to measure complexity versus revenue generated whereby we are able to establish a value for that option. It is easy to determine which parts a customer wants and what we charge for it—and in these cases we can do a pretty good job of passing it on with a nice margin.*[8]

Product design is the right time to consider simplification and standardization, although continuous improvement efforts can later alter existing designs. Many companies use value-engineering techniques during product design to reduce part count and cost. Some of the other policies used to improve design simplification and reduce complexity are as follows:

Establish Premium Pricing for Customization

Many companies are loath to develop premium pricing options. However, this practice can assist in shaping customer demand and can even, in some cases, drive additional margin into the business if required. Many companies are now recognizing that there is a cost to complexity and that customers should be willing to pay more to offset these costs.

Establish Geographic-Specific Options and Standards

Companies are also working to establish regional requirements based on regional customer preferences and designing supply chain configurations around these regional requirements. This approach must be orchestrated carefully with plants and suppliers to ensure success and accommodate appropriate order-to-delivery lead time promises aligned with this design. For example, one manufacturing company noted the following:

> *We are also standardizing certain configurations around certain regions of the country where our plants are. Our plants are from Seattle to Montreal, to the Midwest, Canada, and Mexico to the Southwest and Southeast—and the options are very distinct. Texas truckers like shiny stuff, Midwestern ones, not so much. So we configure by plant and by region. If someone wants an option in one area, they [sic] have to go to a different plant. This is managed by our order fulfillment group that allows us to maintain good plant focus for certain options and configurations[9].*

Maintain a Database of Option Requests

One company has dedicated a formal approach to maintaining complexity and has identified this as a core element, even though it acknowledged the problems associated with managing the business in this manner and the pain inflicted on the supply chain.

The order fulfillment manager described the emotional decisions and backroom wars that took place when they were bought out and the buyer sought to standardize components of their product line, considered to be a company trademark:

We track active options and custom unpublished options. We track usage, and if we have a group of options that has no usage over time, we will try to eliminate them from the available product offerings and get them out of the maintenance mode. On the other hand, if we have some customized options showing increasing usage, we will promote them to a published standard as it is becoming a popular item. In that case we will look closely at the design to see if it is designed for higher volume, to get some cost out of the process.[10]

Do Not Eliminate Frequently Requested Options

The importance of maintaining a company's trademark requirements in product design can be an important counterpoint to the standardization argument. An organization needs to carefully evaluate the standardization decision and ensure it does not design out elements that are critical to its product branding and positioning.

Utilize Business Modeling and TCO Tools to Support Complexity Reduction Decisions

Many companies are developing more formal approaches to managing complexity and have developed business modeling and TCO approaches to developing a business case with tools associated with the decision. For example, Dell Computer utilizes a template of decision criteria against which product design decisions are baselined:

1. Will the item be sole, single, or multisourced?
2. Does the new offering involve a new technology risk item (this could signal a potential quality yield risk)?
3. Who are the manufacturers, and who are the integrators for the parts?
4. Where are all the suppliers located, and what is the logistics plan?
5. Where are these parts used in the industry today and in future, which could affect overall demand?
6. What are the expected cost takedown rates?
7. What does the product road map look like in terms of possible product substitutes?
8. Are there any key alliances that need to be considered from key suppliers/competitors?
9. What is the flexibility to use a particular part in other product lines, or is this part leveraged from another product?
10. Can these parts be sold as aftermarket options or service parts?[11]

Leverage Companywide Purchase Volumes

The consolidation or leveraging of common items and services across buying locations has increased dramatically over the last 10 years, including across worldwide units.[12] This has resulted in major savings as leveraged agreements lead to lower material costs. Lower material costs can significantly reduce the amount of capital committed to inventory over the life of an agreement.

Besides seeking a lower unit cost in leveraged agreements, buyers often pursue other nonprice issues that affect inventory investment. One such issue is **consignment**, which the

APICS Dictionary defines as the process of a supplier placing goods at a customer location without receiving payment until after the buyer uses the goods. The advantage of consignment to the buyer is the ability to defer ownership and avoid committing working capital and incurring carrying charges. This reduces the average amount of inventory a buyer owns, as well as improving velocity.

Use Suppliers for On-Site Inventory Management

Almost all organizations use distributors to provide at least some portion of their inventory requirements, particularly maintenance, repair, and operating supplies. A distributor may stock and sell a full range of items from different manufacturers. If the purchaser has enough volume, then the distributor may be willing to locate an employee at the purchaser's facility to manage the inventory.

Purchasers are increasingly entering partnerships or formal agreements with distributors featuring on-site support. Besides the on-site support, these agreements stipulate that a supplier/distributor will stock a wider range of items and provide agreed-upon service levels. The buyer, in exchange for purchasing solely from the distributor, no longer stocks inventory for items under contract.

The on-site representative orders on an as-needed basis, often directly into the distributor's order-processing system. This reduces the amount of paperwork required to submit an order. A buying firm avoids stocking or managing this inventory, whereas the distributor benefits from a higher share of a purchaser's total purchase requirements. Not stocking the items relieves the purchaser of carrying inventory.

The purchase of most MRO items is a nuisance because (1) they require a disproportionate amount of a buyer's time and (2) this often involves lower-value items. A formal agreement providing on-site supplier support can reduce the MRO ordering problem. These arrangements offer an opportunity to control a category of inventory that usually does not receive enough attention.

Reduce Supplier-Buyer Cycle Times

Shortening the material pipeline in terms of time between suppliers and a buyer can reduce the average amount of inventory in a system. One area of emphasis will be to support reduced order-cycle times with suppliers. A reduced (and reliable) order-cycle time positively affects inventory investment by allowing frequent orders received in smaller quantities. Planning horizons are also shorter, which reduces the need to carry safety stock.

Several actions support reduced order-cycle time with suppliers:

- Expanded electronic capability. The electronic exchange of information in a supply chain supports paperless procurement, faster data movement, and increased information accuracy. Electronic data interchange has the potential to reduce order-cycle times by 15 to 40 percent from current levels.
- Supplier development support. Supplier development means working directly with suppliers to improve performance. This support may include working directly at a supplier's facilities to speed order entry, production, and delivery through the removal of waste.
- Order-cycle time measurement. Tracking order-cycle times helps identify areas of improvement. We expect to see greater emphasis on the development of performance measures that are time oriented.

- Focus on second- and third-tier suppliers. Total supply chain management requires working with first-, second-, and even third-tier suppliers. The ability of a purchaser to reduce order-cycle time and inventory with its immediate suppliers is partly a function of a supplier being able to work with its suppliers. Suppliers located two and three tiers from the buyer will increasingly capture the interest of supply chain managers.

The activities described here are not the only actions that supply chain managers can or will emphasize to manage inventory investment. This discussion points out, however, that there are creative approaches for the system-wide control and management of inventory investment.

Delivering the Perfect Customer Order

Managing inventory investment is not only important from a financial perspective. If a firm can balance the right supply of inventory with the demand for inventory across a supply chain, it increases the probability that it can deliver the perfect order to customers. Simply put, the perfect customer order is one that is delivered on time, accurately, and in perfect condition. "The perfect order metric is especially valuable because it is a comprehensive measure of demand-fulfillment capability and acts as a lightning rod for all the deficiencies in a company's operations," said Debra Hoffman, a Boston-based consultant.[13] Although most companies measure different elements contained in the perfect order measure, only 40 percent have a perfect customer order measure.[14]

A number of factors can cause an order not to be perfect, some of which are inventory related. Orders may be late because of supplier delivery problems, stockouts or manufacturing delays, or in-transit or delivery delays to customers. An order that arrives at the customer may not meet specifications because of inaccurate quantities, poor quality of finished goods, damage during transit, or incorrect or missing documentation. Any of these conditions can result in a less-than-perfect order.

The following identifies various planning systems and ways that progressive companies bring all parts of the supply chain together to pursue the perfect customer order.

Material Requirements Planning System

When we discuss systems that forecast future demand for products or services we sell, we are referring to independent demand systems. This means that demand for an item is not directly dependent on the demand for any other item that we produce. Systems that plan at the independent demand level are critical for achieving the perfect customer order.

A major task of the materials manager, however, is to control the inventory of items whose demand is dependent on the production of other items. A riding lawn mower is an example of an independent demand item. Demand for the final part is independent—expected orders determine the final amount produced. The demand for the steering wheel or tires that go on the mower, for example, are dependent on the demand for the mower. The component or subassembly demand is simply a function of the production schedule for the final part number.

A widely used system that controls dependent demand inventory is the material requirements planning system. An MRP system takes a period-by-period set of master production schedule requirements (anticipated or booked customer orders) and produces a time-phased set of material, component, and subassembly requirements timed to support an expected build schedule. This system relies on production schedules developed for final part numbers in the master production schedule to determine the timing and quantities of materials required for components or subassemblies. If supplier quality and lead times are reliable, planners can time the arrival of components just before production of the final part number.

Component requirements and quantities required to produce or assemble a final part number appear on a bill of material file. The bill of material file details the components or subassemblies and the quantity required to produce a final part number or end item. In some systems, the bill of material also indicates if any components require components themselves. Components that require components are subassemblies of the final part number. An MRP system links directly to the bill of material file and recognizes what components or subassemblies must go into the final item or package. The system will also recognize how many of each part may already be on hand.

Distribution Resource Planning System

Distribution resource planning (DRP) systems attempt to make the most effective use of finished-goods inventories. These systems, which are concerned with inventory that has left the work-in-process status and is working its way through a channel of distribution toward the customer, perform many functions:

- Forecasting finished-goods inventory requirements
- Establishing correct inventory levels at each stocking location
- Determining the timing and replenishment of finished-goods inventories
- Allocating items in short supply
- Transportation planning and vehicle load scheduling

A DRP system, combined with upstream supply chain planning systems such as MRP, can provide a total supply chain perspective.

Supply Chain Inventory Planners

The establishment of a supply chain or logistical planner position responsible for working with supply chain planning and execution systems is gaining popularity as a way to pursue the perfect customer order. A supply chain planner, a position often organized along product lines, manages the flow of inventory and information from suppliers through end customers. This position ties together the requirements of purchasing/materials management, production, inventory control, and product distribution.

The planner coordinates the movement and placement of inventory throughout the supply, production, and distribution channel. This position also acts as the liaison among various groups in the supply chain. Other assignments include developing smooth production schedules, establishing production targets from marketing forecasts, determining inventory deployment at field warehouses, and continuously evaluating inventory safety stock levels. The supply chain planner works closely with purchasing to coordinate material requirements to support production targets and with marketing and sales to meet customer order requirements. The performance of the planner is often measured against his or her ability to ensure that customers receive a perfect order.

Automated Inventory Tracking Systems

Automated inventory control systems involve computerized material and electronic data interchange systems that track the flow of inventory throughout the entire supply chain. This approach electronically connects suppliers, production plants, field distribution centers, and even customers. A customer may be a retail outlet or an independent distributor.

An integrated systems approach relies on new forms of information technology, such as VPN barcodes and RFID, to link the entire supply chain electronically. Walmart, for example, has benefited greatly from automated inventory tracking systems, using bar code technology to capture data at the point of sale and sending this up the supply chain to suppliers. Tracking sales allows Walmart to identify what is selling and to replenish shelves quickly. Automated tracking systems present an opportunity for controlling inventory investment throughout the entire supply chain. Increasingly, producers and channel members use radio frequency identification tags to track material movement across the supply chain. Real-time visibility to inventory across the supply chain makes planning for the perfect customer order that much easier.

Good Practice Example	*Applying Lean Thinking to the Clinical Trials Supply Chain*

Increased globalization of clinical trial materials (CTM) has made effective management of the CTM supply chain an ever more crucial component of the drug-development process. The greater complexity inherent with increased globalization, combined with higher levels of outsourcing, has raised the bar in organizational and operational performance for CTM supply for both sponsor companies and contract manufacturers supplying CTM.

The level of outsourcing in CTM supply is increasing because of a variety of factors. Pharmaceutical and biopharmaceutical companies are reluctant to increase internal headcounts and see increased outsourcing as a means to reduce and manage costs. In the face of increased numbers of clinical programs over the next two years, it is important for companies to evaluate and address problems in both clinical operations and the supply chain to avoid delays in the drug-development process.

A recent book by Robert Handfield documents a clinical supply chain maturity assessment to examine the current challenges and critical success factors in CTM supply. Proper planning between clinical operations and supply chain managers is critical, and the assessment analyzed input from clinical operations and supply chain managers to understand the factors from each area that contribute to problems in CTM supply and resulting delays in the drug-development process.

Supply chain managers point to several problems in clinical operations. These include: failures to provide accurate patient-enrollment forecasts by clinical operations; a lack of resources and capacity in clinical operations and distribution; a lack of processes and distribution lanes for new country distribution; and poor clinical visibility and interactive voice response system (IVRS) performance.

In turn, clinical operations personnel point to several supply chain weaknesses. A key problem relates to the increased globalization of clinical trials and resulting problems in rest-of-world distribution management that cause delays in receiving CTM on time. These problems involve delays in the customs-clearance processes, a lack of distribution capacity, and poorly established distribution lanes. Other problems in the supply chain include poor planning processes in clinical contract manufacturing that can cause delays as well as long lead times for comparator sourcing.

Managers in clinical operations and supply chain also point to some common problems. These involve the necessity of having to re-order production quantities of active pharmaceutical ingredients (APIs), leading to delays of trials; inherited small-molecule programs that are not well-developed and resulting delays in trials; and problems with controlling shipping-temperature excursions. Problems in cold-chain management are of growing importance as the level of biopharmaceuticals in clinical development increases.

The poor handoff among clinical research, clinical logistics, and supply chain managers is a major reason for delays. Effectively managing the interface between clinical operations and supply chain managers, whether it is done internally or through third-party suppliers in an outsourced relationship is key to successful outcomes.

To avoid these problems, Handfield recommends that regularly scheduled tactical forecasting and planning meetings be held to update clinical trials information and to ensure alignment among planning, contract manufacturing, and logistics. Planning is a critical lynchpin in the clinical supply chain and relies on effective forecasting, communication, and capacity analysis. Using tools such as country-risk analysis to prioritize planning requirements and lead times in clinical trials and more importantly, establishing defined roles and responsibilities for staffing in pharmaceutical operations and technology and clinical operations is crucial. There needs to be a discipline that is driven by metrics and changes in behaviors, with consequences for a lack of compliance to the planning process.

Another cause for delay in CTM supply is related to securing internal approvals for sourcing and contract-manufacturing arrangements. A lack of framework and direction on approval rules and policies can cause undue delays. To address these problems, companies must start defining more clearly and streamlining the approval process through improved documentation, the use of contract manufacturing and sourcing approval coordinators, and automation of the approval process.

Tools for improving the planning and implementation of clinical logistics are also of great importance. A common problem involves missed deliveries to a clinical trial site. Time is spent in trying to determine what went wrong with a shipment, locating a shipment, and then trying to get the material delivered. Limited use of capabilities of IVRS inventory and order tracking, poor coordination in notifying logistics of changes in schedules or trial locations, a lack of performance metrics for logistics, and inadequate resources for staffing and training in logistics are some common problems encountered in clinical logistics. Designing and building a logistics tracking and planning system that effectively uses IVRS capabilities for inventory control and replenishment systems is critical. Another important strategy is to establish local country logistics planning coordinators that can monitor market and government developments, manage local depots and supplier relationships, and troubleshoot shipments and supervise depots.

Source: Handfield, Robert, Patient-Focused Network Integration in BioPharma: Strategic Imperatives for the Years Ahead, Boca Raton, FL: Taylor & Francis, June, 2013.

CONCLUSION

The dollars committed to inventory represent a major investment. Like any investment, careful management will help ensure the investment provides an adequate return. Lean supply chain management requires the involvement of multiple parties within the organization, including senior leadership, operational executives and line managers, supply chain managers, logistics, transportation, finance, and other key players, all of whom play an important role in the management of inventory investment. The goal of this chapter is to create an awareness of: (1) the function of inventory; (2) the operational problems that tempt firms to increase inventory levels; (3) the major approaches used to manage inventory investment; and (4) the role of lean thinking in managing inventory. As firms continue to outsource more of their operational and manufacturing requirements, the inclusion of inventory cost within the total cost of ownership equation will also continue to be a challenge and will cause supply chain executives to continue to update their strategies in light of different requirements for trading off supply chain risk, inventory investment, customer responsiveness, and financial performance.

KEY TERMS

consignment, 648

lean, 622

Flow, 622

Pull, 622

kanban system, 643

striving for excellence, 622

waste, 638

DISCUSSION QUESTIONS

1. What does it mean to say that higher inventory levels often disguise underlying problems? What types of problems does this indicate?

2. How is purchasing directly and indirectly involved in the control of a firm's inventory investment?

3. What are some of the operational problems that excessive work-in-process inventory might indicate?

4. Discuss several reasons why managers often neglect the true costs of holding physical inventory. What has happened to change our perspective about holding physical inventory?

5. Why is the control of maintenance, repair, and operating inventory typically a difficult task for most companies?

6. What are the benefits of calculating the total cost of ownership associated with carrying physical inventory?

7. Of the following functions of physical inventory, select the one that purchasing is most likely to be directly involved in: (a) support of production requirements, (b) support of operational requirements, or (c) support of customer service requirements. Explain your choice.

8. Describe the actions that purchasing can take to reduce uncertainty associated with (a) supplier quality, (b) supplier delivery, (c) long order-cycle times, (d) extended material pipelines, and (e) inaccurate demand forecasts.

9. What problems does overforecasting demand create within a supply chain? What problems does underforecasting demand create? What can a company do to resolve the problem of forecasting inaccuracy?

10. The chapter presented various approaches for the control of inventory investment. Discuss three additional approaches not included that might involve supply chain managers.

11. What is a lean supply chain? Explain the three primary elements of a lean system.

12. What are the main characteristics of a lean supply system? What are the barriers to a lean supply system?

13. What is a closed-loop transportation system? Why does such a system require dedicated or contracted transportation carriers?

14. When putting in place a lean supply system, what changes typically occur in the ordering and transportation system between buyer and seller?

15. Discuss the advantages of taking a system-wide approach to the control of inventory investment. Are there any disadvantages? If yes, discuss the disadvantages.

16. What is the perfect order? Why do so few companies measure the perfect order?

ADDITIONAL READINGS

Bernard, P. (1999), *Integrated Inventory Management,* New York: John Wiley & Sons.

Bonney, M. C. (1994), "Trends in Inventory Management," *International Journal of Production Economics,* 35(1–3), 107–114.

Briscoe, A., Pancerella, M. B., and Pleskunas, G. (1997), "The Perfect Order Initiative," *Pharmaceutical Executive,* 17(7), 82–85.

Dong, Y., and Xu, K. (2002), "A Supply Chain Model of Vendor Managed Inventory, Transportation Research," *Part E: Logistics and Transportation Review,* 38(2), 75–95.

Fazel, F. (1997), "A Comparative Analysis of Inventory Costs of JIT and EOQ Purchasing," *International Journal of Physical Distribution and Logistics Management,* 27(2), 496.

Germain, R., and Droge, C. (1998), "The Context, Organization, Design, and Performance of JIT Buying versus Non-JIT Buying Firms," *International Journal of Purchasing and Materials Management,* 34(2), 12–18.

Gould, L. (2003), "Automotive Supply Chain Management: As Good as It Gets?" *Automotive Design and Production,* 115(2), 60–62.

Handfield, R. (2013, June), *Patient-Focused Network Integration in BioPharma: Strategic Imperatives for the Years Ahead,* Boca Raton, FL: Taylor & Francis.

Handfield, R. (2012, June), *Biopharmaceutical Supply Chains, Distribution, Regulatory, Systems, and Structural Changes Ahead,* Boca Raton, FL: Taylor & Francis.

Handfield, R., Straube, F., Pfohl, H.-C., and Wieland, A. (2013), *Trends and Strategies in Logistics and Supply Chain Management,* Berlin: BVL International.

Lewis, C. (1998), *Demand Forecasting and Inventory Control: A Computer Aided Learning Approach,* New York: John Wiley & Sons.

Minner, S. (2003), "Multiple-Supplier Inventory Models in Supply Chain Management: A Review," *International Journal of Production Economics,* 81–82, 265–279.

Narasimhan, S. L. (1995), *Production Planning and Inventory Control,* Englewood Cliffs, NJ: Prentice Hall.

Orlicky, J. (1994), *Materials Requirements Planning,* New York: McGraw-Hill.

Silver, E. A. (1998), *Inventory Management and Production Planning and Scheduling,* New York: John Wiley & Sons.

Stundza, T. (2001), "Buyers Save Money with Smart Inventory Programs," *Purchasing,* 130(23), 8B1–8B6.

Wild, T. (1998), *Best Practice in Inventory Management,* New York: John Wiley & Sons.

Witt, C. E. (2003), "Economic Strategies: Inventory Management," *Material Handling Management,* 58(5), 31–40.

Zipkin, P. H. (2000), *Foundations of Inventory Management,* New York: McGraw-Hill.

ENDNOTES

1. John Shook, as quoted in Liker, J. K. (Ed.). (1998), *Becoming Lean,* Portland, OR: Productivity Press.

2. Womack, J. P., and Jones, D. T. (1996), *Lean Thinking,* New York: Simon & Schuster.

3. Handfield, R. (1993), "Distinguishing Attributes of JIT Systems in the Make-to-Order/Assemble-to-Order Environment," *Decision Sciences Journal,* 24(3), 581–602.

4. This example is based directly on interviews with company managers.

5. This section is drawn from Bozarth, C., and Handfield, R. (2008), *Operations and Supply Chain Management* (2nd ed.), Upper Saddle River, NJ: Prentice Hall.

6. From Womack, J., Jones, D., and Roos, D. D. (1991), *The Machine That Changed the World: The Story of Lean Production,* New York: HarperCollins.

7. Adapted from Doan, A. (1999, November 1), "Vitamin Efficiency," *Forbes,* 179–186.

8. Handfield, R., Bozarth, C., McCreery, J., and Edwards, S. (2006, November), "Design for Order Fulfillment," Working Paper, Supply Chain Resource Cooperative, North Carolina State University.

9. Handfield et al.

10. Handfield et al.

11. Handfield et al.

12. Trent, R. J., and Monczka, R. M. (1998, November), "Purchasing and Supply Management: Trends and Changes Throughout the 1990s," *International Journal of Purchasing and Materials Management,* 2–9.

13. "The Perfect Order: How Does Your Demand Fulfillment Stack Up?" (2003, November), *MSI,* 37.

14. Keebler, J. S., et al. (1999), *Keeping Score: Measuring the Business Value of Logistics in the Supply Chain,* Oak Brook, IL Council of Logistics Management, 59.

Purchasing Services

Learning Objectives

After completing this chapter, you should be able to

- Understand the financial and operating impact of indirect spending on company performance
- Understand the fundamentals of transportation management and how these services can be sourced efficiently and effectively
- Comprehend the fundamentals and growing role of third-party logistics providers in effective and efficient supply chain management practices
- Discuss best practices in managing indirect spending and purchasing of services

Chapter Outline

Procuring Fleet Management Services

According to Bob Stone, Director of Supply Management, General Procurement for Hartford, Connecticut-based United Technologies Corporation, "No spend category is impacted more by the current economy than fleet management services." He indicates that the elements of the current economy that make effective fleet management problematic include: the financial credit crisis, challenges in the automotive industry, rapidly increasing fuel prices, and environmentally related concerns. Many supply management departments that have not historically managed fleet operations procurement are now being asked to do so. He also indicates that it can typically cost between $600 and $1,000 per month to keep a single vehicle on the road.

Fleet management issues include procurement of the vehicle itself (either purchased or leased), insurance, fuel, maintenance and repairs, and tolls, as well as taxes, title, license, and registration fees, which can vary substantially between using locations. A variety of operational complexities can impact fleet operations. The life cycle of fleet vehicles can typically range from three to five years. The number of vehicles maintained in the fleet is dynamic and can change from month to month. Additionally, the number of suppliers in the supply base can often include literally hundreds of repair shops, towing companies, and gas and service stations spread out over a wide area. Fleet vehicles can include automobiles, delivery and maintenance vans, and light pickup trucks, up to and including larger trucks.

Mark Smith, Strategic Consulting Services Leader for GE Fleet Services, says "[T]hat purchasing is in a unique position to take a holistic view of the spend." This exists because of the rigor that a supply management department already exercises in managing spend for other categories, including direct materials, indirect materials, and professional services. Some buyers have decided to manage fleet operations internally, whereas others, who consider fleet management to not be strategic or a core competency, have decided to outsource fleet management services to qualified service providers. These service providers can manage all phases of the entire process, including leasing, need identification, financing, remarketing, and disposal of the vehicle.

Supply management can add value to its companies' fleet management operations by negotiating directly with the vehicle manufacturers for the desired vehicles and then actually leasing them through a fleet management provider. In addition to the lease cost, the fleet management company then adds a fee of 2–5 percent for the management services that are provided. These lease agreements should include a firm guarantee that the fleet management company's fees will not increase throughout the term of the contract.

The following is a list of widely held industry best practices for procurement of fleet management services:

- Fleet management services is a unique category of indirect spend, requiring a RFP that represents its distinctive characteristics.
- Collaborate with internal users and stakeholders to define specific requirements.
- Use a total cost of ownership model to identify relevant and controllable costs.
- Focus on long-term fleet cost drivers such as fuel, maintenance, accidents, and depreciation.
- Set up and conduct quarterly or annual service provider performance reviews.
- Select smaller, lighter vehicles with less engine displacement that still meet user requirements.
- Adopt driver productivity tools, such as global positioning systems and routing systems to reduce total miles driven.

Source: Adapted from Avery, S. (2009, June), "Purchasing Takes the Wheel to Control Fleet Costs," *Purchasing*, 54–56.

Introduction

Indirect spending continues to receive growing attention from top management at both large and small corporations alike. This spend category can be defined as the sum of all purchased goods and services that are not a direct, identifiable part of products or services delivered to the customer. In many cases it is not uncommon for indirect spend to equal 50 percent or more of a company's total purchases, particularly for non-manufacturing organizations. Unfortunately, a substantial amount of indirect spend is not normally purchased through the organization's formal sourcing structure or using well-established supply management processes. However, many companies are now aggressively measuring and attacking the often substantial costs of indirect and services procurement. Senior management now realize that reducing or minimizing their firms' indirect and services spend offers substantial opportunity to radically reduce a company's costs. Common examples of indirect spend include transportation and logistics services, professional and consulting services, utilities, travel and entertainment, maintenance, repair, operating (MRO) supplies, advertising and promotion spending, and employee benefits. Note, however, that because of widespread industry differences, one company's indirect spend may be considered as direct spend for another.

Historically, expenditures for indirect materials and services have not received the same level of management scrutiny as have those for direct materials. Indirect expenditures are often controlled and spent from outside the supply management hierarchy even though the actual dollar amount of such expenditures can be a fairly significant percentage of total purchases. As such, many organizations have overlooked a substantial opportunity to effectively reduce cost in the services supply chain.[1]

A sizable area of indirect spend that will ultimately affect customers is the procurement of transportation and logistics services. Companies are increasingly using third-party logistics (3PL) companies to create a competitive marketplace advantage from which their customers will benefit. Without effective sourcing of transportation services, getting the right product to the right place in the right condition at the right time and the right cost becomes problematic. Selecting an appropriate transportation and third-party logistics provider can be as critical as any other supplier evaluation and selection decision, perhaps even more so.

In this chapter, we begin by describing the role that supply management plays in organizing and managing an organization's indirect spend. We discuss that role in managing transportation, then describe other areas of indirect spending (such as professional services) where supply management can also have a major impact on the cost structure and performance of organizations of all types today.

Transportation Management

The Council of Supply Chain Management Professionals defines **logistics** management as "that part of supply chain management that plans, implements, and controls the efficient, effective forward and reverse flow and storage of goods, services, and related information between the point of origin and the point of consumption to meet customers' requirements."[2] Transportation is a central part of logistics and distribution management, and logistics management, in turn, is a key element of supply chain management.[3]

Transportation service providers support the four major linkages throughout a typical supply chain shown in Exhibit 17.1: (1) inbound logistics, (2) intraorganizational movements, (3) outbound logistics, and (4) recovery and recycling (or reverse logistics). The first link includes all inbound shipments moving from a supplier to a buyer. This element is

Exhibit 17.1	Types of Logistics/Transportation Links

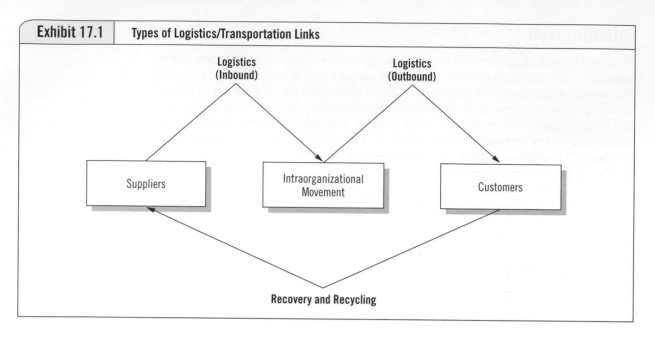

most often included in sourcing negotiations and can be a substantial part of determining the appropriate contractual terms discussed earlier in, Chapter 14.

Companies with multiple production and warehouse locations usually have a second major transportation link— intraorganizational movement. This element includes movement and handling of materials between production facilities within the same organization as well as movement into and out of intermediary storage facilities. A storage facility may be located in the same manufacturing complex as the production facility or at some other geographic location, which another company may actually control. Some companies directly control the movement of goods within this link through the use of company-owned or leased transportation vehicles, for example, its private trucking fleet. Others are increasingly bypassing this link by producing material only when they have a firm customer order, which allows direct shipment to the customer and thus reduces the need for multiple handlings through costly warehouse and distribution network facilities, saving both time and money.

The third link—outbound logistics—represents the link between a company and its customers. Historically, this was referred to as physical distribution, where the transportation department controlled the movement of outbound goods and suppliers arranged the movement of inbound freight to the buyer. Since deregulation of the U.S. transportation industry beginning in the late 1970s and continuing through the 1980s, supply management's involvement with the control of all three transportation links has increased greatly. The fourth link is one that companies are increasingly becoming concerned with when designing and operating sustainable supply chains—recovery, reselling, remanufacturing, and/or recycling of obsolete products, repairable items, used packaging, and reusable shipping containers. This reverse logistics flow requires companies to find innovative methods of recovering and recycling products to minimize potential negative impacts on the natural environment. This activity may also include the shipment of repairable items back to maintenance facilities for refurbishment and ultimate return to usable or salable condition. Companies find that they now have to consider two-way movement of products, packaging, and other ancillary materials when designing and operating their supply chain networks.

As organizations continue to focus more and more on their internal core competencies and outsource non-core activities, they have come to recognize that many of these necessary transportation and logistics services can, and should be, outsourced to expert companies specializing in transportation and logistics services. When these services are outsourced to qualified third parties, supply management must now assume the responsibility of managing these external relationships. Without effective and efficient sourcing and management of transportation and logistics services, world-class supply chain management can never be readily achieved. To describe these processes, we begin by briefly discussing a brief history of deregulation of the transportation industry in the United States, supply management's growing role in sourcing transportation and logistics services, and an effective decision-making framework for developing an effective transportation strategy. We will then focus specifically on how to manage third-party logistics providers.

Deregulation of Transportation and Supply Management's New Role

Transportation Deregulation

Federal legislation passed in the United States during the late 1970s and 1980s, designed to open up economic competition among transportation providers, also encouraged supply management's involvement in the procurement and management of transportation and logistics services. Congress passed the Air Cargo Deregulation Act in 1977, the Air Passenger Deregulation Act in 1978, and the Negotiated Rates Act in 1993. Additionally, the Motor Carrier Act of 1980 and the Staggers Rail Act of 1980 became law. Other major deregulation legislation in the United States includes the Transportation Industry Regulation Reform Act of 1994, the ICC Termination Act of 1995 (creating the Surface Transportation Board), and the Ocean Shipping Reform Act of 1998, which reduced the Federal Maritime Commission's authority.[4]

The primary objective of deregulation in the United States was to make its domestic transportation systems more efficient by dramatically increasing marketplace competition within the transportation and logistics industry and reducing burdensome economic regulation. From the buyer's perspective, these laws offered new opportunities to negotiate lower transportation rates and higher service levels with individual carriers and logistics service providers. From the carrier's perspective, these laws took away a comfortable blanket of government protection and significantly reduced profit margins on almost all freight contracts. Carriers had to learn how to compete day-to-day in a deregulated market, along with becoming more cost efficient in the process. Many long-standing carriers in all modes that were unable to do so simply went out of business or merged with other, more efficient, carriers to survive in this new, open, and highly competitive, market-based global economy.

Transportation carriers and logistics service providers now had to compete openly and aggressively against new entrants, existing carriers, and competition from other modes of transportation. They also had to contend with requests for substantial discounts from their published tariff rates by their customers, although filing published tariff rates with the federal government was no longer required. These legislative changes vastly reshaped the U.S. transportation landscape. Both supply and transportation managers discovered they now had the power to influence both transportation costs and corresponding service levels. Buyers became increasingly involved in the buying of transportation services, something that did not occur frequently when the U.S. transportation industry was highly regulated economically.

If Congress had not deregulated the transportation industry, it is likely that supply management would not have taken as great an interest in the identification, evaluation, selection, and control of transportation and logistics service providers. Although each new piece of federal legislation created more uncertainty for both shippers and carriers, deregulation legislation also created substantial economic opportunities for innovative buyers to add new value through the professional procurement of transportation and logistics services.

Effective procurement of transportation and logistics services is important for several reasons. First, transportation is a major cost center at most manufacturing and many service companies. On average, transportation costs easily comprise ten percent or more of a product's total cost. For many firms, logistics expenses are second only to material costs in terms of their impact on the cost of goods sold, and logistics expenditures represent one of the largest expenditures in international commerce.

Perhaps even more important than cost savings is the direct impact transportation has on operations. Transportation performance dramatically affects production and scheduling systems, inventory levels and carrying costs, warehousing, packaging and materials handling, and customer order management. Companies that do not effectively manage their transportation and logistics activities will experience increased waste, higher costs, and reduced competitiveness. Although often taken for granted, transportation and logistics activities can encounter serious consequences if not managed properly. However, when managed properly, world-class transportation systems can satisfy end-customer needs more quickly and at a lower cost.

A New Role for Supply Management

As more supply management professionals take an active role in transportation and logistics procurement, what exactly duties do they now assume? Supply management can effectively support the procurement of inbound, outbound, and ancillary transportation services just as it supports the purchase of other goods, materials, and services. As supply managers take a more active role in overall transportation decision making, they often become intimately involved with identifying, evaluating, and selecting inbound transportation carriers and logistics service providers, although greater involvement with outbound transportation providers is becoming more common in best-in-class firms.

Supply management can also negotiate favorable long-term freight contracts and evaluate carrier performance similarly to evaluating suppliers of purchased goods (see Chapters 7 and 9 for additional information). The traditional transportation department, if one still exists, now usually involves itself with day-to-day management of the overall transportation system or the development of transportation strategies that need not involve supply management. These non-procurement-related activities may include day-to-day scheduling of pickups and deliveries, processing damage and loss claims, tracing and expediting shipments, coordinating inbound, interplant, and outbound movements, auditing freight bills, and determining plant and warehouse locations.

Both the supply management and transportation departments need to combine their individual expertise when developing transportation strategies. Transportation-related decisions should not be made in a vacuum apart from the rest of the organization. Typical transportation and logistics management activities and processes that are potential candidates for outsourcing include the following:[5]

- Contract management
- Load and routing optimization
- Mode selection

- Shipment execution
- Carrier payment
- Yard and dock management
- Tracking and tracing services
- Supplier and carrier management
- Reverse logistics
- Loss and damage claims management
- Service level reporting
- Carrier and 3PL performance management

A Decision-Making Framework for Developing a Transportation Strategy

The development of an effective transportation strategy typically involves a series of related tactical and strategic decisions. Exhibit 17.2 outlines a general framework of the normal decisions and issues that a supply manager faces when helping to formulate the organization's transportation and logistics strategy. How a firm's transportation network is designed and organized may vary greatly depending on the commodity or material, as well as locations served. For example, transporting bulk raw material usually requires rail or barge movement, whereas small, costly, time-sensitive components may use faster but more expensive modes such as airfreight and package delivery services. No single approach or strategy covers the overall transportation needs of a company.

Determine When and Where to Control Transportation

The initial decision regarding transportation service requirements involves determining how, when, and where to control shipments. A significant amount of inbound domestic materials, for example, are still shipped FOB destination. This means the supplier retains title to the goods and controls the shipment until it is physically received and off-loaded at the consignee's dock. Unless otherwise negotiated, this also means that the supplier is responsible for scheduling the movement of the goods, paying the carrier's freight bill, and filing any loss and damage claims against the carrier. Title of the goods does not transfer to the buyer or consignee until the goods are unloaded at the ultimate destination. In this case, freight costs are included in the invoiced unit price to the buying company. More effective control of inbound shipment costs usually requires purchasing goods under a shipping designation of FOB origin. Here, the buyer, or consignee, is now responsible for choosing the carrier, arranging for the physical movement of the goods, paying the freight bill, and filing loss and damage claims. The title for the goods passes when the goods are tendered to the carrier at the loading site. A savvy buyer will want to control these costs internally instead of simply allowing the shipper to pass them along in the form of a delivered price. FOB origin is more complicated than buying goods with a FOB delivered price, but the buyer can more effectively monitor its freight costs and delivery performance and take corrective action as required. Note that shipping terms for international shipments are far more complicated and covered under INCOTERMS, which are discussed more fully in Chapter 10.

Whenever a supplier includes transportation charges as part of the unit cost of a good (i.e., FOB destination), the buyer often loses the ability to track or control its inbound transportation expenses. This also artificially increases the value of the buyer's inventory because the inbound transportation costs are hidden inside the purchase price, which may have tax and other related financial implications. Even when a supplier assumes responsibility for

| Exhibit 17.2 | Transportation Strategy Development Decision-Making Process |

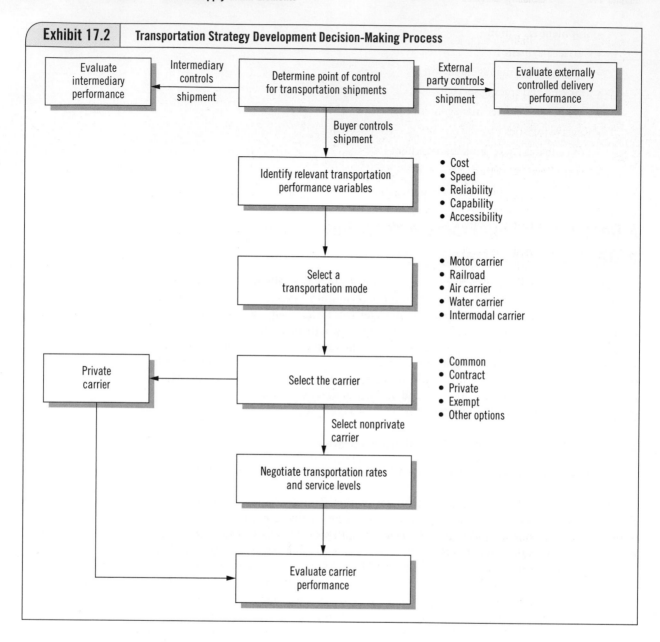

controlling its transportation costs, buyers may require the supplier to identify and itemize transportation-related costs separately from material costs on the invoice.

Exhibit 17.3 compares these two primary domestic FOB shipping designations as well as listing the Uniform Commercial Code (UCC) sections that apply to domestic transportation movements.

The choice of insourcing or outsourcing transportation services is similar to the typical make-or-buy decision in manufacturing. A buyer who chooses to have an external party, such as a supplier or third-party logistics provider, arrange and control its shipments has essentially abdicated its ability to control further decisions regarding the movement of the goods. For some shipments, such as low-volume, infrequent shipments, a buyer may determine it

Exhibit 17.3	**Defining Domestic Transportation Shipping Terms**

CARRIER

SHIPPER'S FACILITY FOB ORIGIN	**BUYER'S FACILITY FOB DESTINATION**

WHAT DOES FOB ORIGIN MEAN?
• Buyer controls or directs shipment
• Buyer assumes title to goods and risk of loss at seller's shipping point, unless agreed to otherwise (UCC Section 2–401)
• Seller has certain responsibilities (UCC Section 2–504):
  • To put the goods in the possession of the carrier
  • To make a proper contract for the transportation of the goods, taking into consideration the nature of the goods and other circumstances
  • To obtain and promptly deliver to the buyer any documents necessary for the buyer to take possession of the goods
  • To promptly notify the buyer of the shipment
	WHAT DOES FOB DESTINATION MEAN?
	• Seller is required at own risk and expense to transport goods to that place and there tender deliver (UCC Section 2–319)
	• Seller assumes title to goods and risk of loss until satisfactory delivery to buyer's facility, unless agreed to otherwise (UCC Section 2–401)

is not worth the time and energy necessary to arrange and manage its own transportation arrangements. When this is the case, an option is to provide suppliers with a list of preapproved or otherwise acceptable carriers, freight consolidators, or 3PLs. The buyer may even have a contract in place with a specific carrier for discounted freight rates based on combined volume. A buyer who relinquishes control of inbound transportation to a supplier or 3PL should still periodically evaluate the delivery performance of externally arranged shipments.

Another option here involves the use of a third-party transportation broker or intermediary, such as a freight forwarder or consolidator. Although this also means giving up direct control of shipments, a buyer may realize additional benefits. The preferred broker or intermediary must have the buyer's best interests in mind, as the buyer is the intermediary's immediate customer. In effect, the broker or intermediary acts as the buyer's agent when arranging transportation. The intermediary can also consolidate a buyer's shipments with those from other customers to achieve a lower total transportation cost. Intermediaries can also perform other value-added services, such as expediting customs, negotiating freight rates directly with carriers, providing temporary storage, mixing, labeling, kitting, or performing light assembly and manufacturing services. This option is popular for small- to mid-sized organizations lacking the internal resources or experience to closely manage their own transportation systems. It is also an appropriate option for small or infrequent shipments.

Identify Key Transportation Performance Variables

Different carrier or 3PL performance variables must be carefully considered and evaluated when developing effective transportation strategy. Data on the following set of performance variables should be collected and analyzed when comparing competing transportation modes as well as specific carriers within the same mode. Typical criteria used to measure and evaluate transportation performance are shown in Exhibit 17.4. The buyer should develop a list of specific key performance indicators (or KPIs) that measure and track relevant actual carrier or 3PL performance. Some typical transportation and logistics KPIs include freight rates (by lane, carrier, or commodity), number of pickups and deliveries (by lane, point of origin, or destination), percent on-time delivery, percent of claims-free shipments, percent of tendered loads accepted by carrier, and average time to settle loss and damage claims.

Exhibit 17.4	Criteria Used to Measure Transportation Performance
PERFORMANCE MEASURE	**DESCRIPTION**
Total Cost	In addition to the fee charges, total cost includes the cost of extra inventory, warehousing, buffer stock, and, in the case of international shipments, broker fees, customs, etc. Other cost factors such as extra managerial time may also have to be factored in.
Speed	Measured as time from when the shipment is released at the supplier's facility to the time of receipt at the buyer's receiving dock.
Reliability	Sometimes described as fill rate. Refers to the ability to deliver on time. Can be measured in different ways, but is typically a window of time when the delivery must be made. The measure is thus the percentage of deliveries made within the specified window.
Capability	Refers to the ability of the carrier to move the material, including special materials, hazardous materials, etc.
Accessibility	Refers to whether the carrier is capable of picking up the shipment and delivering it door to door.

Total Cost

Total cost plays a major role in the transportation decision-making framework. If costs were unimportant, more shipments would arrive via air carrier instead of by truck, barge, or rail. Cost, however, is only one of several key variables. Selecting a mode or carrier based solely on the lowest freight cost ignores the total cost and customer service implications of the decision, not to mention potential loss and damage of transported goods. The lowest-cost mode, carrier, or 3PL may not provide reliable delivery or other value-added services that separate marginal from exceptional logistics service providers. The cost variable, although important, should not be the sole variable used to select, measure, or evaluate transportation and service providers. Furthermore, any cost evaluation must always be in a total cost context, not merely using the charges from the freight bill. An apparently low-cost carrier may actually end up costing far more than a seemingly higher-cost carrier when the total associated costs are identified and calculated. Note, however, that the typical cost accounting system, particularly at small- to medium-sized companies, may not fully identify where all of the costs are derived. Costs may also change over time, as market conditions change. For example, during the recession of 2008, changes in carrier shipping capacity, container availability, and fuel costs dramatically altered the way that carriers operated—forcing supply managers to adapt to adverse conditions.

Speed

This variable refers to the in-transit time for a mode or carrier. For some items, such as bulk raw materials, transport speed may not be an important factor. For producers operating in a time-sensitive or just-in-time environment, speed may be the critical factor for either inbound shipments from suppliers or outbound shipments to customers. Companies that ship products directly to customers after receiving an order are more likely to be focused on speed as a key performance variable.

Critical items that must arrive as soon as possible from a supplier or reach a customer quickly will likely require the choice of a different mode of transportation from other, more commodity-like items. For example, high-value or time-sensitive items, such as pharmaceuticals, cut flowers, and semiconductor chips, are more likely to be shipped via higher-speed priority carriers. Their crucial value to the buyer is such that delaying them in transit is not economically wise. Certain items will always arrive by the same type of transportation mode simply because of their physical nature, such as rail shipments of coal, iron ore, fertilizers, cement, or ethanol. When this is the case, a lack of transportation flexibility regarding the speed variable is something that must be managed by a buyer.

Reliability

A critical performance variable for any mode or carrier is service reliability, which refers to the accuracy and on-time consistency of the transportation service provided, arriving neither late nor early. It also relates to a carrier's ability to deliver a shipment in a pristine or undamaged condition.

For example, if a carrier says a shipment will arrive at 9:00 a.m. on Monday morning, the consignee should expect that the shipment will actually arrive at the promised date and time, within a small time window. Note that reliability differs from speed—it is the measure of actual arrivals against planned arrivals. A reliable carrier requiring a longer in-transit time is oftentimes preferable to an unreliable carrier with a faster average in-transit time that is more variable, particularly from an operational planning perspective. The buyer requires less inventory and safety stock to cover lower delivery variability from the more reliable carrier.

Capability

This variable refers to a mode or carrier's ability to tender the proper equipment and provide the appropriate services for a given product movement. This variable has several dimensions. First, does the mode or carrier have the physical capability to transport an item? For example, can the carrier legally and safely transport a hazardous material, such as nuclear waste or corrosive products, or handle and transport large quantities of bulk products, such as agricultural combines or wind turbine blades and towers? Second, does the carrier have the necessary equipment in the right location at the right time to perform the requested movement? Having the right equipment but in the wrong place at the time it is needed does not promote capability. Lastly, does the carrier have the equipment and resources to transport multiple, frequent shipments for a specific traffic lane? Carriers will typically consider the availability of backhauls when quoting one-way freight rates on a particular traffic lane—no available backhaul, the higher the freight rates for the headhaul, or initial freight movement, because the carrier will have substantial empty mileage until it can find another load. Capability is important because it affects a mode or carrier's ability to provide consistent transportation service or provide a requested service at a reasonable price.

Accessibility

Transportation accessibility refers to a mode's or carrier's ability to provide service over a specific geographic area. A totally accessible mode or carrier is capable of picking up a shipment from anywhere and delivering it directly to its final destination. Geographic constraints, however, restrict some modes. Inland water carriers, for example, are usually not accessible for most shippers, as lakes, rivers, and canals cannot be readily accessed unless the shipper and/or consignee are located nearby. Use of this mode often requires another mode, such as motor carrier or pipeline, for pickup and delivery to and from the waterway. Note that a carrier that cannot offer total accessibility for its customers is not necessarily all bad. However, each time a shipment changes hands, additional handling occurs, and a longer lead time must be accounted for. Also, the risk of freight loss and damage increases.

A carrier may not have the appropriate authority or travel the physical routes necessary to transport goods between two points or to operate in a specific geographic region. Carriers lacking legal authority to move goods directly between two points are considered inaccessible. Motor carriers sometimes market their services on the basis of their authority to operate in the 48 contiguous states. Instead of using different carriers for different shipments around the country, one full-service carrier may be capable of meeting an organization's total transportation requirements, that is, a "one-stop shop."

Select a Transportation Mode

There must be a close match between those key transportation performance variables identified in the previous section and the ability of the different modes or carriers to satisfy these variables. For some items, this is not a difficult decision to make. For example, overseas shipments are usually transported in shipping containers via ocean vessel or, in a limited number of products, by air carrier. Bulk dry or liquid commodities, such as coal or chemicals, usually ship via rail. The most common domestic modal decisions involve comparisons and cost and service tradeoffs between rail and motor carrier, rail and inland water, or motor and air carrier. The most common modal decision for international shipments is between oceangoing vessels and aircraft.

There are five principal modes of transportation available to buyers of transportation services: (1) motor carrier, (2) rail, (3) air, (4) water, and (5) pipeline. A summary of the major advantages and disadvantages of each is shown in Exhibit 17.5.

Exhibit 17.5	Advantages and Disadvantages of Transportation Modes	
TRANSPORTATION MODE	**ADVANTAGES**	**DISADVANTAGES**
Motor Carrier	• High flexibility • Good speed • Good reliability • Good for JIT delivery • Can negotiate rates	• High cost • Limited to domestic or regional transportation • Cannot be used for large volumes
Rail Carrier	• Lower cost • Can handle wide range of items • Piggyback service can increase flexibility • Direct between major cities • Greater intermodal service • Safe for hazardous materials	• Limited access to rail line or spur • Longer in-transit lead times • Less flexible—may not have rails to all locations
Air Carrier	• Quick and reliable • Good for light/small, high-value shipments (e.g., electronics) • Good for expediting/emergency situations	• Very high cost • Location of large airports limits shipping points • Cannot be used for large, bulky, or hazardous shipments
Water Carrier	• Good for bulk commodities (inland) and heavy, large items (international) • Can handle most types of freight • Low cost	• Limited flexibility • Seasonal availability • Very long lead times • Poor reliability (may encounter delays at ports, etc.)
Pipeline	• Good for high-volume liquids and gases • Low cost once installed	• High up-front installation costs • Limited to only certain items

Motor Carriers

The greatest competition between domestic transportation modes involves rail and motor carriers. The availability of modern trucking equipment, the advent of the U.S. interstate highway system after World War II, and the inherent door-to-door flexibility of motor carriage has resulted in the rapid growth of motor transportation, much at the expense of rail carriers. However, greater labor and fuel costs, increased road congestion, and concern about the adverse environmental impact of motor carriers have led to a recent resurgence in the use of rail carriers. Statistics provided by the Association of American Railroads indicate that a typical freight train can take the equivalent of 280 or more trucks off the roads.[6]

It should come as no surprise that over-the-road motor carriers are a popular transportation option. They uniquely provide direct door-to-door service, making it the most highly flexible mode of transportation. In addition, motor carriers are ideal for carrying smaller-volume, or less-than-truckload (LTL), shipments, involving multiple shippers and multiple consignees. A well-established motor carrier network exists for the movement of LTL shipments throughout the United States, using a hub-and-spoke arrangement, whereas it is far more difficult for a rail carrier to accommodate less-than-carload (LCL) shipments. Motor carriers also have an inherent advantage of speed and reliability over the other modes, particularly for full truckload (TL) shipments.

The most significant disadvantage of a motor carrier is its relatively higher variable cost. On average, motor carrier transportation is more expensive than rail on a volume basis and far more expensive than inland water. Also, motor carriers have limited ability to transport large quantities of bulk commodities as compared to rail, inland water, and pipeline carriers. There are minimal economies of scale in motor carriers; you cannot simply add additional cargo-carrying capacity because of weight, width, length, and infrastructure constraints.

Motor carriers are characterized by high variable costs (totaling approximately 70–90 percent of total cost) because of labor, fuel, maintenance, tolls, operating fees, and other costs resulting from compliance with rules and regulations.[7] Limits to the amount of weight a motor carrier can transport at one time also make variable costs higher. These limits are often reduced as a result of seasonal weather conditions and the condition of the road infrastructure. Furthermore, each trailer, or set of tandem trailers, requires a separate power unit (tractor) and operator. A motor carrier does not have the inherent volume flexibility of a rail carrier, which can add more railcars to increase its hauling capacity.

Rail Carriers

A major advantage of a rail carrier is the wide range of items it is capable of hauling. Although most rail freight today consists of bulk commodities, such as coal, ethanol, and agricultural products, a railcar can handle virtually any type of shipment, including manufactured goods. Another advantage of rail, and perhaps its primary one, is its relatively low cost. The ability to move huge amounts of freight over long distances at a per-pound cost that is lower than other transportation modes is the main reason that rail still commands a large share of all intercity ton-mile shipments. It not unusual for a shipper to tender an entire shipment of the same commodity moving as a unit train, such as coal, iron ore, or even automobiles.

The costs associated with owning and operating their own equipment, switchyards, terminals, and rights-of-way mean that rail carriers have comparatively high fixed costs as compared to motor carriers. However, their low variable cost structure allows rail carriers to move freight at a relatively low rate per mile. As described earlier, additional railcars can be added to a freight train with only a minimal increase in its total variable cost, absent any limitations on train length.

Firms that rely on rail shipments must have site access to a rail line or spur unless they are willing to use motor carriers to perform pickup and delivery functions to and from the railhead. This physical constraint limits the use of rail in many instances and highlights perhaps the major disadvantage of rail carriers—limited accessibility. Rail carriers have attempted to overcome this inherent limitation through intermodal shipments involving shipping truck trailers (TOFC) or containers (COFC) directly on flat cars, which is also referred to as piggyback service, a form of intermodalism.

Another disadvantage of rail carriers, and one that motor carriers have successfully exploited, is long and variable in-transit and handling times. A two-day shipment by truck can often take a week or more by rail because of the extra handling involved. Few trains move as a single unit over long distances. Rail carriers ship loaded cars between cities by attaching them to an outbound train moving in the general direction of the consignee's facility. As such, a cross-country journey may require several movements of a customer's railcar at various switching yards. Each switch increases total shipping and handling time and costs. At the destination city, a local locomotive moving only a few cars at a time makes the final delivery to the consignee and then returns at some time in the future to pick up the empty railcars.

In recent years, the railroad industry has engaged in significant consolidation and merger activities, a process that has eliminated thousands of miles of duplicate trackage from the rail infrastructure system. In addition, less competitive rail companies have merged together to share infrastructure and improve their operations and financial condition. There has also been an increase in the number of smaller railroads that seek to serve only limited regions and lanes.

Rail carriers will always be the mode of choice for certain commodities. Rail movement is particularly economical for the shipment of agricultural products, output from extractive industries (e.g., coal or chemicals), or products from heavy manufacturing industries, such as steel, agricultural equipment, and automobiles.

Air Carriers

Air carriers haul the least amount of commercial freight because of the relatively high cost of air travel and the limited amounts, sizes, and types of freight that an aircraft can carry. Historically, a major reason for using airfreight has been to satisfy short lead time and emergency requirements. For example, a mining machine breakdown overseas may require a replacement part to be delivered as soon as possible to get the equipment back into productive use. The buyer is far less concerned about the high cost of airfreight when an expensive mining machine is sitting idle because of a broken or defective part. In this case, an air carrier may be the only option capable of meeting the performance variable of speed. Plus, the shape of the aircraft's fuselage dramatically limits the size and weight of the containers used.

Many firms are evaluating air transportation in relation to their just-in-time inventory and manufacturing systems. Shipping a high-priced component via air may actually be a cost-effective option, particularly if the material does not require much space, because of high inventory carrying costs. Some companies actually ship live lobsters or fresh-cut flowers via air to maintain their freshness. A significant amount of competition for most traffic lanes exists among air carriers today, which supports lower rates and increased service levels. Airlines have largely responded by removing excess capacity from the network in an attempt to stabilize prices and profitability, although passenger capacity has increased slightly in 2010 as some air carriers have returned to modest profitability.

Higher freight cost per pound is the primary disadvantage to the increased use of air transportation. Air has a high variable-cost-to-fixed-cost ratio because of the high costs of operating a flight, such as fuel and labor. Because of the need to cover substantial variable costs, airfreight rates are much higher than those of other modes. Air carriers also suffer from limited capacity and flexibility. The dimensions of the plane itself limit the size, shape, and weight of a shipment. In addition, if the airline has to make a decision on whether to carry freight or take on another fare-paying passenger, the freight will usually be off-loaded for a later flight. Furthermore, the location of larger airports limits the shipping points available to an air carrier, unless a local pickup-and-delivery network with motor carriers is utilized. Even then, most airports are located in high traffic congestion areas, increasing total transit time and negating its time advantage. Once an air shipment arrives, a motor carrier almost always makes the final delivery to the consignee.

Water Carrier

This transportation mode includes both inland water (river, canal, and lake) and ocean-going vessels. Inland water carriers typically transport low-value, large-quantity items, such as bulk commodities and raw materials (e.g., ores, chemicals, sand, rocks, cement, and agricultural products). For example, it is common to see freighters moving raw materials, such as coke and iron ore required for steel production, from Minnesota to steel mills in northwestern Indiana. This material moves via the Great Lakes inland waterway system. However, this mode is closed down during the winter, requiring large inventories to cover the season or the use of more expensive alternative modes.

Inland water carriers rarely transport finished or semifinished products because of the lengthy in-transit time. The main advantage of water transportation is the large volume an inland barge or transoceanic ship can move at one time, as well as the relatively low cost per pound of freight. The primary disadvantages include limited flexibility of shipping and receiving points, seasonal shipment in some inland areas of the country, slow speed, and the potential for natural disasters such as oil spills, which can have devastating effects on the natural environment.

Growth in international trade has increased the amount of freight moving on ocean-going vessels. If a buyer purchases from an international supplier, the modal decision is usually straightforward. Most global shipments move across the ocean on deepwater containerships or tankers, and to a lesser extent via air carrier. Ocean carriers are capable of handling virtually any type of freight or raw material. Although mode selection is usually not an issue for international ocean shipments, as in all strategic supplier selection decisions, carrier selection within the mode is still paramount. The possibility of encountering customs delays because of increased security inspection and documentation requirements at ocean ports is another looming disadvantage of ocean carriers (see Sourcing Snapshot: Maritime Supply Chain Security).

Sourcing Snapshot

Maritime Supply Chain Security

Several government and industry initiatives have been introduced to improve the security of the supply chain segment that deals with shipping containers that travel across the waterways of the world. Many of the world's 2,700 container ships travel through the ports of America each day, unloading more than 17,000 shipping containers. These containers carry more than 80 percent of all

U.S. imports. These shipping containers and ports must be protected to ensure the nation's security. A security attack on a U.S. port would cost the economy several orders of magnitude (in billions of dollars) more than the cost to prevent such an attack. Because of the sheer size and scope of maritime shipping, any attack on the maritime supply chain would effectively suspend international trade, while stopping or slowing shipping interests around the world.

One of the most significant security programs is the Container Security Initiative (CSI). The CSI is a U.S. Customs and Border Protection initiative that encourages foreign governments to inspect and screen container shipments before leaving port to detect possible security problems. This program sets up the exchange of customs officers between countries so that outbound shipments will be inspected by that country's customs officers. The CSI focuses on 20 ports around the world where most imported products originate. The aim is to reduce the risk of security problems on vessels and prevent an explosion or other incident in a port before the vessel can be unloaded. Once a vessel departs the originating port, security initiatives must be in place to prevent tampering with containers while in transit. In addition, an Automated Targeting System (ATS) is being put in place, whereby U.S. Customs requires shippers to send a detailed description of cargo being loaded on a vessel destined for the United States at least 24 hours in advance of loading. Vessels will not be allowed into U.S. ports without this advance notice. The U.S. Customs and Border Protection uses the ATS as an advanced screening tool to determine which potentially suspicious shipments need to be inspected on arrival.

Finally, to increase security and improve the supply chain, the U.S. government is also encouraging companies to streamline their documentation and materials handling processes through the Customs-Trade Partnership Against Terrorism (C-TPAT) program. The C-TPAT is a program for manufacturers, suppliers, importers, and carriers to analyze their own supply chain security processes. It encourages them to improve supply chain security plans, communicate security plans with their trading partners and suppliers, and monitor and improve security measures on a routine basis. Once these companies are C-TPAT-certified by the U.S. government, their products will be able to proceed through ports and border crossings more quickly. They will also develop a closer working relationship with U.S. Customs and Border Protection and other C-TPAT-certified companies. The U.S. C-TPAT program enables companies to avoid increased transportation costs associated with border delays; reduce inventory needs by having a secure, reliable supply chain; and improve supply chain relationships and communication between suppliers and customers. More than 500 companies have joined the C-TPAT program to improve their supply chain security processes.

Sources: Edmonson, R.G. (2003, August 25), "Beyond Calculation," *Journal of Commerce,* 18–22. Lee, H. L, and Wolfe, M. (2003, January/February), "Supply Chain Security without Tears," *Supply Chain Management Review,* 23–35. McGuire, M., Cousineau, H., and Stephanou, M. (2002, November), "The New Era of International Supply Chain Security," *World Trade,* and *Securing the Global Supply Chain* (2004), Washington, D.C.: U.S. Customs and Border Protection.

Pipeline

The use of a pipeline is usually not part of the decision tradeoff between transportation modes. Pipelines primarily transport crude oil, refined petroleum products, natural gas, or coal in a slurry condition. Even if a buyer purchases these products, it is not likely the individual supply manager will make the decision to use a pipeline for transportation of these commodities. Because of the huge quantities involved, deciding on the use of pipeline is rarely something a buyer needs to consider. Individual buyers may buy railcar or truckload quantities of these products from a terminal but not directly from a pipeline. This discussion mentions pipeline only because it is a legitimate mode of transportation.

The total cost structure of pipelines is similar to rail carriers as the equipment, rights-of-way, and physical pipeline have a high fixed cost and a low variable operating cost.

Labor and direct operating costs are relatively low for this mode. Although pipeline movement is low cost and reliable, it is extremely slow and can only be used in one direction, for example, no backhauls are available.

Intermodal Transportation

As discussed earlier, a single mode of transportation may prove inadequate for a specific shipment. For example, a typical surface shipment of material to the United States from China may require a variety of modes and carriers to complete the movement. Once the material is produced in China, it will need to be loaded into a container, which is then transported by either motor carrier or railroad to the port of departure. From there, it will be loaded onto a deepwater containership. Once the container ship docks at the U.S. port of arrival, it will be off-loaded onto another motor carrier's or railroad's equipment to be moved to its final destination. Note that each element in this complex move may be performed by a different carrier.

If the shipper or consignee were to deal individually with each mode and carrier, the administrative cost and effort would be prohibitive and inefficient. To resolve this complexity and provide better service, many global carriers now offer one-stop shopping, where the shipper or consignee contracts with one carrier, which then coordinates and manages the entire intermodal shipment, regardless of carrier or mode, and also provides a single point of contact and a unified freight bill. The underlying idea of intermodal transportation is to utilize the inherent advantages of each mode along with minimizing its relative disadvantages, resulting in a seamless movement to the customer.

Exhibit 17.6 presents the relative ranking of the different transportation modes against our five performance criteria. Examining the relative rankings from the chart, it is easy to see why the popularity of motor carrier has increased with domestic transportation service

Exhibit 17.6	Relative Ranking of Domestic Transportation Modes				
	Lowest per-Unit Cost	Speed	Reliability	Capability	Accessibility
Air	5	1	4	3	3
Rail	3	3	3	1	2
Pipeline	1	4	1	5	5
Motor	4	2	2	2	1
Inland Water	2	5	5	4	4

1 = Highest rated compared to other modes
5 = Lowest rated compared to other modes

buyers. In total, motor carriers often hold a distinct advantage over other modes when taking a systems approach to these performance variables.

Select the Carrier

Once the buyer determines which transportation mode is best suited to move a given product or commodity, the next step involves evaluating and selecting the carrier that will provide the physical movement. A supply manager has several options available besides simply contacting a for-hire company and arranging shipment. Shippers can select a common (or public) carrier, negotiate for services with a contract or exempt carrier, arrange shipments on company-owned vehicles (private carrier), or use a third-party logistics provider to select and manage the carrier. The most common decision is whether to use a common, contract, or exempt carrier (see Exhibit 17.7).

Common Carriers

By law, a common carrier must serve the general public without discrimination based on published rates for specific goods.[8] Part of a common carrier's operating authority comes from its obligation to serve transportation users in a fair and nondiscriminatory manner. Besides its duty not to discriminate, a common carrier must offer reasonable rates, although rates are not published in the same manner as they were during the days of economic regulation. In addition, it is not always apparent what "reasonable" rates are. A buyer deciding to use a common carrier, particularly a motor carrier, often has a wide choice of carriers within a geographic region. Prime examples of common carriers in the United States include YRC Worldwide, J.B. Hunt, and Schneider National (recognized for its bright orange trucks). Note that some common carriers may also serve as contract carriers or 3PLs.

Contract Carriers

Shippers that rely heavily on precise and frequent transportation might consider the use of a contract carrier. A contract carrier does not hold itself out to serve the general public, as does a common carrier. The contract carrier serves a shipper (i.e., a buyer) under specific, negotiated contract terms. A contract carrier, sometimes referred to as a dedicated carrier, serves the transportation requirements of the party with which it has a legal agreement and provides only those services that have been negotiated with the shipper at a mutually agreed upon price.

Contract carriers can offer many benefits to the transportation buyer. Besides negotiating a favorable freight rate based on movement frequency, volume, and/or traffic lane, a buyer can usually receive a higher level of service than might otherwise be expected because the carrier and shipper have a continuous contractual relationship.

Private Carriers

A private carrier is a manufacturer or distributor that controls and manages its own transportation equipment, whether owned or leased. Typically, a private carrier moves goods between suppliers, in-house facilities, or customers. Private carrier backhauls may include inbound finished goods, packaging, components, and raw materials to provide better utilization of transportation assets by providing a backhaul opportunity. Besides offering greater control of its inbound and outbound freight, a private carrier can increase the utilization of company-owned assets. Some companies operate their own private fleets to maintain delivery reliability or to more effectively understand and manage those costs that outside carriers incur, thereby making them a better informed buyer of transportation services. Private carriers may also be

Exhibit 17.7 | Overview of Interstate Motor Carrier Industry

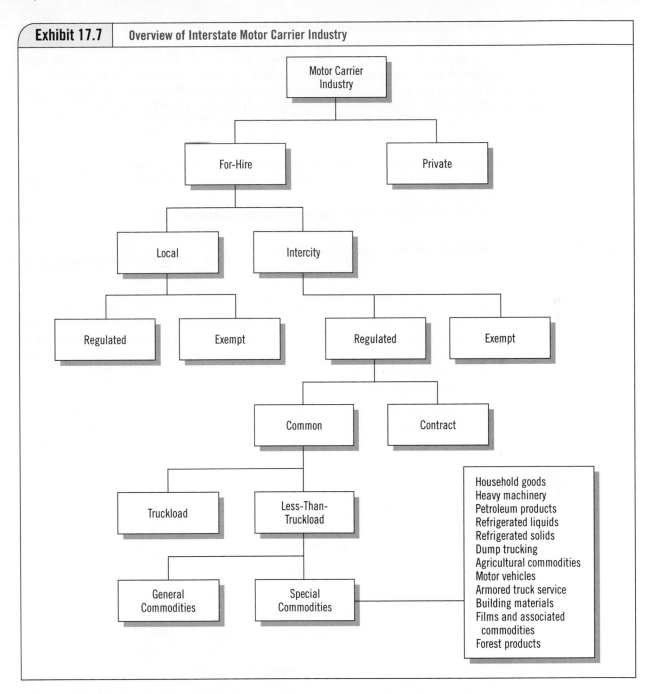

utilized to make daily "milk runs," picking up smaller amounts of materials from a series of nearby suppliers to be used in a just-in-time or lean manufacturing environment.

Perhaps the greatest drawback to using a private fleet for inbound shipments is a lack of scale and/or dedication to this task. For example, it might be difficult to arrange shipments from a supplier's facility on a regular basis using company-controlled vehicles. Practical experience with a number of firms indicates the use of private carriers for inbound shipments is often the exception rather than the rule, although this is beginning to change as more sophisticated transportation management systems (TMS) are installed. When firms use a private carrier for receiving purchased items, it is usually the result of a geographically convenient arrangement between a purchaser and supplier such as the milk runs described earlier. A company operating a private fleet must ensure that it balances the utilization of its equipment for both inbound and outbound shipments. Otherwise, a high level of empty miles reduces the cost-effectiveness of operating a private fleet.

Exempt Carriers

Exempt carriers are free of any economic regulation by the Surface Transportation Board (STB). They gain this status because of the type of commodities they haul and the nature of their operation. These carriers usually transport seasonal agricultural products, newspapers, livestock, or fish and a low probability of finding backhauls. Exempt carriers are primarily local water carriers of bulk items. The presence of exempt carriers ensures a supply of available transportation in markets where only one-way traffic exists (e.g., from an agricultural area during the harvest season). Goods move one way but not the other.

Negotiate Transportation Rates and Service Levels

A buyer with substantial transportation needs across its supply chain will likely negotiate directly with a single carrier or a small number of preferred carriers for dedicated or contracted services. This does not mean that buyers must negotiate only with contract carriers. Negotiation can also occur with a common carrier, particularly regarding transportation rates and service requirements.

A major outcome from transportation economic deregulation has been the shift of pricing information garnered from published tariffs and rate bureaus to the negotiating table. A buyer can negotiate specific services and required service levels, whereas the carrier can indicate what freight volumes are necessary to support a particular service level or rate. This negotiation process can address a number of topics:[9]

- The carrier's service performance guarantees with penalties and rewards based on actual performance
- The shipper's commitment to ship a minimum amount of volume during the life of the contract
- How the parties handle freight loss and damage claims
- The type and quantity of equipment utilized by the carrier
- Frequency and timing of shipments
- Establishment of information-sharing systems
- Freight rates and discounts
- Creative and innovative joint cost reduction activities

A shipper does not necessarily negotiate a contract with every carrier it uses, particularly if it is considered a small or infrequent shipper. A smart buyer, however, can take advantage of the various opportunities offered in today's transportation environment by consolidating its transportation volumes with fewer carriers to achieve greater shipping economies of scale.

Current Transportation Issues

Several current transportation issues exist that can negatively affect a supply manager's supply chain efficiency and effectiveness. Perhaps the most pressing current transportation issue has to do with supply chain security. Dealing with the threat and potential aftermath of terrorism following 9/11 continues to be a contentious issue with growing levels of governmental oversight and regulation around the world. Kathleen Sweet, author of *Transportation and Cargo Security: Threats and Solutions*, describes the potential impact of terrorism in this way, "Keeping passengers and cargo secure is arguably the overall responsibility of governments; however, safely transporting them involves many participants, including manufacturers, shippers, freight forwarders, truckers, facility operators, cruise lines, and air carriers."[10] In response to the substantial threat posed by terrorist activities, many governments have enacted substantial cargo and passenger screening requirements, including the U.S. government's Certified Cargo Screening Program (CCSP) and the SAFE Port Act of 2006, among others.

For air cargo transported aboard passenger aircraft, the CCSP requires 100 percent screening of all cargo originating in the United States at the individual piece level no later than August 2010. However, this federal mandate has not yet been met. The Transportation Security Administration (TSA) has been tasked with ensuring the following standards for Certified Cargo Screening Facilities (CCSFs). These standards dictate the activities to which certified screening locations must adhere:[11]

- Physical access controls—procedures and mechanisms must be in place to prevent unauthorized entry to facilities where certified cargo is screened, prepared, and stored; maintain control of employees, contractors and visitors; and protect company assets.

- Personnel security—processes must be in place to screen prospective employees and contractors to TSA standards, and to periodically check current employees with unfettered access to passenger air cargo.

- Procedural security—security measures must be in place to ensure the integrity and security of processes relevant to the transportation, handling, and storage of cargo throughout the supply chain.

- Physical security—cargo handling and storage facilities must have physical barriers and deterrents that guard against unauthorized access.

- Information technology security—processes must be in place that provide for password protection of user accounts and identify improper access or the altering of data on automated systems.

- Facility validation—allow initial and recurring validations by TSA or a TSA approved organization.

In addition, participants in the certified air cargo supply chain must maintain certain chain of custody standards as follows:

- Documentation—information must be documented and must travel with the shipment.

- Application—tamper evident measures must be applied to cargo or conveyance method prior to departure.

- Authentication—documentation must be authenticated on receipt at each regulated party and processing point in the chain of custody.

The Security and Accountability for Every Port Act of 2006 enabled the U.S. Bureau of Customs and Border Protection (CBP) to establish the so-called "10 + 2" rule, more formally known as the Importer Security Filing (the "10") and Additional Carrier Requirements (the "2") rule that affects only ocean container freight.[12] The "10" refers to ten data elements that importers must transmit electronically to the CBP at least 24 hours before loading any container onto a ship destined for the United States, whereas the "2" refers to two data files that the ocean vessel must submit to the CBP, including a vessel stowage plan indicating where a given container is stowed aboard the ship and container status messages that provide additional details on the movement and status changes on the container itself.

The cumulative effect of these various security-related legislation and administrative rules on supply managers is that documentation and handling requirements have been increased dramatically, adding to the already complex documentation and security activities required in international commerce. If the required documentation is not provided in a timely fashion or if certain security activities are not fulfilled, then a shipment can be significantly delayed. Additionally, the cost of international shipments has increased as well. See Chapter 10 for additional information on worldwide sourcing.

A second current transportation issue that affects the supply manager is concerned with infrastructure condition and traffic congestion. For example, many seaports cannot handle the newer mega-containerships being built because of their deeper draft and overall width. The Panama and Suez Canals are also limited to older and smaller cargo ships because of their size limitations, although the Panama Canal is currently being upgraded to handle larger vessels. In terms of air carriers, ground traffic congestion and additional cargo screening as described earlier can add significantly to the delivery time of air cargo, thereby reducing the time advantage of why freight movement by air was selected in the first place. Because of the recent recession, many airlines began to reduce capacity by taking older, less efficient aircraft out of service. Additionally, the existing U.S. air traffic control system is ominously outdated and overworked, which often requires aircraft to fly inefficient routes. The change to a more efficient GPS-facilitated air traffic control system has been slow in gaining acceptance. For motor carriers, crumbling highways and bridges have forced greater public investment in repairs. Around many U.S. metropolitan areas, traffic congestion has caused inordinate delays for both passenger autos and trucks. Rail freight carriers must compete for space on existing rail lines with existing and proposed high-speed and regular passenger rail routes. The container handling capacity at many seaports has not kept pace with the volume of container shipments. River barge traffic must contend with an antiquated locks and dams system that does not allow longer units to pass through without stopping and breaking down the tow into multiple, shorter groupings that must pass through the lock one at a time and then rejoined on the other side of the lock. Although it is an incomplete response to these challenges, the U.S. American Recovery and Reinvestment Act of 2009 sought to address many of these critical issues by investing more than $105 billion in infrastructure-related projects across all modes of transportation. However, substantial future public investment must still be committed to continue maintenance, improvement, and expansion of the aging U.S. transportation infrastructure.

Performance-Based Logistics[13]

Performance-based logistics (PBL) is an emerging collaborative business model that seeks to move away from the traditional transaction-based model toward meeting the mutual interests of both the buyer and logistics service provider. Under the traditional transaction-based model, logistics service providers are typically compensated for each and every transaction conducted. As such, there is little motivation for the logistics service provider to become more efficient, as any expenditure for operational improvement will negatively impact its revenue stream. This business model generally results in the lowest cost for each individual transaction but does not promote an efficient, low-total-cost logistics system. Therefore, the underlying interests of the buyer and logistics service provider are at odds with each other. In addition, the onus for any cost and efficiency improvement is placed strictly on the buyer, who must then negotiate performance improvements and revised pricing with the logistics service provider.

In comparison, a performance-based logistics system seeks to drive the logistics service provider's performance by clearly delineating the buyer's preferred outcomes, not by transaction, but in terms of provider value added and overall systems cost. In PBL, the logistics service provider is compensated by how well it enables the buyer to achieve these outcomes. Compensation is structured to reward the logistics service provider with longer-term contracts and performance incentives, leading to increased profitability. In order for PBL to work, both the buyer and logistics service provider must explicitly agree as to what the buyer's desired outcomes, goals, and objectives are and how the logistics service provider can help meet them.

Following the determination of, and agreement to, the buyer's goals and objectives, a key factor to consider here is the development of timely, accurate, and cost-effective metrics designed to measure key performance variables (e.g., who measures the logistics service provider's performance, how and where it is measured, how often it is measured, and how the data will be utilized).

Use of PBL is not without its concerns. For example, performance measurement is often difficult to define, let alone accomplish. There can be disagreement regarding the buyer's perception of the logistics service provider's performance and the efficacy of the metrics used to determine its level of performance. Research conducted by the University of Tennessee indicates that total logistics system risk can actually be reduced for both buyer and logistics service provider through the collaboration made possible by PBL.

To date, the single largest proponent of PBL has been the U.S. Department of Defense (DoD), which uses PBL contracts to procure logistics support for its various major weapons systems. Based on its previous successes with PBL, the DoD began mandating its use in all of its major acquisition categories beginning in 2006. Performance-based logistics offers significant promise in the private sector but has not yet been widely adopted.

However, a comparable sourcing strategy, the service-level agreement (SLA), has been used in a number of spend categories, including travel and entertainment, software and technology, and back-office operations. Application of an SLA allows the buyer to specify target or minimum performance and service levels that the supplier is expected to provide for the fee charged. As with PBL, the key is to develop key performance indicators (KPIs) that outline specific performance criteria that a supplier is expected to meet.

An effective PBL system requires the logistics service provider to take a far more proactive role in interacting with the buyer to jointly manage the buyer's supply chain. Requirements for implementation of a successful PBL project include the following:

- Commitment to mutual collaboration and alignment of interests
- Creation of a win-win environment for the buyer and logistics service provider, focused on the value added by the logistics service provider
- Development of a sound sourcing strategy, including close alignment of the buyer's goals and objectives with the logistics service provider's compensation and incentive structure

- Application of an effective checks and balances system utilizing timely and ac curate data collection and multiple metrics, including a formal reporting and review process[14]

Outsourcing Logistics to Third-Party Logistics Providers

A buyer can initiate various actions to improve transportation service and delivery performance throughout the supply chain. One of the most common actions is to outsource logistics to an integrated third-party logistics provider that is responsible for managing all of the buyer's inbound and outbound transportation, as well as providing other logistics, material handling, and storage services, such as warehousing and cross-docking. The use of 3PLs is increasingly becoming a viable option for smaller shippers and infrequent shipments. Third-party logistics providers can furnish convenient, low-cost, and reliable transportation and logistics services, whereas the shipper may not have sufficient volume for economies of scale or available expertise on staff to provide them internally. These service providers also offer linked information systems that provide readily accessible visibility to their services, providing a substantial competitive advantage. For this reason, many distributors and mail-order companies use FedEx and UPS as their primary transportation provider as well as for other logistics services.

Select Providers

Supply managers should be very careful in selecting 3PLs, which may pass themselves off as "integrated global logistics service providers," claiming to offer complete end-to-end supply chain services even when they are incapable of doing so. In a global marketplace, there are many different elements of transportation and logistics that can be managed by a 3PL, including the following:

- Customs brokers
- Freight brokers (both air and surface)
- Warehousing and distribution center operations
- Packaging and export documentation
- Delivery services
- Local sourcing and purchasing
- International trade management and compliance
- Global transportation optimization
- Supply chain planning
- Export packaging services

It is rare in practice to find a single 3PL company that is fully capable of providing world-class services in all of these areas simultaneously. Therefore, supply management should be leery of companies that claim that they are integrated world-class providers in all of these areas. To avoid selecting 3PL providers that cannot meet the shipper's requirements, savvy buyers should consider using the following approach:

1. **Plan**
   - Define specific logistics service requirements and how they will be measured and evaluated.

- Confirm the selection process.
- Involve key stakeholders to ensure internal buy-in.
- Remove barriers to success.

2. **Select**
   - Target best-in-class logistics service providers.
   - Select 3PL, consolidator, or contractor.
   - Negotiate mutually beneficial agreement.

3. **Implement**
   - Share supply chain information to deliver superior value.
   - Build relationships.
   - Work jointly to resolve start-up issues.

4. **Improve**
   - Exchange performance measures to identify improvement opportunities.
   - Encourage cross-organization training and project activities.

5. **Partner**
   - Develop supply chain alliances to agree on tradeoffs and share risks.
   - Involve 3PL partners in joint strategic planning and decision making.

Some of the advantages and disadvantages of considering a third-party logistics provider are shown in Exhibit 17.8.

When identifying, selecting, and qualifying 3PLs, buyers should consider the following elements of performance and determine whether a given provider can effectively execute them. Again, recall the previous discussion about supplier selection and evaluation from Chapter 7.

Exhibit 17.8	**Third-Party Logistics**

Advantages	**Disadvantages**
• Economies of scale and increased flexibility • Improve service performance levels • Release capital from sale of assets • Release running costs • Concentrate on core business activities	• Relinquish control, ownership, and expertise • Loss of integration between sales and supply • Changeover costs and operational problems • Loss of dedicated in-house managed staff • Sacrifice key business service differentiation

Merchandise	Cross Docking	VMI
Marshalling	Transport	Export Packaging
Postponement	FG Pull Expediting	Spares (Returns and Repairs)
Installation Test Fit	Inventory Control	Reverse Flow

Shared Resources or Dedicated Resources?

Gain Access to Critical and Timely Data

Access to accurate and timely information represents power to a decision maker. It is difficult to manage material shipments without the ability to identify, collect, and analyze critical transportation-related cost and performance data. Ideally, the following logistics information should be readily available and should be reported by the 3PL to the buyer. An inability to quickly and accurately provide this information in a usable format may indicate that the 3PL is not capable of effectively managing the buyer's supply network.

- Number of carriers providing inbound, intraorganizational, and outbound transportation services
- Total transportation expenditures by specific carrier and mode of transportation
- Number of suppliers shipping material (e.g., the number of shipping points)
- Volume and transportation costs associated with shipments by supplier
- Breakdown of volumes by commodity or type of material
- Performance statistics and ratings for individual carriers
- Percentage of shipments arranged by suppliers versus buyers (e.g., FOB destination versus FOB origin)

Develop Systems Visibility to Material Shipments

Real-time information concerning the status and location of shipments can provide at least partial visibility that is required for effective material control. The need for visibility and control supports the development of electronic data and communications systems between carrier and buyer. Third-party logistics companies should be able to provide immediate access to information on shipment status, whether on motor carriers linked electronically with shippers through global positioning systems or on a ship, aircraft, or customs location.

Many 3PLs offer detailed shipment tracking systems to provide current status updates. Several levels of complexity exist in these systems. One-way information systems allow a buyer to gain information about the location of a shipment on a real-time basis. A buyer simply requests data directly from a carrier's information system, now often provided via the carrier's website.

However, many 3PLs now utilize event-based systems. These provide status alerts, via e-mail, text message, fax, pager, and so on, to a buyer or salesperson that a particular shipment has been delayed and that this may affect other entities in the supply chain (e.g., manufacturing plants, warehouse locations, and customers). Even though problematic events cannot always be prevented, early warning signals and using an event-management system can help sourcing companies deal with the problem in a more timely manner.

Develop Closer Relationships with Fewer Providers

A common theme throughout this book is that buyers and suppliers often benefit from closer, more collaborative relationships. This logic also applies to 3PL relationships. Transportation buyers are increasingly reducing the number of 3PLs with which they do business on a companywide basis with the intention of working more collaboratively with those remaining. This strategy allows a buyer to realize improved service and greater benefits that otherwise might not be available through a traditional, arm's-length business relationship.

For example, a buyer may receive a guarantee that specific carrier equipment will be available when and where needed. Controlling and managing the movement of goods is easier and more efficient when a buyer selects only the best 3PLs available that meet its specific needs and develops a closer working relationship with them.

Establish Companywide Contracts

Real and substantial cost and service improvements are possible when transportation volumes between facilities, divisions, or business units are aggregated for increased purchasing leverage and put under the jurisdiction of a limited number of highly capable 3PLs and/or 4PLs.

One clear trend is that many carriers no longer market themselves simply as providers of physical transportation services. For complex freight movements—those movements involving multiple parties or additional handling—many carriers now perform those duties that previously required the use of specialized in-house personnel or third parties. Full-service providers, in addition to picking up and delivering goods, may consolidate shipments, provide simplified billing, ship just-in-time from local storage points, handle complex overseas shipments, coordinate shipments with other carriers or modes, or configure final products for direct shipment to end customers. This allows a transportation buyer to focus on strategy development, whereas the full-service carrier manages the day-to-day details of the transportation network.

There are many examples of using service providers for more than just transportation. For example, UPS handles all the worldwide aftermarket spare parts business for Allison Engine. Internet-based services provided by carriers are expanding as well. Most overnight package delivery companies provide full tracking of packages via software that allows users to arrange for, track, and complete entire shipping transactions over the Internet.

Purchasing Services and Indirect Items[15]

Over the past several years, supply management departments in high-performing, best-in-class companies have made great strides in reducing the price of direct material inputs. Because procurement of direct materials is often associated with distinct strategic business units (SBUs), managing this spend is usually accomplished through centralized commodity groups, with sourcing decisions and contract administration occurring at the SBU level. More companies, however, now realize that, until they can capture the benefits of including indirect spending under the umbrella of their company's overall sourcing strategy, a large percentage of indirect spend will not be managed effectively.

We can define **indirect spend** as any purchased good or service that does not end up in the product or service delivered to a customer. This component can be a significant percentage of a company's expenditures. Research on Fortune 500 companies found that services spending accounted for 11 percent of total revenue and 30 percent of total purchase spend. Indirect spending averaged 9 percent of revenue and 23 percent of total purchases. By comparison, direct spending (where the attention of supply management is most often focused) accounted for 18 percent of total revenue and 44 percent of total spend. Another important indicator was that participants expected services spend to increase by 13 percent in the next five years, an indication that the Western world is outsourcing more and more activities to external service organizations. A breakout of the average percentage of total purchasing spending by category is provided in Exhibit 17.9.

Exhibit 17.9	Average Services Spend Activity

SERVICES SPEND CATEGORY	PERCENTAGE OF TOTAL PURCHASE SPEND (NORMALIZED)
Manufacturing	20.24
Inventory	7.93
Professional services	7.61
Construction/engineering	6.04
Information technology	5.24
Marketing	5.13
Logistics	4.94
Real estate	4.25
Advertising	3.00
Project-based services	2.81
Human resources	2.04
Telecommunications	2.00
Travel	1.79
Facilities management	1.86
Printing/copying	1.51
Legal	1.45
Administrative services	1.15
Temporary staffing	0.97
Research and development	0.78
Call center	0.76
Accounting services	0.40
Finance	0.29
Warehouse management	0.14
Other	8.49

Source: CAPS Research, 2003.

With continued growth in outsourcing of non-core capabilities, the expansion of the services sector, and increasing cost pressure, the importance of effectively managing an organization's indirect spend is increasing. However, because of the decentralized nature and wide variety of goods and services in most indirect spend categories, the problem is more complex from a managerial and administrative standpoint. Issues often arise in identifying, segmenting, and/or allocating indirect spend across or between different functional and budgetary areas. Another common problem is that indirect spend is often hidden in the price of direct materials (e.g., FOB destination). For example, if a supplier pays for shipping, the transportation cost (an indirect service) is usually buried in the invoice price of the direct material.

The CAPS Research Critical Issues Report referred to above found that companies have begun using two distinct methods to identify, manage, and reduce their indirect spend: internal and external methods. An overview of these results is provided as follows.

Internal Methods of Managing Indirect Spend
Data Collection and Consolidation

In many cases, several units within one organization will unknowingly purchase the same goods and/or services from different suppliers (or even the same supplier at different prices). For example, John Deere discovered that it was spending $1.4 million annually on work gloves. This total was represented by 425 separate part numbers purchased from twenty different suppliers. In some instances, a single supplier was supplying the same glove to different Deere manufacturing and distribution facilities at vastly disparate prices. Research showed that consolidating and standardizing this indirect purchase alone with few well-chosen suppliers would result in an annual savings of $500,000.[16] In this situation, Deere encountered higher indirect costs by not leveraging its total volume enterprisewide.

If indirect spend is to be leveraged, supply management must have a clear understanding of exactly what indirect goods and services are being purchased by individual SBUs. As Deere's work glove example above shows, there are many indirect purchases in a typical organization that are not normally recognized as having volume leverage opportunity. Comprehensive data collection and focused analytics allow companies to maximize leverage in their indirect spend and also recognize comparable goods or services that could be standardized and aggregated.

For example, FedEx contracted with a firm specializing in electricity usage audits to collect billing information from each of its 2,000 facilities and review whether the correct tariff rates were used for each facility. These facilities varied in size from over 10,000 employees to as few as two and were located in every state. Based on this approach alone, eliminating overbilling errors from improperly applied utility rates yielded a savings of from 4 to 5 percent of its energy spend after all consulting fees had been paid. The most important component of this strategy was not the upfront cost savings as much as it was determining the overall pattern and volume of electricity consumption across this network of facilities. Once this pattern of consumption was identified and understood, FedEx could initiate a strategy for rationalizing its energy spend in accordance with varying deregulation patterns across the different states. In addition, FedEx was able to modify business processes at its stations and hubs to improve electricity usage efficiency.[17]

Restructuring to Establish Accountability

Establishing a capable supply management structure and setting up accountability for indirect purchases are closely connected with data collection, consolidation, and analysis. By gaining a clear understanding of who is spending what, where, and when, supply management can implement procedures and safeguards that deter and control maverick spend. **Maverick spend** can be defined as that amount of an organization's total procurement budget that is purchased from unauthorized sources. Here is where the supply management organization's delegation of responsibility for cost saving occurs: A chain of command must be established that matches appropriate procurement authority and ensures that correct protocols are followed.

Automating the Requisition/Sourcing Process

Companies have improved their sourcing process by using electronic requisitioning and automating routing, approvals, and purchase order/release creation. Such e-procurement automation also facilitates the receiving function by automatically checking receipts against both the supplier's invoice and the buyer's purchase order, often using scanning and/or RFID technology. Finally, once the supply or service has been delivered or provided and is considered complete, the automated process also authorizes the payment, oftentimes an electronic transfer of funds transaction, which saves both the buyer and supplier time and money. A Miller Brewing executive once pointed out, "This allows procurement managers more time to focus on the strategic areas of buying rather than having to worry about the mundane tasks associated with the various buying procedures."

Standardization

Supporting an automated sourcing system with e-catalogs helps to promote item standardization and big data aggregation of indirect spend. By limiting internal requisitioners to previously approved catalogs of already contracted goods and services from preselected and approved suppliers, volume commitments to approved suppliers can be better achieved and maverick spending reduced. Some companies have gone so far as to establish policies that require every indirect goods purchase made off-catalog to be submitted to an executive for review and approval. This visibility is essential in minimizing unauthorized purchases from nonapproved sources.

External Methods of Managing Indirect Spend

Reverse Auctions

The use of reverse auctions can greatly impact the indirect buying process. Among the many reasons for this is that electronic reverse auctions allow buyers and suppliers to more easily communicate in real time from anywhere in the world via the Internet. Buyers have indicated they are seeing an average price savings of 10 to 20 percent on their initial reverse auctions. However, many buyers are beginning to question the sustainability of such cost savings over time once the initial reductions are made, as the "low-hanging fruit" are identified and terms renegotiated, and the overuse of reverse auctions may often have a negative impact on buyer-supplier relations.

Purchasing Consortia

Another growing trend for improving buyers' leverage is the use of purchasing consortia, which are created by buyers from various businesses to pool their buying power to reduce prices. Some companies, such as Raytheon, have been so successful at building and managing their purchasing consortia that they generate revenue by charging other businesses a service fee for using them. However, one of the challenges faced by purchasing consortia is getting the individual members to agree on exactly what is to be collectively purchased. Because of these coordination difficulties, purchasing consortia are often run by an independent third party, which takes all of the different specifications and develops a joint product list that it feels best matches the needs of all the participants.

Supply Management Outsourcing

Some companies have decided to outsource their indirect spend altogether. For example, Harley-Davidson wanted to manage its indirect spend better, but instead of managing this process internally, it decided to outsource all indirect purchases to three reliable suppliers. To do this, Harley-Davidson's supply management department conducted a lengthy search for those outstanding suppliers thought to be able to handle this task. These three suppliers then became responsible for making sure that all indirect sourcing needs were met, either internally or by procuring externally from another supplier. This saved Harley-Davidson over $4 million in its first year of implementation.

Enabling Tactics and Strategies

The previously mentioned CAPS report notes that several enablers are necessary to successfully implement an indirect spend procurement strategy. These are discussed below.

Zero-Based Budgeting

Tracking and capturing the indirect savings achieved by supply management are very difficult to achieve in most organizations, as responsibility for indirect spend is typically decentralized throughout the organization. In addition, traditional cost accounting systems may not be designed to systematically track and consolidate indirect spend across an organization. This approach forces business units to start with and justify the same indirect budget they had in the previous planning cycle. Once this is prepared, supply management examines the spend categories and looks for cost-savings opportunities. If opportunities are found and result in lower-cost purchases, the business unit must write a check to the CFO for the amount of the savings.

Prebudget Savings

Another approach to capturing negotiated savings in the indirect spend is the use of forced budget reductions. Several companies stated that they forced 5 to 10 percent budget reductions on all indirect items. Business units then had the following option:

- Negotiating price reductions on current volumes
- Aggregating spend within or across business units to gain additional volume-based price concessions
- Decreasing demand for indirect items
- Using a combination of the above methods

Organizational Structure

The debate about centralized, decentralized, and centrally led structures in supply management organizations was discussed earlier in Chapter 5. In many cases, however, it appears that a hybrid organization will allow different regions or business units the requisite flexibility to make their own localized procurement decisions and yet be a good fit with the indirect sourcing needs of most large organizations.

Integrating Accounts Payable into Supply Management

Several companies have integrated their accounts payable processes into the supply management organization, addressing one of the more pressing challenges associated with indirect spend, namely contract compliance. This arrangement gives supply management the authority to not pay for indirect items that were bought off-contract. To have the bill paid, the noncompliant business unit is forced to speak to the CFO, an embarrassing and rarely repeated process, thereby effectively controlling maverick spending.

Power Spenders

This category represents those key individuals or units that control substantial indirect spending and typically have positions of great responsibility within the organization. Because of their level of authority and the sheer volume of the indirect spend they control, supply management often has a hard time getting these power spenders to comply with organization-wide supply management policies. Several companies indicate that properly training these power users is a key to controlling their indirect spend. Training often includes information on general strategic sourcing strategies, as well as specific information on the strategies and tools employed by supply management for effectively controlling the indirect spend. Once trained, enlightened power spenders are usually more willing to comply with preestablished supply management contracts and play an appropriate role in managing their indirect spending.

Supplier-Managed E-Catalogs

E-catalogs, coupled with automated requisitioning and supply management systems described earlier in the chapter, help organizations ensure greater compliance with existing contracts. However, most companies indicate that creating and maintaining up-to-date in-house e-catalogs can be extremely costly and challenging. In general, suppliers should provide and manage the e-catalogs, as they have a vested interest in doing so to create additional sales volume.

Commodity Coding for Indirect Spend

Assigning and maintaining accurate and representative commodity codes for indirect goods and services across an enterprise can prove difficult. Indirect goods can often be logically coded into multiple expense categories, leading to inconsistent coding across units, individual purchases, or perhaps even no coding at all (e.g., indirect expenses are put into a generic catch-all account such as Freight In or General Services). Supplier coding is also a challenge. Suppliers of multiple indirect items can have multiple ship-to and bill-to addresses, resulting in numerous codes being assigned to the same supplier for each item. Many suppliers will simply code these disparate purchases with the same accounting information, effectively masking them from detailed analysis and effective cost management by the indirect buyer. This also disguises the total indirect spend with a given supplier and hinders the buyer from fully leveraging its volume. To help counter these problems, companies should limit their commodity coding system to only a few levels of detail, which makes it easier for the end-user to properly identify commodity purchases and reduce the time for determining the perfect code.

One Commodity Team Assigned to Large Suppliers

There can be many challenges when sourcing from large suppliers with a broad and diverse product offering. These include commodity coding as well as standardizing products, pricing, terms, and conditions. One effective solution is to assign a designated commodity team to work with each large supplier. When another internal buyer is considering using this supplier, a commodity team member already assigned to this supplier is consulted to ensure that existing contracts with the appropriate standardized products, pricing, terms, and conditions are used. This collaborative approach helps the buying company counter the common divide-and-conquer strategy often used by large suppliers.

Outsourcing Indirect Sourcing

Although outsourcing any part of a supply management organization can be controversial, it can often return significant benefits. For example, one company decided to outsource its nonstrategic indirect spend. This bold move had a number of benefits. The first benefit was the development of an up-to-date e-catalog that was implemented quickly. The second was tighter control of the organization's indirect spend accompanied by real-time data. The third was a substantial reduction in the cost of indirect goods and services. And lastly, the company was able to reduce its headcount.

Sourcing Professional Services[18]

In this section, we will review best practices in an area of service procurement facing increasing scrutiny: the sourcing of professional services, including consultants and software development. In buying professional services, incorporating such basic steps as rationalizing and optimizing the supply base, working hand in hand with key suppliers, leveraging volume across business units, implementing better control systems, and developing cost-savings ideas can save companies a substantial amount of money.[19]

Although implementation of these strategies can prove crucial in any typical sourcing scenario, its significance in the cost-effective procurement of professional services is further enhanced by the fact that professional services are often used quite differently among departments or business units. Like many other areas of supply management, the first step should be to perform an internal audit or spend analysis to establish a baseline of just how much the company is currently spending on professional services and where those funds are actually spent. An effective audit process should examine expenditure records to get an approximate estimate of the total value of these services. The audit team should then reclassify these expenditures by description, supplier, and internal user. It should also review the recent procurement history for previously contracted professional services.[20] This determines the current state of the professional services sourcing process and allows the company to decide if change is required. In addition, the following steps are recommended for buying professional services, such as outside consulting.

Have a Clearly Defined Scope

Every project must have a scope that succinctly defines the project to help avoid misunderstandings between the buyer and the service provider. At a minimum, the scope, or statement of work (SOW), should provide detailed guidance to the service provider, including project deliverables, performance metrics, milestones and deadlines, and budget. The scope should also include whether rewards and penalties are appropriate and how risk is to be distributed between the parties as well as detailed instructions describing how major changes to project scope are to be handled to ensure that what was contracted for actually gets accomplished and to avoid "scope creep." In some cases, it may be advisable to renegotiate the agreement if the desired changes are too substantial and materially alter the intent of the original agreement. The scope also needs to include nondisclosure statements (NDAs) to protect the buying company's interest. The buyer may want to insert language that specifies the actual persons, by name, who are supposed to do the work. Finally, the scope needs to include statements as to who has operational control over both internal and external project personnel once the contract is signed.

When using a new professional services supplier, it is a good idea for the buyer to develop a very detailed project scope. However, if the buyer is using a previously established or preferred supplier, the scope of the new project may be less detailed because the buyer already has a long-term relationship and past experience with the service provider. This relationship allows for work to be released with only a phone call or e-mail message. However, even with an established service provider, it is always important to follow up with a written confirmation outlining the understanding of the project, although a highly detailed document may not be necessary.

Move to a Centralized Procurement Structure

Moving to a centralized process for procuring professional services allows the buying company to leverage its corporate buying power to ensure they are sourcing the highest-quality service at the most cost-effective price.[21] According to Anne Millen Porter, "Cost reduction is, hands down, the main reason for bringing sizeable purchasing power to bear in the market place."[22] For example, Dial saved $100 million over five years, including $10 million in 2001, by moving to centralized sourcing.[23] After San Diego Gas and Electric centralized its procurement process, it found many positive results, including greater objectivity, improved negotiation, and better pricing.[24]

Centralization of professional service procurement can also increase the accountability of outside consultants to the buyer by increasing the monitoring and auditing of services provided. Centralized procurement often leads to the buyer's ability to reduce the number of professional service providers, thus gaining additional pricing leverage with each. Additionally, centralization can also reduce service provider redundancy and the likelihood of unnecessary charges.[25] Another advantage of centralized procurement for professional services is that it reduces the risk of business units purchasing redundant or duplicated services.

Although utilizing a centralized procurement process has all of the advantages discussed above, it does have disadvantages. One major disadvantage is that no single consultant or firm is likely to be the qualified expert across a variety of consulting projects, so having a decentralized approach may help tailor the sourcing of professional services to better fit specific needs. Therefore, many companies feel that decentralized procurement of professional services is better for highly diversified companies with many diverse business units.

Develop a Professional Services Database

In order for a professional services database solution to be effective, it should include the following two database elements.

A Cumulative Knowledge Database

A cumulative knowledge database is vital in preventing the sourcing of duplicate or redundant professional services across different departments or business units. In general, this database should contain an organized listing of SOWs and results obtained from past projects, including, but not limited to, user satisfaction level, timely project completion, work quality, accuracy of work delivered, and affordability. This database is useful because it allows employees to search past projects to see if a similar solution has already been delivered. If a similar solution is available on the database, redundant services may not be needed, unless conditions have changed significantly. This increased project record keeping can ultimately save the company a significant amount in professional service expenditures.

A Preferred Supplier List Database

This database, including supplier performance records and related user comments, can be extremely useful for companies considering multiple professional service providers. By having access to a list of preferred suppliers, employees know which professional service providers the company recommends and what professional services are available. These recommendations can be determined by user satisfaction ratings, the existence of long-term contracts, or price discounts. In any event, the preferred supplier list must be easily accessible by employees when they search for potential suppliers on new projects.

The database should also be set up to generate a list of preferred suppliers based on previous project performance criteria. For example, the Intelli-Gage system at Merrill Lynch is designed so that hiring managers can select desired skills from a comprehensive menu of options. Once a search request is completed, the database then provides a prioritized list of appropriate or preferred candidates. The system should also display the supplier's most recent hourly rate and fee structure, as well as other useful information such as performance ratings and previous project user comments. According to Merrill Lynch,

"The ability to track the consultant's performance is an enormous benefit for companies with multiple locations and multiple information technology organizations around the globe. In addition, the system's ability to track individual supplier performance, as well as overall supplier performance, allows us to prevent hiring poor performers who leave one supplier company only to resurface under a different corporate umbrella."[26]

As long as the preferred supplier database is meticulously maintained, and employees are encouraged or required to use the preferred supplier list, companies should see improvements in their sourcing of professional services. Moreover, as new and refined search criteria come along, it is important that these criteria be added to the database. This will allow sourcing managers to easily walk through menus to populate future supplier searches. Performance records, supplier evaluations, and project comments will also need to be continually updated in a timely manner for the database to remain effective. Together, these IT elements should enhance the organization and efficiency of the supply management department.

Develop a Sound Procedure for Evaluation and Selection of Consultants

One of the most important functions in procurement is the initial evaluation and selection of consultants and other professional service providers, such as security and janitorial firms. As such, buyers often commit major resources to perform initial supplier evaluations. Although there are different requirements for each performance area, it is typical to create metrics that evaluate such areas as supplier quality, cost competitiveness, potential delivery performance, and technological capability. To help minimize potential bias, it is essential that a cross-functional team carry out this analysis. Companies report cost savings in the range of 15–25 percent by utilizing a cross-functional team.

Optimize the Supply Base

Once the first cut has eliminated those professional service providers that are not as capable of performing the desired project, the buyer must decide how to evaluate the remaining suppliers, some of which may appear equally capable on the surface. This procedure includes an evaluation drawn from supplier interviews and conversations, as well as the use of a preferred supplier list as discussed before. A preferred supplier list can designate whether a professional service provider's capabilities and quality meet the highest performance and service standards as defined by the users. This list may also take into account any price discount or volume-leveraging opportunities offered by the professional services supplier. Such a list helps to monitor the performance of selected suppliers closely, facilitates organizational visibility in the long run, and avoids duplication of efforts to reevaluate the supplier. This information is a key input in the knowledge database. The buyer and supplier should conduct detailed negotiations to agree upon the specific details of the agreement that can be included in the scope of work.

Although it is important to develop a rationalized supply base so that buying power can be appropriately leveraged, a single-source strategy rarely maximizes the value of professional services. Often, the addition of a single new supplier will greatly enhance the performance of previous suppliers because of increased competition. Using multiple sources for products encourages professional service providers to act more competitively. Although no single supplier should be considered an expert in all areas, using a variety of information sources allows managers to find and tap specific and appropriate expertise for any given project. Use of multiple sources also increases the flow of new ideas and information and reduces the dependence on any single supplier. Additionally, all efforts should be taken to avoid one-stop shopping; most service companies are second rate outside their core businesses. Use professional service providers for their core expertise only.

Develop a Standardized Contract

It is critical for supply managers to develop skills and abilities to understand and manage professional service contracts on a regular basis. It is also important for a standard contract template to be developed in association with the organization's legal department. Some companies have created an online contract template where all the standard professional service clauses are built in. The entire scope and SOW of the project should be clearly and succinctly defined at this level, with emphasis on the various sections of the project scope as additional clauses in the contract. These should include project metrics, deliverables, deadlines and milestones, and budget. If a company utilizes an incentive system to reward or penalize its professional service providers, this should also become part of the final agreement. Finally, the contract should contain a clause that allows for renegotiation or termination in case of major scope changes.

Monitor Results

The company should have a predetermined methodology to gauge the performance of its professional service providers at various stages of their projects. The parameters on which the supplier is evaluated should include, but not be limited to, quality, cost management, delivery, technical support, and wavelength. **Wavelength** can be defined as how easy the professional service provider is to do business with. The results of service provider performance evaluations should be entered into the knowledge database in a timely manner, enabling retrieval both at the time of supplier evaluation and after supplier selection.

The internal customers of any contracted professional service (i.e., the users who are directly impacted), should have an active role in the sourcing and evaluation process. Their participation in defining the detailed scope of the project and providing relevant feedback on services rendered by the service provider should be consistently updated in the knowledge database throughout the life cycle of the project. Finally, the company should monitor its expenses, utilizing an information systems tool where available.

Develop Policy Compliance

For the execution of best practices into a systematic professional services procurement process, the prerequisites are mentioned above. The degree of success for implementation and ongoing management of this process will depend not only on how comprehensive and exhaustive these practices and policies are for a given company but also on whether adequate buy-in has been obtained from affected employees and other internal stakeholders. Top management should consider this completely before defining the final scope of the procurement project. Because the maintenance of best practices is a dynamic process, the organization's information systems and knowledge databases should be checked for the most recent updates.

The Procurement Governance Team at Allstate reduced the number of suppliers for one type of professional service from 300 to 11, resulting in a 20 percent cost reduction. The procurement team handles the complete sourcing process from beginning to end, allowing employees to concentrate on their core responsibilities. This also permits the organization

Sourcing Snapshot

Sourcing Travel

The recent recession has forced many companies to take a serious look at various spend categories to find areas of discretionary expenditures that could be reduced in the short run. For some, this involved taking a hard look at travel and entertainment expenses. Tyco International established four regional travel councils, which are led by Rose Speckmann, Director, Global Travel. She is tasked with providing the regional councils with videoconference updates on corporate travel policies and procedures, as well as supply base changes regarding preferred suppliers. Actual out-of-pocket travel cost is only one of the most important considerations for global travelers. Tyco also considers service to be another key factor and is a major component in Tyco's travel supplier performance review system. The company also includes a service level agreement in its travel provider contracts. This kind of centralized oversight demonstrates to Tyco's business units that the company is serious about containing global travel costs while considering service and security to its travelers on an individual basis.

A special travel report in *Purchasing highlights* a series of considerations that supply managers can use to procure travel services more effectively:

- Review, revise, and tighten travel policies.
- Encourage compliance with preestablished preferred suppliers.
- Encourage greater use of videoconferencing.
- Use a total cost approach, looking at total trip costs, including fees, not just the individual cost components.
- Encourage travelers to eat meals at home before traveling and to stay with friends and family if possible.
- Limit expenses that do not require a receipt.
- Look for bargains in unexpected places, like luxury hotels and limousine services.
- Negotiate volume discounts with airlines, rental car agencies, and hotel chains.
- Look for meeting venues that are willing to cut prices to attract more visitors.

Sources: Avery, S. (2009, September), "Travel Procurement Gets a Bigger Role at Tyco," *Purchasing*, 41–42. and "How to Source Travel for 2010" (2009, September), *Purchasing*, 32–33.

to operate more efficiently and receive a greater benefit. According to the vice president and head of procurement governance, effective demand management of professional services depends on establishing clear usage policies, then monitoring and reporting compliance with these policies. Realizing actual savings requires compliance throughout the entire company.[27]

Service Supply Chain Challenges

Research indicates that effectively managing an organization's services supply chain is fraught with challenges.[28] Many service sourcing agreements are characterized by imprecise, indefinite, and unclear specifications in the statement of work. Without clear and concise specifications and work descriptions, it is unlikely that a buyer can properly determine whether a service has actually been performed to the satisfaction of the internal customer. Not having a well-thought-out and thoroughly defined set of performance and outcome expectations can lead to reduced customer satisfaction with the user. Second, in trying to write specific service requirements, many buyers and users find out that clear and accurate service specifications are very difficult to delineate; for example, what determines satisfactory progress on the development of a software program, preparation of a consulting report, or a definition of "clean?"

Likewise, professional service providers can often take advantage of unsuspecting buyers when service performance specifications are unclear or ill-defined. More than one service provider has been able to expand the scope of a contract (and its corresponding fees) through a series of change orders. Without exception, scope creep unfairly favors the service provider, not the buyer. Completion of the service provided is oftentimes also difficult to clearly define. What constitutes the terms "completion" or "level of effort"?

Good Practice Example	*Tetra Pak's Drive to Strategically Manage Its Global Transportation Network*

Tetra Pak, a food processing equipment and packaging division of Tetra Laval, based in Lausanne, Switzerland, faced a daunting task—how to effectively manage its freight flows across multiple international markets along with recognizing the substantial differences between local and regional transportation networks. In 2008, Tetra Pak decided to install a global transportation management system (TMS) designed to incorporate greater visibility of its supply chain and control of its traffic movements throughout the 165 countries in which it does business in real time via the World Wide Web. The TMS system that Tetra Pak chose was provided by Transportation Management Center (TMC), a Chicago-based division of C. H. Robinson, one of the largest non-asset-based 3PLs in the world. Implementation began in early 2009.

The TMS is based on the concept of a "control tower," which provides a customized IT package designed to fit Tetra Pak's unique global operating environment. The steps involved in creating this TMS were similar to its existing freight procurement process managed by the corporate headquarters in Sweden. Tetra Pak's standard freight sourcing process consisted of a qualification phase where the potential carrier prepared a response to a RFI that evaluated it in five performance areas: health, safety, environmental performance, quality, and service. Once qualified, Tetra Pak would then send out its RFQ containing parameters such as volume, routes, and rates. Negotiations with the potential carriers were then conducted between the Swedish headquarters and individual factory shipping departments. Following the evaluation of this phase, the carriers are requested to submit a second offer. The Swedish headquarters, with the cooperation of the local factories, then selected the carriers and negotiated appropriate contracts. Relationships with the suppliers were jointly managed with local factories and the centralized procurement office in Sweden. In the case of the TMS provided by TMC, Tetra Pak also specified its target price for the desired 3PL services.

Tetra Pak and TMC created two superordinate goals for the TMS: (1) standardize how its individual factories and regions manage their transportation networks, and (2) improve visibility in the supply chain. Under the old system, there was no way to integrate systems with their carriers. In addition, certain key events, such as delivery performance, causes of delays, and other service disruptions, were not sufficiently visible to Tetra Pak or its carriers.

Tetra Pak believed that no single 3PL could deliver improved performance on a global basis. However, it worked with TMC to expand its existing capabilities to include more of the world's markets.

For example, TMC manages Tetra Pak's North American transportation system from its Chicago headquarters along with creating another control tower in the Netherlands to cover Europe. Additional control towers will be added to the TMS as required. One of the inherent major advantages to outsourcing its TMS is that Tetra Pak does not have to make a substantial upfront investment in improving and expanding its IT resources, and the learning curve is also shortened because of TMC's expertise. Reporting is updated daily, whereas information can be accessed via the World Wide Web in real time. Although initial information flows among Tetra Pak, TMC, and the system of carriers, eventually Tetra Pak's customers will be brought into the information loop through Tetra Pak's existing e-business system.

Tetra Pak's transportation provider supply base consists of about 130 carriers, which have historically provided performance and operating data in disparate ways. By incorporating a single web-based portal, the TMS system allows Tetra Pak to gather and analyze its data more consistently and in new ways that will allow it to more effectively manage its transportation spend. Future plans include the sharing of best practices among countries, regions, and carriers. Tetra Pak's Kristian Malm, Global Procurement Road Freight, indicates that Tetra Pak will be able to consolidate carrier invoices through TMC, as well as provide for the consolidation of freight. Additionally, the control tower concept allows Tetra Pak to better identify and evaluate systematic risks originating from localized service disruptions.

Source: "Tetra Pak Takes Control of Global Transportation" (2009, January), *MIT-CTL Supply Chain Strategy*, 5(1), 1–4.

CONCLUSION

In studying the best practices used in the procurement of transportation and logistics services, indirect spending, and other professional services, several common themes pervade the discussion. These include the following:

- Link transportation, logistics, and other service activities directly to corporate strategy.

- Organize transportation, logistics, and indirect spending activities under a single executive-level manager, if possible, utilizing a hybrid procurement structure if the indirect spend is spread across several diverse business units.

- Expand and use the power of information and information-processing technology to capture spending behaviors, costs associated with procuring transportation and services, and maverick spending.

- Establish buy-in from senior executive management to the strategy, particularly from the chief financial officer, who is instrumental in overseeing compliance with the strategy.

- Tie cost savings directly to actual spending in business units and be sure to capture the savings either through a zero-based budget or through other appropriate means.

- Form partnerships or alliances with fewer professional service, transportation, and logistics providers to improve collaboration and cost-savings opportunities, along with leveraging the indirect spend volume of the organization.

- Measure transportation, logistics, and service provider performance to drive and sustain superior performance.

- Establish benchmarks against which suppliers and providers are expected to perform and regularly review supplier performance against predetermined goals.

- Establish a detailed project scope up front, and follow up routinely to ensure that it is met in a reasonable and cost-effective manner.

- Review and reevaluate indirect procurement strategies periodically to ensure that user requirements and expectations are being met, along with cost targets.

Supply management's growing involvement in sourcing transportation and professional services, although fairly recent, is expected to continue. Excellent opportunities exist for the supply management professional to make major contributions in this important, but often overlooked, arena. Supply management professionals tasked with sourcing indirect materials and services must strive to become experts in these categories to manage and control them effectively. In addition, it is imperative for supply management professionals to take into account user needs and tailor the sourcing process to adequately accommodate them. A recent joint research paper by CAPS Research and A. T. Kearney, Inc. sums up the importance of procuring services best: "As companies seek to outsource additional non-strategic, non-core activities, outsourcers will have to learn how to serve and add value in addition to landing initial contracts."[29]

KEY TERMS

indirect spend, 683   Maverick spend, 685

logistics, 659   Wavelength, 692

DISCUSSION QUESTIONS

1. Discuss the business and legislative changes that resulted in an increased awareness of the sourcing of transportation and logistics activities.

2. What are the benefits associated with maintaining control and visibility of transportation shipments?

3. Discuss the impact that current transportation issues may have on supply managers.

4. What are some of the key items you should plan on reviewing with a transportation or logistics service provider during a negotiation?

5. Give a definition of a third-party logistics provider. What function does it serve?

6. Discuss the conditions under which a buyer might prefer that a third-party logistics provider arrange and control the transportation and storage of purchased items.

7. Compare and contrast the relative costs and service advantages and disadvantages of air, motor, water, pipeline, and rail carriers.

8. What are the major differences between a common and a contract carrier? Can a buyer negotiate with a common carrier? Why or why not?

9. How can an indirect buyer effectively use performance-based logistics or service-level agreements to control the costs of procuring services?

10. What are the different types of performance metrics used to measure transportation providers? Could this same list be used for a third-party logistics provider? Why or why not?

11. One of the benefits often cited by third-party logistics providers is their ability to provide access to critical performance and operating data. Explain what is meant by this statement.

12. Provide some examples of spending that would fall under the category of services versus indirect spending. What is the difference between the two?

13. One of the biggest problems cited by supply management executives in managing their indirect spend is identifying where and how the spending is taking place. Why do you think this is the case? How can an indirect buyer collect and use this data?

14. Why is it so important to have senior executive support when implementing an indirect spend procurement strategy?

15. Discuss the importance of defining expectations and using standardized contracts when sourcing professional services. Why is this different from sourcing direct materials and components?

16. Can you provide some examples of power spenders of indirect spending and services? How can training help to deploy an indirect spending strategy?

ADDITIONAL READINGS

Ballou, R. H. (2004), *Business Logistics/Supply Chain Management: Planning, Organizing, and Controlling the Supply Chain* (5th ed.), Upper Saddle River, NJ: Pearson Prentice Hall.

Bowersox, D. J., Closs, D. J., and Cooper, M. B. (2010), *Supply Chain Logistics Management*, 3rd ed., New York: McGraw-Hill Irwin.

Carter, P. L., Beall, S., Rossetti, C., and Leduc, E. (2003), *Indirect Spend*, Tempe, AZ: CAPS Research.

Carter, P. L., Carter, J. R., Monczka, R. M., Blascovich, J. D., Slaight, T. H., and Markham, W. J. (2007), *Succeeding in a Dynamic World: Supply Management in the Decades Ahead*, Tempe, AZ: CAPS Research.

Coyle, J. J., Novak, R. A., Gibson, B. J., and Bardi, E. J. (2011), *Transportation: A Supply Chain Perspective*, 7th ed., Mason, OH: South-Western Cengage Learning.

David, P., and Stewart, R. (2008), *International Logistics: The Management of International Trade Operations*, 2nd ed., Mason, OH: Thomson.

Ellram, L. M., Tate, W. L., and Billington, C. (2004), "Understanding and Managing the Services Supply Chain," *Journal of Supply Chain Management*, 40(3), 17–32.

Fender, K. J., and Pierce, D. A. (2013), *An Analysis of the Operational Costs of Trucking: 2013 Update*, Arlington, VA: American Transportation Research Institute.

Frazell, E. H. (2002), *World-Class Warehousing and Material Handling*, New York: McGraw-Hill.

Future Supply Chain 2016: Serving Consumers in a Sustainable Way (2008), Paris: Capgemini.

Johnson, E. (2013), *Transportation Procurement Benchmark Study: Flat Market, Tactical Focus*, Jacksonville, FL: American Shipper (Howard Publications, Inc.).

Moore, P. D., Mullen, H., Guess, L., and Van Boven, A. (2010), *Unpacking Transportation Pricing: A White Paper Challenging Transportation Pricing Models*, Knoxville, TN: University of Tennessee Center for Executive Education.

Murphy, Jr., P. R., and Wood, D. F. (2011), *Contemporary Logistics*, 10th ed., Upper Saddle River, NJ: Prentice Hall.

Stock, J. R., and Lambert, D. M. (2001), *Strategic Logistics Management*, 4th ed., New York: McGraw-Hill.

Sweet, K. M. (2006), *Transportation and Cargo Security: Threats and Solutions*, Upper Saddle River, NJ: Pearson Prentice Hall.

Vitasek, K., and Geary, S. (2007, Summer), "Performance-Based Logistics: The Next Big Thing?" *ProLogis Supply Chain Review*, 1–12.

Vitasek, K., and Ledyard, M. (2009), *Performance-Based Outsourcing: The Next Generation of Outsourcing*, Knoxville, TN: University of Tennessee, Center for Executive Education.

Wade, D. S. (2003), *Managing Your "Services Spend" in Today's Services Economy*, Tempe, AZ: CAPS Research.

ENDNOTES

1. Ellram, L. M., Tate, W. L., and Billington, C. (2004), "Understanding and Managing the Services Supply Chain," *Journal of Supply Chain Management*, 40(3), 20.

2. Retrieved from http://cscmp.org/aboutcscmp/about.asp, June 2008.

3. A complete discussion of transportation and logistics is beyond the scope of this book. For a more complete discussion of the topic, see Bowersox, D. J., Closs, D. J., and Cooper, M. B. (2010), *Supply Chain Logistics Management*, 3rd ed., New York: McGraw-Hill Irwin; Stock, J. R., and Lambert, D. M. (2001), *Strategic Logistics Management*, 4th ed., New York: McGraw-Hill; and Coyle, J. J., Novack, R. A., Gibson, B. J., and Bardi, E. J. (2011), *Transportation*, 7th ed., Mason, OH: South-Western Cengage Learning.

4. Coyle et al., pp. 62–63; and Bowersox et al., pp. 200–202.

5. *Collaborative Outsourcing: Powerful Ideas for Freight Management* (2009), Eden Prairie, MN: C. H. Robinson Worldwide, Inc., p. 8.

6. *Freight Railroads Help Reduce Greenhouse Gas Emissions* (2010). Retrieved from http://www.aar.org/environment/~/media/aar/backgroundpapers/freightrailroadsoffersmarteffectivewaytoreducegreenhousegasemissions.ashx, accessed August 6, 2010.

7. Coyle, et al., p. 179.

8. Coyle, et al., p. 47.

9. Dillon, T. F. (1988, September), "Trends Facing Transportation Buyers/Carriers," *Purchasing World*, 32–34.

10. Sweet, K. M. (2006), *Transportation and Cargo Security: Threats and Solutions*, Upper Saddle River, NJ: Pearson Prentice Hall, pp. xv–xvi.

11. *TSA Certified Cargo Screening Program: Information Bulletin* (2008), Washington, DC: Transportation Security Administration. Retrieved from http://www.expeditors.com/pdf/TSA_Certified_Cargo_Screening_Program_Forums.pdf, accessed August 6, 2010.

12. *Preparing for U. S. Customs "10+2" Importer Security Filing Rule* (2008). Retrieved from http://www.apl.com/security/documents/10+2Advisory_23may08.pdf, accessed August 6, 2010.

13. Adapted from Vitasek, K., and Geary, S. (2007, Summer), "Performance-Based Logistics: The Next Big Thing?" *ProLogis Supply Chain Review*, 1–12.

14. Vitasek and Geary, pp. 5–7.

15. Based on the following reports: Carter, P., Beall, S., Rossetti, C., and Leduc, E. (2003), *Indirect Spend*, Tempe, AZ: CAPS Research. Retrieved from www.capsresearch.org; and Wade, D. S. (2003), *Managing Your "Services Spend" in Today's Services Economy*, Tempe, AZ: CAPS Research.

16. Patterson, J. L. (2000), "Glove Story at John Deere," in *Case Book: Supply Management Cases*, Tempe, AZ: National Association of Purchasing Management, pp. 43–49.

17. Handfield, R. (2004), "The Impact of Energy Deregulation on Sourcing Strategy," *Journal of Supply Chain Management*, 40(2), 38–48.

18. Based on a best practices report by the Supply Chain Resource Consortium (2002, August), North Carolina State University, Raleigh.

19. Reilly, C. (2002), "Central Sourcing Strategy Saves Dial $100M," *Purchasing Online*, January 17.

20. The Global Procurement and Supply Chain Benchmark Institute (1998).

21. Avery, S. (2000), "Allstate Leverages Sourcing to Better Serve Customers," *Purchasing*, 128(2), 12–14.

22. Porter, A. M. (2001), "Big Companies Struggle to Act Their Size," *Purchasing*, 130(21), 24–25.

23. Reilly.

24. "Using Purchasing to Procure Professional Services" (1988), *Purchasing World*, 32(5), 54–56.

25. Baker, W. E., and Faulkner, R. R. (2003), *Strategies for Managing Suppliers of Professional Services*, Tempe, AZ: CAPS Research.

26. Porter, A. M. (2000), "How One Firm Automated Its Professional Services Buy," *Purchasing*, 129(5), S52.

27. Avery, pp. 12–14.

28. Ellram et al., pp. 27–29.

29. Carter, P. L., Carter, J. R., Monczka, R. M., Blascovich, J. D., Slaight, T. H., and Markham, W. J. (2007), *Succeeding in a Dynamic World: Supply Management in the Decades Ahead*, Tempe, AZ: CAPS Research and A.T. Kearney, pp. 107–108.

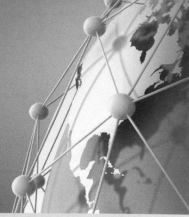

Supply Chain Information Systems and Electronic Sourcing

CHAPTER 18

Learning Objectives

After completing this chapter, you should be able to

- Understand how e-supply chain systems have evolved over time
- Identify the key types of information required in purchasing and supply chains
- Gain an appreciation for the drivers underlying increased use of e-SCM systems
- Understand the primary elements of ERP systems and purchasing databases
- Identify the components of SRM focused e-sourcing suites
- Develop a broad knowledge of social networking blogs, and cloud computing
- Understand the impacts on big data on business models
- Understand why collaboration and information visibility is important in the supply chain

Chapter Outline

MyFloridaMarketPlace: Streamlining Buying and Selling Through E-Sourcing

Ms. Shireen Sackreiter has a unique and ideal skill set for her position. Her skills span the worlds' of information technology and procurement. Shireen is a 1996 graduate of Florida State University in Computer Science and MIS. For the last 9 years she has been at MyFloridaMarketPlace and currently serves as the Managing Director of the program. The following is an interview with Ms. Sackreiter that details the scope and activity she is responsible for in managing this large electronic marketplace in the nation's third largest state.

What is MyFloridaMarketplace?

MyFloridaMarketPlace (MFMP) is the electronic marketplace for the State of Florida. It serves as procurement vehicle for goods and services purchased by the State of Florida government agencies, along with providing a central vendor registration system for suppliers interested in doing business with the State. The program automates the State's requisition, order, approval, invoicing and payment process, making the procurement cycle more cost effective and time efficient than a traditional paper based system. Additionally, MFMP provides electronic tools to streamline the development and execution of solicitations, as well as the award and management of contracts. Online certification of minority vendors, online catalog shopping, and online quoting are also key features of the system.

This web-based e-Procurement system contains the following modules: (1) strategic sourcing (spend analysis, commodity segmentation, and sourcing select commodities); (2) vendor information portal; and (3) procurement applications. In addition to the modules there is a Help Desk that supports both buyers and suppliers.

Could you provide some key facts about MyFloridaMarketPlace?

The Florida State Government supports 19.32 million residents with an estimated 102,000 State employees and an annual budget of approximately $71 billion. The buying activity that is run through the MFMP continues to grow. Our latest figures show the following information about business run through MFMP:

- $11.4B in purchase orders created
- 92,000 registered suppliers
- 370,000 customer interactions
- 17,000 system users
- 495 catalogs loaded
- 93,000 SKUs

What were some of the challenges faced when implementing MyFloridaMarketPlace?

There were numerous challenges faced during our initial implementation and rollout. First, we could not directly tie into existing supplier networks that were available from software providers. Given the State of Florida's unique public sector purchasing requirements, we had to establish our own separate portal for vendor registration and performance. Once this portal was established we were able to link into other software provider networks. Currently, we are heavily tied to the Ariba network.

In addition to the system challenges, we had to enact change management and reengineer business processes. Additionally we had to convince users to move from the old manual, paper based system to the electronic platform. In parallel with the change in mindset, we had to standardize inconsistent procedures and policies across different state agencies. There are 32 state agencies and to this day they maintain some autonomous agency policy differences. We continue to work to standardize their processes. Often times, these "agency unique processes" will result in different approval rules, which can add significant length to the cycle time from requisition to purchase order to receipt of goods or services. This continues to be an area of opportunity for us to work with the agencies and drive real business value.

Organizationally, the central state purchasing group was re-organized to support enhanced procurement business in a more flexible and responsive manner. It was important to improve their collaboration abilities with other state agencies. Finally spend visibility was constrained and there was difficulty monitoring and enforcing compliance on the majority of purchases.

What is the process a user goes through when interacting with MyFloridaMarketPlace?

Let's take a simple example. Suppose a user needs "yearly appointment calendars" for a hundred person office. They can source this need from several supplier online catalogues. The system is setup to mimic "best-in-class" online shopping experiences, leveraging many of the same features experienced by users on the internet. Users can use search filters, display side by side comparisons, and receive pricing totals. Once the user selects the desired item, the system populates the requisition with item information and user defined budget information. The requisition then goes through the approval process, which varies by state agency. The length of the approval process remains a key indicator of how efficient the procurement process is for an organization.

How is the MyFloridaMarketPlace paid for?

The project is self-funded, supported by a 1 percent fee paid by vendors selling to the State. The fee funds the Division of State Purchasing operations, the Office of Supplier Diversity operations, other miscellaneous purchasing related functions and the MFMP Project. Revenue remaining after program funding returns to the State's Purchasing Oversight Operating Trust Fund.

What are the benefits gained by using MyFloridaMarketPlace portal?

There are multiple transactional and strategic sourcing benefits. From the transactional perspective, we have found that order accuracy has increased significantly. Second, the user cycle times to acquire and fulfill their needs have decreased. The average cycle time has dropped from over 7 days to 3.4 days. Third, suppliers are paid on a timely basis and as a result are willing to offer more favorable terms and in some cases lower prices. Finally, the audit trail provided is comprehensive and readily available for each transaction.

The strategic benefits really provide the basis to transform purchasing. The spend visibility from collecting the data and grouping it into spend categories provides a new lens to allow procurement to develop more collaborative relationships and leverage spend. This is accomplished through the spend analysis tool. In addition, this visibility allows purchasing to quickly adjust to changing market needs and user demands. For example, if user preference's switch to notebooks from laptops, this trend is spotted and contract negotiations are initiated with the appropriate suppliers. This visibility also allows procurement to see where contract usage has plummeted and may result in contract termination. Visibility also enhances procurement's ability to improve its demand management capabilities.

Another strategic benefit is the supplier performance data. Actual real-time data on performance is provided. This allows purchasing to monitor variations in supplier lead times, quality and pricing. It also provides another input into upcoming negotiations and a tool to evaluate price-cost tradeoffs. Service-level agreements also underlay the measurement of the MFMP. Two examples of these include: (1) 99 percent systems availability to users; (2) Help desk response to user phone calls within 60–90 seconds. Finally visibility into the stages and cycle times of the transactions allow managers to identify potential improvements for systems and personnel. For example, they can view how long a particular requisition sits on an individual's desk for approval. If one employee's average cycle time for requisition approval is 10 days, whereas another's is 4 days, then a further investigation can be undertaken to analyze root cause.

The MFMP program performance is measured by a set of comprehensive service-level agreements that cover a variety of program functions, inclusive of system and business metrics. For example, underlying applications that support program must be available 99 percent of the time and calls to the help desk must be answered within a certain amount of time. These metrics help maintain focus on key strategic areas of the operations and provide a guideline for measurable results of program performance.

What are the chances of MyFloridaMarketPlace moving to the cloud?*

We are always looking at the economics of such a move. Typically, if you have standardized processes and don't require a lot of customization the cloud provides tremendous benefit. However, where significant customizations are needed to meet the business requirements, the cloud is usually not advantageous. Software providers will often limit or prohibit customization on applications in the cloud. Moving the core procurement functionality of MFMP to the cloud at this time is not economical given the diversity of buying entities and processes in the State of Florida. Additionally, the security of the state's data is a concern as the location of many cloud-computing servers is outside of the United States. However, we continually monitor the environment and economics of cloud computing.

Source: Interview with Ms. Shireen Sackreiter February, 2014.

*For further discussion of cloud computing, see discussion later in this chapter and

Introduction

The electronic revolution continues to impact the supply chain. As can be seen from the chapter opening vignette and throughout this chapter, exciting new software tools are emerging to help supply managers in the future. The opportunities to utilize web-based supply chain (e-SCM) solutions have never been more promising. There are many competent suppliers in a better position to offer value in e-SCM solutions. On the buying side, organizations are becoming much more focused and sophisticated in making decisions involving investments in e-SCM systems. Business cases can provide solid justifications to support a need for these systems. Today, software providers possess increased capabilities, and the cycle time from system design to implementation is shorter. Users demand mobility today and want 24/7 unlimited access. As a result software providers are changing their business models to offer Software as a service (Saas), which in some cases are hosted on the cloud.

As was illustrated in the opening vignette, these systems are no longer the exclusive domain of the private sector. This increased acceptance by users and competitive pressures creates an environment where market providers are giving their customers better pricing and terms. These factors make economic justification of e-SCM systems even more favorable. Overall, e-SCM software uses are growing in application and sophistication.

In conjunction with these advanced purchasing specific solutions, has been the maturation and development of social networking software for business purposes. It is now finding its way into the business world. B2B marketers are using these tools as a way to identify purchasers and assist in starting, building and maintaining relationships. Supply managers who join professional networks can expand their relationships not only within their organization, but also in the general buying community, and build relationships with selling organizations through this new media. Finally, the challenges of managing all this data has created a term "big data" that needs to be managed within and across organizations.

This chapter is not a technical presentation of web-based information systems. Instead, it focuses on a host of issues that managers in the supply chain must be aware of to appreciate the role of both internal information systems (IS) and web-based technologies in purchasing. Many purchasers will at some point become involved in the development and selection of different types of purchasing information systems. Thus knowledge of information systems applications is necessary in order for future managers to realize their purchasing performance objectives.

The chapter begins with a discussion of the evolution of e-SCM systems, provides an overview of supply chain information systems, and then discusses the business drivers for implementing these systems. This is followed by a discussion of internal information systems consisting of enterprise systems, purchasing databases, and data warehouses. Next is a discussion of external information systems, focusing on web-based e-sourcing suites used to manage the entire supply cycle, including a discussion of integrated systems as well as traditional EDI. Next we explore the impact of social media, blogs, and clouds and introduce the concept of big data. Finally, the concept of information visibility and collaboration via these technologies is discussed.

Evolution of E-SCM Systems

Today, supply managers expect powerful solutions to their business problems. However, organizations did not always have sophisticated systems at their disposal. Exhibit 18.1 traces the evolution of e-SCM systems. Early uses of information systems were in the

Exhibit 18.1	The Evolution of E-SCM Systems		
SOLUTION	**TIME PERIOD**	**FOCUS**	**PRIMARY USE OF SYSTEM**
MRP-DRP	1970s	Internal/managing inventory	Inventory planning, inventory control, and distribution efficiencies
EDI	1980s	External	Electronic transmission of purchase orders
ERP	1990s	Internal	Integration of all business functions for processing and reporting
SRM and CRM	2000s	External	Managing and controlling the interface between buyers, suppliers, and customers
Collaboration	2000s	External-internal	CPFR systems permit constant communication within the supply chain via RFID and point of sale systems
Advanced Sourcing Analytics & Social Networking	2010 and beyond	External-internal	Sourcing analytics and computerized negotiations Social Networks help build relationships

accounting and financial areas. However, beginning in the 1970s, more IT resources and software solutions were allocated to purchasing, operations, and distribution. Organizations installed systems such as material requirements planning (MRP) and distribution requirements planning (DRP). These systems were used to improve the planning and control of inventory in manufacturing (MRP) and distribution (DRP).

Because MRP and DRP systems were primarily internal, an electronic linkage to suppliers and customers was needed. Led by efforts of the railroad and retail sectors, electronic data interchange (EDI) was developed as a solution to electronically transfer customer and supplier information in the late 1980s and early 1990s. Though EDI is now mostly web based, it is still used by many large organizations.

Although these early efforts provided efficiencies in the supply chain, intense competition in the final two decades of the twentieth century forced firms to reengineer their business processes to become even leaner. During this period, almost every major Fortune 500 company went through some form of restructuring, as thousands of workers and managers were shed in an effort to increase productivity and reduce costs. In conjunction with this change, organizations further increased their information systems to perform tasks previously done by these workers. Thus enterprise resource planning (ERP) systems became the rage of the late 1990s, and they continue today. The goal of ERP systems is to integrate all business function planning and processing, and to avoid data interruption to make better business decisions and run the business more effectively and efficiently. Ideally, all the different functions in the organization have access to and are working with the same data. Supply managers were at the center of this trend and were challenged to develop accurate databases to improve their decision making.

The next era in electronic commerce was the development of web-based systems on the Internet. ERP systems were primarily internal and lacked the linkage to suppliers and customers. The Internet provided the bridge, and because of its low cost, software providers developed systems that could link customers and suppliers into the ERP system. These e-Sourcing suites are often termed "supplier relationship management (SRM)." On the marketing side they are termed "customer relationship management (CRM)" systems.

Today, software solutions are aimed at collaboration among supply chain partners through point of sale systems, RFID, and other information-sharing systems. Other applications that assist supply management include, product life cycle software, bid optimization, and computerized negotiation models. These increasingly powerful tools will be linked to an e-mobile environment with smaller laptop computers, mobile devices (e.g., Apple's iPad and Microsoft's Surface 2), and increasingly powerful cell phones (e.g., Apple's iPhone, and Samsung's Android), allowing supply managers to have data access on a 24/7 basis irrespective of geographic location. Social networking, blogs, and cloud computing further increase information visibility and can improve both relationships and efficiencies in the buyer-seller process. Finally, managing all this data is a challenge as firms struggle with how to manage this "big data" proliferation.

An Overview of the E-Supply Chain[1]

In this section we present an overview of the e-supply chain that characterizes some of this fast-changing marketplace. Although the players in this industry have changed and will continue to change over time, the areas of functionality and linkages will not.

Supply Chain Information Flows

Supply chain information flows (and the information systems that embody them) serve six major functions:

- Record and retrieve critical data
- Execute and control physical and monetary flows
- Automate routine decisions
- Support planning activities
- Support higher-level tactical and strategic decision making
- Move and share information across firms and among users

Levels of Functionality

Note from the list above how information flows cover everything from relatively low-level functionality (record and retrieve data) to sophisticated analytical support tools. In addition, some of these information flows take place with little or no human intervention, whereas others provide more of a support role to higher-level planning and decision making.

At the most basic level, information flows record and retrieve critical data, then execute and control physical and monetary flows. This is sometimes referred to as **transaction processing**. For example, your credit card company has a record that includes your address, credit limit, payment history, and most recent balance. As time goes on and you pay (or do not pay!) your monthly bills, these records are updated automatically. Another example of transaction processing would be a bar code system to track the actual location of a package in the distribution network.

At a somewhat higher level of functionality, information systems are often used to support **routine decision making**. In many cases, these decisions are automated, with exceptions dealt with manually. Suppose, for example, you are a retailer with 60,000 items to manage. Do you want to manually forecast, calculate the correct order quantities, establish reorder points for all these items, and kick off an order when needed? Of course not. In cases like this, companies often depend on automated inventory management systems to make the decisions for them. Of course, companies can always override the information system's decisions when the situation warrants.

Beyond these transactions and routine decisions, information systems also play a critical role in supply chain planning and strategic decision making in sourcing and supply. As an example of the former, a company will decide on the technologies that may be required for the next generation of products or services, and identify the requirements in terms of the supply base, forecasted demand, production decisions, and projected cash flows. The strategic planning systems can provide critical information and provide it in a way that is meaningful to marketing, operations, purchasing, and finance personnel.

In such cases, information systems can support **strategic decision making** Here, sophisticated analytical tools are often used to search for patterns or relationships in the data. Examples include customer segment analysis, product life cycle forecasting, and what-if analyses regarding long-term product or capacity decisions. These information systems have to be highly flexible in how they manipulate and present the data because the strategic question of interest may change from one situation to the next. Such information systems are generally referred to as **decision support systems (DSSs)**. The name emphasizes the fact that these systems support, but do not *make,* the decision.

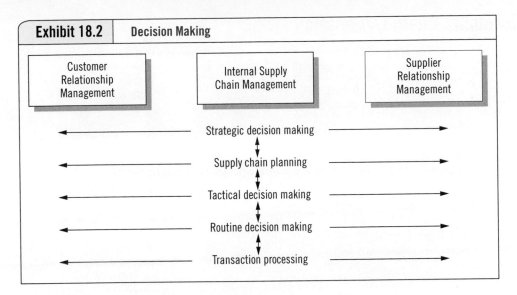

Exhibit 18.2 | Decision Making

Customer Relationship Management

Internal Supply Chain Management

Supplier Relationship Management

Strategic decision making

Supply chain planning

Tactical decision making

Routine decision making

Transaction processing

Directions of Information Linkages

To fully understand the role of information flows in a supply chain, we have to consider not only the level of functionality, but also the direction of the linkages. For example, there are information flows that link a firm with its customers, broadly referred to as customer relationship management flows, and those that link a firm with its suppliers, known as supplier relationship management flows (Exhibit 18.2). There are also flows that link higher-level planning and decision making with lower-level activities within the firm. Chopra and Meindl have termed this "internal supply management"[2] Later we will describe some of the specific IS applications found in the CRM and SRM areas.

A Map of SCM Systems

The map of SCM systems was first laid out in 1999 by Steven Kahl,[3] then a software industry analyst at Piper Jaffray. Kahl's map was later refined by Chopra and Meindl.[4] These authors applied the labels "customer relationship management," "supplier relationship management," and "internal supply chain management" to various areas of the map.

Our map (Exhibit 18.3) distinguishes the various applications by the level of functionality (strategic, planning/tactical, and execution) and the direction of linkages (suppliers, internal supply chain, and customers). We have added an additional column labeled "Logistics." Logistics applications deal with warehousing and transportation issues, such as determining warehouse locations, optimizing transportation systems, and controlling the movement of materials between supply chain partners. Most businesses do not do a good job of integrating these applications with the other applications. We will return to this point later in the chapter.

Enterprise resource planning systems are large, integrated business transaction processing and reporting systems. The primary advantage of ERP systems is that they pull together all of the classic business functions such as accounting, finance, sales, and operations, to name a few, into a single, tightly integrated package that uses a common database (Exhibit 18.4 on p. 712).

The deal breaker was integration of individual systems. In pre-ERP environments every functional area had its own set of software applications, often running on completely

Exhibit 18.3	SCM Systems

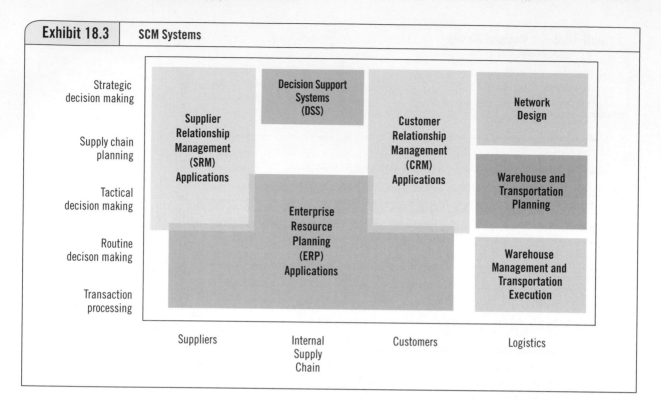

different systems. Sharing information (such as forecasts or customer information) among systems was a nightmare. To make matters worse, the same information often was entered multiple times in different ways.

Sourcing Snapshot

The Top Supply Chain Management Software Providers and Trends

The market for supply chain management software, maintenance and services continued its upward trajectory in 2012, generating $8.3 billion of revenue, including sales of applications for procurement software. This amount represented a 7.1 percent increase over 2011 revenues, according to Chad Eschinger, vice president of supply chain for research firm Gartner.

Taking out procurement, the market generated $5.528 billion, a $333 million jump over 2011 revenues for the group of applications involving supply chain planning and supply chain execution applications such as warehouse management (WMS) and transportation management (TMS).

"We're seeing interest in greater visibility, greater insight into the variability of demand and in satisfying the end customer. Those are all areas where supply chain software plays a pivotal role," Eschinger says. Looking forward, Gartner is predicting a compound annual growth rate (CAGR) for SCM software, excluding procurement, of 9.9 percent for the next five years. The top five software providers in the SCM space for 2012 survey were SAP ($1.721 billion) and Oracle ($1.453 billion). The two market leaders were followed by JDA Software ($426 million) and Manhattan Associates ($160 million). Epicor took the No. 5 spot with $138 million. The Big Three of SAP, Oracle and JDA accounted for 48.5 percent of the total supply chain management software market. It should be noted that the rankings are based on Gartner's estimates of a provider's annual sales for 2012. Gartner's estimates are based on revenues related to supply chain management software excluding vendor-generated services and hardware and not a company's total revenues. Those are the reasons, for example, that Gartner credits Manhattan Associates with $160 million when the company's overall revenues are more than double that amount. The study focuses on supply chain applications in the following areas: (1) ERP and supply chain planning (SCP); (2) warehouse management (WMS); (3); transportation management (TMS); and (4) manufacturing execution (MES) systems. It presents a good picture of the supply chain without procurement.

The list below summarizes the trends Gartner is seeing in the future for SCM software.

The lines between supply chain execution and supply chain planning providers are no longer clearly drawn. ERP providers supply WMS and supply chain execution providers supply planning and optimization solutions.

The number of software providers continues to shrink. According to a Dwight Klappich of Gartner, "Not that long ago, there were at least 75 stand-alone WMS vendors, including RedPrairie and Manhattan Associates." "After the merger, Manhattan is the last, large free-standing WMS vendor."

ERP suppliers are moving into WMS and Supply Chain Execution Applications. "When we look at the numbers, we estimate that SAP, Oracle and Infor (7th place on Gartner list) alone will have more than 50 percent of the market in terms of the numbers of customers," says Klappich. "They will not have the same level of revenues as the best-of-breed providers like Manhattan and RedPrairie, because many of the ERP vendors include WMS as part of a broader deal." Klappich says there are about 250,000 warehouses in North America that can benefit from a WMS system and in 200,000 of these ERP functionality is applicable."

Supply chain collaboration has received increased attention year after year. Now may be its time. "In almost every conversation I had with clients, there was interest in collaboration," Eschinger says. Supply chain software platforms that allow trading partners to share plans and processes will enable this trend.

Sales and Operations Planning applications are growing at 20 percent per year. This is the software application, which ties supply chain activities closely to marketing and sales efforts. The most important trend is the addition of analytics that allow users to create what-if scenarios as part of their planning activities.

Supply Chain Planning software is a growing market especially inventory optimization. This software is growing at roughly 6 percent a year. "Organizations are trying to satisfy their customers and improve service along with simplifying the complexity of their supply chain nodes," says Eschinger.

Growth of the mid-market for Transportation Management Software (TMS): Mid-size shippers are composed of those spending $25 million to $100 million a year on freight. "Software providers are creating solutions for companies that don't have the complexity of someone shipping $200 million a year, but who want to control their freight" says Klappich. The market for transportation management software grew by 14 percent in 2011, posting revenues of about $735 million.

Cloud computing continues to get traction: However, in many instances, it is geographically based. "We're seeing the cloud take off in Latin America," says Eschinger. One reason is that emerging markets don't already have a legacy of on-premises installations to deal with.

Growing interest in the cloud and software-as-a-service (SaaS): As noted by Eschinger, there is interest in cloud applications across the SCM landscape. WMS is no different. The factor holding back deployments has been a concern about whether the performance of the systems would be affected by the cloud. Those concerns appear not to be as serious as once thought.

Supply chain execution convergence versus independent processes: Too often, companies optimize their processes within silos, such as the warehouse or transportation department. Instead, the real savings come from orchestrating those processes in a way that optimizes them across silos. "We're not there yet, but over the next five or so years, we believe you'll be able to optimize warehousing and transportation as one end-to-end process," states Klappich.

Source: Bob Trebilcock, Executive Editor, Summarized from "Top 20 SCM Software Suppliers, 2013" Modern Material Handling July 1, 2013.

As Exhibit 18.4 suggests, ERP's traditional strengths lie in routine decision making and transaction processing. ERP systems collect raw data needed to support higher-level planning and strategic decision making, with a focus primarily on internal operations.

SRM and CRM applications, in contrast, are directly focused on planning and managing the firm's external linkages. Exhibit 18.5 shows how Chopra and Meindl give examples of the types of functionality provided by these applications.

Currently, vendors specializing in CRM and SRM tend to provide higher levels of functionality in their chosen areas than do the ERP vendors. As a result, many firms choose a standard ERP package for routine decision making and transaction processing, and use bolt-on CRM and SRM applications to manage external relationships.

However, this situation is changing as the major ERP vendors, such as SAP and Oracle, look for ways to increase the CRM and SRM functionality of their own systems. Whether the specialized CRM and SRM vendors can maintain enough of a functionality lead to justify a separate system remains to be seen.

The last set of supply chain IS applications we will discuss are those dealing directly with logistics decisions. These applications can be divided into three main categories: network design applications, transportation and warehouse planning systems, and execution systems.

Network design applications address such long-term, strategic questions as where should we locate warehouses, and how large should our transportation fleet be? These applications often make use of simulation and optimization modeling.

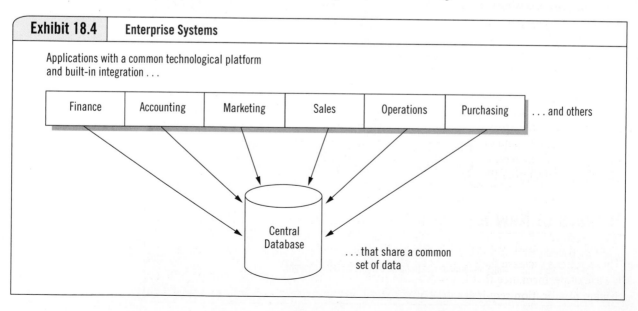

Exhibit 18.4	**Enterprise Systems**

Applications with a common technological platform and built-in integration . . .

| Finance | Accounting | Marketing | Sales | Operations | Purchasing | . . . and others |

Central
Database

. . . that share a common set of data

Exhibit 18.5	SRM/CRM Applications	

SRM APPLICATIONS	CRM APPLICATIONS
Design collaboration	Market analysis
Sourcing decisions	Sell process
Negotiations	Order management
Buy process	Call/service center management
Supply collaboration	

Transportation and warehouse planning systems attempt to allocate fixed logistics capacity in the best possible way, given business requirements. For example, such a system could help you decide how many units to ship from each warehouse to each demand point. To find the optimal answer, the system would allow you to build an optimization model that used data on warehouse capacities, demand levels, and shipping costs to generate the lowest-cost solution.

Execution systems kick off and control the movement of materials among supply chain partners. Within a warehouse, for example, sophisticated execution systems tell workers where to store items, where to go to pick them up, and how many to pick. Similarly, bar code systems and global positioning systems have dramatically changed the ability of businesses to manage actual movements in the distribution system. This enables trucking firms can tell their customers the exact location of a shipment and the arrival time within hours, if not minutes.

As important as these logistics applications are, the level of integration between these applications and those in the other areas of the map can be improved. For example, many supply chain decisions, such as when to order materials and when to ship customer orders, are often made without considering the impact on logistics. Let us look at the experiences of one firm.

Buyers were ordering materials from suppliers whenever they needed them, without considering the shipping costs. The result was many small, expensive shipments. Although inventory costs were low, transportation costs were out of control. The company determined that by releasing a batch of orders over several days, they could place bigger orders with the suppliers. The suppliers, in turn, could make larger shipments. As a result of these actions shipping costs were cut by nearly 70 percent. An unexpected benefit was that the firm also had fewer invoices to deal with, because the supplier would send one invoice with each shipment, whether there were 10 items or 100 items listed.

Increasing the level of integration between logistics and other SCM applications presents firms with both technical and organizational hurdles. On the technical side, efforts to integrate decisions across sales, operations, and distribution increase the complexity of the optimization and simulation models currently used by logistics managers. On the organizational side, firms have to get used to involving logistics personnel earlier in the decision-making process, rather than just calling on them when it is time to make a shipment.

Drivers of New Supply Chain Systems and Applications

Facing increased cost pressure, organizations rely more on systems to replace people. These actions increase the productivity of the remaining workers. Productivity is a critical metric of performance that is driving companies to integrate new information systems. System justification requires developing a solid business case and justifying the benefits and payback of investments. The primary drivers of e-SCM systems include: (1) internal and external integration, (2) globalization and communications, (3) data information management, (4) new business processes, (5) replacement of legacy or obsolete systems, and (6) strategic cost management.

Internal and External Strategic Integration

As supply chain members increasingly work together, integration is required between internal functions (purchasing, engineering, manufacturing, marketing, logistics, accounting, and so on) and external stakeholders (end customers, third-party logistics firms, retailers, distributors, warehouses, transportation providers, suppliers, agents, financial institutions, and so on). Internal strategic integration through an ERP system provides a single integrated master record across business sites and functions. External integration is needed to forecast demand and balance the levels of supply and demand at different points in the supply chain. Systems used to integrate external supply chain members include Internet linkages, network communications, and e-sourcing applications.

Globalization and Communication

Although the notion of a global market is easy to envision, carrying out business in different cultures and geographies is an extremely challenging proposition. Companies require systems that enable them to manage suppliers and customers in all corners of the world, calculate total global logistics costs, increase leverage and component standardization worldwide, and improve communication of strategies across global business units and supply chain partners.

Data Information Management

New forms of servers, telecommunication and wireless applications, and software are enabling companies to do things that were once thought impossible. These systems raise the accuracy, frequency, and speed of communication between suppliers and customers, as well as for internal users. Information systems must be able to effectively filter, analyze, and mine an abundance of data to enable effective decision making. Users must be able to extract from databases the information they need to make better supply chain decisions. This is often achieved through data warehouse systems (described later in the chapter) and associated decision support systems.

New Business Processes

Business processes are constantly being changed in response to a rapidly shifting external environment. Such processes—which include supplier evaluation and selection, negotiation, contracting, co-design efforts, and inventory management—are being mapped, studied, and changed to reduce redundancies, delays, and waste. In so doing, organizations can create a rapid response capability that allows them to quickly adapt to their customers' changing needs and control costs whenever possible. Linking SRM, ERP, and CRM enables companies to coordinate and manage these processes more effectively.

Replacement of Legacy Systems

Historically companies adopted a piecemeal approach to system usage, such that each function (accounting, purchasing, and engineering) used its own stand-alone system.

These obsolete systems (often called **legacy systems**) have now been integrated into a single ERP system used by everyone in the supply chain. Newer systems are being adopted to exploit the new hardware technologies in the areas of computer networking, telecommunications, Web 2.0, and cloud-based applications.

Strategic Cost Management

Throughout the complete supply chain cycle, from order fulfillment back to purchasing and order payment, millions of transactions take place between different parties. In the past, these transactions were all done on paper. Systems have the ability to automate data captured across the supply chain and automate the transactions in the traditional procurement cycle. Not only will this reduce the administrative costs of operating purchasing and logistics departments, but it will also result in reductions of inventory held in warehouses and stockrooms throughout the entire supply chain.

In the remainder of the chapter, we discuss ERP systems, purchasing databases, data warehouses, electronic data interchange (EDI) and e-sourcing suites. We conclude with a discussion of SCM information visibility through social networking, blogs, and cloud computing. This chapter provides an introduction to the above topics, with the understanding that continual learning and evolution of user needs in these systems is required.

Internal Information Systems—Enterprise Resource Planning (ERP)

The ERP system is an integrated transaction processing and reporting system. The different software applications and forms of ERP support the reengineering of business processes. Expressed in simpler terms, **ERP systems** provide the means for tracking organizational resources, including people, processes, and technology. The system serves as the backbone to the organization in terms of providing the information and support required for making decisions.

ERP systems add a process logic to an organizational information system and create a fundamental discipline in business processes. Whereas in the past managers and staff were free to make decisions independent of other functional areas, ERP systems effectively force people to interact together in a single system, even if they would prefer not to. As shown in Exhibit 18.6, ERP systems also create a process logic among the closely related areas of customer order management, manufacturing planning and execution, purchasing processes, and financial management and accounting.

In effect, ERP systems enable employees in these very different parts of the business to communicate with one another. In an ideal case of moving information across the supply chain, sales representatives enter customer orders directly into their company's ERP via a laptop computer desktop computer or mobile device. The sales reps can access the sales order planning and master production schedule. Once the orders are input in the system, the sales reps can provide an available-to-promise report and can inform customers when they can expect order delivery. The master production schedule drives the material requirements system, which automatically generates purchase orders. This ensures that suppliers will deliver parts, components, and services in time to meet the customer's order request.

The material requirements planning (MRP) module converts material requirements into purchase requisitions that purchasing places with selected suppliers. When the supplier delivers the components, this information is passed through to the scheduling system,

Exhibit 18.6	**Enterprise Resource Planning Systems**

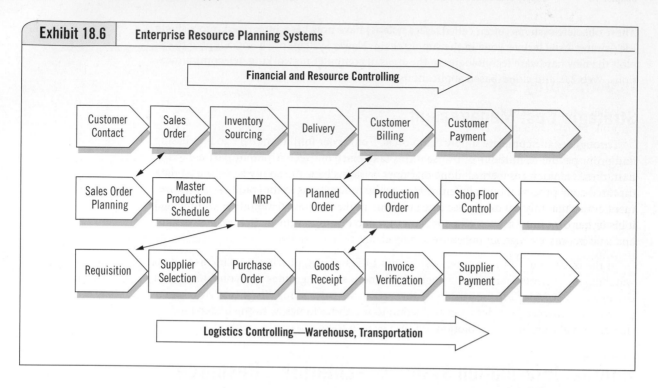

which ensures that the components are linked to the specific production order on the shop floor. Once production begins, the salesperson in the field also knows that the order will soon be delivered to the customer. Once delivered, customer billing and payment are also automatically generated by the ERP system.

A typical ERP system is designed around four primary business processes (see Exhibit 18.6):

1. Selling a product or service. Customer order management process
2. Making a product. Production planning and execution process
3. Buying a product. Procurement process
4. Costing, paying the bills, collecting. Financial/management accounting and reporting process (integrated across the prior three processes)

ERP systems facilitate the integration of these processes by adopting a single customer, product, and supplier database. One master record is used for the enterprise with multiple views. All processes use a common database, and information is captured only once, essentially eliminating the possibility of inaccurate data entering the database. Information is rolled down to the affected business process in real time, eliminating delays of information sharing. Visibility of specific transactions taking place in each business process is accessible to everyone in the organization; theoretically, anyone wanting to find out information, such as where an order is in the process or whether a supplier has been paid, can obtain the latest updates by going through the system (instead of making phone calls). In addition, all business processes are linked with the work flow through the use of templates for entering information about transactions at every step.

The actual process of implementing a new ERP system in an environment where people have grown accustomed to using their single, familiar legacy system has proved to be a monumental task in many organizations. Many implementation efforts have turned into multimillion-dollar projects involving consultants residing on-site for months and even years. Why is the task of ERP implementation proving to be so difficult and expensive?

Implementing ERP Systems

When businesses implement an ERP system, they must by definition adhere to a more rigorous set of business processes. Chapter 12 discusses process mapping as a tool to identify exactly what happens within any given business process. Before organizations actually implement ERP, they must first create a process map for every process shown in Exhibit 18.6. When companies map what they believe a process looks like, they discover that the actual process is quite different from what they thought it would look like. In some cases, no formal process exists, because everyone in the functional organization has done it his or her own unique way. When it comes time to create an information system around business processes, many companies discover that they must also reengineer or change their business processes before they can build an information system around them. In some cases, changing these business processes requires a major organizational and cultural shift. Although ERP consultants can effectively create a system around a well-defined business process, they cannot create a system around a business process that has not been well defined or explained to them by employees.

To effectively implement an ERP system, a company must go through four steps to ensure that the business processes are effectively reengineered and improved:

1. Define the current process "*as is.*" An ERP implementation team of subject-matter experts (SMEs) document what the current process looks like.

2. Define what the best-in-class business process "*should be.*" At this point, the team must have a clear understanding of what the final objective of the process is. Further, they must understand what the ERP system will replace and how the benefits are likely to occur.

3. Develop the system. This is an iterative process in which SMEs work in conjunction with those managers who are most familiar with the business processes in question.

4. Work through all final bugs and then flip the switch. A danger that often exists when flipping the switch—switching over from the old system to the new system—is that the company may not be ready for the change, or the system may not be completely configured to handle the specific activities that keep the business running.

The Sourcing Snapshot: A Consultant's Views on Navigating ERP Implementations provides a detailed implementation strategy from the perspective of one ERP consulting firm. The seven-stage process provides the basis for implementing these complex systems.

Sourcing Snapshot

A Consultant's Views on Navigating ERP Implementations

Abide Consulting, a Florida-based consulting firm, has worked with several organizations to assist in the transition from disparate legacy-based systems to an integrated ERP system. Currently, Abide is working with a consumer products organization to coordinate the worldwide implementation of an ERP system. What follows is a detailed look at one strategy for ERP implementation.

Exhibit 18.7	**ERP Implementation Life Cycle**

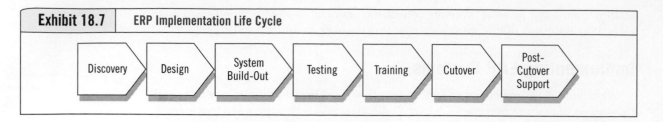

The typical life cycle of an ERP implementation utilizes a seven-stage process. The cycle involves the following phases: (1) discovery, (2) design, (3) system build-out, (4) testing, (5) end-user training, (6) cutover, and (7) post-cutover support. The stages are shown in Exhibit 18.7. In the discovery phase, a core team is assembled, consisting of both internal and external subject-matter experts. Teams are typically grouped into work streams of the functional areas being implemented in the ERP system (e.g., operations, inventory management, finance, sourcing). Training sessions familiarize the team with the: (1) strategic objectives of the project, (2) timelines for implementation, (3) project organization and process, and (4) functionality of the new software. The team then begins a detailed analysis and review of the existing business processes.

On larger, more complex ERP implementations, it is also recommended that significant attention be focused on the data that support the ERP systems. Data integrity (consistency of data within or across systems) and data quality (accuracy and completeness of data) are critical components of an ERP implementation and can often be overlooked. For example, at a previous client, it was discovered the first day live on the new ERP system that the weight data for the finished product were inaccurate and in many cases missing altogether. Thus, correct weights for shipping manifests could not be calculated. The situation brought outbound shipping to a standstill. Trucks and product sat idle in the shipping docks for days until the issue was resolved.

In the *design phase*, the new processes "to be" required to support the ERP system are developed and process flow maps are created. Any process requiring IT involvement is documented in a functional specification. These include reports, integrations, conversions, and enhancements (RICE) elements. Next a *fit/gap analysis* is conducted, which involves isolating the specific differences between the existing system(s) and the new ERP design. Finally, once the core team has identified and resolved the fit/gaps, it is able to define and document the detailed ERP process solution required for the business.

The third step is the *system build-out phase*. In this phase, the IT team begins to take a larger role in the implementation. The ERP system is configured with functional parameters and customized business data (e.g., company branch plants, financial chart of accounts, and purchase orders). The IT team completes the initial development of the RICE elements that were defined in the design phase.

Following build-out is the *testing phase*, which involves several iterations of testing business processes and RICE elements associated with the new ERP system. Unit testing and quality assurance (QA) testing involve executing scripts isolated to a specific business process or RICE element. If the tests are successful, then an integrated quality assurance (QA) check is performed. The QA involves executing end-to-end scripts across business processes and work streams. For example, one script would involve the process of moving from the planning of the product to actually making it, and a second major process would go from making the product to delivering it. Finally, key users of the system are given access to test their business processes in the new system. This is referred to as User Acceptance Testing (UAT). Key users involve many functional departments along the supply chain, including sourcing, inventory control, production planning, and customer service.

The *end-user training phase* can be performed exclusively by outside consultants, using both consultants and internal personnel, or totally internally within the organization. The deciding factor for the specific training method is the extent of ERP implementations at other business units and whether there are internal personnel willing to conduct the training. Oftentimes, to bridge this gap, consultants will perform a train-the-trainers program to initialize the training and build a cadre of trainers within the organization.

During the *cutover phase*, the organization begins to take greater ownership of the ERP system. Throughout the implementation, the organization must have internal champions, who are experts that have the backing of top management to drive the implementation. As with any other change initiative, ERP involves changing people's behavior, and ensuring such behavioral change occurs most often where there is strong top management support. In the cutover phase, both customers and suppliers are contacted to ensure that any and all outstanding issues have been addressed. All too often, unplanned issues surface internally or at the supplier and customer end immediately after the cutover. Precautionary steps can be taken well in advance of the actual cutover to limit risk to business processes. Suppliers, customers, and business partners are notified of the activity to prepare them for any issues or changes. Safety stocks of components and ingredients can be increased. Additionally, some organizations choose to initially pre-build finished stock, by ramping up production in excess of normal demand. This buildup mitigates unplanned surprises such as those created by poor data integrity or other system problems.

The last phase of ERP implementation *is post-cutover support*. During this phase the core implementation team resolves post-implementation problems and software failures, and conducts process upgrades. It is important that the organization discuss the expected role of the consultants and the software provider in the post-cutover phase during contract negotiations.

In summary, successful ERP implementation is a journey, not a destination. There are several key issues that will enhance the experience of the journey and reduce both costs and risks. These include the following:

- Develop a good understanding of the existing business process.
- Develop improved future business process designs.
- Identify inconsistencies and poor quality in existing data.
- Ensure that business processes conform to ERP system parameters.
- Insist that users replace redundant legacy systems.
- Stagger implementations of ERP systems across regions and business locations.
- Schedule cutover during off-peak seasons.
- Determine how much additional safety stock is necessary.
- Develop and train a core team of internal personnel as resources.
- Execute rigorous and structured testing cycles.

Source: Interview with Matthew Giunipero, President, Abide Consulting, and Karina Jarzec, Vice President Sales, Operations, and Planning, January 2014 and July 2010.

Purchasing Databases and Data Warehouses

A prerequisite needed before introducing any type of ERP system that manipulates data is the development of a reliable **database**—an integrated collection of computer files capable of storing operational data essential for managing a department.

Databases are highly efficient in the storage and retrieval of data because there is minimal overlapping of information among the files. Reduced redundancy of information among files allows different systems to cross-reference and efficiently use the data contained in all files.[5] ERP systems are allowing more users from functional groups other than purchasing to access these files.

Although definitions vary, a **data warehouse** is generally thought of as a decision support tool for collecting information from multiple sources and making that information available to end-users in a consolidated, consistent manner. Rather than trying to develop one unified system or linking all systems in terms of processing, a data warehouse provides the means to combine the data in one place and make it available to all of the systems.

In most cases, a data warehouse is a consolidated database maintained separately from an organization's production system databases. Many organizations have multiple databases, often containing duplicate data. A data warehouse, in theory, is organized around *informational subjects* rather than specific business processes. The data warehouse stores, in a format that is readily accessible by end-users, data fed to it from multiple production databases. Data held in data warehouses are time-dependent, historical data; they may also be aggregated. For example, separate production systems may track sales and coupon mailings. Combining data from these different systems may yield insights into the effectiveness of coupon sales promotions that would not be immediately evident from the output data of either system alone. Integrated within a data warehouse, however, such information could easily be extracted.

Purchasing processes require a variety of information maintained on different databases, which make data warehouses very useful. The purchasing system must be able to pull data from and store data into the host data file. If a proposed purchasing system requires nonexistent data, then a new database must collect and store the information.

A basic purchasing system requires, at a minimum, access to a number of databases or files. A file may be a collection of specific data, sorted in alphanumeric order or by criteria chosen by the user. Examples of some of these files include the following:

- *Part file.* Records the part numbers or stock keeping units (SKUs) that all firms rely on to identify the thousands of unique purchased entities within a system. The actual content of the part file is a function of a firm's specific informational requirements. The time required to capture information on part numbers and enter them into a database can be significant.

- *Supplier name and address file.* Contains the names and addresses (including e-mail addresses) of every supplier with which a firm does business.

- *Historical usage file.* Stores historical usage by part number and using location. This information supports inventory analysis and updating of material forecasts with actual historical data.

- *Open-order and past-due file.* Maintains the status of open material releases and stores an order as pending until a firm physically receives the scheduled release. Any orders not received by their due date become past due. This file provides data that a buyer or material planner requires to maintain visibility and control of the material pipeline.

- *Bill of material file.* Details the component requirements of a part number. It is an integral part of the material requirements planning system. If the material system generates a release for an end-item or subassembly part number, then the system must also generate releases for all components as well. This file also provides visibility about sourcing requirements for new parts with components.

- *Engineering requirements file.* Provides visibility to the specific engineering requirements and specifications for a part number. May also include updates or engineering change orders detailing changes to specific SKUs or requirements over time.

- *Forecasted demand file.* Calculates anticipated demand requirements for each part number in the part file. It relies on the historical usage file to update and calculate projected future requirements.

These databases support the development of both basic and sophisticated purchasing and material information systems. Although purchasing is not responsible for directly maintaining all of the data on these files, it must have access to the data to support its operating requirements.

Electronic Data Interchange (EDI)—Pioneering External Electronic Communication

Up until now, we have discussed elements of purchasing information and data flows that reside primarily within the enterprise. An early approach to facilitating transactions electronically with suppliers was electronic data interchange (EDI)—a communications standard that supports inter-organizational electronic exchange of common business documents and information. EDI was implemented in the 1980s, and represented a cooperative effort between buyers and sellers to become more competitive by streamlining the communication process through eliminating many of the steps involved in traditional inter-organizational information flows. The basic components of an EDI system include the following:

1. *A standard form (EDI standards).* Includes the basic rules of formatting and syntax agreed upon by the users in the network. The American National Standards Institute ACS X12 series of EDI standards was one of the first adopted by many companies.

2. *A translation capability (EDI software).* Translates the company-specific database information into EDI standard format for transmission.

3. *A mail service (EDI network).* Responsible for the transmission of the document, usually in the form of a direct network or through a third-party provider. Such a value-added network (VAN) serves as an intermediary post office for the systems.

The Electronic Order Process

Electronically transmitted purchase orders in either web-based or EDI formats follow a similar process that is described below:

1. The computer in the buying company monitors the real-time inventory status of the item purchased using technologies such as bar code scanners.

2. When it is determined, according to a predefined reorder criterion, that there is a need to order more of the item, the application program notifies the translation software.

3. An electronic purchase order is created and released against a prenegotiated blanket amount, and the purchase order is sent to the supplier.

4. The supplier's computer receives the order, and the software translates the order into the supplier's format.

5. A functional acknowledgment, which indicates receipt of the order is automatically generated and transmitted back to the buyer.

6. When the original electronic purchase order is created, a number of additional electronic transactions may occur. Bridging software transmits the relevant data to the buyer's accounts payable application, to the buyer's receiving file, to the supplier's warehouse or factory file, and to the supplier's invoicing file.

7. Once the order is filled from the supplier's warehouse or factory, a shipping notice is created and transmitted to the buyer. This shipping notice may require some manual data entry by the shipper. However, this is the first time that any manual keystrokes are required in the entire process.

8. Upon receipt of the goods, a shipping notice is electronically entered into the receiving file. Although additional keying may be required, technology often eliminates this step as well.

9. The receipt notice is transmitted through bridging software to the accounts payable application and to the supplier's invoicing application, whereupon an invoice is electronically generated and transmitted to the buyer.

10. Once the invoice is received by the buyer's computer, it is translated into the buyer's format; then the invoice, receiving notice, and purchase order are electronically reconciled (eliminating the need for an accounting audit).

11. A payment authorization is electronically created and transmitted to accounts payable, the receivables application is updated to indicate an open receivable, and payment is transmitted electronically from the buyer's bank to the supplier's bank.

12. An electronic remittance advice is transmitted to the supplier, and upon receipt, this information is translated into accounts receivable and the buyer is given credit for payment.

Within this process, there are only three instances of manual data entry. In traditional information flows, each step would require that paperwork be completed and filed by clerical staff. Electronically generated purchase orders save money in two categories. First, administrative savings are realized through the elimination of paperwork, lower error rates, faster transmission to suppliers, and lower clerical costs. Second, productivity is enhanced, as the buyer spends less time on clerical work. The time savings can be used to pursue more innovative and value adding activities such as building supplier relationships and contributing to cost savings.

EDI and the Internet

EDI is a technology that required significant investment by companies to implement. EDI required investment in application-specific hardware that could not be used for other purposes. Smaller suppliers in particular found it difficult to justify the investment in EDI technology and struggled with the demands placed on them from different companies to adopt differing EDI systems. Finally, EDI was never considered an interactive mode of communication. Each time a transmission was sent, it implied that a decision had been made: an order for a fixed amount placed, a forecast of future demand fixed, a lead time for delivery specified. There was never any means for the buying and supplying parties to actually interact, collaborate, and reach a decision through joint, bilateral communication.

The evolution of Web-based EDI provides numerous benefits over traditional hardwired EDI. First it is much less expensive than a traditional EDI and presents fewer standards issues. On the other hand it typically requires that all parties use a common platform (e.g., common ERP systems). EDI continues to be used by many firms today. For example, RailInc.com is a software provider that supports railroads, equipment owners, and rail industry suppliers along every link of the supply chain. It delivers more than nine million messages each day over its EDI network, including transportation waybills, advance lists of cars making up a train, requests and responses to grouping blocks of cars and rail trip plans.[6] Though EDI is still popular, the increased sophistication of web-based service providers make e-Sourcing an alternative for supply managers to communicate electronically with suppliers.

E-Sourcing Basics

Since EDI required an investment and administration, it was often initially limited to large companies. The advent of Internet-based EDI extended the reach to mid-sized firms. However, the evolution of web-based e-sourcing models trumped EDI in many organizations, especially those communicating electronically for the first time. It was comparable to someone who adopted a cell phone and never owned a traditional land line phone. Many e-sourcing providers have appeared and disappeared in the past decade. This turnover makes it critical that supply managers perform due diligence on these firms prior to committing resources. The good news is that there is an abundance of viable firms who provide e-sourcing tools that can add value to the process. We will now discuss the basic models then move into the e-sourcing suites and the components of those suites.

E-Sourcing Models—The External Information Systems

There are basically two major types of e-sourcing business models: (1) sell-side systems, (2) buy-side systems, and (3) third-party marketplaces. A brief explanation of each is presented in the following paragraphs.

Sell-side systems contain the products or services of one or more suppliers. Registration on sell-side sites is usually free, and the supplier guarantees the security of the site.[7] Most suppliers today have a web presence, and many offer the ability to place orders on their sites. Sell-side systems have the advantages of no investment by the buyer, ease of access, and the availability of many suppliers. Drawbacks include the inability to track or control spending by the buying organization and varying degrees of security.[8] A much-used sell-side site in the MRO area is www.grainger.com. Many of the sell-side systems offer "**punchouts**." A punchout is one of several names given to the technical "protocols" or "routines" that allow the selling firm to directly connect its product catalogs to the buyer's e-procurement systems.

Buy-side systems are controlled by buyers and are tied into their intranets and extra-nets. These buy-side systems can be self-developed or acquired through third-party software providers of e-sourcing suites.[9] Buy-side systems allow the supply manager to manage the sourcing cycle, track spend, and exert control over contract management, in a secure environment. They do require an investment by the buying organization and need periodic updating as well as training for users. They are the dominant form of e-sourcing systems used by organizations today.

Third-party marketplaces are independent firms that neither buy nor sell goods but seek to facilitate the electronic purchasing process through value enhancement. These organizations proliferated during the dot com boom era of 1999–2001. Essentially, they sought to be an electronic marketplace for the needs of organizational purchasers. Their idea was to bring buyers and sellers together in cyberspace the way Amazon.com did in the consumer world. One group specialized in a commodity such as chemicals or steel; they were termed **vertical portals**. The other group provided a broad category of services, for example, office supplies or MRO items; they were called **horizontal portals**. Though a few of these portals remain, their value has faded as traditional business firms developed a web presence through sell-side sites (e.g., Grainger.com, officedepot.com, and mcmastercarr.com).

E-Sourcing Suites—General

E-tools used by purchasers can be used to communicate within and outside the organization. As we have studied in previous chapters, a major goal of purchasing is to communicate effectively with external suppliers to be able to source items; share information, forecasts, and updates; make payments; and so on. Traditional information flows between buyers and suppliers often necessitate a lengthy sequential process composed of multiple steps required to service as well as fulfill the order. Examples of these information flows include: (1) transmission of the product specifications from buyer to supplier, (2) submission of a bid, (3) acceptance of the contract, (4) inspection and receiving documents associated with the shipment, (5) accounting audits, and (6) submission of payment. Some of the problems that occur within these traditional information flows include increased transaction time, low accuracy because of data-handling errors, high utilization of staff time and resources, and increased uncertainty in the form of both mailing and processing delays.

E-sourcing tools are defined as a set of tools employed by supply managers to streamline processes and leverage technology to meet the needs of the organization.[10] **Supplier relationship management software** are e-sourcing tools that allow the purchaser to manage the external linkage with suppliers. Although earlier versions of e-sourcing tools were directed more toward process efficiencies (streamlining the purchase order process), SRM tools are focused on managing the entire purchasing cycle from recognition of need through contract management and supplier evaluation. A discussion of these SRM tools will be covered followed by a discussion of basic e-sourcing tools.

E-Sourcing Suites—Supplier Relationship Management (SRM)

SRM systems are typically organized around specific E-Sourcing Suite modules that interact with different elements of the purchasing database, elements of the enterprise resource system, and integration of data obtained through external EDI or web-based communications with suppliers or customers. Although ERP systems such as SAP and Oracle generally manage the internal transactions that take place in processing invoices and purchase orders (as described in Chapter 2), e-sourcing systems are focused on decision support around a broader group of transactions that are specific to certain business processes.

SRM systems have capabilities to allow purchasers to make improved decisions. Decision support systems use both data and structured mathematical models to support the decision-making process. A set of SRM sourcing modules act as an interactive system designed to support purchasing managers in making effective decisions concerning supplier selection, contract management, contract compliance, and so on.

This section describes some typical characteristics of SRM driven e-sourcing suites, which may nevertheless be used by all functions in the organization. Exhibit 18.8 shows our classification of the primary components of SRM e-sourcing suites. Various software providers will title these components differently and even combine some into a single module. We now proceed to discuss each of the components shown of E-Sourcing Suites shown in Exhibit 18.8.

Spend Analysis

Spend analysis is the determination of the dollar amount and volume of expenditures that an organization makes to provide its products and services and support its operations. The goal of spend analysis is to determine what goods and services are purchased, what

Exhibit 18.8	"E-Sourcing Suites"

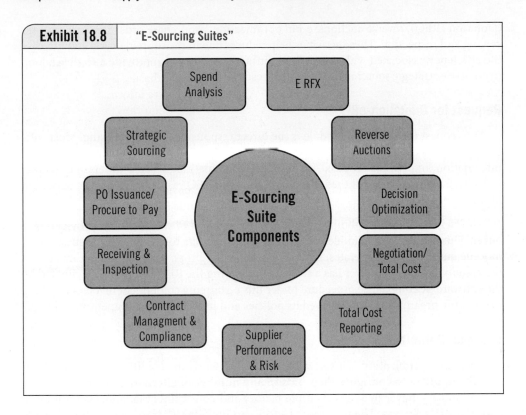

suppliers they are purchased from, and where the demand for the items originates in the organization. Once a baseline of spending is established, the organization can effectively look at opportunities to reduce spending. Such spending reduction occurs through multiple strategies such as (1) consolidation of similar purchases; (2) reduction in the number of suppliers; (3) reduction of maverick spend; (4) reduction of spend not directly managed by purchasing such as human resources, marketing, and finance; (5) increased use of more efficient contracting methods; and (6) the development of contracting methods to reduce risk and increase supply assurance.

Spend analysis data is usually derived from a combination of existing purchase orders, accounts payables and supplier records. Typically, organizations (1) collect at least one year of spend data, (2) develop similar categories of spend, (3) assign spend to the categories, and (4) develop various strategies. Once collected, these data are entered into the spend analysis module and can be analyzed in an unlimited number of ways.

A final application for spend analysis is the compliance aspect. Though most applications revolve around identifying savings opportunities, another function is to make sure that the organization is buying within the parameters of the contract. This is to check for off-contract spend where users are not buying the items specified in the contract, but ordering another brand or item, which hurts contract volume and usually costs more. A second compliance issue involves checking to see if suppliers are billing at contract rates.

Sourcing

When combined with spend analytics platforms this software allows the purchaser to construct a strategic sourcing plan driven by data analysis. Once this strategic plan is constructed the sourcing module provides the implementation vehicle for the plan. Sourcing modules usually contain several phases of the sourcing process, including the request for quotation (RFQ), reverse auctions, e-bid optimization, e-purchase order issuance, and receiving and inspection. These activities help reduce time in the sourcing cycle and increase the efficiency associated with processing transactions. They also provide a feedback loop to compare strategic sourcing plan to actual results.

Request for Quotation-eRFx

The request for quotation module is the direct responsibility of purchasing. Most software providers call this process the eRFx module. The eRFx module includes a request for information, request for proposal, and request for quotation. Because different organizations have alternate uses for these terms, we will use "RFQ" as our term for the quotation module.

An **RFQ** is a request to submit a proposal based on a set of specifications provided by a buyer. This module assists in identifying qualified suppliers to receive RFQ requests. This module automatically generates, issues, and tracks the progress of the RFQs throughout the system. Usually the buyer has a strategy underlying the RFQ that will be facilitated by the software. A compliance procedure under this e-sourcing component involves checking to see if the organization has followed its policies and procedures on competitive bidding.

Decision Optimization

Decision optimization is a software tool that extends the traditional bid process to permit suppliers to configure their bids in any number of alternative ways. Optimization allows the buyer to assess multiple factors and constraints that address both price and non-price factors. The non-price factors can include risk, product quality, internal business rules (e.g., each business unit must have two sources), supplier qualification costs, switching costs etc. Decision optimization enables purchasers to make better supplier award decisions faster, split awards and uncover the real cost impact of sourcing decisions.

This flexible bidding process is often termed **expressive bidding** because suppliers can bid in ways that emphasize their strengths. Traditionally, suppliers have had to quote per the buyer's request or the bid would be ruled nonresponsive. Decision optimization is an advanced sourcing solution that provides a tool for buyers to increase their analytical capabilities in reviewing bids and in realizing more optimal solutions. This software module uses a basic set of mathematical algorithms to assist a buyer when evaluating different supply and cost scenarios.

Much success has been realized by companies using this technology, particularly in the area of transportation sourcing. Transportation buys are complex in the number of shipping lanes serviced per carrier as well as the differing capabilities of carriers. For example, one large organization identified 600 ocean shipping lanes for which it required transportation. Each lane could have three container sizes (20-foot, 40-foot, and 60-foot high), resulting in the equivalent of 1,800 lane/items. Eighteen suppliers were invited to participate, and suppliers could bid on whatever lanes they wanted. Optimization software allows expressive bidding (which suppliers like) on a problem of this scale. It allows purchasers to quickly analyze a problem of this scale and respond to the supplier, creating a dynamic feedback loop allowing for improved sourcing solution.[11] For additional information on this optimization technology, readers are encouraged to visit the websites of SciQuest (www.sciquest.com), IBM/Emptoris (www.ibm.com), and Iasta (www.iasta.com). Overall, decision optimization software allows the buyers to consider many more sourcing alternatives along with allowing the suppliers to bid to their strengths.

Reverse Auctions

Of all the technologies that have impacted e-sourcing, none are more publicized or controversial than **reverse auctions** Suppliers claim that buyers evaluate them solely on price and forget all the other non-price benefits they have provided over time. This need not be the case; Sourcing Snapshot: Reverse Auctions and Buyer-Seller Relationships summarizes research that shows that buyers can use reverse auctions and have relationships with suppliers. Reverse auctions are electronic processes where multiple sellers of a product are vying for the business of a single buyer, resulting in intense price competition among sellers. Bidding continues until a preestablished bidding period ends or until no seller is willing to bid any lower, whichever comes first.

There are two basic types of reverse auctions termed (1) regular and (2) rank. In a **regular reverse auction** prices are completely visible and revealed to all sellers. Only the identity of the competitors remains anonymous to the sellers. In a **rank reverse auction** sellers are only told their relative rank and thus are not aware of their competitors' prices. As sellers change prices they can only see how or if the price change affects their overall rank. Rank auctions are good in situations where the buyer wishes to keep competitors prices more confidential.

It is widely acknowledged by buyers that reverse auctions have led to significant cost savings for various buying requirements. Proponents of reverse auctions state that the tool: (1) is inexpensive; (2) connects buyers and sellers worldwide; (3) supports a more efficient form of competitive bidding; and (4) drives the price of the item to its true market value.

It is very critical that the reverse auction tool be well integrated with the strategic sourcing process to harness its full potential. The procurement process should be robust enough to: adapt to any changes, incorporate financial controls, drive down costs, and eliminate waste. A successful e-auction requires the development of a pre-auction strategy, which sets goals, targets specific potential partners, and clearly lays out the applicable rules to be followed throughout. The process normally follows these steps:[12]

Sourcing Snapshot

Reverse Auctions and Buyer-Seller Relationships

Reverse auctions (R/As) have been used in the sourcing process since the late 1990s, bursting onto the scene led by a new Pittsburgh-based venture appropriately named Free Markets. Suddenly, buyers had a new tool to establish prices during the bidding cycle. Essentially, a reverse auction is a buyer-initiated bidding event utilizing electronic software that permits price or rank visibility to sellers. The process is conducted in a secure, online environment within a specified time frame with the goal of obtaining a rational market price for the commodity or service being procured.

The reverse auction has been touted as a means of reducing the time associated with the supplier selection and award process. One of the major benefits of the time savings associated with reverse auction use is the ability of the supply management professional to devote more effort to strategic sourcing activities. Some of these activities include making in- and outsourcing decisions, strategic cost management, benchmarking, and supplier development. In addition, it is commonly held that the use of reverse auctions results in a reduction in prices paid for products and services.

Despite the proposed benefits associated with reverse auction technology, managers and academicians alike have expressed concern regarding how its use impacts, and is impacted by, buyer-supplier relationships. Some fear the use of reverse auctions tells suppliers that the buying firm is simply looking to extract price reductions without regard to existing or future business relationships, thereby breeding mistrust and lack of cooperation.

Research with 142 experienced purchasing managers (averaging 12 years of experience) was recently conducted to assess the impact of R/As on relationships. The respondents' annual sales ranged from $4.5 million to $45 billion. Total annual purchase expenditures ranged from $1 million to $17 billion. Respondents reported more than 30 different lines of business. Forty-one percent of the sample were managers, which is indicative of their experience level; 59 percent of the sample were nonmanagers. All had experience with reverse auction use, averaging 22 reverse auctions. Respondents used reverse auctions fairly consistently for both standardized direct materials and indirects (MRO, services, and so on).

The research provided some positive results related to a major concern that reverse auctions threaten buyer-supplier relationships. The results suggest that firms that place higher levels of strategic importance on the relationships with their suppliers opt for relational-type structures to govern the subsequent contract. This supports previous writings that indicate that the offer and execution stages of the reverse auction process should be independent. In the offer phase of the reverse auction process, explaining the rules accurately to the parties, prior to conducting the actual R/A event, increases the chances of a successful reverse auction. Once the R/A has been completed, the selection of the appropriate form of contract to govern the relationship becomes an independent decision. Thus, purchasers must evaluate the strategic importance of their existing supplier relationship prior to using a reverse auction, clearly explain the rules of the engagement, and establish the appropriate contract form after completing the R/A and selecting the desired supplier.

Price should be a very important element of the R/A selection process but not the only one. The research supports a relational approach when using reverse auctions for relationships that are strategically important. Supplier cooperation was significantly related to a relational type of contract structure when using reverse auctions. It appears that the supplier's level of cooperation is contingent, at least in part, on its expectation of continued interaction with the buying firm. When both parties involved in a business relationship expected it to last for an extended period of time, the relationship was characterized by a pattern of cooperation.

Price is the most controversial element of the reverse auction phenomenon. The research strongly supported the view that relational contract structures are negatively related to purchase price reduction. Organizations pursuing a more market-based (bid-and-buy) approach will realize greater savings using reverse auctions than those looking to develop or maintain relationships. Consequently, firms must assess the tradeoff between obtaining lower prices (that may or may not be sustainable) and the opportunity cost of not choosing suppliers that can provide assistance in vital non-price-related areas (e.g., product design) when designing the appropriate R/A structure.

The use of reverse auctions will provide the buyer time savings, which could be used to pursue higher value-added or more strategic activities. However, these additional time savings will be mitigated by the increased time required to build and maintain relationships. Given the need to perform more value-added duties, purchasers must carefully select suppliers with whom they enter into relational governance. What the purchaser chooses to do with the time savings realized by reverse auction use is important because employing a relational form of governance structure is time consuming. Consequently, not all suppliers can be managed using a relational approach. Many reverse auctions will continue to be conducted for the sole purpose of obtaining lower prices and will be governed in a transactional mode.

Overall, the research model has demonstrated that purchasers can implement relational governance mechanisms and still use reverse auctions. These relational governance mechanisms will ensure increased levels of supplier cooperation. However, this increased cooperation comes at a cost to the buyer: lower purchase price savings and time savings. If the time savings attributed to reverse auction use is dedicated to building improved relationships, which ultimately lead to lower costs, better service, and higher quality, then both parties win. Conversely, if the purchaser uses reverse auctions to pursue a more market-based bid-and-buy strategy, firms will benefit from increased purchase price savings and realize greater time savings, but this will be at the expense of supplier cooperation. Hence, much of this time savings may be used to monitor the supplier's performance to ensure that the actual savings attributed to reduced purchases prices are realized. Overall, much of the interest in reverse auctions is because of their ability to result in price reductions for the buying firm; the model indicates there are relational benefits that may outweigh temporary reductions in purchase price.

Source: Pearcy, D., Giunipero, L, and Wilson, A. (2007, Winter), "A Model of Relational Governance in Reverse Auctions," *Journal of Supply Chain Management*, 4–15.

1. The purchasing company decides which contracts (products, materials, and services) would benefit from reverse auction procurement.

2. Suppliers are initially evaluated and invited to participate in the bidding process. The list of suppliers contains companies formally accepted through quality and performance criteria, along with potential suppliers that have been researched and approved. The company writes and distributes the request for quotation to all qualified suppliers. Accompanying the RFQ is other pertinent information such as when and where the bidding will take place and auctioning rules and etiquette.

3. The bidding process begins at a certain time and usually lasts no more than 30 minutes. This portion can be open, where all competitors can see other bids, or it can be closed, where buyers are not able to see other bids. The supplier identities are always kept confidential during bidding.

4. The company then analyzes the auction and awards the business to the chosen supplier. This supplier is not necessarily the lowest bidder.

Reverse auction technology is readily available from a number of sources. It can be *self-service,* where the technology is downloaded from the software provider. The buying organization trains the suppliers, sets up the auction, and conducts the auction itself.

A *full-service* model is also available from software providers. In this model the software provider helps the organization with selection of the commodity, assists in qualifying suppliers, conducts training, and runs the reverse auction for the firm. The relative level of experience with reverse auctions is the single most important factor in whether to use a self-service or full-service model.

Total Cost & Negotiation Support Models

Different e-sourcing systems can aid purchasers to estimate the total cost of ownership for products and services. These models incorporate shipping, freight, duty, imports and tariffs, inventory costs, and quality costs. Purchasers can then use this data to negotiate with suppliers in a fact based format.

Procure-to-Pay and Purchase Order

As was previously discussed in Chapter 2, Procure-to-Pay systems encompass the entire purchasing process. The process starts with a requisition from internal users, which is transformed into a purchase order by purchasing, then the goods/services are received upon shipment/task completion by the supplier. Next the process requires invoice reconciliation, and management of suppliers and finally payment. Procure-to-Pay software comprehensively automates all of these processes, which allow for efficient processing, receipt, payment and management of the process.

The purchase order module supports the generation of purchase orders, which involves the automatic assignment of purchase order numbers for selected items, along with the transfer of purchase order information to the proper database(s). This module provides purchasing with visibility to current purchase orders on file.

Receiving and Inspection

The receiving and inspection module updates system records upon receipt of an item. Most systems hold a received item in a protected state (unavailable for use) until all inbound processing is complete. Sophisticated systems are able to do this via a bar code reader that automatically transmits all necessary information to the database. This processing includes tasks such as inspection (if required), material transfer, and stockkeeping. Systems can also send alerts to key stakeholders when there are potential stockouts or imminent shortages.

Contract Management and Compliance

Contract management and compliance provides oversight of the back end of the sourcing process. Once a source is selected and the contract terms are negotiated, there is a need to manage the contract to ensure that suppliers and users are in compliance with established contract terms. Other challenges faced with manual contract management systems are pricing compliance, changes in terms, volume discount thresholds, payment schedules, due dates, and contingencies for nonperformance. Reliable contract management systems provide the ability to keep these issues current with real-time data collection capabilities. These real-time capabilities ensure that the buying organization will realize the full potential of the negotiated terms of the contract.

Software provider IBM-Emptoris describes its contract management tool as combining powerful contract authoring, negotiation, and approval processes with contract administration, enterprise reporting, and proven controls, in an easy-to-use interface. It enables companies to optimize contract management processes along with managing payment obligations and capitalizing on profit opportunities to ensure that supplier management strategies are achieving their full potential.[13]

Risk Management and Supplier Performance Measurement

A recent Forrester study indicated supplier risk and performance management (SRPM) to be one of the highest growth areas of all e-Purchasing Applications with a 2009–2014 compounded growth rate of 16 percent versus 11 percent for all e-Purchasing applications.[14] Most software providers address risk management, however their risk programs often focus on one area of the four areas identified. Currently for example, Ariba stresses the *procurement risk,* at Bravo Solutions it is *vendor management risk,* Citicus stresses *supply chain risk,* and Aravo *governance, risk and compliance.* All of these software providers as well as others interviewed in the Forrester study have been filling out their functionality to develop a complete suite that addresses all four risks. Providers indicated their future offerings would merge the four risk areas into a more unified approach to supplier risk and performance management module.

The traditional performance measurement module provides visibility to open-item status, and measures and analyzes supplier performance. The supplier scorecards may also be updated electronically. The key features include automatic inquiry of item status, monitoring of order due dates, and analysis of supplier performance. This module should have the capability to monitor planned receipts against due dates, provide immediate visibility to past-due items, and flag those items likely to become past due. The system should generate summary reports of supplier performance compared against predetermined performance criteria, which may include due-date compliance, quality ratings, price variances, quantity discrepancies, and total transportation charges.

Key performance indicators are developed that can highlight hidden additional costs created by poor quality, delivery, and service issues. Supplier performance modules provide several benefits including: (1) providing input into supplier selection considering total costs, not just price; (2) isolating supplier process inefficiencies; (3) improving total cycle times; and (4) providing suppliers with reliable feedback on their historical performance.

Total Cost Reporting

A well-designed e-sourcing system has the ability to generate timely management reports, providing visibility to the entire materials process. In creating these total cost reports, more and more companies are turning to data warehouses (described earlier).

Most systems have the capability to generate new reports, assuming data are available or can be generated by using other data. Another capability of a well-designed system is that the frequency of data reporting and system updating matches a user's operational needs. A system that operates in a real-time environment provides the most current data. **Real-time updating** is a process in which all data files that include a specific address are automatically updated within the system. In contrast to real-time updating is the **data bucket**—a process of storing each transaction in a temporary file and updating the system at scheduled times throughout the day or on a weekly basis. **Batch updating** refers to the process of downloading all data buckets into the main system on a regularly scheduled basis.

Price forecasting is an important area under total cost reporting. It requires the construction of a model to identify the variables affecting an item's price, including the length of an item's product life cycle, the life cycle stage the item is in, and the item's price history. Life cycle cost curves can forecast expected price performance through time. Purchasing can use these projections to develop budget projections as well as periodic management reports.

Internal and External Systems Integration[15]

As was mentioned, integration will be a factor in the selection of future e-sourcing suites. ERP systems will no longer be able to be independent of decisions made by managers using the e-Sourcing suites to order materials and transmit forecasts. There will be increased integration between ERP systems, the SRM driven e-sourcing suites, and the systems that communicate information along the supply chain between customers and the buying organization and its suppliers. This convergence will extend upstream in the supply chain to customer relationship management (CRM) systems and internal ERP production schedules which then translate requirements to supplier relationship management systems (SRM). These integrated systems will help ensure that future supplier capacity requirements will be in place to meet future demand requirements for new products and services. In effect, these linked systems will enable a single view of the entire supply chain.

Sales representatives in the field will be able to promise exact delivery dates to customers using an available-to-promise module, a system that allows salespeople to access plant schedules and determine if enough capacity is available to produce the product for the customer by a certain date, and also whether suppliers will be able to deliver the materials in time to produce it. A distribution planning module will help identify the transportation requirements and distribution center inventory levels in time to meet customers' delivery requirements. A demand planning module will help identify whether long-term capacity requirements will be sufficient to meet the demand for new products. We will next discuss general information visibility available through newer tools such as social and professional networking as well as blogs, tweets, and cloud computing. Then we will discuss supply chain information visibility.

Social Networking Software in SCM—Improving Collaboration and Visibility

Perhaps no one web-based application has had a greater impact on more people than social networking. Though most of the applications to date have been at the individual level, purchasing and supply chain professionals will be increasingly affected by these networks. A *social network* is a group of individuals who share something in common such as friendship, relationship (e.g., relatives), geographic area, common interests (e.g., purchasing), political preferences, beliefs, and so forth. Social networks have existed throughout time but in a more physical form. Joining or belonging to organizations such as churches, professional associations, and clubs is a way to link with other people who shared similar interests and values. However, most of these organizations required a physical presence via meetings or events such as the Institute for Supply Management's (ISM) annual International Conference.

With the increasing sophistication of the Internet applications, *social service providers* emerged, and their websites became a focal point for individuals to share their experiences in a virtual setting. Users can now interact over the Internet, via e-mail, or through instant messaging on a variety of platforms from computers to mobile devices. Perhaps the most well-known of these social service providers is Facebook.com. Mark Zuckerberg created Facebook at Harvard in 2004 to connect students on a more personal level. Zuckerberg wanted students to be able to express themselves and share information with other students from within their university. The site grew from six Harvard students in a dorm room to over 10,000 Harvard students in one month and was then extended to other universities. By February of 2007, the site had more than 17 million members. On December 31, 2013 Facebook reported it had 1.23 billion monthly users worldwide.[16] Certainly the number of users can be debated, but the overall growth is impressive.

There is a general perception that Facebook is strictly for individuals, this is not necessarily the case. For example, HubSpot is a B2B company that delivers software primarily to other B2B marketers. (See Sourcing Snapshot) The Facebook page at HubSpot has over 350000 users. The page is linked to a blog, which is a prominent destination for HubSpot's potential customers who are B2B marketers. HubSpot website offers its Facebook followers e-books, marketing guides, and white papers, which takes users directly to a lead-capture form. Once they have captured an e-mail address, they're able to use their marketing automation software to nurture the lead. HubSpot also amplifies the distribution of their posts by utilizing Facebook advertising to reach an even wider audience.[17]

Sourcing Snapshot

Calculating the Value of Social Media Followers

As social media moves more into the domain of the business environment, metrics become more important. What follows is a brief description from B2B Hub Spot's formula for calculating the value of social media followers.

HubSpot develops and markets a software-as-a-service product for inbound marketing for the Business to Business segment. The software platform helps clients attract visitors, convert leads and close customers. HubSpot believes inbound marketing is a necessity in the B2B world today. Inbound marketing is promoting a company through social media marketing, blogs, podcasts, e-newsletters, whitepapers, and other forms of content marketing, which serve to bring customers in closer to the brand. In contrast, outbound or traditional marketing garners buying attention through direct sales calls, printed brochures, trade journal advertising, trade shows and exhibits and even TV and radio advertisements. The HubSpot website illustrates the inefficiency of certain outbound marketing techniques by stating that 44 percent of Direct mail is never opened, that 86 percent of people skip commercials, and that there are over 200 million people on don't call lists.

Dan Zarrella of Hub Spot put together a formula to calculate a metric that he calls VOAL or the Value Of A Like. Zarrella feels that once an organization knows the VOAL, social media efforts can be undertake with confidence that they will generate a positive ROI.

Below is the formula and how it breaks down:

$$L/UpM \cdot (LpD \cdot 30) \cdot (C/L) \cdot CR \cdot ACV = \text{Value of a Like}$$

L (Total Likes) The total number of audience members connected to the organization, group or individual's social media account. On Facebook these are the Likes of your page and on Twitter the followers.

UpM (Unlikes-per-Month) The average number of fans who "unlike" your social network account each month. On Facebook, this is an "unlike," and on Twitter, this is an "unfollow".

LpD (Links-per-Day) The average number of times you're posting links, and potentially converting links driven from your social media account. On Facebook, this is the number of posts you're making, per day, that lead to a page on your website. On Twitter, this is the number of times, per day, you're tweeting these kinds of links.

C (Average Clicks) The average number of clicks on the links to your site you're posting on your social media accounts.

CR (Conversion Rate) The average conversion rate of your website, from visit to sale or visit to lead. This can be an overall average, but for increased accuracy, use the conversion rate measured from traffic coming from the social network you're calculating.

ACV (Average Conversion Value) The average value of each "conversion." In this context, a "conversion" is the action you've used to measure CR for. It could be average sale price or average lead value. For increased accuracy, use the average conversion value of traffic coming from the specific social network.

Located on Website along with Zarrella's formula printed above is a calculator to easily allow an organization, group or individual to calculate its VOAL. I highly recommend you give it a try!

Merely go to the below URL address to access the calculator and figure out your VOAL.

http://blog.hubspot.com/blog/tabid/6307/bid/33871/How-to-Calculate-the-Value-of-Your-Social-Media-Followers-CALCULATOR.aspx

Sources: www.hubspot.com Dan Zarrella, "How to Calculate the Value of your Social Media Followers (Calculator)" at www.hubspot.com

According to Clara Shih, author of *The Facebook Era* B2B marketers are using Facebook and other social networking providers such as LinkedIn to facilitate the sales process.[18] Shih discusses how B2B sales representatives can accelerate the process of building trust by using social networking sites to: (1) convey their qualifications; (2) understand the profile of the ideal target prospect; (3) do a better job on the first call of understanding the prospect's key responsibilities, accomplishments and past experience to tailor the call, versus making a generic pitch.

Salesforce.com has a cloud-based app exchange page that allows members to link directly to the LinkedIn for salesforce and buying profiles from LinkedIn displayed alongside the salesperson's account information. LinkedIn (www.linkedin.com) is a very popular site that many professionals on both organizational selling and buying sides have joined. Seller can use LinkedIn to prospect and make initial contact. Then Salesforce for Twitter and Facebook is another App that is part of Salesforce.com, allows a direct link to Twitter and Facebook, providing more detailed information on the contact such as schools attended, past employers, favorite books, interests, and so forth.[19] This information can help make the sales call much more personal and relevant.

Another popular application from Salesforce.com is "Inside View." Proponents say the information helps target accounts shapes marketing strategy and execution. The tool provides key information on companies, including the latest news, and key players including c-level executives and VPs.[20] The "Inside View" app data is integrated seamlessly into the Salesforce.com platform.

Supply managers need to be aware that B2B marketers using such social networking and CRM tools will be able to target their specific needs better, thus making the buyer-seller interface much more efficient. In the future, supply managers may post a list of their major items purchased on Facebook or another App, allowing sellers to quickly determine if there is a fit between the buying company's needs and the seller's capabilities.

Professional Networking Software in SCM

Whereas current Facebook applications are more geared to B2B marketers, LinkedIn is a social networking provider whose goal is to help business professionals network. According to the website, it began operations in May 2003 and by February 2014, had more than 277 million registered users of which 84 million resided in the United States. LinkedIn users spanned more than 200 countries and territories worldwide, with content in 20 different languages. LinkedIn company pages display 1.2 million products/services and there are over 2.1 million LinkedIn groups that members can join.[21]

Supply managers are able to link with other supply managers, both within and outside their organizations in the "my connections" part of the site. Questions can be posted to one's network and opinions obtained. Individuals seeking advancement or new opportunities can scan the job section by searching under "purchasing," "supply management," or "supply chain management."

Professional development opportunities are available through joining various groups. For example, there are 1874 groups listed under "purchasing," 1166 under "supply chain management" and 206 under "supply management." Familiar national organizations such as the Institute for Supply Management (ISM) and the International Federation of Purchasing and Supply Management (IFPSM) and local groups, such as the Purchasing Management Association of Boston (PMA Boston), ISM-Philadelphia, Inc. and ISM Connecticut are listed under the group site. By industry category there are sites for utility purchasing managers, fashion buyers and designers, travel procurement professionals, and others. Finally, there are specialty group forums; for example, under the category "global sourcing" a supply manager can choose to join 135 groups including the "Global Sourcing Council," "Global Sourcing and Outsourcing Trade Council," and "Global and Textile and Apparel Sourcing." Included in each of the group's listing is a statistic with the number of members who currently belong to the group, as well as members from your network who are in the group.

Though finding the right group may involve some search time, the big advantage of these groups is that the supply manager is able to target an interest group that meets his/her specific needs. For example, the Global Sourcing Council is a nonprofit organization for people and organizations with an interest in the social and economic effects of sourcing. The mission of the Global Sourcing Council is to promote an exchange of ideas and information among businesses, trade organizations, government agencies, and academics; to discuss and define practices in global sourcing; and to encourage progressive economic growth leading to increased trade, investment, and social good, all with the aim of increasing knowledge, deepening trade relations, and broadening commercial and cultural ties among nations.[22]

Blogs, Tweets, and Cloud Computing

In addition to social networking there are millions of blog sites on sourcing. A **blog** is a type of website that is either independent or tied into another website. Blogs are maintained by an organization or individual and regularly post articles, comments, and questions, list upcoming events, and so forth. Participants in blog sites are free to post their reactions, and individuals can respond to other participants' responses. Blogs are a very popular part of the Internet and can be found on almost any topic. It is a good way for purchasers to remain current on different topics pertaining to their work.

Two examples of e-sourcing blogs are presented here. A source of many blogs can be found from e-software providers. One of these is managed by Iasta (www.iasta.com) and can be found at www.esourcing forum.com. E-Sourcing Forum is designed to keep sourcing, procurement and supply chain professionals up-to-date with collaborative discussions about trends, best practices, and industry news through postings of articles of interest to supply managers.[23] These articles are then categorized by subject, for example, project management, global sourcing, E-sourcing marketplace, interviews and the like. There is also a section with ties to other blogs.

Another popular blog site devoted to supply management is www.spendmatters.com. It focuses on a broad spectrum of solution areas in supply management and the companies within these areas. Selected areas of coverage include: e-Procurement, group purchasing organizations (GPOs), leveraged buying/leveraged contracts, supplier enablement, supplier networks, supplier information management, vendor management, supply chain risk, services procurement (general), services procurement (category specific), strategic sourcing, and others. In addition to reporting, the Managing Director (Jason Busch) and Chief Research Officer (Pierre Mitchell) offer general opinions and broader editorial pertaining the overall procurement environment, trade and economic issues. The blog is marketed to everyone from junior analysts to the most seasoned CPOs, COOs, and CFOs.[24]

Twitter is a social networking service created in 2006 by Jack Dorsey. Twitter allows users to send and read messages. These messages are called **tweets**. Tweets are text-based and have a maximum limit of 140 characters. B2B applications for Twitter are still in their infancy, but most blogs are tied into Twitter and allow users to follow tweets as they are posted. Since the tweets are limited to 140 characters, some of the responses are often termed *microblogs*. Blog sites such as spendmatters.com allow tweets in response to blogs.

Cloud computing is Internet-based, and users share software and other information that is provided to computers and mobile devices on demand. Exact definitions vary from source to source. Individual users and corporations no longer have need for expertise in, or control over, the technology infrastructure "in the cloud." Cloud computing providers such as Google, H-P, and Microsoft deliver common business applications online and are accessed from their Web service or software; the data are stored on their servers. In essence, cloud computing encompasses any subscription-based or pay-per-use service that is in real time and over the Internet.[25]

As is explained in our good practice example of collaboration, the cloud-based model provides a more economical way for software providers to deliver their service. Under the older application service provider model users were charged an upfront licensing fee plus a hosting fee to run the software and then an 18–20 percent maintenance fee. Typically the software was a "one off" meaning the service provider had done some customization for the client. With cloud or "software as a service (SaaS)" the service provider utilizes one software solution for many clients thus lowering their cost model and these commonalities in the software solution enable the cloud providers to realize efficiencies of scale and lower their price to the client.

A cloud service has three distinct characteristics that differentiate it from traditional hosting. It is sold on demand, typically by the minute or the hour; it is elastic—users can have as much or as little of a service as they want at any given time; and the service is fully managed by the provider. As long as the consumer has Internet access a connection is established. Significant innovations in virtualization and distributed computing, as well as improved access to high-speed Internet and need to reduce cost in software, storage and retrieval will continue to drive growth in cloud computing.

A cloud can be private or public. A public cloud sells services to anyone on the Internet. Currently, Amazon Web Services is the largest public cloud provider. A private cloud is a proprietary network or a data center that supplies hosted services to a limited number of people. When a service provider uses public cloud resources to create their private cloud, the result is called a virtual private cloud. Private or public, the goal of cloud computing is to provide easy, scalable access to computing resources and IT services.

As with any system potential users need to weigh the potential challenges. First, companies lose a certain amount of control since they do not have ownership of the equipment hosting the cloud environment. Second, and most controversial is the issue of security, cloud providers state they have secure environments for data and have undergone security audits. Apple co-founder Steve Wozniak said he's worried about the "horrendous" problems cloud computing could cause as users yield control of their data to service providers. "I say, the more we transfer everything onto the web, onto the cloud, the less we're going to have control over it," stated Wozniak[26] Users of public cloud services must also integrate with an architecture defined by the cloud provider, using its specific parameters for working with cloud components. Uptime, reliability and capacity are other issues concerning some critics.

Supply managers should ask for security provisions or certifications that cloud providers have implemented. Two standards are Statement on Auditing Standards (SAS 70) and ISO 27001, which cover information security management but at this point are not cloud specific. Given the cost advantages and flexibility on balance it appears the trend to move the software applications beyond the firewall and provide more pay-per-use service will continue.

Information Visibility in SCM

Information visibility within the supply chain is the process of sharing critical data required to manage the flow of products, services, and information in real time between suppliers and customers. If information is available but cannot be accessed by the parties most able to react to a given situation, its value degrades exponentially. Increasing information visibility among supply chain participants can help all parties reach their overall goal of increased stockholder value through revenue growth, asset utilization, and cost reduction. To improve responsiveness across their supply chains, companies are exploring the use of collaborative models that share information across multiple tiers of participants in the supply chain: from their supplier's supplier to their customer's customer. These trading partners need to share forecasts, manage inventories, schedule labor, and optimize deliveries, and in so doing they reduce costs, improve productivity, and create greater value for the final customer in the chain. Software programs for business process optimization and for collaborative planning, forecasting, and replenishment are evolving to help companies forecast and plan among partners, manage customer relations, and improve product life cycles and maintenance.

Some of the considerations that must be planned for in implementing an information visibility system include the size of the supply base and customer base with which to share information, the criteria for implementation, the content of information shared, and the technology used to share it. Clarifying these issues will help to ensure that all participants have access to the information required to effectively control the flow of materials, manage the level of inventory, fulfill service-level agreements, and meet quality standards as agreed upon in the relationship performance metrics.

Benefits of Information Visibility

The most important benefit of a visibility system is not that the system is able to correct a supply chain problem, but that it allows people to become aware of problems earlier and thus take corrective actions more quickly than they would otherwise. The benefits of information visibility include reduced lead times, improved constraint management, better decision making, lower costs, and increased profits. Although problems such as shortages, changes in customer orders, engineering changes, obsolete inventory, and equipment failures can still occur with a visibility system in place, the effects of these problems are less than if the participants in the supply chain were not made aware of these problems until a later date. In other words, without visibility systems, a $5,000 problem could turn into a $500,000 problem.

When implemented properly, a visibility solution results in the following additional benefits that promote improved supply chain performance:

- Breaks organizational barriers and enables sharing of mission-critical information about business activities and interaction on a near-real-time basis across the supply chain.
- Builds visibility into the supply chain and provides people with a real-time snapshot of supply chain performance metrics.
- Manages by metrics, aligns performance metrics with cross-organizational business processes, and assigns ownership of processes and metrics to specific individuals.
- Reduces the decision cycle process and allows an upstream or downstream participant to respond to market or customer demand in hours or days, not weeks or months.
- Encourages decision-making collaboration and facilitates the ability to make decisions collaboratively on the Internet, bringing relevant internal and external stakeholders into the process.
- Reduces opportunity and problem resolution latency, and measures and monitors supply chain activities iteratively, allowing people to respond to events quickly as they occur.

Conversely, the dangers of poor execution of supply chain processes include increased lead and cycle times, higher costs, and less informed decision making. For example, in the apparel industry to lower the risk of a fashion miss, more retailers and apparel companies are pressing their suppliers to crank out small orders quickly—allowing them to test styles in stores—and then fill reorder requests even faster. This strategy, known as chasing demand requires a level of visibility that the apparel industry does not have and, as a result, is creating tension between retailers and their suppliers. The increased pressures are leading factories to set limits on the work they are willing to do at a given time and demand that orders be placed far in advance.[27]

Information Visibility in the Cloud

As illustrated in the above example, in the apparel industry time latency is one of the core problems associated with forecasting. Inaccuracies also plague moving to demand-based planning as the apparel industry would like. However, cloud computing could improve visibility by reducing this latency at all tiers of the supply chain. For example, a key piece of equipment breaks and cannot be repaired until a special-order part is obtained. Many parties are affected by this problem and will not, or cannot, adjust until manually notified. Suppliers continue to send material to feed the broken machine, and customers waiting for product must either find a substitute or do without the product. In a cloud-enabled value chain, customers and suppliers would have visibility into the process since they learn of the breakdown as it happens and can begin their response activities immediately. Ideally, the machine itself has the technology embedded to transmit the information to supply chain participants automatically. The cloud could also allow value chain participants to monitor an array of predictive signals such as order levels and frequency, weather issues, and the like to reduce latency and improve both supplier response and end-customer service. Of course, cloud computing will require a level of trust and open-ness between parties in the value chain as well as changing and modifying processes.[28]

Collaboration and Big Data

In this chapter we have seen the importance of e-sourcing, information visibility and the ever widening access to this information through blogs, social media, and cloud com-puting. Increasingly organizations will grapple with managing this increased information load that is growing exponentially. All of us experience "information overload" and desire a need to manage data to make effective decisions. From a supply management standpoint we face the need to extend these information linkages externally. Making information vis-ible requires a degree of collaboration between the parties.[29] Today this collaboration on the type of information exchanged must be managed and in some cases compartmental-ized because of sensitivity or competitor concerns.

Technology greatly affects the way supply managers collaborate, share information and interface across organizations. The following is a brief discussion of one proposed model (SMAC) that summarizes the convergence of four powerful forces that will shape the fu-ture of our work. The convergence of these four technologies is in large part responsible for the generation of all this information now called **big data**.

SMAC is an acronym for what is happening around our electronic world today. SMAC represents four aspects of our Web driven world and includes: (1) Social; (2) Mobile; (3) Analytics; and (4) Cloud. These four elements will have a large impact on the way we work and play. SMAC is the 5th phase of IT deployment, which began with the (1) main-frame era that was then followed by the (2) minicomputer, (3) distributed pc, (4) Internet pc, and now (5) SMAC. The SMAC technologies add a new dimension the organization's business model and enable us to further increase our productivity. One source states, SMAC is the new enterprise IT model delivering an organization that is more connective, collaborative, real-time, and productive.[30] The final snapshot in this chapter discusses col-laboration in the era of these technologies.

Big data is a topic gaining more attention in the literature and certainly affects supply management. E-provider Cognizant estimates that by 2020, as many as 100 billion com-puting devices will be connected to the Web, and corporations will be managing 50 times the data they do currently.[31] Meanwhile global market intelligence firm IDC states that world information doubles every one and one-half years.

Though term big data seems to have been invented recently, it was recognized by a Meta Group analyst in 2001. Doug Laney defined data growth challenges and opportunities as being three-dimensional, that is, increasing volume (amount of data), velocity (speed of data in and out), and variety (range of data types and sources).[32] Subsequently Gartner Group acquired Meta and in 2012 updated their definition to read: "**Big data** is high vol-ume, high velocity, and/or high variety information assets that require new forms of pro-cessing to enable enhanced decision making, insight discovery and process optimization."[33]

As more organizations come to grips with collecting and analyzing this data those in supply management can begin to use it to increase their effectiveness. Of course the first thing that comes to mind is that we need to analyze these large data sets to make better de-cisions. Thus analytical skills using quantitative and predictive modeling will be in demand for the future supply managers. One of the uses of this data can be for predictive ana-lytics. For example, Walmart constantly gathers information from its 18000 suppliers in 18 countries allowing it to drill down and analyze customer needs. It knows that before a hurricane customers stock up on convenience items that don't require cooking. Data shows Pop Tarts are one of the most popular items and of those Pop Tarts strawberry filled ones are the highest seller. This information enables Walmart to work with its suppliers to have the right amount on the shelves in hurricane prone areas. When members of the supply chain have linked their information systems, it increases visibility. Such visibility provides data to determine lead times, inventory needs, transportation costs and other key information.[34]

Firms are developing quantitative models to take advantage and make sense of this big data. However, one researcher has found that managers "intuition" was better than quantitative models in times of instability, but that models performed well in more stable environments.[35] Big data can be collected from numerous sources, several firms use external sources or other managed providers of data (D&B, LexisNexis, etc.) that can integrate and enhance data provided from enterprise systems.[36] Whatever the use experts agree that "big data" efforts are not stand-alone, but should tie into and support overall organizational goals.

Good Practice Example	*Future Trends to Develop Best Practices*

Good Practice Example: The Future: The Evolution of Collaboration-Moving to Networks

Chris Sawchuk is a Principal in the Hackett Group and holds the position of Global Procurement Advisory Practice Leader. Chris has many years of experience in the procurement world and now spends much of his time advising procurement leaders how to effectively position their businesses to meet their global objectives. Patrick Connaughton is the Director of Global Research and Technology for the Hackett Group. Patrick leads the research and technology areas for Hackett and was previously a Principal Industry Analyst at Forrester Research. Given their extensive experiences in, procurement, technology and research they were ideal candidates to discuss collaboration.

A General Introduction to Collaboration

In Chapter 4 we defined collaboration as the process by which two or more parties adopt a high level purposeful cooperation to maintain a trading relationship over time. Collaboration is characterized by an open exchange of information. The information could include new products, cost data, forecasts, production data etc. In essence collaboration is characterized by an exchange of mutually beneficial information that allows for the development of deeper relationships with stakeholders. Both of our interviewees have seen a great interest from their clients on improving collaboration. What follows, is a discussion of collaboration and a sample of the e-tools that firms are using to implement collaborative efforts.

What do you see as Newer Trends in Collaboration?

Moving from sequential one on one relationships to networks. Traditionally collaboration in supply management has been *sequential* through one-one interfaces between buyers and sellers. In the future it will be more complex and involve *networks*. An example of this is in the area of transportation procurement. Supply Managers have discovered that transportation networks can help them save money on their total transportation spend. These networks consist of transportation firms who often are direct competitors. These organizations voluntarily join forces to provide the customer improved service along with filling more of their excess capacity. For example, one carrier may be preferred on the Boston to Atlanta route but is currently has no excess capacity. A competitor carrier does have capacity and is able to provide the service for the customer in that particular shipping lane. By collaborating the customer is served and the network has received revenue and individual carriers increased both their shipments volumes and increased capacity utilization.

Collaborative networks can also be formed on the buying side. For example, a consumer products firm that ships facial tissue and paper towels faced a problem of shipments filling the trailer cube volume wise but facing a high tariff because of the light weight. In other words, though the product filled the trailer space it was light and therefore expensive to ship. The company found a shipper in their geographic area who was in the beverage business. This firm had the opposite problem. Its product was high in weight but didn't fully utilize the trailer's cube capacity. Now the beverages are layered on the bottom of the trailer and the paper products on top. The two firms now collaborate and coordinate shipping schedules when feasible and both have realized lower rates.

Collaboration beyond the buyer-seller to the customer. The traditional documents that were exchanged by the parties in a collaborative arrangement included specifications, production schedules and forecasts. Most parties who collaborate have become quite good at this. In the future collaboration will expand both horizontally to either more tiers of the supply chain and downstream to the customer. Our research indicates that firms are interested increased future collaboration. New collaborative opportunities will extend not only to the customer but with common challenges faced by firms dealing with their business environment. For example, a group of firms faced similar challenge in meeting a regulatory problem. They collaborated voluntarily to find the best method to meet the regulations. Rather than 15 different approaches to meeting the requirements of the statute they were able to find one best method and apply it across the board.

Though everyone is a customer in a supply chain, the final or end customer triggers the orders for the rest of the supply chain, knowing what this customer demands and the timing associated with those demands are crucial. Here again collaboration along the supply chain with the customer will benefit all participants in the chain. Consortiums of various types are also another area for collaboration between firms.

Which Applications and Providers do you see Assisting Organizations in Performing Tasks that Allow Collaboration?

Though there are many competent providers in the collaboration area you first need to categorize the major application areas. We would break this down into major areas listed below.

New Product Design. Product life cycle management (PLM) software fits this category and includes software that is used to facilitate product development globally in many organizations.

Procurement/supply management. Software that enables varying degrees of collaboration between buyers and sellers. Hubwoo is one provider in this space. According to their website the Hubwoo business network provides an efficient way for buyers and sellers to search, connect, and collaborate. It drives spend compliance and invoice automation, offering users access to a community of over one million businesses.

Logistics Procurement. This very specialized area of procurement allows firms to analyze the various ways to collaborate and optimize their procurement of transportation and determine optimal rates.

Supply Chain Planning. Focuses on traditional collaboration of information on inventory optimization, forecasting and demand scheduling. A long time provider in this space is JDA-I2 technologies. As stated on their website, their advanced planning and scheduling application allows collaboration by considering actual production constraints to improve the flow of materials within a factory and offers more sophisticated monitoring, decision-support and execution capabilities. Applying technology and best practices to eliminate inefficiencies in business processes.

Capital and Maintenance Repair and Operating Items. These enterprise asset management (EAM) software programs allow users to identify: (1) the assets do they have in their operations; (2) where the assets are located; (3) how the devices are configured and connected; and 4) the repair history.

Internal Collaboration. Though most people think of collaboration between organizations, internal collaboration is needed for effective external collaboration. Solutions such as Share Point and Intranets have been assisting internal collaboration.

What if any Impact has the Cloud-Computing Movement had on Collaboration?

The cloud is now hosting many software solutions. This development has created a *"software as a service"* (SAAS) model. The cloud model is different from the traditional *"applications service provider"* model (ASP). Under the ASP model organizations could customize their software to meet their exact needs. However, this customization produced expensive solutions. Firms were required to pay an upfront licensing fee, a hosting fee for the ASP to run the software and then a yearly maintenance agreement that ran 18–20 percent of the licensing fee.

In a cloud-based solution the software provider offers a generic solution that is leased to users on a contract basis. Prices for software are lower and each firm adopting the solution receives a similar solution. The key difference is that under the ASP model the customer had one instance of their own (very often customized) software being hosted by the software provider. In SAAS customers receive a single application (multi-tenant), which drives down the software providers cost model.

Ideally the SAAS model lowers the customer's switching costs. However, these lower switching costs are predicated on the ability of the firm to get their data out of the system. This means that firms must negotiate pre-contract clause on how this data will be transitioned to the buyer. If an organization decides to switch providers the entire data set must be available to the organization. While many firms have reservations about the security of their data that is being stored by cloud-based providers, most software providers undergo security audits. One of the most popular is SAS 70, which ensures that the organization the necessary internal controls to insure security. The cloud will become the preferred way that collaborative software is delivered to customers.

Will Social Networking have any Impact on Collaboration?

Social networking is commonly thought of as Linked In, Facebook and Twitter, however we see enterprise social networking as a way to establish internal collaboration and eventually extend this to external collaboration. Internally firms can provide improved collaboration through either intranets or sites such as Yammer.

For example, at one organization, everyone interested in key suppliers can subscribe to a "supplier group" that allows individuals to see posts about specific suppliers. These focused sites allow internal stakeholders to directly target their specific interests and keep up-to-date on what is happening with suppliers that directly affect their job performance. Posting information can include contract details, volume commitments and changes in key supplier personnel. This information is particularly critical for global organizations who attempt to coordinate sourcing strategies in various areas of the world.

One application that is particularly promising in this area is the force.com application offered by CVM Solutions (www.cvmsolutions.com). Force.com is a platform that companies can use to develop software tools. The solution includes gathering missing or incomplete data, removing duplicate suppliers, standardized categories, and mapping corporate family linkages. It allows organizations to consolidate data across different operating units, establish corporate family linkages and calculate supplier dependencies. Providing more opportunity to leverage global spend. Such information is shared with internal stakeholders to given them more information about supply management's supply strategies.

Questions

1. What are some of the areas of social media or apps you feel could be used in the future to help supply managers?
2. Discuss what roadblocks exist to collaboration and how you would implement a change management plan to gain acceptance of this technology.

Source: Interview Chris Sawchuk and Patrick Connaughton of the Hackett Group, February, 2014

CONCLUSION

Supply managers must expand their use of technology to increase both individual and functional performance. The use of web-based applications, ERP systems, and e-sourcing suites can help professional buyers shift attention from routine to strategic tasks. For example, e-sourcing suites that support the making of better supplier selection decisions—one of a firm's most strategic tasks—can reduce or eliminate future supply-base problems. Also, a system that monitors supplier performance can provide timely visibility toward mitigating potential supply risks.

Ordering and implementing new ERP systems requires systematic planning coupled with process and behavioral changes. The final decision about any system usually represents a long-term commitment to the selected software and equipment. The development of cloud computing applications will allow supply managers of the future to use software as a service (Saas), matching their needs with the software system requirements. If cloud computing performs as advertised, it will enable much more efficient IT operations at a lower overall cost to the organization. Care must be taken to insure the data will be properly secured by the cloud provider.

Supply managers can access a broad range of e-sourcing solutions and must extensively research available tools and software providers and build case studies to support justification for acquiring these systems. It is important to identify systems that not only meet current operating requirements but also have capabilities to meet future needs.

Emerging technologies are supplementing and, in some cases, replacing current technologies. Many of the strategies being pursued within supply chain organizations will rely on end-to-end supply chain solutions that:

- Integrate suppliers and distributors
- Outsource low touch/ high volume transactional purchases
- Share information across the supply chain
- Link CRM, ERP, and SRM systems to increase visibility

- Enable ease of use by all functional groups in the organization
- Facilitate supplier relations, contract and performance management

These strategies will require e-business applications to enable information sharing and, most importantly, provide an effective order fulfillment process with rapid delivery. Many companies lack the fundamental supply chain infrastructure required to be able to apply these technologies across multiple tiers of customers and suppliers.

In learning to crawl before walking, and then running, organizations must address the flawed designs of their existing supply chains and only then build these applications around their reengineered networks. An e-sourcing application cannot fix the problems associated with an unmanaged or poorly performing supply base, characterized by adversarial relationships, lack of trust, and an unwillingness to share information. Success in e-sourcing requires management commitment, supply management skills that foster strategic sourcing capabilities, key relationship management, and changes to outdated processes that have been embedded in the organizational culture.

Progressive supply managers should always be looking five years ahead to identify future trends that will improve their technology applications at lower costs and provided new ways to collaborate for competitive advantage. Supply managers are now increasing their use of social media for professional applications. The use of social networking and blogs is another way to locate information to enable the supply manager to make informed decisions about technology that contribute to the firm's objectives. Managing all this data is a challenge and as supply managers become more comfortable, effective, and efficient with all this data they will look back and realize the way they work has changed dramatically. The key is to manage and use this information in such a way to convince upper management to provide the physical and human resources to develop world-class web-based systems supported by leading-edge technology.

KEY TERMS

batch updating, 729	**E-sourcing tools**, 722	**Sell-side systems**, 721
big data, 737	**expressive bidding**, 724	**Spend Analysis**, 722
blog, 733	**horizontal portals**, 721	**strategic decision making**, 706
Buy-side systems, 721	**legacy systems**, 713	
Cloud computing, 734	**punchouts**, 721	**Supplier Relationship Management software**, 722
database, 717	**rank reverse auction**, 725	
data bucket, 729	**Real-time updating**, 729	**Third-party marketplaces**, 721
data warehouse, 718	**regular reverse auction**, 725	**transaction processing**, 706
decision support systems (DSSs), 706	**reverse auctions**, 725	**tweets**, 734
	RFQ, 724	**Twitter**, 734
ERP systems, 713	**routine decision making**, 706	**vertical portals**, 721

DISCUSSION QUESTIONS

1. Why do you believe there has been so much emphasis on technology in supply management in the twenty-first century?

2. How can purchasing make use of social networking software (e.g., Facebook and LinkedIn) to improve their daily job performance?

3. Why are ERP systems not typically considered a means to improve external integration?

4. Discuss the seven-stage ERP implementation model. What are some of the barriers that would hinder or lengthen actual ERP implementation time?

5. Find at least three blog sites that would help purchasers in managing their spend, sourcing globally, using e-sourcing and outsourcing or off-shoring.

6. An executive made this comment: "Many of our suppliers are too small to implement ERP systems." Do you think that this situation may change in the future?

7. Why do you believe that reverse auctions are so controversial? Why would you participate in one as a seller? Why would you organize one as a buyer?

8. Find an article that provides an example how firms are using and managing "big data" to improve their business model.

9. Explore the websites of Iasta, IBM-Emptoris, and SciQuest; then explain what you feel each provides in the way of decision optimization software.

10. Discuss the difference between traditional software models delivered by Application Service Providers (ASPs) and Software as a service delivered via the cloud.

11. Imagine walking into the purchasing office of the future. How might you go about completing your tasks for the day using future information technologies?

ADDITIONAL READINGS

Beall, S., Carter, C., Carter, P., Germer, T., Hendrick, T., Jap, S., Kaufmann, R., Maciejewski, D., Monczka, R., and Peterson, K. (2003), *The Role of Reverse Auctions in Strategic Sourcing*, Tempe, AZ: CAPS Research.

Giunipero, L., and Carter, P. (2009), *The Role of Optimization in Strategic Sourcing*, Tempe, AZ: CAPS Research.

Griffith, E. (2013, March 13), "What Is Cloud Computing," *PC Magazine*. Retrieved from http://www.pcmag.com/article2/0,2817,2372163,00.asp

Kimball, R., and Ross M. (2013), *The Data Warehouse Toolkit: The Definitive Guide to Dimensional Modeling*, Indianapolis, IN: John Wiley and Sons.

Lamoureux, M. (2008), *The E-Sourcing Handbook.* Retrieved from www.esourcingforum.com

Neef, D. (2001), *E-Procurement: From Strategy to Implementation*, Saddle River, NJ: Prentice Hall.

Pearcy, D., Giunipero, L., and Wilson, A. (2007, Winter), "A Model of Relational Governance in Reverse Auctions," *Journal of Supply Chain Management*, 4–15.

Schonberger, V. M., and Cukier, K. (2014), *Big Data: A Revolution That Will Transform How We Live, Work and Think*, London England: John Murray Publishers.

Shih, Clara. (2011), *The Facebook Era*, Boston, MA: Pearson Education.

Teague, P. E. (March 1, 2007), "PLM Gets Buyers under the Hood," *Purchasing*. Retrieved from http://www.purchasing.com/article/CA6419151.html

Turner, N. (2001), "Choosing the Most Appropriate Warehouse Management System," *Corby*, 3(7), 30–33.

ENDNOTES

1. Bozarth, C., and Handfield, R. (2007), *Operations and Supply Chain Management*, Upper Saddle River, NJ: Prentice Hall.

2. Chopra, S., and Meindl, P. (2007), "Information Technology and the Supply Chain," in *Supply Chain Management: Strategy, Planning and Operation*, Upper Saddle River, NJ: Prentice Hall, Chapter 16.

3. Kahl, S. (1999), "What's the 'Value' of Supply Chain Software?" *Supply Chain Management Review,* 2(4), 59–67.

4. Chopra and Meindl.

5. Bradley, J. (1987), *Introduction to Data Base Management,* New York: Holt, Rinehart and Winston, p. 7.

6. https://www.railinc.com/rportal/web/guest/overview

7. Antonette, G., Giunipero, L., and Sawchuk, C. (2002), *ePurchasingPlus,* Goshen, NY: JGC Enterprises, p. 56.

8. Antonette et al., p. 57.

9. Antonette et al., p. 58.

10. Antonette et al., p. 86.

11. Giunipero, L., and Carter, P. (2009), *The Role of Optimization in Strategic Sourcing,* Tempe, AZ: CAPS Research.

12. Handfield, R., Straight, S., and Sterling, W. (2002, November), "Reverse Auctions: How Do Suppliers Really Feel about Them?" *Inside Supply Management,* 28–32.

13. http://www-03.ibm.com/software/products/en/contract-management-buy-side/

14. Ross Ferrusi, C. (2013, November 4), "Understanding Software Options for Managing Vendor Risk," Forrester Research Report.

15. Benchmarking report developed by Edwards, S., Lakshman, M., members of the Supply Chain Resource Consortium, and other undergraduate students at North Carolina State University.

16. Retrieved from http://www.theguardian.com/news/datablog/2014/feb/04/facebook-in-numbers-statistics

17. Pickering, B. (2012, December 12), "How B2B Marketers Are Successfully Using Facebook," *Social Media Examiner.* Retrieved from http://www.socialmediaexaminer.com/b2b-marketers-successfully-using-facebook/

18. Shih, Clara. (2011), *The Facebook Era,* Boston, MA: Pearson Education.

19. Retrieved from https://appexchange.salesforce.com/popular

20. Retrieved from https://appexchange.salesforce.com/listingDetail?listingId=a0N3000000178fnEAA

21. Smith, C. (2014, February 9), "By the Numbers: 70 Amazing LinkedIn Statistics," *Digital Marketing Ramblings.* Retrieved from http://expandedramblings.com/index.php/by-the-numbers-a-few-important-linkedin-stats/#.Ux4UHFXD9dg

22. Global Sourcing Council Website. Retrieved from http://www.gscouncil.org/

23. Iasta blog. Retrieved from www.esourcingforum.com

24. Retrieved from http://spendmatters.com/about/coverage/

25. Knorr, E., and Gruman, G. (2008, April 7), "What Cloud Computing Really Means," *Info World.* Retrieved from http://www.infoworld.com/d/cloud-computing/what-cloud-computing-really-means-031

26. Butler, B. (2012, August 6), "Wozniak: Cloud Could Create Horrendous Problems," *Network World.* Retrieved from http://www.networkworld.com/news/2012/080612-wozniak-cloud-261428.html

27. Holmes, E. (2010, July 16), "Tug of War in Apparel World," *Wall Street Journal.* p. B.1.

28. Standley, D. (2010, July), "Take to the Clouds," *Inside Supply Management,* 12–13.

29. Handfield, R., and Nichols, E. L. (2003), *Supply Chain Redesign,* Upper Saddle River, NJ: Prentice Hall.

30. Retrieved from http://www.cognizant.com/smac

31. Ibid.

32. Laney, D. (2001, February 6), "3D Data Management: Controlling Data Volume, Velocity and Variety," Meta Group.

33. Laney, D. (2012, June 21), "The Importance of 'Big Data': A Definition," Gartner Group.

34. Siegfried, M. (2014, January/February), "Find the Big Picture in Big Data," *Inside Supply Management*, 18–23.

35. Ibid., p 22.

36. *e-Soucing Forum* (2014, January 31), "Analytics on the Brain." Retrieved from http://www.esourcingforum.com/archives/2014/01/31/analytics-on-the-brain-in-2014/

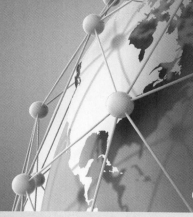

Performance Measurement and Evaluation

CHAPTER 19

Learning Objectives

After completing this chapter, you should be able to

- Create a purchasing and supply measurement framework
- Review and provide insight into key purchasing and supply measurements
- Review benchmarking and its importance
- Identify key characteristics of effective measurement systems

Chapter Outline

Measuring Purchasing and Supply Performance at a Global Automotive Parts Manufacturer

Overview

This multibillion-dollar diversified manufacturer of electrical and electromechanical components and systems has worldwide operations, markets, and suppliers. Purchasing is done at the corporate, division/business, and regional levels. Global coordination is achieved through the corporate headquarters in the United States. Major operating locations are in North America, Europe, Asia/Pacific, and South America.

Purchasing is organized with companywide product and non-product purchasing directors reporting to the vice president of global purchasing. Global commodity directors and business unit leaders also report to the vice president or to the product/non-product purchasing directors. Also at corporate headquarters are purchasing staff groups, including lean operations, organization and employee development, supplier development, supplier quality, minority supplier development, strategic planning, finance, communications, e-systems, strategy and process, and risk management.

Staff number in the hundreds and are located worldwide. Annual spend is in billions of dollars. The vice president of global purchasing reports to an executive vice president. The overall strategic intent of global purchasing is to provide the corporation with a competitive advantage through achieving extended supply chain performance excellence. Achieving this extended supply chain excellence on a worldwide basis requires vertical and horizontal integration, detailed business plans, and an integrated set of metrics to drive and measure behaviors.

The measurement system is aligned vertically and horizontally with corporate goals and other functions and business units through the strategic global purchasing plan. The plan is integrated with the critical competitive requirements through the company's executive committee. Critical drivers are cost, quality, and availability. In addition, minority purchasing spend, effective product launches, and a competitive supply base are also important.

The global purchasing plan is structured around the strategic intent of global purchasing, and key contributing elements include supplier development, cost, sourcing strategically, quality, e-systems, people, supplier relations, and accelerated change. Horizontal linkage is achieved by establishing a multiyear strategy and annual business plans. The strategy and business plans focus on the current and desired state and link together the corporate, commodity, regional, and business unit strategies and plans.

This strategy and planning process clearly provides for effective communication, project planning, and horizontal and vertical alignment with goals and resulting measurements. An extensive set of integrated financial and nonfinancial measures are in place to guide behavior and review performance. The most significant are discussed here.

Cost Management

Two measures are most critical: (1) year-over-year price performance based on contract prices for the same or similar items, and (2) material cost improvement that can be achieved through various approaches such as design change, process improvement, packaging, and so forth.

In addition, the company's overall financial plan includes cost-reduction levels that need to be achieved by purchasing. Revenues of the firm, as they increase or decrease, influence the purchasing cost-reduction target because of the need to protect margin. The finance group makes final judgments regarding validation of purchasing cost savings. Other important measures in use include the following:

- Quality and quality improvement based on parts per million (PPM) defective determination
- On-time delivery and availability
- Flawless on-time launch of new products
- Minority supplier spend targets
- "Rightsizing" the supply base based on an objective measurement of the appropriate number of suppliers
- Environmental sustainability
- Supplier relationships and development via scorecards
- People development based on number of hours of training per year
- Cost management models
- E-system applications
- Lean projects

This company regularly reviews all measures above. Goals and specific targets are modified regularly, based on business needs. Examples include enhancing cost improvement and flawlessly launching new products to ensure timely introduction to the market.

Targets can be reset at any time the business requires a change. Reviews are at least monthly. There is a heavy emphasis on cost improvement. Targets are aggressive in nature, going beyond what has normally been achieved, and are in place at all purchasing levels and business units.

The purchasing performance measures are organized around the contributing key elements identified earlier as part of the global purchasing plan. The strategies by strategy areas and metrics are in place for the current and future states. The global purchasing business plan forces a linkage across the key elements of the corporation, including divisions, commodity teams, and regional purchasing groups.

Measured performance is regularly reported to all appropriate personnel companywide. Owners of performance across the company are established at all levels with project plans in place with appropriate metrics. For example, supplier development may include project steps and metrics for cost savings, developing supplier engineers, and implementing a supplier council.

Personal business priorities, which drive performance, are based primarily on team recognition rather than personal rewards. However, appraisals are done at the individual level, and people are expected to perform at high performance levels to gain the most significant financial and nonfinancial rewards. Incentive compensation is based on overall achievement of the company's business plan and is primarily awarded at the executive level.

Significant resources are committed to the global purchasing business planning process and related measurements. Strategy and process personnel at the corporate level have lead roles in the planning process.

Purchasing personnel across the organization have execution responsibility, with specific personnel assigned to measurement systems input, data integrity, and enhanced systems development. Finance staff work to ensure the accuracy and validity of cost savings. Cost management personnel are developing cost models against which to evaluate purchasing and supplier performance.

Current systems provide significant support for the measurements. Cost and cost improvement are tracked and reported at all organizational levels and by division and product in considerable detail. Finance validates cost-reduction and purchasing performance to the financial plan for both direct and indirect procurement. Various other metrics are provided by SAP and internal systems models for performance monitoring.

In addition, e-systems are being enhanced and will include advanced supplier profiling and score-cards, a supplier suggestion system, and cost management.

The performance of purchasing (both direct and indirect) is critical to the financial success of the company. Top executives regularly review the performance of purchasing and the supply base, with a keen focus on cost, quality, availability, and launch. Companywide and purchasing executives drive the measurement system and critical metrics, using them to guide behavior and to reward performance.

Source: Adapted from "Strategic Performance Measurement for Purchasing and Supply" (2005), CAPS Research, 42–44.

Note: This case discusses an extensive purchasing and supply measurement system. It is organized around key principles of measurement.

Introduction

This chapter begins with a basic overview of performance measurement and evaluation, including the reasons to measure performance and the problems associated with measurement and evaluation. Next, there is a discussion of the most common purchasing and supply chain measurement categories, with specific examples of performance measures presented. The third section discusses the development of a performance measurement and evaluation system. The fourth section discusses performance benchmarking, which is a process involving comparisons against leading firms to establish performance plans and objectives. The next section discusses the balanced scorecard. The chapter concludes with observations about performance measurement and evaluation.

Purchasing and Supply Chain Performance Measurement and Evaluation

A purchasing and supply chain performance evaluation system represents a formal, systematic approach to monitor, assess, and improve purchasing performance. Although this sounds easy, it is often difficult to develop measures that direct behavior or activity exactly as intended. Some firms still rely on measures that could be harmful, depending on performance objectives, rather than supporting long-term performance. For example, the ability to win significant price concessions from a supplier is still a major objective for certain price/cost performance measures. However, if a purchaser primarily and continually squeezes short-term price reductions from a supplier, will that supplier have the financial resources or the commitment to invest in longer-term performance improvements?

Modern purchasing and supply chain performance measurement and evaluation systems contain a variety of measures. Most of these measures fall into two broad categories: effectiveness measures and efficiency measures. **Effectiveness** refers to the extent to which, by choosing a certain course of action, management can meet a previously established goal or standard. **Efficiency** refers to the relationship between planned and actual resources applied to achieve a previously agreed-upon goal.[1] Efficiency measures usually relate some input to a performance output.

Almost all measures include a standard or target against which to evaluate performance results or outcomes. It is incomplete to say, for example, that a measure will track improvement in supplier quality. Actual improvement still needs to be compared against a preestablished target or objective. Meeting this target, which is presumably based on world-class performance levels, will bring value to an organization. Each performance measure should include actual performance levels and a targeted performance level.

Why Measure Performance?

There are a number of reasons for measuring and evaluating purchasing and supply chain activity and performance.

Measure Contributions to Company Competitive Performance

Purchasing and supply chain management is increasingly being asked to contribute to a company's overall performance. CEOs, COOs and CFOs are looking for major contributions in cost, asset utilization, cash flow, innovation, and revenue improvements. Appropriate measurements can determine contribution levels to company competitiveness and financial performance.

Support Better Decision Making

Measurement can lead to better decisions by making performance and results visible. It is difficult to develop performance improvement plans without understanding the areas in which performance falls short. Measurement provides a track record of purchasing performance over time and directly supports decision-making activity by management.

Support Better Communication

Performance measurement can result in better communication across the supply chain, including within purchasing, between departments, with suppliers, and with executive management. For example, a purchaser must clearly communicate performance expectations to suppliers. The measures that quantify supplier performance reflect a purchaser's expectations.

Provide Performance Feedback

Measurement provides the opportunity for performance feedback, which supports the prevention or correction of problems identified during the performance measurement process. Feedback also provides insight into how well a buyer, department, team, or supplier is meeting its performance objectives over time.

Motivate and Direct Behavior

Measurement motivates and directs behavior toward desired end results. A measurement system can accomplish this in several ways. First, the selection of performance categories and objectives indicates to purchasing personnel those activities that an organization considers critical. Second, management can motivate and influence behavior by linking the attainment of performance objectives to organizational rewards, such as pay increases.

Problems with Purchasing and Supply Chain Measurement and Evaluation

Measuring and evaluating performance, including purchasing and supply chain performance, historically has had certain problems and limitations. Mark Brown, an expert on performance measurement, argued that most managers and professionals today are like a pilot trying to fly a plane with only half the instruments needed and many additional instruments that measure irrelevant data.[2] He states that practically every organization has some type of problem with its measurement system.

Too Much Data and Wrong Data

Having too much data is the most common problem an organization has with its measurement system. A second and more serious problem is that the data that managers pay attention to are often the wrong data. The metrics are selected because of history or a feeling that the measure is related to success, which may not be the case at all. In fact, measures that managers follow may sometimes be in conflict with measures used in other units or functional areas. As a general rule, employees should monitor no more than a dozen measures, with half of those being the most critical.

Measures That Are Short-Term Focused

Many small- and medium-sized organizations have a problem of relying on measures and data that are short-term focused. Typically the only data they collect are financial and operating data. In purchasing, this would mean a short-term focus on workload and supply chain activities, while ignoring the longer-range or strategic measures.

Lack of Detail

At times the data that are reported are summarized so much as to make the information meaningless. A measure that reports on a single measure of monthly supplier quality probably lacks detail. A supply manager will want to know what the specific types of defects the supplier is experiencing are, what the defects cost the buyer's company, and the supplier's quality performance over time.

An operations manager at a major automotive regional parts distribution facility receives a monthly measure of the facility's quality as measured by claims made by customers. However, he also receives reports that detail the following:

- The type of errors that are occurring (wrong part picked, damage, shortages, missed shipments, and so on)
- Which customers are making the quality claims
- Which employees are responsible for the quality errors
- The total cost of the quality claims against the facility
- The part numbers that have quality claims against them

With this information the manager can take action that will attack the root causes of the quality problems at his facility.

Drive the Wrong Performance

Unfortunately, many measures drive behavior that is not what was intended or needed. If buyers are measured on the number of purchase orders written, then they will make sure to split orders among suppliers to generate as many purchase orders as possible. Part of this is because of the fact that measuring intellectual work is difficult. However, organizations still want to look for factors that can be measured and reported. These factors may not, however, always be the right ones.

Measures of Behavior versus Accomplishments

The problem with measuring behavior is there is no guarantee the behavior will lead to desired results. For example, a behavioral measure that tracks the amount of purchase volume covered by corporatewide contracts is becoming increasingly common. A better measure, however, is one that tracks the total savings because of the use of corporatewide contracts.

Another example of a behavioral measure is one that measures the number of meetings held by a commodity team each quarter. A better set of measures will track the performance results that occurred because of the team's actions. Although some set of behavioral measures will always be present, measures that capture accomplishments are the ones that really matter.

Purchasing and Supply Chain Performance Measurement Categories

As part of a company-focused purchasing and supply chain measurement approach, firms should follow a systematic process to maximize results and achieve vertical and horizontal alignment of purpose. Exhibit 19.1 on p. 755 illustrates the process. As indicated, company objectives drive specific company strategies such as being the low-cost producer or technology leader. These company strategies should then drive appropriate and prioritized purchasing and supply chain objectives and specific strategies.

Alignment of strategies, measures, and actions will bring together top-down direction and bottom-up targeting to produce positive contributions. In a single enterprise, this could deliver competitive advantage. Integrated purchasing and supply chain management can also produce competitive advantage for the end-to-end supply chain level, improving effectiveness and reducing overhead.

There are hundreds of purchasing and supply chain measures. Perhaps the best way to summarize the vast number of separate measures is by developing performance measurement categories as shown in Exhibit 19.1. Within each category, many separate measures relate to each general category. Most purchasing and supply chain measures fall into one of the following categories:

- Price performance
- Cost-effectiveness
- Revenue
- Quality
- Time/delivery/responsiveness
- Technology and innovation
- Environmental Sustainability
- Asset and integrated supply chain management

Exhibit 19.1   Integrated Company/Purchasing Measurement Process

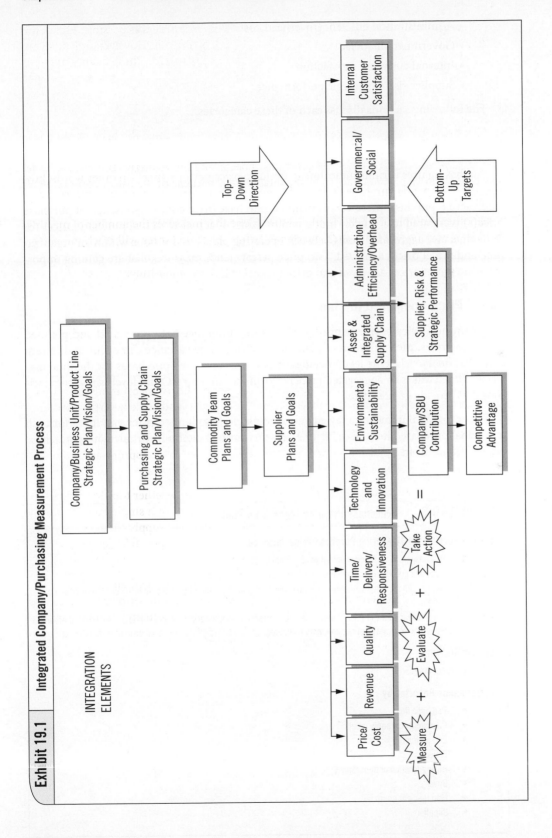

- Administration efficiency/overhead cost
- Governmental/social
- Internal customer satisfaction
- Supplier risk & strategic performance

The following sections discuss each of these categories.

Price Performance Measures

Purchasing uses various indicators to evaluate price performance—in other words, how effectively it spends purchase dollars. The most common price performance measures include actual purchase price versus planned purchase price comparisons, actual purchase price(s) compared to a market index, comparisons of actual-to-actual purchase prices for individual and aggregated items between operating plants or divisions within an organization, and target prices achieved. Two price performance measures that are gaining importance are target prices achieved and price to market index comparisons.

Actual Price Compared to Plan

A common price performance measure is the difference between actual and planned purchase prices. Measurement of planned purchase price variance can occur at different organizational levels. One level includes actual versus planned purchases for the total material budget; this is an aggregated price performance measure. Other levels show comparisons that provide greater detail.

For example, purchasing may calculate actual versus planned price variances for each individual purchased item. Exhibit 19.2 presents various methods for calculating purchase price variance from a plan.

Exhibit 19.2	Purchase Price Variance from Plan

Various Formats for Measuring Purchase Price Variance

1. Purchase price variance = Actual price − Planned price
2. Purchase price variance percentage = Actual price/Planned price
3. Total purchase price variance = (Actual price − Planned price) × Purchase quantity or estimated annual volume
4. Current year dollar impact of purchase price variance = (Actual price − Planned price) × (Estimated annual volume × Percentage of requirements remaining)

Units of Measure

Dollars or percentages

Performance Reported by

- Purchase item
- Commodity or family group
- End product
- Project
- Buying location or department
- Buyer
- Management group
- Supplier

Actual Prices versus Market Index

Purchase price versus market index measures provide information about the relationship between actual prices and published market prices. These measures are most appropriate for market-based products where pricing is primarily a function of supply and demand. This also applies to standard and readily available products. Index measures take into account the difference between a published index number over a designated period (such as a quarter) and the change in the actual price paid. The following illustrates this concept:

1a.	Market-based index for Item X	March 31, 2014	= 125
1b.	Market-based index for Item X	June 30, 2014	= 128
1c.	Market index change	= (128 − 125)/125	= 2.4% increase
2a.	Actual price paid for Item X	March 31, 2014	= $150
2b.	Actual price paid for Item X	June 30, 2014	= $152
2c.	Price paid change rate	= ($152 − $150)/$150	= 1.3% increase
3.	Comparison to market	2.4% − 1.3%	= Better by 1.1%

Price Comparisons among Operations

Actual prices for similar items are also compared between plants, divisions, or business units. These comparisons provide an opportunity to identify purchase price differences within a firm. This provides visibility as to which unit is negotiating or securing the best purchase price. The comparison activity can also help identify commonly purchased items between units for purchase consolidation. A number of firms also attempt actual-to-actual price comparisons among companies to determine true price competitiveness.

Although firms are increasingly focusing on cost versus price, price performance measures are still very important, especially with firms that lack detailed cost data. Price performance measures are also commonly used when purchasing raw materials, other commodity or standard-type items, components, systems, and contract services.

Sourcing Snapshot

Chrysler Speeds Supplier Payday

Chrysler Group is paying suppliers more quickly for some engineering, design, and development work and taking other actions to improve relations with suppliers.

The new policies—to be fully implemented by the end of January—will apply primarily to parts Chrysler will buy for compact and mid-sized cars.

The company also will use the approach on other new programs.

Under new, Fiat-led management, Chrysler is taking a series of steps to reverse its reputation as the worst of the major North American automakers in dealing with suppliers.

"It's no fun to work in a business where you're fighting your supply base," Dan Knott, Chrysler head of purchasing, told *Automotive News*, "We need a healthy supply base."

The changes, which Chrysler has discussed with its advisory council, include:

- Paying selected suppliers upfront for costly advance engineering, design, and development work on certain new Chrysler programs.
- Resolving outstanding payment claims faster.

Unresolved claims can be costly to suppliers and affect other programs. A supplier still waiting for payment for one Chrysler program might be reluctant to take on future work.

- Paying suppliers in chunks at predetermined milestones in the life of the program.

Knott's plan is to pay suppliers at certain milestones a percentage of what they are owed, a sharp departure from the piece-payments approach of the past.

Source: Wernie, B., and Sherefkin, R. (January 18, 2010) "Chrysler Speeds Supplier Payday," *Automotive News*, 1, 29.

Target Prices Achieved

Target pricing is the process of determining what the external customer is willing to pay for a product or service and then assigning specific cost targets to the components, assemblies, and systems that make up the product or service. Target costing uses the following formula to determine allowable costs:

$$\text{Target Price} - \text{Profit Target} = \text{Allowable Cost}$$

Allowable cost is then allocated to various elements that make up the final product or service.

Cost-Effectiveness Measures

The measures in this category focus attention on efforts to reduce purchase costs. Cost-effectiveness measures fall into two general categories: cost changes and cost avoidance. The use of cost-effectiveness measures requires a word of caution. The method used to achieve cost reductions is critical. A cost reduction based on mutual cooperation is the same, on paper, as a cost reduction resulting from heavy-handed pressure on a supplier. Although the end result (i.e., a cost reduction) appears to be the same, the process used to achieve that result can have longer-term implications. Cooperation may reduce costs through joint improvement, whereas heavy-handed cost pressure may force a supplier to cut corners, thereby reducing profits, possibly to unsustainable levels, resulting in poor quality.

Cost Changes

A cost-change measure compares the actual cost of an item or family of items over a period of time. A cost change is the increase or decrease in cost resulting from a change in purchasing strategy or practice brought about by an individual or a group.

The primary measure of concern to companies is cost reduction achieved, which is calculated by taking (New price – Prior price) multiplied by estimated volume. For example, if the new price was $9/unit and the prior price was $10/unit with an estimated volume of 10,000 units for the next budget period, there would be a projected cost reduction of $10,000. Actual usage would determine the final cost reduction achieved.

Cost Avoidance

Cost avoidance represents the difference between a price paid and a potentially higher price (which might have occurred if purchasing had not obtained the lower price through a specific effort or action). For example, assume that purchasing paid $5.00 per unit for an item in the past, but the supplier has now quoted a price of $5.50 per unit. If the buyer negotiates a price of $5.25 per unit, then he or she has achieved a cost avoidance of $0.25 per unit, even though the price was still $0.25 higher than the prior price. Unfortunately, finance often argues that cost-avoidance savings rarely show up on a firm's profit line.

Cost-change and cost-avoidance measures differ significantly. Cost change represents an actual change from a prior-period price, whereas cost avoidance refers to the amount that would have been paid minus the amount actually paid. Purchasing departments that require tangible cost improvement should focus more on the cost-change approach. This represents actual changes that can impact a firm's overall profitability.

Cost-avoidance figures almost always require manual calculation and are sometimes subject to exaggeration. As a result, some observers have described cost-avoidance measures and figures as "soft," "funny money," and "easy to manipulate."

Revenue Measures

Revenue measures demonstrate the impact of purchasing and supply strategies and actions on revenues of the firm. For example, purchasing and supply may uncover new supplier technologies before others in the industry do and gain exclusive access, resulting in new-product applications with favorable pricing and volume growth.

In addition, firms have achieved revenue growth because of royalty agreements negotiated with suppliers that have sold jointly developed technologies to other customers. Revenue from royalty generated from licensing patents and other technologies may be measured and reported.

Meeting new-product introduction dates with perfect supplier performance, enabling a first-to-market position with premium pricing, was also linked to revenue growth. Perfect-launch revenue is critical at many firms and is influenced by supplier performance.

Revenue measures for purchasing and supply are important because they link purchasing and supply strategies to the revenue elements of a firm's economic value-add. However, relatively few revenue measures are in use. Apparently, firms have not fully recognized the contribution to revenue generation that purchasing and supply can make, nor how to best determine the contribution. This is the case for direct goods and even more true on the indirect side, where the linkage of purchasing and supply strategy to revenues is less obvious or, perhaps, nonexistent.

Revenue Measure Examples

- Royalty revenues generated from supplier- or buyer-developed technology and patents initiated by purchasing or sourcing
- Supplier contribution as a reason for new business, for example, new business development, unique technology found by purchasing, flexibility in shifting output product or service mix to meet higher profit or revenue, generating customer demand
- Return on licensing technology driven by purchasing or sourcing
- Number of buyer/supplier patents that have led to royalties

- Number of invention disclosure forms filed
- Number of patents granted
- Value of free samples from suppliers

Quality Measures

Parts per Million (PPM)

This measure expresses a maximum number (in absolute or percentage terms) of level of defects allowable for any particular product, assembly, or service. It may be expressed by using one of the following specific definitions or could be the mean time between failures for a plant or equipment item. When applied to products, components, assemblies, or systems, the traditional metric has been parts per million failing to conform to specification. As quality control has improved and the ability to manufacture to tighter tolerances has increased, this metric may also be tightened. In determining the PPM result, there is a need to measure (by factual inspection, testing, or statistically reliable sampling) the incidence of defective or nonconforming parts. The measure demands a reference point such as production, receipt, incoming inspection, or shipment. In addition, quality measures are also being developed and being used for services.

Customer Defects per Supplier

This is a measure of the number of defects from individual suppliers to indicate comparative quality performance among competing suppliers. It is also used as an absolute target for suppliers in total to attain and surpass, often as part of an assessment, certification, and reward approach. Measurement is calculated by inspecting or sampling the number of acceptable components, assemblies, or systems delivered as a proportion of the total number of those parts delivered by that supplier.

It is possible to aggregate this measure across all the different items supplied by any one supplier to arrive at an average number of defects for that supplier. However, the strategic criticality of items is not taken into account.

Field Failure Rates by Purchase Item and by Supplier

This measures the incidence of failures of components, assemblies, and systems or services when actually incorporated into the final product or service and supplied to external customers. As a measure, it indicates failures after sale, and organizations will tend to aim for a zero incidence of such failures. However, in some industries (e.g., equipment rental) this measure becomes a key measure of customer satisfaction.

The metric is calculated by developing a ratio of failures against total installed population. It is used to monitor product performance after sale, manage after-sales support costs, and provide input to supplier improvement, product design improvement, and replacement design by tracking failure rates and their root causes.

Time/Delivery/Responsiveness Measures

Time-to-Market Targets, New Products/Services

This measure is the amount of time (in weeks or months) from concept to first shipment or provision of a product or service to the external customer. The objective is continuous reduction so as to reduce the amount of time it takes to achieve break-even of investment and also to be first to market with the product or service.

On-Time Delivery/Responsiveness

These measures indicate the degree to which suppliers are able to meet customer schedule requirements. Key elements for such measures include the following:

- Due dates, scheduled or promised
- Delivery windows
- Acceptable early or late arrivals to due dates (e.g., minus two days or no days late)

The metrics are typically calculated as the percentage of shipments, services, or individual items on time or late (occasionally early). These measures can be applied in service or manufacturing businesses. Supplier and procurement performance can be measured through indices based on the above measures. These metrics can be further organized by commodity or purchase family. Percentages are calculated by company total on-time to total deliveries, and then further reported by purchase family and supplier.

Achieving New-Product Introduction Ramp-Up Schedules and Introduction Dates

These measures indicate whether procurement and supply chain management and strategic processes and suppliers are achieving necessary available volume goals at milestones and at market introduction dates for the product or service.

Cycle Time Reductions: Order Entry, Manufacturing/Operations, Distribution, and Logistics

These measures should identify total cycle time and its key components. Measures focus on reduction through elimination of delays and delivering continuous improvement to target times. Examples include supplier manufacturing cycle times, order entry, internal operations, transportation, and so forth.

Responsiveness to Schedule Changes, Mix Changes, and Design or Service Changes

These measures indicate how quickly suppliers can respond to demand or use changes, for example, the ability to adjust schedule by 50 percent within two weeks of scheduled delivery. Another measure could be time to achieve design changes to meet scheduled targets. These measures recognize the need for flexibility.

Technology and Innovation Measures

First Insight/Production Outputs of Supplier Technology

This measure would typically link to a contractual agreement whereby, for new technologies, your firm may get insight, some period of time before new technology developments are shared with other organizations. This may be an important focus in dealings with selected key technology suppliers to your firm. A specific metric can be the number of such agreements with key suppliers for critical technologies. Any target would be firm specific. A potential drawback with this measure is that no account is taken of the success or failure arising from such technology insights.

New Innovations Incorporated Into Products or Services

This measure determines the number and/or rate of product/service. Innovations from suppliers, number of frequency, and revenue impact can be determined.

Sourcing Snapshot

Ford Aligned Business Framework

In an Automotive News article, Ford highlighted the need for a smaller supplier network for production parts to provide greater value. In fact, the number of suppliers had shrunk by about two-thirds over recent years. The objective of the Aligned Business Framework (ABF) is to focus significant business on a small group of excellent suppliers so as to become "customers of choice," obtain supplier innovations and technology and improve overall Ford and supplier performance. As part of the aligned business framework, Ford has emphasized improvements in listening and quickly responding to supplier innovations, as well as focusing business with ABF suppliers. As a result, its reputation with suppliers has improved according to third party analysts. According to one supplier, it now has better access to Ford senior executives, is provided more information and insight into Ford's future plans and is more confident about retaining Ford business provided that quality and availability continues to meet performance expectation.

Source: "Ford strengthens bonds with its elite suppliers," Automotive News Insight, August 5, 2013, pg. 24.

Standardization and Use of Industry Standards to Reduce Complexity

These measures focus on achieving standardization of components, systems, and services and application of currently used purchased items or the use of industry-standard versus unique items. Specific measures include reduction of different items used, percentage of new products or services made up of currently purchased items, and number of industry-unique items utilized in a new product or service. The company would establish these and similar measures and link to product- or service-specific goals.

Environmental Sustainability Measures

Companies are tracking the achievement of environmental goals and costs associated with compliance, both voluntary and where legislation enforces compliance. The objective is to drive performance improvement to achieve self-imposed or regulatory goals. For example, from ISM's "Sustainability and Social Responsibility Metrics and Performance Criteria for Sustainability and Social Responsibility Initiatives,"[3] sustainability refers to the ability to meet current needs without hindering the ability to meet the needs of future generations in terms of economic, environmental and social challenges, and measures include:

 a. Use of sustainability criteria in procurement decisions
 b. Processes in place to embed sustainability and social responsibility into supplier qualification and certification decisions
 c. Processes in place to embed sustainability and social responsibility into product design, redesign, and statements of work
 d. Developing processes/knowledge to ensure understanding of sourcing, recycling, and other decisions
 e. Development of relationships with key suppliers to gain access to protected information on chemical makeup of products being purchased

    f. Working with risk management and/or internally to develop, quantify, and base decisions on financial and other risks related to nonconformance with, or lack of support of, sustainability and social responsibility initiatives

    g. Maintain appropriate records to feed into corporate sustainability and social responsibility reporting

Asset and Integrated Supply Chain Management Measures

The measurement of inventory as an asset for a single enterprise may include a number of typical unit or aggregate inventory measures such as the following:

- Dollar value of inventory investment (following appropriate accounting rules)
- Inventory turnover
- Days/weeks/months of supply of inventory

The objective is to reduce inventory cost by increasing the velocity of throughput or reducing inventory carrying cost. A unique use of this measure is its application across inventory throughout various stages within a firm's supply chain and, more importantly, across firms in the aggregate supply chain (external to your firm) with specified future targets.

In addition, it is common to have additional measures that track different aspects of a firm's inventory investment. Examples include percentage of active versus inactive part numbers, total of part numbers, working capital savings, and inventory investment by type of purchased item (for example, production items, maintenance items, and packaging materials).

It is also common to have measures that track the speed or velocity of inventory as it moves through different elements of the supply chain. This includes raw material, work-in-process, and finished-goods inventory turns. The amount of inventory maintained as safety stock is also a common measure. The accuracy of computer records that are part of the inventory location system is also closely tracked.

Transportation Cost Reduction

Transportation measures include tracking actual transportation costs against some pre-established objective, demurrage and detention costs, and premium transportation. Transportation carrier quality, delivery performance levels, and transportation lead time can also be measured.

Cost-reduction measures focus on the total transportation costs incurred per planning period to conduct business and those premium transportation costs incurred where expediting requires a nonstandard transportation method to meet internal or external requirements, for example, using air shipments when trucking is the preferred shipping mode.

Transportation costs can be measured in total dollars and as a percentage of cost of goods sold or sales revenue. Premium transportation can be measured in dollars or percentage of overall transportation costs. These costs can be measured inbound, intracompany, and outbound.

Customer Orders

These measures evaluate how well an organization is satisfying its commitment to downstream customers. Various measures include the percentage of on-time delivery, total time from customer order to customer delivery, returned orders, and warranty claims. Although we have focused primarily on purchasing and upstream supply chain activities, purchasing and materials planners are increasingly responsible for managing inventory from a total supply chain perspective. This may also include downstream activities.

E-Transactions (Number and Percentage of Suppliers/Dollars/Orders)

These measures show some degree of cross-enterprise or supply chain linkage. The magnitude of use of electronic systems that link buyers and suppliers can, for example, be measured by the following:

- Absolute number of suppliers
- Percentage of suppliers
- Dollar value and percentage of orders
- Percentage of advance shipping notices
- Electronic funds transfer
- Meeting customer requirements
- Inventory throughout the supply chain
- Number or dollars of e-reverse auctions and/or e-quote packages
- Other

Pull Systems/Shared Schedules/Supplier Managed Inventory (SMI)

These measures establish the number (or percentage) of suppliers that are sharing schedules and operating in a pull system environment. They may also measure percentages of suppliers that are sharing schedules against those that should be. SMI measures establish the number of suppliers and magnitude of inventory being managed by suppliers for which they have financial responsibility.

Administration Efficiency/Overhead Cost Measures

Management uses administration and efficiency measures to plan purchasing's annual administrative budget and to help control administrative expenses during a budget period. Budgeted expense items commonly include salaries, travel and living expenses, training expenses, e-systems, office supplies, and other miscellaneous expenses. Salaries traditionally take the largest share of the purchasing administrative budget. The two most common methods to establish the administrative budget for purchasing are the current budget plus adjustment and the use of control ratios.

Current Budget Plus Adjustment

The most common method of establishing a budget uses the current administrative budget as a starting point. Management then adjusts the budget for the next period (usually the next fiscal year) upward or downward depending on expected business conditions or other departmental requirements. Budget adjustments reflect management's view about projected purchasing workload and a firm's profitability. Decreasing workload or profits can result in a budget reduction. Conversely, increasing workload or profits may justify a budget increase.

Control Ratios

With the control ratio approach, the administrative budget for purchasing is a percentage of another measure that reflects purchasing's workload. Planned dollar expenditure for direct material is often the selected workload measure.

The historical control ratio as well as negotiation between purchasing and higher management often determines the control ratio percentage used during calculation of the administrative budget. A projection of direct material purchase requirements for the next period then affects the administrative budget. Purchasing workload is assumed to be proportional to planned dollar expenditures for direct material. The purchasing administrative budget becomes the following:

Purchasing Budget = Estimated Expenditures for Direct materials × Control Ratio

Purchasing managers use the total budget figure to allocate resources among different departmental uses. Management must determine how many buyers are required, the size of the clerical support staff, and other budget-related issues.

Other Approaches

Current budget plus adjustment and control ratios are not the only methods used to arrive at an administrative budget for purchasing or efficiency. Purchasing workload such as purchase orders processed, line items processed, and headcount may also be used to measure efficiency. Again, we must warn against emphasizing purchasing efficiency over purchasing effectiveness as a strict indicator of performance.

Governmental/Social Measures

Minority, Women, and Small-Business Enterprise Objectives

In the United States there are social, state, and federal requirements that public and private organizations place a percentage of their business with minority- and women-owned business enterprises (MWBEs). These expenditures are regularly targeted at specific performance levels, tracked, and reported; they are used to drive purchasing strategy. Small-business purchases may also be included. Specific measures may include the following:

- Percentage of spend (the proportion of purchase spend from MWBE suppliers as a percentage of total annual purchase spend), calculated as follows:

$$\frac{\text{Annual Purchase (\$) from MWBE Suppliers}}{\text{Total Annual External Purchases (\$)}} = \%$$

- Number of suppliers in each MWBE category
- Growth of MWBE spend

Safety Measures

These are measures that focus on the safety of employees at suppliers throughout the supply chain. Supplier safety records will influence sourcing decisions. For example, suppliers with a history of poor and unsafe working conditions in emerging countries may not be awarded new business.

Internal Customer Satisfaction Measures

Companies are also applying measures that indicate the degree of satisfaction with purchasing's value-add contribution. This is typically done by surveying internal customers and asking them to indicate their satisfaction with purchasing by responding to a series of check-off and open-ended questions. Supplier satisfaction surveys and measures are also used.

Supplier, Risk, and Strategic Performance Measures

Supplier Performance

Supplier performance measurement is an area in which many firms have made great progress. Supplier scorecards frequently contain many of the measures discussed above. Purchasers generally track supplier quality, cost, and delivery along with other performance areas. Furthermore, firms are beginning to quantify the cost associated with supplier nonperformance. The resulting cost figure represents the total cost of doing business with a supplier. Supplier total cost measures allow direct comparisons among suppliers.

Hewlett-Packard developed a supplier performance evaluation model that evaluates supplier performance (and the teams that manage those suppliers) in the areas of T (technology contribution), Q (quality), R (supplier responsiveness), D (delivery performance), C (cost), and E (environmental performance). The FedEx supplier scorecard featured in Chapter 9 provides additional details about supplier performance measurement systems. These supplier scorecards are increasingly important in selecting, motivating, and developing suppliers.

Risk Measures

Risk is an important Purchasing consideration in sourcing decisions and pervades many areas that impact company performance. Risk measures have been implemented or are planned for implementation by many companies that include new technology development risk, supplier financial risk, logistics disruption risks, supplier physical disaster risks based on geography (typhoons, earthquakes, etc.) and political conditions. Risk measures for the prior mentioned areas typically are rated as high, moderate or low and require mitigation efforts.

Strategic Performance Measures

Purchasing requires measures that reflect its ability to support overall corporate and functional goals, which means a reduced emphasis on pure efficiency measures (e.g., the cost to issue a purchase order or current workload status) and greater emphasis on effectiveness measures (those that reflect purchasing's strategic contribution). Examples of the latter include tracking early supplier involvement in product design, performance gains resulting from direct supplier development efforts, and supplier-provided improvement suggestions. Within most industries, purchasing must shift from measuring itself as an administrative support function to measuring how well it provides strategic value.

Exhibit 19.3 provides examples of key strategic purchasing measures. Notice that these measures are a combination of activity- and results-oriented measures. Emphasis shifts from strict indicators of personnel performance or efficiency to how well the purchasing function supports strategic supply base management goals and objectives. To shift from an operational to a strategic perspective, the purchasing measurement and evaluation system must also shift.

The performance indicators in Exhibit 19.3 are more strategically and externally focused than traditional performance indicators. They are also specified in terms of broader purchasing goals rather than specific activity. For example, a buyer may be responsible for a performance objective stating that 75 percent of the buyer's suppliers will be quality certified by the third quarter of 2014. This differs from a measure that states a buyer must process 10 requests for quotation per day on average.

Exhibit 19.3	Examples of Strategic Purchasing Measurement Indicators

- Percentage of purchasing's operating budget committed to on-site supplier visits
- Proportion of quality-certified suppliers to total suppliers
- Percentage of receipts free of inspection and material defects
- Total number of suppliers overall and considered strategic
- Proportion of suppliers participating in early product design or other joint value-added activities
- Revenue increase as a result of supplier-provided technology that differentiates end products to customers
- Percentage of operating budget allocated to supplier development and training
- Total cost supplier selection and evaluation measures
- Supplier environmental sustainability
- Supplier lead-time indicators
- Purchasing's contribution to return on assets, return on investment, and economic value-added corporate measures
- Purchasing success with achieving cost reductions with Tier 2 and Tier 3 suppliers
- Percentage of purchase dollars committed to longer-term contracts
- Savings achieved from the use of companywide agreements
- Purchasing's contribution to product development cycle time reduction
- Percentage/dollar value of items purchased from single sources
- Percentage of purchase dollars committed to highest-performing suppliers
- Percentage of purchase transactions processed electronically
- Percentage of total receipts on a just-in-time basis
- Supplier quality levels, cost performance, and delivery performance compared with world-class performance targets
- Supplier development costs and benefits
- Continuous supplier performance improvement measures
- Reductions in working capital because of purchasing and supply chain efforts
- Contribution to return on investment and assets realized from strategic outsourcing efforts
- Savings achieved from part number reduction efforts
- Savings achieved from part standardization efforts
- Risk identification and reduction

Developing a Performance Measurement and Evaluation System

The development of a measurement and evaluation system requires the leadership, support, and commitment of executive management, who must commit the financial resources necessary for system development. Management must also require all purchasing locations to use the same system structure, which can reduce duplication of effort and save development and training costs. This does not mean that each location must use the same performance objectives or performance criteria. It only means that the system's basic design should be similar. Executive management support also sends a message about the seriousness of tracking and improving performance.

Development of an effective measurement and evaluation system follows a general sequence of activities. These include determining which performance categories to measure, developing specific performance measures, establishing performance standards for each measure, finalizing system details, and implementing and reviewing the system and each performance measure. Exhibit 19.4 presents an overview of the development of a purchasing and supply chain performance measurement system.

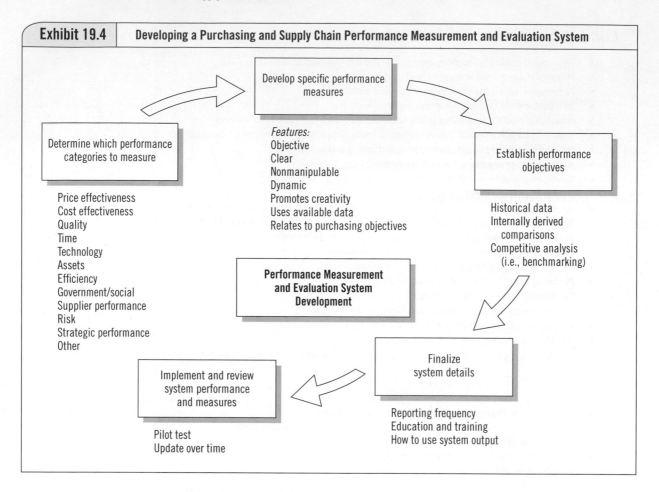

Exhibit 19.4   Developing a Purchasing and Supply Chain Performance Measurement and Evaluation System

Develop specific performance measures

Determine which performance categories to measure

Price effectiveness
Cost effectiveness
Quality
Time
Technology
Assets
Efficiency
Government/social
Supplier performance
Risk
Strategic performance
Other

Features:
Objective
Clear
Nonmanipulable
Dynamic
Promotes creativity
Uses available data
Relates to purchasing objectives

Performance Measurement and Evaluation System Development

Establish performance objectives

Historical data
Internally derived comparisons
Competitive analysis (i.e., benchmarking)

Finalize system details

Reporting frequency
Education and training
How to use system output

Implement and review system performance and measures

Pilot test
Update over time

Determine Which Performance Categories to Measure

A previous section discussed various performance measurement categories. The first step of the development process requires identifying which measurement categories to emphasize. Also, a firm can weight its performance measures and categories differently.

Management does not concern itself with specific performance measures during this phase of system development. The selected performance categories must relate broadly to organizational and purchasing and supply chain goals and objectives.

Selecting the performance measure categories is a critical step prior to developing specific performance measures.

Develop Specific Performance Measures

Developing specific performance measures begins once management identifies the measurement categories it will emphasize. Certain features characterize successful purchasing and supply chain performance measures.

Objectivity

Each measure should be as objective as possible. The measurement system should rely on quantitative data instead of qualitative feelings and assessments. Subjective evaluation can create disagreement between the rater and the individual or group responsible for the performance objective.

Clarity

Personnel must understand a performance measure's requirements to direct performance toward the desired outcome and minimize misunderstandings. All parties must be clear about what each performance measure means, agree on the performance objectives associated with the measure, and understand what it takes to accomplish the measure. Well-understood measures are straightforward and unambiguous.

Use of Accurate and Available Data

Well-defined measures use data that are available and accurate. If a measure requires data that are difficult to generate or unreliable, the probability of using the measure on a consistent basis declines. The cost of generating and collecting the required data should not outweigh the potential benefit of using the performance measure.

Creativity

A common misconception is that a performance evaluation system should measure every possible activity. When this occurs, the measures can stifle individual creativity. The measures control behavior so tightly that the system eliminates room for personal initiative. A successful system measures only what is important along with promoting individual initiative and creativity, which may mean focusing on 5 or 6 important, clearly defined measures instead of 25 vague measures.

Directly Related to Organizational Objectives

Exhibit 19.5 illustrates how corporate goals and objectives influence purchasing goals and objectives. Other functional objectives also can influence purchasing. For example, manufacturing's goals can have a direct impact on purchasing because purchasing supports the manufacturing process. To meet its goals and objectives, purchasing executives develop strategies and action plans. Finally, management develops measures that evaluate the output or performance from the activities required to accomplish purchasing's strategies and plans. The measures serve as indicators of purchasing's progress.

Joint Participation

Joint participation means that the personnel responsible for each measure participate in developing the measure or establishing the measure's performance objective. Joint participation can go a long way toward getting the support of the personnel responsible for achieving the measure.

Dynamic over Time

A dynamic system is one that management reviews periodically, to determine whether existing measures still support purchasing's goals and objectives, if there is a need for new measures, or if performance standards or objectives require updating.

Non-manipulable

A non-manipulable measure is one that personnel cannot inappropriately influence the results of (i.e., the measure is cheat-proof). Ideally, the individual(s) responsible for

Exhibit 19.5 | **Linking Purchasing Measures and Corporate Objectives**

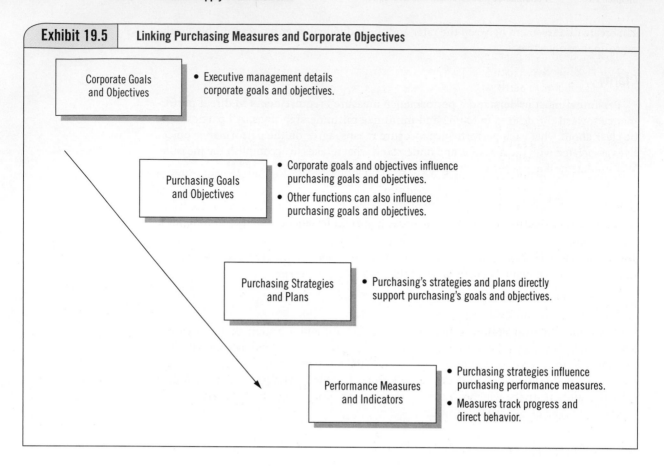

Corporate Goals and Objectives
- Executive management details corporate goals and objectives.

Purchasing Goals and Objectives
- Corporate goals and objectives influence purchasing goals and objectives.
- Other functions can also influence purchasing goals and objectives.

Purchasing Strategies and Plans
- Purchasing's strategies and plans directly support purchasing's goals and objectives.

Performance Measures and Indicators
- Purchasing strategies influence purchasing performance measures.
- Measures track progress and direct behavior.

the measure should not be responsible for supplying the data to the reporting system. This becomes an issue of accountability and integrity. The measure's output should be a true reflection of actual activity or performance results. Systems receiving their input from automated or computerized systems are generally less susceptible to data manipulation.

Establish Performance Objectives for Each Measure

Establishing an objective for each performance measure is critical. Objectives quantify the desired performance target or goal. Management must not specify objectives that are too easy. The too-easy objective can become an accepted performance standard within a department.

Performance standards or objectives must be realistic, which means the measure should be challenging yet achievable through a solid effort. An objective should not be so easy that it requires minimal effort. Conversely, it should not be so difficult that it discourages personnel from even attempting to achieve the objective. The objective must also reflect the realities of a firm's competitive environment. An objective that is challenging internally yet does not reflect the competitive environment is not part of a well-defined measure.

Firms commonly use three methods when establishing performance measure objectives: (1) historical data, (2) internal comparisons, and (3) external analysis.

Historical Data

This method uses past data about an activity as the basis for establishing a formal performance objective. Historical performance is often modified with a performance improvement factor to arrive at a current objective. Purchasing and supply chain managers often use the historical approach with efficiency-related measures.

Relying on historical data can create some problems. The possibility exists that past performance was less than optimal. By establishing an objective based on suboptimal performance, even with an improvement factor, a firm risks continuing suboptimal performance. Also, historical data provide no insight about the performance capabilities of competitors or other leading firms. In addition, the firm's goals, strategies, and financial objectives will drive purchasing and supply goals. Purchasing cannot be a value contributor without contributing to firm success through goal achievement.

Internal Comparisons

A firm can perform internal comparisons between departments or business units. The best internal performance level can become the basis for a companywide performance objective. Firms with multiple business units often compare and rank performance internally across different performance categories.

This approach, which offers some advantages over the historical approach, also has disadvantages. A firm that stresses comparisons between internal units can lose sight of its external competition. Unhealthy rivalry can also develop among internal business units or departments. Furthermore, there is no guarantee that the best-performing internal unit matches the best-performing unit of a direct competitor.

External Analysis

This approach requires examination of the practices and performance objectives of competitors or other leading firms. The advantage of this approach is that it requires an external assessment at very specific levels of detail. A later section discusses benchmarking as a competitive-analysis approach for establishing performance objectives.

Finalize System Details

The next phase of implementation requires management to consider issues such as the frequency of performance reporting, the education and training of system users, and the final determination of how to use system output.

Performance-Reporting Frequency

A sound measurement and evaluation system provides regular reporting of performance results. The actual reporting frequency can differ from measure to measure. Management must determine what frequency supports the most effective use of each measure. A measure that tracks the status of inbound transportation shipments, for example, must be available on a frequent (daily or real-time) basis. A summary measure evaluating overall supplier performance may require only weekly or monthly reporting.

Education and Training

A firm must train its personnel and suppliers to use the performance measurement and evaluation system. Each participant must understand his or her accountability and responsibility under the system and how to use the system's output to improve performance. The measurement and evaluation system is a tool, and like all tools, it requires proper education and training in its use.

Using System Output

Managers use the output of a performance measurement and evaluation system in a number of ways. Some managers rely on the output to directly evaluate the performance of purchasing personnel or suppliers. Managers may use the system to track the effectiveness of individual buyers. System output may also identify better-performing suppliers that deserve future purchase contracts.

Managers must give careful thought to how best to use system output.

Implement and Review System Performance and Measures

All systems have an implementation phase, which may include pilot or trial runs to make sure the system performs as planned. The measurement and evaluation system, along with each performance measure, must be subject to periodic review. Having a system that contains obsolete or inappropriate measures can be more damaging than having no formal system at all.

Performance Benchmarking: Comparing Against the Best

An ongoing approach for establishing performance standards, processes, measurements, and objectives is benchmarking, a process that is not exclusively a purchasing or supply chain practice or approach per se. Rather, it is an approach used by corporate-and functional-level executives and managers. Benchmarking has definite applications, however, when establishing purchasing and supply chain management performance objectives and action plans. Before discussing specific benchmarking applications, we must first gain an understanding of the benchmarking process.

Benchmarking Overview

Benchmarking is the continuous measuring of products, services, processes, activities, and practices against a firm's best competitors or those companies recognized as industry or functional leaders.[4] Formally, the benchmarking process or activity requires measuring performance against that of best-in-class companies, determining how the best-in-class achieve their performance levels, and using that information as the basis for establishing a company's performance targets, strategies, and action plans.[5]

Benchmarking does not always involve comparisons against competitors. Firms often rely on comparisons with non-competitors as a source of information, especially when benchmarking a process or functional activity common to firms across different industries (for example, supply chain management). It is usually easier to obtain benchmarking data and information from a cooperative non-competitor.

Benchmarking is necessary for firms that are not industry leaders. Unfortunately, many U.S. firms did not recognize the need for performance benchmarking until after foreign competitors captured worldwide market share. Industry leaders should also practice performance benchmarking on a regular basis. A firm may not retain market leadership if it is unaware of the actions and capabilities of its competitors.

Types of Benchmarking

There are three basic types of performance benchmarking.[6] The first type is **strategic benchmarking**, which involves a comparison of one firm's market strategies against those of another. Strategic benchmarking usually involves comparisons against leading competitors, allowing a firm to gain an in-depth understanding of their market strategies.[7] With this knowledge, a firm can develop strategies and plans to counter or preempt the competition.

The second type of benchmarking is **operational benchmarking** a process that the purchasing function follows when it performs benchmarking comparisons. Operational benchmarking focuses on different aspects of functional activity and identifies methods to achieve best-in-class performance. Selecting the function and the activities within that function to benchmark are critical to the success of operational benchmarking. Firms should benchmark functional activities that provide the greatest return over time.

The third type of benchmarking is **support-activity benchmarking**. During this process, support functions within an organization demonstrate their cost-effectiveness against external providers of the same support service or activity. Firms are increasingly using support-activity benchmarking as a way of controlling internal overhead and rising costs.

Benchmarking Benefits

There are a number of ways that a company hopes to benefit from actively pursuing performance benchmarking.[8] The benchmarking process helps identify the best business or functional practices to include in a firm's business plans, which can lead directly to performance improvement. Benchmarking can also break down a reluctance to change. Managers begin to see what it takes to maintain corporate or functional leadership by viewing the outside world. Benchmarking can also serve as a source of market intelligence. For example, competitive benchmarking may uncover a previously unrecognized technological breakthrough. Finally, valuable professional contacts between firms can result from the benchmarking process.

Benchmarking Critical Success Factors

Certain factors are critical to benchmarking success. Performance benchmarking must become an accepted process within a firm or function and not simply another fashionable program or fad. Personnel must view performance benchmarking as a permanent part of a system that establishes goals, objectives, and competitive strategies. Executive management support for the process is critical.

A firm must also be willing to commit the necessary legwork to data gathering. A firm must identify which company is the best-in-class for an activity, identify why that company is best, and quantify the benchmarked performance measure. The success of the benchmarking process depends on detailed and accurate benchmarked data and information that becomes part of a firm's action plans and performance objectives.

Managers must view benchmarking as a way to learn from outside companies and improve internal operations on a continuous basis.[9] Some individuals resist the benchmarking process because of a reluctance to recognize the value of a competitor's way of doing business—the "not invented here" syndrome. One way around this syndrome is to benchmark a non-competitor's activities and performance wherever possible. Obviously, strategic benchmarking requires comparisons against direct competitors. For functional activities, however, a firm can study the performance and methods of non-competitors.

Information and Data Sources

A solid source of benchmarking data includes trade journals, other business library resources, and the World Wide Web. Trade journals and other industry publications often feature firms that have distinguished themselves in some way. If this is not adequate, a firm can contact a benchmark target directly to request further information.

Industrywide conferences and professional seminars are also good sources of information, particularly at a functional level. These meetings often serve as a forum for the exchange of ideas about different topics. Leading firms often make presentations at industry trade meetings. These meetings can provide clues about which firms are the most highly regarded in a particular business area or practice.

Suppliers are another source of information. Purchasers can ask suppliers to identify the firms they believe are the best for each benchmark performance area. A firm can also rely on a professional consultant or other industry experts to identify benchmarking candidates.

An ongoing major purchasing benchmarking initiative conducted by CAPS Research (jointly sponsored by the Institute of Supply Management and the W. P. Carey School of Business at Arizona State University) is another important source of information.

This effort includes specific industry-by-industry performance benchmarks and an ongoing study of leading-edge supply strategies. The CAPS Strategic Sourcing and Excellence Model provides the framework for the supply strategy and practice research. Data are collected via focus group visioning sessions, field research, and Internet-based surveys and assessments. Research findings about industry benchmarks and current and future supply chain strategies and practices are available at Knowledge Central, an online database sponsored by CAPS Research (http://www.capsresearch.org).

The Benchmarking Process

Robert Camp noted that there are five distinct steps or phases before a firm fully receives the benefits of the performance benchmarking process.[10] Exhibit 19.6 on p. 775 graphically presents these five phases.

Planning

During this initial phase of the benchmarking process, a firm addresses issues such as which products or functions to benchmark, which companies to select as benchmarking targets (competitors, non-competitors, or both), and how to identify data and information sources. Benchmarking plans should focus on process and methods rather than simply on quantitative performance results. The process and methods cause the quantitative end results.

Analysis

Data and information collection and analysis occur during the second phase. A firm must determine how and why the benchmarked firm is better. A variety of questions should be asked:

- In what product or functional areas is the benchmarked company better?
- Why is the benchmarked company better?

Exhibit 19.6	Benchmarking Implementation Phases

		Characteristics:
Phase 1	Planning	• Determine which products, processes, or functions to benchmark • Identify benchmark target • Determine data and information requirements
Phase 2	Analysis	• Determine how and why benchmark target is better • Determine how to include benchmark company's best practices • Identify future trends and performance levels
Phase 3	Integration	• Communicate benchmark findings to key personnel • Establish operational targets and functional goals based on benchmarking findings
Phase 4	Action	• Include personnel responsible for carrying out plans during formulation of action plans • Develop a schedule for review and updating of goals and plans • Develop system to communicate benchmarking progress
Phase 5	Maturity	• Continuous use of benchmarking at all organizational levels • Continuous performance improvement resulting from the benchmarking process

- How large is the gap between the benchmarked company and our company?
- Can we include the benchmarked company's best practices directly in our operating plans?
- Can we project future performance levels and rates of change?

This phase is critical because it requires management to interpret and understand the benchmarked company's processes, methods, and activities.

Integration

Integration is the process of communicating and gaining acceptance of the benchmarking findings throughout an organization. During this phase, management begins to establish operational targets and functional goals based on the benchmarking findings.

Action

The action phase requires translating the benchmark findings into detailed action plans. Critical items during this phase include having personnel directly responsible for carrying out the plans involved with formulation of the plans, developing a schedule for updating plans and objectives over time, and developing a reporting system to communicate progress toward benchmarking goals.

Maturity

A firm reaches maturity when benchmarking becomes an accepted process for establishing performance plans and objectives. Another indicator of benchmarking maturity occurs when a firm realizes continuous performance improvement as a direct result of performance benchmarking.

A formal process, such as benchmarking, is essential for establishing performance targets and action plans that are externally focused. Without external comparisons, most organizations run the risk of losing sight of what defines best practices or what the competition is doing. Purchasing and supply chain managers must endorse this practice when attempting to establish plans, measures, and objectives that represent best-in-class performance.

Balanced Scorecard for Purchasing and Supply

The balanced scorecard was first presented by Robert S. Kaplan and David P. Norton in 1992. The original premise was that a total reliance on financial measures was leading organizations to make poor decisions. Kaplan and Norton argued that firms must go beyond financial measures, which are lagging indicators, and utilize measures that are leading indicators of performance.

They further suggested that the most appropriate measures that would cause organizations to do the right things would be those metrics that measure the strategy of the firm, its functional activities, and processes.

According to Kaplan and Norton, the balanced scorecard included four key linked performance measurement areas:

1. How do customers see us? (customer satisfaction perspective)
2. What must we excel at? (operational excellence perspective)
3. Can we continue to improve and create value? (innovation perspective)
4. How do we look to shareholders? (financial perspective)

In addition, Kaplan and Norton stressed that measurement itself is not the objective. Measurement and specific metrics provide clarity to general statements and a strategy focus around which to provide performance recognition and rewards.

The balanced scorecard and its related ideas have been adapted by numerous companies and applied to purchasing and supply.

The above Exhibit 19.7 is one example of a balanced scorecard for purchasing and supply. Included are measures related to the following questions:

1. How do we look to shareholders? (financial perspective)
2. How do our customers see us? (internal and external perspectives)
3. What must we excel at? (operational excellence perspective)
4. What do we need to do to improve? (innovation perspective)

Based on the company's purchasing and supply strategies, the balanced scorecard would then be connected to a specific set of appropriate performance measurements. The result will be a scorecard by department or people with specific key performance indicators.

Exhibit 19.7	Case Example of Strategic Performance Measures—Semiconductor Manufacturer

Financial
- Revenue
- Revenue from suppliers based on process improvements
- Royalty revenue from patents
- Cost
- Cost for direct material, indirect spend, and capital spend
- Bill of material cost versus target
- Savings on direct materials used by contract manufacturers
- Administrative costs per headcount
- Maverick spend

Customer Satisfaction
- Internal
- Number of plant shutdowns
- Single-source risk mitigation
- Internal stakeholder survey
- Factory quality incidents
- Supplier business continuity
- Tool performance
- On-time delivery
- Ramp-up readiness
- Percentage of spend with preferred suppliers
- External
- Customer quality incidents

Operational Excellence
- Contract price enforcement
- Audit results and severity of errors
- Payment terms in contracts
- Most favored customer clauses in contracts
- Not to exceed pricing in contracts
- Keeping pricing current in ERP database
- Strategic sourcing plans in place

Innovation
- New-product development
- Performance versus data milestones in the new-product innovation (NPI) process
- Current estimated cost against target in NPI process
- Cost savings initiated by purchasing/supply in the NPI process
- People development
- Training hours
- Leadership development pipeline
- Employee morale

A Summary of Purchasing Measurement and Evaluation Characteristics

A review of purchasing and supply chain performance and measurement systems supports a number of conclusions. These fall into two categories: system characteristics and human resource characteristics.

System Characteristics

1. Measurement is not free. An evaluation system must compare the costs associated with measurement against the benefits. Furthermore, increased measurement does not necessarily mean improved performance. The amount and type of measurement should be enough to achieve the intended result but not enough to cause negative or dysfunctional behavior.

2. Not all aspects of performance lend themselves to quantitative measurement. Negotiating skill and obtaining supplier cooperation are two examples of performance categories that are difficult to quantify.

3. Purchasing and supply chain managers are better served by a few precisely defined and thoroughly understood measures than by many poorly defined measures.

4. An effective measurement system requires a database that provides consistent and reliable data. All personnel must have access to the same data when calculating and reporting purchasing performance indicators.

5. Periodic review of the purchasing and supply chain measurement system should occur to eliminate unimportant or unnecessary performance measures, add new measures as required, and reevaluate performance measure objectives or targets.

6. There is no best way to measure performance. Performance measures differ from firm to firm and industry to industry. No established industry purchasing performance standards have yet emerged. However, the movement toward performance benchmarking does support the development of performance indicators common to more than one firm.

7. Measurement-reporting requirements and content vary by position and level within the organization. Careful planning helps guarantee effective use of the system at each organizational level.

8. A single, overall productivity measure representing purchasing and supply chain performance is not feasible.

9. Many industries need to shift from operational measures focusing on activity to strategic measures assessing a desired end result (for example, increased participation by suppliers during new-product development).

10. The strategies and plans used to produce a performance measure's result are probably more important than the end performance result itself.

11. A balanced scorecard approach is an effective method of measurement and evaluation for purchasing and supply.

Human Resource Characteristics

1. A measurement and evaluation system is not a substitute for effective management. The system is a tool that can be used to assist in the efficient and effective operation of the purchasing and supply chain function.

2. An effective system requires communication. Responsible personnel must clearly understand the performance measure, its performance expectation, and the role of the measure during the performance evaluation process.

3. Measures must reinforce positive behavior and be positively linked to an organization's reward system and not serve as punitive tools. If management uses the measures solely as a means to identify nonperforming individuals, negative, dysfunctional, or beat-the-system behavior may result.

Good Practice Example	*Using Measurement to Drive Continuous Supply Chain Improvement at Accent Industries*

Accent Industries, a U.S.-based consumer goods company, manufactures products for direct shipment to retailers worldwide. This company's strategy is to excel across various operational aspects of service by being the industry leader in price, service, and convenience. Accent has developed a set of organizational objectives that it believes are critical to worldwide success. These objectives include being a low-cost producer; providing the highest quality to customers; and offering the best customer service, delivery, and responsiveness in the industry. The company has also developed a set of purchasing and supply chain performance measures that it believes directly supports its organizational directives.

When implementing its purchasing and supply chain measurement system, Accent followed a series of defined steps:

Step 1: Conduct cross-functional discussions and benchmarking to establish measures, measurement objectives, and performance targets.

Step 2: Formalize measurement objectives into written policy and procedures.

Step 3: Formally communicate measures and objectives to the supply base.

Step 4: Receive feedback from suppliers.

Step 5: Modify, if necessary, performance measures and their objectives.

Step 6: Implement final distribution of the measurement objective and process.

Step 7: Collect and maintain performance data.

Accent relies on a wide range of purchasing and supply chain measures that relate directly to the company's corporate objectives. A sample of the more critical measures include the following:

Quality

- Supplier defects in parts per million
- Internal manufacturing defects in parts per million
- Internal process capability
- Damage
- Number and cost of warranty claims

Price/Cost

- Actual price to market price comparisons
- Price/cost reductions
- Tooling cost management
- Transportation cost management

Cycle Times

- New-product development cycle time

Delivery and Service

- Supplier on-time delivery

Inventory/Forecasting

- Total inventory dollar value over time
- Raw material, work-in-process, and finished-goods inventory turns
- Forecast accuracy

Supplier quality performance is determined during on-site supplier visits and from statistical inferences from product receipts. The frequency of calculation varies with each supplier's current quality levels. Suppliers with known quality problems or higher levels of defects are targeted for more frequent measurement.

Accent uses its performance measurement system to establish and convey performance objectives, track progress, and promote continuous improvement.

Each supplier is provided clear, comprehensive goals and timely feedback. Factors that are critical to effective measurement include a process for establishing aggressive but attainable goals, supplier consensus that the goals are achievable, senior management support, and accurate measurement with regular feedback.

In the future, the company plans to expand its use of total cost of ownership models for supplier evaluation and selection. In addition, Accent wants to pursue the open measurement and sharing of cost elements with its suppliers.

Source: Based on interviews with company managers. Company name has been changed at the request of the company.

CONCLUSION

A purchasing and supply chain performance measurement and management system should directly support corporate goals and objectives. A measurement system that directs behavior and activity away from those goals and objectives is counterproductive and can cause greater harm than good.

There is a need to create measurement systems that are responsive to change. Firms will also increasingly require measures that focus on end results rather than on specific activities. Emphasis will increasingly shift from efficiency measures to effectiveness measures. In addition, executive management must have the ability to distinguish between good and poor purchasing practices and results. A well-developed performance measurement and evaluation system can help provide this distinction. The balanced scorecard is a useful approach to purchasing and supply measurement.

KEY TERMS

benchmarking, 770

effectiveness, 749

efficiency, 749

operational
benchmarking, 771

strategic benchmarking, 771

support-activity
benchmarking, 771

DISCUSSION QUESTIONS

1. What is a purchasing performance measurement and evaluation system? Why would a firm want to measure purchasing performance?

2. Why would a firm want to measure supplier performance? Describe the kinds of measures that can be used to measure supplier performance.

3. What is performance benchmarking? Why is it increasingly being used when establishing purchasing performance goals and objectives?

4. What are the three types of performance benchmarking? Which type is most commonly used by the purchasing function?

5. What is the difference between effectiveness and efficiency measures? When should a firm focus on purchasing effectiveness measures? When should a firm focus on purchasing efficiency measures?

6. Discuss the reasons why measuring and evaluating purchasing performance has historically had certain problems or limitations. Do you think the purchasing function should increase or decrease its effort to measure performance? Why or why not?

7. Consider the following statement: Some firms still rely on measures that harm rather than support purchasing's long-term performance objectives. What does this mean? Provide examples of performance measures that might actually result in a negative longer-term effect on purchasing performance.

8. What is the benefit of developing performance measures that focus on cost versus purchase price?

9. Discuss the major difference between cost-reduction and cost-avoidance measures. Why have some described the reported savings in cost-avoidance measures as "soft," "funny money," and "easy to manipulate"? When can purchasing take credit for a legitimate cost reduction or cost avoidance?

10. Assume you are responsible for developing a benchmarking program. Describe how you would go about establishing the benchmarking process. Be sure to discuss the critical issues you must address.

11. Discuss what is meant by each of the following statements:

    a. Purchasing measurement is not free.
    b. There is no best way to measure purchasing performance.
    c. Many industries need to shift from operational measures focusing on buyer activity to strategic measures focusing on a desired end result.
    d. A purchasing measurement and evaluation system is not a substitute for solid management.

12. Why is it sometimes advantageous to benchmark performance against a non-competitor?

13. Effective performance measurement systems have certain characteristics. Select three characteristics and discuss why a measure should possess that characteristic.

14. Discuss the different uses a manager has for purchasing and supply chain performance data.

15. What is required to establish a balanced scorecard to measure purchasing and supply performance?

ADDITIONAL READINGS

Brown, M. G. (1996), *Keeping Score: Using the Right Metrics to Drive World-Class Performance*, New York: American Management Association, 15–26.

Carter, P. L., Monczka, R. M., and Mosconi, T. (2005), *Strategic Performance Measurement for Purchasing and Supply*, Tempe, AZ: CAPS Research.

Cooper, R., and Kaplan, R. (1988, September–October), "Measure Costs Right: Make the Right Decisions," *Harvard Business Review*, 23–28.

Crain, K. (2008, May 12), "25% is High, but Chrysler Is Wise to Revisit SCORE," *Automotive News*, 12.

D'Avanzo, R., Von Lewinski, H., and Van Wassenhove, L. (2003, November–December), "The Link between Supply Chain and Financial Performance," *Supply Chain Management Review*, 6–7.

Eccles, R. G. (1991, January–February), "The Performance Measurement Manifesto," *Harvard Business Review*, 131–137.

Goentzel, J. (2010, January–February), "Delivering on the Promise of Green Energy," *Supply Chain Management Review*, 10–17.

"Inside Purchasing: Four Pillars of Supply Strategy" (1995), *Purchasing*, 118(10), 13.

Kaplan, R. S., and Norton, D. P. (1992, January–February), "The Balanced Scorecard—Measures That Drive Performance," *Harvard Business Review*, 71–79.

Lauder, Catherine. (2013), "How do you effectively measure cost savings?" *Procurement Leaders Global Intelligence Network*.

Little, Arthur D. (2009), "What CFOs expect from measuring Procurement Success," *Procurement Performance Measurement*, 1–5.

McDowell, C., Monczka, R. M., Carter, P., Trent, R., and Ragatz, G. (2012), *Value Chain Strategies for the Changing Decade: Risk Management Across the Extended Value Chain*, Tempe, AZ: CAPS Research.

Sharman, P. (1995, May), "How to Implement Performance Measurement in Your Organization," *CMA Magazine*, 33–38.

Smeltzer, L. R., and Manship, J. A. (2003, May–June), "How Good Are Your Cost Reduction Measures?" *Supply Chain Management Review*, 3–7.

Timme, S., and Williams-Timme, W. (2000, May–June), "The Financial-SCM Connection," *Supply Chain Management Review*, 33.

Trunick, P. A. (2007, August), "What You Do, Start Measuring," *Logistics Today*, 22–24.

Vitale, R., and Mavrinac, S. C. (1995, August), "How Effective Is Your Performance Measurement System?" *Management Accounting*, 43–47.

Wernie, B., and Sherefkin, R. (2010, January), "Chrysler Speeds Supplier Payday," *Automotive News*, 1 and 29.

ENDNOTES

1. van Wheele, A. J. (1984, Fall), "Purchasing Performance Measurement and Evaluation," *International Journal of Purchasing and Materials Management*, 18–19.

2. Brown, M. G. (1996), *Keeping Score: Using the Right Metrics to Drive World-Class Performance*, New York: American Management Association, 15–26.

3. Novak, P., Chief Executive Officer. (2008), *ISM Principles of Sustainability and Social Responsibility: A Guide to Adoption / Implementation*, Tempe, AZ: Institute for Supply Management.

4. Camp, R. C. (1989, January), "Benchmarking: The Search for Best Practices That Lead to Superior Performance: Part I," *Quality Progress*, 66.

5. Pryor, L. S. (1989, November–December), "Benchmarking: A Self-Improvement Strategy," *Journal of Business Strategy*, 28.

6. Pryor, pp. 29–30.

7. Pryor, p. 29.

8. Camp, R. C. (1989, March), "Benchmarking: The Search for Industry Best Practices That Lead to Superior Performance: Part III," *Quality Progress*, 77–80.

9. Furey, T. R. (1987, September–October), "Benchmarking: The Key to Developing Competitive Advantage," *Planning Review*, 32.

10. Camp, R. C. (1989, February), "Benchmarking: The Search for Best Practices That Lead to Superior Performance: Part II," *Quality Progress*, 71.

Future Directions

Chapter 20   Purchasing and Supply Strategy Trends

Purchasing and Supply Strategy Trends

Learning Objectives

After completing this chapter, you should be able to

- Understand key purchasing and supply strategy directions

- Recognize high-impact strategy areas

- Understand critical characteristics of key strategies

Chapter Outline

Supply Chain Integration Becomes a Reality

Customer-focused supply chains that can better align and link the various firms making up the supply chain are increasingly likely to gain competitive advantage. This can be exemplified by Walmart, Dell, and IBM examples. Supply chain integration with agreement on goals, business strategies, and information transparency can have significant impacts on capacity investment, inventories, design, responsiveness, and support of a firm's worldwide product/service development, operations/manufacturing, and sourcing footprints. An example, discussed here in more detail, is the Motorola supply chain integration. In 2005, Motorola undertook the task of linking the various elements that make up its supply chains worldwide. The objectives were cost, cash, and customer service. Cost competitiveness would enable competitive pricing, cash would enable business investment, and customer service would enable the retention of customers. The challenge was significant, as Motorola operates worldwide. Sales spanned all regions of the globe, and purchases came from suppliers in 47 countries (as of 2004); in the past, the six business units generally did little sharing of resources or facilities. To achieve transformation to an integrated supply chain, the focus was to align and link product design, procurement, manufacturing, logistics, and customer service. In addition, the following six key steps provide a high-level process approach to implement the change:

1. Identify best-in-class processes for duplication throughout the company
2. Develop a supply base that has been right-sized and improve working relationships with key suppliers
3. Establish clear-cut supplier quality expectations and provide performance feedback via a performance scorecard
4. Establish most effective and efficient manufacturing and logistics operations
5. Focus information technology improvement projects to maximize the impact across all business units
6. Create an action-oriented and results-driven culture

The results of the transformation by 2007 were dramatic. Examples are the following:

- Various teams identified best-in-class practices, and the highest-priority practices were implemented worldwide.
- Business units work collaboratively to solicit quotes and award business.
- Suppliers were required to develop "quality renewal plans" to continue to do work with Motorola, and Motorola provided performance data to suppliers.
- Motorola's manufacturing and distribution operation's square footage was reduced by 40 percent by examining its worldwide footprint and consolidating facilities.
- Ninety percent of Motorola's information technology spend is now on systems that are common and help all business units-not just one.
- In addition, a number of achievements as of year-end 2006 include reduced parts per million (PPM) defects from suppliers by 50 percent; achieved customer on-time deliveries of 85 to 92 percent at some business units (up from 30 to 40 percent); improved material expenses, product quality, and manufacturing efficiency by 40 percent; and achieved an 18 percent improvement in inventory turns.

Overall, this example suggests that a focused effort on integrating the vertical or functional silos into a more integrated supply chain(s) can produce performance results. This supply chain integration is a major ongoing challenge and will be the focus of future efforts.

Source: Adapted from Cook, J.A. (2007), "Metamorphosis of a Supply Chain," *CSCMP's Supply Chain Quarterly*, 34–38.

Introduction

A common theme throughout this book is that the functional area called purchasing, along with the activities that support supply chain management, are experiencing dramatic change. Once regarded as a reactive and administrative activity capable only of neutral or negative contribution, purchasing and supply chain leaders and managers must today be at the forefront of responding to and creating change. As a vice president of a large manufacturing firm in the transportation industry commented, "Over 60 percent of our revenue is spent with external suppliers, and effective purchasing and world-class suppliers are absolutely required for us to be successful in the future."[1]

This chapter outlines the real and projected changes and trends that have affected and will continue to affect purchasing and supply chain professionals. These changes and trends appear within eight areas, identified as critical to effective supply management, based on a joint research initiative of CAPS Research, the Institute for Supply Management (ISM), and A.T. Kearney, Inc.[2] Even though this research was completed seven years ago, the findings continue to provide a relevant framework for discussion today. These areas are (1) expanding the mission, goals, and performance expectations of purchasing and supply; (2) developing category strategies; (3) developing and managing suppliers; (4) designing and operating multiple supply networks; (5) leveraging technology enablers; (6) collaborating internally and externally; (7) attracting and retaining supply management talent; and (8) managing and enabling the future supply management organization and measurement systems. Discussion in this chapter is drawn from this study, from other research, and combined with discussions with supply chain leaders. In closing, a series of high-impact strategies are presented.

Expanding the Mission, Goals, and Performance Expectations

Over the recent past and going forward, the mission, goals, and performance contributions required of purchasing and supply by company executives have been expanding and will continue to do so. Increasing contributions in cost reduction, effective asset management, and revenue generation are being required by firms worldwide.

In addition, external forces are continuously changing and will likely impact purchasing and supply management's role and required contributions to a firm's success. These forces at least include the following:

1. Macro-economic, social and political changes
2. Global competition and emerging market growth
3. Mergers, acquisitions, and supply market consolidation
4. Technology advances
5. Increasing customer expectations for products and services
6. Increased governmental regulation and social responsibilities
7. Environmental responsibilities, such as sustainability

Each of these factors individually and in combination will influence change in purchasing and supply strategies and practices, and increase supply complexity. The rate of future business model and purchasing and supply transformations will also likely quicken and impact purchasing and supply mission and goals.

Overall, future purchasing and supply mission and goals will be broader and more aligned with the strategic objectives of the firm. The future focus will be on several supply chain performance areas including the following:

1. Expanding the breadth and depth of cost management efforts in areas such as out-sourcing/insourcing, cost modeling and value chain mapping for identification of cost improvement opportunities, purchase item standardization and complexity reduction.

2. Identifying and mitigating supply risks of any kind to ensure business continu-ity: for example, price volatility, potential supply disruptions, financially troubled suppliers, negative impacts on sustainability and the environment, protection of intellectual properties, and so forth.

3. Leveraging supplier capabilities and know-how to improve performance and estab-lish new sources of revenue: for example, leverage jointly developed technologies with suppliers to enhance revenue generation by being first to market.

4. Increasing the magnitude of worldwide and regional (vs. local) sourcing by com-panies who must find and establish high performance suppliers anywhere in the world to support product/service and customer market segmentation.

5. Accelerating and obtaining more innovation from suppliers.

For example, innovative products, services, and processes will provide increasing compet-itive advantage in the future. Examples include, the use of composites in the Boeing 787; the iPod and iPhone from Apple; side-by-side, front-loading, and colorful washers and dryers on a platform by Whirlpool; and P&G product innovation advances all provide marketplace advantage. In addition, firms recognize that innovation cannot be totally achieved utilizing internal resources alone but must also tap supplier expertise in developing innovations.

Purchasing and supply will also be expected to play a growing role in the sustain-ability efforts of firms, many of which closely involve suppliers. For example, Tyler Elm, Vice President and Senior Director of Corporate Strategy and Business Sustainability at Walmart, recognized that in contrast to early campaigns, their new sustainability strategy would need to be deeply embedded in Walmart's operations and supply chain manage-ment to meet the ambitious goals set in 2005. Elm put it this way: "We recognized early on that we had to look at the entire value chain. If we had focused on just our own opera-tions, we would have limited ourselves to 10 percent of our effect on the environment and eliminated 90 percent of the opportunity that's out there."[3] Purchasers will have to fully understand sustainability issues and make appropriate decisions based on sustainability considerations, which are growing in importance.

In addition, a study by A.T. Kearney shows that overall executive expectations of purchasing/supply are increasing with growing focus on value. See Figure 20.1.

The broadening role of supply management will not reduce the need to continue to con-tribute to cost improvement but also require contributions to other important purchasing objectives, as discussed below and shown in Figures 20.1 and 20.2.

- **Continuous improvement in purchase unit cost, quality, and delivery performance is required.**

A CAPS Research project focused on an "Executive Assessment of Supply,"[4] provides insight into the degree of supply performance achievements across various important per-formance areas in 2013 based on responses from 74 companies to the assessment question shown in Exhibit 20.2. Performance results are shown for cost, inventory, quality, delivery, responsiveness, and supplier diversity.

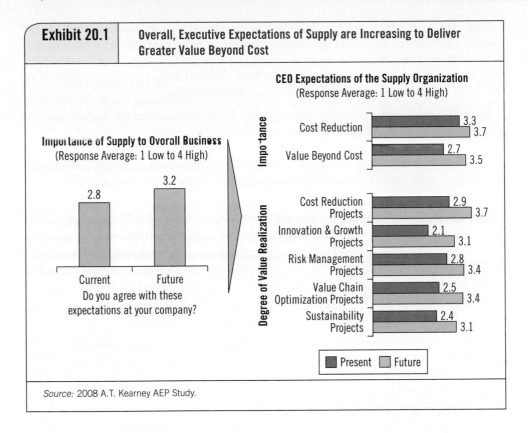

Exhibit 20.1 | **Overall, Executive Expectations of Supply are Increasing to Deliver Greater Value Beyond Cost**

Source: 2008 A.T. Kearney AEP Study.

Providing ongoing purchase price and cost reduction, combined with quality and delivery performance improvement, is the minimum contribution expected of purchasing and supply. Positive results in these areas are required to compete.

- **The reduction of time, particularly during product and process development is especially important.**

Exhibit 20.2 | **2013 Purchasing Supply Performance Achievements**

Assessment Question: "For your most important purchases (80/20 rule) over the past twelve (12) months, indicate the magnitude of measurable performance improvements and/or business unit contribution achieved through sourcing and supply chain strategies at your business unit."

PERFORMANCE AREA	AVERAGE IMPROVEMENT RESULTS
Unit purchase price	3.8%
Transportation and logistics costs	3.0%
Total cost of ownership	3.0%
Performing to Purchasing Price/Cost Objectives	3.8%
Overall inventory investment costs	1.4%
Supplier quality	5.0%
Supplier on-time delivery	2.3%
Supplier responsiveness/flexibility	2.3%
Supplier diversity	3.5%

Source: R. M. Monczka and K. J. Petersen, Supply Strategy Implementation: Current State and Future Opportunities, Tempe, AZ: CAPS Research, 2013.

Although high quality, delivery, and low cost will always be important, time-related capabilities have driven and will continue to drive the next generation of order winners in the eyes of the customer. In particular, product and service support and best customer service with short lead times and the ability to bring new products from concept to customer in the shortest time rival cost and quality as critical market attributes.

Most supply leaders agree that reduced cycle times are essential for market success. Competition is no longer between big and small but rather between fast and agile and slow firms. Purchasing plays an important role in time-based competition because of its ability to affect time-related processes and activities. For example, reducing material delivery cycle times with suppliers can also help reduce internal manufacturing cycle times.

Faster supplier responsiveness supports faster responsiveness to end-customer requirements, particularly as planning horizons become shorter and less certain. Although beyond the scope of this discussion, material ordering cycle time has four components that supply chain practices affect directly: (1) transmission of requirements to suppliers, (2) suppliers' ordering and manufacturing cycle time, (3) delivery from suppliers, and (4) incoming receiving and inspection.

Perhaps the most obvious area where firms are concentrating their time-reduction efforts is during new-product and process development along with achieving innovation. Major changes have occurred in the methods and time required for developing products and processes over the past decade, such as the use of product development teams, rapid prototyping technologies, and computer-aided design systems shared with suppliers. As a result, average product development cycle time has declined and is viewed as significantly important by executive management.

Developing Category Strategies Will Become Broader and More Complex

Strategy Formulation and Selection

In the decade ahead, companies will think differently about purchase category strategies. The overall purpose of a purchase category strategy is to maximize value to the buyer and supplier by leveraging both internal company and external supplier resources and capabilities. In the future, changes in business models, degree of outsourcing, industry structures, technologies, customer demands, environmental regulations, and other factors will change both how value is defined and how external resources can help deliver it.

Companies, in the future, will look beyond cost, quality and delivery as purchase category strategy goals. They will increasingly look for other contributions such as innovation, risk reduction, sustainability and cycle time reduction. "For example, a food manufacturer utilized a flavoring supplier's knowledge and expertise to rationalize its own ingredient base into flavor and additive 'modules' that provide specific taste or texture. Significant savings for the manufacturer and additional sales for the supplier were achieved, also providing for time-to-market reductions, which was critical to business success in their competitive space."[5]

Companies will increasingly use value-focused sourcing approaches to evaluate how a supplier or group of suppliers may be utilized to gain competitive advantage for categories with high business impact. "Value" will become better defined and there will be greater application of total cost sourcing decision-making. There will also be increasing use of value chain mapping, data analytics to better understand industry trends, cost modeling and

Sourcing Snapshot

Global Supply: "Thailand's Turn"

As companies expand their global competitive footprint, emerging markets are becoming an increasing source of customers and production capabilities. For example, Thailand has begun to ship vehicles to the United States and wants to become a global export hub, expanding its' regional scope. Mitsubishi Motors is scheduled to make its first shipment of autos to the United States in August, 2013. Others such as Ford, General Motors, Toyota, Nissan and BMW are tapping into Thailand's production capabilities. If a tariff free trade pact is implemented between Thailand and other countries, including the United States, there will likely be an increased flow of Thai produced vehicles to countries worldwide based on its low costs and government incentives. Exports have increased from less than 10,000 to more than one million vehicles. It is likely that global sourcing for final products, subsystems and components will increase and provide for enhanced competitiveness. However, issues related to quality, responsiveness and logistics will have to be closely evaluated and monitored.

Global Sourcing for Worldwide Competitiveness: "Thailand's Turn?"

Source: Adapted from Greimel, H. (October 14, 2013), "Thailand's turn?," *Automotive News.*

scenario planning techniques to develop, evaluate and select from purchase category strategy alternatives. Category strategy development will cover, at least three to five years and will begin at new-product/service development with broad-based goals being established, for example, innovation, risk reduction, cost, emerging market sourcing, sustainability, collaboration, standardization and so forth. Finally, supply networks (groups of suppliers) will become an increasing focus of purchase category strategies. The strategy consideration will be how to best utilize supplier capabilities, not only individuals, but as part of a supply network.

See *Value Focused Supply: Linking Supply to Competitive Business Strategies* a research report from CAPS Research and A.T. Kearney, Inc. published in 2010 for additional information.[6]

Establishing core competencies and capabilities has influenced the strategic planning process and category strategy development at most firms, and will continue to do so in

Sourcing Snapshot

China Sourcing

General Motors Corporation is increasing the China purchasing staff, which is expected to develop suppliers in China. The purchasing staff will increase from the 200 working with suppliers in Shanghai and the office staff will also increase in Beijing and Guangzhou. GM currently has 198 suppliers in China and is working with over 300 China suppliers to assist them in becoming global suppliers to GM.

Source: Adapted from "GM'son the Hunt for China Suppliers," (December 17, 2007), *Automotive News,* 45.

Sourcing Snapshot

Parts Standardization

Bosch is asking for parts standardization because of significant investment demands being placed on automakers and parts suppliers. Bosch further pointed out that the company made 44 different heads for the ABS speed sensor, as one example of many. The functionality of all of the sensors is basically the same, and the variation could be significantly reduced, yielding economies of scale and possible cost reductions. If there were parts standardization, cost reduction of 5 to 10 percent, and possibly up to 30 percent, could be achieved for certain products. Teamwork between OEMs and suppliers, required to cut costs, is an important consideration. How effective purchasing is in working collaboratively with suppliers in the future will be a competitive differentiator.

Source: Adapted from Shreifkin, R. (January 28, 2008) "Bosch Standardized Parts Can Cut Costs," *Automotive News*, 41.

the years ahead. Because purchasing deals extensively with external sources, it becomes involved with the insourcing/outsourcing decisions. Outsourcing will likely continue, although firms will be carefully examining and sometime rebalancing their insourcing/outsourcing patterns. As logistics costs, major customer locations and automation opportunities (lower labor content) change, opportunities to modify, and sometime insource work will exist. There are a number of reasons, however, why the emphasis on outsourcing will continue:

- Cost-reduction pressures will continue and are forcing organizations to use their productive resources most efficiently. As a result, executive management will rely on well-reasoned (using computer simulations, forecasting software, scenario planning and "What-if" analysis) and data driven insourcing/outsourcing decisions to provide a way to manage and lower costs. Outsourcing to low labor cost areas for high labor cost products/services will generally prevail.

- Firms will increasingly focus more on what they excel at to gain competitive advantage along with outsourcing noncompetitive activities related to both production and administration. Companies are more effectively defining their core competencies to help guide the insourcing/outsourcing decisions and will continue to do so.

- The need for customer responsiveness is increasingly causing companies to decide (insource/outsource) how best to achieve greater flexibility and shorter lead times, for operations and new-product development. Shorter cycle times, frequently, encourage greater outsourcing to firms that are more flexible and responsive to customer requirements.

- Wall Street recognizes and rewards firms that achieve higher return-on-investment. Because insourcing usually requires fixed assets and human capital, financial pressures are causing managers to closely examine insourcing/outsourcing decisions. Avoidance of increased fixed costs is motivating many firms to rely on external rather than internal physical and human assets.

- Globalization and lower-cost suppliers in emerging countries continues to promote outsourcing.

Sourcing Snapshot

Supplier Fumes as Carmakers Take Electric Motors In-House

Motor supplier John Weber should be sitting on a gold mine right now, considering North America's growing interest in hybrids and electric vehicles.

But an odd thing is happening. His potential customers are entering his business.

Core Technology

Toyota Motor Corp., the lead player in the hybrid market so far, and maker of the big-selling Prius, relies on electric motors produced by Toyota itself–not by one of its trusted keiretsu suppliers.

Even General Motors, which has relied on Remy for various products for a century, has decided to eventually bring motor development and production in-house for its Chevrolet Volt plug-in hybrid. GM spun off Remy, then Delco Remy, in 1994.

Duplicated Effort?

But why go through all that trouble for a component that has been a commodity item for decades, powering everything from ceiling fans to dishwashers and windshield wipers?

John Weber is wondering the same thing.

"Does it annoy me that GM's going down this path?" he says. "It annoys the hell out of me. Especially given how much they've crawled around our plants and gone through our supply base."

Weber has heard that automakers' argument–that in the new world of electric-powered vehicles, the motor itself rises to the level of a core technology to the driving experience.

But it is clearly a testy issue for him. He says automakers are declaring motor development to be proprietary even though there is no real breakthrough technology for it on the horizon for anyone–including his own company.

"The strategy driving it is: 'We need to own this technology,' and that doesn't make sense," he says. "Under that argument, they should also get into windshield wiper motors and window motors because they're also part of the vehicle experience. They buy fuel injectors and tires from different people, and yet they're part of the driving experience."

Controlling Costs

Nissan's Mark Perry offers a reasonable explanation for automakers' investment in electric motors. Perry is responsible for the late-2010 launch of the electric Leaf, a model that promises 100 miles of driving per full battery charge.

"The motor touches on everything that's important to us," says Perry, director of product planning for Nissan North America Inc.

"It's central to the car's performance, it's central to system integration, and it's a question of cost control. We want to control all the key elements of the value chain, and how could you do that without producing the motor?"

Source: Adapted from Chappell, L. (June 21, 2010), "Supplier Fumes as Carmakers Take Electric Motors In-House," *Automotive News*, 4, 18.

Concluding Observations

Purchase category strategies that establish goals based on both company and supply objectives are required. Those strategies, at least, include establishing the supply base (internal and external), sourcing allocations globally and to emerging markets, contracting approaches, supplier development, product/service designs, complexity reduction, and physical supply chain considerations. The strategies will require continued development by highly capable global cross-functional and cross-location teams. These strategies, will in the future, focus on obtaining and creating value from and jointly with suppliers and supply networks. Value, as discussed, goes far beyond buying price alone with increasing focus on total cost, innovation and sustainability.

Category strategies will become more complex, be able to be modified as required because of changing conditions and require both internal functional and executive engagement, including review and approval. Strategy development will become more proactive and influence supply market pricing and investment decisions. There will be greater emphasis on risk identification and mitigation, using predictive approaches, as part of strategy development.

Supplier Management Across the Extended Supply Chain

"In the decade ahead, the development of a competitive worldwide supply base and suppliers that collaboratively help to create value in support of the buying company's business models will become the norm. This focus will be driven by global competition, continuous outsourcing, and the need to develop supply chains for innovative products and services to meet unique customer requirements worldwide."[7] Further, the supply base will be viewed not only as tier one suppliers but also as supply networks that extend beyond the tier one suppliers.

Improving Supplier Relationships

As suggested above, significant improvements in supplier management and working relationships with key suppliers across the extended supply chain will be increasingly critical to gain supplier innovation and preferential treatment in the years ahead. Supply base structuring, segmentation and relationship management across the extended supply chain, including identification of strategic suppliers will become the norm.

To enhance future working relationships with important supply chain suppliers, the following are required:

- Supplier segmentation based on company needs and supplier capabilities
- Supplier scorecards and feedback
- Equitable risk/rewards with suppliers
- Supplier councils and conferences
- Process improvement and innovation workshops
- Two-way performance evaluations and satisfaction surveys
- Supplier suggestion systems
- Executive engagement
- Trust

A holistic approach to element implementation is required versus implementation of a limited number of elements.

Further, supply bases will be carefully established based on answers to the following questions:

- What current and future supplier capabilities are required?
- How many suppliers are required to support company needs?
- Which suppliers should we work with and where should they be located?
- Should we establish/require specific suppliers at the Tier 2 and 3 levels?
- For which suppliers do we want collaborative efforts to be established?

These supply bases will be structured to enable business and purchase category strategies.

In addition, companies will increasingly conduct supplier surveys to establish their standing as "best customers" and identify obstacles to improving supplier/buyer approaches, processes and performance. It is also likely that industries will have buyer/supplier surveys, done by independent third parties, to establish levels of buyer/supplier relationships and who the leading companies are. For example, in the auto industry Deloitte Touche Tohmatsu Ltd.[8] conducted a survey of North American automakers to establish the ranking of Automaker Purchasing Operations. Similar supplier surveys have been conducted by Planning Perspectives Inc.[9]

Leading sustainability efforts with suppliers and their suppliers will also increase in importance. IBM recently established a global supply social and environmental management

Sourcing Snapshot

Sustainability and Leadership

Leading sustainability efforts internally and with suppliers will require significant purchasing and supply transformation in the future to ensure competitiveness. Customer buying decisions may become increasingly concerned about how "green" their supplier is. S. C. Johnson's approach provides one example of this transformation.

The company works to improve the environmental impact of the raw materials it purchases. Suppliers and S. C. Johnson work to improve the environment by producing more environmentally friendly ingredients and also improving raw material choices to produce green products.

To support the green efforts, S. C. Johnson developed "Greenlist," an environmental classification system that rates ingredients on four to seven criteria such as biodegradability and aquatic toxicity. Scoring ranges from 3 (best) to 0 indicates that the material is only used with special permission and that a substitute for the raw material must be found.

The results of this effort internally and with suppliers have been very successful. Examples include the following:

- Increased the use of better and best materials significantly by more than 13 million kilograms
- Eliminated millions of kilograms of 0-rated materials

- Phased out chlorine-based external packaging materials worldwide
- Phased out the use of bleached paperboard, which uses elemental chlorine as the bleaching agent

The beneficiary of environmentally favorable philosophies and principles laid down throughout 12 decades of business, S. C. Johnson believes it must still work closely with many organizations that have varying agendas and priorities. However, what is found among a disparate supplier community is widespread and common acceptance of Greenlist and its objectives—and a genuine enthusiasm for helping meet those objectives. The recent scale of successes at S. C. Johnson would not have been possible without the active collaboration of suppliers—and without a clear process to guide collaboration.

Source: Adapted from S. Johnson and D. Long, "The Greening of the Supply Chain," Supply Chain Management Review, May–June 2006, pp. 36–40.

system and rolled-out the strategy to IBM suppliers worldwide. In a letter from IBM's Chief Procurement Officer, John Patterson, IBM suppliers are required to:

- Define, deploy, and sustain a management system that addresses corporate responsibility, including supplier conduct and environmental protection
- Measure performance and establish voluntary environmental goals that are numeric and can be quantified
- Publicly disclose results associated with these voluntary environmental goals and other environmental aspects of the management system

IBM makes the key point that many times a company's inability to develop, integrate and maintain strong employee and environmental programs is the absence of a strong management system that ensures the company (and its suppliers) appropriately addresses responsibilities such as workplace safety, increasing energy efficiency, and reducing waste.

IBM is also requiring its first-tier suppliers to communicate this new set of requirements to their suppliers performing work that is material to the products, parts and/or services being supplied to IBM. This initiative is well aligned with ISM's sustainability and social responsibility efforts and programs.

Sourcing Snapshot

Ford Aligned Business Framework

In 2005, Ford Motor Company established the Aligned Business Framework, an attempt to improve Ford's supplier relations. The plan included reducing the number of suppliers by half and providing longer-term business to those that remained together with early access to new-product programs.

However, at the same time, the financial condition of the firm deteriorated, and much of the purchasing focus was on price reductions. Even though the degree of cooperation that was desired was not fully achieved and supplier relations remained combative, respondents to a supplier survey say that the Aligned Business Framework program has met or exceeded expectations. Access to Ford's senior management has improved, and purchasers and engineers are starting to collaborate. This progress is significant.

Following implementation of the Aligned Business Framework in 2005, Ford in 2013 spends 65 percent of its purchase budget with just 104 preferred suppliers. In addition, Bridget Behrendt, Ford's Vice President of global programs and purchasing operations stated "if you are the preferred customer, the supplier will go to great lengths to work with you and support you." Prior to the ABF, suppliers developing innovations would typically pitch them to other automakers because Ford was slow to implement new technology innovations, according to Behrendt. However, because of implementation of the ABF, this reputation has changed for the better.

Sources: Adapted from "Ford Suppliers' Plan Is Still Just a Work in Progress", (2007, September 10) *Automotive News* and "Ford Strengthens Bonds with its Elite Suppliers," by Neil Bunkley (August 5, 2013), *Automotive News Insight.*

Sourcing Snapshot

Engaging Suppliers Earlier in Product/Service Design and Standardization

Chrysler LLC believed that its interiors lacked refinement in recent years. To change this situation, Chrysler began to bring suppliers into the design process much earlier, some at least two years before the design freeze. The objective was to try more variations and choose the correct materials. It was believed that in the past, suppliers were chosen too late to fully evaluate design options. Now management can make better design decisions and decide what materials to spend money on. This transformation to truly implement the extended enterprise will require that purchasing and supply find innovative suppliers and construct business deals to accelerate supplier innovation for the benefit of the buying company.

Source: Adapted from Wernie, B. (September 17, 2007), "To Aid Interiors, Chrysler Brings in Suppliers Earlier," *Automotive News.*

Concluding Observations

Three dominant themes emerge for the future. First, the purchasing management function will have to establish a supply base and networks going beyond tier one with the capabilities to meet buying company competitive requirements. Increasing information availability worldwide will help in the effort. Second, strategic working relationships between buyers and suppliers will have to improve for increased value creation. Third, the future will require greater focus across the extended supply or value chain to improve customer-focused performance by enhanced leverage of supplier capabilities across the supply chain. This extended focus will require additional information transparency and cooperation among trading partners.

Designing and Operating Multiple Customer-Focused Supply Networks

Customer-focused supply chains, to meet specific needs, will be required to compete effectively and achieve growth and profitability. Supply chain innovation and customer-focused supply chains to meet different customer segments will be required to maximize revenue generation. For example, different supply chains are required for short product life cycle products (cell phones) versus longer product life cycle products (televisions) at consumer electronics firms.

In addition, companies like Dell and Walmart have supply chains that compete not only on cost and quality but also flexibility and responsiveness.

In the future, "Competitive advantage will require agility, whereas supply chain excellence will be defined by the ability to:

- Anticipate changes worldwide in customer requirements, product offerings, supply conditions, regulations, and competitor actions
- Adapt to the changes by reconfiguring existing supply chains or creatively assembling new ones
- Accelerate implementation of the transformed supply chain to capture the new opportunities ahead of the competition"[10]

Make-to-order product/service capabilities will become more important. Multiple global and seamless supply chains will be required for companies to meet needs of different customer segments anywhere in the world. For example, appliance manufacturers have different supply chains for big box retailers versus construction/commercial customers. In addition, Tier 1, 2, and 3 suppliers will become more critical to supply chain performance as quality, cost, availability, and other risks anywhere in the supply chain can cause performance problems.

Risk Considerations

As supply chains become more global and segmented the identification and mitigation of risk becomes a more critical issue. In fact, risk considerations must permeate decisions at new-product/service development, production/operation and distribution. Technology and supplier selection discussion during new-product development affect cost, quality and product/service launch, as well as future production. The choice of suppliers and their global locations affect continuity of supply, quality and cost. Logistics risks of distribution are also impacted.

Sourcing Snapshot

Risk of Global Supply Chain

A massive vehicle recall by four Japanese automakers because of faulty airbags underscores the perils of huge global supply chains as companies increasingly rely on a handful of suppliers for common or similar parts. Toyota, Nissan, Honda, and Mazda are recalling about 3.4 million vehicles worldwide because of airbags supplied by Takata Corp. that are at risk of catching fire or injuring passengers.

Increasingly, groups of carmakers rely on single-source global suppliers for key components. And there are hazards. "It's a huge problem for the industry," said George Magliano, senior auto analyst with HIS Automotive. "The issue today is we can't change the way we do business, because otherwise we just can't operate profitably." Still, he said, "We can't allow failure in the supply chain."

Source: Adapted from "Airbag recall shows risk of global supply chains," (April 15, 2013), *Automotive News*, 6.

Turning the Tide

The traditional adversarial relationship between the Detroit 3 and their suppliers may be turning toward a partnership, especially at Ford Motor Co. Meanwhile, suppliers do not hold Toyota Motor Corp. and other Japanese automakers in the same stratospheric regard that they used to, a supplier survey shows.

If the Detroit 3 can continue to strengthen those partnerships, they will be able to reduce costs, boost efficiency, and bring new technology to market faster. "The way the rankings have changed for the Japanese companies and the U.S. automakers is staggering," said John Henke, CEO of suburban Detroit's Planning Perspectives Inc., which conducts the survey. "Ford is doing everything right," he said. "If Ford continues to improve at the same pace, and Toyota continues falling, Ford could surpass Toyota in the near future."

Tony Brown, Ford group vice president for global purchasing, told *Automotive News*: "We are certainly pleased with the progress, the continuous improvement year over year. But to be clear, we have more work to do. We rely heavily on our supply base for technology, so it is important that we have healthy supplier relations."

Ford began to radically change its ways almost six years ago. It sought fewer suppliers but closer ties with those that it kept. Ford has risen steadily from last place four years ago to third place this year, above Nissan Motor Co.

Source: Adapted from Shreifkin, R. (2010, May), "Turning the Tide" *Automotive News*.

Risk management, therefore, must be an integral part of supply chain management. Formal and systematic approaches must be established and applied for the product/service life cycle.[11]

Concluding Observations

Supply chains not firms compete. Therefore, for companies to be most successful and maximize overall performance they must carefully develop and tailor multiple segmented customer-focused supply chains, beginning at new-product/service development, to meet varying market and specific customer needs. These company supply chains must be cost, quality, delivery, technology competitive and monitored by holistic risk management approaches.

Leveraging E-System Technology Enablers Takes on Additional Focus

There will be ongoing improvements to supply management e-system applications in future years. These improvements, coupled with technological advances that integrate increasingly advanced applications, cloud computing and data should enhance purchasing effectiveness. In addition to basic spend management, e-sourcing, auctions, contract management, purchasing transaction processing and supplier management, "big data" and analytics will play an increasingly important role in purchasing and supply chain management. Big data generally refers to large amounts of data characterized by the "volume" of data that is or can be made available, the "velocity" at which data can be processed and converted into usable information that can be analyzed, and the "variety" of data and data sources that can be incorporated into tactical and strategic analyses leading to improved competitive performance.[12]

"Big data" combined with the capabilities of analytical tools (descriptive statistical analyses, regression, predictive modeling, simulations, and so forth) combined with high talent people will further improve supply analyses and decision-making across many areas. For example, purchasing and supply chain applications will likely include advancement in:

Purchasing/Supply Applications	Supply Chain Applications
• Spend Analyses	• Demand Forecasting
• Risk Analysis	• Inventory Management
• Performance Benchmarking	• Transportation/Logistics Design
• Contract Compliance	• Performance Tracking
• Supplier Performance	• Environmental Monitoring
• Price/Cost Analysis and Modeling	• Value Chain and Supplier Mapping
• Consolidation of Supplier	
• Financial Analyses	

Further, purchasing will more fully move to a digitized and paperless world and tactical activities will become more automated. Also, spend management will continue to increase its flexibility based on data and analytics.

E-systems integration will increase enhancing supply performance. "Contract management software will become more integrated with spend management, particularly in terms of compliance. Collaboration software such as Cisco's TelePresence will also enhance the ability to streamline the contract management process. Performance monitoring and capability mapping will continue to expand supply management's potential. The flexibility provided by user definition and role-based access will enrich the potential for added supply management. E-systems will increasingly provide cross-enterprise visibility and transparency and link to company-wide enterprise resource planning systems."[13]

Sourcing Snapshot

Sourcing E-Tools at Harris

Harris has focused much of its recent transformation attention on the information it needs to determine which suppliers can provide the best-suited products at the lowest overall cost. The company has established a company-wide database infrastructure to capture and store data, processes, and e-system applications.

The e-system transformation took two to three years to somewhat fully develop. Harris now has the ability to view the entire business and drive collaborative decision-making with the capabilities in place.

Harris has implemented numerous buying tools, including an internally developed program called EXPO. This is an enterprisewide portal that connects Harris's four divisions, the ERP programs, and company engineers. The system provides for internal collaboration and billing and enables direct e-system communications with suppliers. EXPO enables Harris to determine parts quality performance, assess whether a part is environmentally safe, view inventory records, identify the type of supplier to which the purchase item is sourced, and so forth.

In addition, Harris uses Oracle's Agile product life cycle management software to help manage product life cycle decisions throughout the company. Harris also uses Indecka's search engine technology to help product development engineers locate parts to meet specific technical requirements. This enables engineers to specify parts that are early in their product life cycle and that meet Harris's cost targets. Harris also uses Dun & Bradstreet's financial alerts to determine the financial status of a supplier and other profile information.

Source: Adapted from Forest, W. (March 2008) "Center-Led Collaboration Powers Harris Sourcing Initiatives," *Purchasing,* 137(3), 14–16.

Concluding Observations

Overall, technology will move from stand-alone, serially connected applications to integrated, collaboration-based, flexible systems. "Big data" and user-defined analytics with a variety of analyses approaches will be emphasized, including knowledge management. Reporting will be on-demand, and the purchasing/supply chain function will become more digitized and paperless. Cross-enterprise transparency will increase, as will collaboration enabled by technology. Finally, additional data and applications will be available through cloud computing.

Collaborating Internally and Externally Will Grow in Strategic Importance

Collaboration with suppliers is quite frequently identified as an important success factor in achieving competitiveness. However, to be successful, a holistic approach is required. Four main themes around collaboration were established by the CAPS, ISM, and A.T. Kearney study:[14]

They were:

1. Internal collaboration and integration must be enhanced to meet future company needs.

2. External collaboration will signal a shift from pure competition to cooperation for some segments of a company's supply base.

3. Technology is required to enable an increase in collaboration—providing for both internal and external information transparency and information sharing.

4. Management of risk and protecting intellectual property may limit collaboration with suppliers (and must be resolved).

Purchasing and supply management, combined with other functional leadership and company executives, will have to establish the company strategy and policies governing collaborative efforts with suppliers (and customers). Significant changes in negative attitudes and limiting strategies, practices, and working relationships will be required.

Obtaining Innovation

Product and service innovations from suppliers will be increasingly important to competitive success. The recent economic downturn resulted in headcount reductions and the outsourcing of non-core competencies increasing reliance on external suppliers. In addition, globalization and growth in emerging markets has been significant. Both trends place greater emphasis on supplier innovation as part of a company's overall innovation strategy. To further facilitate innovation from suppliers, a study was conducted by CAPS Research focused on "Innovation Sourcing" that provided guidelines to what buying companies need to do to accelerate innovations from suppliers.[15] These critical guidelines include approaches to:

- Intellectual property ownership
- Project management
- Trust and communications
- Strategic alignment and risk/reward
- Innovation metrics, supplier capabilities, and performance assessments
- Voice of the customer and supplier
- Cost versus innovation
- Stage-gate processes: from concept to suppliers
- Company innovation culture
- Supply management's role
- Critical problem areas negatively affecting innovation development

Concluding Observations

In the past, supply management has focused on establishing a competitive environment between suppliers. During the next five years, there will be an increased need for systematic approaches for creating and operating collaboratively with strategic suppliers. Suppliers and supply personnel must be convinced that the openness and trust needed in a genuinely collaborative environment will generate positive performance results. In addition, cross-enterprise collaboration will be facilitated by new approaches

Sourcing Snapshot

Chrysler No-Bid

Chrysler Group is piloting a collaborative, no-bid purchasing approach that provides a few preferred suppliers a profit but requires full financial disclosure for the parts supplied. However, no contracts have been signed and significant trust regarding the financials is required between Chrysler and the supplier.

However, pre-sourcing with longer-term no bid contracts provide suppliers with more predictable revenue and profit streams. This may reduce investment risk to suppliers and increase their willingness to provide new technology insights to their best customers. Continuity of supply is also possible for customers. Overall, the approach is a work in process. Some suppliers are reluctant to share their development and production costs. Others are more willing to take their chances in the bidding approach. This innovative approach is championed by Chrysler's Senior Vice President of Purchasing and Supplier Quality, Scott Kunselman who is focused on first working with incumbent suppliers and furthering the development of trust with these suppliers.

Source: Adapted from Vellequette, L.P., "Chrysler Pilots No Bid Contracts on New Mini Van," (August 5, 2013) *Automotive News Insights.*

to incentivize and obtain supplier innovation and by technologies enabling companies to collaborate electronically.

Attracting, Developing, and Retaining Supply Management Talent Will Become a Key Differentiator for Success

"A great deal will be expected of tomorrow's purchasing and supply management professionals, as they will be charged with developing and executing acquisition strategies that find new value in the supply base, deliver value as quickly as possible within the cost parameters defined by the demand market, and maximize the return to the company. To do so, they will need to find and leverage external sources of innovation, contribute to revenue generation, expand efforts to manage costs, and ensure business continuity and sustainability."[16]

Exhibit 20.3 presents an overview of the many skills and capabilities that supply management professionals will need to succeed.

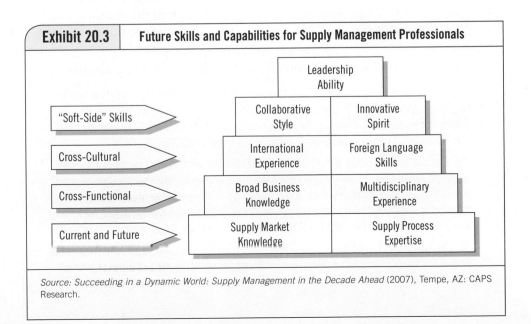

Exhibit 20.3   Future Skills and Capabilities for Supply Management Professionals

Source: Succeeding in a Dynamic World: Supply Management in the Decade Ahead (2007), Tempe, AZ: CAPS Research.

Current and Future Supply Management Skills

Critical skills for supply will require supply market knowledge, including the ability to conduct supply industry, competitive market structure and price and cost analyses. Also required will be the ability to carry out scenario planning based on supply market uncertainties and risks such as natural disasters, emerging market dynamics, sustainability requirements, new suppliers, and technology trends. Overall, supply personnel will be required to perform more complex analyses, using more data, to identify and correct problems, anticipate future issues and trends and establish lead-edge and innovative supply strategies. More holistic and forward looking purchase category strategies will be required.

Cross-Functional and Cross-Cultural Teaming Skills

"Supply management professionals will increasingly need both broader general business knowledge and multidiscipline skills. A working knowledge of business fundamentals including finance, accounting, and business law, and project management skills, as well as exposure to/experience in operations, engineering, product and service development, marketing and sales, and business planning, will help supply professionals to work effectively across functional, organizational and cultural boundaries."[17]

Cross-functional teams will continue to be important to supply management strategy because they provide a broader base of knowledge for decision-making, recognize the needs of major stakeholders in the organization and provide for implementation support. Including internal users on sourcing teams acknowledges their expertise in their particular areas and leads to much better cooperation, which in turn leads to better supplier agreements, in which internal users have a vested interest. Cross-functional teams will increasingly be used in particular for category and supplier strategy development and implementation that leads to product and process innovation.

Sourcing Snapshot

Teamwork and Cooperation Come Slowly between Functions

Companies are taking steps to get different departments to work together effectively, but they are still falling short of the goal. And although most purchasing professionals agree that teamwork and cooperation are the best mechanisms for getting different corporate functions to work together, they also point out that neither attribute exists naturally in a corporate setting.

The results of a recent survey indicate that although there are good signs of cooperation between corporate departments, many companies are not doing enough to foster cooperation between purchasing and other functions. Even worse, many such efforts are actually counterproductive. "There's too much competition among departments," says Ronald Blizzard, materials administrator for Massachusetts-based Guilford Rail System. His response was typical of many purchasers who say that long-standing rivalries between groups do not die easily or quickly.

Most of the survey participants say their companies are not taking the most effective approach to the problem of promoting teamwork and cooperation.

Some survey respondents say that employees themselves are the root of the problem and that staff members simply refuse to play along or work well with others. But the majority of survey respondents lay the responsibility at the feet of management. They say, no matter which process is adopted, it must receive the blessing and support of upper management. Too often, the departments of production, planning, design, quality, and purchasing have different leaders to answer to. Those who have watched this process work well report that their purchasing departments were successfully linked with operations management, logistics and planning, materials, and warehouse receiving/shipping departments.

Management must continually reinforce the common goal of teamwork, reminding employees that they are part of a company, not only a department.

Source: Adapted from Milligan, B. (November 4, 1999), "Despite Attempts to Break Them, Functional Silos Live On," *Purchasing,* 24–26. See also Avery, S. "Rockwell Collins Takes Off," (February 20, 2003), *Purchasing,* 25–28.

Further, as the world shrinks and sourcing to foreign markets globally expands, increasing emphasis will be placed on supply personnel to understand and live in foreign countries, and who are capable of adapting to foreign cultures. Speaking multiple languages will also be important. A broader global perspective and understanding of how to be effective in different cultures will be required.

"Soft-Side" Skills

Strong "soft-side" skills, combined with analytical capabilities, will be a key determinant of success. A collaborative working style, innovative supply approaches and leadership abilities versus. a narrower process view will be necessary to lead supply efforts and achieve results. In addition, the ability to lead virtual, geographically dispersed teams that will include members from different countries and cultures will be critical. These teams will likely include members from multiple functions and geographies.

Acquisition, Development, and Retention

Globalization will require that companies develop specific and tailored approaches to identify and hire foreign nationals. Recognizing differences in potential employee needs by country and region will be required. Supply personnel knowledge and skill development programs will require tailored and focused initiatives by country and region as skill sets worldwide are variable. Retention programs for high talent persons will also have to be tailored, recognizing country/region factors that are important to supply personnel in specific geographies.

Concluding Observations

Companies that are able to attract, develop, and retain talent with the above characteristics will likely be the most competitive. To gain this differential advantage in talent, broader and worldwide hiring practices will have to be enhanced. Tailored development programs that enable people to work independently, on-demand, and in groups to meet development goals are needed. Retention of the best professionals will also grow in importance and require that the company be viewed as a "best" or "interesting" or "exciting" place to work in supply.

Sourcing Snapshot

Establishing Supply Chain Masters at Intel

Intel Corporation, even though a technology leader, recognized in the 1980s and 1990s that it was also the world's largest manufacturer of micro-electronic parts. To compete effectively worldwide, supply chain management had become extremely important to its success. However, until recently, Intel did not have a formal program and career path to develop and advance its supply chain professionals. Existing management and technical career ladders were insufficient to meet long-term needs of supply chain management professionals.

In response, Intel developed a program to attract and retain supply chain professionals who could deal with emerging complex, thorny supply chain issues. It developed a supply chain career path, based on its engineering job ladder. After meeting specific criteria, candidates would receive the title of "supply chain master" or "senior supply chain master."

To achieve these designations, certain levels of supply chain knowledge and expertise had to be demonstrated by candidates. These broadly stated areas of expertise included:

- Customer/supplier collaboration and development
- Negotiation
- Risk management and statistical analysis
- Planning (which could include all types such as commodity strategy planning, transportation network planning, and so forth)
- Supply chain metrics, modeling and development
- Enterprise resource planning/collaborative planning and forecasting
- Business strategy and financial analysis
- Industrial and quality engineering and packaging
- Logistics/distribution

Four criteria were developed to judge the candidates' readiness for the designated titles. The criteria included: (1) depth of knowledge including the development and execution of leading-edge ideas, (2) degree of influence with other internal people and functions so as to implement innovative ideas, (3) ability to influence people and organizations external to Intel such as suppliers, and (4) being a role model and mentor, which establishes the candidate as a thought leader and one who shares their knowledge. "Senior supply chain masters" were required to demonstrate much greater levels of internal and external influence.

Recognition and opportunities are provided to supply chain masters. These include recognition at Intel's quarterly business meeting, additional mentoring and scheduled time to develop their areas of expertise, and participation in a "community-of-practice" (COP) within Intel. This COP provides the opportunity to meet with, exchange information and identify supply chain opportunities and initiatives with other supply chain masters.

The results of the supply chain master program have been significant. They include cost reductions achieved through COP projects and overall satisfaction with and excitement about the supply chain opportunities and careers at Intel.

Source: Adapted from Kellso, J.R. (2009, Q2), "The Making of a Supply Chain Master," *CSCMP's Supply Chain Quarterly* 3(2), 36–41.

Managing and Enabling the Future Supply Management Organization and Measurement Systems

Organization Approaches

The currently dominant center-led model for supply management will continue to be a key strategy, and likely the norm for the foreseeable future. This is true, even as organizations better develop the balance between company-wide advantages because of scale and expertise from center-led approaches and from business unit advantages in providing full product/service needs such as continuity of supply, responsiveness and fast product/service development with perfect launch. In addition, the center-led model will most likely focus on leveraging the scale of common purchases across the company and functional leadership of systems, processes, and talent development. However, unique business unit technology, agility, continuity of supply needs will lead to selected decision-making and activities at the SBU level. In addition, growing pressure for fast new-product development and meeting unique needs of customers will lead to the further integration of purchasing with engineering and a balance between selective decentralization to the business unit combined within the center-led approach.

Another significant issue is how to better integrate purchasing and supply management with the rest of the organization. The most likely scenarios are shown in Exhibit 20.4.

In one scenario, purchasing/supply will become part of a larger supply chain function, which would have responsibility for all functions on both the demand and supply sides of the firm, required to meet customer needs. Specific activities on the demand side that virtually touch the customer would not generally be included.

"In the second likely scenario, supply management will take on a leading role to manage both external and internal supply. The top supply management role will closely resemble

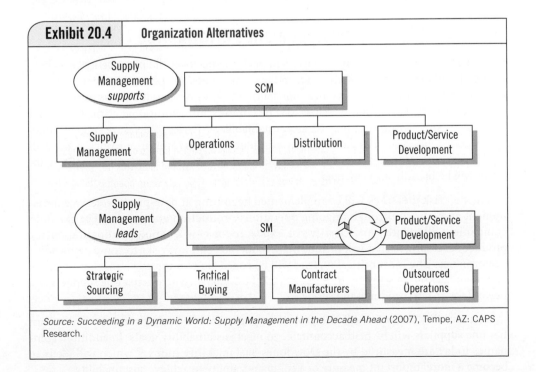

Exhibit 20.4   **Organization Alternatives**

Source: Succeeding in a Dynamic World: Supply Management in the Decade Ahead (2007), Tempe, AZ: CAPS Research.

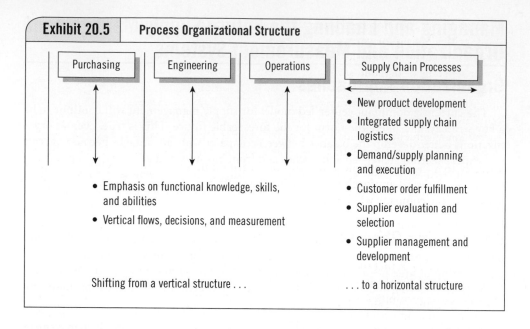

Exhibit 20.5 | Process Organizational Structure

Purchasing   Engineering   Operations   Supply Chain Processes

- New product development
- Integrated supply chain logistics
- Demand/supply planning and execution
- Customer order fulfillment
- Supplier evaluation and selection
- Supplier management and development

- Emphasis on functional knowledge, skills, and abilities
- Vertical flows, decisions, and measurement

Shifting from a vertical structure . . .   . . . to a horizontal structure

today's chief operating officer's job description. In this organizational structure, supply will manage all of the external supply base and contract manufacturers. Required will be a tight integration with operations, engineering, and internal customers to help ensure the proper management of new-product introductions and continuous improvement in the production and distribution of ongoing products and processes. The supply management leader would also act as Chief Cost Management Officer."[18] Exhibit 20.5 further illustrates the increasing focus on horizontal structures integrating various functions. To be competitive in the decade ahead, more cross-functional and customer-focused integration will be necessary.

Measuring Supply Management Performance

Primary measures of supply management performance over the past twenty years have included supplier quality, cost, delivery, and responsiveness. At some companies, measures of supplier technology capability and contribution have also been utilized as have selected social responsibility measures such as MWBE. In the future additional critical measures will include supplier innovation, risk and sustainability. Metrics to measure supplier innovation contribution such as number of new-product/process innovations suggested, product innovations resulting in revenue generation and number of new patents benefiting the buyer will be broadly implemented.

Further, risk measures will be implemented beginning at new-product/service development and launch through ongoing operations/production and service. For example, companies will identify and classify risk exposure for new technology adoption during product development that will include high, moderate, and low risks to company/product performance. The most critical metrics will be rolled-up to a top executive level team to review and act on. In addition, risk metrics will be established across tier one suppliers and beyond for critical products and services.

Sustainability measures will also grow in importance. The buying company and at least tier one suppliers will be held accountable to meet sustainability goals. In addition, companies today are measured by the Dow Jones Sustainability Index,[19] which will likely to become a more important measure of a company's ability to achieve sustainability.

In addition, common metrics across trading partners in the supply chain will become more critical going forward and improvement is needed. Supply measures will also become more customer centric. For example, measuring the ability of the firm to meet customer schedule or demand shifts, fast product redesign needs and performance reliability. In addition, as companies become larger and spread more widely across the globe, relevant and effective metrics will be implemented across far-flung operations to provide an ongoing view, control and improvement of global operations. Further, metrics that clearly link supply management performance to the overall financial and market performance of the company will be implemented. Measurement systems linking purchasing and supply more directly to a firm's economic value-add or return on invested capital will be utilized. A balanced scorecard approach to measuring the contribution of supply management to the success of the company will be in common use.

Concluding Observations

A typical view is that the center-led model provides companies the best opportunities to develop overall supply strategies and effective purchase category strategies that are based on volume opportunities. However, given the global nature of many businesses, especially where customer growth is coming from new and emerging markets, there is an increasing need for a business unit focus to meet unique customer needs. There is need to better balance center-led scale benefits with the agility (technology, demand shifts, specifications) in meeting business unit needs. Strategic business units (SBUs) or regional organizations may become the primary organizational level around which supply activities are managed in the largest organizations. At these levels, the center-led model will continue to predominate, whether at the company or SBU level.

In addition, purchasing and supply will become more integrated with other company functions such as engineering, operations, and finance. Performance measures will become more customer-focused within a balanced scorecard and tightly coupled to a firm's financial performance.

Twelve High-Impact Sourcing and Supply Chain Strategies for 2013–2018

The 2013 Executive Assessment of Supply study conducted by CAPS Research,[20] combined with Succeeding in a Dynamic World: Supply Management in the Decade Ahead, have helped in establishing 12 key purchasing and supply strategies that may be most impactful on a company ability to achieve competitive success in the future. They also provide a focused approach to achieving excellence for leading companies:

1. Continuous outsourcing/insourcing analyses and rebalancing because of globalization and changing product and logistics cost structures

2. A greater focus on risk management because of recent significant supply disruptions caused by natural disasters, combined with economic, industry and supplier (especially financial) uncertainties

3. Enhanced supply chain integration and collaboration with strategic suppliers, including increased information sharing and transparency

4. Sourcing becoming more integrated with other functions, processes, and customers

5. Enhancing the quality, number, and execution of written purchase category/supplier strategies with a focus on value that can be achieved across the total supply network

6. Enhancing global sourcing and supply strategies to maximize competitiveness

7. Requiring suppliers to take a greater cost management role by providing value-adding services in research and development, manufacturing/operations, customer order fulfillment, and system integration

8. Providing common customer-focused measurements and metrics across the supply chain

9. Developing an e-sourcing and supply applications portfolio that includes digitized and paperless supplier invoicing, e-sourcing (with the Internet and global data warehouses providing the backbone), knowledge management systems, and the application of "big data" combined with innovative analytic applications

10. Supply taking a leading role in sustainability and innovation with suppliers

11. Strategic sourcing and supply chain activities primarily center-led, but with appropriate activities being located at SBU sites worldwide to meet unique customer needs, and with decentralized execution of transactions on a global basis

12. Talent strategies with dedicated personnel focusing on identifying, hiring, and developing highly talented, flexible, and globally oriented personnel, who can immediately contribute—a critical success factor

Good Practice Example

Cessna Transforms to Achieve Leading-Edge Sourcing and Supply Status

Charles B. Johnson, President and COO of Cessna, pointed out, "As our supply chain processes house the majority of our cost, it was necessary to create a more strategically aligned supply chain that yielded the most competitive quality, delivery, flexibility, and value." This was a major driver underlying the transformation process at Cessna. Under the leadership of Michael R. Katzorke, Senior Vice President, supply chain management at Cessna has created a long-range strategic plan and cross-functional commodity teams. The purpose was to rationalize the company's supplier base. In addition, Cessna developed a Maturity Path Development tool that aligned suppliers and Cessna strategy. They also revised the company's sales, inventory, and operations plan (SIOP), aimed at improving performance to customer expectations and reducing inventory turns. A value analysis/value engineering process was also introduced, encouraging supplier involvement in removing cost from the supply chain.

Katzorke and the supply chain management team have involved suppliers in supporting Cessna's corporate "High Five" objectives of total customer satisfaction, world quality standards for aviation, breakthrough operating performance, top 10 company to work for, and superior financial results. Clearly, Cessna's sourcing and supply strategy transformation is aimed at contributing to overall company objectives.

"Perhaps the biggest achievement of Katzorke and his team," says Johnson, "has been the transformation from a transactional purchasing organization to an integrated full supply chain process."

Katzorke has stated: "For breakthrough change, we needed the vision, skills, incentives, resources, and action plan fully linked across the entire business."

One of the key transformation elements in achieving an integrated supply chain is cross-functional commodity teams. These teams include representatives of supply chain management, manufacturing engineering, quality engineering, product design engineering, reliability engineering, product support, and finance. The teams work to drive supplier improvement and integration of suppliers into Cessna's design and manufacturing process, thereby integrating critical components of the supply chain. There are six commodity teams for direct materials and one for indirect materials and services. Each team has an annual strategic plan linked to the CEO's strategic objectives.

One key task of the commodity teams was the rationalization of the supply base, from 3,000 to 132 suppliers. Remaining suppliers were then classified into growth suppliers, where Cessna's business will grow; provisional suppliers, whose future prospects are uncertain; and phase-out suppliers, whose business with Cessna is about to end. The teams then formed long-term partnerships with the growth suppliers, aligning the supply base contractually in terms of objectives, strategies, processes and data, and supply chain integration. Today, growth suppliers receive 77 percent of Cessna's business. The teams are also further integrating suppliers into Cessna's design, manufacturing, and other key processes so that they are integrated into Cessna's business.

Cessna also developed a new process that included demand and SIOP processes. Suppliers have clear visibility to production plans and capacity planning interfaces, focusing on end-customer demand. This high-level review of Cessna illustrates the magnitude and company emphasis being placed on developing leading-edge purchasing and supply strategies and processes that contribute to financial performance of the firm.

Source: Adapted from Avery, S. (2003, September 4), "Cessna Soars," Purchasing, 25–35.

CONCLUSION

This chapter—as well as this book—presents purchasing and supply chain management as a dynamic field of study. Surviving in an era of rapid economic and business model change, combined with intense competition requires a commitment to (1) develop the knowledge and skills of purchasing/supply professionals, (2) actively use information technology across the supply chain, (3) pursue activities and practices that capture the full benefit of a world-class supply base, (4) create responsive new organizational structures, and (5) establish the most effective purchasing and supply chain measurement system. Competing today requires purchasing and supply chain managers to play an active role in helping achieve an organization's cost, quality, time, agility, risk, technology, innovation, and sustainability goals—or risk losing market share to competitors that are benefiting from world-class supply chain management.

DISCUSSION QUESTIONS

1. Given the trends described in this chapter, what do you think the future purchasing organization will look like?

2. What are some of the primary skills that purchasing and supply chain managers will need to be successful in the future?

3. What will the role of the Internet, e-systems, big data and analytics be in supporting purchasing and supply chain management activities?

4. Why will there be an increase in using suppliers for product and process technology?

5. Why will the development of global databases increase? What kind of information should a global database provide?

6. Why will global sourcing increase?

7. Do you believe the total number of suppliers within a typical firm's supply bases will increase or decrease? Why?

8. The need to reduce cycle time is important. How can purchasing help in this process?

9. What will an integrated supply chain look like in terms of key elements?

10. How can more innovation from suppliers be achieved? What is required?

11. What is the possible role of purchasing in leading sustainability efforts?

ADDITIONAL READINGS

Arnseth, L. (2013, December), "The Music of True Sustainability," *Inside Supply Management*, 18–21.

Billington, C., and Jager, F. (2008, January), "Procurement: The Missing Link in Innovation," *Supply Chain Management Review*, 22–28.

Carter, P. L., Carter, J. R., Monczka, R. M., Blascovich, J. D., Slaight, T. H., and Markham, W. J. (2007), *Succeeding in a Dynamic World: Supply Management in the Decade Ahead*, Tempe, AZ: CAPS Research.

Chimni, J., and Gupta, A. (2009), "Prioritizing Your Supply Chain Investments," *Supply Chain Management Review*, 13(3), 34.

Davis, E., Collins, J., and Stewart, S. (2013), "Private Equity's New Proving Ground: Operations and Supply Chain," *Supply Chain Management Review*, 18.

Fawcett, S. E. (2009), "An Update on the State of Supply Chain Education," *Supply Chain Management Review*, 13(6), 36.

Goentzel, J. (2010), "Delivering on the Promise of Green Energy," *Supply Chain Management Review*, 14(1), 10.

Harbert, T. (2009), "Why the Leaders Love Value Chain Management," *Supply Chain Management Review*, 13(8), 15.

Hirsch, C., and Barbalho, M. (2003), "Toward World-Class Procurement," *Supply Chain Management Review*, 5(6), 75.

Katzorke, M. (2000), "Cessna Charts a Supply Chain Flight Strategy," *Purchasing*, 129(4), 42.

Kellso, J. R. (2009), "The making of a Supply Chain Master," *CSCMP's Supply Chain Quarterly*, 37.

Kerr, J. (2008), "A New Direction for Executive Education?" *Supply Chain Management Review*, 12(4), 30.

Monczka, R. M., Carter, P. L., Scannell, T. V., and Carter, J. R. (2011), *Innovation Sourcing: Contributing to Company Competitiveness*, Tempe, AZ: CAPS Research.

Monczka, R. M., Carter, P. L., Markham, W. J., Trent, R. J., Hartley, J. L., McDowell, C. P., and Ragatz, G. (2012), *Value Chain Strategies for the Changing Decade: Risk Management Across the Extended Value Chain*, Tempe, AZ: CAPS Research.

Monczka, R. M., Markham, W. J., Carter, J. R., Blascovich, J. D., and Slaight, T. H. (2005), *Outsourcing Strategically for Sustainable Competitive Advantage*, Tempe, AZ: CAPS Research.

Monczka, R. M., and Petersen, K. J. (2012), "The Competitive Potential of Supply Management," *Supply Chain Management Review*, 10, 10.

Monczka, R. M., and Petersen, K. J. (2013), *Supply Strategy Implementation: Current State and Future Opportunities*, Tempe, AZ: CAPS Research.

Monczka, R. M., Petersen, K. J., and Trent, R. J. (2006), *Effective Global Sourcing and Supply for Superior Results,* Tempe, AZ: CAPS Research.

Monczka, R. M., Trent, R. J., and Petersen, K. J. (2008, March), "Getting on Track to Better Global Sourcing," *Supply Chain Management Review,* 46–53.

Olavson, T., Lee, H., and DeNyse, G. (2010), "A Portfolio Approach to Supply Chain Design," *Supply Chain Management Review,* 14, 20.

"One on One: An Interview with Edith Kelly-Green—A Leading Purchasing and Supply Management Professional Shares Her Views on Technology and Trends" (2000), *Journal of Supply Chain Management,* 36(2), 2.

"One on One: An Interview with Gene Richter—A Leading Purchasing and Supply Management Professional Shares His Views on Technology and Trends" (2000), *Journal of Supply Chain Management,* 36(1), 2.

Rudzki, R. A. (2008, March), "Supply Management Transformation: A Leader's Guide," *Supply Chain Management Review,* 12–18.

Slone, R. E., Mentzer, J. T., and Dittmann, P. J. (2007, September), "Are You the Weakest Link in Your Company's Supply Chain?" *Harvard Business Review.* 1–11

Smock, D. A., Rudzki, R. A., and Rogers, S. C. (2007, May), "Sourcing Strategy—The Brains behind the Game," *Supply Chain Management Review,* 42–48.

Timmermans, K., and Pyle, H. (2010), "Snapshot of Today's CPO," *Inside Supply Management,* 31.

Wieland, A., and Handfield, R. (2013), "The Socially Responsible Supply Chain: An Imperative for Global Corporations," *Supply Chain Management Review,* 17(5), 22.

ENDNOTES

1. Interview with R. M. Monczka, 2003.

2. Carter, P. L., Carter, J. R., Monczka, R. M., Blascovich, J. D., Slaight, T. H., and Markham, W. J. (2007), *Succeeding in a Dynamic World: Supply Management in the Decade Ahead,* Tempe, AZ: CAPS Research.

3. Plambeck, E. L. (2007, July–August), "The Greening of Wal-Mart's Supply Chain," *Supply Chain Management Review,* 19.

4. Monczka, R. M., and Petersen, K. J. (2013), *Supply Strategy Implementation: Current State and Future Opportunities,* Tempe, AZ: CAPS Research.

5. Carter et al. p. 43.

6. Monczka, R. M., Blascovich, J. D., Markham, W. J., Parker, L., and Slaight, T. H. (2010), *Value Focused Supply—Linking Supply to Competitive Business Strategies,* Tempe, AZ: CAPS Research and AT. Kearney, Inc.

7. Carter et al. p. 54.

8. Sedgwick, D. (2013, November), "Want suppliers' respect? Bring them in early," *Automotive News,* 3.

9. Walsh, D. (2013, May), "Supplier-automaker relationship gets a grade of "poor" in survey," *Crains Detroit Business,* 23.

10. Carter et al. p. 62.

11. Monczka, R. M., Carter, P. L., Markham, W. J., Trent, R. J., Hartley, J. L., McDowell, C. P., and Ragatz, G. (2012), *Value Chain Strategies for the Changing Decade: Risk Management Across the Extended Value Chain,* Tempe, AZ: CAPS Research.

12. Manyika, J., Chui, M., Brown, B., Dobbs, R., Roxburgh, C., and Byers, A. H. (2011), *Big data: The next frontier for innovation, competition, and productivity,* McKinsey & Company and A.T. Kearney analysis – A.T. Kearney Inc.

13. Carter et al. p. 73.

14. Carter et al. p. 77.

15. Monczka, R. M., Carter, P. L., Carter, J. R., and Scannell, T. V. (2010), *Implementing Supplier Innovation: Case Study Findings*, Tempe, AZ: CAPS Research.

16. Carter et al. p. 81.

17. Carter et al. p. 82.

18. Carter et al. p. 94.

19. RobecoSAM and S&P Dow Jones Sustainability Indices. Annual Review 2013. http://www .sustainability-indices.com/

20. Monczka, R. M., and Petersen, K. J. (2013), *Supply Strategy Implementation: Current State and Future Opportunities 2013*, Tempe, AZ: CAPS Research.

Cases

Avion, Inc.

Susan Dey and Bill Mifflin, procurement managers at Avion, Inc., sat across from each other and reviewed a troubling performance report concerning a key supplier, Foster Technologies. The report detailed the deteriorating performance of Foster Technologies in the areas of material quality and on-time delivery.

Susan: I don't believe what I am seeing. This supplier was clearly a star when we performed our supplier visits before awarding the contract for the new Amrod product line.

Bill: I'm not pleased. I was on the team that performed the audit and site visit. Foster's management was so smooth—they indicated they could meet all our requirements. I feel like we've been misled by this supplier.

Susan: Didn't you look at their processes and quality systems?

Bill: Sure we did. Everything checked out fine. But now every other shipment has some problem, and the delays are hurting our ability to get our product to our customers. What really struck us about this supplier was how innovative they were. Foster's biggest drawback was their size—they lacked some depth at key manufacturing engineering positions. Maybe that's why they are having problems. It could be that someone has left the company.

Susan: We are going to have to address these problems quickly.

Bill: I'll tell you what I am going to recommend. We should begin immediately to look for another supplier. I never was a fan of these single-source contracts. They leave us open to too much risk.

Susan: But won't that take a long time?

Bill: Sure. We'll have to perform another supplier search with team visits. New tooling could really cost, too. This could take months.

Susan: Has anyone talked with the supplier about these problems?

Bill: Kevin went over personally today and talked with the production manager. He didn't have much time to explain, but he indicated on the phone that Foster's production manager said we should accept responsibility for a good part of the problems that are occurring!

Susan: Why should we? I think they are just trying to shift the blame for their poor performance.

At this point, Kevin O'Donnell, another procurement manager, entered the room.

Bill: Kevin, glad you're here. We were just discussing how Foster is trying to blame us for their problems. I think we should dump them fast!

Kevin: Yeah, well, I've got news for you two. I think Foster's production manager is correct. I think I would be frustrated with us, too!

Susan: What are you talking about?

Kevin: I spent a good part of the day over at Foster and learned some interesting things. For example, do either of you remember what we told Foster the monthly volume requirements for the product would be?

Bill: I remember exactly. The volumes were projected to be 2,500 units a month. So what's the problem?

Kevin: We need to talk with our production group more often. The monthly volumes are now over 4,000 units a month! And not only that, our production group now wants material within 10 days of a material release rather than two weeks. We have also been changing the final material release quantities right up to the last minute before delivery.

Bill: Uh oh. I remember on our site visit that the most their production system could handle was 3,500 units a month. And a two-week lead time was about as low as they could go.

Susan: But why didn't they inform us that these changes were causing problems? They still have some explaining to do.

Kevin: Apparently they tried. What did your team tell this supplier about communicating with us after you finished negotiating the contract?

Bill: We said that any operational problems or issues have to go through our materials management people. The team was responsible for evaluating and selecting the supplier, and then negotiating the agreement.

Kevin: Foster's production manager produced a log detailing seven memos and letters outlining the impact of our production and scheduling changes on their operation. He also called us several times with no response. Each of these inquiries received little attention on the part of our materials group. I'm not sure how fond Foster is of us as a customer. I think they are anxious for this contract to wind down so they can dump us!

Susan: What do we do now?

ASSIGNMENT

1. What parts of the supply chain are most closely involved with the situation in this case? What is the responsibility of each part in order to maintain a smooth flow of material?

2. What initially appears to be the problem? What really is the problem(s) in this case?

3. How easy is it to switch suppliers? What could complicate a firm's ability to switch to a new supplier?

4. What does it mean to get to the root cause of a problem?

5. What does it mean to be a good *customer*? Why does a buying firm want to be perceived by a supplier as a good customer? Provide specific examples of what a firm must do to be a good supply chain customer.

6. Explain the role of performance measurement in managing supply chain activities.

7. Why can changes within a supply chain disrupt the normal flow of goods and services within a supply chain?

8. Why might Avion want to reduce the lead times on its purchased materials and components?

9. Why do firms single-source contracts?

10. Develop an action plan for Avion that addresses the issues presented in this case. Be prepared to fully explain your recommendations.

The Global Sourcing Wire Harness Decision

Sheila Austin, a buyer at Autolink, a Detroit-based producer of subassemblies for the automotive market, has sent out requests for quotations for a wiring harness to four prospective suppliers. Only two of the four suppliers indicated an interest in quoting the business: Original Wire (Auburn Hills, MI) and Happy Lucky Assemblies (HLA) of Guangdong Province, China. The estimated demand for the harnesses is 5,000 units a month. Both suppliers will incur some costs to retool for this particular harness. The harnesses will be prepackaged in 24 × 12 × 6-inch cartons. Each packaged unit weighs approximately 10 pounds.

Quote 1

The first quote received is from Original Wire. Auburn Hills is about 20 miles from Autolink's corporate headquarters, so the quote was delivered in person. When Sheila went down to the lobby, she was greeted by the sales agent and an engineering representative. After the quote was handed over, the sales agent noted that engineering would be happy to work closely with Autolink in developing the unit and would also be interested in future business that might involve finding ways to reduce costs. The sales agent also noted that they were hungry for business, as they were losing a lot of customers to companies from China. The quote included unit price, tooling, and packaging. The quoted unit price does not include shipping costs. Original Wire requires no special warehousing of inventory, and daily deliveries from its manufacturing site directly to Autolink's assembly operations are possible.

Original Wire Quote:

- Unit price = $30
- Packing costs = $0.75 per unit
- Tooling = $6,000 one-time fixed charge
- Freight cost = $5.20 per hundred pounds

Quote 2

The second quote received is from Happy Lucky Assemblies of Guangdong Province, China. The supplier must pack the harnesses in a container and ship via inland transportation to the port of Shanghai in China, have the shipment transferred to a container ship, ship material to Seattle, and then have material transported inland to Detroit. The quoted unit price does not include international shipping costs, which the buyer will assume.

HLA Quote:

- Unit price = $19.50
- Shipping lead time = Eight weeks
- Tooling = $3,000

In addition to the supplier's quote, Sheila must consider additional costs and information before preparing a comparison of the Chinese supplier's quotation:

- Each monthly shipment requires three 40-foot containers.
- Packing costs for containerization = $2 per unit.
- Cost of inland transportation to port of export = $200 per container.
- Freight forwarder's fee = $100 per shipment (letter of credit, documentation, etc.).
- Cost of ocean transport = $4,000 per container. This has risen significantly in recent years due to a shortage of ocean freight capacity.
- Marine insurance = $0.50 per $100 of shipment.
- U.S. port handling charges = $1,200 per container. This fee has also risen considerably this year, due to increased security. Ports have also been complaining that the charges may increase in the future.
- Customs duty = 5% of unit cost.
- Customs broker fees per shipment = $300.
- Transportation from Seattle to Detroit = $18.60 per hundred pounds.
- Need to warehouse at least four weeks of inventory in Detroit at a warehousing cost of $1.00 per cubic foot per month, to compensate for lead time uncertainty.

Sheila must also figure the costs associated with committing corporate capital for holding inventory. She has spoken to some accountants, who typically use a corporate cost of capital rate of 15%.

- Cost of hedging currency—broker fees = $400 per shipment
- Additional administrative time due to international shipping = 4 hours per shipment × $25 per hour (estimated)
- At least two five-day visits per year to travel to China to meet with supplier and provide updates on performance and shipping = $20,000 per year (estimated)

The international sourcing costs must be absorbed by Sheila, as the supplier does not assume any of the additional estimated costs and invoice Sheila later, or build the costs into a revised unit price. Sheila feels that the U.S. supplier is probably less expensive, even though it quoted a higher price. Sheila also knows that this is a standard technology that is unlikely to change during the next three years, but which could be a contract that extends multiple years out. There is also a lot of "hall talk" amongst the engineers on her floor about next-generation automotive electronics, which will completely eliminate the need for wire harnesses, which will be replaced by electronic components that are smaller, lighter, and more reliable. She is unsure about how to calculate the total costs for each option, and she is even more unsure about how to factor these other variables into the decision.

ASSIGNMENT

1. Calculate the total cost per unit of purchasing from Original Wire.
2. Calculate the total cost per unit of purchasing from Happy Lucky Assemblies.
3. Based on the total cost per unit, which supplier should Sheila recommend?
4. Are there any other issues besides cost that Sheila should evaluate?
5. Based on this case, do you think international purchasing is more or less complex than domestic purchasing? Why? Is it worth the additional effort?

Managing Supplier Quality: Integrated Devices

Bill Edwards is a quality engineer assigned to the Injected Molding Commodity Team at Integrated Devices. The commodity team is responsible for evaluating, selecting, and negotiating agreements with plastic-injected molding suppliers to be used throughout Integrated Devices. The team is also responsible for improving service quality and material that Integrated Devices receives from its suppliers. Bill's role after supplier selection involves working directly with suppliers that require training or technical assistance concerning quality control and quality improvement.

The company spends about 70% of each sales dollar on purchased goods and services, so suppliers have a major impact on product quality.

Bill just received a call concerning a recurring manufacturing problem at Integrated Devices' Plant No. 3. The plant buyer said the plant is experiencing some quality variability problems with a key plastic-injected molding component supplied by Trexler Plastics. The component is sometimes too short or too long to fit properly with other components within the finished product. On occasion, the bracket snaps, causing end-product failure. Although the unit cost of the plastic-injected molding component is only $1.55, these quality issues (length variability and snapping) are creating production problems that far exceed the component's purchase price.

The local buyer announced he was having difficulty resolving the problem and asked for support from the corporate commodity team. The buyer said, "You corporate guys selected this supplier that we all have to use. The least you can do is to help us out of the jam your supplier choice is causing." The buyer's comment surprised Bill, although Bill would soon come to understand that plant personnel resented not being able to select their own suppliers.

After investigating the problem during a tension-filled meeting with Plant No. 3 personnel, Bill determined he would have to visit the supplier directly. He would work with Trexler's process engineers to address the manufacturing variability caused by the nonconforming component. Bill went back and reviewed his team's actions when selecting a single supplier to provide an entire family of plastic-injected moldings.

Trexler had quoted the lowest price of all competing suppliers and had provided samples that passed Integrated Devices' engineering tests.

Upon his arrival at the supplier, Bill learned that Trexler did not have a dedicated process engineer. One engineer, Steve Smith, was responsible for plant layout, process, quality, and industrial engineering. This individual, who was hired only two months previously, was still becoming familiar with Trexler's procedures. When Bill asked to review the supplier's quality control procedures, Steve had to ask several people before he could locate Trexler's procedures manual.

Bill decided that his first step should be to understand the process responsible for producing the defective component. At an afternoon meeting, Bill asked Steve for actual output data from Trexler's process. Steve explained they did not collect data for process capability studies or for statistical control charting of continuous production. However, he did say that sometimes "things don't seem to be operating well" with the equipment that produces the component. Trexler uses an inspector to examine every finished item to determine if it should be shipped to the customer.

After explaining the basics of process capability to Steve, Bill asked him to collect data from the process that produced the bracket component. Bill requested that Steve take exact measurements periodically from the process so they could draw statistical conclusions. Bill said he would return in three days to examine the data.

Upon his return three days later, Steve shared with Bill the details of the data collection effort (see Exhibit 1).

Exhibit 1		Process Output Data Part #03217666					
4.01	4.02	4.00	3.99	3.98	4.00	4.00	4.03
4.04	4.02	4.07	3.95	3.98	4.01	4.03	4.00
4.00	3.96	3.94	3.98	3.99	4.02	4.01	4.00
4.05	3.98	3.97	4.03	4.07	4.04	4.02	4.01
3.99	3.96	4.00	4.00	4.01	4.02	4.02	4.01
3.98	3.99	3.94	3.93	4.00	4.02	4.00	3.97
3.99	4.02	4.04	4.00	3.96	3.97	4.00	4.01

Component: #03217666

Description: Bracket

Design specification: 4 ± 0.06 inches

Once Bill calculated a preliminary process capability from this data and examined the training and quality control procedures at Trexler, he realized he had some serious work ahead of him.

ASSIGNMENT

1. Calculate the C_p and C_{pk} of the process that produces the component purchased by Integrated Devices. Remember—Process width = 6 times the standard deviation of the sample. Can the process at Trexler satisfy design requirements? What should be a target C_{pk} level?

2. Why is it important to prove that a process is proven capable before developing statistical control limits (i.e., SPC charts)?

3. Is Integrated Devices being reactive or proactive when it comes to managing supplier quality? Why?

4. Discuss the possible advantages of negotiating quality requirements directly into supplier contracts.

5. What is the risk of relying on product samples when selecting suppliers? What is the risk of relying too heavily on unit cost when making the selection decision?

6. Why was it so important for Bill to work with Plant No. 3 personnel before visiting Trexler?

7. The local buyer at Integrated Devices did not seem pleased that a corporate team selected the supplier that the local plants must use. Why do firms use corporate commodity teams to select suppliers? How can firms get support from plant personnel for companywide suppliers?

8. Is quality a major emphasis at this supplier? Why or why not?

9. What are the possible effects if Trexler's inspector approves components for shipment that should be rejected due to nonconformance (Type II error)? What are the possible effects if Trexler's inspector rejects components for shipment that are in conformance with specifications (Type I error)? How can we control error of measurement?

10. When evaluating supplier quality, why is it important to focus on the process that produces the material or service rather than on the material or service itself? What did Integrated Devices rely on?

11. Discuss the likelihood that Bill will resolve the problem(s) with this component.

12. If Integrated Devices decides to continue using Trexler as a supplier, what must both companies do to begin improving Trexler's component quality?

13. Design a supplier quality management process for Integrated Devices that focuses on the prevention of supplier defects. (Hint: Activities performed during supplier evaluation and selection should be part of this process. Process capability analysis may also be part of your supplier quality management process.)

Negotiation—Porto

Due to competitive pressures, firms in the computer industry are constantly looking to reduce costs. Computer manufacturers compete fiercely for contracts based on meeting the technology, quality, and price requirements of customers. Profit margins and return-on-investment targets are almost always under pressure. Dell Computer recently saw its operating margins slip to a slim 7%.

Most computer manufacturers have programs designed to improve quality and reduce the costs associated with their products. One strategy that many producers use is to contract only with high-quality suppliers and develop longer-term buyer-seller relationships. One major computer company, Porto, also initiated a program requesting suppliers to continually improve productivity, which should lead to cost reductions.

The objective of the program was to reduce purchase costs over the foreseeable future. Porto also expects its suppliers to contribute cost-saving ideas whenever possible.

The high-technology industry features high fixed costs due to large investments in plant and equipment. These companies also commit large expenditures to research and development.

Porto currently has a requirement for an electronic component termed "New Prod," which is part of a recently designed product. The estimated volume requirement of New Prod is 200,000 units with additional follow-on orders likely. For the New Prod component, Porto felt there were five to eight highly competitive suppliers capable of producing the item. These suppliers are located primarily along the East and West Coasts of the United States. After a request for quote and preliminary analysis, the buyer for Porto decided to pursue further discussions with Technotronics.

Negotiation Session Requirements

Each negotiator must plan and prepare before conducting the negotiation. The group leader has information packets for the buyer and the seller that provide additional information and assignments required for conducting the negotiation. Buyers and sellers can share as little or as much of the information with each other as they desire during the actual negotiation.

Your negotiation strategy should be developed prior to the negotiation session. If working in groups, all group members should participate in the research planning as well as the actual negotiation. Remember, price is not the only variable subject to negotiation. In highly volatile industries like the computer industry, for example, capacity guarantees from suppliers are often critical. Be creative when crafting your purchase agreement.

822

Purchasing Ethics

Scenario 1

Bryan Janz was just arriving back from lunch when his office phone rang. It was his wife, Nina, calling from home. Nina told Bryan that FedEx had just delivered a package addressed to her. The package contained a beautiful clock, now sitting over the fireplace. In fact, Nina said, "the clock looks absolutely beautiful on our living room fireplace." Thinking the clock was from a family member, Bryan asked who sent the present. She said she did not recognize the name—the clock was from Mr. James McEnroe. Bryan immediately told Nina that she had to repack the clock because it was from a supplier who had been trying to win business from Bryan's company. They definitely could not accept the clock. Nina was very upset and responded that the clock was perfect for the room and, besides, the clock came to their home, not to Bryan's office. Because of Nina's attachment to the clock, Bryan was unsure about what to do.

ASSIGNMENT

1. What should Bryan do about the clock?

2. What does the Institute of Supply Management (ISM) code of ethics say about accepting supplier favors and gifts?

3. Why do you think the supplier sent the clock to Bryan's home and addressed it to his wife?

4. Does the mere act of sending the clock to Bryan mean that Mr. McEnroe is an unethical salesperson?

Scenario 2

Lisa Jennings thought that at long last, her company, Assurance Technologies, was about to win a major contract from Sealgood Instruments. Sealgood, a maker of precision measuring instruments, was sourcing a large contract for component subassemblies. The contract that Assurance Technologies was bidding on was worth at least $2.5 million annually, a significant amount given Assurance's annual sales of $30 million. Her team had spent hundreds of hours preparing the quotation and felt they could meet Sealgood's requirements in quality, cost, delivery, part standardization, and simplification. In fact, Lisa had never been more confident about a quote meeting the demanding requirements of a potential customer.

Troy Smyrna, the buyer at Sealgood Instruments responsible for awarding this contract, called Lisa and asked to meet with her at his office to discuss the specifics of the contract. When she arrived, Lisa soon realized that the conversation was not going exactly as she had expected. Troy informed Lisa that Assurance Technologies had indeed prepared a solid quotation for the contract. However, when he visited Assurance's facility earlier on a prequalifying visit, he was disturbed to see a significant amount of a competitor's product being used by Assurance. Troy explained his uneasiness with releasing part plans and designs to a company that clearly had involvement with a competitor. When Lisa asked what Assurance could do to minimize his uneasiness, Troy replied that he would be more comfortable if Assurance no longer used the competitor's equipment and used

823

Sealgood's equipment instead. Lisa responded that this would mean replacing several hundred thousand dollars worth of equipment. Unfazed, Troy simply asked her whether or not she wanted the business. Lisa responded that she needed some time to think and that she would get back to Troy in a day or so.

ASSIGNMENT

1. Do you think the buyer at Sealgood Instruments, Troy Smyrna, is practicing unethical behavior? First, what is the term for this behavior, and second, defend why you think it is ethical or unethical behavior.

2. What should Lisa do in this situation? Formulate a response.

Scenario 3

Ben Gibson, the purchasing manager at Coastal Products, was reviewing purchasing expenditures for packaging materials with Jeff Joyner. Ben was particularly disturbed about the amount spent on corrugated boxes purchased from Southeastern Corrugated. Ben said, "I don't like the salesman from that company. He comes around here acting like he owns the place. He loves to tell us about his fancy car, house, and vacations. It seems to me he must be making too much money off of us!" Jeff responded that he heard Southeastern Corrugated was going to ask for a price increase to cover the rising costs of raw material paper stock. Jeff further stated that Southeastern would probably ask for more than what was justified simply from rising paper stock costs.

After the meeting, Ben decided he had heard enough. After all, he prided himself on being a results-oriented manager. There was no way he was going to allow that salesman to keep taking advantage of Coastal Products. Ben called Jeff and told him it was time to rebid the corrugated contract before Southeastern came in with a price increase request. Who did Jeff know that might be interested in the business? Jeff replied he had several companies in mind to include in the bidding process. These companies would surely come in at a lower price, partly because they used lower-grade boxes that would probably work well enough in Coastal Products' process. Jeff also explained that these suppliers were not serious contenders for the business. Their purpose was to create competition with the bids. Ben told Jeff to make sure that Southeastern was well aware that these new suppliers were bidding on the contract. He also said to make sure the suppliers knew that price was going to be the determining factor in this quote, because he considered corrugated boxes to be a standard industry item.

ASSIGNMENT

1. Is Ben Gibson acting legally? Is he acting ethically? Why or why not?

2. As the Marketing Manager for Southeastern Corrugated, what would you do upon receiving the request for quotation from Coastal Products?

Scenario 4

Sharon Gillespie, a new buyer at Visionex, Inc., was reviewing quotations for a tooling contract submitted by four suppliers. She was evaluating the quotes based on price, target quality levels, and delivery lead time promises. As she was working, her manager, Dave Cox, entered her office. He asked how everything was progressing and if she needed any help. She mentioned she was reviewing quotations from suppliers for a tooling contract. Dave asked who the interested suppliers were and if she had made a decision. Sharon indicated that one supplier, Apex, appeared to fit exactly the requirements Visionex had specified in the proposal. Dave told her to keep up the good work.

Later that day Dave again visited Sharon's office. He stated that he had done some research on the suppliers and felt that another supplier, Micron, appeared to have the best track record with Visionex. He pointed out that Sharon's first choice was a new supplier to Visionex and there was some risk involved with that choice. Dave indicated that it would please him greatly if she selected Micron for the contract.

The next day Sharon was having lunch with another buyer, Mark Smith. She mentioned the conversation with Dave and said she honestly felt that Apex was the best choice. When Mark asked Sharon who Dave preferred, she answered, "Micron." At that point Mark rolled his eyes and shook his head. Sharon asked what the body language was all about. Mark replied, "Look, I know you're new but you should know this. I heard last week that Dave's brother-in-law is a new part owner of Micron. I was wondering how soon it would be before he started steering business to that company. He is not the straightest character." Sharon was shocked. After a few moments, she announced that her original choice was still the best selection. At that point Mark reminded Sharon that she was replacing a terminated buyer who did not go along with one of Dave's previous preferred suppliers.

ASSIGNMENT

1. What does the Institute of Supply Management code of ethics say about financial conflicts of interest?

2. Ethical decisions that affect a buyer's ethical perspective usually involve the organizational environment, cultural environment, personal environment, and industry environment. Analyze this scenario using these four variables.

3. What should Sharon do in this situation?

6 Insourcing/Outsourcing: The FlexCon Piston Decision

This case addresses many issues that affect insourcing/outsourcing decisions. A complex and important topic facing businesses today is whether to produce a component, assembly, or service internally (insourcing) or purchase that same component, assembly, or service from an external supplier (outsourcing).

Because of the important relationship between insourcing/outsourcing and competitiveness, organizations must consider many variables when considering an insourcing/outsourcing decision. This may include a detailed examination of a firm's competency and costs, along with quality, delivery, technology, responsiveness, and continuous improvement requirements. Because of the critical nature of many insourcing/outsourcing decisions, cross-functional teams often assume responsibility for managing the decision-making process. A single functional group usually does not have the data, insight, or knowledge required to make effective strategic insourcing/outsourcing decisions.

FlexCo'ns Insourcing/Outsourcing of Pistons

FlexCon, a $3 billion maker of small industrial engines, is undergoing a major internal review to decide where the company should focus its product development efforts and strategic investment. Executive management is arguing that too much capacity and talent are being committed to producing simple, commodity-type items that provide small differentiation within the marketplace. FlexCon concluded that in its attempts to preserve jobs, it has insourced parts that are easy to manufacture, while outsourcing those that are complex or challenging. Producing commodity-like components with mature technologies is adding little to what FlexCon's customers consider important. The company has become increasingly dependent on suppliers for critical components and subassemblies that make a major difference in the performance and cost of finished products.

Part of FlexCon's effort at redefining itself involves creating an understanding of insourcing/outsourcing among managers and employees. The company has sponsored workshops and presentations to convey executive management's vision and goals, including educating those who are directly involved in making detailed insourcing/outsourcing recommendations.

One presentation given by an expert in strategic sourcing focused on the changes in the marketplace that are encouraging outsourcing. The expert noted six key trends and changes that influence insourcing/outsourcing decisions:

1. *The pressure for cost reduction is severe and will continue to increase.* Cost reduction pressures are forcing organizations to use their production resources more efficiently. A recent study found that over 70% of firms surveyed expect stable or increasing purchased material costs through 2010. As a result, executive management will increasingly rely on insourcing/outsourcing decisions as a way to manage costs.

2. *Firms are continuing to become more highly specialized in product and process technology.* Increased specialization implies focused investment in a process or technology, which contributes to greater cost differentials between firms.

3. *Firms will increasingly focus on what they excel at while outsourcing areas of nonexpertise.* Some organizations are formally defining their core competencies to help guide the insourcing/outsourcing effort. This has affected decisions concerning what businesses a firm should engage.

4. *The need for responsiveness in the marketplace is increasingly affecting insourcing/outsourcing decisions.* Shorter cycle times, for example, encourage greater outsourcing with less vertical integration. The time to develop a production capability or capacity may exceed the window available to enter a new market.

5. *Wall Street recognizes and rewards firms with higher ROI/ROA.* Because insourcing usually requires an assumption of fixed assets (and increased human capital), financial pressures are causing managers to closely examine sourcing decisions. Avoidance of fixed costs and assets is motivating many firms to rely on supplier assets.

6. *Improved computer simulation tools and forecasting software enable firms to perform insourcing/outsourcing comparisons with greater precision.* These tools allow the user to perform sensitivity analysis (what-if analysis) that permits comparison of different sourcing possibilities.

One topic that interested FlexCon managers was a discussion of how core competencies relate to outsourcing decisions. FlexCon management commonly accepted that a core competency was something the company "was good at." This view, however, is not correct. A core competency refers to skills, processes, or resources *that distinguish a company,* are hard to duplicate, and make that firm unique compared to other firms. Core competencies begin to define a firm's long-run, strategic ability to build a dominant set of technologies or skills that enable it to adapt quickly to changing market opportunities. The presenter argued that three key points relate to the idea of core competence and its relationship to insourcing/outsourcing decisions:

1. A firm should concentrate internally on those components, assemblies, systems, or services that are critical to the finished product and where the firm possesses a distinctive (i.e., unique) advantage valued by the customer.

2. Consider outsourcing components, assemblies, systems, or services when suppliers have an advantage. Supplier advantages may occur because of economies of scale, process-specific investment, higher quality, familiarity with a technology, or a favorable cost structure.

3. Recognize that once a firm outsources an item or service, it usually loses the ability to bring that production capability or technology in-house without committing a significant investment.

The manager or team responsible for making an insourcing/outsourcing decision must develop a true sense of what the core competency of the organization is and whether the product or service under consideration is an integral part of that core competency.

The workshops and presentations have given most participants a greater appreciation of the need to consider factors besides cost when assessing insourcing/outsourcing opportunities. One breakout work session focused exclusively on developing a list of the key factors that may affect the insourcing/outsourcing analysis at FlexCon, which appears in Exhibit 1.

Exhibit 1	Key Factors Supporting Insourcing/Outsourcing Decisions

FACTORS SUPPORT INSOURCING:

1. Cost considerations favor the buyer.
2. A need or desire exists to integrate internal plant operations.
3. Excess plant capacity is available that can absorb fixed overhead.
4. A need exists to exert direct control over production and quality.
5. Product design secrecy is an important issue.
6. A lack of reliable suppliers characterizes the supply market.
7. Firm desires to maintain a stable workforce in a declining market.
8. Item or service is directly part of a firm's core competency, or links directly to the strategic plans of the organization.
9. Item or technology behind making the item is strategic to the firm. The item adds to the qualities customers consider important.
10. Union or other restrictions discourage or even prohibit outsourcing.
11. Outsourcing may create or encourage a new competitor.

FACTORS SUPPORT OUTSOURCING:

1. Cost considerations favor the supplier.
2. Supplier has specialized research and know-how, which creates differentials in cost and quality.
3. Buying firm lacks the technical ability to build an item.
4. Buyer has small volume requirements.
5. Buying firm has capacity constraints while the seller does not.
6. Buyer does not want to add permanent workers.
7. Future volume requirements are uncertain—buyer wants to transfer risk to the supplier.
8. Item or service is routine and available from many competitive sources.
9. Short cycle time requirements discourage new investment by the buyer—using existing supplier assets is logical.
10. Adding capacity at the buyer requires high capital start-up costs.
11. Process technology is mature with minimal likelihood of providing a future competitive advantage to the purchaser.

The Piston Insourcing/Outsourcing Decision

FlexCon is considering outsourcing production of all pistons that are part of the company's "R" series of engines. FlexCon has machined various versions of these pistons for as long as anyone at the company can remember. In fact, the company started fifty years ago as a producer of high-quality pistons. The company grew as customers requested that FlexCon produce a broader line of products. This outsourcing analysis has generated a great deal of interest and emotion among FlexCon engineers, managers, and employees.

FlexCon produces pistons in three separate work cells, which differ according to the type of piston produced. Each cell has six numerically controlled machines in a U-shape layout, with a supervisor, a process engineer, a material handler, and 12 employees assigned across the three cells. Employees, who are cross-trained to perform each job within their cell, work in teams of four. FlexCon experienced a 30% gain in quality and a 20% gain in productivity after shifting from a process layout, where equipment was grouped by similar capabilities, to work cells, where equipment was grouped to support a specific family of products. If FlexCon decides to outsource the pistons, the company will likely dedicate the floor space currently occupied by the work cells to a new product or expansion of an existing product. FlexCon will apply the work cell equipment for other applications, so the outsourcing analysis will not consider equipment write-offs beyond normal depreciation.

Although there are different opinions regarding outsourcing the pistons, FlexCon engineers agreed that the process technology used to produce this family of components is mature. Gaining future competitive advantages from new technology was probably not as great as other process applications within FlexCon's production process. This did not mean, however, that FlexCon could avoid making new investments in process technology if the pistons remained in-house, or that some level of process innovation is not possible.

Differences over outsourcing a component that is critical to the performance of FlexCon's final product threatens to affect the insourcing/outsourcing decision. One engineer threatened to quit if FlexCon outsourced a component that could "bring down" the entire engine in case of quality failure. He also maintained, "Our pistons are known in the industry as first-rate." Another engineer suggested that FlexCon's supply management group, if given support from the engineers, could adequately manage any risk of poor supplier quality. However, a third engineer noted, "Opportunistic suppliers will exploit FlexCon if given the chance—we've seen it before!" This engineer warned the group about suppliers "buying in" to the piston business only to coercively raise prices. Several experienced engineers voiced the opinion that they could not imagine FlexCon outsourcing a component that was responsible for making FlexCon the company it is today. Several newer members of the engineering group suggested they should wait until the outsourcing cost analysis was complete before rendering final judgment.

Management has created a cross-functional team composed of a process engineer, a cost analyst, a quality engineer, a procurement specialist, a supervisor, and a machine cell employee to conduct the outsourcing analysis. A major issue confronting this team involves determining which internal costs to apply to the analysis. Including total variable costs is straightforward because these costs are readily identifiable and vary directly with production levels. Examples of variable costs include materials, direct labor, and transportation.

The team is struggling with whether (or at what level) to include total factory and administrative costs (i.e., fixed costs and the fixed portion of semivariable costs). Factory and administrative costs include utilities, indirect labor, process engineering support, depreciation, corporate office administration, maintenance, and product design charges. Proper allocation of overhead is a difficult, and sometimes subjective, task. The assumptions the team makes about how to allocate total factory and operating costs can dramatically alter the results of the analysis.

The aggregated volume for pistons over the next several years is critical to this analysis. Exhibit 2 provides a monthly forecast of expected piston volumes over the next two years. Total forecasted volume is 300,000 units in Year 1 and 345,000 units in Year 2. The team arrived at the forecast by determining the forecast for FlexCon "R" series engines, which is an independent demand item. Pistons are a dependent demand item (i.e., dependent on the demand for the final product).

Although this is a long-term decision likely to extend beyond ten years, the team has confidence in its projections (including supplier pricing) only through two years. Although maintaining piston production internally would require some level of process investment in Years 3 through 10, the team believes any projections past Year 2 contain too much uncertainty. (Conducting a net present value for expected savings from outsourcing, if they exist, is beyond the scope of this assignment.)

Exhibit 2	Aggregated Two-Year Piston Demand	
	YEAR 1 EXPECTED DEMAND	**YEAR 2 EXPECTED DEMAND**
January	30,000	34,000
February	30,000	34,000
March	30,000	34,000
April	27,000	31,000
May	25,000	28,000
June	25,000	28,000
July	23,000	27,000
August	21,000	26,000
September	22,000	25,000
October	23,000	27,000
November	23,000	27,000
December	21,000	25,000
Total	300,000	345,000

Insourcing Costs

The team has decided that a comprehensive total cost analysis should include all direct and indirect costs incurred to support piston production. FlexCon tracks its materials and labor by completing production worksheets for each job. The team collected data for the previous year, which revealed that the three work cells produced 288,369 pistons.

Direct Materials

FlexCon machines the pistons from a semifinished steel alloy purchased directly from a steel foundry. The foundry ships the alloy to FlexCon in 50 lb. blocks, which cost $195 per block. Each piston requires, on average, 1.1 lb. of semifinished raw material for each finished piston. This figure includes scrap and waste.

The team expects the semifinished raw material price to remain constant over the next two years. Although FlexCon expects greater piston volumes in Years 1 and 2 compared with current demand, the team does not believe additional material economies are available.

FlexCon spent $225,000 last year on other miscellaneous direct materials required to produce the pistons. The team expects to use this figure as a basis for calculating expected Year 1 and 2 costs for miscellaneous direct material requirements.

Direct Work Cell Labor

The direct labor in the three work cells worked a total of 27,000 hours last year. Total payroll for direct labor was $472,500, which includes overtime pay. The average direct labor rate is $17.50 per hour ($472,500 / 27,000 total hours = $17.50 per hour). As a rule of thumb, the team expects to add 40% to direct labor costs to account for benefits (health, dental, pension, etc.). The team also expects direct labor rates to increase 3% a year for the next two years. The team does not expect per-hour production rates to change significantly. The process is well established, and FlexCon has already captured any learning curve benefits.

Work cell employees are responsible for machine setup, so the team decided not to include machine setup as a separate cost category.

Indirect Work Cell Labor

FlexCon assigns a supervisor, material handler, and engineer full-time to the three work cells. Last year, the supervisor earned $52,000, the material handler earned $37,000, and the engineer earned $63,000 in salary. Again, the team expects to apply an additional 40% to these figures to reflect fringe benefits. The team expects these salaries to increase 3% each year.

Factory Overhead and Administrative Costs

This category of costs is, without doubt, the most difficult category of cost to allocate. For example, should the team prorate part of the plant manager's salary to the piston work cells? One team member argued that these costs are present with or without piston production and, therefore, should not be part of the insourcing calculation. Another member maintained that factory overhead supports the factory, and the three work cells are a major part of the factory. Not including these costs would distort the insourcing calculation. She noted that the supplier is most assuredly considering these costs when quoting the piston contract. Another member suggested performing two analyses of insourcing costs. One would include factory overhead and administrative costs, and the other would exclude these costs.

The team divided the factory into six "zones" based on the functions performed throughout the plant. The piston work cells account for 25% of the factory's floor space, 28% of total direct labor hours, and 23% of plant volume. From this analysis, the team has decided to allocate 25% of the factory's overhead and administrative costs to the piston work cells for the analysis that includes these costs. Exhibit 3 presents relevant cost data for the previous year. The team expects these costs to increase 3% each year.

Preventive Maintenance Costs

FlexCon spent $40,250 on preventive maintenance activities on the 18 machines in the three cells last year and expects this to increase by 10% in each of the next two years (due to the increasing age of the equipment).

Machine Repair Costs

An examination of maintenance work orders reveals that the 18 work cell machines, which are each five to seven years old, required total unplanned repair expenses of $37,000 last year. The maintenance supervisor expects this figure to increase by 8% in Year 1 and 12% in Year 2 of the analysis due to increasing age and volumes.

Ordering Costs

Although FlexCon produces pistons in-house, the company still incurs ordering costs for direct materials. The team estimates that each monthly order to the foundry and other suppliers costs FlexCon $1,500 in direct and transaction-related costs.

Semifinished Raw Material Inventory Carrying Costs

FlexCon typically maintains one month of semifinished raw material inventory as safety and buffer stock. The carrying charge assigned to this inventory is 18% annually.

Exhibit 3	Total Factory Overhead and Administrative Costs
COST CATEGORY	**PREVIOUS YEAR EXPENSE/COST**
Administrative staff	$1,200,000
Staff engineering	$ 900,000
Taxes	$ 120,000
Utilities	$1,500,000
Insurance	$ 500,000
Plant Maintenance	$ 800,000
Total	$5,020,000

Inbound Transportation

FlexCon receives a monthly shipment of semifinished alloy that the work cells use to machine the pistons. Total transportation costs for the previous year amounted to $31,500 (which resulted in 288,369 pistons produced).

The team expects transportation charges for other direct materials used in production to be $0.01 per unit in Years 1 and 2 of the analysis.

Consumable Tooling Costs

The machines in the work cell are notorious for "going through tooling." Given the consumable tooling costs realized during the previous year, the team estimates additional tooling expenses of $56,000 in Year 1, and $65,000 in Year 2.

Depreciation

The team has decided to include in its cost calculation normal depreciation expenses for the 18 work cell machines. The depreciation expense for the equipment is $150,000 per year.

Finished Piston Carrying Costs

Because FlexCon coordinates the production of pistons with the production of "R" series engines, any inventory carrying charges for finished pistons are part of the cost of the finished engine and are not considered relevant to this calculation.

Opportunity Costs

The team recognizes that opportunities may exist for achieving a better return on the space and equipment committed to piston production. Unfortunately, the team does not know with any certainty what management's plans may be for the floor space or equipment if FlexCon outsources piston production. The team is confident, however, that management will find a use for the space. If the facility no longer engages in piston production, then FlexCon must allocate fixed factory and overhead costs across a lower base of production. This will increase the average costs of the remaining items produced in the plant, possibly making them uncompetitive compared with external suppliers.

Outsourcing Costs

The following provides relevant information collected by the team as it relates to outsourcing the family of pistons to an external supplier. Although it is beyond the scope of this case, the team has already performed a rigorous assessment of the supply market and has reached consensus on the external supplier in the event the team recommends outsourcing. This was necessary to obtain reliable outsourcing cost data.

Unit Price

The most obvious cost in an outsourcing analysis is the unit price quoted by the supplier. In many respects, outsourcing is an exercise in supplier evaluation and selection. Insourcing/outsourcing requires the evaluation of several suppliers in depth—the internal supplier (FlexCon) and external suppliers (in the marketplace). The supplier that the team favors if FlexCon outsources the pistons quoted an average unit price of $12.20 per piston (recall that this outsourcing decision involves different piston part numbers). The team

believes that negotiation will occur if FlexCon elects to outsource, perhaps resulting in a lower quoted price. Because the team does not yet know the final negotiated price, some members argued that several outsourcing analyses are required to reflect different possible unit prices. Quoted terms are 2/10, net 30. The supplier says it will maintain the negotiated price over the next two years.

Safety Stock Requirements

If the team decides to outsource, FlexCon will hold physical stock from the supplier equivalent to one month's average demand. This results in an inventory carrying charge, which the team must calculate and include in the total cost analysis. Although FlexCon likely will rely on or draw down safety stock levels during the next two years, for purposes of costing the inventory the team has decided not to estimate when this might occur. Inventory carrying charges include working capital committed to financing the inventory, plus charges for material handling, warehousing, insurance and taxes, and risk of obsolescence and damage. FlexCon's inventory carrying charge is 18% annually.

Administrative Support Costs

FlexCon expects to commit the equivalent of one third of a buyer's total time to supporting the commercial issues related to the outsourced family of pistons. The team estimates the buyer's salary at $54,000, with 40% for fringe benefits. The team expects the buyer's compensation to increase by 3% each year.

Ordering Costs

The team expects that FlexCon will order monthly, or twelve material releases a year. Unfortunately, suppliers in this industry have not been responsive to shipping on a just-in-time basis or using electronic data interchange. Although FlexCon would like to pursue a JIT purchasing model, the team feels that assuming lower volume shipments on a frequently scheduled basis is not appropriate. The company expects the supplier to deliver one month of inventory at the beginning of each month. The team estimates the cost to release and receive an order to be $1,500 per order.

Quality-Related Costs

The team has decided to include quality-related costs in its outsourcing calculations. During the investigation of the supplier, a team member collected data on the process that would likely produce FlexCon's pistons. The team estimates that the supplier's defect level, based on process measurement data, will be 1,500 ppm. FlexCon's quality assurance department estimates that each supplier defect will cost the company an average of $250 in nonconformance costs.

Inventory Carrying Charges

FlexCon must assume inventory carrying charges for pistons received at the start of each month and then consumed at a steady rate during the month. For purposes of calculating inventory-carrying costs for finished pistons provided by the supplier, the team expects to use the average inventory method. The formula for determining the average number of units in inventory each month is the following:

$$((\text{Beginning Inventory at the Start of Each Month} + \text{Ending Inventory at the End of Each Month})/2) \times \text{Carrying Cost per Month}$$

For calculation purposes, the team assumes that ending inventory each month is zero units (excluding safety stock, which requires a separate calculation). The team expects production to use all the pistons received at the beginning of each month. The carrying charge applied to inventory on an annual basis is 14% of the unit value of the inventory.[1] Appendices 1 and 2 on pp. 823 and 824 will help in the calculation of monthly carrying charges associated with holding supplier-provided piston inventory.

Transportation Charges

Although it is FlexCon's policy to have suppliers ship goods F.O.B. shipping point, the company does not accept title or ownership of goods until receipt at the buyer's dock. However, the company assumes all transportation-related charges. The team estimates that transportation charges for pistons will average $2,100 per truckload, with fourteen truck-loads expected in Year 1 and sixteen truckloads expected in Year 2. The outsourcing supplier is in the United States, which means the team does not have to consider additional costs related to international purchasing.

Tooling Charges

The supplier said that new tooling charges to satisfy FlexCon's production requirements would be $300,000. The team has decided to depreciate tooling charges over two years, or $150,000 per year.

Supplier Capacity

The team has concluded that the supplier has available capacity to satisfy FlexCon's total piston requirements.

Appendix 3 provides a worksheet to help in the insourcing/outsourcing cost analysis.

Appendix 1	Year1 Inventory Carrying Charges Outsourcing Option			
	BEGINNING INVENTORY	ENDING INVENTORY	AVERAGE INVENTORY	INVENTORY CARRYING COSTS
January	30,000	0		$
February	30,000	0		$
March	30,000	0		$
April	27,000	0		$
May	25,000	0		$
June	25,000	0		$
July	23,000	0		$
August	21,000	0		$
September	22,000	0		$
October	23,000	0		$
November	23,000	0		$
December	21,000	0		$
			Total Inventory Carrying Costs	

Appendix 2	Year 2 Inventory Carrying Charges Outsourcing Option

	BEGINNING INVENTORY	ENDING INVENTORY	AVERAGE INVENTORY	INVENTORY CARRYING COSTS
January	34,000	0		$
February	34,000	0		$
March	34,000	0		$
April	31,000	0		$
May	28,000	0		$
June	28,000	0		$
July	27,000	0		$
August	25,000	0		$
September	25,000	0		$
October	27,000	0		$
November	27,000	0		$
December	25,000	0		$
			Total Inventory Carrying Costs	

Appendix 3	Insourcing/Outsourcing Cost Factors Worksheet

INSOURCING COSTS PER UNIT	YEAR 1	YEAR 2	OUTSOURCING COSTS PER UNIT	YEAR 1	YEAR 2
Direct materials			Purchase cost		
Semifinished					
Other					
Direct labor			Transportation		
Indirect labor			New tooling		
Factory overhead and administrative			Administrative support		
Preventive maintenance			Inventory carrying		
Machine repair			Safety stock		
Ordering			Quality-related costs		
Depreciation			Ordering		
Inventory carrying			Other costs		
Inbound transportation			Total Outsourcing Costs per Unit		
Consumable tooling			Total savings (1)		
Other costs			Less: Taxes on savings (40%)		
Total Insourcing Cost per Unit			Net Outsourcing Savings		

Total Savings = (Total Insourcing Costs − Total Outsourcing Costs) × (Total Volume)
Note that the total savings could be negative if the analysis shows that outsourcing costs are greater than insourcing costs.

ASSIGNMENT

1. Perform a quantitative insourcing/outsourcing analysis using the data provided. What qualitative issues might affect your final decision? Identify any costs or issues that are not part of your analysis that might affect your decision. What is your recommendation regarding what FlexCon should do with its family of pistons? Support your arguments with evidence gathered during your analysis.

2. Assume your group decided to outsource the pistons to the external supplier. Identify a plan that would enable FlexCon to carry out this recommendation. Be as thorough as possible.

3. Discuss the primary reasons when and why insourcing/outsourcing decisions occur.

4. A major challenge with an insourcing/outsourcing analysis involves gathering reliable data. Discuss the various groups that should be involved when conducting an insourcing/outsourcing analysis such as the one presented in this case. What information can each of these groups provide?

5. Discuss the major issues associated with an insourcing/outsourcing analysis and decision.

ENDNOTES

1. The 14% figure is less than the 18% figure applied to safety stock carrying charges. The supplier does not receive payment until at least four weeks after FlexCon receives the pistons. This makes FlexCon's working capital committed to financing production inventory somewhat less than the capital committed to financing safety stock.

Email Exercise

Consider the following email that was sent to you by a Global Procurement Office representative from your satellite office located in New Delhi, who is passing on information he has received on conditions for a new major supplier. Based on the facts provided by this individual, complete a supply risk evaluation, and estimate the dollar impact associated with this supplier. If there is no information available for a particular variable in the model, enter a "1," meaning that it does not pose a significant risk.

To access the Risk Evaluation, go to www.cengage.com/decisionsciences/monczka and select "Risk Evaluation" from the left-hand navigation.

To: Victor Kliossis

From: Anil Patel

Victor,

I was following up on your request to explore sourcing from a castings supplier located in India. I have identified a suitable candidate, the Golden Elephant castings company. As you stated, this is an important decision, as this supplier **will be a single source providing castings for your entire new line of product in the C-series**. As you know, the C-series forecast is $50M in revenue during the first year, growing to $75M in the second year. Based on your process specifications, this is the **only available castings supplier in our supply base with the required heat treat ovens capable of meeting your specifications as well as the cost and price targets you specified**. Essentially, this supplier has the lock on this business for the C-series. He seems to know this.

We visited the supplier's location, and were greeted by the company's owner. He was very pleased with the results that our negotiating team came to terms with, and afterwards boasted with some pleasure that this was going to be a very profitable business deal for Golden Elephant. He noted that the firm was under new management as of six months ago, and that he was taking over management of the factory from the previous owner, who had sold out and gone into retirement. Upon taking a tour of the facility, we found it was well-lit, and workers seemed to know what they were doing. In private, the owner told us that he felt these workers were overpaid, but that he was trying to keep labor costs below the average for New Delhi, and tried to keep his workers in the dark. **We did not see evidence of any statistical quality control charts, but the owner assured us that workers were well-trained in these methods** The owner also noted that they are anxious for this business, as this will **represent an order that will double their current business volume** We met with some of their technical engineers, and they seemed very young. In fact, one of them shared with us that he had just started the day before, and was replacing someone who had lasted only two months in that role.

We met with their purchasing group. Their office was full of paper piled up high to the ceiling, and they emphasized how busy they were processing PO's with their vendors. When we asked who their primary steel suppliers were, we were told that they liked to shop around for the cheapest price, and rarely bought any steel except at spot prices through intensive negotiations. They also noted that there had been some problems in getting steel in some cases, due to the recent shortages being driven by the high demand for steel.

We then identified how shipments would get to your factory location in Omaha, NE. Golden Elephant will arrange for in-land transportation, as the **owner's brother-in-law has a trucking company**. The shipment would then go through the Indian port. **There have been some rumors of union problems with the dockworkers at this location**, but our sources believe that these are only rumors. Once the shipment arrives in the port of Los Angeles, it will be unloaded, put onto a trailer, and driven to the Omaha location. We are still waiting for quotes for shipment times, **as the recent hike in fuel prices means the shipping companies will not commit to a firm transoceanic shipping cost**. This is the **first time this supplier has exported products to the United States**, but the owner has assured me that his administrative assistant has worked on shipping documentation in her former job, so this shouldn't be a problem.

Let me know what your decision is on whether to proceed.

Anil

Index

Note: Page numbers in italics refer to exhibits